PLAYS ONSTAGE

AN ANTHOLOGY

Ronald Wainscott
Indiana University

Kathy Fletcher
Indiana University

Boston New York San Francisco
Mexico City Montreal Toronto London Madrid Munich Paris
Hong Kong Singapore Tokyo Cape Town Sydney

Series Editor: Molly Taylor
Editorial Assistant: Suzanne Stradley
Senior Production Administrator: Donna Simons
Composition Buyer: Linda Cox
Manufacturing Buyer: JoAnne Sweeney
Cover Administrator: Linda Knowles
Editorial-Production Service: Omegatype Typography, Inc.
Electronic Composition: Omegatype Typography, Inc.

For related titles and support materials, visit our online catalog at
www.ablongman.com.

Library of Congress Cataloging-in-Publication Data

Plays onstage : an anthology / [compiled by] Ronald Wainscott, Kathy Fletcher.
     p. cm.
     Includes index.
     ISBN 0-205-40574-6 (paperback)
      1. Drama—Collections. I. Wainscott, Ronald Harold. II. Fletcher, Kathy.

PN6112.P615 2006
808.82—dc22

                                        2005050978

Printed in the United States of America
10 9 8 7 6 5 4 3 2 1   09 08 07 06 05

Contents

Introduction

WHY AN ANTHOLOGY OF PLAYS?

A collection of important plays representing an array of historical periods and playwrights; offering different points of view and variety of characterization; and representing significant genres, structures, and styles can offer the beginning and continuing student of theatre and drama a window on the dramatic expression and theatrical production of the past, including the very recent past. In turn, such a collection addresses our current theatrical practice and play writing, while demonstrating graphically how the theatre has changed as it continues to celebrate its dynamic past. An anthology is something of a monument to dramatic writing and a glimpse into the artistic, social, and political worlds that gave rise to the plays' creation. Plays are the expression of individual artistry and creativity, commentary on the time period in which they were composed, and detailed outlines for theatrical production. Plays make up some of the most memorable clues to theatre art of the past and they can open a myriad of possibilities for the reader's imagination.

WHY THIS ANTHOLOGY?

This dramatic collection has several purposes. It is intended to accompany our introductory theatre textbook entitled *Theatre: Collaborative Acts,* published by Allyn & Bacon. The teaching of the arts contained in the theatre is difficult without also reading and teaching plays. Specific plays become vital examples for understanding the dramatic structure and styles of historical periods, for envisioning theatrical production, and for encountering different approaches to language—especially dialogue, which is so crucial to most theatrical presentation. Specific plays, if well chosen, dem-onstrate the remarkable variety of dramatic possibilities. We hope we have chosen well.

Of course, this anthology can be used for other purposes. It can be read for other kinds of courses in theatre and drama. Or it can simply be enjoyed as a collection of splendid plays.

READING A PLAY

If play-reading is a new or infrequent experience for you, we have a number of suggestions to make your reading more intriguing and efficient. The most important first principle is to bear in mind that nearly all plays are intended for performance. (Occasionally the play form is selected by a writer who never intends the play for production.) Most playwrights hope that their plays will find a home in a theatre with an audience, and not be experienced only by solitary readers. In the case of *Woyzeck* by Georg Büchner, we do not know what he intended for production because his play was not quite finished when he died. The play's first production was not until some seventy-six years after his death.

Generally, however, a playwright's intent to secure a stage production suggests that the reader should imagine the dialogue and stage directions of the play as a detailed outline and guide for performance. In other words, all of the words spoken in the play are typically present on the page, but the stage directions are usually less complete and complex than the text of a novel. What is performed beyond the spoken words is often sketchily included, if at all. Therefore it is up to the reader to fill in possibilities for what is seen and how the dramatic action moves. The reader creates a theatre in his or her head and imaginatively fills in the missing details. If the play takes place in a room, for example, the playwright may simply identify the location as "a room." On the other hand, many realistic playwrights include details for that room, but rarely is every possible description for the subtleties of the room provided. The reader supplies those missing particulars, unless the reader prefers to keep the setting vague.

If the playwright calls attention to a specific item in the room it is likely that the item will be part of prominent action or character development. Within this anthology, for example, the play *Ghosts* by Henrik Ibsen includes considerable interior detail from the playwright. Some of these details, such as specific controversial books on the table, are very important to our understanding of one of the characters. The window called for is also linked to action and discovery, and the placement of doors is significant for sudden entrances, or the overhearing of disturbing offstage dialogue. In *The Conduct of Life* by Maria Irene Fornes, the playwright is very specific about the setting, which represents several rooms all at the same time but at different distances from the audience. Despite her specificity about the space, other stage directions are sparingly provided. On the other hand, in Molière's *The Hypochondriac*, the action again takes place in a single room, but we know very little about it other than that it is apparently the bedroom of the central character. We know that in the original production the playwright, who also played the leading role, frequently used a wheelchair. Generally speaking, Molière gives his interior settings scant, if any, description; the reader's or the theatre artist's imagination is given much freedom. Conversely, a play such as Samuel Beckett's *Act without Words I* has no dialogue at all. In this case, the playwright supplies many precise stage directions, although many of these are open to interpretation.

Besides imagining the physical environment, the reader must fill in many of the emotional possibilities of the characters' action. Often the only clues to a character's emotionality lie in the spoken text. In many cases a playwright may provide emotional hints through stage directions: at different times, José Rivera's *Marisol* stage directions indicate that the protagonist is "frightened," "energized," "a little disappointed," "momentarily relieved," and "filled with new terror." There are many kinds of anger and joy. An actor or a reader's imagination can lead to many possible readings and interpretations of the spoken text. So we suggest that you read and pay attention to the stage directions.

It is important to imagine the play three-dimensionally as you read, but also to understand the passage of time in the play. Literal or figurative time becomes a fourth dimension. Obviously, the time expended by the played action is related to understanding how the play unfolds moment-by-moment. The sweep of the entire action from beginning to end may be continuous and only represent the period of time taken up by the play itself. In Susan Glaspell's *Trifles,* for example, the playing time is unbroken and represents only the real period of time it takes to read or perform it. Many plays, however, represent a longer time period: days, months, or years, skipping over time periodically. August Wilson's *The Piano Lesson* depicts about five days. *Venus* by Suzan-Lori Parks takes place over more than a year. Twenty years pass between the third and fourth scenes of *Color Struck* by Zora Neale Hurston. The anonymous medieval play *The World and the Child* traverses the lifetime of a man, from the cradle to the grave.

The most obvious and essential task in reading a play is to keep the basic action and forward progress of the play in mind. Understanding what happens to the characters and the ultimate import of that action is primary. The play usually has a story, but does not have to. A play could present a series of images, sounds, or dialogue that make cultural, political, or social comments but never create a story. Sometimes the audience or reader is simply drawn to the struggles of a character without following that character's progress through some kind of narrative. We may never know precisely where the characters are.

Regardless of whether the play has a recognizable story, your connection to the characters is often vital to a successful experience with a play. You may closely identify with one or two characters and even imagine yourself in one or more roles. Unless a play is written with an overwhelming focus on one character, such as *Machinal* by Sophie Treadwell, you may find yourself switching your allegiance to different characters as you read the play for the first time. It can be a good exercise to read some of the lines aloud to get a sense of how the dialogue works in real time or to get a feel for the language if it is particularly lyrical, strident, or complex. If at all possible, the first time you read a play, try to read it in one sitting. The best way to get a sense of a play's impact is to read it as if it is being played while you read.

Remember that, unlike most novels and other stories, plays are always in present tense. This quality is a vibrant part of your experience with a play text. Even if there is a narrator guiding you through some of the action, as in David Henry Hwang's *M. Butterfly,* the dramatized scenes are performed as if they are happening at this moment.

EXPERIENCING A PLAY

A play is meant to be performed, so we encourage you to see as many plays as you can in theatres. The more experience you have as an audience member, the more skills you will develop for appreciating and understanding the subtleties, pleasures, and challenges of well written and conceived plays. Of course, reading is vital to your analytical understanding of plays as well. We always see new things or make discoveries that would be missed in a production, and vice-versa. For a thorough understanding of the possibilities of the theatre and playwriting, we must experience live theatre; read plays; and read critical, theoretical, and historical studies of the theatrical event. Any one of these exercises without the others limits our growth as artists or audience members.

There are always discoveries to be made when you read the play on your own. If you see a play only in production and never read it, you are led to think of that play only in terms of the interpretation presented by the artists involved. Furthermore, to see a play or portions of a play only on film, video, or DVD is to see the play not only interpreted by others, but visually focused more narrowly (the eye of the camera as selected by the director) than a theatrical performance, without a real audience and without any three-dimensional aspects so central to the way theatre works. We often use film and

video as a teaching tool, but we must always bear in mind its limitations—it is not theatre, but a related art form. Even if a live performance with an audience is recorded on one of these media, it has been transformed into something new.

CONTEXT OF A PLAY

When a play is first written and produced, it is likely that most of the audience will understand and recognize the context and cultural detail of the play. Contemporary slang will be understood; topical events will be recognized, often humorously or cynically; the environment, costumes, speech, and personal behavior of the characters are all likely to be familiar. When a playwright is writing a new play, many details and issues of the day can be simply mentioned without any explanation. A playwright creating a scene today can have a character utter "9–11" or "World Trade Center" and the audience will automatically conjure up images and intellectual and emotional responses because the recognition of the event is immediate and total. But some fifty years from now it is possible that the term will have lost its emotional trigger for most of its audience. Dion Boucicault's melodrama *The Poor of New York* addresses audiences of his time period by dramatizing financial panics and economic depression particular to their time and place: the mid-nineteenth century. The first act takes place during a real financial panic of 1837 and the rest of the play during a panic of 1857—the year when Boucicault wrote the play. The timeliness was so vital to the playwright/producer in fact, that when he moved the production to another city, he changed the title (*The Streets of Philadelphia,* for example) and some of the details to address the local audience.

Most plays, when first written and produced, address the age in which they were created, even if a play's action is set earlier than the playwright's own time. For example, in Bertolt Brecht's *The Caucasian Chalk Circle,* the opening scene is set in Brecht's time, 1945, in the Caucasian Mountains of Asian Georgia, but subsequent scenes represent the same location centuries earlier. The dramatist uses events of the past to comment on conditions in the present.

Most playwrights are intent on engaging the audiences of their time. Few are writing for posterity—although we suspect that most playwrights hope that their plays will find an audience in the distant future. How shocked Shakespeare would have been to discover that his plays of the late sixteenth and early seventeenth centuries, such as *Romeo and Juliet,* would still be at the heart of theatrical production some four hundred years after he wrote and produced them. He would also be amazed that his plays are popular not just in London, but worldwide. He was writing for local audiences of his moment and place, yet his work has been translated into nearly every language. Fortunately, his plays continue to inspire and entertain the world.

When studying a play long after its composition—whether as a fragment of literature, for the theatre in your head, or for revival on the stage—it is helpful, sometimes vital, for the reader to reach an understanding of the historical context of that play. We may not always know for certain why it was written and what the playwright's precise intent may have been. Few playwrights before the nineteenth century left any record of their intent in writing specific plays. We can, however, learn about the circumstances of the playwright's world and thus have a fuller understanding of the possibilities for the play. We will have a fuller understanding of William Wycherley's *The Country Wife* if we know about fashion, social manners, dress, and slang among the wealthy classes in London in the late 1600s. Without such information, we are still likely to enjoy the play's outrageous comedy. But with an introduction to the context, the characters' social duplicity, seduction, and one-upmanship are even more fun, and the play's social satire becomes more hard-hitting. When producing a play from an earlier historical period, some theatres provide notes and images in printed programs or in lobby displays for the contextual benefit of their audience members.

Theatrical context also helps to open the world of a play from the distant past for the reader of the play. The playwrights knew the kind of theatre for which they were writing. They implicitly understood what kind of performance space would be available, what spatial relationship the audience had to the performance area, what theatrical conventions were prominent, and how the play was likely to be interpreted (at least superficially) by the artists in production. Such things are rarely addressed by the play as written—they are understood by playwrights and theatre artists of the time.

When Arthur Miller wrote *Death of a Salesman,* he knew that it would be performed on a proscenium (picture-frame) stage. When Zeami wrote the Japanese Noh play *Hagoromo* he knew that it would be performed in a raised but open ceremonial space, roofed like a temple, with the audience stage right and center, but not stage left. When Sophocles wrote *Antigone* he knew that the tragedy would appear outdoors under the light of the sun in an open playing space, with a large chorus on stage and musical accompaniment. In *Antigone* all performers would be males wearing masks even though some of the characters are female. In *Hagoromo* only some of the actors would wear masks but all would be male—even though the leading character is a woman. Ibsen's plays, however, were intended for a realistic style—no masks, no music, no cross-dressing. Beyond their original periods, all of these plays have been performed in very different spaces than the original and with different conventions and often with great success. But there is much to be learned about the plays by examining the original theatrical context.

TRANSLATION OF A PLAY

Translation is a tricky problem with plays, but is vital to sharing plays with other language groups and to keeping the plays alive beyond their original time and place. In order to make available plays from many different periods and cultures, it is necessary to secure translations. Seven of the twenty-one plays in this anthology are translations from Greek, Japanese, Spanish, French, German, or Norwegian. We have endeavored to select translations that are not only accurate to the text of the original language version, but playable for the theatre. All translations, however, suffer from the problem that the beauties and subtleties of the original language are lost. No language has an effective word-to-word correspondence that will survive the characteristics of such things as rhythm, rhyme, consonance, alliteration, puns, and idioms. Some translators work very hard for accuracy of content and word choice. Consequently, no translation can be exacting and precise while still capturing the flavor and sounds of the language. This variance is especially obvious if the play, such as *Life Is a Dream* by Calderón de la Barca, was written in verse.

Bearing such problems in mind, many famous plays from the past have a number of available translations that all fall into one of several categories. The translator may strive for accuracy of meaning and maintain all essentials of the story with few or no substitutions of analogy and allusion. Such a translation is very important for study of the play if the reader does not know the original language, but such a version often requires heavy footnoting and can prove to be rather dull when spoken aloud. Unfortunately, such translations are usually not very effective in the theatre and are far less intriguing, theatrical, or artistic than the original. We have tried to avoid this kind of translation.

The translator may also be a poet or artistic linguist who has found a way to create a style that is similar to the original, but the translator is often required to make many substitutions in imagery or even event. If event remains essentially unchanged and the version is very playable for the theatre, then we are attracted to this kind of translation. When event and imagery are heavily amended, then the translation has become more than a translation. It has become an adaptation. We have avoided adaptation wherever possible.

INDIVIDUAL PLAY INTRODUCTIONS

Each of the twenty-one plays that follow has an individual introduction that will provide material to aid the reader with context for the plays. Within each of these introductions, the information is broken into seven sections. The "When the Play Was New" section will identify the dates and circum-

stances of composition and first production (when known), the historical and sociological context of the play, a description of what the theatre was like at the time, and any influential artistic collaborators involved with the play. "The Playwright" will identify the writer, describe his or her connection to the theatre, list other memorable plays by the dramatist, and explain significant recurring ideas and issues in the playwright's work. "Genre, Structure, and Style" will identify the generic type of the play when such an identity is possible and point out what may be unusual or typical about the playwright's approach to form, structure, and style. "Important Elements of Content" will point out things to look for in the story and text of the play that have helped to make this play famous, have contributed to its success in production and study, or have made it unusual in the history of theatre. "The Play in Revival" will note prominent and, when appropriate, recent productions of the play that exemplify unusual or outstanding interpretations of the play. "Special Features" will point to a unique or particularly poignant aspect of the play that makes it significant in theatre history or literature. Finally, each introduction provides an annotated list of resources in the section entitled "Further Reading about the Play, Playwright, and Context."

ACKNOWLEDGMENTS

We wish to thank the following reviewers for their helpful comments: Matt Andrews, Marist College; DeAnna Toten Beard, Baylor University; Andrew M. Hayes, DePauw University; and Scott P. Irelan, SIU–Carbondale.

We also wish to thank the series editor, Molly Taylor, for all of her kind assistance in getting this anthology completed. We continue to appreciate the good people at Omegatype Typography, who are so efficient. As always, we owe a profound debt to our many theatre students who have taught us as we taught theatre history and dramatic literature to them.

Introduction to *Antigone*

WHEN THE PLAY WAS NEW

The first production of Sophocles' *Antigone*, according to tradition, was c. 441 BCE in Athens, Greece. At this point in history, the Greek Classical era, Athens was a powerful city-state, the cultural center of the Greek world, a military power, and the earliest experiment we know of in which a society created a democratic form of government. *Antigone* was presented as part of the Dionysian Festival held annually in the spring. Tragedies were produced as entries in contests. (The Greeks loved competition in many venues—just as many Americans do.) Sophocles won many contests for tragedy and proved to be highly revered in his own time. Each tragedy was produced as one of a set of three tragedies by the same playwright who competed against sets of tragedies by two other playwrights. All was done in honor of the god Dionysus, and the festival was both a religious and a civic affair.

In the time of Sophocles, Greek tragedies usually celebrated received stories from the distant past of Greece: the Trojan War, the exploits and suffering of ancient kings and royal families, and the competitive world of their pantheon of gods. Playwrights seemed to adapt these stories to meet their own inclinations and perhaps the political, moral, and social issues of their time. Often the plays are about duty to family, the state, or the gods. All three levels of duty come into play in *Antigone*.

This tragedy was first performed in a large outdoor theatre holding an audience of thousands. All of the action was lit by the sun and much or most of the action was performed in a large, probably circular, orchestra ("dancing place"). Upstage of the orchestra was a temporary *skene*—a façade with one or more doors and the source of our words *scene, scenery,* and *scenic*. In the case of *Antigone,* the skene represented the palace of Creon in the Greek city of Thebes. Except for the opening scene between Antigone and her sister Ismene, a chorus of probably fifteen men representing influential elders of Thebes and advisors to King Creon were always on stage. Every tragedy had a chorus that spoke, chanted, sang, and danced with musical accompaniment led by a flute player.

Greek tragedies used three speaking actors who often played several roles in each tragedy. In *Antigone* the actor playing Creon interacts with every other character except the briefly presented Eurydice, so it is assumed that this actor performed no other roles. The remaining seven speaking roles, however, were taken by two actors in a scheme something like this:

Actor #2: Antigone, Haimon, Eurydice
Actor #3: Ismene, Watchman, Teiresias, Messenger

The variety required of actors was sometimes astounding. All actors and chorus members wore masks, so scholars believe that when an actor changed roles he changed masks and possibly costumes as well. All performers—including the musicians—were male; women were never allowed to perform publicly in the Theatre of Dionysus. Nonetheless, many important roles in the tragedies are female.

Antigone is often grouped with Sophocles' so-called "Theban" or "Oedipus" plays. *Oedipus the King, Oedipus at Colonus,* and *Antigone* are often presented as a trilogy. Although interesting to see performed together, the plays were written at very different times and were not produced in the same trilogy by the Greeks. If the plays are read or performed in story order, *Antigone* appears last. However, it was written first—more than a decade before *Oedipus the King* and some thirty-five years before *Colonus.*

THE PLAYWRIGHT

We know practically nothing about the personal life of Sophocles (496–406 BCE). It is evident, however, that he was a very successful and popular tragic playwright. Only seven of his tragedies survive, but he is known to have written and produced well over one hundred. He is credited with winning twenty-four Dionysian contests and was highly esteemed in his lifetime as well as in nearly every historical period since, including our own. Tradition tells us that Sophocles, like many of the early Greek playwrights, also performed in his early plays, but discontinued the practice by the time of the surviving plays. We can assume then that he had a thorough understanding of how the theatre of his time functioned since he had an insider's view through practical experience.

Of his surviving plays, the most famous must be *Oedipus the King,* which is often read and studied as an exemplar of the tragic form. His *Electra* is a very important play, in part because its subject is the only one treated by all three Greek tragic playwrights whose works survive today: Aeschylus, Sophocles, and Euripides. A reading of work of the three demonstrates how very differently the familiar ancient stories were treated by the dramatists. *Ajax* by Sophocles is the only surviving Greek tragedy that has a death on stage. In all other plays, a dead figure appears only after the killing, as we see twice in *Antigone.*

Sophocles seemed to love the use of irony, and several ironic themes recur in his plays. Perhaps the most enduring irony is the central character's figurative blindness to what is truthful or necessary. In *Oedipus the King* the title character refuses to see the obvious: He is himself the murderer he seeks to punish. Sophocles enhances the irony by having a blind man—the prophet Teiresias—see clearly, while the sighted Oedipus remains blind until he puts out his own eyes. The blind Teiresias is also used in *Antigone* to work a similar illumination with Creon, who is too stubborn, arrogant, and reactionary to recognize the truth. When he finally does, it is too late to undo his damage.

GENRE, STRUCTURE, AND STYLE

In its most basic definition, *tragedy* is a dramatic genre that is serious and ends unhappily. The Greek philosopher Aristotle in his *Poetics* noted that tragedy evoked the emotions of pity and fear in the audience. Greek tragedy has a number of typical characteristics, some of which it shares with, but also many of which separate it from, other classical tragedy. Tragedies from many historical periods share the same or similar stories and situations. The Romans and seventeenth-century French, for example, borrowed the material of many Greek tragic plays and retold or refocused the events.

Greek tragedy usually, but not strictly, adheres to the unity of time and place. These unities mean that typically all of the action takes place in twenty-four hours or less and in a single location: outside the palace of Creon in *Antigone,* for example. *The Eumenides* by Aeschylus is an example of a Greek tragedy that takes place in two different locations. The tendency toward unity of time, however, is sometimes figurative. The action is played *as if* it occurs continuously, or nearly so. In *Antigone,* for example, the chorus often represents a longer passage of time for offstage events to transpire. In terms of the actual stage time these offstage events occur much more quickly than reality or the length of the choral passage would allow. Therefore the total time passage in *Antigone* could possibly take place in a single day, but it would be a long day, or possibly several days if the playwright were being literal—but he never is. It would be many centuries before playwrights would take a literal approach to time and place.

Sophocles includes an important structural element in *Antigone* that is also important to many other playwrights. All of the scenes in this play are public except the first one, a private, secret scene between Antigone and her sister. With many playwrights who follow Sophocles, this juxtaposition of private and public scenes is a dynamic device, not only for structure, but for development of character. Shakespeare, nearly two thousand years after Sophocles, was a master at contrasting public and private scenes.

Most Greek tragedies include violence—murders, suicides, battles—but typically these events occur offstage and are then reported onstage by a character who witnessed the carnage. The Greek playwrights were probably not squeamish; their society gloried in violence, war, and competition. The plays reflect this preoccupation with gory detail that accompanies many of the murderous reports. The playwrights, however, seemed to think that onstage violence was either not something that could be presented effectively in the theatre, or was not as impactful and meaningful as describing it in the aftermath. They also seemed to put a higher premium on language than spectacle. Therefore audiences focus more on the effect of the violence on the living than the violence itself. The productions further underscored such displacement by showing dead bodies frequently, but not the living body struggling at death. Near the end of *Antigone* we see Creon suffering through a horrible lament over two bodies whose deaths he unintentionally caused. In this respect, Greek theatre was remarkably different than that of Shakespeare or that of our own.

The Greek love of language does not suggest, however, that spectacle did not appear in Greek theatres—dynamic visual images certainly were created. Most of the spectacle appears to have been highly selective or associated with the dance, music, or masks and occasional powerful moments such as flying in a god or goddess at the play's end as we see in *Orestes* by Euripides. One of the most striking visual images in *Antigone* occurs when Antigone (the only female character on stage) stands up to the forceful king Creon, who is surrounded by a chorus of all-male Theban elders. One girl faces off with a group of powerful men, and she never blinks. She is adamant in her resolve. Such images are indispensable to the theatrical event and demonstrate why these plays are meant to be performed, not only read.

IMPORTANT ELEMENTS OF CONTENT

Understanding the family relationships in this play is crucial. Antigone and Ismene are sisters and their two brothers, Eteocles and Polyneices, have just killed each other in battle before the play begins. This battle ended a family feud and fierce civil war. Their father was King Oedipus, now dead, the hapless man who unknowingly killed his father and married his mother, Jocasta; therefore, his children with Jocasta are also his sisters and brothers. King Creon was the brother of Jocasta, thus uncle to the children of Oedipus as well as Oedipus himself. With the deaths of the sons of Oedipus, Creon has just been crowned and made his royal decree not to bury the body of Polyneices. This event leads to the conflict in the play.

Burial of the dead with specific sacrifices, especially the pouring of libations of wine, was a vital ritual in Greek culture and religion. It was believed to be the only way to bring comfort to the dead and help them to the underworld, or afterlife. To deny this ceremonial burial to anyone would be deemed sacreligious. When Creon decrees that Polyneices cannot be buried, he withholds this crucial ritual from a royal prince of the house of Thebes.

The chorus in Greek tragedy often comments on the action, prays to the gods for guidance, and sometimes offers advice to the major characters. If the chorus sees clearly, its advice is often unheeded by the major characters until too late. Early in *Antigone,* at lines 366–367, the chorus provides an observation central to the play's import: "Human laws are frail./Divine laws live in truth."

THE PLAY IN REVIVAL

Antigone had a life in the Greek theatre long after its first production (once the Greeks started regularly reviving plays from the past in the fourth century BCE). After the collapse of Greek political, military, and cultural power, however, the play was probably never performed again until the sixteenth century in Italy, where it was translated and adapted along with other Greek tragedies. *Antigone* was frequently read, studied in schools, and written about, especially in the nineteenth-century Romantic era. In 1841 the Romantic playwright and director Ludwig Tieck revived *Antigone* in Germany and attempted to reconstruct Greek approaches to space and staging. Other European producers (especially in Germany and France) periodically presented Sophocles' *Antigone* or new adaptations of it throughout the nineteenth century. It was in the twentieth century, however, that the Western theatre's interest in this play surged. We have had many famous and not-so-famous adaptations in every decade since the 1920s. Jean Anouilh's French adaptation of 1943, performed during World War II when German forces occupied Paris, has been the most enduring. Carl Orff adapted *Antigone* as an opera in 1949; the Living Theatre's adaptation with a controlling chorus in the 1960s was very political; and in 2004 the Aurora Theatre Company in San Francisco premiered an adaptation by Cherylene Lee set in contemporary China, entitled *Antigone Falun Gong*. But many directors have returned frequently to the text of Sophocles and found new audiences prepared to relate to the generational, gender, familial, and religious struggles in the face-off of Antigone and Creon.

SPECIAL FEATURES

The Greeks left us no stage directions. All stage directions are the logical, assumed, or hoped-for directions of much-later editors of the plays. We like the minimal directions in this translation because they do not intrude on the spoken text; they appear only to clarify entrances and exits. The surviving text is often obvious in terms of basic directions and identity of speaker, but occasional moments are debated by scholars and historians who see very different possibilities in the text.

Most Greek tragedies spend little time dealing with everyday people. *Antigone* is unusual, though not unique, in placing the Watchman, an unnamed common soldier, in the midst of the high-stakes conflict. He is an unwitting partici-pant in events that are beyond his understanding. Nonetheless, this soldier gives us a small window onto the plight of the unprivileged classes of the time of Sophocles as well as an opportunity to put a touch of humor in the production of the play.

A curiosity of this play is that the title character, Antigone, leaves the stage rather early, at line 943, which is a bit beyond two-thirds of the way through. The play continues to line 1346. It must be said that other characters and the chorus continue to talk about her until the catastrophe of multiple deaths. After that point we hear no more about her, but witness the grief and horror of others. The upshot is that we may be most strongly drawn to Antigone and her dilemma, but technically she is not the central character of the play. Of course, without her there is no play at all.

FURTHER READING ABOUT THE PLAY, PLAYWRIGHT, AND CONTEXT

For information on the production of Greek plays in the classical period, see T. B. L. Webster, *Greek Theatre Production*; Peter Arnott, *Greek Scenic Conventions*; and David Wiles, *Greek Theatre Performance*.

For information on later productions of Greek plays, see Oliver Taplin, *Greek Tragedy in Action*, and J. Michael Walton, *Living Greek Theatre*.

For examinations of Sophocles and Greek tragedy, see Harold Bloom, *Sophocles*; Alan H. Sommerstein, *Greek Drama and Dramatists*; and P. E. Easterling, *The Cambridge Companion to Greek Tragedy*.

For historical context, see Eric Csapo and William Slater, *The Context of Ancient Drama*, and Ruth Scodel, *Theater and Society in the Classical World*.

Antigone

BY SOPHOCLES

TRANSLATED BY NICHOLAS RUDALL

CHARACTERS

ANTIGONE sister of Eteocles and Polyneices
ISMENE sister of Antigone
CREON king of Thebes
HAIMON son of Creon
TEIRESIAS a prophet
EURYDICE wife of Creon
WATCHMAN
MESSENGER
CHORUS of male Theban elders
Thebes. Before the palace gate.

ANTIGONE: My sister. My Ismene. We are alive . . .
but the grief, the suffering that Zeus puts on
us I know *must* come from our father's curse.

I have seen it all, the grief, the sense of doom,
the shame, yes, the disgrace, in the eyes of the
world. I have seen it all, your sufferings and
mine.

But now the pain gets worse. This edict . . . the
people say that Creon has proclaimed it to the
whole city. What have you heard?

The wickedness of our enemies will soon destroy our family.

Do you believe me? Do you understand?

ISMENE: My sister. My Antigone. I have heard nothing. Nothing.

Not a word about our friends or family. Not
since that moment when we lost our two
brothers—when our world died as they died,
a double breath, a double death. The Argive
army has left.

I have no further news. There is neither good
nor bad in the air.

ANTIGONE: That is why I brought you from the
house. What I have to say is for your ears
alone.

ISMENE: Tell me all. I see that you are deeply
troubled.

ANTIGONE: My trouble is indeed deep. Creon will
honor one of our brothers in death, *dis*honor
the other.

Eteocles he has buried, respecting all law, all
custom, all sense of justice.

And Eteocles now shares honor with the dead.

But Polyneices is a mere corpse in the sand, a sad
dead body that none can bury, none mourn
for. Bereft of tears, bereft of soothing earth, his
body lies there to fill the hungry eyes and jaws
of scavenging birds.

No one shall touch him. Creon has made this a
law.

And he, the great Creon, comes here now to pro-
claim this law to you and me, specifically to
me . . . and to make its meaning clear to those
citizens who know nothing about it. But there
is more. . . .

He will condemn to death anyone who attempts
to bury Polyneices.

And the death will be by public stoning in the
city.

That is the truth. What will you do? Are you as
noble as your blood?

Or have you fallen, fallen low?

ISMENE: If this is where matters now lie . . . what
can I do?

My poor sister, I can do nothing that will either
help or harm.

ANTIGONE: Then will you join with me in what I
have to do?

ISMENE: What is it that you have to do, what risk
will you take?

ANTIGONE: Will you join with me and bury the body?

ISMENE: Polyneices? . . . but the law forbids . . .

ANTIGONE: He is our brother. Perhaps you wish he was not. *I* will never forsake him.

ISMENE: You are rash, my sister. Creon has passed an edict.

ANTIGONE: Creon cannot keep me from the one I love.

ISMENE: Alas alas. I love you, my sister. But remember how our father died, not only unloved but hated, *hated*. He knew the curse and he put out his own sad eyes.

Remember, my sister, remember his wife, his own mother.

Remember her death, the anguish and the shame. The noose.

Remember the death of brothers.

They murdered and they died.

One day, two deaths. The hands that loved suddenly killed.

And now we are alone. We too will die a painful
60   death—if we ignore the king, forget the law.

Remember that we are women.

Remember that the law belongs to men.

This edict, cruel as it is, must be obeyed.

I ask forgiveness. I ask forgiveness of the dead.

I have no power. I must bow to those who have it.

To make a wild and futile gesture makes no sense.

ANTIGONE: I ask nothing of you. Nothing. Even if you *chose* to join me now . . .
70   I would not permit it. . . . It is too late.

Be what you are.

But I will bury Polyneices. I will do what I must do and I will die an honorable death.

I am his family, his kin, and kin will lie by kin.

Mine will be a holy crime.

I must honor not the living but the dead. For I will spend a longer time with them. There shall I lie forever.

As for you . . . dishonor what the gods have honored.

ISMENE: I will dishonor no one. But I cannot resist the rule of law. I cannot.

ANTIGONE: That easy phrase protects you. I will leave you now . . . to bury my brother whom
80   I love.

ISMENE: Oh my sister. I feel nothing but terror. I fear for you.

ANTIGONE: For me? Feel no fear for me! Put your own life in order.

ISMENE: Tell no one of what you are about to do. Keep silence. And I will do the same.

ANTIGONE: No, scream it aloud. Denounce me. If you are silent I will hate you even more. I want the world to know.

ISMENE: Your heart is burning, but what you have to do is cold as ice.

ANTIGONE: I know to whom my love must flow, and flow deep.

ISMENE: If only it could reach him . . . but your love is impossible.   90

ANTIGONE: When my strength dies, I will die.

ISMENE: But you are wrong from the start . . . to seek what cannot be done.

ANTIGONE: If that is what you believe, I shall be the first to hate you, then the dead, your brother Polyneices, with justice will hate you too. But leave me to my own folly, leave me to the suffering and the terror.

But be sure that I will suffer nothing so shameful as death without honor.

ISMENE: If that is what you believe, then go your way.

But mindless is your journey, though you are rightly loved by all your family.

CHORUS: Oh Light of the Sun,

Oh most glorious light that ever shone

Upon Thebes of the Seven Gates,   100

Across Dirce's streams,

Oh eye of the golden sun,

Oh then did you shine

Upon the Man from Argos

With his Gleaming Armor.

Polyneices!

Running in unbridled fear now

In the harsh blaze of your dawn.

Polyneices!

He had come in bitter quarrel with his brother.

Screaming shrill, like an eagle he flew above our land.

Covered with a wing white as snow

He came, weapons and feathered crests bristling

In the sun.

Polyneices!

He stood above our city's homes, hovered here,
Spears thirsty for blood,
A black circle of death.
And then, before the flames of war could burn
  our tower's crown,
Before he could slake his jaws' thirst with our
  blood,
He was turned back.
120 The war god screamed at his back.
Thebes rose like a dragon behind him.

Zeus hates the boasts of a proud tongue.
And seeing the enemy rolling on like a mighty
  stream
In arrogant clash of gold
He struck the man who rushed to our towers'
  height
Struck him down with a bolt of fire
Before his mouth could scream the cry of
  victory.

Polyneices!
Traitor!

To the echoing ground he fell, twisting hard,
Fire yet in his hand.
This man, who in mad attack had raged
  against us in his hate.
And the War God, flailing blood,
Marked now one, now another for black death.

Seven Captains stood at the Seven Gates,
Seven against Seven.
They lowered their weapons, yielded to
  the might
Of Zeus who turns the battle.

All but those brothers in blood,
Two bred of one father one mother,
They alone hurled their spears
And found a common share of death.

Polyneices!
Eteocles!

Now
Victory whose name is Fame
Dances in the joy of Thebes,
City of warriors.

But   150
Let us forget these rough wars.
Let us worship at the shrines of the gods.
Let us dance through the dark night
And Bacchus will lead us,
God of Thunder, Lord of Thebes.

Ah now comes Creon, son of Menoeceus,
King of Thebes, our new king, appointed
  by this new twist of Fate.
What plan beats in his mind?
Why has he called the Council of Elders?
Why has he summoned us all?   160

CREON: Men of Thebes, the gods, with waves of
  wrath, storm-tossed our Ship of State.
But now they have righted her once more. I have
  summoned you here, from every quarter of
  the city, because I know that I can trust you.
You were loyal to Laius our king.
You were loyal to Oedipus when he restored the
  state.
You were loyal yet again to his descendants
  when he died.

Now it is I who hold the full power of the throne.
  For it descends to me after the double death
  on a single day of the brothers Eteocles and
  Polyneices.
Killer and killed were one flesh, and the flesh
  was polluted by spilled blood.
No king can expect complete loyalty from his
  subjects until he shows his control over government and the law. You cannot know his
  mind, his soul.
For I truly believe that the man who controls
  the state must have a supreme and moral vision for its future. But if he is prone to fear
  and locks his tongue in silence, then he is the
  worst of all who ever led this country or could
  lead it now. I love my country. I love no human being more than my country.   180
Zeus is my god and Zeus sees all. I swear that if
  I saw the state headed for disaster I could not
  keep silent. Her safety is our only hope.
Nor could I call any enemy of this country my
  friend.
For when she sails safe upon an even keel, then
  and only then can we say that we have friends.

These are my principles of government. They will make our city great again.

And that is why I have issued the edict concerning the sons of Oedipus.

Men of Thebes, Eteocles who died defending our city, brave spear in hand, is to be buried with all the honors we bestow on fallen heroes.

But his brother Polyneices who returned from exile to burn and pillage his own father's land, to overturn his native gods, who sought to spill the blood that was his own, who sought to make us his slaves . . . no one in this town may bury him nor mourn for him.

200

Unburied his corpse will feed wild dogs and carrion birds.

This is my command. Never will I honor the wicked at the expense of the just. The man who is loyal to this city, him I will honor in death as in life.

CHORUS: Creon, you have the right to pass this law. You have the power to rule over the living and the dead, the traitor and the patriot.

CREON: See to it that you enforce the law.

CHORUS: We are old. Entrust this to the young.

CREON: That is not what I mean. Sentries watch the corpse.

CHORUS: Then what would you have us do?

CREON: Give no support to anyone who breaks the law.

220 CHORUS: I am not a fool. I have no love of death.

CREON: And the price is death. But there's many a man who has risked his future for money.

(*Enter the* WATCHMAN)

WATCHMAN: My Lord, I'm not saying that I'm out of breath from running.

No, I didn't exactly put my best foot forward. In fact I stopped to think often enough and nearly went back to where I came from.

I kept thinking: "Go there and you'll pay for it! Idiot! Get going!

For if Creon finds out from someone else it'll be even worse."

230

So I kept on thinking and I kept on slowing down.

I haven't come far but it took long enough. So . . . here I am finally.

I will tell you. It may be nonsense . . . but I'll tell you.

My only hope is that I won't be harmed . . . but what's going to happen . . . is going to happen.

CREON: What has made you so uneasy?

WATCHMAN: Let me tell you first about myself . . . I didn't do it.

I didn't see who did it. It's not fair if I get into trouble.

CREON: You know how to protect yourself. You've built a clever defense.

You have some bad news. Speak.

WATCHMAN: It's terrible. I don't know where to begin.

CREON: Out with it and then be off with you!

WATCHMAN: All right. The corpse . . . well, someone's buried it . . . and . . . gone away . . . dry dust sprinkled on the flesh and all the rituals complete.

CREON: Who dared to do this? Who?

WATCHMAN: I don't know! The ground was hard and dry . . . there were no signs of digging . . . no wheel tracks in the dust.

250

Whoever did this left no trace. Nothing. It was the guard who had the morning shift who noticed it first. We felt sick . . . astonished really.

The body was not there as it had been, not *buried* exactly, just a thin layer of dust, just enough to put his ghost at rest . . . no footprints of wild animals . . . no dog tracks . . . nothing. The body was intact.

We began to fight, quarrel, shout at each other. Guard punched guard.

Accusations flew about. No one could stop it.

Everyone had done it. Nobody had done it. We were ready to take red-hot iron in our hands to swear our innocence. We'd walk through fire.

We'd swear by every god we had not done it. We knew nothing.

Not the when or the where. Finally when we had talked all questions through, one man spoke up: it was clear—*you had to be told.*

We all stared at the ground.

270

But there was no other choice, no way out really. No way to hide it.

What he said . . . convinced us. We cast lots. I . . . won. And so I am here.

It's not what I want but I'm here. Not what *you* want either.

Nobody likes the bringer of bad news.

CHORUS: As I listened, I could only think that this was some god's doing.

CREON: Stop! You are fools. Old old fools. Do not risk my anger, for it runs deep.

Some god? Intolerable! The gods care nothing for this corpse.

Or do you think *they* buried him? . . . since he treated them so well.

After all, he did come to burn their temples, overturn their images, pillage their land, and break their laws. Did you ever see the gods honor wicked men? It is not so.

No. From the beginning I knew that some men in this city loathed this edict, formed cabals, whispered together, conspired against me. These are no *subjects.*

290 These men are not loyal to me.

No. These men—oh I can see it, I can see it—they bribed the guards to do this.

Money! There is nothing in this world that corrupts so much as money.

It destroys the state. It drives men from their homes. The honest are corrupted.

And all for money.

300 Money makes evil thrive and wickedness grow fat.

Every man who took bribes and helped in this sealed his own fate there and then.

Now to you. Listen to me carefully. I speak to you under oath, for I swear before great Zeus whom *I* revere: if you don't find the man who laid his hands upon the corpse and bring him here right before my eyes, death will not be enough for you.

I'll string you up alive until you unmask this criminal. Understand?

Perhaps then you'll learn this lesson: sometimes greed exacts a heavy price.

Perhaps in the future you'll think twice about the source of your profit.

You'll see that dirty money destroys more men than it saves.

WATCHMAN: Can I say something? Or should I just turn around and go?

CREON: When you open your mouth you irritate me.

WATCHMAN: *Where* exactly . . . ears or heart?

CREON: Why do you anatomize my discomfort?

WATCHMAN: The man who did it hurts your heart . . . I hurt your ears.

CREON: Talk talk talk! That's all you are fit for! 320

WATCHMAN: Maybe. But I didn't *do* anything.

CREON: This from you who sold his soul for money.

WATCHMAN: It's terrible when you make a guess and the guess is simply not true.

CREON: You and your guesses. Clever talk again.

Look, if you don't bring me the men who did this you'll be *talking* about the punishment that the money inflicted on you.
(*exit* CREON)

WATCHMAN: Well, I pray they catch the man! But whether they do or not . . . that's in the hands of fate. You've seen the last of *me!*

I didn't expect to get away, no I didn't! But thanks be to the gods, I'm safe!
(*exit*)

CHORUS: What a remarkable piece of work is man.
In the tossed waves of winter
He dares the bucking back of the sea
When the swells swirl heavy.

Year in year out he pummels the earth,
Earth, undying, greatest of the goddesses,
Pliant mother,
As the plows turn her soil
And the mules plod on her tireless breast. 340

The birds of the air he nets and brings to earth,
And the wild beasts of the hills.
With nets he traps the tribe of fish from the deep,
Nets fingered with skill.

He is lord over the savage mountain lion,
Masters the long-haired horse and the bull
That has never known the pain of the yoke.

He knows the language of the tongue.
He knows thought that has wings.
He knows the passions that create cities.

And he has found refuge from the arrows
Of rain and hail.

He can do everything. And yet he can
   do nothing,
Nothing in the face of the death that
360   must come.

He has cured disease.
But he cannot cure death.

His mind is rich in thought.
His mind feeds on hope.
But Good comes and Bad comes.

Human laws are frail.
Divine laws live in truth.
Keep the laws of the gods and cities
   stand high.
Cities fall when arrogant excess keeps court.

Never will the transgressor
Break bread at my table.

   (*The* WATCHMAN *enters with* ANTIGONE)

CHORUS: My mind splits in pain.

This is Antigone.

Anguished daughter
Of an anguished father.

380   Oh god, what can this mean?

It cannot be that you have broken the king's
   law!
You are caught in shame, in shame!
WATCHMAN: This is the woman who did it. We
   caught her burying him. Where's the king?
CHORUS: Here. He was waiting.
CREON: Speak to me your Lord. What has
   happened?
WATCHMAN: One should never make a promise you
   can't keep.
You change your mind and you break your
   word.
My Lord, you threatened me. And I swore I
   wouldn't come back.
You terrified me. But I am now a happy man. I
   didn't expect to be.
But I am happy beyond dreams.
I'm back. I swore I'd never come, but I'm back
   and I've brought the girl.
We caught her burying the dead.
This time we didn't have to cast lots. It was mine
   for the taking.

I bring you the news.
O now, my Lord, take her. She's yours. Question
   her. Find out the truth.
Me? I'm free. You can't bring anything against
   me.   400
CREON: Tell me exactly what happened.
WATCHMAN: She was burying him. That's it.
CREON: This is the truth? You understand the con-
   sequences?
WATCHMAN: I saw her burying the body. She was
   breaking your law. Enough?
CREON: Give me details of how she was caught.
WATCHMAN: It was like this: When we got back
   there, terrified by your threats, we brushed
   the dust off the corpse. We cleansed the rot-
   ting flesh.
And we sat on a mound away from the smell.
We kept each other awake, poking, threatening.
   Everyone had to be on the lookout.
We did this for a while. Then it was noon. And
   hot. Sun up above.
Out of nowhere came this wind, twisting, whirl-
   ing, covering the leaves of the trees.
The plain was filled with spinning dust.   420
We shut our eyes, cursed the gods, and sat there.
   It lasted long.
But then suddenly it was gone.
Then we saw the girl.
She screamed, sharp and shrill. Like a bird that
   has lost its young.
She began to groan when she saw the naked
   body, began to curse the ones who had done
   this awful thing.
She took the dry dust in her hands, raised a
   pitcher of bronze and poured libations on the
   corpse, three comforts for the dead.   430
We saw this and we charged down the hill.
We got her. But she was completely calm. We
   said to her:
"You did this and it was you the first time."
She did not say no.
I was so happy.
But it hurt, it hurt.
I'm happy to be found not guilty.
But it hurts to hurt a friend.
However, forget these second thoughts.
I'm glad to be safe.

CREON: You there, you with your head bowed low, do you admit this or do you deny it?

ANTIGONE: I did it. Nothing more.

CREON: (*to the* WATCHMAN) Go! You are free!

CREON: (*to* ANTIGONE) You knew this was against the law? Yes or no?

ANTIGONE: I knew. Of course I knew. Everyone knew.

CREON: And still you did it? You broke the law?

ANTIGONE: It was not god's law. Zeus made no such law.

Nor did justice who lives with the gods below the earth make it a practice for mankind.

You are a mere mortal. And what you decree is as nothing in the face of the laws of god unwritten and beyond truth.

They live not in the now or in the yesterday.

They live in eternity. They come to us time out of mind.

I am not afraid of any man. Man's power means nothing.

I am afraid of the anger of the gods.

And therefore I have kept their laws.

460   I knew that I would die. Of course. But your threats meant nothing.

If I die before my time, I think I win.

For if you live in grief such as mine, what is death but a victory?

So there is no grief in death for me. But if I left my mother's son to rot unburied, I would feel grief, but now I grieve not at all.

You may think me a fool. But folly may be in the eye of the beholder.

CHORUS: The girl speaks bitter words.

She is her father's child.

She fights Fate. So did he.

CREON: People who are proud crack first.

They shatter like iron forged in hot fire.

Hard iron splits and slivers in the heat.

The sliver of a bit reins in the proudest horse.

Pride makes slaves.

And this girl is proud, arrogant.

She broke the law, our city's law.

480   She did it. That was the first thing.

Now she boasts of it. She laughs.

She laughs in my man's face.

She plays the man. And I am nothing if she wins.

She is my sister's child. But if she were my own daughter she would die.

She and her sister. For I accuse Ismene too. She shared in this . . . this burial.

Call her out. I saw her in the house. She was no longer mistress of herself.

Sometimes secret plans become revealed before the plotters work their evil.

I loathe too when the workers of evil try to make what they do some thing of grace.

ANTIGONE: Do you want more than my arrest and my death?

CREON: Nothing. Nothing.

ANTIGONE: What are you waiting for? Nothing you say do I agree with.

I pray I never will.   500

And I know that nothing I say will touch your heart.

But to bury my brother . . . what could feed my glory more?

And these men here, they praise what I did but fear makes them slaves.

But you are free, a king, and you can speak at will.

CREON: That is *not* what they think.

ANTIGONE: That *is* what they think. But in fear they seal their lips.

CREON: You are not ashamed to be the only one who thinks this way?

ANTIGONE: I am not ashamed. When was it a shame to honor your brother?

CREON: But was it not your brother who *killed* him?

ANTIGONE: Yes. My brother. Yes. My mother's son.

CREON: But to bury *him* is a crime, not an act of grace.

ANTIGONE: His dead brother would not say so.

CREON: And you, you make no distinction.

ANTIGONE: No. I do not. For it was a free man who died.

CREON: Making war on his own country! Eteocles died in defense of it.

ANTIGONE: Death is a fair judge. All men are equal.

CREON: The good and the bad are not necessarily equal.

520 ANTIGONE: But who knows if this is eternal truth?

CREON: When a man you hate dies, he does not become your friend.

ANTIGONE: I was born to share in love, not hate.

CREON: Then go down to love the dead below. You are a woman. I am a man . . . that says it all.

CHORUS: Look, Ismene is coming out. She weeps. For she loves her sister. Her cheeks are torn with nails of grief.

CREON: You there, poisonous viper! You hid in the dark of my house and sucked my lifeblood dry. The pair of you were plotting to overthrow the throne, but I was blind. Admit it! You did this together. Or will you swear that you knew nothing?

ISMENE: I did it, if she will allow it. I am her partner. I share the blame.

ANTIGONE: Justice will say no. You had no desire to be my partner. Nor did I allow it.

ISMENE: The journey with you into pain is what I long for.

ANTIGONE: Death and the dead know who did this. I cannot love someone whose love is mere words.

ISMENE: Sister, don't deprive me of honor. Honor for me is to die with you, bringing glory to the dead.

ANTIGONE: You cannot die with me. You chose to live. My death's enough.

ISMENE: When you are gone, what love can there be left?

ANTIGONE: Ask Creon. He is your kinsman and the one you care for.

ISMENE: Why do you hurt me? It does you no 550 good.

ANTIGONE: I hurt too. Even when I laugh at you.

ISMENE: What more can I do for you?

ANTIGONE: Save yourself. I will not begrudge your life.

ISMENE: I am in torment. I cannot share your fate?

ANTIGONE: No. You chose life, I chose death.

ISMENE: But I talked to you. I warned you.

ANTIGONE: In some people's eyes, you were right. In others' wrong.

ISMENE: But we both have lost.

ANTIGONE: Be strong. You will live. My breath died long ago. I joined the dead and I will help them. 560

CREON: Of these sisters, one proved a fool just now. The other was a fool from birth.

ISMENE: Yes, my Lord. When people are in pain, common sense leaves them behind.

CREON: You lost your common sense when you chose to do evil with this evil girl.

ISMENE: What life is there for me to live without her?

CREON: Don't speak of her. She is no more.

ISMENE: Will you kill the future wife of your son?

CREON: Oh, he can plow other fields.

ISMENE: But they were bound together like no other!

CREON: I hate the thought of my son marrying an evil woman.

ANTIGONE: Haimon!—your father robs you of your rights.

CREON: You and your marriage utterly repel me.

CHORUS: You will deprive your son of his bride?

CREON: Death will destroy this marriage.

CHORUS: It is determined then that this girl must die.

CREON: So must you . . . and so must I. (*to slaves*) Move! Slaves, take them inside. They must be watched. They may be women with no means of escape. 580

But even brave men will run away when they see death coming close.

CHORUS: Happy is the man whose life has never tasted pain.
For when a house is shaken by the gods
No generation escapes.
The curse lives, ever surging onward,
Like the wave that swells
When the north winds whip the sea
And the black depths spew their sand
And the storm winds rumble off the
    distant cliffs.

Time out of mind I have seen the sorrows
Of this house, seen them loom and come
Crashing down upon the children.
Grief upon grief.
No generation can escape. A god always
    strikes.

And now the last light is dimmed.
600 The last root of the tree of Oedipus
Is cut by the bloody knife.
The god of death wills it,
Madness and Fury have made it so.

Zeus, no man can surpass the majesty of
 your power.
It is forever young.
Sleep cannot bedim its glory
Nor the endless moving of the months
 of time.
Yours is the kingdom of Olympus's
Shining heights,
Yours the power and the glory
Time past, now, and forever.
But in the life of man
No pride can escape the anger of the gods.
Their breathless wanderings bring some
 men profit,
Some men mere emptiness.
Ambition stalks the ignorant
620 Until knowledge comes through fire.
This saying holds the wisdom of truth:
"The man who believes the bad to be good
Lives in the grip of the curse of god."
His pleasure is brief, his doom eternal.

My Lord, here is your only son, Haimon.
Does he come in grief for Antigone,
In anger for the loss of his bride?
CREON: We have no need of prophets. We shall
 know soon enough.
My son, you have heard my judgment, my last
 word?
Do you come in fury or in deference to the father
 that you love?
HAIMON: Father, I am your son. You have always
 set me on a straight path.
Your wisdom will always be my guide.
I will not sacrifice that for any marriage.
CREON: My son, your heart tells you true.
Never put anything above your father's will.
A father prays that he will breed sons who live
 with him in duty and obedience, hating his
 enemies and honoring his friends.
But when a son proves good for nothing, what
 has a man bred but trouble for himself and
 laughter for his enemies?

My son, do not let desire for a woman rule your
 mind.
This thing in your arms would soon grow cold
 when you knew you had a wicked woman for
 a wife.
A wicked lover in your bed—what knife could
 cut as deep?
No. Spit her out, devil that she is—let her be a
 bride in Hell!

She was the only one of all the city to disobey me.
She was caught in the act. I will not be called a
 liar—she must die.
She can sing a prayer to Zeus, the god of
 kinship.
If I allowed disobedience in my own family, I
 would have to allow it everywhere.
If a man is honest and fair in the home, he will
 gain the public's confidence. 660
I would trust such a man to rule his people well,
 even to *be* ruled well.
In the thick of battle, when the hail of spears fall,
 he will be there, by your side. But if a man
 crosses the law, uses force, makes plans to
 subvert the power of the state, you will never
 find I have a word of praise for him!
Whoever the state has put in power must be
 obeyed—in all things, important unimport-
 ant, just and unjust.
Anarchy! There is nothing worse.
Anarchy destroys great cities and hurls great
 families to the dust.
Anarchy breaks the battle lines of great armies.
If men live decent lives it is because *rule of law* is
 their protector.
We must protect those who live within the law.
I will not be beaten by a woman. If we must lose,
 let it be to a man.
Is a woman to be seen as stronger than we are?
CHORUS: Unless old age has dimmed our wits, we
 believe that you have spoken sensibly and
 well.
HAIMON: My father, the gods have given men the
 power to think.
It is the best thing that we have.
I could not find the words to turn your words
 around.
I have no such skill.

But someone else might argue differently . . . and well.

You cannot know everything that people say or do . . . or how they criticize you.

You frighten them. They are afraid to say things that would annoy you.

But in the darkness I have heard them say that the city grieves for Antigone, grieves for her unjust punishment.

Unjust—to die in shame for what was an act of glory and of justice.

She would not leave her dead brother to lie unburied in the dust, for birds and hungry dogs to make an end of him.

700 She deserves a crown of golden glory.

Beneath the skin of the city that is what you will hear.

My father, your success is my success.

There is no greater pleasure for a son than to see his father prosper and achieve undying respect. And a father wishes the same for his son.

I beg you . . . let your stubbornness die.

You do not alone own truth.

The man who thinks that truth is his alone, who thinks his eloquence and wisdom surpasses all, when his world turns, finds mere emptiness.

A man, intelligent though he be, should never be ashamed of learning more.

His mind must be supple.

When a flood strikes, have you not seen the leaves that submit to the water's rage survive and the resistant trees be swept away? So too the ship that fights the wind, the sail drawn tight resisting, overturns. She comes home, keel on top.

720 No. Soften your anger . . . let the winds pass by.

I am young, I know, but let me say that it would be best if men were created with perfect wisdom. But since this is not so—to learn from others when they speak good sense is no disgrace.

CHORUS: If your son has spoken to the point, you should learn from him, and he from you. Both sides have spoken well.

CREON: At my age I am to be taught by him? I am to be schooled by a boy?

HAIMON: In nothing that is unjust. True, I am young. But look not at my age but at what I *do*.

CREON: Even if what you *do* is to respect anarchy?

HAIMON: I have no respect for those who break the law.

CREON: Is not Antigone so charged?

HAIMON: Your fellow citizens believe her innocent.

CREON: Is the city to tell me how to govern?

HAIMON: Now who is talking like a boy?

CREON: I and I alone give the orders in this city.

HAIMON: It is no city if it belongs to one man.

CREON: The law is that the city is the property of its ruler.

HAIMON: All alone you would be a fine king—of a deserted city.

CREON (*to* CHORUS): He has taken the woman's side.

HAIMON: If you are the woman. It is only you I care for.

CREON: You unspeakable thing you. Contradicting your father!

HAIMON: I must, when you act without justice.

CREON: Is it unjust to respect the duties of my office?

HAIMON: There is no respect. You are trampling on divine law.

CREON: Your mind is poisoned. You have given in to a woman!

HAIMON: I will never give in to what is not right.

CREON: Your whole argument is to protect her.

HAIMON: And you. And me. And the gods under the earth.

CREON: You will not marry her while she is alive.

HAIMON: Then she must die. But her death will bring another death.

CREON: Ah, now your arrogance is in full flood. You threaten me?

HAIMON: It is no threat to try to stop your senseless plans.

CREON: It is you who have lost your senses. And you will regret this argument.

HAIMON: If you weren't my father I would say you were mad.

CREON: Don't call me father. You belong to that woman.

HAIMON: You always want to speak, never to listen.

CREON: Is that so? By god—you will not abuse me like this and get away with it.

(*to the slaves*) Bring the woman out! Bring her here! 760

She shall die right before his eyes. Die in the bridegroom's arms!

HAIMON: No. Never! She will not die in my arms. And you will never set eyes on this face again! Share your madness with others. (*he leaves*) Not with me! Not with me!

CHORUS: My Lord, he is gone. His anger runs deep. Such a state of mind in the young is dangerous.

CREON: Let him go. Let him think, let him *do* whatever his arrogance feeds him. In any case, the girls must die.

CHORUS: Both of them, my Lord?

CREON: No. You are right. Not the one who did not do it.

CHORUS: And what death have you chosen for Antigone?

CREON: She will be taken where no man walks the desert ground. I will seal her in some hollow cave, still alive. She will be given just enough food to clear the city of the guilt of death. Let her pray there to the only god she honors—the god of Death.

Maybe *he* can save her.

Or maybe she will learn, too late, how futile it is to honor those already dead.

780 CHORUS: Love! Invincible god!
You take whatever we possess.
You sleep in the soft bed
Of a young girl's cheeks.
You can cross all oceans,
Move at ease through the wild.
Not the immortal gods,
Not Man who lives but a day
Can escape your embrace.
He who possesses you goes mad.

Even the just man loses his mind.
You twist him into injustice.

You made this quarrel
Of a father and a son,
Provoking shared blood.

Desire shines in the eyes
Of a beautiful bride,
Shines, conquers, and the ordered world
Dissolves.

800 For Aphrodite
Smiles as she kills.

(ANTIGONE *enters in chains or under guard*)

CHORUS: Ah, now *my* world dissolves. I see Antigone
Going to that chamber where all men sleep.
I cannot hold back my tears.

ANTIGONE: Citizens of this my homeland, you see me
Walking the last steps of my life,
Seeing the last rays of the sun.
Then, never again.
In this life I never heard the music
Of the marriage hymn nor the laughter.

Death, in whose arms all men sleep,
Leads me to the cold waters of Acheron
To be his living bride.

CHORUS: But in honor and bright fame
You walk into the darkness.
Untouched by wasting sickness,
Not slain by savage swords,
Head high and alone among mortals
You walk in life down to the house
Of Death.   820

ANTIGONE: I know the story of sad Niobe,
Know the deep pity of her death.
She too was sheathed in stone,
Choked by the mountain's ivied grip.
As she fades from life she is washed
By endless showers and soft snow.
Her grieving eyes shed eternal tears
That soak her cheeks of stone.
I know her story.
Some god has made it mine.

CHORUS: She was a god and born of gods.
We are mortal and born to die.
But in death, like her, you will find fame
For your life and for your death.
You have gone like a god to your fate.

ANTIGONE: Mock me not. Could you not wait till I had gone?
Must you throw insults in my face?   840
O gods of my country, oh my city of Thebes!
I call upon Dirce's holy waters,
Upon this sacred land that protects its people.
Look upon me now! Witness my silent unmourned death.
Remember the law that buries me in a grave of rock.

I am alive!
But soon I will sleep with corpses
Having a home with neither the living nor
the dead.
CHORUS: You risked all, my child.
You climbed to the summit of high Justice.
And you fell, perhaps paying for your father's
pain.
ANTIGONE: My father! Oh you touched the deepest
sorrow of my heart.
Generations have spilled grief upon grief.
There is a doom that haunts our house.
Mother and son breeding life!
860   Breeding death!
These were my parents, I their child.
I go now to be with them.
I did not marry. I did not breed.
That is my curse.
My brother, your life, your death
Have killed me.
CHORUS: You honored the dead.
We honor you. But power cannot be
thwarted.
You chose. You die.
ANTIGONE: No one weeps for me.
No one sings a last wedding song.
I have no friends.
I walk to death,
Last light kissing my eyes.
880   Silence!
        (CREON enters)
CREON: You sing your grief. You mourn your own
death. But you cannot stop its coming.
Now! Take her. Open the tomb. Put her inside.
There, all alone, can she choose death or a
buried life. We are free of guilt. Our hands are
clean.
It is time for her to leave this earth.
ANTIGONE: My tomb, Death's bedroom, where I
shall sleep forever!
Soon I will be with my family, the pale corpses
whom Persephone welcomed.
I am the last and the most accursed. For I have
won death before my time.
But I know I shall see again those that I love—
my dear father, and you my mother, and my
900   brother too.

I washed your bodies, dressed you for the grave,
poured the libations at your tombs.
Oh Polyneices! You know the price I pay for covering your body.
But in the eyes of the wise what I did was right.
        (she turns to the CHORUS)
If a child of mine had died or its father, I would
not have broken the state's decree.
What makes me think this way? If a husband
had died
I might have found another and then given
birth again. But my parents are dead, and I
can never have another brother. That is why I
risked my life for you, my darling Polyneices.
But Creon thought that what I did was wrong,
dreadful and arrogant. And so he marches me
away to death.
I will know no marriage bed, hear no bridal
song, take no husband in my arms nor hold a
baby to my breast.
Now without a friend, cursed by fate, with life
still in me
I go to share darkness with the dead.   920

What law of god have I broken? I have done no
wrong!
Why, in my grief, do I look to the gods for help?
They care nothing for me. I followed the laws of
god and yet I am condemned for ungodliness.
If the gods believe this sentence just,
I will learn the truth in death. But if this man
here is the guilty one, may his punishment
equal mine.
CHORUS: The storm winds of her heart are raging
still.
CREON: Her guards will regret letting her linger
here.
CHORUS: Your words bring death even closer.
CREON: I have no reason to contradict you.
        (CREON leaves)
ANTIGONE: Thebes! My father's city! You gods of old!
I am led away and there is no more time.
Look on me, you men of Thebes.   940
I am the last of this throne of kings.
Remember my suffering and who inflicted it.
Because I would not break the laws of god.
        (ANTIGONE is led away)
CHORUS: My child, my child.

Danae suffered like you,
Locked in a prison of bronze,
Both bedchamber and tomb,
Where the sun could not brush her face.
She was a princess too.
In her, Zeus sowed his seed
950 In a shower of gold.

Fate moves on relentless.
Man cannot hide.
Not Wealth nor War
Nor castle Walls
Can escape its power.

The son of Dryas, quick to anger,
Raged against the god,
Scorned his power.
Dionysus locked him deep
Within a tomb of rock.
And when his madness slowly dripped away,
960 He knew that he had mocked the majesty
Which now had buried him.
For he had tried to stop the ecstasy
And the fire divine,
Stop the haunting music of the hills.

There is a place where black rocks divide
the sea.
Salmydessus.
There the savage god of war
Watched the blood wounds dealt to infant eyes,
Watched the mistress blind her lover's sons,
Plunging the bloody shuttle, gouging deep
Those eyes that never would look on
vengeance.

They wept tears of blood,
Wept for the fate that gave them birth,
Wept for their mother, woeful queen.
980 She was a princess too.
Her father, the North Wind, had raised her
In his far-off cave, cradled by storms,
Never to run free in the sun's warm light.
She shares her endless fate with you,
My child, my child.
(*enter* TEIRESIAS *led by a boy*)
TEIRESIAS: Men of Thebes, we two have come here
together, two with the eyes of one.
For this is how blind men walk.
990 (CREON *enters*)

CREON: Teiresias, what news do you bring me?
TEIRESIAS: I will speak, but you must trust a
prophet's words.
CREON: I have always listened to your advice.
TEIRESIAS: And so you govern our city well.
CREON: I thank you for your help.
TEIRESIAS: But now you walk upon a razor's edge.
CREON: What do you mean? Your words make me
shudder.
TEIRESIAS: You will understand when you have
heard the meaning of my art.
I sat as of old in the secret haven where I listen to
the sacred screams of birds.
I heard bird cries I have never known.
They screeched mad and inarticulate.
I could hear the murderous tearing of their tal-
ons, heard the dying of their wings.
I was afraid. I lit a fire of sacrifice upon the altar.
The flames refused the flesh and a slimy ooze
dripped from the thighs, sputtered, smoked,
and died.
Gall spurted from the bladder and became va-
por in the air.
The fat dripped, dripped. But did not burn. 1010
The meaning of my art is clear. The ritual failed.
This boy was my eyes. As I am yours.
The city is diseased because of your decision.
Every altar in the town is glutted with the
spewed-out flesh of Polyneices, regurgitated
by dogs and birds . . . the son of Oedipus.
The gods will accept no sacrifice from us, not
prayer nor flesh nor flame.
The birds cry in the air, but I do not understand
their cries.
For they are gorged with the oozing blood of the
dead.
Think about these things, my son. All men make
mistakes.
But a wise and determined man will change his
course when he knows that he is wrong. He
will cure the sickness.
Pride breeds disaster. Yield to the dead. Why
kick a corpse?
Why kill the dead a second time?
Listen to me. I speak only for your good.

To learn from such a man as me who knows
  what is right is not a painful thing, especially
  if what he says will do you good.

CREON: Old man! All of you, like archers aiming at
  a target, have turned your bows on me.

I know you and your so-called art. You treat me
  like a piece of merchandise to be bought and
  sold. Make your filthy money, trade in gold
  from India or precious metals from Lydia, if
  that's your business.

But you will never bury that corpse.

Not if eagles were to tear his flesh and leave it
  as an offering at the throne of Zeus. I will not
  give him up. I am not afraid of pollution.

No mortal can pollute the gods. Teiresias, it is
  a shameful thing when wise men sell their
  knowledge, tell lies to make a profit.

TEIRESIAS: Ah, is there no man who can understand
  or tell . . .

CREON: Tell what? What trite pearl of wisdom do
  you have for us?

TEIRESIAS: . . . no man who knows that wisdom is
  better far than gold?

CREON: And that to be a fool is a most dangerous
  thing?

TEIRESIAS: You are the fool. That is your sickness.

CREON: I do not wish to contradict a prophet.

TEIRESIAS: It is too late. You said I lied.

CREON: Prophets! All you think of is money.

TEIRESIAS: Tyrants! All you think of is power.

CREON: Take care. You are talking to a king.

TEIRESIAS: I know. Who helped you to the throne?

CREON: You may be a wise prophet. But you are
  corrupt.

TEIRESIAS: Stop! You will make me say things that
  should remain unspoken.

CREON: Speak! But there should be no profit in this
  for you.

TEIRESIAS: There will be no profit in this for you.

CREON: I will not change. No matter how much
  money changes hands.

TEIRESIAS: Take what I say to heart. Before the passing
  of the sun into its depths, you will give
  corpse for corpse, flesh of your flesh.

You have lost the meaning of the life above and
  the death below.

You send a living breath into a lifeless tomb.

You keep on earth a body which belongs below,
  denying it the grave.

The gods above cannot claim him now. Nor
  you.

He belongs to the gods beneath the earth. And
  so the Furies will track you down, lurking in
  the dark they will pounce upon their prey.

You wish to talk of money now?

Soon within your house you will hear the wailing
  screams of mourning.

You left upon the field of war bodies to rot for
  birds and dogs to bury with their jaws.

The fathers of these sons will rise against you
  now.

The stench of your sin will settle on the earth.

Yes. I am an archer. The arrow of my tongue
  shoots straight into the heart.

Boy! take me home now.

Let him spill his rage on younger men. Let him
  still his angry tongue and learn truth.

(exit TEIRESIAS)

CHORUS: My Lord, these are words of terror. He has
  gone.

But his truth remains. I am old, but never yet has
  he proven false.

CREON: I know this too. . . . It troubles me. To give
  in is hard.

But if my pride breeds stubbornness, then destruction
  is at hand.

CHORUS: Listen to me, hear what I have to say.

CREON: I am ready. I will listen.

CHORUS: Go! Now! Release Antigone. Tear the
  rocks from her tomb.

Bury the waiting dead!

CREON: That is what you think?

CHORUS: There is no time. Gods move as quick as
  light.

Destruction falls heavy upon the fools of this
  earth.

CREON: It is hard to deny what I believe in. But I
  will do it.

I cannot fight with Destiny.

CHORUS: You must do this yourself. You cannot
  leave it to others.

CREON: I am going. Immediately. You! Bring pickaxes
  to lay bare the rock.

Come. Bring other men with you. We must reach
  the cave that lowers upon our house.

I imprisoned her. Shall I set her free?
The laws of the gods are old, mighty, and a man
must serve them till his death.

CHORUS: Dionysus! God of our city! God of many
names!
Oh help us now!
Semele's golden child!
Born of thunder,
Spinner of Mysteries' Dreams!
Bacchus! You wash your body in our
sacred waters.

1120 Women wild with your will within them
Whirl in the night of the seed of dragons!

Help us now!
God of many names!

The nymphs laugh on the hills.
And in the glow of burning torches
You come to us,
You come from the mountains where your
ivy clings
And the waters of Kastalia wash you clean.

We cry your name aloud! *Evoi Evoi.*
You are our god, our Lord of Thebes,
This is your city,
Thebes where your mother birthed and died.

We are sick, diseased.
1140 Heal us now, heal us now.
Come to us across the grieving sea.
You make the stars dance in the black sky
of night.
You hear the echo of eternal silence.
Son of Zeus, bring the whirlwind of your
ecstasy
And help us now.

MESSENGER: Men of Thebes, ancient city of Cad-
mus. I can no longer say of any human life
that it is good or it is bad. Fate can bless a man,
and Fate can ruin the happy or unhappy man
in a single day. No man can know what the
future will bring. Creon was envied once. His
1160 life was good.
He saved this city from its enemies and became
its king. He ruled it well.
And he had noble sons. Now everything has
gone.
When a man has lost all happiness you cannot
say he is alive.

He is a corpse that breathes.
Live your rich life in your palace, sport the trap-
pings of a king, but once your happiness is
gone you are nothing but smoke's shadow in
the sun.

CHORUS: You talk of kings. What grief do you bring
to us?

MESSENGER: They are dead. The living are guilty of
their death.

CHORUS: Who died? Who was the killer? Speak!

MESSENGER: Haimon is dead, killed by his own
hand.

CHORUS: His own or his father's?

MESSENGER: He killed himself, driven mad by the
murder his father had committed.

CHORUS: Teiresias! You saw and told the truth!

MESSENGER: This is my news. You must think of
what to do.

CHORUS: Here is Eurydice, Creon's poor wife.
She may have come outside by chance or she
may have heard something about her son.

EURYDICE: I heard your words as I was coming out
to pray at Athena's shrine.
As I moved the bolts which locked the door, I
heard of my own pain.
I fainted and fell back into my women's arms.
But speak again. I have known grief before.

MESSENGER: Dear lady, I was there. And I will tell
you everything that happened.
I will not try to ease your pain by telling lies.
This is the truth.
I followed your husband to the edge of the plain
where Polyneices' corpse was lying still. It
had been torn apart by wild dogs. . . .
Dear god! We prayed to Hecate and Hades to
speed him on his way and turn their anger to
mercy. We bathed what was left of him with
holy water and burned the flesh on fresh-cut
1220 branches.
Then we covered him with a mound of the earth
of the land where he was born and turned toward the chamber of rock where Antigone lay,
the bride of death. From afar, one of us heard a
voice grieving within that accursed place. He
ran back to tell Creon.
The king approached. All he could hear were
deep groans, the words were unintelligible.
He cried out, "Am I a prophet now? Am I

walking along the saddest path of my wretched life? I hear my son weeping!

Hurry! Go to the tomb and look inside! Tear the
rocks aside.

Look through the crevice and tell me if that is
Haimon's voice I hear or if the gods are deceiving me."

We did what we were told. In the far corner of
the tomb we saw her.

She was hanging by the neck in a noose made of
her own linen veil.

Haimon had his arms around her. He mourned
aloud the death of his bride, her departure
from this life . . . and cursed his father.

When Creon saw him he moaned aloud, moved
toward him, and called out, "What have you
done? My son, speak to me.

What is in your mind? Your suffering is killing you. Come out to me. I beg you. Come to
me!"

Haimon looked at him, his eyes on fire. He spat
in his father's face and then said not a word.

Suddenly he drew his sword and lunged at his
father. Creon leapt aside.

In a fury Haimon turned the sword upon himself, fell upon it hard.

The blade entered his side, half its length pierced
his flesh.

Still conscious he crawled toward the girl and
gently put his arms around her.

Blood spurted from his mouth and stained her
white cheek.

Corpse lay upon corpse. This was their bridal
1240   bed.

The hymns of their marriage are now sung in
the halls of death.

He did not listen to good sense, and in his death
he is a lesson for all mankind.
(EURYDICE *runs into the palace*)

CHORUS: The queen left without a word! What do
you make of this?

MESSENGER: I do not know what to think. We can
only hope that she needs to grieve in private
with her women, away from the general
public.

She knows what is best.

CHORUS: Perhaps. But her silence weighs upon me
more than any cry of grief.

MESSENGER: You may be right. I too fear the
silence.

I will go inside and see if in the wildness of her
heart she means to harm herself.
(MESSENGER *exits*)

CHORUS: Here is the king. Look, he bears his grief
in his arms, brings home his own damnation.

CREON: Oh the sins of my wicked heart!   1260

The murdering crimes of my heart!

You see before you the killer and the son
he killed.

What price to pay for my love of the city!

My son, you died too young, too young.

I was the fool, not you. You died in innocence.

CHORUS: You have learned truth. Too late, too late.

CREON: I learned it in my tears. Some god has
struck me down.

Crushed me with the weight of heaven's curse.

He drove me to this madness,

Pressed his heavy foot upon my happiness.

Oh the sorrow, the pity!
(*the* MESSENGER *returns*)

MESSENGER: You hold one sorrow in your arms.
But there is more.

And you will find it in the palace.   1280

CREON: What further suffering can there be?

MESSENGER: The queen is dead. The mother of this
poor child.

Her wounds bleed still.

CREON: Hades! Where all men must travel, you
have destroyed me now.

I weep in the horror of your words.

I was dead and you have killed me again.

Aaaagh! My son, the queen are dead . . . death
upon death.
(*the doors open and the body of the Queen is
revealed*)

CHORUS: Now you can see. All is in the light.

CREON: Yes, I look upon the second anguish of this
day.

What further pain can strike me now?

Just now I held my son in my arms. And now
I look upon the body of my wife.

Oh pity the mother, pity the son!   1300

MESSENGER: By the altar she fell upon the sword and her eyes embraced the darkness.

She moaned for Megareos, her firstborn, and for this child here.

And as she died she cursed you, the killer of her children.

CREON: Aaaagh! Fear courses through my veins.

Will no one turn their sword on me? Pity this pitiful man by killing him!

MESSENGER: She held you guilty of the death of both her sons.

CREON: Tell me once more of her death.

MESSENGER: When she heard of Haimon's death she thrust the blade through her heart.

CREON: The guilt *is* mine, all mine. I killed you! Shout it loud!

Take me in, take me from the sight of men. I am nothing now.

CHORUS: That is good, if anything can be so called.

It is best to make a quick end of our sorrows.

CREON: Let me go, oh let me go. May my death be soon.

Let me never see another day, another dawn.

CHORUS: That is in the future. We must deal with the present.

What will be is out of our hands.

CREON: All my heart was in that prayer.

CHORUS: Pray no more. No man can escape what Fate has in store for him.

CREON: Lead me away, the man who in his madness killed . . . oh you my son and you my wife.

I did not mean to do it!! Where can I turn, where lay my head to rest?

Whatever my life has touched has turned to dust. A cruel Fate has struck me down.

(CREON *and his attendants go into the palace*)

CHORUS: Wisdom it is that breeds happiness.

The gods take what is theirs.

The words of a proud man are always punished.

Wisdom comes to the old.

1340

Introduction to *Hagoromo*

WHEN THE PLAY WAS NEW

Hagoromo is difficult to date with precision. The play is credited to the Japanese Noh theatre master actor/playwright Zeami (also spelled *Seami* in English), but he was not the first to write and perform it, so parts of this play probably predate him. At any rate Zeami's version dates from the late-fourteenth to early-fifteenth century. We know nothing of the first production, but we know the traditional manner of performance passed down to the modern era.

Noh (also anglicized as Nō) theatre, the first great surviving classical theatrical form of Japan, is often associated with the aristocracy of the Japanese Shogun; his court; and the samurai economic, cultural, and military system. Noh is sometimes described as an esoteric, elite form of drama and performance, but it was also presented for popular audiences. More important than royal patronage, however, is the Noh theatre's strong association with Zen Buddhism—with meditation, reflection, memory, and release from sorrows of the past.

A Noh play was, and is, typically presented as one of a program of plays—usually five or six—each of a different type, mood, or style. *Hagoromo* is considered a woman or "wig" play, often appearing third on a program. The woman play always has a female protagonist. Other plays have female protagonists as well, but many of these are witches or demons, often with onstage transformations. Other categories deal with gods, religious pilgrims, and warriors. The comic form of Noh, Kyogen, usually deals with common people rather than nobility.

The Noh stage for performance seems to have developed from spaces associated with dry river beds (the earliest performance spaces), temples, and court. The traditional arrangement is unusual in the history of the theatre. The main performance space is a raised square stage marked by four pillars surmounted by a temple-like roof. The chorus sits on a stage extension that is stage left of the square (from the audience point of view, to the right of the square), and the musicians sit upstage of the square. Upstage of the square is a wall with a painted pine tree, but three small living pine trees mark the path taken by a bridge (*hashigakari*), which extends stage right (audience left) from the square to the exit to the actor's dressing room (mirror room). There is only one other entrance: a "hurry door" for quick or unnoticed entrances or exits. The raised stage is covered by highly polished wood, and resonating jars are under the stage to enhance stomping sounds made by performers dancing.

Casts of Noh plays are usually small—much smaller than the number of chorus members and musicians. The protagonist of the play is called the *Shite* (pronounced "shtāy"), and he or she is the only character who wears a mask, unless the Shite has silent attendants, who may also be masked. The Shite does not speak or sing; the Shite's words are delivered by the chorus. This gives the Shite a dreamy, spiritual, even unearthly quality that serves the tone of many of the plays, including *Hagoromo*. Each play usually has a conversation or argument between the Shite and a character called the *Waki*, who is unmasked and speaks for himself. The Waki always identifies himself, announces the arrival of others, and addresses the audience directly. In *Hagoromo* the Shite is the angel and the Waki is the fisherman. As in the classical Greek theatre, all of the actors in Noh are male.

THE PLAYWRIGHT

Motokiyo Zeami (1363–1444) is credited with writing forty percent or more of the modern repertory of Noh plays. His father Kan'ami is credited with creating the Noh form as we know it, but Zeami is said to have perfected the Noh form and acting styles. Zeami also left us one of the most valuable documents in theatre history, his *Kadensho,* a secret document meant only for himself and the other Noh actors who trained with him. Actors in this and many other periods carefully guarded their techniques, much as a magician would do today. Within the *Kadensho,* Zeami tells us more about the acting process than we learn from any other source in the ancient world, aside from the *Natyasastra* in India. *Kadensho* also explores the aesthetics of Noh, competition among actors, and the important characteristic of Noh called *yugen,* which defines the actor's task and performance as seeking to create temporary beauty and elegance like a flower (a central image for Zeami). Within the world of Noh the plays themselves are less important than performance—Noh was and is an actors' theatre.

GENRE, STRUCTURE, AND STYLE

The written text is very brief, like a short one-act play, but in performance the time is extended by the use of music and dance. The plays are very lyrical and read much like a poem. Structurally there is typically an introduction by the Waki, who soon welcomes the Shite to the stage and identifies the protagonist. The Shite is usually in agony, seeking revenge, or plagued by terrible memories of an unresolved event in the past. The entire play can give the impression of a memory.

Many Noh plays culminate in a dance. In *Hagoromo,* however, the dance serves a more central dramatic purpose. Except for the Kyogen plays, which were created as a kind of comic relief from a program of Noh, the plays of Noh are typically serious in tone—sometimes even horrific in terms of the deeds of the past—but there is no tragedy. These are plays of reflection, purging, forgiveness, and spiritual enlightenment. In some plays the Shite may be possessed by a demon, but always the demon is exorcised or in some way excised from the dramatic action. The style of performance is typically slow and stately—even the dancing—a condition that often accentuates the

potential of a movement as much or more than the movement itself. The pause is very important to the Noh style.

IMPORTANT ELEMENTS OF CONTENT

Hagaromo is an exception to the reflective nature of most Noh plays in that the angel's dilemma is immediate. She removes her magical feather robe (hagoromo) to bathe in the sea, and hangs it on a tree. The beautiful robe is found by the fisherman who ultimately blackmails the angel before letting her have the robe again. Without the robe she can neither fly nor return to her heavenly home. The fisherman wants to see her dance. Ultimately he is not only entranced by the beauty of her dance but is remorseful for having made her dance to get the robe returned. Therefore, he learns a lesson, but he (like his audience) gets to experience her heavenly dance. Once the angel begins her dance, most of the language (sung or chanted) is in praise of the spiritual life and the glory of the gods. In this respect, the choral presentation resembles that of some of the choruses in Greek tragedy.

THE PLAY IN REVIVAL

Hagoromo continues to be performed regularly in the Noh repertory. Most scholars of Noh consider the line of performance virtually unbroken since the time of Zeami and therefore assume that the approach to performance has remained quite similar for centuries. The basic story of this play, however, appears in many different cultures with variations. Numerous Western playwrights, beginning in the early twentieth century, have adapted the Noh form, specific Noh plays, and Noh aesthetics for their own work. The Irish "Noh" plays of William Butler Yeats are examples, along with modern Kyogen plays created in many different countries and adapted Noh plays produced often in California and on the East Coast. In many Western productions the aesthetics and stories of Noh have been combined with other classical Japanese forms and styles such as Kabuki and the Bunraku puppet plays. Such combinations, however, also have precedent in Japan since both Kabuki and

Bunraku borrowed many things from Noh. Often when traditional Noh plays such as *Hagaromo* tour outside Japan they must be performed in proscenium theatres or other spaces very different than the traditional theatres. When this occurs, a traveling troupe typically brings its own pillars and temporary floor laid out like the hashigakari and Noh stage arrangement.

SPECIAL FEATURE

Many plays, stories, and, more recently, movies and television shows have presented visits to mortals by the gods or angels. It is intriguing to examine the variety of dramatic treatments created for angels interacting with humans. In the case of *Hagoromo*, the loss of a magical garment reduces the angel to near human status (until once again dressed appropriately), thus allowing exchanges otherwise impossible.

FURTHER READING ABOUT THE PLAY, PLAYWRIGHT, AND CONTEXT

For a history of Japanese classical theatre and drama, see Benito Ortolani, *The Japanese Theatre: From Shamanistic Ritual to Contemporary Pluralism*, and Faubion Bowers, *Japanese Theatre*.

For an examination of Noh, see Kunio Kamparu, *The Noh Theatre: Principles and Perspectives*, and Zeami, *Kadensho*.

For collections of Japanese Noh plays, see Donald Keene, *20 Plays of the Nō Theatre*, and Arthur Waley, *The Nō Plays of Japan*.

Hagoromo

By Zeami

Translated by Arthur Waley

NOTE ON HAGOROMO

The story of the mortal who stole an angel's cloak and so prevented her return to heaven is very widely spread. It exists, with variations and complications, in India, China, Japan, the Liu Chiu Islands and Sweden. The story of Hasan in the *Arabian Nights* is an elaboration of the same theme.

The Nō play is said to have been written by [Z]eami, but a version of it existed long before. The last half consists merely of chants sung to the dancing. Some of these (e.g. the words to the Suruga Dance) have no relevance to the play, which is chiefly a framework or excuse for the dances. It is thus a Nō of the primitive type, and perhaps belongs, at any rate in its conception, to an earlier period than such unified dramas as *Atsumori* or *Kagekiyo*. The words of the dances in *Maiguruma* are just as irrelevant to the play as those of the Suruga Dance in *Hagoromo*, but there the plot explains and even demands their intrusion.

The libretto of the second part lends itself very ill to translation, but I have thought it best to give the play in full.

PERSONS

HAKURYŌ   a fisherman
ANGEL
ANOTHER FISHERMAN
CHORUS

FISHERMAN: Loud the rowers' cry
 Who through the storm-swept paths of
  Mio Bay
 Ride to the rising sea.
HAKURYŌ: I am Hakuryō, a fisherman whose home
 is by the pine-woods of Mio.

BOTH: "On a thousand leagues of lovely hill
  clouds suddenly close;
 But by one tower the bright moon shines in a
  clear sky."[1]
A pleasant season, truly: on the pine-wood
 shore
The countenance of Spring;
Early mist close-clasped to the swell of the
 sea;
In the plains of the sky a dim, loitering moon.
Sweet sight, to gaze enticing
Eyes even of us earth-cumbered
Low souls, least for attaining
Of high beauty nurtured.
Oh unforgettable! By mountain paths
Down to the sea of Kiyomi I come
And on far woodlands look,
Pine-woods of Mio, thither
Come, thither guide we our course.

Fishers, why put you back your boats to
 shore,
No fishing done?
Thought you them rising waves, those
 billowy clouds
Wind-blown across sea?
Wait, for the time is Spring and in the trees
The early wind his everlasting song
Sings low; and in the bay
Silent in morning calm the little ships,
Ships of a thousand fishers, ride the sea.
(*The second* FISHERMAN *retires to a position near the leader of the* CHORUS *and takes no further part in the action.*)

---

1. A Chinese couplet quoted from the *Shih Jēn Yü Hsieh* ("Jade-dust of the Poets"), a Sung Dynasty work on poetry which was popular in Japan.

HAKURYŌ: Now I have landed at the pine-wood of Mio and am viewing the beauty of the shore. Suddenly there is music in the sky, a rain of flowers, unearthly fragrance wafted on all sides. These are no common things; nor is this beautiful cloak that hangs upon the pinetree. I come near to it. It is marvellous in form and fragrance. This surely is no common dress. I will take it back with me and show it to the people of my home. It shall be a treasure in my house.

(*He walks four steps towards the Waki's pillar carrying the feather robe.*)

ANGEL (*entering through the curtain at the end of the gallery*): Stop! That cloak is mine. Where are you going with it?

HAKURYŌ: This is a cloak I found here. I am taking it home.

ANGEL: It is an angel's robe of feathers, a cloak no mortal man may wear. Put it back where you found it.

HAKURYŌ: How? Is the owner of this cloak an angel of the sky? Why, then, I will put it in safe keeping. It shall be a treasure in the land, a marvel to men unborn.[2] I will not give back your cloak.

ANGEL: Oh pitiful! How shall I cloakless tread
The wing-ways of the air, how climb
The sky, my home?
Oh, give it back, in charity give it back.

HAKURYŌ: No charity is in me, and your moan
Makes my heart resolute.
Look, I take your robe, hide it, and will not
give it back.

(*Describing his own actions. Then he walks away.*)

ANGEL: Like a bird without wings,
I would rise, but robeless

HAKURYŌ: To the low earth you sink, an angel dwelling
In the dingy world.

ANGEL: This way, that way.
Despair only.

HAKURYŌ: But when she saw he was resolved to keep it . . .

ANGEL: Strength failing.

HAKURYŌ: Help none . . .

CHORUS: Then on her coronet,
Jewelled as with the dew of tears,
The bright flowers drooped and faded.[3]
O piteous to see before the eyes,
Fivefold the signs of sickness
Corrupt an angel's form.

ANGEL: I look into the plains of heaven,
The cloud-ways are hid in mist,
The path is lost.

CHORUS: Oh, enviable clouds,
At your will wandering
For ever idle in the empty sky
That was my home!
Now fades and fades upon my ear
The voice of Kalavink,[4]
Daily accustomed song.
And you, oh you I envy,
Wild-geese clamorous
Down the sky-paths returning;
And you, O seaward circling, shoreward sweeping
Swift seagulls of the bay:
Even the wind, because in heaven it blows,
The wind of Spring I envy.

HAKURYŌ: Listen. Now that I have seen you in your sorrow, I yield and would give you back your mantle.

ANGEL: Oh, I am happy! Give it me then!

HAKURYŌ: Wait. I have heard tell of the dances that are danced in heaven. Dance for me now, and I will give back your robe.

ANGEL: I am happy, happy. Now I shall have wings and mount the sky again.
And for thanksgiving I bequeath
A dance of remembrance to the world,
Fit for the princes of men:
The dance-tune that makes to turn
The towers of the moon,
I will dance it here and as an heirloom leave
it

---

2. *Masse* here means, I think, "future generations," not "this degraded age."

3. When an angel is about to die, the flowers of his crown wither, his feather robe is stained with dust, sweat pours from under the arm-pits, the eyelids tremble, he is tired of his place in heaven.

4. The sacred bird of heaven.

To the sorrowful men of the world.
Give back my mantle, I cannot dance
    without it.
Say what you will, I must first have back
    the robe.
HAKURYŌ: Not yet, for if I give back your robe, not a
    step would you dance, but fly with it straight
    to the sky.
ANGEL: No, no. Doubt is for mortals;
    In heaven is no deceit.
HAKURYŌ: I am ashamed. Look, I give back the robe.
    (*He gives it to her and she takes it in both hands.*)
ANGEL: The heavenly lady puts on her garment,
    She dances the dance of the Rainbow Skirt, of
    the Robe of Feathers.
HAKURYŌ: The sky-robe flutters; it yields to the
    wind.
ANGEL: Sleeve like a flower wet with rain . . .
HAKURYŌ: The first dance is over.
ANGEL: Shall I dance?
CHORUS: The dance of Suruga, with music of the
    East?
    Thus was it first danced.
    (*The* ANGEL *dances, while the* CHORUS *sings the
    words of the dance, an ancient Shintō chant.*)
    "Why name we
    Wide-stretched and everlasting
    The sky of heaven?
    Two gods[5] there came of old
    And built, upon ten sides shut in,
    A measured world for men;
    But without limit arched they
    The sky above, and named it
    Wide-stretched and everlasting."
ANGEL: Thus is the Moon-God's palace:
    Its walls are fashioned
    With an axe of jade.
CHORUS: In white dress, black dress,
    Thrice ten angels
    In two ranks divided,
    Thrice five for the waning,
    Thrice five for nights of the waxing moon,
    One heavenly lady on each night of the moon
    Does service and fulfils
    Her ritual task assigned.

ANGEL: I too am of their number,
    A moon-lady of heaven.
CHORUS: "Mine is the fruit of the moon-tree,[6] yet
    came I to the East incarnate,[7]
    Dwelt with the people of Earth, and gave
    them
    A gift of music, song-dance of Suruga.

    Now upon earth trail the long mists of
    Spring;
    Who knows but in the valleys of the moon
    The heavenly moon-tree puts her blossom
    on?
    The blossoms of her crown win back their
    glory:
    It is the sign of Spring.
    Not heaven is here, but beauty of the wind
    and sky.
    Blow, blow, you wind, and build
    Cloud-walls across the sky, lest the vision
    leave us
    Of a maid divine!
    This tint of springtime in the woods,
    This colour on the headland,
    Snow on the mountain,[8]
    Moonlight on the clear shore,—
    Which fairest? Nay, each peerless
    At the dawn of a Spring day.
    Waves lapping, wind in the pine-trees
    whispering
    Along the quiet shore. Say you, what cause
    Has Heaven to be estranged
    From us Earth-men; are we not children of
    the Gods,
    Within, without the jewelled temple wall,[9]
    Born where no cloud dares dim the waiting
    moon,
    Land of Sunrise?"
ANGEL: May our Lord's life
    Last long as a great rock rubbed
    Only by the rare trailing

---

5. Izanagi and Izanami.

6. The "Katsura" tree, a kind of laurel supposed to grow in the moon.
7. Lit. "dividing my body," an expression used of Buddhist divinities that detach a portion of their godhead and incarnate it in some visible form.
8. Fuji.
9. The inner and outer temples at Ise.

Of an angel's feather-skirt.[10]
Oh, marvellous music!
The Eastern song joined
To many instruments;
Harp, zither, pan-pipes, flute,
Belly their notes beyond the lonely clouds.
The sunset stained with crimson light
From Mount Sumeru's side;[11]
For green, the islands floating on the sea;
For whiteness whirled
A snow of blossom blasted
By the wild winds, a white cloud
Of sleeves waving.
(*Concluding the dance, she folds her hands and prays.*)

NAMU KIMYŌ GWATTEN-SHI: To thee, O Monarch of
    the Moon,
  Be glory and praise,
  Thou son of Seishi Omnipotent![12]

CHORUS: This is a dance of the East.
  (*She dances three of the five parts of the dance
  called "yo no Mai," the Prelude Dance.*)

ANGEL: I am robed in sky, in the empty blue of
    heaven.

CHORUS: Now she is robed in a garment of mist, of
    Spring mist.

10. Quoting an ancient prayer for the Mikado.
11. Sumeru is the great mountain at the centre of the universe. Its west side is of rubies, its south side of green stones, its east side of white stones, etc.
12. Called in Sanskrit Mahāsthāma-prāpta, third person of the Trinity sitting on Amida's right hand. The Moon-God is an emanation of this deity.

ANGEL: Wonderful in perfume and colour, an
    angel's skirt,—left, right, left, left, right.
  (*Springing from side to side.*)
  The skirt swishes, the flowers nod, the
    feathery sleeves trail out and return, the
    dancing-sleeves.
  (*She dances "Ha no Mai" the Broken Dance.*)

CHORUS: She has danced many dances,
  But not yet are they numbered,
  The dances of the East.
  And now she, whose beauty is as the young
    moon,
  Shines on us in the sky of midnight,
  The fifteenth night,
  With the beam of perfect fulfilment,
  The splendour of Truth.
  The vows[13] are fulfilled, and the land we
    live in
  Rich with the Seven Treasures
  By this dance rained down on us,
  The gift of Heaven.
  But, as the hours pass by,
  Sky-cloak of feathers fluttering, fluttering,
  Over the pine-woods of Mio,
  Past the Floating Islands, through the feet
    of the clouds she flies,
  Over the mountain of Ashitaka, the high
    peak of Fuji,
  Very faint her form,
  Mingled with the mists of heaven;
  Now lost to sight.

13. Of Buddha.

Introduction to *The World and the Child*

WHEN THE PLAY WAS NEW

Dating the medieval morality play *The World and the Child* accurately is difficult, but we can get close. Scholars believe that the anonymous play was written in England between 1508 and 1522. It could have been written a little earlier. The only surviving copy from its period, entitled *A Propre Newe Interlude of The Worlde and the Chylde, Otherwyse Called Mundus et Infans,* was published in 1522. Morality plays were usually called either "moralities" or "moral interludes," and publication of plays at the time was unusual. Most morality plays, like an overwhelming amount of literature from the Middle Ages, were of unknown authorship.

Medieval theatre did not develop from the classical tradition of Greece and Rome, and apparently theatrical practitioners and dramatic writers had no awareness of early Asian drama. Christianity dominated both religion and government in Europe after 500 CE. The religion celebrated in morality plays is in the Catholic tradition; the Protestant Reformation in Germany was only just under way, and the Church of England was not created by King Henry VIII until the 1530s. The earliest surviving forms of dramatic expression in medieval Europe occurred in the Church, which had early on—when still smarting from the dominance of the Roman Empire—attacked theatre, actors, and plays as frivolous and dangerous to the Christian faith. Ironically, the Church itself eventually created plays celebrating scripture and belief by retelling biblical stories and connecting them to medieval life and character. Such works were called *mystery plays.*

Many short mystery plays were sometimes performed together as a cycle—dramatizing significant stories from the creation of the world to the last judgment. Cycles became very popular and remained so in churches and civic community productions until the Protestant Reformation beginning in the sixteenth century. They were finally outlawed in England by the government of Queen Elizabeth I in 1570 and in other European countries as well. This banning was initiated either by Protestants because the plays were Catholic, or by the Catholics themselves as part of their Counter-Reformation. Well after the religious cycles were established, secular plays began to appear and created an audience for popular fare outside religious dramaturgy. The secular plays consisted primarily of farces and lightweight domestic or pastoral comedies. When the morality plays appeared beginning in the 1400s they drew on both traditions: the cycles and the secular plays. The morality plays are religious, but not biblical.

We have no specifics about performances of *The World and the Child,* but we have much information regarding medieval performances and productions of morality plays. This play could have been performed indoors or out, but most likely as an interlude at a feast or other entertainment in the house of aristocracy or nobility. Traveling troupes of performers, sometimes professionalized, may have been employed to perform in a space not necessarily designed for plays—in a banquet room or great hall, or on a raised platform in nearly any large room. No formal or permanent theatres existed in England until the 1570s.

What we know about production methods suggests simple or allegorical costumes and stage properties. For example, the World character would probably dress like a king. An image published with the play in 1522 shows the World (Mundus) sitting enthroned, and looking like a monarch with crown, robe, and scepter. Conscience might dress like a priest or monk. As the Manhood character develops from childhood to old age, the actor might add symbolic touches to the costume to suggest the progressing ages of humanity.

THE PLAYWRIGHT

The author of *The World and the Child* is unknown, but is likely to have been either some kind of cleric or ex-priest, or a literate member of a morality troupe of actors. If not a troupe member, the playwright could have been hired by a theatrical troupe to provide a play appropriate for a small cast. Assuming that the playwright was male (likely, but not certain, given the values of the period), he was clearly a poet, conversant with church doctrine, savvy about theatrical doubling of characters, and very familiar with allegorical substitution.

The ideology of *The World and the Child* is similar to other morality plays; the theatricality is simpler than many. One could compare this play to the popular *Everyman,* which also limits most of its dramatic confrontations to two characters at a time. Structurally, however, *Everyman* is quite different from *The World and the Child:* The action in *Everyman* examines activity only at the end of the protagonist's life, while *The World and the Child* covers his entire life span. In this respect the development is more like the familiar *Castle of Perseverance. Castle,* however, has a very large cast and could not have been performed for an intimate audience as would be the case with *The World and the Child.* All of these plays share the idea of man's fall and redemption through repentance and conversion. Always the mankind character falls in with bad characters who dissuade him from living a life of humility and devotion. The fallen man must be redeemed.

GENRE, STRUCTURE, AND STYLE

Although morality plays do not all share a common structure, a similar organization is apparent in many. The typical morality play develops like a journey. We follow the development of a central character, a male protagonist from youth (even infancy) to old age and death. This character is usually given no name other than Mankind, Manhood, Everyman, or a similar appellation. He is meant to represent all of us. Along his journey (or throughout his life) we see emblematic episodes as he develops, grows older, and encounters many other characters. These other characters may be evil or helpful, but they often persuade him to deviate from the Christian path. The secondary characters are frequently more interesting than the protagonist, and are almost always allegorical in nature. They represent a type, a virtue, or an evil. They might be called Friendship or Good Deeds, Conscience or Folly. Sometimes we see demons, wantonness, greed, and good or bad angels. Manhood carries out conversations and dramatic action with the symbolic characters as if they were real. In *Castle of Perseverance* a band of female virtues battles with an army of devils. The virtues win even though their only weapons in the pitched battle are flowers thrown down from the castle at the invading demons. In *Everyman* the protagonist encounters the character Death, and in *The World and the Child* the protagonist converses with the World as if it were a single character. The symbolic substitutions are often fascinating, but they can still be played in a very human way.

Morality plays are serious but are never tragedies. Tragedies were not created during the Middle Ages—perhaps the always-present spiritual redemption prevented such a form from appearing. Italians began writing tragedies about the same time as *The World and the Child*, but British playwrights adopted the tragic form some forty years later, all inspired by the classical tradition of ancient Greece and Rome. Sometimes the moralities include comic material, but it never dominates. The same is true of the biblical cycle plays, which delivered a serious message but included comic action.

IMPORTANT ELEMENTS OF CONTENT

The morality play is drama with a purpose. The play is meant to teach the audience or remind the audience of moral teachings it may have forgotten. When performed well, these plays can be fascinating and engaging, even though the moral teachings are obvious and not likely to be surprising. The moralities reinforced teachings of the Church without telling biblical stories. They dramatize a belief in a continuum of time, as if nothing important has changed since the birth of Christianity.

Nevertheless, these plays always represent the present moment as well. The road of life is full of temptations and mankind too easily falls into folly or sinfulness. The city is seen as a place where moral downfall is more likely; London, especially, is full of traps and attractive diversions from faith. The image of the urban environment as a corrupting one has been common for a long time. Real social and spiritual problems and concerns of the time are central to most of the morality plays. While the morality play had a serious purpose, it was also meant to entertain. In performance, the antics of characters such as Folly, and frequent comments made directly to the audience, lighten the mood and draw the audience into the world of the play.

The use of allegory and personification would have been familiar to audiences in the Middle Ages. The seven deadly sins that humans must avoid at all costs (pride, envy, anger, avarice, sloth, gluttony, and lust) were often given human form, for example, in literature and fine art. The visual images in the moralities are frequently based on iconography that surrounded the medieval audience member. The stages of life, from infancy to old age, were portrayed in stained glass windows, carvings, and illuminated manuscripts.

THE PLAY IN REVIVAL

Revival of *The World and the Child* has not been as frequent as that of *Everyman*, but it has been produced by various organizations since the second decade of the twentieth century. Nugent Monck staged a series of performances in Great Britain beginning in 1910. The play was produced at the University of Chicago in the late 1960s. The Poculi Ludique Societas of the University of Toronto (a group specializing in performance of medieval drama) included the play in its season and took it on tour in 1978–1979. The PLS performance at Indiana University introduced us to the humor and simple humanity of the play. Regardless of one's personal beliefs, seeing this play in performance sparks the imagination and offers possibilities for how such plays may have been performed in their own time.

SPECIAL FEATURE

Perhaps the most unusual feature of this play is the likelihood that it was intended to be performed by only two actors who doubled throughout. Assuming that one actor played the protagonist in all of his manifestations (Infans, Wanton, Lust-and-Liking, Manhood, and Age) then the second actor would play World, Conscience, Folly, and Perseverance.

FURTHER READING ABOUT THE PLAY, PLAYWRIGHT, AND CONTEXT

To read the play in an unmodernized text, see Clifford Davidson and Peter Happé, *The Worlde and the Chylde*.

To examine the morality dramatic form, see Robert Potter, *The English Morality Play*, and Edgar Schell and J. D. Shuchter, *English Morality Plays and Moral Interludes*.

To read about the larger world of medieval theatre and its context, see Glynne Wickham, *The Medieval Theatre*, and Ronald Vince, *A Companion to the Medieval Theatre*.

To experience some of the variety of medieval plays, see Greg Walker, ed., *Medieval Drama: An Anthology*.

The World and the Child

ANONYMOUS

Note: The editors have modernized the most obscure words for ease of reading.

The Interlude of the World and the Child, otherwise called Mundus et Infans, and it showeth of the estate of Childhood and Manhood.

CHARACTERS

MUNDUS "the World"
The major character on the journey of life, called:
INFANS as a baby
WANTON as a child
LUST-AND-LIKING as a teenager
MANHOOD as an adult; also called "Shame" by Folly
AGE as an old man also called "Repentance" by Perseverance
CONSCIENCE
FOLLY
REPENTANCE

Enter MUNDUS

MUNDUS: Sirs, peace of your babbling, what so befall,
    And look yet bow courteously to my bidding,
    For I am ruler of realms, I warn you all,
    And over all lands I am king;
    For I am king and well known in these realms round.
    I have also palace pitched;
    I have steeds in stable stalwart and strong,
    Also streets and strands full strongly prepared.
    For All-the-World-Wide I know is my name;
    All richess readily it runneth in me,
    All pleasure worldly, both mirth and game.
    Myself, seemly in sale, I send with you to be,
    For I am the world I warn you all.

Prince of power and plenty,
He that cometh not when I do him call,
I shall smite with poverty,
For poverty I part in many a place
To them that will not obedient be.
I am a king in every case,
Methinketh I am a god of grace.
The flower of virtue followeth me,
Lo, here I sit seemly,
I command you all obedient be
And with free will ye follow me.
(*Enter* INFANS)
INFANS: Christ our King grant you clearly to know
        ye case,
    To move of this matter that is in my mind.
    Clearly to declare it Christ grant me grace.
    Now seemly sirs, behold on me
    How Mankind doth begin.
    I am a child, as you may see,
    Gotten in game and in great sin.
    Forty weeks my mother me found,
    Flesh and blood my home.
    When I was ripe from her to found
    In peril of death we stood both two.
    Now to seek death I must begin
    For to pass that strait passage,
    For body and soul that shall then twin
    And make a parting of that marriage.
    Forty weeks I was freely fed
    Within my mother's possession,
    Full oft of death she was adread
    When that I should part her from;
    Now into the world she hath me sent,
    Poor and naked as ye may see.
    I am not worthily wrapt nor fed,
    But poorly pricked in poverty.
    Now into the world I will wend,

Some comfort of him for to crave.
All hail, comely crowned King!
God that all made you see and save!
MUNDUS: Welcome fair child, what is thy name?
INFANS: I know not, sir, withouten blame.
  But offtime my mother in her game
  Called me Dalliance.
MUNDUS: Dalliance, my sweet child,
  It is a name that is right wild,
  For when thou waxest old
  It is a name of no substance.
  But my fair child what wouldst thou have?
INFANS: Sir, of some comfort I you crave,
  Meat and clothes my life to save,
  And I your true servant shall be.
MUNDUS: Now fair child, I grant thee thine asking.
  I will thee find, while thou are young,
  So thou wilt be obedient to my bidding.
  These garments gay I give to thee
  And also I give to thee a name,
  And call thee Wanton, in every game,
  Till fourteen year be come and gone,
  And then come again to me.
WANTON: Gramercy World, for mine array,
  For now I purpose me to play.
MUNDUS: Farewell fair child, and have good day,
  All recklessness is kind for thee.
  (Exit)
WANTON: A ha! Wanton is my name
  I can many a quaint game.
  Lo, my top I drive in same,
  See, it turneth round.
  I can with my scourge-stick
  My fellow upon the head hit,
  And boldy from him make a skip,
  And stick out at him my tongue.
  If brother or sister do me chide
  I will scratch and also bite,
  I can cry and also kick,
  And mock them all anew.
  If father or mother will me smite
  I will wring with my lip
  And lightly from him make a skip
  And call my dame a shrew.
  A ha! A new game I have found.
  See this toy, it runneth round;
  And here another have I found

And yet more can I find.
I can scowl at a man
And tell a falsehood well I can
And maintain it right well then.
This cunning came me of kind.
Yea sirs, I can well geld a snail
And catch a cow by the tail,
This is a fair cunning,
I can dance and also skip,
I can play at the cherry pit
And I can whistle you a fit
Sirs, in a willow rind,
Yea sirs, and every day
When I to school shall take the way,
Some good man's garden I will assay,
Pears and plums to pluck.
I can spy a sparrow's nest,
I will not go to school but when I wish,
For there beginneth a sorry fest
When the master should spank my bottom.
But sirs, when I was seven year of age
I was sent to the World to take wage,
And this seven year I have been his page
And kept his commandment.
Now I will go to the World, that worthy
  Emperor.
Hail, Lord of great honor!
This seven year I have served you in hall and
  in bower
With all my true intent.
MUNDUS: Now welcome, Wanton, my darling
  dear,
  A new Name I shall give thee here,
  Love-Lust-Liking in fact
  These thy names they shall be.
  All game and glee and gladness
  All love-longing in lewdness,
  This seven year forsake all sadness
  And then come again to me.
LUST-AND-LIKING: Ah ha! Now Lust-and-Liking is
  my name,
  I am fresh as flowers in May,
  I am seemly shapen in same
  And proudly appareled in garments gay.
  My locks be full lovely to a lady's eye
  And in love-longing my heart is sore set.
  Might I find a place that were fair and free

To lie in hell till doomsday for love I would
  not let.
My love for to win
All game and glee
All mirth and melody
All revel and riot
And of boast will I never cease.
But sirs, now I am nineteen winters old.
Truly, I wax wonder bold.
Now I will go to the World
A higher science to assay,
For the World will me advance,
I will keep his governance,
His pleasing will I pray,
For he is a king in all substance.
All hail, master full of might!
Now I come as I you command.
One and twenty winter is come and gone.
MUNDUS: Now welcome, Love-Lust-and-Liking,
  For thou hast been obedient to my
    bidding.
  I increase thee in all things
  And mightily I make thee a man.
  Manhood Mighty shall be thy name
  Bear thee staked in every game
  And wait well that thou suffer no shame,
  Neither for land nor for rent.
  If any man would weight thee with blame
  Withstand him with thy whole intent,
  Full sharply thou beat him to shame
  With boldness of deed,
  For of one thing, Manhood, I warn thee,
  I am most of bounty
  For seven kings serve me
  Both by day and night.
  One of them is the King of Pride,
  The King of Envy, mighty in deed,
  The King of Wrath, that boldly will abide,
  For great is his might,
  The King of Covetous is the fourth,
  The fifth King he is called Sloth.
  The King of Gluttony hath no jollity
  If poverty is rife.
  Lechery is the seventh King,
  All men in him have great delighting,
  Therefore worship him above all thing
  Manhood, with all thy might.

MANHOOD: Yes, Sir King, without a doubt
  It shall be wrought.
  Had I known of the first King, without lying,
  Well joyous should I be.
MUNDUS: The first King called Pride.
MANHOOD: Ah Lord, with him fain would I bide.
MUNDUS: Yea, but wouldst thou serve him truly in
  every tide?
MANHOOD: Yea sir, and thereto my truth I plight
  That I shall truly Pride present.
  I swear by Saint Thomas of Kent,
  To serve him truly is mine intent,
  With main and all my might.
MUNDUS: Now Manhood I will array thee new
  In robes royal right of good hue,
  And I pray thee principally be true
  And here I dub thee a knight,
  And haunt away to chivalry.
  I give thee grace and also beauty,
  Gold and silver great plenty,
  Of the wrong to make the right.
MANHOOD: Gramercy World, and Emperor,
  Gramercy World, and Governor,
  Gramercy comfort in all color,
  And now I take my leave. Farewell.
MUNDUS: Farewell Manhood, my gentle knight,
  Farewell my son, seemly in sight,
  I give thee a sword and also strength and
    might
  In battle boldly to bear thee well.
MANHOOD: Now I am dubbed a skillful knight
  Wonder wide shall wax my fame,
  To seek adventures now will I wend,
  To please the World in glee and game.
MUNDUS: Lo sirs, I am a prince proved in battle,
  I proved full perilous and powerful;
  As a lord in each land I am beloved,
  Mine eyes do shine as lantern bright,
  I am a creature comely, out of care,
  Emperors and Kings they kneel to my knee,
  Every man is afeard when I do on him stare,
  For all merry middle-earth maketh mention
    of me,
  Yet all is at my handwork, both by down and
    by dale,
  Both the sea and land and fowls that fly,
  And I were once moved, I tell you in tale,

There durst no star steer that standeth in the
    sky,
For I am lord and leader so that in land
All boweth to my bidding courteously about.
Who that stirreth with any strife or weighteth
    me with wrong
I shall mightily make him to stammer and
    stoop
For I am rich in mine array,
I have knights and towers,
I have ladies, brightest in bowers,
Now will I fare on these flowers,
Lordings, have good day.
(*Exit.*)

MANHOOD: Peace now, peace ye fellows all about,
    Peace now, and hearken to my words,
    For I am lord both stalwart and stout.
    All lands are led by my laws,
    Baron was there never born that so well him
      bore,
    A better nor a bold nor a brighter hue,
    For I have might and main over countries far,
    And Manhood Mighty am I named in every
      country,
    For Salerne and Samers and Ynetheloys,
    Calais, Kent and Cornwall I have conquered
      clean,
    Picardy and Punt and gentle Artois,
    Florence, Flanders and France, also
      Gascoyne,
    All I have conquered as a knight.
    There is no emperor so keen
    That dare to anger me
    For lives and limbs I lean
    So greatness is my right.
    For I have boldly blood full piteously
      de-spilled
    There many hath left fingers and feet, both
      head and face.
    I have done harm on heads and knights have
      I killed
    And many a lady for love hath said "Alas,"
    Brigand Ernys I have beaten to back and to
      bones
    And beaten also many a groom to ground.
    Breastplates I have beaten as
    Saint Stephen was with stones

So fierce a fighter in field was there never
    found.
To me no man is nakèd,
For Manhood Mighty that is my name
Many a lord have I made lame
Wonder wide walketh my fame
And many a King's crown have I cracked.
I am worthy and knowing, witty and wise,
I am royal arrayed to ascend under the rise,
I am proudly appareled in purple and blue,
As gold I glisten in gear,
I am stiff, strong, stalwart and stout,
I am royalest, redely, that runneth in
    this rout.
There is no knight so grisly that I dread
    nor doubt
For I am so bravely arrayed that none may
    hurt me dear,
And the King of Pride full prest with all his
    proud presence,
And the King of Lechery lovely his letters
    hath me sent,
And the King of Wrath full worldly with all
    his intent,
They will me maintain with main and all
    their might.
The King of Covetous and the King of
    Gluttony,
The King of Sloth and the King of Envy,
All those send me their livery.
Where is now so worthy a creature?
A creature?
Yea, as a creature witty
Here in this seat sit I
For no love lets I
Here for to sit.
(*Enter* CONSCIENCE)

CONSCIENCE: Christ, as he is crowned king,
    Save all this comely company
    And grant you all his dear blessing,
    That generously saved you on the cross.
    Now pray you earnestly on every side
    To God omnipotent
    To set our enemy sharply on side,
    That is the devil and his convent,
    And all men to have a clear knowing
    Of heaven bliss, that high tower.

Methinketh it is a necessary thing
For young and old, both rich and poor,
Poor Conscience for to know,
For Conscience Clear it is my name,
Conscience counseleth both high and low,
And Conscience commonly beareth great
    blame—
Blame?—
Yea, and oftentimes set in shame,
Wherefore I govern you men, both in earnest
    and in game,
Conscience that ye know,
For I know all the mysteries of man,
They be as simple as they can,
And in every company where I come
Conscience is outcast.
All the world doth conscience hate
Mankind and Conscience be at debate
For if Mankind might Conscience take
My body would they break.
Break, yea, and work me much woe.

MANHOOD: Say how, fellow, who gave thee leave
    this way to go?
What, think thou I dare not come thee to?
Say, thou harlot, whither in haste?

CONSCIENCE: What, let me go, sir. I know you not.

MANHOOD: No, bitched brothel, thou shalt be
    taught,
For I am a knight, if I were sought.
The World hath advanced me.

CONSCIENCE: Why, good sir knight what is your
    name?

MANHOOD: Manhood Mighty, in mirth and in
    game,
All power of Pride have I taken,
I am as gentle as jay on tree.

CONSCIENCE: Sir, though the World have you to
    manhood brought,
To maintain manners ye were never taught;
No conscience clear ye know, right nought,
And this belongeth to a knight.

MANHOOD: Conscience! What the devil man is he?

CONSCIENCE: Sir, a teacher of spirituality.

MANHOOD: Spirituality? What the devil may that
    be?

CONSCIENCE: Sir, all that be leaders into light—

MANHOOD: Light, yea but hark fellow, yet light
    fain would I see!

CONSCIENCE: Will ye so, sir? Then do after me.

MANHOOD: Yea, if to Pride's pleasing be,
I will take thy teaching.

CONSCIENCE: Nay, sir, beware of Pride and you do
    well,
For Pride, Lucifer fell into hell,
Till doomsday there shall he dwell
Without any outcoming,
For Pride, sir, is but a vainglory.

MANHOOD: Peace, thou brothel, and let those
    words be!
For the World and Pride hath advanced me.
To me men bow full low.

CONSCIENCE: And to beware of Pride, sir, I would
    counsel you,
And think on King Robert of Sicily
How he, for pride, in great poverty fell
For he would not Conscience know.

MANHOOD: Yea, Conscience, go forth thy way,
For I love pride, and will go gay.
All thy teaching is not worth a straw
For Pride I call my king.

CONSCIENCE: Sir, there is no king but God above,
That bodily bought us with pain and passion,
Because of man's soul's redemption,
In Scripture thus we find.

MANHOOD: Say, Conscience, since ye wouldst take
    Pride from me,
What sayest thou against the King of
    Lechery?
With all mankind he must be
And with him I love to linger.

CONSCIENCE: Nay Manhood, that may not be.
From lechery fast you flee,
For encumbrance it will bring thee
And all that to him will fall.

MANDHOOD: Say, Conscience, of the King of Sloth.
He hath promised me good faith,
And I may not forsake him,
For with him I think to rest.

CONSCIENCE: Manhood, in Scripture thus we find,
That Sloth is a traitor to heaven king.
Sir knight, if you will keep your birthright
From Sloth keep you away.

MANHOOD: Say, Conscience, the King of Gluttony,
    He saith he will not forsake me
    And I intend his servant to be
    With main and all my might.
CONSCIENCE: Think, Manhood, on substance,
    And put out gluttony, for encumbrance,
    And keep with you good governance
    For this belongeth to a knight.
MANHOOD: What, Conscience, from all my masters
    ye wouldst have me,
    But I will never forsake Envy
    For he is king of company
    Both with more and less.
CONSCIENCE: Nay Manhood, that may not be.
    If ye will cherish Envy
    God will not well pleased be
    To comfort you in that case.
MANHOOD: Aye, aye! From five kings thou has
    counseled me,
    But from the King of Wrath I will never flee,
    For he is in every deed mighty,
    For him dare no man cast out.
CONSCIENCE: Nay Manhood, beware of Wrath,
    For it is but superfluity that cometh and
    goeth,
    Yea, and all men his company hateth,
    For oft they stand in doubt.
MANHOOD: Fie on thee, false flattering friar!
    Thou shalt rue the time that thou came here.
    The devil might set thee on a fire
    That ever I with thee meet,
    For thou counsellest me from all gladness,
    And would me set unto all sadness,
    Before thou bring me in this madness,
    The devil break thy neck!
    But sir friar, (evil might thou be),
    From six kings thou hast counseled me,
    But that day shall thou never see
    To counsel me from Covetous.
CONSCIENCE: No sir, I will not you from Covetous
    bring,
    For Covetous I call a king
    Sir, Covetous, in good doing
    Is good in all wise;
    But, sir knight, will ye do after me,
    And Covetous your king shall be.

MANHOOD: Yea sir, my truth I plight to thee,
    That I will work at thy will.
CONSCIENCE: Manhood, will ye by this word
    stand?
MANHOOD: Yea Conscience, here is my hand.
    I will never take it away,
    Neither under any circumstance.
CONSCIENCE: Manhood, ye must love God above
    all thing;
    His name in idleness ye may not forget;
    Keep your holyday from worldly doing;
    Your father and mother worship aye,
    Covet ye to slay no man
    Nor do no lechery with no woman;
    Your neighbor's good take not by no way,
    And all false witness ye must deny;
    Neither ye must not covet no man's wife
    Nor no good that him belieth.
    This covetise shall keep you out of strife.
    These be the commandments ten
    Mankind, and ye these commandments keep
    Heaven bliss I promise you.
    For Christ's commandments are full sweet
    And full necessary to all men.
MANDHOOD: What, Conscience, is this thy
    Covetous?
CONSCIENCE: Yea Manhood, in all wise,
    And covet to Christ's service,
    Both to matins and to mass.
    Yet must, Manhood, with all your might
    Maintain Holy Church's right,
    For this belongeth to a knight
    Plainly in every place.
MANHOOD: What, Conscience, should I leave all
    game and glee?
CONSCIENCE: Nay Manhood, I do not so wish thee.
    All mirth in measure is good for thee,
    But sir, measure is in all things.
MANHOOD: Measure, Conscience? What thing may
    measure be?
CONSCIENCE: Sir, keep you in charity
    And from all evil company
    For fear of folly doing.
MANHOOD: Folly? What thing callest thou folly?
CONSCIENCE: Sir, it is Pride, Wrath and Envy,
    Sloth, Covetous and Gluttony,

Lechery the seventh is,
These seven sins I call folly.
MANHOOD: What, thou liest! To this
Seven the World delivered me
And said they were kings of great beauty
And most of might and main.
But yet I pray thee sir, tell me
May I not go arrayed honestly?
CONSCIENCE: Yes Manhood, hardily
In all manner of degree.
MANHOOD: But I must have sporting of play.
CONSCIENCE: Certainly, Manhood, I say not nay,
But good governance keep both night and
day
And maintain meekness and all mercy.
MANHOOD: All mercy, Conscience? What may
that be?
CONSCIENCE: Sir, all discretion that God gave thee.
MANHOOD: Discretion I know not, so more need I
thee.
CONSCIENCE: Sir, it is all the wits that God hath
you sent.
MANHOOD: Ah, Conscience, now I know and see,
Thy cunning is much more than mine,
But yet I pray thee sir, tell me
What is most necessary for man in
every time.
CONSCIENCE: Sir, in every time beware of folly;
Folly is full of false flattering.
In what occupation that ever ye be,
Always, or ye begin to think on the ending.
Now farewell Manhood, I must go.
MANHOOD: Now farewell Conscience, mine own
friend.
CONSCIENCE: I pray you, Manhood, have God in
mind
And beware of folly and shame.
(*Exit.*)
MANHOOD: Yes, yes! Ye come wind and rain,
God let him never come here again!
Now he is gone I am right glad,
For in faith, sir, he had near counseled me all
amiss.
Ah, ah, now I have bethought me if I shall
heaven win
Conscience's teachings I must begin
And clean forsake the kings of sin
That the World me taught,

And Conscience's servant will I be
And believe, as he hath taught me,
Upon one God and Persons three
That made all things from nought;
For Conscience Clear I call my king
And I his knight in good doing
For right of reason, as I find,
Conscience's teaching is true.
The World is full of boast
And saith he is of might most,
All his teaching is not worth a cost,
For Conscience he doth refuse.
But yet will I him not forsake,
For Mankind he doth merry make
Though the World and Conscience be at
debate,
Yet the World will I not despise.
For both in church and at market
And in other places being
The World findeth me all things
And doth me great service.
Now here full prest
I think so to rest,
Now mirth is best.
(*Enter* FOLLY)
FOLLY: What, hey ho! now care, away!
My name is Folly, am I not gay?
Is here any man that will say nay,
That runneth in this route?
Ah sir, God give you good eve.
MANHOOD: Stand, utter fellow, where dost
thou thy courtesy prove?
FOLLY: What, I do but claw mine arse, sir, by your
leave.
I pray you, sir, rend me this cloth.
MANHOOD: What, stand out, thou feigned shrew!
FOLLY: By my faith, sir, there the cock crew,
For I call these people to witness
My good luck is near past.
MANHOOD: Now truly, it may well be so.
FOLLY: By God, Sir, yet have I fellows more,
For in every country where I go
Some man his thrift hath lost.
MANHOOD: But hark, fellow, art thou any
craftsman?
FOLLY: Yea sir, I can bind a sieve and tink a pan,
And thereto a curious buckler player I am.
Arise, fellow! Wilt thou assay?

MANHOOD: Now truly sir, I know thou canst but
little skill play.

FOLLY: Yes, by Cock's bones, that I can!
I will never flee for no man
That walketh by the way.

MANHOOD: Fellow, though thou have cunning
I counsel thee, leave thy boasting,
For here thou may thy fellow find
Whether thou wilt at long sword or short.

FOLLY: Come look if thou darest: arise and assay!

MANHOOD: Yea sir, but yet Conscience biddeth me
nay.

FOLLY: No sir, thou darest not, in good faith,
For truly thou failest now, false heart.

MANHOOD: What, sayest thou I have a false heart?

FOLLY: Yea sir, in good faith.

MANHOOD: Manhood will not that, I say nay!
Defend thee, Folly, if that you may,
For in faith, I purpose to find what thou art.
(*They fight.*)
Now, faith, how now Folly, have I not touched
you?

FOLLY: No, indeed, but a little on my pouch.
On all these people I will me vouch
That standeth here about.

MANHOOD: And I take record on all these people
Thou has two touches, though I say but
few.

FOLLY: Yea, this place is not without a shrew
I yield to thee your due.

MANHOOD: But hark fellow, by thy faith, where
was thou born?

FOLLY: By my faith, in England have I dwelled
yore,
And all mine ancestors me before;
But sir, in London is my chief dwelling.

MANHOOD: In London! Where, if a man thee
sought?

FOLLY: Sir, in Holborn I was forth brought
And with the Courtiers I am betaught.
To Westminster I used to go.

MANHOOD: Hark fellow why dost thou to
Westminster draw?

FOLLY: For I am a servant of the law.
Covetous is mine own fellow,
We twain plead for the king,
And poor men that come from upland
We will take their matter in hand

Be it right or be it wrong
Their wealth shall come our way.

MANHOOD: Now hear, fellow, I pray, whither goest
thou then?

FOLLY: By my faith sir, into London I ran,
To the taverns to drink the wine,
And then to the inns I took the way
And there I was not welcome to the hosteler
But I was welcome to the fair tapster
And to all the household I was right dear,
For I have dwelled with her many a day.

MANHOOD: Now I pray ye, whither took ye then
the way?

FOLLY: In faith sir, over London Bridge I ran
And the straight way to the brothels I came,
And took lodging for a night,
And there I found my brother Lechery
There men and women did folly
And every man made of me as worthy
As though I had been a knight.

MANHOOD: I pray thee, yet tell me more of thine
adventures.

FOLLY: In faith, even straight to all the friars,
And with them I dwelled many years
And they crowned Folly a king.

MANHOOD: I pray thee fellow, whither went thou
then?

FOLLY: Sir, all England to and fro,
Into abbeys and nunneries also,
And always Folly doth fellows find.

MANHOOD: Now hark fellow I pray thee, tell me
thy name.

FOLLY: Certainly, I am called Folly and Shame.

MANHOOD: Ah ha! Thou art he that Conscience
did blame
When he me taught.
I pray thee Folly, go hence and follow me not.

FOLLY: Yes good sir, let me your servant be.

MANHOOD: Nay, so wish I thee,
For then a shrew had I caught.

FOLLY: Why good sir, what is your name?

MANHOOD: Manhood Mighty, that beareth no
blame.

FOLLY: By the cross, and Manhood needeth in
every game
Somewhat to cherish Folly.
For Folly is fellow with the World
And greatly beloved with many a lord,

And if ye put me out of your ward
The World right cross will be.

MANHOOD: Yea sir, yet had I rather the World be
    angry
    Than lose the cunning that Conscience me
    gave.

FOLLY: A cuckoo for Conscience, he is but a crow
    He can not else but preach.

MANHOOD: Yea, I pray thee leave thy lewd
    clattering,
    For Conscience is a counselor for a king.

FOLLY: I would not give a straw for his teaching;
    He doth but make men mad.
    But understand thou what I say man?
    By that ilk truth that God me gave,
    Had I that bitched Conscience in this place
    I should so beat him with my staff
    That all his stones should stink.

MANHOOD: I pray thee Folly, go hence and follow
    me not.

FOLLY: Yes sir, so need I thee
    Your servant will I be,
    I ask but meat and drink.

MANHOOD: Peace man, I may not have thee for thy
    name,
    For thou sayest thy name is both Folly and
    Shame.

FOLLY: Sir, here in this cloth I knit Shame,
    And call me but proper Folly.

MANHOOD: Yea Folly, will thou be my true
    servant?

FOLLY: Yea Sir Manhood, here is my bond.

MANHOOD: Now let us drink at this covenant
    For that is courtesy.

FOLLY: Marry master, ye shall have in haste.
    A ha, sirs, let the cat wink,
    For all ye know not what I think.
    I shall draw him such a draft of drink
    That Conscience he shall away cast.
    Have, master, and drink well,
    And let us make revel, revel,
    For I swear by the Church of Saint Michael
    I would we were at brothels,
    For there is nothing but reveling about.
    If we were there I have no doubt
    I should be known all about
    Where Conscience would refuse.

MANHOOD: Peace, Folly my fair friend
    For, by Christ, I would not that Conscience
    should me here find.

FOLLY: Tush master, thereof speak nothing,
    For Conscience cometh no time here.

MANHOOD: Peace, Folly, there is no man that
    knoweth me.

FOLLY: Sir, here my truth I plight to thee
    An thou wilt go thither with me
    For knowledge have thou no care.

MANHOOD: Peace, but it is hence a great way.

FOLLY: Pardon, sir, we may be there on a day.
    Yea, and we shall be right welcome, I dare
    well say.
    In Eastcheap for to dine,
    And then we will with Lombards at Passage
    play,
    And at the Pope's Head sweet wine assay.
    We shall be lodged well, *à fin.*

MANHOOD: What sayest thou, Folly? Is this the
    best?

FOLLY: Sir, all this is manhood, well thou
    knowest.

MANHOOD: Now Folly, go we hence in haste,
    But fain I would change my name,
    For well I know if Conscience meet me in this
    tide
    Right well I know he would me chide.

FOLLY: Sir, for fear of you his face he shall hide.
    I shall call *you* Shame.

MANHOOD: Now gramercy Folly, my fellow
    companion,
    Go we hence, Tarry no longer here,
    Till we be gone me think it seven year.
    I have gold and good to spend.

FOLLY: Ah ha! Master, that is good cheer,
    And before it be past half a year
    I shall shear thee like a lewd friar
    And higher again thee send.

MANHOOD: Folly, go before and teach me
    the way.

FOLLY: Come after, Shame, I thee pray,
    And Conscience Clear ye cast away.
    Lo, sirs, this Folly teacheth aye,
    For where Conscience cometh with his
    cunning
    Yet Folly full featly shall make him blind;

Folly before and Shame behind,
Lo, sirs, thus fareth the world away.
(*Exit.*)
MANHOOD: Now I will follow Folly, for Folly is
    my man,
Yea, Folly is my fellow and hath given me a
    name.
Conscience called me Manhood, Folly calleth
    me Shame,
Folly will lead me to London to learn revel,
Yea, and Conscience is but a flattering
    brothel,
Forever he is carping of "care."
The World and Folly counselleth me to all
    gladness,
Yea, and Conscience counselleth me to all
    sadness,
Yea, too much sadness might bring me into a
    madness.
And now, have good day sirs, to London to
    seek Folly will I fare.
(*Enter* CONSCIENCE)
CONSCIENCE: Say, Manhood friend, whither will
    ye go?
MANHOOD: Nay sir, in faith, my name is not so.
Why brother, what the devil hast thou to do
Whether I go or abide?
CONSCIENCE: Yes sir, I will counsel you for the
    best.
MANHOOD: I will none of thy counsel, so have I
    rest.
I will go whither me list
For thou canst nought else but chide.
(*Exit.*)
CONSCIENCE: Lo, sirs, a great example you may
    see,
The frailness of mankind
How of the falleth in folly
Through temptation of the Fiend,
For when the Fiend and the flesh be at once
    assent
Then Conscience Clear is clean outcast.
Men think not on the great Judgement
That the silly soul shall have at the last,
But would God all men would have in mind
Of the great Day of Doom
How he shall give a great reckoning

Of evil deeds that he hath done.
But nevertheless, since it is so
That Manhood is forth with Folly gone,
To see Perseverance now will I go.
Perseverance's counsel is most clear,
Next to him is Conscience Clear
From sinning.
Now into his presence to Christ I pray
To speed me well in my journey.
Farewell lordlings, and have good day,
To seek Perseverance will I go.
(*Exit.*)
(*Enter* PERSEVERANCE.)
Now Christ our comely creature clearer than
    crystal clean
That craftily made every creature by good
    re-creation,
Save all this company that is gathered here
    together,
And set all your souls into good salvation.
Now good God, that is most wisest and
    wieldy of wits,
This company counsel, comfort and glad,
And save all this audience that seemly here
    sits,
Now good God for His mercy that all men
    made.
Now Mary, mother meekest that I mean,
Shield all this company from evil's inversion
And save you from our enemy, as She is
    bright and clean
And at the last Day of Doom deliver you
    from everlasting damnation.
Sirs, Perseverance is my name,
Conscience's born brother is;
He sent me hither mankind to indoctrinate
That they should to no vices incline,
For oft mankind is governed amiss
And through folly mankind is set in shame.
Therefore in this presence to Christ I pray
Before I hence go away
Some good word that I may say
To borrow man's soul from blame.
(*Enter* MANHOOD *as* AGE)
AGE: Alas, alas, that me is woe!
My life, my liking I have forlorn,
My rents, my riches, it is all gone,

Alas the day that I was born,
For I was born Manhood most of might
Stiff, strong, both stalwart and stout.
The World full worthily hath made me a
    knight,
All bowed to my bidding courteously about
Then Conscience Clear comely and kind
Meekly he met me in seat there I sat,
He learned me a lesson of his teaching,
And the seven deadly sins full loathly he did
    hate.
Pride, Wrath and Envy, and Covetous in
    kind.
The World all these sins delivered me until,
Sloth, Covetous and Lechery that is full of
    false flattering,
All these Conscience reproved both loud and
    still.
To Conscience I held up my hand
To keep Christ's commandments
He warned me of Folly, that traitor, and bade
    me beware,
And thus he went his way.
But I have falsely me foresworn,
Alas the day that I was born,
For body and soul I have forlorn!
I clung as a clod in clay
In London many a day
At the Passage I would play;
I thought to borrow and never pay.
Then was I sought and set in stocks,
In Newgate I lay under locks,
If I said aught I caught many knocks.
Alas, where was Manhood though?
Alas, my lewdness hath me lost.
Where is my body, so proud and prest?
I cough and rough, my body will break,
Age doth follow me so
I stare and stagger as I stand,
I groan grisly upon the ground,
Alas, death, why lettest thou me live so long?
I wander as a creature in woe
And care
For I have done ill
Now go I will
Myself to spill,
I care no whither or where.

PERSEVERANCE: Well met sir, well met, and whither
    away?
AGE: Why, good sir, whereby do ye say?
PERSEVERANCE: Tell me, sir, I you pray
    And I with you will go.
AGE: Why, good sir, what is your name?
PERSEVERANCE: Forsooth sir, Perseverance, the
    same.
AGE: Sir, ye are Conscience's brother that did me
    blame,
    I may not with you linger.
PERSEVERANCE: Yes, yes Manhood, my friend in
    company.
AGE: Nay sir, my name is in another manner,
    For Folly his own self was here
    And hath called me Shame.
PERSEVERANCE: Shame?
    Nay Manhood, let him go,
    Folly and his fellows also,
    For they would thee bring into care
        and woe,
    And all that will follow his game.
AGE: Yea, game who so game
    Folly hath given me a name
    So wherever I go
    He calleth me Shame.
    Now Manhood is gone
    Folly hath followed me so.
    When I first from my mother came
    The World made me a man
    And fast in riches I ran
    Till I was dubbed a knight,
    And then I met with Conscience Clear,
    And he me set in such manner
    Methought his teaching was full dear
    Both by day and night.
    And then Folly met me
    And sharply he beset me
    And from Conscience he fetched me,
    He would not from me go.
    Many a day he kept me
    And to all folks he called me
    Shame,
    And unto all sins he set me
    Alas, that me is woe!
    For I have falsely me forsworn,
    Alas that I was born,

Body and soul I am forlorn,
Me liketh neither glee not game.
PERSEVERANCE: Nay, nay Manhood, say not so,
Beware of Despair, for he is a foe.
A new name I shall give you to,
I call you Repentance,
For, if you here repent your sin
Ye are possible heaven to win,
But with great contrition ye must begin,
And take you to abstinence,
For though a man had done alone
The deadly sins every one,
If he with contrition make his moan
To Christ our heaven king,
God is also glad of him
As of the creature that never did sin.
AGE: Now good sir, how should I contrition
begin?
PERSEVERANCE: Sir, confess aloud, without varying
And another example I shall you show to:
Think on Peter and Paul, and others,
Thomas, James and John also
And also Mary Magdalen,
For Paul did Christ's people great villainy,
And Peter at the Passion forsook Christ
thrice,
And Magdalen lived long in lechery
And Saint Thomas believed not in the
resurrection,
And yet these to Christ are darlings dear,
And now be saints in heaven clear,
And therefore, though ye have trespassed
here
I hope ye be sorry for your sin.
AGE: Yea Perseverance, I you plight,
I am sorry for my sin both day and night,
I would fain learn with all my might
How I should heaven win.
PERSEVERANCE: So to win heaven five necessary
things there be
That must be known to all mankind.
The five wits doth begin
Sir, bodily and spiritually.
AGE: Of the five wits I would have knowing.
PERSEVERANCE: Forsooth sir, hearing, seeing, and
smelling,
The remnant tasting and feeling,

These be the five wits bodily,
And sir, other five wits there be.
AGE: Sir Perseverance I know not them.
PERSEVERANCE: Now Repentance I shall you ken.
They are the powers of the soul:
Clear-in-mind there is one,
Imagination, and all reason,
Understanding and compassion,
These belong unto Perseverance.
AGE: Gramercy Perseverance, for your true
teaching,
But good sir, is there any more behind
That is necessary to all mankind
Freely for to know?
PERSEVERANCE: Yea Repentance, more there be
That every man must on believe.
The twelve Articles of the Faith
That Mankind must know:
The first that God is one substance,
And also that God is in three persons,
Beginning and ending without variance,
And all this world made, of nought;
The second that the Son of God truly
Took flesh and blood of the Virgin Mary
Without touching of men's flesh company,
This must be in every man's thought;
The third, that that same God's Son
Born of that holy Virgin
And after His birth, maiden as She
was before
And clearer in all kind;
Also the fourth, that same Christ, God
and Man,
He suffered pain and passion
Because of man's soul's redemption,
And on a Cross did hang;
The fifth Article I shall you tell—
Then the spirit of Godhead went to hell
And brought out the souls that there
did dwell
By the power of his own might;
The sixth Article I shall you say,
Christ rose upon the third day,
Very God and Man, without a nay,
That all shall deem and ordain.
He sent man's soul into heaven
Aloft all the angels every one,

There is the Father, the Son and that truthful
    Holy Ghost.
The eighth Article we must believe on:
That same God shall come down
And deem men's souls at the Day of Doom,
And on mercy then must we trust.
The ninth Article, without strife,
Every man, maiden and wife
And all the bodies that ever bore life
At the Day of Doom body and soul prepare.
Truly the tenth Article is:
All they that hath kept God's service
They shall be crowned in heaven bliss
As Christ's servants, to him full dear.
The eleventh Article, the truth to say:
All that hath testified falsely to God,
They shall be put into hell pain
There shall be no sin covering.
Sir, after the twelfth we must work,
And believe in all the sacraments of Holy
    Church,
That they be necessary to both last and first,
To all manner of mankind.
Sir, ye must also hear and know the
    commandments ten.

Lo, sir, this is your belief and all men's,
Do after it, and ye shall heaven win
Without doubt I know.

AGE: Gramercy Perseverance, for your true
    teaching,
For in the spirit of my soul well I find
That it is necessary to all mankind
Truly for to know.
Now sirs, take all example by me,
How I was born in simple degree,
The World royal received me
And dubbed me knight,
Then Conscience met me,
So after him came Folly;
Folly falsely deceived me,
Then Shame my name became.

PERSEVERANCE: Yea, and now is your name
    Repentance
Through the grace of God almight,
And therefore without any distance
I take my leave of king and knight
And I pray to Jesus which has made us all
Cover you with his mantle perpetual. Amen.

HERE ENDETH THE INTERLUDE OF MUNDUS ET INFANS.

Introduction to *Romeo and Juliet*

WHEN THE PLAY WAS NEW

Most Shakespearean scholars agree that *Romeo and Juliet* was written between 1594 and 1596. The play definitely appeared on the Elizabethan stage in the 1590s, and has remained an important play in revival ever since. Even when many of Shakespeare's plays of fantasy, such as *A Midsummer Night's Dream*, went out of fashion between 1660 and 1800, *Romeo and Juliet* continued to thrive on the professional stage, although it was done at that time in severely adapted form. The popular film *Shakespeare in Love* offers a fanciful and fictional, though not historically accurate, depiction of the creation of *Romeo and Juliet*.

The play was probably first produced by William Shakespeare's theatre company, the Lord Chamberlain's Men, who would later occupy the famous Globe Theatre and eventually become the King's Men with royal patronage. The company was headed by its leading actor Richard Burbage, who played many of the title roles in Shakespeare's famous tragedies such as *Hamlet* and *King Lear*. Like many plays of the Elizabethan era (1558–1603), *Romeo and Juliet* had a story that Shakespeare received from others. He of course altered and modified the story and created beautiful language for it, but the story was already literary. Shakespeare certainly knew a version first published in 1562 that Arthur Brooke had translated into English from Italian.

Elizabethan society was fascinated with Italian stories and many English plays are set in Italy, just as *Romeo and Juliet* purports to take place in Verona. The geographical shift was also convenient in the volatile times of Queen Elizabeth and King James and King Charles who followed her. During the reign of all three monarchs (up to 1642 when the theatres were closed due to a Puritan revolution) the theatre was very popular and a frequent scene of political and domestic violence and decadence. By frequently setting the action in Italy instead of England, the playwrights could often fend off possible censorship and avoid offending the crown or other powerful people.

The period of Elizabeth was a British Renaissance that was ripe with the arts—especially theatre and poetry—and was something of a golden age for theatre, despite the fact that London was a turbulent and a dangerous place, especially at night. Violence looms large in *Romeo and Juliet*, not only with its sword fights and family feuding, but also with raging language that is a remarkable contrast for the lyrical beauty found in the love affair and language of the two unfortunate lovers who are the protagonists of the play. In this respect, Shakespeare reveals the influence of Roman tragedy as written by Seneca, which gloried in violent acts, depictions of horror, and themes of revenge.

The public theatre of the time where *Romeo and Juliet* was performed was an open, thrust stage with the audience wrapped around three sides of the raised performance space. Upstage of (behind) the stage was a façade with probably two doors and perhaps a central discovery space. Most importantly for this play, the stage had an upper level for split-level performances and the all-important balcony scene. The company probably used little or no scenery since the scenes shifted quickly and were usually defined by language that told the audience the time of day and where the action was taking place. All action was performed in the daytime by the light of the sun. All of the actors were male, and the role of Juliet was taken by a boy. As was true of Greek and Roman society, women in England were not allowed to perform in public. This law would change in 1660, some forty-four years after the death of Shakespeare.

THE PLAYWRIGHT

William Shakespeare (1564–1616) was an actor and dramatist in London early in the 1590s, and he was soon popular as a playwright and made a good living as a member of the professional company in which he held shares. He was later a "householder"—meaning he held part ownership of the Globe Theatre, where most of his plays were performed. *Romeo and Juliet* was an early work and probably his second tragedy after *Titus Andronicus*. Perhaps the single most important fact concerning Shakespeare's artistry is that he was the only playwright of his period who wrote masterpieces in every genre of his time: tragedy, comedy, tragicomedy, and chronicle (history play), as well as the many variations of these types such as romantic tragedy (*Romeo and Juliet*), historical tragedy (*Richard II*), revenge tragedy (*Hamlet*), romantic comedy (*Much Ado About Nothing)*, pastoral (*As You Like It*), and fantasy (*The Tempest*). Lovers of Shakespeare's works often point to *Hamlet* as the peak of his creativity, but one could make a case for many of his plays. Most of Shakespeare's rival playwrights—such as Christopher Marlowe, who created the tragedy *Doctor Faustus,* or Ben Jonson, who wrote the satirical comedy *Volpone*—were lucky to master *one* genre, although they may have written in many. It is no wonder that sometimes people refer to the Elizabethan period as the Shakespearean period. No other playwright enjoys such a distinction.

GENRE, STRUCTURE, AND STYLE

Elizabethan tragedy can be chiefly distinguished from Greek tragedy by its preoccupation with onstage violence, its romantic language (the Greek is very stoic by comparison), and its meandering structure with multiple plot lines, side-issue excursions, and early point of attack. This last feature means that the plot is likely to develop over many days (as in *Romeo and Juliet*), months (*Henry V*), even years: there is a twenty-year gap in the midst of *The Winter's Tale*. The result is an exciting episodic structure in which comic and tragic action combine to produce a mixed tone. A clown can appear in the middle of intense murder as we see in *Macbeth*. In *Romeo and Juliet* the character of Mercutio offers comic and sarcastic language and antics, but he also suffers a painful death. The nurse provides both comic language and humorous

stage business. Although many cultures following the age of Shakespeare avoided such a mixed tone and graphic presentation of violence, it came roaring back to prominence in the nineteenth century, and has remained popular in the theatre and film ever since.

The juxtaposition of private and public scenes that we saw in *Antigone* is here expanded and accelerated. Shakespeare often veers back and forth, and *Romeo and Juliet* is no exception. The very private scenes of the two lovers when they meet at the Capulet party, on the balcony, and later after marriage by Friar Laurence are buttressed by very public brawls, killings, reveling in the streets, and so on. Furthermore, the private scenes are usually interrupted, calling our attention to the danger inherent in the clandestine meetings of the protagonists: Juliet is called from the balcony by her nurse; the household is awakening as Romeo must flee from the bed of Juliet. Throughout the play the mood and basic action changes suddenly, without warning. The result is something of a roller coaster ride. The play's structure imitates the rashness and impetuosity of youth.

Most Elizabethan playwrights, including Shakespeare, wrote their plays in blank verse (unrhymed iambic pentameter). They combined this verse form with rhyming couplets and prose. Such variety in language not only contributed to the mixed tone of the plays, but also aided in the distinction of character, mood, and emotional intensity of a scene. In most of Shakespeare's plays the blank verse serves as a kind of home base to which the playwright will always return. In *Romeo and Juliet* some 70 percent of the lines are blank verse with the remainder being split about evenly between rhyming couplets and prose.[1]

IMPORTANT ELEMENTS OF CONTENT

An all-important feature of *Romeo and Juliet* is the use of misfortune. Right away in the prologue we are told that the protagonists are star-crossed lovers. We suspect that all will not turn out well. The lovers are caught up in a long-standing family

1. Sylvan Barnett, *The Complete Signet Classic Shakespeare* (New York: Harcourt Brace Jovanovich, 1972), p. 20.

feud. Its intensity is demonstrated immediately in the first scene of the play, but its source is never explained. The lack of explanation underscores the absurdity and inflexibility of the senseless hatred. In modern productions, the feud often inspires theatre artists to incorporate racial, ethnic, and religious bigotry along with the family enmity.

The tragedy in the play seems inevitable; the lovers are trapped in their situation. Even if Friar Lawrence's note had reached Romeo in time to avoid disaster, the lovers still could not have lived together happily. The families are so imbued with hatred that reaching an understanding without undergoing some awful carnage and human loss is impossible. In Shakespeare's plays, the fall of the protagonists is hard and usually fatal. The consequences of a character's actions are not only irreversible, but complete. Romeo and Juliet ultimately find themselves alone (even isolated from one another) and the results are catastrophic.

THE PLAY IN REVIVAL

Since its appearance, *Romeo and Juliet* has rarely been out of the professional and amateur repertory, but was often presented in modified form, especially in the eighteenth century. In the mid-eighteenth century, the famous British star actor David Garrick added a scene in the tomb in which both lovers were alive at the same time. A number of variations on this additional shot of pathos have occurred throughout the twentieth century. It seems that each generation has tried to capture the attention of young theatre or filmgoers with an updated version focusing on sexuality, racial conflict, industrial pacing, or the drug culture. These adaptations have often proved successful and brought a new generation to the language and story-telling of Shakespeare. In 1957, Leonard Bernstein and his collaborators adapted *Romeo and Juliet* as the musical *West Side Story,* adding racial conflict to the mix of the play. Many versions of the play are available on film and video, and we continue to see new stage versions every year. Most recently, we saw a streamlined production performed in about nine-ty minutes and using a handful of actors doubling in multiple roles at the Indiana Repertory Theatre in Indianapolis. Although generously cut, this version was very true to Shakespeare's language and effectively stressed the vigor and impetuosity of the young characters.

SPECIAL FEATURE

Perhaps the most distinguishing feature of *Romeo and Juliet* is its famous balcony scene. It stands as an effective symbol of the separation of the protagonists: through much of the scene they are kept apart vertically while yearning to touch. The scene was created to exploit the possibilities of the Elizabethan public theatre, but it also serves the play magnificently. It must be one of the most enduring romantic images in all of the theatre. When one sees an image of *Romeo and Juliet* from nearly any period, it is usually of the balcony scene and, regardless of period style, the play is instantly recognized.

FURTHER READING ABOUT THE PLAY, PLAYWRIGHT, AND CONTEXT

For examinations of Shakespeare's tragedy, and *Romeo and Juliet* in particular, see Harley Granville-Barker, *Prefaces to Shakespeare,* and John Russell Brown, *Shakespeare: The Tragedies.*

For details on Elizabethan theatre, see Glynne Wickham, Herbert Berry, and William Ingram, *English Professional Theatre, 1530–1660,* and Gerald E. Bentley, *The Profession of Player in Shakespeare's Time.*

For cultural study of audiences and values of the period, see Andrew Gurr, *Playgoing in Shakespeare's London.*

For details on playhouses of the period, see Andrew Gurr, *The Shakespearean Stage, 1574–1642.*

For a history of *Romeo and Juliet* in production, see James N. Loehlin, *Romeo and Juliet,* in the Cambridge "Shakespeare in Production" series.

Romeo and Juliet

BY WILLIAM SHAKESPEARE

DRAMATIS PERSONAE

CHORUS

ESCALUS   Prince of Verona.

PARIS   Kinsman of the Prince.

MONTAGUE

CAPULET

AN OLD MAN   of Capulet Family.

ROMEO   Son to Montague.

MERCUTIO   Kinsman to the Prince, Friend to Romeo.

BENVOLIO   Nephew to Montague, Friend to Romeo.

TYBALT   Nephew to Lady Capulet.

FRIAR LAWRENCE   a Franciscan.

FRIAR JOHN   a Franciscan.

BALTHASAR   Servant to Romeo.

SAMPSON   Servant to Capulet.

GREGORY   Servant to Capulet.

PETER   Servant to Juliet's Nurse.

ABRAM   Servant to Montague.

APOTHECARY

THREE MUSICIANS

OFFICER

LADY MONTAGUE   Wife to Montague.

LADY CAPULET   Wife to Capulet.

JULIET   Daughter to Capulet.

NURSE   to Juliet.

CITIZENS OF VERONA, GENTLEMEN AND GENTLEWOMEN, MASKERS, TORCHBEARERS, PAGES, GUARDS, WATCHMEN, SERVANTS, AND ATTENDANTS.

Set in Verona and Mantua in Italy.

THE PROLOGUE

Enter CHORUS.

CHORUS: Two households, both alike in dignity,
In fair Verona, where we lay our scene,
From ancient grudge break to new mutiny,
Where civil blood makes civil hands unclean.
From forth the fatal loins of these two foes
A pair of star-cross'd lovers take their life;
Whose misadventur'd piteous overthrows
Doth with their death bury their parents' strife.
The fearful passage of their death-mark'd love,
And the continuance of their parents' rage,
Which but their children's end naught could remove,
Is now the two hours' traffic of our stage;
The which, if you with patient ears attend,
What here shall miss, our toil shall strive to mend.
(CHORUS *Exit.*)

ACT I

SCENE I   VERONA. A PUBLIC PLACE.

Enter SAMPSON *and* GREGORY *armed with swords and bucklers of the House of Capulet.*

SAMPSON: Gregory, on my word, we'll not carry coals.

GREGORY: No, for then we should be colliers.

SAMPSON: I mean, and we be in choler we'll draw.

GREGORY: Ay, while you live, draw your neck out of collar.

SAMPSON: I strike quickly, being moved.

GREGORY: But thou art not quickly moved to strike.

SAMPSON: A dog of the house of Montague moves me.

GREGORY: To move is to stir; and to be valiant is to stand:
therefore, if thou art moved, thou runn'st away.

SAMPSON: A dog of that house shall move me to stand:

I will take the wall[1] of any man or maid of
    Montague's.
GREGORY: That shows thee a weak slave; for the
    weakest goes to the wall.
SAMPSON: 'Tis True; and therefore women, being
    the weaker vessels, are ever thrust to the wall:
    therefore I will push Montague's men from
    the wall and thrust his maids to the wall.
GREGORY: The quarrel is between our masters and
    us their men.
SAMPSON: 'Tis all one, I will show myself a tyrant:
    when I have fought with the men I will be
    civil with the maids, I will cut off their heads.
GREGORY: The heads of the maids?
SAMPSON: Ay, the heads of the maids, or their
    maidenheads; take it in what sense thou wilt.
GREGORY: They must take it in sense that feel it.
SAMPSON: Me they shall feel while I am able to
    stand;
    And 'tis known I am a pretty piece of flesh.
GREGORY: 'Tis well thou art not fish; if thou hadst,
    thou hadst been Poor John.[2] Draw thy tool!
    Here comes two of the house of Montagues.
    (*Enter* ABRAM *and* BALTHASAR)
SAMPSON: My naked weapon is out: quarrel! I will
    back thee.
GREGORY: How! turn thy back and run?
SAMPSON: Fear me not.
GREGORY: No, marry; I fear thee!
SAMPSON: Let us take the law of our sides; let
    them begin.
GREGORY: I will frown as I pass by; and let them
    take it as they list.
SAMPSON: Nay, as they dare. I will bite my thumb
    at them; which is disgrace to them if they
    bear it.
ABRAM: Do you bite your thumb at us, sir?
SAMPSON: I do bite my thumb, sir.
ABRAM: Do you bite your thumb at us, sir?
SAMPSON: (*Aside*) Is the law of our side if I say ay?
GREGORY: No.
SAMPSON: No, sir, I do not bite my thumb at you,
    sir; but I bite my thumb, sir.

1. To take the wall is to take the safer, cleaner position on
the sidewalk when passing others.
2. Poor man's food.

GREGORY: Do you quarrel, sir?
ABRAM: Quarrel, sir! no, sir.
SAMPSON: But if you do, sir, I am for you: I serve
    as good a man as you.
ABRAM: No better.
SAMPSON: Well, sir.
GREGORY: Say better; here comes one of my
    master's kinsmen.
    (*Enter* BENVOLIO)
SAMPSON: Yes, better, sir.
ABRAM: You lie.
SAMPSON: Draw, if you be men.—Gregory remem-
    ber thy swashing blow.
    (*They fight*)
BENVOLIO: Part, fools! put up your swords; you
    know not what you do.
    (BENVOLIO *draws. Enter* TYBALT)
TYBALT: What, art thou drawn among these heart-
    less hinds?
    Turn thee Benvolio, look upon thy death.
BENVOLIO: I do but keep the peace: put up thy
    sword,
    Or manage it to part these men with me.
TYBALT: What, drawn, and talk of peace! I hate the
    word
    As I hate hell, all Montagues, and thee:
    Have at thee, coward!
    (*They fight*)
    (*Enter an* OFFICER *and others with clubs*)
OFFICER: Clubs, bills, and partisans! strike! beat
    them down!
    Down with the Capulets! Down with the
    Montagues!
    (*Enter* CAPULET *in his gown, and* LADY CAPULET)
CAPULET: What noise is this?—Give me my long
    sword, ho!
LADY CAPULET: A crutch, a crutch!—Why call you
    for a sword?
CAPULET: My sword, I say!—Old Montague is come,
    And flourishes his blade in spite of me.
    (*Enter* MONTAGUE *and* LADY MONTAGUE)
MONTAGUE: Thou villain Capulet!—Hold me not,
    let me go.
LADY MONTAGUE: Thou shalt not stir one foot to
    seek a foe.
    (*Enter* PRINCE ESCALUS *with attendants*)
PRINCE: Rebellious subjects, enemies to peace,

Profaners of this neighbour-stained steel,—
Will they not hear?—What, ho! you men, you
    beasts,
That quench the fire of your pernicious rage
With purple fountains issuing from your
    veins,—
On pain of torture, from those bloody hands
Throw your mistemper'd weapons to the
    ground
And hear the sentence of your moved prince.—
Three civil brawls, bred of an airy word,
By thee, old Capulet, and Montague,
Have thrice disturb'd the quiet of our streets;
And made Verona's ancient citizens
Cast by their grave beseeming ornaments,
To wield old partisans, in hands as old,
Canker'd with peace, to part your canker'd
    hate:
If ever you disturb our streets again,
Your lives shall pay the forfeit of the peace.
For this time, all the rest depart away:—
You, Capulet, shall go along with me;—
And, Montague, come you this afternoon,
To know our farther pleasure in this case,
To old Free-town, our common judgment-
    place.—
Once more, on pain of death, all men depart.
    (*Exeunt all but* MONTAGUE, LADY MONTAGUE *and*
    BENVOLIO)
MONTAGUE: Who set this ancient quarrel new
    abroach?—
    Speak, nephew, were you by when it began?
BENVOLIO: Here were the servants of your
    adversary
    And yours, close fighting ere I did approach:
    I drew to part them: in the instant came
    The fiery Tybalt, with his sword prepar'd;
    Which, as he breath'd defiance to my ears,
    He swung about his head, and cut the winds,
    Who, nothing hurt withal, hiss'd him in scorn:
    While we were interchanging thrusts and
        blows,
    Came more and more, and fought on part and
        part,
    Till the prince came, who parted either part.
LADY MONTAGUE: O, where is Romeo?—saw you
    him to-day?—
    Right glad I am he was not at this fray.

BENVOLIO: Madam, an hour before the worshipp'd
    sun
    Peer'd forth the golden window of the east,
    A troubled mind drave me to walk abroad;
    Where,—underneath the grove of sycamore
    That westward rooteth from the city's side,—
    So early walking did I see your son.
    Towards him I made; but he was ware of me,
    And stole into the covert of the wood:
    I, measuring his affections by my own,—
    Pursu'd my humour, not pursuing his,
    And gladly shunn'd who gladly fled from me.
MONTAGUE: Many a morning hath he there been
    seen,
    With tears augmenting the fresh morning's dew,
    Adding to clouds more clouds with his deep
        sighs:
    But all so soon as the all-cheering sun
    Should in the farthest east begin to draw
    The shady curtains from Aurora's bed,
    Away from light steals home my heavy son,
    And private in his chamber pens himself;
    Shuts up his windows, locks fair daylight out
    And makes himself an artificial night:
    Black and portentous must this humour prove,
    Unless good counsel may the cause remove.
BENVOLIO: My noble uncle, do you know the cause?
MONTAGUE: I neither know it nor can learn of him.
BENVOLIO: Have you importun'd him by any
    means?
MONTAGUE: Both by myself and many other friends;
    But he, his own affections' counsellor,
    Is to himself,—I will not say how true,—
    But to himself so secret and so close,
    So far from sounding and discovery,
    As is the bud bit with an envious worm
    Ere he can spread his sweet leaves to the air,
    Or dedicate his beauty to the sun.
    Could we but learn from whence his sorrows
        grow,
    We would as willingly give cure as know.
BENVOLIO: See, where he comes: so please you
    step aside;
    I'll know his grievance or be much denied.
    (*Enter* ROMEO)
MONTAGUE: I would thou wert so happy by thy stay
    To hear true shrift.—Come, madam, let's away,
    (*Exit* MONTAGUE *and* LADY MONTAGUE)

BENVOLIO: Good morrow, cousin.

ROMEO: Is the day so young?

BENVOLIO: But new struck nine.

ROMEO: Ay me! sad hours seem long.
  Was that my father that went hence so fast?

BENVOLIO: It was.—What sadness lengthens
      Romeo's hours?

ROMEO: Not having that which, having, makes
    them short.

BENVOLIO: In love?

ROMEO: Out,—

BENVOLIO: Of love?

ROMEO: Out of her favour where I am in love.

BENVOLIO: Alas, that love, so gentle in his view,
  Should be so tyrannous and rough in proof!

ROMEO: Alas that love, whose view is muffled still,
    Should, without eyes, see pathways to his will!—
    Where shall we dine?—O me!—What fray was
      here?
    Yet tell me not, for I have heard it all.
    Here's much to do with hate, but more with
      love:—
    Why, then, O brawling love! O loving hate!
    O anything, of nothing first create!
    O heavy lightness! serious vanity!
    Mis-shapen chaos of well-seeming forms!
    Feather of lead, bright smoke, cold fire, sick
      health!
    Still-waking sleep, that is not what it is!—
    This love feel I, that feel no love in this.
    Dost thou not laugh?

BENVOLIO: No, coz, I rather weep.

ROMEO: Good heart, at what?

BENVOLIO: At thy good heart's oppression.

ROMEO: Why, such is love's transgression.—
    Griefs of mine own lie heavy in my breast;
    Which thou wilt propagate, to have it prest
    With more of thine: this love that thou hast
      shown
    Doth add more grief to too much of mine own.
    Love is a smoke made with the fume of sighs;
    Being purg'd, a fire sparkling in lovers' eyes;
    Being vex'd, a sea nourish'd with lovers' tears:
    What is it else? a madness most discreet,
    A choking gall, and a preserving sweet.—
    Farewell, my coz.

BENVOLIO: Soft! I will go along:
  And if you leave me so, you do me wrong.

ROMEO: Tut! I have lost myself; I am not here:
  This is not Romeo, he's some other where.

BENVOLIO: Tell me in sadness who is that you love?

ROMEO: What, shall I groan and tell thee?

BENVOLIO: Groan! why, no;
  But sadly tell me who.

ROMEO: Bid a sick man in sadness make his will,—
  Ah, word ill urg'd to one that is so ill!—
  In sadness, cousin, I do love a woman.

BENVOLIO: I aim'd so near when I suppos'd you
    lov'd.

ROMEO: A right good markman!—And she's fair
    I love.

BENVOLIO: A right fair mark, fair coz, is soonest hit.

ROMEO: Well, in that hit you miss: she'll not be hit
    With Cupid's arrow,—she hath Dian's wit;
    And, in strong proof of chastity well arm'd,
    From love's weak childish bow she lives
      uncharm'd.
    She will not stay the siege of loving terms
    Nor bide th' encounter of assailing eyes,
    Nor ope her lap to saint-seducing gold:
    O, she's rich in beauty; only poor
    That, when she dies, with beauty dies her store.

BENVOLIO: Then she hath sworn that she will still
    live chaste?

ROMEO: She hath, and in that sparing makes huge
    waste;
    For beauty, starv'd with her severity,
    Cuts beauty off from all posterity.
    She is too fair, too wise; wisely too fair,
    To merit bliss by making me despair:
    She hath forsworn to love; and in that vow
    Do I live dead that live to tell it now.

BENVOLIO: Be rul'd by me, forget to think of her.

ROMEO: O, teach me how I should forget to think.

BENVOLIO: By giving liberty unto thine eyes;
  Examine other beauties.

ROMEO: 'Tis the way
    To call hers, exquisite, in question more:
    These happy masks that kiss fair ladies' brows,
    Being black, puts us in mind they hide the fair;
    He that is strucken blind cannot forget
    The precious treasure of his eyesight lost:
    Show me a mistress that is passing fair,
    What doth her beauty serve but as a note
    Where I may read who pass'd that passing fair?
    Farewell: thou canst not teach me to forget.

BENVOLIO: I'll pay that doctrine, or else die in debt.
(*Exeunt*)

SCENE II   A STREET.
Enter CAPULET, PARIS, *and* SERVANT

CAPULET: But Montague is bound as well as I,
  In penalty alike; and 'tis not hard, I think,
  For men so old as we to keep the peace.
PARIS: Of honourable reckoning are you both;
  And pity 'tis you liv'd at odds so long.
  But now, my lord, what say you to my suit?
CAPULET: But saying o'er what I have said before:
  My child is yet a stranger in the world,
  She hath not seen the change of fourteen years;
  Let two more summers wither in their pride
  Ere we may think her ripe to be a bride.
PARIS: Younger than she are happy mothers made.
CAPULET: And too soon marr'd are those so early
    made.
  The earth hath swallowed all my hopes but
    she,—
  She is the hopeful lady of my earth:
  But woo her, gentle Paris, get her heart,
  My will to her consent is but a part;
  An she agreed, within her scope of choice
  Lies my consent and fair according voice.
  This night I hold an old accustom'd feast,
  Whereto I have invited many a guest,
  Such as I love; and you among the store,
  One more, most welcome, makes my number
    more.
  At my poor house look to behold this night
  Earth-treading stars that make dark heaven
    light:
  Such comfort as do lusty young men feel
  When well apparell'd April on the heel
  Of limping winter treads, even such delight
  Among fresh female buds shall you this night
  Inherit at my house; hear all, all see,
  And like her most whose merit most shall be:
  Which, among view of many, mine, being one,
  May stand in number, though in reckoning none.
  Come, go with me.—Go, sirrah, trudge about
  Through fair Verona; find those persons out

Whose names are written there, and to them say,
My house and welcome on their pleasure stay.
  (*Exeunt* PARIS *and* CAPULET)
SERVANT: Find them out whose names are written
  here! It is written that the shoemaker should
  meddle with his yard and the tailor with his
  last, the fisher with his pencil, and the painter
  with his nets; but I am sent to find those
  persons whose names are here writ, and can
  never find what names the writing person
  hath here writ. I must to the learned:—in
  good time!
  (*Enter* BENVOLIO *and* ROMEO)
BENVOLIO: Tut, man, one fire burns out another's
    burning,
  One pain is lessen'd by another's anguish;
  Turn giddy, and be holp by backward turning;
  One desperate grief cures with another's
    languish:
  Take thou some new infection to thy eye,
  And the rank poison of the old will die.
ROMEO: Your plantain-leaf is excellent for that.
BENVOLIO: For what, I pray thee?
ROMEO: For your broken shin.
BENVOLIO: Why, Romeo, art thou mad?
ROMEO: Not mad, but bound more than a mad-
    man is;
  Shut up in prison, kept without my food,
  Whipp'd and tormented and—God-den, good
    fellow.
SERVANT: God gi' go-den.—I pray, sir, can you read?
ROMEO: Ay, mine own fortune in my misery.
SERVANT: Perhaps you have learned it without
    book:
  but I pray, can you read anything you see?
ROMEO: Ay, If I know the letters and the language.
SERVANT: Ye say honestly: rest you merry!
ROMEO: Stay, fellow; I can read. (*Reads*)
  "Signior Martino and his wife and daughters;
    County Anselmo and his beauteous sisters;
    the lady widow of Vitruvio; Signior Placen-
    tio and his lovely nieces; Mercutio and his
    brother Valentine; mine uncle Capulet, his
    wife, and daughters; my fair niece Rosaline;
    Livia; Signior Valentio and his cousin Tybalt;
    Lucio and the lively Helena."
  A fair assembly. Whither should they come?

SERVANT: Up.

ROMEO: Whither? To supper?

SERVANT: To our house.

ROMEO: Whose house?

SERVANT: My master's.

ROMEO: Indeed I should have ask'd you that
before.

SERVANT: Now I'll tell you without asking: my
master is the great rich Capulet; and if you be
not of the house of Montagues, I pray, come
and crush a cup of wine. Rest you merry!
(*Exit*)

BENVOLIO: At this same ancient feast of Capulet's
Sups the fair Rosaline whom thou so lov'st;
With all the admired beauties of Verona.
Go thither; and, with unattainted eye,
Compare her face with some that I shall show,
And I will make thee think thy swan a crow.

ROMEO: When the devout religion of mine eye
Maintains such falsehood, then turn tears to
fires;
And these,—who, often drown'd, could never
die,—
Transparent heretics, be burnt for liars!
One fairer than my love? the all-seeing sun
Ne'er saw her match since first the world
begun.

BENVOLIO: Tut, you saw her fair, none else being
by,
Herself pois'd with herself in either eye:
But in that crystal scales let there be weigh'd
Your lady's love against some other maid
That I will show you shining at this feast,
And she shall scant show well that now seems
best.

ROMEO: I'll go along, no such sight to be shown,
But to rejoice in splendour of mine own.
(*Exeunt*)

SCENE III   ROOM IN CAPULET'S HOUSE.

Enter LADY CAPULET *and* NURSE

LADY CAPULET: Nurse, where's my daughter? call
her forth to me.

NURSE: Now, by my maidenhead,—at twelve year
old,—

I bade her come.—What, lamb! what lady-
bird!—
God forbid!—where's this girl?—what, Juliet!
(*Enter* JULIET)

JULIET: How now, who calls?

NURSE: Your mother.

JULIET: Madam, I am here. What is your will?

LADY CAPULET: This is the matter,—Nurse, give
leave awhile,
We must talk in secret: nurse, come back again;
I have remember'd me, thou's hear our
counsel.
Thou knowest my daughter's of a pretty age.

NURSE: Faith, I can tell her age unto an hour.

LADY CAPULET: She's not fourteen.

NURSE: I'll lay fourteen of my teeth,—
And yet, to my teen be it spoken, I have but
four,—
She is not fourteen. How long is it now
To Lammas-tide?

LADY CAPULET: A fortnight and odd days.

NURSE: Even or odd, of all days in the year,
Come Lammas-eve at night shall she be
fourteen.
Susan and she,—God rest all Christian souls!—
Were of an age: well, Susan is with God;
She was too good for me:—but, as I said,
On Lammas-eve at night shall she be fourteen;
That shall she, marry; I remember it well.
'Tis since the earthquake now eleven years;
And she was wean'd,—I never shall forget it—,
Of all the days of the year, upon that day:
For I had then laid wormwood to my dug,
Sitting in the sun under the dove-house wall;
My lord and you were then at Mantua:
Nay, I do bear a brain:—but, as I said,
When it did taste the wormwood on the nipple
Of my dug and felt it bitter, pretty fool,
To see it tetchy, and fall out with the dug!
Shake, quoth the dove-house: 'twas no need,
I trow,
To bid me trudge.
And since that time it is eleven years;
For then she could stand alone; nay, by the rood
She could have run and waddled all about;
For even the day before, she broke her brow:
And then my husband,—God be with his soul!

'A was a merry man,—took up the child:
"Yea," quoth he, "dost thou fall upon thy face?
Thou wilt fall backward when thou hast
    more wit;
Wilt thou not, Jule?" and, by my holidame,
The pretty wretch left crying, and said "Ay."
To see now how a jest shall come about!
I warrant, an I should live a thousand yeas,
I never should forget it; "Wilt thou not, Jule?"
    quoth he;
And, pretty fool, it stinted, and said "Ay."

LADY CAPULET: Enough of this; I pray thee hold
    thy peace.

NURSE: Yes, madam;—yet I cannot choose but
    laugh,
To think it should leave crying, and say "Ay."
And yet, I warrant, it had upon its brow
A bump as big as a young cockerel's stone;
A parlous knock; and it cried bitterly.
"Yea," quoth my husband, "fall'st upon thy face?
Thou wilt fall backward when thou com'st to
    age;
Wilt thou not, Jule?" it stinted, and said "Ay."

JULIET: And stint thou too, I pray thee, nurse, say I.

NURSE: Peace, I have done. God mark thee to his
    grace!
Thou wast the prettiest babe that e'er I nurs'd:
An I might live to see thee married once, I have
    my wish.

LADY CAPULET: Marry, that marry is the very
    theme
I came to talk of.—Tell me, daughter Juliet,
How stands your disposition to be married?

JULIET: It is an honour that I dream not of.

NURSE: An honour!—were not I thine only nurse,
I would say thou hadst suck'd wisdom from
    thy teat.

LADY CAPULET: Well, think of marriage now:
    younger than you,
Here in Verona, ladies of esteem,
Are made already mothers: by my count
I was your mother much upon these years
That you are now a maid. Thus, then, in brief;—
The valiant Paris seeks you for his love.

NURSE: A man, young lady! lady, such a man
As all the world—why he's a man of wax.[3]

3. Man of good physical form.

LADY CAPULET: Verona's summer hath not such a
    flower.

NURSE: Nay, he's a flower, in faith, a very flower.

LADY CAPULET: What say you? can you love the
    gentleman?
This night you shall behold him at our feast;
Read o'er the volume of young Paris' face,
And find delight writ there with beauty's pen;
Examine every married lineament,
And see how one another lends content;
And what obscur'd in this fair volume lies
Find written in the margent of his eyes.
This precious book of love, this unbound lover,
To beautify him, only lacks a cover:
The fish lives in the sea; and 'tis much pride
For fair without the fair within to hide:
That book in many's eyes doth share the glory,
That in gold clasps locks in the golden story;
So shall you share all that he doth possess,
By having him, making yourself no less.

NURSE: No less! nay, bigger; women grow by men

LADY CAPULET: Speak briefly, can you like of Paris'
    love?

JULIET: I'll look to like, if looking liking move:
But no more deep will I endart mine eye
Than your consent gives strength to make it fly.
    (*Enter* SERVANT)

SERVANT: Madam, the guests are come, supper
    served up, you called, my young lady asked
    for, the nurse cursed in the pantry, and ev-
    erything in extremity. I must hence to wait; I
    beseech you, follow straight.
    (*Exit*)

LADY CAPULET: We follow thee.
Juliet the county stays.

NURSE: Go, girl, seek happy nights to happy days.
    (*Exeunt*)

SCENE IV   A STREET.

Enter ROMEO, MERCUTIO, BENVOLIO, MASKERS, TORCH-
BEARERS

ROMEO: What, shall this speech be spoke for our
    excuse?
Or shall we on without apology?

BENVOLIO: The date is out of such prolixity:
We'll have no Cupid hoodwink'd with a scarf,

Bearing a Tartar's painted bow of lath,
Scaring the ladies like a crow-keeper;
Nor no without-book prologue, faintly spoke
After the prompter, for our entrance:
But, let them measure us by what they will,
We'll measure them a measure, and be gone.

ROMEO: Give me a torch,—I am not for this
   ambling;
Being but heavy, I will bear the light.

MERCUTIO: Nay, gentle Romeo, we must have you
   dance.

ROMEO: Not I, believe me: you have dancing
   shoes,
With nimble soles; I have a soul of lead
So stakes me to the ground I cannot move.

MERCUTIO: You are a lover; borrow Cupid's
   wings,
And soar with them above a common bound.

ROMEO: I am too sore enpierced with his shaft
To soar with his light feathers; and so bound,
I cannot bound a pitch above dull woe:
Under love's heavy burden do I sink.

MERCUTIO: And, to sink in it, should you burden
   love;
Too great oppression for a tender thing.

ROMEO: Is love a tender thing? it is too rough,
Too rude, too boisterous; and it pricks like
   thorn.

MERCUTIO: If love be rough with you, be rough
   with love;
Prick love for pricking, and you beat love
   down.—
Give me a case to put my visage in:
A visor for a visor! what care I
What curious eye doth quote deformities?
Here are the beetle-brows shall blush for me.

BENVOLIO: Come, knock and enter; and no sooner in
But every man betake him to his legs.

ROMEO: A torch for me: let wantons, light of heart,
Tickle the senseless rushes with their heels;
For I am proverb'd with a grandsire phrase,—
I'll be a candle-holder and look on,—
The game was ne'er so fair, and I am done.

MERCUTIO: Tut, dun's the mouse, the constable's
   own word:
If thou art Dun, we'll draw thee from the mire
Of this—sir-reverence—love, wherein thou
   stick'st

Up to the ears.[4]—Come, we burn daylight, ho.

ROMEO: Nay, that's not so.

MERCUTIO: I mean, sir, in delay
We waste our lights in vain, like lamps by day.
Take our good meaning, for our judgment sits
Five times in that ere once in our five wits.

ROMEO: And we mean well, in going to this mask;
But 'tis no wit to go.

MERCUTIO: Why, may one ask?

ROMEO: I dreamt a dream to-night.

MERCUTIO: And so did I.

ROMEO: Well, what was yours?

MERCUTIO: That dreamers often lie.

ROMEO: In bed asleep, while they do dream things
true.

MERCUTIO: O, then, I see Queen Mab hath been
with you.[5]
She is the fairies' midwife; and she comes
In shape no bigger than an agate-stone
On the fore-finger of an alderman,
Drawn with a team of little atomies
Over men's noses as they lie asleep:
Her waggon-spokes made of long spinners'
   legs;
The cover, of the wings of grasshoppers;
The traces, of the smallest spider's web;
The collars, of the moonshine's watery beams;
Her whip, of cricket's bone; the lash, of film;
Her waggoner, a small grey-coated gnat,
Not half so big as a round little worm
Prick'd from the lazy finger of a maid:
Her chariot is an empty hazel-nut,
Made by the joiner squirrel or old grub,
Time out o' mind the fairies' coachmakers.
And in this state she gallops night by night
Through lovers' brains, and then they dream of
   love;
O'er courtiers' knees, that dream on court'sies
   straight;
O'er lawyers' fingers, who straight dream on
   fees;
O'er ladies' lips, who straight on kisses
   dream,—
Which oft the angry Mab with blisters plagues,

4. A game using a horse or substitute.
5. With Queen Mab, a Celtic fairy Queen, Mercutio rambles
bizarre images until he gets out of control.

Because their breaths with sweetmeats tainted
  are:
Sometime she gallops o'er a courtier's nose,
And then dreams he of smelling out a suit;
And sometime comes she with a tithe-pig's
  tail,
Tickling a parson's nose as 'a lies asleep,
Then dreams he of another benefice:
Sometime she driveth o'er a soldier's neck,
And then dreams he of cutting foreign throats,
Of breaches, ambuscadoes, Spanish blades,
Of healths five fathom deep; and then anon
Drums in his ear, at which he starts and wakes;
And, being thus frighted, swears a prayer or
  two,
And sleeps again. This is that very Mab
That plats the manes of horses in the night;
And bakes the elf-locks in foul sluttish hairs,
Which, once untangled, much misfortune
  bodes:
This is the hag, when maids lie on their backs,
That presses them, and learns them first to bear,
Making them women of good carriage:
This is she,—

ROMEO: Peace, peace, Mercutio, peace,
  Thou talk'st of nothing.

MERCUTIO: True, I talk of dreams,
  Which are the children of an idle brain,
  Begot of nothing but vain fantasy;
  Which is as thin of substance as the air,
  And more inconstant than the wind, who
    wooes
  Even now the frozen bosom of the north,
  And, being anger'd, puffs away from thence,
  Turning his side to the dew-dropping south.

BENVOLIO: This wind you talk of blows us from
  ourselves:
  Supper is done, and we shall come too late.

ROMEO: I fear, too early: for my mind misgives
  Some consequence, yet hanging in the stars,
  Shall bitterly begin his fearful date
  With this night's revels; and expire the term
  Of a despised life, clos'd in my breast,
  By some vile forfeit of untimely death:
  But He that hath the steerage of my course
  Direct my sail!—On, lusty gentlemen!

BENVOLIO: Strike, drum.
    (*They march about the stage and exeunt*)

SCENE V   A HALL IN CAPULET'S HOUSE.

Enter SERVANTS

FIRST SERVANT: Where's Potpan, that he helps not
  to take away? he shift a trencher![6] he scrape a
  trencher!

SECOND SERVANT: When good manners shall lie
  all in one or two men's hands, and they
  unwash'd too, 'tis a foul thing.

FIRST SERVANT: Away with the join-stools, remove
  the court-cupboard, look to the plate:—good
  thou, save me a piece of marchpane;[7] and as
  thou loves me, let the porter let in Susan
  Grindstone and Nell, Antony! and Potpan!

SECOND SERVANT: Ay, boy, ready.

FIRST SERVANT: You are looked for and called for,
  asked for and sought for in the great chamber.

SECOND SERVANT: We cannot be here and there
  too.—Cheerly, boys; be brisk awhile, and the
  longer liver take all.
  (*Exeunt*)
  (*Enter* CAPULET, LADY CAPULET, JULIET, TYBALT,
  NURSE, *and all the guests and gentlewomen with
  the* MASKERS)

CAPULET: Welcome, gentlemen! ladies that have
  their toes
  Unplagu'd with corns will have a bout with
    you.—
  Ah ha, my mistresses! which of you all
  Will now deny to dance? she that makes dainty,
    she,
  I'll swear hath corns; am I come near you now?
  Welcome, gentlemen! I have seen the day
  That I have worn a visor; and could tell
  A whispering tale in a fair lady's ear,
  Such as would please;—'tis gone, 'tis gone, 'tis
    gone:
  You are welcome, gentlemen!—Come, musi-
    cians, play.
  A hall—a hall! give room! and foot it, girls.—
    (*Music plays. They dance*)
  More light, you knaves; and turn the tables up,
  And quench the fire, the room is grown too
    hot.—
  Ah, sirrah, this unlook'd-for sport comes well.

---

6. Trencher is a wooden plate.
7. Marzipan.

Nay, sit, nay, sit, good cousin Capulet;
For you and I are past our dancing days;
How long is't now since last yourself and I
Were in a mask?

SECOND CAPULET: By'r Lady, thirty years.

CAPULET: What, man! 'tis not so much, 'tis not so
    much:
'Tis since the nuptial of Lucentio,
Come Pentecost as quickly as it will,
Some five-and-twenty years; and then we
    mask'd.

SECOND CAPULET: 'Tis more, 'tis more: his son is
    elder, sir;
His son is thirty.

CAPULET: Will you tell me that?
His son was but a ward two years ago.

ROMEO: What lady is that, which doth enrich the
    hand
Of yonder knight?

SERVANT: I know not, sir.

ROMEO: O, she doth teach the torches to burn
    bright!
It seems she hangs upon the cheek of night
Like a rich jewel in an Ethiop's ear;
Beauty too rich for use, for earth too dear!
So shows a snowy dove trooping with crows
As yonder lady o'er her fellows shows.
The measure done, I'll watch her place of stand
And, touching hers, make blessed my rude
    hand.
Did my heart love till now? forswear it, sight!
For I ne'er saw true beauty till this night.

TYBALT: This, by his voice, should be a
    Montague.—
Fetch me my rapier, boy:—what, dares the
    slave
Come hither, cover'd with an antic face,
To fleer and scorn at our solemnity?
Now, by the stock and honour of my kin,
To strike him dead I hold it not a sin.

CAPULET: Why, how now, kinsman! wherefore
    storm you so?

TYBALT: Uncle, this is a Montague, our foe;
A villain, that is hither come in spite,
To scorn at our solemnity this night.

CAPULET: Young Romeo, is it?

TYBALT: 'Tis he, that villain, Romeo.

CAPULET: Content thee, gentle coz, let him alone,

'A bears him like a portly gentleman;
And, to say truth, Verona brags of him
To be a virtuous and well-govern'd youth:
I would not for the wealth of all the town
Here in my house do him disparagement:
Therefore be patient, take no note of him,—
It is my will; the which if thou respect,
Show a fair presence and put off these frowns,
An ill-beseeming semblance for a feast.

TYBALT: It fits, when such a villain is a guest:
I'll not endure him.

CAPULET: He shall be endur'd:
What, goodman boy!—I say he shall;—go to;
Am I the master here, or you? go to.
You'll not endure him!—God shall mend my
    soul,
You'll make a mutiny among my guests!
You will set cock-a-hoop! you'll be the man!

TYBALT: Why, uncle, 'tis a shame.

CAPULET: Go to, go to!
You are a saucy boy. Is't so, indeed?—
This trick may chance to scathe you,—I know
    what:
You must contrary me! marry, 'tis time.—
Well said, my hearts!—You are a princox;[8] go:
Be quiet, or—More light, more light!—For
    shame!
I'll make you quiet. What!—cheerly, my hearts.

TYBALT: Patience perforce with wilful choler
    meeting
Makes my flesh tremble in their different
    greeting.
I will withdraw: but this intrusion shall,
Now seeming sweet, convert to bitter gall.
    (*Exit*)

ROMEO (*To* JULIET.): If I profane with my unworthi-
    est hand
This holy shrine, the gentle fine is this,—
My lips, two blushing pilgrims, ready stand
To smooth that rough touch with a tender kiss.

JULIET: Good pilgrim, you do wrong your hand
    too much,
Which mannerly devotion shows in this;
For saints have hands that pilgrims' hands do
    touch,
And palm to palm is holy palmers' kiss.

---

8. Young arrogant upstart.

ROMEO: Have not saints lips, and holy palmers
too?

JULIET: Ay, pilgrim, lips that they must use in prayer.

ROMEO: O, then, dear saint, let lips do what hands
do;

They pray, grant thou, lest faith turn to despair.

JULIET: Saints do not move, though grant for
prayers' sake.

ROMEO: Then move not while my prayer's effect
I take.

Thus from my lips, by thine my sin is purg'd.
(*Kisses her*)

JULIET: Then have my lips the sin that they have
took.

ROMEO: Sin from my lips? O trespass sweetly urg'd!
Give me my sin again.

JULIET: You kiss by the book.

NURSE: Madam, your mother craves a word with
you.

ROMEO: What is her mother?

NURSE: Marry, bachelor,

Her mother is the lady of the house.

And a good lady, and a wise and virtuous:

I nurs'd her daughter that you talk'd withal;

I tell you, he that can lay hold of her

Shall have the chinks.[9]

ROMEO: Is she a Capulet?

O dear account! my life is my foe's debt.

BENVOLIO: Away, be gone; the sport is at the best.

ROMEO: Ay, so I fear; the more is my unrest.

CAPULET: Nay, gentlemen, prepare not to be gone;

We have a trifling foolish banquet towards.—

Is it e'en so? why then, I thank you all;

I thank you, honest gentlemen; good-night.—

More torches here!—Come on then, let's to bed.

Ah, sirrah, by my fay, it waxes late;

I'll to my rest.

(*Exeunt all but* JULIET *and* NURSE)

JULIET: Come hither, nurse. What is yond
gentleman?

NURSE: The son and heir of old Tiberio.

JULIET: What's he that now is going out of door?

NURSE: Marry, that, I think, be young Petruchio.

JULIET: What's he that follows there, that would
not dance?

NURSE: I know not.

9. Lots of money.

JULIET: Go ask his name: if he be married,
My grave is like to be my wedding-bed.

NURSE: His name is Romeo, and a Montague;
The only son of your great enemy.

JULIET: My only love sprung from my only hate!
Too early seen unknown, and known too late!
Prodigious birth of love it is to me,
That I must love a loathed enemy.

NURSE: What's this? What's this?

JULIET: A rhyme I learn'd even now
Of one I danc'd withal.
(*One calls within,* "*Juliet.*")

NURSE: Anon, anon!
Come, let's away; the strangers all are gone.
(*Exeunt*)

ACT II

Enter CHORUS

CHORUS: Now old desire doth in his deathbed lie,
And young affection gapes to be his heir;
That fair for which love groan'd for, and would
die,
With tender Juliet match'd, is now not fair.
Now Romeo is belov'd, and loves again,
Alike bewitched by the charm of looks;
But to his foe suppos'd he must complain,
And she steal love's sweet bait from fearful
hooks:
Being held a foe, he may not have access
To breathe such vows as lovers us'd to swear;
And she as much in love, her means much less
To meet her new beloved anywhere:
But passion lends them power, time means, to
meet,
Tempering extremities with extreme sweet.
(*Exit*)

SCENE I   AN OPEN PLACE ADJOINING CAPULET'S GARDEN.

Enter ROMEO

ROMEO: Can I go forward when my heart is here?
Turn back, dull earth, and find thy centre out.
(*Enter* BENVOLIO *and* MERCUTIO)

BENVOLIO: Romeo! my cousin Romeo!

MERCUTIO: He is wise;
  And, on my life, hath stol'n him home to bed.
BENVOLIO: He ran this way, and leap'd this or-
    chard wall:
  Call, good Mercutio.
MERCUTIO: Nay, I'll conjure too.—
  Romeo! humours! madman! passion! lover!
  Appear thou in the likeness of a sigh:
  Speak but one rhyme, and I am satisfied;
  Cry but "Ah me!" pronounce but Love and
    dove;
  Speak to my gossip Venus one fair word,
  One nickname for her purblind son and heir,
  Young Abraham Cupid, he that shot so trim
  When King Cophetua lov'd the beggar-maid!—
  He heareth not, he stirreth not, he moveth not;
  The ape is dead, and I must conjure him.—
  I conjure thee by Rosaline's bright eyes,
  By her high forehead and her scarlet lip,
  By her fine foot, straight leg, and quivering
    thigh,
  And the demesnes[10] that there adjacent lie,
  That in thy likeness thou appear to us!
BENVOLIO: An if he hear thee, thou wilt anger
    him.
MERCUTIO: This cannot anger him: 'twould anger
    him
  To raise a spirit in his mistress' circle,
  Of some strange nature, letting it there stand
  Till she had laid it, and conjur'd it down;
  That were some spite: my invocation
  Is fair and honest, and, in his mistress' name,
  I conjure only but to raise up him.
BENVOLIO: Come, he hath hid himself among
    these trees,
  To be consorted with the humorous night:
  Blind is his love, and best befits the dark.
MERCUTIO: If love be blind, love cannot hit the
    mark.
  Now will he sit under a medlar tree,
  And wish his mistress were that kind of fruit
  As maids call medlars when they laugh
    alone.—
  Romeo, good night.—I'll to my truckle-bed;
  This field-bed is too cold for me to sleep:
  Come, shall we go?

BENVOLIO: Go then; for 'tis in vain
  To seek him here that means not to be found.
    (*Exeunt*)

SCENE II   CAPULET'S GARDEN.
Enter ROMEO

ROMEO: He jests at scars that never felt a wound.—
    (JULIET *appears above at a window*)
  But soft! what light through yonder window
    breaks?
  It is the east, and Juliet is the sun!—
  Arise, fair sun, and kill the envious moon,
  Who is already sick and pale with grief,
  That thou her maid art far more fair than she:
  Be not her maid, since she is envious;
  Her vestal livery is but sick and green,
  And none but fools do wear it; cast it off.—
  It is my lady; O, it is my love!
  O, that she knew she were!—
  She speaks, yet she says nothing: what of that?
  Her eye discourses, I will answer it.—
  I am too bold, 'tis not to me she speaks:
  Two of the fairest stars in all the heaven,
  Having some business, do entreat her eyes
  To twinkle in their spheres till they return.
  What if her eyes were there, they in her head?
  The brightness of her cheek would shame those
    stars,
  As daylight doth a lamp; her eyes in heaven
  Would through the airy region stream so bright
  That birds would sing and think it were not
    night.—
  See how she leans her cheek upon her hand!
  O that I were a glove upon that hand,
  That I might touch that cheek!
JULIET: Ah me!
ROMEO: She speaks:—
  O, speak again, bright angel! for thou art
  As glorious to this night, being o'er my head,
  As is a winged messenger of heaven
  Unto the white-upturned wondering eyes
  Of mortals that fall back to gaze on him
  When he bestrides the lazy-puffing clouds
  And sails upon the bosom of the air.
JULIET: O Romeo, Romeo! wherefore art thou
    Romeo?
  Deny thy father and refuse thy name;

10. Domains.

Or, if thou wilt not, be but sworn my love,
And I'll no longer be a Capulet.

ROMEO (*Aside*): Shall I hear more, or shall I speak
    at this?

JULIET: 'Tis but thy name that is my enemy;—
    Thou art thyself, though not a Montague.
    What's Montague? It is nor hand, nor foot,
    Nor arm, nor face, nor any other part
    Belonging to a man. O, be some other name!
    What's in a name? that which we call a rose
    By any other name would smell as sweet;
    So Romeo would, were he not Romeo call'd,
    Retain that dear perfection which he owes
    Without that title:—Romeo, doff thy name;
    And for that name, which is no part of thee,
    Take all myself.

ROMEO: I take thee at thy word:
    Call me but love, and I'll be new baptiz'd;
    Henceforth I never will be Romeo.

JULIET: What man art thou that, thus bescreen'd in
    night,
    So stumblest on my counsel?

ROMEO: By a name
    I know not how to tell thee who I am:
    My name, dear saint, is hateful to myself,
    Because it is an enemy to thee.
    Had I it written, I would tear the word.

JULIET: My ears have yet not drunk a hundred
    words
    Of that tongue's utterance, yet I know the
    sound;
    Art thou not Romeo, and a Montague?

ROMEO: Neither, fair saint, if either thee dislike.

JULIET: How cam'st thou hither, tell me, and
    wherefore?
    The orchard walls are high and hard to climb;
    And the place death, considering who thou art,
    If any of my kinsmen find thee here.

ROMEO: With love's light wings did I o'erperch
    these walls;
    For stony limits cannot hold love out:
    And what love can do, that dares love attempt;
    Therefore thy kinsmen are no stop to me.

JULIET: If they do see thee, they will murder thee.

ROMEO: Alack, there lies more peril in thine eye
    Than twenty of their swords: look thou but
    sweet,
    And I am proof against their enmity.

JULIET: I would not for the world they saw thee
    here.

ROMEO: I have night's cloak to hide me from their
    sight;
    And, but thou love me, let them find me here.
    My life were better ended by their hate
    Than death prorogued,[11] wanting of thy love.

JULIET: By whose direction found'st thou out this
    place?

ROMEO: By love, that first did prompt me to
    enquire;
    He lent me counsel, and I lent him eyes.
    I am no pilot; yet, wert thou as far
    As that vast shore wash'd with the furthest sea,
    I would adventure for such merchandise.

JULIET: Thou knowest the mask of night is on my
    face;
    Else would a maiden blush bepaint my cheek
    For that which thou hast heard me speak to-
    night.
    Fain would I dwell on form, fain, fain deny
    What I have spoke; but farewell compliment!
    Dost thou love me, I know thou wilt say Ay;
    And I will take thy word: yet, if thou swear'st,
    Thou mayst prove false; at lovers' perjuries,
    They say Jove laughs. O gentle Romeo,
    If thou dost love, pronounce it faithfully:
    Or if thou thinkest I am too quickly won,
    I'll frown, and be perverse, and say thee nay,
    So thou wilt woo: but else, not for the world.
    In truth, fair Montague, I am too fond;
    And therefore thou mayst think my 'haviour
    light:
    But trust me, gentleman, I'll prove more true
    Than those that have more cunning to be
    strange.
    I should have been more strange, I must con-
    fess,
    But that thou overheard'st, ere I was 'ware,
    My true-love passion: therefore pardon me;
    And not impute this yielding to light love,
    Which the dark night hath so discovered.

ROMEO: Lady, by yonder blessed moon I swear,
    That tips with silver all these fruit-tree tops,—

JULIET: O, swear not by the moon, the inconstant
    moon,

11. Delayed.

That monthly changes in her circled orb,
Lest that thy love prove likewise variable.
ROMEO: What shall I swear by?
JULIET: Do not swear at all;
Or if thou wilt, swear by thy gracious self,
Which is the god of my idolatry,
And I'll believe thee.
ROMEO: If my heart's dear love,—
JULIET: Well, do not swear: although I joy in thee,
I have no joy of this contract to-night;
It is too rash, too unadvis'd, too sudden;
Too like the lightning, which doth cease to be
Ere one can say It lightens. Sweet, good night!
This bud of love, by summer's ripening breath,
May prove a beauteous flower when next we
meet.
Good night, good night! as sweet repose and rest
Come to thy heart as that within my breast!
ROMEO: O, wilt thou leave me so unsatisfied?
JULIET: What satisfaction canst thou have to-night?
ROMEO: The exchange of thy love's faithful vow
for mine.
JULIET: I gave thee mine before thou didst request
it;
And yet I would it were to give again.
ROMEO: Would'st thou withdraw it? for what
purpose, love?
JULIET: But to be frank and give it thee again.
And yet I wish but for the thing I have;
My bounty is as boundless as the sea,
My love as deep; the more I give to thee,
The more I have, for both are infinite.
I hear some noise within: dear love, adieu!—
(NURSE calls within)
Anon, good nurse!—Sweet Montague, be true.
Stay but a little, I will come again.
(Exit)
ROMEO: O blessed, blessed night! I am afeard,
Being in night, all this is but a dream,
Too flattering-sweet to be substantial.
(Enter JULIET above)
JULIET: Three words, dear Romeo, and good night
indeed.
If that thy bent of love be honourable,
Thy purpose marriage, send me word to-morrow,
By one that I'll procure to come to thee,
Where and what time thou wilt perform the rite;
And all my fortunes at thy foot I'll lay

And follow thee, my lord, throughout the
world.
NURSE (Within): Madam!
JULIET: I come anon.—But if thou meanest not
well,
I do beseech thee,—
NURSE (Within): Madam!
JULIET: By-and-by I come:—
To cease thy strife and leave me to my grief:
To-morrow will I send.
ROMEO: So thrive my soul,—
JULIET: A thousand times good night!
(Exit)
ROMEO: A thousand times the worse, to want thy
light!—
Love goes toward love as schoolboys from their
books;
But love from love, towards school with heavy
looks.
(Re-enter JULIET, above)
JULIET: Hist! Romeo, hist!—O for a falconer's
voice
To lure this tassel-gentle back again!
Bondage is hoarse and may not speak aloud;
Else would I tear the cave where Echo lies,
And make her airy tongue more hoarse than
mine
With repetition of my Romeo's name.
ROMEO: It is my soul that calls upon my name:
How silver-sweet sound lovers' tongues by
night,
Like softest music to attending ears!
JULIET: Romeo!
ROMEO: My sweet?
JULIET: At what o'clock to-morrow
Shall I send to thee?
ROMEO: At the hour of nine.
JULIET: I will not fail: 'tis twenty years till then.
I have forgot why I did call thee back.
ROMEO: Let me stand here till thou remember it.
JULIET: I shall forget, to have thee still stand there,
Remembering how I love thy company.
ROMEO: And I'll still stay, to have thee still forget,
Forgetting any other home but this.
JULIET: 'Tis almost morning; I would have thee
gone:
And yet no farther than a wanton's bird;
That lets it hop a little from her hand,

Like a poor prisoner in his twisted gyves,[12]
And with a silk thread plucks it back again,
So loving-jealous of his liberty.

ROMEO: I would I were thy bird.

JULIET: Sweet, so would I:
Yet I should kill thee with much cherishing.
Good night, good night! parting is such sweet
   sorrow
That I shall say good night till it be morrow.
   (Exit)

ROMEO: Sleep dwell upon thine eyes, peace in thy
   breast!—
Would I were sleep and peace, so sweet to rest!
Hence will I to my ghostly father's cell,
His help to crave and my dear hap to tell.
   (Exit)

SCENE III   FRIAR LAWRENCE'S CELL.

Enter FRIAR LAWRENCE with a basket

FRIAR: The grey-ey'd morn smiles on the frowning
   night,
Chequering the eastern clouds with streaks of
   light;
And flecked darkness like a drunkard reels
From forth day's path and Titan's fiery wheels:
Now, ere the sun advance his burning eye,
The day to cheer and night's dank dew to dry,
I must up-fill this osier cage of ours
With baleful weeds and precious-juiced
   flowers.
The earth, that's nature's mother, is her tomb;
What is her burying grave, that is her womb:
And from her womb children of divers kind
We sucking on her natural bosom find;
Many for many virtues excellent,
None but for some, and yet all different.
O, mickle[13] is the powerful grace that lies
In plants, herbs, stones, and their true qualities:
For naught so vile that on the earth doth live
But to the earth some special good doth give;
Nor aught so good but, strain'd from that fair
   use,
Revolts from true birth, stumbling on abuse:

Virtue itself turns vice, being misapplied;
And vice sometimes by action dignified.
Within the infant rind of this small flower
Poison hath residence, and medicine power:
For this, being smelt, with that part cheers each
   part;
Being tasted, slays all senses with the heart.
Two such opposed kings encamp them still
In man as well as herbs,—grace and rude will;
And where the worser is predominant,
Full soon the canker death eats up that plant.
   (Enter ROMEO)

ROMEO: Good morrow, father!

FRIAR: Benedicite!
What early tongue so sweet saluteth me?—
Young son, it argues a distemper'd head
So soon to bid good morrow to thy bed:
Care keeps his watch in every old man's eye,
And where care lodges sleep will never lie;
But where unbruised youth with unstuff'd
   brain
Doth couch his limbs, there golden sleep doth
   reign:
Therefore thy earliness doth me assure
Thou art uprous'd with some distemperature;
Or if not so, then here I hit it right,—
Our Romeo hath not been in bed to-night.

ROMEO: That last is true; the sweeter rest was mine.

FRIAR: God pardon sin! wast thou with Rosaline?

ROMEO: With Rosaline, my ghostly father? no;
I have forgot that name, and that name's woe.

FRIAR: That's my good son: but where hast thou
   been then?

ROMEO: I'll tell thee ere thou ask it me again.
I have been feasting with mine enemy;
Where, on a sudden, one hath wounded me
That's by me wounded. Both our remedies
Within thy help and holy physic lies;
I bear no hatred, blessed man; for, lo,
My intercession likewise steads my foe.

FRIAR: Be plain, good son, and homely in thy drift;
Riddling confession finds but riddling shrift.

ROMEO: Then plainly know my heart's dear love
   is set
On the fair daughter of rich Capulet:
As mine on hers, so hers is set on mine;
And all combin'd, save what thou must
   combine

12. Chains.
13. Much.

By holy marriage: when, and where, and how
We met, we woo'd, and made exchange of vow,
I'll tell thee as we pass; but this I pray,
That thou consent to marry us to-day.
FRIAR: Holy Saint Francis! what a change is here!
Is Rosaline, that thou didst love so dear,
So soon forsaken? young men's love, then, lies
Not truly in their hearts, but in their eyes.
Jesu Maria, what a deal of brine
Hath wash'd thy sallow cheeks for Rosaline!
How much salt water thrown away in waste,
To season love, that of it doth not taste!
The sun not yet thy sighs from heaven clears,
Thy old groans ring yet in mine ancient ears;
Lo, here upon thy cheek the stain doth sit
Of an old tear that is not wash'd off yet:
If e'er thou wast thyself, and these woes thine,
Thou and these woes were all for Rosaline;
And art thou chang'd? Pronounce this sentence
then,—
Women may fall, when there's no strength in
men.
ROMEO: Thou chidd'st me oft for loving Rosaline.
FRIAR: For doting, not for loving, pupil mine.
ROMEO: And bad'st me bury love.
FRIAR: Not in a grave
To lay one in, another out to have.
ROMEO: I pray thee chide not: she whom I love now
Doth grace for grace and love for love allow;
The other did not so.
FRIAR: O, she knew well
Thy love did read by rote, that could not spell.
But come, young waverer, come go with me,
In one respect I'll thy assistant be;
For this alliance may so happy prove,
To turn your households' rancour to pure love.
ROMEO: O, let us hence; I stand on sudden haste.
FRIAR: Wisely, and slow; they stumble that run fast.
(*Exeunt*)

SCENE IV   A STREET.

Enter BENVOLIO *and* MERCUTIO

MERCUTIO: Where the devil should this Romeo
be?—
Came he not home to-night?
BENVOLIO: Not to his father's; I spoke with his man.

MERCUTIO: Ah, that same pale hard-hearted
wench, that Rosaline,
Torments him so that he will sure run mad.
BENVOLIO: Tybalt, the kinsman to old Capulet,
Hath sent a letter to his father's house.
MERCUTIO: A challenge, on my life.
BENVOLIO: Romeo will answer it.
MERCUTIO: Any man that can write may answer a
letter.
BENVOLIO: Nay, he will answer the letter's master,
how he dares, being dared.
MERCUTIO: Alas, poor Romeo, he is already dead!
stabbed with a white wench's black eye; shot
through the ear with a love song; the very
pin of his heart cleft with the blind bow-boy's
butt-shaft: and is he a man to encounter
Tybalt?
BENVOLIO: Why, what is Tybalt?
MERCUTIO: More than prince of cats, I can tell you.
O, he's the courageous captain of compliments. He fights as you sing prick-song—
keeps time, distance, and proportion; rests
me his minim rest, one, two, and the third in
your bosom: the very butcher of a silk button,
a duellist, a duellist; a gentleman of the very
first house,—of the first and second cause: ah,
the immortal passado! the punto reverso! the
hay.—
BENVOLIO: The what?
MERCUTIO: The pox of such antic, lisping, affecting
fantasticoes; these new tuners of accents!—
"By Jesu, a very good blade!—a very tall
man!—a very good whore!"—Why, is not this
a lamentable thing, grandsire, that we should
be thus afflicted with these strange flies, these
fashion-mongers, these pardonnez-moi's, who
stand so much on the new form that they cannot sit at ease on the old bench? O, their bones,
their bones!
BENVOLIO: Here comes Romeo, here comes
Romeo!
MERCUTIO: Without his roe, like a dried herring.—
O flesh, flesh, how art thou fishified!—Now
is he for the numbers that Petrarch flowed
in: Laura, to his lady, was but a kitchen
wench,—marry, she had a better love to
be-rhyme her; Dido, a dowdy; Cleopatra, a
gypsy; Helen and Hero, hildings and

harlots; Thisbe, a gray eye or so, but not to the purpose,—

(*Enter* ROMEO)

Signior Romeo, bon jour! there's a French salutation to your French slop. You gave us the counterfeit fairly last night.

ROMEO: Good morrow to you both. What counterfeit did I give you?

MERCUTIO: The slip, sir, the slip; can you not conceive?

ROMEO: Pardon, good Mercutio, my business was great; and in such a case as mine a man may strain courtesy.

MERCUTIO: That's as much as to say, such a case as yours constrains a man to bow in the hams.

ROMEO: Meaning, to court'sy.

MERCUTIO: Thou hast most kindly hit it.

ROMEO: A most courteous exposition.

MERCUTIO: Nay, I am the very pink of courtesy.

ROMEO: Pink for flower.

MERCUTIO: Right.

ROMEO: Why, then is my pump well-flowered.

MERCUTIO: Well said: follow me this jest now till thou hast worn out thy pump; that, when the single sole of it is worn, the jest may remain, after the wearing, sole singular.

ROMEO: O single-soled jest, solely singular for the singleness!

MERCUTIO: Come between us, good Benvolio; my wits faint.

ROMEO: Swits and spurs, swits and spurs; or I'll cry a match.

MERCUTIO: Nay, if thy wits run the wild-goose chase, I have done; for thou hast more of the wild-goose in one of thy wits than, I am sure, I have in my whole five: was I with you there for the goose?

ROMEO: Thou wast never with me for anything when thou wast not there for the goose.

MERCUTIO: I will bite thee by the ear for that jest.

ROMEO: Nay, good goose, bite not.

MERCUTIO: Thy wit is a very bitter sweeting; it is a most sharp sauce.

ROMEO: And is it not, then, well served in to a sweet goose?

MERCUTIO: O, here's a wit of cheveril, that stretches from an inch narrow to an ell broad!

ROMEO: I stretch it out for that word broad: which added to the goose, proves thee far and wide a broad goose.

MERCUTIO: Why, is not this better now than groaning for love? now art thou sociable, now art thou Romeo; not art thou what thou art, by art as well as by nature: for this drivelling love is like a great natural,[14] that runs lolling up and down to hide his bauble in a hole.

BENVOLIO: Stop there, stop there.

MERCUTIO: Thou desirest me to stop in my tale against the hair.

BENVOLIO: Thou wouldst else have made thy tale large.

MERCUTIO: O, thou art deceived; I would have made it short: for I was come to the whole depth of my tale; and meant indeed to occupy the argument no longer.

ROMEO: Here's goodly gear!

(*Enter* NURSE *and her servant* PETER)

MERCUTIO: A sail, a sail, a sail!

BENVOLIO: Two, two; a shirt and a smock.

NURSE: Peter!

PETER: Anon.

NURSE: My fan, Peter.

MERCUTIO: Good Peter, to hide her face; for her fan's the fairer face.

NURSE: God ye good morrow, gentlemen.

MERCUTIO: God ye good-den, fair gentlewoman.

NURSE: Is it good-den?

MERCUTIO: 'Tis no less, I tell ye; for the bawdy hand of the dial is now upon the prick of noon.

NURSE: Out upon you! what a man are you!

ROMEO: One, gentlewoman, that God hath made for himself to mar.

NURSE: By my troth, it is well said; "for himself to mar," quoth 'a?—Gentlemen, can any of you tell me where I may find the young Romeo?

ROMEO: I can tell you: but young Romeo will be older when you have found him than he was when you sought him: I am the youngest of that name, for fault of a worse.

NURSE: You say well.

MERCUTIO: Yea, is the worst well? very well took, i' faith; wisely, wisely.

14. Fool or idiot.

NURSE: If you be he, sir, I desire some confidence with you.

BENVOLIO: She will indite him to some supper.

MERCUTIO: A bawd, a bawd, a bawd! So ho!

ROMEO: What hast thou found?

MERCUTIO: No hare, sir; unless a hare, sir, in a lenten pie, that is something stale and hoar ere it be spent.

(*Sings*)

> An old hare hoar,
> And and old hare hoar,
> An old hare hoar,
> And an old hare hoar,
> Is very good meat in Lent;
> But a hare that is hoar
> Is too much for a score
> When it hoars ere it be spent.

Romeo, will you come to your father's? we'll to dinner thither.

ROMEO: I will follow you.

MERCUTIO: Farewell, ancient lady; farewell,—
(*singing*) lady, lady, lady.

(*Exeunt* MERCUTIO *and* BENVOLIO)

NURSE: Marry, farewell!—I pray you, sir, what saucy merchant was this that was so full of his ropery?

ROMEO: A gentleman, nurse, that loves to hear himself talk; and will speak more in a minute than he will stand to in a month.

NURSE: And 'a speak anything against me, I'll take him down, and 'a were lustier than he is, and twenty such Jacks; and if I cannot, I'll find those that shall. Scurvy knave! I am none of his flirt-gills; I am none of his skains-mates.— And thou must stand by too, and suffer every knave to use me at his pleasure!

PETER: I saw no man use you at his pleasure; if I had, my weapon should quickly have been out, I warrant you: I dare draw as soon as another man, if I see occasion in a good quarrel, and the law on my side.

NURSE: Now, afore God, I am so vexed that every part about me quivers. Scurvy knave!—Pray you, sir, a word: and, as I told you, my young lady bid me enquire you out; what she bade me say I will keep to myself: but first let me tell ye, if ye should lead her into a fool's paradise, as they say, it were a very gross kind of behaviour, as they say: for the gentlewoman is young; and, therefore, if you should deal double with her, truly it were an ill thing to be offered to any gentlewoman, and very weak dealing.

ROMEO: Nurse, commend me to thy lady and mistress. I protest unto thee,—

NURSE: Good heart, and i' faith I will tell her as much: Lord, Lord, she will be a joyful woman.

ROMEO: What wilt thou tell her, nurse? thou dost not mark me.

NURSE: I will tell her, sir,—that you do protest: which, as I take it, is a gentlemanlike offer.

ROMEO: Bid her devise some means to come to shrift
This afternoon;
And there she shall at Friar Lawrence' cell
Be shriv'd and married. Here is for thy pains.

NURSE: No, truly, sir; not a penny.

ROMEO: Go to; I say you shall.

NURSE: This afternoon, sir? well, she shall be there.

ROMEO: And stay, good nurse, behind the abbey-wall:
Within this hour my man shall be with thee,
And bring thee cords made like a tackled stair;
Which to the high top-gallant of my joy
Must be my convoy in the secret night.
Farewell; be trusty, and I'll quit thy pains:
Farewell; commend me to thy mistress.

NURSE: Now God in heaven bless thee!—Hark you, sir.

ROMEO: What say'st thou, my dear nurse?

NURSE: Is your man secret? Did you ne'er hear say,
Two may keep counsel, putting one away?

ROMEO: I warrant thee, my man's as true as steel.

NURSE: Well, sir; my mistress is the sweetest lady.—Lord, Lord! when 'twas a little prating thing,—O, there's a nobleman in town, one Paris, that would fain lay knife aboard; but she, good soul, had as lief see a toad, a very toad, as see him. I anger her sometimes, and tell her that Paris is the properer man; but I'll warrant you, when I say so, she looks as pale as any clout[15] in the versal world.[16] Doth not rosemary and Romeo begin both with a letter?

ROMEO: Ay, nurse; what of that? both with an R.

---

15. Cloth.
16. Universe.

NURSE: Ah, mocker! that's the dog's name. R is for
    the dog: no; I know it begins with some other
    letter:—and she hath the prettiest sententious
    of it, of you and rosemary, that it would do
    you good to hear it.

ROMEO: Commend me to thy lady.

NURSE: Ay, a thousand times. (*Exit* ROMEO)—Peter!

PETER: Anon?

NURSE: Peter, take my fan, and go before.
    (*Exeunt*)

SCENE V   CAPULET'S GARDEN.

Enter JULIET

JULIET: The clock struck nine when I did send the
    nurse;
  In half an hour she promis'd to return.
  Perchance she cannot meet him: that's not so.—
  O, she is lame! love's heralds should be
    thoughts,
  Which ten times faster glide than the sun's
    beams,
  Driving back shadows over lowering hills:
  Therefore do nimble-pinion'd doves draw love,
  And therefore hath the wind-swift Cupid
    wings.
  Now is the sun upon the highmost hill
  Of this day's journey; and from nine till twelve
  Is three long hours,—yet she is not come.
  Had she affections and warm youthful blood,
  She'd be as swift in motion as a ball;
  My words would bandy her to my sweet love,
  And his to me:
  But old folks, many feign as they were dead;
  Unwieldy, slow, heavy and pale as lead.—
  O God, she comes!
    (*Enter* NURSE *and* PETER)
  O honey nurse, what news?
  Hast thou met with him? Send thy man away.

NURSE: Peter, stay at the gate.
    (*Exit* PETER)

JULIET: Now, good sweet nurse,—O Lord, why
    look'st thou sad?
  Though news be sad, yet tell them merrily;
  If good, thou sham'st the music of sweet news
  By playing it to me with so sour a face.

NURSE: I am aweary, give me leave awhile;—

  Fie, how my bones ache! what a jaunt have I
    had!

JULIET: I would thou hadst my bones, and I thy
    news:
  Nay, come, I pray thee speak;—good, good
    nurse, speak.

NURSE: Jesu, what haste? can you not stay awhile?
  Do you not see that I am out of breath?

JULIET: How art thou out of breath, when thou
    hast breath
  To say to me that thou art out of breath?
  The excuse that thou dost make in this delay
  Is longer than the tale thou dost excuse.
  Is thy news good or bad? answer to that;
  Say either, and I'll stay the circumstance:
  Let me be satisfied, is't good or bad?

NURSE: Well, you have made a simple choice; you
    know not how to choose a man: Romeo! no,
    not he; though his face be better than any
    man's, yet his leg excels all men's; and for a
    hand and a foot, and a body,—though they
    be not to be talked on, yet they are past com-
    pare: he is not the flower of courtesy,—but
    I'll warrant him as gentle as a lamb.—Go thy
    ways, wench; serve God.—What, have you
    dined at home?

JULIET: No, no: but all this did I know before.
  What says he of our marriage? what of that?

NURSE: Lord, how my head aches! what a head
    have I!
  It beats as it would fall in twenty pieces.
  My back o' t' other side,—O, my back, my
    back!—
  Beshrew your heart for sending me about
  To catch my death with jauncing up and down!

JULIET: I' faith, I am sorry that thou art not well.
  Sweet, sweet, sweet nurse, tell me, what says
    my love?

NURSE: Your love says, like an honest gentleman,
  And a courteous, and a kind, and a handsome;
  And, I warrant, a virtuous,—Where is your
    mother?

JULIET: Where is my mother?—why, she is within;
  Where should she be? How oddly thou repliest!
  Your love says, like an honest gentleman,—
  Where is your mother?

NURSE: O God's lady dear!
  Are you so hot? marry, come up, I trow;

Is this the poultice for my aching bones?
Henceforward, do your messages yourself.
JULIET: Here's such a coil!—come, what says
      Romeo?
NURSE: Have you got leave to go to shrift[17] to-day?
JULIET: I have.
NURSE: Then hie you hence to Friar Lawrence' cell;
    There stays a husband to make you a wife:
    Now comes the wanton blood up in your
      cheeks,
    They'll be in scarlet straight at any news.
    Hie you to church; I must another way,
    To fetch a ladder, by the which your love
    Must climb a bird's nest soon when it is dark:
    I am the drudge, and toil in your delight;
    But you shall bear the burden soon at night.
    Go; I'll to dinner; hie you to the cell.
JULIET: Hie to high fortune!—honest nurse,
      farewell.
      (*Exeunt*)

SCENE VI   FRIAR LAWRENCE'S CELL.

Enter FRIAR LAWRENCE *and* ROMEO

FRIAR: So smile the heavens upon this holy act
    That after-hours with sorrow chide us not!
ROMEO: Amen, amen! but come what sorrow can,
    It cannot countervail the exchange of joy
    That one short minute gives me in her sight:
    Do thou but close our hands with holy words,
    Then love-devouring death do what he dare,—
    It is enough I may but call her mine.
FRIAR: These violent delights have violent ends,
    And in their triumph die; like fire and powder,
    Which, as they kiss, consume: the sweetest
      honey
    Is loathsome in his own deliciousness,
    And in the taste confounds the appetite:
    Therefore love moderately: long love doth so;
    Too swift arrives as tardy as too slow.
        (*Enter* JULIET)
    Here comes the lady:—O, so light a foot
    Will ne'er wear out the everlasting flint:
    A lover may bestride the gossamer
    That idles in the wanton summer air

And yet not fall; so light is vanity.
JULIET: Good-even to my ghostly confessor.
FRIAR: Romeo shall thank thee, daughter, for us
      both.
JULIET: As much to him, else is his thanks too much.
ROMEO: Ah, Juliet, if the measure of thy joy
    Be heap'd like mine, and that thy skill be more
    To blazon it, then sweeten with thy breath
    This neighbour air, and let rich music's tongue
    Unfold the imagin'd happiness that both
    Receive in either by this dear encounter.
JULIET: Conceit, more rich in matter than in words,
    Brags of his substance, not of ornament:
    They are but beggars that can count their worth;
    But my true love is grown to such excess,
    I cannot sum up sum of half my wealth.
FRIAR: Come, come with me, and we will make
      short work;
    For, by your leaves, you shall not stay alone
    Till holy church incorporate two in one.
      (*Exeunt*)

ACT III

SCENE I   A PUBLIC PLACE.

Enter MERCUTIO, BENVOLIO, *and others*

BENVOLIO: I pray thee, good Mercutio, let's
      retire:
    The day is hot, the Capulets abroad,
    And, if we meet, we shall not scape a brawl;
    For now, these hot days, is the mad blood
      stirring.
MERCUTIO: Thou art like one of these fellows
      that, when he enters the confines of a tavern,
      claps me his sword upon the table, and
      says "God send me no need of thee!" and
      by the operation of the second cup draws
      him on the drawer, when indeed there is no
      need.
BENVOLIO: Am I like such a fellow?
MERCUTIO: Come, come, thou art as hot a Jack
      in thy mood as any in Italy; and as soon
      moved to be moody, and as soon moody to
      be moved.
BENVOLIO: And what to?

17. Confession.

MERCUTIO: Nay, an there were two such, we should
have none shortly, for one would kill the other.
Thou! why, thou wilt quarrel with a man that
hath a hair more or a hair less in his beard
than thou hast. Thou wilt quarrel with a man
for cracking nuts, having no other reason but
because thou hast hazel eyes;—what eye but
such an eye would spy out such a quarrel?
Thy head is as full of quarrels as an egg is full
of meat; and yet thy head hath been beaten
as addle as an egg for quarrelling. Thou hast
quarreled with a man for coughing in the
street, because he hath wakened thy dog that
hath lain asleep in the sun. Didst thou not fall
out with a tailor for wearing his new doublet
before Easter? With another for tying his new
shoes with an old riband? and yet thou wilt
tutor me from quarrelling!

BENVOLIO: An I were so apt to quarrel as thou art,
any man should buy the fee simple of my life
for an hour and a quarter.

MERCUTIO: The fee simple! O simple!

BENVOLIO: By my head, here come the Capulets.

MERCUTIO: By my heel, I care not.

(*Enter* TYBALT *and others*)

TYBALT: Follow me close, for I will speak to
them.—Gentlemen, good-den: a word with
one of you.

MERCUTIO: And but one word with one of us?
Couple it with something; make it a word
and a blow.

TYBALT: You shall find me apt enough to that, sir,
an you will give me occasion.

MERCUTIO: Could you not take some occasion
without giving?

TYBALT: Mercutio, thou consortest with Romeo,—

MERCUTIO: Consort! what, dost thou make us
minstrels? An thou make minstrels of us,
look to hear nothing but discords: here's my
fiddlestick; here's that shall make you dance.
Zounds, consort!

BENVOLIO: We talk here in the public haunt of men:
Either withdraw unto some private place,
And reason coldly of your grievances,
Or else depart; here all eyes gaze on us.

MERCUTIO: Men's eyes were made to look, and let
them gaze;
I will not budge for no man's pleasure, I.

TYBALT: Well, peace be with you, sir.—Here comes
my man.

(*Enter* ROMEO)

MERCUTIO: But I'll be hanged, sir, if he wear your
livery:
Marry, go before to field, he'll be your follower;
Your worship in that sense may call him man.

TYBALT: Romeo, the love I bear thee can afford
No better term than this,—Thou art a villain.

ROMEO: Tybalt, the reason that I have to love thee
Doth much excuse the appertaining rage
To such a greeting. Villain am I none;
Therefore farewell; I see thou know'st me not.

TYBALT: Boy, this shall not excuse the injuries
That thou hast done me; therefore turn and draw.

ROMEO: I do protest I never injur'd thee;
But love thee better than thou canst devise
Till thou shalt know the reason of my love:
And so good Capulet,—which name I tender
As dearly as mine own,—be satisfied.

MERCUTIO: O calm, dishonourable, vile submission!
Alla stoccata[18] carries it away. (*Draws.*)
Tybalt, you rat-catcher, will you walk?

TYBALT: What wouldst thou have with me?

MERCUTIO: Good king of cats, nothing but one
of your nine lives; that I mean to make bold
withal, and, as you shall use me hereafter,
dry-beat the rest of the eight. Will you pluck
your sword out of his pitcher by the ears?
make haste, lest mine be about your ears ere
it be out.

TYBALT: I am for you. (*Drawing*)

ROMEO: Gentle Mercutio, put thy rapier up.

MERCUTIO: Come, sir, your passado.

(*They fight*)

ROMEO: Draw, Benvolio; beat down their
weapons.—
Gentlemen, for shame! forbear this outrage!—
Tybalt,—Mercutio,—the prince expressly hath
Forbid this bandying in Verona streets.—
Hold, Tybalt!—good Mercutio!—

(MERCUTIO *stabbed under* ROMEO's *arm*)

(*Exeunt* TYBALT *with his Partisans*)

MERCUTIO: I am hurt;—
A plague o' both your houses!—I am sped.—
Is he gone, and hath nothing?

18. Fencing term.

BENVOLIO: What, art thou hurt?

MERCUTIO: Ay, ay, a scratch, a scratch; marry, 'tis enough.—

Where is my page?—go, villain, fetch a surgeon.
(*Exit* PAGE)

ROMEO: Courage, man; the hurt cannot be much.

MERCUTIO: No, 'tis not so deep as a well, nor so wide as a church door; but 'tis enough, 'twill serve: ask for me to-morrow, and you shall find me a grave man. I am peppered, I warrant, for this world.—A plague o' both your houses!—Zounds, a dog, a rat, a mouse, a cat, to scratch a man to death! a braggart, a rogue, a villain, that fights by the book of arithmetic!—Why the devil came you between us? I was hurt under your arm.

ROMEO: I thought all for the best.

MERCUTIO: Help me into some house, Benvolio,
Or I shall faint.—A plague o' both your houses!
They have made worms' meat of me:
I have it, and soundly too.—Your houses!
(*Exit* MERCUTIO *and* BENVOLIO)

ROMEO: This gentleman, the prince's near ally,
My very friend, hath got his mortal hurt
In my behalf; my reputation stain'd
With Tybalt's slander,—Tybalt, that an hour
Hath been my kinsman.—O sweet Juliet,
Thy beauty hath made me effeminate
And in my temper soften'd valour's steel.
(*Enter* BENVOLIO)

BENVOLIO: O Romeo, Romeo, brave Mercutio's dead!
That gallant spirit hath aspir'd the clouds,
Which too untimely here did scorn the earth.

ROMEO: This day's black fate on more days doth depend;
This but begins the woe others must end.

BENVOLIO: Here comes the furious Tybalt back again.

ROMEO: Alive in triumph! and Mercutio slain!
Away to heaven respective lenity,
And fire-ey'd fury be my conduct now!—
(*Enter* TYBALT)
Now, Tybalt, take the 'villain' back again
That late thou gavest me; for Mercutio's soul
Is but a little way above our heads,
Staying for thine to keep him company.
Either thou or I, or both, must go with him.

TYBALT: Thou, wretched boy, that didst consort him here,
Shalt with him hence.

ROMEO: This shall determine that.
(*They fight.* TYBALT *falls*)

BENVOLIO: Romeo, away, be gone!
The citizens are up, and Tybalt slain.—
Stand not amaz'd. The prince will doom thee death
If thou art taken. Hence, be gone, away!

ROMEO: O, I am fortune's fool!

BENVOLIO: Why dost thou stay?
(*Exit* ROMEO)
(*Enter* CITIZENS)

FIRST CITIZEN: Which way ran he that kill'd Mercutio?
Tybalt, that murderer, which way ran he?

BENVOLIO: There lies that Tybalt.

FIRST CITIZEN: Up, sir, go with me;
I charge thee in the prince's name obey.
(*Enter* PRINCE, MONTAGUE, CAPULET, *their Wives, and others*)

PRINCE: Where are the vile beginners of this fray?

BENVOLIO: O noble prince. I can discover all
The unlucky manage of this fatal brawl:
There lies the man, slain by young Romeo,
That slew thy kinsman, brave Mercutio.

LADY CAPULET: Tybalt, my cousin! O my brother's child!—
O prince!—O husband!—O, the blood is spill'd
Of my dear kinsman!—Prince, as thou art true,
For blood of ours shed blood of Montague.—
O cousin, cousin!

PRINCE: Benvolio, who began this bloody fray?

BENVOLIO: Tybalt, here slain, whom Romeo's hand did slay;
Romeo, that spoke him fair, bid him bethink
How nice the quarrel was, and urg'd withal
Your high displeasure.—All this,—uttered
With gentle breath, calm look, knees humbly bow'd,—
Could not take truce with the unruly spleen
Of Tybalt, deaf to peace, but that he tilts
With piercing steel at bold Mercutio's breast;
Who, all as hot, turns deadly point to point,
And, with a martial scorn, with one hand beats
Cold death aside, and with the other sends
It back to Tybalt, whose dexterity

Retorts it: Romeo he cries aloud,
"Hold, friends! friends, part!" and swifter than
　his tongue,
His agile arm beats down their fatal points,
And 'twixt them rushes; underneath whose arm
An envious thrust from Tybalt hit the life
Of stout Mercutio, and then Tybalt fled:
But by-and-by comes back to Romeo,
Who had but newly entertain'd revenge,
And to 't they go like lightning; for, ere I
Could draw to part them was stout Tybalt slain;
And as he fell did Romeo turn and fly.
This is the truth, or let Benvolio die.

LADY CAPULET: He is a kinsman to the Montague,
Affection makes him false, he speaks not true:
Some twenty of them fought in this black strife,
And all those twenty could but kill one life.
I beg for justice, which thou, prince, must give;
Romeo slew Tybalt, Romeo must not live.

PRINCE: Romeo slew him; he slew Mercutio:
Who now the price of his dear blood doth owe?

MONTAGUE: Not Romeo, prince; he was Mercutio's
　friend;
His fault concludes but what the law should end,
The life of Tybalt.

PRINCE: And for that offence
Immediately we do exile him hence:
I have an interest in your hate's proceeding,
My blood for your rude brawls doth lie
　a-bleeding;
But I'll amerce[19] you with so strong a fine
That you shall all repent the loss of mine:
I will be deaf to pleading and excuses;
Nor tears nor prayers shall purchase out abuses,
Therefore use none: let Romeo hence in haste,
Else, when he is found, that hour is his last.
Bear hence this body, and attend our will:
Mercy but murders, pardoning those that kill.
　(*Exeunt*)

SCENE II   CAPULET'S HOUSE.

Enter JULIET

JULIET: Gallop apace, you fiery-footed steeds,
Towards Phoebus' lodging; such a waggoner
As Phaeton would whip you to the west

19. Punish.

And bring in cloudy night immediately.—
Spread thy close curtain, love-performing night!
That rude eyes may wink, and Romeo
Leap to these arms, untalk'd of and unseen.—
Lovers can see to do their amorous rites
By their own beauties: or, if love be blind,
It best agrees with night.—Come, civil night,
Thou sober-suited matron, all in black,
And learn me how to lose a winning match,
Play'd for a pair of stainless maidenhoods:
Hood my unmann'd blood, bating in my cheeks,
With thy black mantle; till strange love, grown
　bold,
Think true love acted simple modesty.
Come, night;—come, Romeo;—come, thou day
　in night;
For thou wilt lie upon the wings of night
Whiter than new snow upon a raven's back.—
Come, gentle night;—come, loving, black-
　brow'd night,
Give me my Romeo; and, when he shall die,
Take him and cut him out in little stars,
And he will make the face of heaven so fine
That all the world will be in love with night,
And pay no worship to the garish sun.—
O, I have bought the mansion of a love,
But not possess'd it; and, though I am sold,
Not yet enjoy'd: so tedious is this day
As is the night before some festival
To an impatient child that hath new robes,
And may not wear them. O, here comes my
　nurse,
And she brings news; and every tongue that
　speaks
But Romeo's name speaks heavenly
　eloquence.—
　(*Enter* NURSE, *with cords*)
Now, nurse, what news? What hast thou there?
　the cords
That Romeo bid thee fetch?

NURSE: Ay, ay, the cords.

JULIET: Ah me! what news? why dost thou wring
　thy hands?

NURSE: Ah, well-a-day! he's dead, he's dead, he's
　dead!
We are undone, lady, we are undone!—
Alack the day!—he's gone, he's kill'd, he's
　dead!

JULIET: Can heaven be so envious?

NURSE: Romeo can,

Though heaven cannot.—O Romeo, Romeo!—
Who ever would have thought it?—Romeo!

JULIET: What devil art thou, that dost torment me thus?

This torture should be roar'd in dismal hell.
Hath Romeo slain himself? say thou but I,
And that bare vowel I shall poison more
Than the death-darting eye of cockatrice:
I am not I if there be such an I;
Or those eyes shut that make thee answer I.
If he be slain, say I; or if not, no:
Brief sounds determine of my weal or woe.

NURSE: I saw the wound, I saw it with mine eyes,—
God save the mark!—here on his manly breast.
A piteous corse,[20] a bloody piteous corse;
Pale, pale as ashes, all bedaub'd in blood,
All in gore-blood;—I swounded at the sight.

JULIET: O, break, my heart!—poor bankrout,[21] break at once!

To prison, eyes; ne'er look on liberty!
Vile earth, to earth resign; end motion here;
And thou and Romeo press one heavy bier!

NURSE: O Tybalt, Tybalt, the best friend I had!
O courteous Tybalt! honest gentleman!
That ever I should live to see thee dead!

JULIET: What storm is this that blows so contrary?
Is Romeo slaughter'd, and is Tybalt dead?
My dear-lov'd cousin, and my dearer lord?—
Then, dreadful trumpet, sound the general doom!
For who is living, if those two are gone?

NURSE: Tybalt is gone, and Romeo banished;
Romeo that kill'd him, he is banished.

JULIET: O God!—did Romeo's hand shed Tybalt's blood?

NURSE: It did, it did; alas the day, it did!

JULIET: O serpent heart, hid with a flowering face!
Did ever dragon keep so fair a cave?
Beautiful tyrant! fiend angelical!
Dove-feather'd raven! wolvish-ravening lamb!
Despised substance of divinest show!
Just opposite to what thou justly seem'st,
A damned saint, an honourable villain!—

20. Corpse.
21. Bankrupt.

O nature, what hadst thou to do in hell
When thou didst bower the spirit of a fiend
In mortal paradise of such sweet flesh?—
Was ever book containing such vile matter
So fairly bound? O, that deceit should dwell
In such a gorgeous palace!

NURSE: There's no trust,
No faith, no honesty in men; all perjur'd,
All forsworn, all naught, all dissemblers.—
Ah, where's my man? Give me some aqua vitae.—
These griefs, these woes, these sorrows make me old.
Shame come to Romeo!

JULIET: Blister'd be thy tongue
For such a wish! he was not born to shame:
Upon his brow shame is asham'd to sit;
For 'tis a throne where honour may be crown'd
Sole monarch of the universal earth.
O, what a beast was I to chide at him!

NURSE: Will you speak well of him that kill'd your cousin?

JULIET: Shall I speak ill of him that is my husband?
Ah, poor my lord, what tongue shall smooth thy name,
When I, thy three-hours' wife, have mangled it?—
But wherefore, villain, didst thou kill my cousin?
That villain cousin would have kill'd my husband:
Back, foolish tears, back to your native spring;
Your tributary drops belong to woe,
Which you, mistaking, offer up to joy.
My husband lives, that Tybalt would have slain;
And Tybalt's dead, that would have slain my husband:
All this is comfort; wherefore weep I, then?
Some word there was, worser than Tybalt's death,
That murder'd me: I would forget it fain;
But O, it presses to my memory
Like damned guilty deeds to sinners' minds:
"Tybalt is dead, and Romeo banished."
That "banished," that one word "banished,"
Hath slain ten thousand Tybalts. Tybalt's death
Was woe enough, if it had ended there:
Or, if sour woe delights in fellowship,

And needly will be rank'd with other griefs,—
Why follow'd not, when she said Tybalt's dead,
Thy father, or thy mother, nay, or both,
Which modern lamentation might have
  mov'd?
But with a rear-ward following Tybalt's death,
"Romeo is banished"—to speak that word
Is father, mother, Tybalt, Romeo, Juliet,
All slain, all dead: "Romeo is banished,"—
There is no end, no limit, measure, bound,
In that word's death; no words can that woe
  sound.—
Where is my father and my mother, nurse?
NURSE: Weeping and wailing over Tybalt's corse:
  Will you go to them? I will bring you thither.
JULIET: Wash they his wounds with tears: mine
  shall be spent,
  When theirs are dry, for Romeo's banishment.
  Take up those cords. Poor ropes, you are
  beguil'd,
  Both you and I; for Romeo is exil'd:
  He made you for a highway to my bed;
  But I, a maid, die maiden-widowed.
  Come, cords; come, nurse; I'll to my wedding-
  bed;
  And death, not Romeo, take my maidenhead!
NURSE: Hie to your chamber. I'll find Romeo
  To comfort you: I wot well where he is.
  Hark ye, your Romeo will be here at night:
  I'll to him; he is hid at Lawrence' cell.
JULIET: O, find him! give this ring to my true
  knight,
  And bid him come to take his last farewell.
  (*Exeunt*)

SCENE III   FRIAR LAWRENCE'S CELL.

Enter FRIAR LAWRENCE

FRIAR: Romeo, come forth; come forth, thou fear-
  ful man.
  Affliction is enamour'd of thy parts,
  And thou art wedded to calamity.
  (*Enter* ROMEO)
ROMEO: Father, what news? what is the prince's
  doom
  What sorrow craves acquaintance at my hand,
  That I yet know not?

FRIAR: Too familiar
  Is my dear son with such sour company:
  I bring thee tidings of the prince's doom.
ROMEO: What less than doomsday is the prince's
  doom?
FRIAR: A gentler judgment vanish'd from his lips,—
  Not body's death, but body's banishment.
ROMEO: Ha, banishment? be merciful, say death;
  For exile hath more terror in his look,
  Much more than death; do not say banishment.
FRIAR: Hence from Verona art thou banished:
  Be patient, for the world is broad and wide.
ROMEO: There is no world without Verona walls,
  But purgatory, torture, hell itself.
  Hence-banished is banish'd from the world,
  And world's exile is death,—then banished
  Is death mis-term'd: calling death banishment,
  Thou cutt'st my head off with a golden axe,
  And smil'st upon the stroke that murders me.
FRIAR: O deadly sin! O rude unthankfulness!
  Thy fault our law calls death; but the kind
  prince,
  Taking thy part, hath brush'd aside the law,
  And turn'd that black word death to banishment:
  This is dear mercy, and thou see'st it not.
ROMEO: 'Tis torture, and not mercy: heaven is
  here,
  Where Juliet lives; and every cat, and dog,
  And little mouse, every unworthy thing,
  Live here in heaven, and may look on her;
  But Romeo may not.—More validity,
  More honourable state, more courtship lives
  In carrion flies than Romeo: they may seize
  On the white wonder of dear Juliet's hand,
  And steal immortal blessing from her lips;
  Who, even in pure and vestal modesty,
  Still blush, as thinking their own kisses sin;
  But Romeo may not; he is banished,—
  This may flies do, when I from this must fly.
  And sayest thou yet that exile is not death!
  Hadst thou no poison mix'd, no sharp-ground
  knife,
  No sudden mean of death, though ne'er so
  mean,
  But banished to kill me; banished?
  O friar, the damned use that word in hell;
  Howlings attend it: how hast thou the heart,
  Being a divine, a ghostly confessor,

A sin-absolver, and my friend profess'd,
To mangle me with that word banishment?
FRIAR: Thou fond mad man, hear me speak a
    little,—
ROMEO: O, thou wilt speak again of banishment.
FRIAR: I'll give thee armour to keep off that word;
    Adversity's sweet milk, philosophy,
    To comfort thee, though thou art banished.
ROMEO: Yet banished? Hang up philosophy!
    Unless philosophy can make a Juliet,
    Displant a town, reverse a prince's doom,
    It helps not, it prevails not,—talk no more.
FRIAR: O, then I see that madmen have no ears.
ROMEO: How should they, when that wise men
    have no eyes?
FRIAR: Let me dispute with thee of thy estate.
ROMEO: Thou canst not speak of that thou dost
    not feel:
    Wert thou as young as I, Juliet thy love,
    An hour but married, Tybalt murdered,
    Doting like me, and like me banished,
    Then mightst thou speak, then mightst thou
        tear thy hair,
    And fall upon the ground, as I do now,
    Taking the measure of an unmade grave.
        (*Knocking within*)
FRIAR: Arise; one knocks. Good Romeo, hide
    thyself.
ROMEO: Not I; unless the breath of heartsick
    groans,
    Mist-like infold me from the search of eyes.
        (*Knocking*)
FRIAR: Hark, how they knock!—Who's there?—
    Romeo, arise;
    Thou wilt be taken.—Stay awhile;—Stand up;
        (*Knocking*)
    Run to my study.—By-and-by!—God's will!
    What simpleness is this.—I come, I come!
        (*Knocking*)
    Who knocks so hard? whence come you?
    what's your will?
NURSE: (*Within*) Let me come in, and you shall
    know my errand;
    I come from Lady Juliet.
FRIAR: Welcome then.
        (*Enter* NURSE)
NURSE: O holy friar, O, tell me, holy friar,
    Where is my lady's lord, where's Romeo?

FRIAR: There on the ground, with his own tears
    made drunk.
NURSE: O, he is even in my mistress' case,—
    Just in her case!
FRIAR: O woeful sympathy!
    Piteous predicament!
NURSE: Even so lies she,
    Blubbering and weeping, weeping and
        blubbering.—
    Stand up, stand up; stand, an you be a man:
    For Juliet's sake, for her sake, rise and stand;
    Why should you fall into so deep an O?[22]
ROMEO: Nurse!
NURSE: Ah sir! ah sir!—Well, death's the end of all.
ROMEO: Spakest thou of Juliet? how is it with her?
    Doth not she think me an old murderer,
    Now I have stain'd the childhood of our joy
    With blood remov'd but little from her own?
    Where is she? and how doth she? and what
        says
    My conceal'd lady to our cancell'd love?
NURSE: O, she says nothing, sir, but weeps and
        weeps;
    And now falls on her bed; and then starts up,
    And Tybalt calls; and then on Romeo cries,
    And then down falls again.
ROMEO: As if that name,
    Shot from the deadly level of a gun,
    Did murder her; as that name's cursed hand
    Murder'd her kinsman.—O, tell me, friar, tell
        me,
    In what vile part of this anatomy
    Doth my name lodge? tell me, that I may sack
    The hateful mansion.
        (*Drawing his sword*)
FRIAR: Hold thy desperate hand:
    Art thou a man? thy form cries out thou art;
    Thy tears are womanish; thy wild acts denote
    The unreasonable fury of a beast;
    Unseemly woman in a seeming man!
    Or ill-beseeming beast in seeming both!
    Thou hast amaz'd me: by my holy order,
    I thought thy disposition better temper'd.
    Hast thou slain Tybalt? wilt thou slay thyself?
    And slay thy lady, too, that lives in thee,
    By doing damned hate upon thyself?

22. Moaning.

Why rail'st thou on thy birth, the heaven, and
earth?
Since birth and heaven and earth, all three do
meet
In thee at once; which thou at once wouldst lose.
Fie, fie, thou sham'st thy shape, thy love, thy wit;
Which, like a usurer, abound'st in all,
And usest none in that true use indeed
Which should bedeck thy shape, thy love, thy
wit:
Thy noble shape is but a form of wax,
Digressing from the valour of a man;
Thy dear love sworn, but hollow perjury,
Killing that love which thou hast vow'd to
cherish;
Thy wit, that ornament to shape and love,
Mis-shapen in the conduct of them both,
Like powder in a skilless soldier's flask,
Is set a-fire by thine own ignorance,
And thou dismember'd with thine own defence.
What, rouse thee, man! thy Juliet is alive,
For whose dear sake thou wast but lately dead;
There art thou happy: Tybalt would kill thee,
But thou slewest Tybalt; there art thou happy
too:
The law, that threaten'd death, becomes thy
friend,
And turns it to exile; there art thou happy:
A pack of blessings lights upon thy back;
Happiness courts thee in her best array;
But, like a misbehav'd and sullen wench,
Thou pout'st upon thy fortune and thy love:—
Take heed, take heed, for such die miserable.
Go, get thee to thy love, as was decreed,
Ascend her chamber, hence and comfort her:
But, look, thou stay not till the watch be set,
For then thou canst not pass to Mantua;
Where thou shalt live till we can find a time
To blaze[23] your marriage, reconcile your friends,
Beg pardon of the prince, and call thee back
With twenty hundred thousand times more joy
Than thou went'st forth in lamentation.—
Go before, nurse: commend me to thy lady;
And bid her hasten all the house to bed,
Which heavy sorrow makes them apt unto.
Romeo is coming.

23. Announce.

NURSE: O Lord, I could have stay'd here all the night
To hear good counsel: O, what learning is!—
My lord, I'll tell my lady you will come.
ROMEO: Do so, and bid my sweet prepare to chide.
NURSE: Here, sir, a ring she bid me give you, sir:
Hie you, make haste, for it grows very late.
(*Exit*)
ROMEO: How well my comfort is reviv'd by this!
FRIAR: Go hence; good night! and here stands all
your state:
Either be gone before the watch be set,
Or by the break of day disguis'd from hence.
Sojourn in Mantua; I'll find out your man,
And he shall signify from time to time
Every good hap to you that chances here:
Give me thy hand; 'tis late; farewell; good
night.
ROMEO: But that a joy past joy calls out on me,
It were a grief so brief to part with thee:
Farewell.
(*Exeunt*)

SCENE IV   A ROOM IN CAPULET'S HOUSE.
Enter CAPULET, LADY CAPULET, *and* PARIS

CAPULET: Things have fallen out, sir, so unluckily
That we have had no time to move our daughter:
Look you, she lov'd her kinsman Tybalt dearly,
And so did I; well, we were born to die.
'Tis very late; she'll not come down to-night:
I promise you, but for your company,
I would have been a-bed an hour ago.
PARIS: These times of woe afford no tune to woo.—
Madam, good night: commend me to your
daughter.
LADY CAPULET: I will, and know her mind early
to-morrow;
To-night she's mew'd up to her heaviness.
CAPULET: Sir Paris, I will make a desperate tender
Of my child's love: I think she will be rul'd
In all respects by me; nay more, I doubt it
not.—
Wife, go you to her ere you go to bed;
Acquaint her here of my son Paris' love;
And bid her, mark you me, on Wednesday
next,—
But, soft! what day is this?

PARIS: Monday, my lord.

CAPULET: Monday! ha, ha! Well, Wednesday is too
    soon,
  Thursday let it be;—a Thursday, tell her,
  She shall be married to this noble earl.—
  Will you be ready? do you like this haste?
  We'll keep no great ado,—a friend or two;
  For, hark you, Tybalt being slain so late,
  It may be thought we held him carelessly,
  Being our kinsman, if we revel much:
  Therefore we'll have some half a dozen friends,
  And there an end. But what say you to
    Thursday?

PARIS: My lord, I would that Thursday were
    tomorrow.

CAPULET: Well, get you gone: o' Thursday be it
    then.—
  Go you to Juliet, ere you go to bed,
  Prepare her, wife, against this wedding-day.—
  Farewell, my lord.—Light to my chamber, ho!—
  Afore me, it is so very very late
  That we may call it early by and by.—
  Good night.
    (*Exeunt*)

SCENE V JULIET'S CHAMBER, ABOVE.

Enter ROMEO *and* JULIET

JULIET: Wilt thou be gone? it is not yet near day:
  It was the nightingale, and not the lark,
  That pierc'd the fearful hollow of thine ear;
  Nightly she sings on yond pomegranate tree:
  Believe me, love, it was the nightingale.

ROMEO: It was the lark, the herald of the morn,
  No nightingale: look, love, what envious
    streaks
  Do lace the severing clouds in yonder east:
  Night's candles are burnt out, and jocund day
  Stands tiptoe on the misty mountain tops.
  I must be gone and live, or stay and die.

JULIET: Yond light is not daylight, I know it, I:
  It is some meteor that the sun exhales
  To be to thee this night a torch-bearer
  And light thee on the way to Mantua:
  Therefore stay yet, thou need'st not to be gone.

ROMEO: Let me be ta'en, let me be put to death;
  I am content, so thou wilt have it so.

I'll say yon gray is not the morning's eye,
  'Tis but the pale reflex of Cynthia's brow;
  Nor that is not the lark whose notes do beat
  The vaulty heaven so high above our heads:
  I have more care to stay than will to go.—
  Come, death, and welcome! Juliet wills it so.—
  How is't, my soul? let's talk,—it is not day.

JULIET: It is, it is!—hie hence, be gone, away!
  It is the lark that sings so out of tune,
  Straining harsh discords and unpleasing
    sharps.
  Some say the lark makes sweet division;
  This doth not so, for she divideth us:
  Some say the lark and loathed toad change
    eyes;
  O, now I would they had chang'd voices too!
  Since arm from arm that voice doth us affray,
  Hunting thee hence with hunt's-up to the day.
  O, now be gone; more light and light it grows.

ROMEO: More light and light,—more dark and
    dark our woes!
    (*Enter* NURSE)

NURSE: Madam!

JULIET: Nurse?

NURSE: Your lady mother is coming to your
    chamber:
  The day is broke; be wary, look about.
    (*Exit*)

JULIET: Then, window, let day in, and let life out.

ROMEO: Farewell, farewell! one kiss, and I'll
    descend.
    (*Descends*)

JULIET: Art thou gone so? my lord, my love, my
    friend!
  I must hear from thee every day i' the hour,
  For in a minute there are many days:
  O, by this count I shall be much in years
  Ere I again behold my Romeo!

ROMEO: Farewell!
  I will omit no opportunity
  That may convey my greetings, love, to thee.

JULIET: O, think'st thou we shall ever meet again?

ROMEO: I doubt it not; and all these woes shall
    serve
  For sweet discourses in our time to come.

JULIET: O God! I have an ill-divining soul!
  Methinks I see thee, now thou art below,
  As one dead in the bottom of a tomb:

Either my eyesight fails, or thou look'st pale.

ROMEO: And trust me, love, in my eye so do you:
Dry sorrow drinks our blood. Adieu, adieu!
(*Exit below*)

JULIET: O fortune, fortune! all men call thee fickle:
If thou art fickle, what dost thou with him
That is renown'd for faith? Be fickle, fortune;
For then, I hope, thou wilt not keep him long
But send him back.

LADY CAPULET (*Within*): Ho, daughter! are you
up?

JULIET: Who is't that calls? is it my lady mother?
Is she not down so late, or up so early?
What unaccustom'd cause procures her hither?
(*Enter* LADY CAPULET)

LADY CAPULET: Why, how now, Juliet?

JULIET: Madam, I am not well.

LADY CAPULET: Evermore weeping for your
cousin's death?
What, wilt thou wash him from his grave with
tears?
An if thou couldst, thou couldst not make him
live;
Therefore have done: some grief shows much
of love;
But much of grief shows still some want of wit.

JULIET: Yet let me weep for such a feeling loss.

LADY CAPULET: So shall you feel the loss, but not
the friend
Which you weep for.

JULIET: Feeling so the loss,
I cannot choose but ever weep the friend.

LADY CAPULET: Well, girl, thou weep'st not so
much for his death
As that the villain lives which slaughter'd him.

JULIET: What villain, madam?

LADY CAPULET: That same villain Romeo.

JULIET: Villain and he be many miles asunder.—
God pardon him! I do, with all my heart;
And yet no man like he doth grieve my heart.

LADY CAPULET: That is because the traitor murderer lives.

JULIET: Ay, madam, from the reach of these my
hands.
Would none but I might venge my cousin's
death!

LADY CAPULET: We will have vengeance for it, fear
thou not:

Then weep no more. I'll send to one in
Mantua,—
Where that same banish'd runagate[24] doth
live,—
Shall give him such an unaccustom'd dram
That he shall soon keep Tybalt company:
And then I hope thou wilt be satisfied.

JULIET: Indeed I never shall be satisfied
With Romeo till I behold him—dead—
Is my poor heart so for a kinsman vex'd:
Madam, if you could find out but a man
To bear a poison, I would temper it,
That Romeo should, upon receipt thereof,
Soon sleep in quiet. O, how my heart abhors
To hear him nam'd,—and cannot come to him,—
To wreak the love I bore my cousin Tybalt
Upon his body that hath slaughter'd him!

LADY CAPULET: Find thou the means, and I'll find
such a man.
But now I'll tell thee joyful tidings, girl.

JULIET: And joy comes well in such a needy time:
What are they, I beseech your ladyship?

LADY CAPULET: Well, well, thou hast a careful
father, child;
One who, to put thee from thy heaviness,
Hath sorted out a sudden day of joy
That thou expect'st not, nor I look'd not for.

JULIET: Madam, in happy time, what day is that?

LADY CAPULET: Marry, my child, early next Thurs-
day morn
The gallant, young, and noble gentleman,
The County Paris, at St. Peter's Church,
Shall happily make thee there a joyful bride.

JULIET: Now by Saint Peter's Church, and Peter
too,
He shall not make me there a joyful bride.
I wonder at this haste; that I must wed
Ere he that should be husband comes to woo.
I pray you, tell my lord and father, madam,
I will not marry yet; and when I do, I swear
It shall be Romeo, whom you know I hate,
Rather than Paris:—these are news indeed!

LADY CAPULET: Here comes your father: tell him so
yourself,
And see how he will take it at your hands.
(*Enter* CAPULET *and* NURSE)

---

24. Renegade.

CAPULET: When the sun sets, the air doth drizzle
  dew;
But for the sunset of my brother's son
It rains downright.—
How now! a conduit, girl? what, still in tears?
Evermore showering? In one little body
Thou counterfeit'st a bark, a sea, a wind:
For still thy eyes, which I may call the sea,
Do ebb and flow with tears; the bark thy body is,
Sailing in this salt flood; the winds, thy sighs;
Who,—raging with thy tears and they with
  them,—
Without a sudden calm, will overset
Thy tempest-tossed body.—How now, wife!
Have you deliver'd to her our decree?

LADY CAPULET: Ay, sir; but she will none, she gives
  you thanks.
I would the fool were married to her grave!

CAPULET: Soft! take me with you, take me with
  you, wife.
How! will she none? doth she not give us
  thanks?
Is she not proud? doth she not count her bles'd,
Unworthy as she is, that we have wrought
So worthy a gentleman to be her bridegroom?

JULIET: Not proud you have; but thankful that you
  have:
Proud can I never be of what I hate;
But thankful even for hate that is meant love.

CAPULET: How now, how now, chop-logic! What
  is this?
Proud,—and, I thank you,—and I thank you
  not;—
And yet not proud:—mistress minion, you,
Thank me no thankings, nor proud me no
  prouds,
But fettle your fine joints 'gainst Thursday next
To go with Paris to Saint Peter's Church,
Or I will drag thee on a hurdle thither.
Out, you green-sickness carrion! out, you
  baggage!
You tallow-face!

LADY CAPULET: Fie, fie! what, are you mad?

JULIET: Good father, I beseech you on my knees,
Hear me with patience but to speak a word.

CAPULET: Hang thee, young baggage! disobedient
  wretch!
I tell thee what,—get thee to church o' Thursday,
Or never after look me in the face:
Speak not, reply not, do not answer me;
My fingers itch.—Wife, we scarce thought us
  bles'd
That God had lent us but this only child;
But now I see this one is one too much,
And that we have a curse in having her:
Out on her, hilding![25]

NURSE: God in heaven bless her!—
You are to blame, my lord, to rate her so.

CAPULET: And why, my lady wisdom? hold your
  tongue,
Good prudence; smatter with your gossips, go.

NURSE: I speak no treason.

CAPULET: O, God ye good-en!

NURSE: May not one speak?

CAPULET: Peace, you mumbling fool!
Utter your gravity o'er a gossip's bowl,
For here we need it not.

LADY CAPULET: You are too hot.

CAPULET: God's bread! it makes me mad:
Day, night, hour, time, tide, work, play,
Alone, in company, still my care hath been
To have her match'd, and having now provided
A gentleman of noble parentage,
Of fair demesnes, youthful, and nobly train'd,
Stuff'd, as they say, with honourable parts,
Proportion'd as one's heart would wish a
  man,—
And then to have a wretched puling fool,
A whining mammet,[26] in her fortune's tender,
To answer, "I'll not wed,—I cannot love,
I am too young,—I pray you pardon me:"—
But, an you will not wed, I'll pardon you:
Graze where you will, you shall not house with
  me:
Look to 't, think on't, I do not use to jest.
Thursday is near; lay hand on heart, advise:
An you be mine, I'll give you to my friend;
An you be not, hang, beg, starve, die i' the
  streets,
For, by my soul, I'll ne'er acknowledge thee,
Nor what is mine shall never do thee good:
Trust to 't, bethink you, I'll not be forsworn.
  (Exit)

25. Worthless human being.
26. Puppet.

JULIET: Is there no pity sitting in the clouds,
  That sees into the bottom of my grief?
  O, sweet my mother, cast me not away!
  Delay this marriage for a month, a week;
  Or, if you do not, make the bridal bed
  In that dim monument where Tybalt lies.
LADY CAPULET: Talk not to me, for I'll not speak a
  word;
  Do as thou wilt, for I have done with thee.
  (*Exit*)
JULIET: O God!—O nurse! how shall this be
  prevented?
  My husband is on earth, my faith in heaven;
  How shall that faith return again to earth,
  Unless that husband send it me from heaven
  By leaving earth?—comfort me, counsel me.—
  Alack, alack, that heaven should practise
  stratagems
  Upon so soft a subject as myself!—
  What say'st thou? hast thou not a word of joy?
  Some comfort, nurse.
NURSE: Faith, here 'tis; Romeo
  Is banished; and all the world to nothing
  That he dares ne'er come back to challenge
  you;
  Or if he do, it needs must be by stealth.
  Then, since the case so stands as now it doth,
  I think it best you married with the county.
  O, he's a lovely gentleman!
  Romeo's a dishclout to him; an eagle, madam,
  Hath not so green, so quick, so fair an eye
  As Paris hath. Beshrew my very heart,
  I think you are happy in this second match,
  For it excels your first: or if it did not,
  Your first is dead; or 'twere as good he were,
  As living here, and you no use of him.
JULIET: Speakest thou this from thy heart?
NURSE: And from my soul too;
  Or else beshrew them both.
JULIET: Amen!
NURSE: What?
JULIET: Well, thou hast comforted me marvellous
  much.
  Go in; and tell my lady I am gone,
  Having displeas'd my father, to Lawrence' cell,
  To make confession and to be absolv'd.
NURSE: Marry, I will; and this is wisely done.
  (*Exit*)

JULIET: Ancient damnation! O most wicked fiend!
  Is it more sin to wish me thus forsworn,
  Or to dispraise my lord with that same tongue
  Which she hath prais'd him with above
    compare
  So many thousand times?—Go, counsellor;
  Thou and my bosom henceforth shall be
    twain.—
  I'll to the friar to know his remedy;
  If all else fail, myself have power to die.
  (*Exit*)

ACT IV

SCENE I   FRIAR LAWRENCE'S CELL.

Enter FRIAR LAWRENCE *and* PARIS

FRIAR: On Thursday, sir? the time is very short.
PARIS: My father Capulet will have it so;
  And I am nothing slow to slack his haste.
FRIAR: You say you do not know the lady's mind:
  Uneven is the course; I like it not.
PARIS: Immoderately she weeps for Tybalt's death,
  And therefore have I little talk'd of love;
  For Venus smiles not in a house of tears.
  Now, sir, her father counts it dangerous
  That she do give her sorrow so much sway;
  And, in his wisdom, hastes our marriage,
  To stop the inundation of her tears;
  Which, too much minded by herself alone,
  May be put from her by society:
  Now do you know the reason of this haste.
FRIAR (*Aside*): I would I knew not why it should
  be slow'd.—
  Look, sir, here comes the lady toward my cell.
  (*Enter* JULIET)
PARIS: Happily met, my lady and my wife!
JULIET: That may be, sir, when I may be a wife.
PARIS: That may be must be, love, on Thursday
  next.
JULIET: What must be shall be.
FRIAR: That's a certain text.
PARIS: Come you to make confession to this
  father?
JULIET: To answer that, I should confess to you.
PARIS: Do not deny to him that you love me.
JULIET: I will confess to you that I love him.

PARIS: So will ye, I am sure, that you love me.

JULIET: If I do so, it will be of more price,
Being spoke behind your back than to your
face.

PARIS: Poor soul, thy face is much abus'd with
tears.

JULIET: The tears have got small victory by that;
For it was bad enough before their spite.

PARIS: Thou wrong'st it more than tears with that
report.

JULIET: That is no slander, sir, which is a truth;
And what I spake, I spake it to my face.

PARIS: Thy face is mine, and thou hast slander'd
it.

JULIET: It may be so, for it is not mine own.—
Are you at leisure, holy father, now;
Or shall I come to you at evening mass?

FRIAR: My leisure serves me, pensive daughter,
now.—
My lord, we must entreat the time alone.

PARIS: God shield I should disturb devotion!—
Juliet, on Thursday early will I rouse you:
Till then, adieu; and keep this holy kiss.
(*Exit*)

JULIET: O, shut the door! and when thou hast
done so,
Come weep with me; past hope, past cure, past
help!

FRIAR: Ah, Juliet, I already know thy grief;
It strains me past the compass of my wits:
I hear thou must, and nothing may prorogue[27] it,
On Thursday next be married to this county.

JULIET: Tell me not, friar, that thou hear'st of this,
Unless thou tell me how I may prevent it:
If, in thy wisdom, thou canst give no help,
Do thou but call my resolution wise,
And with this knife I'll help it presently.
God join'd my heart and Romeo's, thou our
hands;
And ere this hand, by thee to Romeo's seal'd,
Shall be the label to another deed,
Or my true heart with treacherous revolt
Turn to another, this shall slay them both:
Therefore, out of thy long-experienc'd time,
Give me some present counsel; or, behold,
'Twixt my extremes and me this bloody knife

27. Delay.

Shall play the empire; arbitrating that
Which the commission of thy years and art
Could to no issue of true honour bring.
Be not so long to speak; I long to die,
If what thou speak'st speak not of remedy.

FRIAR: Hold, daughter. I do spy a kind of hope,
Which craves as desperate an execution
As that is desperate which we would prevent.
If, rather than to marry County Paris
Thou hast the strength of will to slay thyself,
Then is it likely thou wilt undertake
A thing like death to chide away this shame,
That cop'st with death himself to scape from it;
And, if thou dar'st, I'll give thee remedy.

JULIET: O, bid me leap, rather than marry Paris,
From off the battlements of yonder tower;
Or walk in thievish ways; or bid me lurk
Where serpents are; chain me with roaring
bears;
Or shut me nightly in a charnel-house,
O'er-cover'd quite with dead men's rattling
bones,
With reeky shanks and yellow chapless skulls;
Or bid me go into a new-made grave,
And hide me with a dead man in his shroud;
Things that, to hear them told, have made me
tremble;
And I will do it without fear or doubt,
To live an unstain'd wife to my sweet love.

FRIAR: Hold, then; go home, be merry, give consent
To marry Paris: Wednesday is to-morrow;
To-morrow night look that thou lie alone,
Let not thy nurse lie with thee in thy chamber:
Take thou this vial, being then in bed,
And this distilled liquor drink thou off:
When, presently, through all thy veins shall run
A cold and drowsy humour; for no pulse
Shall keep his native progress, but surcease:
No warmth, no breath, shall testify thou livest;
The roses in thy lips and cheeks shall fade
To paly ashes; thy eyes' windows fall,
Like death, when he shuts up the day of life;
Each part, depriv'd of supple government,
Shall, stiff and stark and cold, appear like
death:
And in this borrow'd likeness of shrunk death
Thou shalt continue two-and-forty hours,
And then awake as from a pleasant sleep.

Now, when the bridegroom in the morning
    comes
To rouse thee from thy bed, there art thou dead:
Then,—as the manner of our country is,—
In thy best robes, uncover'd, on the bier,
Thou shalt be borne to that same ancient vault
Where all the kindred of the Capulets lie.
In the mean time, against thou shalt awake,
Shall Romeo by my letters know our drift;
And hither shall he come: and he and I
Will watch thy waking, and that very night
Shall Romeo bear thee hence to Mantua.
And this shall free thee from this present shame,
If no inconstant toy nor womanish fear
Abate thy valour in the acting it.
JULIET: Give me, give me! O, tell not me of fear!
FRIAR: Hold; get you gone, be strong and prosperous
    In this resolve: I'll send a friar with speed
    To Mantua, with my letters to thy lord.
JULIET: Love give me strength! and strength shall
    help afford.
    Farewell, dear father.
    (*Exeunt*)

SCENE II   HALL IN CAPULET'S HOUSE.

Enter CAPULET, LADY CAPULET, NURSE, *and* SERVANTS

CAPULET: So many guests invite as here are writ.—
    (*Exit* SERVANT)
    Sirrah, go hire me twenty cunning cooks.
SERVANT: You shall have none ill, sir; for I'll try if
    they can lick their fingers.
CAPULET: How canst thou try them so?
SERVANT: Marry, sir, 'tis an ill cook that cannot lick
    his own fingers: therefore he that cannot lick
    his fingers goes not with me.
CAPULET: Go, begone.—
    (*Exit* SECOND SERVANT)
    We shall be much unfurnish'd for this time.—
    What, is my daughter gone to Friar Lawrence?
NURSE: Ay, forsooth.
CAPULET: Well, be may chance to do some good on
    her:
    A peevish self-will'd harlotry it is.
NURSE: See where she comes from shrift with
    merry look.
    (*Enter* JULIET)

CAPULET: How now, my headstrong! where have
    you been gadding?
JULIET: Where I have learn'd me to repent the sin
    Of disobedient opposition
    To you and your behests; and am enjoin'd
    By holy Lawrence to fall prostrate here,
    To beg your pardon:—pardon, I beseech you!
    Henceforward I am ever rul'd by you.
CAPULET: Send for the county; go tell him of this:
    I'll have this knot knit up to-morrow morning.
JULIET: I met the youthful lord at Lawrence' cell;
    And gave him what becomed love I might,
    Not stepping o'er the bounds of modesty.
CAPULET: Why, I am glad on't; this is well,—stand
    up,—
    This is as't should be.—Let me see the county;
    Ay, marry, go, I say, and fetch him hither.—
    Now, afore God, this reverend holy friar,
    All our whole city is much bound to him.
JULIET: Nurse, will you go with me into my closet,
    To help me sort such needful ornaments
    As you think fit to furnish me to-morrow?
LADY CAPULET: No, not till Thursday; there is time
    enough.
CAPULET: Go, nurse, go with her.—We'll to church
    to-morrow.
    (*Exeunt* JULIET *and* NURSE)
LADY CAPULET: We shall be short in our provision:
    'Tis now near night.
CAPULET: Tush, I will stir about,
    And all things shall be well, I warrant thee, wife:
    Go thou to Juliet, help to deck up her;
    I'll not to bed to-night;—let me alone;
    I'll play the housewife for this once.—What, ho!—
    They are all forth: well, I will walk myself
    To County Paris, to prepare him up
    Against to-morrow: my heart is wondrous light
    Since this same wayward girl is so reclaim'd.
    (*Exeunt*)

SCENE III   JULIET'S CHAMBER.

Enter JULIET *and* NURSE

JULIET: Ay, those attires are best:—but, gentle
    nurse,
    I pray thee, leave me to myself to-night;
    For I have need of many orisons

To move the heavens to smile upon my state,
Which, well thou know'st, is cross and full of sin.
   (*Enter* LADY CAPULET)
LADY CAPULET: What, are you busy, ho? need you
      my help?
JULIET: No, madam; we have cull'd such necessaries
   As are behoveful for our state to-morrow:
   So please you, let me now be left alone,
   And let the nurse this night sit up with you;
   For I am sure you have your hands full all
   In this so sudden business.
LADY CAPULET: Good night:
   Get thee to bed, and rest; for thou hast need.
      (*Exeunt* LADY CAPULET *and* NURSE)
JULIET: Farewell!—God knows when we shall
      meet again.
   I have a faint cold fear thrills through my veins
   That almost freezes up the heat of life:
   I'll call them back again to comfort me;—
   Nurse!—What should she do here?
   My dismal scene I needs must act alone.—
   Come, vial.—
   What if this mixture do not work at all?
   Shall I be married, then, to-morrow morning?—
   No, No!—this shall forbid it:—lie thou there.—
      (*Laying down her dagger*)
   What if it be a poison, which the friar
   Subtly hath minister'd to have me dead,
   Lest in this marriage he should be dishonour'd,
   Because he married me before to Romeo?
   I fear it is: and yet methinks it should not,
   For he hath still been tried a holy man:—
   I will not entertain so bad a thought.—
   How if, when I am laid into the tomb,
   I wake before the time that Romeo
   Come to redeem me? there's a fearful point!
   Shall I not then be stifled in the vault,
   To whose foul mouth no healthsome air
      breathes in,
   And there die strangled ere my Romeo comes?
   Or, if I live, is it not very like
   The horrible conceit of death and night,
   Together with the terror of the place,—
   As in a vault, an ancient receptacle,
   Where, for this many hundred years, the bones
   Of all my buried ancestors are pack'd;
   Where bloody Tybalt, yet but green in earth,
   Lies festering in his shroud; where, as they say,

At some hours in the night spirits resort;—
Alack, alack, is it not like that I,
So early waking,—what with loathsome smells,
And shrieks like mandrakes torn out of the earth,
That living mortals, hearing them, run mad;—
O, if I wake, shall I not be distraught,
Environed with all these hideous fears?
And madly play with my forefathers' joints?
And pluck the mangled Tybalt from his shroud?
And, in this rage, with some great kinsman's
   bone,
As with a club, dash out my desperate brains?—
O, look! methinks I see my cousin's ghost
Seeking out Romeo, that did spit his body
Upon a rapier's point:—stay, Tybalt, stay!—
Romeo, I come! this do I drink to thee.
   (*Throws herself on the bed.*)

SCENE IV   HALL IN CAPULET'S HOUSE.
Enter LADY CAPULET *and* NURSE

LADY CAPULET: Hold, take these keys and fetch
      more spices, nurse.
NURSE: They call for dates and quinces in the pastry.
      (*Enter* CAPULET)
CAPULET: Come, stir, stir, stir! The second cock
      hath crow'd,
   The curfew bell hath rung, 'tis three o'clock:—
   Look to the bak'd meats, good Angelica;
   Spare not for cost.
NURSE: Go, you cot-quean,[28] go,
   Get you to bed; faith, you'll be sick to-morrow
   For this night's watching.
CAPULET: No, not a whit: what! I have watch'd ere
      now
   All night for lesser cause, and ne'er been sick.
LADY CAPULET: Ay, you have been a mouse-hunt[29]
      in your time;
   But I will watch you from such watching now.
      (*Exeunt* LADY CAPULET *and* NURSE)
CAPULET: A jealous-hood, a jealous-hood!—Now,
      fellow,
      (*Enter* SERVANTS, *with spits, logs and baskets*)
   What's there?

---

28. A man doing women's work.
29. Prowling at night.

FIRST SERVANT: Things for the cook, sir; but I know
    not what.

CAPULET: Make haste, make haste. (*Exit* FIRST
    SERVANT.)
    —Sirrah, fetch drier logs:
    Call Peter, he will show thee where they are.

SECOND SERVANT:
    I have a head, sir, that will find out logs
    And never trouble Peter for the matter.
        (*Exit*)

CAPULET: Mass, and well said; a merry whoreson,
    ha!
    Thou shalt be logger-head.—Good faith, 'tis day.
    The county will be here with music straight,
    For so he said he would:—I hear him near.
        (*Music within*)
    Nurse!—wife!—what, ho!—what, nurse, I say!
        (*Enter* NURSE)
    Go, waken Juliet; go and trim her up;
    I'll go and chat with Paris:—hie, make haste,
    Make haste; the bridegroom he is come already:
    Make haste, I say.
        (*Exeunt*)

SCENE V   JULIET'S CHAMBER; JULIET ON THE BED.

Enter NURSE

NURSE: Mistress!—what, mistress!—Juliet!—fast, I
    warrant her, she:—
    Why, lamb!—why, lady!—fie, you slug-abed!—
    Why, love, I say!—madam! sweetheart!—why,
    bride!—
    What, not a word?—you take your penny-
    worths now;
    Sleep for a week; for the next night, I warrant,
    The County Paris hath set up his rest
    That you shall rest but little.—God forgive me!
    Marry, and amen, how sound is she asleep!
    I needs must wake her.—Madam, madam,
    madam!—
    Ay, let the county take you in your bed;
    He'll fright you up, i' faith.—Will it not be?
    What, dress'd! and in your clothes! and down
    again!
    I must needs wake you.—lady! lady! lady!—
    Alas, alas!—Help, help! My lady's dead!—

O, well-a-day that ever I was born!—
    Some aqua-vitae, ho!—my lord! my lady!
        (*Enter* LADY CAPULET)

LADY CAPULET: What noise is here?

NURSE: O lamentable day!

LADY CAPULET: What is the matter?

NURSE: Look, look! O heavy day!

LADY CAPULET: O me, O me!—my child, my only
    life!
    Revive, look up, or I will die with thee!—
    Help, help!—call help.
        (*Enter* CAPULET)

CAPULET: For shame, bring Juliet forth; her lord is
    come.

NURSE: She's dead, deceas'd, she's dead; alack the
    day!

LADY CAPULET: Alack the day, she's dead, she's
    dead, she's dead!

CAPULET: Ha! let me see her:—out alas! she's cold;
    Her blood is settled, and her joints are stiff;
    Life and these lips have long been separated:
    Death lies on her like an untimely frost
    Upon the sweetest flower of all the field.
    Accursed time! unfortunate old man!

NURSE: O lamentable day!

LADY CAPULET: O woful time!

CAPULET: Death, that hath ta'en her hence to make
    me wail,
    Ties up my tongue and will not let me speak.
        (*Enter* FRIAR LAWRENCE *and* PARIS *with* MUSICIANS)

FRIAR: Come, is the bride ready to go to church?

CAPULET: Ready to go, but never to return:—
    O son, the night before thy wedding day
    Hath death lain with thy bride:—there she lies,
    Flower as she was, deflowered by him.
    Death is my son-in-law, death is my heir;
    My daughter he hath wedded: I will die.
    And leave him all; life, living, all is death's.

PARIS: Have I thought long to see this morning's
    face,
    And doth it give me such a sight as this?

LADY CAPULET: Accurs'd, unhappy, wretched,
    hateful day!
    Most miserable hour that e'er time saw
    In lasting labour of his pilgrimage!
    But one, poor one, one poor and loving child,
    But one thing to rejoice and solace in,
    And cruel death hath catch'd it from my sight!

NURSE: O woe! O woeful, woeful, woeful day!
  Most lamentable day, most woeful day
  That ever, ever, I did yet behold!
  O day! O day! O day! O hateful day!
  Never was seen so black a day as this:
  O woeful day! O woeful day!
PARIS: Beguil'd, divorced, wronged, spited, slain!
  Most detestable death, by thee beguil'd,
  By cruel cruel thee quite overthrown!—
  O love! O life!—not life, but love in death!
CAPULET: Despis'd, distressed, hated, martyr'd,
    kill'd!—
  Uncomfortable time, why cam'st thou now
  To murder, murder our solemnity?—
  O child! O child!—my soul, and not my child!—
  Dead art thou, dead!—alack, my child is dead;
  And with my child my joys are buried!
FRIAR: Peace, ho, for shame! confusion's cure lives
    not
  In these confusions. Heaven and yourself
  Had part in this fair maid; now heaven hath all,
  And all the better is it for the maid:
  Your part in her you could not keep from death;
  But heaven keeps his part in eternal life.
  The most you sought was her promotion;
  For 'twas your heaven she should be advanc'd:
  And weep ye now, seeing she is advanc'd
  Above the clouds, as high as heaven itself?
  O, in this love, you love your child so ill
  That you run mad, seeing that she is well:
  She's not well married that lives married long:
  But she's best married that dies married young.
  Dry up your tears, and stick your rosemary
  On this fair corse; and, as the custom is,
  In all her best array bear her to church;
  For though fond nature bids us all lament,
  Yet nature's tears are reason's merriment.
CAPULET: All things that we ordained festival
  Turn from their office to black funeral:
  Our instruments to melancholy bells;
  Our wedding cheer to a sad burial feast;
  Our solemn hymns to sullen dirges change;
  Our bridal flowers serve for a buried corse,
  And all things change them to the contrary.
FRIAR: Sir, go you in,—and, madam, go with
    him;—
  And go, Sir Paris;—every one prepare
  To follow this fair corse unto her grave:

The heavens do lower upon you for some ill;
Move them no more by crossing their high will.
  (*Exeunt* CAPULET, LADY CAPULET, PARIS, FRIAR)
FIRST MUSICIAN: Faith, we may put up our pipes
  and be gone.
NURSE: Honest good fellows, ah, put up, put up;
  For well you know this is a pitiful case.
  (*Exit*)
FIRST MUSICIAN: Ay, by my troth, the case may be
  amended.
  (*Enter* PETER)
PETER: Musicians, O, musicians, "Heart's ease,"
  "Heart's ease":
  O, an you will have me live, play "Heart's ease."
FIRST MUSICIAN: Why "Heart's ease"?
PETER: O, musicians, because my heart itself plays
  "My heart is
  full of woe": O, play me some merry dump to
  comfort me.
FIRST MUSICIAN: Not a dump we: 'tis no time to
  play now.
PETER: You will not then?
FIRST MUSICIAN: No.
PETER: I will then give it you soundly.
FIRST MUSICIAN: What will you give us?
PETER: No money, on my faith; but the gleek,—I
  will give you the minstrel.
FIRST MUSICIAN: Then will I give you the serving-
  creature.
PETER: Then will I lay the serving-creature's dag-
  ger on your pate. I will carry no crotchets: I'll
  re you, I'll fa you: do you note me?
FIRST MUSICIAN: An you re us and fa us, you note
  us.
SECOND MUSICIAN: Pray you put up your dagger,
  and put out your wit.
PETER: Then have at you with my wit! I will dry-
  beat you with an iron wit, and put up my
  iron dagger.—Answer me like men:

      "When griping grief the heart doth wound,
      And doleful dumps the mind oppress,
      Then music with her "silver sound"—

why "silver sound"? why "music with her
  silver sound"?—
What say you, Simon Catling?
FIRST MUSICIAN: Marry, sir, because silver hath a
  sweet sound.

PETER: Pretty!—What say you, Hugh Rebeck?

SECOND MUSICIAN: I say "silver sound" because musicians sound for silver.

PETER: Pretty too!—What say you, James Sound-post?

THIRD MUSICIAN: Faith, I know not what to say.

PETER: O, I cry you mercy; you are the singer: I will say for you.

It is "music with her silver sound" because musicians have

no gold for sounding:—

"Then music with her silver sound
    With speedy help doth lend redress."

(*Exit*)

FIRST MUSICIAN: What a pestilent knave is this same!

SECOND MUSICIAN: Hang him, Jack!—Come, we'll in here; tarry for the mourners, and stay dinner.

(*Exeunt*)

ACT V

SCENE I   MANTUA. A STREET.

Enter ROMEO

ROMEO: If I may trust the flattering eye of sleep,
My dreams presage some joyful news at hand;
My bosom's lord sits lightly in his throne;
And all this day an unaccustom'd spirit
Lifts me above the ground with cheerful thoughts.
I dreamt my lady came and found me dead,—
Strange dream, that gives a dead man leave to think!—
And breath'd such life with kisses in my lips,
That I reviv'd, and was an emperor.
Ah me! how sweet is love itself possess'd,
When but love's shadows are so rich in joy!
    (*Enter* BALTHASAR)
News from Verona!—How now, Balthasar?
Dost thou not bring me letters from the friar?
How doth my lady? Is my father well?
How fares my Juliet? that I ask again;
For nothing can be ill if she be well.

BALTHASAR: Then she is well, and nothing can be ill:
Her body sleeps in Capel's monument,
And her immortal part with angels lives.

I saw her laid low in her kindred's vault,
And presently took post to tell it you:
O, pardon me for bringing these ill news,
Since you did leave it for my office, sir.

ROMEO: Is it even so? then I defy you, stars!—
Thou know'st my lodging: get me ink and paper,
And hire post-horses. I will hence to-night.

BALTHASAR: I do beseech you, sir, have patience:
Your looks are pale and wild, and do import
Some misadventure.

ROMEO: Tush, thou art deceiv'd:
Leave me, and do the thing I bid thee do.
Hast thou no letters to me from the friar?

BALTHASAR: No, my good lord.

ROMEO: No matter: get thee gone,
And hire those horses; I'll be with thee straight.
    (*Exit* BALTHASAR)
Well, Juliet, I will lie with thee to-night.
Let's see for means;—O mischief, thou art swift
To enter in the thoughts of desperate men!
I do remember an apothecary,—
And hereabouts he dwells,—which late I noted
In tatter'd weeds, with overwhelming brows,
Culling of simples;[30] meagre were his looks,
Sharp misery had worn him to the bones;
And in his needy shop a tortoise hung,
An alligator stuff'd, and other skins
Of ill-shaped fishes; and about his shelves
A beggarly account of empty boxes,
Green earthen pots, bladders, and musty seeds,
Remnants of packthread, and old cakes of roses,
Were thinly scatter'd, to make up a show.
Noting this penury, to myself I said,
An if a man did need a poison now,
Whose sale is present death in Mantua,
Here lives a caitiff wretch would sell it him.
O, this same thought did but forerun my need;
And this same needy man must sell it me.
As I remember, this should be the house:
Being holiday, the beggar's shop is shut.—
What, ho! apothecary!
    (*Enter* APOTHECARY)

APOTHECARY: Who calls so loud?

ROMEO: Come hither, man.—I see that thou art poor;

---

30. Collecting herbs.

Hold, there is forty ducats: let me have
A dram of poison; such soon-speeding gear
As will disperse itself through all the veins
That the life-weary taker may fall dead;
And that the trunk may be discharg'd of breath
As violently as hasty powder fir'd
Doth hurry from the fatal cannon's womb.
APOTHECARY: Such mortal drugs I have; but
  Mantua's law
Is death to any he that utters them.
ROMEO: Art thou so bare and full of wretchedness
And fear'st to die? famine is in thy cheeks,
Need and oppression starveth in thine eyes,
Contempt and beggary hangs upon thy back,
The world is not thy friend, nor the world's
  law:
The world affords no law to make thee rich;
Then be not poor, but break it and take this.
APOTHECARY: My poverty, but not my will
  consents.
ROMEO: I pay thy poverty, and not thy will.
APOTHECARY: Put this in any liquid thing you will,
And drink it off; and, if you had the strength
Of twenty men, it would despatch you straight.
ROMEO: There is thy gold; worse poison to men's
  souls,
Doing more murders in this loathsome world
Than these poor compounds that thou mayst
  not sell:
I sell thee poison; thou hast sold me none.
Farewell: buy food and get thyself in flesh.—
Come, cordial and not poison, go with me
To Juliet's grave; for there must I use thee.
  (*Exeunt*)

SCENE II   FRIAR LAWRENCE'S CELL.
Enter FRIAR JOHN

FRIAR JOHN: Holy Franciscan friar! brother, ho!
  (*Enter* FRIAR LAWRENCE)
FRIAR LAWRENCE: This same should be the voice of
  Friar John.
Welcome from Mantua: what says Romeo?
Or, if his mind be writ, give me his letter.
FRIAR JOHN: Going to find a barefoot brother out,
One of our order, to associate me,
Here in this city visiting the sick,

And finding him, the searchers of the town,
Suspecting that we both were in a house
Where the infectious pestilence did reign,
Seal'd up the doors, and would not let us forth;
So that my speed to Mantua there was stay'd.
FRIAR LAWRENCE: Who bare my letter, then, to
  Romeo?
FRIAR JOHN: I could not send it,—here it is
  again,—
Nor get a messenger to bring it thee,
So fearful were they of infection.
FRIAR LAWRENCE: Unhappy fortune! by my
  brotherhood,
The letter was not nice, but full of charge
Of dear import; and the neglecting it
May do much danger. Friar John, go hence;
Get me an iron crow[31] and bring it straight
Unto my cell.
FRIAR JOHN: Brother, I'll go and bring it thee.
  (*Exit*)
FRIAR LAWRENCE: Now must I to the monument
  alone;
Within this three hours will fair Juliet wake:
She will beshrew me much that Romeo
Hath had no notice of these accidents;
But I will write again to Mantua,
And keep her at my cell till Romeo come;—
Poor living corse, clos'd in a dead man's tomb!
  (*Exit*)

SCENE III   A CHURCHYARD; IN IT A MONUMENT BELONGING TO THE CAPULETS.
Enter PARIS *and his* PAGE *bearing flowers and a torch*

PARIS: Give me thy torch, boy: hence, and stand
  aloof;—
Yet put it out, for I would not be seen.
Under yond yew tree lay thee all along,
Holding thine ear close to the hollow ground;
So shall no foot upon the churchyard tread,—
Being loose, unfirm, with digging up of
  graves,—
But thou shalt hear it: whistle then to me,
As signal that thou hear'st something approach.
Give me those flowers. Do as I bid thee, go.

31. Crowbar.

PAGE (*Aside*): I am almost afraid to stand alone
  Here in the churchyard; yet I will adventure.
    (*Retires*)
PARIS: Sweet flower, with flowers thy bridal bed I
    strew:
  O woe! thy canopy is dust and stones!
  Which with sweet water nightly I will dew;
  Or, wanting that, with tears distill'd by moans:
  The obsequies that I for thee will keep,
  Nightly shall be to strew thy grave and weep.
    (*The* PAGE *whistles*)
  The boy gives warning something doth
    approach.
  What cursed foot wanders this way to-night,
  To cross my obsequies and true love's rite?
  What, with a torch! muffle me, night, awhile.
    (*Retires*)
    (*Enter* ROMEO *and* BALTHASAR *with a torch and
    tools*)
ROMEO: Give me that mattock and the wrenching
    iron.
  Hold, take this letter; early in the morning
  See thou deliver it to my lord and father.
  Give me the light; upon thy life I charge thee,
  Whate'er thou hear'st or seest, stand all aloof
  And do not interrupt me in my course.
  Why I descend into this bed of death
  Is partly to behold my lady's face,
  But chiefly to take thence from her dead finger
  A precious ring,—a ring that I must use
  In dear employment: therefore hence, be gone:—
  But if thou, jealous, dost return to pry
  In what I further shall intend to do,
  By heaven, I will tear thee joint by joint,
  And strew this hungry churchyard with thy
    limbs:
  The time and my intents are savage-wild;
  More fierce and more inexorable far
  Than empty tigers or the roaring sea.
BALTHASAR: I will be gone, sir, and not trouble you.
ROMEO: So shalt thou show me friendship.—Take
  thou that:
  Live, and be prosperous: and farewell, good
    fellow.
BALTHASAR (*Aside*): For all this same, I'll hide me
  hereabout:
  His looks I fear, and his intents I doubt.
    (*Exit*)

ROMEO: Thou detestable maw,[32] thou womb of
  death,
  Gorg'd with the dearest morsel of the earth,
  Thus I enforce thy rotten jaws to open,
    (*Breaking open the door of the monument*)
  And, in despite, I'll cram thee with more food!
PARIS: This is that banish'd haughty Montague
  That murder'd my love's cousin,—with which
    grief,
  It is supposed, the fair creature died,—
  And here is come to do some villanous shame
  To the dead bodies: I will apprehend him.—
    (*Advances*)
  Stop thy unhallow'd toil, vile Montague!
  Can vengeance be pursu'd further than death?
  Condemned villain, I do apprehend thee;
  Obey, and go with me; for thou must die.
ROMEO: I must indeed; and therefore came I
    hither.—
  Good gentle youth, tempt not a desperate man;
  Fly hence and leave me:—think upon these gone;
  Let them affright thee.—I beseech thee, youth,
  Put not another sin upon my head
  By urging me to fury: O, be gone!
  By heaven, I love thee better than myself;
  For I come hither arm'd against myself:
  Stay not, be gone;—live, and hereafter say,
  A madman's mercy bid thee run away.
PARIS: I do defy thy conjurations,
  And apprehend thee for a felon here.
ROMEO: Wilt thou provoke me? then have at thee,
  boy!
    (*They fight*)
PAGE: O lord, they fight! I will go call the watch.
    (*Exit*)
PARIS: O, I am slain! (*Falls.*) If thou be merciful,
  Open the tomb, lay me with Juliet.
    (*Dies*)
ROMEO: In faith, I will.—Let me peruse this face:—
  Mercutio's kinsman, noble County Paris!—
  What said my man, when my betossed soul
  Did not attend him as we rode? I think
  He told me Paris should have married Juliet:
  Said he not so? or did I dream it so?
  Or am I mad, hearing him talk of Juliet,
  To think it was so?—O, give me thy hand,

---

32. Stomach.

One writ with me in sour misfortune's book!
I'll bury thee in a triumphant grave;—
A grave? O, no, a lanthorn, slaught'red youth,
For here lies Juliet, and her beauty makes
This vault a feasting presence full of light.
Death, lie thou there, by a dead man interr'd.
(*Laying* PARIS *in the monument*)
How oft when men are at the point of death
Have they been merry! which their keepers call
A lightning before death: O, how may I
Call this a lightning?—O my love! my wife!
Death, that hath suck'd the honey of thy breath,
Hath had no power yet upon thy beauty:
Thou art not conquer'd; beauty's ensign yet
Is crimson in thy lips and in thy cheeks,
And death's pale flag is not advanced there.—
Tybalt, liest thou there in thy bloody sheet?
O, what more favour can I do to thee
Than with that hand that cut thy youth in twain
To sunder his that was thine enemy?
Forgive me, cousin!—Ah, dear Juliet,
Why art thou yet so fair? Shall I believe
That unsubstantial death is amorous;
And that the lean abhorred monster keeps
Thee here in dark to be his paramour?
For fear of that I still will stay with thee,
And never from this palace of dim night
Depart again: here, here will I remain
With worms that are thy chambermaids: O, here
Will I set up my everlasting rest;
And shake the yoke of inauspicious stars
From this world-wearied flesh.—Eyes, look
   your last!
Arms, take your last embrace! and, lips, O you
The doors of breath, seal with a righteous kiss
A dateless bargain to engrossing death!—
Come, bitter conduct, come, unsavoury guide!
Thou desperate pilot, now at once run on
The dashing rocks thy sea-sick weary bark!
Here's to my love! (*Drinks*)—O true apothecary!
Thy drugs are quick.—Thus with a kiss I die.
(*Dies*)
(*Enter* FRIAR LAWRENCE *with a lantern, crow, and
spade*)
FRIAR: Saint Francis be my speed! how oft to-night
   Have my old feet stumbled at graves!—Who's
   there?
   Who is it that consorts, so late, the dead?

BALTHASAR: Here's one, a friend, and one that
   knows you well.
FRIAR: Bliss be upon you! Tell me, good my friend,
   What torch is yond that vainly lends his light
   To grubs and eyeless skulls? as I discern,
   It burneth in the Capels' monument.
BALTHASAR: It doth so, holy sir; and there's my
   master,
   One that you love.
FRIAR: Who is it?
BALTHASAR: Romeo.
FRIAR: How long hath he been there?
BALTHASAR: Full half an hour.
FRIAR: Go with me to the vault.
BALTHASAR: I dare not, sir;
   My master knows not but I am gone hence;
   And fearfully did menace me with death
   If I did stay to look on his intents.
FRIAR: Stay then; I'll go alone:—fear comes upon me;
   O, much I fear some ill unlucky thing.
BALTHASAR: As I did sleep under this yew tree here,
   I dreamt my master and another fought,
   And that my master slew him.
FRIAR: Romeo! (*Advances.*)
   Alack, alack! what blood is this which stains
   The stony entrance of this sepulchre?—
   What mean these masterless and gory swords
   To lie discolour'd by this place of peace?
   Romeo! O, pale!—Who else? what, Paris too?
   And steep'd in blood?—Ah, what an unkind
   hour
   Is guilty of this lamentable chance!—The lady
   stirs.
   (JULIET *wakes*)
JULIET: O comfortable friar! where is my lord?—
   I do remember well where I should be,
   And there I am:—where is my Romeo?
   (*Noise within*)
FRIAR: I hear some noise.—Lady, come from that
   nest
   Of death, contagion, and unnatural sleep:
   A greater power than we can contradict
   Hath thwarted our intents:—come, come away!
   Thy husband in thy bosom there lies dead;
   And Paris too:—come, I'll dispose of thee
   Among a sisterhood of holy nuns:
   Stay not to question, for the watch is coming.
   Come, go, good Juliet—I dare no longer stay.

JULIET: Go, get thee hence, for I will not away.—
  (*Exit* FRIAR LAWRENCE)
What's here? a cup, clos'd in my true love's
  hand?
Poison, I see, hath been his timeless end:—
O churl! drink all, and left no friendly drop
To help me after?—I will kiss thy lips;
Haply some poison yet doth hang on them,
To make me die with a restorative.
  (*Kisses him*)
Thy lips are warm!

FIRST WATCHMAN (*within*): Lead, boy:—which
  way?

JULIET: Yea, noise?—Then I'll be brief.—O happy
  dagger!
  (*Takes* ROMEO's *dagger*)
This is thy sheath; (*stabs herself*) there rest, and
  let me die.
  (*Falls and dies*)
  (*Enter* WATCH *with* PAGE *of* PARIS)

PAGE: This is the place; there, where the torch doth
  burn.

FIRST WATCHMAN: The ground is bloody; search
  about the churchyard:
Go, some of you, whoe'er you find attach.
  (*Exeunt some of the* WATCH)
Pitiful sight! here lies the county slain;—
And Juliet bleeding; warm, and newly dead,
Who here hath lain this two days buried.—
Go, tell the prince;—run to the Capulets,—
Raise up the Montagues,—some others
  search:—
  (*Exeunt others of the* WATCH)
We see the ground whereon these woes do lie;
But the true ground of all these piteous woes
We cannot without circumstance descry.
  (*Enter some of the* WATCH *with* BALTHASAR)

SECOND WATCHMAN: Here's Romeo's man; we
  found him in the churchyard.

WATCHMAN: Hold him in safety till the prince
  come hither.
  (*Enter others of the* WATCH *with* FRIAR LAWRENCE)

THIRD WATCHMAN: Here is a friar, that trembles,
  sighs, and weeps:
We took this mattock and this spade from him
As he was coming from this churchyard side.

WATCHMAN: A great suspicion: stay the friar too.
  (*Enter the* PRINCE *and* ATTENDANTS)

PRINCE: What misadventure is so early up,

That calls our person from our morning's rest?
  (*Enter* CAPULET, LADY CAPULET, *and others*)

CAPULET: What should it be, that they so shriek
  abroad?

LADY CAPULET: The people in the street cry Romeo,
  Some Juliet, and some Paris; and all run,
  With open outcry, toward our monument.

PRINCE: What fear is this which startles in our ears?

WATCHMAN: Sovereign, here lies the County Paris
  slain;
And Romeo dead; and Juliet, dead before,
Warm and new kill'd.

PRINCE: Search, seek, and know how this foul
  murder comes.

WATCHMAN: Here is a friar, and slaughter'd
  Romeo's man,
With instruments upon them fit to open
These dead men's tombs.

CAPULET: O heaven!—O wife, look how our
  daughter bleeds!
This dagger hath mista'en,—for, lo, his house
Is empty on the back of Montague,—
And it mis-sheathed in my daughter's bosom!

LADY CAPULET: O me! this sight of death is as a bell
  That warns my old age to a sepulchre.
  (*Enter* MONTAGUE *and others*)

PRINCE: Come, Montague; for thou art early up,
  To see thy son and heir more early down.

MONTAGUE: Alas, my liege, my wife is dead to-
  night;
Grief of my son's exile hath stopp'd her breath:
What further woe conspires against mine age?

PRINCE: Look, and thou shalt see.

MONTAGUE: O thou untaught! what manners is in
  this,
To press before thy father to a grave?

PRINCE: Seal up the mouth of outrage for a while,
  Till we can clear these ambiguities,
And know their spring, their head, their true
  descent;
And then will I be general of your woes,
And lead you even to death: meantime forbear,
And let mischance be slave to patience.—
Bring forth the parties of suspicion.

FRIAR: I am the greatest, able to do least,
  Yet most suspected, as the time and place
Doth make against me, of this direful murder;
And here I stand, both to impeach and purge
Myself condemned and myself excus'd.

PRINCE: Then say at once what thou dost know in this.

FRIAR: I will be brief, for my short date of breath
Is not so long as is a tedious tale.
Romeo, there dead, was husband to that Juliet;
And she, there dead, that Romeo's faithful wife:
I married them; and their stol'n marriage day
Was Tybalt's doomsday, whose untimely death
Banish'd the new-made bridegroom from this city;
For whom, and not for Tybalt, Juliet pin'd.
You, to remove that siege of grief from her,
Betroth'd, and would have married her perforce,
To County Paris:—then comes she to me,
And with wild looks, bid me devise some means
To rid her from this second marriage,
Or in my cell there would she kill herself.
Then gave I her, so tutored by my art,
A sleeping potion; which so took effect
As I intended, for it wrought on her
The form of death: meantime I writ to Romeo
That he should hither come as this dire night,
To help to take her from her borrow'd grave,
Being the time the potion's force should cease.
But he which bore my letter, Friar John,
Was stay'd by accident; and yesternight
Return'd my letter back. Then all alone
At the prefixed hour of her waking
Came I to take her from her kindred's vault;
Meaning to keep her closely at my cell
Till I conveniently could send to Romeo:
But when I came,—some minute ere the time
Of her awaking,—here untimely lay
The noble Paris and true Romeo dead.
She wakes; and I entreated her come forth
And bear this work of heaven with patience:
But then a noise did scare me from the tomb;
And she, too desperate, would not go with me,
But, as it seems, did violence on herself.
All this I know; and to the marriage
Her nurse is privy: and if ought in this
Miscarried by my fault, let my old life
Be sacrific'd, some hour before his time,
Unto the rigour of severest law.

PRINCE: We still have known thee for a holy man.—
Where's Romeo's man? what can he say in this?

BALTHASAR: I brought my master news of Juliet's death;
And then in post he came from Mantua
To this same place, to this same monument.
This letter he early bid me give his father;
And threaten'd me with death, going in the vault,
If I departed not, and left him there.

PRINCE: Give me the letter,—I will look on it.—
Where is the county's page that rais'd the watch?—
Sirrah, what made your master in this place?

BOY: He came with flowers to strew his lady's grave;
And bid me stand aloof, and so I did:
Anon comes one with light to ope the tomb;
And by-and-by my master drew on him;
And then I ran away to call the watch.

PRINCE: This letter doth make good the friar's words,
Their course of love, the tidings of her death:
And here he writes that he did buy a poison
Of a poor 'pothecary, and therewithal
Came to this vault to die, and lie with Juliet.—
Where be these enemies?—Capulet,—Montague,—
See what a scourge is laid upon your hate,
That heaven finds means to kill your joys with love!
And I, for winking at your discords too,
Have lost a brace of kinsmen:—all are punish'd.

CAPULET: O brother Montague, give me thy hand:
This is my daughter's jointure, for no more
Can I demand.

MONTAGUE: But I can give thee more:
For I will raise her statue in pure gold;
That while Verona by that name is known,
There shall no figure at such rate be set
As that of true and faithful Juliet.

CAPULET: As rich shall Romeo's by his lady's lie;
Poor sacrifices of our enmity!

PRINCE: A glooming peace this morning with it brings;
The sun for sorrow will not show his head.
Go hence, to have more talk of these sad things;
Some shall be pardon'd, and some punished;
For never was a story of more woe
Than this of Juliet and her Romeo.
(*Exeunt*)

Introduction to *Life Is a Dream*

WHEN THE PLAY WAS NEW

Calderón de la Barca, along with Lope de Vega, represents the pinnacle of dramatic achievement in the Spanish Golden Age between c. 1550 and 1650. This period in Spain is often compared to the Elizabethan period in England for its vibrant professional theatre and remarkable output of important and lasting plays. Much of this work continues to be performed regularly in Spanish-speaking cultures. The most famous plays are regularly revived in translation throughout the world and are central, not only to the history of the theatre, but to students of dramatic literature nearly everywhere.

Life Is a Dream (*La vida es sueño*) was probably written and first produced in the late 1620s. We are uncertain of its first production, but it was certainly popular by 1636 when Calderón published it. Like many of his Spanish contemporaries, Calderón was preoccupied with dramatizing the complex and inflexible code of honor. The code was very important to the nobility and upper classes of Spain and, by extension, the Spanish-speaking world, which was considerable because this was a time of global expansion for Spain. Artistically, this period was extraordinary in theatre, painting (El Greco), and literature (Cervantes) as well. Although Calderón sets *Life Is a Dream* in Poland, it is really Spanish culture and values that he is addressing: a Catholic country with a strong Moorish heritage. Women's rights were severely curtailed and unmarried girls were strictly sheltered, yet Calderón created intrepid female characters.

When writing for the public, professional theatre of Madrid, Calderón knew that the performance space—called a corral—would be outdoors, lit by the sun. The elevated stage was set at one end of a courtyard (patio). The audience stood in the patio below the stage or sat on the sides of the courtyard on three levels of balconies and boxes. Except for the lack of a thrust stage, the general arrangement was similar to that in Elizabethan England. Unlike England, however, unmarried or unaccompanied women and girls were segregated from the men and had to sit behind a lattice-work screen in a balcony called the *cazuela,* which was well away from the stage. The corral had a façade with doors or doorways, sometimes a discovery space at stage level, and an upper level for performance—similar to the Elizabethan public theatre.

The most remarkable difference between the Spanish and English stages, however, was the presence of actresses in Spain. Women's roles were played by women, which is surprising given that women in Spanish society were much more restricted than in England. Women were professionally licensed for the stage as early as 1587. Like the men in England, the actresses sometimes cross-dressed. We see an example of this with Rosaura in *Life Is a Dream.* Both actors and actresses, however, were denied the sacraments of the Church because their profession was considered reprehensible. This prohibition was not lifted until the twentieth century.

THE PLAYWRIGHT

Pedro Calderón de la Barca (1600–1681) was university-educated and prepared for the priesthood, which he eventually joined in 1651 after many personal losses in mid-life. By 1623 he was an established playwright who wrote for professional theatres, religious festivals (the Feast of Corpus Christi always included plays), and performances at court for the royalty of Spain. Even after becoming a priest he still wrote plays occasionally. He also used the title *Life Is a Dream* for one of his religious dramas. This prolific playwright is credited with writing more than seventy religious plays and more than 110 secular plays for the professional theatres. Of the professional works, his most famous after *Life Is a Dream* is *The Constant Prince* (1629), an examination of self-sacrifice. In a war between the Moors and the Christians, a captured prince rejects his own forces' attempt to ransom him—an act that amazes both his countrymen and his captors. Calderón was fascinated with cosmic themes, large symbols, allegory, fantasy, and unsolvable problems. He seriously examines the code of honor in terms of marital infidelity and murder of passion in *Painter of His Own Dishonor* (c. 1648). Even though such acts as murder and rape occur with frequency in his plays, Calderón always created a happy ending in which order is restored and the oppressed and honorable characters are rewarded.

GENRE, STRUCTURE, AND STYLE

Life Is a Dream is written in comedia form. This genre of play was perfected by Lope de Vega, whose career began well before, but overlapped, that of Calderón. The comedia in Spain was a tragicomedy in three acts. It was always of a mixed tone like Elizabethan plays but, unlike the works of Shakespeare and his contemporaries, never ended in tragedy. Often the comedia action was very serious and entered dramatic territory that could have easily turned tragic, but did not. In this respect, the comedia bears some resemblance to melodrama. Spanish comedias often centered on a conflict of love and honor, as we see in *Life Is a Dream*. The restoration of order and a happy or socially and politically appropriate ending seems to have been required and no doubt contributed to the comedia's popularity.

The action in this play is supposed to occur in Poland, which may seem an odd choice now. At the time in Spain, however, Poland would seem impossibly distant and unknown—an exotic, fairy-tale land. The play alternates formality with crudeness, and the contrast is underscored by having all of the action take place at court or not far from the court of Basilio, the King of Poland. Astolfo and Estrella seem obsessed with formality in both language and behavior. When the uncouth Segismundo is thrust upon them, however, we experience dissonance and humor: This prince has been kept a prisoner all of his life and is suddenly pushed into the middle of a gracious court. Further contrast is achieved by placing a clown (Clarín) in so much of the action. His end is also startling and perhaps distressing to the audience, and demonstrates a bit of the real world in the midst of a power struggle.

Restoration of order at the play's end is accompanied by a final pairing off that modern audiences may not find so satisfying as contemporaries of Calderón probably did. For us, however, that pairing provides tension and uneasiness, which can give the play a new edge in revival. The same is true of the fate of the rebellious soldier who aids Segismundo. These are topics that can lead to interesting discussions of the conclusions of the comedia. Calderón seems to reveal some of the unfairness of war, but also underscores his belief in the sanctity and power of the crown.

IMPORTANT ELEMENTS OF CONTENT

The code of honor in Spain of the Golden Age was very complex, but there are a few characteristics to keep in mind. The code provided a way to accept untimely death: Within the belief system, a noble person dishonored does not really live; therefore, the person working to avenge dishonor will willingly face and accept death. It is also imperative that honor be restored by fighting the person who violated the honor. Rosaura absolutely must get revenge on Astolfo. Curiously, however, it is not necessary that Astolfo die—only that a serious attempt is made to get revenge.

This play has a curious device that reappears in plays and other literature from time to time. The device is *voix du sang* (call of the blood), which occurs here between Rosaura and Clotaldo. The notion, believed by many, was that blood ties were so strong that people related by blood would be automatically drawn to one another, even if they had never met. Sometimes this phenomenon is first interpreted as romantic as we see in the popular *Star Wars* films. Early on, Luke and Leia are attracted to one another before they realize that they are siblings.

At the heart of this play are several ideas and questions that propel the play into the philosophical realm. The plight of Segismundo raises the primal question of "Why do I suffer?" He has endured years of torturous pain and isolation because of the fears of his father. It is no wonder that his release causes such problems. Calderón seems to ask his audience to explore the concept of free will versus predestination. And the titular question of dreaming versus waking dominates much of the play's thought.

Some of the action with Segismundo is probably meant to be comic, especially his inablility to function socially and the attempts of the servants to dress him. His response to women, whom he is seeing for the first time, is comic and bizarre. He has no idea how to act in front of them and also does not understand his feelings. He is adolescent, childish, boorish, and beastial at once. Calderón turns Clarin, the clown, into Segismundo's confidant deep into the play.

Before the action moves into the palace of Basilio, Calderón calls for a mountainous terrain and a tower that opens up. This effect would not have been done with literal scenery in the seventeenth century; the upper level of the façade would be used as the mountain, and the tower would be created with the discovery space. Like the plays of Shakespeare, Calderón's comedias allow the language to suggest where the action is taking place. Most contemporary translations of *Life Is a Dream*, like the one included here, have modernized the language and typically include modern allusions as well.

THE PLAY IN REVIVAL

The plays of Calderón have remained very popular in the Spanish-speaking world; during the romantic era of the nineteenth century, many other cultures rediscovered his plays and began to translate and stage them—especially *Life Is a Dream*. The romantics took his locations and images literally and often created vast, complex settings for the action of the play. Closer to our own time, the play has enjoyed many professional productions in England and the United States, including one by the Royal Shakespeare Company in 1983, an unusual interpretation by Anne Bogart at the American Repertory Theatre in 1989, and one by JoAnne Akalaitis at the Court Theatre in Chicago in 2004. One can see this play either on a university or professional stage nearly every season.

SPECIAL FEATURE

The cross-dressing of Rosaura in *Life Is a Dream* is managed in an unusual way. In the first act she is dressed as a man and passes as such. Only her servant knows her true identity. In Act II she appears as a woman at court—a complete visual and social shift. In the final act, however, she is dressed as half-man/half-woman—a hybrid—as she has prepared herself for battle yet does not deny her sex.

FURTHER READING ABOUT THE PLAY, PLAYWRIGHT, AND CONTEXT

For studies of theatre in the Spanish Golden Age, see Melveena McKendrick, *Theatre in Spain, 1490–1700*, and N. D. Shergold, *A History of the Spanish Stage: From Medieval Times until the End of the Seventeenth Century*.

For examinations of Spanish plays, including Calderón, see Charles Ganelin and Howard Mancing, *The Golden Age Comedia: Text, Theory and Performance*, and Margaret Wilson, *Spanish Drama of the Golden Age*.

For a study of Spanish society, see Melveena McKendrick, *Women and Society in the Spanish Drama of the Golden Age*.

For an examination of the Spanish corral, see John Allen, *The Reconstruction of a Spanish Golden Age Playhouse*.

Life Is a Dream

By Pedro Calderón de la Barca

Translated by John Clifford

CHARACTERS

ROSAURA lady
CLARIN comedian
SEGISMUNDO prince
CLOTALDO old man
ASTOLFO prince
ESTRELLA princess
BASILIO king
GUARD 1 /SOLDIER 1 /COURTIER 1
MUSICIANS

ACT ONE

A noise off. ROSAURA *falls onto the stage. She is dressed as a man.*

ROSAURA: Call yourself a horse! You hippogriff!
  Violently running, fast as the wind,
  Then falling like a meteor crashing
  Into the labyrinth, into the maze,
  Of these naked mountain crags.
  You're a thunderbolt with a limp!
  A bird without wings. A fish without scales.
  Stay in this mountain. You be its Phaeton
  You be so foolish and fall from the sky!
  Abandon me! Leave me here, desperate, alone
  With no map or path to guide me
  Nothing but the working of blind chance
  As I struggle randomly through the tangled
    hair
  On the head of this giant mountain.
  Whose furrowed ridges frown at the sun.
  And this is Poland! You vile country!
  Viciously greeting this stranger
  Writing your greeting in letters of blood.
  I've hardly arrived. Such a hard arrival.
  Where can I find pity in my pitiless fate
  Arriving in anguish. Greeted with hate.
    (*Enter* CLARIN.)

CLARIN: Wait a minute. "Where can I find pity?"
  What about me? Why not "Where can we . . . "
  Where can we find pity? That's a better line.
  After all, it was the two of us left home,
  Looking for adventure, us two,
  Sadly and madly reaching this god forsaken
    place.
  Us two rolling half way down this mountain
  Us two sharing disaster and pain
  So it's us two who get to complain.
ROSAURA: Listen, Clarin, I didn't mention you in
    my speech
  Because I didn't want to deprive you of your
    opportunity
  To make your own. To lament your misfortune,
  Find consolation in your grief. Remember the
    philosopher
  Who said that to complain was such a pleasure
  That misfortunes should be looked for, like a
    moral treasure.
CLARIN: Lady, your philosopher's an idiot and I
    wish he was here
  So I could kick his head in. Only then I'd have
    to hear him
  Complaining about my utterly amazing skill in
    kicking.
  But, lady, look at us. Look at the state we're in.
  On foot, completely and utterly lost
  In a totally deserted mountain
  With night falling like a guillotine.
  Even the sun's deserting us.
  We're completely on our own.
ROSAURA: Is there anyone who's ever seen anything
  So utterly extraordinary and strange?
  And it could be my eyes are deceiving me
  Or my imagination's playing tricks on my fear-
    ful mind
  But in the faint cold light of the dying day
  I think I can see a building.

CLARIN: That's what I want to see
   And if it turns out not to be actually there
   I'll destroy the scenery.
ROSAURA: The mountains are so high
   And the building is so low
   It's as if the sun's hardly able to see it.
   Its construction is so crude
   It could be one of the rocks that surround it
   Rocks casting such fierce shadows
   It's as if they hurt the sunlight.
CLARIN: Lady, I think we're talking too much
   here,
   Why don't we get a little closer
   So that the kind people who live round here
   Can welcome us with food and wine
   And let us sit by a roaring fire to warm
   ourselves?
ROSAURA: The door—no. I could put that better—
   this black mouth . . .
   Its sinister jaws yawn open, and the dark night
   within
   Engenders a deeper darkness.
   (Chains sound inside.)
CLARIN: Good grief what's that?
ROSAURA: I cannot move. I'm a block of fire and
   ice.
   Burning with curiosity. Frozen with fear.
CLARIN: It's just someone been to the loo
   And is pulling at the chain.
SEGISMUNDO (within): All I know of life is pain!
ROSAURA: What sadness in that voice. What
   desperation!
   I'm left struggling with new grief and pain.
CLARIN: Me with new fear.
ROSAURA: Clarin!
CLARIN: My lady!
ROSAURA: Let's run from the terrors
   Of this evil and enchanted tower.
CLARIN: Lady, when it comes down to it,
   I'm too petrified to even run.
ROSAURA: Is that a light, that feeble exhalation,
   That pale and trembling star,
   That pulse so weakly beating
   In so obscure and dubious a dwelling
   That, far from lightening,
   Appears to darken it.
   In its dim light I can barely see
   A dark prison lit by a single flame

The burial place of a living corpse.
And as if that were not amazing enough
There's a man chained like an animal
A lonely man with one small light.
   (SEGISMUNDO *is discovered. He is dressed in ani-*
   mal skins, with a chain on his leg, in such a way
   that he can get up and walk when his cue comes. He
   speaks the whole speech sitting on the ground.)
SEGISMUNDO: All I know of life is pain
   And I don't understand
   Why I must live like this.
   What crime did I commit?
   The worst thing I do is to exist.
   When I think of that I understand
   A human's greatest crime is to be born!
   But there's still something to be explained
   The bitter dregs left to be drained.
   And I still don't really understand
   I must have done something else
   For life to treat me like this.
   Aren't other beings born?
   What privilege is it they possess?
   And what is it I so badly lack?
   When a bird is born, it is so beautiful
   Its feathers like the petals of a flower
   It can barely fly before it leaves
   The kind safety of its parents nest
   And then it's gliding, freely gliding
   Through the vast halls of the empty sky.
   I have more soul than a bird
   Why should I have less liberty?
   When a beast is born, its skin becomes
   A mirror of the patterns of the stars.
   It can barely walk before human need
   Stalks it, captures it, teaches it cruelty:
   And then it's hunting with vicious greed
   Through the endless tunnels of nature's
   maze.
   I have more feeling than a brute,
   Why should I have less liberty?
   When a fish is born, it does not breathe,
   It's an abortion of mud and slime.
   It can barely swim before it glides
   Like a ship of fins and scales
   And then it's sailing in immensity
   Through the vast cold heart of the endless sea.
   I have more freewill than a fish
   Why should I have less liberty?

When a stream is born, it's like a snake
Uncoiling its length past rocks and flowers
Like a silver serpent it begins to glide
And its waters sing as they break on the stones,
Celebrating the kindness of the life-giving sky.
I have more life than a stream
Why should I have less liberty?
And when I reach this moment
My heart burns like a volcano.
I want to tear it from my chest
And rip it into pieces!
How can it be justified
And how can it be right
For God to give freedom
—Sweet and beautiful freedom—
To give it to a stream, a fish,
A brute and a bird
And deny it to a human being!

ROSAURA: Your words fill me with pity and fear.

SEGISMUNDO: Who was it heard me?
Was it Clotaldo?

CLARIN: Say yes.

ROSAURA: No. It was a lonely cry of grief
Lost in these cold vaults of stone
Feeling for your sadness.
    (SEGISMUNDO *grabs her.*)

SEGISMUNDO: Then I'll kill you.
I can't have you knowing
I know you know my weakness.
Just because you heard me weep
These strong arms of mine
Will tear you into pieces.

CLARIN: I'm stone deaf. I never heard a word.

ROSAURA: You were born a human being.
It will be enough to touch your heart
Enough to fall helpless at your feet
For you to free me.

SEGISMUNDO: Your voice could fill me with
    tenderness
Your presence could fill me with . . . what?
I hesitate; I look at you with . . . awe.
Who are you? I know so little of the world.
This tower is my cradle and my grave.
Since the day I was born,
If this is really what it is to live,
All I've known is this desert place,
This bare mountain, where I live in misery
Like a skeleton which walks

Like a corpse which breathes.
There's only one man I've ever spoken to or
    seen.
He feels for me in my misfortune.
He brings me news of earth and heaven.
Be amazed at me, call me a monster,
I'm an animal, and I am a man.
I am a man, and I'm an animal.
Amidst all this misfortune, all this grief
Even though I've studied politics
Just by observing the wild beasts
And being taught by the flight of birds,
And though I've measured the perfect circles
Of the motions of the harmonious stars,
I've never seen in anyone
The perfect beauty that I see in you.
What force and what authority
Do you possess since you . . .
You, you alone have caused to halt
My fury at my wrongs
And filled my ears with pity?
Each time I look at you you amaze me more.
The more I look at you
The more I want to see you again and again.
My eyes must have a kind of rabies
For even when it's death to drink
They want to drink in more and more
And even though I understand
That seeing is a kind of death
I am still dying to see more.

ROSAURA: It so moves me to hear you
It amazes me to see you
And I don't know what to say to you
And I don't know what to ask you.
All I'll say is that somehow fate
Must have guided me here to find comfort,
If anyone unhappy really can be comforted
In seeing someone more unhappy still.
I know a story of a wise philosopher
Who was so deeply sunk in poverty
That all he could find to eat
Were wild herbs he picked off the roadside.
Can there possibly be anyone, he wondered,
Who's as poor and as wretched as me?
And then he looked back, and then he saw
Another wise philosopher
Eating the leaves that he had thrown away.
And there I was, full of self-pity

Wondering if there could be anyone
So miserable and wretched as I.
And you have given me your sad reply.
For after listening to your story
I find my griefs have disappeared.
You have gathered them, and turned them into
   happiness.
Perhaps my misfortunes can help relieve your
   pain.
So I'll tell my story. Take from it
All my superfluous grief. I am—
CLOTALDO: Guards of this tower,
   Are you cowards?
   Are you asleep?
   Two intruders
   Have broken into the tower!
ROSAURA: Now new confusion fills me.
SEGISMUNDO: That is Clotaldo, my jailer.
   There is still no end to all my sufferings.
CLOTALDO: Stir yourselves! Capture or kill them
   Before they can defend themselves!
CLARIN: Guards of the tower,
   Just remember he's offering you a choice
   You can capture us or kill us.
   Capturing is so much easier.
      (*Enter* CLOTALDO *and* SOLDIERS.)
CLOTALDO: Hide your faces. No-one should know
   us.
CLARIN: Ooh it's a masked ball.
CLOTALDO: Ignorant fools, you've trespassed
   On forbidden ground, broken the king's decree
   Which forbids anyone to view or see
   This dangerous monster imprisoned here.
   Surrender: or this gun, like a metal cobra,
   Will spit two balls of poisoned fire
   Through the terrified and frozen air.
SEGISMUNDO: You monster of injustice,
   I'll die before I see you touch
   Or harm them, I'll tear myself to pieces
   With these chains, these rocks,
   With my own teeth before I consent
   To their suffering or weep for their pain!
CLOTALDO: God decreed, Segismundo, you should
   die
   Before you were even born. That's how
   monstrous
   Are your misfortunes. You know that.
   And you also know you need these chains
   To hold back the proud fury of your rage.

So why make idle boasts? Take him back
   To his cell: lock him in. Hide him
   From our sight.
SEGISMUNDO: God in heaven
   How wise you are to deprive me
   Of my freedom! For otherwise
   I'd tear down the mountains
   To build a ladder of stone.
   I'd climb up to attack the sky!
   I'd be a giant and destroy the sun
   And I'd smash heaven's crystal spheres!
      (*They overpower* SEGISMUNDO *and lock him back in
      his cell.*)
CLOTALDO: Perhaps it's to prevent you
   That you suffer such misfortune.
ROSAURA: Obviously pride offends you. I'll try
   humility,
   Fall at your feet, and beg for my life.
   It would be remarkable cruelty
   If humbleness offended you as much as pride.
CLARIN: I don't expect you to be impressed by
   either.
   Humility and pride are both unbelievably dull,
   And besides they've both had parts
   In endless allegorical dramas. So I won't be
   humble,
   And I won't be proud. I'm kind of in between
   the two
   And ask you nicely to be kind.
CLOTALDO: You!
GUARD: My lord!
CLOTALDO: Take their weapons and blindfold their
   eyes.
ROSAURA: This is my sword. It can only be given
   to you,
   For you are the noblest here, and it will refuse
   To be taken by anyone of less nobility.
CLARIN: My sword isn't fussy. Any shit can have it.
   You take it.
ROSAURA: All I ask is that you take good care of it
   For the sake of the man who once wore it.
      (*When* CLOTALDO *takes* ROSAURA'S *sword, he is
      disturbed.*)
CLOTALDO (*aside*): (God help me, I know this sword.
   Holding it fills my heart with pain.
   And it's hard to believe that this is true
   And not part of some appalling dream.)
   Who are you?
ROSAURA: A stranger.

CLOTALDO: Obviously, since you did not know
　This place was forbidden you.
ROSAURA: Even if I had known it, there was
　　nothing I could do.
　This mad horse of mine tried to be some kind
　　of bird,
　Threw me off its back and left me stranded in
　　misfortune.
CLOTALDO: Where you from?
ROSAURA:　　　　　　　Moscow.
CLOTALDO:　　　　　　　　　I have many ties
　With that nation. Why have you come?
ROSAURA: I have been insulted. I lost my self-
　　respect.
　I have come to seek revenge.
CLOTALDO:　　　　　　　(Oh God
　Each new moment adds to my unhappiness.)
ROSAURA: And so I beg you, keep this sword safe;
　　for if
　By any freak of chance I am spared this sentence
　And allowed to live, then this sword will regain
　My honour; for although I do not understand
　What secret this sword contains, I know
　It holds one. Though it could well be
　That I deceive myself, and only value it
　Because it is the only object I possess
　That was once my father's.
CLOTALDO:　　　　　　　Who was he?
ROSAURA: I never knew him.
CLOTALDO:　　　　　　How do you know
　This sword contains a secret?
ROSAURA: The one who gave it me said: "Go to
　　Poland
　Be secret, careful, skilful, and make sure
　The leaders there see you with this sword.
　For I know that one of them will show you favour
　And will safeguard you. Or will, if he still lives.
　But for now, in case he's dead,
　I'll hide his name in silence."
CLOTALDO: (My heart like a prisoner hammers
　At the bars of its cell. Like a moth,
　It beats its wings. It flies up
　To the window to look out in the street.
　And so I feel tears in my eyes
　Weeping at the window of my soul.
　I gave this sword to my lover,
　The beautiful Violante, and I told her
　Anyone who wore it would find me
　A kind and loving father to my own son.

But I don't know what favour or help
I can give him, when I'm supposed to drive
The sword's point into his chest.
What can I do? What can I do?
If I take him to the king
I am taking him to die.
But that is what my duty commands.
My hands are tied by duty,
My heart is driven by love.
But I should be in no doubt.
They say that loyalty to the king
Matters more than honour, more
Than life itself. So let duty live,
Let love die. They also say
That anyone who has lost their honour
And their self respect cannot be noble.
He tells me he's my son. It cannot be true.
He cannot have my noble blood.
But all that's happened to him is a danger
No-one can escape, because honour
Is so fragile, it's broken with a single blow.
It's shattered by a breath of wind.
And he, with anger and with courage,
Is seeking revenge. What else can anyone do?
He is my son, his boldness proves it.
What can I do? Take courage!
The best thing is to take him to the king,
Tell him he's my son and should be killed.
Perhaps the extreme loyalty I'll show him
Will oblige him to show mercy; if not,
If the king is constant in his cruelty, then the boy
Will die without knowing he is my son.)
Foreigners, come this way, and don't imagine
You're alone in your misfortunes.
In dilemmas like these it's hard to tell
Which is the greater misfortune: to die or live.
　(*Exit.*)
　(*A sound of trumpets and drums; enter, on one
　side,* ASTOLFO *accompanied by* SOLDIERS, *and* ES-
　TRELLA *on the other accompanied by* WOMEN.)
ASTOLFO: Your eyes are like comets, madam.
　They announce the death of kings.
　Your exquisite beauty inspires these trumpets.
　To greet you they become metal birds.
　Their mouthpieces sprout feathers
　And fly through the air. Cannons salute you
　As empress; the palace fountains greet you
　As the goddess of spring; the trumpets
　Greet you as the goddess of war, and the birds

Greet you as the goddess of dawn.
Day has come to send the night to exile
But you are more radiant still
In joyfulness you are the dawn
In beauty you are the spring
In anger you are war itself
And you are the ruler of my soul.

ESTRELLA: What we say must correspond
With what we do. I think it wrong
For you to flatter me in such courteous terms
When your words are so plainly contradicted
By your obvious preparations for war.
I'm not afraid to fight against them, Prince,
For the flatteries I hear do not correspond
To the hostility I see before me. Remember,
Prince, how vile it is to flatter with the tongue,
But kill with the intention.

ASTOLFO: Estrella you are ill-informed
If you doubt that I'm sincere
In praising you. I beg you listen.
When the last king of Poland died
He left two daughters and his son
Basilio to inherit the throne.
Your mother was the eldest daughter,
Mine the youngest. She married in Moscow,
Of whose state I am now Prince.
As for Basilio, he is the victim
Of advancing old age; and he has always cared
More for his studies than for women or vice.
Since he is childless, we are both entitled to
   inherit:
You as the offspring of the elder child,
And myself because I am a man.
We told our uncle of our competing claims
And he promised to meet us here, today,
And satisfy us both. That is why I left Moscow.
That is why I came here; not to make war on
   you
But so you could lay loving siege to my heart.
Dear princess, I pray the god of love be wise
And that the common people, the only true
   astrologer,
May bless this union and crown you queen
—Queen, that is, of my tender heart.

ESTRELLA: Such extraordinary courtesy is exactly
What my high rank deserves, and of course
It would be the most enormous pleasure
For me to gain the imperial crown,

Solely to hand it over to you.
But I know you have come here to deceive me
Because the flattery of your words
Is undermined by the girl
Whose portrait you wear round your neck.
   (*A drum beats.*)

ASTOLFO: How greatly I regret that sound
For it prevents me explaining
And proclaims the arrival of the King!
   (*Drums beat. Enter* KING BASILIO, *an an old man,
   and his court.*)

ESTRELLA: Allow me to tenderly embrace

ASTOLFO: Allow me to tenderly entwine

ESTRELLA: My arms around your feet in humble
   coils.

ASTOLFO: My arms like ivy round your majestic
   trunk.

BASILIO: Nephew, niece, embrace me. I know you
   love me,
Because you have faithfully obeyed
My loving request with such kind words
And I want to leave neither unsatisfied
And both of you on equal terms.
You know my knowledge has earned me
The title of Basilio the wise.
The sciences I love the most
And engage in with a subtle and discerning
   mind
Are those which foretell the future,
Which steal the function of passing time
To tell us what happens with each day that
   comes.
For I can look at astrological tables
And I can foresee the future in the present.
The planets revolve in circles of snow
The stars spread out a canopy of diamonds
These are the subjects of my studies,
The sky is like a book to me, a book
Of diamond paper, with sapphire binding,
Written in letters of gold, hieroglyphics
I can read and easily decipher. And so I know
What the future holds for each of us, for good
   or bad.
But I wish to God that my own life
Had been the first target of the heaven's anger,
Long before I learnt to interpret its messages
And learnt to understand its signs.
For when a man is unfortunate

Even his gifts stab him in the back
And a man whose knowledge harms him
Murders his own self! This I can tell you,
Though in the events of my sad life
It is still better told. So once again
It is for silence that I ask you.
Clorilene my wife gave birth to a son.
The omens of his birth were so many, and so
    dreadful
They exhausted the skies. While the baby still
    lay
In the womb's living grave, far from the beauti-
    ful light
Of day, she dreamt again and again of her belly
    torn open
By a monster in the shape of a man.
And on the day that he was born, the sun itself
Engaged in blood-soaked battle with the moon
With the earth as the battlefield. This was the
    worst eclipse
The world has suffered since weeping for the
    death of Christ.
The sun was smothered in living fire,
The heavens darkened, palaces trembled,
The clouds rained stones and the rivers ran
    with torrents of blood.
And it was under this sign
My son Segismundo was born.
He foretold his future in the manner of his
    birth,
For in being born he killed his mother
And so boasted with male ferocity:
"Look: I am human and this how
We humans repay those who do us good."
I ran to my books, and in them I read
Segismundo would be the most brutal man,
The cruellest prince, the most vicious
    monarch.
That under him his kingdom would become
Divided, split, torn by civil wars:
I saw him inspired by fury.
I saw him driven on by rage.
I saw him defeat and overcome me.
I saw me lying vanquished at his feet.
I saw me humiliated, helpless,
And forced to be his wretched slave.
His feet—and how it shames me to confess it—
Would make a carpet out of my white hairs.

Self love plays such a part in science
And when despite of it science predicts
So dire an outcome, we must believe it.
We know that evil is far more likely to occur
    than good
And good endings are never as plausible as
    bad.
I had to believe such frightening predictions
I had to try to avert the evil that seemed sure to
    come.
I had to see if wisdom can help a human over-
    come the stars.
So I prepared a tower, hidden in the mountains,
Where the daylight scarcely dares enter.
I passed strict laws and edicts,
I forbade anyone to enter
And I had it announced that the prince was
    born dead.
There Segismundo lives, chained like a beast,
Imprisoned in poverty and misery.
Only Clotaldo has spoken to him and seen him;
He has taught him divine law and human
    knowledge
And been the only witness of his unhappy life.
Three things must be considered here. The first
That I love my country, and I must do all I can
To rescue it from the prospect of a cruel vindic-
    tive king.
The second is that we are talking of my son.
He has the right to freedom, he has the right to
    rule.
To deprive him of these rights would be a
    crime,
A crime I cannot justify,
Even if what I intend is the good of all.
The third is that we know we should not too
    easily believe
That what is predicted will unavoidably occur.
Even the most evil omen, even the worst
    horoscope
Can only incline the will. It cannot force it.
And so my friends you must imagine me
Struggling for many months with these dilemmas
Until today, when I have finally found
A solution that will utterly amaze you.
Tomorrow I will place my son on the throne
I will not tell him that he is my son, or that he is
    your king

But he will govern you, and you will swear
    obedience.
Now think what that this achieves.
It resolves the three issues I have set before you.
One: I love my country, and if I give you a king
Who rules with justice, wisdom and goodwill
Then the stars' predictions are defeated, and
    you enjoy
The government of your rightful king.
Second: I will not commit a crime
Because if he acts unjustly, cruelly,
Gives free rein to viciousness and vice
Then I can depose him and imprison him again
And that will not be cruelty but just punishment.
Third, if the horoscope is right it can all still be
    remedied
If I marry Estrella to Astolfo, set them on the
    throne
And give you rulers who will be worthy of the
    task.
This I command you as your king
This I ask you as a father,
This I request you as a philosopher
And if what Seneca said is really true,
And the king really is the slave of his own
    kingdom
Then this I humbly beg you as your slave.
ASTOLFO: It is my duty to reply to this
    As the one whose interests are most at stake
    In the name of all I say:
    Bring us Segismundo, for he is your son.
    And that is enough for all of us.
ALL: Give us our Prince
    for we ask him to be our king!
BASILIO: Vassals, I respect and thank you
    For this generous act. Accompany
    These two pillars of the state to their rooms
    For tomorrow you will see him.
ALL: Long live the great king Basilio!
    (*Exit all. Before the* KING *exits,* CLOTALDO *enters
    with* ROSAURA *and* CLARIN *and stops the* KING.)
CLOTALDO: Can I speak to you?
BASILIO: Oh Clotaldo, you are most welcome!
CLOTALDO: Coming into your presence, majesty,
    Always fills me with joy, but today
    An angry twist of vicious destiny
    Has robbed a law of its privilege
    And a custom of its joy.

BASILIO: What troubles you?
CLOTALDO: A misfortune, your majesty, has
    occurred;
    Although it should have been a source of joy.
BASILIO: Go on.
CLOTALDO: This young man, your majesty,
    And it is hard to repress my tears
    He entered the tower, and saw the prince.
    And he is—
BASILIO: Do not trouble yourself Clotaldo.
    Even if this happened through carelessness
    You have no need to excuse it
    I have just revealed the secret
    And it does not matter he should know it.
    See me afterwards, because I have much to tell
        you
    And there is much for you to do for me;
    For I must tell you you are to be the instrument
    Of the most amazing event the world has ever
        seen.
    As for these prisoners, so that you know
    I do not punish in them your carelessness
    I forgive them. Let them go.
        (*Exit* BASILIO.)
CLOTALDO: Great king, may you live a thousand
    centuries!
    (My poor heart, the first ordeal is over.
    Now let the next ordeal begin.)
    Foreign travellers, you are free.
ROSAURA: I kiss your feet a thousand times.
CLARIN: I'll make do with a couple of hundred.
    A few kisses more or less
    Won't matter between friends.
ROSAURA: My lord, you have given me my life.
    I will for ever be your grateful slave.
CLOTALDO: You're wrong. I never gave you life.
ROSAURA: Why not?
CLOTALDO: A man of noble birth who's been
    dishonoured
    Does not truly live. And since you have come
    To avenge an insult, that obviously applies to
        you.
    I could not have given you life
    For living in dishonour is no life at all.
    (I hope that I encourage him to speak.)
ROSAURA: I admit for now I have no proper life
    Even though I receive it from you.
    But when I take my revenge

I will regain my self-respect.
My life then without any doubt at all
Will seem like a gift from you.
CLOTALDO: Don't go without a weapon.
Take this sword you brought
For I know it will suffice for your revenge
And will be stained with your enemy's blood;
For this blade will know how to revenge you
I know, for it once was mine—or rather,
Mine for this instant, for this brief time
I have held it in my power.
ROSAURA: And so for the second time in your
name
I put on this sword and swear to obtain revenge
However powerful my enemy may be.
CLOTALDO: And is he?
ROSAURA: So powerful, I will not disclose his
name;
For I would not wish to lose your friendship.
CLOTALDO: But if you were to tell me
It would strengthen my concern for you,
For it would make it impossible
For me to help your enemy.
(Oh I wish I knew who it was.)
ROSAURA: So you do not think I place a low value
on the trust
You place in me, you must know my enemy
Is no less than Astolfo, the duke of Moscow.
CLOTALDO: (It's hard not to be overcome by grief.
The affair is far worse than I imagined.
Let's investigate a little further.)
If you were born a Muscovite
Then your natural lord could not insult you
Even if (anxiety will drive me mad!)
He called you a liar in public.
ROSAURA: I know that even though he was my
prince
He could still offend me.
CLOTALDO: He could not, even though he slapped
you in the face.
(My God!)
ROSAURA: What I suffered was far worse!
CLOTALDO: Then tell it now, because you cannot
say more
Than what I already imagine.
ROSAURA: I look at you with a respect I do not
understand.
I look on to you with such deep regard,

And I hold you in such great esteem,
That I hardly dare tell you
That how I appear is a disguise,
That I am not whom I appear to be.
Be alert; reflect;
If I am not who I seem
And Astolfo came here to marry Estrella,
Think how he could offend me.
I have already said too much.
      (*Exit* ROSAURA *and* CLARIN.)
CLOTALDO: Stop wait come back!
What tangled labyrinth is this
Where reason cannot find the thread?
My honour is offended;
The enemy is powerful;
I am his vassal; she is my daughter.
May heaven find some solution
Although I doubt it can
In so deep a pit of confusion
The whole sky is an omen
The whole world a prodigious portent.
      (*Exit.*)

                    END OF ACT ONE.

ACT TWO

CLOTALDO: Everything you ordered
Has been accomplished.
BASILIO: Tell me what happened.
CLOTALDO: This is how it was.
You ordered me to make a tranquillising drink,
A drink made of herbs whose secret power
Is to deprive a man of reason, to rob
And dispossess him of awareness and of con-
scious will.
In short: transform him to a living corpse.
We don't need to convince anyone this is
possible;
For medicine, your majesty, is full of natural
secrets;
There is no animal, no plant, no stone
That does not possess its own determined quality.
And if we start to examine the thousand poisons
Human malice uses to give death,
It should come as no surprise to find
That since there are poisons that can kill
Once their destructive power is diluted,
They should also bring sleep.

Still, your majesty, leaving aside this fascinating
    question,
Of whether it is possible for such a thing to
    occur
—Since it is already proved by reason and
    empirical evidence—
I went down to Segismundo with the drink
In which were mixed opium, henbane and
    belladona,
And there, in his small cell, I spoke to him
Of the human knowledge taught him by dumb
    nature,
Nature his mother, who in these learned
    solitudes
Has taught him the politics of the beasts and
    birds.
In order to elevate his spirits for your
    enterprise
I allowed him to see a royal eagle's soaring
    flight
Despising the sphere of the wind and rising
To the highest regions of fire, where it flew
Like a bright comet or a feathered lightning
    bolt.
I praised its proud flight, saying: "In the end
You are king of the birds, and so it is right
That you should fly high above them all."
That was enough; for when he thinks of
    kingship,
He thinks with ambition and with pride
—For he has a kind of blood in him
That inspires, moves, and spurs him on to great
    things—
And he said: "To think that even in the unquiet
    republic of birds
There should be one to whom they swear
    obedience!"
When I saw how this occupied his mind
And it is the constant theme of his suffering.
I toasted him with the potion, and hardly
Had the liquid passed from glass to stomach
When he surrendered his strength to the power
    of sleep.
A cold sweat ran down through his veins and
    limbs,
So cold, that if I had not known this was pre-
    tended death,
I would have feared for his life.

At that moment the people came
In whom you have entrusted
The secret of this experiment.
They carried him to a coach, and then to your
    room
Where is prepared the greatness and majesty
Merited by his position. There they put him to
    bed
And there, once the drowsiness has lost its
    power,
There they will serve him as they would serve
    you,
Just as you ordered. And if having obeyed you
    in every respect
Makes me worthy of any slight reward
Then all I would ask you
—forgive my indiscretion—
Is that you tell me what you intend
In bringing Segismundo here to the palace.
BASILIO: Clotaldo, that is a very good question
    And to you alone will I answer it in full.
    You already know that the influence of the stars
    On my son Segismundo threatens us all
    With endless misfortunes and tragic events.
    It is impossible for the heavens to lie
    And they have given us so many proofs of their
        veracity—
    But I want to examine whether it is possible
    For the heavens to relent a little or mitigate
        their harshness
    Or to see whether with boldness and prudence
    They can be contradicted, whether human
        beings
    Have power over their own destiny.
    This is what I want to investigate,
    And this is why I have brought him here:
    So he may be told he is my son,
    And to have his ability put to the test.
    If he has the greatness of spirit to overcome
        himself,
    Then he will be king; but if he shows himself to
        be cruel,
    Or indulges in the abuse of power,
    I'll return him to his chains.
    Now you're going to ask, why, to determine
        this,
    Was it necessary to drug him first?
    I want to satisfy you in every respect.

If he knew now today that he was my son,
And then tomorrow saw himself reduced again
To prison and to misery, it is certain that he
    would
Despair in his condition. For having known
    who he really is
What consolation could he possibly find?
I wanted to leave him a remedy for future misery
By telling him that everything he saw
Was no more than a dream. So this achieves
    two ends:
Firstly his disposition, since while he is awake
He behaves exactly as he imagines and thinks.
Secondly his consolation, because even though
    he sees himself
Obeyed now and then returned to his chains,
He could still believe he dreamt it all
And that will be a good understanding for him
    to have,
Because in this world, Clotaldo,
Everyone who lives is dreaming.
CLOTALDO: I can think of many reasons
    To demonstrate you are mistaken
    But now it is all too late
    For the signs are that he has woken,
    And he is coming this way.
BASILIO: I shall withdraw; you are his tutor,
    You go up to him. His mind will be full
    Of confusion. So tell him the truth.
CLOTALDO: You mean tell him who he is?
BASILIO: Yes; for it could be if he knows it
    He will recognise his danger
    And be more inclined to overcome himself.
        (*Exit* BASILIO. *Enter* CLARIN.)
CLARIN: Getting in here isn't cheap is it?
    This man standing at the door
    Wanted to see my ticket. I said
    You won't catch me buying one of those.
    The price they are nowadays
    Do you think I'm stupid?
    I don't need a ticket. I've got my eyes.
    Keep them wide open
    And you can see anything.
CLOTALDO: (O god, that's Clarin, the servant of
        that woman
    That dealer in misfortune
    Who has carried my shame into Poland.)
    Clarin, what's new?

CLARIN: What's new, sir, is that your enormous
        kindness
    Always so ready to avenge Rosaura's wrongs,
    Has advised her to dress as her own sex.
CLOTALDO: Of course. So as not to cause a scandal.
CLARIN: And what's also new sir is that she's
        changed her name,
    And is now known as your niece.
CLOTALDO: I'm taking responsibility for her
        reputation.
    What else?
CLARIN: Now she's a lady in waiting for the
    Extraordinary Estrella, and she's waiting for you
    To find the time and place to achieve her
        revenge.
CLOTALDO: That's as it should be. For all these things
    Will be set right in time.
CLARIN: And the other thing, sir, is that she is living
    In luxury, she is being treated like a queen
    And is the favourite of the princess,
    Whereas I, her faithful companion and friend
    Am dying of hunger, and everyone forgets me
    And forgets that I'm Clarin, and that Clarin
    —For the benefit of the ignorant—means
        trumpet.
    It's from the Latin. Clarinus. Or clarion.
    As in call. Clarion call. And I could call
    The king, Astolfo, and Estrella, to tell them
    Just what is going on and just who your niece
    Really is and what she's hoping to do here.
CLOTALDO: I think I understand you, and I'm sure
    That we'll get on. You work for me,
    And here's an advance on your wages.
CLARIN: And here comes Segismundo.
        (*Enter as many as can be afforded, dressing* SEGIS-
        MUNDO, *who is now wearing beautiful clothes. He
        is amazed by everything, and walks around while
        the* MUSICIANS *sing.*)
SEGISMUNDO: God help me! What do I see?
    God help me! What do I touch!
    I look at it with wonder!
    I see it with amazement!
    Me in this beautiful palace!
    Me wearing satin and silk!
    Me surrounded by all these
    Elegant looking servants!
    Me waking up to find myself
    In that gorgeous feather bed!

I can't be. I'm dreaming;
I know I'm awake.
Aren't I still Segismundo?
Look just tell me, God,
What's supposed to be going on!
I mean what could have happened
To me while I was fast asleep?
What is it that I'm seeing now?
Well, whatever it is, why should
That bother me? Why worry?
I'll just let myself be waited on
And then just see what happens.
SERVANT 1: He's so preoccupied.
SERVANT 2: After what's happened to him
Who wouldn't be?
CLARIN: I wouldn't be. I'd be jumping for joy.
SERVANT 1: Go and talk to him.
SERVANT 2: Should they sing again?
SEGISMUNDO: No,
I don't want any more singing.
SERVANT 2: I just wanted to entertain you.
You seem so preoccupied.
SEGISMUNDO: No, I
Don't think music helps me, really.
All I like are brass bands.
CLOTALDO: Your Highness, Great Lord,
Allow me to kiss your hand.
I will be honoured to be the first
To swear obedience to you as Lord.
SEGISMUNDO: (That's Clotaldo. What's he doing?
Why's he being so polite?
When I was in prison he treated me like a pig.
What is happening to me?)
CLOTALDO: Your life has so suddenly changed
And your heart and mind will be filled
With confusion and doubts.
And if I can, I want to help you understand.
(He becomes grave.)
Great lord, you have to understand
That you are Prince of Poland.
You will inherit the throne.
You've been hidden in a tower
Because the stars foretold
A most terrible tragedy
Would occur when you were crowned.
But if he makes use of the power
Of reason a good-hearted man
Can overcome the stars

We must trust that truth.
And that is why, while you were sleeping
You were taken from the tower
And brought to this palace.
My lord, the king your father,
Will come here soon and from him
You'll learn the rest.
SEGISMUNDO: You wicked foul betrayer
I've nothing else to learn.
I know all I need to know.
I've got pride now, I've got power
And I know you betrayed your country
Because you hid me and you denied me
My rightful place in the world!
CLOTALDO: (Oh no!)
SEGISMUNDO: You broke the law, you lied to the
king
And you were cruel to me. And so
We all agree, the king, the law, and me
That you're condemned to death.
And I'm going to kill with these hands.
SERVANT 1: My lord!
SEGISMUNDO: Don't try to protect him. Don't
waste your time
And listen, you, I swear to God,
If you get in my way
I'll chuck you out the window.
SERVANT 2: Clotaldo run!
CLOTALDO: You sad deluded fool, so savage in
your pride
Without understanding that you're dreaming!
(Exit CLOTALDO.)
SERVANT 2: Just take note—
SEGISMUNDO: You keep out of this!
SERVANT 2: He was only obeying orders.
SEGISMUNDO: You shouldn't obey orders when
they're wrong.
And anyway I'm his prince.
SERVANT 2: But it wasn't up to him to think
He just did what he was told.
SEGISMUNDO: So why don't you do the same?
Instead of answering me back all the time!
CLARIN: Everything the Prince says is completely
right
And everything you say is completely wrong!
SERVANT 2: Who said you could speak like this?
CLARIN: I did.
SEGISMUNDO: Who are you?

CLARIN: I poke my nose into palaces.
I step on official's toes.
I destroy protocol.

SEGISMUNDO: In this strange new world
You're the only one I like.

CLARIN: My lord, I'm the greatest Segismundo-pleaser
In the whole wide world.
(Enter ASTOLFO.)

ASTOLFO: Happy a thousand times this august day
Dear prince, when you arrive to fill the world
From west to east with joy and gladness.
You rise like the sun from behind the savage mountains;
Rise then; and although the laurel wreath
(He puts on his hat.)
Is crowning your Imperial self a little late
May its freshness be as late in fading.

SEGISMUNDO: Morning.
God keep you.
(He turns his back.)

ASTOLFO: It's clear that you don't know me, and so
I'll excuse you, this once, for not showing me
more honour.
My name is Astolfo, I'm by birth a Duke,
And ruler of the principality of Moscow.
From you I anticipate more respect.

SEGISMUNDO: I said "God keep you." Isn't God
Good enough for you? Apparently not
Since you're boasting about how important you are.
Well next time we meet I'll ask God
To shit on you instead!

SERVANT 2: Your Highness must bear in mind
That he comes from the mountains
And doesn't know any better.
I'm sure, your grace, Astolfo would prefer . . .

SEGISMUNDO: It really annoyed me the way he just
turned up
And didn't bow to me. Instead he put his hat on.

SERVANT 2: He's a Great Man. He can do that.
He's one of the Great and Good.

SEGISMUNDO: I'm greater. And I'm gooder.

SERVANT 2: Of course your grace, but none the less
It would be fitting for your relationships
To have a little more decorum—

SEGISMUNDO: And
What's it got to do with you?
(Enter ESTRELLA.)

SEGISMUNDO: You there,
Come here, tell me, who is that?
That gorgeous woman, that divine beauty
Even the sun itself must bow down
To kiss her amazingly beautiful feet.

CLARIN: That's your cousin, lord. Her name's
Estrella.
That means star.

SEGISMUNDO: What an appropriate name.

ESTRELLA: We are all of us eager to greet you,
Highness,
And accept you as our king; and we hope
That in spite of difficulties, you are King
Not simply for years but for many centuries.

SEGISMUNDO: I thank you for making me welcome
But the best thing that's happened to me
Has been seeing you. I could forgive my father
If I'd had you in the mountain with me.
What could possibly be more cruel
Than deny a man the joy of seeing a woman?
Especially of seeing you, Estrella, you star
Whose rising puts the sun in the shade.

ESTRELLA: I think you should show a little more
tact.

ASTOLFO: (If he says he loves her, then I am done
for.)

SERVANT 2: (I understand Astolfo's trouble
And I want to set his mind at ease.)
My lord, you shouldn't say Estrella
Pleases you, because she's to marry
Astolfo—

SEGISMUNDO: Didn't I tell you to keep out my
way?

SERVANT 2: Yes, but Astolfo's here—

SEGISMUNDO: That's enough!

SERVANT 2: All I'm saying is what I know is
right—

SEGISMUNDO: It can't be right if I don't like it!

SERVANT 2: But I thought I heard you tell me
The right thing was to do what you're told.

SEGISMUNDO: I thought I also told you
That anyone who angered me
Would be chucked out the nearest window!

SERVANT 2: But you can't do that to people like
me.

SEGISMUNDO: Oh can't I? Let's find out!
(He picks him up and exits with him, returning
soon after.)

ASTOLFO: What is happening?

ESTRELLA: Someone go and help him!

SEGISMUNDO: Thank you God it could be done.
He fell from the balcony into the sea.

ASTOLFO: Nonetheless you should take more care
And think before committing a cruelty.
A mountain is not the same as a palace.
A human is not the same as a beast.

SEGISMUNDO: Perhaps you should take more care
as well
Or you'll find you don't have a head to put a
hat on.
(*Exit* ASTOLFO *and* ESTRELLA. *Enter the* KING.)

BASILIO: What's happened?

SEGISMUNDO: Nothing. Someone made me angry.
I chucked him out the window.

CLARIN: Careful. This is the king.

SEGISMUNDO: So what?

BASILIO: On your first day you kill a man!

SEGISMUNDO: He told me it couldn't be done.
So I proved him wrong.

BASILIO: It saddens me to see you
Acting with such cruelty.
I'm horrified your first action
Is to commit a cruel homicide.
I was hoping that you'd conquered destiny
And would be standing like an enlightened
man
Triumphant over the prediction of the stars.
How can I come and embrace you now
When I know your hands are stained with
blood
And that you have learnt the skill of murder?
Is there anyone here who wouldn't be afraid?
It's like seeing a dagger that's carried out a
murder.
It's like seeing the spot where someone's been
killed.
It makes you shiver. Self-preservation has to be
The strongest impulse. So when I look at your
arms
I see a dagger, I see a place that's stained with
blood,
And I recoil, disgusted. I was going to embrace
you,
But now I turn my back, frightened and appalled.

SEGISMUNDO: Why should I care if you don't
embrace me?
I've had to live without it up to now,

With a father who brings me up with such
cruelty
He locks me in a tower, treats me like an
animal,
And tries to have me killed. Your embraces
really
Do not count for much. What matters is
You stopped me being human!

BASILIO: I wish to God I'd never given you life
So I wouldn't have to hear your voice
Or feel your vile ingratitude.

SEGISMUNDO: If you'd never given me life I
wouldn't be complaining.
But you gave me life and then took it away
from me.
Giving's the most amazing, noble act.
But to give and then to take away
That is the most contemptible.

BASILIO: You used to be a poor and helpless
prisoner.
Now you're a rich and powerful prince.
Why don't you show some gratitude?

SEGISMUNDO: What have I to be grateful for?
You took away my freedom.
And now you're old and tired and dying
And all you're giving me is what is already
mine.
You're my father, you're my king,
So although I'm now a prince
That's nothing to do with you.
That's the law of nature. I'm not
In debt to you, you're in debt to me!
You owe me all the years you took from me
When you stole my freedom and you stole my
life!
Remember: You owe me. You be grateful.
Be grateful I don't make you pay.

BASILIO: You shameless barbarian. You proud,
ignorant fool.
You're everything the stars predicted.
And even though you know who you are
And find yourself preferred above all
Remember this: you be humble, you be kind
Perhaps you're dreaming, as you'll find
When you wake up in your right mind.
(*Exit* BASILIO.)

SEGISMUNDO: I can't be dreaming. I can see and
touch
All I have been and all I am.

And you may be sorry now for what you've
    done.
And you may sigh and sorely regret it.
But you are helpless because what you cannot
    take
From me is the fact I am prince and must in-
    herit your throne.
And if once you saw me give up and accept my
    chains,
Despairing of the struggle,
That was because I didn't know who I was
But now my eyes are opened and I know who
    I am:
Half human half wild animal.
    (*Enter* ROSAURA, *dressed as a woman.*)

ROSAURA (*aside*): (I've come in search of Estrella
And I'm terrified of meeting Astolfo
For Clotaldo wants him not to see me
And not to know who I really am
Clotaldo, to whom I owe this comfort,
This safety, this soft life.)

CLARIN: Of all the things you've seen and admired
What's the one that has pleased you most?

SEGISMUNDO: Nothing has amazed me at all;
For I was ready for everything
But if there's one thing I admire in this world
It has to be woman's beauty. I read once,
In one of the books I was given,
That in the whole creation the one thing
God worked the hardest to make was man,
Because man is the whole world in miniature.
But I think he must have worked harder creat-
    ing woman
Because women are much more beautiful,
Women are a replica of heaven.
Especially when she's the woman I see now.

ROSAURA (*aside*): (The prince is here; I must go back.)

SEGISMUNDO: Wait woman, stop! Don't run away.
Don't be sunrise and sunset both at once.
Night shouldn't come as soon as the sun rises
Or the days would be unbearably short.
(But who is this?)

ROSAURA: (I can't believe what I am seeing. Yet I
    must . . .)

SEGISMUNDO: (I have seen this beauty somewhere
    else.)

ROSAURA: (I have seen this power in chains.)

SEGISMUNDO: (I have found my life.)
Woman . . . just to call you woman

Is the greatest compliment I can pay you.
Who are you, for I know
I've never seen you before, and yet
I know that once you felt something
For me, and I felt joy in seeing you?

ROSAURA: (It's important I hide who I am.)
I'm a sad lady, waiting on Estrella.

SEGISMUNDO: Don't say that; Estrella's just a star,
But you're the sun itself. She gets her light from
    you.
When I looked at the beautiful kingdom of
    flowers
I saw them governed by the beauty of the rose.
When I looked at the academy of stones
I saw them led by the brilliance of the diamond.
When I looked at the unquiet republic of stars
I found Venus to be the brightest of planets.
And when I looked at the harmony of plan-
    etary spheres
I saw the sun was the most beautiful of all.
So when I look at you, I just don't understand
How you, amidst flowers, amidst stars
Amidst spinning planets and precious stones
Could be serving someone of less beauty,
When you are the most beautiful
Diamond, sun, Venus, rose.
    (*Enter* CLOTALDO.)

CLOTALDO (*aside*): (I want to help Segismundo see
    reason.
I brought him up. I feel responsible.
But what's happening now?)

ROSAURA: I'm moved by your compliments, but
May silence make a speech for me.
My reasoning feels clumsy, lord,
And silence must be my best reply.

SEGISMUNDO: No wait, you mustn't go away.
Why do you want to leave me in darkness?

ROSAURA: I ask permission to do so from your
    Highness.

SEGISMUNDO: If you're going to ask permission
You should wait for my reply.
For leaving before I give it, isn't
Asking permission, but taking it.

ROSAURA: If you're not going to give permission
Then I will take it.

SEGISMUNDO: Then you'll make me change.
Instead of being courteous, I'll be violent.
Resistance is a poison kills my patience.

ROSAURA: This poison may well destroy

All patience and self-restraint,
Charged with fury, inhumanity
And rage. But it wouldn't dare
Force my consent. Nor could it.

SEGISMUNDO: Perhaps I could.
I'm getting curious to see. You're making me
Lose all respect and fear of your beauty.
Besides, I love doing what they tell me
Can't be done. And only today
I threw a man out the window
Because he told me I couldn't do it.
And right now I feel most inclined
To throw your honour out the window too.

CLOTALDO: (The situation's getting worse.
What can I do, for heaven's sake,
When yet again a mad desire
Endangers my reputation.)

ROSAURA: They were obviously right to prophesy
your cruelty
And say that if you ruled this poor kingdom, it
would suffer
Betrayal, murder, treachery and civil war.
But what else do you expect from a man
A man so inhuman and so cruel, so vicious
Violent and unrestrained, a man
Human only in name, born and bred among
wild animals?

SEGISMUNDO: I didn't want you to insult me like
that.
And I was trying to be courteous.
I thought that might make you treat me better.
But now you call me an animal
And I didn't deserve that. But now,
By Christ! I'll show you what it means.
Get out. Leave us alone. Let no-one in.
Bolt the door!
    (*Exit* CLARIN.)

ROSAURA: Listen.

SEGISMUNDO: I'm an animal, remember? I'm not
human any more.
It's no use trying to make me change my
mind.

CLOTALDO: (What a dreadful situation. Even if he
kills me,
I must still prevent him.)
My Lord, wait, think . . .

SEGISMUNDO: You feeble mad old man
You're provoking me again.

Do you really think so little of my cruelty and
rage?
How did you get in here?

CLOTALDO: This voice called me. That's what
brought me here.
I came to tell you not to be so proud
Not to be so wild. If you want to be king,
Rule peaceably. You may think you're the mas-
ter here
But don't be cruel. It may turn out to be a dream.

SEGISMUNDO: When you talk of ending illusions,
When you talk of ending dreams,
You touch a kind of light in me
And it maddens me with rage!
But I know how I'll find out if this is true.
I'll find out by killing you.
    (*As he pulls out his dagger,* CLOTALDO *stops him,*
    falling onto his knees.)

CLOTALDO: This is how I'll save myself.

SEGISMUNDO: Let go!

CLOTALDO: Until people come
Who can restrain
Your anger and rage
I won't let go!

SEGISMUNDO: Let go, feeble mad old man
Or I'll kill you.
    (*They struggle.*)

ROSAURA: Quick, someone!
The prince is killing Clotaldo!
    (*Exit* ROSAURA.)
    (*Enter* ASTOLFO *just as* CLOTALDO *falls at his feet.*
    He stands between him and SEGISMUNDO.)

ASTOLFO: What are you doing, Prince?
Staining your noble sword
With an old man's cold blood?
Put your sword away.

SEGISMUNDO: Only when I see it stained
With this man's filthy blood.

ASTOLFO: He's fallen at my feet. He's asked for
sanctuary.
I'll make sure it does him good.

SEGISMUNDO: All it'll do is cause your death.
And I'll get my revenge
On the way that you insulted me.

ASTOLFO: This isn't treason. This is self-defence.
    (*They draw their swords. Enter* BASILIO *and* ESTRELLA.)

CLOTALDO: Astolfo, don't attack him.

BASILIO: Are these drawn swords?

ESTRELLA (*aside*): (It's Astolfo. And I'm attacked by
  a grief
That's filled with rage!)
BASILIO: What happened?
ASTOLFO: Nothing, my lord, now you are here.
SEGISMUNDO: This isn't nothing, even if you are here.
  I was trying to kill this old man . . .
BASILIO: Have you no respect for his age?
CLOTALDO: Your majesty, remember it's only me.
  It really does not matter.
SEGISMUNDO: You expect me to respect old age?
  Don't waste your time. Even you, old fool
  You could find yourself one day
  Begging for mercy at my feet.
  You brought me up so cruelly
  One day I'll get revenge.
      (*Exit* SEGISMUNDO.)
BASILIO: Before that day comes
  You'll go back to sleep
  And when you wake up
  You'll believe everything
  You've seen and felt
  Like all the world's good things
  Were just a dream.
      (*Exit* BASILIO *and* CLOTALDO. ESTRELLA *and* ASTOLFO
      remain.)
ASTOLFO: My dear Estrella, how sad life is.
  When a horoscope predicts
  Misfortunes, it's generally correct:
  Any evil it predicts is certain:
  Any good it predicts is dubious.
  This can be absolutely proven
  In the case of Segismundo and myself,
  For the opposite was predicted for each.
  For him was foretold unpleasantness,
    misfortune
  Deaths. And we can see for ourselves
  How all of it is coming true.
  The prognosis was bad, its accuracy excellent.
  As for myself, I was predicted
  Good fortune, happiness, pleasure, glory.
  But one glance from your extraordinary eyes
  Whose brilliance dims the sun and makes even
    the sky
  A pale reflection of its former glory
  Make me understand, dear lady, all too well,
  The prognosis was excellent, but its accuracy
    dubious.

ESTRELLA: I'm absolutely sure these flatteries
  Are utterly and totally sincere
  But meant for someone else.
  Perhaps for the lady whose portrait
  You carried round your neck
  When you first came to see me.
  And so, obviously, these gorgeous compliments
  Deserve to be heard by her.
  You should go and make sure she returns them
  For in love's counting house, Astolfo,
  I'm afraid they count as forgeries
  Bills of love made out in someone else's name
    (*Enter* ROSAURA, *where the other characters cannot
    see her.*)
ROSAURA (*aside*): (My misfortunes have reached
  the absolute limit!
  And thank god for that, for any lover who sees
    this happen
  Has seen the worst and has nothing more to
    fear.)
ASTOLFO: In the presence of a diamond,
  A magnet loses its strength.
  In the presence of an emerald
  A poison loses its venom
  And, confronted with the sun,
  A star loses its splendour.
  And so, my lady, that portrait
  When it came and saw you, lost
  All strength, power and loveliness
  Because your beauty conquered it.
ESTRELLA: If I had really conquered it, Astolfo,
  It would run away when it saw me
  For the vanquished always run
  From the place where they are defeated.
ASTOLFO: Then I will ensure it leaves this place
  And then, like a defeated slave,
  Kneels and kisses your delightful feet.
  (Beautiful Rosaura, forgive me
  For demeaning you. But for men and women
  Who are separated, this is faithfulness.)
    (*Exit* ASTOLFO.)
ROSAURA (*aside*): (I was so worried about being
  seen I never heard a thing!)
ESTRELLA: Astrea.
ROSAURA: My lady.
ESTRELLA: I'm so pleased it is you. For you are the
  only one
  To whom I dare entrust this secret.

ROSAURA: My lady, you honour me. I am ready to
    obey you.
ESTRELLA: In the little time I have known you
    You have won the key to my soul.
    For this reason, and because you are,
    The person that you are, I now entrust to you
    A secret that so often I have feared to disclose
    Even to myself.
ROSAURA: Tell me your wish.
ESTRELLA: Well . . .
    To be brief . . . my cousin Astolfo,
    To say he's my cousin is more than enough . . .
    There are things one should express
    Only in thought . . . he is to marry me.
    Or at least he will if the world allows
    One piece of good fortune to remove
    So many other sources of grief.
    It hurt me to see hanging round his neck
    The portrait of another lady.
    I asked him for it courteously;
    He is polite and wishes well.
    He went to fetch it and will bring it here
    It will embarrass me if he comes here
    And gives it to me face to face.
    Please tell him to give it you, and . . .
    I'll say no more. You are beautiful
    And you are also discreet.
    You know what love is very well.
        (*Exit* ESTRELLA.)
ROSAURA: And I wish I didn't know a thing about
    it!
    God help me! Who could ever be clever enough
    To know what advice to give herself
    In such an impossible situation!
    Can there be anyone in the whole world
    Attacked by so much misfortune
    Besieged by so much pain?
    What will I do in such confusion
    Where it seems impossible to find
    Any reason to comfort me
    Or any comfort to console me?
    After the first misfortune
    There is no happening or event
    That isn't another source of grief!
    One after another they keep coming.
    One gives birth to the next
    Like the phoenix, each new misfortune
    Arises from the ashes of the one before!

    And they never get cold in their graves.
    Someone said once that misfortunes
    Are cowards because you never see any
    On their own. I say they're brave.
    They always keep advancing
    And never turn their back.
    Clotaldo tells me to keep quiet,
    My shame tells me to wait.
    Estrella tells me to be a go-between,
    Love tells me to sort it out.
    And I know jealousy's
    Something it's impossible to conceal.
    So what can I do to straighten out
    Such a tangled knotted mess!
    But what's the use of trying to prepare
    Or thinking what I ought to do or say.
    It's obvious that when the moment comes
    Grief will do what it must,
    For there's no-one anywhere in the world
    That can ever control their anguish?
    Well, since my soul does not dare decide
    What must be done, let my grief go on
    As far as it dares or can, and let my pain
    Travel to its far extreme and so leave me free
    Free from doubts and wondering what to do.
    But till then—God help me. Heaven give me
    strength!
        (*Enter* ASTOLFO.)
ASTOLFO: This is the portrait, my lady . . .
ROSAURA: Why does your highness hesitate?
    Why does your highness stand amazed?
ASTOLFO: Amazed to see you, Rosaura, and to
    hear you speak.
ROSAURA: Why are you calling me Rosaura?
    Your Highness is mistaken, and takes me
    For some other lady. For I am Astrea,
    And in my humble state do not deserve
    The great happiness of seeing you so
    perturbed.
ASTOLFO: Rosaura, that's enough deception.
    The soul never lies
    And although I see you as Astrea
    I love you as Rosaura.
ROSAURA: All I can tell you is that Estrella
    —But perhaps I should call her Aphrodite!—
    Asked me to await you here
    And to tell you on her behalf
    To hand over that portrait

Of the lady who once passed through your life.
That is what Estrella wants
And even in the smallest things
She must always be obeyed
Even when they cause me grief.
ASTOLFO: However hard you try, Rosaura,
How badly you pretend! Tell your eyes
To harmonise their music with your voice;
For it's an instrument that's out of tune,
Full of discord and dissonance,
Trying in vain to conceal the gulf
Between the falsehood that it speaks
And the deep truth it feels.
ROSAURA: All I can say to you is
That I'm waiting for the portrait.
ASTOLFO: Well if you wish to continue this deception
I'll continue it in my reply.
Astrea, you will tell the princess
That I so greatly esteem her that
When she asked me for a portrait
It seemed to me so small a thing
To send it on its own, and so,
Because I esteem and value her,
I'm sending the original.
ROSAURA: When there's something that a man
    intends
And he's decisive, proud and brave
He has to find what he's resolved to
Or he turns back covered in shame.
I came for a portrait, and it's true
I do possess an original worth far more.
I'll still return a failure if I return alone
And so, your highness, give me the miniature
For I refuse to leave without it.
ASTOLFO: But how do you propose to take it
If I don't intend to give it?
ROSAURA: Like this.
    (*She tries to take it from him.*)
You betrayed me! Let it go!
ASTOLFO: It's no use struggling.
ROSAURA: I swear to God I'll never see it
In that woman's hands! I'd rather die!
ASTOLFO: You're
    frightening.
ROSAURA: You're disgusting!
ASTOLFO: Rosaura my dear, that's quite enough.
ROSAURA: I'm not yours. You liar!
    (*Enter* ESTRELLA.)

ESTRELLA: Astrea, Astolfo, what is this?
ASTOLFO: (Oh God, here comes Estrella!)
ROSAURA: (God of love be kind. Give me cunning.)
If you want to know what's happening, my
    lady,
I will tell you.
ASTOLFO: (Now she's done for!)
ROSAURA: You asked me to wait here
For Astolfo, and ask him for a miniature.
I was alone for a moment, and since in the
    mind
One thing leads to another so easily,
As you spoke of miniatures, I remembered
I had one of my own in this sleeve.
I've never met my father, and I had it made for
    him.
I wanted to see it for when one's alone.
It's always trivial things that pass the time.
It fell from my hand onto the floor.
Astolfo, coming to give you the other miniature,
Picked it up, and is so unwilling to give you
The thing you ask of him, that instead of giving
One picture, he wished to take another.
And when I asked him, and tried to persuade
    him
To return it me, he refused point blank.
I became angry and impatient
And tried to take it.
That's my portrait he holds in his hand;
As to whether if it's a likeness,
Take it and see for yourself.
ESTRELLA: Astolfo, give me that picture!
    (*She takes it from him.*)
ASTOLFO: My lady!
ESTRELLA: It's flattering.
ROSAURA: Is it not mine?
ESTRELLA: What doubt could there possibly be?
ROSAURA: Well, since this picture's mine,
Tell him to give you the other one.
ESTRELLA: Take your picture and be gone.
ROSAURA: (I've got my picture back;
I don't care what happens now.)
    (*Exit* ROSAURA.)
ESTRELLA: Now you give me the picture
That I asked from you. For although
I no longer have any plans
To see you or speak to you again,
I still definitely do not want

To see it in your power even if
Simply because I embarrassed myself
In asking for it.

ASTOLFO: Lady, please take note.

ESTRELLA: There's nothing I have to note.
You have to give me the picture.

ASTOLFO: (How can I get out of this?)
Beautiful Estrella, I would dearly love
To serve you and obey you, I still cannot
Give you the portrait, because . . .

ESTRELLA: How gross!
I don't want you to give it to me now
Because I don't ever want you to remind me
That I ever asked you for it.
      (*Exit* ESTRELLA.)

ASTOLFO: No stop, listen, wait!
When, where and how, Rosaura,
Have you managed to come here
To destroy us both!
      (*Exit* ASTOLFO.)
      (SEGISMUNDO *is discovered as at the beginning,
      dressed in skins, bound with chains, asleep on
      the ground. Enter* CLOTALDO, CLARIN *and* TWO
      SERVANTS.)

CLOTALDO: This is where
You leave him
And pride ends
Where it began.

SERVANT 1: I've just tied him to the chain
Like he was before.

CLARIN: Segismundo, don't wake up.
Don't find yourself
With your good fortune turned to bad.
Don't see how all your glory was a sham,
A shadow of life,
A flame of death.

CLOTALDO: Anyone who can speak like that
Needs to have a space prepared
Where he has lots of room to argue in.
This is the one you have to seize
And lock up in that cell.

CLARIN: Why me?

CLOTALDO: Because it's important to
      imprison
A Clarin who knows so many secrets
In case he starts to sing.

CLARIN: No wait a minute. Did I try to kill my
      father?

Did I throw anyone out the window
To see if they might fly?
Am I a King's son?
Am I dreaming? Am I awake?
Why lock me up?

CLOTALDO: You're Clarin.

CLARIN: From the Latin. Clarion.
All right I'll be a cornet, and shut up,
Or the man with the little triangle that sits at
      the back
And never gets to play a note.
      (*They carry him off.*)
      (*Enter* KING BASILIO, *muffled in a cloak.*)

BASILIO: Clotaldo?

CLOTALDO: Your majesty! You have come here?

BASILIO: I felt a foolish curiosity to see
What will happen to Segismundo
And I felt a foolish grief.

CLOTALDO: Look at him now returned
To his old state of misery.

BASILIO: My sad unfortunate prince,
Born at the wrong time!
Go and wake him now
For the drug you gave him
Must surely have lost its strength.

CLOTALDO: My lord, he is restless
He's speaking in his sleep.

BASILIO: What will he be dreaming of?
Let's listen.

SEGISMUNDO (*in his dreams*): A good king should
      punish injustice.
It's my duty to kill Clotaldo.
I must make my father my slave.

CLOTALDO: He threatens me with death.

BASILIO: He threatens me with servitude.

CLOTALDO: He wants to kill me.

BASILIO: He wants me to be his slave.

SEGISMUNDO: Returning to stage by popular
      demand,
Featuring in the great theatre of the world
The courageous prince Segismundo
Who takes revenge on his wicked father!
      (*He wakes up.*)
Where am I? Oh no . . . no!

BASILIO: He must not see me.
You know what you must do.
I'll be listening from here.
      (*The* KING *withdraws.*)

SEGISMUNDO: Is this me?
  Is this really me?
  Back in chains again.
  Back in my prison.
  Back in my grave.
  Yes. God help me.
  Dear God, the things I've dreamed!
CLOTALDO (*aside*): (And now I'm supposed to complete the deception.)
  So it's time to wake up, is it?
SEGISMUNDO: Yes, it's time to wake up.
CLOTALDO: Are you going to sleep the whole day?
  You mean you've been sleeping since the time
  We spoke of that proud eagle's flight?
SEGISMUNDO: Yes
  Clotaldo, and I think I'm still asleep.
  And I can't be that far wrong
  For if everything was a dream
  Everything I saw and touched for sure
  Then anything could be a dream,
  Everything I see and touch just now.
  And it seems very possible now
  Now I am so utterly defeated
  That even though I'm sleeping I can still see
  That even though I'm waking I can still dream.
CLOTALDO: Tell me what you dreamed.
SEGISMUNDO: Supposing that it was a dream
  I won't tell you what I dreamt, Clotaldo.
  I'll tell you what I saw.
  I woke up and found myself—
  And this was a lie, Clotaldo,
  A cruel and flattering lie! Because
  I was in a bed so brightly coloured
  It could have been a bed of flowers
  Woven by the goddess of spring.
  A thousand nobles bowed down to me,
  Called me their prince, and served me
  With perfumes, jewels, and fine clothes.
  My senses were in turmoil;
  You turned them into joy
  By telling me my good fortune.
  For even though this is how I am
  There I was a Prince of Poland.
CLOTALDO: And did you reward me for this good
  news?
SEGISMUNDO: No. Because you were a traitor
  I summoned up all my bold courage
  And I killed you twice.

CLOTALDO: You hated me so much?
SEGISMUNDO: I was lord of all
  And took my revenge on everyone.
  I only loved one woman
  And I think that love was true
  Because everything else ended.
  But that love goes on and on.
    (*Exit the* KING.)
CLOTALDO: (The king was moved by what he
  heard, and left.)
  It's because we spoke about
  That eagle, you dreamt of empires;
  But even dreaming it's a good idea to treat me
  well
  Because I've done my best to bring you up
  And Segismundo, even when you're dreaming.
  The good you do is never lost.
    (*Exit.*)
SEGISMUNDO: What if he's right? What if we
  suppressed
  This ferocity, this ambition and this rage
  Just in case it is a dream.
  Yes, let's do that, for this life's so strange
  Living it is just a dream.
  That's what experience teaches me:
  That everyone who lives is only dreaming
  Who they are till they awake.
  The king dreams he is a king, and lives
  Governing under this deception,
  Making laws and ruling;
  And the applause, which he receives,
  He gets it as a loan, and it's written in the wind
  And death turns it all to ashes.
  And that's such a terrible thing!
  Is there anyone who'd want to rule
  Knowing that they must wake up
  Wake up in the sleep of death!
  The rich man dreams of his riches
  Which just offer him more cares.
  The poor man dreams he suffers
  His misery and poverty.
  The one who tries to get on in life is dreaming
  The one who ambitiously and obsessively strives
  The one who hurts, insults and offends
  And in this world, in the end,
  Everyone dreams they are who they are
  Although no-one understands this.
  I dream that I am here

Bound down by these heavy chains
And I dreamed that once I lived differently
And was happy.
What is life? A frenzy.
Life's an illusion.
Life's a shadow, a fiction,
And the greatest good is worth nothing at all,
For the whole of life is just a dream
And dreams . . . dreams are only dreams.
                  END OF ACT TWO.

ACT THREE

Enter CLARIN, *on his own, in the dark.*

CLARIN: Here I am. Locked up in a magic tower
  Imprisoned for what I know.
  So what about what I don't know?
  What'll they do to me for that?
  They'll kill me. They're killing me already.
  For someone as hungry as me
  Is slowly but surely dying.
  I feel sorry for myself.
  I know you're all going to think
  "Well I'm not at all surprised"
  And you're right. It's all terribly predictable.
  It's terrible to have a name like Clarin
  And be silent. Clarin. You know. From the Latin.
  And I'm all alone with no-one to talk to
  But spiders and rats. And their conversation
  Leaves a lot to be desired.
  And my poor head's full of dreams.
  I keep dreaming of trumpets.
  And people whipping themselves
  In processions, and other people
  Watching them and fainting.
  And some go up and some go down
  And I just stay in the same place
  Fainting for lack of food.
  I'm on a starvation diet
  And it's worse than the diet of Worms.
  If I were a philosopher,
  I'd be in the anorexic school of thought.
  And I don't get any holidays or feast days
  Or anydays but hungry days.
  I'm all dazed. And I deserve it:
  Because I had a bit of knowledge and I didn't
    share it.

Servants are meant to talk in plays
  And I haven't said a word.
    (*There's a sound of drums within, and shouting.*)
SOLDIER 2: Here he is. This is the tower.
  Kick in the door!
  Come on in.
CLARIN: Christ they must be looking for me.
  They've just said here I am.
  What do they want me for?
  Are these people looking for me?
    (*Enter as many* SOLDIERS *as possible.*)
SOLDIER 1: Come on!
SOLDIER 2: Here he is!
CLARIN: No he isn't.
ALL: Your majesty!
CLARIN: Are they drunk?
SOLDIER 2: You are our Prince
  For we don't want and we won't accept
  Anyone except our own real prince
  And we don't want any foreigner.
ALL: Long live our great prince!
CLARIN: I think they really mean it!
  Maybe in this kingdom it's the custom
  Maybe they take someone every day, make him
    prince
  And then lock him up again?
  They did it yesterday. I saw them.
  So this is them doing it today.
  I'd better play the part.
SOLDIERS: Allow us to kiss your feet.
CLARIN: No I can't do that, I haven't washed them.
  Anyway they're my feet and I like them.
  Don't want anyone fooling around with them
  Footling around with them.
  It would be footless. Fruitless.
  But thank you anyway.
SOLDIER 2: We all went to your father and we told
    him
  You're the only prince we'll recognise
  And not that foreigner from Moscow.
CLARIN: Are you telling me you were rude to my
    dad?
  You're a lot of rotten shits.
SOLDIER 1: We only did it out of loyalty.
CLARIN: Oh well if it was loyalty, I forgive you.
SOLDIER 2: Come out and restore your Empire!
  Long live Segismundo!
ALL: Long live Segismundo!

CLARIN: Are they calling me Segismundo? Oh well.
Obviously they call all their fake princes Segis-
mundo.
(*Enter* SEGISMUNDO.)
SEGISMUNDO: Who calls for me?
CLARIN: That's the end of me as prince.
Now I'm the artist formerly known as Blank.
SOLDIER 2: So who is Segismundo?
SEGISMUNDO: Me.
SOLDIER 2: So what were you doing, you stupid,
rash fool
Calling yourself Segismundo?
CLARIN: How dare you. I never did. Call myself
Segismundo . . .
You were the ones who were Segismundo-ing
me.
So you're the ones who's stupid and rash.
SOLDIER 1: Great prince Segismundo
Your father, king Basilio, was afraid
Of some prophecy which said
He would find himself helpless at your feet.
He wants to take away from you your power
And your right to rule
And give it all to Astolfo, Duke of Moscow.
That's what he told his court, and the people
got to know of this
And once we knew we have a real king
We don't want to be ruled by a foreigner.
And so we've come to find you
Where they're keeping you prisoner.
We bring you weapons and an army
So you can lead a revolution
To depose a tyrant and restore yourself
As rightful ruler. Come then:
For out in this wasteland a huge army
Is waiting to acclaim you.
Freedom awaits you Prince:
Hear its shouts.
VOICES (*within*): Long live Segismundo!
SEGISMUNDO: Yet again am I supposed to dream
Another vision of greatness and power
Which will be destroyed by time?
Yet again am I supposed to see
Dimly amidst mists and shadows
Another vision of pompous majesty?
Yet again am I supposed to feel
The pain of disillusionment and loss
That all human power is subject to

And must humbly live and alertly watch for?
I won't do it. I won't. I won't!
Go away you figments! You illusions
Deceiving my dead senses
With the appearance of bodies and voices
When you have no body and you have no
voice!
I don't want false power.
I don't want false majesty!
You fantastical illusions
That will disappear at the first breath of dawn,
You're like the blossom on the almond tree
Who flowers so foolishly soon
And then withers, fades, and loses
From its rosy buds all beauty,
All delight, all ornament,
Blown away by the first breath of winter wind.
You see I know you now
I know it's just the same with you
And with anyone who's dreaming.
Now there's no way I can be deceived
My eyes are opened, I have no illusions
And I know life is just a dream.
SOLDIER 2: You think we're fooling you
And it just isn't true. Turn your eyes
And look up at that proud mountain.
You'll see there's a crowd of people there
Waiting to do whatever you tell them.
SEGISMUNDO: I saw all that before, and it looked
As clear and as distinct
As everything that I see now
And it was all a dream.
SOLDIER 1: When great things happen, lord, they
always come with premonitions
And that's what that was, if you dreamed it
first.
SEGISMUNDO: You're right; it was a premonition
(And so just in case it is true
And since life is a dream,
Let's dream, my soul,
Let's dream again but this time with attention
And bearing in mind that at some fine time
We're going to wake up from this pleasure.
Because if we know that
It'll all come as less of a shock.
And it's always best to be one step ahead
Of pain. So, taking this precaution,
And knowing that all power is on loan

And will have to be given back to its owner
Let's dare to do everything.
Friends, I appreciate your loyalty.
You'll find in me
Someone clever enough and brave enough
To free you from foreign rule.
Call to arms! Prepare to march!
My courage will never be defeated!
I will fight my own father and defeat him!
I will make the prophecy come true!
And he will be lying helpless at my feet!
(But if before this I wake up
   wouldn't it be better not to say it
   since I'm not going to do it?)
ALL: Long live Segismundo!
  Long live freedom!
    (*Enter* CLOTALDO.)
CLOTALDO: What is this?
SEGISMUNDO: Clotaldo!
CLOTALDO: My lord!
  (I expect I'll be the first target of his cruelty.)
CLARIN: (I bet he throws him off the mountain.)
    (*Exit.*)
CLOTALDO: I kneel before you. I know I shall die.
SEGISMUNDO: Father, get up, don't stay on your
   knees.
  I want you to guide me
  In what I have to do.
  I know I owe my upbringing
  To your love and loyalty.
  Embrace me.
CLOTALDO: What are you saying?
SEGISMUNDO: I am dreaming and I want to do
   good.
  For the good you do is never lost,
  Not even in dreams.
CLOTALDO: Well, my lord, if doing good
  Is what you now intend, then obviously
  It won't offend you if I try to do the same.
  You are about to make war on your father;
  I can't advise you in a war against my king
  Or be of any use to you.
  Here I am at your feet: kill me.
SEGISMUNDO: You peasant, you wretch, you
   traitor,
  (God I need to control myself!)
  I'm not even sure if I'm awake!
  It's like putting a brake on all my rage

This thought that I'm going to wake up
And find myself without this power!)
SOLDIER 2: All this loyalty's a waste of time.
  What you're really doing is ignoring the com-
   mon good.
  We're the ones that are loyal because we're
   making sure
  That it's our real prince who governs us.
CLOTALDO: That would be fine once the king was
   dead
  But the king is still alive and must be obeyed
  As our only ruler; and nothing can ever
   justify
  His vassals taking arms against him.
SOLDIER 2: Well we'll soon see Clotaldo
  How much this loyalty is worth.
CLOTALDO: The main thing is to obey orders
SEGISMUNDO: That's enough!
CLOTALDO: My lord.
SEGISMUNDO: Clotaldo, I envy you your bravery
  And I'm grateful for it.
  Go and serve the king.
  We'll meet on the battlefield.
  But let's not argue
  Whether it's a good thing or a bad.
  We all have our sense of honour.
CLOTALDO: I won't forget my gratitude.
    (*Exit.*)
SEGISMUNDO: You, beat the drum for war
  And march in good order.
  Head for the king's palace!
ALL: Long live our great prince!
SEGISMUNDO: Fortune, we're going to be king.
  Don't wake me up, if I'm dreaming;
  If it's real, then don't send me back to sleep.
  But whether it's real or whether it's a dream
  Doing good is all that matters
  If it's real, then just because;
  If it's a dream, to win friends
  For when we wake up again.
    (*They exit. Drums beat.*)
    (*Enter* BASILIO *and* ASTOLFO.)
BASILIO: When a horse goes mad and starts to run
  Is there anyone strong enough to halt it?
  Can anyone stop a raging river on a slope
  Tumbling wildly down jagged rocks to the sea?
  Can anyone stop a torn off mountain crag
  Crashing uncontrollably to the valley below?

All these things would be easier to control
Than the fierce energy of the common people.
All we see and hear attests this truth.
The shouts of opposing factions echo across the
  valleys.
Some call out "Segismundo" some "Astolfo".
The throne room has become a side show
A dismal theatre, an empty auditorium
Where fortune mounts tragedies no-one wants
  to see.

ASTOLFO: All rejoicing has to be postponed,
All applause brought to a sudden halt
Every good fortune promised by your fortunate
  hand,
For if Poland—which I hope to rule—
Now resists the obedience it owes me
It is simply so I can earn the right to it.
Bring me a horse, and, full of pride,
I'll boast like thunder and descend
Like a bolt of lightning.
  (*Exit* ASTOLFO.)

BASILIO: Nothing can be done against the infal-
  libly true.
There is great danger in tampering with the
  foreseen.
If something has to happen, nothing can pre-
  vent it,
And the more you try to stop it
The more you make it actually occur.
How harsh a law. How terrifying a fact. How
  cruel a universe.
Anyone who thinks they are avoiding a risk
Is in fact walking right into it. Trying to save
  myself,
I have dug my own grave.
I tried to overcome a danger
And I have brought it about.
I tried to save my country
And I have destroyed it.
  (*Enter* ESTRELLA.)

ESTRELLA: Great king, you have to prevent this riot
Breaking out among rival mobs, tearing
Each other apart in the city streets.
Otherwise your kingdom will drown in blood
An ocean of bloodshed will overwhelm it.
For now in the streets walks nothing but
  misfortune.
Now in the streets screams nothing but tragedy.

So great is the ruin of your empire
So great the rage and thirst for blood
All eyes are filled with terror
All ears with the wounded's screams.
The sun is darkened, the wind breathes fear,
Each stone marks a grave
Each flower a funeral wreath
Each building a cemetery
And each soldier a living skeleton.
  (*Enter* CLOTALDO.)

CLOTALDO: Thank god I'm alive to fall at your feet!

BASILIO: Clotaldo! What news of Segismundo?

CLOTALDO: The people, like a blinded monster
A boulder rolling down a mountain,
Have reached the tower and set him free.
For the second time, he finds himself honoured
And treated like a king, and has sworn
To dethrone you, fiercely declaring
That he will make heaven's prophecies come
  true.

BASILIO: Then bring me a horse, and my weary
  old age
Will ride out to subdue a rebellious son.
And when it comes to defending my throne,
Perhaps where science failed, violence will
  prevail.

ESTRELLA: I have fought a fierce battle against
  jealousy
So a battlefield for me holds no terrors.
I'll ride after you and swing my sword
Striking men dead with each fierce blow.
  (*Exit* BASILIO *and* ESTRELLA.)

ROSAURA: All is war. And I know your courage
Screams within you to urge you join it, but
Please hear me. I came here poor, lonely and
  humiliated.
Out of nobility you sheltered and took pity on
  me.
I was obliged to you, obliged to follow
Your advice, dress as a woman, live
In the palace, conceal my true self
And serve Estrella, my beautiful enemy.
Astolfo saw me, knows who I am
And acts with such utter disregard of me
He has made an assignation with Estrella
For tonight in the palace garden.
I have the key. You can enter it.
With pride, courage and determination

You can end my shame.
I know you have already decided
To avenge me by killing him.
Take your chance. I want his death.
Kill the man who has betrayed me.
CLOTALDO: It's true that I did find myself inclined
Rosaura, from the moment I first saw you,
Inclined towards doing all I could to help you
And your weeping was the witness.
I intended to help you take revenge.
The first step I took was to have you change
     your clothes
So that if Astolfo saw you, he would see you
Dressed as a woman, and so would not judge
Your absurd rashness as a sign of promiscuity.
At that time I was trying to find the means
To recover your lost honour, and did even
     consider
—And judge from this how far my concern was
     taking me—
Killing Astolfo. What an absurd notion!
Even though, given he is not my King
I could contemplate his murder without
     astonishment
Or dismay. I was about to kill him when
     Segismundo
Tried to kill me. Astolfo came, showed courage,
Ignored his own safety, and saved my life.
So how am I supposed to repay
This man who gave me life
By giving him death in return?
I don't know what to do. I want
To give you an honourable life
And that pulls me one way;
But I am obliged to him for the fact
That I'm still living at all.
Torn between giving and receiving,
I am an agent, and a patient too:
Caught in the slipstream, uncertain, undecided,
A person who acts; a soul who suffers.
ROSAURA: You know perfectly well that it's nobler
To give than it is to receive. Giving
Puts you in a position of strength:
Receiving puts you at a disadvantage.
So think of the difference between him and me.
I have enabled you to give, and strengthened you
But he has forced you to receive, and weakened
     you.

So you are more beholden to me; not him,
And in this dangerous time you must
Come over to me. For I take precedence,
Just as giving is nobler than receiving.
CLOTALDO: I agree the act of giving is noble. But
It calls for gratitude from the receiver.
A reputation for generosity I already possess;
Allow me now to gain what I lack:
A reputation for gratitude.
ROSAURA: You gave me life; but you told me
     yourself
That life without self-respect, life
Lived under the weight of insult,
Is not life at all. It's a kind of death.
You say you want to be generous.
So be generous. Give me life.
The only true life: life free from dishonour.
Be generous first. You can be grateful
     afterwards.
CLOTALDO: Rosaura, I'm sure you're right.
Generosity matters more.
So I'll give you all my property
So you can enter a convent and there live in
     peace.
This resolves the situation, for it
Gives you refuge from your shame.
And with the whole kingdom
In a state of civil war, I refuse
To kill Astolfo, my prince, and so add
To my country's deep misfortunes.
You see this solves everything:
I can be loyal to my country,
Show generosity to you and
Gratitude to Astolfo.
So it's important you agree,
For I could hardly do more,
For heavens sake!—if I was your father.
ROSAURA: If you were my father
I might put up with this.
But since you're not, I won't.
CLOTALDO: So what do you intend to do?
ROSAURA: Kill Astolfo.
CLOTALDO: Can a girl who's never known her
     father
Have the courage to do such a thing?
ROSAURA: Yes.
CLOTALDO: What drives you on?
ROSAURA: My self-respect.

CLOTALDO: Remember you have to see Astolfo—

ROSAURA: As the man who's insulted and
betrayed me.

CLOTALDO: —As your king and husband to
Estrella.

ROSAURA: That will never be. I swear to God.

CLOTALDO: This is madness.

ROSAURA: I know.

CLOTALDO: Then overcome it.

ROSAURA: I cannot.

CLOTALDO: Then you will lose . . .

ROSAURA: Yes.

CLOTALDO: Life and honour.

ROSAURA: I know.

CLOTALDO: What are you hoping to achieve?

ROSAURA: My death.

CLOTALDO: This is worse than desperate.

ROSAURA: It is honour.

CLOTALDO: It's madness.

ROSAURA: Bravery.

CLOTALDO: It's sheer lunacy.

ROSAURA: It's anger, it's rage.

CLOTALDO: You're possessed by a hatred
You won't even try to control?

ROSAURA: No.

CLOTALDO: Who will help you?

ROSAURA: I'll help myself.

CLOTALDO: Is there no alternative?

ROSAURA: No.

CLOTALDO: There has to be. Rosaura please.
There has to be another way.

ROSAURA: Another way to destroy myself!
(*Exit* ROSAURA.)

CLOTALDO: Daughter!
Well, if you insist on being destroyed,
Let's destroy ourselves together!
(*Exit* CLOTALDO.)
(*They beat the drum, and enter* SEGISMUNDO,
dressed in skins, with CLARIN *and* MARCHING
SOLDIERS.)

SEGISMUNDO: I wish the Roman Emperors could
see me now
Dressed like an animal, leading an army
Ready for anything! I could defeat the sky!
No. Wait, don't get too ambitious. Don't aim so
high
Don't make it all disappear, or this dream of
greatness

Will hurt me when I wake up and find it gone.
The less I have to lose, the less I suffer when it
disappears.

CLARIN: There's a man with his eyes wide open
But still living in the dark. It's madness.
He can see everything, but can't make sense of it.
And I'm as bad. Here's me, seeing him,
And not making sense of him at all.
(*A clarion call within. Drums.*)

SEGISMUNDO: What's that?

CLARIN: A swift horse. And, I'm
sorry,
But I have to describe it. It's my cue.
It's a horse on which the learned can see a map.
For its body is the earth,
The fire its soul all locked up in its chest
The sea is the foam that's all spewed up at its
mouth
And the air's its panting breath.
Now this is confusing and extremely chaotic
For in its soul, foam, body and breath
It's a monster of fire, water, wind and earth,
A piebald monster, dappled all over, bridled
and spurred
By the person who's riding her
And who doesn't just gallop but flies
Into your presence and is a woman

SEGISMUNDO: Whose beauty blinds me.

CLARIN: For goodness sake it's Rosaura!
(*Exit* CLARIN.)

SEGISMUNDO: Fate has brought her back to me.
Everything I dreamed of is coming true.
(*Enter* ROSAURA *wearing a gorgeous dress, a sword
and a dagger.*)

ROSAURA: Segismundo, noble prince, rising
Like the sun after years of darkness
Rising, crowned and majestic,
In the arms of dawn,
Glittering like a jewel,
On flowers, roses, mountain tops,
The flecks of foam on the crests of the waves:
I know you will help me because you are noble
And I am a woman in need of assistance.
This is the third time you have seen and ad-
mired me
Yet the third time you do not know me
For each time we meet I have appeared
In a different shape, dress and form.

The first time you saw me you were held in
   chains.
You saw me in your prison and you thought
   me a man
And you helped me through a time of dark
   misfortune.
The second time you saw me you were treated
   as a king.
I was dressed as a woman, you were admiring
   of my beauty
In your illusory dream of power and majesty.
Today is the third time and I'm a kind of
   monster
Carrying man's weapons, but wearing wom-
   en's clothes
And so that you may now take pity
And be spurred on the better to help me
I must tell you my sad story.
They say beauty and misfortune go hand in
   hand.
My mother was unfortunate enough
To be most beautiful. She was a noble Muscovite;
A man fell in love with her,
A man I cannot name because I do not know it.
I know he had courage, because I have courage
   too.
And in my grief at the circumstance of my birth
I would imagine him to be a kind of god,
Those you find in the ancient stories
And whose victims weep, like Danae, like
   Leda,
Because gods, like men, forget the women
Who once gave them pleasure.
I was afraid I was lengthening my story
By quoting all these ancient, frivolous tales.
But now I've discover that I've told it all.
My mother was as beautiful as any
And as unhappy as them all.
It was a promise of marriage,
That same old stupid story,
Which took such a hold on her mind.
She still expects it to be fulfilled.
The man was like Aeneas in the siege of Troy,
So great a betrayer of faith
That he even left his sword behind.
I'll sheathe it here and when the story ends
The time will come to show it naked to the
   world.

The promise of marriage is like a knot
That's been badly tied, it does not bind,
It gives no shelter nor protection,
But I was born from it. Born so like my mother
If not in beauty, then at least
In how I lived and suffered
And what I allowed happen to me.
The man who wrecked my reputation
And destroyed my self-respect
Is . . . Astolfo. My face flares up,
And the simple act of naming him
Fills my heart with anger and with rage
Which is exactly what you would expect
When you name a vicious enemy.
Astolfo was the wretched man
Who forgot all of our love's glories
Just like you'd forget the name
Of some chance acquaintance,
Betrayed me, left for Poland
Aiming for another conquest,
This time with the beautiful Estrella.
She was the guide for my descent into
   darkness.
If it really was a star
That brought us together as lovers.
How ironic that now Estrella
Should be the unlucky star to divide us.
He lied to me. He insulted me.
He left me drowning in madness and grief.
Inside me boiled the confusion of Babylon
And burned the pitiless fires of hell.
I never spoke of this. Some griefs
Are best spoken of in silence.
Until one day alone with my mother,
I broke down their prison door
And they all burst out at once
Tripping over each other in their haste.
I will not shame myself repeating them;
But I could freely speak to her
Because I knew she had suffered similar pain.
Sometimes a bad example is of some use.
She took pity on me in my tears,
Consoled me with her own, forgave me.
Forgiveness is easy when you have also sinned.
Learning a lesson from her own life story
—for she had left it all to be sorted out by time,
And had been left alone with her misfortunes—
She thought it best that I follow Astolfo

And having found him, force him to repay his
   debt.
To try to lessen the damage to my battered
   reputation.
She thought it best I go dressed as a man.
She took down an ancient sword,
The one that I am now wearing
—And it is time I fulfilled my promise
And unsheathed its naked blade—
And there she told me "Go to Poland
Rosaura, dressed as a man,
And there make sure the noblest men
See you with this sword. For it could be
That in one you will find a friend
To take pity on your griefs
And remedy your misfortunes".
And so I came to Poland.
I won't describe how a maddened horse
Led me to your prison where you languished
In chains and darkness, and there first saw me.
I won't describe how Clotaldo
Became so passionately involved in my
   misfortune
How the king spares my life for him;
How, once I'd told him who I am,
Clotaldo persuades me to put on women's
   clothes
And serve Estrella, where I'm clever enough
To disturb Astolfo's wooing.
I won't describe how you saw me there,
Admiring me, confused because you'd seen me
Wearing clothes of two different forms.
But now I'll tell you that Clotaldo
Became convinced that it matters
That Astolfo and the beautiful Estrella marry
And become rulers of Poland together.
And so he advised me to drop my claim,
And live in a convent and there languish
Sad and inconsolable. But now,
Brave Segismundo, now that fate
Has set you free from your dark prison
That place where you have been
Like a wild animal in your fierce anger
And like an unbroken rock of patient suffering
Now you have the chance to take revenge.
And seeing this, I have decided to join you,
Wearing both the gorgeous dress of Aphrodite
And the god of war's impenetrable steel.

Both adorn me as we meet for this third time.
And I've come both to oblige you and assist
   you
Coming as a woman to persuade you
To help me regain my honour
And coming as a man to assist you
To help you regain your throne.
As a woman I come to inspire your pity
When I beg you at your feet
As a man I come to serve you with courage
When your army enters the fight
As a woman I come so you can rescue me
In my insult and my dishonour
And as a man I have come to fight for you
With my sword and my fierce presence.
And so it seems to me that today
If I fall in love with you as a woman
As a man I will die for you
Fiercely defending my honour.
It matters to us both, brave leader,
That this arranged wedding does not take
   place.
It matters to me so that the man
Who calls himself my husband does not marry;
It matters to you because you need to prevent
The union of their powers which may put in
   doubt
Our own inevitable victory.
As a woman, I come to persuade you
To take up arms in defence of my honour;
As a man I come to encourage you
To recover your lost sceptre.
As a woman, I come to beg for your pity
When I fall helpless at your feet.
As a man I come to aid you
With my sword and my fierce courage.
If you love me as a woman
As a man I'll fight to the death.
To regain honour and self-respect,
I'll be a woman and fill your heart with
   tenderness
And I'll be a man to gain respect.
SEGISMUNDO: God if it's true I'm dreaming
   Then stop me remembering
   For it's not possible for so many things
   All to fit into the one dream!
   God help me! Is there anyone
   Who could solve all those dilemmas

Or else turn his back on all of them!
All the things she said . . . !
If I was really dreaming I was king
Then how come that woman saw me
And can tell me about it in such detail?
So it has to have been true.
It can't have been a dream.
But if it was true, then it just makes
Everything far more confusing.
Because how come I think
My life's a dream? I mean,
Are wonderful experiences so like dreams
That what's real can be utterly dreamlike
And what's unreal can be taken to be true?
Which means, which means it must be obvious
That this dream is what life is
And that this life is really just a dream.
So if that's true, and all this greatness
All this majesty, all this power,
If it's all going to disappear as if it never was
The thing to do is make the most of what we've
   got.
I've got Rosaura in my power
And I love her incredible beauty
So let's make the most of it.
It's true she trusts me, she, expects me to help
   her
But I want her. And love and desire
Break all rules of confidence and trust.
If everything's just a dream,
Then let's dream, my soul,
Let's dream of happiness
Because we know it will soon be grief.
But I've just gone and made myself
Change my mind. There has to be
A kind of happiness that lasts for ever.
And who'd want to destroy that
Just for a moment's pleasure?
Every past happiness is just a dream.
Is there anyone here who hasn't
Thought back to some happy time
And thought: "It all feels like
It was just a dream?" There's a thought
That kills all illusion, there's a thought
Makes every pleasure seem like a candle flame
Easily blown out by the first breath of wind.
I have to look for more than that
I have to look for something that lasts for ever

Some living, ever-burning flame
Where happiness never ends
And great things are not forgotten.
And anyway, when I look at Rosaura . . .
I'm more in love with her than ever,
But I don't know . . . Her story's placed
Some kind of poison in my soul.
It's the thought her body's already been
   enjoyed
By someone else. What a vile thing
It must be in this world to love
Someone another has forgotten, to love
Someone another still enjoys! Besides,
Rosaura has been dishonoured.
A good prince should not dishonour her more
A good prince should give her honour back.
For God's sake, that's what I should try to
   regain
That's more important than gaining power!
But I'll have to turn my back on this
   opportunity
Because it's just so very attractive . . .
Sound to arms! We'll fight the battle today!
To arms! To arms!

ROSAURA:　　　　My lord
   Why do you turn your back on me?
   Don't all my troubles even earn
   A single word? How can you bear
   To turn your back on me?
   Not to look at me or hear me?
   Won't you even turn a moment
   Won't you even give me a single glance?

SEGISMUNDO: Rosaura, I want to show you pity
   So for now I must be cruel.
   I want to answer with my actions
   I dare not answer with my voice.
   I cannot look at you because
   In such uncertain, dangerous times
   Anyone who wants to think about your honour
   Cannot afford to gaze upon your beauty.
       (*Exit* SEGISMUNDO *and the* SOLDIERS.)

ROSAURA: O for god's sake! What's that supposed
   to be about!
   After all I've gone through
   And I've still got to cope
   With such incomprehensible replies?
       (*Enter* CLARIN.)

CLARIN: My lady, can I see you?

ROSAURA: Oh Clarin! Where have you been?

CLARIN: Locked up in a tower. Playing cards with
    death.

  She almost played me a nasty trick
  And I was very nearly disappeared.

ROSAURA: Why?

CLARIN: Because I know the secret of who you are
  And your father is. And that in fact Clotaldo . . .
    (*Drums beat within.*)
  But what is that appalling noise?

ROSAURA: What can it be?

CLARIN: Oh it's just an armed regiment coming
    out
  Of the besieged palace to try to beat
  The fearsome army of fierce Segismundo.

ROSAURA: Then what am I doing standing here like
    a coward?
  Why aren't I out there fighting beside him
  Scandalising the entire world
  When there's so much violence and cruelty
  Tearing the world apart without order and law?
    (*Exit.*)

WITHIN SOME VOICES: Long live our King!

WITHIN SOME OTHER VOICES: Long live our freedom!

CLARIN: Long live our freedom! And long live the
    king!
  Let them both live very happily together
  Because nothing's going to bother me at all
  Just as long as I'm on the winning side at the
    end.
  But just for now I think I'll make myself scarce.
  I don't fancy playing a soldier at all.
  I think I'll play Nero instead.
  I'll just buy a violin second hand
  And play fiddle while Poland burns.
  And I really won't care what happens
  Just as long as it all leaves me alone.
  There's a little snug crevice here
  In among these rocks.
  To hell with death.
  She'll never find me here.
    (*He hides. We hear the sound of clashing weapons,
    and then enter the* KING, CLOTALDO *and* ASTOLFO, *all
    running away.*)

BASILIO: Was there ever a more unfortunate king?
  Was there ever a more mistreated father?

CLOTALDO: Your defeated army flees without
    order or discipline.

ASTOLFO: The battlefield belongs to the rebellious
    traitors.

BASILIO: In battles like these, Astolfo,
  The loyal subjects are those who win
  The rebellious traitors are those who lose.
    (*A shot within.* CLARIN *falls, wounded, from where
    he is.*)

BASILIO: Who is it?

ASTOLFO: Who is this wretched soldier
  Falling at our feet
  Wounded and covered in blood?

CLARIN: I'm someone who wanted to run from
    death
  But all I did was find it.
  That's how it is; you run
  From the thing you're afraid of
  And you run right into it.
  You try to avoid it, but
  Instead you make it happen.
  You're trying to escape death
  On the battlefield by running
  Deep into the deserted mountains
  But turn back. Turn back!
  You're safer among gunshots
  In less danger from sword thrusts
  Than in the remotest valley.
  There is nowhere safe, nowhere
  To escape the reach of death.
  Remember you're going to die
  If God says your hour has come.
    (*He falls within.*)

BASILIO: Remember that you're going to die
  If God says your hour has come.
  O God how well this speaking corpse
  How well this wounded bleeding mouth
  Persuades us of our ignorance and error.
  His trail of blood is like a tongue
  Teaching us that when we try to resist a higher
    power
  Everything we do is wasted effort.
  I tried to prevent my country suffering
  Rebellion bloodshed and civil war
  And all I've done is to create the very suffering
  I worked so hard to try to prevent.

CLOTALDO: My lord, it's true that death knows
    every path
  But a good Christian does not despair
  And say there's no escaping evil destiny.

It isn't true; the wise and prudent man
Can control his destiny, can control his fate.
At the moment you are not at all protected
From danger and calamity; so you must take
   steps
And find a place where you can be safe.
ASTOLFO: Clotaldo, my lord, speaks to you
  As a prudent man of advancing age.
  I speak to you as a brave young man
  Who has kept a fast horse hidden in the
    mountain.
  It's a swift abortion of the dawn:
  Take it and ride away on it;
  For I will guard your back.
BASILIO: If God has decreed I die
  Or if death lies in wait for me
  I want to meet it here.
  And meet death face to face.
    (*Weapons clash; enter* SEGISMUNDO *and the whole*
    company.)
SEGISMUNDO: The king is hiding in the mountains
  In the thick branches of the forest.
  Follow him. Search the forest
  Tree by tree and leaf by leaf.
CLOTALDO: Your majesty, run!
BASILIO: Why?
ASTOLFO: What do you intend to do?
BASILIO: Get back Astolfo!
CLOTALDO: What do you intend?
BASILIO: To do the thing that I must do.
  If it's me you're looking for
  Then here I am. I kneel before you.
  I lie on the ground and I'm helpless at your feet.
  Here I am. Trample me in the mud.
  Use me as your slave.
  And after so many attempts to evade it
  Let the will of fate be done
  Let the decree of heaven be fulfilled.
SEGISMUNDO: Famous court of Poland
  Witness of so many amazing events
  Listen to me: I speak to you as your Prince.
  God writes our stories with his finger in the sky
  And he writes with letters of silver and gold
  On the beautiful azure of heaven's mysteries.
  God never lies; the man who lies,
  The man who deceives,
  Is the man who deciphers these mysteries
  And then makes wrong use of them.

Look at my father, who feared my rage
And then did everything to provoke it.
He made me wild beast, a brute, when
Everything in my heritage
Predisposed me to be gentle and courteous.
But because he treated me like an animal
I became a savage beast.
What kind of wisdom was that!
If someone said to you:
"Be careful of that animal. Its lucky it's sleeping
Because it's savage and cruel
And would certainly kill you
If you wake it." Would it be wise
To take a sharpened stick and poke it?
If someone said to you:
"Be careful of that sword you're wearing
Or its sharp blade will kill you"
Would it be wise to unsheathe it
And hold its naked point against your chest?
And what if someone said:
"Be careful of the ocean deeps:
Or its depths will be your gravestone"
Would it be wise to take a boat
And set out from harbour in the middle of a
  storm?
My rage was that sleeping beast
My fury that sheathed sword
My cruelty that stormy sea.
If life threatens you with evil
It cannot be overcome
By acting with injustice and cruelty
For that only increases its malice.
It can only be defeated
By courage intelligence and strength,
Daring to meet evil face to face.
All of you: observe the downfall of this king
Witness this extraordinary spectacle
Let it fill you with fear and amazement.
My father did everything he could
To escape an evil that threatened him
And failed. So how can I
Not so old as he, not so brave and not so wise
How can I do any better?
Father please get up, don't lie there on the
  ground.
Give me your hand, and now
Heaven and the world have shown you your
  mistakes

I bow my head, I kneel at your feet
And I place myself at your mercy.

BASILIO: My son, in your nobility you are reborn.
You are prince; the laurel and the palm of
victory
Are yours. You overcame. Your achievements
Give you victory.

ALL: Long live Segismundo!

SEGISMUNDO: There are more victories I need to
win
And they all require great courage.
I'll start with the hardest: to overcome myself.
I have decided to restore Rosaura's honour:
So Astolfo you must marry her at once.

ASTOLFO: Although it's true I owe her obligations
I have to say her father is unknown.
Clearly it would be baseness and infamy
For me to marry such a woman.

CLOTALDO: Stop. That's enough, don't go on.
For Rosaura is as noble as you are,
And my sword will defend her in a duel.
She's my daughter. That's all that need be said.

ASTOLFO: What?

CLOTALDO: Until she was married and
honourable
I didn't want to reveal who she was.
The story of this is very long
But there you are. She is my daughter.

ASTOLFO: Well, if that's the case I'll keep my
promise.

ROSAURA: In one day, I've found a double
happiness.

SEGISMUNDO: And so I need to marry Estrella
To a Prince of equal rank and worth.
I'll marry you myself. Give me your hand.

ESTRELLA: I seem to have got myself a better
husband.

SEGISMUNDO: And Clotaldo, as a reward for
loyalty,
Will be my Chief Minister.

SOLDIER 1: So if you're rewarding all these people
Who fought against you and did you harm
What will you give me, who started this
rebellion
Set you free from the tower and made you
king?

SEGISMUNDO: The tower. And there you'll stay
Chained up until you die.
For once the moment of betrayal's past
It's important to get rid of the traitor.

ASTOLFO: How very wise!

BASILIO: What statesmanship!

CLOTALDO: How much you've changed!

ROSAURA: How clever you've become!

SEGISMUNDO: Why are you all so amazed? I still
live in dread
I'm going to wake up and find myself in prison
again.
My teacher was a dream
A dream that destroys illusions
And tells me life's just a sweet lie
And when we wake up from it
We find it's nothing. Empty air.
It's how it is for an actor,
One minute he's a king
And the next he's at your mercy.
When the play comes to its end
He humbly begs your pardon
And asks you to forgive mistakes.

                            END.

Introduction to *The Hypochondriac*

WHEN THE PLAY WAS NEW

The Hypochondriac (*Le malade imaginaire*), also translated as *The Imaginary Invalid,* was the last play written and produced by Molière in the year of his death, 1673. This actor/playwright, who often took the leading role in the plays he wrote, became sick on stage a week or so after the play opened and soon died. Ironically, he fell fatally ill while pretending to be a hypochondriac.

French drama in the seventeenth century was typically written in a neoclassical style. Consequently, most French plays of Molière's era adhered to the Italian rules of unity of place (all action in one location), unity of time (all of the action takes place in twenty-four hours or less), and unity of action (no subplots unless directly related to the central conflict). Also, all action was reality based (no fantasy or supernatural activity onstage), and the play was supposed to teach a moral lesson. Such an approach to drama was expected of playwrights at the time and Molière usually accommodated these expectations. In the three major acts of *The Hypochondriac,* Molière follows the prescription, but in the prologue and interludes the neoclassical rules are suspended.

The profession of doctors and the study and practice of medicine were in a very sorry state when Molière was active in the theatre. Because of his own preoccupation with the dangers inherent in the medical profession, Molière frequently attacked doctors and apothecaries in plays such as *A Doctor in Spite of Himself* (1666) and *The Flying Doctor* (c. 1648). Any time Molière found dishonesty in a social or professional field important, he ambushed the perpetrators with his comedy. In the case of medicine, he did not have to push the absurdities too far from reality to get the ridiculousness that we see dramatized. With the focus on the patient, however, the satire extends well beyond the medical profession and comments on compulsive, unreasoned behavior.

Molière wrote for a proscenium (picture frame) theatre based on the Italian model, which had had a great impact on the French theatre. Many of his plays are set in interiors, usually a generic semi-public room in a house that is a logical location for many people to come and go throughout the action of the play. *The Hypochondriac* is unusual in that the action appears to take place in a private room of Argan. His private room becomes public since it is supposed to be a sickroom of the "invalid." In this play and others, however, few properties or furniture are used for any of the interiors. Only those vital to the action were carried into the space. If it were necessary that characters sit, the call for chairs is often found in the dialogue. Otherwise, Molière's comedies were "stand-up" theatre with the actors working on the stage apron close to the audience. Much of the dialogue—and certainly all of the asides—were delivered directly to the house. The theatre was also a noisy place, fully lit throughout. Audience members ate, talked, and moved about. Very good actors would, of course, arrest their attention.

Like the theatre of Spain, French theatre companies also cast women, who became prominent company members. Women had performed periodically in France since the medieval period, but with the rise of professionalism in the 1600s they became a standard element of the theatre. Once Molière married, he often played opposite his wife, the actress Armande Béjart. The Béjart family of actors was extremely important to Molière, who worked with many and wrote roles for at least five Béjarts during his career.

THE PLAYWRIGHT

Molière (1622–1673) is the stage name of Jean-Baptiste Poquelin, who—like many actors and actresses in France—changed his name when he decided to embark on a career in the theatre beginning in 1643. He had a rough apprenticeship in the theatre and even spent some time in debtor's prison. For well over a decade he toured provincial French cities and towns. He became the manager as well as the leading actor and playwright of his theatre company, which was eventually centered in Paris by 1658. Molière also won the favor of King Louis XIV, who permitted Molière's company to perform with the Italian commedia dell'arte company (an important influence on Molière's comedy) before moving him into the Palais-Royal a few years later. This theatre became the site of Molière's finest work, and he often gave performances at court as well. Molière wrote many different kinds of plays but he clearly excelled at comedy. His most successful and frequently revived comedies are comedies of manners and character wherein typically the central male character (played by Molière) is a character of excess who suffers from an obsession. This excess is at the heart of the conflict in this play.

In *The Hypochondriac* the protagonist Argan is fixated on the idea that he is dying of multiple diseases. In *Tartuffe* (1669) the credulous protagonist is obsessed with a charlatan who represents the worst in religious fraud; in *The Misanthrope* (1666) the central character despises humankind and finds serious fault with everyone—even the woman he loves. The preoccupation in *The Miser* (1668) is made obvious by the title. In *The Learned Ladies* (1672) Molière focuses on obsession in women rather than men. Learning from Italian comedies, he also excelled at farce and created musical forms as well. His attempts at tragedy were less successful. Throughout his career Molière made it clear that he understood best how to demonstrate the absurdities of the human condition and poked fun at nearly everyone, including himself. He married an actress at least twenty years his junior and promptly pointed out the folly of this situation in his play *The School for Wives* (1662).

GENRE, STRUCTURE, AND STYLE

Typically, a full-length neoclassical play was written in five acts as we see in Molière's *Tartuffe* and *The Misanthrope*. Molière used the three-act form with interludes in *The Hypochondriac*. This format

was due to the play's secondary purpose of incorporating a musical celebration with song, dance, and pageantry in honor of King Louis XIV, the "Sun King," returning from military engagement. You will notice references to the king and the sun in the prologue. With the exception of the musical final scene, the play can be and sometimes is performed in modern revival without the musical interludes. They are included in this edition, however, because we want you to see the original dramatic context of the play. The interludes also aid the logic of the finale—without the interludes, the concluding pageant would seem to come out of the blue to help restore order at the play's end. Molière created similar forced resolutions when a happy ending (if thinking of the action realistically) would be highly unlikely. Such a manipulation occurs at the end of *Tartuffe* when the king unexpectedly intervenes to save a family from ruin. Contrived endings may suggest to the audience that, in reality, the consequences of such excessive, compulsive decisions would lead to disaster.

Like so many of Molière's comedies, *The Hypochondriac* is structured around an obsessive character who cannot recognize the ridiculousness of his fixations. When others try to talk sense into him he either argues unreasonably or ignores them. The playwright usually creates one or more supporting character who represents a "voice of reason" and tries to make the protagonist see the folly of his choices. This voice in *The Hypochondriac* is Béralde, Argan's brother. Ultimately, Béralde is important in bringing about the happy conclusion. Toinette also interjects common sense, but she is crucial to much of the comic action as well: She makes fun of Argan while at the same time trying to make him see the light. Her antic behavior in tormenting her employer is also a favorite device of Molière's, which we also see in *Tartuffe*.

In Molière's plays, the obsessive protagonist typically does not reform or he simply shifts to a new compulsion at the end of the play. He does not really learn. In this respect Molière flirted with breaking the tenet of neoclassicism that a play should teach a moral lesson. The lack of reform is more like a lesson in reality than a moral lesson. At the conclusion of *The Hypochondriac*, Argan simply refocuses his energies away from seeking cures, and toward becoming a charlatan doctor himself. At least he won't waste so much money on the imposters.

IMPORTANT ELEMENTS OF CONTENT

Eccentricity rules the day in this play and in nearly all the works of Molière. The playwright always makes his most comic characters—such as Toinette—outrageous, but ultimately logical and loyal. His less attractive but necessary characters—such as the parade of stupid, greedy doctors and the avaricious, duplicitous, and scheming wife Béline—are either very eccentric or absurd caricatures. Placed in obvious relief to these grotesques and eccentrics, we see much more normal characters, people very likely to exist, such as Béralde, Cléante, and Angélique. The daughter especially is very normal and well-behaved. Angélique knows how to obey her father, yet she is adamant in her resolve to marry Cléante; that is the sensible and romantically appropriate thing for her to do. The playwright wants us to root for this unfairly oppressed young woman of beauty, youthful vigor, and common sense. Naturally she wins.

Conversely, the stupid and dishonest characters never win in the end, even though they may be successful throughout much of the play. The doctors Lillicrap and Purgeon have their way with Argan until the final act, and Béline is very successful at manipulating Argan until, through the trickery of the clear-thinking people, she condemns herself out of her own mouth. Molière was fond of self-incrimination as a dramatic device and used it in other plays as well. The stupid and deceptive characters are always banished from the play before the action ends, and the stage remains peopled by the protagonist and the good characters who helped to save the day.

THE PLAY IN REVIVAL

Since *The Hypochondriac* was a new play when Molière died suddenly in 1673, the play got much immediate attention and the King sponsored a revival of the play at the Palace of Versailles in honor of Molière the very next year. After the death of Molière, the theatre scene in Paris was thrown into turmoil with different companies jockeying for dominance. The crown settled the problems in 1680 by creating a state-sponsored Comédie Française, which has always had the major plays of Molière, including *The Hypochondriac*, in its repertory. In fact the Comédie Française is unofficially known as the "House of Molière." Outside of France, the play is regularly revived, but typically without the prologue and interludes.

SPECIAL FEATURE

Cross-dressing is not a typical device for Molière, but he uses it in *The Hypochondriac* in a transparent yet effective way. When Toinette disguises herself as a ninety-year-old doctor, no one is fooled. The overcredulous Argan protests at the switch but ultimately seems to accept it. Toinette's ruse heightens Argan's obsession to unbelievable absurdity and gives her character something of a star turn as she takes over the scene.

FURTHER READING ABOUT THE PLAY, PLAYWRIGHT, AND CONTEXT

For examination of Molière's plays and *The Hypochondriac* in particular, see Virginia Scott, *Molière: A Theatrical Life*, and Peter Nurse, *Molière and the Comic Spirit*.

For a study of Molière's original company and methods of production, see Roger Herzel, *The Original Casting of Molière's Plays*.

For information on French theatre in the period, see W. D. Howarth, et al., *French Theatre in the Neo-Classical Era, 1550–1789*, and T. E. Lawrenson, *The French Stage and Playhouse in the Seventeenth Century: A Study in the Advent of the Italian Order*.

The Hypochondriac

By Molière

Translated by Martin Sorrell

CHARACTERS

ARGAN   who imagines himself ill
BÉLINE   Argan's second wife
ANGÉLIQUE   Argan's elder daughter, in love with
    Cléante
LOUISON   Argan's younger daughter
BÉRALDE   Argan's brother
CLÉANTE   in love with Angélique
TOINETTE   Argan's servant
DR LILLICRAP (Diafoirus)   doctor of medicine
THOMAS LILLICRAP (Diafoirus)   his son, and
    would-be fiancé of Angélique
DR PURGEON (Purgon)   Argan's personal doctor
MR FLORID (Fleurant)   apothecary
MR GOODFELLOW (Bonnefoi)   notary
The action takes place in Paris

PROLOGUE

After the victorious campaigns of our Great King,
it is appropriate that anyone whose business is
writing should set about either celebrating or
entertaining him. This has been the aim of the
play printed here; and this prologue is an attempt
to sing the praises of our monarch. It serves as an
introduction to the comedy of *The Hypochondriac*,
which has been written for the purpose of entertaining him and of giving him some distraction
after his wonderful exploits.

A delightful, rural setting.

ECLOGUE

Dance and music.

FLORA, PAN, CLIMÈNE, DAPHNÉ, TIRCIS, DORILAS, ZEPHYRS,
SHEPHERDS, SHEPHERDESSES.

FLORA: Nymphs and shepherds, come away!
    Leave sheep and lambs at play.
    I've news to delight you,
    News to excite you,
    So, nymphs and shepherds, come away!
CLIMÈNE AND DAPHNÉ: Flora calls us, come away!
    Leave sheep and lambs at play.
TIRCIS AND DORILAS: Wait! Heart of stone—
TIRCIS: My love, my own—
DORILAS: I beg, I pray—
CLIMÈNE AND DAPHNÉ: Now come, now come
        away!
TIRCIS AND DORILAS: One little word, we beg you,
        say—
TIRCIS: One word, no more—
DORILAS: I beg, implore—
CLIMÈNE AND DAPHNÉ: Now come, now come away!
    *(Dance and music. The shepherds and shepherd-
    esses gather round* FLORA*)*
CLIMÈNE: Great goddess, Flora, speak—
    Delight each listening ear.
DAPHNÉ: Your news we seek—
DORILAS: We shake, we ache—
ALL: We pant, we quake—
FLORA: Be quiet, then. You'll hear.
    Your prayers are heard,
    Each anxious word.
    Let joy abound:
    He's safe and sound,
    King LOUIS, home. All danger's past,
    And peace has broken out at last.
ALL: He's safe and sound
    Let joy abound.
    All danger's past.
    We've peace at last.
    *(Shepherds and shepherdesses express their joy in
    dance.)*
FLORA: Play music, dance and sing,
    Salute this happy day.

Let woods with joy now ring,
All Nature, leap and play.
ALL: Salute this happy day.
All Nature, leap and play.
FLORA: Sing now, be glad, rejoice,
Be heard each shepherd's voice.
Your rival songs now test.
Step forward, improvise.
Your monarch's glory praise,
This happiest of days.
We'll hear, we'll choose the best:
His song will win the prize.
CLIMÈNE: If Tircis's song is best—
DAPHNÉ: If Dorilas wins the test—
CLIMÈNE: I'll be his for life—
DAPHNÉ: His loving wife.
TIRCIS: Expectation—
DORILAS: Agitation—
BOTH: For such a theme, with such a prize,
Let music play! Sweet voices rise!
(*The orchestra plays to urge on the two shepherds.*
FLORA, *as judge, goes to the foot of a tree centre-stage. She is accompanied by two zephyrs. The others go to the edges of the stage to watch.*)
TIRCIS: The melting winter snow
Makes rushing rivers flow,
Sweeps forests in its dance.
But cities, dams, chateaux,
Must yield their place and go
When LOUIS, Sun of France,
Begins his dread advance.
(*Dancing on* TIRCIS's *side to mark approval.*)
DORILAS: Loud thunder fill the air!
Bright lightning split the sky!
Black darkness gloom and glower!
Draw back! Bow down! Despair!
King LOUIS comes! His hour
Is now! His praise, his power
Bedazzles every eye.
(*Dancing on* DORILAS's *side.*)
TIRCIS: Our lord's great victory
Begins all history.
His lance! His spear! His sword!
The trembling foreign horde!
That fiery, glowing glance!
Our LOUIS, Sun of France!
(*More dancing on* TIRCIS's *side.*)

DORILAS: His triumph sing, his praise!
Salute these golden days,
Our enemies struck dumb,
For centuries to come.
They run away; they hide;
Shout out his name with pride.
(*More dancing on* DORILAS's *side.*)
PAN (*accompanied by six Fauns*): Hush, shepherds,
sing no more.
Lay down the rustic flute.
Join hands, bow down, implore
Apollo with his lute
To sing great LOUIS's fame,
To praise his royal name.

To hymn such great renown
With humble, mortal strain
Is flying too near the Sun:
You'll fall, you'll sink, you'll drown.
Now silence, everyone!
Let others entertain.
ALL: Give up this humble strain.
Let others entertain.
FLORA: Too much to ask,
Too great a task,
To sing such triumphs. Hear
The verdict. Both have won.
No loser, none.
You'll share the prize.
No shame—
Both nobly played the game.
(*The two zephyrs dance holding garlands of flowers. They crown the two shepherds.*)
CLIMÈNE AND DAPHNÉ (*each offering their hand*): You'll
share the prize. No shame.
Both nobly played the game.
TIRCIS AND DORILAS: We share the victor's
crown—
FLORA AND PAN: Sing LOUIS's great renown.
THE FOUR LOVERS: We'll serve him all we
may—
FLORA AND PAN: Until your dying day.
ALL: His mighty deeds require
We sing his peerless reign.
We'll praise and praise you, Sire,
In this our poor refrain.
(*Dance. Fauns, shepherds, shepherdesses, join and mingle, then exit to gel ready for the Play.*)

ALTERNATIVE PROLOGUE
Shepherdess's lament.

SHEPHERDESS: Doctors, you're rogues, own up,
          come on!
    Your so-called learning's a great big con.
    Those strings of words like macaroni
    Are indigestible. You're phoney!

    Your laxatives, your syrups, potions
    Won't find a place in my emotions.
    I'll suffer in silence, out of reach.
    You prate and lecture, rant and preach—
    It's rubbish, a con, it's a try-on.
    You'll never be a shoulder to die on!

    Some dummies believe all your rot,
    They're born every minute.
    But the dimmest, the worst of the lot
    Is on stage now. It's our play, and he's in it.

ACT ONE

1. ARGAN.

ARGAN (*alone in his room, checking his consultants'
bills and accounts, using counters*): Three and
two make five, plus five ten, and ten more
make twenty. Three and two make five. "In
addition, on the twenty-fourth last, one ex-
ploratory, preparatory and emollient enema,
for the purpose of softening, moistening and
refreshing Monsieur Argan's lower bowel".
I like Mr Florid, my apothecary. His bills are
phrased so politely. "M. Argan's lower bowel,
thirty sous". Yes.... All very well being polite, Mr Florid, but you have to be fair too; you
can't go stinging patients like that. Thirty sous
for an enema! Got to be some movement there,
that'll have to drop down. Otherwise, you
know what you can do with it.... You've only
charged twenty sous up till now, and when an
apothecary says twenty sous, it's ten he's got
in mind. There we are then, ten. "In addition,
on the same date, a strong detergent enema
made up of diacatholicon, rhubarb, an edul-
corated rose-water infusion, and other preparations as per prescription, for the purpose of
cleaning, washing and scrubbing M. Argan's

gut, thirty sous". Ten sous again, if you don't
mind. "In addition, on the evening of the
same date, a hepatic, soporific, somniferous
julep to help M. Argan sleep, thirty-five sous".
No complaints about that one, it did the trick.
Ten, fifteen, sixteen, seventeen and a half sous.
"In addition, on the twenty-fifth, a tonic pur-
gative made up of fresh cascara and Levantine
senna, as prescribed by Dr Purgeon, to expel
and evacuate M. Argan's bile, four francs".
Ah! Mr Florid, I'm not taking that lying down!
Patients have rights. Dr Purgeon didn't autho-
rise you to charge four francs. Three francs it
should be. Yes, put three francs down, and I'll
pay . . . half. "In addition, on the same date,
a lenitive and astringent potion to make M.
Argan sleep, thirty sous". All right, that's one
ten-sous piece, one fifteen-sous. "In addition,
on the twenty-sixth, a carminative emetic to
expel M. Argan's wind, thirty sous". Is this a
joke? Ten. "In addition, M. Argan's enema, repeat dose, same evening. Thirty sous". What
does he take me for? Ten! "In addition, on the
twenty-seventh, a double-strength laxative to
invade, break up, and evacuate M. Argan's
foul humours, three francs". So, that's half,
plus one thirty-sous piece. Now you're talking sense. "In addition, on the twenty-eighth,
a single dose of skimmed and sweetened
whey, to cleanse, mollify and lenify M. Argan's blood, twenty sous". Ten—right away.
"In addition, a fortified cordial made up
of half a gramme of bezoar, with essence of
lemon and pomegranate, as per prescription,
five francs". Steady on, doctor, that's a touch
excessive. If you go on like this, nobody'll
want to be ill any more. Why don't you settle
for half, and I'll add two twenty-sous pieces?
Three plus two, five, another five equals ten,
and ten is twenty. Let's see again: two twenty-
sous pieces, six ten-sous, one fifteen-sous. . . .
That's sixty-three francs four and a half sous.
So that means this month I must have taken
one, two, three, four, five, six, seven, eight lots
of medicine, and one, two, three, four, five, six,
seven, eight, nine, ten, eleven, twelve enemas.
Last month it came to twelve lots of medicine
and twenty enemas. Hmm! Not in the least

surprising, that. I haven't been so well this month as last. I'll tell Dr Purgeon, he'll have to get stuck in and do something about it. (*Shouting.*) Somebody come and clear all this away! . . . Nobody there? As usual, I'm wasting good breath. I'm always telling them that I mustn't be left on my own, ever. No use. (*Rings a little bell to summon his servants.*) They don't hear, or don't want to. This damn thing isn't loud enough! Ting-a-ling, ting-a-ling. (*Pause.*) Deafening silence. Ting-a-ling, ting-a-ling. (*Pause.*) There's none so deaf as those who . . . Ting-a-ling, ting-a-ling, where the blazes is everyone? Toinette, ting-a-ling. Just as if I didn't exist. She's a pain in the . . . , she really is! Ting-a-ling. Selfish cow! Ting-a-ling. On top of everything else they want me to burst an artery! (*No longer rings bell, just shouts.*) Ting-a-ling, ting-a-ling, ting-a-ling. She can go to hell, for all I care. Hey, monkey-face, you can't just leave invalids on their own, unattended! Unbelievable. Ting-a-ling, ting-a-ling, ting-a-ling. For crying out loud! Baboon-bum, where are you? Ting-a-ling, ting-a-ling, ting-a-ling. I don't believe this, they *are* going to let me die! Ting-a-ling, ting-a-ling, ting-a-ling!

2. TOINETTE, ARGAN.

TOINETTE (*entering* ARGAN's *room*): Here I am!

ARGAN: Ah! You little . . .

TOINETTE (*pretending to have hit her head*): All right, all right. . . . Now look what you've made me do, you're so bloody impatient. I was in such a hurry to get here, I hit my head on the corner of a shutter.

ARGAN (*angry*): D'you expect me to believe? . . .

TOINETTE (*to shut him up each time*): Ouch!

ARGAN: I've been waiting . . .

TOINETTE: Ouch!

ARGAN: A whole hour . . .

TOINETTE: Ouch!

ARGAN: And nobody . . .

TOINETTE: Ouch!

ARGAN: Shut up, will you. I'm trying to reduce you to a quivering wreck.

TOINETTE: Oh charming, that's really nice. Just what I need after what I've done to myself.

ARGAN: What about me! I've almost lost my voice, shouting.

TOINETTE: And I've almost lost my head, thanks to you. I call that quits. Agreed?

ARGAN: By God, you *are* a little . . .

TOINETTE: If you go on, I'll cry.

ARGAN: But you just left me for . . .

TOINETTE: Bloody hell!

ARGAN: Foulmouth! . . . . Do you want me to? . . .

TOINETTE: Ouch!

ARGAN: Shut up, will you! She won't even give me the pleasure of telling her off!

TOINETTE: Tell me off as much as you like. See if I care.

ARGAN: You won't let me get going. Every time I start, you interrupt.

TOINETTE: Look, if your pleasure's yelling at me, yell. Whatever blows your frock up. But my pleasure's howling, so let me howl.

ARGAN: All right, all right. Truce. Now, get rid of all of this. (*Gets up from his chair.*) Has today's enema taken?

TOINETTE: Taken?

ARGAN: Yes, yes. Did I produce much bile?

TOINETTE: How should I know, for crying out loud? I don't stick my nose into that. That's for your Mr Florid. He's the one that's making the killing.

ARGAN: I've got to take another one in a minute. Go and get some hot water.

TOINETTE: These two . . . medicos, Florid and Purgeon, are having a high old time with you. They're making mincemeat out of you. I'd like to know exactly what sort of illness it is that needs so many medicines.

ARGAN: Don't meddle. This is too hard for you. Fetch my daughter, will you, I want a word with her about a little matter.

TOINETTE: Talk of the devil . . . she must be psychic.

3. ANGÉLIQUE, TOINETTE, ARGAN.

ARGAN: I was just thinking about you, Angélique. Come over here, I want a little word.

ANGÉLIQUE: I'm listening, father.

ARGAN (*hurrying off to toilet*): Just one moment. Pass me my stick. Back in a jiff.

TOINETTE (*mocking*): Hurry, sir, hurry. Goodness, that Mr Florid certainly knows how to get things out of people. The way he worms it out. Talk about time and motion!

4. ANGÉLIQUE, TOINETTE.

ANGÉLIQUE (*lovelorn expression, confiding*): Toinette!

TOINETTE: Yes?

ANGÉLIQUE: Look at me.

TOINETTE: I'm looking.

ANGÉLIQUE: Toinette!

TOINETTE: That's me. Well?

ANGÉLIQUE: Can't you guess?

TOINETTE: Oh, I expect I can. That young man of yours. That's the one subject we keep coming back to. For a whole week now, my dear, you've refused to talk of anything else.

ANGÉLIQUE: I know you think I've got a one-track mind. Why don't you bring the subject up first, instead of me?

TOINETTE: You never give me the chance. You're straight in, wham, every time.

ANGÉLIQUE: It's true, I can't stop thinking about him and talking about him. You do understand, Toinette? I just can't help it. You're not cross with me?

TOINETTE: Of course I'm not.

ANGÉLIQUE: It can't be wrong to feel the way I do about him?

TOINETTE: I never said it was.

ANGÉLIQUE: He's got such a way with words!

TOINETTE: Charms birds off trees.

ANGÉLIQUE: Do you think I should make myself deaf to all the lovely things he says to me?

TOINETTE: Of course I don't.

ANGÉLIQUE: Don't you think it was Destiny that brought us together? Don't you think we were simply meant for each other? It just had to be!

TOINETTE: Oh yes.

ANGÉLIQUE: Don't you think it was just so chivalrous the way he leapt to my defence without even knowing who I was? What a gentleman!

TOINETTE: Who said the age of romance was dead?

ANGÉLIQUE: Don't you think he's gallant?

TOINETTE: Oh yes.

ANGÉLIQUE: Don't you think he's the most handsome man you've ever seen?

TOINETTE: Oh yes.

ANGÉLIQUE: And so winning?

TOINETTE: Oh yes.

ANGÉLIQUE: And such a gentleman.

TOINETTE: Born and bred.

ANGÉLIQUE: Every word he says is so romantic.

TOINETTE: Oh yes.

ANGÉLIQUE: And isn't it the cruellest thing you ever heard, that we're not allowed to meet and get to know each other properly and show each other our feelings?

TOINETTE: Oh it is.

ANGÉLIQUE: But Toinette, listen, do you think he loves me as much as he says he does?

TOINETTE: Ah, yes, well, these things aren't always what they seem. With some people, real love and make-believe look the same. I've certainly seen some dab-hands in my time.

ANGÉLIQUE: Oh, Toinette, don't say that! He says such lovely things to me, he can't be lying, he can't be!

TOINETTE: You'll find out soon enough. He wrote to you yesterday, didn't he, to tell you he's going to ask permission to marry you? Let's see if he sticks to it. The proof of the pudding . . .

ANGÉLIQUE: Oh, Toinette, if he's lying to me, I'll never believe anything any man says ever again.

TOINETTE: Shh! Your father . . .

5. ARGAN, ANGÉLIQUE, TOINETTE.

ARGAN (*sitting down in his chair*): Well now, Angélique, I'm going to tell you something which I dare say you've not been expecting. I've received an offer of marriage for you. There, what do you think of that? It makes you smile? Lovely word, marriage, isn't it? Definitely a favourite with the girls. Ah, human nature! . . . Anyway, from what I can see, I don't really need to ask if you want to get married.

ANGÉLIQUE: My duty is to obey you always, father.

ARGAN: That's my girl. I've agreed on your behalf, everything's been settled.

ANGÉLIQUE: I must do what you say, father.

ARGAN: Your step-mother thinks I should put you both in a convent, you and your little sister. She's quite adamant it's the best idea.

TOINETTE (*aside*): For her, yes.

ARGAN: She wouldn't agree to this marriage at first. But I've won her round at last, and now it's official.

ANGÉLIQUE: Father, I do want you to know how much I appreciate your kindness.

TOINETTE: Credit where credit's due. I have to hand it to you, this is the most sensible thing I've ever seen you do.

ARGAN: I haven't met the young man yet. But I'm told that we'll be very satisfied with him, both of us.

ANGÉLIQUE: Oh father, I know we will.

ARGAN: How do you know? Have you seen him already?

ANGÉLIQUE: As you've agreed to our marriage, I can tell you . . . everything. We met six days ago, quite by chance. We were instantly attracted towards each other, straightaway. That's why he's asked for my hand.

ARGAN: That's not exactly how it was reported to me, but no matter, if that's what happened, so be it, and everyone can be happy. Apparently he's a good-looking boy, tall.

ANGÉLIQUE: Yes, father.

ARGAN: Good bones, organs. Steady pulse.

ANGÉLIQUE: Undoubtedly.

ARGAN: Pleasant sort of cove.

ANGÉLIQUE: Oh yes.

ARGAN: Strong athletic build.

ANGÉLIQUE: Very athletic.

ARGAN: Steady. Good family background.

ANGÉLIQUE: Couldn't be better.

ARGAN: Reliable.

ANGÉLIQUE: Utterly.

ARGAN: Good command of Latin and Greek.

ANGÉLIQUE: That I couldn't say.

ARGAN: And he's sitting his final medical exams at the moment. He'll be a qualified doctor in a month or so.

ANGÉLIQUE: A doctor?

ARGAN: A doctor, yes. Hasn't he told you?

ANGÉLIQUE: No he hasn't. Who told you?

ARGAN: Dr Purgeon.

ANGÉLIQUE: Does Dr Purgeon know him then?

ARGAN: He ought to, he's his nephew.

ANGÉLIQUE: Cléante, the nephew of Dr Purgeon?

ARGAN: Who's Cléante? We're talking about the young man who wants to marry you.

ANGÉLIQUE: That's what I thought.

ARGAN: The one who wants to marry you is Dr Purgeon's nephew, the son of his brother-in-law, Dr Lillicrap. The lad's name is Thomas, not Cléante. Thomas Lillicrap. We fixed up your marriage this morning, the three of us, Dr Purgeon, Mr Florid and myself. Tomorrow, your fiancé's being brought over by his father to see me. What's the matter? You seem a little surprised.

ANGÉLIQUE: I think we've been talking at cross-purposes. We've been talking about different people.

TOINETTE: It's a farce, sir, this scheme. With all the money you've got, you don't need to marry her off to a doctor.

ARGAN: That's exactly what I'm going to do. You keep out of this, it doesn't concern you.

TOINETTE: Shhh, calm down. Can't we discuss the matter like reasonable, grownup people? For example, perhaps you'd be kind enough to explain to us the reasons behind your decision?

ARGAN: Reasons? You know how I'm suffering. Every illness in the book. I need a doctor for a son-in-law. Even better if he's from a medical family. That way I can have a team of specialists permanently on call. I'll have a whole dispensary available day and night as well . . . absolutely essential if I'm to turn the corner.

TOINETTE: Well, there, that's nice and clear. And logical. You see, nobody had to get steamed up. But, come on now, sir, hand on heart, you're not really ill, are you? Not really, eh?

ARGAN: Not ill? Me? Not ill? How can you . . . ? Of course I'm ill! Don't ever say that again!

TOINETTE: Sorry, sorry. Yes you're ill, no question. Don't let's argue. Very ill, I absolutely agree. Seriously ill. Totally ill. Even iller than you think, if that's possible. A basket of maladies. But your daughter should please herself who she marries. She's not ill, and there's no earthly reason why she should marry a doctor.

ARGAN: It's for my sake that I'm giving her to a doctor. A proper daughter, with proper feelings, would be only too delighted to marry someone who'd be good for her poor father's health.

TOINETTE: I don't know, sir, really I don't. Can I give you a piece of friendly advice?

ARGAN: Depends what it is.

TOINETTE: Put this ridiculous marriage right out of your feverish, addled old noddle.

ARGAN: Why?

TOINETTE: Because your daughter won't do it.

ARGAN: She won't?

TOINETTE: She won't.

ARGAN: Angélique?

TOINETTE: Angélique. She'll tell you that she's got no time for Dr Lillicrap. Or his son Thomas. Or for any other Lillicrap you come up with.

ARGAN: Well, I've got time for this plan because it's going to work out better than you may think. Dr Lillicrap's son is his only heir, and on top of that Dr Purgeon has no children of his own, and intends to leave everything he has to the children of this marriage. Do you know how much he's worth? Eight thousand francs, no less.

TOINETTE: He must have polished of a lot of patients to make that kind of money.

ARGAN: Eight thousand. Not to be sneezed at. And there's the father's estate too. We mustn't forget that.

TOINETTE: That's all well and good, sir, but I come back to my point. I really would advise you to find her another husband. She's just not cut out to be Mrs Lillicrap.

ARGAN: I say she is.

TOINETTE: Don't.

ARGAN: Don't what?

TOINETTE: Say.

ARGAN: Why shouldn't I?

TOINETTE: People will say you've gone off your head.

ARGAN: They can say what they like. I'm telling you, I insist. She'll keep the promise I've made.

TOINETTE: She won't.

ARGAN: I'll make her.

TOINETTE: I'm telling you she won't.

ARGAN: I'll put her in a convent.

TOINETTE: You wouldn't.

ARGAN: I would.

TOINETTE: Ha!

ARGAN: What do you mean, ha?

TOINETTE: You'd never put her in a convent.

ARGAN: I'd never put her in a convent?

TOINETTE: You'd never put her in a convent.

ARGAN: Never?

TOINETTE: Never.

ARGAN: Ha ha ha! Very droll. I won't put my own daughter in a convent if I want to?

TOINETTE: That's what I said.

ARGAN: Who'll stop me?

TOINETTE: You will.

ARGAN: I will?

TOINETTE: You haven't the heart.

ARGAN: Oh yes I have.

TOINETTE: Who are you kidding?

ARGAN: I'm serious.

TOINETTE: You're too much of a daddy.

ARGAN: I'm not.

TOINETTE: One or two big rolling tears; arms around your neck; "daddykins" in your ear; you'll be putty in her hands.

ARGAN: I won't be caught like that.

TOINETTE: You will, you will.

ARGAN: I shan't give an inch.

TOINETTE: You're a fool, sir.

ARGAN: Mind what you're saying!

TOINETTE: I know you. You're a softie, you can't help it.

ARGAN (getting worked up): I am not a softie. I can be tough any time I want. Tough. Tough. Oh yes.

TOINETTE: Easy, sir. Remember you're not well.

ARGAN: She'll marry the man I say she'll marry. That's final. She'd better start getting used to it.

TOINETTE: She won't. You'd better start getting used to that.

ARGAN: What's the world coming to? Staff speaking to quality like that!

TOINETTE: When the quality doesn't see the cockup he's making, he's got to be sorted out.

ARGAN (running after TOINETTE): You cheeky little . . . ! Now you've gone too far!

TOINETTE (fleeing): You pay me to stop you doing things you'll only be sorry for.

ARGAN (angrily chasing her around his chair, waving his stick): Come here! Wait! I'll teach you to talk like that!

TOINETTE (*fleeing, and dodging around Argan's chair*): I only want to make you see sense.

ARGAN: Meddler!

TOINETTE: I'll never give my consent to this marriage.

ARGAN: Pig-head!

TOINETTE: I won't have her marrying Thomas Lillicrap.

ARGAN: Feminist!

TOINETTE: She'll do what I say, not you.

ARGAN: Angélique, help me, will you. Stop her.

ANGÉLIQUE: Calm down, daddy, you'll only make yourself ill.

ARGAN: If you don't stop her wicked schemes, Angélique, I'll have nothing further to do with you.

TOINETTE: And if she obeys you, I'll cut her off without a penny.

ARGAN (*slumps into his chair, exhausted by the chase*): Ouf! Ouf! I can't go on. This'll be the death of me.

6. BÉLINE, ANGÉLIQUE, TOINETTE, ARGAN.

ARGAN: Ah, here's my wife! Come here, come here.

BÉLINE: What's the matter, you poor thing?

ARGAN: You've saved my life.

BÉLINE: What's been happening, petal?

ARGAN: Sweetie.

BÉLINE: Babykins.

ARGAN: They've been getting me all upset.

BÉLINE: There, there! Poor darling. Tell mummy all about it.

ARGAN: That nasty horrid Toinette's getting cheekier than ever.

BÉLINE: Don't get upset.

ARGAN: She makes me so angry.

BÉLINE: Shhh! Sweetums.

ARGAN: She's been arguing with everything I say. For a whole hour!

BÉLINE: Try and calm down.

ARGAN: She had the nerve to say I'm not ill.

BÉLINE: What a cheek.

ARGAN: You know how bad I am, don't you, dearest?

BÉLINE: Yes, yes, she was very naughty.

ARGAN: She'll drive me to an early grave.

BÉLINE: Shhh.

ARGAN: She's the cause of all these bilious attacks.

BÉLINE: Don't get upset.

ARGAN: I've been asking you for heaven knows how long to get rid of her.

BÉLINE: But, poppet, the servant without some sort of shortcoming hasn't been invented. Some are bad, and others are not so bad, and you have to put up with it. Toinette's good at her work, she's careful and conscientious, and above all she's not on the fiddle. Servants like that you don't grow on trees. . . . Toinette!

TOINETTE: Madame.

BÉLINE: Why have you been upsetting my husband?

TOINETTE (*sugary*): Me, madame? I'm sure I don't know what you mean. I try to serve Monsieur Argan in every possible way.

ARGAN: Little liar!

TOINETTE: He told us he wanted to marry his daughter to Dr Lillicrap's son. I said it would be a very good catch for her, but that he still ought to put her in a convent.

BÉLINE: I see nothing wrong in that. Toinette's right.

ARGAN: You don't really mean that. She's wicked, and she's behaved atrociously to me.

BÉLINE: All right, darling, I believe you. There, crisis over. It's not a drama. Toinette, you must understand that if you upset my husband again, I shall dismiss you. Give me his dressing gown and some pillows. I'll settle him into his chair. You don't look at all comfortable. Pull your night-cap down. The surest way to catch cold is through the ears.

ARGAN: My angel. How can I ever show you how grateful I am? All your care and attention.

BÉLINE (*arranging* ARGAN's *pillows*): Sit up a moment, so I can put these under you. This one to lean on here, and this one on here. Lie back on this one, and we'll pop the last one under your head.

TOINETTE (*putting a pillow firmly down on his head, then running off*): And this one to keep the mildew away.

ARGAN (*getting up and throwing all the pillows at* TOINETTE): So now you're a murderer?

BÉLINE: What's the matter?

ARGAN (*out of breath; falls into his chair*): I can't stand it!

BÉLINE: Why do you get so worked up? She was only trying to help.

ARGAN: You don't understand how tricky she is, my love. Now I'm in a state again. I'll need at least eight prescriptions and twelve enemas to sort this out.

BÉLINE: There, there, my little lamb, don't fret so.

ARGAN: Oh Béline, you're my only consolation.

BÉLINE: Poor little martyr!

ARGAN: Listen, pussikin, I want to do one big, special thing, a monument of my love for you. I've mentioned it before, I'm going to make my will.

BÉLINE: Oh no, oh dear no, let's have none of that. I don't want to hear that kind of talk, I don't even want to think about it. The mere mention of wills makes me shudder.

ARGAN: I did ask you to have a word with our notary, didn't I?

BÉLINE: He's here. I brought him along with me.

ARGAN: Show him in. What are we waiting for? (*Pause.*) Well?

BÉLINE: I'm sorry, my darling. It's just that when one loves one's husband as much as I do, one doesn't think straight.

7. MR GOODFELLOW, BÉLINE, ARGAN.

ARGAN: Come in, Mr Goodfellow, come in. Have a seat. My wife has told me all about you. I'd like both of your opinions on the will I propose to make.

BÉLINE: Oh no, please! Leave me out of this, I don't understand any of it.

MR GOODFELLOW: Your good wife has explained your intentions to me, what it is you have in mind for her. I have to tell you that you can't leave her anything in your will.

ARGAN: Why not?

MR GOODFELLOW: It's prohibited here in Paris under an ancient law. It would be another matter, of course, in those legislative areas where the new family law operates. But here, your will would be null and void. The only provision a man and wife can make for each other is by mutual gift during the lifetime of both. On top of that, there must be no children, whether by that marriage or any previous one contracted by either party, at the time of the decease of the testatur.

ARGAN: What kind of law is that, not allowing a husband to leave anything to a wife who's been loving and devoted? I'll look for a lawyer, a barrister, anyone, and find a way out of this.

MR GOODFELLOW: I wouldn't recommend it. They're usually extremely strict about this kind of thing, they're concerned with the letter of the law, not the spirit. They see things in black and white, there's nothing grey about it. There are other people you could speak to who are more amenable, who know all about the grey areas. They don't actually break any law, they're just broad-minded about the rules. You see what I'm trying to say. Ah well, where would we be without them? Live and let live. If there was no leeway in this profession one would simply starve.

ARGAN: My wife told me what a clever man you are, very above board. Tell me what I should do, then, to make sure she inherits all my estate. My children mustn't get their hands on it.

MR GOODFELLOW: What do you do? You choose a reliable friend of your wife, say nothing about it, and put all you can in trust to him or her. Then, at an appropriate date, that friend transfers it to your wife. Conversely, you could contract a large number of obligations to various creditors. They'd allow their names to be used on your wife's behalf, at the same time giving her a written guarantee that they're legally making her a gift. Or, thirdly, you could simply give her cash instalments, using different accounts. It's quite simple.

BÉLINE: Don't go on! If anything happened to this little mite, I wouldn't want to go on living. Really, I wouldn't, my love.

ARGAN: My treasure!

BÉLINE: My world would fall apart if I lost you.

ARGAN: What a wonderful wife you are!

BÉLINE: Life wouldn't be worth that to me!

ARGAN: Angel!

BÉLINE: I'd follow you to the grave just to prove how much I loved you!

ARGAN: Dear darling, you'll break my heart. Don't get so upset, please don't.

MR GOODFELLOW: Tears aren't necessary, we haven't reached that stage yet.

BÉLINE: Oh, Mr Goodfellow, you don't know what it is to love a husband as I love mine.

ARGAN: If I die, the only regret I'll have, my love, is that you and I never had a child. Dr Purgeon did promise me that he'd make sure I could do it.

MR GOODFELLOW: I'm sure you can rise to the occasion.

ARGAN: I must make out my will, precious, the way Mr Goodfellow recommends. But as a precaution I'm going to give you twenty thousand francs in gold. They're under the floorboards in my study. I'll give you a couple of bonds as well, which you can cash in whenever you choose.

BÉLINE: I don't want it . . . How much did you say was under the floorboards?

ARGAN: Twenty thousand francs, my dumpling.

BÉLINE: I won't hear any more talk of money . . . How much are the bonds worth?

ARGAN: Four thousand francs one, six thousand the other, sweetheart.

BÉLINE: Money! You can be swimming in the stuff for all I care, but if you haven't got love, you're the poorest person in the world.

ARGAN: That came straight from the heart, my precious.

MR GOODFELLOW: Shall we get on with the will?

ARGAN: We'd be more comfortable in my study. Your arm, my love.

BÉLINE: Come along, cabbage.

8. ANGÉLIQUE, TOINETTE.

TOINETTE: They're in there with the notary. I heard them mention the word 'will'. Your step-mother doesn't miss a trick. I bet that at this precise moment she's separating you and Louison from your inheritance.

ANGÉLIQUE: He can do what he likes with his money, I really don't care. Just so long as he doesn't tell me who to marry. . . . But that's exactly what he *is* doing, Toinette. It's dreadful. Help me, please, tell me what to do. I can't bear it.

TOINETTE: I'll help you, silly thing, you know you can always rely on me. To be perfectly honest, I've never had any time for your step-mother, always trying to get round me. Well, it doesn't wash, I'm on your side. I'll have to change tactics, though, if I'm to help you. I'll pretend I don't care what happens to you. I'll go along with the plot your father and step-mother are hatching.

ANGÉLIQUE: And please find some way to tell Cléante what's happening.

TOINETTE: I could get my . . . friend, the one I call Mr Punchinello, to take a message. I'll have to whisper some sweet nothings in his ear, but, ah well, for you. . . . It's a bit late today, but first thing tomorrow I'll find him and I'm sure he'll be delighted.

BÉLINE: Toinette!

TOINETTE: Her Ladyship calls. Bye. Count on me.

FIRST INTERLUDE

Change to street scene. PUNCHINELLO *enters, to serenade his lady under cover of dark. He is interrupted first by violins, making him angry; then by the night-watch, made up of dancers and musicians.*

PUNCHINELLO: Oh, love, love, love! Punchinello, have you gone raving mad? What's your game? What are you playing at? You never do a day's work these days, your business is going down the plug. You can't eat, can't drink, can't sleep, and for what? For a dragon, a tyrant who walks all over you, whatever you do or say. Oh, no self-pity. I'm caught in the tender trap. Love's a madness, a disease. Not exactly ideal for a man of my age, but there you go! You can't be sensible at the snap of a finger. A pensioner can fall head over heels as much as a teenager. I've come to try to tame my jungle-cat with a serenade. Sometimes a lump-in-the-throat lament outside her door can melt a sweet lover. I'll strum along on this. (*Picks up an instrument*) Night, o gentle night, slide my song of love up under her bedclothes! (*Sings*)

Night and day, you are the one,
Oh please say yes, or I'm undone!

But say no and I'll go.
I'll moan at the moon
And howl at the sun.

I live in hope,
I watch the clock.
It's such a shock:
How can I cope?

I dream that I'm crooning
Your name to the stars.
I'm in my bed swooning,
But I'm still behind bars
In your prison of love!

Night and day, you are the one,
Oh please say yes, or I'm undone!
But say no and I'll go.
I'll moan at the moon
And howl at the sun.

If you can't sleep,
Come and have a peep
At the all-over bruise
You've made of me,
My loving, tender Muse!

Say you've been wrong
To use me so.
One word and I'll go.

Night and day, you are the one,
Oh please say yes, or I'm undone!
But say no and I'll go.
I'll moan at the moon
And howl at the sun.

(*An old woman appears at the window and makes fun of* PUNCHINELLO *as she sings:*)

OLD WOMAN: Ah! You young men, you're all the
    same,
    Faithful for just one day!
    For you it's one big game,
    Then pack bags and creep away.
    Trust men?
    I won't again.
    It's the morals of the pig-sty.
    A girl should have a good think why
    She'd believe a single word you said.
    Better dead than bed
    With a sack of testosterone.
    Want some advice, girls?

Keep yourself to yourself, it's more fun
    on your own.

(*Dance and music. Orchestra punctuates the next speech.*)

PUNCHINELLO: What was that cacophony? Violins, shhh! Let me have a nice and private moan about my gut-wrenching love. Knock it off, will you? Shut it! Did you hear me? Oi! Is this some kind of a joke? You'll bust my ear-drums. Hey! I'll get upset. And I'm not a pretty sight when I get upset. . . . Thank God!. . . . What, again? Bloody violins! Put out the cat! (PUNCHI-NELLO *sings to drown out violins.*) La, la la la, la. (*Pretending to play an instrument.*) Plink, plank, plonk. Well, this is fun. I'll show you, scrapers and pluckers. This'll shut you up. Musicians are bastards. Right, now, before my piece of resistance, I must tune up properly. Plink, plank, plonk. No, wind's in the wrong direction. Plink, plank, plonk. The weather's got at the strings. Plink, plank, plonk. . . . Someone's coming. Just let me put this down . . .

CONSTABLES (*coming down the street, singing*): Who goes there? Who goes there?

PUNCHINELLO: Who the hell is this, now? Am I in some sort of opera?

CONSTABLES: Who goes there? Who goes there? Who goes there?

PUNCHINELLO (*alarmed*): It's me! It's me!

CONSTABLES: Who's me, exactly?

PUNCHINELLO: Just me. I told you: me.

CONSTABLES: And who are *you*?

PUNCHINELLO: Me, me, me, me, me, me!

CONSTABLES: Name, rank, number! Jump to it!

PUNCHINELLO (*swaggering*): My name's . . . Count . . . Yerblessings.

CONSTABLES: Over here, lads! That joker's over here.

(*Dance. The night-watch hunt for* PUNCHINELLO. *Next speech is punctuated by music and dance.*)

PUNCHINELLO: Who goes there? Hark, do I hear fairies? This way, my people. I'm coming to get you now. Save yourselves while you can! I'll cut you to ribbons! Messrs Champagne, Poitevin, Picard, Basque and Breton! Pass me my musket. (*Pretends to fire it.*) Bang! (*They all fall, get up and flee.*) Ha ha ha! That showed 'em. I'm scared of them; they're petrified of me! If you're going

to tell porkies, make 'em big and juicy. What saved my bacon? Putting on the lardy-da.
(CONSTABLES *move in close, hear what he says, and grab him.*)
CONSTABLES: Got him! Give us a hand here, lads.
(*Dance. The whole night-watch approach, carrying lanterns.*)
CONSTABLES: You bastard, tried to frighten us? You dog-breath, snot-rag, turd-sack, bog-pile, piss-pant—frighten us!
PUNCHINELLO: Gentlemen, I was plastered.
CONSTABLES: Plastered, did you hear him, boys? Well now, we're going to do the plastering. You wait. In jug for starters.
PUNCHINELLO: I've done nothing.
CONSTABLES: Clink.
PUNCHINELLO: What *have* I done?
CONSTABLES: Cooler.
PUNCHINELLO: Let go, if you'd be so good.
CONSTABLES: No.
PUNCHINELLO: Please.
CONSTABLES: No.
PUNCHINELLO: Go on.
CONSTABLES: No.
PUNCHINELLO: Just move your arms.
CONSTABLES: No.
PUNCHINELLO: A fraction.
CONSTABLES: No.
PUNCHINELLO: If I ask you nicely?
CONSTABLES: No.
PUNCHINELLO: If I smile sweetly?
CONSTABLES: No.
PUNCHINELLO: You wouldn't hurt an old man?
CONSTABLES: Stuff it! Not another word!
We'll teach you. You heard.
You're doing bird.
PUNCHINELLO: Gentlemen, is there no arrangement you can think of . . . to oil this particular lock?
CONSTABLES: Well, we're not hard men. In fact,
A softer touch would be hard to find.
A handful of banknotes might swing it.
PUNCHINELLO: Search me, gentlemen, no wallet.
CONSTABLES: Oh dear, oh dear!
The choice is clear.
It's pinchin' and pokin',
Or every bone broken.
PUNCHINELLO: Let's see. . . . Erm, yes. Pinchin' and pokin'.

CONSTABLES: Brace yourself.
(*Dance. The* CONSTABLES *push him about, pinch him etc. to the music.*)
PUNCHINELLO: One, two, three, four, five, six, seven, eight, nine, ten, eleven, twelve, and thirteen and fourteen makes fifteen.
CONSTABLES: I think we missed one. Start again.
PUNCHINELLO: Ooh ooh! My head! It's splitting. Do my bones instead. I'll go for broke . . .

Just a joke.

CONSTABLES: Fair enough, whatever you say.
(*Dance. The* CONSTABLES *beat him in rhythm.*)
PUNCHINELLO: All right, all right. Oh look, I've found my wallet!
CONSTABLES: Now there's a decent bloke.
And he does like a joke.
PUNCHINELLO: Gentlemen, goodnight.
CONSTABLES: Ta ta.
PUNCHINELLO: Au reservoir.
CONSTABLES: Toodloo.
PUNCHINELLO: Till we meet again.
CONSTABLES: Don't know where, don't know when.
But why not, some rainy day?

ACT TWO

1. TOINETTE, CLÉANTE.

TOINETTE: What is it you want, sir?
CLEANTE: Who? Want? Me?
TOINETTE: Oh, it's you. What are you doing here?
CLÉANTE: Discovering my fate. And I want to talk to my darling Angélique. Those mad marriage plans I've been hearing about. I must know how she feels.
TOINETTE: All right. But don't go charging in, all guns blazing, not with Angélique. You've got to be subtle, play it, play it. . . . You know they're watching her like hawks, for a start? She's not allowed out, nobody can talk to her and she can talk to nobody. In fact, it's only because her auntie's got a soft spot for her that we were able to go to the theatre that evening, when you two first set eyes on each other. And we've made very sure not to mention that.
CLÉANTE: And that's precisely why I'm not here now as Cléante, the man in love with her, but

as a friend of her music teacher. He's said I can stand in for him.

TOINETTE: Here comes her father. Go over there, by the door, and I'll announce you.

2. ARGAN, TOINETTE, CLÉANTE.

ARGAN: Dr Purgeon told me to stride up and down my room every morning, twelve times. But I forgot to ask if he meant lengths or widths.

TOINETTE: Sir, there's a . . .

ARGAN: Not so loud! Stupid woman, you'll split my head open. Don't you know that the sick must always be addressed in a whisper?

TOINETTE: I wanted to tell you . . .

ARGAN: I told you, in a whisper.

TOINETTE: Sir . . . (*She pretends to speak; no sound.*)

ARGAN: What?

TOINETTE: I said . . . (*Pretending to speak; no sound.*)

ARGAN: What are you saying?

TOINETTE (*aloud*): I said there's someone here who wants to speak to you.

ARGAN: Show him in.

(TOINETTE *gestures* CLÉANTE *to come closer.*)

CLÉANTE: Sir . . .

TOINETTE (*mocking*): Shhh, not so loud. You'll split his head.

CLÉANTE: Sir, I'm delighted to see that you're up and about and obviously so much better.

TOINETTE (*pretending to be angry*): What do you mean, better? What rubbish! Sir? Sir's always ill.

CLÉANTE: Someone said his honour was in better health, and if looks are anything to go by, he certainly looks well.

TOINETTE: What d'you mean, "looks well"? He looks awful, and anyone who says anything else is a troublemaker. His honour's never been as bad as this.

ARGAN: She's right.

TOINETTE: He may eat, drink, walk and sleep like anyone else. But don't be fooled, he's ill.

ARGAN: That's a fact.

CLÉANTE: I'm terribly sorry. I'm here on behalf of your daughter's music teacher. He's had to leave town for a day or two, and I'm here in his place. I'm a very dear friend. He's concerned that there shouldn't be any gaps in your daughter's lessons, in case she forgets what she's already learnt.

ARGAN: Good, good. Fetch Angélique.

TOINETTE: Don't you think, sir, it would be a better idea to take this gentleman to her room instead?

ARGAN: No, no, bring her here.

TOINETTE: He can't give her proper lessons unless they're alone.

ARGAN: Oh yes he can.

TOINETTE: Your head will only start spinning, and you know you mustn't have any excitement in your present state. We mustn't bludgeon your poor old brains.

ARGAN: You heard what I said. I like music, and I'd find it very. . . . Ah! here she comes. Toinette, go and see if my wife's got dressed yet.

3. ARGAN, ANGÉLIQUE, CLÉANTE.

ARGAN: Come here, child. Your music teacher has gone off somewhere out of town. This is his replacement. He'll give you your lesson.

ANGÉLIQUE: Oh my God!

ARGAN: What's the matter?

ANGÉLIQUE: It's . . .

ARGAN: It's what?

ANGÉLIQUE: It's . . . very odd.

ARGAN: Go on.

ANGÉLIQUE: Last night, I dreamt I was in the most awful situation, and that someone who was the spitting image of this gentleman appeared. I asked him to help me, and he sorted everything out. So you can see what an amazing coincidence it is . . . the person who filled my thoughts all night long . . . in this very room.

CLÉANTE: Awake or asleep, I'm delighted to fill Mademoiselle's thoughts. My happiness would be total if she asked me to sort out all her problems. Ask anything you like, I'd—

4. TOINETTE, CLÉANTE, ANGÉLIQUE, ARGAN.

TOINETTE (*mocking*): Sir, I must swallow my words and go back on what I was saying yesterday. I'm now entirely on your side. Messrs Lillicrap father and son have just arrived. You won't be so much losing a daughter as gaining a . . . You're about to see before you the most gorgeous, the wittiest young man you've ever clapped eyes on. He only had to speak half a sentence and I was mesmerised! What a specimen! I almost fainted. Your daughter won't know what hit her.

ARGAN (*to* CLÉANTE, *who is on the point of leaving*): Please don't go. I've decided that my daughter should get married, and the person we're talking about is her fiancé. She hasn't met him yet.

CLÉANTE: You're doing me too great an honour, asking me to be present at such a joyful first encounter.

ARGAN: He's the son of a magnificent doctor. The wedding's in four days.

CLÉANTE: So happy for you.

ARGAN: Do tell her music teacher. He must come.

CLÉANTE: I shall.

ARGAN: And you're invited as well.

CLÉANTE: How kind.

TOINETTE: Come on, everyone in their places. They're here.

5. DR LILLICRAP, THOMAS, ARGAN, ANGÉLIQUE, CLÉANTE, TOINETTE.

ARGAN (*putting his hand on his nightcap without taking it off*): Dr Purgeon has strictly forbidden me to uncover my head, gentlemen. Dr Lillicrap, what would happen if I did?

DR LILLICRAP: Professionally or socially, all our visits are designed to help the sick, not to inconvenience them.

ARGAN: It's a great pleasure for me . . .

DR LILLICRAP: We're here today . . .

ARGAN: To welcome you today . . .

DR LILLICRAP: My son Thomas and I . . .

ARGAN: The honour you're doing us . . .

DR LILLICRAP: To show you, sir . . .

ARGAN: I would have wished . . .

DR LILLICRAP: The great pleasure it gives us both . . .

ARGAN: I'd have paid you a visit . . .

DR LILLICRAP: That you have graciously consented . . .

ARGAN: To assure you of the strength . . .

DR LILLICRAP: To welcome us here . . .

ARGAN: But you know . . .

DR LILLICRAP: To honour . . .

ARGAN: That being so sick . . .

DR LILLICRAP: The union of our . . .

ARGAN: I've no choice but . . .

DR LILLICRAP: Let me assure you . . .

ARGAN: To tell you here . . .

DR LILLICRAP: That in all medical matters which may arise . . .

ARGAN: That I'll miss no opportunity . . .

DR LILLICRAP: And indeed in any other . . .

ARGAN: To let you know . . .

DR LILLICRAP: We'll always be, sir . . .

ARGAN: That I'm entirely at your service . . .

DR LILLICRAP: At your service. (*Turns to his son.*) Thomas, walk this way. Introduce yourself properly. Say your piece.

THOMAS (*a gawky oaf straight out of school; gauche and clumsy*): I start with the father, don't I?

DR LILLICRAP: That's right.

THOMAS: Sir, I am here to salute, to recognise, cherish and revere a second father. That second father is you, to whom I would go as far as saying that I owe an even greater debt than to the first. The first gave me corporeal existence, but you have chosen me. He took me out of ineluctable necessity, you accepted me out of nothing less than pure grace. I am the fruit of his loins; but you have exercised your will when you chose to create me. And, in the very way that the spiritual faculties are superior to those of the body, so I owe you the greater debt, and esteem all the more precious this future filiation, for the creation of which I have come today to offer in advance my profound, my humble gratitude.

TOINETTE: Long live higher education!

THOMAS: All right, father?

DR LILLICRAP: Optime.

ARGAN (*to* ANGÉLIQUE): Don't just stand there. Curtsey.

THOMAS: Do I kiss her now?

DR LILLICRAP: Yes, yes.

THOMAS (*to* ANGÉLIQUE): Madame, it is with its unerring justice that Providence has bestowed upon you the name of mother-in-law, since one . . .

ARGAN: That's not my wife, it's my daughter.

THOMAS: Where's the wife?

ARGAN: She'll be here.

THOMAS: Father, should I wait till she gets here?

DR LILLICRAP: Get on with the speech to the young lady.

THOMAS: Mademoiselle, even as the statue of Memnon issued forth a harmonious note whenever the sun's shafts bathed it in light, so in a like manner do I feel myself brought to life by a gentle rapture in the presence of your golden, radiant charms. And, just as naturalists have observed that the heliotrope, the aptly named sunflower, ceaselessly turns towards the star of day, so my heart from this day forward shall always turn towards the two splendid heavenly bodies which are your eyes, as if towards the magnetic pole insistently drawing to itself that organ, my heart. Permit me, mademoiselle, to lay on the altar of your beauty the gift of this, my heart, which beats with no other ambition than to be, mademoiselle, your very humble, very obedient servant, wedded henceforth and until death us do part, to you.

TOINETTE (*mocking*): What a way with words! Scholar and poet, rolled into one!

ARGAN: Hey, you, what d'you say to that?

CLÉANTE: The gentleman is a linguistic sorcerer, and if he's as fine a doctor as he is an orator, it'll be a remarkable experience to be one of his patients.

TOINETTE: If he writes prescriptions the way he talks . . .

ARGAN: Now then, get me my chair, quick. Everyone sit down. You there, Angélique. Dr Lillicrap, you can see how your boy's impressed us. All I can say is, you're lucky indeed to have a lad like him.

DR LILLICRAP: My dear sir, it's not because I happen to be his father that I can say I'm well pleased with him. Everyone finds him quite . . . transparent. He's never been burdened with what you might call an over-lively imagination. He's not as quick-witted as some folk. But that's precisely what gives me faith in his sound good sense—a quality essential, after all, in our profession. Even when he was still a little boy, he wasn't silly and impertinent. No, no, no. He was docile, gentle. Kept his own counsel. Never went in for what people call "children's games". He was . . . unhurried in learning to read, and in fact he was nine before he mastered his ABC. "Never mind", I said to myself, "late flowering trees bring forth the best fruit. It's harder to write on marble than on sand; but what's written on marble lasts, while insubstantial sand soon vanishes. This drip-feed way of learning, this caution of the imagination surely mark a subtle and certain mind in the making". When I sent him to medical school, he struggled a little. But he soon got the bit between his teeth, and his teachers made a point of praising his industry and application. Anyway, by dint of sheer perseverance he passed his exams, and I can tell you in all objectivity that for the final two years of his studies there has been no candidate more in the thick of the intellectual fray than Thomas. He's become a formidable debater, fearsome in his passion to argue against any proposition at all. His arguments are watertight, he's a lion in his defence of principles, he won't be shaken from his opinions, he pursues his dialectical reasoning with punishing, ruthless logic. But what pleases me most of all—and this is where you can see that he's the true son of his father—is that he has an absolute and blind faith in the old school of medicine. He won't have any truck with those so-called new discoveries, all that rubbish about blood circulating, and other "scientific facts" of the same kidney.

THOMAS (*taking a large rolled-up thesis which he presents to* ANGÉLIQUE): I've had this thesis accepted. It attacks the charlatans of the circulation school. With your permission, sir, I'd like to present it to mademoiselle. In the burgeoning harvest of my intellect, this is the first crop.

ANGÉLIQUE: It's of no use to me, sir. I wouldn't understand a thing.

TOINETTE: Oh, give it to me. Yes, crop's the word. Nice drawings too. Shall we paper the bedroom wall with this crop, with this . . . thesis?

THOMAS: Again with your permission, sir, may I invite mademoiselle one day soon to the hospital to see a woman being dissected? I could explain the various stages of the process.

TOINETTE: Enchanting. Captivating. Some men take the women in their life to theatres of another sort. But to see a body sliced up, well, that's so much more seductive. I mean, what woman wouldn't swoon?

DR LILLICRAP: Let me add that as far as the prerequisites for marriage and the propagation of the species are concerned, you may rest assured that he's exactly as anyone would desire. I've been through our medical checklist. In the reproduction department, he's entirely equipped. The balances, levels and counts to make healthy babies are spot on.

ARGAN: Isn't it your intention, sir, to launch him at court and to establish him as a doctor there?

DR LILLICRAP: To be absolutely frank with you, it's never seemed desirable to me to practise our craft among the great and the famous. I've always felt that we were much better employed serving the general public. They're so much more accommodating. You don't have to answer to anybody for anything you do, and so long as you go by the book, there's no need to worry about any comeback. What's so irritating about upper-class patients is that whenever they fall ill, they insist that their doctors get them well again.

TOINETTE: That really takes the biscuit! Who do they think they are, demanding that you actually cure them? No, your job is to write prescriptions and collect your fees; theirs is to get better if they can. That's the proper division of labour.

DR LILLICRAP: Our one obligation is to follow the code of practice.

ARGAN (*to* CLÉANTE): Now sir, why don't you get my daughter to sing to us?

CLÉANTE: Delighted. I thought it might amuse you all if I were to join the young lady in a duet from the latest cantata. (*To* ANGÉLIQUE, *giving her a sheet of paper.*) This is your part.

ANGÉLIQUE: For me?

CLÉANTE (*aside*): Don't ask questions. Just go along with it, and I'll explain what we're going to sing. Read between the lines. (*Aloud.*) You must bear with me, I'm not the world's greatest singer. The main thing is to listen to mademoiselle.

ARGAN: I hope it tells a nice story.

CLÉANTE: It's a kind of improvised operetta in what you might call rhythmic prose, free verse,

something like that. The kind of spontaneous language you'd expect of two people who have to use every subterfuge to get across how they feel about each other.

ARGAN: Subterfuge? Good. We're listening.

CLÉANTE (*using the name of a shepherd, he tells his love how he fell in love with her at first sight, and then in song they tell each other their feelings*): This is the subject of the interlude. A young shepherd is watching the opening scene of a theatrical entertainment. He is distracted by a disturbance nearby. He turns round and sees some lout insulting a young woman. Instantly he goes to the rescue of what men like to call the weaker sex. He sees off this lout. Then he turns to look at the girl. What he sees is a young thing with the most beautiful eyes imaginable, shedding the most wonderful tears in the world! He is outraged by the abuse aimed at such a creature, moved by her tears, beautiful, beautiful tears. He wants to dry them for her. The young lady thanks him for his timely intervention, but in such a charming, such a warm way, with such feeling, that the young shepherd positively melts. Her every glance, her every word, burns into his soul. "Did I", he asks, "did I really do anything to deserve such sweet thanks? Any man would be only too enchanted, run any risk, go to any lengths, to earn such a display of gratitude". The whole of the performance he has come to see goes by unnoticed. Its only drawback is that it doesn't last long enough. From that first encounter, from that very first moment, he is in the grip of a wild love, as if it had already existed for years and years. He wanders round in a daze. Without her, without this one being, the world is empty, nobody exists. He does all he can to find her but is thwarted at every turn. The young lady is kept well away from prying eyes. But his need is so urgent that he manages to get a note to her. He has written her a marriage proposal. She accepts. But at the same time he hears that her father has arranged for her to marry someone else. Apparently everything is in place for the wedding ceremony. You can imagine how the shepherd feels! The pain, the desolation! Desperate with jealousy, he devises a scheme to get himself invited into her house. He must find out what she herself thinks, what the future holds for him. His worst fears are confirmed. The wedding preparations have been made. He witnesses his rival's entrance, a preposterous young man who owes his good luck entirely to the capriciousness of her father. To see such a travesty of justice, to see the natural order stood on its head, makes him so angry that he almost explodes. He darts looks of anguish at the girl, but out of respect for her and because her father is there, that's absolutely all he can do. In the end, he throws caution to the wind, and bursting with love, sings these words to her:

(*Singing.*)

"Fair Phyllis, this silence is killing me,
  Speak, say something, say what you
    think of me,
  Tell me my destiny!
  What will become of me?"

ANGÉLIQUE (*also singing*):
  "Look how I am, Tircis—disconsolate.
  This nightmare marriage I must
    consummate.
  Yet I only have eyes for you.
  I sigh, I cry, I look to the sky.
  If I have to go through with it, I'll die."

ARGAN: Well, well, well, who'd have thought my daughter could sight-read so easily!

CLÉANTE: "Alas! Fairest Phyllis,
  How could love-sick Tircis
  Know that for him
  There was room
  In your bosom?"

ANGÉLIQUE: "Indeed there's room, more than ever
    before.
  Oh Tircis, Tircis, it's you I adore!"

CLÉANTE: "Oh words so full of delight!
  Dearest Phyllis, did I hear you right?
  Say it again, just to make double sure."

ANGÉLIQUE: "Yes, Tircis, it's you I adore.
  I love you."

CLÉANTE: "Oh God! Again!"

ANGÉLIQUE: "I love you."

CLÉANTE: "Again and again and again. Don't stop."

ANGÉLIQUE: "I love you, I love you, I love you.
  Dear Tircis, have I told you I love you?"

CLÉANTE: "Kings, lords, princes, gods, up there on
    your thrones,
  You've never tasted happiness like my
    own!
  But sweetest Phyllis, there's a vile
    infection
  Which will plunge me into black
    dejection.
  That other man, that rival . . . "

ANGÉLIQUE: "Ah! I loathe him! Everything about
    him's evil.
  A plague-ridden rat that's crawled up a
    drain!
  His very existence causes me pain.
  Let's deal with this rat. . . . Do I make
    myself plain?"

CLÉANTE: "Plain, my belovèd, yet never so fair.
  But when I hear your father declare . . . "

ANGÉLIQUE: "Let him declare!
  I'd rather die
  Than comply,
  Much rather die, much rather, rather,
  Much rather die, die, die, my father,
  Than . . . "

ARGAN: And what does the father have to say in all this?

CLÉANTE: Nothing.

ARGAN: What kind of father is that? What a fool, to put up with this nonsense without saying a word!

CLÉANTE: "Ah! My belovèd, my . . . "

ARGAN: Yes, quite, we heard you the first time. This little play sets a very bad example. The shepherd Tircis is impertinent, and that Phyllis lacks heart, she shows none of the normal care and consideration due to a father. Show me that bit of paper. Aha, now where exactly do I find the words you were singing? All I can see here are musical notes.

CLÉANTE: But surely you know, sir, that a new system of writing words into the music has just been invented.

ARGAN: If you say so, I must believe you. I bid you good day, and I must say we could have done without your impertinent little cantata.

CLÉANTE: I was only trying to please.

ARGAN: Stupidity is never pleasing. Ah, here's my wife.

6. BÉLINE, ARGAN, TOINETTE, ANGÉLIQUE, DR LILLICRAP, THOMAS.

ARGAN: My love, let me introduce Dr Lillicrap's son.

THOMAS (*begins a compliment he has learnt, but his memory fails him, and he cannot finish it.*): Madame, it is with unerring justice that Providence has bestowed upon you the name of mother-in-law, since one beholds on your face . . .

BÉLINE: Young man, I'm happy to have arrived in time to give myself the pleasure of meeting you.

THOMAS: . . . since one beholds on your face . . . since one beholds on your face. . . . Madame, you've broken into my flow. I've lost my place.

DR LILLICRAP: Thomas, save it for another occasion.

ARGAN: I wish you'd been here earlier, dear.

TOINETTE: Oh yes, madame, you missed out on the "second father", and the "statue of Memnon", and the "flower called the heliotrope".

ARGAN: Now then, Angélique, you and the young gentleman should join hands and make a promise.

ANGÉLIQUE: Oh father!

ARGAN: Now why that tone of voice?

ANGÉLIQUE: Don't rush things, please. Give us time to get to know each other and be sure that the right feelings are there. You can't have a perfect union without right feelings.

THOMAS: I've got them already. Why delay?

ANGÉLIQUE: It may have been easy for you, sir, but, well, your own merits don't quite, well, leap out and hit one in the face, at least not mine.

ARGAN: Oh, that. Plenty of time for that after you're married.

ANGÉLIQUE: Please, father, please, I need time. Marriage is a once-in-a-lifetime thing, nobody should be forced into it. If Mr Lillicrap is a real gentleman, he won't want someone who's marrying him against her will.

THOMAS: Non sequitur. I can be a gentleman and at the same time agree to accept your hand from your father.

ANGÉLIQUE: How can you try to get someone to love you by force and pressure? It's immoral!

THOMAS: If you read Classical literature, you'll find that the custom was to take intended brides away from their fathers' houses by force, so as to give the impression that they weren't falling into some man's arms out of choice.

ANGÉLIQUE: Ancient writers are ancient. We belong to our own times. Now. We don't need to play these silly games. When a marriage is an attractive prospect, we know perfectly well how to say yes. Why put pressure on us? There's no need. Be patient for a while. If you love me, you should want what I want.

THOMAS: I quite agree. But only where there's no conflict with the requirements of my own position. My love, I mean.

ANGÉLIQUE: But surely the best proof of love is to put the woman you love first. Me.

THOMAS: Two remarks, if you permit. Primo: I concede your point in respect of all matters outside a husband's ownership of his wife. But, secundo: a husband has an absolute right to possession of the said wife.

TOINETTE: Don't waste your breath, honestly. The gentleman has had the benefit of higher education. He'll run rings round you, always. Anyway, why not accept gracefully? You could bask in the reflected glory of being a doctor's appendage.

BÉLINE: Perhaps Angélique has someone else in mind?

ANGÉLIQUE: If I had, madame, it would be an honest and sincere choice.

ARGAN: Excuse me. Would you like a referee?

BÉLINE: In your shoes, my sweet, I wouldn't force her into this marriage. I know what I'd do instead.

ANGÉLIQUE: I know exactly what you have in mind, madame, just as I know how you feel towards me. But your advice may get turned down.

BÉLINE: Clever, educated girls like you don't care these days if they obey their fathers or not. It was different in my day.

ANGÉLIQUE: A daughter's duty goes only so far, madame. There are some demands which can simply not be met.

BÉLINE: What you mean is that you're willing to get married but you insist on choosing your husband yourself.

ANGÉLIQUE: If my father won't give me a husband I like, then at least let me plead with him not to force on me one I can't stand.

ARGAN: Gentlemen, do please excuse all this.

ANGÉLIQUE: Everyone has their individual reasons for marrying. For me, I want to marry a man I can love truly and properly for the rest of my life. Yes, I confess, I want to choose him myself, with great care. Other women may look to marriage as an escape from their parents. All they want is freedom to do exactly as they please. There are some women, madame, who consider marriage solely in terms of financial gain. They marry one old wreck after another just to gather in their inheritances. As matter-of-fact as that. No irrelevances like feelings. Money, just money makes their world go around.

BÉLINE: You're rather argumentative today, young lady. I'm not too sure what you're trying to imply.

ANGÉLIQUE: Imply? Nothing. I'm saying what I think.

BÉLINE: Well, you're making no sense at all, and I don't think we need detain you any longer.

ANGÉLIQUE: If you're trying to provoke me, it won't work. I shan't give you the pleasure. I shall count to ten.

BÉLINE: I don't have to put up with this impertinence.

ANGÉLIQUE: Excuse me, madame, I've only got to three.

BÉLINE: You're full of stupid pride, impertinence, arrogance. The whole world will turn its back on you.

ANGÉLIQUE: This will get us nowhere. I'm going to go on behaving calmly and rationally, whatever you may say or do. You want to put me in a straitjacket? You'll have to catch me first.

ARGAN: You listen here, my girl, I'm not going to argue with you. The choice is clear. Either you marry this young man, or I put you in a convent. Understand? You've got precisely four days to decide. (*To* BÉLINE.) Don't worry yourself, she'll see sense.

BÉLINE: I hate to leave you, my sugar, but I have urgent business in town. It won't wait. Back soon.

ARGAN: Off you go now, and don't forget your visit to the notary. You know why.

BÉLINE: Bye bye, chicken.

ARGAN: Bye bye, treasure. . . . Now there's a woman who knows the meaning of love. I can hardly believe my luck.

DR LILLICRAP: Monsieur Argan, if you'll excuse us, we'll take our leave as well.

ARGAN: Umm, before you go, you couldn't just give me a check-up? A teeny weeny examination?

DR LILLICRAP (*taking his pulse*): Come along, Thomas, take Monsieur Argan's other wrist. See if you can do an accurate diagnosis. . . . And your verdict?

THOMAS: I'd say the sick gentleman's sick pulse is the pulse of a sick man.

DR LILLICRAP: Ah, quod erat demonstrandum.

THOMAS: I'd say the pulse is pulsating a touch impulsively. We've caught it in flagrante.

DR LILLICRAP: Very good.

THOMAS: Enough élan vital to repulse my finger.

DR LILLICRAP: Bene.

THOMAS: The beat is even a mite compulsive.

DR LILLICRAP: Melius.

THOMAS: Which indicates, ipso facto, sound cardiac propulsion. There is, however, an imbalance in the splenetic parenchyma, videlicet, the spleen.

DR LILLICRAP: Optime.

ARGAN: But Dr Purgeon says it's my liver.

DR LILLICRAP: Well, naturally, he would. But remember, the parenchyma and the liver are fundamentally the same thing. That's because they are cognatively connected by means of the vas breve, the pylorus, and even in certain circumstances, the meatus cholidichi. . . . Dr Purgeon has doubtless told you to eat plenty of roast beef?

ARGAN: No, boiled. Boiled beef.

DR LILLICRAP: Obviously. Boiled, roast, it's the same thing. He's an excellent doctor, you couldn't ask for better. He knows what he's doing.

ARGAN: Doctor, how many grains of salt should I put on my egg?

DR LILLICRAP: Six, eight, ten, but always even numbers. It's the same with drops and pills, except that they must always be odd numbers.

ARGAN: Gentlemen, I bid you good day.

7. BÉLINE, ARGAN.

BÉLINE: I thought I'd better have a quick word with you, my little object of desire, before going out. Only I think you should be warned. I was passing Angélique's room and I caught a glimpse of a young man who disappeared when he saw I'd spotted him.

ARGAN: A man with my daughter!

BÉLINE: Exactly. Her little sister Louison was with them. She might be able to tell you more.

ARGAN: Fetch her, my love, fetch her this instant. Ah! What a schemer! No wonder she won't obey me. I see it all now.

8. LOUISON, ARGAN.

LOUISON: Hello papa. Step-mamma said you want to see me. Why, papa?

ARGAN: Come over here. Come on. Here. That's it. Turn round. Look at me. So?

LOUISON: What, papa?

ARGAN: Eh?

LOUISON: What do you mean?

ARGAN: Haven't you got something to tell me?

LOUISON: If you want, I can recite the story of the Ass's Skin, or the Fable of The Crow and The Fox. I've just learnt them.

ARGAN: No, that's not what I want to hear.

LOUISON: What then?

ARGAN: Little fox! You know exactly what I mean.

LOUISON: I don't, papa.

ARGAN: Is this how you obey and respect your father?

LOUISON: What do you mean?

ARGAN: Haven't I said you must always come and tell me everything you see?

LOUISON: Yes, papa.

ARGAN: And have you?

LOUISON: Yes, papa. I've come and told you everything I've seen.

ARGAN: And have you seen anything today?

LOUISON: No, papa.

ARGAN: No?

LOUISON: No, papa.

ARGAN: You're sure?

LOUISON: I'm sure.

ARGAN: Right, now it's my turn to show you something!

(*He grabs a cane.*)

LOUISON: Oh papa, please don't!

ARGAN: So, you little adder. I haven't heard you tell me there was a man in your sister's room.

LOUISON: Papa!

ARGAN: This'll teach you to lie to me!

LOUISON (*falling to her knees*): Oh, please, please, I'm sorry. It's Angélique's fault. She told me not to tell you, but I will, I will.

ARGAN: First, you must be caned. We'll talk after.

LOUISON: Papa, I'm sorry, truly I am.

ARGAN: Bend over.

LOUISON: Don't hurt me.

ARGAN: I will, I must.

LOUISON: Please, don't.

ARGAN (*taking hold of her*): Come on!

LOUISON: Oh papa, that hurt. I think you've killed me. (*She pretends to die.*)

ARGAN: Hey! Louison! Wake up! My little girl, my Louison! Oh God, what have I done? Damn cane! Stupid cane! Louison, darling! Louison, Louison!

LOUISON: Shhh, there there, papa, I'm not a hundred per cent dead.

ARGAN: What? You crafty thing! All right, I'll let you off so long as you tell me everything you know. Is that fair?

LOUISON: Oh yes.

ARGAN: But remember: this little finger knows everything and it'll tell me the moment you start lying again.

LOUISON: Please, papa, please don't tell Angélique I told.

ARGAN: I won't. Promise.

LOUISON: What happened is that a man came into her room when I was there.

ARGAN: And?

LOUISON: I said, "Can I help you?", and he said he was Angélique's music teacher.

ARGAN: Did he, indeed? Then what?

LOUISON: Angélique said, "Please leave, please, please! Oh, you'll be the death of me!"

ARGAN: And?

LOUISON: He wouldn't leave.

ARGAN: What did he say to her?

LOUISON: Lots and lots of things.

ARGAN: What else happened?

LOUISON: He went on saying things, like how he had these feelings about her, and how she was the most beautiful girl he'd ever seen in his whole life.

ARGAN: Then what?

LOUISON: He knelt down in front of her.

ARGAN: Then what?

LOUISON: He started kissing her hands.

ARGAN: Then what?

LOUISON: Step-mamma came to the door, so he went out quickly.

ARGAN: Anything else?

LOUISON: No, papa.

ARGAN: Now then, this little finger's twitching. I think it wants to tell me something. (*Puts his finger to his ear.*) Yes? Ah? Oh! Really? Really! My little finger says you've left something out.

LOUISON: Papa, your little finger's telling fibs.

ARGAN: Careful!

LOUISON: No, papa, honestly. It's fibbing, don't believe a word it says.

ARGAN: We'll see. Off you go now, but be careful. Run along. . . . Ah, children aren't children any more. What a business! I haven't been able to concentrate on my illness in all this. I'm drained. (*Falls into his chair.*)

9. BÉRALDE, ARGAN.

BEÉRALDE: Greetings, Argan. And how's my one and only brother today?

ARGAN: Bad.

BÉRALDE: How d'you mean, bad?

ARGAN: I'm so weak . . .

BÉRALDE: That's terrible.

ARGAN: Scarcely strength to speak.

BÉRALDE: Argan, I think I've found a solution to this Angélique business.

ARGAN (*suddenly energetic and angry, getting up from his chair*): Don't mention that name to me! You know what she is, don't you? There's a word for it, but I shan't soil my mouth. She's going into a convent in the next forty-eight hours.

BÉRALDE: That's the spirit! I'm delighted to see you've recovered a bit. Glad my visit's cheered you up. We'll speak about serious things in a moment. But first, I thought you might like to meet some theatre folk I ran into today. They're a bit . . . unexpected, but very entertaining. They'll take your mind off things. Just hear them. Songs, dances. I'm sure ten minutes with them is worth a cupboard-ful of Dr Purgeon's pills and potions. What do you say?

SECOND INTERLUDE

ARGAN'*s brother brings on several Egyptians in Moorish costume, to entertain him with a mixture of songs and dance.*

1ST MOORISH WOMAN:

Gather rosebuds while you may.
Youth must decay.
The time for love is now.

Without passion's bright flame,
Life's an empty game.
The time for love is now.
Gather rosebuds while you may.
Youth must decay.
The time for love is now.

The sun's shining, make hay!
Good looks go,
Liver-spots grow,
Beauty won't stay,
We all decay.

Make hay, you'll soon forget how!
Gather rosebuds while you may.
Youth must decay.
The time for love is now.

2ND MOORISH WOMAN:

What is this thing called love?
It's so urgent when we're young.
It's ready, steady, go!
Who ever says no?
Yet we're told all the time
It's a sin, a crime.
We're young, let's have the pleasure.
After, we'll have time to count the cost,
Repent at leisure.

3RD MOORISH WOMAN:

I feel charming,
He's disarming,
He can be my lover . . .
Now, he's had his wicked way
There's a price to pay.
It's the same the whole world over.

4TH MOORISH WOMAN:

> They steal inside our clothes,
> And then steal out again.
> But the stealing I loathe,
> The theft that causes most pain,
> It's when they steal our heart,
> Every time they steal our heart.

2ND MOORISH WOMAN:

> How can we recognise
> A lurking Don Juan?

4TH MOORISH WOMAN:

> We've known lots already.
> We've had masses to chew on.

ALL: No, we can't fight it.

> Oh, the delight it
> Is to touch, stroke, caress,
> Be touched, stroked, caressed.
>
> Mothers, cleaners, scrubbers, cooks,
> That's how our husbands define us.
> Girls, while we've still got our looks,
> There're others to wine us and dine us!
>
> Overgrown children, all aches and great
>   pains,
> Their bruised shins and egos, their ter-
>   rible sprains,
> Their poor battered pride and their tickly
>   throats . . .
> Well, let's have no more, girls, we all
>   want our oats!

(*Dance, accompanied by performing monkeys.*)

ACT THREE

1. BÉRALDE, ARGAN, TOINETTE.

BÉRALDE: So, Argan, what did you think of that? Better than pumping things up your bottom, eh?

TOINETTE: The Lillicrap solution, ha ha.

BÉRALDE: Now then, I think we should have a talk.

ARGAN: You'll have to wait a bit. I'll be back.

TOINETTE: Hey, not so fast. Remember you can't walk without a stick.

ARGAN: Oh yes.

2. BÉRALDE, TOINETTE.

TOINETTE: You won't forget to speak up for your niece, will you?

BÉRALDE: Indeed I won't. I'll do all I can for her.

TOINETTE: This lunatic marriage must be stopped at all costs. What I thought was this: let's get a doctor on our side. He could turn your brother away from that Dr Purgeon and bring him to his senses. The problem is, I couldn't think of anyone, so I'm working on a scheme of my own.

BÉRALDE: Yes?

TOINETTE: It's a bit . . . elaborate . . . but it should be fun. And it certainly ought to work. Let me work on it. Ah, careful, he's coming back.

3. ARGAN, BÉRALDE.

BÉRALDE: Now, before we start our conversation, I want you to promise me you won't lose your temper.

ARGAN: I promise.

BÉRALDE: You'll stay cool and calm, whatever I say.

ARGAN: Promise.

BÉRALDE: We'll have a sober, rational discussion. There are important things to sort out.

ARGAN: I promise. Look, never mind the overture, Béralde. Say what you have to say.

BÉRALDE: All right. Why is it that a wealthy man like you, with only one daughter—the little one doesn't really count—can think of putting her into a convent?

ARGAN: Why is it that the head of a household has to justify himself?

BÉRALDE: Your wife doesn't miss an opportunity to tell you what a good thing it would be if you were rid of both your girls. She'd love to see them safely inside a convent.

ARGAN: Ahah, that's what it's all about! You want to drag my poor wife into it. She's the villain of the piece, don't tell me. Universal scapegoat.

BÉRALDE: Let's leave her out of it. I'm sure she has the very best of intentions for all of you. She never considers herself, she worships the ground you stand on, and her warmth and kindness to your children are legendary. Not another word about her. Let's get back to Angélique. You want her to marry a doctor's son. Where's the logic in that?

ARGAN: The logic is that I need a son-in-law who'll be useful to me.

BÉRALDE: With respect, that's scarcely relevant to your daughter. But there is another candidate, as it happens, and a much better one from her point of view.

ARGAN: Not from mine.

BÉRALDE: Who's getting married, you or her?

ARGAN: Both. In my family, I'll only tolerate people I need.

BÉRALDE: By that token, if Louison were old enough, you'd make her marry an apothecary?

ARGAN: Why not?

BÉRALDE: How long will this obsession with doctors and apothecaries go on, for heaven's sake? You want to be ill, you take no notice of your friends or of Nature itself.

ARGAN: What exactly are you implying?

BÉRALDE: I'm implying, my dear brother, that I've never seen anyone as fit as you. I'd love to have your constitution. You're in great shape. If you want proof of what I'm saying, look at the way you've stood up to all that barrage of cures, remedies and treatments.

ARGAN: But that's the point! If I didn't see Dr Purgeon every three days, I'd succumb. That's what he says.

BÉRALDE: At this rate, he'll still be looking after you in the life everlasting.

ARGAN: This is ridiculous. You don't believe in medicine, do you?

BÉRALDE: No, frankly, I don't. I don't believe that it promotes good health.

ARGAN: You refuse to believe in well-established scientific facts?

BÉRALDE: Absolutely not. I'd go even further. Between you, me and the bedpost, I'd say that medicine is one of the daftest bits of nonsense ever dreamt up by humankind. Scientific facts? Mumbo-jumbo! It's ridiculous to think one person can cure another.

ARGAN: I see. And why is that?

BÉRALDE: Human beings are too complex and enigmatic. We may want to delude ourselves, but we understand precious little. Nature didn't intend us to.

ARGAN: So, according to you, doctors know nothing?

BÉRALDE: Oh yes they do. They've got degrees, they know all the jargon, all the patter. Huge medical dictionaries. But what they haven't got is any way of making people better.

ARGAN: They still get nearer than the rest of us.

BÉRALDE: What they're expert at is frightening us. Latin and Greek words as long as a waiting-list. Always promises, never results.

ARGAN: Rubbish. There are some people in medicine today, every bit as clever as you. In any case, if all doctors were useless, nobody would see them, would they?

BÉRALDE: I'm afraid that says more about human gullibility than anything else.

ARGAN: But doctors must believe what they're doing is right, since they do it to themselves.

BÉRALDE: Some of them are stupid enough to believe in it, like their patients. And they do nicely out of it, thank you very much. Others make a packet without believing a single word. Your Dr Purgeon is in the former camp. A no-bones sort of doctor, uncomplicated as you like, who's swallowed the lot, hook, line and sinker. He'd go to the stake rather than take an objective look at medical 'truth'. For him, medicine's about certainties, certainties and . . . certainties. He's coarse, he's blunt, he's blind, and he doesn't care. He goes around sticking needles in here, enemas there, as if there were no tomorrow. You can't really hold it against him, it's not malice on his part. But he'll finish you off in the absolute conviction he's doing wonders for you. No cloud of self-doubt will ever darken the sky of his complacency. It's not only his patients; he'd just as cheerfully despatch his wife, his children, himself even.

ARGAN: You don't like him, do you? Tell me, what should people do when they're ill?

BÉRALDE: Nothing.

ARGAN: Nothing?

BÉRALDE: Nothing. Rest, let Nature take its course. Nature sorts things out. It's our impatience, our anxiety, which wreck everything. Most people die of cures, not illnesses.

ARGAN: Oh, surely you'd concede that Nature can be helped along?

BÉRALDE: No, people like to hang on to comforting ideas and fantasies because it's soothing. But because something's soothing doesn't mean it's true. Doctors'll tell you how they help Nature, encourage it, speed it up, restore the balance, get everything working again. They'll go on and on about thin blood, thick blood, lower bowel, upper bowel, here a gland, there a gland, everywhere a quack quack. And what are they really doing? I'll tell you. They're quoting from the Collected Novels, Short Stories and Fairy Tales of that fertile old hack called Medicine. Visit your local bookshop, look under "F" for Fiction. . . . dreams, doctors are pedlars of dreams. And when you wake up from a dream, too often you wish you hadn't had it in the first place.

ARGAN: I bow to your superior knowledge and wisdom. Of course you know more than all the doctors put together.

BÉRALDE: Hear doctors pronounce, their intelligence is off the end of the scale. But watch them at work, they haven't got a single clue.

ARGAN: Oh, you're too clever for me. I wish one of these poor useless doctors were here to defend himself. He'd put you in your place, like that.

BÉRALDE: I'm not interested. Let people go on thinking what they want. This conversation was for our ears only. But I'd love to open your eyes, even so. Look, there's a comedy by Molière on at the moment. That would explain better than I can.

ARGAN: Molière! One of those arty-farty people. He's got no business making fun of medicine. It's far too serious.

BÉRALDE: He's not mocking medicine. It's the abuse of it he finds laughable.

ARGAN: He still shouldn't stick his oar in. He's no right to ridicule his betters. Medicine's not the right subject for a night out at the theatre.

BÉRALDE: But what else can he put on stage except what humans do? You see plenty of plays about kings and queens. So why not doctors?

ARGAN: Dammit, if I were a doctor, I'd soon sort out that Molière. I'd let him die slowly if he were ill. He could plead for medicines, treatment, but let him whistle. "Die, go on, die," I'd say, "another time you'll know better than to make fun of these . . . these saints".

BÉRALDE: You have got it for him!

ARGAN: He's a fool, and he's dangerous. Doctors would do well to take my advice.

BÉRALDE: I'm sure he'd outsmart your doctors. He'd never seek their help.

ARGAN: He'd be the one to suffer.

BÉRALDE: He says you need to be as strong as an ox to fight off both an illness and its cure. For his part, he's only got enough resistance for the illness.

ARGAN: Bizarre logic! Look, we must stop this. My pulse is going wild again.

BÉRALDE: Right, agreed. Let's talk of something else. I really don't think you can shut your daughter up in a convent simply because she's fighting one of your batty schemes. It's really going too far. Surely a woman has the right to choose her husband? After all, it's for life, and it's Angélique who's doing the marrying, not you.

4. MR FLORID *carrying a syringe,* ARGAN, BÉRALDE.

ARGAN: Ah, Béralde, excuse me one moment.

BÉRALDE: What's the matter?

ARGAN: I've got to take something for my bowels. Mr Florid specialises in bowel disorders.

BÉRALDE: Are you completely crazy? Can't one single moment pass without an enema or a sedative or some damn pill? Please, just this once, say no. What about tomorrow?

ARGAN: Mr Florid, what about this evening or tomorrow morning?

MR FLORID (*to* BÉRALDE): I must ask Monsieur not to interfere. I know what I'm doing. Monsieur does not. Keep out of this.

BÉRALDE (*pointing to his own face*): With the greatest respect, Monsieur, this is a face you're addressing, not a backside. A little common courtesy, if you please.

MR FLORID: You're wasting my time. You can't play around with medical people like this. The attitude in this house is frivolous, and I shall report back to Dr Purgeon that I was prevented from following his instructions. You'll hear more of this . . . (*Exits*).

ARGAN: I don't think he's pleased.

BÉRALDE: What a tragedy, refusing Purgeon's laxative. No, Argan, you've got to get over this love affair you're having with medicine. It's beyond a joke.

ARGAN: It's easy for you, you're not sick. I wish you were in my shoes, you'd soon change your tune.

BÉRALDE: What exactly is it that's wrong with you?

ARGAN: What's wrong? What's wrong! Béralde, sometimes I wonder about you. . . . Ah, here's Dr Purgeon.

5. DR PURGEON, ARGAN, BÉRALDE, TOINETTE.

DR PURGEON: What's this I've just been hearing? You won't take my prescriptions, you're laughing at my diagnoses?

ARGAN: Doctor, it's not . . .

DR PURGEON: And what gives a patient the right to question his doctor?

TOINETTE: It's an outrage.

DR PURGEON: I took great pains making up that enema.

ARGAN: Not my fault.

DR PURGEON: I used the best formula. Tried and tested.

TOINETTE: Beneath contempt.

DR PURGEON: You'd have had blissful bowels.

ARGAN: Béralde . . .

DR PURGEON: Sending my man packing like that!

ARGAN: It was Béralde.

DR PURGEON: Quite unforgivable.

TOINETTE: Straight from the horse's mouth.

DR PURGEON: You're out to . . . to murder medicine.

ARGAN: My brother . . .

DR PURGEON: It's . . . civil disobedience.

TOINETTE: Not lèse majesty, lèse quackery.

DR PURGEON: I'll have to strike you off my list.

ARGAN: It was my brother.

DR PURGEON: I want nothing more to do with you.

TOINETTE: Very wise.

DR PURGEON: I'm winding everything up, including the deed of covenant I took out for my nephew as his wedding gift. (*Tears up a deed.*)

ARGAN: It's all my brother's fault.

DR PURGEON: Spurn my suppositories!

ARGAN: Please bring them back, I'll take the lot!

DR PURGEON: I'd have seen to you once and for all.

TOINETTE: He doesn't deserve it.

DR PURGEON: I'd have irrigated everything, left your insides squeaky clean.

ARGAN: Ah, Béralde!

DR PURGEON: It would only have needed a dozen or so bottles for a perfect evacuation.

TOINETTE: He's not worthy of such attention.

DR PURGEON: Still, as you obviously don't wish me to be the one . . .

ARGAN: It's not my fault.

DR PURGEON: As all the time you were the dark angel rebelling against his Father . . .

TOINETTE: This must be punished.

DR PURGEON: As you've committed the sin of disobedience . . .

ARGAN: No, I haven't, no!

DR PURGEON: All I say to you is that I cast you adrift, I abandon you to your boiling arteries, your stinking entrails, your filthy blood, your sour bile, your puffy skin, your starchy flesh, your corrupt, evil body!

TOINETTE: Well done.

ARGAN: Oh, my God!

DR PURGEON: And I hope that in less than a week your illness becomes terminal.

ARGAN: God, help me!

DR PURGEON: That you fall into bradepepsia.

ARGAN: Doctor!

DR PURGEON: From bradepepsia into dyspepsia.

ARGAN: Doctor!

DR PURGEON: From dyspepsia into apepsia.

ARGAN: Doctor Purgeon!

DR PURGEON: From apepsia into diarrhoea.

ARGAN: Doctor!

DR PURGEON: From diarrhoea into dysentery.

ARGAN: Doctor!

DR PURGEON: From dysentry into dropsy.

ARGAN: Doctor Purgeon!

DR PURGEON: And from dropsy into the complete and utter extinction of your life! Hanging's too good for you!

6. ARGAN, BÉRALDE.

ARGAN: Oh, Béralde, I've had it, I'm done for. And it's all your fault.

BÉRALDE: Let's not exaggerate.

ARGAN: It's the end. Medicine is avenged.

BÉRALDE: Frankly, you're off your head. I wish with every bone in my body that you'd snap out of this. Get a grip. Think straight. Stop letting your imagination get the better of you.

ARGAN: Did you hear him, though? Those terrible illnesses I'm certain to get?

BÉRALDE: Are you that naïve?

ARGAN: I've got less than a week to live, he said.

BÉRALDE: He isn't God. He can't shorten or lengthen your life at a stroke. Your life's in your own hands, no-one else's. Dr Purgeon's anger won't kill you, any more than his medicines will keep you alive. I'd have thought this experience would turn you against doctors forever. If you refuse to change your ways, at least find someone who's less of a tyrant.

ARGAN: But Dr Purgeon knows me inside out. He knows exactly what to do.

BÉRALDE: Sometimes I don't have the faintest idea how you see the world. Are you wearing the right glasses?

7. TOINETTE, ARGAN, BÉRALDE.

TOINETTE: Sir, there's a doctor here, says he wants to see you.

ARGAN: Which doctor?

TOINETTE: Not a witch doctor, a proper one.

ARGAN: What's his name?

TOINETTE: Don't know. Funnily enough, he's the spitting image of yours truly. I know my mother's been the model widow since her old man passed away, but, well, it makes you wonder.

ARGAN: Show him in.

BÉRALDE: Your dream's come true. Out goes one doctor, in comes another.

ARGAN: You've really put the cat among the pigeons, haven't you!

BÉRALDE: Don't start again.

ARGAN: I can't stop thinking about those hundreds of undiagnosed complaints I've got.

8. TOINETTE *disguised as doctor*, ARGAN, BÉRALDE.

TOINETTE: Good day to you. Thank you for agreeing to see me. Allow me to offer you my varied and expert services. I can do you an excellent blood-letting, nice and smooth, or I've a wide range of purgatives, including the very latest on the market.

ARGAN: How kind. . . . But this is Toinette's double.

TOINETTE: One moment, sir, if you don't mind. I must pop out to tell my personal assistant something. Back in two shakes of a wooden leg.

ARGAN: It is Toinette.

BÉRALDE: A striking resemblance, I grant you. But these things happen.

ARGAN: It's amazing.

9. TOINETTE, ARGAN, BÉRALDE.

TOINETTE (*she has taken off her doctor's gown so quickly that it is difficult to believe she was a doctor a moment ago*): Yes, sir?

ARGAN: Pardon?

TOINETTE: Didn't you call?

ARGAN: No.

TOINETTE: Sorry, must be hearing things.

ARGAN: Now you're here, you can see just how much you look like this new doctor.

TOINETTE (*leaving*): Yes, yes. I'm busy. I've seen all I want to see of him.

ARGAN: If I hadn't seen them separately, I'd say they were one and the same person.

BÉRALDE: There's quite a substantial literature on this phenomenon. Even the experts have been fooled.

ARGAN: Well, I'd have been fooled by this pair. I'd have sworn they were the same person.

10. TOINETTE *disguised as doctor*, ARGAN, BÉRALDE.

TOINETTE: My apologies.

ARGAN: Unbelievable.

TOINETTE: I hope you'll forgive my curiosity, but I wanted to see for myself this incredibly famous invalid. Your reputation stretches far and wide.

ARGAN: This is a great pleasure for me, sir.

TOINETTE: Why are you staring at me like that? Wondering about my age? How old do you think?

ARGAN: Oh, twenty-six, twenty-seven.

TOINETTE: Ahah! Ninety.

ARGAN: Ninety?

TOINETTE: Ninety. That's one effect of my medical skills, to stay permanently young and lively.

ARGAN: Well indeed, what a fine . . . geriatric!

TOINETTE: No, no. Not geriatric. Peripatetic. I wander from town to town, district to district, bringing my gifts to a public who might not otherwise get the benefit. I sniff out illnesses worthy of my concern, the complicated, mysterious ones, none of your common-or-garden colds, aches and pains, rheumatism, migraine, athlete's foot. No, I want the big ones, raging fevers for weeks on end, wild delirium. I want plagues, dropsy, pleurisy, collapsed and/or missing lungs, that kind of thing. I'd really love it, sir, if you were suffering from any combination of all these, even better if you were at death's door, the despair of every ordinary doctor, so that I could take charge and get to work with my re-markable cures. Oh, how I could sort you out!

ARGAN: Thanks very much.

TOINETTE: Give me your hand, let's check this naughty little pulse, shall we? Ahah, ahah, oh dear, oh dear me, not good, not right at all. But we'll soon have you ticking properly. It's a cheeky little pulse, got a will of its own. Settle, settle! Down boy! You mustn't be afraid of me. (*To* ARGAN.) Who's your doctor?

ARGAN: Dr Purgeon.

TOINETTE: Can't say I know him. Hasn't made any sort of a name for himself. What does he say's wrong with you?

ARGAN: He says it's my liver. The others say it's spleen.

TOINETTE: Amateurs! Lungs, that what it is. Lungs.

ARGAN: Lungs?

TOINETTE: Lungs. What are your symptoms?

ARGAN: Headaches.

TOINETTE: Exactly. Lungs.

ARGAN: Sometimes my eyes feel all swimmy.

TOINETTE: Lungs.

ARGAN: Then again I feel sick.

TOINETTE: Lungs.

ARGAN: My legs give way.

TOINETTE: Lungs.

ARGAN: My stomach aches.

TOINETTE: Lungs. Do you have a hearty appetite?

ARGAN: Yes, doctor.

TOINETTE: Lungs. Do you enjoy an occasional drink or two?

ARGAN: Yes, doctor.

TOINETTE: Lungs. Do you take forty winks of an afternoon?

ARGAN: Yes, doctor.

TOINETTE: Lungs, no question. What food does your doctor recommend?

ARGAN: Soup.

TOINETTE: Fool.

ARGAN: Breast of chicken.

TOINETTE: Idiot.

ARGAN: Veal cutlets.

TOINETTE: Cretin.

ARGAN: Meat broth.

TOINETTE: Charlatan.

ARGAN: New-laid eggs, chicken or duck.

TOINETTE: Quack.

ARGAN: And last thing at night, stewed prunes. Regularly.

TOINETTE: Moron.

ARGAN: And, most important he says I must al-ways water down my wine.

TOINETTE: Ignoramus maximus crapulous! He's suffering from what us doctors called stupid-ity. You have to take your drink neat. Your blood needs thickening. What you need is generous helpings of roast beef, thick bacon rashers, a good selection of dairy produce, cheeses, porridge, oatmeal, rice puddings, chestnuts, pancakes, that sort of thing. You need to clot that watery blood. Your doctor's on another planet. I'll send one of my partners round, he'll keep an eye on you for the dura-tion of my stay.

ARGAN: I'd be most grateful.

TOINETTE: What's wrong with that arm?

ARGAN: I beg your pardon.

TOINETTE: I'd have it amputated this minute, if I were you.

ARGAN: Why?

TOINETTE: Can't you see it's hogging all the nour-ishment and making the other shrivel up?

ARGAN: But I need both arms.

TOINETTE: Oh dear, now that right eye, I'd have it surgically removed without delay.

ARGAN: Lose an eye!

TOINETTE: Can't you see it's a parasite? It's steal-ing all the other one's sustenance. Believe me, have it whipped out, and you'll see a whole lot better out of the left one.

ARGAN: Could I have a second opinion?

TOINETTE: Sorry, must dash. Got an important meeting. We're discussing the treatment for a patient who died yesterday.

ARGAN: A patient who died?

TOINETTE: Indeed. We want to determine what we should have done to save him. Good day.

ARGAN: Do you mind seeing yourself out? I'm not feeling so good.

BÉRALDE: Now that doctor seemed pretty much on the ball to me.

ARGAN: But he's so hasty in his conclusions.

BÉRALDE: All specialists are the same.

ARGAN: I don't know, cut off my arm, remove an eye for the sake of the others! What sort of medical ethics is that? I think I prefer to let them muddle along as they are!

11. TOINETTE, ARGAN, BÉRALDE.

TOINETTE (*off-stage*): All right, all right, no funny business. I won't, that's all, I just won't.

ARGAN: Won't what?

TOINETTE: Won't have my pulse taken by that doctor, dirty old man.

ARGAN: Is that what he was doing? At ninety?

BÉRALDE: Changing the subject, Argan, I think we should talk about my niece. Now that you've fallen out with Purgeon, there's another offer we should consider.

ARGAN: No, I've told you, she's earned a convent and that's what she's getting. How dare she oppose me? I fancy there's some love affair at the bottom of this. You may think I don't notice certain things, but I do.

BÉRALDE: All right, and what if there is a little matter of mutual affection, is that so criminal? Why are you so furious? It would be prefectly normal if it led to marriage.

ARGAN: Be that as it may, she's going into the convent, and that's that.

BÉRALDE: This isn't about Angélique, is it? Someone else is behind this.

ARGAN: Ah, I know what you're driving at. My wife. She gets up your nose, doesn't she?

BÉRALDE: Your words, not mine. But yes, it is your wife I mean. I have to say that you're as blind and stubborn about her as you are about medicine. You fall into every trap she sets, and I can't bear to see it.

TOINETTE: Oh, Monsieur Béralde, you shouldn't talk about madame like that. If ever a woman loved her husband deeply and sincerely, it's madame. . . . You shouldn't say such things!

ARGAN: Tell him how affectionate she can be.

TOINETTE: Oh yes.

ARGAN: How my illness is upsetting her.

TOINETTE: Oh yes.

ARGAN: All those little kindnesses.

TOINETTE: Oh yes. (*To* BÉRALDE): Shall I show you how much she loves him? Do you want to see for yourself? (*To* ARGAN.) Let's show him.

ARGAN: Now what are you up to?

TOINETTE: Madame will be back any moment. Slump down in the chair, pretend you're dead. We'll soon see how devastated she is when she hears the news.

ARGAN: Well, if you say so.

TOINETTE (*To* BÉRALDE): You hide over there.

ARGAN: Is it . . . life-threatening to pretend to be dead?

TOINETTE: No, no, of course it isn't. Go on, stretch out. (*Whispers.*) We'll enjoy showing your brother up. Here she comes.

12. BÉLINE, TOINETTE, ARGAN, BÉRALDE.

TOINETTE: Oh, my God! Help! Something's happened.

BÉLINE: What is it, Toinette?

TOINETTE: Oh, madame!

BÉLINE: What on earth's the matter?

TOINETTE: Your husband's dead.

BÉLINE: Dead?

TOINETTE: Dead. The poor man's dead.

BÉLINE: Are you sure?

TOINETTE: Absolutely certain. I was here on my own with him, and he just passed away in my arms. Look at him there, in that chair.

BÉLINE: Heaven be praised! At last I'm rid of him. Stupid great lump! Cheer up, Toinette, it's a relief all round.

TOINETTE: I thought, madame, we might actually cry.

BÉLINE: Cry? No, no, no. Frankly, who's going to miss him? What a futile existence! A pain, a nuisance to everyone. A disgusting, smelly carcass. Those endless purges, those pills, those syrups. All that moaning. Beyond endurance, believe me. Blowing his nose, coughing, spitting and worse.

TOINETTE: What a touching obituary.

BÉLINE: I've got a plan, Toinette, and you must help me. You won't go away empty-handed. Does anyone know yet that the old boy's dead? Good. Let's get him into his bed, and keep things quiet for the moment. We'll play for time. I need to get my hands on his papers and his money. I won't have spent the best years of my life in this living hell for nothing. Come on, Toinette, let's find his keys.

ARGAN (*getting up suddenly*): Just one moment, if you don't mind.

BÉLINE: Aah!

ARGAN: So, wife, this is what you call love?

TOINETTE: Ah! Oh! The corpse isn't dead.

ARGAN (*to* BÉLINE *as she leaves*): I'm moved by the depth of your feelings for me. And I'm delighted I didn't miss your touching little eulogy. You've certainly taught me a few things. I'll be very different from now on.

BÉRALDE (*emerging from his hiding place*): So, Argan, what do you make of that?

TOINETTE: Who would have thought! But I can hear Angélique. Get back in that chair like you were before. Let's see how she takes your death. It's not a bad idea to find out what the whole family thinks while we're about it.

13. ANGÉLIQUE, ARGAN, TOINETTE, BÉRALDE.

TOINETTE: Oh, no, no, no! This is the worst day of my life!

ANGÉLIQUE: What's the matter, Toinette?

TOINETTE: Very bad news.

ANGÉLIQUE: What? What news?

TOINETTE: Your father's dead.

ANGÉLIQUE: Dead?

TOINETTE: Dead. There. Look. In that chair. He suddenly went all faint, and that was that.

ANGÉLIQUE: Oh my God! My heavens! It can't be true, it can't be! This is awful. I can't bear it. He was all I had in the world, he was still angry with me when he . . . when he. . . . I'll never forgive myself! I want to die! Oh, papa, papa!

14. CLÉANTE, ANGÉLIQUE, ARGAN, TOINETTE, BÉRALDE.

CLÉANTE: My Angélique, what's happened? Why are you like this?

ANGÉLIQUE: I've lost the dearest thing in my life. I've lost my father.

CLÉANTE: Oh, what a dreadful thing! What a terrible shock! I was coming here to introduce myself to him, now that he'd heard about me from your uncle. I was hoping I'd convince him, that he'd see I was serious about marrying you.

ANGÉLIQUE: Cléante, we can't think about any of that now. No more talk of marriage, please. I can't, not now. I'll do what he wanted, and go into a convent. Papa, I'll try to make up for everything, just a little. I promise. Please, please, try to forgive me just a little bit.

ARGAN: Ah, my little girl.

ANGÉLIQUE: Aah!

ARGAN: Come closer, don't be frightened. I'm not dead. You are my flesh and blood. You are real. I'm so glad I've seen who you really are, so full of natural goodness.

ANGÉLIQUE: Oh, papa, papa, I don't understand any of this, but it doesn't matter, it's wonderful you're back. A miracle. Can I ask you just one favour? If you won't let me marry Cléante, please don't make me marry anyone else. That's the only thing I'll ever ask.

CLÉANTE (*falling to his knees*): Please sir, please listen to two people who are desperately in love. Listen to us both.

BÉRALDE: So, Argan, how long are you going to hold out?

TOINETTE: All this love, doesn't it give you even the tiniest warm feeling in the tummy?

ARGAN: I'll agree.... If ... he becomes a doctor. Yes, let him become a doctor, and they can get married.

CLÉANTE: Willingly. If that's all that's needed to become your son-in-law, I'll do it. I'll become anything you want, apothecary, anything. You name it, I'll become it.

BÉRALDE: I've just had a thought, Argan. Why don't you become a doctor yourself? Patient and healer, one and the same person? Much more convenient.

TOINETTE: What a brilliant idea! You'll always recover. Guaranteed. What illness would be fool enough to stand up to a doctor?

ARGAN: Might you possibly be laughing at me? Anyway, I'm too old to start studying.

BÉRALDE: Studying, that's just a word. You're as clever as any student. I'd go so far as to say most of them are less intelligent than you.

ARGAN: But I don't know any of the language, all that Latin and Greek. I'd have to learn thousands of illnesses and cures.

BÉRALDE: That'll come, as soon as you put on cap and gown.

ARGAN: As soon as?

BÉRALDE: As soon as. A nice long gown, headgear to go with it, and the whole world will believe anything you say. Make it up as you go along, they'll worship you.

TOINETTE: What about a neat beard? Very distinguished. With the right beard, you're halfway there.

CLÉANTE: For me, I'm game, whatever you all decide.

BÉRALDE: Shall we do it now?

ARGAN: What, straightaway?

BÉRALDE: Why not? Here, now.

ARGAN: Here? In this house?

BÉRALDE: I've got a friend who knows some people in the School of Medicine. I'm sure they could be here in two minutes, perform the ceremony. It won't cost you a penny.

ARGAN: What must I do? Are there special things I have to say?

BÉRALDE: They'll tell you. It's easy. You'll have your lines written down for you. Go and get ready, and I'll fetch them.

ARGAN: All right. I'll get ready.

CLÉANTE: What have you got in mind? Who exactly are these friends of yours?

TOINETTE: Yes, do explain.

BÉRALDE: Shall we have a bit of fun tonight? We deserve it. Apparently there's a theatre company here who've been rehearsing a piece about a man who's just passed his medical exams. It's a whole ceremony, with music and dancing. I thought we could all have a part in it, with my brother starring as the doctor.

ANGÉLIQUE: Don't you think you're sending my poor father up a bit too much?

BÉRALDE: Not sending him up: indulging his fantasy. Anyway, don't give it away. We can all have some innocent fun, no harm in that. It is carnival time. So, let's get everything ready.

CLÉANTE (*to* ANGÉLIQUE): Is this all right?

ANGÉLIQUE: I suppose so, if uncle says so.

THIRD INTERLUDE

A burlesque ceremony to instal a new doctor, in words, music and dance.

The scene-shifters organise the stage accompanied by music. Then enter the whole gathering, comprising eight syringe-bearers, six apothecaries, twenty-two doctors, and the candidate with ten surgeons, eight dancing and two singing. All take up their places, allotted by rank.

PRESIDENT: Distinguissimi doctores,
Molto learnèd professores,
Sumus gathered here today
To welcome our new protégé.
Will you each please raise your glass!
Drink! In vitro veritas!
Remember our motto,
Before you get blotto ...
"Per laxative ad astra,
Totum scrotum est".
Personally dicto,
I've huge admiratio
For our respected professio.
Let us recall, ergo,
The words of our logo ...
"Mens sauna in corpore sano".

For medecina there's a vogue now,
No doctor's quack or cheat or rogue now,
We state the cure; you'd better heed it.
You've got the cash, and don't we
    need it!
The whole world likes to babble
    bunkum,
The sick, let's kick 'em up the rectum.
We own the mundus, look, we're gods,
We cure all ills with sennapods.

For omnes nos, necesse est
To do our constant, level best,
To tell the kind of stories
That win us new doctores.
Take note of our motto
Before you get blotto . . .
"Clever descriptions, unheard-of ills,
Expensive prescriptions, enormous great
    bills".

Now standing here before us
Monsieur Argan, who adores us.
Hey presto, hocus pocus,
He'll join our magnum opus.
Our feeling's pro, not anti.
Rise, doctore debutante!

FIRST DOCTOR: Cum your kind permissione,
        Can I ask him one questione?
        We make our pills as white as snow;
        What's the reason, do you know?
ARGAN: They have to be bright
        To stand out at night.
CHORUS: Bene, bene replicata.
        It's clear you've learnt the data.
        We'll grant to you the Charter.
SECOND DOCTOR: And next, cum great respect,
        How would you expect
        To deal with dropsy?
ARGAN: That's easy. Dropsy?
        Enema, khazi, plopsy.
CHORUS: Bene, bene replicata.
        It's clear you've learnt the data.
        We'll grant to you the Charter.
THIRD DOCTOR: If the doctors will permit me,
        I'll ask our learnèd toff
        How he'd deal with a coff.
ARGAN: For anything asthmatic,
        Try an emetic.

CHORUS: Bene, bene replicata.
        It's clear you've learnt the data.
        We'll grant to you the Charter.
FOURTH DOCTOR: One last question, if I may.
        What do you think you'd have to say
        To those malingerers
        Who come to see us
        With breathing dificultates?
ARGAN: For things respiratory,
        Suppository.
FIFTH DOCTOR: What if it endures?
ARGAN: No other cures.
        Don't clean it or wash it or boil it.
        Smile nicely, and point to the toilet.
CHORUS: Bene, bene replicata.
        It's clear you've learnt the data.
        We'll grant to you the Charter.
PRESIDENT: Make sure your great fame runs
        Through every land and border,
        And swear to keep all bums
        In perfect running order.
ARGAN: I swear.
PRESIDENT: The next commandment here is . . .
        Poo-poo the latest theories.
ARGAN: Poo-poo? I will.
PRESIDENT: Never leave them in the lurch
        Till they drop off the perch.
ARGAN: I swear.
PRESIDENT: With this bonnet I thee wed,
        I now pronounce you doctor.
        You have been profoundly
        And venerably doctored.
        By the power of Almighty Medicine,
        You may go forth and medicate,
        Dilate, inflate, berate, truncate, pontificate.
        You may purge, inject, cleanse,
        Bleed, dry and finish off . . .
        Anywhere in the world.
        And ego to absolvo of all responsibilitate!
        (Dance. All the surgeons and apothecaries pay
        their respects, accompanied by music.)
ARGAN: Doctores of doctoring,
        Royals of flushing,
        Scourges of amnesia,
        Milkmen of magnesia,
        By Saint Syrup of Figs, the Puller of
            Chains,
        I'd be daft to pit my brains

Against your massive cerebella.
You're the great light, I'm a dim fellah.
You're the first bright day of Spring,
The sea, the stars, that kind of thing.
All my life I'll be in your debt,
Doctors, the ne plus ultra violet.
Thanks to my pater familias
I have fundamentum gravitas
Ego sum so . . . compost mentis,
But I'll serve as your apprentice.
I am now so allegretto
That my heart sings out falsetto,
I'll wear with pride the gown and cap-o,
I'll be like Doctor Lillicrap-o!

CHORUS: Long live the nova doctor!
He parley well! A lovely speaker!
May he eat and drink his fill,
Bleed, drain, purge, evacuate and kill.
Three cheers for Dr Argan!
Take a long deep breath . . .
Hip, hip, hip, hip, hip hooray!
Our newest Doctor Death!

(*Dance. The surgeons and apothecaries dance to the sound of instruments, singing, clapping and apothecaries' mortars.*)

FIRST SURGEON: May he find the magic cures
In time-honoured style.
May he make such a killing
The banks will be willing
To sit on his pile.

CHORUS: Long live the nova doctor!
He parley well! A lovely speaker!

May he eat and drink his fill,
Bleed, drain, purge, evacuate and kill.
Three cheers for Dr Argan!
Take a long deep breath . . .
Hip, hip, hip, hip, hip hooray!
Our newest Doctor Death!

SECOND SURGEON: May he have a succession,
An endless procession
Of pox, plague and fever!
May he drink and be merry,
Get good dysentery,
Our Argan, Believer, Reliever!

CHORUS: Long live the nova doctor!
He parley well! A lovely speaker!
May he eat and drink his fill,
Bleed, drain, purge, evacuate and kill.
May fatal illness cheer him up!
Raise your glasses, bottoms up!
A little purge to loosen up!
Raise your glasses, bottoms up!
May the hard bowel soften up!
Raise your glasses, bottoms up!
The patient's number's coming up!
Raise your glasses, bottoms up!
One last drink now, bottoms up!
Just raise your glasses, BOTTOMS UP!

(*Final dance. Doctors, surgeons, apothecaries exit by rank with the same ceremony as when they entered.*)

THE END

Introduction to *The Country Wife*

WHEN THE PLAY WAS NEW

The Country Wife was performed in London by the King's Company at the Theatre Royal in 1675, was probably written in 1673–1674, and was first published in 1675. The play proved very popular and was often revived, but its morality soon became a subject of debate and remains so today. The play is a model of the style and wit of the era in London, but also dramatizes the hypocritical, duplicitous nature of typical behavior of the moneyed classes. Clearly the play is satirical, but some critics also see it as a celebration of amorality. Audiences and readers must reach their own conclusions.

The Restoration Period, 1660–1700, is named for the restoration of the king to the English throne. King Charles I had been defeated and later executed by a Puritan-controlled Parliament in 1642. The country was without a monarch for some eighteen years, during which theatre and many other pleasures were outlawed. In 1660 the king's son, Charles II, returned to England from exile in France to be crowned, and many previous social activities and entertainments were also restored, including the theatre.

Although the new Restoration theatre activity borrowed from the older Elizabethan practices and revived plays from the past, much about the Restoration theatre was new and more reflective of French and Italian tastes and styles than Elizabethan ones. The most dynamic changes were the introduction of actresses to the professional theatre, a proscenium stage, and a revitalized comedy of manners.

The addition of actresses to professional performance was controversial, but it was also one of the most dynamics changes in the British theatre ever. Cross-dressing did not cease with the arrival of the women, but its very nature altered, as we can see in *The Country Wife*. Playwrights began to write with actresses in mind, and many older plays were reconceived and severely modified, both to update them and bring them in line with French practice, but also to accommodate the elements that women would bring to a performance. The earliest actresses must have been intrepid and they often suffered bad social reputations, just as they did in both Spain and France. We know little about the first actresses of *The Country Wife* except that Elizabeth Boutell, who played Margery Pinchwife, was blonde, small in stature, and very popular in breeches (cross-dressing) roles, which she performs in this play. Both actors and actresses wore contemporary, fashionable dress, even when reviving a play from the past. Everything was "modern dress."

The new theatres featured a proscenium (picture frame) stage with an extensive playing apron about as deep as the stage inside the proscenium frame. On each side of the proscenium, the stage also had functioning doors that were used for both interior and exterior exits. There is an especially effective use of these doors in the "china" scene in the fourth act of *The Country Wife*. Despite the use of real doors within the theatre architecture, the scenery on stage was not three dimensional. Flat, painted scenery (called wing and drop scenery) could be changed very quickly and efficiently. Like the theatres of seventeenth-century France, the audiences were noisy, fully lit, and sometimes competitive with each other and occasionally the actors. Food vendors moved about the house, much like at sporting events today.

THE PLAYWRIGHT

William Wycherley (c. 1641–1715) was an occasional playwright beginning with a successful first play, *Love in a Wood*, in 1671. He was the author of only four plays, including *The Gentleman Dancing*

Master (1672), all written and first produced while he was in his thirties. Wycherley moved in aristocratic circles and was a favorite at the court of Charles II while writing his comedies of manners. Wycherley did not write or work in the theatre for a living, but as a fashionable outsider. He was not alone in this practice.

Wycherley was very aware of classical plays and strongly influenced by the comedies of Molière. We can see bits that Wycherley gleaned from Molière's *The School for Wives* and *The School for Husbands* in *The Country Wife*. Wycherley's biting social satire is also reminiscent of Shakespeare's contemporary, Ben Jonson, whose satires, such as *Volpone,* were a much stronger influence on Wycherley and his contemporaries than the comedies of Shakespeare. Wycherley was very modern—he explored not just the recent past, but his precise moment in social history. Despite other literary influences, *The Country Wife* is original and remains a classic Restoration comedy of manners.

Wycherley's final play, *The Plain Dealer* (1676), was also a social satire and a scathing attack on elements of the legal profession (Wycherley had trained for the bar but never practiced). The playwright references himself and a controversy over the previous season's *The Country Wife* by having his characters argue about the immorality or justification of *The Country Wife*.

Unfortunately, after his brief playwriting career, but probably not because of it, Wycherley's economic and social fortunes began to decline. He made a bad marriage, grew out of favor at court, and ended up in debtor's prison for years. His attempts at other kinds of writing, such as poetry, failed. His theatrical career was like a shooting star—but a very bright one, whose fame lives on in four plays, and *The Country Wife* in particular.

GENRE, STRUCTURE, AND STYLE

The Country Wife is a nearly perfect example of a comedy of manners, the most enduring genre of play from the Restoration. Some critics view this period as having created the model for the ages. A comedy of manners examines the behavior of people of a particular class, usually the economic upper echelons. The conflict is typically centered in characters whose desires are at odds with social expectations. Wycherley exposes the hypocrisy of characters pretending to follow social expectations, while really doing just the opposite, but he does so with elegant language, courtly manners, and outrageous fun.

Like the plays of Molière, the Restoration comedies of manners were neoclassical except that they did not teach moral lessons and manipulated some of the rules, such as unity of place and action. While adhering to unity of time (all action in twenty-four hours or less), the British approach to unity of place was any location that could be reached in that twenty-four hours. Hence the scenery changed frequently, offering both indoor and outdoor settings in the same play. In *The Country Wife* the action takes place in Horner's house, Pinchwife's house, an outdoor exchange (an open outdoor mall), a bedchamber, and a piazza (an outdoor square). Unity of action was also liberally interpreted by the British, who, like the Elizabethans, remained very fond of subplots and carried on several lines of action simultaneously. Consequently, the plots of Restoration comedies are much more complex than their French counterparts.

Wycherley and his colleagues were very attracted to sexual intrigue and trickery. Characters love to talk about their exploits, but the hypocrites among them pretend otherwise. Unlike all of the plays appearing before this one in this collection, *The Country Wife* is written in prose. When writing comedies, the Restoration playwrights wrote typically in prose unless a character quotes a favorite line of poetry. In fact, people in this period were very fond of quotation—both in life as well as in plays. The play is also generously laced with asides like those we see in Shakespeare. Here the characters are often taking the audience into their confidence—as if the audience is a conspirator with their trickery and hypocrisy.

IMPORTANT ELEMENTS OF CONTENT

Characters in *The Country Wife* who are clever and intelligent win. Those who are stupid fools, such as Jasper Fidget and Sparkish, or characters who cannot control their emotions, such as Pinchwife and his too-young wife Margery, lose. Controlling one's emotions was critical in this society (at least among the upper classes). It was a period of self-protection because so many people were eager to take advantage of the weaknesses of others. Unlike contemporary social behavior in the United States, Restoration society had no interest in public confession. In keeping with this state of affairs, virtue does not arise at all in the plays as something to be pursued. There is little poetic justice, but a kind of comic reality in terms of the victories and defeats of the characters. The play is not realism, but it is reality-based and very contemporary. Despite this lack of sentimentality, Wycherley still manages to unite two characters (Alithea and Harcourt), who truly love one another. So the playwright injected just a touch of poetic justice.

The Country Wife, like other comedies of its time, has a rake for a hero. Horner is witty, clever, self-serving, and nearly brutal in his efforts to make sexual conquests. His machinations and scheming seem nearly effortless, as does his florid, adept language, fashionable carriage, and perfect manners. Such characters are always rewarded in Restoration comedies. The audience is apparently expected to admire the rake's skills and deportment. Therefore we cannot be certain that Wycherley intended Horner as an object of satire: The playwright may have been celebrating his exploits.

Wycherley is also attracted to disguises (forced or otherwise). Margery is required by her maniacal husband, Pinchwife, to dress as a boy if she is to see the city. The plan of course backfires as the rakes recognize at once that Margery is a woman, yet they court her while pretending that she is a boy. Harcourt also adopts a disguise as a priest in order to bring about the marriage he desires with Alithea. The disguises create intrigue while also complicating the comic action of the play.

The courtship of Alithea and Harcourt stands in sharp contrast to the sexual pursuits of Horner, Lady Fidget and her "virtuous gang," and even the ingenuous Margery. The result is a sharp juxtaposition of the pursuit of sex (especially executed secretly like a clandestine sport), with nurturing, genuine love. Ironically the real love with the objective of marriage must also be pursued secretly due to obstacles set up by others.

Most of the Restoration comedies of manners have a clown. The example in *The Country Wife* is typical of the genre and results in one of the most memorable characters of the Restoration, Mr. Sparkish. Playwrights and audiences loved to make fun of fops—"wanna-be" rakes who emphatically and sometimes desperately, but always ineffectually, emulate the real wits and stylish characters such as Horner and Harcourt. Sparkish slavishly follows the rakish model cosmetically, but with totally different effects. The clown is self-conscious about style and grace; the rake seems to do it without effort, as if it is natural. Sparkish consequently becomes the butt of many jokes and usually seems oblivious to the ridicule of those characters in the know.

Consistent with this kind of mockery is contempt for Puritans and for anyone who hails from the country and is thus unsophisticated, ingenuous, and foolish. Margery fits this country bumpkin model and is often the object of jokes by the sophisticates. The model of superiority is the urban, fashionable wit, who moves easily in high society and knows how to negotiate all the traps laid by worldly social types.

In most cases in Restoration comedy, many of the characters are given emblematic names that indicate to the audience the inclinations or weaknesses of the characters. In *The Country Wife* Pinchwife tries to keep his wife a prisoner and ignorant of the world, Lady Fidget is anxious to move about in her hypocritical lechery, Horner is very sexually active and intent on putting cuckold's horns on a variety of husbands, and the Squeamish ladies are exactly what their name implies.

THE PLAY IN REVIVAL

During the twenty-five remaining years of the Restoration period, *The Country Wife* was frequently performed and it continued to be revived throughout the eighteenth century in England but usually in a modified, "safer" form. The nineteenth century saw a sharp decline in revival since the play was considered by many to be immoral. By the mid-twentieth century, however, revival became frequent again. It had a Broadway production in 1965 and an off-Broadway production in 1982 by the Acting Company. In more recent times companies find the play challenging to perform well, but it is produced nearly every season in the United Kingdom and throughout the world by professionals and amateurs, and in the United States by professional companies and universities. Recent interesting revivals include a modern dress production in Britain by the Touring Partnership in 1997, and a very realistically staged version by the Shakespeare Theatre in Washington, D.C., in 2000. At almost any moment you can find a production of this play somewhere in North America.

SPECIAL FEATURE

The most famous event in this play is the "china" scene (Act IV, Scene 3) in which Lady Fidget has sex with Horner while talking through the door to her unwitting husband. She pretends that she is examining Horner's china, which becomes a euphemism for sex. After the event Lady Fidget says to her husband and other women: "we women of quality never think we have china enough." Through it all, her husband, Sir Jasper, is completely duped—and remains so.

FURTHER READING ABOUT THE PLAY, PLAYWRIGHT, AND CONTEXT

For more about Wycherley, this play, and Restoration comedy, see William Chadwick, *The Four Plays of William Wycherley* and Joseph Wood Krutch, *Comedy and Conscience after the Restoration.*

For more on theatre in the Restoration, see Robert Hume, *The London Theatre World, 1660–1800* and Deborah Fisk, *The Cambridge Companion to English Restoration Theatre.*

For more on Restoration comedy in production, see J. L. Styan, *Restoration Comedy in Performance* and Simon Callow, *Acting in Restoration Comedy.*

The Country Wife

BY WILLIAM WYCHERLEY

CHARACTERS

MR. HORNER
MR. HARCOURT
MR. DORILANT
MR. PINCHWIFE
SIR JASPER FIDGET
MRS. MARGERY PINCHWIFE
MRS. ALITHEA
MY LADY FIDGET
MRS. DAINTY FIDGET
MRS. SQUEAMISH
OLD LADY SQUEAMISH
WAITERS, SERVANTS, AND ATTENDANTS
A BOY
A QUACK
LUCY   Alithea's maid
The Scene: London

ACT I

SCENE I   HORNER'S LODGING

Enter HORNER, *and* QUACK *following him at a distance.*

HORNER (*aside*): A quack is as fit for a pimp as a midwife for a bawd; they are still but in their way both helpers of nature.—Well, my dear doctor, hast thou done what I desired?

QUACK: I have undone you forever with the women, and reported you throughout the whole town as bad as a eunuch, with as much trouble as if I had made you one in earnest.

HORNER: But have you told all the midwives you know, the orange-wenches[1] at the playhouses, the city husbands, and old fumbling keepers of this end of the town? For they'll be the readiest to report it.

QUACK: I have told all the chambermaids, waiting-women, tire-women, and old women of my acquaintance; nay, and whispered it as a secret to 'em, and to the whisperers of Whitehall; so that you need not doubt 'twill spread, and you will be as odious to the handsome young women as—

HORNER: As the smallpox. Well—

QUACK: And to the married women of this end of the town as—

HORNER: As the great ones; nay, as their own husbands.

QUACK: And to the city dames as aniseed Robin of filthy and contemptible memory;[2] and they will frighten their children with your name, especially their females.

HORNER: And cry, "Horner's coming to carry you away." I am only afraid 'twill not be believed. You told 'em 'twas by an English-French disaster, and an English-French surgeon, who has given me at once not only a cure but an antidote for the future against that damned malady, and that worse distemper, love, and all other women's evils?

QUACK: Your late journey into France has made it the more credible, and your being here a fortnight before you appeared in public looks as if you apprehended the shame, which I wonder you do not. Well, I have been hired by young gallants to belie 'em t'other way; but you are the first would be thought a man unfit for women.

HORNER: Dear Mr. Doctor, let vain rogues be contented only to be thought abler men than they are, generally 'tis all the pleasure they have; but mine lies another way.

QUACK: You take, methinks, a very preposterous way to it, and as ridiculous as if we operators

---

1. Serving women in the theatre.

2. Real hermaphrodite of the time.

in physic should put forth bills to disparage our medicaments, with hopes to gain customers.

HORNER: Doctor, there are quacks in love as well as physic, who get but the fewer and worse patients for their boasting; a good name is seldom got by giving it oneself, and women no more than honor are compassed by bragging. Come, come, doctor, the wisest lawyer never discovers the merits of his cause till the trial; the wealthiest man conceals his riches, and the cunning gamester his play. Shy husbands and keepers, like old rooks, are not to be cheated but by a new unpracticed trick; false friendship will pass now no more than false dice upon 'em; no, not in the city.

(*Enter* BOY.)

BOY: There are two ladies and a gentleman coming up.

(*Exit.*)

HORNER: A pox! some unbelieving sisters of my former acquaintance, who, I am afraid, expect their sense should be satisfied of the falsity of the report. No—this formal fool and women!

(*Enter* SIR JASPER FIDGET, LADY FIDGET, *and* MRS. DAINTY FIDGET.)

QUACK: His wife and sister.

SIR JASPER FIDGET: My coach breaking just now before your door, sir, I look upon as an occasional reprimand to me, sir, for not kissing your hands, sir, since your coming out of France, sir; and so my disaster, sir, has been my good fortune, sir; and this is my wife and sister, sir.

HORNER: What then, sir?

SIR JASPER FIDGET: My lady, and sister, sir.—Wife, this is Master Horner.

LADY FIDGET: Master Horner, husband!

SIR JASPER FIDGET: My lady, my Lady Fidget, sir.

HORNER: So, sir.

SIR JASPER FIDGET: Won't you be acquainted with her, sir?—(*Aside.*) So, the report is true, I find, by his coldness or aversion to the sex; but I'll play the wag with him.—Pray salute my wife, my lady, sir.

HORNER: I will kiss no man's wife, sir, for him, sir; I have taken my eternal leave, sir, of the sex already, sir.

SIR JASPER FIDGET (*aside*): Ha, ha, ha! I'll plague him yet.—Not know my wife, sir?

HORNER: I do know your wife, sir; she's a woman, sir, and consequently a monster, sir, a greater monster than a husband, sir.

SIR JASPER FIDGET: A husband! how, sir?

HORNER: So, sir; but I make no more cuckolds, sir. (*Makes horns.*[3])

SIR JASPER FIDGET: Ha, ha, ha! Mercury, Mercury![4]

LADY FIDGET: Pray, Sir Jasper, let us be gone from this rude fellow.

MRS. DAINTY FIDGET: Who, by his breeding, would think he had ever been in France?

LADY FIDGET: Foh! he's but too much a French fellow, such as hate women of quality and virtue for their love to their husbands, Sir Jasper; a woman is hated by 'em as much for loving her husband as for loving their money. But pray let's be gone.

HORNER: You do well, madam, for I have nothing that you came for. I have brought over not so much as a bawdy picture, new postures, nor the second part of the *École des Filles*,[5] nor—

QUACK: (*apart to* HORNER): Hold, for shame, sir! What d'ye mean? You'll ruin yourself forever with the sex—

SIR JASPER FIDGET: Ha, ha, ha! He hates women perfectly, I find.

MRS. DAINTY FIDGET: What pity 'tis he should.

LADY FIDGET: Ay, he's a base, rude fellow for't; but affectation makes not a woman more odious to them than virtue.

HORNER: Because your virtue is your greatest affectation, madam.

LADY FIDGET: How, you saucy fellow! Would you wrong my honor?

HORNER: If I could.

LADY FIDGET: How d'ye mean, sir?

SIR JASPER FIDGET: Ha, ha, ha! No, he can't wrong your ladyship's honor, upon my honor; he, poor man—hark you in your ear—a mere eunuch.

LADY FIDGET: O filthy French beast! foh, foh! Why do we stay? Let's be gone; I can't endure the sight of him.

---

3. HORNER makes the sign of a cuckold.
4. Mercury was a treatment for syphilis.
5. A pornographic book.

SIR JASPER FIDGET: Stay but till the chairs[6] come; they'll be here presently.

LADY FIDGET: No, no.

SIR JASPER FIDGET: Nor can I stay longer. 'Tis—let me see, a quarter and a half quarter of a minute past eleven; the council will be sat, I must away. Business must be preferred always before love and ceremony with the wise, Mr. Horner.

HORNER: And the impotent, Sir Jasper.

SIR JASPER FIDGET: Ay, ay the impotent, Master Horner, ha ha ha!

LADY FIDGET: What, leave us with a filthy man alone in his lodgings?

SIR JASPER FIDGET: He's an innocent man now, you know. Pray stay. I'll hasten the chairs to you.— Mr. Horner, your servant; I should be glad to see you at my house. Pray come and dine with me, and play at cards with my wife after dinner; you are fit for women at that game yet, ha, ha!—(*Aside.*) 'Tis as much a husband's prudence to provide innocent diversion for a wife as to hinder her unlawful pleasures, and he had better employ her than let her employ herself.—Farewell.

HORNER: Your servant, Sir Jasper.

(*Exit* SIR JASPER.)

LADY FIDGET: I will not stay with him, foh!

HORNER: Nay, madam, I beseech you stay, if it be but to see I can be as civil to ladies yet as they would desire.

LADY FIDGET: No, no, foh! You cannot be civil to ladies.

MRS. DAINTY FIDGET: You as civil as ladies would desire?

LADY FIDGET: No, no, no! foh, foh, foh!

(*Exeunt* LADY FIDGET *and* MRS. DAINTY.)

QUACK: Now, I think, I, or you yourself rather, have done your business with the women.

HORNER: Thou art an ass. Don't you see already, upon the report and my carriage, this grave man of business leaves his wife in my lodgings, invites me to his house and wife, who before would not be acquainted with me out of jealousy?

QUACK: Nay, by this means you may be the more acquainted with the husbands, but the less with the wives.

HORNER: Let me alone; if I can but abuse the husbands, I'll soon disabuse the wives. Stay—I'll reckon you up the advantages I am like to have by my stratagem: First, I shall be rid of all my old acquaintances, the most insatiable sorts of duns, that invade our lodgings in a morning. And next to the pleasure of making a new mistress is that of being rid of an old one, and of all old debts; love, when it comes to be so, is paid the most unwillingly.

QUACK: Well, you may be so rid of your old acquaintances, but now will you get any new ones?

HORNER: Doctor, thou wilt never make a good chemist, thou are so incredulous and impatient. Ask but all the young fellows of the town if they do not lose more time, like huntsmen, in starting the game than in running it down; one knows not where to find 'em, who will or will not. Women of quality are so civil you can hardly distinguish love from good breeding, and a man is often mistaken; but now I can be sure she that shows an aversion to me loves the sport, as those women that are gone, whom I warrant to be right.[7] And then the next thing is, your women of honor, as you call 'em are only chary of their reputations, not their persons, and 'tis scandal they would avoid, not men. Now may I have, by the reputation of a eunuch, the privileges of one; and be seen in a lady's chamber in a morning as early as her husband; kiss virgins before their parents or lovers; and may be, in short, the *passe partout*[8] of the town. Now, doctor.

QUACK: Nay, now you shall be the doctor; and your process is so new that we do not know but it may succeed.

HORNER: Not so new, neither; *probatum est,*[9] doctor.

QUACK: Well, I wish you luck and many patients whilst I go to mine.

(*Exit* QUACK.

Enter HARCOURT *and* DORILANT *to* HORNER.)

---

6. A means of transportation; a covered chair attached to poles which was carried by two porters.

7. Women who are loose.
8. Pass key.
9. Proven.

HARCOURT: Come, your appearance at the play yesterday has, I hope, hardened you for the future against the women's contempt and the men's raillery; and now you'll abroad as you were wont.

HORNER: Did I not bear it bravely?

DORILANT: With a most theatrical impudence; nay, more than the orange-wenches show there, or a drunken vizard-mask,[10] or a great-bellied actress; nay, or the most impudent of creatures, an ill poet; or what is yet more impudent, a secondhand critic.

HORNER: But what say the ladies? Have they no pity?

HARCOURT: What ladies? The vizard-masks, you know, never pity a man when all's gone, though in their service.

DORILANT: And for the women in the boxes,[11] you'd never pity them when 'twas in your power.

HARCOURT: They say, 'tis pity but all that deal with common women should be served so.

DORILANT: Nay, I dare swear they won't admit you to play at cards with them, go to plays with 'em, or do the little duties which other shadows of men are wont to do for 'em.

HORNER: Who do you call shadows of men?

DORILANT: Half-men.

HORNER: What, boys?

DORILANT: Ay, your old boys, old *beaux garcons*,[12] who, like superannuated stallions, are suffered to run, feed, and whinny with the mares as long as they live, though they can do nothing else.

HORNER: Well, a pox on love and wenching! Women serve but to keep a man from better company; though I can't enjoy them, I shall you the more. Good fellowship and friendship are lasting, rational, and manly pleasures.

HARCOURT: For all that, give me some of those pleasures you call effeminate too; they help to relish one another.

HORNER: They disturb one another.

HARCOURT: No, mistresses are like books. If you pore upon them too much, they doze you and make you unfit for company; but if used discreetly, you are the fitter for conversation by 'em.

DORILANT: A mistress should be like a little country retreat near the town, not to dwell in constantly, but only for a night and away, to taste the town the better when a man returns.

HORNER: I tell you, 'tis as hard to be a good fellow, a good friend, and a lover of women, as 'tis to be a good fellow, a good friend, and a lover of money. You cannot follow both, then choose your side. Wine gives you liberty, love takes it away.

DORILANT: Gad, he's in the right on't.

HORNER: Wine gives you joy; love, grief and tortures, besides the surgeon's. Wine makes us witty; love, only sots. Wine makes us sleep; love breaks it.

DORILANT: By the world, he has reason, Harcourt.

HORNER: Wine makes—

DORILANT: Ay, wine makes us—makes us princes; love makes us beggars, poor rogues, egad—and wine—

HORNER: So, there's one converted.—No, no, love and wine, oil and vinegar.

HARCOURT: I grant it; love will still be uppermost.

HORNER: Come, for my part I will have only those glorious, manly pleasures of being very drunk and very slovenly.

(*Enter* BOY.)

BOY: Mr. Sparkish is below, sir.

(*Exit.*)

HARCOURT: What, my dear friend! a rogue that is fond of me only, I think, for abusing him.

DORILANT: No, he can no more think the men laugh at him than that women jilt him, his opinion of himself is so good.

HORNER: Well, there's another pleasure by drinking I thought not of; I shall lose his acquaintance, because he cannot drink; and you know 'tis a very hard thing to be rid of him, for he's one of those nauseous offerers at wit, who, like the worst fiddlers, run themselves into all companies.

HARCOURT: One that, by being in the company of men of sense, would pass for one.

HORNER: And may so to the shortsighted world, as a false jewel amongst true ones is not discerned at a distance. His company is as troublesome to us as a cuckold's when you have a mind to his wife's.

---

10. A masked woman.
11. The most expensive place to sit in the theatre.
12. Male escorts.

HARCOURT: No, the rogue will not let us enjoy one another, but ravishes our conversation, though he signifies no more to't than Sir Martin Mar-all's[13] gaping, and awkward thrumming upon the lute, does to his man's voice and music.

DORILANT: And to pass for a wit in town shows himself a fool every night to us, that are guilty of the plot.

HORNER: Such wits as he are, to a company of reasonable men, like rooks to the gamesters who only fill a room at the table, but are so far from contributing to the play that they only serve to spoil the fancy of those that do.

DORILANT: Nay, they are used like rooks too, snubbed, checked, and abused; yet the rogues will hang on.

HORNER: A pox on 'em, and all that force nature, and would be still what she forbids 'em! Affectation is her greatest monster.

HARCOURT: Most men are the contraries to that they would seem. Your bully, you see, is a coward with a long sword; the little, humbly fawning physician, with his ebony cane, is he that destroys men.

DORILANT: The usurer, a poor rogue possessed of moldy bonds and mortgages; and we they call spendthrifts are only wealthy who lay out his money upon daily new purchases of pleasure.

HORNER: Ay, your arrantest cheat is your trustee, or executor; your jealous man, the greatest cuckold; your churchman, the greatest atheist; and your noisy, pert rogue of a wit, the greatest fop, dullest ass, and worst company, as you shall see. For here he comes.

(*Enter* SPARKISH *to them.*)

SPARKISH: How is't, sparks, how is't? Well, faith, Harry, I must rally thee a little, ha, ha, ha! upon the report in town of thee, ha, ha, ha! I can't hold i'faith; shall I speak?

HORNER: Yes, but you'll be so bitter then.

SPARKISH: Honest Dick and Frank here shall answer for me, I will not be extreme bitter, by the universe.

HARCOURT: We will be bound in ten thousand pound bond, he shall not be bitter at all.

DORILANT: Nor sharp, nor sweet.

HORNER: What, not downright insipid?

SPARKISH: Nay then, since you are so brisk and provoke me, take what follows. You must know, I was discoursing and rallying with some ladies yesterday, and they happened to talk of the fine new signs in town.

HORNER: Very fine ladies, I believe.

SPARKISH: Said I, "I know where the best new sign is." "Where?" says one of the ladies. "In Covent Garden," I replied. Said another, "In what street?" "In Russell Street," answered I. "Lord," says another, "I'm sure there was ne'er a fine new sign there yesterday." "Yes, but there was," said I again, "and it came out of France, and has been there a fortnight."

DORILANT: A pox! I can hear no more, prithee.

HORNER: No, hear him out; let him tune his crowd[14] a while.

HARCOURT: The worst music, the greatest preparation.

SPARKISH: Nay, faith, I'll make you laugh. "It cannot be," says a third lady. "Yes, yes," quoth I again. Says a fourth lady—

HORNER: Look to't, we'll have no more ladies.

SPARKISH: No—then mark, mark, now. Said I to the fourth, "Did you never see Mr. Horner? He lodges in Russell Street, and he's a sign of a man, you know, since he came out of France." He, ha, he!

HORNER: But the devil take me, if thine be the sign of a jest.

SPARKISH: With that they all fell a-laughing, till they bepissed themselves! What, but it does not move you, methinks? Well, I see one had as good go to law without a witness, as break a jest without a laugher on one's side. Come, come, sparks, but where do we dine? I have left at Whitehall an earl to dine with you.

DORILANT: Why, I thought thou hadst loved a man with a title better than a suit with a French trimming to't.

HARCOURT: Go to him again.

SPARKISH: No, sir, a wit to me is the greatest title in the world.

HORNER: But go dine with your earl, sir; he may be exceptious. We are your friends, and will not take it ill to be left, I do assure you.

---

13. A character in a play by John Dryden who pretends to serenade his mistress when someone else is actually singing.

14. A fiddle.

HARCOURT: Nay, faith, he shall go to him.

SPARKISH: Nay, pray, gentlemen.

DORILANT: We'll thrust you out, if you wo'not. What, disappoint anybody for us?

SPARKISH: Nay, dear gentlemen, hear me.

HORNER: No, no, sir, by no means; pray go, sir.

SPARKISH: Why, dear rogues—

DORILANT: No, no.

(*They all thrust him out of the room.*)

ALL: Ha, ha, ha!

(SPARKISH *returns.*)

SPARKISH: But, sparks, pray hear me. What, d'ye think I'll eat then with gay, shallow fops and silent coxcombs? I think wit as necessary at dinner as a glass of good wine, and that's the reason I never have any stomach when I eat alone.—Come, but where do we dine?

HORNER: Even where you will.

SPARKISH: At Chateline's?

DORILANT: Yes, if you will.

SPARKISH: Or at the Cock?

DORILANT: Yes, if you please.

SPARKISH: Or at the Dog and Partridge?

HORNER: Ay, if you have mind to't, for we shall dine at neither.

SPARKISH: Pshaw! with your fooling we shall lose the new play; and I would no more miss seeing a new play the first day than I would miss sitting in the wits' row. Therefore I'll go fetch my mistress and away.

(*Exit* SPARKISH.

Manent HORNER, HARCOURT, DORILANT. *Enter to them* MR. PINCHWIFE.)

HORNER: Who have we here? Pinchwife?

PINCHWIFE: Gentlemen, your humble servant.

HORNER: Well, Jack, by thy long absence from the town, the grumness of thy countenance, and the slovenliness of thy habit, I should give thee joy, should I not, of marriage?

PINCHWIFE (*aside*): Death! does he know I'm married too? I thought to have concealed it from him at least.—My long stay in the country will excuse my dress, and I have a suit of law, that brings me up to town, that puts me out of humour; besides, I must give Sparkish tomorrow five thousand pound to lie with my sister.

HORNER: Nay, you country gentlemen, rather than not purchase, will buy anything; and he is a cracked title, if we may quibble. Well, but am I to give thee joy? I heard thou wert married.

PINCHWIFE: What then?

HORNER: Why, the next thing that is to be heard is, thou'rt a cuckold.

PINCHWIFE (*aside*): Insupportable name!

HORNER: But I did not expect marriage from such a whoremaster as you, one that knew the town so much, and women so well.

PINCHWIFE: Why, I have married no London wife.

HORNER: Pshaw! that's all one; that grave circumspection in marrying a country wife is like refusing a deceitful, pampered Smithfield jade[15] to go and be cheated by a friend in the country.

PINCHWIFE (*aside*): A pox on him and his simile!— At least we are a little surer of the breed there, know what her keeping has been, whether foiled or unsound.

HORNER: Come, come, I have known a clap gotten in Wales; and there are cousins, justices' clerks, and chaplains in the country. I won't say coachmen. But she's handsome and young?

PINCHWIFE (*aside*): I'll answer as I should do.—No, no, she has no beauty but her youth; no attraction but her modesty; wholesome, homely, and housewifely; that's all.

DORILANT: He talks as like a grazier[16] as he looks.

PINCHWIFE: She's too awkward, ill-favored, and silly to bring to town.

HARCOURT: Then methinks you should bring her, to be taught breeding.

PINCHWIFE: To be taught! No, sir, I thank you. Good wives and private soldiers should be ignorant.—(*Aside.*) I'll keep her from your instructions, I warrant you.

HARCOURT (*aside*): The rogue is as jealous as if his wife were not ignorant.

HORNER: Why, if she be ill-favored, there will be less danger here for you than by leaving her in the country; we have such variety of dainties that we are seldom hungry.

DORILANT: But they have always coarse, constant, swingeing[17] stomachs in the country.

15. An old horse.
16. A cattleman.
17. Big.

HARCOURT: Foul feeders indeed.

DORILANT: And your hospitality is great there.

HARCOURT: Open house, every man's welcome.

PINCHWIFE: So, so, gentlemen.

HORNER: But, prithee, why wouldst thou marry her? If she be ugly, ill-bred, and silly, she must be rich then.

PINCHWIFE: As rich as if she brought me twenty thousand pound out of this town; for she'll be as sure not to spend her moderate portion as a London baggage would be to spend hers, let it be what it would; so 'tis all one. Then, because she's ugly, she's the likelier to be my own; and being ill-bred, she'll hate conversation; and since silly and innocent, will not know the difference betwixt a man of one-and-twenty and one of forty.

HORNER: Nine—to my knowledge; but if she be silly, she'll expect as much from a man of forty-nine as from him of one-and-twenty. But methinks wit is more necessary than beauty, and I think no young woman ugly that has it, and no handsome woman agreeable without it.

PINCHWIFE: 'Tis my maxim, he's a fool that marries, but he's a greater that does not marry a fool. What is wit in a wife good for, but to make a man cuckold?

HORNER: Yes, to keep it from his knowledge.

PINCHWIFE: A fool cannot contrive to make her husband a cuckold.

HORNER: No, but she'll club with a man that can; and what is worse, if she cannot make her husband a cuckold, she'll make him jealous, and pass for one, and then 'tis all one.

PINCHWIFE: Well, well, I'll take care for one, my wife shall make me no cuckold, though she had your help, Mr. Horner; I understand the town, sir.

DORILANT (*aside*): His help!

HARCOURT (*aside*): He's come newly to town, it seems, and has not heard how things are with him.

HORNER: But tell me, has marriage cured thee of whoring, which it seldom does?

HARCOURT: 'Tis more than age can do.

HORNER: No, the word is, I'll marry and live honest; but a marriage vow is like a penitent gamester's oath, and entering into bonds and penalties to stint himself to such a particular small sum at play for the future, which makes him but the more eager, and not being able to hold out, loses his money again, and his forfeit to boot.

DORILANT: Ay, ay, a gamester will be a gamester whilst his money lasts, and a whoremaster whilst his vigor.

HARCOURT: Nay, I have known 'em, when they are broke and can lose no more, keep a-fumbling with the box[18] in their hands to fool with only, and hinder other gamesters.

DORILANT: That had wherewithal to make lusty stakes.

PINCHWIFE: Well, gentlemen, you may laugh at me, but you shall never lie with my wife; I know the town.

HORNER: But prithee, was not the way you were in better? Is not keeping better than marriage?

PINCHWIFE: A pox on't! The jades would jilt me; I could never keep a whore to myself.

HORNER: So then you only married to keep a whore to yourself. Well, but let me tell you, women, as you say, are like soldiers, made constant and loyal by good pay rather than by oaths and covenants. Therefore I'd advise my friends to keep rather than marry, since too I find, by your example, it does not serve one's turn; for I saw you yesterday in the eighteen-penny place[19] with a pretty country wench.

PINCHWIFE (*aside*): How the devil! Did he see my wife then? I sat there that she might not be seen. But she shall never go to a play again.

HORNER: What, dost thou blush at nine-and-forty, for having been seen with a wench?

DORILANT: No, faith I warrant 'twas his wife, which he seated there out of sight, for he's a cunning rogue and understands the town.

HARCOURT: He blushes. Then 'twas his wife, for men are now more ashamed to be seen with them in public than with a wench.

PINCHWIFE (*aside*): Hell and damnation! I'm undone, since Horner has seen her, and they know 'twas she.

18. For throwing dice.
19. A cheap seat in the theatre.

HORNER: But prithee, was it thy wife? She was exceedingly pretty; I was in love with her at that distance.

PINCHWIFE: You are like never to be nearer to her. Your servant, gentlemen.

(*Offers to go.*)

HORNER: Nay, prithee stay.

PINCHWIFE: I cannot, I will not.

HORNER: Come, you shall dine with us.

PINCHWIFE: I have dined already.

HORNER: Come, I know thou hast not. I'll treat thee, dear rogue; thou shalt spend none of thy Hampshire money today.

PINCHWIFE (*aside*): Treat me! So, he uses me already like his cuckold.

HORNER: Nay, you shall not go.

PINCHWIFE: I must, I have business at home.

(*Exit* PINCHWIFE.)

HARCOURT: To beat his wife; he's as jealous of her as a Cheapside husband of a Covent Garden wife.

HORNER: Why, 'tis as hard to find an old whoremaster without jealousy and the gout, as a young one without fear or the pox.

As gout in age from pox in youth proceeds,
So wenching past, then jealousy
 succeeds,
The worse disease that love and wenching
 breeds.

(*Exeunt.*)

ACT II

SCENE I PINCHWIFE'S HOUSE

MRS. MARGERY PINCHWIFE *and* ALITHEA.
MR. PINCHWIFE *peeping behind at the door.*

MRS. PINCHWIFE: Pray, sister, where are the best fields and woods to walk in, in London?

ALITHEA: A pretty question! Why, sister, Mulberry Garden and St. James's Park; and for close walks, the New Exchange.

MRS. PINCHWIFE: Pray, sister, tell me why my husband looks so grum here in town, and keeps me up so close, and will not let me go a-walking, nor let me wear my best gown yesterday.

ALITHEA: Oh, he's jealous, sister.

MRS. PINCHWIFE: Jealous? What's that?

ALITHEA: He's afraid you should love another man.

MRS. PINCHWIFE: How should he be afraid of my loving another man, when he will not let me see any but himself?

ALITHEA: Did he not carry you yesterday to a play?

MRS. PINCHWIFE: Ay, but we sat amongst ugly people; he would not let me come near the gentry, who sat under us, so that I could not see 'em. He told me none but naughty women sat there, whom they toused and moused. But I would have ventured for all that.

ALITHEA: But how did you like the play?

MRS. PINCHWIFE: Indeed, I was a-weary of the play, but I liked hugeously the actors; they are the goodliest, properest men, sister!

ALITHEA: Oh, but you must not like the actors, sister.

MRS. PINCHWIFE: Ay, how should I help it, sister? Pray, sister, when my husband comes in, will you ask leave for me to go a-walking?

ALITHEA (*aside*): A-walking! Ha, ha! Lord, a country gentlewoman's leisure is the drudgery of the foot-post; and she requires as much airing as her husband's horses.

(*Enter* MR. PINCHWIFE *to them.*)

But here comes your husband; I'll ask, though I'm sure he'll not grant it.

MRS. PINCHWIFE: He says he won't let me go abroad for fear of catching the pox.

ALITHEA: Fie! the smallpox you should say.

MRS. PINCHWIFE: O my dear, dear bud, welcome home! Why dost thou look so fropish? Who has nangered thee?

PINCHWIFE: You're a fool.

(MRS. PINCHWIFE *goes aside and cries.*)

ALITHEA: Faith, so she is, for crying for no fault, poor tender creature!

PINCHWIFE: What, you would have her as impudent as yourself, as arrant a jill-flirt, a gadder, a magpie, and to say all, a mere, notorious town-woman?

ALITHEA: Brother, you are my only censurer; and the honor of your family shall sooner suffer in your wife there than in me, though I take the innocent liberty of the town.

PINCHWIFE: Hark you, mistress, do not talk so before my wife. The innocent liberty of the town!

ALITHEA: Why, pray, who boasts of any intrigue with me? What lampoon has made my name notorious? What ill women frequent my lodgings? I keep no company with any women of scandalous reputations.

PINCHWIFE: No, you keep the men of scandalous reputations company.

ALITHEA: Where? Would you not have me civil? answer 'em in a box at the plays, in the drawing room at Whitehall, in St. James's park, Mulberry Garden, or—

PINCHWIFE: Hold, hold! Do not teach my wife where the men are to be found! I believe she's the worse for your town documents already. I bid you keep her in ignorance, as I do.

MRS. PINCHWIFE: Indeed, be not angry with her, bud; she will tell me nothing of the town, though I ask her a thousand times a day.

PINCHWIFE: Then you are very inquisitive to know, I find!

MRS. PINCHWIFE: Not I, indeed, dear; I hate London. Our place-house in the country is worth a thousand of't; would I were there again!

PINCHWIFE: So you shall, I warrant. But were you not talking of plays and players when I came in?—(*To* ALITHEA.) You are her encourager in such discourses.

MRS. PINCHWIFE: No, indeed, dear; she chid me just now for liking the playermen.

PINCHWIFE (*aside*): Nay, if she be so innocent as to own to me her liking them, there is no hurt in't.—Come, my poor rogue, but thou lik'st none better than me?

MRS. PINCHWIFE: Yes indeed, but I do; the playermen are finer folks.

PINCHWIFE: But you love none better than me?

MRS. PINCHWIFE: You are mine own dear bud, and I know you; I hate a stranger.

PINCHWIFE: Ay, my dear, you must love me only, and not be like the naughty town-women, who only hate their husbands and love every man else, love plays, visits, fine coaches, fine clothes, fiddles, balls, treats, and so lead a wicked town-life.

MRS. PINCHWIFE: Nay, if to enjoy all these things be a town-life, London is not so bad a place, dear.

PINCHWIFE: How! If you love me, you must hate London.

ALITHEA (*aside*): The fool has forbid me discovering to her the pleasures of the town, and he is now setting her agog upon them himself.

MRS. PINCHWIFE: But, husband, do the town-women love the playermen too?

PINCHWIFE: Yes, I warrant you.

MRS. PINCHWIFE: Ay, I warrant you.

PINCHWIFE: Why, you do not, I hope?

MRS. PINCHWIFE: No, no, bud; but why have we no playermen in the country?

PINCHWIFE: Ha!—Mrs. Minx, ask me no more to go to a play.

MRS. PINCHWIFE: Nay, why, love? I did not care for going; but when you forbid me, you make me, as 'twere, desire it.

ALITHEA (*aside*): So t'will be in other things, I warrant.

MRS. PINCHWIFE: Pray let me go to a play, dear.

PINCHWIFE: Hold your peace, I wo'not.

MRS. PINCHWIFE: Why, love?

PINCHWIFE: Why, I'll tell you.

ALITHEA (*aside*): Nay, if he tell her, she'll give him more cause to forbid her that place.

MRS. PINCHWIFE: Pray, why, dear?

PINCHWIFE: First, you like the actors, and the gallants may like you.

MRS. PINCHWIFE: What, a homely country girl? No, bud, nobody will like me.

PINCHWIFE: I tell you, yes, they may.

MRS. PINCHWIFE: No, no, you jest—I won't believe you, I will go.

PINCHWIFE: I tell you then that one of the lewdest fellows in town, who saw you there, told me he was in love with you.

MRS. PINCHWIFE: Indeed! Who, who pray who was't?

PINCHWIFE (*aside*): I've gone too far, and slipped before I was aware. How overjoyed she is!

MRS. PINCHWIFE: Was it any Hampshire gallant, any of our neighbors? I promise you, I am beholding to him.

PINCHWIFE: I promise you, you lie; for he would but ruin you, as he has done hundreds. He has no other love for women but that; such as he look upon women, like basilisks, but to destroy 'em.

MRS. PINCHWIFE: Ay, but if he loves me, why should he ruin me? Answer me to that. Methinks he should not; I would do him no harm.

ALITHEA: Ha, ha, ha!

PINCHWIFE: 'Tis very well; but I'll keep him from doing you any harm, or me either.
(*Enter* SPARKISH *and* HARCOURT.)
But here comes company; get you in, get you in.

MRS. PINCHWIFE: But pray, husband, is he a pretty gentleman that loves me?

PINCHWIFE: In, baggage, in. (*Thrusts her in; shuts the door.*)—(*Aside.*) What, all the lewd libertines of the town brought to my lodging by this easy coxcomb! 'Sdeath, I'll not suffer it.

SPARKISH: Here, Harcourt, do you approve my choice?—(*To* ALITHEA.) Dear little rogue, I told you I'd bring you acquainted with all my friends, the wits, and—
(HARCOURT *salutes her.*)

PINCHWIFE (*aside*): Ay, they shall know her, as well as you yourself will, I warrant you.

SPARKISH: This is one of those, my pretty rogue, that are to dance at your wedding tomorrow; and him you must bid welcome ever to what you and I have.

PINCHWIFE (*aside*): Monstrous!

SPARKISH: Harcourt, how dost thou like her, faith?— Nay, dear, do not look down; I should hate to have a wife of mine out of countenance at anything.

PINCHWIFE (*aside*): Wonderful!

SPARKISH: Tell me, I say, Harcourt, how dost thou like her? Thou hast stared upon her enough to resolve me.

HARCOURT: So infinitely well that I could wish I had a mistress too, that might differ from her in nothing but her love and engagement to you.

ALITHEA: Sir, Master Sparkish has often told me that his acquaintance were all wits and railleurs, and now I find it.

SPARKISH: No, by the universe, madam, he does not rally now; you may believe him. I do assure you, he is the honestest, worthiest, true-hearted gentleman—a man of such perfect honor, he would say nothing to a lady he does not mean.

PINCHWIFE (*aside*): Praising another man to his mistress!

HARCOURT: Sir, you are so beyond expectation obliging that—

SPARKISH: Nay, egad, I'm sure you do admire her extremely; I see't in your eyes.—He does admire you, madam.—By the world, don't you?

HARCOURT: Yes, above the world, or the most glorious part of it, her whole sex; and till now I never thought I should have envied you, or any man about to marry, but you have the best excuse for marriage I ever knew.

ALITHEA: Nay, now, sir, I'm satisfied you are of the society of the wits and railleurs, since you cannot spare your friend, even when he is but too civil to you; but the surest sign is, since you are an enemy to marriage, for that, I hear, you hate as much as business or bad wine.

HARCOURT: Truly, madam, I never was an enemy to marriage till now, because marriage was never an enemy to me before.

ALITHEA: But why, sir, is marriage an enemy to you now? Because it robs you of your friend here? For you look upon a friend married as one gone into a monastery, that is, dead to the world.

HARCOURT: 'Tis indeed because you marry him; I see, madam, you can guess my meaning. I do confess heartily and openly, I wish it were in my power to break the match; by heavens I would.

SPARKISH: Poor Frank!

ALITHEA: Would you be so unkind to me?

HARCOURT: No, no, 'tis not because I would be unkind to you.

SPARKISH: Poor Frank! No, gad, 'tis only his kindness to me.

PINCHWIFE (*aside*): Great kindness to you indeed! Insensible fop, let a man make love to his wife to his face!

SPARKISH: Come, dear Frank, for all my wife there that shall be, thou shalt enjoy me sometimes, dear rogue. By my honor, we men of wit condole for our deceased brother in marriage as much as for one dead in earnest. I think that was prettily said of me, ha, Harcourt? But come, Frank, be not melancholy for me.

HARCOURT: No, I assure you I am not melancholy for you.

SPARKISH: Prithee, Frank, dost think my wife that shall be there a fine person?

HARCOURT: I could gaze upon her till I became as blind as you are.

SPARKISH: How, as I am? How?

HARCOURT: Because you are a lover, and true lovers are blind, stock blind.

SPARKISH: True, true; but by the world, she has wit too, as well as beauty. Go, go with her into a corner, and try if she has wit; talk to her anything; she's bashful before me.

HARCOURT: Indeed, if a woman wants wit in a corner, she has it nowhere.

ALITHEA: (*aside to* SPARKISH): Sir, you dispose of me a little before your time—

SPARKISH: Nay, nay, madam, let me have an earnest of your obedience, or—go, go, madam—
(HARCOURT *courts* ALITHEA *aside*.)

PINCHWIFE: How, sir! If you are not concerned for the honor of a wife, I am for that of a sister; he shall not debauch her. Be a pander to your own wife, bring men to her, let 'em make love before your face, thrust 'em into a corner together, then leave 'em in private! Is this your own town wit and conduct?

SPARKISH: Ha, ha, ha! A silly wise rogue would make one laugh more than a stark fool, ha, ha! I shall burst. Nay, you shall not disturb 'em; I'll vex thee, by the world.
(*Struggles with* PINCHWIFE *to keep him from* HARCOURT *and* ALITHEA.)

ALITHEA: The writings are drawn, sir, settlements made: 'tis too late, sir, and past all revocation.

HARCOURT: Then so is my death.

ALITHEA: I would not be unjust to him.

HARCOURT: Then why to me so?

ALITHEA: I have no obligation to you.

HARCOURT: My love.

ALITHEA: I had his before.

HARCOURT: You never had it; he wants, you see, jealousy, the only infallible sign of it.

ALITHEA: Love proceeds from esteem; he cannot distrust my virtue; besides, he loves me, or he would not marry me.

HARCOURT: Marrying you is no more sign of his love than bribing your woman, that he may marry you, is a sign of his generosity. Marriage is rather a sign of interest than love; and he that marries a fortune covets a mistress, not loves her. But if you take marriage for a sign of love, take it from me immediately.

ALITHEA: No, now you have put a scruple in my head; but, in short, sir, to end our dispute, I must marry him, my reputation would suffer in the world else.

HARCOURT: No, if you do marry him, with your pardon, madam, your reputation suffers in the world, and you would be thought in necessity for a cloak.

ALITHEA: Nay, now you are rude, sir.—Mr. Sparkish, pray come hither, your friend here is very troublesome, and very loving.

HARCOURT (*aside to* ALITHEA): Hold, hold!—

PINCHWIFE: D'ye hear that?

SPARKISH: Why, d'ye think I'll seem to be jealous, like a country bumpkin?

PINCHWIFE: No, rather be a cuckold, like a credulous cit.[20]

HARCOURT: Madam, you would not have been so little generous as to have told him.

ALITHEA: Yes, since you could be so little generous as to wrong him.

HARCOURT: Wrong him! No man can do't, he's beneath an injury, a bubble, a coward, a senseless idiot, a wretch so contemptible to all the world but you that—

ALITHEA: Hold, do not rail at him, for since he is like to be my husband, I am resolved to like him. Nay, I think I am obliged to tell him you are not his friend.—Master Sparkish, Master Sparkish!

SPARKISH: What, what?—Now, dear rogue, has not she wit?

HARCOURT (*speaks surlily*): Not so much as I thought, and hoped she had.

ALITHEA: Mr. Sparkish, do you bring people to rail at you?

HARCOURT: Madam—

SPARKISH: How! No, but if he does rail at me, 'tis but in jest. I warrant; what we wits do for one another, and never take any notice of it.

ALITHEA: He spoke so scurrilously of you, I had no patience to hear him; besides, he has been making love to me.

HARCOURT (*aside*): True, damned, telltale woman!

SPARKISH: Pshaw! to show his parts—we wits rail and make love often but to show our parts; as we have no affections, so we have no malice; we—

---

20. Citizen of a town.

ALITHEA: He said you were a wretch, below an injury.

SPARKISH: Pshaw!

HARCOURT (*aside*): Damned, senseless, impudent, virtuous jade! Well, since she won't let me have her, she'll do as good, she'll make me hate her.

ALITHEA: A common bubble.

SPARKISH: Pshaw!

ALITHEA: A coward!

SPARKISH: Pshaw, pshaw!

ALITHEA: A senseless, driveling idiot.

SPARKISH: How! Did he disparage my parts? Nay, then my honor's concerned; I can't put up that, sir, by the world. Brother, help me to kill him.—(*Aside.*) I may draw[21] now, since we have the odds of him. 'Tis a good occasion, too, before my mistress—

(*Offers to draw.*)

ALITHEA: Hold, hold!

SPARKISH: What, what?

ALITHEA (*aside*): I must not let 'em kill the gentleman neither, for his kindness to me; I am so far from hating him that I wish my gallant had his person and understanding. Nay, if my honor—

SPARKISH: I'll be thy death.

ALITHEA: Hold, hold! Indeed, to tell the truth, the gentleman said after all that what he spoke was but out of friendship to you.

SPARKISH: How! Say I am—I am a fool, that is, no wit, out of friendship to me?

ALITHEA: Yes, to try whether I was concerned enough for you, and made love to me only to be satisfied of my virtue, for your sake.

HARCOURT (*aside*): Kind, however—

SPARKISH: Nay, if it were so, my dear rogue, I ask thee pardon; but why would not you tell me so, faith?

HARCOURT: Because I did not think on't, faith.

SPARKISH: Come, Horner does not come; Harcourt, let's be gone to the new play.—Come, madam.

ALITHEA: I will not go if you intend to leave me alone in the box and run into the pit, as you use to do.

SPARKISH: Pshaw! I'll leave Harcourt with you in the box to entertain you, and that's as good; if I sat in the box, I should be thought no judge, but of trimmings.—Come away, Harcourt, lead her down.

(*Exeunt* SPARKISH, HARCOURT, *and* ALITHEA.)

PINCHWIFE: Well, go thy ways, for the flower of the true town fops, such as spend their estates before they come to 'em, and are cuckolds before they're married. But let me go look to my own freehold.—How!—

(*Enter* MY LADY FIDGET, MRS. DAINTY FIDGET, *and* MRS. SQUEAMISH.)

LADY FIDGET: Your servant, sir; where is your lady? We are come to wait upon her to the new play.

PINCHWIFE: New play!

LADY FIDGET: And my husband will wait upon you presently.

PINCHWIFE (*aside*): Damn your civility.—Madam, by no means; I will not see Sir Jasper here till I have waited upon him at home; nor shall my wife see you till she has waited upon your ladyship at your lodgings.

LADY FIDGET: Now we are here, sir—

PINCHWIFE: No, madam.

MRS. DAINTY FIDGET: Pray, let us see her.

MRS. SQUEAMISH: We will not stir till we see her.

PINCHWIFE (*aside*): A pox on you all! (*Goes to the door, and returns.*)—She has locked the door, and is gone abroad.

LADY FIDGET: No, you have locked the door, and she's within.

MRS. DAINTY FIDGET: They told us below she was here.

PINCHWIFE (*aside*): Will nothing do?—Well, it must out then. To tell you the truth, ladies, which I was afraid to let you know before, lest it might endanger your lives, my wife has just now the smallpox come out upon her. Do not be frightened; but pray, be gone, ladies; you shall not stay here in danger of your lives; pray get you gone, ladies.

LADY FIDGET: No, no, we have all had 'em.

MRS. SQUEAMISH: Alack, alack!

MRS. DAINTY FIDGET: Come, come, we must see how it goes with her; I understand the disease.

LADY FIDGET: Come.

PINCHWIFE (*aside*): Well, there is no being too hard for women at their own weapon, lying; therefore I'll quit the field.

(*Exit* PINCHWIFE.)

---

21. Draw a sword.

MRS. SQUEAMISH: Here's an example of jealousy.

LADY FIDGET: Indeed, as the world goes, I wonder there are no more jealous, since wives are so neglected.

MRS. DAINTY FIDGET: Pshaw! as the world goes, to what end should they be jealous?

LADY FIDGET: Foh! 'tis a nasty world.

MRS. SQUEAMISH: That men of parts, great acquaintance, and quality should take up with and spend themselves and fortunes in keeping little playhouse creatures, foh!

LADY FIDGET: Nay, that women of understanding, great acquaintance, and good quality should fall a-keeping too of little creatures, foh!

MRS. SQUEAMISH: Why, it's the men of quality's fault; they never visit women of honor and reputation, as they used to do; and have not so much as common civility for ladies of our rank, but use us with the same indifferency and ill-breeding as if we were all married to 'em.

LADY FIDGET: She says true; 'tis an arrant shame women of quality should be so slighted. Methinks birth—birth should go for something; I have known men admired, courted, and followed for their titles only.

MRS. SQUEAMISH: Ay, one would think men of honor should not love, no more than marry, out of their own rank.

MRS. DAINTY FIDGET: Fie, fie upon 'em! They are come to think crossbreeding for themselves best, as well as for their dogs and horses.

LADY FIDGET: They are dogs and horses for't.

MRS. SQUEAMISH: One would think, if not for love, for vanity a little.

MRS. DAINTY FIDGET: Nay, they do satisfy their vanity upon us sometimes; and are kind to us in their report, tell all the world they lie with us.

LADY FIDGET: Damned rascals! That we should be only wronged by 'em; to report a man has had a person, when he has not had a person, is the greatest wrong in the whole world that can be done to a person.

MRS. SQUEAMISH: Well, 'tis an arrant shame noble persons should be so wronged and neglected.

LADY FIDGET: But still 'tis an arranter shame for a noble person to neglect her own honor, and defame her own noble person with little inconsiderable fellows, foh!

MRS. DAINTY FIDGET: I suppose the crime against our honor is the same with a man of quality as with another.

LADY FIDGET: How! No, sure, the man of quality is likest one's husband, and therefore the fault should be the less.

MRS. DAINTY FIDGET: But then the pleasure should be the less.

LADY FIDGET: Fie, fie, fie, for shame, sister! Whither shall we ramble? Be continent in your discourse, or I shall hate you.

MRS. DAINTY FIDGET: Besides, an intrigue is so much the more notorious for the man's quality.

MRS. SQUEAMISH: 'Tis true, nobody takes notice of a private man, and therefore with him 'tis more secret, and the crime's the less when 'tis not known.

LADY FIDGET: You say true; I'faith, I think you are in the right on't. 'Tis not an injury to a husband till it be an injury to our honors; so that a woman of honor loses no honor with a private person; and to say truth—

MRS. DAINTY FIDGET (*apart to* MRS. SQUEAMISH): So, the little fellow is grown a private person—with her—

LADY FIDGET: But still my dear, dear honor.

(*Enter* SIR JASPER, HORNER, DORILANT.)

SIR JASPER FIDGET: Ay, my dear, dear of honor, thou hast still so much honor in thy mouth—

HORNER (*aside*): That she has none elsewhere.

LADY FIDGET: Oh, what d'ye mean to bring in these upon us?

MRS. DAINTY FIDGET: Foh! these are as bad as wits.

MRS. SQUEAMISH: Foh!

LADY FIDGET: Let us leave the room.

SIR JASPER FIDGET: Stay, stay; faith, to tell you the naked truth—

LADY FIDGET: Fie, Sir Jasper! Do not use that word "naked."

SIR JASPER FIDGET: Well, well, in short, I have business at Whitehall, and cannot go to the play with you, therefore would have you go—

LADY FIDGET: With those two to a play?

SIR JASPER FIDGET: No, not with t'other but with Mr. Horner; there can be no more scandal to go with him than with Mr. Tattle, or Master Limberham.

LADY FIDGET: With that nasty fellow! No—no!

SIR JASPER FIDGET: Nay, prithee, dear, hear me.
   (*Whispers to* LADY FIDGET.)

HORNER: Ladies—
   (HORNER, DORILANT *drawing near* MRS. SQUEAMISH
   and MRS. DAINTY.)

MRS. DAINTY FIDGET: Stand off.

MRS. SQUEAMISH: Do not approach us.

MRS. DAINTY FIDGET: You herd with the wits, you
   are obscenity all over.

MRS. SQUEAMISH: And I would as soon look upon a
   picture of Adam and Eve, without fig leaves,
   as any of you, if I could help it; therefore keep
   off, and do not make us sick.

DORILANT: What a devil are these?

HORNER: Why, these are pretenders to honor, as
   critics to wit, only by censuring others; and as
   every raw, peevish, out-of-humored, affected,
   dull, tea-drinking arithmetical fop sets up for
   a wit by railing at men of sense, so these for
   honor by railing at the Court, and ladies of as
   great honor as quality.

SIR JASPER FIDGET: Come, Mr. Horner, I must desire
   you to go with these ladies to the play, sir.

HORNER: I, sir!

SIR JASPER FIDGET: Ay, ay, come, sir.

HORNER: I must beg your pardon, sir, and theirs; I
   will not be seen in women's company in public again for the world.

SIR JASPER FIDGET: Ha, ha! strange aversion!

MRS. SQUEAMISH: No, he's for women's company
   in private.

SIR JASPER FIDGET: He—poor man—he! Ha, ha, ha!

MRS. DAINTY FIDGET: 'Tis a greater shame amongst
   lewd fellows to be seen in virtuous women's
   company than for the women to be seen with
   them.

HORNER: Indeed, madam, the time was I only hated
   virtuous women, but now I hate the other too;
   I beg your pardon, ladies.

LADY FIDGET: You are very obliging, sir, because we
   would not be troubled with you.

SIR JASPER FIDGET: In sober sadness, he shall go.

DORILANT: Nay, if he wo'not, I am ready to wait upon
   the ladies; and I think I am the fitter man.

SIR JASPER FIDGET: You, sir, no, I thank you for
   that—Master Horner is a privileged man
   amongst the virtuous ladies; 'twill be a great
   while before you are so, he, he, he! He's my

wife's gallant, he, he, he! No, pray withdraw,
   sir, for as I take it, the virtuous ladies have no
   business with you.

DORILANT: And I am sure he can have none with them.
   'Tis strange a man can't come amongst virtuous
   women now but upon the same terms as men
   are admitted into the Great Turk's seraglio; but
   heavens keep me from being an ombre[22] player
   with 'em! But where is Pinchwife?
   (*Exit* DORILANT.)

SIR JASPER FIDGET: Come, come, man; what, avoid
   the sweet society of womankind? that sweet,
   soft, gentle, tame, noble creature, woman,
   made for man's companion—

HORNER: So is that soft, gentle, tame and more noble
   creature a spaniel, and has all their tricks—can
   fawn, lie down, suffer beatings, and fawn the
   more; barks at your friends when they come
   to see you; makes your bed hard; gives you
   fleas, and the mange sometimes. And all the
   difference is, the spaniel's the more faithful
   animal, and fawns but upon one master.

SIR JASPER FIDGET: He, he, he!

MRS. SQUEAMISH: Oh, the rude beast!

MRS. DAINTY FIDGET: Insolent brute!

LADY FIDGET: Brute! Stinking, mortified, rotten
   French wether,[23] to dare—

SIR JASPER FIDGET: Hold, an't please your ladyship.—For shame, Master Horner, your mother
   was a woman.—(*Aside.*) Now shall I never reconcile 'em.—(*Aside to* LADY FIDGET.) Hark you,
   madam, take my advice in your anger. You
   know you often want one to make up your
   drolling pack of ombre players; and you may
   cheat him easily, for he's an ill gamester, and
   consequently loves play. Besides, you know,
   you have but two old civil gentlemen, with
   stinking breaths too, to wait upon you abroad;
   take in the third into your service. The other
   are but crazy; and a lady should have a super-
   numerary gentleman-usher, as a supernumer-
   ary coach-horse, lest sometimes you should
   be forced to stay at home.

LADY FIDGET: But are you sure he loves play, and
   has money?

22. Card game
23. A ram incapable of reproduction.

SIR JASPER FIDGET: He loves play as much as you, and has money as much as I.

LADY FIDGET: Then I am contented to make him pay for his scurrility; money makes up in a measure all other wants in men.—(*Aside.*) Those whom we cannot make hold for gallants, we make fine.

SIR JASPER FIDGET (*aside*): So, so; now to mollify, to wheedle him.—Master Horner, will you never keep civil company? Methinks 'tis time now, since you are only fit for them. Come, come, man, you must e'en fall to visiting our wives, eating at our tables, drinking tea with our virtuous relations after dinner, dealing cards to 'em, reading plays and gazettes to 'em, picking fleas out of their shocks[24] for 'em, collecting receipts, new songs, women, pages and footmen for 'em.

HORNER: I hope they'll afford me better employment, sir.

SIR JASPER FIDGET: He, he he! 'Tis fit you know your work before you come into your place; and since you are unprovided of a lady to flatter and a good house to eat at, pray frequent mine, and call my wife mistress, and she shall call you gallant, according to the custom.

HORNER: Who, I?

SIR JASPER FIDGET: Faith, thou shalt for my sake; come, for my sake only.

HORNER: For your sake—

SIR JASPER FIDGET (*to* LADY FIDGET): Come, come here's a gamester for you; let him be a little familiar sometimes; nay, what if a little rude? Gamesters may be rude with ladies, you know.

LADY FIDGET: Yes, losing gamesters have a privilege with women.

HORNER: I always thought the contrary, that the winning gamester had lost privilege with women; for when you have lost your money to a man, you'll lose anything you have, all you have, they say, and he may use you as he pleases.

SIR JASPER FIDGET: He, he, he! Well, win or lose, you shall have your liberty with her.

LADY FIDGET: As he behaves himself; and for your sake I'll give him admittance and freedom.

24. Hair.

HORNER: All sorts of freedom, madam?

SIR JASPER FIDGET: Ay, ay, ay, all sorts of freedom thou canst take and so go to her, begin thy new employment; wheedle her, jest with her, and be better acquainted one with another.

HORNER (*aside*): I think I know her already, therefore may venture with her, my secret for hers. (HORNER *and* LADY FIDGET *whisper.*)

SIR JASPER FIDGET: Sister, cuz, I have provided an innocent playfellow for you there.

MRS. DAINTY FIDGET: Who, he!

MRS. SQUEAMISH: There's a playfellow indeed!

SIR JASPER FIDGET: Yes, sure; what, he is good enough to play at cards, blindman's buff, or the fool with sometimes.

MRS. SQUEAMISH: Foh! we'll have no such playfellows.

MRS. DAINTY FIDGET: No, sir, you shan't choose playfellows for us, we thank you.

SIR JASPER FIDGET: Nay, pray hear me. (*Whispering to them.*)

LADY FIDGET (*aside to* HORNER): But, poor gentleman, could you be so generous, so truly a man of honor, as for the sakes of us women of honor, to cause yourself to be reported no man? No man! And to suffer yourself the greatest shame that could fall upon a man, that none might fall upon us women by your conversation? Bud indeed, sir, as perfectly, perfectly, the same man as before your going into France, sir? As perfectly, perfectly, sir?

HORNER: As perfectly, perfectly, madam. Nay, I scorn you should take my word; I desire to be tried only, madam.

LADY FIDGET: Well, that's spoken again like a man of honor; all men of honor desire to come to the test. But, indeed, generally you men report such things of yourselves, one does not know how or whom to believe; and it is come to that pass we dare not take your words, no more than your tailor's, without some staid servant of yours be bound with you. But I have so strong a faith in your honor, dear, dear, noble sir, that I'd forfeit mine for yours at any time, dear sir.

HORNER: No, madam, you should not need to forfeit it for me; I have given you security already to save you harmless, my late reputation being so well known in the world, madam.

LADY FIDGET: But if upon any future falling out, or upon a suspicion of my taking the trust out of your hands, to employ some other, you yourself should betray your trust, dear sir? I mean, if you'll give me leave to speak obscenely, you might tell, dear sir.

HORNER: If I did, nobody would believe me; the reputation of impotency is as hardly recovered again in the world as that of cowardice, dear madam.

LADY FIDGET: Nay then, as one may say, you may do your worst, dear, dear sir.

SIR JASPER FIDGET: Come, is your ladyship reconciled to him yet? Have you agreed on matters? For I must be gone to Whitehall.

LADY FIDGET: Why, indeed, Sir Jasper, Master Horner is a thousand, thousand times a better man than I thought him. Cousin Squeamish, Sister Dainty, I can name him now; truly, not long ago, you know, I thought his very name obscenity, and I would as soon have lain with him as have named him.

SIR JASPER FIDGET: Very likely, poor madam.

MRS. DAINTY FIDGET: I believe it.

MRS. SQUEAMISH: No doubt on't.

SIR JASPER FIDGET: Well, well—that your ladyship is as virtuous as any she, I know, and him all the town knows—he, he, he! Therefore, now you like him, get you gone to your business together; go, go to your business, I say, pleasure, whilst I go to my pleasure, business.

LADY FIDGET: Come, then, dear gallant.

HORNER: Come away, my dearest mistress.

SIR JASPER FIDGET: So, so; why 'tis as I'd have it.

(*Exit* SIR JASPER.)

HORNER: And as I'd have it.

LADY FIDGET: Who for his business from his wife will run,
    Takes the best care to have her business done.

(*Exeunt omnes.*)

ACT III

SCENE I PINCHWIFE'S HOUSE

ALITHEA *and* MRS. PINCHWIFE.

ALITHEA: Sister, what ails you? You are grown melancholy.

MRS. PINCHWIFE: Would it not make anyone melancholy, to see you go every day fluttering about abroad, whilst I must stay at home like a poor, lonely, sullen bird in a cage?

ALITHEA: Ay, sister, but you came young and just from the nest to your cage, so that I thought you liked it, and could be as cheerful in't as others that took their flight themselves early, and are hopping abroad in the open air.

MRS. PINCHWIFE: Nay, I confess I was quiet enough till my husband told me what pure lives the London ladies live abroad, with their dancing, meetings, and junketings, and dressed every day in their best gowns; and I warrant you, play at ninepins every day of the week, so they do.

(*Enter* MR. PINCHWIFE.)

PINCHWIFE: Come, what's here to do? You are putting the town pleasures in her head, and setting her a-longing.

ALITHEA: Yes, after ninepins; you suffer none to give her those longings, you mean, but yourself.

PINCHWIFE: I tell her of the vanities of the town like a confessor.

ALITHEA: A confessor! Just such a confessor as he that, by forbidding a silly ostler to grease the horse's teeth, taught him to do't.

PINCHWIFE: Come, Mistress Flippant, good precepts are lost when bad examples are still before us; the liberty you take abroad makes her hanker after it, and out of humour at home. Poor wretch! she desired not to come to London; I would bring her.

ALITHEA: Very well.

PINCHWIFE: She has been this week in town, and never desired, till this afternoon, to go abroad.

ALITHEA: Was she not at a play yesterday?

PINCHWIFE: Yes, but she ne'er asked me; I was myself the cause of her going.

ALITHEA: Then, if she ask you again, you are the cause of her asking, and not my example.

PINCHWIFE: Well, tomorrow night I shall be rid of you; and the next day, before 'tis light, she and I'll be rid of the town, and my dreadful apprehensions.—(*To* MRS. PINCHWIFE.) Come, be not melancholy, for thou shalt go into the country after tomorrow, dearest.

ALITHEA: Great comfort!

MRS. PINCHWIFE: Pish! what d'ye tell me of the country for?

PINCHWIFE: How's this! What, pish at the country?

MRS. PINCHWIFE: Let me alone, I am not well.

PINCHWIFE: Oh, if that be all—what ails my dearest?

MRS. PINCHWIFE: Truly, I don't know; but I have not been well since you told me there was a gallant at the play in love with me.

PINCHWIFE: Ha!—

ALITHEA: That's by my example, too!

PINCHWIFE: Nay, if you are not well, but are so concerned because a lewd fellow chanced to lie, and say he liked you, you'll make me sick too.

MRS. PINCHWIFE: Of what sickness?

PINCHWIFE: Oh, of that which is worse than the plague, jealousy.

MRS. PINCHWIFE: Pish, you jeer! I'm sure there's no such disease in our receipt-book at home.

PINCHWIFE: No, thou never met'st with it, poor innocent.—(*Aside.*) Well, if thou cuckold me, 'twill be my own fault—for cuckolds and bastards are generally makers of their own fortune.

MRS. PINCHWIFE: Well, but pray, bud, let's go to a play tonight.

PINCHWIFE: 'Tis just done, she comes from it. But why are you so eager to see a play?

MRS. PINCHWIFE: Faith, dear, not that I care one pin for their talk there; but I like to look upon the playermen, and would see, if I could, the gallant you say loves me; that's all, dear bud.

PINCHWIFE: Is that all, dear bud?

ALITHEA: This proceeds from my example.

MRS. PINCHWIFE: But if the play be done, let's go abroad, however, dear bud.

PINCHWIFE: Come, have a little patience, and thou shalt go into the country on Friday.

MRS. PINCHWIFE: Therefore I would see first some sights, to tell my neighbors of. Nay, I will go abroad, that's once.

ALITHEA: I'm the cause of this desire too.

PINCHWIFE: But now I think on't, who was the cause of Horner's coming to my lodging today? That was you.

ALITHEA: No, you, because you would not let him see your handsome wife out of your lodging.

MRS. PINCHWIFE: Why, O Lord! Did the gentleman come hither to see me indeed?

PINCHWIFE: No, no.—You are not the cause of that damned question too, Mistress Alithea?—(*Aside.*) Well, she's in the right of it. He is in love with my wife—and comes after her—'tis so—but I'll nip his love in the bud; lest he should follow us into the country, and break his chariot-wheel near our house on purpose for an excuse to come to't. But I think I know the town.

MRS. PINCHWIFE: Come, pray, bud, let's go abroad before 'tis late; for I will go, that's flat and plain.

PINCHWIFE (*aside*): So! The obstinacy already of a town-wife, and I must, whilst she's here, humour her like one.—Sister, how shall we do, that she may not be seen or known?

ALITHEA: Let her put on her mask.

PINCHWIFE: Pshaw! A mask makes people but the more inquisitive, and is as ridiculous a disguise as a stage-beard; her shape, stature, habit will be known. And if we should meet with Horner, he would be sure to take acquaintance with us, must wish her joy, kiss her, talk to her, leer upon her, and the devil and all. No, I'll not use her to a mask, 'tis dangerous; for masks have made more cuckolds than the best faces that ever were known.

ALITHEA: How will you do then?

MRS. PINCHWIFE: Nay, shall we go? The Exchange will be shut, and I have a mind to see that.

PINCHWIFE: So—I have it—I'll dress her up in the suit we are to carry down to her brother, little sir James; nay, I understand the town tricks. Come, let's go dress her. A mask! No—a woman masked, like a covered dish, gives a man curiosity and appetite, when, it may be, uncovered, 'twould turn his stomach; no, no.

ALITHEA: Indeed your comparison is something a greasy one. But I had a gentle gallant used to say, "A beauty masked, like the sun in eclipse, gather together more gazers than if it shined out." (*Exeunt.*)

SCENE II

The scene changes to the New Exchange.[25]
Enter HORNER, HARCOURT, DORILANT.

DORILANT: Engaged to women, and not sup with us?

HORNER: Ay, a pox on 'em all!

25. A fashionable shopping area.

HARCOURT: You were much a more reasonable man in the morning, and had as noble resolutions against 'em as a widower of a week's liberty.

DORILANT: Did I ever think to see you keep company with women in vain?

HORNER: In vain! No—'tis, since I can't love 'em, to be revenged on 'em.

HARCOURT: Now your sting is gone, you looked in the box, amongst all those women, like a drone in the hive, all upon you. Shoved and ill-used by 'em all, and thrust from one side to t'other.

DORILANT: Yet he must be buzzing amongst 'em still, like other old beetle-headed, liquorish drones. Avoid 'em, and hate 'em as they hate you.

HORNER: Because I do hate 'em, and would hate 'em yet more, I'll frequent 'em; you may see by marriage, nothing makes a man hate a woman more than her constant conversation. In short, I converse with 'em, as you do with rich fools, to laugh at 'em and use 'em ill.

DORILANT: But I would no more sup with women, unless I could lie with 'em, than sup with a rich coxcomb, unless I could cheat him.

HORNER: Yes, I have known thee sup with a fool for his drinking; if he could set out your hand that way only, you were satisfied, and if he were a wine-swallowing mouth 'twas enough.

HARCOURT: Yes, a man drinks often with a fool, as he tosses with a marker, only to keep his hand in ure.[26] But do the ladies drink?

HORNER: Yes, sir, and I shall have the pleasure at least of laying 'em flat with a bottle, and bring as much scandal that way upon 'em as formerly t'other.

HARCOURT: Perhaps you may prove as weak a brother amongst 'em that way as t'other.

DORILANT: Foh! drinking with women is as unnatural as scolding with 'em; but 'tis a pleasure of decayed fornicators, and the basest way of quenching love.

HARCOURT: Nay, 'tis drowning love instead of quenching it. But leave us for civil women too!

DORILANT: Ay, when he can't be the better for 'em. We hardly pardon a man that leaves his friend for a wench, and that's a pretty lawful call.

HORNER: Faith, I would not leave you for 'em, if they would not drink.

DORILANT: Who would disappoint his company at Lewis's for a gossiping?

HARCOURT: Foh! Wine and women, good apart, together as nauseous as sack and sugar. But hark you, sir, before you go, a little of your advice; an old maimed general, when unfit for action, is fittest for counsel. I have other designs upon women than eating and drinking with them. I am in love with Sparkish's mistress, whom he is to marry tomorrow. Now how shall I get her? (*Enter* SPARKISH, *looking about.*)

HORNER: Why, here comes one will help you to her.

HARCOURT: He! He, I tell you is my rival, and will hinder my love.

HORNER: No, a foolish rival and a jealous husband assist their rival's designs; for they are sure to make their women hate them, which is the first step to their love for another man.

HARCOURT: But I cannot come near his mistress but in his company.

HORNER: Still the better for you, for fools are most easily cheated when they themselves are accessories; and he is to be bubbled of his mistress, as of his money, the common mistress, by keeping him company.

SPARKISH: Who is that, that is to be bubbled? Faith, let me snack,[27] I haven't met with a bubble since Christmas. Gad, I think bubbles are like their brother woodcocks, go out with cold weather.

HARCOURT (*apart to* HORNER): A pox! he did not hear all I hope.

SPARKISH: Come, you bubbling rogues you, where do we sup?—Oh, Harcourt, my mistress tells me you have been making fierce love to her all the play long, ha ha! But I—

HARCOURT: I make love to her?

SPARKISH: Nay, I forgive thee; for I think I know thee, and I know her, but I am sure I know myself.

HARCOURT: Did she tell you so? I see all women are like these of the Exchange, who, to enhance the price of their commodities, report to their fond customers offers which were never made 'em.

HORNER: Ay, women are as apt to tell before the intrigue as men after it, and so show them-

---

26. References to gaming.

27. Let me in on the joke.

selves the vainer sex. But hast thou a mistress, Sparkish? 'Tis as hard for me to believe it as that thou ever hadst a bubble, as you bragged just now.

SPARKISH: Oh, your servant, sir; are you at your raillery, sir? But we were some of us beforehand with you today at the play. The wits were something bold with you, sir; did you not hear us laugh?

HORNER: Yes, but I thought you had gone to the plays to laugh at the poet's wit, not at your own.

SPARKISH: Your servant, sir; no, I thank you. Gad, I go to a play as to a country treat; I carry my own wine to one, and my own wit to t'other, or else I'm sure I should not be merry at either. And the reason why we are so often louder than the players is because we think we speak more wit, and so become the poet's rivals in his audience. For to tell you the truth, we hate the silly rogues; nay, so much that we find fault even with their bawdy upon the stage, whilst we talk nothing else in the pit as loud.

HORNER: But why shouldst thou hate the silly poets? Thou hast too much wit to be one, and they, like whores, are only hated by each other; and thou dost scorn writing, I'm sure.

SPARKISH: Yes I'd have you to know I scorn writing; but women, women, that make men do all foolish things, make 'em write songs too; everybody does it. 'Tis even as common with lovers as playing with fans; and you can do no more help rhyming to your Phyllis than drinking to your Phyllis.

HARCOURT: Nay, poetry in love is no more to be avoided than jealousy.

DORILANT: But the poets damned your songs, did they?

SPARKISH: Damn the poets! They turned 'em into burlesque, as they call it. That burlesque is a hocus-pocus trick they have got, which by the virtue of *hictius doctius, topsy-turvy,* they make a wise and witty man in the world a fool upon the stage, you know not how; and 'tis therefore I hate 'em too, for I know not but it may be my own case; for they'll put a man into a play for looking asquint. Their predecessors were contented to make serving-men only

their stage-fools, but these rogues must have gentlemen, with a pox to 'em, nay, knights. And indeed, you shall hardly see a fool upon the stage, but he's a knight; and to tell you the truth, they have kept me these six years from being a knight in earnest, for fear of being knighted in a play, and dubbed a fool.

DORILANT: Blame 'em not; they must follow their copy, the age.

HARCOURT: But why shouldst thou be afraid of being in a play, who expose yourself every day in the playhouses, and at public places?

HORNER: 'Tis but being on the stage, instead of standing on a bench in the pit.

DORILANT: Don't you give money to painters to draw you like? And are you afraid of your pictures at length in a playhouse, where all your mistresses may see you?

SPARKISH: A pox! Painters don't draw the smallpox or pimples in one's face. Come, damn all your silly authors whatever, all books and booksellers, by the world, and all readers, courteous or uncourteous.

HARCOURT: But who comes here, Sparkish?
(*Enter* MR. PINCHWIFE, *and his wife in man's clothes,* ALITHEA, LUCY *her maid.*)

SPARKISH: Oh, hide me! There's my mistress too.
(SPARKISH *hides himself behind* HARCOURT.)

HARCOURT: She sees you.

SPARKISH: But I will not see her. 'Tis time to go to Whitehall, and I must not fail the drawing room.

HARCOURT: Pray, first carry me, and reconcile me to her.

SPARKISH: Another time; faith, the King will have supped.

HARCOURT: Not with the worse stomach for thy absence; thou art one of those fools that think their attendance at the King's meals as necessary as his physicians', when you are more troublesome to him than his doctors, or his dogs.

SPARKISH: Pshaw! I know my interest, sir; prithee, hide me.

HORNER: Your servant, Pinchwife.—What, he knows us not!

PINCHWIFE (*to his wife aside*): Come along.

MRS. PINCHWIFE (*to a* BOOKSELLER): Pray, have you any ballads? Give me sixpenny worth.

BOOKSELLER: We have no ballads.

MRS. PINCHWIFE: Then give me *Covent Garden Drollery*, and a play or two—Oh, here's *Tarugo's Wiles*, and *The Slighted Maiden*, I'll have them.

PINCHWIFE (*apart to her*): No, plays are not for your reading. Come along; will you discover yourself?

HORNER: Who is that pretty youth with him, Sparkish?

SPARKISH: I believe his wife's brother, because he's something like her; but I never saw her but once.

HORNER: Extremely handsome; I have seen a face like it too. Let us follow 'em.

(*Exeunt* PINCHWIFE, MRS. PINCHWIFE, ALITHEA, LUCY, HORNER, DORILANT, *following them.*)

HARCOURT: Come, Sparkish, your mistress saw you, and will be angry you go not to her. Besides, I would fain be reconciled to her, which none but you can do, dear friend.

SPARKISH: Well, that's a better reason, dear friend. I would not go near her now, for hers or my own sake, but I can deny you nothing; for though I have known thee a great while, never go, if I do not love thee as well as a new acquaintance.

HARCOURT: I am obliged to you indeed, dear friend. I would be well with her, only to be well with thee still; for these ties to wives usually dissolve all ties to friends. I would be contented she should enjoy you a-night, but I would have you to myself a-days, as I have had, dear friend.

SPARKISH: And thou shalt enjoy me a-days, dear, dear friend, never stir; and I'll be divorced from her sooner than from thee. Come along.

HARCOURT (*aside*): So, we are hard put to't when we make our rival our procurer; but neither she nor her brother would let me come near her now. When all's done, a rival is the best cloak to steal to a mistress under, without suspicion; and when we have once got to her as we desire, we throw him off like other cloaks.

(*Exit* SPARKISH, *and* HARCOURT *following him. Re-enter* MR. PINCHWIFE, MRS. PINCHWIFE *in man's clothes.*)

PINCHWIFE (*to* ALITHEA): Sister, if you will not go, we must leave you.—(*Aside.*) The fool her gallant and she will muster up all the young saunterers of this place, and they will leave their dear seamstress to follow us. What a swarm of cuckolds, and cuckold-makers are here!—Come, let us be gone, Mistress Margery.

MRS. PINCHWIFE: Don't you believe that, I han't half my bellyful of sights yet.

PINCHWIFE: Then walk this way.

MRS. PINCHWIFE: Lord, what a power of brave signs are here! Stay—the Bull's-Head, the Ram's Head, and the Stag's-Head, dear—

PINCHWIFE: Nay, if every husband's proper sign here were visible, they would be all alike.

MRS. PINCHWIFE: What d'ye mean by that, bud?

PINCHWIFE: 'Tis no matter—no matter, bud.

MRS. PINCHWIFE: Pray tell me; nay, I will know.

PINCHWIFE: They would be all bulls', stags', and rams' heads.

(*Exeunt* MR. PINCHWIFE, MRS. PINCHWIFE. *Re-enter* SPARKISH, HARCOURT, ALITHEA, LUCY *at t'other door.*)

SPARKISH: Come, dear madam, for my sake you shall be reconciled to him.

ALITHEA: For your sake I hate him.

HARCOURT: That's something too cruel, madam, to hate me for his sake.

SPARKISH: Ay indeed, madam, too, too cruel to me, to hate my friend for my sake.

ALITHEA: I hate him because he is your enemy; and you ought to hate him too, for making love to me, if you love me.

SPARKISH: That's a good one; I hate a man for loving you! If he love you, 'tis but what he can't help; and 'tis your fault, not his, if he admires you. I hate a man for being of my opinion! I'll ne'er do't, by the world.

ALITHEA: Is it for your honor or mine, to suffer a man to make love to me, who am to marry you tomorrow?

SPARKISH: It is for your honor or mine, to have me jealous? That he makes love to you is a sign you are handsome; and that I am not jealous is a sign you are virtuous. That, I think, is for your honor.

ALITHEA: But 'tis your honor too I am concerned for.

HARCOURT: But why, dearest madam, will you be more concerned for his honor than he is himself? Let his honor alone, for my sake and his. He, he has no honor—

SPARKISH: How's that?

HARCOURT: But what my dear friend can guard himself.

SPARKISH: O ho—that's right again.

HARCOURT: Your care of his honor argues his neglect of it, which is no honor to my dear friend here; therefore once more, let his honor go which way it will, dear madam.

SPARKISH: Ay, ay, were it for my honor to marry a woman whose virtue I suspected, and could not trust her in a friend's hands?

ALITHEA: Are you not afraid to lose me?

HARCOURT: He afraid to lose you, madam! No, no—you may see how the most estimable and most glorious creature in the world is valued by him. Will you not see it?

SPARKISH: Right, honest Frank, I have that noble value for her that I cannot be jealous of her.

ALITHEA: You mistake him, he means you care not for me, nor who has me.

SPARKISH: Lord, madam, I see you are jealous. Will you wrest a poor man's meaning from his words?

ALITHEA: You astonish me, sir, with your want of jealousy.

SPARKISH: And you make me giddy, madam, with your jealousy and fears, and virtue and honor. Gad, I see virtue makes a woman as troublesome as a little reading or learning.

ALITHEA: Monstrous!

LUCY (*behind*): Well, to see what easy husbands these women of quality can meet with; a poor chambermaid can never have such lady-like luck. Besides, he's thrown away upon her; she'll make no use of her fortune, her blessing; none to a gentleman for a pure cuckold, for it requires good breeding to be a cuckold.

ALITHEA: I tell you then plainly, he pursues me to marry me.

SPARKISH: Pshaw!

HARCOURT: Come, madam, you see you strive in vain to make him jealous of me; my dear friend is the kindest creature in the world to me.

SPARKISH: Poor fellow.

HARCOURT: But his kindness only is not enough for me, without your favor; your good opinion, dear madam, 'tis that must perfect my happiness. Good gentleman, he believes all I say; would you would do so. Jealous of me! I would not wrong him nor you for the world.

SPARKISH: Look you there; hear him, hear him, and do not walk away so.

(ALITHEA *walks carelessly to and fro.*)

HARCOURT: I love you, madam, so—

SPARKISH: How's that! Nay—now you begin to go too far indeed.

HARCOURT: So much, I confess, I say I love you, that I would not have you miserable, and cast yourself away upon so unworthy and inconsiderable a thing as what you see here.

(*Clapping his hand on his breast, points at* SPARKISH.)

SPARKISH: No, faith, I believe thou wouldst not; now his meaning is plain. But I knew before thou wouldst not wrong me nor her.

HARCOURT: No, no, heavens forbid the glory of her sex should fall so low as into the embraces of such a contemptible wretch, the last of mankind—my dear friend here—I injure him!

(*Embracing* SPARKISH.)

ALITHEA: Very well.

SPARKISH: No, no, dear friend, I knew it.—Madam, you see he will rather wrong himself than me, in giving himself such names.

ALITHEA: Do you not understand him yet?

SPARKISH: Yes, how modestly he speaks of himself, poor fellow.

ALITHEA: Methinks he speaks imprudently of yourself, since—before yourself too; insomuch that I can no longer suffer his scurrilous abusiveness to you, no more than his love to me.

(*Offers to go.*)

SPARKISH: Nay, nay, madam, pray stay—his love to you! Lord, madam, has he not spoke yet plain enough?

ALITHEA: Yes, indeed, I should think so.

SPARKISH: Well then, by the world, a man can't speak civilly to a woman now but presently she says he makes love to her. Nay, madam, you shall stay, with your pardon, since you have not yet understood him, till he has made an *éclaircissement* of his love to you, that is, what kind of love it is.—(*To* HARCOURT.) Answer to thy catechism. Friend, do you love my mistress here?

HARCOURT: Yes, I wish she would not doubt it.

SPARKISH: But how do you love her?

HARCOURT: With all my soul.

ALITHEA: I thank him; methinks he speaks plain enough now.

SPARKISH (*to* ALITHEA): You are out still.—But with what kind of love, Harcourt?

HARCOURT: With the best and truest love in the world.

SPARKISH: Look you there then, that is with no matrimonial love, I'm sure.

ALITHEA: How's that? Do you say matrimonial love is not best?

SPARKISH: Gad, I went too far ere I was aware. But speak for thyself, Harcourt; you said you would not wrong me nor her.

HARCOURT: No, no, madam, e'en take him for heaven's sake—

SPARKISH: Look you there, madam.

HARCOURT: Who should in all justice be yours, he that loves you most.
(*Claps his hand on his breast.*)

ALITHEA: Look you there, Mr. Sparkish, who's that?

SPARKISH: Who should it be?—Go on, Harcourt.

HARCOURT: Who loves you more than women titles, or fortune fools.
(*Points at* SPARKISH.)

SPARKISH: Look you there, he means me still, for he points at me.

ALITHEA: Ridiculous!

HARCOURT: Who can only match your faith and constancy in love.

SPARKISH: Ay.

HARCOURT: Who knows, if it be possible, how to value so much beauty and virtue.

SPARKISH: Ay.

HARCOURT: Whose love can no more be equaled in the world than that heavenly form of yours.

SPARKISH: No.

HARCOURT: Who could no more suffer a rival than your absence, and yet could no more suspect your virtue than his own constancy in his love to you.

SPARKISH: No.

HARCOURT: Who, in fine, loves you better than his eyes, that first made him love you.

SPARKISH: Ay—nay, madam, faith, you shan't go till—

ALITHEA: Have a care, lest you make me stay too long—

SPARKISH: But till he has saluted you; that I may be assured you are friends, after his honest advice and declaration. Come, pray, madam, be friends with him.
(*Enter* MR. PINCHWIFE, MRS. PINCHWIFE.)

ALITHEA: You must pardon me, sir, that I am not yet so obedient to you.

PINCHWIFE: What, invite your wife to kiss men? Monstrous! Are you not ashamed? I will never forgive you.

SPARKISH: Are you not ashamed that I should have more confidence in the chastity of your family than you have? You must not teach me; I am a man of honor, sir, though I am frank and free; I am frank, sir—

PINCHWIFE: Very frank, sir, to share your wife with your friends.

SPARKISH: He is an humble, menial friend, such as reconciles the differences of the marriage bed. You know man and wife do not always agree; I design him for that use, therefore would have him well with my wife.

PINCHWIFE: A menial friend! you will get a great many menial friends by showing your wife as you do.

SPARKISH: What then? It may be I have a pleasure in't, as I have to show fine clothes at a playhouse the first day, and count money before poor rogues.

PINCHWIFE: He that shows his wife or money will be in danger of having them borrowed sometimes.

SPARKISH: I love to be envied, and would not marry a wife that I alone could love; loving alone is as dull as eating alone. Is it not a frank age? And I am a frank person. And to tell you the truth, it may be I love to have rivals in a wife, they make her seem to a man still but as a kept mistress; and so good night, for I must to Whitehall.—Madam, I hope you are now reconciled to my friend; and so I wish you a good night, madam, and sleep if you can, for tomorrow you know I must visit you early with a canonical gentleman. Good night, dear Harcourt.
(*Exit* SPARKISH.)

HARCOURT: Madam, I hope you will not refuse my visit tomorrow, if it should be earlier, with a canonical gentleman, than Mr. Sparkish's.

PINCHWIFE: This gentlewoman is yet under my care; therefore you must yet forbear your freedom with her, sir.

(*Coming between* ALITHEA *and* HARCOURT.)

HARCOURT: Must, sir!

PINCHWIFE: Yes, sir, she is my sister.

HARCOURT: 'Tis well she is, sir—for I must be her servant, sir.—Madam—

PINCHWIFE: Come away, sister; we had been gone, if it had not been for you, and so avoided these lewd rakehells, who seem to haunt us.

(*Enter* HORNER, DORILANT *to them.*)

HORNER: How now, Pinchwife!

PINCHWIFE: Your servant.

HORNER: What! I see a little time in the country makes a man turn wild and unsociable, and only fit to converse with his horses, dogs, and his herds.

PINCHWIFE: I have business, sir, and must mind it; your business is pleasure; therefore you and I must go different ways.

HORNER: Well, you may go on, but this pretty young gentleman—

(*Takes hold of* MRS. PINCHWIFE.)

HARCOURT: The lady—

DORILANT: And the maid—

HORNER: Shall stay with us, for I suppose their business is the same with ours, pleasure.

PINCHWIFE (*aside*): 'Sdeath, he knows her, she carries it so sillily! Yet if he does not, I should be more silly to discover it first.

ALITHEA: Pray, let us go, sir.

PINCHWIFE: Come, come—

HORNER (*to* MRS. PINCHWIFE): Had you not rather stay with us?—Prithee, Pinchwife, who is this pretty young gentleman?

PINCHWIFE: One to whom I'm a guardian.—(*Aside.*) I wish I could keep her out of your hands.

HORNER: Who is he? I never saw anything so pretty in all my life.

PINCHWIFE: Pshaw! do not look upon him so much; he's a poor bashful youth, you'll put him out of countenance.—Come away, brother.

(*Offers to take her away.*)

HORNER: Oh, your brother.

PINCHWIFE: Yes, my wife's brother.—Come, come, she'll stay supper for us.

HORNER: I thought so, for he is very like her I saw you at the play with, whom I told you I was in love with.

MRS. PINCHWIFE (*aside*): O jeminy! Is this he that was in love with me? I am glad on it, I vow, for he's a curious fine gentleman, and I love him already too.—(*To* MR. PINCHWIFE.) Is this he, bud?

PINCHWIFE (*to his wife.*): Come away, come away.

HORNER: Why, what haste are you in? Why won't you let me talk with him?

PINCHWIFE: Because you'll debauch him; he's yet young and innocent, and I would not have him debauched for anything in the world.—(*Aside.*) How she gazes on him! The devil!

HORNER: Harcourt, Dorilant, look you here; this is the likeness of that dowdy he told us of, his wife. Did you ever see a lovelier creature? The rogue has reason to be jealous of his wife, since she is like him, for she would make all that see her in love with her.

HARCOURT: And as I remember now, she is as like him here as can be.

DORILANT: She is indeed very pretty, if she be like him.

HORNER: Very pretty? A very pretty commendation!—she is a glorious creature, beautiful beyond all things I ever beheld.

PINCHWIFE: So, so.

HARCOURT: More beautiful than a poet's first mistress of imagination.

HORNER: Or another man's last mistress of flesh and blood.

MRS. PINCHWIFE: Nay, now you jeer, sir; pray don't jeer me.

PINCHWIFE: Come, come.—(*Aside.*) By heavens, she'll discover herself!

HORNER: I speak of your sister, sir.

PINCHWIFE: Ay, but saying she was handsome, if like him, made him blush.—(*Aside.*) I am upon a rack!

HORNER: Methinks he is so handsome he should not be a man.

PINCHWIFE (*aside*): Oh, there 'tis out! He has discovered her! I am not able to suffer any longer.—(*To his wife.*) Come, come away, I say.

HORNER: Nay, by your leave, sir, he shall not go yet.—(*To them*) Harcourt, Dorilant, let us torment this jealous rogue a little.

HARCOURT, DORILANT: How?

HORNER: I'll show you.

PINCHWIFE: Come, pray let him go, I cannot stay fooling any longer; I tell you his sister stays supper for us.

HORNER: Does she? Come then, we'll all go sup with her and thee.

PINCHWIFE: No, now I think on't, having stayed so long for us, I warrant she's gone to bed.— (*Aside.*) I wish she and I were well out of their hands.—Come, I must rise early tomorrow, come.

HORNER: Well then, if she be gone to bed, I wish her and you a good night. But pray, young gentleman, present my humble service to her.

MRS. PINCHWIFE: Thank you heartily, sir.

PINCHWIFE (*aside*): 'Sdeath! She will discover herself yet in spite of me.—He is something more civil to you, for your kindness to his sister, than I am, it seems.

HORNER: Tell her, dear sweet little gentleman, for all your brother there, that you revived the love I had for her at first sight in the playhouse.

MRS. PINCHWIFE: But did you love her indeed, and indeed?

PINCHWIFE (*aside*): So, so.—Away I say.

HORNER: Nay, stay. Yes, indeed, and indeed, pray do you tell her so, and give her this kiss from me.

(*Kisses her.*)

PINCHWIFE (*aside*): O heavens! what do I suffer! Now 'tis too plain he knows her, and yet—

HORNER: And this, and this—

(*Kisses her again.*)

MRS. PINCHWIFE: What do you kiss me for? I am no woman.

PINCHWIFE (*aside*): So—there, 'tis out.—Come, I cannot nor will stay any longer.

HORNER: Nay, they shall send your lady a kiss too. Here, Harcourt, Dorilant, will you not?

(*They kiss her.*)

PINCHWIFE (*aside*): How! do I suffer this? Was I not accusing another just now for this rascally patience, in permitting his wife to be kissed before his face? Ten thousand ulcers gnaw away their lips!—Come, come.

HORNER: Good night, dear little gentleman; madam, good night; farewell, Pinchwife.—(*Apart to* HARCOURT *and* DORILANT.) Did not I tell you I would raise his jealous gall?

(*Exeunt* HORNER, HARCOURT, *and* DORILANT.)

PINCHWIFE: So, they are gone at last; stay, let me see first if the coach be at this door.

(*Exit.*)

(HORNER, HARCOURT, DORILANT *return.*)

HORNER: What, not gone yet? Will you be sure to do as I desired you, sweet sir?

MRS. PINCHWIFE: Sweet sir, but what will you give me then?

HORNER: Anything. Come away into the next walk.

(*Exit* HORNER, *haling away* MRS. PINCHWIFE.)

ALITHEA: Hold, hold! What d'ye do?

LUCY: Stay, stay, hold—

HARCOURT: Hold, madam, hold! let him present him, he'll come presently; nay, I will never let you go till you answer my question.

LUCY: For God's sake, sir, I must follow 'em.

DORILANT: No, I have something to present you with too; you shan't follow them.

(ALITHEA, LUCY *struggling with* HARCOURT *and* DORILANT. PINCHWIFE *returns.*)

PINCHWIFE: Where?—how?—what's become of— gone!—whither!

LUCY: He's only gone with the gentleman, who will give him something, an't please your worship.

PINCHWIFE: Something!—give him something, with a pox!—where are they?

ALITHEA: In the next walk only, brother.

PINCHWIFE: Only, only! Where, where?

(*Exit* PINCHWIFE, *and returns presently, then goes out again.*)

HARCOURT: What's the matter with him? Why so much concerned? But dearest madam—

ALITHEA: Pray let me go, sir; I have said and suffered enough already.

HARCOURT: Then you will not look upon, nor pity, my sufferings?

ALITHEA: To look upon 'em, when I cannot help 'em, were cruelty, not pity; therefore I will never see you more.

HARCOURT: Let me then, madam, have my privilege of a banished lover, complaining or railing, and giving you but a farewell reason why, if you cannot condescend to marry me, you should not take that wretch, my rival.

ALITHEA: He only, not you, since my honor is engaged so far to him, can give me a reason why I should not marry him; but if he be true, and what I think him to me, I must be so to him. Your servant, sir.

HARCOURT: Have women only constancy when 'tis a vice, and, like fortune, only true to fools?

DORILANT (*to* LUCY, *who struggles to get away from him*): Thou shalt not stir, thou robust creature; you see I can deal with you, therefore you should stay the rather, and be kind.
(*Enter* PINCHWIFE.)

PINCHWIFE: Gone, gone, not to be found! quite gone! Ten thousand plagues go with 'em! Which way went they?

ALITHEA: But into t'other walk, brother.

LUCY: Their business will be done presently sure, an't please your worship; it can't be long in doing, I'm sure on't.

ALITHEA: Are they not there?

PINCHWIFE: No; you know where they are, you infamous wretch, eternal shame of your family, which you do not dishonor enough yourself, you think, but you must help her to do it too, thou legion of bawds!

ALITHEA: Good brother—

PINCHWIFE: Damned, damned sister!

ALITHEA: Look you here, she's coming.
(*Enter* MRS. PINCHWIFE *in man's clothes, running, with her hat under her arm, full of oranges and dried fruit.* HORNER *following.*)

MRS. PINCHWIFE: O dear bud, look you here what I have got, see!

PINCHWIFE (*aside, rubbing his forehead*): And what I have got here too, which you can't see.

MRS. PINCHWIFE: The fine gentleman has given me better things yet.

PINCHWIFE: Has he so?—(*Aside.*) Out of breath and colored! I must hold yet.

HORNER: I have only given your little brother an orange, sir.

PINCHWIFE (*To* HORNER): Thank you, sir.—(*Aside.*) You have only squeezed my orange, I suppose, and given it me again; yet I must have a city patience.—(*To his wife.*) Come, come away.

MRS. PINCHWIFE: Stay, till I have put up my fine things, bud.
(*Enter* SIR JASPER FIDGET)

SIR JASPER FIDGET: Master Horner, come, come, the ladies stay for you; your mistress, my wife, wonders you make not more haste to her.

HORNER: I have stayed this half hour for you here, and 'tis your fault I am not now with your wife.

SIR JASPER FIDGET: But pray, don't let her know so much; the truth on't is, I was advancing a certain project to his Majesty about—I'll tell you.

HORNER: No, let's go, and hear it at your house.— Good night, sweet little gentleman. One kiss more; you'll remember me now, I hope.
(*Kisses her.*)

DORILANT: What, Sir Jasper, will you separate friends? He promised to sup with us; and if you take him to your house, you'll be in danger of our company too.

SIR JASPER FIDGET: Alas, gentlemen, my house is not fit for you; there are none but civil women there, which are not for your turn. He, you know, can bear with the society of civil women now, ha, ha, ha! Besides, he's one of my family—he's—he, he, he!

DORILANT: What is he?

SIR JASPER FIDGET: Faith, my eunuch, since you'll have it, he, he, he!
(*Exeunt* SIR JASPER FIDGET, *and* HORNER.)

DORILANT: I rather wish thou wert his, or my cuckold. Harcourt, what a good cuckold is lost there for want of a man to make him one! Thee and I cannot have Horner's privilege, who can make use of it.

HARCOURT: Ay, to poor Horner 'tis like coming to an estate at three-score, when a man can't be the better for't.

PINCHWIFE: Come.

MRS. PINCHWIFE: Presently, bud.

DORILANT: Come, let us go too.—(*To* ALITHEA.) Madam, your servant.—(*To* LUCY.) Good night, strapper.

HARCOURT: Madam, though you will not let me have a good day or night, I wish you one; but dare not name the other half of my wish.

ALITHEA: Good night, sir, forever.

MRS. PINCHWIFE: I don't know where to put this here, dear bud, you shall eat it; nay, you shall have part of the fine gentleman's good things, or treat as you call it, when we come home.

PINCHWIFE: Indeed, I deserve it, since I have furnished the best part of it. (*Strikes away the orange.*)

> The gallant treats, presents, and gives the ball;
> But 'tis the absent cuckold pays for all.

(*Exeunt.*)

ACT IV

SCENE I

In PINCHWIFE's *house in the morning.*
LUCY, ALITHEA *dressed in new clothes.*

LUCY: Well—madam, now have I dressed you, and set you out with so many ornaments, and spent upon you ounces of essence and pulvilio;[28] and all this for no other purpose but as people adorn and perfume a corpse for a stinking secondhand grave; such or as bad I think Master Sparkish's bed.

ALITHEA: Hold your peace.

LUCY: Nay, madam, I will ask you the reason why you would banish poor Master Harcourt forever from your sight. How could you be so hardhearted?

ALITHEA: 'Twas because I was not hardhearted.

LUCY: No, no; 'twas stark love and kindness, I warrant.

ALITHEA: It was so; I would see him no more because I love him.

LUCY: Hey-day, a very pretty reason!

ALITHEA: You do not understand me.

LUCY: I wish you may yourself.

ALITHEA: I was engaged to marry, you see, another man, whom my justice will not suffer me to deceive or injure.

LUCY: Can there be a greater cheat or wrong done to a man than to give him your person without your heart? I should make a conscience of it.

ALITHEA: I'll retrieve it for him after I am married a while.

LUCY: The woman that marries to love better will be as much mistaken as the wencher that marries to live better. No, madam, marrying to increase love is like gaming to become rich; alas, you only lose what little stock you had before.

ALITHEA: I find by your rhetoric you have been bribed to betray me.

LUCY: Only by his merit, that has bribed your heart, you see, against your word and rigid honor. But what a devil is this honor! 'Tis sure a disease in the head, like the megrim, or falling sickness, that always hurries people away to do themselves mischief. Men lose their lives by it; women what's dearer to 'em, their love, the life of life.

ALITHEA: Come, pray talk you no more of honor, nor Master Harcourt. I wish the other would come to secure my fidelity to him and his right in me.

LUCY: You will marry him then?

ALITHEA: Certainly; I have given him already my word, and will my hand too, to make it good when he comes.

LUCY: Well, I wish I may never stick pin more if he be not an arrant natural[29] to t'other fine gentleman.

ALITHEA: I own he wants the wit of Harcourt, which I will dispense withal for another want he has, which is want of jealousy, which men of wit seldom want.

LUCY: Lord, madam, what should you do with a fool to your husband? You intend to be honest, don't you? Then that husbandly virtue, credulity, is thrown away upon you.

ALITHEA: He only that could suspect my virtue should have cause to do it; 'tis Sparkish's confidence in my truth that obliges me to be so faithful to him.

LUCY: You are not sure his opinion may last.

ALITHEA: I am satisfied 'tis impossible for him to be jealous after the proofs I have had of him. Jealousy in a husband—Heaven defend me from it! It begets a thousand plagues to a poor woman, the loss of her honor, her quiet, and her—

LUCY: And her pleasure.

ALITHEA: What d'ye mean, impertinent?

LUCY: Liberty is a great pleasure, madam.

ALITHEA: I say, loss of her honor, her quiet, nay her life sometimes; and what's as bad almost, the loss of this town; that is, she is sent into the country, which is the last ill usage of a husband to a wife, I think.

---

28. Scented powder.

29. Slow-witted person.

LUCY (*aside*): Oh, does the wind lie there?—Then, of necessity madam, you think a man must carry his wife into the country, if he be wise. The country is as terrible, I find, to our young English ladies as a monastery to those abroad; and on my virginity, I think they would rather marry a London jailer than a high sheriff of a county, since neither can stir from his employment. Formerly women of wit married fools for a great estate, a fine seat, or the like; but now 'tis for a pretty seat only in Lincoln's Inn Fields, St. James's Fields, or the Pall Mall.

(*Enter to them* SPARKISH, *and* HARCOURT *dressed like a parson.*)

SPARKISH: Madam, your humble servant, a happy day to you, and to us all.

HARCOURT: Amen.

ALITHEA: Who have we here?

SPARKISH: My chaplain, faith. O madam, poor Harcourt remembers his humble service to you, and in obedience to your last commands, refrains coming into your sight.

ALITHEA: Is not that he?

SPARKISH: No, fie, no; but to show that he ne'er intended to hinder our match, has sent his brother here to join our hands. When I get me a wife, I must get her a chaplain, according to the custom; this is his brother, and my chaplain.

ALITHEA: His brother?

LUCY (*aside*): And your chaplain, to preach in your pulpit then.

ALITHEA: His brother!

SPARKISH: Nay, I knew you would not believe it.— I told you, sir, she would take you for your brother Frank.

ALITHEA: Believe it!

LUCY (*aside*): His brother! ha, ha, he! He has a trick left still, it seems.

SPARKISH: Come, my dearest, pray let us go to church before the canonical hour is past.

ALITHEA: For shame, you are abused still.

SPARKISH: By the world, 'tis strange now you are so incredulous.

ALITHEA: 'Tis strange you are so credulous.

SPARKISH: Dearest of my life, hear me. I tell you this is Ned Harcourt of Cambridge, by the world; you see he has a sneaking college look. 'Tis true he's something like his brother Frank,

and they differ from each other no more than in their age, for they were twins.

LUCY: Ha, ha, he!

ALITHEA: Your servant, sir; I cannot be so deceived, though you are. But come, let's hear, how do you know what you affirm so confidently?

SPARKISH: Why, I'll tell you all. Frank Harcourt coming to me this morning, to wish me joy and present his service to you, I asked him if he could help me to a parson; whereupon he told me he had a brother in town who was in orders, and he went straight away and sent him you see there to me.

ALITHEA: Yes, Frank goes and puts on a black coat, then tells you he is Ned; that's all you have for't.

SPARKISH: Pshaw, pshaw! I tell you by the same token, the midwife put her garter about Frank's neck to know 'em asunder, they were so like.

ALITHEA: Frank tells you this too.

SPARKISH: Ay, and Ned there too; nay, they are both in a story.

ALITHEA: So, so; very foolish!

SPARKISH: Lord, if you won't believe one, you had best try him by your chambermaid there, for chambermaids must needs know chaplains from other men, they are so used to 'em.

LUCY: Let's see; nay I'll be sworn he has the canonical smirk, and the filthy, clammy palm of a chaplain.

ALITHEA: Well, most reverend doctor, pray let us make an end of this fooling.

HARCOURT: With all my soul, divine, heavenly creature, when you please.

ALITHEA: He speaks like a chaplain indeed.

SPARKISH: Why, was there not "soul," "divine," "heavenly," in what he said?

ALITHEA: Once more, most impertinent black coat, cease your persecution, and let us have a conclusion of this ridiculous love.

HARCOURT (*aside*): I had forgot; I must suit my style to my coat, or I wear it in vain.

ALITHEA: I have no more patience left; let us make once an end of this troublesome love, I say.

HARCOURT: So be it, seraphic lady, when your honor shall think it meet and convenient so to do.

SPARKISH: Gad, I'm sure none but a chaplain could speak so, I think.

ALITHEA: Let me tell you, sir, this dull trick will not serve your turn; though you delay our marriage, you shall not hinder it.

HARCOURT: Far be it from me, munificent patroness, to delay your marriage. I desire nothing more than to marry you presently, which I might do, if you yourself would; for my noble, good-natured and thrice generous patron here would not hinder it.

SPARKISH: No, poor man, not I, faith.

HARCOURT: And now, madam, let me tell you plainly, nobody else shall marry you; by heavens, I'll die first, for I'm sure I should die after it.

LUCY (*aside*): How his love has made him forget his function, as I have seen it in real parsons!

ALITHEA: That was spoken like a chaplain too! Now you understand him, I hope.

SPARKISH: Poor man, he takes it heinously to be refused; I can't blame him, 'tis putting an indignity upon him not to be suffered. But you'll pardon me, madam, it shan't be, he shall marry us; come away, pray, madam.

LUCY: Ha, ha, he! More ado! 'Tis late.

ALITHEA: Invincible stupidity! I tell you he would marry me as your rival, not as your chaplain.

SPARKISH: Come, come, madam.

(*Pulling her away.*)

LUCY: I pray, madam, do not refuse this reverend divine the honor and satisfaction of marrying you; for I dare say he has set his heart upon't, good doctor.

ALITHEA: What can you hope, or design by this?

HARCOURT (*aside*): I could answer her, a reprieve for a day only often revokes a hasty doom; at worst, if she will not take mercy on me and let me marry her, I have at least the lover's second pleasure, hindering my rival's enjoyment, though but for a time.

SPARKISH: Come, madam, 'tis e'en twelve o'clock, and my mother charged me never to be married out of the canonical hours. Come, come; Lord, here's such a deal of modesty, I warrant, the first day.

LUCY: Yes, an't please your worship, married women show all their modesty the first day, because married men show all their love the first day.

(*Exeunt* SPARKISH, ALITHEA, HARCOURT, *and* LUCY.)

SCENE II

The scene changes to a bedchamber, where appear PINCHWIFE, MRS. PINCHWIFE.

PINCHWIFE: Come, tell me, I say.

MRS. PINCHWIFE: Lord! han't I told it an hundred times over?

PINCHWIFE (*aside*): I would try if, in the repetition of the ungrateful tale, I could find her altering it in the least circumstance; for if her story be false, she is so too.—Come, how was't, baggage?

MRS. PINCHWIFE: Lord, what pleasure you take to hear it, sure!

PINCHWIFE: No, you take more in telling it, I find; but speak, how was't?

MRS. PINCHWIFE: He carried me up in to the house next to the Exchange.

PINCHWIFE: So; and you two were only in the room.

MRS. PINCHWIFE: Yes, for he sent away a youth that was there, for some dried fruit and China oranges.

PINCHWIFE: Did he so? Damn him for it—and for—

MRS. PINCHWIFE: But presently came up the gentlewoman of the house.

PINCHWIFE: Oh, 'twas well she did; but what did he do whilst the fruit came?

MRS. PINCHWIFE: He kissed me an hundred times, and told me he fancied he kissed my fine sister, meaning me, you know, whom he said he loved with all his soul, and bid me be sure to tell her so, and to desire her to be at her window by eleven of the clock this morning, and he would walk under it at that time.

PINCHWIFE: And he was as good as his word, very punctual; a pox reward him for't.

MRS. PINCHWIFE: Well, and he said to me if you are not within, he would come up to her, meaning me, you know, bud, still.

PINCHWIFE (*aside*): So—he knew her certainly; but for this confession, I am obliged to her simplicity.—But what, you stood very still when he kissed you?

MRS. PINCHWIFE: Yes, I warrant you; would you have had me discovered myself?

PINCHWIFE: But you told me he did some beastliness to you, as you called it; what was't?

MRS. PINCHWIFE: Why, he put—

PINCHWIFE: What?

MRS. PINCHWIFE: Why, he put the tip of his tongue between my lips, and so mousled me—and I said I'd bite it.

PINCHWIFE: An eternal canker seize it, for a dog!

MRS. PINCHWIFE: Nay, you need not be so angry with him neither, for to say truth, he has the sweetest breath I ever knew.

PINCHWIFE: The devil!—you were satisfied with it then, and would do it again.

MRS. PINCHWIFE: Not unless he should force me.

PINCHWIFE: Force you, changeling! I tell you no woman can be forced.

MRS. PINCHWIFE: Yes, but she may sure by such as he, for he's a proper, goodly strong man; 'tis hard, let me tell you, to resist him.

PINCHWIFE (aside): So, 'tis plain she loves him, yet she has not love enough to make her conceal it from me; but the sight of him will increase her aversion for me and love for him, and that love instruct her how to deceive me and satisfy him, all idiot as she is. Love! 'Twas he gave women first their craft, their art of deluding; out of nature's hands they came plain, open, silly, and fit for slaves, as she and Heaven intended 'em; but damned love—well—I must strangle that little monster whilst I can deal with him.—Go fetch pen, ink, and paper out of the next room.

MRS. PINCHWIFE: Yes, bud.

(Exit MRS. PINCHWIFE.)

PINCHWIFE (aside): Why should women have more invention in love than men? It can only be because they have more desires, more soliciting passions, more lust, and more of the devil.

(MRS. PINCHWIFE returns.)

Come, minx, sit down and write.

MRS. PINCHWIFE: Ay, dear bud, but I can't do't very well.

PINCHWIFE: I wish you could not at all.

MRS. PINCHWIFE: But what should I write for?

PINCHWIFE: I'll have you write a letter to your lover.

MRS. PINCHWIFE: O Lord, to the fine gentleman a letter!

PINCHWIFE: Yes, to the fine gentleman.

MRS. PINCHWIFE: Lord, you do but jeer; sure you jest.

PINCHWIFE: I am not so merry; come, write as I bid you.

MRS. PINCHWIFE: What, do you think I am a fool?

PINCHWIFE (aside): She's afraid I would not dictate any love to him, therefore she's unwilling.—But you had best begin.

MRS. PINCHWIFE: Indeed, and indeed, but I won't, so I won't!

PINCHWIFE: Why?

MRS. PINCHWIFE: Because he's in town; you may send for him if you will.

PINCHWIFE: Very well, you would have him brought to you; is it come to this? I say, take the pen and write, or you'll provoke me.

MRS. PINCHWIFE: Lord, what d'ye make a fool of me for? Don't I know that letters are never writ but from the country to London, and from London into the country? Now he's in town, and I am in town too; therefore I can't write to him, you know.

PINCHWIFE (aside): So, I am glad it is no worse; she is innocent enough yet.—Yes, you may, when your husband bids you, write letters to people that are in town.

MRS. PINCHWIFE: Oh, may I so? Then I'm satisfied.

PINCHWIFE: Come, begin.—(Dictates.) "Sir"—

MRS. PINCHWIFE: Shan't I say, "Dear Sir"? You know one says always something more than bare "sir."

PINCHWIFE: Write as I bid you, or I will write "whore" with this penknife in your face.

MRS. PINCHWIFE: Nay, good bud—(She writes.) "Sir"—

PINCHWIFE: "Though I suffered last night your nauseous, loathed kisses and embraces"—Write.

MRS. PINCHWIFE: Nay, why should it say so? You know I told you he had a sweet breath.

PINCHWIFE: Write!

MRS. PINCHWIFE: Let me but put out "loathed."

PINCHWIFE: Write, I say!

MRS. PINCHWIFE: Well then.

(Writes.)

PINCHWIFE: Let's see, what have you writ?—(Takes the paper, and reads.) "Though I suffered last night your kisses and embraces"—Thou impudent creature! Where is "nauseous" and "loathed"?

MRS. PINCHWIFE: I can't abide to write such filthy words.

PINCHWIFE: Once more write as I'd have you, and question it not, or I will spoil thy writing with this. (*Holds up the penknife.*) I will stab out those eyes that cause my mischief.

MRS. PINCHWIFE: O Lord, I will!

PINCHWIFE: So—so—let's see now!—(*Reads.*) "Though I suffered last night your nauseous, loathed kisses and embraces"—go on—"Yet I would not have you presume that you shall ever repeat them."—So.

(*She writes.*)

MRS. PINCHWIFE: I have writ it.

PINCHWIFE: On then.—"I then concealed myself from your knowledge, to avoid your insolencies."—

(*She writes.*)

MRS. PINCHWIFE: So—

PINCHWIFE: "The same reason, now I am out of your hands"—

(*She writes.*)

MRS. PINCHWIFE: So—

PINCHWIFE: "Makes me own to you my unfortunate, though innocent frolic, of being in man's clothes"—

(*She writes.*)

MRS. PINCHWIFE: So—

PINCHWIFE: "That you may forevermore cease to pursue her, who hates and detests you"—

(*She writes on.*)

MRS. PINCHWIFE: So—heigh!

(*She sighs.*)

PINCHWIFE: What, do you sigh?—"detests you—as much as she loves her husband and her honor."

MRS. PINCHWIFE: I vow, husband, he'll ne'er believe I should write such a letter.

PINCHWIFE: What, he'd expect a kinder from you? Come, now your name only.

MRS. PINCHWIFE: What, shan't I say, "Your most faithful, humble servant till death"?

PINCHWIFE: No, tormenting fiend!—(*Aside.*) Her style, I find, would be very soft.—Come, wrap it up now, whilst I go fetch wax and a candle; and write on the backside, "For Mr. Horner."

(*Exit* PINCHWIFE.)

MRS. PINCHWIFE: "For Mr. Horner."—So, I am glad he has told me his name. Dear Mr. Horner! But why should I send thee such a letter that will vex thee, and make thee angry with me?—

Well, I will not send it—Ay, but then my husband will kill me—for I see plainly he won't let me love Mr. Horner—but what care I for my husband?—I won't, so I won't send poor Mr. Horner such a letter—But then my husband—But oh, what if I writ at bottom, my husband made me write it?—Ay, but then my husband would see't—Can one have no shift? Ah, a London woman would have had a hundred presently. Stay—what if I should write a letter, and wrap it up like this, and write upon't too? Ay, but then my husband would see't—I don't know what to do—but yet y'vads[30] I'll try, so I will—for I will not send this letter to poor Mr. Horner, come what will on't.

(*She writes, and repeats what she hath writ.*)

"Dear, sweet Mr. Horner:—so—"My husband would have me send you a base, rude, unmannerly letter—but I won't"—so—"and would have me forbid you loving me—but I won't"—so—"and would have me say to you, I hate you, poor Mr. Horner—but I won't tell a lie for him"—there—"for I'm sure if you and I were in the country at cards together"—so—"I could not help treading on your toe under the table"—so—"or rubbing knees with you, and staring in your face till you saw me"—very well—"and then looking down, and blushing for an hour together"—so—"but I must make haste before my husband come; and now he has taught me to write letters, you shall have longer ones from me, who am, dear, dear, poor, dear Mr. Horner, your most humble friend, and servant to command till death, Margery Pinchwife."

Stay, I must give him a hint at bottom—so—now wrap it up just like t'other—so—now write, "For Mr. Horner"—But oh now, what shall I do with it? For here comes my husband.

(*Enter* PINCHWIFE.)

PINCHWIFE (*aside*): I have been detained by a sparkish coxcomb, who pretended a visit to me; but I fear 'twas to my wife.—What, have you done?

MRS. PINCHWIFE: Ay, ay, bud, just now.

---

30. In faith.

PINCHWIFE: Let's see't; what d'ye tremble for? What, you would not have it go?

MRS. PINCHWIFE: Here.—(*Aside.*) No, I must not give him that, so I had been served if I had given him this.

PINCHWIFE (*He opens, and reads the first letter.*): Come, where's the wax and seal?

MRS. PINCHWIFE (*aside*): Lord, what shall I do now? Nay, then, I have it.—Pray let me see't. Lord, you think me so arrant a fool I cannot seal a letter; I will do't, so I will.

(*Snatches the letter from him, changes it for the other, seals it, and delivers it to him.*)

PINCHWIFE: Nay, I believe you will learn that, and other things too, which I would not have you.

MRS. PINCHWIFE: So, han't I done it curiously?— (*Aside.*) I think I have; there's my letter going to Mr. Horner, since he'll needs have me send letters to folks.

PINCHWIFE: 'Tis very well; but I warrant you would not have it go now?

MRS. PINCHWIFE: Yes, indeed, but I would, bud, now.

PINCHWIFE: Well, you are a good girl then. Come, let me lock you up in your chamber till I come back; and be sure you come not within three strides of the window when I am gone, for I have a spy in the street.

(*Exit* MRS. PINCHWIFE. PINCHWIFE *locks the door.*) At least, 'tis fit she think so. If we do not cheat women, they'll cheat us; and fraud may be justly used with secret enemies, of which a wife is the most dangerous; and he that has a handsome one to keep, and a frontier town, must provide against treachery rather than open force. Now I have secured all within, I'll deal with the foe without with false intelligence.

(*Holds up the letter.*)

(*Exit* PINCHWIFE.)

SCENE III

The scene changes to HORNER's *lodgings.* QUACK *and* HORNER.

QUACK: Well, sir, how fadges the new design? Have you not the luck of all your brother projectors, to deceive only yourself at last?

HORNER: No, good domine doctor, I deceive you, it seems, and others too; for the grave matrons and old, rigid husbands think me as unfit for love as they are; but their wives, sisters, and daughters know some of 'em better things already.

QUACK: Already!

HORNER: Already, I say. Last night I was drunk with half a dozen of your civil persons, as you call 'em, and people of honor, and so was made free of their society and dressing rooms forever hereafter; and am already come to the privileges of sleeping upon their pallets, warming smocks, tying shoes and garters, and the like, doctor, already, already, doctor.

QUACK: You have made use of your time, sir.

HORNER: I tell thee, I am now no more interruption to 'em when they sing, or talk bawdy, than a little squab French page who speaks no English.

QUACK: But do civil persons and women of honor drink, and sing bawdy songs?

HORNER: Oh, amongst friends, amongst friends. For your bigots in honor are just like those in religion; they fear the eye of the world more than the eye of Heaven, and think there is no virtue but railing at vice, and no sin but giving scandal. They rail at a poor, little, kept player, and keep themselves some young, modest pulpit comedian to be privy to their sins in their closets, not to tell 'em of them in their chapels.

QUACK: Nay, the truth on't is, priests amongst the women now have quite got the better of us lay confessors, physicians.

HORNER: And they are rather their patients, but—

(*Enter* MY LADY FIDGET, *looking about her.*) Now we talk of women of honor, here comes one. Step behind the screen there, and but observe if I have not particular privileges with the women of reputation already, doctor, already.

(QUACK *steps behind screen.*)

LADY FIDGET: Well, Horner, am I not a woman of honor? You see I'm as good as my word.

HORNER: And you shall see, madam, I'll not be behindhand with you in honor; and I'll be as good as my word too, if you please but to withdraw into the next room.

LADY FIDGET: But first, my dear sir, you must promise to have a care of my dear honor.

HORNER: If you talk a word of your honor, you'll make me incapable to wrong it. To talk of honor in the mysteries of love is like talking of Heaven or the Deity in an operation of witchcraft, just when you are employing the devil; it makes the charm impotent.

LADY FIDGET: Nay, fie! let us not be smutty. But you talk of mysteries and bewitching to me; I don't understand you.

HORNER: I tell you, madam, the word "money" in a mistress's mouth, at such a nick of time, is not a more disheartening sound to a younger brother than that of "honor" to an eager lover like myself.

LADY FIDGET: But you can't blame a lady of my reputation to be chary.

HORNER: Chary! I have been chary of it already, by the report I have caused of myself.

LADY FIDGET: Ay, but if you should ever let other women know that dear secret, it would come out. Nay, you must have a great care of your conduct; for my acquaintance are so censorious (oh, 'tis a wicked, censorious world, Mr. Horner!), I say, are so censorious and detracting that perhaps they'll talk, to the prejudice of my honor, though you should not let them know the dear secret.

HORNER: Nay, madam, rather than they shall prejudice your honor, I'll prejudice theirs; and to serve you, I'll lie with 'em all, make the secret their own, and then they'll keep it. I am a Machiavel in love, madam.

LADY FIDGET: Oh, no, sir, not that way.

HORNER: Nay, the devil take me if censorious women are to be silenced any other way.

LADY FIDGET: A secret is better kept, I hope, by a single person that a multitude; therefore pray do not trust anybody else with it, dear, dear Mr. Horner.

(*Embracing him.*)

(*Enter* SIR JASPER FIDGET.)

SIR JASPER FIDGET: How now!

LADY FIDGET (*aside*): Oh, my husband!—prevented—and what's almost as bad, found with my arms about another man—that will appear too much—what shall I say?

Sir Jasper, come hither. I am trying if Mr. Horner were ticklish, and he is ticklish as can be; I love to torment the confounded toad; let you and I tickle him.

SIR JASPER FIDGET: No, your ladyship will tickle him better without me, I suppose. But is this your buying china? I thought you had been at the china house.

HORNER (*aside*): China house! That's my cue, I must take it.—A pox! can't you keep your impertinent wives at home? Some men are troubled with the husbands, but I with the wives. But I'd have you to know, since cannot be your journeyman by night, I will not be your drudge by day, to squire your wife about and be your man of straw, or scarecrow, only to pies and jays, that would be nibbling at your forbidden fruit; I shall be shortly the hackney gentleman-usher of the town.

SIR JASPER FIDGET (*aside*): He, he, he! Poor fellow, he's in the right on't, faith; to squire women about for other folks is as ungrateful an employment as to tell money for other folks.—He, he, he! Ben't angry, Horner.

LADY FIDGET: No, 'tis I have more reason to be angry, who am left by you to go abroad indecently alone; or, what is more indecent to pin myself upon such ill-bred people of your acquaintance as this is.

SIR JASPER FIDGET: Nay, prithee what has he done?

LADY FIDGET: Nay, he has done nothing.

SIR JASPER FIDGET: But what d'ye take ill, if he has done nothing?

LADY FIDGET: Ha, ha, ha! Faith, I can't but laugh, however; why, d'ye think the unmannerly toad would come down to me to the coach? I was fain to come up to fetch him, or go without him, which I was resolved not to do; for he knows china very well, and has himself very good, but will not let me see it lest I should beg some. But I will find it out, and have what I came for yet.

(*Exit* LADY FIDGET, *and locks the door, followed by* HORNER *to the door.*)

HORNER (*apart to* LADY FIDGET): Lock the door, madam.—so she has got into my chamber, and locked me out. Oh, the impertinency of womankind! Well, Sir Jasper, plain dealing is a jewel; if ever you suffer your wife to trouble me again here, she shall carry you home a pair of horns, by my Lord Mayor she shall; though I cannot furnish you myself, you are sure, yet I'll find a way.

SIR JASPER FIDGET (*aside*): Ha, ha, he! At my first coming in and finding her arms about him, tickling him it seems, I was half jealous, but now I see my folly.—He, he, he! Poor Horner.

HORNER: Nay, though you laugh now, 'twill be my turn ere long. Oh, women, more impertinent, more cunning, and more mischievous than their monkeys, and to me almost as ugly! Now is she throwing my things about and rifling all I have, but I'll get in to her the back way, and so rifle her for it.

SIR JASPER FIDGET: Ha, ha, ha! Poor angry Horner.

HORNER: Stay here a little; I'll ferret her out to you presently, I warrant.

(*Exit* HORNER *at t'other door.*)

SIR JASPER FIDGET: Wife! My Lady Fidget! Wife! He is coming in to you the back way.

(SIR JASPER *calls through the door to his wife; she answers from within.*)

LADY FIDGET: Let him come, and welcome, which way he will.

SIR JASPER FIDGET: He'll catch you, and use you roughly, and be too strong for you.

LADY FIDGET: Don't you trouble yourself, let him if he can.

QUACK (*behind*): This indeed I could not have believed from him, nor any but my own eyes.

(*Enter* MRS. SQUEAMISH.)

MRS. SQUEAMISH: Where's this woman-hater, this toad, this ugly, greasy, dirty sloven?

SIR JASPER FIDGET (*aside*): So, the women all will have him ugly; methinks he is a comely person, but his wants make his form contemptible to 'em; and 'tis e'en as my wife said yesterday, talking of him, that a proper handsome eunuch was as ridiculous a thing as a gigantic coward.

MRS. SQUEAMISH: Sir Jasper, your servant. Where is the odious beast?

SIR JASPER FIDGET: He's within in his chamber, with my wife; she's playing the wag with him.

MRS. SQUEAMISH: Is she so? And he's a clownish beast, he'll give her no quarter, he'll play the wag with her again, let me tell you. Come, let's go help her.—What, the door's locked?

SIR JASPER FIDGET: Ay, my wife locked it.

MRS. SQUEAMISH: Did she so? Let us break it open then.

SIR JASPER FIDGET: No, no, he'll do her no hurt.

MRS. SQUEAMISH: No.—(*Aside.*) But is there no other way to get in to 'em? Whither goes this? I will disturb 'em.

(*Exit* MRS. SQUEAMISH *at other door.*)

(*Enter* OLD LADY SQUEAMISH.)

OLD LADY SQUEAMISH: Where is this harlotry, this impudent baggage, this rambling tomrig?[31] O Sir Jasper, I'm glad to see you here, did you not see my vile grandchild come in hither just now?

SIR JASPER FIDGET: Yes.

OLD LADY SQUEAMISH: Ay, but where is she then? where is she? Lord, Sir Jasper, I have e'en rattled myself to pieces in pursuit of her. But can you tell what she makes here? They say below, no woman lodges here.

SIR JASPER FIDGET: No.

OLD LADY SQUEAMISH: No! What does she here then? Say, if it be not a woman's lodging, what makes she here? But are you sure no woman lodges here?

SIR JASPER FIDGET: No, nor man neither; this is Mr. Horner's lodging.

OLD LADY SQUEAMISH: Is it so, are you sure?

SIR JASPER FIDGET: Yes, yes.

OLD LADY SQUEAMISH: So; then there's no hurt in't, I hope. But where is he?

SIR JASPER FIDGET: He's in the next room with my wife.

OLD LADY SQUEAMISH: Nay, if you trust him with your wife, I may with my Biddy. They say he's a merry harmless man now, e'en as harmless a man as ever came out of Italy with a good voice,[32] and as pretty harmless company for a lady as a snake without his teeth.

SIR JASPER FIDGET: Ay, ay, poor man.

(*Enter* MRS. SQUEAMISH.)

MRS. SQUEAMISH: I can't find 'em.—Oh, are you here, Grandmother? I followed, you must know, my Lady Fidget hither; 'tis the prettiest lodging, and I have been staring on the prettiest pictures.

---

31. A loose woman.
32. A male singer castrated to achieve a high voice.

(*Enter* LADY FIDGET *with a piece of china in her hand, and* HORNER *following.*)

LADY FIDGET: And I have been toiling and moiling for the prettiest piece of china, my dear.

HORNER: Nay, she has been too hard for me, do what I could.

MRS. SQUEAMISH: O Lord, I'll have some china too. Good Mr. Horner, don't think to give other people china, and me none; come in with me too.

HORNER: Upon my honor, I have none left now.

MRS. SQUEAMISH: Nay, Nay, I have known you deny your china before now, but you shan't put me off so. Come.

HORNER: This lady had the last there.

LADY FIDGET: Yes, indeed, madam, to my certain knowledge he has no more left.

MRS. SQUEAMISH: Oh, but it may be he may have some you could not find.

LADY FIDGET: What, d'ye think if he had had any left, I would not have had it too? For we women of quality never think we have china enough.

HORNER: Do not take it ill, I cannot make china for you all, but I will have a rol-waggon[33] for you too, another time.

MRS. SQUEAMISH: Thank you, dear toad.

LADY FIDGET (*to* HORNER, *aside*): What do you mean by that promise?

HORNER (*apart to* LADY FIDGET): Alas, she has an innocent, literal understanding.

OLD LADY SQUEAMISH: Poor Mr. Horner! He has enough to do to please you all, I see.

HORNER: Ay, madam, you see how they use me.

OLD LADY SQUEAMISH: Poor gentleman, I pity you.

HORNER: I thank you, madam. I could never find pity but from such reverend ladies as you are; the young ones will never spare a man.

MRS. SQUEAMISH: Come, come, beast, and go dine with us, for we shall want a man at ombre after dinner.

HORNER: That's all their use of me, madam, you see.

MRS. SQUEAMISH: Come, sloven, I'll lead you, to be sure of you.
(*Pulls him by the cravat.*)

OLD LADY SQUEAMISH: Alas, poor man, how she tugs him! Kiss, kiss her; that's the way to make such nice women quiet.

HORNER: No, madam, that remedy is worse than the torment; they know I dare suffer anything rather than do it.

OLD LADY SQUEAMISH: Prithee kiss her, and I'll give you her picture in little, that you admired so last night; prithee do.

HORNER: Well, nothing but that could bribe me; I love a woman only in effigy and good painting, as much as I hate them. I'll do't, for I could adore the devil well painted.
(*Kisses* MRS. SQUEAMISH.)

MRS. SQUEAMISH: Foh, you filthy toad! Nay, now I've done jesting.

OLD LADY SQUEAMISH: Ha, ha, ha! I told you so.

MRS. SQUEAMISH: Foh! a kiss of his—

SIR JASPER FIDGET: Has no more hurt in't than one of my spaniel's.

MRS. SQUEAMISH: Nor no more good neither.

QUACK (*behind*): I will now believe anything he tells me.
(*Enter* MR. PINCHWIFE.)

LADY FIDGET: O Lord, here's a man! Sir Jasper, my mask, my mask! I would not be seen here for the world.

SIR JASPER FIDGET: What, not when I am with you?

LADY FIDGET: No, no, my honor—let's be gone.

MRS. SQUEAMISH: Oh grandmother, let us be gone; make haste, make haste, I know not how he may censure us.

LADY FIDGET: Be found in the lodging of anything like a man! Away!
(*Exeunt* SIR JASPER, LADY FIDGET, OLD LADY SQUEAMISH, MRS. SQUEAMISH.)

QUACK (*behind*): What's here? another cuckold? He looks like one, and none else sure have any business with him.

HORNER: Well, what brings my dear friend hither?

PINCHWIFE: Your impertinency.

HORNER: My impertinency!—Why, you gentlemen that have got handsome wives think you have a privilege of saying anything to your friends, and are as brutish as if you were our creditors.

PINCHWIFE: No, sir, I'll ne'er trust you any way.

---

33. A phallic-shaped piece of china.

HORNER: But why not, dear Jack? Why diffide[34] in me thou know'st so well?

PINCHWIFE: Because I do know you so well.

HORNER: Han't I been always thy friend, honest Jack, always ready to serve thee, in love or battle, before thou wert married, and am so still?

PINCHWIFE: I believe so; you would be my second now indeed.

HORNER: Well then, dear Jack, why so unkind, so grum, so strange to me? Come, prithee kiss me, dear rogue. Gad, I was always, I say, and am still as much thy servant as—

PINCHWIFE: As I am yours, sir. What, you send a kiss to my wife, is that it?

HORNER: So, there 'tis—a man can't show his friendship to a married man, but presently he talks of his wife to you. Prithee, let thy wife alone, and let thee and I be all one, as we were wont. What, thou are as shy of my kindness as a Lombard Street alderman[35] of a courtier's civility at Locket's.

PINCHWIFE: But you are overkind to me, as kind as if I were your cuckold already; yet I must confess you ought to be kind and civil to me, since I am so kind, so civil to you, as to bring you this. Look you there sir.
(*Delivers him a letter.*)

HORNER: What is't?

PINCHWIFE: Only a love letter, sir.

HORNER: From whom? How! this is from your wife!—hum—and hum—

PINCHWIFE: Even from my wife, sir. Am I not wondrous kind and civil to you now too?—(*Aside.*) But you'll not think her so.

HORNER (*aside*): Ha! Is this a trick of his or hers?

PINCHWIFE: The gentleman's surprised, I find. What, you expected a kinder letter?

HORNER: No, faith, not I, how could I?

PINCHWIFE: Yes, yes, I'm sure you did; a man so well made as you are must needs be disappointed if the women declare not their passion at first sight or opportunity.

HORNER (*aside*): But what should this mean? Stay, the postscript.

34. Distrust.
35. A businessman would suspect a polite courtier of asking for a loan.

—(*Reads aside.*) "Be sure you love me whatsoever my husband says to the contrary, and let him not see this, lest he should come home and pinch me, or kill my squirrel."—(*Aside.*) It seems he knows not what the letter contains.

PINCHWIFE: Come, ne'er wonder at it so much.

HORNER: Faith, I can't help it.

PINCHWIFE: Now, I think, I have deserved your infinite friendship and kindness, and have showed myself sufficiently an obliging kind friend and husband; am I not so, to bring a letter from my wife to her gallant?

HORNER: Ay, the devil take me, art thou the most obliging, kind friend and husband in the world, ha, ha!

PINCHWIFE: Well, you may be merry, sir; but in short I must tell you, sir, my honor will suffer no jesting.

HORNER: What dost thou mean?

PINCHWIFE: Does the letter want a comment? Then know, sir, though I have been so civil a husband as to bring you a letter from my wife, to let you kiss and court her to my face, I will not be a cuckold, sir, I will not.

HORNER: Thou art mad with jealousy. I never saw thy wife in my life but at the play yesterday, and I know not if it were she or no. I court her, kiss her!

PINCHWIFE: I will not be a cuckold, I say; there will be danger in making me a cuckold.

HORNER: Why, wert thou not well cured of thy last clap?

PINCHWIFE: I wear a sword.

HORNER: It should be taken from thee lest thou shouldst do thyself a mischief with it; thou art mad, man.

PINCHWIFE: As mad as I am, and as merry as you are, I must have more reason from you ere we part. I say again, though you kissed and courted last night my wife in man's clothes, as she confesses in her letter—

HORNER (*aside*): Ha!

PINCHWIFE: Both she and I say, you must not design it again, for you have mistaken your woman, as you have done your man.

HORNER (*aside*): Oh—I understand something now.—Was that thy wife? Why wouldst thou not tell me 'twas she? Faith, my freedom with her was your fault, not mine.

PINCHWIFE (*aside*): Faith, so 'twas.

HORNER: Fie! I'd never do't to a woman before her husband's face, sure.

PINCHWIFE: But I had rather you should do't to my wife before my face than behind my back, and that you shall never do.

HORNER: No—you will hinder me.

PINCHWIFE: If I would not hinder you, you see by her letter, she would.

HORNER: Well, I must e'en acquiesce then, and be contented with what she writes.

PINCHWIFE: I'll assure you 'twas voluntarily writ; I had no hand in't, you may believe me.

HORNER: I do believe thee, faith.

PINCHWIFE: And believe her too, for she's an innocent creature, has no dissembling in her; and so fare you well, sir.

HORNER: Pray, however, present my humble service to her, and tell her I will obey her letter to a tittle, and fulfill her desires, be what they will, or with what difficulty soever I do't, and you shall be no more jealous of me, I warrant her and you.

PINCHWIFE: Well then, fare you well and play with any man's honor but mine, kiss any man's wife but mine, and welcome.

(*Exit* MR. PINCHWIFE.)

HORNER: Ha, ha, ha! doctor.

QUACK: It seems he has not heard the report of you, or does not believe it.

HORNER: Ha, ha! Now, doctor, what think you?

QUACK: Pray let's see the letter—hum—(*Reads the letter.*) "for—dear—I love you"—

HORNER: I wonder how she could contrive it! What say's thou to't? 'Tis an original.

QUACK: So are your cuckolds, too, originals, for they are like no other common cuckolds, and I will henceforth believe it not impossible for you to cuckold the Grand Signior amidst his guards of eunuchs, that I say.

HORNER: And I say for the letter, 'tis the first love letter that ever was without flames, darts, fates, destinies, lying and dissembling in't.

(*Enter* SPARKISH, *pulling in* MR. PINCHWIFE.)

SPARKISH: Come back, you are a pretty brother-in-law, neither go to church, nor to dinner with your sister bride!

PINCHWIFE: My sister denies her marriage, and you see is gone away from you dissatisfied.

SPARKISH: Pshaw! upon a foolish scruple, that our parson was not in lawful orders, and did not say all the Common Prayer; but 'tis her modesty only, I believe. But let women be never so modest the first day, they'll be sure to come to themselves by night, and I shall have enough of her then. In the meantime, Harry Horner, you must dine with me; I keep my wedding at my aunt's in the Piazza.

HORNER: Thy wedding! What stale maid has lived to despair of a husband, or what young one of a gallant!

SPARKISH: Oh, your servant, sir—this gentleman's sister then—no stale maid.

HORNER: I am sorry for't.

PINCHWIFE (*aside*): How comes he so concerned for her?

SPARKISH: You sorry for't? Why, do you know any ill by her?

HORNER: No, I know none but by thee; 'tis for her sake, not yours, and another man's sake that might have hoped, I thought.

SPARKISH: Another man! another man! What is his name?

HORNER: Nay, since 'tis past he shall be nameless.—(*Aside.*) Poor Harcourt! I am sorry thou hast missed her.

PINCHWIFE (*aside*): He seems to be much troubled at the match.

SPARKISH: Prithee tell me—nay, you shan't go, brother.

PINCHWIFE: I must of necessity, but I'll come to you to dinner.

(*Exit* PINCHWIFE.)

SPARKISH: But, Harry, what, have I a rival in my wife already? But with all my heart, for he may be of use to me hereafter; for though my hunger is now my sauce, and I can fall on heartily without, but the time will come when a rival will be as good sauce for a married man to a wife as an orange to veal.

HORNER: O thou damned rogue! Thou has set my teeth on edge with thy orange.

SPARKISH: Then let's to dinner—there I was with you again. Come.

HORNER: But who dines with thee?

SPARKISH: My friends and relations, my brother Pinchwife, you see, of your acquaintance.

HORNER: And his wife?

SPARKISH: No, gad, he'll ne'er let her come amongst us good fellows. Your stingy country coxcomb keeps his wife from his friends, as he does his little firkin of ale for his own drinking, and a gentleman can't get a smack on't; but his servants, when his back is turned, broach it at their pleasures, and dust it away, ha ha ha! Gad I am witty. I think, considering I was married today, by the world; but come—

HORNER: No, I will not dine with you, unless you can fetch her too.

SPARKISH: Pshaw! what pleasure canst thou have with women now, Harry.

HORNER: My eyes are not gone; I love a good prospect yet, and will not dine with you unless she does too. Go fetch her, therefore, but do not tell her husband 'tis for my sake.

SPARKISH: Well, I'll go try what I can do; in the meantime come away to my aunt's lodging, 'tis in the way to Pinchwife's.

HORNER: The poor woman has called for aid, and stretched forth her hand, doctor; I cannot but help her over the pale out of the briars.

(*Exeunt* SPARKISH, HORNER, QUACK.)

SCENE IV

The scene changes to PINCHWIFE's *house.* MRS. PINCHWIFE *alone, leaning on her elbow. A table, pen, ink, and paper.*

MRS. PINCHWIFE: Well, 'tis e'en so, I have got the London disease they call love; I am sick of my husband, and for my gallant. I have heard this distemper called a fever, but methinks 'tis liker an ague, for when I think of my husband, I tremble and am in a cold sweat and have inclinations to vomit; but when I think of my gallant, dear Mr. Horner, my hot fit comes and I am all in a fever, indeed, and as in other fevers my own chamber is tedious to me, and I would fain be removed to his, and then methinks I should be well. Ah, poor Mr. Horner! Well, I cannot, will not stay here; therefore I'll make an end of my letter to him, which shall be a finer letter than my last, because I have studied it like anything. Oh sick, sick!

(*Takes the pen and writes.*)

(*Enter* MR. PINCHWIFE, *who seeing her writing steals softly behind her, and looking over her shoulder, snatches the paper from her.*)

PINCHWIFE: What, writing more letters?

MRS. PINCHWIFE: O Lord, bud! Why d'ye fright me so?

(*She offers to run out; he stops her, and reads.*)

PINCHWIFE: How's this! Nay, you shall not stir, madam. "Dear, dear, dear, Mr. Horner"—very well—I have taught you to write letters to good purpose—but let's see't.

"First, I am to beg your pardon for my boldness in writing to you, which I'd have you to know I would not have done had not you said first you loved me so extremely, which if you do, you will never suffer me to lie in the arms of another man, whom I loathe, nauseate, and detest."—Now you can write these filthy words. But what follows?—"Therefore I hope you will speedily find some way to free me from this unfortunate match, which was never, I assure you, of my choice, but I'm afraid 'tis already too far gone. However, if you love me, as I do you, you will try what you can do, but you must help me away before tomorrow, or else, alas, I shall be forever out of your reach, for I can defer no longer our—our" (*The letter concludes.*)—What is to follow "our"?— Speak, what? Our journey into the country, I suppose—Oh, woman, damned woman! and love, damned love, their old tempter! for this is one of his miracles; in a moment he can make those blind that could see, and those see that were blind, those dumb that could speak, and those prattle who were dumb before; nay, what is more than all, make these dough-baked, senseless, indocile animals, women, too hard for us, their politic lords and rulers, in a moment. But make an end of your letter, and then I'll make an end of you thus and all my plagues together.

(*Draws his sword.*)

MRS. PINCHWIFE: O Lord, O Lord, you are such a passionate man, bud.

(*Enter* SPARKISH.)

SPARKISH: How now, what's here to do?

PINCHWIFE: This fool here now!

SPARKISH: What, drawn upon your wife? You should never do that but at night in the dark, when you can't hurt her. This is my sister-in-law, is it not? (*Pulls aside her handkerchief.*) Ay, faith, e'en our country Margery; one may know her. Come, she and you must go dine with me; dinner's ready, come. But where's my wife? Is she not come home yet? Where is she?

PINCHWIFE: Making you a cuckold; 'tis that they all do, as soon as they can.

SPARKISH: What, the wedding day? No, a wife that designs to make a cully of her husband will be sure to let him win the first stake of love, by the world. But come, they stay dinner for us; come, I'll lead down our Margery.

MRS. PINCHWIFE: No—so, go, we'll follow you.

SPARKISH: I will not wag without you.

PINCHWIFE (*aside*): This coxcomb is a sensible torment to me amidst the greatest in the world.

SPARKISH: Come, come, Madam Margery.

PINCHWIFE: No, I'll lead her my own way. What, would you treat your friends with mine, for want of your own wife? (*Leads her to t'other door, and locks her in, and returns.*)—(*Aside.*) I am contented my rage should take breath.

SPARKISH (*aside*): I told Horner this.

PINCHWIFE: Come now.

SPARKISH: Lord, how shy you are of your wife! But let me tell you, brother, we men of wit have amongst us a saying that cuckolding, like the smallpox, comes with a fear, and you may keep your wife as much as you will out of danger of infection, but if her constitution incline her to't, she'll have it sooner or later, by the world, say they.

PINCHWIFE (*aside*): What a thing is a cuckold, that every fool can make him ridiculous!—Well, sir—but let me advise you, now you are come to be concerned, because you suspect the danger, not to neglect the means to prevent it, especially when the greatest share of the malady will light upon your own head, for

> Hows'e'er the kind wife's belly comes to swell,
> The husband breeds for her, and first is ill.

(*Exeunt* PINCHWIFE *and* SPARKISH.)

ACT V

SCENE I   MR. PINCHWIFE'S HOUSE.

Enter MR. PINCHWIFE *and* MRS. PINCHWIFE. *A table and candle.*

PINCHWIFE: Come, take the pen and make an end of the letter, just as you intended; if you are false in a tittle, I shall soon perceive it, and punish you with this as you deserve. (*Lays his hand on his sword.*) Write what was to follow—let's see—"You must make haste and help me away before tomorrow, or else I shall be forever out of your reach, for I can defer no longer our"—What follows "our"?

MRS. PINCHWIFE: Must all out then, bud? (MRS. PINCHWIFE *takes the pen and writes.*) Look you there then.

PINCHWIFE: Let's see—"For I can defer no longer our—wedding—Your slighted Alithea." What's the meaning of this? My sister's name to't. Speak, unriddle!

MRS. PINCHWIFE: Yes, indeed, bud.

PINCHWIFE: But why her name to't? Speak—speak, I say!

MRS. PINCHWIFE: Ay, but you'll tell her then again; if you would not tell her again—

PINCHWIFE: I will not—I am stunned, my head turns around. Speak.

MRS. PINCHWIFE: Won't you tell her indeed, and indeed?

PINCHWIFE: No, speak, I say.

MRS. PINCHWIFE: She'll be angry with me, but I had rather she should be angry with me than you, bud; and to tell you the truth, 'twas she made me write the letter, and taught me what I should write.

PINCHWIFE (*aside*): Ha! I thought the style was somewhat better than her own.—But how could she come to you to teach you, since I had locked you up alone?

MRS. PINCHWIFE: Oh, through the keyhole, bud.

PINCHWIFE: But why should she make you write a letter for her to him, since she can write herself?

MRS. PINCHWIFE: Why, she said because—for I was unwilling to do it.

PINCHWIFE: Because what—because?

MRS. PINCHWIFE: Because, lest Mr. Horner should be cruel, and refuse her; or vain afterwards, and show the letter, she might disown it, the hand not being hers.

PINCHWIFE (*aside*): How's this? Ha!—then I think I shall come to myself again. This changeling could not invent this lie; but if she could, why should she? She might think I should soon discover it—stay—now I think on't too, Horner said he was sorry she had married Sparkish, and her disowning her marriage,[36] to me makes me think she has evaded it for Horner's sake. Yet why should she take this course? But men in love are fools; women may well be so.—But hark you, madam, your sister went out in the morning, and I have not seen her within since.

MRS. PINCHWIFE: Alackaday, she has been crying all day above, it seems, in a corner.

PINCHWIFE: Where is she? Let me speak with her.

MRS. PINCHWIFE (*aside*): O Lord, then he'll discover all!—Pray hold, bud; what, d'ye mean to discover me? She'll know I have told you then. Pray, bud, let me talk with her first.

PINCHWIFE: I must speak with her, to know whether Horner ever made her any promise, and whether she be married to Sparkish or no.

MRS. PINCHWIFE: Pray, dear bud, don't, till I have spoken with her and told her that I have told you all, for she'll kill me else.

PINCHWIFE: Go then, and bid her come out to me.

MRS. PINCHWIFE: Yes, yes, bud.

PINCHWIFE: Let me see—

MRS. PINCHWIFE (*aside*): I'll go, but she is not within to come to him. I have just got time to know of Lucy her maid, who first set me on work, what lie I shall tell next, for I am e'en at my wit's end.

(*Exit* MRS. PINCHWIFE.)

PINCHWIFE: Well, I resolve it; Horner shall have her. I'd rather give him my sister than lend him my wife, and such an alliance will prevent his pretensions to my wife, sure. I'll make him of kin to her, and then he won't care for her.

(MRS. PINCHWIFE *returns.*)

MRS. PINCHWIFE: O Lord, bud! I told you what anger you would make me with my sister.

PINCHWIFE: Won't she come hither?

MRS. PINCHWIFE: No, no, alackaday, she's ashamed to look you in the face, and she says, if you go in to her, she'll run away downstairs, and shamefully go herself to Mr. Horner, who has promised her marriage, she says, and she will have no other, so she won't.

PINCHWIFE: Did he so—promise her marriage?—then she shall have no other. Go tell her so, and if she will come and discourse with me a little concerning the means, I will about it immediately. Go.

(*Exit* MRS. PINCHWIFE.)

His estate is equal to Sparkish's, and his extraction as much better than his as his parts are; but my chief reason is, I'd rather be of kin to him by the name of brother-in-law than that of cuckold.

(*Enter* MRS. PINCHWIFE.)

Well, what says she now?

MRS. PINCHWIFE: Why, she says she would only have you lead her to Horner's lodging—with whom she first will discourse the matter before she talk with you, which yet she cannot do; for alack, poor creature, she says she can't so much as look you in the face, therefore she'll come to you in a mask; and you must excuse her if she make you no answer to any question of yours, till you have brought her to Mr. Horner; and if you will not chide her, nor question her, she'll come out to you immediately.

PINCHWIFE: Let her come; I will not speak a word to her, nor require a word from her.

MRS. PINCHWIFE: Oh, I forgot; besides, she says she cannot look you in the face through a mask, therefore would desire you to put out the candle.

PINCHWIFE: I agree to all; let her make haste—there, 'tis out.

(*Puts out the candle.*)

(*Exit* MRS. PINCHWIFE.)

—My case is something better. I'd rather fight with Horner for not lying with my sister than for lying with my wife, and of the two I had rather find my sister too forward than my wife; I expected no other from her free education, as she calls it, and her passion for the

---

36. Pinchwife thinks that Alithea claims her marriage is invalid so she can be with Horner.

town. Well—wife and sister are names which make us expect love and duty, pleasure and comfort, but we find 'em plagues and torments, and are equally, though differently, troublesome to their keeper; for we have as much ado to get people to lie with our sisters as to keep 'em from lying with our wives.

(*Enter* MRS. PINCHWIFE *masked, and in hoods and scarves and a nightgown and petticoat of* ALITHEA'S, *in the dark.*)

What, are you come, Sister? Let us go then—but first let me lock up my wife.—Mrs. Margery, where are you?

MRS. PINCHWIFE: Here, bud.

PINCHWIFE: Come hither, that I may lock you up; get you in.

(*Locks the door.*)—come, sister, where are you now?

(MRS. PINCHWIFE *gives him her hand, but when he lets her go, she steals softly on t'other side of him, and is led away by him for his sister* ALITHEA.)

SCENE II

The scene changes to HORNER'S *lodging.*

QUACK, HORNER.

QUACK: What, all alone? Not so much as one of your cuckolds here, nor one of their wives! They use to take their turns with you, as if they were to watch you.

HORNER: Yes, it often happens that a cuckold is but his wife's spy, and is more upon family duty when he is with her gallant abroad, hindering his pleasure, than when he is at home with her, playing the gallant. But the hardest duty a married woman imposes upon a lover is keeping her husband company always.

QUACK: And his fondness wearies you almost as soon as hers.

HORNER: A pox! keeping a cuckold company, after you have had his wife, is as tiresome as the company of a country squire to a witty fellow of the town, when he has got all his money.

QUACK: And as at first a man makes a friend of the husband to get the wife, so at last you are fain to fall out with the wife to be rid of the husband.

HORNER: Ay, most cuckold-makers are true courtiers; when once a poor man has cracked his credit for 'em, they can't abide to come near him.

QUACK: But at first, to draw him in, are so sweet, so kind, so dear, just as you are to Pinchwife. But what becomes of that intrigue with his wife?

HORNER: A pox! he's as surly as an alderman that has been bit, and since he's so coy, his wife's kindness is in vain, for she's a silly innocent.

QUACK: Did she not send you a letter by him?

HORNER: Yes, but that's a riddle I have not yet solved. Allow the poor creature to be willing, she is silly too, and he keeps her up so close—

QUACK: Yes, so close that he makes her but the more willing, and adds but revenge to her love, which two, when met, seldom fail of satisfying each other one way or other.

HORNER: What! here's the man we are talking of, I think.

(*Enter* MR. PINCHWIFE, *leading in his wife, masked, muffled, and in his sister's gown.*)

Pshaw!

QUACK: Bringing his wife to you is the next thing to bringing a love letter from her.

HORNER: What means this?

PINCHWIFE: The last time, you know, sir, I brought you a love letter; now you see, a mistress. I think you'll say I am a civil man to you.

HORNER: Ay, the devil take me, will I say thou art the civilest man I ever met with, and I have known some. I fancy I understand thee now better than I did the letter; but hark thee, in thy ear—

PINCHWIFE: What?

HORNER: Nothing but the usual question, man: is she sound, on thy word?

PINCHWIFE: What, you take her for a wench, and me for a pimp?

HORNER: Pshaw! wench and pimp, paw words. I know thou art an honest fellow, and hast a great acquaintance among the ladies, and perhaps hast made love for me rather than let me make love to thy wife.

PINCHWIFE: Come, sir, in short, I am for no fooling.

HORNER: Nor I neither; therefore prithee let's see her face presently. Make her show, man; art thou sure I don't know her?

PINCHWIFE: I am sure you do know her.

HORNER: A pox! why dost thou bring her to me then?

PINCHWIFE: Because she's a relation of mine—

HORNER: Is she, faith, man? Then thou are still more civil and obliging, dear rogue.

PINCHWIFE: Who desired me to bring her to you.

HORNER: Then she is obliging, dear rogue.

PINCHWIFE: You'll make her welcome for my sake, I hope.

HORNER: I hope she's handsome enough to make herself welcome. Prithee, let her unmask.

PINCHWIFE: Do you speak to her; she would never be ruled by me.

HORNER: Madam—(MRS. PINCHWIFE *whispers to* HORNER.)—She says she must speak with me in private. Withdraw, prithee.

PINCHWIFE (*aside*): She's unwilling, it seems, I should know all her undecent conduct in this business.—Well then, I'll leave you together, and hope when I am gone you'll agree; if not, you and I shan't agree, sir.

HORNER (*aside*): What means the fool?—If she and I agree, 'tis no matter what you and I do.

(*Whispers to* MRS. PINCHWIFE, *who makes signs with her hand for* PINCHWIFE *to be gone.*)

PINCHWIFE: In the meantime, I'll fetch a parson, and find out Sparkish and disabuse him. You would have me fetch a parson, would you not? Well then—now I think I am rid of her, and shall have no more trouble with her. Our sisters and daughters, like usurers' money, are safest when put out; but our wives, like their writings, never safe but in our closets under lock and key.

(*Exit* MR. PINCHWIFE.)

(*Enter* BOY.)

BOY: Sir Jasper Fidget, sir, is coming up.

(*Exit.*)

HORNER: Here's the trouble of a cuckold, now, we are talking of. A pox on him! Has he not enough to do to hinder his wife's sport, but he must other women's too?—Step in here, madam.

(*Exit* MRS. PINCHWIFE.)

(*Enter* SIR JASPER.)

SIR JASPER FIDGET: My best and dearest friend.

HORNER (*aside to* QUACK): The old style, doctor.— Well, be short, for I am busy. What would your impertinent wife have now?

SIR JASPER FIDGET: Well guessed, i'faith, for I do come from her.

HORNER: To invite me to supper. Tell her I can't come; go.

SIR JASPER FIDGET: Nay, now you are out, faith; for my lady and the whole knot of the virtuous gang, as they call themselves, are resolved upon a frolic of coming to you tonight in a masquerade, and are all dressed already.

HORNER: I shan't be at home.

SIR JASPER FIDGET (*aside*): Lord, how churlish he is to women!—Nay, prithee don't disappoint 'em; they'll think 'tis my fault; prithee don't. I'll send in the banquet and the fiddles. But make no noise on't, for the poor virtuous rogues would not have it known for the world that they go a-masquerading, and they would come to no man's ball but yours.

HORNER: Well, well—get you gone, and tell 'em if they come, 'twill be at the peril of their honor and yours.

SIR JASPER FIDGET: He, he, he!—we'll trust you for that; farewell.

(*Exit* SIR JASPER.)

HORNER: Doctor, anon you too shall be my guest, But now I'm going to a private feast.

(*Exeunt.*)

SCENE III

The scene changes to the Piazza of Covent Garden.
SPARKISH, PINCHWIFE.

SPARKISH (*with the letter in his hand*): But who would have thought a woman could have been false to me? By the world, I could not have thought it.

PINCHWIFE: You were for giving and taking liberty; she has taken it only, sir, now you find in that letter. You are a frank person, and so is she, you see there.

SPARKISH: Nay, if this be her hand—for I never saw it.

PINCHWIFE: 'Tis no matter whether that be her hand or no; I am sure this hand at her desire, led her to Mr. Horner, with whom I left her just now, to go fetch a parson to 'em, at their desire too, to deprive you of her forever, for it seems yours was but a mock marriage.

SPARKISH: Indeed, she would needs have it that 'twas Harcourt himself in a parson's habit that married us, but I'm sure he told me 'twas his brother Ned.

PINCHWIFE: Oh, there 'tis out, and you were deceived, not she, for you are such a frank person—but I must be gone. You'll find her at Mr. Horner's; go and believe your eyes.

(*Exit* MR. PINCHWIFE.)

SPARKISH: Nay, I'll to her, and call her as many crocodiles, sirens, harpies, and other heathenish names as a poet would do a mistress who had refused to hear his suit, nay more, his verses on her.—But stay, is not that she following a torch at t'other end of the Piazza? And from Horner's certainly—'tis so.

(*Enter* ALITHEA, *following a torch, and* LUCY *behind.*)

You are well met, madam, though you don't think so. What, you have made a short visit to Mr. Horner, but I suppose you'll return to him presently; by that time the parson can be with him.

ALITHEA: Mr. Horner, and the parson, sir!

SPARKISH: Come, madam, no more dissembling, no more jilting, for I am no more a frank person.

ALITHEA: How's this?

LUCY (*aside*): So 'twill work I see.

SPARKISH: Could you find out no easy country fool to abuse? none but me, a gentleman of wit and pleasure about the town? But it was your pride to be too hard for a man of parts, unworthy false woman! false as a friend that lends a man money to lose; false as dice, who undo those that trust all they have to 'em.

LUCY (*aside*): He has been a great bubble by his similes, as they say.

ALITHEA: You have been too merry, sir, at your wedding dinner, sure.

SPARKISH: What, d'ye mock me too?

ALITHEA: Or you have been deluded.

SPARKISH: By you.

ALITHEA: Let me understand you.

SPARKISH: Have you the confidence—I should call it something else, since you know your guilt—to stand my just reproaches? You did not write an impudent letter to Mr. Horner! who I find now has clubbed with you in deluding me with his aversion for women, that I might not, forsooth, suspect him for my rival.

LUCY (*aside*): D'ye think the gentleman can be jealous now, madam?

ALITHEA: I write a letter to Mr. Horner!

SPARKISH: Nay, madam, do not deny it; your brother showed it me just now, and told me likewise he left you at Horner's lodging to fetch a parson to marry you to him, and I wish you joy, madam, joy, joy! And to him, too, much joy, and to myself more joy for not marrying you.

ALITHEA (*aside*): So, I find my brother would break off the match, and I can consent to't, since I see this gentleman can be made jealous.—O Lucy, by his rude usage and jealousy, he makes me almost afraid I am married to him. Art thou sure 'twas Harcourt himself and no parson that married us?

SPARKISH: No, madam, I thank you. I suppose that was a contrivance too of Mr. Horner's and yours, to make Harcourt play the parson; but I would as little as you have him one now, no, not for the world, for shall I tell you another truth? I never had any passion for you till now, for now I hate you. 'Tis true I might have married your portion, as other men of parts of the town do sometimes, and so your servant; and to show my unconcernedness, I'll come to your wedding, and resign you with as much joy as I would a stale wench to a new cully; nay, with as much joy as I would after the first night, if I had been married to you. There's for you, and so your servant, servant.

(*Exit* SPARKISH.)

ALITHEA: How was I deceived in a man!

LUCY: You'll believe then, a fool may be made jealous now? For that easiness in him that suffers him to be led by a wife will likewise permit him to be persuaded against her by others.

ALITHEA: But marry Mr. Horner! My brother does not intend it, sure; if I thought he did, I would take thy advice, and Mr. Harcourt for my husband. And now I wish that if there be any overwise woman of the town, who, like me, would marry a fool for fortune, liberty, or title, first, that her husband may love play, and be a cully to all the town but her, and suffer none but fortune to be mistress of his purse; then, if for liberty, that he may send her into the country under the conduct of some housewifely mother-in-law; and if for title, may the world give 'em none but that of cuckold.

LUCY: And for her greater curse, madam, may he not deserve it.

ALITHEA: Away, impertinent!—Is not this my old Lady Lanterlu's?

LUCY: Yes, madam.—(*Aside.*) And here I hope we shall find Mr. Harcourt.

(*Exeunt* ALITHEA, LUCY.)

SCENE IV

The scene changes again to HORNER'S *lodging.* HORNER, LADY FIDGET, MRS. DAINTY FIDGET, MRS. SQUEAMISH. *A table, banquet, and bottles.*

HORNER (*aside*): A pox! they are come too soon—before I have sent back my new mistress. All I have now to do is to lock her in, that they may not see her.

LADY FIDGET: That we may be sure of our welcome, we have brought our entertainment with us, and are resolved to treat thee, dear toad.

MRS. DAINTY FIDGET: And that we may be merry to purpose, have left Sir Jasper and my old Lady Squeamish quarreling at home at backgammon.

MRS. SQUEAMISH: Therefore let us make use of our time, lest they should chance to interrupt us.

LADY FIDGET: Let us sit then.

HORNER: First, that you may be private, let me lock this door and that, and I'll wait upon you presently.

LADY FIDGET: No, sir, shut 'em only and your lips forever, for we must trust you as much as our women.

HORNER: You know all vanity's killed in me; I have no occasion for talking.

LADY FIDGET: Now, ladies, supposing we had drank each of us our two bottles, let us speak the truth of our hearts.

MRS. DAINTY FIDGET AND MRS. SQUEAMISH: Agreed.

LADY FIDGET: By this brimmer, for truth is nowhere else to be found.—(*Aside to* HORNER.) Not in thy heart, false man!

HORNER (*aside to* LADY FIDGET): You have found me a true man, I'm sure.

LADY FIDGET (*aside to* HORNER): Not every way.—But let us sit and be merry.

(LADY FIDGET *sings.*)

1

Why should our damn'd tyrants oblige
   us to live
On the pittance of pleasure which they
   only give?
We must not rejoice
With wine and with noise.
In vain we must wake in a dull bed
   alone,
Whilst to our warm rival, the bottle,
   they're gone.
Then lay aside charms,
And take up these arms.

2

'Tis wine only gives 'em their courage
   and wit;
Because we live sober, to men we submit.
If for beauties you'd pass,
Take a lick of the glass,
'Twill mend your complexions, and
   when they are gone,
The best red we have is the red of the
   grape.
Then, sisters, lay't on.
And damn a good shape.

MRS. DAINTY FIDGET: Dear brimmer! Well, in token of our openness and plain-dealing, let us throw our masks over our heads.

HORNER: So, 'twill come to the glasses anon.

MRS. SQUEAMISH: Lovely brimmer! Let me enjoy him first.

LADY FIDGET: No, I never part with a gallant till I've tried him. Dear brimmer, that mak'st our husband shortsighted.

MRS. DAINTY FIDGET: And our bashful gallants bold.

MRS. SQUEAMISH: And for want of a gallant, the butler lovely in our eyes.—Drink, eunuch.

LADY FIDGET: Drink, thou representative of a husband. Damn a husband!

MRS. DAINTY FIDGET: And, as it were a husband, an old keeper.

MRS. SQUEAMISH: And an old grandmother.

HORNER: And an English bawd, and a French surgeon.

LADY FIDGET: Ay, we have all a reason to curse 'em.

HORNER: For my sake ladies?

LADY FIDGET: No, for our own, for the first spoils all young gallants' industry.

MRS. DAINTY FIDGET: And the other's art makes 'em bold only with common women.

MRS. SQUEAMISH: And rather run the hazard of the vile distemper amongst them than of a denial amongst us.

MRS. DAINTY FIDGET: The filthy toads choose mistresses now as they do stuffs, for having been fancied and worn by others.

MRS. SQUEAMISH: For being common and cheap.

LADY FIDGET: Whilst women of quality, like the richest stuffs, lie untumbled and unasked for.

HORNER: Ay, neat, and cheap, and new, often they think best.

MRS. DAINTY FIDGET: No, sir, the beasts will be known by a mistress longer than by a suit.

MRS. SQUEAMISH: And 'tis not for the cheapness neither.

LADY FIDGET: No, for the vain fops will take up druggets[37] and embroider 'em. But I wonder at the depraved appetites of witty men; they use to be out of the common road, and hate imitation. Pray tell me, beast, when you were a man, why you rather chose to club with a multitude in a common house for an entertainment than to be the only guest at a good table.

HORNER: Why, faith, ceremony and expectation are unsufferable to those that are sharp bent; people always eat with the best stomach at an ordinary, where every man is snatching for the best bit.

LADY FIDGET: Though he get a cut over the fingers.—But I have heard people eat most heartily of another man's meat, that is, what they do not pay for.

HORNER: When they are sure of their welcome and freedom, for ceremony in love and eating is as ridiculous as in fighting; falling on briskly is all should be done in those occasions.

LADY FIDGET: Well, then, let me tell you, sir, there is nowhere more freedom than in our houses, and we take freedom from a young person as a sign of good breeding, and a person may be as free as he pleases with us, as frolic, as gamesome, as wild as he will.

HORNER: Han't I heard you all declaim against wild men?

LADY FIDGET: Yes, but for all that, we think wildness in a man as desirable a quality as in a duck or rabbit; a tame man, foh!

HORNER: I know not, but your reputations frightened me, as much as your faces invited me.

LADY FIDGET: Our reputation! Lord, why should you not think that we women make use of our reputation, as you men of yours, only to deceive the world with less suspicion? Our virtue is like the statesman's religion, the Quaker's word, the gamester's oath, and the great man's honor—but to cheat those that trust us.

MRS. SQUEAMISH: And that demureness, coyness, and modesty that you see in our faces in the boxes at plays, is as much a sign of a kind woman as a vizard-mask in the pit.

MRS. DAINTY FIDGET: For, I assure you, women are least masked when they have the velvet vizard on.

LADY FIDGET: You would have found us modest women in our denials only.

MRS. SQUEAMISH: Our bashfulness is only the reflection of the men's.

MRS. DAINTY FIDGET: We blush when they are shamefaced.

HORNER: I beg your pardon, ladies; I was deceived in you devilishly. But why that mighty pretense to honor?

LADY FIDGET: We have told you. But sometimes 'twas for the same reason you men pretend business often, to avoid ill company, to enjoy the better and more privately those you love.

HORNER: But why would you ne'er give a friend a wink then?

LADY FIDGET: Faith, your reputation frightened us as much as ours did you, you were so notoriously lewd.

HORNER: And you so seemingly honest.

LADY FIDGET: Was that all that deterred you?

HORNER: And so expensive—you allow freedom, you say—

LADY FIDGET: Ay, ay.

37. Cheap fabric.

HORNER: That I was afraid of losing my little money, as well as my little time, both which my other pleasures required.

LADY FIDGET: Money, foh! You talk like a little fellow now; do such as we expect money?

HORNER: I beg your pardon, madam; I must confess, I have heard that great ladies, like great merchants, set but the higher prices upon what they have, because they are not in necessity of taking the first offer.

MRS. DAINTY FIDGET: Such as we make sale of our hearts?

MRS. SQUEAMISH: We bribed for our love? Foh!

HORNER: With your pardon, ladies, I know, like great men in offices, you seem to exact flattery and attendance only from your followers; but you have receivers about you, and such fees to pay, a man is afraid to pass your grants.[38] Besides we must let you win at cards, or we lose your hearts; and if you make an assignation, 'tis at a goldsmith's, jeweler's, or china house, where, for your honor you deposit to him, he must pawn his to the punctual cit, and so paying for what you take up, pays for what he takes up.

MRS. DAINTY FIDGET: Would you not have us assured of our gallant's love?

MRS. SQUEAMISH: For love is better known by liberality than by jealousy.

LADY FIDGET: For one may be dissembled, the other not.—(*Aside.*) But my jealousy can be no longer dissembled, and they are telling ripe. —Come, here's to our gallants in waiting whom we must name, and I'll begin. This is my false rogue. (*Claps him on the back.*)

MRS. SQUEAMISH: How!

HORNER (*aside*): So, all will out now.

MRS. SQUEAMISH (*aside to* HORNER): Did you not tell me, 'twas for my sake only you reported yourself no man?

MRS. DAINTY FIDGET (*aside to* HORNER): Oh wretch! Did you not swear to me, 'twas for my love and honor you passed for that thing you do?

HORNER: So, so.

LADY FIDGET: Come, speak, ladies; this is my false villain.

MRS. SQUEAMISH: And mine too.

MRS. DAINTY FIDGET: And mine.

HORNER: Well then, you are all three my false rogues too, and there's an end on't.

LADY FIDGET: Well then, there's no remedy; sister sharers, let us not fall out, but have a care of our honor. Though we get no presents, no jewels of him, we are savers of our honor, the jewel of most value and use, which shines yet to the world unsuspected, though it be counterfeit.

HORNER: Nay, and is e'en as good as if it were true, provided the world think so; for honor, like beauty now, only depends on the opinion of others.

LADY FIDGET: Well, Harry Common, I hope you can be true to three. Swear—but 'tis no purpose to require your oath, for you are as often forsworn as you swear to new women.

HORNER: Come, faith, madam, let us e'en pardon one another, for all the difference I find betwixt we men and you women, we forswear ourselves at the beginning of an amour, you as long as it lasts.

(*Enter* SIR JASPER FIDGET, *and* OLD LADY SQUEAMISH.)

SIR JASPER FIDGET: Oh, my Lady Fidget, was this your cunning, to come to Mr. Horner without me? But you have been nowhere else, I hope.

LADY FIDGET: No, Sir Jasper.

OLD LADY SQUEAMISH: And you came straight hither, Biddy?

MRS. SQEAMISH: Yes, indeed, Lady Grandmother.

SIR JASPER FIDGET: 'Tis well, 'tis well; I knew when once they were thoroughly acquainted with poor Horner, they'd ne'er be from him. You may let her masquerade it with my wife and Horner, and I warrant her reputation safe. (*Enter* BOY.)

BOY: Oh, sir, here's the gentleman come whom you bid me not suffer to come up without giving you notice, with a lady too, and other gentlemen.

HORNER: Do you all go in there, whilst I send 'em away, and, boy, do you desire 'em to stay below till I come, which shall be immediately. (*Exeunt* SIR JASPER, LADY SQUEAMISH, LADY FIDGET, MRS. DAINTY, MRS. SQUEAMISH.)

BOY: Yes, sir. (*Exit.*)

---

38. Is afraid to believe you.

(*Exit* HORNER *at t'other door, and returns with* MRS. PINCHWIFE.)

HORNER: You would not take my advice to be gone home before your husband came back; he'll now discover all. Yet pray, my dearest, be persuaded to go home, and leave the rest to my management; I'll let you down the back way.

MRS. PINCHWIFE: I don't know the way home, so I don't.

HORNER: My man shall wait upon you.

MRS. PINCHWIFE: No, don't you believe that I'll go at all; what, are you weary of me already?

HORNER: No, my life, 'tis that I may love you long, 'tis to secure my love, and your reputation with your husband; he'll never receive you again else.

MRS. PINCHWIFE: What care I? D'ye think to frighten me with that? I don't intend to go to him again; you shall be my husband now.

HORNER: I cannot be your husband, dearest, since you are married to him.

MRS. PINCHWIFE: Oh, would you make me believe that? Don't I see every day, at London here, women leave their first husbands, and go and live with other men as their wives? Pish, pshaw! you'd make me angry, but that I love you so mainly.

HORNER: So, they are coming up—in again, in, I hear 'em.

(*Exit* MRS. PINCHWIFE.)

Well, a silly mistress is like a weak place, soon got, soon lost, a man has scarce time for plunder; she betrays her husband first to her gallant, and then her gallant to her husband.

(*Enter* PINCHWIFE, ALITHEA, HARCOURT, SPARKISH, LUCY, *and a* PARSON.)

PINCHWIFE: Come, madam, 'tis not the sudden change of your dress, the confidence of your asseverations, and your false witness there, shall persuade me I did not bring you hither just now; here's my witness, who cannot deny it, since you must be confronted.—Mr. Horner, did not I bring this lady to you just now?

HORNER: Now must I wrong one woman for another's sake, but that's no new thing for me; for in these cases I am still on the criminal side, against the innocent.

ALITHEA: Pray, speak sir.

HORNER (*aside*): It must be so—I must be impudent, and try my luck; impudence uses to be too hard for truth.

PINCHWIFE: What, you are studying an evasion or excuse for her. Speak, sir.

HORNER: No, faith, I am something backward only to speak in women's affairs or disputes.

PINCHWIFE: She bids you speak.

ALITHEA: Ay, pray, sir, do; pray satisfy him.

HORNER: Then truly, you did bring that lady to me just now.

PINCHWIFE: Oh ho!

ALITHEA: How, sir!

HARCOURT: How, Horner!

ALITHEA: What mean you, sir, I always took you for a man of honor.

HORNER (*aside*): Ay, so much a man of honor that I must save my mistress, I thank you, come what will on't.

SPARKISH: So, if I had had her, she'd have made me believe the moon had been made of a Christmas pie.

LUCY (*aside*): Now could I speak, if I durst, and solve the riddle, who am the author of it.

ALITHEA: O unfortunate woman! A combination against my honor, which most concerns me now, because you share in my disgrace, sir, and it is your censure, which I must now suffer, that troubles me, not theirs.

HARCOURT: Madam, then have no trouble, you shall now see 'tis possible for me to love too, without being jealous; I will not only believe your innocence myself, but make all the world believe it.—(*Apart to* HORNER). Horner, I must now be concerned for this lady's honor.

HORNER: And I must be concerned for a lady's honor too.

HARCOURT: This lady has her honor, and I will protect it.

HORNER: My lady has not her honor, but has given it me to keep, and I will preserve it.

HARCOURT: I understand you not.

HORNER: I would not have you.

MRS. PINCHWIFE (*peeping in behind*): What's the matter with 'em all?

PINCHWIFE: Come, come, Mr. Horner, no more disputing; here's the parson. I brought him not in vain.

HARCOURT: No, sir, I'll employ him, if this lady please.

PINCHWIFE: How! what d'ye mean?

SPARKISH: Ay, what does he mean?

HORNER: Why, I have resigned your sister to him; he has my consent.

PINCHWIFE: But he has not mine, sir; a woman's injured honor, no more than a man's can be repaired or satisfied by any but him that first wronged it; and you shall marry her presently, or—

(*Lays his hand on his sword.*
Enter to them MRS. PINCHWIFE.)

MRS. PINCHWIFE (*aside*): O Lord, they'll kill poor Mr. Horner! Besides, he shan't marry her whilst I stand by and look on; I'll not lose my second husband so.

PINCHWIFE: What do I see?

ALITHEA: My sister in my clothes!

SPARKISH: Ha!

MRS. PINCHWIFE (*to* MR. PINCHWIFE): Nay, pray now don't quarrel about finding work for the parson; he shall marry me to Mr. Horner; for now, I believe you have enough of me.

HORNER (*aside*): Damned, damned, loving changeling!

MRS. PINCHWIFE: Pray, sister, pardon me for telling so many lies of you.

HARCOURT: I suppose the riddle is plain now.

LUCY: No, that must be my work. Good sir, hear me.

(*Kneels to* MR. PINCHWIFE, *who stands doggedly, with his hat over his eyes.*)

PINCHWIFE: I will never hear woman again, but make 'em all silent thus—

(*Offers to draw upon his wife.*)

HORNER: No, that must not be.

PINCHWIFE: You then shall go first, 'tis all one to me.

(*Offers to draw on* HORNER; *stopped by* HARCOURT.)

HARCOURT: Hold!

(*Enter* SIR JASPER FIDGET, LADY FIDGET, LADY SQEAMISH, MRS. DAINTY FIDGET, MRS. SQUEAMISH.)

SIR JASPER FIDGET: What's the matter? What's the matter? Pray, what's the matter, sir? I beseech you communicate, sir.

PINCHWIFE: Why, my wife has communicated, sir, as your wife may have done too, sir, if she knows him, sir.

SIR JASPER FIDGET: Pshaw! with him! Ha, ha, he!

PINCHWIFE: D'ye mock me, sir, a cuckold is a kind of a wild beast; have a care, sir.

SIR JASPER FIDGET: No, sure you mock me, sir—he cuckold you! It can't be, ha, ha, he! Why, I'll tell you, sir—

(*Offers to whisper.*)

PINCHWIFE: I tell you again, he has whored my wife, and yours too, if he knows her, and all the women he comes near; 'tis not his dissembling, his hypocrisy, can wheedle me.

SIR JASPER FIDGET: How! does he dissemble? Is he a hypocrite? Nay, then—how—wife—sister, is he a hypocrite?

OLD LADY SQEAMISH: An hypocrite! A dissembler! Speak, young harlotry, speak, how?

SIR JASPER FIDGET: Nay, then—oh, my head too!—O thou libidinous lady!

OLD LADY SQUEAMISH: O thou harloting harlotry! Hast thou done't then?

SIR JASPER FIDGET: Speak, good Horner, art thou a dissembler, a rogue? Hast thou—

HORNER: Soh!

LUCY: (*apart to* HORNER): I'll fetch you off, and her too, if she will but hold her tongue.

HORNER (*apart to* LUCY): Canst thou? I'll give thee—

LUCY (*to* MR. PINCHWIFE): Pray have but patience to hear me, sir, who am the unfortunate cause of all this confusion. Your wife is innocent, I only culpable; for I put her upon telling you all these lies concerning my mistress, in order to the breaking off the match between Mr. Sparkish and her, to make way for Mr. Harcourt.

SPARKISH: Did you so, eternal rotten tooth? Then, it seems, my mistress was not false to me, I was only deceived by you.—Brother that should have been, now, man of conduct, who is a frank person now? To bring your wife to her lover—ha!

LUCY: I assure you, sir, she came not to Mr. Horner out of love, for she loves him no more.

MRS. PINCHWIFE: Hold, I told lies for you, but you shall tell none for me, for I do love Mr. Horner with all my soul, and nobody shall say me nay; pray, don't you go to make poor Mr. Horner believe to the contrary, 'tis spitefully done of you, I'm sure.

HORNER (*aside to* MRS. PINCHWIFE): Peace, dear idiot.

MRS. PINCHWIFE: Nay, I will not peace.

PINCHWIFE: Not till I make you.

(*Enter* DORILANT, QUACK.)

DORILANT: Horner, your servant; I am the doctor's guest, he must excuse our intrusion.

QUACK: But what's the matter, gentlemen? For heaven's sake, what's the matter?

HORNER: Oh, 'tis well you are come. 'Tis a censorious world we live in; you may have brought me a reprieve, or else I had died for a crime I never committed, and these innocent ladies had suffered with me; therefore pray satisfy these worthy, honorable, jealous gentlemen—that—

(*Whispers.*)

QUACK: Oh, I understand you; is that all?—(*whispers to* SIR JASPER.) Sir Jasper, by heavens and upon the word of a physician, sir—

SIR JASPER FIDGET: Nay, I do believe you truly.—Pardon me, my virtuous ladies, and dear of honor.

OLD LADY SQUEAMISH: What, then all's right again?

SIR JASPER FIDGET: Ay, ay, and now let us satisfy him too.

(*They whisper with* MR. PINCHWIFE.)

PINCHWIFE: An eunuch! Pray, no fooling with me.

QUACK: I'll bring half the surgeons in town to swear it.

PINCHWIFE: They!—they'll swear a man bled to death through his wounds died of an apoplexy.

QUACK: Pray hear me, sir—why all the town has heard the report of him.

PINCHWIFE: But does all the town believe it?

QUACK: Pray inquire a little, and first of all these.

PINCHWIFE: I'm sure when I left the town he was the lewdest fellow in't.

QUACK: I tell you, sir, he has been in France since; pray ask but these ladies and gentlemen, your friend Mr. Dorilant.—Gentlemen and ladies han't you all heard the late sad report of poor Mr. Horner?

ALL THE LADIES: Ay, ay, ay.

DORILANT: Why, thou jealous fool, dost thou doubt it? Here's an arrant French capon.

MRS. PINCHWIFE: 'Tis false, sir, you shall not disparage poor Mr. Horner, for to my certain knowledge—

LUCY: Oh, hold!

MRS. SQUEAMISH (*aside to* LUCY): Stop her mouth!

LADY FIDGET (*to* PINCHWIFE): Upon my honor, sir, 'tis as true—

MRS. DAINTY FIDGET: D'ye think we would have been seen in his company?

MRS. SQUEAMISH: Trust our unspotted reputations with him!

LADY FIDGET (*aside to* HORNER): This you get, and we too, by trusting your secret to a fool.

HORNER: Peace, madam.—(*Aside to* QUACK.) Well, doctor, is not this a good design, that carries a man on unsuspected, and brings him off safe?

PINCHWIFE (*aside*): Well, if this were true, but my wife—

(DORILANT *whispers with* MRS. PINCHWIFE.)

ALITHEA: Come, brother, your wife is yet innocent, you see; but have a care of too strong an imagination, lest like an overconcerned, timorous gamester, by fancying an unlucky cast, it should come. Women and fortune are truest still to those that trust 'em.

LUCY: And any wild thing grows but the more fierce and hungry for being kept up, and more dangerous to the keeper.

ALITHEA: There's doctrine for all husbands, Mr. Harcourt.

HARCOURT: I edify, madam, so much that I am impatient till I am one.

DORILANT: And I edify so much by example I will never be one.

SPARKISH: And because I will not disparage my parts I'll ne'er be one.

HORNER: And I, alas, can't be one.

PINCHWIFE: But I must be one—against my will, to a country wife, with a country murrain[39] to me.

MRS. PINCHWIFE (*aside*): And I must be a country wife still too, I find, for I can't, like a city one, be rid of my musty husband and do what I list.

HORNER: Now, sir, I must pronounce your wife innocent, though I blush whilst I do it, and I am the only man by her now exposed to shame, which I will straight drown in wine, as you shall your suspicion, and the ladies' troubles

---

39. Plague.

we'll divert with a ballet.—Doctor, where are your maskers?

LUCY: Indeed, she's innocent, sir, I am her witness; and her end of coming out was but to see her sister's wedding, and what she has said to your face of her love to Mr. Horner was but the usual innocent revenge on a husband's jealousy—was it not, madam? Speak.

MRS. PINCHWIFE (*aside to* LUCY *and* HORNER): Since you'll have me tell more lies—Yes, indeed, bud.

PINCHWIFE: For my own sake fain I would all believe;
>   Cuckolds, like lovers, should themselves deceive.

But—(*Sighs.*)
His honor is least safe, too late I find
Who trusts it with a foolish wife or friend.
  (*A dance of cuckolds.*)

HORNER: Vain fops but court, and dress, and keep a pother,
To pass for women's men with one another;
But he who aims by women to be priz'd,
First by the men, you see, must be despis'd.

                    FINIS

Introduction to *Woyzeck*

WHEN THE PLAY WAS NEW

The German play *Woyzeck* was written in 1836–1837, but its playwright Georg Büchner died before completing the play. It lay unfinished and unpublished until 1875 when it appeared with the wrong title (*Wozzeck*), and it was not produced on the stage until 1913 when it was presented professionally in Munich. The play's real title was not restored until 1922. With the belated realization of this remarkable play on the stage, *Woyzeck* finally emerged as a modern classic. The entire play, surviving in a badly damaged manuscript, was not restored for publication and production until 1967.

In the 1830s Germany was experiencing considerable political unrest. Local and regional reactionary governments often ruled the day. Revolutionary rumblings were frequent in the 1830s and 1840s, and many people anticipated a revolution as had occurred in France. Although this never quite happened, Büchner emerged as a political insurgent who supported working class and peasant uprisings.

The movement of romanticism, which began in the late eighteenth century in Germany, was a dynamic influence on art and literature at the time of Büchner. Shakespeare was an important model for the romantics, and the works of Lenz, Schiller, and Goethe in Germany were important to Büchner. Some elements of romantic plays and theatre definitely had their effect on Büchner's plays, such as episodic dramatic structure; historically accurate scenery and costuming, which exploded in importance after the 1820s; literalness in terms of location in staging; and a focus on the internal struggles of the protagonist. All of these seem to have played a role in his work.

Büchner, however, was not a true romantic. Although the plays he wrote reflect some elements of the romantic, for the most part they stand alone.

None of his plays were produced in his lifetime, but the subject matter of each clearly represents his era. We do not know if he intended for his plays to be produced or simply read. If produced at the time, they would have been presented on a proscenium stage with two-dimensional wing and drop scenery, and lit by candles and oil lamps or possibly gas light, which had recently made its way into some theatres. Given the state of the German theatre at the time, he may have considered the plays appropriate for reading only.

THE PLAYWRIGHT

Georg Büchner (1813–1837) was a young, brilliant academic who was drawn to science, trained as a doctor, and quickly made his mark in research in comparative anatomy. He was fascinated with evolutionary theory in those pre-Darwin days, and was exposed to the medical profession early on—his father and many ancestors were doctors before him. Heredity, environment, and social conditions all proved important to his development of character. Such choices, however, came long before other playwrights of the movement of realism made those elements primary to their play development. Büchner was appointed to the faculty of the University of Zurich, but not long thereafter he contracted typhus and died at the untimely age of 23. Both the scientific and the theatrical worlds lost one of their most promising practitioners.

Büchner is difficult to categorize. His first play, *Danton's Death* (1835), has to be one of the finest first dramas written in any period. Like Calderón before him, Büchner explored the question, "Why do I suffer?" but for very different purposes. Creating a huge cast of characters, the playwright dramatizes the aftereffects of the French Revolution during the Reign of Terror. He followed this play in 1836 with *Leonce and Lena*, a satirical comedy that is a radical departure from *Danton*. He was working on *Woyzeck* when he died, and he apparently wrote a fourth play, which is lost.

During his three years of writing plays, Büchner also pursued scientific studies and ducked German authorities because of his political dissidence: He wrote a dangerous pamphlet entitled *The Hessian Courier*, which called for rebellion by the poor. He also wrote a wonderful but incomplete story (labeled by some as a novella) on the German playwright Jacob Lenz, who apparently suffered from schizophrenia. The description of the action in the story is so dramatic and visually stimulating that Büchner seems to have a mind like a modern stage or film director. Schizophrenia also appears to be at work in the character of Woyzeck. Some critics label Büchner as premodern, or a precursor of modernism. His plays were a powerful influence on expressionism and the work of Bertolt Brecht (both theory and practice) and probably many modern movements such as Theatre of the Absurd—any theatrical work that features characters cut off from one another and stranded in a strange and hostile world. He was not interested in painting life as it ought to be, but life as it truly is. He once wrote that a playwright should not just be entertaining or painting a picture of previous events, but he should be creating history for a second time.

GENRE, STRUCTURE, AND STYLE

Woyzeck is often referred to as a fragment. Clearly it is incomplete, but complete enough to be read and staged coherently. It is one of the most enigmatically structured plays to be found until deep into the twentieth century. The action is loosely based on real events in 1824: A deranged man named Woyzeck stabbed to death a woman with whom he had an illegitimate child.

Because the surviving text is incomplete, it is open to interpretation. The scenes were left unnumbered in the manuscript, so we are unsure of their order. How was the play meant to end? Perhaps some of the written scenes would have been cut and probably many would have been fleshed out or at least revised. Because *Danton's Death* is

very carefully written and not nearly as schematic as *Woyzeck*, some scenes would probably have been added by the playwright. As the play exists, however, *Woyzeck* must be structured or adapted by a writer or director. There is so much that is moving, disturbing, and dramatically viable in *Woyzeck* that the play is worthy of study and production. It is a wonderful collection of possibilities. No matter how the play is organized, the play's climax is clear—the stabbing at the pond.

Woyzeck is essentially a working-class tragedy. The hero is a victim, yet he is also guilty of a crime. In our own era, defense attorneys would have a field day with Woyzeck's history of being abused and manipulated. He would probably be acquitted or sent to an institution. At the time, of course, he would have been executed. (The real Woyzeck was beheaded in 1824.) Those irresponsible people (the Doctor and Captain, for example) who "created" the character Woyzeck would never have been punished or even challenged by the authorities in the 1830s. But Büchner challenges them. He was appalled by the typical practice of medicine and all of the ridiculous, irresponsible experiments that passed for real science and research.

One aspect of character becomes a structural device as well. Büchner works so hard at creating an alienated, misunderstood protagonist that nearly all of the action keeps returning to this isolation. As an audience, we focus on Woyzeck's suffering, confusion, and the steady abuse heaped on him to such a degree that even major characters like Marie (another victim) pale in comparison to this tightly focused study of a man who does not know who he is or understand what is happening to him. With this innovative character development, Büchner created a new take on the tragic act for his time and place. Some critics see this as the first truly modern tragedy.

IMPORTANT ELEMENTS OF CONTENT

The character of Woyzeck was not the first lower-class tragic hero in drama, but he is certainly the poorest and most pitifully drawn up to that time in history. Perhaps it is more appropriate to call him an anti-hero, but not in the villainous mode that had existed before in the likes of Richard III.

We see an ignorant man used as an experimental animal as Büchner combines his knowledge of dramatic literature and contemporary science. The inept society and military life surrounding Woyzeck are corrupt—but society also comprises a sea of ignorance, abuse, and primal instincts out of control. Büchner attacks irresponsible education, faulty science, and charlatans of all sorts—even at the side show, where he introduces ideas of evolution. The small mindedness of small-town life is satirized through behavior, gossip, and drinking. Büchner sprinkles the play with antisemitic moments that can lead to a variety of interpretations. The most prevalent imagery, however, is the knife. The word and the image are repeated many times throughout the play, almost like a choral refrain. The motif of the knife seems to overwhelm the suffering protagonist. We repeatedly see Woyzeck fail to understand what is happening to him. His psychosis goes undiagnosed—almost ignored—and the results are catastrophic.

THE PLAY IN REVIVAL

Two German productions finally occurred in 1913 followed in 1921 by a celebrated production by Max Reinhardt. A version for opera entitled *Wozzeck* by Alban Berg was first produced in 1925 and continues to be revived regularly. The famous auteur director Robert Wilson created another musical version in 2002. The play is also frequently revived in university and professional productions worldwide—for example, at the Gaiety Theatre in Dublin (2001), by the New York Public Theatre directed by JoAnne Akalaitis with music by Phillip Glass (1992), and as an off-Broadway production reset at a U.S. military base in the 1950s (1997). The play has been adapted for television and as at least three feature films in Germany, Hungary, and Great Britain—most famously by Werner Herzog with the wonderfully cast Klaus Kinski as Woyzeck.

SPECIAL FEATURE

The most unusual feature of *Woyzeck* is that the unfinished state of the manuscript and the myriad of possibilities for ordering the scenes lead translators and directors to structure the action in a variety of ways. Some have also written a conclusion or expanded some very short surviving fragments to make sense of them. Even if no scenes are written or expanded, the translator or director is left with a fascinating task. Some versions begin with Woyzeck shaving the Captain. Others commence with Woyzeck and Andres doing work. Many versions end with the scene of Woyzeck's return to the pond. Others construct a trial for Woyzeck, or place his body in a morgue. It can be challenging and fun to come up with your own structure.

FURTHER READING ABOUT THE PLAY, PLAYWRIGHT, AND CONTEXT

For information on German theatre, see George Brandt, *German and Dutch Theatre, 1600–1848.*

For examination of German plays, see F. J. Lamport, *German Classical Drama: Theatre, Humanity, and Nation, 1750–1870,* and Michael Patterson, *The First German Theatre: Schiller, Goethe, Kleist, and Büchner in Performance.*

For information on Büchner, see David Richards, *Georg Büchner's* Woyzeck: *A History of Its Criticism;* John Reddick, *Georg Büchner: The Shattered Whole;* and Maurice Benn, *The Drama of Revolt: A Critical Study of Georg Büchner.*

For a discussion of the romantic movement, see Walter Bruford, *Theatre, Drama and Audience in Goethe's Germany,* and Siobhan Donovan, *Music and Literature in German Romanticism.*

Woyzeck

By Georg Büchner
Translated by Carl Richard Mueller

CHARACTERS

WOYZECK
MARIE
CAPTAIN
DOCTOR
DRUM MAJOR
SERGEANT
ANDRES
MARGRET
PROPRIETOR OF THE BOOTH
CHARLATAN
OLD MAN WITH BARREL-ORGAN
JEW
INNKEEPER
APPRENTICES
KATHY
KARL THE TOWN IDIOT
GRANDMOTHER
POLICEMAN
SOLDIERS, STUDENTS, YOUNG MEN AND GIRLS, CHIL-
DREN, JUDGE, COURT CLERK, PEOPLE

SCENE I

AT THE CAPTAIN'S

The CAPTAIN *in a chair.* WOYZECK *shaving him.*

CAPTAIN: Not so fast, Woyzeck, not so fast! One thing at a time! You're making me dizzy. What am I to do with the ten extra minutes that you'll finish early today? Just think, Woyzeck: you still have thirty beautiful years to live! Thirty years! That makes three hundred and sixty months! And days! Hours! Minutes! What do you think you'll do with all that horrible stretch of time? Have you ever thought about it, Woyzeck?

WOYZECK: Yes, Sir, Captain.

CAPTAIN: It frightens me when I think about the world . . . when I think about eternity. Busy-
ness, Woyzeck, busyness! There's the eternal: that's eternal, that is eternal. That you can understand. But then again it's not eternal. It's only a moment. A mere moment. Woyzeck, it makes me shudder when I think that the earth turns itself about in a single day! What a waste of time! Where will it all end? Woyzeck, I can't even look at a mill wheel any more without becoming melancholy.

WOYZECK: Yes, sir, Captain.

CAPTAIN: Woyzeck, you always seem so exasperated! A good man isn't like that. A good man with a good conscience, that is. Well, say something, Woyzeck! What's the weather like today?

WOYZECK: Bad, Captain, sir, bad: wind!

CAPTAIN: I feel it already. Sounds like a real storm out there. A wind like that has the same effect on me as a mouse. (*Cunningly.*) I think it must be something out of the north-south.

WOYZECK: Yes, Sir, Captain.

CAPTAIN: Ha! Ha! Ha! North-south! Ha! Ha! Ha! Oh, he's a stupid one! Horribly stupid! (*Moved.*) Woyzeck, you're a good man, but (*With dignity.*) Woyzeck, you have no morality! Morality, that's when you have morals, you understand. It's a good word. You have a child without the blessings of the Church, just like our Right Reverend Garrison Chaplain says: "Without the blessings of the Church." It's not *my* phrase.

WOYZECK: Captain, sir, the good Lord's not going to look at a poor worm just because they said Amen over it before they went at it. The Lord said: "Suffer little children to come unto me."

CAPTAIN: What's that you said? What kind of strange answer's that? You're confusing me with your answers!

WOYZECK: It's us poor people that . . . You see, Captain, sir . . . Money, money! Whoever hasn't got money . . . Well, who's got morals when he's bringing something like me into the world? We're flesh and blood, too. Our kind is miserable only once: in this world and in the next. I think if we ever got to Heaven we'd have to help with the thunder.

CAPTAIN: Woyzeck, you have no virtue! You're not a virtuous human being! Flesh and blood? Whenever I rest at the window, when it's finished raining, and my eyes follow the white stockings along as they hurry across the street . . . Damnation, Woyzeck, I know what love is, too, then! I'm made of flesh and blood, too. But, Woyzeck: Virtue! Virtue! How was I to get rid of the time? I always say to myself: "You're a virtuous man (*Moved*), a good man, a good man."

WOYZECK: Yes, Captain, sir: Virtue. I haven't got much of that. You see, us common people, we haven't got virtue. That's the way it's got to be. But if I could be a gentleman, and if I could have a hat and a watch and a cane, and if I could talk refined, I'd want to be virtuous, all right. There must be something beautiful in virtue, Captain, sir. But I'm just a poor good-for-nothing!

CAPTAIN: Good, Woyzeck. You're a good man, a good man. But you think too much. It eats at you. You always seem so exasperated. Our discussion has affected me deeply. You can go now. And don't run so! Slowly! Nice and slowly down the street!

SCENE II

AN OPEN FIELD. THE TOWN IN THE DISTANCE

WOYZECK *and* ANDRES *cut twigs from the bushes.* ANDRES *whistles.*

WOYZECK: Andres? You know this place is cursed? Look at that light streak over there on the grass. There where the toadstools grow up. That's where the head rolls every night. One time somebody picked it up. He thought it was a hedgehog. Three days and three nights and he was in a box. (*Low.*) Andres, it was the Freemasons, don't you see, it was the Freemasons!

ANDRES (*sings*): Two little rabbits sat on a lawn
　　Eating, oh, eating the green green grass . . .

WOYZECK: Quiet! Can you hear it, Andres? Can you hear it? Something moving!

ANDRES (*sings*): Eating, oh, eating the green green grass
　　Till all the grass was gone.

WOYZECK: It's moving behind me! Under me! (*Stamps on the ground.*) Listen! Hollow! It's all hollow down there! It's the Freemasons!

ANDRES: I'm afraid.

WOYZECK: Strange how still it is. You almost want to hold your breath. Andres!

ANDRES: What?

WOYZECK: Say something! (*Looks about fixedly.*) Andres! How bright it is! It's all glowing over the town! A fire's sailing around the sky and a noise coming down like trumpets. It's coming closer! Let's get out of here! Don't look back! (*Drags him into the bushes.*)

ANDRES (*after a pause*): Woyzeck? Do you still hear it?

WOYZECK: It's quiet now. So quiet. Like the world's dead.

ANDRES: Listen! I can hear the drums inside. We've got to go!

SCENE III

THE TOWN

MARIE *with her* CHILD *at the window.* MARGRET. *The Retreat passes,* THE DRUM MAJOR *at its head.*

MARIE (*rocking* THE CHILD *in her arms*): Ho, boy! Da-da-da-da! Can you hear? They're coming! There!

MARGRET: What a man! Built like a tree!

MARIE: He walks like a lion. (THE DRUM MAJOR *salutes* MARIE.)

MARGRET: Oh, what a look he threw you, neighbor! We're not used to such things from you.

MARIE (*sings*): Soldiers, oh, you pretty lads . . .

MARGRET: Your eyes are still shining.

MARIE: And if they are? Take *your* eyes to the Jew's and let him clean them for you. Maybe he can shine them so you can sell them for a pair of buttons!

MARGRET: Look who's talking! Just look who's talking! If it isn't the Virgin herself! I'm a respectable person. But you! Everyone knows you could stare your way through seven layers of leather pants!

MARIE: Slut! (*Slams the window shut.*) Come, boy! What's it to them, anyway! Even if you are just a poor whore's baby, your dishonorable little face still makes your mother happy! (*Sings.*)

> I have my trouble and bother
> But, baby dear, where is your father?
> Why should I worry and fight
> I'll hold you and sing through the night:
> Heio popeio, my baby, my dove
> What do I want now with love?

(*A knock at the window.*) Who's there? Is it you, Franz? Come in!

WOYZECK: Can't. There's roll call.

MARIE: Did you cut wood for the Captain?

WOYZECK: Yes, Marie.

MARIE: What is it, Franz? You look so troubled.

WOYZECK: Marie, it happened again, only there was more. Isn't it written: "And there arose a smoke out of the pit, as the smoke of a great furnace"?

MARIE: Oh, Franz!

WOYZECK: Shh! Quiet! I've got it! The Freemasons! There was a terrible noise in the sky and everything was on fire! I'm on the trail of something, something big. It followed me all the way to the town. Something that I can't put my hands on, or understand. Something that drives us mad. What'll come of it all?

MARIE: Franz!

WOYZECK: Don't you see? Look around you! Everything hard and fixed, so gloomy. What's moving back there? When God goes, everything goes. I've got to get back.

MARIE: And the child?

WOYZECK: My God, the boy!—Tonight at the fair! I've saved something again.

(*He leaves.*)

MARIE: That man! Seeing things like that! He'll go mad if he keeps thinking that way! He frightened me! It's so gloomy here. Why are you so quiet, boy? Are you afraid? It's growing so dark. As if we were going blind. Only that street lamp shining in from outside. (*Sings.*)

> And what if your cradle is bad
> Sleep tight, my lovey, my lad.

I can't stand it! It makes me shiver!

(*She goes out.*)

SCENE IV

FAIR BOOTHS. LIGHTS. PEOPLE

OLD MAN *with a* CHILD, WOYZECK, MARIE, CHARLATAN, WIFE, DRUM MAJOR, *and* SERGEANT

OLD MAN (*sings while* THE CHILD *dances to the barrel-organ*):

> There's nothing on this earth will last,
> Our lives are as the fields of grass,
> Soon all is past, is past.

WOYZECK: Ho! Hip-hop there, boy! Hip-hop! Poor man, old man! Poor child, young child! Trouble and happiness!

MARIE: My God, when fools still have their senses, then we're all fools. Oh, what a mad world! What a beautiful world!

(*They go over to* THE CHARLATAN *who stands in front of a booth, his* WIFE *in trousers, and a monkey in costume*)

CHARLATAN: Gentlemen, gentlemen! You see here before you a creature as God created it! But it is nothing this way! Absolutely nothing! But now look at what Art can do. It walks upright. Wears coat and pants. And even carries a saber. This monkey here is a regular soldier. So what if he *isn't* much different! So what if he *is* still on the bottom rung of the human ladder! Hey there, take a bow! That's the way! Now you're a baron, at least. Give us a kiss! (*The monkey trumpets.*) This little customer's musical, too. And, gentlemen, in here you will see the astronomical horse and the little lovebirds. Favorites of all the crowned heads of Europe. They'll tell you anything: how old you are, how many children you have, what your ailments are. The performance is about to begin. And at the beginning. The beginning of the beginning!

WOYZECK: You know, I had a little dog once who kept sniffing around the rim of a big hat, and I thought I'd be good to him and make it easier for him and sat him on top of it. And all the people stood around and clapped.

GENTLEMEN: Oh, grotesque! How really grotesque!

WOYZECK: Don't you believe in God either? It's an honest fact I don't believe in God.—You call that grotesque? I like what's grotesque. See

that? That grotesque enough for you? (*To* MA-
RIE.) You want to go in?

MARIE: Sure. That must be nice in there. Look at the
tassels on him! And his wife's got pants on!
(*They go inside.*)

DRUM MAJOR: Wait a minute! Did you see her?
What a piece!

SERGEANT: Hell, she could whelp a couple regi-
ments of cavalry!

DRUM MAJOR: *And* breed drum majors!

SERGEANT: Look at the way she carries that head!
You'd think all that black hair would pull her
down like a weight. And those eyes!

DRUM MAJOR: Like looking down a well . . . or up a
chimney. Come on, let's go after her!

SCENE V

INTERIOR OF THE BRIGHTLY
LIGHTED BOOTH

MARIE, WOYZECK, PROPRIETOR OF THE BOOTH, SERGEANT,
and DRUM MAJOR

MARIE: All these lights!

WOYZECK: Sure, Marie. Black cats with fiery eyes.

PROPRIETOR OF THE BOOTH (*bringing forward a horse*):
Show your talent! Show your brute reason! Put
human society to shame! Gentlemen, this animal you see here, with a tail on its torso, and
standing on its four hoofs, is a member of all
the learnèd societies—as well as a professor at
our university where he teaches students how
to ride and fight. But that requires simple intelligence. Now think with your double reason!
What do you do when you think with your
double reason? Is there a jackass in this learnèd
assembly? (*The nag shakes its head.*) How's that
for double reasoning? That's physiognomy for
you. This is no dumb animal. This is a person! A
human being! But still an animal. A beast. (*The
nag conducts itself indecently.*) That's right, put
society to shame. As you can see, this animal
is still in a state of Nature. Not ideal Nature, of
course! Take a lesson from him! But ask your
doctor first, it may prove highly dangerous!
What we have been told by this is: Man must
be natural! You are created of dust, sand, and
dung. Why must you be more than dust, sand,

and dung? Look there at his reason. He can figure even if he can't count it off on his fingers.
And why? Because he cannot express himself,
can't explain. A metamorphosed human being.
Tell the gentlemen what time it is! Which of you
ladies and gentlemen has a watch? A watch?

SERGEANT: A watch? (*He pulls a watch imposingly
and measuredly from his pocket.*) There you are,
my good man!

MARIE: I want to see this. (*She clambers down to the
first row of seats;* THE SERGEANT *helps her.*)

DRUM MAJOR: What a piece!

SCENE VI

MARIE'S ROOM

MARIE *with her* CHILD

MARIE (*sitting, her* CHILD *on her lap, a piece of mirror
in her hand*): He told Franz to get the hell out,
so what could he do! (*Looks at herself in the mirror.*) Look how the stones shine! What kind
are they, I wonder? What kind did he say they
were? Sleep, boy! Close your eyes! Tight! Stay
that way now. Don't move or he'll get you!
(*Sings*)

> Hurry, lady, close up tight
> A gypsy lad is out tonight
> And he will take you by the hand
> And lead you into gypsyland.

(*Continues to look at herself in the mirror.*) They
must be gold! I wonder how they'll look on me
at the dance? Our kind's got only a little corner
in the world and a piece of broken mirror. But
my mouth is just as red as any of the fine ladies
with their mirrors from top to bottom, and their
handsome gentlemen that kiss their hands for
them! I'm just a poor common piece! (THE CHILD
sits up.) Quiet, boy! Close your eyes! There's the
sandman! Look at him run across the wall! (*She
flashes with the mirror.*) Eyes tight! Or he'll look
into them and make you blind!
(WOYZECK *enters behind her. She jumps up, her
hands at her ears.*)

WOYZECK: What's that?

MARIE: Nothing.

WOYZECK: There's something shiny in your hands.

MARIE: An earring. I found it.

WOYZECK: I never have luck like that! Two at a time!

MARIE: Am I human or not?

WOYZECK: I'm sorry, Marie.—Look at the boy asleep. Lift his arm, the chair's hurting him. Look at the shiny drops on his forehead. Everything under the sun works! We even sweat in our sleep. Us poor people! Here's some money again, Marie. My pay and something from the Captain.

MARIE: God bless you, Franz.

WOYZECK: I've got to get back. Tonight, Marie! I'll see you tonight!

(*He goes off.*)

MARIE (*alone, after a pause*): I *am* bad, I *am*! I could run myself through with a knife! Oh, what a life, what a life! We'll all end up in hell, anyway, in the end: man, woman, and child!

SCENE VII

AT THE DOCTOR'S

THE DOCTOR *and* WOYZECK

DOCTOR: I don't believe it, Woyzeck! And a man of your word!

WOYZECK: What's that, Doctor, sir?

DOCTOR: I saw it all, Woyzeck. You pissed on the street! You were pissing on the wall like a dog! And here I'm giving you three groschen a day plus board! That's terrible, Woyzeck! The world's becoming a terrible place, a terrible place!

WOYZECK: But, Doctor, sir, when Nature . . .

DOCTOR: When Nature? When Nature? What has Nature to do with it? Did I or did I not prove to you that the *musculus constrictor vesicae* is controlled by your will? Nature! Woyzeck, man is free! In Mankind alone we see glorified the individual's will to freedom! And you couldn't hold your water! (*Shakes his head, places his hands behind the small of his back, and walks back and forth.*) Have you eaten your peas today, Woyzeck? Nothing but peas! *Cruciferae!* Remember that! There's going to be a revolution in science! I'm going to blow it sky-high! *Urea Oxygen.* Ammonium hydrochloratem hyperoxidic. Woyzeck, couldn't you just *try* to piss again? Go in the other room there and make another try.

WOYZECK: Doctor, sir, I can't.

DOCTOR (*disturbed*): But you could piss on the wall. I have it here in black and white. Our contract is right here! I saw it. I saw it with these very eyes. I had just stuck my head out the window, opening it to let in the rays of the sun, so as to execute the process of sneezing. (*Going toward him.*) No, Woyzeck, I'm not going to vex myself. Vexation is unhealthy. Unscientific. I'm calm now, completely calm. My pulse is beating at its accustomed sixty, and I am speaking to you in utmost cold-bloodedness. Why should I vex myself over a man, God forbid! A man! Now if he were a Proteus, it would be worth the vexation! But, Woyzeck, you really shouldn't have pissed on the wall.

WOYZECK: You see, Doctor, sir, sometimes a person's got a certain kind of character, like when he's made a certain way. But with Nature it's not the same, you see. With Nature (*He snaps his fingers.*), it's like *that*! How should I explain, it's like—

DOCTOR: Woyzeck, you're philosophizing again.

WOYZECK (*confidingly*): Doctor, sir, did you ever see anything with double nature? Like when the sun stops at noon, and it's like the world was going up in fire? That's when I hear a terrible voice saying things to me!

DOCTOR: Woyzeck, you have an *aberratio!*

WOYZECK (*places his finger at his nose*): It's in the toadstools, Doctor, sir, that's where it is. Did you ever see the shapes the toadstools make when they grow up out of the earth? If only somebody could read what they say!

DOCTOR: Woyzeck, you have a most beautiful *aberratio mentalis partialis* of a secondary order! And so wonderfully developed! Woyzeck, your salary is increased! *Idée fixe* of a secondary order, and with a generally rational state. You go about your business normally? Still shaving the Captain?

WOYZECK: Yes, sir.

DOCTOR: You eat your peas?

WOYZECK: Just as always, Doctor, sir. My wife gets the money for the household.

DOCTOR: Still in the army?

WOYZECK: Yes, sir, Doctor.

DOCTOR: You're an interesting case. Patient Woyzeck, you're to have an increase in salary. So behave yourself! Let's feel the pulse. Ah yes.

SCENE VIII

MARIE'S ROOM

DRUM MAJOR *and* MARIE

DRUM MAJOR: Marie!

MARIE (*looking at him, with expression*): Go on, show me how you march!—Chest broad as a bull's and a beard like a lion! There's not another man in the world like that! And there's not a prouder woman than me!

DRUM MAJOR: Wait till Sunday when I wear my helmet with the plume and my white gloves! Damn, that'll be a sight for you! The Prince always says: "My God, there goes a real man!"

MARIE (*scoffing*): Ha! (*Goes toward him.*) A man?

DRUM MAJOR: You're not such a bad piece yourself! Hell, we'll plot a whole brood of drum majors! Right? (*He puts his arm around her.*)

MARIE (*annoyed*): Let go!

DRUM MAJOR: Bitch!

MARIE (*fiercely*): You just touch me!

DRUM MAJOR: There's devils in your eyes.

MARIE: Let there be, for all I care! What's the difference!

SCENE IX

STREET

CAPTAIN *and* DOCTOR. THE CAPTAIN *comes panting along the street, stops; pants, looks about.*

CAPTAIN: Ho, Doctor, don't run so fast! Don't paddle the air so with your stick! You're only courting death that way! A good man with a good conscience never walks as fast as that. A good man . . . (*He catches him by the coat.*) Doctor, permit me to save a human life!

DOCTOR: I'm in a hurry, Captain, I'm in a hurry!

CAPTAIN: Doctor, I'm so melancholy. I have such fantasies. I start to cry every time I see my coat hanging on the wall.

DOCTOR: Hm! Bloated, fat, thick neck: apoplectic constitution. Yes, Captain, you'll be having *apoplexia cerebria* any time now. Of course you could have it on only one side. In which case you'll be paralyzed down that one side. Or if things go really well you'll be mentally disabled so that you can vegetate away for the rest of your days. You may look forward to something approximately like that within the next four weeks! And, furthermore, I can assure you that you give promise of being a most interesting case. And if it is God's will that only one half of your tongue become paralyzed, then we will conduct the most immortal of experiments.

CAPTAIN: Doctor, you mustn't scare me that way! People are said to have died of fright. Of pure, sheer fright. I can see them now with lemons in their hands. But they'll say: "He was a good man, a good man." You devil's coffinnail-maker!

DOCTOR (*extending his hat toward him*): Do you know who this is, Captain? This is Sir Hollowhead, my most honorable Captain Drill-theirassesoff!

CAPTAIN (*makes a series of folds in his sleeve*): And do you know who this is, Doctor? This is Sir Manifold, my dear devil's coffinnail-maker! Ha! Ha! Ha! But no harm meant! I'm a good man, but I can play, too, when I want to, Doctor, when I want to . . .

(WOYZECK *comes toward them and tries to pass in a hurry.*)

CAPTAIN: Ho! Woyzeck! Where are you off to in such a hurry? Stay awhile, Woyzeck! Running through the world like an open razor, you're liable to cut someone. He runs as if he had to shave a castrated regiment and would be hung before he discovered and cut the longest hair that wasn't there. But on the subject of long beards . . . What was it I wanted to say? Woyzeck, why was I thinking about beards?

DOCTOR: The wearing of long beards on the chin, remarks Pliny, is a habit of which soldiers must be broken—

CAPTAIN (*continues*): Ah, yes, this thing about beards! Tell me, Woyzeck, have you found any long hairs from beards in your soup bowl lately? Ho, I don't think he understands! A hair from a human face, from the beard of an engineer, a sergeant, a . . . a drum major? Well, Woyzeck? But then he's got a good wife. It's not the same as with the others.

WOYZECK: Yes, sir, Captain! What was it you wanted to say to me, Captain, sir?

CAPTAIN: What a face he's making! Well, maybe not in his soup, but if he hurries home around the corner I'll wager he might still find one on a certain pair of lips. A pair of lips, Woyzeck. I know what love is, too, Woyzeck. Look at him, he's white as chalk!

WOYZECK: Captain, sir, I'm just a poor devil. And there's nothing else I've got in the world but her. Captain, sir, if you're just making a fool of me . . .

CAPTAIN: A fool? Me? Making a fool of you, Woyzeck?

DOCTOR: Your pulse, Woyzeck, your pulse! Short, hard, skipping, irregular.

WOYZECK: Captain, sir, the earth's hot as coals in hell. But I'm cold as ice, cold as ice. Hell is cold. I'll bet you. I don't believe it! God! God! I don't believe it!

CAPTAIN: Look here, you, how would you . . . how'd you like a pair of bullets in your skull? You keep stabbing at me with those eyes of yours, and I'm only trying to help. Because you're a good man, Woyzeck, a good man.

DOCTOR: Facial muscles rigid, taut, occasionally twitches. Condition strained, excitable.

WOYZECK: I'm going. Anything's possible. The bitch! Anything's possible.—The weather's nice, Captain, sir. Look, a beautiful, hard, gray sky. You'd almost like to pound a nail in up there and hang yourself on it. And only because of that little dash between Yes and Yes again . . . and No. Captain, sir: Yes and No: did No make Yes or Yes make No? I must think about that.

(*He goes off with long strides, slowly at first, then faster and faster.*)

DOCTOR (*shouting after him*): Phenomenon! Woyzeck, you get a raise!

CAPTAIN: I get so dizzy around such people. Look at him go! Long-legged rascals like him step out like a shadow running away from its own spider. But short ones only dawdle along. The long-legged ones are the lightning, the short ones the thunder. Haha . . . Grotesque! Grotesque!

SCENE X

MARIE'S ROOM

WOYZECK *and* MARIE

WOYZECK (*looks fixedly at her and shakes his head*): Hm! I don't see it! I don't see it! My God, why can't I see it, why can't I take it in my fists!

MARIE (*frightened*): Franz, what is it?—You're raving, Franz.

WOYZECK: A sin so swollen and big—it stinks to smoke the angels out of Heaven! You have a red mouth, Marie! No blisters on it? Marie, you're beautiful as sin. How can mortal sin be so beautiful?

MARIE: Franz, it's your fever making you talk this way!

WOYZECK: Damn you! Is this where he stood? Like this? Like this?

MARIE: While the day's long and the world's old a lot of people can stand in one spot, one right after the other.—Why are you looking at me so strange, Franz! I'm afraid!

WOYZECK: It's a nice street for walking, uh? You could walk corns on your feet! It's nice walking on the street, going around in society.

MARIE: Society?

WOYZECK: A lot of people pass through this street here, don't they! And you talk to them—to whoever you want—but that's not my business!—Why wasn't it me!

MARIE: You expect me to tell people to keep off the streets—and take their mouths with them when they leave?

WOYZECK: And don't you ever leave your lips at home, they're too beautiful, it would be a sin! But then I guess the wasps like to light on them, uh?

MARIE: And what wasp stung you! You're like a cow chased by hornets!

WOYZECK: I saw him!

MARIE: You can see a lot with two eyes while the sun shines!

WOYZECK: Whore! (*He goes after her.*)

MARIE: Don't you touch me, Franz! I'd rather have a knife in my body than your hands touch me. When I looked at him, my father didn't dare lay a hand on me from the time I was ten.

WOYZECK: Whore! No, it should show on you! Something! Every man's a chasm. It makes you dizzy when you look down in. It's got to show! And she looks like innocence itself. So, innocence, there's a spot on you. But I can't prove it—can't prove it! Who can prove it? (*He goes off.*)

SCENE XI

THE GUARDHOUSE
WOYZECK *and* ANDRES

ANDRES (*sings*):

> Our hostess she has a pretty maid
> She sits in her garden night and day
> She sits within her garden . . .

WOYZECK: Andres!

ANDRES: Hm?

WOYZECK: Nice weather.

ANDRES: Sunday weather.—They're playing music tonight outside the town. All the whores are already there. The men stinking and sweating. Wonderful, uh?

WOYZECK (*restlessly*): They're dancing, Andres, they're dancing!

ANDRES: Sure. So what? (*Sings.*)

> She sits within her garden
> But when the bells have tollèd
> Then she waits at her garden gate
> Or so the soldiers say.

WOYZECK: Andres, I can't keep quiet.

ANDRES: You're a fool!

WOYZECK: I've got to go out there. It keeps turning and turning in my head. They're dancing, dancing! Will she have hot hands, Andres? God damn her, Andres! God damn her!

ANDRES: What do you want?

WOYZECK: I've got to go out there. I've got to see them.

ANDRES: Aren't you ever satisfied? What's all this for a whore?

WOYZECK: I've got to get out of here! I can't stand the heat!

SCENE XII

THE INN
The windows are open. Dancing. Benches in front of the inn. APPRENTICES

FIRST APPRENTICE (*sings*):

> This shirt I've got on, it is not mine
> And my soul it stinketh of brandywine . . .

SECOND APPRENTICE: Brother, let me be a real friend and knock a hole in your nature! Forward! I'll knock a hole in his nature! Hell, I'm as good a man as he is; I'll kill every flea on his body!

FIRST APPRENTICE: My soul, my soul stinketh of brandywine!—And even money passeth into decay! Forget me not, but, the world's a beautiful place! Brother, my sadness could fill a barrel with tears! I wish our noses were two bottles so we could pour them down one another's throats.

THE OTHERS (*in chorus*):

> A hunter from the Rhine
> Once rode through a forest so fine
> Hallei-hallo, he called to me
> From high on a meadow, open and free
> A hunter's life for me.

(WOYZECK *stands at the window.* MARIE *and* THE DRUM MAJOR *dance past without noticing him.*)

WOYZECK: Both of them! God damn her!

MARIE (*dancing past*): Don't stop! Don't stop!

WOYZECK (*seats himself on the bench, trembling, as he looks from there through the window*): Listen! Listen! Ha, roll on each other, roll and turn! Don't stop, don't stop, she says!

IDIOT: Pah! It stinks!

WOYZECK: Yes, it stinks! Her cheeks are red, red, why should she stink already? Karl, what is it you smell?

IDIOT: I smell, I smell blood.

WOYZECK: Blood? Why are all things red that I look at now? Why are they all rolling in a sea of blood, one on top of the other, tumbling, tumbling! Ha, the sea is red!—Don't stop! Don't stop! (*He starts up passionately, then sinks down again onto the bench.*) Don't stop! Don't stop! (*Beating his hands together.*) Turn and roll and roll and turn! God, blow out the sun and let them roll on each other in their lechery! Man and woman and man and beast! They'll do it in the light of the sun! They'll do it in the palm of your hand like flies! Whore! That whore's red as coals, red as coals! Don't stop! Don't stop! (*Jumps up.*) Watch how the bastard takes hold of her! Touching her body! He's holding her now, holding her . . . the way I held her once. (*He slumps down in a stupor.*)

FIRST APPRENTICE (*preaching from a table*): I say unto you, forget not the wanderer who standeth leaning against the stream of time, and who giveth himself answer with the wisdom of God, and saith: What is Man? What is Man? Yea, verily I say unto you: How should the farmer, the cooper, the shoemaker, the doctor, live, had not God created Man for their use? How should the tailor live had not God endowed Man with the need to slaughter himself? And therefore doubt ye not, for all things are lovely and sweet! Yet the world with all its things is an evil place, and even money passeth into decay. In conclusion, my belovèd brethren, let us piss once more upon the Cross so that somewhere a Jew will die!

(*Amid the general shouting and laughing* WOYZECK *wakens.* PEOPLE *are leaving the inn.*)

ANDRES: What are you doing there?

WOYZECK: What time is it?

ANDRES: Ten.

WOYZECK: Is that all it is? I think it should go faster— I want to think about it before night.

ANDRES: Why?

WOYZECK: So it'd be over.

ANDRES: What?

WOYZECK: The fun.

ANDRES: What are you sitting here by the door for?

WOYZECK: Because it feels good, and because I know—a lot of people sit by doors, but they don't know—they don't know till they're dragged out of the door feet first.

ANDRES: Come with me!

WOYZECK: It feels good here like this—and even better if I laid myself down . . .

ANDRES: There's blood on your head.

WOYZECK: *In* my head, maybe. If they all knew what time it was they'd strip themselves naked and put on a silk shirt and let the carpenter make their bed of wood shavings.

ANDRES: He's drunk.

(*Goes off with the others.*)

WOYZECK: The world is out of order! Why did the street-lamp cleaner forget to wipe my eyes— everything's dark. Devil damn you, God! I lay in my own way: jump over myself. Where's my shadow gone? There's no safety in the kennels any more. Shine the moon through my legs again to see if my shadow's here. (*Sings.*)

  Eating, oh, eating the green green grass
  Eating, oh, eating the green green grass
  Till all the grass was go-o-one.

What's that lying over there? Shining like that? It's making me look. How it sparkles. I've got to have it.

(*He rushes off.*)

SCENE XIII

AN OPEN FIELD

WOYZECK

WOYZECK: Don't stop! Don't stop! Hishh! Hashh! That's how the fiddles and pipes go.—Don't stop! Don't stop!—Stop your playing! What's that talking down there? (*He stretches out on the ground.*) What? What are you saying? What? Louder! Louder! Stab? Stab the goat-bitch dead? Stab? Stab her? The goat-bitch dead? Should I? Must I? Do I hear it there, too? Does the wind say so, too? Won't it ever stop, ever stop? Stab her! Stab her! Dead! Dead!

SCENE XIV

A ROOM IN THE BARRACKS. NIGHT

ANDRES *and* WOYZECK *in a bed.*

WOYZECK (*softly*): Andres! (ANDRES *murmurs in his sleep. Shakes* ANDRES.) Andres! Hey, Andres!

ANDRES: Mmmmm! What do you want?

WOYZECK: I can't sleep! When I close my eyes everything turns and turns. I hear voices in the fiddles: Don't stop! Don't stop! And then the walls start to talk. Can't you hear it?

ANDRES: Sure. Let them dance! I'm tired. God bless us all, Amen.

WOYZECK: It's always saying: Stab! Stab! And then when I close my eyes it keeps shining there, a big, broad knife, on a table by a window in a narrow, dark street, and an old man sitting behind it. And the knife is always in front of my eyes.

ANDRES: Go to sleep, you fool!

WOYZECK: Andres! There's something outside. In the ground. They're always pointing to it. Don't you hear them now, listen, now, knocking on the walls? Somebody must have seen me out the window. Don't you hear? I hear it all day long. Don't stop. Stab! Stab the—

ANDRES: Lay down. You ought to go to the hospital. They'll give you a schnapps with a powder in it. It'll cut your fever.

WOYZECK: Don't stop! Don't stop!

ANDRES: Go to sleep!

(*He goes back to sleep.*)

SCENE XV

THE DOCTOR'S COURTYARD

STUDENTS *and* WOYZECK *below,* THE DOCTOR *in the attic window.*

DOCTOR: Gentlemen, I find myself on the roof like David when he beheld Bathsheba. But all I see are the Parisian panties of the girls' boarding school drying in the garden.

Gentlemen, we are concerned with the weighty question of the relationship of the subject to the object. If, for example, we were to take one of those innumerable things in which we see the highest manifestation of the self-affirmation of the Godhead, and examine its relationship to space, to the earth, and to the planetary constellations . . . Gentlemen, if we were to take this cat and toss it out the window: how would this object conduct itself in conformity with its own instincts towards its *centrum gravitationis?* Well, Woyzeck? (*Roars.*) Woyzeck!

WOYZECK (*picks up the cat*): Doctor, sir, she's biting me!

DOCTOR: Damn, why do you handle the beast so tenderly! It's not your grandmother! (*He descends.*)

WOYZECK: Doctor, I'm shaking.

DOCTOR (*utterly delighted*): Excellent, Woyzeck, excellent! (*Rubs his hands, takes the cat.*) What's this, gentlemen? The new species of rabbit louse! A beautiful species . . . (*He pulls out a magnifying glass; the cat runs off.*) Animals, gentlemen, simply have no scientific instincts. But in its place you may see something else. Now, observe: for three months this man has eaten nothing but peas. Notice the effect. Feel how irregularly his pulse beats! And look at his eyes!

WOYZECK: Doctor, sir, everything's going dark! (*He sits down.*)

DOCTOR: Courage, Woyzeck! A few more days and then it will all be over with. Feel, gentlemen, feel! (*They fumble over his temples, pulse, and chest.*)

DOCTOR: Apropos, Woyzeck, wiggle your ears for the gentlemen! I've meant to show you this before. He uses only two muscles. Let's go, let's go! You stupid animal, shall I wiggle them for you? Trying to run out on us like the cat? There you are, gentlemen! Here you see an example of the transition into a donkey: frequently the result of being raised by women and of a persistent usage of the Germanic language. How much hair has your mother pulled out recently for sentimental remembrances of you? It's become so thin these last few days. It's the peas, gentlemen, the peas!

SCENE XVI

THE INN

WOYZECK. THE SERGEANT

WOYZECK (*sings*):
Oh, daughter, my daughter
And didn't you know
That sleeping with coachmen
Would bring you low?

What is it that our Good Lord God cannot do? What? He cannot make what is done undone. Ha! Ha! Ha!—But that's the way it is, and that's the way it should be. But to make things better is to make things better. And a respectable man loves his life, and a man who loves his life has no courage, and a virtuous man has no courage. A man with courage is a dirty dog.

SERGEANT (*with dignity*): You're forgetting yourself in the presence of a brave man.

WOYZECK: I wasn't talking about anybody, I wasn't talking about anything, not like the Frenchmen do when they talk, but it was good of you.—But a man with courage is a dirty dog.

SERGEANT: Damn you! You broken mustache cup! You watch or I'll see you drink a pot of your own piss and swallow your own razor!

WOYZECK: Sir, you do yourself an injustice! Was it *you* I talked about? Did I say *you* had courage? Don't torment me, sir! My name is science. Every week for my scientific career I get half a guilder. You mustn't cut me in two or I'll go hungry. I'm a *Spinosa pericyclia;* I have a Latin behind. I am a living skeleton. All Mankind studies me.—What is Man? Bones! Dust, sand, dung. What is Nature? Dust, sand, dung. But poor, stupid Man, stupid Man! We must be friends. If only you had no courage, there would be no science. Only Nature, no amputation, no articulation. What is this? Woyzeck's arm, flesh, bones, veins. What is this? Dung. Why is it rooted is dung? Must I cut off my arm? No, Man is selfish, he beats, shoots, stabs his own kind. (*He sobs.*) We must be friends. I wish our noses were two bottles that we could pour down each other's throats. What a beautiful place the world is! Friend! My friend! The world! (*Moved.*) Look! The sun coming through the clouds—like God emptying His bedpan on the world. (*He cries.*)

SCENE XVII

THE BARRACKS YARD

WOYZECK. ANDRES

WOYZECK: What have you heard?
ANDRES: He's still inside with a friend.
WOYZECK: He said something.
ANDRES: How do you know? Why do I have to be the one to tell you? Well, he laughed and then he said she was some piece. And then something or other about her thighs—and that she was hot as a red poker.
WOYZECK (*quite coldly*): So, he said that? What was that I dreamed about last night? About a knife? What stupid dreams we get!
ANDRES: Hey, friend! Where you off to?
WOYZECK: Get some wine for the Captain. Andres, you know something? There aren't many girls like she was.
ANDRES: Like who was?
WOYZECK: Nothing. I'll see you. (*Goes off.*)

SCENE XVIII

THE INN

DRUM MAJOR, WOYZECK, *and* PEOPLE

DRUM MAJOR: I'm a man! (*He pounds his chest.*) A man, you hear? Anybody say different? Anybody who's not as crocked as the Lord God Himself better keep off. I'll screw his nose up his own ass! I'll . . . (*To* WOYZECK.) You there, get drunk!

I wish the world was schnapps, schnapps! You better start drinking! (WOYZECK *whistles.*) Son-of-a-bitch, you want me to pull your tongue out and wrap it around your middle? (*They wrestle;* WOYZECK *loses.*) You want I should leave enough wind in you for a good old lady's fart? Uh! (*Exhausted and trembling,* WOYZECK *seats himself on the bench.*) The son-of-a-bitch can whistle himself blue in the face for all I care. (*Sings.*)

Brandy's all my life, my life
Brandy gives me courage!

A MAN: He sure got more than he asked for.
ANOTHER: He's bleeding.
WOYZECK: One thing after another.

SCENE XIX

PAWNBROKER'S SHOP

WOYZECK *and* THE JEW

WOYZECK: The pistol costs too much.
JEW: So you want it or not? Make up your mind.
WOYZECK: How much was the knife?
JEW: It's straight and sharp. What do you want it for? To cut your throat? So what's the matter? You get it as cheap here as anywhere else. You'll die cheap enough, but not for nothing. What's the matter? It'll be a cheap death.
WOYZECK: This'll cut more than bread.
JEW: Two groshen.
WOYZECK: There! (*He goes out.*)
JEW: There, he says! Like it was nothing! And it's real money!—Dog!

SCENE XX

MARIE'S ROOM

THE IDIOT. THE CHILD. MARIE

IDIOT (*lying down, telling fairy tales on his fingers*): This one has the golden crown. He's the Lord King. Tomorrow I'll bring the Lady Queen her child. Bloodsausage says: Come, Liversausage . . .
MARIE (*paging through her Bible*): "And no guile is found in his mouth." Lord God, Lord God! Don't look at me! (*Paging further.*) "And the Scribes and Pharisees brought unto him a

woman taken in adultery, and set her in the midst . . . And Jesus said unto her: Neither do I condemn thee; go, and sin no more." (*Striking her hands together.*) Lord God! Lord God! I can't. Lord God, give me only so much strength that I may pray. (THE CHILD *presses himself close to her.*) The child is a sword in my heart. (*To* THE IDIOT.) Karl!—I've strutted it in the light of the sun, like the whore I am—my sin, my sin! (THE IDIOT *takes* THE CHILD *and grows quiet.*) Franz hasn't come. Not yesterday. Not today. It's getting hot in here! (*She opens the window and reads further.*) "And stood at his feet weeping, and began to wash his feet with tears, and did wipe them with the hairs of her head, and anointed them with ointment." (*Striking her breast.*) Everything dead! Saviour! Saviour! If only I might anoint Your feet!

SCENE XXI

AN OPEN FIELD

WOYZECK

WOYZECK (*buries the knife in a hole*): Thou shalt not kill. Lay here! I can't stay here! (*He rushes off.*)

SCENE XXII

THE BARRACKS

ANDRES. WOYZECK *rummages through his belongings.*

WOYZECK: Andres, this jacket's not part of the uniform, but you can use it, Andres.
ANDRES (*replies numbly to almost everything with*): Sure.
WOYZECK: The cross is my sister's. And the ring.
ANDRES: Sure.
WOYZECK: I've got a Holy Picture, too: two hearts—they're real gold. I found it in my mother's Bible, and it said:
　　O Lord with wounded head so sore
　　So may my heart be evermore.
My mother only feels now when the sun shines on her hands . . . that doesn't matter.
ANDRES: Sure.

WOYZECK (*pulls out a paper*): Friedrich Johann Franz Woyzeck. Soldier. Rifleman, Second Regiment, Second Battalion, Fourth Company. Born: the Feast of the Annunciation, twentieth of July. Today I'm thirty years old, seven months and twelve days.
ANDRES: Go to the hospital, Franz. Poor guy, you've got to drink some schnapps with a powder in it. It'll kill the fever.
WOYZECK: You know, Andres—when the carpenter puts those boards together, nobody knows who it's made for.

SCENE XXIII

THE STREET

MARIE *with little* GIRLS *in front of the house door.*
GRANDMOTHER. *Later* WOYZECK

GIRLS (*singing*):
　　The sun shone bright on Candlemas Day
　　And the corn was all in bloom
　　And they marched along the meadow way
　　They marched by two and two.
　　The pipers marched ahead
　　The fiddlers followed through
　　And their socks were scarlet red . . .
FIRST CHILD: I don't like that one.
SECOND CHILD: Why do you always want to be different?
FIRST CHILD: *You* sing for us, Marie!
MARIE: I can't.
SECOND CHILD: Why?
MARIE: Because.
SECOND CHILD: But *why* because?
THIRD CHILD: Grandmother, *you* tell us a story!
GRANDMOTHER: All right, you little crab apples!—Once upon a time there was a poor little girl who had no father and no mother. Everyone was dead, and there was no one left in the whole wide world. Everyone was dead. And the little girl went out and looked for someone night and day. And because there was no one left on the earth, she wanted to go to Heaven. And the moon looked down so friendly at her. And when she finally got to the moon, it was a piece of rotten wood. And so she went to the sun, and it was a faded sunflower. And when she got to the stars, they were little golden flies, stuck up

there as if they were caught in a spider's web. And when she wanted to go back to earth, the earth was an upside-down pot. And she was all alone. And she sat down there and she cried. And she sits there to this day, all, all alone.

WOYZECK (*appears*): Marie!

MARIE (*startled*): What!

WOYZECK: Let's go. It's getting time.

MARIE: Where to?

WOYZECK: How should I know?

SCENE XXIV

A POND BY THE EDGE OF THE WOODS

MARIE *and* WOYZECK

MARIE: Then the town must be out that way. It's so dark.

WOYZECK: You can't go yet. Come, sit down.

MARIE: But I've got to get back.

WOYZECK: You don't want to run your feet sore.

MARIE: What's happened to you?

WOYZECK: You know how long it's been, Marie?

MARIE: Two years from Pentecost.

WOYZECK: You know how much longer it'll last?

MARIE: I've got to get back. Supper's not made yet.

WOYZECK: Are you freezing, Marie? And still you're so warm. Your lips are hot as coals! Hot as coals, the hot breath of a whore! And still I'd give up Heaven just to kiss them again. Are you freezing? When you're cold through, you won't freeze any more. The morning dew won't freeze you.

MARIE: What are you talking about?

WOYZECK: Nothing. (*Silence.*)

MARIE: Look how red the moon is! It's rising.

WOYZECK: Like a knife washed in blood.

MARIE: What are you going to do? Franz, you're so pale. (*He raises the knife.*)

MARIE: Franz! Stop! For Heaven's sake! Help me! Help me!

WOYZECK (*stabbing madly*): There! There! Why can't you die? There! There! Ha, she's still shivering! Still not dead? Still not dead? Still shivering? (*Stabbing at her again.*) Are you dead? Dead! Dead! (*He drops the knife and runs away.*) (*Two* MEN *approach.*)

FIRST MAN: Wait!

SECOND MAN: You hear something? Shh! Over there!

FIRST MAN: Whhh! There! What a sound!

SECOND MAN: It's the water, it's calling. It's a long time since anyone drowned here. Let's go! I don't like hearing such sounds!

FIRST MAN: Whhh! There it is again! Like a person, dying!

SECOND MAN: It's uncanny! So foggy, nothing but gray mist as far as you can see—and the hum of beetles like broken bells. Let's get out of here!

FIRST MAN: No, it's too clear, it's too loud! Let's go up this way! Come on! (*They hurry on.*)

SCENE XXV

THE INN

WOYZECK, KATHY, INNKEEPER, IDIOT, *and* PEOPLE

WOYZECK: Dance! Everybody! Don't stop! Sweat and stink! He'll get you all in the end! (*Sings.*)
Oh, daughter, my daughter
And didn't you know
That sleeping with coachmen
Would bring you low?
(*He dances.*) Ho, Kathy! Sit down! I'm so hot, so hot! (*Takes off his coat.*) That's the way it is: the devil takes one and lets the other get away. Kathy, you're hot as coals! Why, tell me why? Kathy, you'll be cold one day, too. Be reasonable.—Can't you sing something?

KATHY (*sings*):
That Swabian land I cannot bear
And dresses long I will not wear
For dresses long and pointed shoes
Are clothes a chambermaid never should choose.

WOYZECK: No shoes, no shoes! We can get to hell without shoes.

KATHY (*sings*): To such and like I'll not be prone
Take back your gold and sleep alone.

WOYZECK: Sure, sure! What do I want to get all bloody for?

KATHY: Then what's that on your hand?

WOYZECK: Me? Me?

KATHY: Red! It's blood! (PEOPLE *gather round him.*)

WOYZECK: Blood? Blood?

INNKEEPER: Blood!

WOYZECK: I think I cut myself. Here, on my right hand.

INNKEEPER: Then why is there blood on your elbow?

WOYZECK: I wiped it off.

INNKEEPER: Your right hand and you wiped it on your right elbow? You're a smart one!

IDIOT: And then the Giant said: "I smell, I smell the flesh of Man." Pew, it stinks already!

WOYZECK: What do you want from me? Is it your business? Out of my way or the first one who . . . Damn you! Do I look like I murdered somebody? Do I look like a murderer? What are you looking at? Look at yourselves! Look! Out of my way! (*He runs off.*)

SCENE XXVI

AT THE POND

WOYZECK, *alone.*

WOYZECK: The knife! Where's the knife? I left it here. It'll give me away! Closer! And closer! What is this place? What's that noise? Something's moving! It's quiet now.—It's got to be here, close to her. Marie? Ha, Marie! Quiet. Everything's quiet! Why are you so pale, Marie? Why are you wearing those red beads around your neck? Who was it gave you that necklace for sinning with him? Your sins made you black, Marie, they made you black! Did I make you so pale? Why is your hair uncombed? Did you forget to twist your braids today? The knife, the knife! I've got it! There! (*He runs toward the water.*) There, into the water! (*He throws the knife into the water.*) It dives like a stone into the black water. No, it's not out far enough for when they swim! (*He wades into the pond and throws it out farther.*) There! Now! But in the summer when they dive for mussels? Ha, it'll get rusty, who'll ever notice it! Why didn't I break it first! Am I still bloody? I've got to wash myself. There, there's a spot, and there's another . . . (*He goes farther out into the water.*)

SCENE XXVII

THE STREET

CHILDREN

FIRST CHILD: Let's go find Marie!

SECOND CHILD: What happened?

FIRST CHILD: Don't you know? Everybody's out there. They found a body!

SECOND CHILD: Where?

FIRST CHILD: By the pond, out in the woods.

SECOND CHILD: Hurry, so we can still see something. Before they bring it back.
(*They rush off.*)

SCENE XXVIII

IN FRONT OF MARIE'S HOUSE

IDIOT. CHILD. WOYZECK.

IDIOT (*holding* THE CHILD *on his knee, points to* WOYZECK *as he enters*): Looky there, he fell in the water, he fell in the water, he fell in the water!

WOYZECK: Boy! Christian!

IDIOT (*looks at him fixedly*): He fell in the water.

WOYZECK (*wanting to embrace* THE CHILD *tenderly, but it turns from him and screams*): My God! My God!

IDIOT: He fell in the water.

WOYZECK: I'll buy you a horsey, Christian. There, there. (THE CHILD *pulls away. To the* IDIOT). Here, buy the boy a horsey! (THE IDIOT *stares at him.*) Hop! Hop! Hip-hop, horsey!

IDIOT (*shouting joyously*): Hop! Hop! Hip-hop, horsey! Hip-hop, horsey!
(*He runs off with* THE CHILD. WOYZECK *is alone.*)

SCENE XXIX

THE MORGUE

JUDGE, COURT CLERK, POLICEMAN, CAPTAIN, DOCTOR, DRUM MAJOR, SERGEANT, IDIOT, *and others.* WOYZECK

POLICEMAN: What a murder! A good, genuine, beautiful murder! Beautiful a murder as you could hope for! It's been a long time since we had one like this!
(WOYZECK *stands in their midst, dumbly looking at the body of* MARIE; *he is bound, the dogmatic atheist, tall, haggard, timid, good-natured, scientific.*)

Introduction to *The Poor of New York*

WHEN THE PLAY WAS NEW

The Poor of New York by Dion Boucicault opened at Wallack's Theatre in New York in 1857 during a catastrophic financial panic that scarred many people during those economically unregulated times. Although the setting for the opening scene is an earlier financial panic in 1837, the rest of the play occurs in the financially troubling moment experienced by the audience watching the play. This very topical play was also a sensational melodrama, so the audience was entertained at the same time that it was reminded of the disturbing current events.

Wallack's Theatre specialized in British plays at the time. In fact, the American theatre was dominated by British plays from the beginning of professional theatre in the American colonies in 1752 up until the first decade of the twentieth century (1909) when for the first time a season in New York City had more American than British plays. The popularity of British imports has remained a staple of American theatre, whether the fare is Shakespeare (whose plays were a dominant element of all Western theatre in the nineteenth century) or contemporary plays.

Aside from Shakespeare, however, nineteenth-century theatres were predominantly occupied by melodrama—the most popular type of contemporary play on American and European stages. The romantic movement, which began in Europe, included melodrama in its dramatic arsenal. Even after the makers of melodrama became enamored of realistic visual detail and "local color" (the use of contemporary recognizable events, settings, costumes, authentic locations, and language—especially slang), many of the elements of melodrama remained romantic and idealized. The American theatre seems to have remained more romantic for many decades than any of its European forebears.

The theatres for which Boucicault wrote were always proscenium stages, lit by gas, using both two-dimensional wing and drop scenery and many three-dimensional elements. One of the most dynamic changes in scenery beginning around 1830 was the use of the box set—a completely enclosed interior setting representing a room with furniture, decorations, functioning doors, and sometimes windows. By mid-century the box set was nearly standard, and several were probably used in *The Poor of New York*. The mixture of two-dimensional and three-dimensional scenery is evident in the stage directions surviving for *The Poor of New York*.

By the mid-nineteenth century, many American theatre managers and starring actors (especially touring stars) were beginning to give more direction to the acting company. Before this time most actors were independent performers who usually made their own decisions regarding movement and staging. The increased staging and scenic details called for in melodrama, and a few years later in realism, made the role of director as we think of it, not an option, but a necessity. Except for acting stars, many actors were also losing the traditional practice of costuming themselves.

THE PLAYWRIGHT

Dion Boucicault (c. 1820–1890) was born in Dublin, Ireland, with the name Dionysius Lardner Boursiquot. His theatrical career commenced in London as an actor, but he soon made his mark as a playwright with the popular comedy of manners entitled *London Assurance* (1841). Ultimately he could be claimed by Ireland, England, and the United States. The subject matter of his plays was centered in all three countries, and his career was split between Britain and the United States. Toward the end of his career he became a U.S. citizen. As a playwright he wrote more than 100 plays, and some critics and historians credit him with up to 400. He remained a successful character actor throughout his career, often creating supporting, and occasionally leading roles for himself as well as for his popular actress wife, Agnes Robertson. At various times in his theatrical life he was also a producer, director, and theatre manager. His approach to directing is evident in his detailed stage directions.

Although some of his plays were based on original material, most of his work was based on novels (chiefly British and French, including those of Charles Dickens) and other plays (primarily adaptations of French dramas such as *The Poor of New York*). His most famous plays include *Belle Lamar* (1874), the first successful drama set during the U.S. Civil War, which established the formula with a southern heroine and a northern hero that marked so many Civil War plays, novels, and movies for the next century. His Irish melodramas such as *The Colleen Bawn* (1860) dominated Irish dramatic expression until the Irish Renaissance in the early twentieth century. He took up the U.S. slavery issue with *The Octoroon* (1859), popular on both sides of the Atlantic. His version of *Rip Van Winkle* (1865) was the preferred stage version for half a century. *The Flying Scud* (1866) launched a series of popular horse-racing melodramas that continue to appear periodically in film. In fact, film rather than theatre is the ultimate beneficiary of Dion Boucicault's style and methods.

GENRE, STRUCTURE, AND STYLE

The Poor of New York is what Boucicault called at the time a "sensation" melodrama—that is, a melodrama dominated by extraordinary events, spectacle, and confrontations. The climax was meant to startle the audience and make them wonder how the special effects were done. The general characteristics typical of nineteenth-century melodrama are:

1. The action is often fast-paced and suspenseful. Most mysteries and thrillers are melodramas. Boucicault's *The Octoroon* features an extended chase scene, a device we now associate with film.

2. The conflict in the play is one of good and evil, usually personified in an unmistakable hero and/or heroine versus one or more villains. The names of villains are typically obvious: In *The Poor of New York* we have Gideon Bloodgood and Badger.

3. The plotting and intrigue are much more clearly developed than the characters. In other words, one could easily substitute many different characters for those who find themselves in the conflict. Events are rarely caused by the internal distress or ethical choices made by the characters.

4. The action is punctuated by big discoveries and reversals of the immediate fortunes of the hero/heroine. These events are usually life and death situations—high stakes problems in which characters must act in extraordinary ways in order to overcome the villainy of the bad guys. In *The Colleen Bawn* the heroine tries to commit suicide by drowning but is saved at the last minute. In *The Octoroon* the villain's act of murder is caught accidentally by the new technology of photography.

5. The hero/heroine is likely to have a comic or homespun sidekick who provides comic relief periodically. The villain may also have a comic sidekick who sometimes repents by the play's end as we see in *The Poor of New York*.

6. The climax of the play often has a spectacular event like an earthquake, volcanic eruption, sinking ship, or burning building (which we see in *The Poor of New York*). In *The Octoroon* a steamboat catches fire and sinks on stage.

7. Although the conflict is serious, the play has a happy ending with poetic justice for all.

IMPORTANT ELEMENTS OF CONTENT

The Poor of New York was adapted from a French melodrama entitled *Les Pauvres de Paris* by Édouard Brisebarre and Eugène Nus. While borrowing from the original, Boucicault altered locations, language, and many details. This play was his first "photographic" melodrama (to use his word). He set the action during real events: one from twenty years earlier, the Panic of 1837, and another in process when the play opened, the Panic of 1857. For local color Boucicault selected real locations in New York—famous ones such as Five Points, a park near Tammany Hall, and Union Square—all places that his audience was likely to recognize, along with recognizable language, events, and urban street types. Real newspapers—the New York *Herald* and *The Police Gazette*—are quoted and referred to. The firefighters, hard at work during the climactic scene, use slang and paraphernalia based on reality.

In order to make the play current, and therefore seem vital and immediately relevant to the audience, Boucicault inserts social comments that could be heard on the street, but he is careful not to side with any point of view that could be seen as radical. Ultimately, like other popular writers of melodrama of the time, Boucicault is topical but ultimately supportive of the reigning ethical and economic system. For example, he gives language of respectability to his upper class characters, even after they have fallen economically. They are always treated with respect by those of lower classes, even though the "humbler" people now have more money than the formerly rich. The idea is that breeding and patrician "blood" will always rise when the chips are down. *The Poor of New York* are not those born into poverty, but those who have temporarily fallen into it.

In many melodramas, as well as other popular literature throughout the history of the United States, the city is presented as a center of corruption and crime. The city itself is often seen as not only a hotbed of criminal elements and a crucible for poverty, but even one of the causes of such conditions. This urban image remains poignant in American literature and journalism.

THE PLAY IN REVIVAL

After its New York premiere in 1857, Boucicault continued to revive *The Poor of New York* and to adapt it to the settings and local color of any city where he mounted the play: Philadelphia, Boston, Dublin, London, Liverpool, and other cities. The play continued in its popularity for at least thirty years, and it even evolved as a musical form. We are not aware of modern revivals of this play, but this is not surprising. The play's importance lies in its historical development and its influence on later melodrama (especially "sensation" melodrama) in film and television—dramatic venues that have essentially taken over the production of the genre.

SPECIAL FEATURE

Boucicault went to great lengths to pull off the authentic presentation of a huge tenement fire in *The Poor of New York.* He published a partial account of the effects in a magazine at the time and revealed that the building was made of painted flats designed in irregular pieces that could fall to the stage floor on cue. He used steam for smoke, some painted flames in motion upstage, but also real fire under controlled conditions using chemicals and scenic elements soaked in flammable liquids. Obviously such methods would never be allowed today. It is not surprising that the nineteenth century had more theatre fires than any other period; all stage lighting in the era was gas, and this often led to damaging fires. Despite Boucicault's efforts, which seem dangerous to us, he was also instrumental in creating fireproofing methods for stage scenery.

FURTHER READING ABOUT THE PLAY, PLAYWRIGHT, AND CONTEXT

For material on Boucicault and melodrama, see Richard Fawkes, *Dion Boucicault*, and Frank Rahill, *The World of Melodrama.*

For commentary on this play and historical context, see Don B. Wilmeth and Christopher Bigsby, *The Cambridge History of American Theatre*, vol 1., and Bruce McConachie, *Melodramatic Formations.*

For other studies of nineteenth-century melodrama beyond Boucicault, see Jeffrey Mason, *Melodrama and the Myth of America*, and David Grimstead, *Melodrama Unveiled.*

For Boucicault's descripton of the tenement fire, see "Illusions of the Stage," *Scientific American*, (1881), pp. 4265–4266. Part of this description is also published in Don B. Wilmeth, *Staging the Nation*, pp. 4–5.

The Poor of New York

By Dion Boucicault

DRAMATIS PERSONAE

CAPTAIN FAIRWEATHER

GIDEON BLOODGOOD

BADGER

MARK LIVINGSTONE

PAUL

PUFFY

DAN

DANIELS

EDWARDS

MRS. FAIRWEATHER

MRS. PUFFY

ALIDA

LUCY

Scene: The first act occurs during the Commercial Panic of 1837. The remainder of the drama takes place during the panic of 1857.

ACT I: THE PANIC OF 1837

The private office of a banking house in New York; door at back, leading to the Bank; Door leading to a side street; GIDEON BLOODGOOD seated, at desk.

Enter EDWARDS, with a sheet of paper.

EDWARDS: The stock list, sir;—second board of brokers.

BLOODGOOD (*Rising eagerly*): Let me see it. Tell the cashier to close the Bank on the stroke of three, and dismiss the clerks. (*Reads.*)

(*Exit EDWARDS.*)

So—as I expected, every stock is down further still, and my last effort to retrieve my fortune has plunged me into utter ruin? (*Crushes up the paper.*) To-morrow, my drafts to the amount of eighty thousand dollars will be protested. Tomorrow, yonder street, now so still, will be filled with a howling multitude, for the house of Bloodgood, the Banker, will fail, and in its fall will crush hundreds, thousands, who have their fortunes laid up here.

(*Re-enter EDWARDS.*)

EDWARDS: Here are the keys of the safe, sir and the vault. (*Leaves keys on desk and shows a check to BLOODGOOD.*) The building committee of St. Peter's new church have applied for your donation. It is a thousand dollars.

BLOODGOOD: Pay it. (*Exit EDWARDS.*) To-morrow, New York will ring from Union Square to the Battery with the news—"Bloodgood has absconded"—but to-morrow I shall be safe on board the packet for Liverpool—all is prepared for my flight with my only care in life, my only hope—my darling child—her fortune is secure—(*Rises.*) The affair will blow over; Bloodgood's bankruptcy will soon be forgotten in the whirl of New York trade, but Alida, my dear Alida will be safe from want. (*Re-enter EDWARDS.*)

EDWARDS: Here, sir, are the drafts on the Bank of England, 7,000 dollars. (*Hands papers to BLOODGOOD, who places them in his pocketbook.*)

BLOODGOOD: Are the clerks all gone?

EDWARDS: All, sir, except Mr. Badger.

BLOODGOOD: Badger! the most negligent of all! That is strange.

EDWARDS: His entries are behindhand, he says, and he is balancing his books.

BLOODGOOD: Desire him to come to me. (*Sits. Exit EDWARDS.*)

(*Enter BADGER, smoking cigar.*)

BADGER: You have asked for me.

BLOODGOOD: Yes, you are strangely attentive to business to-day, Mr. Badger.

BADGER: Everything has a beginning.

BLOODGOOD: Then you will please begin to-morrow.

BADGER: To-morrow! no, sir, my business must be done to-day. *Carpe diem*—make most of to-day—that's my philosophy.

BLOODGOOD: Mr. Badger, Philosophy is not a virtue in a banker's clerk.

BADGER: Think not?

BLOODGOOD (*Impatiently*): Neither philosophy nor impertinence. You are discharged from my employment.

BADGER: Pardon me! I do not catch the precise word.

BLOODGOOD (*Sternly*): Go, sir, go! I discharge you.

BADGER: Go!—discharge me? I am still more in the dark, I can understand my services not being required in a house that goes on, but where the house is ready to burst up the formality of telling a clerk he is discharged, does seem an unnecessary luxury.

BLOODGOOD (*Troubled*): I do not understand you, sir.

BADGER (*Seating himself on a desk, deliberately dangling his legs*): No! well I'll dot my i's and cross my t's and make myself plain to the meanest capacity. In business there are two ways of getting rich, one hard, slow and troublous: this is called labor;—

BLOODGOOD: Sir!

BADGER: Allow me to finish. The other easy, quick and demanding nothing but a pliant conscience and a daring mind—is now pleasantly denominated financiering—but when New York was honest, it was called fraudulent bankruptcy, that was before you and I were born.

BLOODGOOD: What do you mean?

BADGER: I mean that for more than two years I have watched your business transactions; when you thought me idle, my eyes were everywhere: in your books, in your safe, in your vaults; if you doubt me question me about your operations for the last three months.

BLOODGOOD: This is infamous!

BADGER: That is precisely the word I used when I came to the end of your books.

EDWARDS (*Outside*): This way, sir.

(*Enter* EDWARDS, *with* CAPTAIN FAIRWEATHER.)

BLOODGOOD (*To* BADGER, *in alarm*): Not a word.

BADGER: All right.

EDWARDS (*Introducing* CAPTAIN FAIRWEATHER): This is Mr. Bloodgood.

CAPTAIN: Glad to see you, sir. You will pardon my intruding at an hour when the bank, I am told, is closed.

BLOODGOOD: I am at your service, sir.

(*He makes a sign for* BADGER *to retire, but the latter remains.*)

BADGER (*To* CAPTAIN): You may speak, sir; Mr. Bloodgood has no secrets from me. I am in his confidence.

CAPTAIN (*Sits*): I am a sea-captain, in the India Trade. My voyages are of the longest, and thus I am obliged to leave my wife and two children almost at the mercy of circumstances. I was spending a happy month with my darlings at a little cozy place I have at Yonkers while my ship was loading, when this infernal commercial squall set in—all my fortune, 100,000 dollars, the fruits of thirty years' hard toil—was invested in the United States Bank—it was the livelihood of my wife—the food of my little children—I hurried to my brokers and sold out. I saved myself just in time.

BLOODGOOD: I admire your promptitude.

CAPTAIN: To-morrow I sail for China; for the last three weeks I have worried my brains to think how I should bestow my money—to-day I bethought me of your house—the oldest in New York—your name stands beyond suspicion, and if I leave this money in your hands, I can sleep nightly with the happy assurance that whatever happens to me, my dearest ones are safe.

BADGER: You may pull your nightcap over your ears with that established conviction.

CAPTAIN: Now, I know your bank is closed, but if you will accept this money as a special deposit, I will write to you how I desire it to be invested hereafter.

BLOODGOOD (*Pensive*): You have a family.

CAPTAIN: Don't talk of them—tears of joy come into my eyes whenever I think of those children—and my dear wife, the patient, devoted companion of the old sailor, whose loving voice murmurs each evening a prayer for those who are on the sea; and my children, sir, two little angels; one a fair little thing—we call her Lucy—she is the youngest—all red and white like a little bundle of flowers; and my eldest—my son Paul—we named him after Paul Jones—a sailor's whim; well, sir, when the ship is creaking and groaning under my feet, when the squall drives the hail and sleet across my face, amidst the thunder,

I only hear three voices—through the gloom I can see only three faces, pressed together like three angels waiting for me in heaven, and that heaven is my home. But, how I do talk, sir—forgetting that these things can't interest you.

BLOODGOOD: They do, more than you imagine. I, too, have a child—only one—a motherless child!

CAPTAIN: Ain't it good to speak of the little beings? Don't it fill the heart like a draught of sweet water? My darling torments, here is their fortune—I have it in my hand—it is here—I have snatched it from the waves; I have won it across the tempest; I have labored, wrestled and suffered for it; but it seemed nothing, for it was for them. Take it, sir. (*He hands* BLOODGOOD *a pocketbook.*) In this pocketbook you will find one hundred thousand dollars. May I take your receipt and at once depart for my vessel?

BADGER (*Aside*): This is getting positively interesting.

BLOODGOOD: Your confidence flatters me. You desire to place this money with me as a special deposit?

CAPTAIN: If you please. Will you see that the amount is correct?

BLOODGOOD (*Counting*): Mr. Badger, prepare the receipt.

BADGER (*Writing*): "New York, 13th of December, 1837. Received, on special deposit, from—" (*To* CAPTAIN.) Your name, sir?

CAPTAIN: Captain Fairweather, of the ship Paul and Lucy, of New York.

BADGER (*Writing*): Captain Fairweather, of the ship—

BLOODGOOD: One hundred thousand dollars—quite correct.

BADGER (*Handing receipt to* BLOODGOOD, *and watching him closely as he takes the pen*): Please sign the receipt. (*Aside.*) His hand does not tremble, not a muscle moves. What a magnificent robber!

BLOODGOOD (*To* CAPTAIN): Here is your receipt.

CAPTAIN: A thousand thanks. Now I am relieved of all trouble.

BADGER (*Aside*): That's true.

CAPTAIN: I must return in haste to the Astor House, where I dine with my owners at four—I fear I am late. Good-day, Mr. Bloodgood.

BLOODGOOD: Good-day Captain, and a prosperous voyage to you. (*Exit* CAPTAIN FAIRWEATHER. BADGER *opens ledger.*) What are you doing, Mr. Badger?

BADGER: I am going to enter that special deposit in the ledger.

BLOODGOOD: Mr. Badger!

BADGER: Mr. Bloodgood!

BLOODGOOD (*Brings him down*): I have been deceived in you. I confess I did not know your value.

BADGER (*Modestly*): Patience and perseverance, sir, tells in the long run.

BLOODGOOD: Here are one thousand dollars—I present them to you for your past services.

BADGER (*Takes the money, and walks over to the ledger on the desk, which he closes significantly*): And for the present service?

BLOODGOOD: What do you mean?

BADGER: My meaning is as clear as Croton.[1] I thought you were going to fail—I see I was wrong—you are going to abscond.

BLOODGOOD: Mr. Badger! this language—

BADGER: The deposit is special; you dare not use it in your business; your creditors cannot touch it—ergo, you mean to make a raise, and there's but one way—absconsion! absquatulation.

BLOODGOOD (*Smiling*): It is possible that this evening I may take a little walk out of town.

BADGER: In a steamboat?

BLOODGOOD: Meet me at Peck Slip, at five o'clock, and I will hand you double the sum I gave you.

BADGER (*Aside*): In all three thousand dollars. (*Re-enter* EDWARDS.)

EDWARDS: Your daughter, sir; Miss Alida is in the carriage at the door and is screaming to be admitted.

BLOODGOOD: Tell the nurse to pacify her for a few moments.

EDWARDS: She dare not, sir; Miss Alida has torn the nurse's face in a fearful manner already. (*Exit.*)

BADGER: Dear, high-spirited child! If she is so gentle now, what will she be when she is twenty, and her nails are fully developed?

---

1. Water supply for New York.

BLOODGOOD (*Takes hat*): I will return immediately. (*Exit.*)

BADGER (*Following* BLOODGOOD *with his eyes*): Oh, nature, wonderful mistress! Keep close to your daughter, Bloodgood, for she is your master! Ruin, pillage, rob fifty families to make her rich with her misery, happy in their tears. I watched him as he received the fortune of that noble old sailor—not a blink—his heart of iron never quailed, but in his heart of iron there is a straw, a weakness by which it may be cracked, and that weakness is his own child—children! They are the devil in disguise. I have not got any except my passions, my vices—a large family of spoilt and ungrateful little devils, who threaten their loving father with a prison.

EDWARDS (*Outside*): I tell you, sir, he is not in.

CAPTAIN (*Outside*): Let me pass I say. (*He enters very much agitated.*) Where is he? Where is he?

BADGER (*Surprised*): What is the matter, sir?

CAPTAIN: Mr. Bloodgood—I must see him—speak to him this instant. Do you not hear me?

BADGER: But—

CAPTAIN: He has not gone.

BADGER: Sir—

CAPTAIN: Ah! he is here!
    (*Re-enter* BLOODGOOD.)

BLOODGOOD: What is the meaning of this.

CAPTAIN: Ah! you—it is you—(*Trying to restrain his emotion.*) Sir, I have changed my mind; here is your receipt; have the goodness to return me the deposit I—I—left with you.

BLOODGOOD: Sir!

CAPTAIN: I have another investment for this sum, and I—beg you to restore it to me.

BLOODGOOD: Restore it! you have a very strange way, sir of demanding what is due to you.

CAPTAIN: It is true; pardon me but I have told you it is all I possess. It is the fortune of my wife, of my children, of my brave Paul, and my dear little Lucy. It is their future happiness, their life! Listen, sir; I will be frank with you. Just now, on returning to my hotel, I found the owners of my ship waiting dinner for me, well, they were speaking as merchants will speak of each other—your name was mentioned—I listened—and they said—It makes

me tremble even now—they said there were rumors abroad to-day that your house was in peril.

BLOODGOOD: I attach no importance, sir, to idle talk.

CAPTAIN: But I attach importance to it, sir. How can I leave the city with this suspicion on my mind that perhaps I have compromised the future of my family.

BLOODGOOD: Sir!

CAPTAIN: Take back your receipt, and return me my money.

BLOODGOOD: You know, sir, that it is after banking hours. Return to-morrow.

CAPTAIN: No. You received my deposit after banking hours.

BLOODGOOD: I am not a paying teller, to count out money.

CAPTAIN: You did not say so, when you counted it in.
    (*Enter* EDWARDS.)

EDWARDS: The driver says you will be late for the—

BLOODGOOD (*Trying to stop him*): That will do.
    (*Exit* EDWARDS.)

CAPTAIN: What did he say? (*Runs to the window.*) A carriage at the door—

BADGER (*Aside*): Things are getting complicated here.

CAPTAIN: Yes—I see it all. He is going to fly with the fortunes and savings of his dupes! (*Tearing his cravat.*) Ah! I shall choke! (*Furiously to* BLOODGOOD.) But I am here, villain, I am here in time.

BLOODGOOD: Sir.

CAPTAIN: To-morrow, you said—return to-morrow—but to-morrow you will be gone. (*Precipitates himself on* BLOODGOOD.) My money, my money. I will have it this instant! Do not speak a word, it is useless, I will not listen to you. My money, or I will kill you as a coward should be killed. Robber! Thief!

BADGER (*Aside*): Hi! hi! This is worth fifty cents—reserved seats extra.

BLOODGOOD (*Disengaging himself*): Enough of this scandal. You shall have your money back again.

CAPTAIN: Give it me—ah!—(*In pain.*) My head! (*To* BLOODGOOD.) Be quick, give it to me, and let me go. (*Staggering and putting his hands to face.*) My God! what is this strange feeling that overcomes me.

BADGER: He is falling, what's the matter of him? (CAPTAIN *falls in chair.*)

BLOODGOOD: His face is purple. (*Takes pocketbook and commences to county out money.*)
(*Soft music to end of act.*)

CAPTAIN: I am suffocating; some air. I cannot see; everything is black before my eyes. Am I dying? O, no, no! it cannot be, I will not die. I must see them again. Some water—quick! Come to me—my wife—my children! Where are they that I cannot fold them in my arms! (*He looks strangely and fearfully into the face of* BLOODGOOD *for an instant, and then breaks into a loud sob.*) Oh, my children—my poor, poor little children! (*After some convulsive efforts to speak his eyes become fixed.*)

BLOODGOOD (*Distracted*): Some one run for help. Badger a doctor quick.

BADGER (*Standing over* CAPTAIN): All right, sir, I have studied medicine—that's how I learned most of my loose habits. (*Examines the* CAPTAIN's *pulse and eyes.*) It is useless sir. He is dead.

BLOODGOOD (*Horrified*): Dead! (BLOODGOOD's *attitude is one of extreme horror. This position gradually relaxes as he begins to see the advantages that will result from the* CAPTAIN's *death.*) Can it be possible?

BADGER (*Tearing open the* CAPTAIN's *vest. The receipt falls on the ground.*): His heart has ceased to beat—congestion in all its diagnostics.

BLOODGOOD: Dead!

BADGER: Apoplexy—the systems well developed—the causes natural, overexcitement and sudden emotion.

BLOODGOOD (*Relaxing into an attitude of cunning*): Dead!

BADGER: You are spared the agony of counting out his money.

BLOODGOOD: Dead!

BADGER (*Sees receipt on ground*): Ha! here is the receipt! Signed by Bloodgood. As a general rule never destroy a receipt—there is no knowing when it may yet prove useful. (*Picks it up, and puts it in his pocket.*)

TABLEAU.

(*A lapse of twenty years is supposed to intervene between the first and second acts.*)

ACT II: THE PANIC OF 1857

SCENE I
The Park, near Tammany Hall.

Enter LIVINGSTONE.

LIVINGSTONE: Eight o'clock in the morning! For the last hour I have been hovering round Chatham street—I wanted to sell my overcoat to some enterprising Israelite, but I could not muster the courage to enter one of those dens. Can I realize the fact? Three months ago, I stood there the fashionable Mark Livingstone, owner of the Waterwitch yacht, one of the original stock-holders in the Academy of Music, and now, burst up, sold out, and reduced to breakfast off this coat. (*Feels in pocket.*) What do I feel? a gold dollar—undiscovered in the Raglan of other days! (*Withdraws his hand.*) No; 'tis a five-cent piece!
(*Enter* PUFFY, *with a hot-potato arrangement.*)

PUFFY: Past eight o'clock! I am late this morning.

LIVINGSTONE: I wonder what that fellow has in his tin volcano—it smells well. Ha! what are those funny things? Ah!

PUFFY: Sweet potatoes, sir.

LIVINGSTONE: Indeed! (*Aside.*) If the Union Club saw me—(*Looks around.*) No; I am incog—hunger cries aloud. Here goes.

PUFFY: Why, bless me, if it ain't Mr. Livingstone!

LIVINGSTONE: The devil! He knows me—I dare not eat a morsel.

PUFFY: I'm Puffy, sir; the baker that was—in Broadway—served you sir, and your good father afore you.

LIVINGSTONE: Oh, Puffy—ah, true. (*Aside.*) I wonder if I owe him anything.

PUFFY: Down in the world now, sir—over speculated like the rest on 'em. I expanded on a new-fangled oven, that was to bake enough bread in six hours to supply the whole United States—got done brown in it myself—subsided into Bowery—expanded again on waffles, caught a second time—obliged to contract into a twelve foot front on Division street. Mrs. P. tends the indoor trade—I do a locomotive business in potatoes, and we let our second floor. My son Dan sleeps with George Washington No. 4,[2] while Mrs. P. and I make out under the counter; Mrs. P., bein' wide, objects some, but I says—says I, "My dear, everybody must contract themselves in these here hard times."

LIVINGSTONE: So you are poor now, are you? (*Takes a potato, playfully.*)

PUFFY: Yes sir; I ain't ashamed to own it—for I hurt nobody but myself. Take a little salt, sir. But, Lord bless you, sir, poverty don't come amiss to me—I've got no pride to support. Now, there's my lodgers—

LIVINGSTONE: Ah, your second floor.

PUFFY: A widow lady and her two grown children—poor as mice, but proud, sir—they was grand folks once; you can see that by the way they try to hide it. Mrs. Fairweather is a—

LIVINGSTONE: Fairweather—the widow of a sea captain, who died here in New York twenty years ago.

PUFFY: Do you know my lodgers?

LIVINGSTONE: Three months ago, they lived in Brooklyn—Paul had a clerkship in the Navy Yard.

PUFFY: But when the panic set in, the United States government contracted—it paid off a number of employees, and Mr. Paul was discharged.

LIVINGSTONE: They are reduced to poverty and I did not know it.—No, how could I? (*Aside.*) Since my ruin I have avoided them. (*Aloud.*) And Lucy—I mean Miss Fairweather?—

PUFFY: She works at a milliner's in Broadway—bless her sweet face and kind smile—me and my wife, we could bake ourselves into bread afore she and they should come to want; for as my boy Dan—talk of going through fire and water for her—he does that every night for nothing. Why, sir, you can't say "Lucy," but a big tear will come up in his eye as big as a cartwheel, and then he'll let out an almighty cuss, that sounds like a thousand o'brick.

2. Name of a fire engine.

(*Enter* PAUL *and* MRS. FAIRWEATHER, *dressed in black.*)

LIVINGSTONE: Oh! (*In confusion, hides the potato in his pocket, and hums an air as she walks away. Aside.*) I wonder if they know me.

MRS. FAIRWEATHER: Ah, Mr. Puffy.

PUFFY: What, my second floor. Mrs. Fairweather—good morning, Mr. Paul; I hope no misfortune as happened—you are dressed in mourning.

MRS. FAIRWEATHER: This is the anniversary of my poor husband's death; this day, twenty years ago, he was taken away from us—we keep it sacred to his memory.

PAUL: It was a fatal day for us. When my father left home he had 100,000 dollars on his person—when he was found lying dead on the sidewalk of Liberty Street, he was robbed of all.

MRS. FAIRWEATHER: From that hour misfortune has tracked us—we have lost our friends.

PUFFY: Friends—that reminds me—why where is Mr. Livingstone—there's his coat—Livingstone!

PUFFY: We were talking of you, when you came up. He slipped away.

(*Re-enter* LIVINGSTONE.)

LIVINGSTONE: I think I dropped my coat. (*Recognizing them.*) Paul—am I mistaken?

MRS. FAIRWEATHER: No, Mr. Livingstone.

PAUL: Good morning, sir.

LIVINGSTONE: Sir!—Mr. Livingstone—have I offended you?

PAUL: We could not expect you to descend to visit us in our poor lodging.

MRS. FAIRWEATHER: We cannot afford the pleasure of your society.

LIVINGSTONE: Let me assure you that I was ignorant of your misfortune—and if I have not called—it was because—a—because—(*Aside.*) What shall I say. (*Aloud.*)—I have been absent from the city; may I ask how is your sister?

PAUL: My sister Lucy is now employed in a millinery store in Broadway—she sees you pass the door every day.

LIVINGSTONE (*Aside*): The devil—I must confess my ruin, or appear a contemptible scoundrel.

PAUL: Livingstone—I cannot conceal my feelings, we were schoolmates together—and I must speak out.

LIVINGSTONE (*Aside*): I know what's coming.

PAUL: I'm a blunt New York boy, and have something of the old bluff sailor's blood in my veins—so pardon me if I tell you that you have behaved badly to my sister Lucy.

LIVINGSTONE: For many months I was a daily visitor at your house—I loved your sister.

PAUL: You asked me for Lucy's hand—I gave it, because I loved you as a brother—not because you were rich.

LIVINGSTONE (*Aside*): To retrieve my fortunes so that I might marry—I speculated in stocks and lost all I possessed. To enrich Lucy and her family, I involved myself in utter ruin.

PAUL: The next day I lost my clerkship—we were reduced to poverty, and you disappeared.

LIVINGSTONE: I can't stand it—I will confess all—let me sacrifice every feeling but Lucy's love and your esteem—

MRS. FAIRWEATHER: Beware, Mr. Livingstone, how you seek to renew our acquaintance; recollect my daughter earns a pittance behind a counter—I take in work, and Paul now seeks the poorest means of earning an honest crust of bread.

LIVINGSTONE: And what would you say if I were not better off than yourselves—if I were poor—if I—

PUFFY: You, poor, you who own a square mile of New York?

(*Enter* BLOODGOOD.)

LIVINGSTONE: Mr. Bloodgood!

BLOODGOOD: Ah, Livingstone—why do you not call to see us? You know our address—Madison square—my daughter Alida will be delighted.—By the way—I have some paper of yours at the bank, it comes due to-day—ten thousand dollars, I think—you bank at the Chemical?

LIVINGSTONE: Yes, I do—that is did,—bank there.

BLOODGOOD: Why don't you bank with me, a rich and careless fellow like you—with a large account.

LIVINGSTONE: Yes—I—(*Aside*.) He is cutting the ground from under my feet.

PAUL: Mr. Bloodgood—pardon me, sir, but I was about to call on you today to solicit employment.

BLOODGOOD: I'm full, sir,—indeed I think of reducing salaries, everybody is doing so.

LIVINGSTONE: But you are making thousands a week?

BLOODGOOD: That is no reason that I should not take advantage of the times—(*Recognizing* PUFFY.) Ah, Mr. Puffy, that note of yours.

PUFFY: Oh Lord! It is the note Mrs. Fairweather gave me for her rent.

BLOODGOOD: My patience is worn out.

PUFFY: It's all right sir.

BLOODGOOD: Take care it is.

(*Exit.*)

PUFFY: There goes the hardest cuss that ever went to law.

LIVINGSTONE: Paul—my dear friend—will you believe me—my feelings are the same towards you—nay more tender, more sincere than ever—but there are circumstances I cannot explain.

MRS. FAIRWEATHER: Mr. Livingstone, say no more. We ask no explanation.

LIVINGSTONE: But I ask something—let me visit you—let me return to the place that I once held in your hearts.

PUFFY: 219 Division street—Puffy, Baker. Dinner at half past one—come to-day, sir—do, sir.

PAUL: We cannot refuse you.

MRS. FAIRWEATHER: I'll go to Lucy's store and let her know. Ah! Mr. Livingstone—she has never confessed that she loved you—but you will find her cheek paler than it used to be.

(*Exit.*)

PAUL: And now to hunt for work—to go from office to office pleading for employment—to be met always with the same answer—"we are full"—or "we are discharging hands"—Livingstone, I begin to envy the common laborer who has no fears, no care beyond his food and shelter—I am beginning to lose my pity for the poor.

LIVINGSTONE: The poor!—whom do you call the poor? Do you know them? Do you see them? They are frequently found under a black coat than under a red shirt. The poor man is the clerk with a family, forced to maintain a decent suit of clothes, paid for out of the hunger of his children. The poor man is the artist who is obliged to pledge the tools of his trade to buy medicines for his sick wife. The lawyer who, craving for employment, buttons up his thin paletot to hide his shirtless breast. These needy wretches are poorer than the poor, for they are obliged to conceal their poverty with the false mask of content—smoking a cigar to disguise their hunger—they drag from their pockets their last quarter, to cast it with studied carelessness, to the beggar, whose mattress at home is lined with gold. These are the most miserable poor of the Poor of New York.

(*A small crowd has assembled round* LIVINGSTONE *during this speech; they take him for an orator, one of them takes down what he says on tablets.*)

(*Enter* POLICEMAN.)

PUFFY AND CROWD: Bravo—Bravo—Hurray—get on the bench!

POLICEMAN: Come—I say—this won't do.

LIVINGSTONE: What have I done.

POLICEMAN: No stumping to the population allowed in the Park.

LIVINGSTONE: Stumping!!

REPORTER: Oblige me with your name, sir, for the *Herald.*

LIVINGSTONE: Oh!

(*Rushes off followed by* PAUL.)

SCENE II

Exterior of BLOODGOOD's *Bank, Nassau Street.*

Enter BLOODGOOD.

BLOODGOOD (*Looking at papers*): Four per cent a month—ha! if this panic do but last, I shall double my fortune! Twenty years ago this very month—ay, this very day—I stood in yonder bank, a ruined man. Shall I never forget that day—when I and my accomplice carried out the body of the old sailor and laid it there. (*Points.*) I never pass the spot without a shudder. But his money—that founded my new fortune.

(*Enter* ALIDA.)

Alida, my dear child, what brings you to this part of the city?

ALIDA: I want two thousand dollars.

BLOODGOOD: My dearest child, I gave you five hundred last week.

ALIDA: Pooh! what's five hundred? You made ten thousand in Michigan Southern last week—I heard you tell Mr. Jacob Little so.

BLOODGOOD: But—

ALIDA: Come, don't stand fooling about it, go in and get the money—I must have it.

BLOODGOOD: Well, my darling, if you must. Will you step in?

ALIDA: Not I. I'm not going into your dirty bank. I've seen all your clerks—they're not worth looking at.

BLOODGOOD: I'll go and fetch it.

(*Exit.*)

ALIDA: This is positively the last time I will submit to this extortion. (*Opens a letter and reads.*) "My adored Alida—I fly to your exquisite feet; I am the most wretched of men. Last night, at Hall's I lost two thousand dollars—it must be paid before twelve o'clock. Oh, my queen! My angel! Invent some excuse to get this money from your father, and meet me at Maillard's at half-past eleven. When shall we meet again alone, in that box at the opera, where I can press my lips to your superb eyes, and twine my hands in your magnificent hair? *Addio carissima!* The Duke of Calcavella." I wonder if he showed that to any of his friends before he sent it!

(*Re-enter* BLOODGOOD, *followed by* PUFFY.)

BLOODGOOD: I tell you, sir, it must be paid. I have given you plenty of time.

PUFFY: You gave me the time necessary for you to obtain execution in the Marine Court.

BLOODGOOD: Alida, my love, there is a draft for the money. (*Gives her notes. She takes them.*) And now, will you do me a favor? Do not be seen about so much, in public, with that foreign Duke.

ALIDA: I never ask you for a draft but you always give me a pill to take with it.

BLOODGOOD: I don't like him.

ALIDA: I do—bye-bye.

(*Exit.*)

BLOODGOOD: How grand she looks! That girl possesses my whole heart.

PUFFY: Reserve a little for me, sir. This here note, it was give to me by my 2d floor in payment for rent. It's as good as gold, sir—when they are able to pay it. I'd sooner have it—

BLOODGOOD: My Puffy, you are the worst kind of man; you are a weak honest fool. You are always failing—always the dupe of some new swindler.

PUFFY: Lord love you, sir! if you was to see the folks you call swindlers—the kindest, purest, 2d floor as ever drew God's breath. I told them that this note was all right—for if they know'd I was put about, long of it, I believe they'd sell the clothes off their backs to pay it.

BLOODGOOD (*Aside*): This fellow is a fool. But I see, if I levy execution the note will be paid. (*Aloud.*) Very good, Mr. Puffy. I will see about it.

PUFFY: You will! I knew it—there—when folks says you're a hard man—I says—no—no mor'n a rich man's got to be.

BLOODGOOD: Very good. (*Aside.*) I'll put an execution on his house at once. (*Aloud.*) Good morning, Mr. Puffy.

PUFFY: Good morning, sir. So, I'm floated off that mud bank. Lord! if he had seized my goods and closed me up—I'd never a dared to look Mrs. Fairweather in the face again. (*Exit.*)

SCENE III

The interior of PUFFY's *house. A poor but neat room—window at back.* MRS. FAIRWEATHER *is arranging dinner.*

Enter LUCY, *with a box.*

LUCY: My dear mother.

MRS. FAIRWEATHER: My darling Lucy. Ah, your eye is bright again. The thought of seeing Mark Livingstone has revived your smile.

LUCY: I have seen him. He and Paul called at Madame Victorine's.

MRS. FAIRWEATHER: Is your work over, Lucy, already?

LUCY: What we expected has arrived, mother. This dress is the last I shall receive from Madame Victorine—she is discharging her hands.

MRS. FAIRWEATHER: More misfortunes—and Paul has not been able to obtain employment.

(*A knock. Enter* MRS. PUFFY.)

MRS. PUFFY: May I come in? it's only Mrs. Puffy. I've been over the oven for two hours! Knowing you had company—I've got a pigeon pie—such a pie—um—oo—mutton kidneys in it—and hard boiled eggs—love ye!—then I've got a chicken, done up a way of my own! I'll get on a clean gown and serve it up myself.

MRS. FAIRWEATHER: But my dear Mrs. Puffy—really we did not mean to incur any expense—

MRS. PUFFY: Expense! why, wasn't them pigeons goin' to waste—they was shot by Dan—and we can't abide pigeons, neither Puffy nor I. Then the rooster was running round—always raisn' hereafter early in the mornin'—a noosance, it was—

(*Enter* DAN)

DAN: Beg pardon, ladies—I just stepped in—

LUCY: Good day, Dan.

DAN: Day, Miss!—(*Aside to* MRS. PUFFY.) Oh! mother ain't she pootty this morning.

MRS. PUFFY (*Smoothing her hair*): What have you go there, Dan'el?

DAN: When I was paying the man for them birds—(MRS. PUFFY *kicks him.*)—Creation! mother—you're like the stocks—you can't move a'though crushin' somebody—well, he'd got this here pair o'boots ornder his arm—why, ses I, if ever der was a foot created small enough to go into them thar, it is Miss Lucy's—so I brought them back for you to look at.

LUCY: They are too dear for me, Dan, pray give them back.

DAN: Well, ye see—the man has kinder gone, Miss—he said he'd call again—some time next fall—

MRS. FAIRWEATHER: Dan—Mrs. Puffy—you are good, kind, dear souls—when the friends of our better days have deserted us—when the rich will scarcely deign to remember us—you, without any design, but with the goodness of God in your hearts—without any hope but that of hiding your kindness, you help me. Give me your hands—I owe you too much already—but you must bestow on us no more out of your poverty.

MRS. PUFFY: Lord, Mr.! just as if me and Puffy could bestow anything—and what's Dan fit for?

DAN: Yes—what's I'm fit for?

MRS. FAIRWEATHER: Well, I will accept your dinner to-day on one condition—that you will dine with us.

MRS. PUFFY: Oh—my! Dine with up-town folks!

LUCY: Yes indeed, Dan, you must.

DAN: Lord, miss! I sent no account at dinin' with folks—I take my food on the fust pile of bricks, anyhow.

MRS. PUFFY: I'm accustomed to mine standin', behind the counter.

DAN: We never set down to it, square out—except on Sundays.

MRS. PUFFY: Then it don't seem natural—we never eat, each of us is employed a-helping of the other.

DAN: I'll fix it! Father and mother, and I, will all wait on you.

LUCY (*Laughing*): That's one way of dining together, certainly.

(*Enter* PAUL *and* LIVINGSTONE.)

LIVINGSTONE: Here we are. Why, what a comfortable little cage this is!

DAN: Let me take your coat and hat, sir.

LIVINGSTONE: Thank you. (*Exit* DAN *and* MRS. PUFFY.) How like the old times, eh, Lucy? (*Sits by her.*)

MRS. FAIRWEATHER (*Aside to* PAUL): Well, Paul, have you obtained employment?

PAUL: No, mother; but Livingstone is rich—he must have influence, and he will assist me.

MRS. FAIRWEATHER: Heaven help us! I fear that the worst is not come.

PAUL: Nonsense, mother—cheer up! Is there anything you have concealed from me?

MRS. FAIRWEATHER: No—nothing you need to know. (*Aside.*) If he knew that for five weeks we have been subsisting on the charity of these poor people.

(*Enter* MRS. PUFFY *with a pie, followed by* DAN *with a roast chicken and* PUFFY, *loaded with plates and various articles of dinner service.*)

MRS. PUFFY: Here it is.

LUCY: Stay—we must lay more covers; help me, Paul.

LIVINGSTONE: Let me assist you. (*They join another table to the first.*)

MRS. FAIRWEATHER: Mr. and Mrs. Puffy and Dan dine with us.

PAUL: Bravo!

LIVINGSTONE: Hail Columbia! (DAN *begins dancing about.*)

LUCY: Why, Dan—what's the matter?

DAN: Oh, nothing, miss.

LUCY: How red your face is!

DAN: Don't mind, miss.

MRS. PUFFY: Oh Lord! I forgot that dish; it has been in the oven for an hour.

DAN: It ain't at all hot. (PAUL *touches it and jumps away.*) It's got to burn into the bone afore George Washington No. 4 gives in.

(*Lays down the plate—they all sit.*)

PUFFY: Now, this is agreeable—I have not felt so happy since I started my forty horse power oven.

LIVINGSTONE: This pie is magnificent.

(MRS. PUFFY *rises.*)

MRS. PUFFY: Oh, sir, you make me feel good.

DAN (*Holding the table*): Mother can't express her feelings without upsetting the table.

(*Enter two* SHERIFF'S OFFICERS.)

PAUL: What persons are these?

PUFFY: What do you want?

FIRST SHERIFF'S OFFICER: I am the Deputy Sheriff—I come at the suit of Gideon Bloodgood, against Susan Fairweather and Jonas Puffy—amount of debt and costs, one hundred and fifty dollars.

PAUL: Mother!

PUFFY: He said he would see about it—Oh, Mrs. Fairweather—I hope you will forgive me—I couldn't help it.

DEPUTY SHERIFF: I do not want to distress you; Mr. Livingstone will perhaps pay the debt—or give me his check.

PAUL: Livingstone!

LIVINGSTONE (*After a pause.*): I cannot help you. Yes, I will rather appear what I am a ruined man, than seem a contemptible one—I am penniless, broken—for weeks I have been so—but I never felt poverty until now.

TABLEAU

ACT III

A room in the house of GIDEON BLOODGOOD; *the furniture and ornaments are in a style of exaggerated richness, white satin and gold.* BLOODGOOD *is discovered writing at a table on one side,* ALIDA *seated reading a newspaper on the other.*

BLOODGOOD: What are you reading?

ALIDA: The New York *Herald.*

BLOODGOOD: You seem interested in it?

ALIDA: Very. Shall I read aloud?

BLOODGOOD: Do. (*Goes on writing.*)

ALIDA (*Reads*): "Wall street is a perch, on which a row of human vultures sit, whetting their beaks, ready to fight over the carcass of a dying enterprise. Amongst these birds of prey, the most vulturous is perhaps Gid Bloodgood. This popular financier made his fortune in the lottery business. He then dabbled a little in the slave trade, as the Paraquita case proved,—last week by a speculation in flour he made fifty thousand dollars, this operation raised the price of bread four cents a loaf, and now there are a thousand people starving in the hovels of New York—we nominate Gid for Congress, expense to be paid by the admiring crowd—send round the hat." Father! (*Rises.*) Are you not rich?

BLOODGOOD: Why do you ask?

ALIDA: Because people say that riches are worshipped in New York, that wealth alone graduates society. This is false, for I am young, handsome and your heiress—yet I am refused admission into the best families here whose intimacy I have sought.

BLOODGOOD: Refused admission! Is not Fifth Avenue open to you?

ALIDA: Fifth Avenue! that jest is stale. Fifth Avenue is a shop where the richest fortunes are displayed like the dry goods in Stewart's windows, and like them, too, are changed daily. But why do we not visit those families at whose names all men and all journals bow with respect, the Livingstones, the Astors, Van Renssalaers. Father, these families receive men less rich than you—and honor many girls who don't dress as well as I do, nor keep a carriage.

BLOODGOOD: Is not the Duke of Calcavella at my feet?

ALIDA: The Duke de Calcavella is an adventurer to whom you lend money, who escorts me to my box at the opera that he may get in free.

BLOODGOOD: You minx, you know you love him.

ALIDA: I am not speaking of love—but of marriage.

BLOODGOOD: Marriage!

ALIDA: Yes, marriage! This society in New York which has shut its doors against me, it is from amongst these families that I have resolved to choose a husband.

BLOODGOOD (*Rising*): Alida, do you already yearn to leave me? For you alone I have hoarded my wealth—men have thought me miserly, when I have had but one treasure in the world and that was you, my only child. To the rest of my fellow creatures I have been cold and calculating, because in you alone was buried all the love my heart could feel—my fortune, take it, gratify your caprices—take it all, but leave me your affection.

ALIDA: You talk as if I were still a child.

BLOODGOOD: I would to God you were! Oh, Alida, if you knew how fearful a thing it is for a man like me to lose the only thing in the world that ties him to it!

ALIDA: Do you wish me to marry the Duke de Calcavella?

BLOODGOOD: A *roué,* a gambler! Heaven forbid!

ALIDA: Besides, they say he has a wife in Italy.

BLOODGOOD: I shall forbid him the house.

ALIDA: No you won't.

BLOODGOOD: His reputation will compromise yours.

ALIDA: Judge my nature by your own—I may blush from anger—never from shame.
(*Enter* EDWARDS.)

EDWARDS: Mr. Mark Livingstone.

ALIDA: Livingstone! This is the first time that name has ever been announced in this house.

BLOODGOOD: He comes on business. Tell Mr. Livingstone I cannot see him. Beg him to call at my office to-morrow.

ALIDA: Show him up.

BLOODGOOD: Alida!

ALIDA (*Sharply to* EDWARDS): Do you hear me?

BLOODGOOD: This is tyranny—I—I—(*In a rage to* EDWARDS.) Well, blockhead, why do you stand staring there? Don't you hear the order? Show him up.

(*Exit* EDWARDS.)

ALIDA: Livingstone!

(*Enter* MARK LIVINGSTONE.)

LIVINGSTONE: Mr. Bloodgood—Miss Bloodgood—(*Bows.*) I am most fortunate to find you at home.

ALIDA: I trust that Mrs. Livingstone, your mother, and Miss Livingstone your sister, are well.

LIVINGSTONE (*Coldly*): I thank you. (*Gaily.*) Allow me to assure you that you were the belle of the opera last night.

ALIDA: Yet you did not flatter me with your presence in our box.

LIVINGSTONE: You noticed my absence! You render me the happiest and proudest member of my club.

ALIDA: By the way, papa, I thought you were going to be a member of the Union.

LIVINGSTONE: Ahem! (*An awkward silence.*) He was black-balled last week.

BLOODGOOD: I think, Mr. Livingstone you have some business with me.

ALIDA: Am I in the way?

LIVINGSTONE: Not at all—the fact is, Miss Bloodgood—my business can be explained in three words.

BLOODGOOD: Indeed!

LIVINGSTONE: I am ruined.

ALIDA: Ruined!

LIVINGSTONE: My father lived in those days when fancy stocks were unknown, and consequently was in a position to leave me with a handsome fortune. I spent it—extravagantly—foolishly. My mother, who loves me "not wisely but too well," heard that my name was pledged for a large amount,—Mr. Bloodgood held my paper—she sold out all her fortune without my knowledge, and rescued my credit from dishonor.

BLOODGOOD: Allow me to observe, I think she acted honorably, but foolishly.

LIVINGSTONE (*Bows to* BLOODGOOD): She shared my father's ideas on these matters; well (*Turns to* ALIDA.) finding I was in such good pay, your father lent me a further sum of money, with which I speculated in stocks to recover my mother's loss—I bulled the market—lost—borrowed more—the crisis came—I lost again—until I found myself ruined.

BLOODGOOD (*Rising*): Mr. Livingstone, I anticipate the object of your present visit—you desire some accommodation—I regret that it is out of my power to accord it. If you had applied to me a few days earlier I might have been able to—but—a—at the present moment it is quite impossible.

LIVINGSTONE (*Aside*): Impossible—the usual expression—I am familiar with it. (*Rising—aloud.*) I regret exceedingly that I did not fall on the more fortunate moment to which you allude—a thousand pardons for my untimely demand—

BLOODGOOD: I hope you believe I am sincere when I say—

LIVINGSTONE: Oh! I am sure of it. Accept my thanks—good morning, Miss Bloodgood.

BLOODGOOD (*Ringing the bell*): I trust you will not be put to serious inconvenience.

LIVINGSTONE: Oh, no. (*Aside.*) A revolver will relieve me of every difficulty. (*Aloud.*) Good day, Mr. Bloodgood.

(*Exit.*)

BLOODGOOD: I like his impudence! To come to me for assistance! Let him seek it of his aristocratic friends—his club associates who blackballed me last week.

ALIDA (*Who has been seated writing at table*): Father, come here.

BLOODGOOD: What is it?

ALIDA: I am writing a letter which I wish you to sign.

BLOODGOOD: To whom?

ALIDA: Mr. Livingstone.

BLOODGOOD: Mr. Livingstone!

GALIDA: Read it.

BLOODGOOD (*Reads*): "My dear sir, give yourself no further anxiety about your debt to me; I will see that your notes are paid—and if the loan of ten thousand dollars will serve you, I beg to hold that amount at your service, to be repaid at your convenience. Yours truly." (*Throwing down letter.*) I will write nothing of the kind.

ALIDA: You are mistaken—you will write nothing else.

BLOODGOOD: With what object?

ALIDA: I want to make a purchase.

BLOODGOOD: Of what?

ALIDA: A husband—a husband who is a gentleman—and through whom I can gain that position you cannot with all your wealth obtain—you see—the thing is cheap—there's the pen. (*She rings a bell.*)

BLOODGOOD: Is your mind so set on this ambition?

ALIDA: If it cost you half your fortune. (BLOODGOOD *signs.*)

(*Enter* EDWARDS.)

(*To servant.*) Deliver this letter immediately.

EDWARDS (*Takes the letter and is going out, when he runs against* BADGER, *who is coolly entering*): I have told you already that my master is not to be seen.

BADGER: So you did—but you see how mistaken you were. There he is—I can see him distinctly.

BLOODGOOD: Badger! (*To* EDWARDS.) You may go, Edwards.

BADGER (*To* EDWARDS): James—get out.

BLOODGOOD: What can he want here?

BADGER: Respected Gideon, excuse my not calling more promptly, but since my return from California, this is my first appearance in fashionable society.

ALIDA (*Proudly*): Who is this fellow?

BADGER: Ah, Alida, how is the little tootles? You forget me.

ALIDA: How can I recollect every begging imposter who importunes my father.

BADGER: Charming! The same as ever—changed in form, but the heart, my dear Gideon, the same as ever, is hard and dry as a biscuit.

ALIDA: Father, give this wretch a dollar and let him go.

BADGER: Hullo! Miss Bloodgood, when I hand round the hat it is time enough to put something in it. Gideon, ring and send that girl of yours to her nurse.

ALIDA: Is this fellow mad?

BLOODGOOD: Hush! my dear!

ALIDA: Speak out your business—I am familiar with all my father's affairs.

BADGER: All? I doubt it.

(*Enter* EDWARDS, *followed by* LUCY.)

EDWARDS: This way, Miss. (*To* ALIDA.) Here is your dress maker.

ALIDA (*Eyeing* LUCY): Ha! you are the young person I met this morning walking with Mr. Livingstone?

LUCY: Yes, Madam.

ALIDA: Hum! follow me, and let me see if you can attend on ladies as diligently as you do on gentlemen.

(*Exeunt* ALIDA *and* LUCY.)

BLOODGOOD (*Looking inquiringly at* BADGER): So you are here again. I thought you were dead.

BADGER: No; here I am—like a bad shilling, come back again. I've been all over the world since we parted company twenty years ago. Your 3,000 dollars lasted me for some months in California. Believe me, had I known that instead of absconding, you remained in New York, I would have hastened back again ten years ago, to share your revived fortunes.

BLOODGOOD: I am at a loss to understand your allusions, sir—nor do I know the object of your return to this city. We have plenty of such persons as you in New York.

BADGER: The merchants of San Francisco did not think so, for they subscribed to send me home.

BLOODGOOD: What do you mean?

BADGER: I mean the Vigilance Committee.

BLOODGOOD: What do you intend to do here?

BADGER: Reduced in circumstance and without character, the only resource I have left to me is to start a bank.

BLOODGOOD: Well, Mr. Badger; I cannot see in what way these things can affect me!

BADGER: Can't you? Ahem! Do you ever read the Sunday papers?

BLOODGOOD: Never.

BADGER: I've got a romance ready for one of them—allow me to give you a sketch of it.

BLOODGOOD: Sir—

BADGER: The scene opens in a bank on Nassau street. Twenty years ago a very respectable old sea captain, one winter's night, makes a special deposit of one hundred thousand dollars—nobody present but the banker and one clerk. The old captain takes a receipt and goes on his way rejoicing—but lo! and behold you!—in half an hour he returns—having ascertained a fact or two, he demands his money back, but while receiving it he is seized by a fit of apoplexy, and he dies on the spot. End of Chapter One.

BLOODGOOD: Indeed Mr. Badger, your romance is quite original.

BADGER: Ain't it! never heard it before, did you?—no! Good! Chapter Two. (*Pointedly.*) The banker and his clerk carried the body out on the sidewalk, where it was discovered, and the next day the Coroner's Jury returned a verdict accordingly. The clerk receiving 3,000 dollars hush money left for parts unknown. The banker remained in New York, and on the profits of his plunder established a colossal fortune. End of Part No. 1—to be continued in our next.

BLOODGOOD: And what do you suppose such a romance will be worth?

BADGER: I've come to you to know.

BLOODGOOD: I am no judge of that.

BADGER: Ain't you?—well—in Part No. 2, I propose to relate that this history is true in every particular, and I shall advertise for the heirs of the dead man.

BLOODGOOD: Ha! you know his name then?

BADGER: Yes, but I see you don't. I wrote the acknowledgement you signed—you had not even the curiosity then to read the name of your victim.

MR BLOODGOOD: Really, Mr. Badger, I am at a loss to understand you. Do you mean to insinuate that this romance applies in any way to me?

BADGER: It has a distance reference.

BLOODGOOD: Your memory is luxurious—perhaps it can furnish some better evidence of this wonderful story than the word of a convict ejected from California as a precaution of public safety.

BADGER: You are right—my word is not worth much.

BLOODGOOD: I fear not.

BADGER: But the receipt, signed by you, is worth a great deal.

BLOODGOOD (*Starting*): Ha! you lie!

BADGER: Let us proceed with my romance. When the banker and his clerk searched for the receipt, they could not find it—a circumstance which only astonished one of the villains—because the clerk had picked up the document and secured it in his pocket. I don't mean to insinuate that this applies in any way to you.

BLOODGOOD: Villain!

BADGER: Moral: As a general rule, never destroy receipts—it is no knowing when they may not prove useful.

BLOODGOOD: Were it so, this receipt is of no value in your hands—the heirs of the dead man can alone establish a claim.

BADGER (*Rising*): That's the point—calculate the chance of my finding them, and let me know what it is worth.

BLOODGOOD: What do you demand?

BADGER: Five thousand dollars.

BLOODGOOD: Five thousand devils!

BADGER: You refuse?

BLOODGOOD: I defy you—find the heir if you can. (*Enter* EDWARDS.)

EDWARDS: Mr. Paul Fairweather!
(*Enter* PAUL. BADGER *starts, then falls laughing in a chair.*)

BLOODGOOD: Your business, sir, with me.

PAUL: Oh, pardon me, Mr. Bloodgood—but the officers have seized the furniture of our landlord—of your tenant—for a debt owned by my mother. I come to ask your mercy—utter ruin awaits two poor families.

BADGER: Oh, Supreme Justice! there is the debtor.

PAUL: My mother—my sister—I plead for them, not for myself.

BLOODGOOD: I have waited long enough.

BADGER (*Rising*): So have I. (*To* PAUL.) Have you no friends or relations to help you?

PAUL: None, sir: My father is dead.
(BLOODGOOD *returns to his table.*)

BLOODGOOD: Enough of this. (*Rings the bell.*)

BADGER: Not quite; I feel interested in this young gentleman—don't you?

BLOODGOOD: Not at all; therefore my servant will show you both out—so you may talk this matter over elsewhere.

BADGER (*To* PAUL): Your name is familiar to me—was your father in trade?

PAUL: He was a sea captain.

BADGER: Ah! he died nobly in some storm, I suppose—the last to leave his ship?

PAUL: No, sir, he died miserably! Twenty years ago, his body was found on the side walk on Liberty street, where he fell dead by apoplexy.

BLOODGOOD (*Rising*): Ah!

(*Enter* EDWARDS.)

BADGER: James, show us out—we'll talk over this matter elsewhere.

BLOODGOOD: No—you—you can remain. Leave us, Edwards.

BADGER: Ah, I told you that the young man was quite interesting. Alphonse, get out.

(*Exit* EDWARDS.)

BLOODGOOD: My dear Mr. Badger, I think we have a little business to settle together?

BADGER: Yes, my dear Gideon. (*Aside to him.*) Stocks have gone up—I want fifty thousand dollars for that receipt.

BLOODGOOD: Fifty thousand!

BADGER (*Aside*): You see the effect of good news on the market—quite astonishing; ain't it.

BLOODGOOD: If you will step down to the dining-room, you will find lunch ready—refresh yourself, while I see what can be done for this young man.

BADGER (*Aside*): What are you up to? You want to fix him—to try some game to euchre me. Go it! I've got the receipt; you're on the hook—take out all the line you want. (*Calls.*) Ho! without there!

(*Enter* EDWARDS.)

Maximilian, vamos! Show me to the banqueting-hall.

(*Exit, with* EDWARDS.)

BLOODGOOD: Your situation interests me; but surely, at your age—you can find employment.

PAUL: Alas, sir, in these times, it is impossible. I would work, yes, at any kind of labor—submit to anything, if I could save my mother and sister from want.

BLOODGOOD: Control your feelings; perhaps I can aid you.

PAUL: Oh, sir, I little expected to find in you a benefactor.

BLOODGOOD: My correspondents at Rio Janeiro require a book-keeper—are you prepared to accept this situation? But there is a condition attached to this employment that may not suit you—you must start by the vessel which sails tomorrow.

PAUL: To-morrow!

BLOODGOOD: I will hand you a thousand dollars in advance of salary, to provide for your mother and sister; they had better leave this city until they can follow you. You hesitate.

PAUL: Oh, sir, 'tis my gratitude that renders me silent.

BLOODGOOD: You accept? the terms are two thousand dollars a year.

PAUL (*Seizing his hand*): Mr. Bloodgood, the prayers of a family whom you have made happy, will prosper your life. God bless you, sir! I speak not for myself, but for those still more dear to me.

BLOODGOOD: Call again in an hour, when your papers of introduction and the money shall be ready.

PAUL: Farewell, sir, I can scarcely believe my good fortune.

(*Exit.*)

BLOODGOOD: So, now to secure Badger. (*Sitting down and writing.*) He must, at any risk, be prevented from communicating with the mother and daughter until they can be sent into some obscure retreat. I doubt that he is in possession of this receipt, (*Rings a bell*) but I will take an assurance about that. (*Rings.*)

(*Enter* LUCY.)

LUCY: I will do my best, miss, to please you. Oh, let me hasten from this house!

(*Enter* MARK LIVINGSTONE.)

LIVINGSTONE: Lucy!

LUCY: Mark!

LIVINGSTONE: What brings you here?

LUCY: What brings the poor into the saloons of the rich?

(*Enter* ALIDA, *unseen by the others.*)

ALIDA (*Aside*): Mr. Livingstone here, and with this girl!

LIVINGSTONE: My dear Lucy, I have news, bright news, that will light up a smile in your eyes—I am once more rich. But before I relate my good fortune, let me hear from you the consent to share it.

LUCY: What do you mean?

LIVINGSTONE: I mean, dearest one, that I love you—I love you with all my reckless, foolish, worthless heart.

ALIDA (*Advancing*): Mr. Livingstone, my father is waiting for you in his study.

LIVINGSTONE: A thousand pardons, Miss Blood-good; I was not aware—excuse me. (*Aside.*) I wonder if she overheard me. (*To* LUCY.) I will see you again this evening.
(*Exit.*)

ALIDA (*To* LUCY, *who is going*): Stay; one word with you. Mr. Livingstone loves you? Do not deny it, I have overheard you.

LUCY: Well, Miss Bloodgood, I have no account to render you in this matter.

ALIDA: I beg your pardon—he is to be my husband.

LUCY: Your husband?

ALIDA: Be quiet and listen. Mr. Livingstone is ruined—my father has come to his aid; but one word from me, and the hand, extended to save him from destruction, will be withdrawn.

LUCY: But you will not speak that word?

ALIDA: That depends—

LUCY: On what? his acceptance of your hand? he does not love you.

ALIDA: That is not the question.

LUCY: You have overheard that he loves *me*.

ALIDA: That is no concern of mine.

LUCY: And you will coldly buy this man for a husband, knowing that you condemn him to eternal misery!

ALIDA: You are candid, but not complimentary. Let us hope that in time he will forget you, and learn to endure me.

LUCY: Oh, you do not love him. I see, it is his name you require to cover the shame which stains your father's, and which all his wealth cannot conceal. Thank Heaven! his love for me will preserve him from such a cowardly scheme.

ALIDA: I will make him rich. What would you make him?

LUCY: I would make him happy.

ALIDA: Will you give him up?

LUCY: Never!

ALIDA: Be it so.
(*Re-enter* LIVINGSTONE.)

LIVINGSTONE: Lucy, dear Lucy, do you see that lady?—she is my guardian angel. To her I owe my good fortune—Mr. Bloodgood has told me all, and see, this letter is in her own handwriting; now, let me confess, Miss Bloodgood, that

had I not been thus rescued from ruin, I had no other resource but a Colt's revolver.

LUCY: Mark!

LIVINGSTONE: Yes, Lucy—I had resolved I could not endure the shame and despair which beset me on all sides. But let us not talk of such madness—let us only remember that I owe her my life.

ALIDA (*Aside*): And I intend to claim the debt.

LIVINGSTONE: More than my life—I owe to her all the happiness which you will bestow upon me.

LUCY: Me! me!—Mark—No, it is impossible.

LIVINGSTONE: Impossible!

LUCY: I cannot be your wife.

LIVINGSTONE: What mean you, Lucy?

LUCY (*With supreme effort*): I—I do not love you.

LIVINGSTONE: You jest, Lucy—yet, no—there are tears in your eyes.

LUCY (*Looking away*): Did I ever tell you that I loved you?

LIVINGSTONE: No, it is true—but your manner, your looks, I thought—

LUCY: You are not angry with me, are you?

LIVINGSTONE: I love you too sincerely for that, and believe me I will never intrude again on your family, where my presence now can only produce pain and restraint; may I hope, however, that you will retain enough kindness towards me, as to persuade your mother to accept my friendship? It will soothe the anguish you have innocently inflicted, if your family will permit me to assist them. Have you the generosity to make this atonement? I know it will pain you all—but you owe it to me. (LUCY *falls, weeping, in a chair.*) Pardon me, Miss Bloodgood. Farewell, Lucy. (*To* ALIDA.) I take my leave.

ALIDA: He has gone—you may dry your eyes.

LUCY: Oh! I know what starvation is—I have met want face-to-face, and I have saved him from that terrible extremity.

ALIDA: He offered you money; I should prefer that my husband should not have pecuniary relations with you—at least not at present—so, as you are in want—here is some assistance. (*Offers her purse to* LUCY.)

LUCY (*Rising*): You insult me, Miss Bloodgood.

ALIDA: How can an offer of money insult anybody?

LUCY: You thought I sold my heart—no—I gave it. Keep your gold, it would soil my poverty;

you have made two fellow-beings unhappy for life—God forgive you!

(*Exit.*)

(*Re-enter* BLOODGOOD.)

BLOODGOOD: What is the matter, Alida?

(*Re-enter* BADGER.)

BADGER: Your cook is perfect, your wine choice. (*He pockets the napkins.*) Well, now suppose we do a little business.

BLOODGOOD (*Rings bell*): It is time we began to understand each other.

(*Enter* EDWARDS.)

Has that letter been delivered?

(EDWARDS *bows, and at a sign from* BLOODGOOD, *exits.*)

BADGER: Do you wish to enter into particulars in the presence of this charming creature?

BLOODGOOD: Her presence will not affect our business.

(*Re-enter* EDWARDS, *and two* POLICE OFFICERS.)

BADGER: Just as you please. What proposition have you to make?

BLOODGOOD: I propose to give you into custody for an attempt to extort money by threats and intimidation.

FIRST POLICEMAN: You are our prisoner.

BADGER: Arrested!

BLOODGOOD: Let him be searched; on his person will be found a receipt signed by me which he purloined from my desk yonder.

BADGER: Well played, my dear Gideon, but, knowing the character of the society into which I was venturing, I left the dear document safe at home. Good morning, Gid—Miss Bloodgood, yours. General—Colonel—take care of me. (*Goes off with* POLICEMEN.)

ACT IV

SCENE I

Union Square—Night. The snow falls.

PUFFY *discovered, with a pan of roasting chestnuts.* PAUL *crouches in a corner of the street.*

PUFFY: Lord! how cold it is. I can't sell my chestnuts. I thought if I posted myself just there, so as to catch the grand folks as they go to the opera, they might fancy to take in a pocketfull, to eat during the performance.

(*Enter* DAN, *with two trunks on his shoulder, followed by a* GENTLEMAN.)

DAN: There is the hotel. I'll wait here while you see if you can get a room.

(*Exit* GENTLEMAN, into the hotel.)

PUFFY: Dan, my boy, what cheer?

DAN: This is the first job I've had to-day.

PUFFY: I've not taken a cent.

DAN: Have you been home to dinner?

PUFFY: No; I took a chestnut. There wasn't more than enough for the old woman and you, so I dined out.

DAN: I wasn't hungry much, so I boried a bit o'bacca.

PUFFY: Then the old woman had all the dinner, that's some comfort—

DAN: I don't know, father—she's just ugly enough to go and put it by for our supper.

(*Enter* MRS. PUFFY, *with a tin can.*)

PUFFY: Here she is.

MRS. PUFFY: Ain't you a nice pair? For five mortal hours I've been carryin' this dinner up and down Broadway.

DAN: I told you so.

MRS. PUFFY: You thought to give old mother the slip, you undootiful villin—but I've found ye both. Come—here's your suppers—I've kept it warm under my cloak.

PUFFY: Lay the table on the gentleman's trunk.

DAN (*Looking into the tin can*): A splendid lump of bread, and a chunk of beef!

PUFFY: Small feed for three human beings.

DAN: Here goes.

PUFFY: Stay, Dan. (*Placing his hand over the bread.*) God bless us, and pity the Poor of New York. Now I'll share the food in three.

DAN (*Pointing to* PAUL): Father, that cuss in the corner there looks kinder bad—suppose you have the food in four.

MRS. PUFFY: I don't want more. Give him mine—I ain't at all cold.

DAN: Mother, there's a tear on the end of your nose—let me break it off.

MRS. PUFFY: Get out.

DAN (*Takes a piece of bread, and goes to* PAUL): Hello, stranger! He's asleep.

MRS. PUFFY: Then don't wake him. Leave the bread in his lap. (DAN *places the bread, softly, beside* PAUL, *and rejoins the party—they eat.*)

(*Enter a gentleman, followed by* BADGER.)

BADGER (*Very ragged, with some opera books in one hand, and boxes of matches in the other*): Book of the opera, sir? take a book, sir—they will charge you double inside. Well, buy a box of lucifers—a hundred for three cents. (*Dodging in front of him to prevent him passing.*) Genuine Pollak's—try one. (*Exit gentleman—*BADGER *changes his tone, and calls after him.*) If you're short of cash, I'll lend you a shilling. He wants all he has got to pay his omnibus. Jerusha! ain't it cold! Tum-iddy-tum-iddy-tum. (*Performs a short dance, while he hums a banjo melody.*) I could play the banjo on my stomach, while all my shivering anatomy would supply the bones.

(*Enter* MRS. FAIRWEATHER.)

MRS. FAIRWEATHER: I cannot return to our miserable home without food for my children. Each morning, we separate in search of work, in search of food, only to meet again at night—their poor faces thin with hunger. (*She clasps her hands in anguish.*) Ah! what's here? yes, this remains—it is gold!

BADGER (*Overhearing her last word*): Gold! Book of the opera, ma'am?

MRS. FAIRWEATHER: Tell me, friend, where can I buy a loaf of bread at this hour?

BADGER: There's a saloon open in the 4th Avenue. (*Aside.*) Gold—she said gold.

MRS. FAIRWEATHER: Will they accept this pledge for some food? (*Shows a ring to* BADGER.)

BADGER (*Eagerly*): Let me see it. (*Looks around.*)

MRS. FAIRWEATHER: It is my wedding ring.

(BADGER *examines it by the light of the Druggist's window.*)

BADGER (*Aside*): I can easily make off with it. (*Rubs his nose with the ring while he considers.*)

MRS. FAIRWEATHER: My children are starving—I must part with it to buy them bread.

BADGER (*Whistles—hesitates—and returns the ring*): Go along, go buy your children food, start, and don't show that ring to anybody else. You deserve to lose it for showing it to such a blackguard as I am.

(*Exit* MRS. FAIRWEATHER.)

(*Enter* BLOODGOOD.)

BLOODGOOD: What's the time? The opera must be nearly over. (*Looks at his watch by the light of the Druggist's window.*)

BADGER: Book of the opera, sir—only authorized edition. (*Recognizing him.*) Bloodgood!

BLOODGOOD: Badger! (*They advance.* BLOODGOOD *puts his hand into the breast of his coat.*)

BADGER: Ah, my dear Gideon—(*Suddenly.*) Take your hand out of your breast—come! none of that—I've a knife up my sleeve that would rip you up like a dried codfish before you could cock that revolver you have there so handy.

BLOODGOOD (*Withdrawing his hand*): You are mistaken.

BADGER: Oh, no! I am not. I have not been ten years in California for nothing—you were just thinking that you could blow out my brains, and swear that I was trying to garrote you.

BLOODGOOD: What do you want?

BADGER: I want your life—but legally. A week ago, I came out of prison—you had removed the Fairweather family—I could not find a trace of them but I found the receipt where I had concealed it. Tomorrow I shall place it in the hands of the District Attorney with my confession of our murder of the Sea Captain.

BLOODGOOD: Murder—

BADGER: Only think what a fine wood cut for the *Police Gazette* we shall make, carrying out the dead body between us.

BLOODGOOD: Demon!

BADGER: There will be a correct plan of your back office in the *Herald*—headed—the "Bloodgood Tragedy."

BLOODGOOD: Come to my house to-morrow and bring that document with you.

BADGER: No, sir-ee! once caught twice shy. You owe a call. Come to my house to-night—and alone.

BLOODGOOD: Where do you live?

BADGER: Nineteen and a half Cross Street, Five Points—fifth floor back—my name is on the door in chalk.

BLOODGOOD: In an hour I will be there.

BADGER: In an hour. Don't forget to present my compliments to your charming daughter—

sweet creature! the image of her father—how I should like to write something in her album. (*Exit* BLOODGOOD. *Enter two gentlemen from Hotel—they talk. Cries.*) Here's lucifers—three cents a hundred. (*Gentlemen shake hands and separate. Following one off.*) Here's this miscellaneous stock of lumber, just imported from Germany, to be sold out—an alarming sacrifice, in consequence of the present state of the money market. (*Exit importuning the gentleman, who tries to escape.*)

PUFFY: Come mother, we must get home—

MRS. PUFFY: Dan, have you seen nothing of poor Mrs. Fairweather and her children?

DAN: No, mother—I can't find out where they have gone to—I guess they've quit New York.

MRS. PUFFY: God help them—wherever they are!

PUFFY: Come, mother.

(*Music*—PUFFY *and* MRS. PUFFY *go out*—DAN *goes up and speaks with a* GENTLEMAN.)

(*Enter* LUCY.)

LUCY: This is the place. The sisters of charity in Houston Street told me that I might find work at this address. (*Reads paper.*) 14th Street. Oh, Heaven! be merciful to me, this is my last hope. (*Exit.*)

(PAUL *rises and comes forward.*)

PAUL: My limbs are powerless. How long have I slept there?—another long day has passed—I have crept around the hotels—the wharves—I have begged for work—but they laughed at my poor thin form—the remnant of better days hung in tatters about me—and I was thrust from the door, by stronger wretches than I. To-day I applied to get employment as a waiter in a hotel—but no, I looked too miserable. Oh, my mother! my poor mother! my dear sister! Were it not for you, I would lie down here and die where I was born, in the streets of New York.

DAN: All right, sir—to the Brevoort House. Here, you lazy cuss, shoulder this trunk, and earn a quarter—

(*Enter a* PORTER.)

PAUL: Yes—oh, gladly!—

PORTER: It's myself will do that same. (PAUL *and the* PORTER *seize the trunk.*) Lave yer hoult—you dandy chap wid the black coat.

PAUL: He called to me.

PORTER: It is the likes of you—that ud be takin' the bread out of the mouths of honest folks.

PAUL: God help me! I have not tasted bread for two days.

PORTER: The Lord save us! why didn't ye say so?—take the trunk and welkim. (PAUL *trying to lift it. Exit* DAN.)

GENTLEMAN: Come along, quick!

(*Exit* GENTLEMAN.)

PAUL (*Unable to lift it, staggers back*): I—I—can't—I am too weak from hunger.

PORTER: Look at this, my jewel. (*Tossing the trunk on his shoulder.*) That's the way of—id—all right, yer honor! (*Exit* PORTER.)

PAUL (*Falling against the lamp-post in despair, on his knees*): Oh, God—you who have refused to me the force to earn my bread, give me the resignation to bear your will.

(*Re-enter* LUCY.)

LUCY: The lady was from home—they told me to call next week—oh, could I see some kindly face—I would beg, yes—I would ask alms.

(*Enter a* GENTLEMAN.)

Sir—pardon me—would you—

GENTLEMAN: Eh?

LUCY (*Stammering*): I—I—I—

GENTLEMAN: What do you want?

LUCY (*Faintly*): The—the—Bowery—if—if—you please—

GENTLEMAN: Just turn to the right and keep straight on.

LUCY: Oh coward! coward!—I have not the courage to beg.

(*Enter* MRS. FAIRWEATHER.)

MRS. FAIRWEATHER: They refused to take my ring—they said I had stolen it—they drove me from the house. To what have I come!—to beg in the streets—yes, for them, for my children!

LUCY (*Covering her face with one hand, and holding out the other*): For pity's sake—give me the price of—

PAUL: Mother!!

LUCY: My Brother!

MRS. FAIRWEATHER: My Son!

} (*Together.*)

PAUL: Oh, mother! my own Lucy! my heart is broken! (*They embrace.*) Have you concealed from me the extent of your misery?

MRS. FAIRWEATHER: My son! my poor children! I cannot see you die of hunger and cold!

PAUL: Take Lucy home, mother—and I will bring you food.

MRS. FAIRWEATHER: Paul, promise me that nothing will tempt you to a dishonorable act.

PAUL: Do not fear, mother; the wretched have always one resource—they can die! Do not weep, Lucy—in an hour I will be with you.
(*Exeunt* LUCY *and* MRS. FAIRWEATHER.)
I will go and await the crowd as they leave the Academy of Music—amongst them Heaven will inspire some Christian heart to aid me.

SCENE II

The vestibule of the Academy of Music.

Enter ALIDA *and* LIVINGSTONE. *Music within.*

ALIDA: How strange that my father has not returned.

LIVINGSTONE: Allow me to look for the carriage.

ALIDA: I will remain here. (*Exit* LIVINGSTONE.) At last I have won the husband I desire. He is entangled in my father's debt; in one month hence I shall be Livingstone's wife. Our box is now crowded with the first people in New York.— The dear Duke still makes love to me—to which Livingstone appears indifferent—so much the better—once Mrs. Livingstone he may do as he likes and so will I.
(*Enter* PAUL.)

PAUL: Ah 'tis she—Alida Bloodgood.

ALIDA: I wonder they permit such vagabonds to hang about the opera.
(*Re-enter* LIVINGSTONE.)

LIVINGSTONE: The carriage is ready—(*Recognizing* PAUL.) Paul!

PAUL: Livingstone!

LIVINGSTONE: Great heaven! In what condition do I find you.

PAUL: We are poor—we are starving.

ALIDA: Give the poor fellow a dollar, and send him away.

LIVINGSTONE: My dear Alida, you do not know—this is a school fellow—an old friend.

ALIDA: I know that you are keeping me in the cold—ah! I see the Duke of Calcavella on the steps yonder, smoking a cigar. He will see me home, don't let me take you from your old friend.
(*Exit.*)

LIVINGSTONE (*Aside*): Cold—heartless girl! (*Aloud.*) Come, Paul, come quickly, bring me to where I shall find your mother—your sister—stay, let me first go home, and get money, I will meet you at your lodgings—where do you live?

PAUL: Number nineteen and a half Cross Street— Five Points—I will wait for you at the door.

LIVINGSTONE: In less than an hour I shall be there.
(*Exeunt.*)

SCENE III

No. 19½ Cross Street—Five Points. Two adjoining attic rooms; that of BADGER, *that of the* FAIRWEATHER *family. Music.* LUCY *is seated and* MRS. FAIRWEATHER *is kneeling.*

LUCY: Surely an hour has passed and Paul has not returned.

MRS. FAIRWEATHER: Oh, merciful father! protect my poor children!
(*Enter* BADGER *in his attic with his box of matches. He scrapes several which do not light.* MRS. FAIRWEATHER *rises and goes to window.*)

BADGER: One hundred matches like that for one cent. (*Lighting one.*) Oh, lucky chance! here's one that condescends. (*Lights a candle in a bottle.*)

MRS. FAIRWEATHER: Day after day goes by—no hope—the future worse than the present— dark—dark. Oh! this load of wretchedness is too much to bear.

LUCY: The candle is going out.

MRS. FAIRWEATHER: So much the better, I shall not be able to see your tears. (LUCY *rests her face on her hands.*)

BADGER (*Taking a bottle from his pocket*): There's the concentrated essence of comfort—the poor man's plaster for the inside.

LUCY (*Aside*): Is there no way to end this misery? None but death.

BADGER (*Taking from pocket a slice of bread and meat wrapped in a bit of newspaper*): Here's my supper. (*Addressing an imaginary servant.*) James, lay the table—spread the table cloth.— "Yes sa"—(*Places the newspaper over the table.*) It's cold here, there's a draught in this room, somewhere.—James, champagne. Thank you, James. (*Drinks and eats.*)

MRS. FAIRWEATHER (*Aside, coming down*): If Paul had only Lucy to support, they might live—why should I prolong my life only to hasten theirs.

BADGER: The draught comes from—(*Examining the wall.*)—yes there are great chinks in the wall— I must see my landlord and solicit repairs. A new family moved into the room, yesterday; I wonder who they are?

LUCY: The wretched always have one resource— they can die!

BADGER (*At his table eating—he has taken the blanket from his bed and wrapped it about his shoulders*): Now let us do a little business. James, turn up the gas. Yes sa!—(*He snuffs the candle with his fingers.*) Thank you. Ahem! James, Bloodgood is coming for the receipt bequeathed to me by the old sailor. What price shall we set upon it, James?

LUCY (*Aside*): When I am gone, there will be one mouth less to feed—Paul will have but one care to provide for.

MRS. FAIRWEATHER (*Aside*): In this room, we had some charcoal—there is enough left to bestow on me an easy death.

(MRS. FAIRWEATHER *exits.*)

BADGER: I think $50,000 would be the figure—Oh, what a prospect opens before me—50,000 dollars—I should resume specie payments.

LUCY (*Looks into room*): What is mother doing? ah, she is lighting the pan of charcoal on which we prepare our food—ah!—the thought!—could I induce her to leave me alone. Hem.—the deadly fumes of that fuel will bestow on me an easy death.

MRS. FAIRWEATHER (*Re-enters*): It is there—now, now, while I have the courage of despair.

BADGER: 50,000 dollars! I'll have a pair of fast trotters, and dine at Delmonico's. James, more champagne. (*Takes a drink from the bottle.*) Thank you—

LUCY & MRS. FAIRWEATHER (*Together*): Mother— Lucy.

LUCY: Dear mother—I have just thought of a friend—a—a—fellow work girl, from whom I may get assistance—

MRS. FAIRWEATHER: Go, then, my child—yes—go at once.

LUCY: I fear to go alone. Come with me, you can wait at the corner of the street until I come out.

MRS. FAIRWEATHER (*Putting on her bonnet. Aside*): When she is out of sight, I can return and accomplish my purpose.

LUCY (*Casting a cloak over her head. Aside*): I will come back by another way.

MRS. FAIRWEATHER: Come, Lucy.

LUCY: I am ready, mother. (*Aside.*) She does not think that we are about to part forever.

MRS. FAIRWEATHER (*Aside*): My poor child!

LUCY: Kiss me—mother, for my heart is cold. (*They embrace.*)

BADGER (*Cogitating*): 50,000 dollars! I'll have a box at Grace Church and a pew at the opera.

LUCY: Mother, I am ready.

(*Exeunt.*)

BADGER (*Finding his bottle empty*): What's the news? Let us consult my table cloth. What journal have we here. (*Reads.*) "Chevalier Greely has got a new hat."—It's the *Herald*—What's here?—(*Reads*) "You lie—villainy—you lie, and you know it." No! it's the *Tribune*.

(*Enter* BLOODGOOD.)

BLOODGOOD: Ah, Mr. Badger.

BADGER: Please wipe your feet, before you come in—my carpet is new. I am glad to see you. Take a seat upon the sofa. (*Pointing to the bed.*)

BLOODGOOD: Come, sir; to business. You have the receipt with you, I suppose?

BADGER: You know I've got it, or you would not have come.

BLOODGOOD: How much do you want for it?

BADGER: Stay a moment. Let us see. You have had for twenty years in your possession, the sum of $100,000, the profits of one robbery—well, at eight per cent, this sum would be doubled.

BLOODGOOD: Let me see the document, and then we can estimate its value.

BADGER (*Drawing receipt from pocket*): Here it is.

BLOODGOOD (*Springing towards him*): Let me have it.

BADGER: Hands off!

BLOODGOOD (*Drawing pistol*): That paper, give it me, or I'll blow your brains out!

BADGER (*Edging slowly towards the bed*): Ah! that's your calculation.

BLOODGOOD: Now you are in my power.

BADGER: It's an old dodge, but ineffective. Come, no violence—I'll give you the paper.

BLOODGOOD: A bullet is a good argument.

BADGER (*Drawing from beneath his pillow, two enormous pistols*): A brace of bullets are better still!

BLOODGOOD: Damnation!

BADGER: Derringer's self-cocking. Drop your hand, or I'll blow you into pieces—So, you took me for a fool;—that's where you made a mistake. I took you for a thorough rascal, that's where I did *not* make a mistake. Now, to business.

BLOODGOOD (*Surlily*): How much do you want?

BADGER: Fifty thousand dollars!

BLOODGOOD: Be it so.

BADGER: In gold, or Chemicals.

BLOODGOOD: Very well. To-morrow—

BADGER: No—to-night.

BLOODGOOD: To-night!

BADGER: Yes; I wish to purchase a brown stone house on the avenue early in the morning.

BLOODGOOD: Come with me to my house in Madison Square.

BADGER: No thank you. I'll expect you here in an hour with the money.

BLOODGOOD (*Aside*): He has me in his power—I must yield. (*Aloud.*) I will return, then, in an hour.

BADGER: Let me light you out. Mind the banister—don't break your precious neck, at least not to-night. No, go in front, will you? I prefer it.

BLOODGOOD: What for?

BADGER (*With pistol and candle*): A fancy of mine—a want of confidence. A want of confidence, in fact, pervades the community.

(*Exeunt.*)

(*Re-enter* LUCY.)

LUCY: I took a cross street, and ran rapidly home. Now I am alone; the fumes of the charcoal will soon fill this small room. They say it is an easy death—but let me not hesitate—let me sleep the long sleep where there are no more tears, no more suffering.

(*Exit into closet.*)

(*Re-enter* BADGER.)

BADGER: So! that is settled. I hope he will be cautious and escape the garroters. James, my chibouque. (*Takes his pipe.*)

(*Re-enter* MRS. FAIRWEATHER.)

MRS. FAIRWEATHER: Poor Lucy! I dared not look back upon her as we parted forever. Despair hastened my steps. My poor children! I have given you all I had, and now I hope my wretched life will serve you in your terrible need. Come, courage; let me prevent the fresh air from entering. (*Takes bits of linen and stops window and door.*)

BADGER (*Snuffing*): I smell charcoal—burning charcoal—where can it come from?

MRS. FAIRWEATHER: Now let me stop the door.

BADGER (*Smoking*): It's very odd; I've a queer feeling in my head; let me lie down awhile. (*Lies on his bed.*)

(*Enter* LUCY, *with a brazier of charcoal, alight.*)

MRS. FAIRWEATHER: That's done. (*Going towards closet, and meeting* LUCY.) Now the hour has come.

LUCY: Now the moment has arrived. (*Sets down the brazier.*)

MRS. FAIRWEATHER: Lucy!

LUCY: Mother!

MRS. FAIRWEATHER: My child, what is this for? For what purpose are you here?

LUCY: And you, mother, why have you fastened those apertures so closely? Like me, you wish to die!

MRS. FAIRWEATHER: No, no, you shall not die! my darling child—you are young—life is before you—hope—happiness.

LUCY: The future! what is it? The man I love will soon wed another. I have no future, and the present is a torture.

MRS. FAIRWEATHER: Hush, my child, hush!

LUCY: Is it not better to die thus, than by either grief or hunger?

MRS. FAIRWEATHER (*Falling in a chair*): Already my senses fail me. Lucy my child, live, live!

LUCY (*Falls at her feet*): No; let us die together—thus, mother—as often I knelt to you as a child, let me pray for those we love.

MRS. FAIRWEATHER: Oh, merciful Judge in heaven, forgive us—forgive my child—and let—your anger fall—on me—alone—

LUCY: God bless my dear brother—and you my dear Mark, may—you be—hap—(*Murmurs the rest of the prayer.*)

BADGER: It's very cold! I feel quite sleepy. I must not go to sleep. (*Sings in a low voice.*) "Oh, down in ole Virginny."

PAUL (*Without, knocking*): Mother, open the door, why is the door locked? Mother, mother! Open, mother, open! (*Knocks violently.* MRS. FAIRWEATHER, *arising, tries to reach the door, but cannot, and falls.* PAUL *bursts open the door and enters with* LIVINGSTONE; *they start back*—LIVINGSTONE *breaks the window, and* PAUL *runs to his mother.*) Too late! too late! They have committed suicide!

LIVINGSTONE: They live still. Quick, bear them outside into the air. (*Carries* LUCY *out while* PAUL *assists his mother into the next room.*)

BADGER (*Starting up*): How hot it is here—I cannot breathe. Have I drunk too much? Nonsense! I could drink a dozen such bottles. Let me try my legs a bit—where's the door? I can't see it—my head spins round—come, Badger, no nonsense now. God! I'm suffocating! Am I going to die, to die like that old sea captain? (*Tears off his cravat.*) Justice of Heaven! I am strangling. Help! Help! Bloodgood will return and find me helpless, then he will rob me of the receipt, as I robbed the old sailor—I know him of old—he is capable of it, but he shall not have it! There in its nook, if I have the strength to reach it—it is safe—safe. (*Drags himself along the floor, lifts up a loose board, puts the receipt beneath it and falls exhausted.*) There!

PAUL (*Entering the room*): I heard smothered cries for help—they came from this floor.
(*Exit.*)
(*Enter* BLOODGOOD.)

BLOODGOOD: Here I am, Badger. (*Starts back, suffocated.*) What a suffocating atmosphere! where is he? ha! is he intoxicated?

PAUL (*Entering room*): Perhaps the cry came from here, dead?

BLOODGOOD: Paul Fairweather!

PAUL: Gideon Bloodgood!

BADGER (*Raising his head*): What names were those? Both of them! Together, here! (*To* PAUL.) Listen—while I yet have breath to speak—listen! Twenty years ago, that man robbed your father of $100,000!

PAUL: Robbed!

BLOODGOOD: Scoundrel!

BADGER: I've got the proofs.

PAUL: The proofs?

BADGER: I have 'em safe—you'll find 'em—th—ah—(*Falls backward insensible;* PAUL *and* BLOODGOOD *stand aghast.*)

ACT V

SCENE 1

Brooklyn Heights, overlooking the city of New York and its harbors. The stage is occupied by a neat garden, on a natural terrace of the heights—a frame cottage stands, prettily built—a table with breakfast laid, at which MRS. FAIRWEATHER *and* PAUL *are seated.*

Enter MRS. PUFFY, *from the cottage, with a teapot.*

MRS. PUFFY: There's the tea. Bless me, how hot it is to-day! Who would think that we were in the month of February? (*Sits.*)

MRS. FAIRWEATHER: Your husband is late to breakfast.

PAUL: Here he comes.
(*Enter* PUFFY, *gaily.*)

PUFFY: How is everybody? And above everybody, how is Miss Lucy this morning? (*Sits at table.*)

MRS. FAIRWEATHER: Poor child! her recovery is slow—the fever has abated, but she is still very weak.

PAUL: Her life is saved, for a whole month she hovered over the grave.

PUFFY: But how is it we never see Mr. Livingstone? Our benefactor is like Santa Claus—he showers benefits and blessings on us all, yet never shows us his face.

MRS. FAIRWEATHER: He brought us back to this, our old home—he obtained employment for Paul in the Navy Yard.

PUFFY: He set me up again in my patent oven, and got me a government contract for Navy biscuit.

MRS. PUFFY: He is made of the finest flour that heaven ever put into human baking; he'll die of over-bigness of heart.

MRS. FAIRWEATHER: That's a disease hereditary in your family.

PAUL (*Rising*): I will tell you why Livingstone avoids our gratitude. Because my sister refused his love—because he sold his hand to Alida Bloodgood—and he has given us the purchase money.

PUFFY: And amongst those who have served us, don't let us forget poor Badger.

(*Enter* BADGER, *behind.*)

BADGER: They are talking of me.

MRS. FAIRWEATHER (*Rising*): Forget him! Forget the man who watched Lucy during her illness, with more than the tenderness of a brother! A woman never can forget anyone who has been kind to her children.

MRS. PUFFY: Them's my sentiments to a hair.

BADGER: You shan't have cause to change them.

PAUL: Badger!

BADGER: Congratulate me. I have been appointed to the police. The commissioners wanted a special service to lay on to Wall Street's savagery, it seems has concentrated there, and we want to catch a big offender.

MRS. PUFFY: They all go to Europe.

PUFFY: That accounts for the drain of specie.

(MR. AND MRS. PUFFY *take off the breakfast table.*)

MRS. FAIRWEATHER: I will tell Lucy that her nurse has come. (*Exit into cottage.*)

PAUL: Now, Badger, the news.

BADGER: Bad, sir. To-night. Mr. Livingstone is to be married to Alida Bloodgood.

PAUL: What shall I do? I dare not accuse Bloodgood of this robbery, unless you can produce the proofs—and perhaps the wretch has discovered and destroyed them.

BADGER: I think not. When I recovered from the effects of the charcoal, the day after my suffocation, I started for my lodging—I found the house shut up, guarded by a servant of Bloodgood's—the banker had bought the place. But I had concealed the document too cunningly; he has not found it.

PAUL: But knowing this man to be a felon, whom we may be able at any hour to unmask, can we allow Livingstone to marry his daughter?

(*Enter* LIVINGSTONE.)

LIVINGSTONE: Paul, I have come to bid you farewell, and to see Lucy for the last time—

(*Enter* LUCY.)

LUCY: For the last time, why so—(PAUL *and* BADGER *run to assist her forward.*)

LIVINGSTONE: Lucy, dear Lucy.

BADGER: Now take care—sit down—

LUCY: Ah, my good kind nurse. (*She sits.*) You are always by my side.

BADGER: Always ready with a dose of nasty medicine, ain't I—well now I've got another dose ready—do you see this noble kind heart, Lucy; it looks through two honest blue eyes into your face—well tell me what you see there—

LUCY: Why do you ask me? (*Troubled.*)

BADGER: Don't turn your eyes away—the time has come when deception is a crime, Lucy—look in his face and confess the infernal scheme by which Alida Bloodgood compelled you to renounce your love.

LIVINGSTONE: Alida!

LUCY: Has she betrayed me—

BADGER: No! you betrayed yourself—one night in the ravings of your fever, when I held your hands in the paroxysm of your frenzy, I heard the cries that came from your poor wounded heart; shall I repeat the scene.

LUCY (*Hiding her face in her hands*): No, no.

LIVINGSTONE: Paul, is this true? have I been deceived?

PAUL: You have—Lucy confessed to me this infamous bargain, extorted from her by Alida Bloodgood; and to save you from ruin, she sacrificed her love—

LIVINGSTONE: Lucy! dear Lucy, look up. It was for your sake alone that I accepted this hated union—to save you and yours from poverty—but whisper one word, tell me that ruin of fortune is better than ruin of the heart. (LUCY *falls upon his neck.*)

BADGER: Hail Columbia! I know a grand party at Madison Square that will cave in to-night—hi!—I shall be there to congratulate that sweet girl. (*Enter* DAN.)

DAN: Mother! mother! where's my hat, quick, there's a fire in New York.

(*He runs into the house and re-enters with a telescope, looks off toward the city.*)

BADGER: Yes, and there is a fire here, too, but one we don't want to put out.

PAUL: Now Mark, I can confess to you that documents exist—proofs of felony against Bloodgood, which may at any moment consign him to the State Prison and transfer to our family his ill-gotten wealth.

LIVINGSTONE: Proofs of felony?

DAN: The fire is in Chatham Street.

PAUL: Twenty years ago he robbed my father of 100,000 dollars.

BADGER: And I was his accomplice in the act; we shared the plunder between us—

DAN: No it isn't Chatham Street—I see plainly—it is in Cross Street, Five Points.

BADGER (*Starting*): Cross Street—where, where—(*Runs up.*)

LIVINGSTONE: But if these proofs—these documents exist, where are they?

DAN: It is the tenement house two doors from the corner.

BADGER: Damnation! it is our old lodging! you ask where are these proofs, these documents? They are yonder, in the burning house—fired by Bloodgood to destroy the papers he could not find—curses on him!

(*Enter* MRS. PUFFY, *with* DAN's *hat.*)

MRS. PUFFY: Here's your hat, Dan.

BADGER: Quick! Dan, my son—for our lives! Dan! the fortunes of Lucy and Paul and the old woman are all in that burning house.

(DAN *begins to thrust his trousers into his boots. Enter* MRS. FAIRWEATHER *and* PUFFY.)

BADGER: I mean to save it or perish in the flames.

DAN: Count me in. (*They run out.*)

TABLEAU.

SCENE II

*Stage dark. The exterior of the tenement house, No. 19½ Cross Street, Five Points—the shutters of all the windows are closed. A light is seen through the round holes in the shutters of the upper windows—presently a flame rises—it is extinguished—then revives. The light is seen to descend as the bearer of it passes down the staircase, the door opens cautiously—*BLOODGOOD, *disguised, appears—he looks round—closes the door again—locks it.*

BLOODGOOD: In a few hours this accursed house will be in ruins. The receipt is concealed there—and it will be consumed in flames. (*The glow of the fire is seen to spread from room to room.*) Now Badger—do your worst—I am safe! (*Exit.*)

(*The house is gradually enveloped in fire, a cry outside is heard "Fi-er!" "Fi-er!" It is taken up by other voic-es more distant. The tocsin sounds—other churches take up the alarm—bells of Engines are heard. Enter a crowd of persons. Enter* BADGER, *without coat or hat—he tries the door—finds it fast; seizes a bar of iron and dashes in the ground-floor window, the interior is seen in flames. Enter* DAN.)

DAN (*Seeing* BADGER *climbing into the window*): Stop! Stop! (BADGER *leaps in and disappears. Shouts from the mob;* DAN *leaps in—another shout,* DAN *leaps out again black and burned, staggers forward and seems overcome by the heat and smoke. The shutters of the garret fall and discover* BADGER *in the upper floor. Another cry from the crowd, a loud crash is heard,* BADGER *disappears as if falling with the inside of the building. The shutters of the windows fall away, and the inside of the house is seen, gutted by the fire; a cry of horror is uttered by the mob.* BADGER *drags himself from the ruins, and falls across the sill of the lower window.* DAN *and two of the mob run to help him forward but recoil before the heat; at length they succeed in rescuing his body—which lies center stage.* LIVINGSTONE, PAUL, *and* PUFFY, *rush on.* DAN *kneels over* BADGER *and extinguishes the fire which clings to parts of his clothes.*)

SCENE III

The Drawing-Room in BLOODGOOD's *mansion, in Madison Square—illuminated. Music within.*

Enter BLOODGOOD.

BLOODGOOD: The evidence of my crime is destroyed—no power on earth can reveal the past. (*Enter* ALIDA *dressed as a bride.*) My dearest child, tonight you will leave this roof; but from this home in your father's heart, none can displace you.

ALIDA: Oh, dear pap, do take care of my flounces—you men pat one about as if a dress was put on only to be rumpled.

BLOODGOOD: The rooms below are full of company. Has Livingstone arrived?

ALIDA: I did not inquire. The duke is there, looking the picture of misery, while all my female friends pretend to congratulate me—but I know they are dying with envy and spite.

BLOODGOOD: And do these feelings constitute the happiest day of your life? Alida, have you no heart?

ALIDA: Yes, father, I have a heart—but it is like yours. It is an iron safe in which are kept the secrets of the past.

(*Enter* EDWARDS.)

EDWARDS: The clergyman is robed, sir, and ready to perform the ceremony.

BLOODGOOD: Let the bridesmaids attend Miss Bloodgood. (*The curtains are raised, and the* BRIDESMAIDS *enter.* BLOODGOOD *goes up and off, and immediately returns with the bridal party.*) Welcome, my kind friends. (ALIDA *speaks aside with the duke.*) Your presence fills me with pride and joy—but where is the bridegroom? Has no one seen my son-in-law?

EDWARDS (*Announcing*): Mr. Mark Livingstone.

(*Enter* LIVINGSTONE.)

BLOODGOOD: Ah! at last. What a strange costume for a bridegroom.

ALIDA (*Turns, and views* LIVINGSTONE): Had I not good reasons to be assured of your sincerity, Mr. Livingstone, your appearance would lead me to believe that you looked upon this marriage as a jest, or a masquerade.

LIVINGSTONE: As you say, Miss Bloodgood, it is a masquerade—but it is one where more than one mask must fall.

BLOODGOOD (*Aside*): What does he mean?

ALIDA: You speak in a tone of menace. May—

BLOODGOOD: Perhaps I had better see Mr. Livingstone alone—he may be under some misapprehension.

LIVINGSTONE: I am under none, sir—although I believe you may be; and what I have to say and do, demands no concealment. I come here to decline the hand of your daughter. (*Movement amongst the crowd.*)

BLOODGOOD: You must explain this public insult.

LIVINGSTONE: I am here to do so, but I do not owe this explanation to you; I owe it to myself, and those friends I see here, whose presence under your roof is a tribute to the name I bear. My friends, I found myself in this man's debt; he held in pledge all I possessed—all but my name; that name he wanted to shelter the infamy in which is own was covered, and I was vile enough to sell it.

BLOODGOOD: Go on, sir; go on.

LIVINGSTONE: With your leave, I will.

ALIDA: These matters you were fully acquainted with, I presume, when you sought my hand.

LIVINGSTONE: But I was not acquainted with the contents of these letters—written by you to the Duke of Calcavella.

BLOODGOOD: Do you dare insinuate that they contain evidence derogatory to the honor of my child?

LIVINGSTONE: No, sir; but I think Miss Bloodgood will agree with me, that the sentiments expressed in these letters entitle her to the hand of the duke rather than to mine. (*He hands letters to* ALIDA.)

ALIDA: Let him go, father.

LIVINGSTONE: Not yet. You forget that my friends are here assembled to witness a marriage, and all we require is a bride.

BLOODGOOD: Yes; a bride who can pay your debts.

(*Enter* PAUL, LUCY, *and* MRS. FAIRWEATHER.)

PAUL: No, sir; a bride who can place the hand of a pure and loving maiden in that of a good and honest man.

BLOODGOOD: How dare you intrude in this house?

PAUL: Because it is mine; because your whole fortune will scarcely serve to pay the debt you owe the widow and children of Adam Fairweather!

BLOODGOOD: Is my house to be invaded by beggars like these! Edwards send for the police. Is there no law in New York for ruffians?

(*Enter* BADGER, *in the uniform of an officer of police.*)

BADGER: Yes, plenty—and here's the police.

BLOODGOOD: Badger!

BADGER: What's left of him.

BLOODGOOD (*Wildly*): Is this a conspiracy to ruin me?

BADGER: That's it. We began it twenty years ago; we've been hatching it ever since; we let you build up a fortune; we tempted you to become an incendiary; we led you on from misdemeanor to felony—and that's what I want you for.

BLOODGOOD: What do you mean?

BADGER: My meaning is set forth very clearly in an affidavit, on which the Recorder, at this very late hour for business, issued this warrant for your arrest.

(*Enter two* POLICEMEN. ALIDA *falls in a chair.*)

BLOODGOOD: Incendiary! Dare you charge a man of my standing in this city, with such a crime, without any cause?

BADGER: Cause! you wanted to burn up this receipt, which I was just in time to rescue from the flames!

BLOODGOOD (*Drawing a knife*): Fiend! You escaped the flames here—now go to those hereafter!

BADGER: Hollo! (*Disarms* BLOODGOOD *and slips a pair of handcuffs on him.*) Gideon—my dear Gideon—don't lose your temper. (*Throws him back, manacled, on the sofa.*)

PAUL: Miss Bloodgood, let me lead you from this room.

ALIDA (*Rises, and cross to her father*): Father.

BLOODGOOD: Alida, my child.

ALIDA: Is this true? (*A pause.*) It is—I read it in your quailing eye—on your paling lips. And it was for this that you raised me to the envied position of the rich man's heiress—for this you roused my pride—for this you decked me in jewels—to be the felon's daughter. Farewell.

BLOODGOOD: Alida—my child—my child—it was for you alone I sinned—do not leave me.

ALIDA: What should I do in this city? can I earn my bread? what am I fit for—with your tainted name and my own sad heart? (*Throws down her bride's coronet.*) I am fit for the same fate as yours—infamy.
(*Exit.*)

BADGER: Duke, you had better see that lady out. (*Exit* DUKE.) Gideon, my dear, allow me to introduce you to two friends of mine, who are anxious to make your acquaintance.

BLOODGOOD: Take me away; I have lost my child— my Alida; take me away; hide me from all the world.

PAUL: Stay! Mr. Bloodgood, in the midst of your crime there was one virtue; you loved your child; even now your heart deplores her ruin—not your own. Badger, give me that receipt. (*Takes the receipt from* BADGER.) Do you acknowledge this paper to be genuine?

BLOODGOOD: I do.

PAUL (*Tears it*): I have no charge against you. Let him be released. Restore to me my fortune, and take the rest; go, follow your child; save her from ruin, and live a better life.

BLOODGOOD: I cannot answer you as I would. (*Turns aside in tears and goes out with* POLICEMEN *and* BADGER, *who releases* BLOODGOOD.)

LIVINGSTONE: That was nobly done, Paul. Now my friends, since all is prepared for my marriage, let the ceremony proceed.

MRS. FAIRWEATHER: But where is Mrs. Puffy?

BADGER: Here they are, outside, but they won't come in.

PAUL: Why not?

BADGER: They are afraid of walking on the carpets.

LIVINGSTONE: Bring them in.

BADGER: That's soon done.

MRS. FAIRWEATHER: Poor, good, kind people—the first to share our sorrow, the last to claim a part in our joy.
(*Enter* BADGER *and* DAN—PUFFY *and one* POLICEMAN—MRS. PUFFY *and the other* POLICEMAN.)

BADGER: They wouldn't come—I was obliged to take 'em in custody.

DAN: Oh! mother, where's this?

MRS. PUFFY: I'm walkin' on a feather bed.

PUFFY: He wouldn't let me wipe my shoes.

LIVINGSTONE: Come in—these carpets have never been trodden by more honest feet, these mirrors have never reflected kinder faces—come in—breathe the air here—you will purify it.

MRS. PUFFY: Oh, Dan, what grand folks—ain't they?

DAN: Canvas backs[3] every one on 'em.

LIVINGSTONE: And now, Lucy, I claim your hand. (*Music inside.*) All is ready for the ceremony.

BADGER: You have seen the dark side of life—you can appreciate your fortune, for you have learned the value of wealth.

MRS. FAIRWEATHER: No, we have learned the value of poverty. (*Gives her hand to* PUFFY.) It opens the heart.

PAUL (*To the public*): Is this true? have the sufferings we have depicted in this mimic scene, touched your hearts, and caused a tear of sympathy to fill your eyes? If so, extend to us your hands.

MRS. FAIRWEATHER: Not to us—but when you leave this place, as you return to your homes, should you see some poor creatures, extend your hands to them, and the blessings that will follow you on your way will be the most grateful tribute you can pay to the Poor of New York.

END.

---

3. A garment with the back made of canvas; i.e., something that is elegant from the front but cheap from the back.

Introduction to *Ghosts*

WHEN THE PLAY WAS NEW

Ghosts, the third of Henrik Ibsen's realistic plays, along with *A Doll House,* launched a worldwide sensation for the movement of realism in theatre and drama. Because the subject matter seemed so severe and disturbing to many people, *Ghosts* at first had a larger reading than viewing audience, but eventually the play became the standard bearer for many new independent theatres that championed realism and naturalism.

When *Ghosts* appeared, complex, character-driven novels such as *Madame Bovary* by Flaubert and *Anna Karenina* by Tolstoy dominated the literary world, and science was in often fierce conflict with dominant religious and social values. People argued about Darwin and the appropriate position of humankind in the natural world. Social Darwinism was very much on the minds of many writers, including Ibsen, who insisted on drawing his characters in terms of heredity and environment. This approach to characterization became the heart of realistic playwriting and eventually acting as well. Most large urban areas in Europe saw the appearance of new realistic playwrights, directors, and theatre companies during and just after the mature career of Ibsen, who became their inspiration.

Ibsen was part of a revolt against the excesses and hyperbole of melodrama and romanticism. To accompany the increasing social awareness and recognition of the plight of the working class in the late part of the nineteenth century, realism focused on depicting real people in authentic domestic environments struggling with everyday but serious problems—not the cosmic or spectacular struggles of romanticism and melodrama. Most realistic drama did not end happily. This was precisely the opposite of the resolutions for melodrama and one of the things that made Ibsen's plays so controversial. Ibsen never offered answers for complicated problems. He was determined to set the stage for argument and ignite the search for solutions.

The theatre for which Ibsen wrote, however, was not so different than that of melodrama. All theatres had prosceniums. Throughout the first part of Ibsen's career the stages were lit by gas. Toward the end electric light was the standard. Directors were fully in charge for most of his career, and most called for authentic-appearing box sets and very detailed exteriors. Scenery of the professional theatre continued to grow more literal and detailed in its creation until about the time of World War I. Some exceptions appeared after 1890 among avant-garde theatres, but such symbolic and emblematic settings would not become the norm until much later. Partially in response to the needs and popularity of Ibsen's plays, a number of actors worked to achieve a more reality-based approach to characterization. Actresses such as Eleanora Duse in Italy and Minnie Maddern Fiske and Mary Shaw in the United States became strongly identified with Ibsen and Bernard Shaw (who was in turn inspired by Ibsen). An approach to realistic acting eventually became systematized at the Moscow Art Theatre in Russia under Konstantin Stanislavsky.

THE PLAYWRIGHT

Henrik Ibsen (1828–1906) wrote many plays before stunning the world with *A Doll House* (1879) and *Ghosts.* As early as 1850 he was writing, directing, designing, and producing plays in Norway and remained an important fixture in Scandinavian theatre. By 1864, Ibsen, who was in his mid-thirties, was an expatriate living and writing in Germany and Italy. Nearly all of his famous plays were written in exile. He always set his plays in Norway, however, and continued to explore provincial life outside the major cities of Europe he came to know. Although his settings were regional, the social issues and conflicts of his characters seemed universal to Europeans and later North Americans. He captured and explored many problems plaguing late nineteenth-century people, but many of his dramatizations remained relevant long beyond his time.

The most important of Ibsen's early poetic dramas, *Brand* (1866) and *Peer Gynt* (1867), appeared as twin pillars of his dramatic philosophy, juxtaposing two protagonists, one who would compromise nothing and the other who would compromise anything. These extremes are played out more subtly in all of the plays he wrote thereafter. Also, all of his plays from *Catiline* in 1850 to *When We Dead Awaken* in 1899 are about buried secrets (literal or figurative)—something hidden in the past comes back to haunt one or more of the characters in the present. Consequently, as we have heard it said, all of his plays could have been entitled *Ghosts*.

His variations with this theme, however, lend great variety to his plays. Characters often meddle in the business of others with typically catastrophic results, such as the death of a young girl in *The Wild Duck* (1884). In many of his plays Ibsen explores the plight of women in society, most famously in *A Doll House* but more intriguingly in *Lady from the Sea* (1888). Ibsen attacked inflexible social and religious rules that seemed horribly antiquated and oppressive to him. Consequently, his characters frequently suffer with guilt as we see in *Rosmersholm* (1886). All of these issues are in play in *Ghosts*. *Ghosts* is also typical of Ibsen's realism in that all of the action takes place in a single interior to focus on the environment of his central characters. This is not a rule for Ibsen, but a recurring practice which he last invokes with *Hedda Gabler* (1890).

GENRE, STRUCTURE, AND STYLE

When directing plays in Norway in the 1850s and 1860s, Ibsen directed more plays by Eugène Scribe than any other playwright. Scribe was notable in the early nineteenth century for popularizing the well-made play. The well-made play—usually a comedy or melodrama—includes carefully crafted exposition presented early (all of which is important to the plot) followed by introduction of the conflict that involves a secret. The conflict rises in intensity and suspense to a climactic moment of tension at the end of each act. The fortunes of the hero or heroine typically reverse several times before the appearance of an "obligatory" scene, or *scène à faire*, in which the secret is revealed. The resolution is always logical based on all that has gone before and ties up neatly at the end. Although the playwright may include surprises, they are logical surprises.

Scribe and popular melodrama were influential on Ibsen, who adopted parts of them but modified or severely altered many dramatic devices. Ibsen loved startling, climactic curtains at the ends of acts, and he provided a wealth of exposition. He typically undermined the customary conclusion by startling his audience again and providing an ending both unexpected and contrary to traditional values. Most of all, Ibsen disturbed his audiences with his controversial subject matter. He engaged his audience by using parts of the conventional structure, then shocked them by denying the expected conclusion. Combining the familiar with the unfamiliar was a secret to his ultimate success, but it also condemned him in the eyes of many who found his plays dangerous. The danger was further underscored by creating such convincing contemporary realism in character, dialogue, situation, and location. All of the action seemed very authentic and was usually played out with only two or three characters at a time so he could create dynamic argument and private scenes likely to make some audiences uncomfortable. At the conclusion of *Ghosts*, Ibsen denies resolution altogether so that the audience must decide what the next action after the curtain falls is likely to be.

IMPORTANT ELEMENTS OF CONTENT

One way of viewing *Ghosts* is to see it in part as an answer to the furor Ibsen created in his previous play, *A Doll House*. Many of his critics were distressed that Ibsen had his character Nora Helmer walk out of her marriage, leaving both her husband and small children at the conclusion of the play; her exit is proverbially referred to as "the door slam heard round the world." In *Ghosts* Ibsen seems to ask, "What would happen if a woman in an unhappy or inappropriate marriage decided not to leave her husband?" The characters are very different here, but the plight of Mrs. Alving resonates in terms of Nora.

What really disturbed many people, however, was the undisguised subject of sexually transmitted disease in *Ghosts.* Ibsen hinted at this in *A Doll House,* but brought it out into the light in his next play. Because we are now so accustomed to frank talk about sex and sexually transmitted diseases, the subject seems partially veiled in *Ghosts;* in 1881, however, Ibsen was accused of creating an open sewer in the theatre. Many bookstores refused to carry the play or sent copies back to the publisher once they knew the subject. At the same time, many directors and audience members found the play a rallying cry. Ibsen went even further by including a near-incest scene, a subject essentially absent from the Western stage since the seventeenth century. With Mrs. Alving and Pastor Manders, Ibsen explores liberal and progressive ideas in conflict with the traditional church. The burning of the orphanage sets up the brothel as the true monument to the memory or ghost of Captain Alving, which lingers over much of the action of the play. Ibsen also presents the allure of the outside urban world (here symbolized by Paris) to the confined and sheltered inhabitants such as Regina of the backwaters of Norway—a theme played out many times since in plays and other literature dealing with unsophisticated characters of limited experience.

THE PLAY IN REVIVAL

Ghosts premiered in 1882 in Chicago, rather than in Europe where it was first published a year earlier. The play has been regularly revived. Its European premiere occurred in 1883 with a Scandinavian tour. Soon thereafter the play appeared in independent theatres in France, Germany, and elsewhere. In the United States the play's early great champion was the actress Mary Shaw who regularly performed in the play as Mrs. Alving from

1899 until at least 1922. The play has never been absent from professional production and it can be seen somewhere every season in professional and university theatres. Recent revivals include The Arizona Theatre Company's 2003 production directed by Marshall Mason in a new translation by Lanford Wilson; a 2003 production directed by the legendary Ingmar Bergman in Sweden and London; and a 2003 production by the Shakespeare Theatre in Washington, D.C., adapted and directed by Edwin Sherin and starring Jane Alexander as Mrs. Alving, in which the action was updated to 1981 in Maine.

SPECIAL FEATURE

Although Ibsen was preoccupied with ghosts, he did not literally bring them on the stage in his realistic plays, but in some figurative way. The ghost of a dead wife is often "felt" by living characters. The ghosts of Captain Alving and Regina's mother appear once again in the characters of their children, Oswald and Regina. This reanimation is not seen on stage, however, but only heard by the audience and Mrs. Alving. Its offstage occurrence becomes very powerful and brings to a climax the rising action of Act I.

FURTHER READING ABOUT THE PLAY, PLAYWRIGHT, AND CONTEXT

For theatrical context of Ibsen's plays, see Oscar Brockett and Robert Findlay, *Century of Innovation.*

For Ibsen's plays as seen when new, see Bernard Shaw, *The Quintessence of Ibsenism,* and Michael Meyer, *Ibsen: A Biography.*

For recent criticism of Ibsen's plays, see Theoharis C. Theoharis, *Ibsen's Drama: Right Action and Tragic Joy,* and Michael Goldman, *Ibsen: The Dramaturgy of Fear.*

For a complete edition of all of Ibsen's realistic plays and commentary, see *Ibsen: The Complete Major Prose Plays,* translated by Rolf Fjelde.

Ghosts

By Henrik Ibsen

Translated by Rolf Fjelde

THE CHARACTERS

MRS. HELENE ALVING   widow of Captain Alving, late Court Chamberlain

OSVALD ALVING   her son, a painter

PASTOR MANDERS

ENGSTRAND   a carpenter

REGINA ENGSTRAND   in service with MRS. ALVING

The action takes place on MRS. ALVING'S *country estate by a large fjord in West Norway.*

ACT ONE

A large garden room, with a door in the left-hand wall, and two doors in the wall to the right. In the middle of the room a round table with chairs grouped about it; on the table lie books, magazines, and newspapers. In the left foreground, a window, and next to it a small sofa with a sewing table in front of it. In the background, the room is extended into a somewhat smaller greenhouse, whose walls are great panes of glass. From the right side of the greenhouse, a door leads into the garden. Through the glass walls a somber fjord landscape can be glimpsed, half hidden by the steady rain.

ENGSTRAND is standing by the garden door. His left leg is partly deformed; under his bootsole he has a wooden block. REGINA, with an empty garden syringe in her hand, is trying to keep him from entering.

REGINA (*in a low voice*): What do you want? Just stay where you are. Why, you're dripping wet.

ENGSTRAND: It's God's own rain, my girl.

REGINA: The devil's rain, it is!

ENGSTRAND: Jeez, how you talk, Regina. (*Hobbles a few steps into the room.*) But now, what I wanted to say—

REGINA: Stop stomping about with that foot, will you! The young master's sleeping upstairs.

ENGSTRAND: Still sleeping? In broad daylight?

REGINA: That's none of your business.

ENGSTRAND: I was out on a binge last night—

REGINA: I can imagine.

ENGSTRAND: Yes, because we mortals are weak, my girl—

REGINA: Yes, so we are.

ENGSTRAND: And temptations are manifold in this world, you see— But for all of that, I was on the job, so help me God, five thirty this morning early.

REGINA: All right now, get out of here. I'm not going to stand around, having a rendezvous with you.

ENGSTRAND: You're not going to have any what?

REGINA: I'm not going to have anyone meeting you here. So—on your way.

ENGSTRAND (*a few steps closer*): Damned if I'll go before I've had my say with you. This afternoon I'll be done with my work down at the schoolhouse, and then I'll rip right back to town by the night boat.

REGINA (*mutters*): Pleasant trip!

ENGSTRAND: Thank you, my girl. Tomorrow they'll be dedicating the orphanage, and there'll probably be all kinds of carrying-on here, with hard liquor, you know. And nobody's going to say about Jacob Engstrand that he can't put temptation behind him.

REGINA: Ha!

ENGSTRAND: Yes, because you know a lot of the best people'll be here tomorrow. Pastor Manders is expected from town.

REGINA: He's coming today.

ENGSTRAND: There, you see. And I'll be damned if he's going to get anything on me.

REGINA: Ah, so *that's* it!

ENGSTRAND: What do you mean, *that*?

REGINA (*looks knowingly at him*): Just what are you out to trick him into this time?

ENGSTRAND: Shh, are you crazy? Would *I* trick the pastor into anything? Oh no, Pastor Manders, he's been much too good to me for that. But it's what I wanted to talk to you about, see—that I'll be leaving for home then, tonight.

REGINA: The sooner the better.

ENGSTRAND: Yes, but I want you along with me, Regina.

REGINA (open-mouthed): You want me along—? What did you say?

ENGSTRAND: I'm saying I want you back home with me.

REGINA (scornfully): Back home with you? Never. Not a chance!

ENGSTRAND: Oh, we'll see about that.

REGINA: Yes, you can bet we will, all right. I, who've been brought up by Mrs. Alving—? Been taken in like one of the family—? I should move back with you? To a house like that? Pah!

ENGSTRAND: What the devil is this? You trying to cross your own father, you slut?

REGINA (mutters, without looking at him): You've always said I had no part of you.

ENGSTRAND: Ahh, never mind about that—

REGINA: How many times haven't you cursed me and called me a—fi donc!

ENGSTRAND: So help me God if I've ever used such a dirty word.

REGINA: Oh, I haven't forgotten the word you used.

ENGSTRAND: Yes, but that was only when I had some drink in me—hm. Temptations are manifold in this world, Regina.

REGINA: Ugh!

ENGSTRAND: And when your mother got nasty, see—then I had to find something to needle her with. Always made herself so refined. (Mimics.) "Let go of me, Engstrand! Leave me be! I've been three years in service to Chamberlain Alving at Rosenvold!" (Laughs.) Jeez, that was something she never could forget—that the captain was made a chamberlain while she was in service there.

REGINA: Poor mother—you bullied the life out of her soon enough.

ENGSTRAND (with a shrug): Yes, that's right; I get the blame for everything.

REGINA (in an undertone, as she turns away): Ugh—! And that leg.

ENGSTRAND: What did you say, my girl?

REGINA: Pied de mouton.

ENGSTRAND: What's that—German?[1]

REGINA: Yes.

ENGSTRAND: Oh yes, you got some learning out here, and that's going to come in handy now, Regina.

REGINA (after a short silence): And what was it you wanted with me in town?

ENGSTRAND: How can you ask what a father wants with his only child? Aren't I a lonely, forsaken widower?

REGINA: Oh, don't give me that garbage. Why do you want me in town?

ENGSTRAND: All right, I'll tell you—I've been thinking of striking into something new.

REGINA (with a snort): You've done that so often, and it always goes wrong.

ENGSTRAND: Ah, but this time, Regina, you wait and see! Hell's bells—!

REGINA (stamps her foot): Stop swearing!

ENGSTRAND: Sh, sh! Perfectly right you are, my girl! I only wanted to say—I've put by a nice piece of change out of the work on this new orphanage.

REGINA: Have you? Well, that's good for you.

ENGSTRAND: Because what can you spend your money on here, out in the country?

REGINA: Well, so?

ENGSTRAND: Yes, so you see, I thought I might put the money into something that'd turn a profit. It was going to be a sort of hotel for seamen—

REGINA: Ugh-ah!

ENGSTRAND: A regular, first-class inn, you understand—not just any old pigsty for sailors. No, damn it all—it's going to be for ship captains and mates and—and real fine people, you understand.

REGINA: And how do I—?

ENGSTRAND: You? You get to help, see. Just for the look of things, if you follow me. There wouldn't be so damn much to do. You can have it just like you want it.

REGINA: I'll bet!

ENGSTRAND: But there've got to be women on the premises, that's clear as day. Because we want a little life in the evenings—singing and dancing

1. "English," in the original, which loses meaning in an English translation.

and that sort of thing. You have to remember, these are wayfaring seamen on the ocean of life. (*Comes nearer.*) Now don't be stupid and hold yourself back, Regina. What can you come to out here? What good can it do you, all this learning Mrs. Alving's paid out for? You're supposed to take care of the children, I hear, in the new orphanage. Is *that* anything for you, uh? Have you such a hunger to run yourself ragged for the sake of those filthy brats?

REGINA: No, if things go the way *I* want, then— And it could happen, all right. Yes, it could!

ENGSTRAND: What could?

REGINA: None of your business. Is it—quite a bit of money you made out here?

ENGSTRAND: Between this and that, I'd say up to seven, eight hundred crowns.

REGINA: That's not so bad.

ENGSTRAND: It's enough for a start, my girl.

REGINA: Don't you think you might give me some of that money?

ENGSTRAND: No, I don't think I might!

REGINA: Don't you think you could send me at least some cloth for a dress?

ENGSTRAND: Just come with me into town, and you'll have dresses to burn.

REGINA: Pah! I can do as well on my own, if I care to.

ENGSTRAND: No, but it goes better, Regina, with a father's guiding hand. There's a nice house I can get now in Little Harbor Street. They don't want too much money down; and it could make some kind of seamen's home, all right.

REGINA: But I don't want to stay with you! I've got no business with you. Get out!

ENGSTRAND: You wouldn't stay so damn long with me, girl. No such luck—if you know how to show off yourself. A wench as good-looking as you've turned out these last two years—

REGINA: Yes—?

ENGSTRAND: It wouldn't be long before some ship's officer—maybe even a captain—

REGINA: I'm not marrying any of those. Sailors don't have any *savoir-vivre*.

ENGSTRAND: They don't have any what?

REGINA: Let me tell you, I know about sailors. They aren't any sort to marry.

ENGSTRAND: Then forget about getting married. That can pay just as well. (*More confidential-*

ly.) Him—the Englishman—the one with the yacht—he gave three hundred dollars, he did—and she was no better looking than you.

REGINA (*advancing on him*): Get out of here!

ENGSTRAND (*steps back*): Easy now, you don't want to hit me.

REGINA: Don't I! Talk about Mother, and you'll find out. Get out of here, I said! (*She forces him back toward the garden door.*) And no slamming doors; young Mr. Alving—

ENGSTRAND: Yes, he's asleep. It's something all right, how you worry about young Mr. Alving—(*Dropping his voice.*) Ho-ho! It just wouldn't be that *he*—?

REGINA: Out of here, quick! You're all mixed up! No, not that way. There's Pastor Manders coming. Down the kitchen stairs.

ENGSTRAND (*moving to the right*): All right, I'm going. But you talk with *him* that's coming in. He's the one who'll tell you what a child owes her father. Because, after all, I *am* your father, you know. I can prove it in the parish register.

(*He goes out by the farther door, which* REGINA *has opened, closing it after him. She hurriedly glances at herself in the mirror, fans herself with her handkerchief and straightens her collar, then busies herself with the flowers.* PASTOR MANDERS, *in an overcoat, carrying an umbrella along with a small traveling bag on a strap over his shoulder, comes through the garden door into the greenhouse.*)

MANDERS: Good morning, Miss Engstrand.

REGINA (*turning with a pleasantly surprised look*): Why, Pastor Manders, good morning! The boat's already come?

MANDERS: It just arrived. (*Entering the room.*) It's certainly tedious weather we've been having these days.

REGINA (*following him*): It's a godsend for the farmers, Pastor.

MANDERS: Yes, you're quite right. That's something we townspeople hardly think of. (*He starts taking his overcoat off.*)

REGINA: Oh, let me help you—that's it. My, how wet it is! I'll just hang it up in the hall. And the umbrella, too—I'll leave it open to dry.

(*She goes out with the things through the farther door on the right.* MANDERS *removes his traveling bag and sets it and his hat down on a chair, as* RE-GINA *returns.*)

MANDERS: Ah, but it's good to be indoors. So—everything's going well out here?

REGINA: Yes, thank you.

MANDERS: But terribly busy, I suppose, getting ready for tomorrow?

REGINA: Oh yes, there's plenty to do.

MANDERS: And, hopefully, Mrs. Alving's at home?

REGINA: Why, of course. She just went upstairs to bring the young master some hot chocolate.

MANDERS: Yes, tell me—I heard down at the pier that Osvald was supposed to have come.

REGINA: He got in the day before yesterday. We hadn't expected him before today.

MANDERS: In the best of health, I hope?

REGINA: Yes, just fine, thank you. But awfully tired after his trip. He came straight from Paris without a break—I mean, he went the whole route without changing trains. I think he's sleeping a little now, so we should talk just a tiny bit softer.

MANDERS: Shh! We'll be so quiet.

REGINA (*as she moves an armchair up to the table*): Please now, do sit down, Pastor, and make yourself comfortable. (*He sits; she slips a footstool under his feet.*) That's it! Is that all right, Pastor?

MANDERS: Just perfect, thank you. (*Regarding her.*) You know, Miss Engstrand, I definitely think you've grown since I saw you last.

REGINA: Do you think so, Pastor? Mrs. Alving says that I've filled out, too.

MANDERS: Filled out—? Well, yes, maybe a little—but acceptably. (*A short pause.*)

REGINA: Shall I tell Mrs. Alving you're here?

MANDERS: Oh, thank you, there's no hurry, my dear child—well, uh—but tell me now, Regina, how's it been going for your father out here?

REGINA: Fairly well, Pastor, thank you.

MANDERS: He was in to see me when he was last in town.

REGINA: Really? He's always so happy when he can talk with you.

MANDERS: And you make it your rule, of course, to look in on him daily.

REGINA: I? Oh, yes, of course—whenever I have some time—

MANDERS: Your father is not very strong in character, Miss Engstrand. He's woefully in need of a guiding hand.

REGINA: Yes, I'm sure of that.

MANDERS: He needs to have someone around him that he can love, and whose judgment carries some weight. He confessed as much quite frankly when he was last up to see me.

REGINA: Yes, he said something like that to me. But I don't know if Mrs. Alving could spare me—especially now, when we've got the new orphanage to manage. And then I'd be so awfully unhappy to leave Mrs. Alving—she's always been so kind to me.

MANDERS: But, my dear girl, a daughter's duty—Naturally, we'd first have to obtain Mrs. Alving's consent.

REGINA: But I don't know if it would do for me, at my age, to keep house for a single man.

MANDERS: What! But, my dear Miss Engstrand, this is your own father we're speaking of!

REGINA: Yes, maybe so, but all the same—you see, if it were a *good* house, with a real gentleman—

MANDERS: But, my dear Regina—

REGINA: One I could care and look up to, almost like a daughter—

MANDERS: Yes, but my dear child—

REGINA: Because I'd like so much to live in town. Out here it's terribly lonely—and you know yourself, Pastor, what it is to stand alone in the world. And I think I can say that I'm both capable and willing. Mr. Manders, don't you know of a place like that for me?

MANDERS: I? No, I don't, for the life of me.

REGINA: But dear, dear Mr. Manders—you will think of me, in any case, if ever—

MANDERS (*getting up*): Yes, I'll remember, Miss Engstrand.

REGINA: Yes, because if I—

MANDERS: Perhaps you'll be good enough to tell Mrs. Alving I've come.

REGINA: I'll go call her right away, Pastor.

(*She goes out left.* MANDERS *paces back and forth in the room a couple of times, then stands for a moment at the far end of the room, hands behind his back, looking out into the garden. He then returns to the table, picks up a book and looks at the title page, starts, and inspects several others.*)

MANDERS: Hm—aha! Well!

(MRS. ALVING *comes in by the door, left. She is followed by* REGINA, *who immediately goes out by the nearer door to the right.*)

MRS. ALVING (*extending her hand*): So good to see you, Mr. Manders.

MANDERS: Good morning, Mrs. Alving. Here I am, just as I promised.

MRS. ALVING: Always on the dot.

MANDERS: But you can imagine, it was touch and go for me, getting away. All those blessed boards and committees—

MRS. ALVING: All the more kind of you to come so promptly. Now we can get our business done before dinner. But where do you have your bags?

MANDERS (*hurriedly*): My things are down at the general store—I took a room there for tonight.

MRS. ALVING (*repressing a smile*): You can't be persuaded even yet to spend the night here in my house?

MANDERS: No, no, really; thank you so much, but I'll stay down there as usual. It's so convenient to the boat.

MRS. ALVING: Well, you do as you wish. But I really thought instead that two old people like us—

MANDERS: Gracious me, the way you joke! Yes, of course you're in rare spirits today. First the celebration tomorrow, and then you've got Osvald home.

MRS. ALVING: Yes, can you imagine how happy I am! It's more than two years since he was home last. And then he's promised to stay with me this whole winter.

MANDERS: No, has he really? That's certainly a nice gesture for a son to make—because there must be other, quite different attractions to life in Rome and Paris, I'm sure.

MRS. ALVING: Yes, but he has his mother here at home, you see. Oh, that dear, blessed boy—he still has room in his heart for me!

MANDERS: It would really be tragic if distance and devotion to anything like art should dull his natural feelings.

MRS. ALVING: You're perfectly right. But there's no chance at all of that with him. Oh, I'm going to be so curious to see if you still recognize him.

He'll be down shortly; he's just stretched out to rest a little on the sofa upstairs. But now, my dear Mr. Manders—do sit down.

MANDERS: Thank you. It *is* convenient, then—?

MRS. ALVING: Why, of course. (*She sits at the table.*)

MANDERS: Good. Then let's have a look—(*Goes over to the chair where his bag lies, takes out a sheaf of papers, sits at the opposite side of the table, and searches for a space to lay the papers out.*) Now here, first, we have—(*Breaks off.*) Tell me, Mrs. Alving, where did these books come from?

MRS. ALVING: These books? I'm reading them.

MANDERS: You read this sort of thing?

MRS. ALVING: Yes, of course I do.

MANDERS: Do you feel you've grown any better or happier for this kind of reading?

MRS. ALVING: I think it makes me feel more secure.

MANDERS: That's astonishing. What do you mean?

MRS. ALVING: Well, I find it clarifies and reinforces so many ideas I've been thinking out all to myself. Yes, that's the strange part, Mr. Manders—there's actually nothing really new in these books, nothing beyond what most people think and believe. It's simply that most people don't like to face these things, or what they imply.

MANDERS: Oh, my dear God! You don't seriously consider that most people—?

MRS. ALVING: Yes, I certainly do.

MANDERS: Well, but not here in our society? Not among us?

MRS. ALVING: Yes, definitely—among us, too.

MANDERS: Well, I must say, really—!

MRS. ALVING: But what exactly do you object to in these books?

MANDERS: Object to? You surely don't think I waste my time exploring that kind of publication?

MRS. ALVING: In other words, you know nothing of what you're condemning?

MANDERS: I've read quite enough about these writings to disapprove of them.

MRS. ALVING: Yes, but your own opinion—

MANDERS: My dear Mrs. Alving, there are many circumstances in life where one has to entrust oneself to others. That's the condition of this world, and it's all for the best. How else could society function?

MRS. ALVING: That's true; maybe you're right.

MANDERS: Besides, I wouldn't deny that there's a certain fascination about such writings. And I can't blame you either for wanting to become acquainted with the intellectual currents that, I hear, are quite prevalent in the larger world—where you've let your son wander so long. But—

MRS. ALVING: But—?

MANDERS (*dropping his voice*): But one needn't talk about it, Mrs. Alving. One doesn't have to recount to all and sundry everything one reads and thinks within one's own four walls.

MRS. ALVING: No, of course not. I agree.

MANDERS: Remember your obligations to the orphanage, which you decided to found at a time when your attitude toward things of the mind and spirit was so very different from now—at least as *I* see it.

MRS. ALVING: Yes, I admit it, completely. But it was about the orphanage—

MANDERS: It was about the orphanage we wanted to speak, yes. All the same—prudence, my dear Mrs. Alving! And now, let's turn to business. (*Opens a folder and takes out some papers.*) You see these?

MRS. ALVING: The deeds?

MANDERS: The whole set—in perfect order. You can imagine it hasn't been easy to get them in time. I actually had to apply some pressure. The authorities are almost painfully scrupulous when it comes to decisions. But here they are, in any case. (*Leafing through the papers.*) See, here's the duly recorded conveyance of title of the Solvik farm, said property being part of the Rosenvold estate, together with all buildings newly erected thereon, including the schoolhouse, the staff residence, and the chapel. And here's the official charter for the institution—and the by-laws governing its operation. You see— (*Reads.*) "By-laws governing the Captain Alving Memorial Orphan's Home."

MRS. ALVING (*looking at the papers for a long moment*): So—there it is.

MANDERS: I chose "Captain" for the title, rather than "Court Chamberlain." "Captain" seems less ostentatious.

MRS. ALVING: Yes, whatever you think.

MANDERS: And here you've got the bankbook showing interest on capital reserved to cover the running expenses of the orphanage.

MRS. ALVING: Thank you—but please, won't you hold onto it, for convenience' sake?

MANDERS: Yes, gladly. I think we can leave the money in the bank for a time. It's true, the interest rate isn't very attractive: four percent, with a six-month withdrawal notice. If we could come across a good mortgage later on—naturally, it would have to be a first mortgage, of unquestionable security—then we could reconsider the situation.

MRS. ALVING: Yes, dear Mr. Manders, you know best about all that.

MANDERS: Anyway, I'll keep an eye out. But now there's one more thing I've meant several times to ask you.

MRS. ALVING: And what's that?

MANDERS: Should the orphanage be insured or not?

MRS. ALVING: Why, of course, it has to be insured.

MANDERS: Ah, not too fast, Mrs. Alving. Let's study this question a bit.

MRS. ALVING: Everything I own is insured—buildings, furniture, crops, livestock.

MANDERS: Obviously, when it's your own property. I do the same, naturally. But here, you see, it's a very different matter. This orphanage is going to be, so to say, consecrated to a higher calling.

MRS. ALVING: Yes, but if—

MANDERS: From my personal standpoint, I wouldn't find the slightest objection to insuring us against all eventualities—

MRS. ALVING: No, I wouldn't either.

MANDERS: But how would that sit with the public opinion hereabouts? You know better than I.

MRS. ALVING: Public opinion, hm—

MANDERS: Is there any considerable segment of opinion—I mean, really important opinion—that might take offense?

MRS. ALVING: Well, what do you mean, exactly, by important opinion?

MANDERS: I was thinking mainly of people of such independent and influential position that one could hardly avoid giving their opinions a certain weight.

MRS. ALVING: There are a few like that here who might possibly take offense if—

MANDERS: There, you see! In town we have any number of them. The congregations of other churches, for example. It would be the easiest thing in the world for them to construe this as neither you nor I having adequate faith in Divine Providence.

MRS. ALVING: But, my dear Mr. Manders, as long as you know to your own satisfaction—

MANDERS: Yes, I know, I know—I have my own inner conviction, quite so. But the fact remains that we wouldn't be able to counter a false and damaging impression—and that, in turn, could easily hamper the work of the orphanage.

MRS. ALVING: Well, if that's the case, then—

MANDERS: Also, I can hardly ignore the difficult—I might just as well say, painful—position I'd probably be in myself. Among the best circles in town there's a good deal of interest in the orphanage. After all, it's partly being established to benefit the town as well, and hopefully it's going to have a sizable effect in lowering our local public welfare taxes. But since I've been your adviser in this and made all the business arrangements, I'm afraid those bigots would concentrate all their fire on me—

MRS. ALVING: No, you shouldn't be exposed to that.

MANDERS: Not to mention the charges that would doubtless be leveled against me in certain papers and magazines that—

MRS. ALVING: Enough, Mr. Manders; that settles it.

MANDERS: Then you won't want the insurance?

MRS. ALVING: No, we'll let that be.

MANDERS (leaning back in his chair): But now, if there *should* be an accident—one never knows, after all—would you be able to make good the losses?

MRS. ALVING: I can tell you right now, I absolutely wouldn't.

MANDERS: Ah, but you know, Mrs. Alving—then it's a grave responsibility we're taking on.

MRS. ALVING: But what else do you see that we *can* do?

MANDERS: No, that's just the thing: we *can't* do anything else. We shouldn't expose ourselves to unfavorable opinion; and we certainly have no right to stir dissension in the community.

MRS. ALVING: Especially you, as a clergyman.

MANDERS: And also I really do believe that we can depend on a project like this carrying some luck along with it—standing, so to say, under a special protection.

MRS. ALVING: Let's hope so, Mr. Manders.

MANDERS: Then we'll leave things as they are?

MRS. ALVING: Yes, of course.

MANDERS: Right. As you wish. (Jotting a note.) No insurance.

MRS. ALVING: It's strange you happened to speak about this just today—

MANDERS: I've often thought to ask you about it—

MRS. ALVING: Because yesterday we nearly had a fire down there.

MANDERS: What!

MRS. ALVING: Well, there wasn't anything to it, really. Some shavings caught fire in the carpenter shop.

MANDERS: Where Engstrand works?

MRS. ALVING: Yes. They say he's often so careless with matches.

MANDERS: He has so much on his mind, that man—so many tribulations. Praise be to God, he's now making a real effort to lead a blameless life, I hear.

MRS. ALVING: Oh? Who's been saying that?

MANDERS: He's assured me of it himself. And he's a capable workman, too.

MRS. ALVING: Why, yes, as long as he's sober—

MANDERS: Ah, that distressing weakness! But he tells me he frequently has to resort to it for the sake of his ailing leg. Last time he was in town, I really was quite moved by him. He stopped in and thanked me so sincerely for getting him this work out here, so he could be together with Regina.

MRS. ALVING: But he hardly ever sees her.

MANDERS: No, he speaks with her every day—he told me that himself.

MRS. ALVING: Yes—well, it's possible.

MANDERS: He feels so positively that he needs someone there who can restrain him when temptation looms. That's what's so engaging about Jacob Engstrand, the way he comes to one so utterly helpless and accuses himself and admits his faults. Just this last time that he talked to me—Mrs. Alving, if it became a vital necessity for him to have Regina home with him again—

MRS. ALVING (*rising impulsively*): Regina!

MANDERS: Then you mustn't set yourself against it.

MRS. ALVING: Yes, I'm decidedly set against it. And besides—Regina will have a position at the orphanage.

MANDERS: But remember, he *is* her father—

MRS. ALVING: I know all too well what kind of father he's been to her. No, she'll never have my blessings to go to him.

MANDERS (*rising*): But my dear Mrs. Alving, don't take it so violently. It's such a pity, the way you misjudge Engstrand. Really, it's as if you were somehow afraid—

MRS. ALVING (*more calmly*): Never mind about that. I've taken Regina in here, and she'll stay here with me. (*Listens.*) Shh, now! Dear Mr. Manders, let's not talk of this anymore. (*Her face radiating joy.*) Hear that! Osvald's coming downstairs. Now we'll think only of him.

(OSVALD ALVING, *wearing a light overcoat, hat in hand, and smoking a large meerschaum pipe, comes in through the door to the left.*)

OSVALD (*pausing in the doorway*): Oh, I'm sorry—I thought you were in the study. (*Comes in.*) Good morning, Pastor Manders.

MANDERS (*stares at him*): Ah—! That's amazing—!

MRS. ALVING: Yes, what do you think of him, Mr. Manders?

MANDERS: Well, I must say—no, but—is it really—?

OSVALD: Yes, really—the prodigal son, Pastor.

MANDERS: But my dear boy—

OSVALD: Well, the homecoming son, anyway.

MRS. ALVING: Osvald's thinking of the time when you were so against his becoming a painter.

MANDERS: From our human viewpoint, you know, many a step looks doubtful that later turns out—(*Shaking his hand.*) Ah, welcome, welcome back! Imagine, my dear Osvald—may I still call you by your first name?

OSVALD: What else could you think of calling me?

MANDERS: Good. What I meant to say, my dear Osvald—was that you mustn't suppose that I categorically condemn the artist's life. I as-

sume there are quite a few who keep their inner selves uncorrupted even in those circumstances.

OSVALD: Let's hope so.

MRS. ALVING (*beaming with pleasure*): I know one who's kept both his inner and outer selves incorruptible. You only have to look at him, Mr. Manders.

OSVALD (*pacing about the room*): Yes, all right, Mother dear—that's enough.

MANDERS: Completely so—that's undeniable. And you've already begun to make your name. You're often mentioned in the papers—and most favorably, too. Though lately, I should say, there seems to be less.

OSVALD (*near the greenhouse*): I haven't been painting so much lately.

MRS. ALVING: Even artists need a rest now and then.

MANDERS: That I can understand. A time to prepare oneself and gather strength for the great work to come.

OSVALD: Yes. Mother, are we eating soon?

MRS. ALVING: In just half an hour. He certainly has an appetite, thank goodness.

MANDERS: And likes his tobacco, too.

OSVALD: I found Father's pipe upstairs in the bedroom—

MANDERS: Ah, that explains it!

MRS. ALVING: What?

MANDERS: When Osvald came through the door there with that pipe in his mouth, it was as if I saw his father in the flesh.

OSVALD: Really?

MRS. ALVING: Oh, how can you say that? Osvald takes after me.

MANDERS: Yes, but there's a look around the corners of the mouth, something about the lips, that's the very picture of Alving—especially now that he's smoking.

MRS. ALVING: No, it's nothing like him, not at all. To me, Osvald has more of a minister's look about the mouth.

MANDERS: Yes. Yes, a number of my colleagues have a similar expression.

MRS. ALVING: But put the pipe down, dear. I don't want smoking in this room.

OSVALD (*sets the pipe down*): All right. I only thought I'd try it because I'd once smoked it as a child.

MRS. ALVING: You?

OSVALD: Yes. I was very small then. And I remember going up to Father's room one evening when he was in such a marvelous humor.

MRS. ALVING: Oh, you don't remember anything from those years.

OSVALD: Oh yes, I distinctly remember him taking me on his knee and letting me smoke his pipe. "Smoke, boy," he said, "smoke it for real!" And I smoked for all I was worth, till I felt myself go pale, and the great drops of sweat stood out on my forehead. Then he shook all over with laughter—

MANDERS: That's most peculiar.

MRS. ALVING: I'm sure it's just something that Osvald dreamed.

OSVALD: No, Mother, it was definitely no dream. Because—don't you remember—then you came in and carried me off to the nursery. I was sick then, and I could see you were crying. Did Father often play such tricks?

MANDERS: When he was young he was always full of life—

OSVALD: And still he got so much accomplished—so much that was good and useful, for all that he died so early.

MANDERS: Yes, Osvald Alving—it's a strong and worthy name you've inherited. Well, let's hope it'll inspire you—

OSVALD: It certainly ought to.

MANDERS: And it was good of you to come home for the ceremonies in his honor.

OSVALD: It's the least I could do for Father.

MRS. ALVING: And that he'll remain with me here so long—that's the best of his goodness.

MANDERS: Yes, I hear you're staying all winter.

OSVALD: I'll be staying on indefinitely, Pastor. Oh, it's wonderful to be home again!

MRS. ALVING (radiant): Yes, how true!

MANDERS (looks sympathetically at him): You were out in the world quite early, Osvald, weren't you?

OSVALD: Yes. I wonder sometimes if it wasn't too early.

MRS. ALVING: Nonsense! There's nothing better for a healthy boy, especially when he's an only child. He shouldn't be kept home and coddled by his mother and father.

MANDERS: That's a highly debatable proposition, Mrs. Alving. A child's rightful place is and always will be his parental home.

OSVALD: I have to agree with Mr. Manders there.

MANDERS: Now take your own son, for instance. Yes, we can discuss this in front of him. What effect has this had on him? He's grown to age twenty-six or -seven without any chance to experience a normal home life.

OSVALD: Excuse me, Mr. Manders—but you're quite wrong about that.

MANDERS: Really? I thought you'd been moving almost entirely in artistic circles.

OSVALD: I have.

MANDERS: And mainly among the younger artists.

OSVALD: Yes.

MANDERS: But I thought most of those people hadn't the means to start a family and make a home.

OSVALD: It's true that a number of them haven't the means to get married—

MANDERS: Well, that's what I'm saying.

OSVALD: But they can still have a home life. And several of them do—one that's quite normal and pleasant.

(MRS. ALVING, following attentively, nods but says nothing.)

MANDERS: But it's not a bachelor life I'm talking about. By home life I mean a family home, where a man lives with his wife and his children.

OSVALD: Yes, or with his children and his children's mother.

MANDERS (jolted, clasping his hands together): Merciful God—!

OSVALD: What—?

MANDERS: Lives together with—his children's mother!

OSVALD: Well, would you rather have him abandon her?

MANDERS: But you're talking about illicit relations! About plain, irresponsible free love!

OSVALD: I've never noticed anything particularly irresponsible about the way these people live.

MANDERS: But how is it possible that—that even moderately decent young men or women could accept living in that manner—before the eyes of the world!

OSVALD: But what else can they do? A poor young artist—a poor young girl—and marriage so expensive. What can they do?

MANDERS: What they can do? Well, Mr. Alving, I'll tell you what they can do. They ought to keep each other at a distance right from the start—that's what they ought to do!

OSVALD: You won't get very far with that advice among warm-blooded young people in love.

MRS. ALVING: No, you certainly won't!

MANDERS (*persisting*): And to think the authorities tolerate such things! That it's allowed to go on openly. (*To* MRS. ALVING.) You see what good reason I've had to be concerned about your son. In circles where immorality is flaunted, and even seems to be prized—

OSVALD: Let me tell you something, Pastor. I've been a frequent Sunday guest in a couple of these so-called unconventional homes—

MANDERS: Sunday, no less!

OSVALD: Yes, the day of rest and relaxation—and yet I've never once heard an offensive word, nor have I ever witnessed anything that could be called immoral. But do you know when and where I *have* met immorality among artists?

MANDERS: No, thank God, I don't!

OSVALD: Well, then let me tell you. I've met it when one or another of our exemplary husbands and fathers—on a trip away from home and out to see a little life—did the artists the honor of dropping in on them in their poor cafés. Then we had our ears opened wide. Those gentlemen could tell us about things and places we never dreamed existed.

MANDERS: What? Are you suggesting that respectable men from here at home would—?

OSVALD: Have you never—when these same respectable men came home from their trips—have you never heard them carrying on about the monstrous immorality abroad?

MANDERS: Why, of course—

MRS. ALVING: I have, too.

OSVALD: Well, you can trust their word for it—they're experts, many of them. (*Clasps his head.*) Oh, that the beautiful freedom of that life—could be made so foul!

MRS. ALVING: You mustn't provoke yourself, Osvald. It's not good for you.

OSVALD: No, you're right, Mother. It's bad for my health. It's this damnable fatigue, you know. Well, I'll go for a little walk now before dinner. I'm sorry, Pastor. You can't share my feelings about this—but it's the way I see it. (*He goes out through the farther door to the right.*)

MRS. ALVING: My poor boy—!

MANDERS: Yes, you can well say that. How far he's strayed! (MRS. ALVING *looks at him, saying nothing.* MANDERS *paces up and down.*) He called himself the prodigal son. Yes, it's sad—sad! (MRS. ALVING *continues to look at him.*) And what do you say to all this?

MRS. ALVING: I say Osvald was right in every word that he said.

MANDERS (*stops short*): Right? Right! With such principles?

MRS. ALVING: Here in my solitude I've come to the same conclusions, Mr. Manders—though I've never dared breathe a word of it. All well and good—my boy can speak for me now.

MANDERS: You're a woman much to be pitied, Mrs. Alving. Now I must talk seriously with you. It's no longer as your business adviser, nor as your and your husband's childhood friend, that I'm standing before you now—but as your priest, exactly as I once did at the most bewildered hour of your life.

MRS. ALVING: And what does my priest have to tell me?

MANDERS: First, let me call up some memories. It's a suitable moment. Tomorrow is the tenth anniversary of your husband's death; tomorrow the memorial will be unveiled in his honor; tomorrow I'll be speaking to all those assembled—but today I want to speak to you alone.

MRS. ALVING: All right, Mr. Manders—speak!

MANDERS: Do you recall how, after barely a year of marriage, you stood on the very edge of the abyss? That you left house and home—deserted your husband—yes, Mrs. Alving, deserted, deserted, and refused to go back to him, for all that he begged and implored you to?

MRS. ALVING: Have you forgotten how unutterably miserable I was that first year?

MANDERS: But this is the very essence of the rebellious spirit, to crave happiness here in this life. What right have we human beings to happiness? No, we must do our duty, Mrs. Alving! And your duty was to stand by that man you once had chosen, and to whom you were joined by a sacred bond.

MRS. ALVING: You know well enough what kind of life Alving led in those days—and the appetites he indulged.

MANDERS: I know quite well the rumors that circulated about him; and to the extent that those rumors were true, I'd be the last to condone such conduct as his then. But a wife isn't required to be her husband's judge. It was your proper role to bear with a humble heart that cross that a higher will saw fit to lay upon you. But instead, you rebelliously cast away the cross, left the groping soul you should have aided, went off and risked your good name and reputation and—nearly ruined other reputations in the bargain.

MRS. ALVING: Other reputations? Just one, I think you mean.

MANDERS: It was exceedingly thoughtless of you to seek refuge with me.

MRS. ALVING: With our pastor? With an old, close friend?

MANDERS: Yes, for that very reason. You should thank Almighty God that I had the necessary inner strength—that I got you to drop your hysterical plans, and that it was given me to lead you back to the path of duty, and home to your lawful husband.

MRS. ALVING: Yes, Pastor Manders, that certainly was your doing.

MANDERS: I was only a humble instrument directed by a higher power. And that I bent your will to duty and obedience—hasn't that grown as a great blessing, from that time on, in all the days of your life? Didn't it go the way I foretold? Didn't Alving turn away from his depravities, as a man must, and take up a loving and blameless life with you right to the end? Didn't he become a benefactor of the community, and uplift you as well into his own sphere of activities to share them all? And how effectively you shared them, too—that I know, Mrs. Alving; I'll give you *that* credit. But now I come to the next great mistake in your life.

MRS. ALVING: What do you mean?

MANDERS: Just as you once evaded the duties of a wife, you've since evaded those of a mother.

MRS. ALVING: Ah—!

MANDERS: All your life you've been governed by an incorrigible spirit of willfulness. Instinctively you've been drawn to all that's undisciplined and lawless. You never can bear the least constraint. Everything that inconveniences your life you've carelessly and irresponsibly thrown aside—as if it were baggage you could leave behind if you chose. It didn't agree with you to be a wife any longer, so you left your husband. You found it troublesome to be a mother, so you put your child out with strangers.

MRS. ALVING: Yes, it's true—that's what I did.

MANDERS: And for that same reason you've become a stranger to him.

MRS. ALVING: No, no, I'm *not*!

MANDERS: You are. You had to be! And what sort of son have you gotten back? Think well, Mrs. Alving. You were terribly unfair to your husband—you admit as much by raising this monument to him. Now admit as well how unfair you've been to your son; there may still be time to lead him back from the paths of error. Change your ways—and save what's still left to be saved in him. For truly, Mrs. Alving— (*With an admonishing forefinger.*)—you're profoundly guilty as a mother! I've considered it my duty to tell you this.

(*Silence.*)

MRS. ALVING (*deliberately, controlling herself*): You've said your piece, Pastor; and tomorrow you'll be speaking publicly in my husband's memory. Tomorrow I'll make no speeches; but now I want to say something to you, exactly as you've just spoken to me.

MANDERS: Naturally, you want to make excuses for your conduct—

MRS. ALVING: No. Only to tell a few facts.

MANDERS: Well—?

MRS. ALVING: All that you've been saying here about me and my husband and our life together—after, as you put it, you led me back to the path of duty—all this is something you don't know the least thing about at firsthand.

From that moment on, you, our dearest friend, never set foot in our house again.

MANDERS: But you and your husband moved out of town right after that.

MRS. ALVING: Yes, and you never came out here to see us while my husband was living. It was business that impelled you to visit me, since you were involved with the orphanage, too.

MANDERS (*in a low, hesitant voice*): Helene—if that's meant as a reproach, then I ask you to consider—

MRS. ALVING: The respect you owed to your calling, yes. And I, after all, was a runaway wife. One can never be careful enough with such reckless women.

MANDERS: Dear—Mrs. Alving, that is a flagrant exaggeration—

MRS. ALVING: Yes, yes, all right, then forget that. I simply wanted to say that when you make judgments on my married life, you're basing them on no more than common gossip.

MANDERS: Granted. Well, what of it?

MRS. ALVING: But now, Mr. Manders, now I'll tell you the truth! I swore to myself that one day you were going to hear it—you alone.

MANDERS: And what, then, is the truth?

MRS. ALVING: The truth is—that my husband died just as dissolute as he'd lived every day of his life.

MANDERS (*groping for a chair*): What did you say?

MRS. ALVING: After nineteen years of marriage, just as dissolute—in his desires, in any case—as he was before you married us.

MANDERS: But these mistakes of his youth, these confusions—dissipations, if you want—you call them a dissolute life?

MRS. ALVING: It's the phrase our doctor used.

MANDERS: I don't understand you.

MRS. ALVING: You don't have to.

MANDERS: It makes my head spin. You mean the whole of your marriage—all those many years together with your husband—were nothing more than a hollow mockery?

MRS. ALVING: Exactly. Now you know.

MANDERS: This—I find this so hard to believe. I can't understand it! It doesn't make sense! But how was it possible to—? How could it be kept a secret?

MRS. ALVING: That was the constant battle I had, day after day. When Osvald was born, I thought things might go better with Alving—but it didn't last long. So then I had to redouble my efforts, fight with a vengeance so no one would know what kind of a man my child's father was. And you know, of course, how charming Alving could be. No one thought anything but good of him. He was one of those people whose lives never detract from their reputations. But then, Mr. Manders—and this you also have to hear—then came the most sickening part of the whole business.

MANDERS: More sickening than what you've told me!

MRS. ALVING: I'd borne with him, even though I knew very well what was going on in secret away from this house. But when the infection came right within our own four walls—

MANDERS: You mean—here!

MRS. ALVING: Yes, here in our own house. In there—(*Pointing to the nearer door on the right.*)—in the dining room, that was where I first discovered it. I had something to get inside, and the door was ajar. I heard the maid come up from the garden with water for the plants—

MANDERS: And—?

MRS. ALVING: A moment later I heard Alving come in after her. I could hear him saying something to her. And then I heard—(*With an abrupt laugh.*)—oh, I can hear it still, as something both so shattering and so ludicrous—my own maid whispering: "Let go of me, Captain Alving! Leave me be!"

MANDERS: How terribly gross and thoughtless of him! Oh, but Mrs. Alving, it was no more than a moment's thoughtlessness, believe me.

MRS. ALVING: I soon learned what to believe. The captain had his way with the girl—and that affair had its after-effects, Pastor Manders.

MANDERS (*as if stunned into stone*): And all that in this house! In this house!

MRS. ALVING: I've endured a lot in this house to keep him home in the evenings—and nights, I had to become his drinking companion as he got sodden over his bottle, holed up in his room. There I had to sit alone with him, forcing myself through his jokes and toasts and all his maundering, abusive talk, and then fight him bare-handed to drag him into bed—

MANDERS (*shaken*): That you were able to bear all that!

MRS. ALVING: I had my little boy, and I bore it for him—at least until that final humiliation, when my own maid—! Then I swore to myself: that was the end! So I took charge of the house—complete charge—over him and everything else. Because now, you see, I had a weapon against him; he couldn't let out a word of protest. It was then I sent Osvald away. He was going on seven and starting to notice things and ask questions, the way children do. All that was too much for me, Manders. I thought the child would be poisoned just breathing this polluted air. That's why I sent him away. And now you can understand, too, why he never set foot in this house as long as his father lived. No one will know what that cost me.

MANDERS: What a trial your life has been!

MRS. ALVING: I could never have gotten through it if it hadn't been for my work. And *I have* worked, I can tell you. All the additions to the property, all the improvements and technical innovations that Alving got fame and credit for—do you think those were *his* doing? *He,* sprawled all day on the sofa, reading old government journals! No, I can tell you as well; it was *I* who got him moving whenever he had his lucid moments; and it was I who had to pull the whole load when he fell back in his old wild ways or collapsed in groveling misery.

MANDERS: And for this man, you're raising a monument!

MRS. ALVING: There's the power of a bad conscience.

MANDERS: A bad—? What do you mean?

MRS. ALVING: It always seemed inevitable to me that the truth would have to come out someday and be believed. So the orphanage was meant to spike all the rumors and dispel the doubts.

MANDERS: Well, you've certainly accomplished that, Mrs. Alving.

MRS. ALVING: And I had still another reason. I didn't want Osvald, my own son, to inherit the least little thing from his father.

MANDERS: Then it's with Alving's money that—?

MRS. ALVING: Yes. The sums I've contributed year after year to the orphanage add up to just the amount—I've figured it out exactly—just the amount that made Lieutenant Alving such a good catch at the time.

MANDERS: Then, if I understand you—

MRS. ALVING: It was my selling price. I don't want that money passing into Osvald's hands. Everything my son inherits will come from me, and no one else.

(OSVALD *enters by the farther door to the right. He has left his hat and overcoat outside.*)

MRS. ALVING (*moving toward him*): You back again, dear?

OSVALD: Yes. What can anyone do outside in this interminable rain? But I hear dinner's ready. That's good news!

(REGINA *enters from the dining room with a package.*)

REGINA: A parcel just came for you, ma'am. (*Handing it to her.*)

MRS. ALVING (*with a quick look at* MANDERS): The choir music for tomorrow, most likely.

MANDERS: Hm—

REGINA: And dinner is served.

MRS. ALVING: Good. We'll be along in a moment; I just want to— (*Starts opening the package.*)

REGINA (*to* OSVALD): Will Mr. Alving have red wine, or white?

OSVALD: Both, Miss Engstrand.

REGINA: *Bien.* Very good, Mr. Alving. (*She goes into the dining room.*)

OSVALD: I better help her uncork the bottles—(*He follows her into the dining room, the door swinging half shut behind him.*)

MRS. ALVING (*who has unwrapped the package*): Yes, quite so—it's the choir music, Mr. Manders.

MANDERS (*with folded hands*): How I'll ever be able to give my speech tomorrow with any conviction—!

MRS. ALVING: Oh, you'll manage all right.

MANDERS (*softly, so as not to be heard in the dining room*): Yes, we musn't stir up any scandal.

MRS. ALVING (*in a quiet, firm voice*): No. And then this long, horrible farce will be over. After tomorrow, it will really seem as if the dead had never lived in this house. There'll be no one else here but my son and me.

(From the dining room comes the sound of a chair knocked over, along with REGINA's *voice in a sharp whisper.)*

REGINA: Osvald! Are you crazy? Let me go!

MRS. ALVING *(starting in terror)*: Ah—!

(She stares distractedly at the half-open door. OSVALD *is heard to cough within and start humming. A bottle is uncorked.)*

MANDERS *(shaken)*: But what happened, Mrs. Alving? What was that?

MRS. ALVING *(hoarsely)*: Ghosts. Those two from the greenhouse—have come back.

MANDERS: You mean—! Regina—? Is *she*—?

MRS. ALVING: Yes. Come. Not a word—!

(She grips PASTOR MANDER's *arm and moves falteringly toward the dining room.)*

ACT TWO

The same room. A thick mist still veils the landscape. MANDERS *and* MRS. ALVING *enter from the dining room.*

MRS. ALVING: Why, you're very welcome, Mr. Manders. *(Speaking into the dining room.)* Aren't you joining us, Osvald?

OSVALD *(from within)*: No, thanks; I think I'll go out for a while.

MRS. ALVING: Yes, do that. It's clearing a little now. *(She shuts the dining room door, goes over to the hall door and calls.)* Regina!

REGINA *(from without)*: Yes, ma'am.

MRS. ALVING: Go down to the laundry room and help out with the decorations.

REGINA: Very good, ma'am.

*(*MRS. ALVING *makes certain* REGINA *has gone, then shuts the door.)*

MANDERS: You're sure he can't hear us in there?

MRS. ALVING: Not with the door closed. Anyway, he's going out soon.

MANDERS: I'm still in a daze. I can't understand how I ever managed to devour one morsel of that heavenly meal.

MRS. ALVING *(pacing up and down, suppressing her anxiety)*: Nor I, either. But what's to be done?

MANDERS: Yes, what's to be done? Believe me, I just don't know; I'm so utterly inexperienced in such matters.

MRS. ALVING: I'm convinced nothing serious has happened so far.

MANDERS: God forbid! But it's still an unsavory business.

MRS. ALVING: It's just a foolish fancy of Osvald's, you can be sure of that.

MANDERS: Well, as I said, I'm not really up on these things; but it definitely seems to me—

MRS. ALVING: She'll have to get out of this house. Immediately. That's clear as day—

MANDERS: Yes, that's obvious.

MRS. ALVING: But where? We can't simply—

MANDERS: Where? Home to her father, of course.

MRS. ALVING: To whom, did you say?

MANDERS: To her—ah, but of course, Engstrand isn't—! Good Lord, Mrs. Alving, how is this possible? You must be mistaken, really.

MRS. ALVING: Unfortunately, I'm not the least bit mistaken. Joanna had to confess everything to me—and Alving couldn't deny it. There was nothing else to do, then, but have the whole thing hushed up.

MANDERS: Yes, that was essential.

MRS. ALVING: The girl was turned out at once and given a fairly sizable amount to keep quiet. She managed the rest for herself when she got back to town. She revived an old friendship with Engstrand—probably dropped a few hints, I would guess, about all the money she had—and spun him some tale of a foreigner on a yacht berthed here for the summer. So she and Engstrand were married straight off—well, you married them yourself.

MANDERS: But I don't see how—? I distinctly remember when Engstrand came to arrange the wedding. He was so woefully penitent, accusing himself so bitterly of the casual ways he and his fiancée had allowed themselves.

MRS. ALVING: Well, naturally he had to take the blame himself.

MANDERS: But the hypocrisy of the man! And with *me!* I absolutely never would have believed that of Jacob Engstrand. Well, I'll have to be very severe with him; he better be ready for that. And the immorality of such a marriage—all for money! How much did the girl get?

MRS. ALVING: Three hundred dollars.

MANDERS: Yes, can you imagine—to go and get married to a fallen woman for a paltry three hundred dollars!

MRS. ALVING: Then what's your opinion of me, who let herself be married to a fallen man?

MANDERS: God of mercy, what are you saying? A fallen man!

MRS. ALVING: Do you think my husband was any better when I went with him to the altar than Joanna when Engstrand married her?

MANDERS: But—there's a world of difference between you and her—

MRS. ALVING: Much less than a world, I think. There was a considerable difference in price—a paltry three hundred dollars as against a whole fortune.

MANDERS: But there's just no comparison here. After all, you'd listened to the counsels of your own heart, and those of your family.

MRS. ALVING (*not looking at him*): I thought you understood where I'd lost what you call my heart at the time.

MANDERS (*withdrawn*): If I'd understood any such thing, I would never have become a regular visitor in your husband's house.

MRS. ALVING: Anyway, one thing is clear: I never really listened to myself.

MANDERS: Well, to your nearest of kin then, as it's ordained you should: your mother and your two aunts.

MRS. ALVING: Yes, how true. The three of them wrote up my bill of sale. Oh, it's amazing how neatly they figured it out, that it would be stark madness to turn down an offer like that. If Mother could come back and see me now, where all those splendors got me.

MANDERS: No one's responsible for the outcome. At least there's this to be said: your marriage was carried through with every respect for law and order.

MRS. ALVING (*at the window*): Yes, always law and order! I often think they're the root of all our miseries on earth.

MANDERS: Mrs. Alving, that's a sinful thought.

MRS. ALVING: Yes, perhaps it is. But I can't stand it any longer, with all these webs of obligation. I can't stand it! I've got to work my way out to freedom.

MANDERS: What do you mean by that?

MRS. ALVING (*drumming on the windowpane*): I never should have covered up Alving's life. It was all I dared do then—not only for Osvald, but to spare myself. What a coward I was!

MANDERS: Coward?

MRS. ALVING: If people had known anything of what went on, they would have said: "Poor man, it's no wonder he strays at times; his wife ran away, you know."

MANDERS: And they could say that with some right, too.

MRS. ALVING (*looking straight at him*): If I were all I should have been, I would have taken Osvald aside and said: "Listen, my boy, your father was a degenerate human being—"

MANDERS: Good Lord—!

MRS. ALVING: Then I ought to have told him everything—word for word as I've told it to you.

MANDERS: I find you almost frightening, Mrs. Alving.

MRS. ALVING: I'm aware of that. Yes, I'm quite aware! I frighten myself by the thought. (*Coming away from the window.*) That's the coward I am.

MANDERS: And you call it cowardice to do your bounden duty? Have you forgotten that a child should love and honor his father and mother?

MRS. ALVING: Oh, don't let's talk abstractions! Why don't we ask, should Osvald love and honor Captain Alving?

MANDERS: Isn't there something that tells you, as a mother, not to destroy your son's ideals?

MRS. ALVING: Yes, but what of the truth—?

MANDERS: Yes, but what of his ideals—?

MRS. ALVING: Oh—ideals, ideals! If I only weren't the coward I am!

MANDERS: Don't demolish ideals, Mrs. Alving— that can have cruel repercussions. And especially now, with Osvald. He hasn't too many ideals, sad to say—but as far as I can make out, his father is some sort of ideal to him.

MRS. ALVING: Yes, you're right about that.

MANDERS: And the impressions he has you've instilled and nourished yourself, through your letters.

MRS. ALVING: Yes, I felt it was my duty and obligation—so year after year, I've gone on lying to my own child. Oh, what a coward—what a coward I've been!

MANDERS: You've built up a beautiful image in your son's imagination—and that's something you mustn't take lightly.

MRS. ALVING: Hm—who knows how good that's been, after all. But, in any case, I'm not going to have any trifling with Regina. He's not going to get that poor girl in trouble.

MANDERS: Good God, that would be dreadful!

MRS. ALVING: If I knew he was serious about it, and that it would make him happy—

MANDERS: Yes? Then what?

MRS. ALVING: But it wouldn't work out. Regina just isn't the type.

MANDERS: How so? What do you mean?

MRS. ALVING: If I weren't such a wretched coward, then I'd say to him: "Marry her, or live any way you like—but just be honest together."

MANDERS: Heavens above—! A legal marriage, no less! That would be barbarous—! It's unheard of—!

MRS. ALVING: Unheard of, you say? Word of honor, Pastor Manders—haven't you heard that, out here in the country, there are numbers of married couples who are just as closely related?

MANDERS: I really don't understand you.

MRS. ALVING: Oh yes you do, very well.

MANDERS: Well, you mean cases where possibly they—? Yes, unfortunately family life isn't always as pure as it ought to be, that's true. But what you're referring to is hardly ever known—at least, not conclusively. But here, instead—you, the mother, are willing to let your own—!

MRS. ALVING: But I'm not willing. I don't want to encourage it for anything in the world—that's just what I was saying.

MANDERS: No, because you're a coward, as you put it. But if you weren't a coward—! Almighty God—what a monstrous union!

MRS. ALVING: Well, as far as that goes, it's been rumored that we're all descended from a similar union. And who was it who thought up that arrangement, Pastor?

MANDERS: I will not discuss such questions with you, Mrs. Alving—because you're not in the proper state of mind. But, that you can dare call it cowardice on your part—!

MRS. ALVING: You have to understand what I mean by that. I'm anxious and fearful because of the ghosts that haunt me, that I can't get rid of.

MANDERS: Because of—what did you say?

MRS. ALVING: Ghosts. When I heard Regina and Osvald in there, it was as if I was seeing ghosts. But I almost believe we *are* ghosts, all of us, Pastor. It's not only what we inherit from our fathers and mothers that keeps on returning in us. It's all kinds of old dead doctrines and opinions and beliefs, that sort of thing. They aren't alive in us; but they hang on all the same, and we can't get rid of them. I just have to pick up a newspaper, and it's as if I could see the ghosts slipping between the lines. They must be haunting our whole country, ghosts everywhere—so many and thick, they're like grains of sand. And there we are, the lot of us, so miserably afraid of the light.

MANDERS: Ah! So this is the outgrowth of all your reading. Fine fruit, I must say! Oh, these disgusting, insidious freethinking books!

MRS. ALVING: My dear Mr. Manders, you're wrong. It was you yourself who set me to thinking—and for that I'll always be grateful.

MANDERS: *I?*

MRS. ALVING: Yes, when you made me give in to what you called duty and obligation; when you praised as right and proper what I rebelled against heart and soul as something loathsome—that's when I started going over your teachings, seam by seam. I just wanted to pull out a single thread; but after I'd worked it loose, the whole design fell apart. And then I realized it was only basted.

MANDERS (*quietly, with feeling*): Is that all that was won by the hardest battle of my life?

MRS. ALVING: You mean your most shameful defeat.

MANDERS: It was the greatest victory I've known, Helene—victory over myself.

MRS. ALVING: It was a crime against us both.

MANDERS: That I entreated you by saying, "Woman, go home to your lawful husband," when you came to me distracted, crying, "Here I am, take me!" Was that a crime?

MRS. ALVING: Yes, I think so.

MANDERS: We two don't understand each other.

MRS. ALVING: Not anymore, at least.

MANDERS: Never—never, in even my most secret thoughts, have I seen you as anything but another man's wife.

MRS. ALVING: You believe that?

MANDERS: Helene—!

MRS. ALVING: One forgets so easily.

MANDERS: I don't. I'm the same as I always was.

MRS. ALVING (*shifting her tone abruptly*): Yes, yes, well—let's stop talking about the old days. Now you're up to your ears in boards and committees; and I go around here struggling with ghosts, inside me and outside both.

MANDERS: At least I can help you manage the outer ones. After all the disturbing things I've heard from you today, my conscience won't suffer a defenseless young girl to remain in this house.

MRS. ALVING: It would be best, don't you think, if we could see her established? I mean, decently married.

MANDERS: Undoubtedly. I'd say it's desirable for her in, every respect. Regina's already at an age when—of course, I'm really no judge of these things, but—

MRS. ALVING: Regina matured quite early.

MANDERS: Yes, didn't she, though? It's my impression she was unusually well developed physically when I was preparing her for confirmation. But temporarily, in all events, she ought to go home, under her father's supervision—ah, but of course, Engstrand isn't—to think that he—that *he* could conceal the truth from me like that! (*There is a knock at the hall door.*)

MRS. ALVING: Who can that be? Come in!

(ENGSTRAND, *in his Sunday clothes, appears in the doorway.*)

ENGSTRAND: I beg your pardon most humbly, but—

MANDERS: Aha! Hm—

MRS. ALVING: Oh, it's you, Engstrand.

ENGSTRAND: There were none of the maids about, so I made myself so bold as to give a knock.

MRS. ALVING: Well, all right, come in. You want to talk to me about something?

ENGSTRAND (*coming in*): No, thanks all the same. It was the pastor, actually, I wanted to have a little word with.

MANDERS (*walking up and down*): Oh, yes? You want to talk to me? Is that it?

ENGSTRAND: Yes, I'd be grateful no end—

MANDERS (*stopping in front of him*): Well, may I ask what this is about?

ENGSTRAND: See, it's like this, Pastor; we've gotten paid off down there now—with all thanks to you, ma'am—and now we've finished everything up. And so I was thinking how nice and fitting it'd be if all us honest craftsmen who've been working together all this time— I was thinking, we ought to round things off with a little prayer meeting this evening.

MANDERS: A prayer meeting? Down at the orphanage?

ENGSTRAND: Yes. But of course if the pastor's not agreeable, then—

MANDERS: Oh, it's a splendid thought, but—hm—

ENGSTRAND: I've been holding a few evening prayers down there myself now and then—

MRS. ALVING: You have?

ENGSTRAND: Yes, now and then. Just a little meditation, so to speak. But then I'm a common, ordinary man, with no special gifts, God help me—and so I was thinking, since the pastor was out here—

MANDERS: Now look, Engstrand, first I have to ask you a question. Are you in a proper frame of mind for this kind of meeting? Do you feel your conscience is free and clear?

ENGSTRAND: Oh, Lord help us, Pastor, there's no point going on talking about my conscience.

MANDERS: Ah, but it's exactly what we *are* going to talk about. Well, what's your answer?

ENGSTRAND: My conscience? Yes, that can be pretty nasty at times, it can.

MANDERS: Well, at least you're owning up to it. Now will you tell me, without any subterfuge—just what is your relationship to Regina?

MRS. ALVING (*quickly*): Mr. Manders!

MANDERS (*calming her*): If you'll leave it to me—

ENGSTRAND: To Regina! Jeez, you gave me a turn there! (*Looking at* MRS. ALVING.) There's nothing wrong with Regina, is there?

MANDERS: We hope not. What I mean is, just exactly how are you related to her? You pass for her father, don't you? Well?

ENGSTRAND (*vaguely*): Why—hm—you know, Pastor, this business with me and poor Joanna.

MANDERS: Stop bending the truth. Your late wife told Mrs. Alving everything before she left her service.

ENGSTRAND: But it's supposed to—! She did that, really?

MANDERS: So your secret's out, Engstrand.

ENGSTRAND: And after she swore on a stack of Bibles—!

MANDERS: She swore—!

ENGSTRAND: I mean, she gave me her word. But with such sincerity.

MANDERS: And all these years you've hidden the truth from me. From *me*, who put my absolute trust in you.

ENGSTRAND: Yes, I'm afraid that's just what I've done.

MANDERS: Have I deserved this from you, Engstrand? Haven't I always been ready to help you out in every way, so far as I possibly could? Answer! Haven't I?

ENGSTRAND: There's plenty of times things would've looked pretty bad for me, if it wasn't for Pastor Manders.

MANDERS: And this is the way you pay me back. Get me to make false entries in the parish register, and for years after withhold information you owed as a matter of respect both to me and the plain truth. Your conduct has been unpardonable, Engstrand: and from now on we're through with each other.

ENGSTRAND (*with a sigh*): Well, that's it, I guess.

MANDERS: Yes. Because how can you ever justify yourself?

ENGSTRAND: But how could she go around shaming herself the more by talking about it? If you could just imagine, Pastor, yourself in the same trouble as poor Joanna—

MANDERS: I!

ENGSTRAND: Jeez now, I don't mean the very same. But I mean, supposing you had something to be ashamed of in the eyes of the world, as they say. We menfolk oughtn't to judge a poor woman too hard, Pastor.

MANDERS: But that's not what I'm doing. It's you that I blame.

ENGSTRAND: If I might ask your Reverence one tiny little question—?

MANDERS: Yes, go ahead.

ENGSTRAND: Isn't it right and proper of a man that he raises up the fallen?

MANDERS: Why, of course.

ENGSTRAND: And isn't a man obliged to keep his word of honor?

MANDERS: Certainly he is, but—

ENGSTRAND: At the time Joanna had her downfall at the hands of that Englishman—or maybe it was an American, or a Russian, or whatever—well, it was then she came back to town. Poor thing, she'd turned me down once or twice already; she only had eyes for the handsome ones, see—and I had this crook in my leg. Yes, you remember, Pastor, how I once took it on myself to go into a dance hall where common seamen were rioting in drink and dissipation, like they say. And when I tried to arouse them to seek out a better life—

MRS. ALVING (*over by the window*): Hm—

MANDERS: Yes, I know, Engstrand; those ruffians threw you downstairs. You've told me that before. Your disability does you great credit.

ENGSTRAND: I'm not priding myself on it, Pastor. But what I wanted to say was that then she came and confessed the whole thing to me, streaming down tears and gnashing her teeth. And I have to say, Pastor, it just about ripped the heart out of me to listen.

MANDERS: All of *that*, Engstrand. Well! Then what?

ENGSTRAND: Yes, so I said to her: that American, he's beating over the seas of the world, he is. And you, Joanna, I said—you've had your downfall, and you're a sinful, fallen creature. But Jacob Engstrand, I said, he stands on two stout legs—yes, I meant it like a manner of speaking, Pastor.

MANDERS: Yes, I quite understand. Go on.

ENGSTRAND: Well, so that's how I raised her up and gave her an honorable marriage, so no one'd ever find out about her wild carrying-on with foreigners.

MANDERS: That was all quite commendable of you. What I cannot approve is that you could bring yourself to accept money—

ENGSTRAND: Money? I? Not a penny.

MANDERS (*with an inquiring glance at* MRS. ALVING): But—?

ENGSTRAND: Oh, yes—just a minute; now I remember. Joanna did have a little odd change, all right—but I wanted nothing of *that*. Faugh! I said: Mammon, that's the wages of sin, it is.

We'll take that greasy gold—or banknotes, whatever it was—and heave it back into the American's face, I said. But he was off and gone over the rolling sea, Pastor.

MANDERS: Was that it, my dear Engstrand?

ENGSTRAND: That's right. So I and Joanna agreed that the money ought to be put toward the child's bringing up, and that's where it went; and I can give a true reckoning of every penny.

MANDERS: But that changes things substantially.

ENGSTRAND: That's the way it worked out, Pastor. And I'll be bold enough to say I've been a real father to Regina, as far as it lay in my power—for I have to admit, I'm only a poor, frail mortal.

MANDERS: There, there, Engstrand—

ENGSTRAND: But I will say that I brought up the child and looked after my poor, dear Joanna and made them a home, like the gospel says. But it never would have occurred to me to go up to Pastor Manders, priding myself and making much out of a good deed done in this world. No, when that sort of thing happens to Jacob Engstrand, he keeps it to himself, he does. Though it happens none too often, sorry to say. No, when I come to see Pastor Manders, then it's all I can do just to talk out my sins and errors. Because to say what I said before—my conscience does turn pretty nasty at times.

MANDERS: Give me your hand, Jacob Engstrand.

ENGSTRAND: Oh, Jeez, Pastor—

MANDERS: No fuss now. (*Grasping his hand.*) There!

ENGSTRAND: And if I can dare to beg your pardon, Pastor, most humbly—

MANDERS: You? Quite the contrary, I'm the one who should beg your pardon—

ENGSTRAND: Oh, no, no!

MANDERS: Yes, definitely. And I do, with all my heart. Forgive me that I could so misjudge you. If only I could give you some sign of my sincere regret, and the goodwill I have toward you—

ENGSTRAND: You'd like that, Pastor?

MANDERS: It would please me no end.

ENGSTRAND: Because there's a real good opportunity for that right now. With the bit of honest coin I've put aside from my work out here, I was thinking of founding a kind of seaman's home back in town.

MRS. ALVING: *You?*

ENGSTRAND: Yes, it'd be sort of a refuge for the orphans of the sea, so to speak. Temptations are so manifold for a sailor when he comes wandering ashore. But in this house of mine he could live like under a father's protection, that was my thought.

MANDERS: What do you say to that, Mrs. Alving?

ENGSTRAND: It's not much I have to begin with, Lord knows; but if I could just take hold of a helping hand—

MANDERS: Yes, yes, we have to consider this further. Your project interests me enormously. But now, go on down and get things ready—and light some candles, to give it a ceremonial touch. And then we'll have our devotional hour together, my dear Engstrand, for now I'm sure you're in the right frame of mind.

ENGSTRAND: I really do think so, yes. So good-bye, Mrs. Alving, and thanks for everything. And take good care of Regina for me. (*Brushes a tear from his eye.*) Poor Joanna's child—um, isn't it amazing—but it's just as if that girl had grown a part of my very heart. Yes, sir, and that's a fact. (*He bows and goes out.*)

MANDERS: Well, what do you think of the man now, Mrs. Alving? That's quite a different picture of things we got from him.

MRS. ALVING: Yes, quite so, indeed.

MANDERS: There you see how scrupulously careful one has to be about judging one's fellowman. But it's also a wonderful joy to discover one's made a mistake. Well, what do you say?

MRS. ALVING: I say you are and you always will be a big baby, Manders.

MANDERS: I?

MRS. ALVING (*placing both hands on his shoulders*): And I say I could easily wrap you up in a great, big hug.

MANDERS (*pulling back quickly*): Oh, bless you, no! What an impulse!

MRS. ALVING (*with a smile*): Oh, don't be afraid of me.

MANDERS (*by the table*): You sometimes have the most outrageous way of expressing yourself. Now I first want to collect these documents together and put them in my bag. (*Doing so.*)

There now. And so good-bye for the moment. Keep your eye on Osvald when he comes back. I'll be looking in on you later.

(*He takes his hat and goes out by the hall door.* MRS. ALVING *sighs, gazes a moment out of the window, straightens the room up a bit and starts into the dining room, then stops with a stifled cry in the doorway.*)

MRS. ALVING: Osvald! Are you still at the table?

OSVALD (*from the dining room*): I'm just finishing my cigar.

MRS. ALVING: I thought you'd gone for a walk.

OSVALD: In such weather?

(*The chink of a glass and decanter.* MRS. ALVING *leaves the door open and settles down with her knitting on the sofa by the window.*)

OSVALD: Wasn't that Pastor Manders who left just now?

MRS. ALVING: Yes, he went down to the orphanage.

OSVALD: Hm.

(*Again, the chink of glass and decanter.*)

MRS. ALVING (*with an anxious glance*): Osvald dear, you ought to go easy with the liqueur. It's strong.

OSVALD: It keeps the dampness out.

MRS. ALVING: Wouldn't you rather come in here with me?

OSVALD: But I can't smoke in there.

MRS. ALVING: Now you know a cigar is all right.

OSVALD: Oh, well, then I'll come in. Just a tiny drop more—ah, there. (*He enters, smoking his cigar, and shuts the door after him. Short silence.*) Where'd the pastor go?

MRS. ALVING: I told you, he went down to the orphanage.

OSVALD: Oh yes, that's right.

MRS. ALVING: You shouldn't go on sitting at the table so long, Osvald.

OSVALD (*holding his cigar behind his back*): But I think it's so cozy, Mother. (*Patting and fondling her.*) Imagine—what it is for me, coming home, to sit at my mother's own table, in my mother's room, and enjoy her delectable meals.

MRS. ALVING: My dear, dear boy!

OSVALD (*somewhat impatiently, walking about and smoking*): And what else am I going to do here? I can't accomplish anything—

MRS. ALVING: Can't you?

OSVALD: In all this murk? Not a glimmer of sunlight the whole day long? (*Pacing about.*) Oh, this—! This not being able to work—!

MRS. ALVING: Perhaps it wasn't such a good idea for you to come home.

OSVALD: No, Mother, that was essential.

MRS. ALVING: Because I'd ten times rather give up the joy of having you home with me, if it meant that you—

OSVALD (*stops by the table*): Now tell me, Mother—is it really such a great joy for you to have me home?

MRS. ALVING: What a question to ask!

OSVALD (*crumbling a newspaper*): I should have thought it hardly mattered to you whether I was here or not.

MRS. ALVING: You have the heart to say that to your mother, Osvald?

OSVALD: But you lived without me very well before.

MRS. ALVING: Yes, I've lived without you—that's true.

(*Silence. The twilight gradually deepens.* OSVALD *paces the floor, back and forth. He has set his cigar down.*)

OSVALD (*stops by* MRS. ALVING): Do you mind if I sit beside you on the sofa?

MRS. ALVING (*making room for him*): Please sit down, dear.

OSVALD (*sitting*): There's something I have to tell you, Mother.

MRS. ALVING (*nervously*): What?

OSVALD (*staring ahead into space*): Because I can't go on bearing it any longer.

MRS. ALVING: Bearing what? What is it?

OSVALD (*as before*): I couldn't bring myself to write you about it; and ever since I came home—

MRS. ALVING (*gripping his arm*): But, Osvald, what is it?

OSVALD: All yesterday and today I've been trying to drive these thoughts away—and free myself. But it doesn't work.

MRS. ALVING (*rising*): You've got to speak out, Osvald!

OSVALD (*drawing her down on the sofa again*): Sit still, and I'll try to tell you—I've been complaining so about my tiredness after the trip here—

MRS. ALVING: Yes? Well?

OSVALD: But that isn't what's wrong with me, not any ordinary tiredness—

MRS. ALVING (*starts to rise*): Osvald, you're not ill!

OSVALD (*draws her down again*): Sit still, Mother. Just be calm about it. I'm not exactly ill—at least not ill in the ordinary sense. (*Puts his hands to his head.*) Mother, it's my mind that's broken down—out of control—I'll never be able to work again! (*Hands over his face, he throws himself down in her lap and bursts into deep sobs.*)

MRS. ALVING (*pale and trembling*): Osvald! Look at me! No, no, it isn't true.

OSVALD (*looks up despairingly*): Never able to work again! Never—never! It's like a living death! Mother, can you imagine anything as horrible?

MRS. ALVING: My poor boy! How did this awful thing happen to you?

OSVALD (*sitting up again*): That's just what I don't understand. I can't figure it out. I've never lived a wild life—not in any respect. You have to believe me, Mother—that's something I've never done!

MRS. ALVING: I believe you, Osvald.

OSVALD: And yet it's come on me—this horrible thing!

MRS. ALVING: Oh, but dearest, it's going to be all right. It's no more than nervous exhaustion, believe me.

OSVALD (*heavily*): That's what I thought at first— but it's not so.

MRS. ALVING: Tell, me everything, right from the start.

OSVALD: Yes, I want to.

MRS. ALVING: When did you first notice anything?

OSVALD: It was just after my last visit home, and I'd returned to Paris. I began having such tremendous pains in my head—mostly toward the back, it seemed. It felt like a tight iron band squeezing me from my neck up—

MRS. ALVING: Go on.

OSVALD: At first I thought they were nothing more than the old, familiar headaches I've been bothered by ever since I was little.

MRS. ALVING: Yes, yes—

OSVALD: But I soon found out: that wasn't it. I couldn't work any longer. I wanted to start a new large painting, but it was as if all my talents had flown, and all my strength was paralyzed; I couldn't focus any of my thoughts;

everything swam—around and around. Oh, it was a terrifying state to be in! Finally I sent for a doctor—and through him I discovered the truth.

MRS. ALVING: What do you mean?

OSVALD: He was one of the foremost doctors down there. He had me describe exactly what I was feeling; and then he began asking me a whole lot of questions that didn't seem to bear at all. I couldn't grasp what he was after—

MRS. ALVING: So—?

OSVALD: At last he said: Right from your birth, your whole system has been more or less worm-eaten. The actual expression he used was *vermoulu*.

MRS. ALVING (*anxiously*): What did he mean by that?

OSVALD: I didn't understand either, so I asked him to be more specific. And then that old cynic said—(*Clenching his fist*). Oh—!

MRS. ALVING: What—?

OSVALD: He said: The sins of the fathers are visited upon the children.

MRS. ALVING (*slowly stands up*): The sins of the fathers—!

OSVALD: I almost hit him in the face.

MRS. ALVING (*moving across the room*): The sins of the fathers—

OSVALD (*smiles sadly*): Yes, can you imagine? Of course I assured him that was absolutely out of the question. But do you think he gave way? No, he had his mind made up; and it was only when I brought out your letters and translated all the parts to him that dealt with Father—

MRS. ALVING: What then—?

OSVALD: Well, then naturally he had to admit he'd been on the wrong track; and that's when I learned the truth—the incredible truth: that this beautiful, soul-stirring life with my young artist friends was something I should never have entered. It was too much for my strength. So—everything's my own fault.

MRS. ALVING: Osvald, no! You mustn't believe that!

OSVALD: There was no other way to explain it, he said. *That's* the worst of it. The whole of my life ruined beyond repair—all because of my own carelessness. So much that I wanted to do in this world—I don't dare think of it any-more—I'm not *able* to think of it. Oh, if I only could live my life over—and wipe out what I've done!

(*He throws himself face down on the sofa.* MRS. ALVING *wrings her hands and walks silently back and forth, locked in inner struggle. After a moment,* OSVALD *looks up, propping himself on his elbows.*)

OSVALD: If it had only *been* something inherited—something that wasn't my fault. But this! In a shameful, mindless, trivial way, to have thrown away health, happiness, a world of possibility—my future, my life—!

MRS. ALVING: No, no, my own dearest—it can't be! (*Bending over him.*) Things aren't as desperate as you think.

OSVALD: Oh, you don't know—(*Leaps to his feet.*) And then all the pain that I'm causing you, Mother! How often I could almost hope and wish you wouldn't care for me so much.

MRS. ALVING: Oh, Osvald, my only boy! You're all I have in this world, and all I care to have.

OSVALD (*grasps both her hands and kisses them*): Yes, yes, now I see. When I'm home I see it so well. And it's part of what weighs on me—Any-way, now you know the whole story. And let's not talk about it anymore today. I can't bear thinking about it very long. (*Walking about the room.*) Give me something to drink, Mother!

MRS. ALVING: To drink? What do you want to drink now?

OSVALD: Oh, anything. You must have some cold punch in the house.

MRS. ALVING: Oh, but Osvald dear—!

OSVALD: Don't refuse me that, Mother. Be good now! I've got to have something to drown all these gnawing thoughts. (*Goes into the green-house.*) And how—how dark it is here!

(MRS. ALVING *goes over to the bellpull, right, and rings.*)

OSVALD: And this interminable rain. Week after week it can go on; whole months at a time. In all my visits home, I never once remember seeing the sun shine.

MRS. ALVING: Osvald—you're thinking of leaving me!

OSVALD: Hm—(*Sighs deeply.*) I'm not thinking of anything. I can't think of anything! (*In a low tone.*) I've given that up.

REGINA (*entering from the dining room*): You rang, ma'am?

MRS. ALVING: Yes, bring the lamp in.

REGINA: Right away, ma'am. It's already lit. (*Goes out.*)

MRS. ALVING (*going over to* OSVALD): Osvald, don't keep anything from me.

OSVALD: I won't, Mother. (*Moves to the table.*) I've told you a lot, I think.

(REGINA *comes in with the lamp and sets it on the table.*)

MRS. ALVING: Yes, and Regina, you might bring us a half bottle of champagne.

REGINA: Yes, ma'am. (*Goes out again.*)

OSVALD (*clasping* MRS. ALVING *about the neck*): That's the way it should be. I knew you wouldn't let your boy go thirsty.

MRS. ALVING: Ah, my poor dear Osvald—how could I refuse you anything now?

OSVALD (*buoyantly*): Is that true, Mother? You mean it?

MRS. ALVING: Mean what—?

OSVALD: That you won't refuse me *anything*?

MRS. ALVING: But Osvald dear—

OSVALD: Shh!

(REGINA *returns with a half bottle of champagne and two glasses on a tray, which she sets down on the table.*)

REGINA: Should I open it—?

OSVALD: No, thanks, I'll do it.

(REGINA *goes out again.*)

MRS. ALVING (*seating herself at the table*): What did you mean—that I shouldn't refuse you?

OSVALD (*busy opening the bottle*): First a glass—may-be two.

(*The cork pops; he fills one glass and is about to pour the second.*)

MRS. ALVING (*holds her hand over it*): Thanks—not for me.

OSVALD: Well, for me then. (*He drains the glass, refills it, drains it again, then sits down at the table.*)

MRS. ALVING (*expectantly*): Well?

OSVALD (*not looking at her*): Say, tell me—I thought you and Mr. Manders looked so strange—hm, so quiet during lunch.

MRS. ALVING: You noticed that?

OSVALD: Yes. Hm—(*A short silence.*) Tell me, what do you think of Regina?

MRS. ALVING: What do I think?

OSVALD: Yes, isn't she splendid?

MRS. ALVING: Osvald dear, you don't know her as well as I do—

OSVALD: So—?

MRS. ALVING: It's too bad Regina lived at home for so long. I should have taken her in earlier.

OSVALD: Yes, but she's magnificent to look at, isn't she, Mother?

MRS. ALVING: Regina has a good many serious flaws—

OSVALD: Oh, but what does that matter? (*He drinks again.*)

MRS. ALVING: Even so, I'm fond of her; and I'm responsible for her. I wouldn't for the world want anything to hurt her.

OSVALD (*springing to his feet*): Mother, Regina's my only hope!

MRS. ALVING (*rising*): What do you mean by that?

OSVALD: I can't bear this anguish all by myself.

MRS. ALVING: But you have your mother to help you bear it, don't you?

OSVALD: Yes, I thought so—and that's why I came home to you. But it won't work that way. I can see; it won't work. I can't make a life out here.

MRS. ALVING: Osvald!

OSVALD: I have to live differently, Mother. So I will have to leave you. I don't want you to see all this.

MRS. ALVING: Oh, my miserable child! But, Osvald, when you're sick as you are—

OSVALD: If it were only the illness, I'd stay with you, Mother—I would. For you're my best friend in this world.

MRS. ALVING: Yes, it's true; I am, aren't I?

OSVALD (*striding restlessly about*): But it's all the torment, agony, remorse—and the great deathly fear. Oh—this hideous fear!

MRS. ALVING (*following him*): Fear? What fear? What do you mean?

OSVALD: Oh, don't ask me anymore about it. I don't know. I can't describe it to you.

(MRS. ALVING *crosses to the bell-pull, right, and rings.*)

OSVALD: What do you want?

MRS. ALVING: I want my boy to be happy, that's what. He mustn't go around brooding. (*To* REGINA, *who has appeared at the door.*) More champagne. A whole bottle.

(REGINA *goes.*)

OSVALD: Mother!

MRS. ALVING: Don't you think, in the country too, we know how to live?

OSVALD: Isn't she magnificent-looking? The figure she has! And the glow of her health!

MRS. ALVING: Sit down, Osvald, and let's have a quiet talk.

OSVALD (*sits*): You wouldn't know this, Mother, but I have a wrong to make right with Regina.

MRS. ALVING: You!

OSVALD: Or a little indiscretion—you might call it. Quite innocent, actually. When I was home last—

MRS. ALVING: Yes?

OSVALD: She asked me so many times about Paris, and I told her bits and pieces about the life down there. And I remember that one day I chanced to say, "Wouldn't you like to go there yourself?"

MRS. ALVING: Well?

OSVALD: I could see her blushing all shades of red, and then she said, "Yes, I'd very much like to." "All right," I said, "I expect that can be arranged"—or something like that.

MRS. ALVING: Oh?

OSVALD: Of course I forgot the whole thing completely; but then the day before yesterday I happened to ask her if she was glad I'd be staying so long at home this time—

MRS. ALVING: Yes?

OSVALD: And she gave me such a peculiar look and said, "But what about my trip to Paris?"

MRS. ALVING: Her trip!

OSVALD: And then I got it out of her that she'd taken the whole thing seriously, that she'd been thinking of me all this while, and that she'd even started to learn some French—

MRS. ALVING: So that's why—

OSVALD: Mother—when I saw her there in front of me, that splendid girl, so alive with health and beauty—it was as if I'd never noticed her before—but now she was standing there as if her arms were simply waiting to take me in—

MRS. ALVING: Osvald!

OSVALD: Then it struck me that in her was my salvation, because I saw how the joy of life was in her.

MRS. ALVING (*with a start*): The joy of life—? Is there salvation in that?

REGINA (*entering from the dining room with a bottle of champagne*): I'm sorry for taking so long, but I had to go down in the cellar— (*Sets the bottle down on the table.*)

OSVALD: And get one more glass.

REGINA (*looks at him in surprise*): But Mrs. Alving has her glass.

OSVALD: Yes, but bring one for yourself, Regina. (REGINA *looks startled and flashes a quick, shy glance at* MRS. ALVING.)

OSVALD: Well?

REGINA (*her voice low and hesitant*): Is that your wish, Mrs. Alving—?

MRS. ALVING: Get the glass, Regina. (REGINA *goes out into the dining room.*)

OSVALD (*his eyes following her*): Can you see the way she walks? So firm and fearless.

MRS. ALVING: Osvald, this can't happen—!

OSVALD: The thing is settled. You must see that. There's no use denying it. (REGINA *returns with an empty glass in her hands.*)

OSVALD: Sit down, Regina. (REGINA *looks uncertainly at* MRS. ALVING.)

MRS. ALVING: Sit down. (REGINA *sits on a chair by the dining-room door, still holding the empty glass in her hand.*)

MRS. ALVING: What were you saying, Osvald, about the joy of life?

OSVALD: Yes, the joy of life, Mother—you don't know much about that here at home. I never feel it here.

MRS. ALVING: Not even with me?

OSVALD: Not when I'm home. But how could you understand that?

MRS. ALVING: Oh, yes, yes. I think I'm beginning to understand—now.

OSVALD: That—and the joy of work. Yes, they're really the same thing, basically. But no one understands that here, either.

MRS. ALVING: Maybe you're right. Go on, I want to hear more of this.

OSVALD: I mean, here everyone's brought up to believe that work is a curse and a punishment, and that life is a miserable thing that we're best off to be out of as soon as possible.

MRS. ALVING: A vale of tears, yes. And we ingeniously manage to make it that.

OSVALD: But they won't hear of such things down there. Nobody abroad believes in that sort of outlook anymore. Down there, simply to be alive in the world is held for a kind of miraculous bliss. Mother, have you noticed how everything I've painted is involved with this joy of life? Always and invariably, the joy of life. With light and sun and holiday scenes—and faces radiant with human content. That's why I'm afraid to stay on at home with you.

MRS. ALVING: Afraid? What are you afraid of here with me?

OSVALD: I'm afraid that everything that's most alive in me will degenerate into ugliness here.

MRS. ALVING (*looking fixedly at him*): Would *that* happen, do you think?

OSVALD: I'm sure it would. Live here the same as down there—and it still wouldn't be the same life.

MRS. ALVING (*who has been listening intently, rises, her eyes large and thoughtful*): Now I see how it all fits together.

OSVALD: What do you see?

MRS. ALVING: I see it now, for the first time. And now I can speak.

OSVALD (*getting up*): I don't understand you, Mother.

REGINA (*who has also gotten up*): Shouldn't I go?

MRS. ALVING: No, stay here. Now I can speak. Now, my son, you have to know everything—and then you can choose. Osvald! Regina!

OSVALD: Quiet! The pastor—

MANDERS (*entering by the hall door*): Well, we've really had a heart-warming session together.

OSVALD: We also.

MANDERS: Engstrand needs help with his seaman's home. Regina will have to move back and accommodate him—

REGINA: No, thank you, Pastor.

MANDERS (*just noticing her*): What—? Here—with a glass in your hand!

REGINA (*hurriedly putting the glass down*): *Pardon*—!

OSVALD: Regina's leaving with me, Pastor.

MANDERS: Leaving—with you!

OSVALD: Yes, as my wife—if she wants that.

MANDERS: Merciful heavens—!

REGINA: It wasn't my doing, Mr. Manders.

OSVALD: Or she'll stay here if I stay.

REGINA (*involuntarily*): Here!

MANDERS: You petrify me, Mrs. Alving.

MRS. ALVING: Neither one nor the other will happen—because now I can speak out freely.

MANDERS: But you can't do that! No, no, no!

MRS. ALVING: I both can and will. And without demolishing any ideals.

OSVALD: Mother, what is it you're hiding from me?

REGINA (listening): Mrs. Alving! Listen! People are shouting out there. (She goes into the greenhouse and looks out.)

OSVALD (moving toward the window, left): What's going on? What's that light in the sky?

REGINA (cries out): The orphanage—it's burning!

MRS. ALVING (hurrying to the window): Burning!

MANDERS: Burning? Impossible. I was just down there.

OSVALD: Where's my hat? Oh, never mind—! Father's orphanage—! (He runs out through the garden door.)

MRS. ALVING: My shawl, Regina! It's all ablaze!

MANDERS: How awful! Mrs. Alving, this is God's fiery judgment on a wayward house!

MRS. ALVING: Yes, no doubt. Come along, Regina. (She and REGINA hurry out the hall door.)

MANDERS (clasping his hands together): And then—no insurance! (He follows them out.)

ACT THREE

The room as before. All the doors stand open. The lamp is still burning on the table. It is dark outside, with only a faint red glow in the background to the left. MRS. ALVING, with a large shawl over her head, is standing in the greenhouse, gazing out. REGINA, also with a shawl about her, stands slightly behind her.

MRS. ALVING: Completely burned out—right to the ground.

REGINA: It's burning still in the basement.

MRS. ALVING: Why Osvald doesn't come up—? There's nothing to save.

REGINA: Should I go down to him with his hat?

MRS. ALVING: He hasn't even got his hat?

REGINA (pointing into the hall): No, it's hanging in there.

MRS. ALVING: Oh, leave it be. He has to come up soon. I'll look for him myself. (She goes into the garden.)

MANDERS (entering from the hall): Isn't Mrs. Alving here?

REGINA: She just went into the garden.

MANDERS: This is the most frightful night I've ever experienced.

REGINA: Yes, it's a terrible catastrophe, isn't it, Pastor?

MANDERS: Oh, don't speak of it! I can hardly think of it even.

REGINA: But how could it have happened—?

MANDERS: Don't ask me, Miss Engstrand. How should I know? You're not also going to—? Isn't it enough that your father—?

REGINA: What about him?

MANDERS: He's got me completely confused.

ENGSTRAND (entering from the hall): Pastor—!

MANDERS (turning away, appalled): Are you after me even here!

ENGSTRAND: Yes, God strike me dead, but I have to—! Good grief, what a mess this is, Pastor!

MANDERS (pacing back and forth): Dreadful, dreadful!

REGINA: What's going on?

ENGSTRAND: Oh, it was on account of this here meeting, see? (In an undertone.) Now we've got the old bird snared, my girl. (Aloud.) And to think it's all my fault that it's Pastor Manders' fault for something like this!

MANDERS: But I assure you, Engstrand—

ENGSTRAND: But there was nobody besides the pastor who messed around with the candles down there.

MANDERS (stopping): Yes, that's what you say. But I absolutely cannot remember ever having a candle in my hand.

ENGSTRAND: And I saw so plainly how the pastor took that candle and pinched it out with his fingers and flicked the tip of the wick down into those shavings.

MANDERS: You saw me do that?

ENGSTRAND: Plain as day, I saw it.

MANDERS: I just don't understand it. It's never been a habit of mine to snuff a candle in my fingers.

ENGSTRAND: Yes, it did look pretty sloppy to me, all right. But could it really do that much damage, Pastor?

MANDERS (walking restlessly back and forth): Oh, don't ask me.

ENGSTRAND (*walking along with him*): And then your Reverence hadn't insured it either, had you?

MANDERS (*keeps walking*): No, no, no—you heard me.

ENGSTRAND (*keeps following him*): Not insured. And then to go straight over and set the whole works afire. Lord love us—what awful luck!

MANDERS (*wiping the sweat from his brow*): Yes, you can say that again, Engstrand.

ENGSTRAND: And to think it would happen to a charitable institution that was meant to serve the whole community, so to speak. The papers'll handle you none too gently, Pastor, I can bet.

MANDERS: No, that's just what I've been thinking about. That's almost the worst part of the whole business—all these vicious attacks and innuendoes—! Oh, it's too upsetting to think about!

MRS. ALVING (*coming from the garden*): I can't pull him away from the embers.

MANDERS: Ah, you're back, Mrs. Alving.

MRS. ALVING: So you got out of making your speech, Mr. Manders.

MANDERS: Oh, I would have been only too glad—

MRS. ALVING (*her voice subdued*): It's best that it went like this. This orphanage was never made for anyone's benefit.

MANDERS: You think it wasn't?

MRS. ALVING: You think it was?

MANDERS: It was a frightful misfortune, in any case.

MRS. ALVING: Let's discuss it purely as a business arrangement—Are you waiting for the pastor, Engstrand?

ENGSTRAND (*by the hall door*): Well, actually I was.

MRS. ALVING: Then sit down and rest a moment.

ENGSTRAND: Thanks. I can stand all right.

MRS. ALVING (*to* MANDERS): I suppose you'll be leaving by the steamer?

MANDERS: Yes. It goes an hour from now.

MRS. ALVING: Would you be so good as to take all the papers back with you. I don't want to hear another word about this thing. I've got other matters to think about—

MANDERS: Mrs. Alving—

MRS. ALVING: I'll shortly be sending you power of attorney to settle everything however you choose.

MANDERS: I'll be only too glad to take care of it. Of course the original terms of the bequest will have to be changed completely now, I'm afraid.

MRS. ALVING: That's understood.

MANDERS: Just offhand, it strikes me that I might arrange it so the Solvik property is made over to the parish. The land itself can hardly be written off as worthless; it can always be put to some use or other. And the interest on the balance of capital in the bank—I could probably apply that best to support some project or other that might be considered of benefit to the town.

MRS. ALVING: Whatever you wish. The whole thing's utterly indifferent to me now.

ENGSTRAND: Think of my seaman's home, Pastor!

MANDERS: Yes, definitely, that's a possibility. Well, it will bear some investigation.

ENGSTRAND: The hell with investigating—oh, Jeez!

MANDERS (*with a sigh*): And then too, unfortunately I have no idea how long I'll be able to handle these affairs—or if public opinion won't force me to drop them. That depends entirely on the results of the inquest into the fire.

MRS. ALVING: What are you saying?

MANDERS: And those results aren't predictable in advance.

ENGSTRAND (*approaching him*): Oh yes, they are! Because here's old Jacob Engstrand, right beside you.

MANDERS: Yes, but—?

ENGSTRAND (*lowering his voice*): And Jacob Engstrand's not the man to go back on a worthy benefactor in his hour of need, as the expression goes.

MANDERS: Yes, but my dear fellow—how can you—?

ENGSTRAND: Jacob Engstrand's sort of like your guardian angel, Pastor, see?

MANDERS: No, no, that I absolutely cannot accept.

ENGSTRAND: Oh, it's how it's going to be, anyway. It's not like somebody here hasn't taken the blame for somebody else before, you know.

MANDERS: Jacob! (*Grasps his hand.*) You're a rare individual. Well, you're going to have every bit of help you need for your seaman's home, you can count on that.

(ENGSTRAND *tries to thank him, but is overcome by emotion.*)

MANDERS (*slipping the strap of his traveling bag over his shoulder*): Well, time to be off. We can travel together.

ENGSTRAND (*by the dining-room door*): Come along with me, wench! You'll live soft as a yoke in an egg.

REGINA (*tossing her head*): Merci! (*She goes out in the hall and fetches* MANDERS' *overcoat and umbrella.*)

MANDERS: Good-bye, Mrs. Alving. And may the spirit of law and order soon dwell again in this house.

MRS. ALVING: Good-bye, Manders. (*She goes into the greenhouse as she notices* OSVALD *coming in through the garden door.*)

ENGSTRAND (*as he and* REGINA *help* MANDERS *on with his coat*): Good-bye, my girl. And if you're ever in any trouble, well, you know where to find Jacob Engstrand. (*Quietly.*) Little Harbor Street, hm—! (*To* MRS. ALVING *and* OSVALD.) And my house for wayfaring seamen—that's going to be known as "Captain Alving's Home," yes. And if I get to run that house after my own devices, I think I can promise you it'll be truly worthy of that great man's memory, bless him.

MANDERS (*in the doorway*): Hm—hm! Come along, my dear Engstrand. Good-bye, good-bye! (*He and* ENGSTRAND *go out the hall door.*)

OSVALD (*going toward the table*): What is this house he was speaking of?

MRS. ALVING: It's some sort of home that he and the pastor want to establish.

OSVALD: It'll burn up like all this here.

MRS. ALVING: Why do you say that?

OSVALD: Everything will burn. There'll be nothing left in memory of Father. And here I'm burning up, too. (REGINA *stares perplexed at him.*)

MRS. ALVING: Osvald! Poor boy, you shouldn't have stayed down there so long.

OSVALD (*sitting at the table*): I guess you're right.

MRS. ALVING: Let me dry your face, dear; you're dripping wet.

OSVALD (*gazing indifferently into space*): Thank you, Mother.

MRS. ALVING: Aren't you tired, Osvald? Perhaps you could sleep?

OSVALD (*anxiously*): No, no—not sleep! I never sleep; I only pretend to. (*Dully.*) That comes soon enough.

MRS. ALVING (*looking worriedly at him*): You know, dearest, you really are ill.

REGINA (*tensely*): Is Mr. Alving ill?

OSVALD (*impulsively*): And shut all the doors! This racking fear—!

MRS. ALVING: Shut them, Regina. (REGINA *shuts the doors and remains standing by the hall door.* MRS. ALVING *removes her shawl;* REGINA *does the same.*)

MRS. ALVING (*draws a chair over beside* OSVALD *and sits by him*): There, now I'll sit with you—

OSVALD: Yes, do that. And Regina must stay here too. I always want her close to me. You'll give me your help, Regina—won't you?

REGINA: I don't understand—

MRS. ALVING: Help?

OSVALD: Yes—when it's needed.

MRS. ALVING: Osvald, don't you have your mother to give you help?

OSVALD: You? (*Smiles.*). No, Mother, that kind of help you'd never give me (*With a mournful laugh.*) You! Ha, ha! (*Looks soberly at her.*) Although you're the obvious choice. (*Vehemently.*) Regina, why are you so reserved toward me? Why can't you call me Osvald?

REGINA (*softly*): I don't think Mrs. Alving would like it.

MRS. ALVING: You'll have every right to soon—so won't you sit down with us here? (*After a moment,* REGINA *sits down with shy dignity at the other side of the table.*)
  And now, my poor, troubled boy, I'm going to take all this weight off your mind—

OSVALD: You, Mother?

MRS. ALVING: Everything you call the agony of remorse and self-reproach.

OSVALD: Do you think you can?

MRS. ALVING: Yes, Osvald, now I can. You were speaking earlier about the joy of life; and as you said those words, it was as if a new light had been shed over the whole of my life.

OSVALD (*shaking his head*): I don't understand this.

MRS. ALVING: You should have known your father when he was just a young lieutenant. *He* had the joy of life, he did!

OSVALD: Yes, I know.

MRS. ALVING: It was like a holiday just to look at him. And all the energy, the unquenchable power that was in him!

OSVALD: Well—?

MRS. ALVING: And then, so full of that very joy, this child—because he *was* like a child then, really—had to make a life here in a mediocre town that had no joys to offer—only distractions. He had to get along here with no real goal in life—only a routine job to hold down. He never found any activity he could throw himself in heart and soul—only business affairs. He never had one single friend with the slightest sense of what the joy of life can mean—no one but drifters and drunkards—

OSVALD: Mother—!

MRS. ALVING: And finally the inevitable happened.

OSVALD: The inevitable?

MRS. ALVING: You said yourself, earlier this evening, what would happen to you if you stayed at home.

OSVALD: You're saying that Father—?

MRS. ALVING: Your poor father never found any outlet for the overpowering joy of life that he had. And I'm afraid I couldn't make his home very festive, either.

OSVALD: You, too?

MRS. ALVING: They'd drilled me so much in duty and things of that kind that I went on here all too long putting my faith in them. Everything resolved into duties—*my* duties, and *his* duties, and—I'm afraid I made this home unbearable for your poor father.

OSVALD: Why didn't you ever write me any of this?

MRS. ALVING: I've never seen it before as anything I could mention to you—his son.

OSVALD: And how, then, did you see it?

MRS. ALVING (*slowly*): I only saw the one thing: that your father was a ravaged man before you were born.

OSVALD (*with a strangled cry*): Ah—! (*He stands up and goes to the window.*)

MRS. ALVING: And then day after day I had only one thought on my mind: that Regina in reality belonged here in this house—just as much as my own son.

OSVALD (*wheeling about*): Regina—!

REGINA (*brought shaken to her feet, in a choked voice*): I—!

MRS. ALVING: Yes, now you both know.

OSVALD: Regina!

REGINA (*to herself*): So that's what she was.

MRS. ALVING: Your mother was decent in many ways, Regina.

REGINA: Yes, but she was that kind, all the same. Well, I sometimes thought so, but—then, Mrs. Alving, if you don't mind, may I leave right away, at once?

MRS. ALVING: Do you really want to, Regina?

REGINA: Yes, of course I want to.

MRS. ALVING: Naturally you can do as you wish, but—

OSVALD (*going over to* REGINA): Leave now? But you belong here.

REGINA: *Merci*, Mr. Alving—yes, I guess I can call you Osvald now. But it's certainly not the way I wanted to.

MRS. ALVING: Regina, I haven't been straightforward with you—

REGINA: That's putting it mild! If I'd known that Osvald was sick, why—And now that there isn't a chance of anything serious between us—No, I really can't stay out in the country and run myself ragged for invalids.

OSVALD: Not even for someone this close to you?

REGINA: Not on your life, I can't! A poor girl's only got her youth; she'd better use it—or else she'll find herself barefoot at Christmas before she knows it. And I've got this joy of life too, Mrs. Alving—in *me*!

MRS. ALVING: Yes, I'm afraid so. Only don't throw yourself away, Regina.

REGINA: Oh, things go as they go. If Osvald takes after his father, then I take after my mother, I guess. May I ask, Mrs. Alving, if Pastor Manders knows all this about me?

MRS. ALVING: Pastor Manders knows everything.

REGINA (*busy putting on her shawl*): Then I really better see if I can catch the boat out of here as quick as I can. The pastor's so nice to deal with, and I definitely think I've got just as much right to some of that money as he does—that rotten carpenter.

MRS. ALVING: You're quite welcome to it, Regina.

REGINA (*looking sharply at her*): You know, Mrs. Alving, you could have raised me as a gentleman's daughter—and I would've been a lot better off. (*Tossing her head.*) But, hell—what's the difference! (*With a bitter glance at the unopened bottle.*) I'll get my champagne in society yet, just see if I don't.

MRS. ALVING: If you ever need a home, Regina, you can come to me.

REGINA: No, thank you, ma'am. Pastor Manders'll look out for me, all right. And if things really go wrong, I still know a house where I'll do just fine.

MRS. ALVING: Where?

REGINA: In "Captain Alving's Home."

MRS. ALVING: Regina—I can see now—you'll go to your ruin!

REGINA: Ahh, ffft! *Adieu.* (*She curtsies and goes out the hall door.*)

OSVALD (*standing at the window, looking out*): Has she gone?

MRS. ALVING: Yes.

OSVALD (*murmuring to himself*): I think it's insane, all this.

MRS. ALVING (*goes over behind him, placing her hands on his shoulders*): Osvald, dear—has this disturbed you terribly?

OSVALD (*turning his face toward her*): All that about Father, you mean?

MRS. ALVING: Yes, about your poor father. I'm afraid it's been too much of a shock for you.

OSVALD: Why do you think so? It came as quite a surprise, of course; but basically it can hardly make any difference to me.

MRS. ALVING (*withdrawing her hands*): No difference! That your father was so enormously unhappy!

OSVALD: Naturally I can feel sympathy for him as for any human being, but—

MRS. ALVING: Nothing more—for your own father—!

OSVALD (*impatiently*): Yes, Father—Father! I never knew a father. My only memory of him is that he once got me to vomit.

MRS. ALVING: That's a dreadful thought! Surely a child ought to feel some love for his father, no matter what.

OSVALD: When that child has nothing to thank him for? Hasn't even known him? Do you really hang on to that old superstition—you, so enlightened in everything else?

MRS. ALVING: And is that just a superstition—!

OSVALD: Yes, you must realize that, Mother. It's one of these ideas that materialize in the world for a while, and then—

MRS. ALVING (*with a shudder*): Ghosts!

OSVALD (*pacing the floor*): Yes, you could very well call them ghosts.

MRS. ALVING (*in an outcry*): Osvald—you don't love me either!

OSVALD: I know you, at least—

MRS. ALVING: Yes, I know—but is that all?

OSVALD: And I know how much you care for me, and I have to be grateful to you for that. And you can be especially useful to me, now that I'm ill.

MRS. ALVING: Yes, I can, Osvald, can't I? Oh, I could almost bless this illness that forced you home to me, because it's made me see you're really not mine; you still have to be won.

OSVALD (*impatiently*): Yes, yes, yes, that's all just a manner of speaking. You have to remember I'm a sick man, Mother. I can't be concerned very much with others; I have enough just thinking about myself.

MRS. ALVING (*softly*): I'll be patient and forebearing.

OSVALD: And cheerful, Mother!

MRS. ALVING: Yes, dearest, you're right. (*Going over to him.*) Now have I taken away all your remorse and self-reproach?

OSVALD: Yes, you have. But who'll take away the fear?

MRS. ALVING: The fear?

OSVALD (*pacing about the room*): Regina would have done it for the asking.

MRS. ALVING: I don't understand. What is all this about fear—and Regina?

OSVALD: Is it very late, Mother?

MRS. ALVING: It's nearly morning. (*Looking out through the greenhouse.*) There's the first light of dawn already on the mountains. It's going to be clear, Osvald! In a little while you'll see the sun.

OSVALD: I look forward to that. Oh, there can be so much still to look forward to, and live for—!

MRS. ALVING: I'm sure there will be!

OSVALD: And even though I can't work, I'll—

MRS. ALVING: Oh, my dearest, you'll find yourself working again so soon. Because now you won't have these worrisome, depressing thoughts to brood on any longer.

OSVALD: Yes, it was good that you could rid me of all those fantasies of mine. And now, if I can only face this one thing more—(*Sits down on the sofa.*) Mother, we have to talk together—

MRS. ALVING: Yes, let's. (*She pushes an armchair over by the sofa and sits beside him.*)

OSVALD: And meanwhile the sun will rise. And by then, you'll know—and I won't have this fear any longer.

MRS. ALVING: Tell me, what will I know?

OSVALD (*not listening*): Mother, didn't you say earlier this evening that there wasn't anything in the world you wouldn't do for me if I asked you?

MRS. ALVING: Why, yes, of course!

OSVALD: And you meant it, Mother?

MRS. ALVING: That you can depend on. You're my one and only boy; I have nothing else to live for but you.

OSVALD: All right, then listen. You have a strong, resilient mind, I know that. I want you to sit very quiet as I tell this.

MRS. ALVING: But what is it that's so terrible—?

OSVALD: You mustn't scream. Do you hear? Promise me that? We're going to sit and speak of it quietly. Mother, promise me?

MRS. ALVING: Yes, yes, I promise—just tell me!

OSVALD: Well, then you've got to realize that all this about tiredness—and my incapacity for thinking in terms of my work—isn't the real illness—

MRS. ALVING: What is the real illness?

OSVALD: The one that I inherited, the illness—(*Points to his forehead and speaks very softly.*)—that's seated here.

MRS. ALVING (*nearly speechless*): Osvald! No—no!

OSVALD: Don't scream; I can't bear it. Yes, it sits in here and waits. And any day, at any time, it can strike.

MRS. ALVING: Oh, how horrible—!

OSVALD: Just stay calm. So, that's how things are with me.

MRS. ALVING (*springing to her feet*): It's not true, Osvald! It's impossible! It can't be!

OSVALD: I had one attack down there. It soon passed off—but when I found out how things stood

with me, then this anxiety took hold, racking me like a cold fever; and with that, I started home here to you as fast as I could.

MRS. ALVING: So that's the fear—!

OSVALD: Yes, I can't tell you how excruciating it is. Oh, if it only had been some ordinary disease that would kill me—I'm not so afraid of dying, though I want to live as long as I can.

MRS. ALVING: Yes, yes, Osvald, you must!

OSVALD: But the thought of it *is* excruciating. To revert back to a helpless child again. To have to be fed, to have to be—oh, it's unspeakable.

MRS. ALVING: My child has his mother to nurse him.

OSVALD (*leaps up*): No, never! That's just what I won't have! I can't abide the thought of lying here like that for years—turning old and gray. And in the meantime you might die before me. (*Sits in* MRS. ALVING's *chair.*) Because the doctor surd it needn't be fatal at once. He called it a kind of "softening of the brain"—some phrase like that. (*Smiles sadly.*) I think that expression sounds so nice. It always makes me think of cherry-red velvet draperies—something soft to stroke.

MRS. ALVING (*screams*): Osvald!

OSVALD (*leaps up again and paces the floor*): And now you've taken Regina away from me! If I'd only had her. She would have helped me out, I'm sure.

MRS. ALVING (*going over to him*): My dear boy, what do you mean? Is there any help in this world that I wouldn't willingly give you?

OSVALD: After I'd recovered from the attack down there, the doctor told me that, when it struck again—and it *would* strike—there'd be no more hope.

MRS. ALVING: That he could be so heartless—

OSVALD: I demanded it of him. I told him I had certain arrangements to make. (*With a shy smile.*) And so I had. (*Brings out a small box from his inner breast pocket.*) Mother, you see this?

MRS. ALVING: What's that?

OSVALD: Morphine pills.

MRS. ALVING (*looks at him in horror*): Osvald—my child!

OSVALD: I've saved up twelve of them—

MRS. ALVING (*snatching at it*): Give me the box, Osvald!

OSVALD: Not yet, Mother. (*He returns the box to his pocket.*)

MRS. ALVING: I can't live through this!

OSVALD: You'll have to. If I'd had Regina here now, I'd have told her what state I was in—and asked for her help with this one last thing. She'd have helped me, I'm positive of that.

MRS. ALVING: Never!

OSVALD: If this horrible thing struck me down, and she saw me lying there like an infant child, helpless, and beyond help, lost, hopeless—incurable—

MRS. ALVING: Regina never would have done that!

OSVALD: Yes, she would have. Regina was so wonderfully lighthearted. She soon would have gotten tired of tending an invalid like me.

MRS. ALVING: Then thank God Regina's not here!

OSVALD: So now, Mother, you've got to give me that help.

MRS. ALVING (*in a loud outcry*): I!

OSVALD: What more obvious choice than you?

MRS. ALVING: I! Your mother!

OSVALD: Exactly the reason.

MRS. ALVING: I, who gave you life!

OSVALD: I never asked you for life. And what is this life you gave me? I don't want it! You can take it back!

MRS. ALVING: Help! Help! (*She runs out into the hall.*)

OSVALD (*right behind her*): Don't leave me! Where are you going?

MRS. ALVING (*in the hall*): To get the doctor, Osvald! Let me out!

OSVALD (*also in the hall*): You don't leave. And no one comes in.

(*The sound of a key turning in a lock.*)

MRS. ALVING (*coming in again*): Osvald—Osvald—my child!

OSVALD (*following her*): Have you no mother-love for me at all—to see me suffer this unbearable fear!

MRS. ALVING (*after a moment's silence, controlling her voice*): Here's my hand on it.

OSVALD: Then you will—?

MRS. ALVING: If it becomes necessary. But it won't be necessary. No, no, that's simply impossible!

OSVALD: Well, that we can hope. And now let's live together as long as we can. Thank you, Mother.

(*He settles down in the armchair that* MRS. ALVING *had moved over to the sofa. The day is breaking; the lamp still burns on the table.*)

MRS. ALVING: Now do you feel all right?

OSVALD: Yes.

MRS. ALVING (*bending over him*): What a fearful nightmare this has been for you, Osvald—but it was all a dream. Too much excitement—it hasn't been good for you. But now you can have your rest, at home with your mother near, my own, my dearest boy. Anything you want you can have, just like when you were a little child. There now, the pain is over. You see how quickly it went. Oh, I knew it would—And look, Osvald, what a lovely day we'll have. Bright sunlight. Now you really can see your home.

(*She goes to the table and puts out the lamp. Sunrise. The glaciers and peaks in the background shine in the brilliant light of morning. With his back toward the distant view,* OSVALD *sits motionless in the armchair.*)

OSVALD (*abruptly*): Mother, give me the sun.

MRS. ALVING (*by the table, looks at him, startled*): What did you say?

OSVALD (*repeats in a dull monotone*): The sun. The sun.

MRS. ALVING (*moves over to him*): Osvald, what's the matter?

(OSVALD *appears to crumple inwardly in the chair; all his muscles loosen; the expression leaves his face; and his eyes stare blankly.*)

MRS. ALVING (*shaking with fear*): What is it? (*In a shriek.*) Osvald! What's wrong! (*Drops to her knees beside him and shakes him.*) Osvald! Osvald! Look at me! Don't you know me?

OSVALD (*in the same monotone*): The sun—the sun.

MRS. ALVING (*springs to her feet in anguish, tears at her hair with both hands and screams*): I can't bear this! (*Whispers as if paralyzed by fright.*) I can't bear it! Never! (*Suddenly.*) Where did he put them? (*Her hand skims across his chest.*) Here! (*She shrinks back several steps and shrieks.*) No, no, no!—Yes!—No, no! (*She stands a few steps away from him, her fingers thrust into her hair, staring at him in speechless horror.*)

OSVALD (*sitting motionless, as before*): The sun—the sun.

Introduction to *Trifles*

WHEN THE PLAY WAS NEW

Susan Glaspell wrote *Trifles* specifically to be performed in a tiny converted wharf building in Provincetown, Massachusetts, in 1916. As a founding member (since 1915) of the Provincetown Players, an amateur company that was dedicated to producing original plays under the direction or oversight of the playwright, she felt obligated to serve well the intentions and abilities of this fledgling theatre company as well as offer a one-act play that addressed issues of her time.

Trifles opened to a small but engaged audience at the tiny Lewis Wharf at the edge of the water in Provincetown on August 8, 1916, along with two other one-act plays now all but forgotten. Glaspell's play soon emerged as one of the best plays created by the Provincetown Players and has stood the test of time as a brilliant example of the one-act play form. In that first production, Glaspell, who served as one of the group's best and most reliable actresses from 1915 to 1922, played the role of Mrs. Hale. The Provincetown Players took on all jobs in seeing their plays reach the stage. Although the play had a single author, the production was a group effort by an artistic collective. The members of Provincetown had every confidence that their work could help change the value of plays to the American theatre. And they were right. The Provincetown Players moved to Greenwich Village in New York in the fall of 1916 and opened their Playwrights' Theatre first in a brownstone, then in a converted stable; *Trifles* was performed there along with early plays by Eugene O'Neill, Edna St. Vincent Millay, and many other writers, more than forty percent of whom were women.

While a journalist, Susan Glaspell covered a trial in Iowa, an event that contributed to the backstory of the play. According to her own account, she developed the story and action of the play by sitting alone in the small theatrical space and staring at the stage—envisioning it as a kitchen, and then a kitchen that two neighbor women were reluctant to enter since the woman who lived there had been arrested and taken away. They view it as another woman's space, not their own. Their husbands and the sheriff, however, barge right in looking for clues to a murder. Her account suggests that Glaspell was almost asking the space to reveal its possibilities to her.

Glaspell was very concerned with the roles of women in modern American society. In her usual manner she exposed the marked differences in the sexes often subtly, but effectively, without preaching to the audience or haranguing society for its inconsistencies and gendered double standards. The playwright's voice is gentle, but firm. She reveals the problems and, like Henrik Ibsen before her, leaves the audience to ponder or discuss the problems without offering her own solutions. The issue is raised; it is up to the audience to act. At the time of the first production men and women in American society were continuing to struggle with equal rights for women, women's suffrage, the role of child rearing, birth control, and a host of gender-specific issues on the minds and tongues of many modern citizens. Rather than make speeches from a soapbox, Glaspell dramatized in *Trifles*, as well as in most of her plays, the battle of the sexes played out often in observation, silence, or whispers. The effect is simple, but stunning.

At the time of the composition of the play, Europe was fighting World War I, but the United States had not yet entered the action. Many Americans were worried about the war, but the artistic, intellectual, and journalistic communities were also very concerned with new issues surrounding psychoanalysis, escalating divorce, and urbanization. In 1916 the United States was on the verge of becoming an urban majority—a fact verified by the census of 1920. The world was changing rapidly and Glaspell's plays address a number of those changes as they affected women and what was appropriate as "women's work."

Chief among Glaspell's artistic collaborators with this and many of her plays in production was her husband, George Cram Cook, who served as artistic director of the Provincetown Players and performed in the first production of *Trifles*.

THE PLAYWRIGHT

Susan Glaspell (1876?–1948), in addition to being a playwright, was a novelist and, early in her career, a journalist in Iowa where she was born. After her marriage to George Cram Cook, also a co-founder of the Provincetown Players, Glaspell spent much of her adult life in New York and New England. Besides *Trifles*, Glaspell wrote or co-wrote a number of satirical one act plays. *Suppressed Desires* (1915), a collaboration with Cook, was on the first bill of plays produced by the Provincetowners; it offered a tongue-in-cheek examination of the furor over psychoanalysis raging in the United States at the time. Alone she wrote a number of full-length plays culminating in *Alison's House* (1930). Although not her finest work, this study of the poet Emily Dickinson won the Pulitzer Prize for Glaspell. It was probably a belated award for her earlier work such as *Inheritors* (1921), a poignant exploration of conscientious objection to war and liberal thinking in a reactionary time—an appeal for tolerance. Her most fascinating full-length play is arguably *The Verge* (1921), an early American experiment in expressionistic technique, and a vibrant examination of a talented woman's journey into insanity within a world controlled by men. All of these plays (except *Alison's House*) were first produced by the Provincetown Players, who disbanded in 1922. The later Provincetown Playhouse in New York (beginning in 1924) was the same theatre building but a different professional production organization.

GENRE, STRUCTURE, AND STYLE

Trifles is essentially a murder mystery. Two women have come to the scene of a crime to collect some personal things for a woman who is accused of murdering her husband and is now in jail. The male sheriff and his sidekicks (the women's husbands) search the premises looking for clues, but they find nothing. The men do not know how to examine a woman's sphere with understanding and sensitivity. They can find no motive; it is the women who know how to read the scene and decipher the clues. The style is realistic, but quiet in its development and very tightly focused on the task at hand. Ultimately, this play is about the importance of environment and the underlying differences in the ways women and men look at the world. It depicts the suffering of women when forced to live with men who never attempt to understand their emotional and intellectual worlds. In many ways *Trifles* is a window on most of Glaspell's later plays.

IMPORTANT ELEMENTS OF CONTENT

Glaspell draws the audience's attention to the ability of the sensitive women to unravel the mystery by examining the domestic environment. Because of the experiences they share in tasks such as quilting and cooking, and an understanding of the treatment of women by brusque men, Mrs. Peters and Mrs. Hale can spot the clues left by Minnie Wright, the wife accused of murdering her husband. A woman's sphere and her pain are revealed in the carefully selected stage properties. The presence of Minnie looms large in the play, despite the fact that she never appears on stage. This device of unseen presence is explored in several of Glaspell's plays and reveals the dramatic power of absence in staged work. The ultimate decision of the onstage women is often identified by critics as effective passive resistance.

THE PLAY IN REVIVAL

After the first performance in 1916 in Massachusetts, the Provincetown Players revived the play in New York, and it has continued to be revived throughout the country and abroad. It was a staple item for many little theatres (community-based amateur and professional theatres) in the 1920s and 1930s. It continues in regular performances at colleges, universities, and community theatres. Professional revival is infrequent; due to the play's short length it must usually be performed on a program with other plays. *Trifles,* nonetheless, is a modern classic. If you attend the theatre often it is likely that you will encounter this play in performance.

SPECIAL FEATURE

Trifles features the lack of meaningful communication between the men and women. Assumptions on the part of men, and sometimes women, of the cultural and domestic dominance of the male in society, lead the women in this play to undercut the men's inept attempts to see that justice is done. The women quietly render their own insightful interpretation and silent justice.

FURTHER READING ABOUT THE PLAY, PLAYWRIGHT, AND CONTEXT

For additional material on Susan Glaspell's life and times, see Barbara Ozieblo, *Susan Glaspell: A Critical Biography;* Elaine Partnow, *The Female Dramatist;* and Susan Glaspell, *The Road to the Temple.*

For accounts of the Provincetown Players, including the contributions of Susan Glaspell, see Robert Karoly Sarlos, *Jig Cook and the Provincetown Players;* Helen Deutsch and Stella Hanau, *The Provincetown: A Story of the Theatre;* Cheryl Black, *The Women of Provincetown;* and Edna Kenton, *The Provincetown Players and the Playwrights' Theatre, 1915–1922.*

For other plays by Glaspell see Susan Glaspell, *Plays,* edited by C. W. E. Bigsby.

For analysis of the work of Glaspell, see Veronica Makowsky, *Susan Glaspell's Century of American Women,* and J. Ellen Gainor, *Susan Glaspell in Context.*

For history of the American theatre at the time of Glaspell, see Ronald Wainscott, *The Emergence of the Modern American Theatre,* and Don B. Wilemeth and C. W. E. Bigsby, ed., *The Cambridge History of American Theatre,* vol. 2.

Trifles

❧

By Susan Glaspell

CHARACTERS

GEORGE HENDERSON   County Attorney
HENRY PETERS   Sheriff
LEWIS HALE   A neighboring farmer
MRS. PETERS
MRS. HALE

Scene: The kitchen is the now abandoned farmhouse of JOHN WRIGHT, *A GLOOMY KITCHEN, AND LEFT WITHOUT HAVING BEEN PUT IN ORDER—UNWASHED PANS UNDER THE SINK, A LOAF OF BREAD OUTSIDE THE BREAD-BOX, A DISH-TOWEL ON THE TABLE—OTHER SIGNS OF INCOMPLETED WORK. AT THE REAR THE OUTER DOOR OPENS AND THE* SHERIFF *comes in followed by the* COUNTY ATTORNEY *and* HALE. *The* SHERIFF *and* HALE *are men in middle life, the* COUNTY ATTORNEY *is a young man; all are much bundled up and go at once to the stove. They are followed by the two women—the* SHERIFF'S WIFE *first; she is a slight wiry woman, a thin nervous face.* MRS. HALE *is larger and would ordinarily be called more comfortable looking, but she is disturbed now and looks fearfully about as she enters. The women have come in slowly, and stand close together near the door.*

COUNTY ATTORNEY (*rubbing his hands*): This feels good. Come up to the fire, ladies.

MRS. PETERS (*after taking a step forward*): I'm not—cold.

SHERIFF (*unbuttoning his overcoat and stepping away from the stove as if to mark the beginning of official business*): Now, Mr. Hale, before we move things about, you explain to Mr. Henderson just what you saw when you came here yesterday morning.

COUNTY ATTORNEY: By the way, has anything been moved? Are things just as you left them yesterday?

SHERIFF (*looking about*): It's just the same. When it dropped below zero last night I thought I'd better send Frank out this morning to make a fire for us—no use getting pneumonia with a big case on, but I told him not to touch anything except the stove—and you know Frank.

COUNTY ATTORNEY: Somebody should have been left here yesterday.

SHERIFF: Oh—yesterday. When I had to send Frank to Morris Center for that man who went crazy—I want you to know I had my hands full yesterday. I knew you could get back from Omaha by today and as long as I went over everything here myself—

COUNTY ATTORNEY: Well, Mr. Hale, tell just what happened when you came here yesterday morning.

HALE: Harry and I had started to town with a load of potatoes. We came along the road from my place and as I got here I said, "I'm going to see if I can't get John Wright to go in with me on a party telephone." I spoke to Wright about it once before and he put me off, saying folks talked too much anyway, and all he asked was peace and quiet—I guess you know about how much he talked himself; but I thought maybe if I went to the house and talked about it before his wife, though I said to Harry that I didn't know as what his wife wanted made much difference to John—

COUNTY ATTORNEY: Let's talk about that later, Mr. Hale. I do want to talk about that, but tell now just what happened when you got to the house.

HALE: I didn't hear or see anything; I knocked at the door, and still it was all quiet inside. I knew they must be up, it was past eight o'clock. So I knocked again, and I thought I heard somebody say, "Come in." I wasn't sure, I'm not sure yet, but I opened the door—this door (*indicating the door by which the two women are still standing*) and there in that rocker—(*pointing to it*) sat Mrs. Wright.

(*They all look at the rocker.*)

COUNTY ATTORNEY: What—was she doing?

HALE: She was rockin' back and forth. She had her apron in her hand and was kind of—pleating it.

COUNTY ATTORNEY: And how did she—look?

HALE: Well, she looked queer.

COUNTY ATTORNEY: How do you mean—queer?

HALE: Well, as if she didn't know what she was going to do next. And kind of done up.

COUNTY ATTORNEY: How did she seem to feel about your coming?

HALE: Why, I don't think she minded—one way or other. She didn't pay much attention. I said, "How do, Mrs. Wright it's cold, ain't it?" And she said, "Is it?"—and went on kind of pleating at her apron. Well, I was surprised; she didn't ask me to come up to the stove, or to set down, but just sat there, not even looking at me, so I said, "I want to see John." And then she—laughed. I guess you would call it a laugh. I thought of Harry and the team outside, so I said a little sharp: "Can't I see John?" "No," she says, kind o' dull like. "Ain't he home?" says I. "Yes," says she, "he's home." "Then why can't I see him?" I asked her, out of patience. "Cause he's dead," says she. "*Dead?*" says I. She just nodded her head, not getting a bit excited, but rockin' back and forth. "Why—where is he?" says I, not knowing what to say. She just pointed upstairs—like that (*himself pointing to the room above*). I got up, with the idea of going up there. I walked from there to here—then I says, "Why, what did he die of?" "He died of a rope round his neck," says she, and just went on pleatin' at her apron. Well, I went out and called Harry. I thought I might—need help. We went upstairs and there he was lyin'—

COUNTY ATTORNEY: I think I'd rather have you go into that upstairs, where you can point it all out. Just go on now with the rest of the story.

HALE: Well, my first thought was to get that rope off. It looked . . . (*stops, his face twitches*) . . . but Harry, he went up to him, and he said, "No, he's dead all right, and we'd better not touch anything." So we went back down stairs. She was still sitting that same way. "Has anybody been notified?" I asked. "No," says she unconcerned. "Who did this, Mrs. Wright?" said Har-

ry. He said it business-like—and she stopped pleatin' of her apron. "I don't know," she says. "You don't *know?*" says Harry. "No," says she. "Weren't you sleepin' in the bed with him?" says Harry. "Yes," says she, "but I was on the inside." "Somebody slipped a rope round his neck and strangled him and you didn't wake up?" says Harry. "I didn't wake up," she said after him. We must 'a looked as if we didn't see how that could be, for after a minute she said, "I sleep sound." Harry was going to ask her more questions but I said maybe we ought to let her tell her story first to the coroner, or the sheriff, so Harry went fast as he could to Rivers' place, where there's a telephone.

COUNTY ATTORNEY: And what did Mrs. Wright do when she knew that you had gone for the coroner?

HALE: She moved from that chair to this one over here (*pointing to a small chair in the corner*) and just sat there with her hands held together and looking down. I got a feeling that I ought to make some conversation, so I said I had come in to see if John wanted to put in a telephone, and at that she started to laugh, and then she stopped and looked at me—scared. (*The* COUNTY ATTORNEY, *who has had his notebook out, makes a note.*) I dunno, maybe it wasn't scared. I wouldn't like to say it was. Soon Harry got back, and then Dr Lloyd came, and you, Mr. Peters, and so I guess that's all I know that you don't.

COUNTY ATTORNEY (*looking around*): I guess we'll go upstairs first—and then out to the barn and around there. (*to the* SHERIFF) You're convinced that there was nothing important here—nothing that would point to any motive.

SHERIFF: Nothing here but kitchen things.

(*The* COUNTY ATTORNEY, *after again looking around the kitchen, opens the door of a cupboard closet. He gets up on a chair and looks on a shelf. Pulls his hand away, sticky.*)

COUNTY ATTORNEY: Here's a nice mess.

(*The women draw nearer.*)

MRS. PETERS (*to the other woman*): Oh, her fruit; it did freeze. (*to the* LAWYER) She worried about that when it turned so cold. She said the fire'd go out and her jars would break.

SHERIFF: Well, can you beat the women! Held for murder and worryin' about her preserves.

COUNTY ATTORNEY: I guess before we're through she may have something more serious than preserves to worry about.

HALE: Well, women are used to worrying over trifles. (*The two women move a little closer together.*)

COUNTY ATTORNEY (*with the gallantry of a young politician*): And yet, for all their worries, what would we do without the ladies? (*The women do not unbend. He goes to the sink, takes a dipperful of water from the pail and pouring it into a basin, washes his hands. Starts to wipe them on the roller-towel, turns it for a cleaner place.*) Dirty towels! (*kicks his foot against the pans under the sink.*) Not much of a housekeeper, would you say, ladies?

MRS. HALE (*stiffly*): There's a great deal of work to be done on a farm.

COUNTY ATTORNEY: To be sure. And yet (*with a little bow to her*) I know there are some Dickson county farmhouses which do not have such roller towels. (*He gives it a pull to expose its length again.*)

MRS. HALE: Those towels get dirty awful quick. Men's hands aren't always as clean as they might be.

COUNTY ATTORNEY: Ah, loyal to your sex, I see. But you and Mrs. Wright were neighbors. I suppose you were friends, too.

MRS. HALE (*shaking her head*): I've not seen much of her of late years. I've not been in this house—it's more than a year.

COUNTY ATTORNEY: And why was that? You didn't like her?

MRS. HALE: I liked her all well enough. Farmers' wives have their hands full, Mr. Henderson. And then—

COUNTY ATTORNEY: Yes—?

MRS. HALE (*looking about*): It never seemed a very cheerful place.

COUNTY ATTORNEY: No—it's not cheerful. I shouldn't say she had the homemaking instinct.

MRS. HALE: Well, I don't know as Wright had, either.

COUNTY ATTORNEY: You mean that they didn't get on very well?

MRS. HALE: No, I don't mean anything. But I don't think a place'd be any cheerfuller for John Wright's being in it.

COUNTY ATTORNEY: I'd like to talk more of that a little later. I want to get the lay of things upstairs now. (*He goes to the left, where three steps lead to a stair door.*)

SHERIFF: I suppose anything Mrs. Peters does'll be all right. She was to take in some clothes for her, you know, and a few little things. We left in such a hurry yesterday.

COUNTY ATTORNEY: Yes, but I would like to see what you take, Mrs. Peters, and keep an eye out for anything that might be of use to us.

MRS. PETERS: Yes, Mr. Henderson. (*The women listen to the men's steps on the stairs, then look about the kitchen.*)

MRS. HALE: I'd hate to have men coming into my kitchen, snooping around and criticising. (*She arranges the pans under sink which the LAWYER had shoved out of place.*)

MRS. PETERS: Of course it's no more than their duty.

MRS. HALE: Duty's all right, but I guess that deputy sheriff that came out to make the fire might have got a little of this on. (*Gives the roller towel a pull.*) Wish I'd thought of that sooner. Seems mean to talk about her for not having things slicked up when she had to come away in such a hurry.

MRS. PETERS (*who has gone to a small table in the left rear corner of the room, and lifted one end of a towel that covers a pan*): She had bread set. (*Stands still.*)

MRS. HALE (*eyes fixed on a loaf of bread beside the bread-box, which is on a low shelf at the other side of the room. Moves slowly toward it*): She was going to put this in there. (*Picks up loaf, then abruptly drops it. In a manner of returning to familiar things.*) It's a shame about her fruit. I wonder if it's all gone. (*Gets up on the chair and looks.*) I think there's some here that's all right, Mrs. Peters. Yes—here; (*holding it toward the window*) this is cherries, too. (*looking again*) I declare I believe that's the only one. (*Gets down, bottle in her hand. Goes to the sink and wipes it off on the outside.*) She'll feel awful bad after all her hard work in the hot weather. I remember the afternoon I put up my cherries last summer.

(*She puts the bottle on the big kitchen table, center of the room. With a sigh, is about to sit down in* the rocking-chair. Before she is seated realizes what chair it is; with a slow look at it, steps back. The chair which she has touched rocks back and forth.)

MRS. PETERS: Well, I must get those things from the front room closet, (She goes to the door at the right, but after looking into the other room, steps back.) You coming with me, Mrs. Hale? You could help me carry them.

(They go in the other room; reappear, MRS. PETERS carrying a dress and skirt, MRS. HALE following with a pair of shoes.)

MRS. PETERS: My, it's cold in there.

(She puts the clothes on the big table, and hurries to the stove.)

MRS. HALE (examining the skirt): Wright was close. I think maybe that's why she kept so much to herself. She didn't even belong to the Ladies Aid. I suppose she felt she couldn't do her part, and then you don't enjoy things when you feel shabby. She used to wear pretty clothes and be lively, when she was Minnie Foster, one of the town girls singing in the choir. But that—oh, that was thirty years ago. This all you was to take in?

MRS. PETERS: She said she wanted an apron. Funny thing to want, for there isn't much to get you dirty in jail, goodness knows. But I suppose just to make her feel more natural. She said they was in the top drawer in this cupboard. Yes, here. And then her little shawl that always hung behind the door. (Opens stair door and looks.) Yes, here it is.

(Quickly shuts door leading upstairs.)

MRS. HALE (abruptly moving toward her): Mrs. Peters?

MRS. PETERS: Yes, Mrs. Hale?

MRS. HALE: Do you think she did it?

MRS. PETERS (in a frightened voice): Oh, I don't know.

MRS. HALE: Well, I don't think she did. Asking for an apron and her little shawl. Worrying about her fruit.

MRS. PETERS (starts to speak, glances up, where footsteps are heard in the room above. In a low voice): Mr. Peters says it looks bad for her. Mr. Henderson is awful sarcastic in a speech and he'll make fun of her sayin' she didn't wake up.

MRS. HALE: Well, I guess John Wright didn't wake when they was slipping that rope under his neck.

MRS. PETERS: No, it's strange. It must have been done awful crafty and still. They say it was such a—funny way to kill a man, rigging it all up like that.

MRS. HALE: That's just what Mr. Hale said. There was a gun in the house. He says that's what he can't understand.

MRS. PETERS: Mr. Henderson said coming out that what was needed for the case was a motive; something to show anger, or—sudden feeling.

MRS. HALE (who is standing by the table): Well, I don't see any signs of anger around here. (She puts her hand on the dish towel which lies on the table, stands looking down at table, one half of which is clean, the other half messy.) It's wiped to here. (Makes a move as if to finish work, then turns and looks at loaf of bread outside the breadbox. Drops towel. In that voice of coming back to familiar things.) Wonder how they are finding things upstairs. I hope she had it a little more red-up[1] up there. You know, it seems kind of sneaking. Locking her up in town and then coming out here and trying to get her own house to turn against her!

MRS. PETERS: But Mrs. Hale, the law is the law.

MRS. HALE: I s'pose 'tis. (unbuttoning her coat) Better loosen up your things, Mrs. Peters. You won't feel them when you go out.

(MRS. PETERS takes off her fur tippet,[2] goes to hang it on hook at back of room, stands looking at the under part of the small corner table.)

MRS. PETERS: She was piecing a quilt. (She brings the large sewing basket and they look at the bright pieces.)

MRS. HALE: It's log cabin pattern. Pretty, isn't it? I wonder if she was goin' to quilt it or just knot it?

(Footsteps have been heard coming down the stairs. The SHERIFF enters followed by HALE and the COUNTY ATTORNEY.)

SHERIFF: They wonder if she was going to quilt it or just knot it! (The men laugh, the women look abashed.)

COUNTY ATTORNEY (rubbing his hands over the stove): Frank's fire didn't do much up there, did it? Well, let's go out to the barn and get that cleared up. (The men go outside.)

1. Tidy.
2. Shoulder cape.

MRS. HALE (*resentfully*): I don't know as there's anything so strange, our takin' up our time with little things while we're waiting for them to get the evidence. (*She sits down at the big table smoothing out a block with decision.*) I don't see as it's anything to laugh about.

MRS. PETERS (*apologetically*): Of course they've got awful important things on their minds.
(*Pulls up a chair and joins* MRS. HALE *at the table.*)

MRS. HALE (*examining another block*): Mrs. Peters, look at this one. Here, this is the one she was working on, and look at the sewing! All the rest of it has been so nice and even. And look at this! It's all over the place! Why, it looks as if she didn't know what she was about!
(*After she has said this they look at each other, then start to glance back at the door. After an instant* MRS. HALE *has pulled at a knot and ripped the sewing.*)

MRS. PETERS: Oh, what are you doing, Mrs. Hale?

MRS. HALE (*mildly*): Just pulling out a stitch or two that's not sewed very good. (*threading a needle*) Bad sewing always made me fidgety.

MRS. PETERS (*nervously*): I don't think we ought to touch things.

MRS. HALE: I'll just finish up this end. (*suddenly stopping and leaning forward*) Mrs. Peters?

MRS. PETERS: Yes, Mrs. Hale?

MRS. HALE: What do you suppose she was so nervous about?

MRS. PETERS: Oh—I don't know. I don't know as she was nervous. I sometimes sew awful queer when I'm just tired. (MRS. HALE *starts to say something, looks at* MRS. PETERS, *then goes on sewing*) Well I must get these things wrapped up. They may be through sooner than we think. (*putting apron and other things together*) I wonder where I can find a piece of paper, and string.

MRS. HALE: In that cupboard, maybe.

MRS. PETERS (*looking in cupboard*): Why, here's a bird-cage. (*holds it up*) Did she have a bird, Mrs. Hale?

MRS. HALE: Why, I don't know whether she did or not—I've not been here for so long. There was a man around last year selling canaries cheap, but I don't know as she took one; maybe she did. She used to sing real pretty herself.

MRS. PETERS (*glancing around*): Seems funny to think of a bird here. But she must have had one, or why would she have a cage? I wonder what happened to it.

MRS. HALE: I s'pose maybe the cat got it.

MRS. PETERS: No, she didn't have a cat. She's got that feeling some people have about cats—being afraid of them. My cat got in her room and she was real upset and asked me to take it out.

MRS. HALE: My sister Bessie was like that. Queer, ain't it?

MRS. PETERS (*examining the cage*): Why, look at this door. It's broke. One hinge is pulled apart.

MRS. HALE (*looking too*): Looks as if someone must have been rough with it.

MRS. PETERS: Why, yes.
(*She brings the cage forward and puts it on the table.*)

MRS. HALE: I wish if they're going to find any evidence they'd be about it. I don't like this place.

MRS. PETERS: But I'm awful glad you came with me, Mrs. Hale. It would be lonesome for me sitting here alone.

MRS. HALE: It would, wouldn't it? (*dropping her sewing*) But I tell you what I do wish, Mrs. Peters. I wish I had come over sometimes when *she* was here. I—(*looking around the room*)—wish I had.

MRS. PETERS: But of course you were awful busy, Mrs. Hale—your house and your children.

MRS. HALE: I could've come. I stayed away because it weren't cheerful—and that's why I ought to have come. I—I've never liked this place. Maybe because it's down in a hollow and you don't see the road. I dunno what it is, but it's a lonesome place and always was. I wish I had come over to see Minnie Foster sometimes. I can see now—(*shakes her head*)

MRS. PETERS: Well, you mustn't reproach yourself, Mrs. Hale. Somehow we just don't see how it is with other folks until—something comes up.

MRS. HALE: Not having children makes less work—but it makes a quiet house, and Wright out to work all day, and no company when he did come in. Did you know John Wright, Mrs. Peters?

MRS. PETERS: Not to know him; I've seen him in town. They say he was a good man.

MRS. HALE: Yes—good; he didn't drink, and kept his word as well as most, I guess, and paid his debts. But he was a hard man, Mrs. Peters. Just to pass the time of day with him—(*shivers*) Like a raw wind that gets to the bone. (*pauses, her eye falling on the cage*) I should think she would 'a wanted a bird. But what do you suppose went with it?

MRS. PETERS: I don't know, unless it got sick and died. (*She reaches over and swings the broken door, swings it again, both women watch it.*)

MRS. HALE: You weren't raised round here, were you? (MRS. PETERS *shakes her head*) You didn't know—her?

MRS. PETERS: Not till they brought her yesterday.

MRS. HALE: She—come to think of it, she was kind of like a bird herself—real sweet and pretty, but kind of timid and—fluttery. How—she—did—change. (*silence; then as if struck by a happy thought and relieved to get back to everyday things*) Tell you what, Mrs. Peters, why don't you take the quilt in with you? It might take up her mind.

MRS. PETERS: Why, I think that's a real nice idea, Mrs. Hale. There couldn't possibly be any objection to it, could there? Now, just what would I take? I wonder if her patches are in here—and her things.

(*They look in the sewing basket.*)

MRS. HALE: Here's some red. I expect this has got sewing things in it. (*brings out a fancy box*) What a pretty box. Looks like something somebody would give you. Maybe her scissors are in here. (*Opens box. Suddenly puts her hand to her nose.*) Why—(MRS. PETERS *bends nearer, then turns her face away.*) There's something wrapped up in this piece of silk.

MRS. PETERS: Why, this isn't her scissors.

MRS. HALE (*lifting the silk*): Oh, Mrs. Peters—it's—
(MRS. PETERS *bends closer.*)

MRS. PETERS: It's the bird.

MRS. HALE (*jumping up*): But, Mrs. Peters—look at it! It's neck! Look at its neck! It's all—other side *to.*

MRS. PETERS: Somebody—wrung—its—neck.
(*Their eyes meet. A look of growing comprehension, of horror. Steps are heard outside.* MRS. HALE *slips box under quilt pieces, and sinks into her chair. Enter* SHERIFF *and* COUNTY ATTORNEY. MRS. PETERS *rises.*)

COUNTY ATTORNEY (*as one turning from serious things to little pleasantries*): Well ladies, have you decided whether she was going to quilt it or knot it?

MRS. PETERS: We think she was going to—knot it.

COUNTY ATTORNEY: Well, that's interesting, I'm sure. (*seeing the birdcage*) Has the bird flown?

MRS. HALE (*putting more quilt pieces over the box*): We think the—cat got it.

COUNTY ATTORNEY (*preoccupied*): Is there a cat?
(MRS. HALE *glances in a quick covert way at* MRS. PETERS.)

MRS. PETERS: Well, not now. They're superstitious, you know. They leave.

COUNTY ATTORNEY (*to* SHERIFF PETERS, *continuing an interrupted conversation*): No sign at all of anyone having come from the outside. Their own rope. Now let's go up again and go over it piece by piece. (*they start upstairs*) It would have to have been someone who knew just the—
(MRS. PETERS *sits down. The two women sit there not looking at one another, but as if peering into something and at the same time holding back. When they talk now it is in the manner of feeling their way over strange ground, as if afraid of what they are saying, but as if they can not help saying it.*)

MRS. HALE: She liked the bird. She was going to bury it in that pretty box.

MRS. PETERS (*in a whisper*): When I was a girl—my kitten—there was a boy took a hatchet, and before my eyes—and before I could get there—(*covers her face an instant*) If they hadn't held me back I would have—(*catches herself, looks upstairs where steps are heard, falters weakly*)—hurt him.

MRS. HALE (*with a slow look around her*): I wonder how it would seem never to have had any children around. (*pause*) No, Wright wouldn't like the bird—a thing that sang. She used to sing. He killed that, too.

MRS. PETERS (*moving uneasily*): We don't know who killed the bird.

MRS. HALE: I knew John Wright.

MRS. PETERS: It was an awful thing was done in this house that night, Mrs. Hale. Killing a man while he slept, slipping a rope around his neck that choked the life out of him.

MRS. HALE: His neck. Choked the life out of him.
(*Her hand goes out and rests on the bird-cage.*)

MRS. PETERS (*with rising voice*): We don't know who killed him. We don't *know.*

MRS. HALE (*her own feeling not interrupted*): If there'd been years and years of nothing, then a bird to sing to you, it would be awful—still, after the bird was still.

MRS. PETERS (*something within her speaking*): I know what stillness is. When we homesteaded in

Dakota, and my first baby died—after he was two years old, and me with no other then—

MRS. HALE (*moving*): How soon do you suppose they'll be through, looking for the evidence?

MRS. PETERS: I know what stillness is. (*pulling herself back*) The law has got to punish crime, Mrs. Hale.

MRS. HALE (*not as if answering that*): I wish you'd seen Minnie Foster when she wore a white dress with blue ribbons and stood up there in the choir and sang. (*a look around the room*) Oh, I *wish* I'd come over here once in a while! That was a crime! That was a crime! Who's going to punish that?

MRS. PETERS (*looking upstairs*): We mustn't—take on.

MRS. HALE: I might have known she needed help! I know how things can be—for women. I tell you, it's queer, Mrs. Peters. We live close together and we live far apart. We all go through the same things—it's all just a different kind of the same thing. (*brushes her eyes, noticing the bottle of fruit, reaches out for it*) If I was you, I wouldn't tell her her fruit was gone. Tell her it *ain't.* Tell her it's all right. Take this in to prove it to her. She—she may never know whether it was broke or not.

MRS. PETERS (*takes the bottle, looks about for something to wrap it in; takes petticoat from the clothes brought from the other room, very nervously begins winding this around the bottle. In a false voice*): My, it's a good thing the men couldn't hear us. Wouldn't they just laugh! Getting all stirred up over a little thing like a—dead canary. As if that could have anything to do with—with—wouldn't they *laugh!*

(*The men are heard coming down stairs.*)

MRS. HALE (*under her breath*): Maybe they would—maybe they wouldn't.

COUNTY ATTORNEY: No, Peters, it's all perfectly clear except a reason for doing it. But you know juries when it comes to women. If there was some definite thing. Something to show—something to make a story about—a thing that would connect up with this strange way of doing it—

(*The women's eyes meet for an instant. Enter* HALE *from outer door.*)

HALE: Well, I've got the team around. Pretty cold out there.

COUNTY ATTORNEY: I'm going to stay here a while by myself. (*to the* SHERIFF) You can send Frank out for me, can't you? I want to go over everything. I'm not satisfied that we can't do better.

SHERIFF: Do you want to see what Mrs. Peters is going to take in?

(*The* LAWYER *goes to the table, picks up the apron, laughs.*)

COUNTY ATTORNEY: Oh, I guess they're not very dangerous things the ladies have picked out. (*Moves a few things about, disturbing the quilt pieces which cover the box. Steps back.*) No, Mrs. Peters doesn't need supervising. For that matter, a sheriff's wife is married to the law. Ever think of it that way, Mrs. Peters?

MRS. PETERS: Not—just that way.

SHERIFF (*chuckling*): Married to the law. (*moves toward the other room*) I just want you to come in here a minute, George. We ought to take a look at these windows.

COUNTY ATTORNEY (*scoffingly*): Oh, windows!

SHERIFF: We'll be right out, Mr. Hale.

(HALE *goes outside. The* SHERIFF *follows the* COUNTY ATTORNEY *into the other room. Then* MRS. HALE *rises, hands tight together, looking intensely at* MRS. PETERS, *whose eyes make a slow turn, finally meeting* MRS. HALE's. *A moment* MRS. HALE *holds her, then her own eyes point the way to where the box is concealed. Suddenly* MRS. PETERS *throws back quilt pieces and tries to put the box in the bag she is wearing. It is too big. She opens box, starts to take bird out, cannot touch it, goes to pieces, stands there helpless. Sound of a knob turning in the other room.* MRS. HALE *snatches the box and puts it in the pocket of her big coat. Enter* COUNTY ATTORNEY *and* SHERIFF.)

COUNTY ATTORNEY (*facetiously*): Well, Henry, at least we found out that she was not going to quilt it. She was going to—what is it you call it, ladies?

MRS. HALE (*her hand against her pocket*): We call it—knot it, Mr. Henderson.

CURTAIN

Introduction to *Color Struck*

WHEN THE PLAY WAS NEW

Zora Neale Hurston wrote *Color Struck* (1925–1926), as well as her other plays, as part of a movement of theatrical and literary activity usually identified as the Harlem Renaissance. This movement was very active in the 1910s and 1920s and launched many important voices such as Langston Hughes, Marita Bonner, and Georgia Douglas Johnson, all of whom wrote plays as well as other forms. Hurston probably had little hope of professional productions of her plays, but she certainly believed that her plays in exploration and celebration of the African American experience in the United States would find a reading audience. Indeed, a first version of *Color Struck* was published in the African American periodical *Opportunity* in 1925, and a second version in 1926. Hurston found both reading and theatre audiences, but productions were few in her lifetime, and usually limited to amateur productions in little theatres and colleges.

THE PLAYWRIGHT

Zora Neale Hurston (1891–1960) emerged as one of the most influential women of the Harlem Renaissance. Born in Alabama, she grew up in Florida, and was educated in Baltimore, at Howard University in Washington, D.C., and at Barnard College in New York, where she received a B. A. in anthropology. She studied and wrote about African American folklore, drawing on experiences and travels through the south and her work at Barnard. Her literary works include one-act and full-length plays, musical revues, short stories, and essays. In addition she created nonfiction and novels, most notably *Their Eyes Were Watching God* (1937). By 1924, Hurston was living and writing in Harlem and had stories and plays published in African American periodicals such as *Opportunity*

and *Crisis*. She created sketches for and performed in a Broadway revue entitled *Fast and Furious* in 1931 at the New Yorker Theatre. The same year she collaborated with Langston Hughes on the play *Mule Bone: A Comedy of Negro Life* and a short-lived experimental literary journal entitled *Fire!*, which included *Color Struck*. Unfortunately Hurston and Hughes quarreled bitterly, resulting in *Mule Bone* being shelved until long after the deaths of both writers. It was finally revived on Broadway in 1991 and subsequently published. Another major musical play by Hurston in collaboration with Dorothy Waring, *Polk County* (c. 1944), was rediscovered in the Library of Congress in 1997 and has had numerous professional productions since. Although well known in the 1920s and 1930s, Hurston fell into obscurity thereafter until a revival of interest in her work in the 1980s. The U.S. Postal Service commemorated her life and work with a stamp in 2003.

GENRE, STRUCTURE, AND STYLE

Although unusual in subject matter and distinctive in language, *Color Struck* is typical of many American plays of the early twentieth century in that it avoids a specific generic label by having a very serious intent, but a decidedly mixed tone. The material is ultimately sad, ending with the death of a sick child, but it is not a tragedy. It is a study in racial obsession, jealousy, and missed opportunities. The center of the play's action is a love triangle involving John, "a light brown-skinned man," Emmaline, "a black woman," and Effie, "a mulatto girl." Despite the dramatic conflict, the play often features humor, especially in the first three scenes.

Although technically a one-act due to its overall length, *Color Struck* is presented in four scenes with four different interior settings, including a "Jim Crow" segregated railway car, a dance hall, an outer compartment of the hall, and a one-room shack. There is also a passage of seventeen years between scenes three and four, necessitating significant makeup and costume changes. The cast is also large for a one-act: seven principal characters and many extras, especially for the railway travel and the cake walk. Consequently, the production needs are far greater than a typical one-act play. Another factor that probably limited production when the play was new was the racially mixed cast. A white doctor appears near the end of the play.

IMPORTANT ELEMENTS OF CONTENT

Color Struck is a study in manners, courtship, jealousy, and color distinctions among African Americans at the time. Much is essentially universal about the human condition, but some problems are quite distinctive in terms of geographical location and racial consciousness. Consequently, it would be nearly impossible to reconceive this play in an earlier or later period, anywhere other than the American south, or played by anyone other than an African American cast. Like a historical artifact, this play is locked into its moment. In its time it was identified as a "folk" play.

THE PLAY IN REVIVAL

Despite the inherent theatricality, vivid conflict, and strongly delineated characters in *Color Struck,* we are unable to uncover any evidence of this play being produced professionally, but it has probably been produced by amateur groups. The most important revival audience for *Color Struck* is apparently an ongoing reading audience. The play was probably not intended as a closet play, but that seems to be its essential fate.

SPECIAL FEATURE

Aside from the principal dramatic activity involving impassioned attraction, sexual flirtation, gender conflict, and an important racial issue of its time, *Color Struck* focuses on and serves as a wonderful evocation of a social activity often misunderstood or barely recognized in later periods. The cake walk activity alone makes the play an important historical document, laying out the procedure and activity of the cake walk as practiced in the American south as both a contest and a social event. The usual braggadocio and hyperbole associated with competitions of all sorts underscores much of the pre-contest banter, and helps the audience understand the importance of winning to the characters involved. There are no individual winners, only a winning male–female couple as selected by judges—not unlike modern ice-skating pairs. The couple's style is just as important as skill. More ominous than this often attractive and comic activity, however, is the prejudice and stereotyping of some of the characters in terms of varying degrees of blackness and what that signifies to them. Ultimately, the consequences of colorism are awful.

FURTHER READING ABOUT THE PLAY, PLAYWRIGHT, AND CONTEXT

For additional material on Hurston's life and times, see Zora Neale Hurston, *Dust Tracks on the Road* (autobiography); Elizabeth Brown-Guillory, *Their Place on the Stage*; David Krasner, *A Beautiful Pageant: African American Theatre, Drama, and Performance in the Harlem Renaissance*; and Errol Hill and James Hatch, *History of African American Theatre.*

For other plays by Hurston, see Kathy A. Perkins, *Black Female Playwrights: An Anthology of Plays Before 1950,* and Jennifer Burton, *Zora Neale Hurston, Eulalie Spence, Marita Bonner, and Others.*

For analysis of the work of Hurston, see David Krasner, "Migration, Fragmentation, and Identity: Zora Neale Hurston's *Color Struck* and the Geography of the Harlem Renaissance," *Theatre Journal* 53, 4 (December 2001): 533–550.

Color Struck: A Play in Four Scenes

By Zora Neale Hurston

PERSONS

JOHN   a light brown-skinned man

EMMALINE   a black woman

WESLEY   a boy who plays an accordion

EMMALINE'S DAUGHTER   a very white girl

EFFIE   a mulatto girl

A RAILWAY CONDUCTOR

A DOCTOR

SEVERAL WHO PLAY MOUTH ORGANS, GUITARS,
    BANJOS.

DANCERS, PASSENGERS, ETC.

Time: Twenty years ago and present.

Place: A Southern City.

Setting: Early night. The inside of a "Jim Crow" railway coach. The car is parallel to the footlights. The seats on the down stage side of the coach are omitted. There are the luggage racks above the seats. The windows are all open. There are exits in each end of the car—right and left.

Action: Before the curtain goes up there is the sound of a locomotive whistle and a stopping engine, loud laughter, many people speaking at once, good-natured shrieks, strumming of stringed instruments, etc. The ascending curtain discovers a happy lot of Negroes boarding the train dressed in the gaudy, tawdry best of 1900. They are mostly in couples—each couple bearing a covered-over market basket which the men hastily deposit in the racks as they scramble for seats. There is a little friendly pushing and shoving. One pair just miss a seat three times, much to the enjoyment of the crowd. Many "plug" silk hats are in evidence, also sun flowers in button holes. The women are showily dressed in the manner of the time, and quite conscious of their finery. A few seats remain unoccupied.

Enter EFFIE *(left) above, with a basket.*

ONE OF THE MEN *(standing, lifting his "plug" in a grand manner)*: Howdy do, Miss Effie, you'se lookin' jes lak a rose. (EFFIE *blushes and is confused. She looks up and down for a seat.)* Fack is, if you wuzn't walkin' long, ah'd think you *wuz* a rose—*(he looks timidly behind her and the others laugh).* Looka here, where's Sam at?

EFFIE *(tossing her head haughtily)*: I don't know an' I don't keer.

THE MAN *(visibly relieved)*: Then lemme scorch you to a seat. *(He takes her basket and leads her to a seat center of the car, puts the basket in the rack and seats himself beside her with his hat at a rakish angle.)*

MAN *(sliding his arm along the back of the seat)*: How come Sam ain't heah—y'll on a bust?

EFFIE *(angrily)*: A man dat don't buy me nothin tuh put in *mah* basket, ain't goin' wid *me* tuh no cake walk. *(The hand on the seat touches her shoulder and she thrusts it away)* Take yo' arms from 'round me, Dinky! Gwan hug yo' Ada!

MAN *(in mock indignation)*: Do you think I'd look at Ada when Ah got a chance tuh be wid you? Ah always wuz sweet on you, but you let ole Mullet-head Sam cut me out.

ANOTHER MAN *(with head out of the window)*: Just look at de darkies coming! *(With head inside coach.)* Hey, Dinky! Heah come Ada wid a great big basket.

*(*DINKY *jumps up from beside* EFFIE *and rushes to exit right. In a moment they re-enter and take a seat near entrance. Everyone in coach laughs.* DINKY'S *girl turns and calls back to* EFFIE.)*

GIRL: Where's Sam, Effie?

EFFIE: Lawd knows, Ada.

GIRL: Lawd a mussy! Who you gointer walk de cake wid?

EFFIE: Nobody, Ah reckon. John and Emma gointer win it nohow. They's the bestest cake-walkers in dis state.

ADA: You'se better than Emma any day in de week. Cose Sam cain't walk lake John. *(She stands up and scans the coach.)* Looka heah, ain't John an' Emma going? They ain't on heah!

(The locomotive bell begins to ring.)

EFFIE: Mah Gawd, s'pose dey got left!

MAN (*with head out of window*): Heah they come, nip and tuck—whoo-ee! They'se gonna make it! (*He waves excitedly.*) Come on Jawn! (*Everybody crowds the windows, encouraging them by gesture and calls. As the whistle blows twice, and the train begins to move, they enter panting and laughing at left. The only seat left is the one directly in front of* EFFIE.)

DINKY (*standing*): Don't y'all skeer us no mo' lake dat! There couldn't be no cake walk thout y'all. Dem shad-mouf St. Augustine coons would win dat cake and we would have tuh kill 'em all bodaciously.

JOHN: It was Emmaline nearly made us get left. She says I wuz smiling at Effie on the street car and she had to get off and wait for another one.

EMMA (*removing the hatpins from her hat, turns furiously upon him*): You wuz grinning at her and she wuz grinning back jes lake a ole chessy cat!

JOHN (*positively*): I wuzn't.

EMMA (*about to place her hat in rack*): You wuz. I seen you looking jes lake a possum.

JOHN: I wuzn't. I never gits a chance tuh smile at nobody—you won't let me.

EMMA: Jes the same every time you sees a yaller face, you *takes* a chance. (*They sit down in peeved silence for a moment.*)

DINKY: Ada, les we all sample de basket. I bet you got huckleberry pie.

ADA: No I aint, I got peach an' tater pies, but we aint gonna tetch a thing tell we gits tuh de hall.

DINKY (*mock alarm*): Naw, don't do dat! It's all right tuh save the fried chicken, but pies is *always* et on trains.

ADA: Aw shet up! (*He struggles with her for a kiss. She slaps him but finally yields.*)

JOHN (*looking behind him*): Hellow, Effie, where's Sam?

EFFIE: Deed, I don't know.

JOHN: Y'all on a bust?

EMMA: None ah yo' bizness, you got enough tuh mind yo'own self. Turn 'round!
(*She puts up a pouting mouth and he snatches a kiss. She laughs just as he kisses her again and there is a resounding smack which causes the crowd to laugh. And cries of "Oh you kid!" "Salty dog!"*)

(*Enter conductor left calling tickets cheerfully and laughing at the general merriment.*)

CONDUCTOR: I hope somebody from Jacksonville wins this cake.

JOHN: You live in the "Big Jack"?

CONDUCTOR: Sure do. And I wanta taste a piece of that cake on the way back tonight.

JOHN: Jes rest easy—them Augustiners ain't gonna smell it. (*Turns to* EMMA.) Is they, baby?

EMMA: Not if Ah kin help it.
(*Somebody with a guitar sings:* "Ho babe, mah honey taint no lie.")
(*The* CONDUCTOR *takes up tickets, passes on and exits right.*)

WESLEY: Look heah, you cake walkers—y'all oughter git up and limber up yo' joints. I heard them folks over to St. Augustine been oiling up wid goose-grease, and over to Ocala they been rubbing down in snake oil.

A WOMAN'S VOICE: You better shut up, Wesley, you just joined de church last month. Somebody's going to tell the pastor on you.

WESLEY: Tell it, tell it, take it up and smell it. Come on out you John and Emma and Effie, and limber up.

JOHN: Naw, we don't wanta do our walking steps—nobody won't wanta see them when we step out at the hall. But we kin do something else just to warm ourselves up.
(*WESLEY* begins to play "Goo Goo Eyes" on his accordion, the other instruments come in one by one and *JOHN* and *EMMA* step into the aisle and "parade" up and down the aisle—*EMMA* holding up her skirt, showing the lace on her petticoats. They two-step back to their seat amid much applause.*)

WESLEY: Come on out, Effie! Sam aint heah so you got to hold up his side too. Step on out. (*There is a murmur of applause as she steps into the aisle.* WESLEY *strikes up "I'm gointer live anyhow till I die." It is played quite spiritedly as* EFFIE *swings into the pas-me-la*—)

WESLEY (*in ecstasy*): Hot stuff I reckon! Hot stuff I reckon! (*The musicians are stamping. Great enthusiasm. Some clap time with hands and feet. She hurls herself into a modified Hoochy Koochy, and finishes up with an ecstatic yell.*)
(*There is a babble of talk and laughter and exultation.*)

JOHN (*applauding loudly*): If dat Effie can't step nobody can.

EMMA: Course you'd say so cause it's her. Everything she do is pretty to you.

JOHN (*caressing her*): Now don't say that, Honey. Dancing is dancing no matter who is doing it. But nobody can hold a candle to you in nothing.

(*Some men are heard tuning up—getting pitch to sing. Four of them crowd together in one seat and begin the chorus of "Daisies Won't Tell." JOHN and EMMA grow quite affectionate.*)

JOHN (*kisses her*): Emma, what makes you always picking a fuss with me over some yaller girl. What makes you so jealous, nohow? I don't do nothing.

(*She clings to him, but he turns slightly away. The train whistle blows, there is a slackening of speed. Passengers begin to take down baskets from their racks.*)

EMMA: John! John, don't you want me to love you, honey?

JOHN (*turns and kisses her slowly*): Yes, I want you to love me, you know I do. But I don't like to be accused o' ever light colored girl in the world. It hurts my feeling. I don't want to be jealous like you are.

(*Enter at right* CONDUCTOR, *crying "St. Augustine, St. Augustine." He exits left. The crowd has congregated at the two exits, pushing good-naturedly and joking. All except* JOHN *and* EMMA. *They are still seated with their arms about each other.*)

EMMA (*sadly*): Then you don't want my love, John, cause I can't help mahself from being jealous. I loves you so hard, John, and jealous love is the only kind I got.

(JOHN *kisses her very feelingly.*)

EMMA: Just for myself alone is the only way I knows how to love.

(*They are standing in the aisle with their arms about each other as the curtain falls.*)

SCENE II

Setting: A weather-board hall. A large room with the joists bare. The place has been divided by a curtain of sheets stretched and a rope across from left to right. From behind the curtain there are occasional sounds of laughter, a note or two on a stringed instrument or accordion. General stir. That is the dance hall. The front is the ante-room where the refreshments are being served. A "plank" seat runs all around the hall, along the walls. The lights are kerosene lamps with reflectors. They are fixed to the wall. The lunch-baskets are under the seat. There is a table on either side upstage with a woman behind each. At one, ice cream is sold, at the other, roasted peanuts and large red-and-white sticks of peppermint candy.

People come in by twos and three, laughing, joking, horse-plays, gauchily flowered dresses, small waists, bulging hips and busts, hats worn far back on the head, etc. People from Ocala greet others from Palatka, Jacksonville, St. Augustine, etc.

Some find seats in the ante-room, others pass on into the main hall.

Enter the Jacksonville delegation, laughing, pushing proudly.

DINKY: Here we is, folks—here we *is*. Gointer take dat cake on back tuh Jacksonville where it belongs.

MAN: Gwan! Whut wid you mullet-head Jacksonville Coons know whut to do wid a cake. It's gointer stay right here in Augustine where de good cake walkers grow.

DINKY: Taint no "Walkers" never walked till John and Emmaline prance out—you mighty come a tootin'.

(*Great laughing and joshing as more people come in.* JOHN *and* EMMA *are encouraged, urged on to win.*)

EMMA: Let's we git a seat, John, and set down.

JOHN: Sho will—nice one right over there.

(*They push over to wall seat, place basket underneath, and sit. Newcomers shake hands with them and urge them on to win.*)

(*Enter* JOE CLARKE *and a small group. He is a rotund, expansive man with a liberal watch chain and charm.*)

DINKY (*slapping* CLARKE *on the back*): If you don't go 'way from here! Lawdy, if it aint Joe.

CLARKE (*jovially*): Ah thought you had done forgot us people in Eatonville since you been living up here in Jacksonville.

DINKY: Course Ah aint. (*Turning.*) Looka heah folks! Joe Clarke oughta be made chairman uh dis meetin'—Ah mean Past Great-Grand Master of Ceremonies, him being the onliest mayor of de onliest colored town in de state.

GENERAL CHORUS: Yeah, let him be—thass fine, etc.

DINKY (*setting his hat at a new angle and throwing out his chest*): And *Ah'll* scorch him to the platform. Ahem!

(*Sprinkling of laughter as* JOE CLARKE *is escorted into next room by* DINKY.)

(*The musicians are arriving one by one during this time. A guitar, accordion, mouth organ, banjo, etc. Soon there is a rapping for order heard inside and the voice of* JOE CLARKE.)

JOE CLARKE: Git yo' partners one an' all for de gran' march! Git yo' partners, gent-mens!

A MAN (*drawing basket from under bench*): Let's we all eat first.

(JOHN *and* EMMA *go buy ice-cream. They coquettishly eat from each other's spoons.* OLD MAN LIZZIMORE *crosses to* EFFIE *and removes his hat and bows with a great flourish.*)

LIZZIMORE: Sam ain't here t'night, is he, Effie.

EFFIE (*embarrassed*): Naw suh, he aint.

LIZZ: Well, you like chicken? (*Extends arm to her.*) Take a wing!

(*He struts her up to the table amid the laughter of the house. He wears no collar.*)

JOHN (*squeezes* EMMA'S *hand*): You certainly is a ever loving mamma—when you aint mad.

EMMA (*smiles sheepishly*): You oughtn't to make me mad then.

JOHN: Ah don't make you! You makes yo'self mad, den blame it on me. Ah keep on tellin' you Ah don't love nobody but you. Ah knows heaps uh half-white girls Ah could git ef Ah wanted to. But (*he squeezes her hard again*) Ah jus' wants *you!* You know what they say! De darker de berry, de sweeter de taste!

EMMA (*pretending to pout*): Oh, you tries to run over me an' keep it under de cover, but Ah won't let yuh. (*Both laugh.*) Les' we eat our basket!

JOHN: All right. (*He pulls the basket out and she removes the table cloth. They set the basket on their knees and begin to eat fried chicken.*)

MALE VOICE: Les' everybody eat—motion's done carried. (*Everybody begins to open baskets. All have fried chicken. Very good humor prevails. Delicacies are swapped from one basket to the other.* JOHN *and* EMMA *offer the man next them some sup-*

per. *He takes a chicken leg.* EFFIE *crosses to* JOHN *and* EMMA *with two pieces of pie on a plate.*)

EFFIE: Y'll have a piece uh mah blueberry pie—it's might nice! (*She proffers it with a timid smile to* EMMA *who "freezes" up instantly.*)

EMMA: Naw! We don't want no pie. We got cocoanut layer-cake.

JOHN: Ah—Ah think ah'd choose a piece uh pie, Effie. (*He takes it.*) Will you set down an' have a snack wid us? (*He slides over to make room.*)

EFFIE (*nervously*): Ah, naw, Ah got to run on back to mah basket, but ah thought maybe y'll mout' want tuh taste mah pie. (*She turns to go.*)

JOHN: Thank you, Effie. It's mighty good, too. (*He eats it.* EFFIE *crosses to her seat.* EMMA *glares at her for a minute, then turns disgustedly away from the basket.* JOHN *catches her shoulder and faces her around.*)

JOHN (*pleadingly*): Honey, be nice. Don't act lak dat!

EMMA (*jerking free*): Naw, you done ruint mah appetite now, carryin' on wid dat punkin-colored ole gal.

JOHN: Whut kin Ah do? If you had a acted polite Ah wouldn't a had nothin' to say.

EMMA: Naw, youse jus' hog-wile ovah her cause she's half-white! No matter whut Ah say, you keep carryin' on wid her. Act polite? Naw Ah aint gonna be deceitful an' bust mah gizzard fuh nobody! Let her keep her dirty ole pie ovah there where she is!

JOHN (*looking around to see if they are overheard*): Sh-sh! Honey, you mustn't talk so loud.

EMMA (*louder*): Ah-Ah aint gonna bite mah tongue! If she don't like it she can lump it. Mah back is broad—(JOHN *tries to cover her mouth with his hand*). She calls herself a big cigar, but *I* kin smoke her!

(*The people are laughing and talking for the most part and pay no attention.* EFFIE *is laughing and talking to those around her and does not hear the tirade. The eating is over and everyone is going behind the curtain.* JOHN *and* EMMA *put away their basket like the others, and sit glum. Voice of Master-of-ceremonies can be heard from beyond curtain announcing the pas-me-la contest. The contestants, mostly girls, take the floor. There is no music except the clapping of hands and the shouts of "Parse-me-lah" in time with the hand-clapping. At the end Master, announces winner. Shadows seen on curtain.*)

MASTER: Mathilda Clarke is winner—if she will step forward she will receive a beautiful wook fascinator. (*The girl goes up and receives it with great hand-clapping and good humor.*) And now since the roosters is crowin' foah midnight, an' most of us got to git up an' go to work tomorrow, The Great Cake Walk will begin. Ah wants de floor cleared, cause de representatives of de several cities will be announced an' we wants 'em to take de floor as their names is called. Den we wants 'em to do a gran' promenade roun' de hall. An' they will then commence to walk fuh de biggest cake ever baked in dis state. Ten dozen eggs—ten pounds of flour—ten pounds of butter, and so on and so forth. Now then—(*he strikes a pose*) for St. Augustine—Miss Lucy Taylor, Mr. Ned Coles.
(*They step out amid applause and stand before stage.*)
For Daytona—
Miss Janie Bradley, Enoch Nixon
(*Same business.*)
For Ocala—
Miss Docia Boger, Mr. Oscar Clarke
(*Same business.*)
For Palatka—
Miss Maggie Lemmons, Mr. Senator Lewis
(*Same business.*)
And for Jacksonville the most popular "walkers" in de state—
Miss Emmaline Beazeley, Mr. John Turner.
(*Tremendous applause.* JOHN *rises and offers his arm grandiloquently to* EMMA.)

EMMA (*pleadingly, and clutching his coat*): John let's we all don't go in there with all them. Let's we all go on home.

JOHN (*amazed*): Why, Emma?

EMMA: Cause, cause all them girls is going to pulling and hauling on you, and—

JOHN (*impatiently*): Shucks! Come on. Don't you hear the people clapping for us and calling our names? Come on!
(*He tries to pull her up—she tries to drag him back.*)
Come on, Emma! Taint no sense in your acting like this. The band is playing for us. Hear 'em? (*He moves feet in a dance step.*)

EMMA: Naw, John, Ah'm skeered. I loves you—I—.
(*He tries to break away from her. She is holding on fiercely.*)

JOHN: I got to go! I been practising almost a year—I—we done come all the way down here. I can walk the cake, Emma—we got to—I got to go in! (*He looks into her face and sees her tremendous fear.*) What you skeered about?

EMMA (*hopefully*): You won't go it—You'll come on go home with me all by ourselves. Come on John. I can't, I just can't go in there and see all them girls—Effie hanging after you—.

JOHN: I got to go in—(*he removes her hand from his coat*)—whether you come with me or not.

EMMA: Oh—them yaller wenches! How I hate 'em! They gets everything they wants—.

VOICE INSIDE: We are waiting for the couple from Jacksonville—Jacksonville! Where is the couple from—.
(WESLEY *parts the curtain and looks out.*)

WESLEY: Here they is out here spooning! You all can't even hear your names called. Come on John and Emma.

JOHN: Coming. (*He dashes inside.* WESLEY *stands looking at* EMMA *in surprise.*)

WESLEY: What's the matter, Emma? You and John spatting again? (*He goes back inside.*)

EMMA (*calmly bitter*): He went and left me. If we is spatting we done had our last one. (*She stands and clenches her fists.*) Ah, mah God! He's in there with her—Oh, them half whites, they gets everything, they gets everything everybody else wants! The men, the jobs—everything! The whole world is got a sign on it. Wanted: Light colored. Us blacks was made for cobble stones. (*She muffles a cry and sinks limp upon the seat.*)

VOICE INSIDE: Miss Effie Jones will walk for Jacksonville with Mr. John Turner in place of Miss Emmaline Beazeley.

SCENE III

DANCE HALL

EMMA *springs to her feet and flings the curtains wide open. She stands staring at the gay scene for a moment defiantly, then creeps over to a seat along the wall and shrinks into the spanish Moss, motionless.*

Dance hall decorated with palmetto leaves and Spanish Moss—a flag or two. Orchestra consists of guitar, mandolin, banjo, accordion, church organ and drum.

MASTER (*on platform*): Couples take yo' places! When de music starts, gentlemen parade yo' ladies once round de hall, den de walk begins. (*The music begins. Four men come out from behind the platform bearing a huge chocolate cake. The couples are "prancing" in their tracks. The men lead off the procession with the cake—the contestants make a grand slam around the hall.*)

MASTER: Couples to de floor! Stan' back, ladies an' gentlemen—give 'em plenty room.
(*Music changes to "Way Down in Georgia." Orchestra sings.* EFFIE *takes the arm that* JOHN *offers her and they parade to the other end of the hall. She takes her place.* JOHN *goes back upstage to the platform, takes off his silk hat in a graceful sweep as he bows deeply to* EFFIE. *She lifts her skirts and curtsies to the floor. Both smile broadly. They advance toward each other, meet midway, then, arm in arm, begin to "strut."* JOHN *falters as he faces her, but recovers promptly and is perfection in his style. (Seven to nine minutes to curtain. Fervor of spectators grows until all are taking part in some way—either hand-clapping or singing the words. At curtain they have reached frenzy.)*

QUICK CURTAIN

(*It stays down a few seconds to indicate ending of contest and goes up again on* JOHN *and* EFFIE *being declared winners by judges.*)

MASTER (*on platform, with* JOHN *and* EFFIE *on the floor before him*): By unanimous decision de cake goes to de couple from Jacksonville!
(*Great enthusiasm. The cake is set down in the center of the floor and the winning couple parade around it arm in arm.* JOHN *and* EFFIE *circle the cake happily and triumphantly. The other contestants, and then the entire assembly fall in behind and circle the cake, singing and clapping. The festivities continue. The Jacksonville quartet step upon the platform and sing a verse and chorus of "Daisies won't tell." Cries of "Hurrah for Jacksonville! Glory for the big town," "Hurrah for Big Jack."*)

MAN (*seeing* EMMA): You're from Jacksonville, aint you? (*He whirls her around and around.*) Aint you happy? Whoopee! (*He releases her and she drops upon a seat. She buries her face in the moss.*)
(*Quartet begins on chorus again. People are departing, laughing, humming, with quartet cheer-ing.* JOHN, *the cake, and* EFFIE *being borne away in triumph.*)

SCENE IV

Time: present. The interior of a one-room shack in an alley. There is a small window in the rear wall upstage left. There is an enlarged crayon drawing of a man and woman—man sitting cross-legged, woman standing with her hand on his shoulder. A center table, red cover, a low, cheap rocker, two straight chairs, a small kitchen stove at left with a wood-box beside it, a water-bucket on a stand close by. A hand towel and a wash basin. A shelf of dishes above this. There is an ordinary oil lamp on the center table but it is not lighted when the curtain goes up. Some light enters through the window and falls on the woman seated in the low rocker. The door is center right. A cheap bed is against the upstage wall. Someone is on the bed but is lying so that the back is toward the audience.

Action: As the curtain rises, the woman is seen rocking to and fro in the low rocker. A dead silence except for the sound of the rocker and an occasional groan from the bed. Once a faint voice says "water" and the woman in the rocker arises and carries the tin dipper to the bed.

WOMAN: No mo' right away—Doctor says not too much. (*Returns dipper to pail.—Pause.*) You got right much fever—I better go git the doctor agin.
(*There comes a knocking at the door and she stands still for a moment, listening. It comes again and she goes to door but does not open it.*)

WOMAN: Who's that?

VOICE OUTSIDE: Does Emma Beasely live here?

EMMA: Yeah—(*pause*)—who is it?

VOICE: It's me—John Turner.

EMMA (*puts hands eagerly on the fastening*): John? did you say John Turner?

VOICE: Yes, Emma, it's me.
(*The door is opened and the man steps inside.*)

EMMA: John! Your hand (*she feels for it and touches it*). John flesh and blood.

JOHN (*laughing awkwardly*): It's me all right, old girl. Just as bright as a basket of chips. Make a light quick so I can see how you look. I'm crazy to see you. Twenty years is a long time to wait, Emma.

EMMA (*nervously*): Oh, let's we all just sit in the dark awhile. (*Apologetically.*) I wasn't expecting nobody and my house aint picked up. Sit down. (*She draws up the chair. She sits in rocker.*)

JOHN: Just to think! Emma! Me and Emma sitting down side by each. Know how I found you?

EMMA (*dully*): Naw. How?

JOHN (*brightly*): Soon's I got in town I hunted up Wesley and he told me how to find you. That's who I come to see, you!

EMMA: Where you been all these years, up North somewheres? Nobody round here could find out where you got to.

JOHN: Yes, up North. Philadelphia.

EMMA: Married yet?

JOHN: Oh yes, seventeen years ago. But my wife is dead now and so I came as soon as it was decent to find *you*. I wants to marry you. I couldn't die happy if I didn't. Couldn't get over you—couldn't forget. Forget me, Emma?

EMMA: Naw, John. How could I?

JOHN (*leans over impulsively to catch her hand*): Oh, Emma, I love you so much. Strike a light honey so I can see you—see if you changed much. You was such a handsome girl!

EMMA: We don't exactly need no light, do we, John, tuh jus' set an' talk?

JOHN: Yes, we do, Honey. Gwan, make a light. Ah wanna see you. (*There is a silence.*)

EMMA: Bet you' wife wuz some high-yaller dickty-doo.

JOHN: Naw she wasn't neither. She was jus' as much like you as Ah could get her. Make a light an' Ah'll show you her pictcher. Shucks, ah gotta look at mah old sweetheart. (*He strikes a match and holds it up between their faces and they look intently at each other over it until it burns out.*) You aint changed none atall, Emma, jus' as pretty as a speckled pup yet.

EMMA (*lighter*): Go long, John! (*Short pause*) 'member how you useter bring me magnolias?

JOHN: Do I? Gee, you was sweet! 'Member how Ah useter pull mah necktie loose so you could tie it back for me? Emma, Ah can't see to mah soul how we lived all this time, way from one

another. 'Member how you useter make out mah ears had done run down and you useter screw 'em up agin for me? (*They laugh.*)

EMMA: Yeah, Ah useter think you wuz gointer be mah husban' then—but you let dat ole—

JOHN: Ah aint gonna let you alibi on me lak dat. Light dat lamp! You cain't look me in de eye and say no such. (*He strikes another match and lights the lamp.*) Course, ah don't wanta look too bossy, but ah b'lieve you got to marry me tuh git rid of me. That is, if you aint married.

EMMA: Naw, Ah aint. (*She turns the lamp down.*)

JOHN (*looking about the room*): Not so good, Emma. But wait till you see dat little place in Philly! Got a little "Rolls-Rough," too—gointer teach you to drive it, too.

EMMA: Ah been havin' a hard time, John, an' Ah lost you—oh, aint nothin' been right for me! Ah aint never been happy. (JOHN *takes both of her hands in his.*)

JOHN: You gointer be happy now, Emma. Cause Ah'm gointer make you. Gee Whiz! Ah aint but forty-two and you aint forty yet—we got plenty time. (*There is a groan from the bed.*) Gee, what's that?

EMMA (*ill at ease.*): Thass mah chile. She's sick. Reckon ah bettah see 'bout her.

JOHN: You got a chile? Gee, that great! Ah always wanted one, but didn't have no luck. Now we kin start off with a family. Girl or boy?

EMMA (*slowly*): A girl. Comin' tuh see me agin soon, John?

JOHN: Comin' agin? Ah aint gone yet! We aint talked, you aint kissed me an' nothin', and you aint showed me our girl. (*Another groan, more prolonged.*) She must be pretty sick—let's see. (*He turns in his chair and* EMMA *rushes over to the bed and covers the girl securely, tucking her long hair under the covers, too—before he arises. He goes over to the bed and looks down into her face. She is mulatto. Turns to* EMMA, *teasingly.*) Talkin' 'bout *me* liking high-yallers—yo husband musta been pretty near *white*.

EMMA (*slowly*): Ah, never wuz married, John.

JOHN: It's all right, Emma. (*Kisses her warmly.*) Everything is going to be O.K. (*Turning back to the bed.*) Our child looks pretty sick, but she's pretty. (*Feels her forehead and cheek.*) Think she oughter have a doctor.

EMMA: Ah done had one. Course Ah cain't git no specialist an' nothin' lak dat. (*She looks about the room and his gaze follows hers.*) Ah aint got a whole lot lak you. Nobody don't git rich in no white-folks' kitchen, nor in de washtub. You know Ah aint no school-teacher an' nothin' lak dat.

(JOHN *puts his arm about her.*)

JOHN: It's all right, Emma. But our daughter is bad off—run out an' git a doctor—she needs one. Ah'd go if Ah knowed where to find one—you kin git one the quickest—hurry, Emma.

EMMA (*looks from* JOHN *to her daughter and back again*): She'll be all right, Ah reckon, for a while. John, you love me—you really want me sho' nuff?

JOHN: Sure Ah do—think Ah'd come all de way down here for nothin'? Ah wants to marry agin.

EMMA: Soon, John?

JOHN: Real soon.

EMMA: Ah wuz jus' thinkin', mah folks is away now on a little trip—be home day after tomorrow—we could git married tomorrow.

JOHN: All right. Now run on after the doctor—we must look after our girl. Gee, she's got a full suit of hair! Glad you didn't let her chop it off. (*Looks away from bed and sees* EMMA *standing still.*)

JOHN: Emma, run on after the doctor, honey. (*She goes to the bed and again tucks the long braids of hair in, which are again pouring over the side of the bed by the feverish tossing of the girl.*) What's our daughter's name?

EMMA: Lou Lillian. (*She returns to the rocker uneasily and sits rocking jerkily. He returns to his seat and turns up the light.*)

JOHN: Gee, we're going to be happy—we gointer make up for all them twenty years (*another groan*). Emma, git up an' gwan git dat doctor. You done forgot Ah'm de boss uh dis family now—gwan, while Ah'm here to watch her whilst you're gone. Ah got to git back to mah stoppin'-place after a while.

EMMA: You go git one, John.

JOHN: Whilst Ah'm blunderin' round tryin' to find one, she'll be gettin' worse. She sounds pretty bad—(*takes out his wallet and hands her a bill*)—get a taxi if necessary. Hurry!

EMMA (*does not take the money, but tucks her arms and hair in again, and gives the girl a drink*): Reckon Ah better go git a doctor. Don't want nothin' to happen to *her*. After you left, Ah useter have such a hurtin' in heah (*touches bosom*) till she come an' eased it some.

JOHN: Here, take some money and get a good doctor. There must be some good colored ones around here now.

EMMA (*scornfully*): I wouldn't let one of 'em tend my cat if I had one! But let's we don't start a fuss.

(JOHN *caresses her again. When he raises his head he notices the picture on the wall and crosses over to it with her—his arm still about her.*)

JOHN: Why, that's you and me!

EMMA: Yes, I never could part with that. You coming tomorrow morning, John, and we're gointer get married, aint we? Then we can talk over everything.

JOHN: Sure, but I aint gone yet. I don't see how come we can't make all our arrangements now.

(*Groans from bed and feeble movement.*)

Good lord, Emma, go get that doctor!

(EMMA *stares at the girl and the bed and seizes a hat from a nail on the wall. She prepares to go but looks from* JOHN *to bed and back again. She fumbles about the table and lowers the lamp. Goes to door and opens it.* JOHN *offers the wallet. She refuses it.*)

EMMA: Doctor right around the corner. Guess I'll leave the door open so she can get some air. She won't need nothing while I'm gone, John. (*She crosses and tucks the girl in securely and rushes out, looking backward and pushing the door wide open as she exits.* JOHN *sits in the chair beside the table. Looks about him—shakes his head. The girl on the bed groans, "water," "so hot."* JOHN *looks about him excitely. Gives her a drink. Feels her forehead. Takes a clean handkerchief from his pocket and wets it and places it upon her forehead. She raises her hand to the cool object. Enter* EMMA *running. When she sees* JOHN *at the bed she is full of fury. She rushes over and jerks his shoulder around. They face each other.*)

EMMA: I knowed it! (*She strikes him.*) A half white skin. (*She rushes at him again.* JOHN *staggers back and catches her hands.*)

JOHN: Emma!

EMMA (*struggles to free her hands*): Let me go so I can kill you. Come sneaking in here like a pole cat!

JOHN (*slowly, after a long pause*): So this is the woman I've been wearing over my heart like a rose for twenty years! She so despises her own skin that she can't believe any one else could love it! (EMMA *writhes to free herself.*)

JOHN: Twenty years! Twenty years of adoration, of hunger, of worship! (*On the verge of tears he crosses to door and exits quietly, closing the door after him.*)

(EMMA *remains standing, looking dully about as if she is half asleep. There comes a knocking at the door. She rushes to open it. It is the* DOCTOR. *White. She does not step aside so that he can enter.*)

DOCTOR: Well, shall I come in?

EMMA (*stepping aside and laughing a little*): That's right, doctor, come in.

(DOCTOR *crosses to bed with professional air. Looks at the girl, feels the pulse and draws up the sheet over the face. He turns to her.*)

DOCTOR: Why didn't you come sooner. I told you to let me know of the least change in her condition.

EMMA (*flatly*): I did come—I went for the doctor.

DOCTOR: Yes, but you waited. An hour more or less is mighty important sometimes. Why didn't you come?

EMMA (*passes hand over face*): Couldn't see.

DOCTOR: (*Looks at her curiously, then sympathetically takes out a small box of pills, and hands them to her.*) Here, you're worn out. Take one of these every hour and try to get some sleep. (*He departs.*)

(*She puts the pill-box on the table, takes up the low rocking chair and places it by the head of the bed. She seats herself and rocks monotonously and stares out of the door. A dry sob now and then. The wind from the open door blows out the lamp and she is seen by the little light from the window rocking in an even, monotonous gait, and sobbing.*)

Introduction to *Machinal*

WHEN THE PLAY WAS NEW

As *Machinal* by Sophie Treadwell opened at the Plymouth Theatre in New York on September 7, 1928, Broadway theatres and the American business world had been enjoying an exhilarating upward ride. But the bubble was about to burst. Before the next year ended, the stock market crash would propel the country into its worst financial depression ever and, along with widespread poverty and business collapses, change the face of American theatre and entertainment.

In 1928 it appeared that commercialism and big business were the monarchs of America even though dissenting voices punctuated the decade. Writers expressed alarm over the problems associated with urbanization. The United States had become an urban majority by 1920 and divisiveness was apparent on many social, political, and economic fronts. Many of the warnings were launched by novelists and playwrights. Most of the latter, like Treadwell, were attracted to the artistic movement of expressionism, which had begun in Germany before World War I. Although serving as a critique of the dehumanizing impact of industry, commercialism, and war, a number of expressionistic plays enjoyed commercial productions in Broadway theatres. Producer–director Arthur Hopkins launched several of these, including *Machinal*, which starred an unknown actress, Zita Johann, as the Young Woman and a young, not-yet-movie-star Clark Gable as her insensitive lover. Hopkins produced and directed more plays by women playwrights than any other Broadway producer of the 1920s, and was instrumental in maintaining dissenting voices in the commercial venue.

THE PLAYWRIGHT

Although a prolific writer, Sophie Treadwell (1885–1970), the author of some forty plays and a number of novels, is noted primarily for one play, *Machinal*. Treadwell—who was born and spent much of her life in California and was educated at the University of California, Berkeley—was drawn early to the theatre through acting, but during her lifetime she had most of her professional success as a journalist and novelist. As a journalist, especially after moving to New York in 1915, she covered many important events for major newspapers and magazines, including a stint as war correspondent in France during World War I (an unusual assignment for a woman at the time). She was very active in the struggle for women's rights and suffrage, and her position is evident in much of her work. In 1921 she scored a journalistic coup by spending two days in Mexico with the notorious Pancho Villa, resulting in a feature news story and her play *Gringo* (1922).

A few of Treadwell's plays had minor productions in her native California and at universities or community theatres in the west. Seven of her plays reached Broadway production. Arthur Hopkins also directed *Plumes in the Dust* (1936), a study of Edgar Alan Poe; the accomplished Guthrie McClintic directed *Gringo*; the prestigious Theatre Guild produced *Hope for a Harvest* (1941), a semi-autobiographical play, and Treadwell directed several of the plays. Nonetheless, all productions in New York, save *Machinal*, failed to maintain a successful run. Beginning with *Gringo* in 1922 and extending to *Hope for a Harvest* in 1941, the disappointing production runs were only three to thirty-eight performances. Perhaps recognizing the difficulties, Treadwell actively engaged in novel writing by 1931 and wrote little for the theatre after 1941. Some of her plays and stories made their way to television productions between 1953 and 1960, and most of her later life was spent in California and Arizona. It is doubtful that she could have envisioned the resurgence in popularity of *Machinal* after her death.

GENRE, STRUCTURE, AND STYLE

Machinal is one of the last of the plays in either Germany or the United States to be identified with the movement of expressionism. Partially modeled on or inspired by such plays as Georg Kaiser's *From Morn to Midnight* (1916) and Ernst Toller's *Man and the Masses* (1921) from Germany, and Susan Glaspell's *The Verge* (1921), Eugene O'Neill's *The Hairy Ape* (1922), and Elmer Rice's *The Adding Machine* (1923) in the United States, Treadwell's play uses a form reminiscent of medieval morality plays such as *The World and the Child,* which are episodic, following something of a journey motif. We observe the central character (often an "everyman" character) at critical stations of his life. By selecting a woman as the protagonist, however, Treadwell makes an unusual choice for this form and style, seen earlier only in *Man and the Masses* and *The Verge*. Rice had written *Subway*—an expressionistic play with a female protagonist—in 1923, but he could not get it produced until 1929 after the success of *Machinal*. Whether male or female, however, all of the expressionistic plays end in destruction of the protagonist. All are victims of society, war, or the industrial complex; in the case of *Machinal,* the Young Woman is a victim of the oppression of men as well.

In expressionist plays, most or all of the characters are given generic names such as Mother, Young Man, Stenographer, with little or no identity. Even the protagonist is known only as the Young Woman until late in the play when she is finally identified as Helen Jones. Much of the activity of the play is geared to stylized movement, often heavily choreographed, filled with repetition and the dehumanization of mechanized work and lifestyles. The dialogue is often shortened, poeticized, or simplified as are the short phrases of advertising and meaningless or codified interaction and cross talk in everyday conversation. In other words, little successful communication between characters ever takes place. Much is communicated to the audience, but little to the characters through conversation. The result in many of the plays is a series of monologues by the protagonist giving us vital information about how the character feels—especially frustration and a sense of not belonging anywhere. In *Machinal* these characteristics are most evident in the dialogue at the office, the cross talk in the speakeasy, and the monologues of the Young Woman. Treadwell probably wants us to recognize both workplace and domestic settings as having become unnatural environments.

IMPORTANT ELEMENTS OF CONTENT

Much of this play is about confinement—especially the confinement and claustrophobic feelings of a woman. Note that all settings are interiors with few doors. Of the nine settings, the last five interiors have only one way out. Everyone suppresses the Young Woman, including other women who follow the lead of the male characters. The Young Woman has no sense of ownership—either figuratively or literally. Least of all does she seem to own herself. Like the male protagonist in O'Neill's *The Hairy Ape,* she can't find anywhere she belongs. The business world oppresses her through its repetition and coldness. The Young Woman is trapped not only by society and circumstances, but by the environment. The play seems to say that the Young Woman, and by extension women in general, are swamped by mediocrity and loneliness whether in the deadening workplace or an uninspired marriage.

Although not a replication of real events, the play is partially based on a 1927 murder trial—the Ruth Snyder case, in which a woman and her lover murdered her husband. In the case of the Young Woman (not Snyder) the murder is apparently her attempt in her crisis to free herself, but it ends ironically with her demise, not her freedom. Ruth Snyder was the first woman to be executed by electrocution. In the first production in 1928, the Young Woman's execution was represented by pulsating red lights and the screams of the protagonist "Somebody!" In 1928 juries were all-male, so the trial scene in the original production had one woman onstage surrounded by twenty men. This predicament is reminiscent of Antigone facing the all-male chorus and Creon when she is condemned to death. Unlike the Greek tragedy, however, in *Machinal* the Young Woman's pain goes unrecognized by her oppressors. Her confusion is never understood.

THE PLAY IN REVIVAL

After premiering in New York in 1928, *Machinal* was revived in London's West End in 1931, and in two different productions in Moscow, Russia, in 1933. Things were quiet with this play until an off-Broadway production in 1960, and another thirty years passed until a resurgence of theatrical activity in the 1990s. Probably inspired by republication of the play in the 1980s along with significant scholarly attention, especially by feminist writers, a dynamic production in New York in 1990 by the New York Shakespeare Festival led to revivals at the American Conservatory Theatre in San Francisco (1996–1997); the National Theatre in London (1993), for which Fiona Shaw as the Young Woman won the Olivier Award for Best Actress; and numerous other European and U.S. regional productions including a 2003 revival in Chicago by the Hypocrites theatre company. Many college, university, and community productions have followed this renewal of the play.

SPECIAL FEATURE

Machinal is unusual for its time in its introduction of the abortion issue and homosexuality in the speakeasy scene, labeled "Episode 5: Prohibited." Treadwell may have been striving to shock her audience with topics rarely even vaguely suggested on the American stage at the time, but we should note that this was also a sly way to introduce other types of oppression and gender rights issues parallel to the oppression of the Young Woman, and issues unable to get a full hearing on the stage in the 1920s.

FURTHER READING ABOUT THE PLAY, PLAYWRIGHT, AND CONTEXT

For material on the life and times of Treadwell and criticism of her plays, see Jerry Dickey, *Sophie Treadwell: A Research and Production Sourcebook;* Brenda Murphy, *The Cambridge Companion to American Women Playwrights;* and Elaine Partnow, *The Female Dramatist.* Jerry Dickey also contributed to a helpful and accurate website on Treadwell at the University of Arizona: http://dizzy.library.arizona.edu/branches/spc/treadwell/sthome.html.

For detailed criticism of Treadwell's plays and career, see two dissertations: Nancy Wynn, "Sophie Treadwell: The Career of a Twentieth Century American Feminist Playwright," and Louise Heck-Rabi, "Sophie Treadwell: Subjects and Structures in 20th Century American Drama."

For historical and theatrical context for Treadwell and *Machinal,* see Ronald Wainscott, *The Emergence of the Modern American Theatre,* and Don Wilmeth and Christopher Bigsby, *The Cambridge History of American Theatre,* volume 2.

Machinal

By Sophie Treadwell

CHARACTERS

YOUNG WOMAN
TELEPHONE GIRL
STENOGRAPHER
FILING CLERK
ADDING CLERK
MOTHER
HUSBAND
BELLBOY
NURSE
DOCTOR
YOUNG MAN
GIRL
MAN
BOY
MAN
ANOTHER MAN
WAITER
JUDGE
LAWYER FOR DEFENSE
LAWYER FOR PROSECUTION
COURT REPORTER
BAILIFF
REPORTER
SECOND REPORTER
THIRD REPORTER
JAILER
MATRON
PRIEST

THE PLOT

The story of a woman who murders her husband—an ordinary young woman, any woman.

THE PLAN

To tell this story by showing the different phases of life that the woman comes in contact with, and in none of which she finds any place, any peace. The woman is essentially soft, tender, and the life around her is essentially hard, mechanized. Business, home, marriage, having a child, seeking pleasure—all are difficult for her—mechanical, nerve nagging. Only in an illicit love does she find anything with life in it for her, and when she loses this, the desperate effort to win free to it again is her undoing.

The story is told in nine scenes. In the dialogue of these scenes there is the attempt to catch the rhythm of our common city speech, its brassy sound, its trick of repetition, etc.

Then there is, also, the use of many different sounds chosen primarily for their inherent emotional effect (steel riveting, a priest chanting, a Negro singing, jazz band, etc.), but contributing also to the creation of a background, an atmosphere.

THE HOPE

To create a stage production that will have "style", and at the same time, by the story's own innate drama, by the directness of its telling, by the variety and quick changingness of its scenes, and the excitement of its sounds, to create an interesting play.

SCENICALLY

This play is planned to be handled in two basic sets (or in one set with two backs).

The first division—the first Four Episodes—needs an entrance at one side, and a back having a door and a large window. The door gives, in

EPISODE 1—to Vice President's office.
EPISODE 2—to hall.
EPISODE 3—to bathroom.
EPISODE 4—to corridor.

And the window shows, in

EPISODE 1—An opposite office.
EPISODE 2—An inner apartment court.
EPISODE 3—Window of a dance casino opposite.
EPISODE 4—Steel girders. (Of these, only the ca-
    sino window is important. Sky could be used
    for the others.)

*The second division—the last Five Episodes—has the
same side entrance, but the back has only one opening—
for a small window (barred).*

EPISODE 5—window is masked by electric piano.
EPISODE 6—window is disclosed (sidewalk outside).
EPISODE 7—window is curtained.
EPISODE 8—window is masked by Judge's bench.
EPISODE 9—window is disclosed (sky outside).

*There is a change of furniture, and props for each epi-
sode—only essential things, full of character. For Episode 9, the room is closed in from the sides, and there is
a place with bars and a door in it, put straight across
stage down front (back far enough to leave a clear passageway in front of it).*
        *Lighting concentrated and intense.—Light and
shadow—bright light and darkness.—This darkness,
already in the scene, grows and blacks out the light for
dark stage when the scene changes are made.*

OFFSTAGE VOICES
Characters in the Background Heard, but Unseen:
A JANITOR
A BABY
A BOY AND A GIRL
A HUSBAND AND WIFE
A HUSBAND AND WIFE
A RADIO ANNOUNCER
A NEGRO SINGER

MECHANICAL OFFSTAGE SOUNDS
A SMALL JAZZ BAND
A HAND ORGAN
STEEL RIVETING
TELEGRAPH INSTRUMENTS
AEROPLANE ENGINE

MECHANICAL ONSTAGE SOUNDS
OFFICE MACHINES (TYPEWRITERS, TELEPHONES, ETC.)
ELECTRIC PIANO.

CHARACTERS
*In the Background Seen, Not Heard (Seen, off the main
set, i.e., through a window or door)*
COUPLES OF MEN AND WOMEN DANCING
A WOMAN IN A BATHROBE
A WOMAN IN A WHEEL CHAIR
A NURSE WITH A COVERED BASIN
A NURSE WITH A TRAY
THE FEET OF MEN AND WOMEN PASSING IN THE STREET

EPISODE I

TO BUSINESS
*Scene: An office: a switchboard, filing cabinet, adding
machine, typewriter and table, manifold machine.*

*Sounds: Office machines: typewriters, adding machine,
manifold, telephone bells, buzzers.*

Characters and their machines: A YOUNG WOMAN *(typewriter);* A STENOGRAPHER *(typewriter);* A FILING CLERK
(filing cabinet and manifold); AN ADDING CLERK *(adding
machine);* TELEPHONE OPERATOR *(switchboard);* JONES

*Before the curtain: Sounds of machines going. They con-
tinue throughout the scene, and accompany the* YOUNG
WOMAN's *thoughts after the scene is blacked out.*

*At the rise of the curtain: All the machines are disclosed,
and all the characters with the exception of the* YOUNG
WOMAN.

Of these characters, the YOUNG WOMAN, *going any day
to any business. Ordinary. The confusion of her own
inner thoughts, emotions, desires, dreams cuts her off
from any actual adjustment to the routine of work. She
gets through this routine with a very small surface of
her consciousness. She is not homely and she is not
pretty. She is preoccupied with herself—with her person. She has well kept hands, and a trick of constantly
arranging her hair over her ears.*

The STENOGRAPHER *is the faded, efficient woman office
worker. Drying, dried.*

The ADDING CLERK *is her male counterpart.*

The FILING CLERK *is a boy not grown, callow adolescence.*

The TELEPHONE GIRL, *young, cheap and amorous.*

Lights come up on office scene. Two desks right and left.

Telephone booth back right center. Filing cabinet back of center. Adding machine back left center.

ADDING CLERK (*in the monotonous voice of his monotonous thoughts; at his adding machine*): 2490, 28, 76, 123, 36842, 1, ¼, 37, 804, 23 ½, 982.

FILING CLERK (*in the same way—at his filing desk*): Accounts—A. Bonds—B. Contracts—C. Data—D. Earnings—E.

STENOGRAPHER (*in the same way—left*): Dear Sir—in re—your letter—recent date—will state—

TELEPHONE GIRL: Hello—Hello—George H. Jones Company good morning—hello hello—George H. Jones Company good morning—hello.

FILING CLERK: Market—M. Notes—N. Output—O. Profits—P—! (*Suddenly*) What's the matter with Q?

TELEPHONE GIRL: Matter with it—Mr. J.—Mr. K. wants you—What you mean matter? Matter with what?

FILING CLERK: Matter with Q.

TELEPHONE GIRL: Well—what is? Spring 1726?

FILING CLERK: I'm asking yuh—

TELEPHONE GIRL: Well?

FILING CLERK: Nothing filed with it—

TELEPHONE GIRL: Well?

FILING CLERK: Look at A. Look at B. What's the matter with Q?

TELEPHONE GIRL: Ain't popular. Hello—Hello—George H. Jones Company.

FILING CLERK: Hot dog! Why ain't it?

ADDING CLERK: Has it personality?

STENOGRAPHER: Has it Halitosis?

TELEPHONE GIRL: Has it got it?

FILING CLERK: Hot dog!

TELEPHONE GIRL: What number do you want? (*Recognizing but not pleased.*) Oh—hello—sure I know who it is—tonight? Uh, uh—(*Negative, but each with a different inflection.*) You heard me—No!

FILING CLERK: Don't you like him?

STENOGRAPHER: She likes 'em all.

TELEPHONE GIRL: I do not!

STENOGRAPHER: Well—pretty near all!

TELEPHONE GIRL: What number do you want? Wrong number. Hello—hello—George H. Jones Company. Hello, hello—

STENOGRAPHER: Memorandum—attention Mr. Smith—at a conference of—

ADDING CLERK: 125—83 ¾—22—908—34—¼—28593.

FILING CLERK: Report—R, Sales—S, Trade—T.

TELEPHONE GIRL: Shh—! Yes, Mr. J.—? No—Miss A. ain't in yet—I'll tell her, Mr. J.—just the minute she gets in.

STENOGRAPHER: She's late again, huh?

TELEPHONE GIRL: Out with her sweetie last night, huh?

FILING CLERK: Hot dog.

ADDING CLERK: She ain't got a sweetie.

STENOGRAPHER: How do you know?

ADDING CLERK: I know.

FILING CLERK: Hot dog.

ADDING CLERK: She lives alone with her mother.

TELEPHONE GIRL: Spring 1876? Hello—Spring 1876. Spring! Hello, Spring 1876? 1876! Wrong number! Hello! Hello!

STENOGRAPHER: Director's meeting semi-annual report card.

FILING CLERK: Shipments—Sales—Schedules—S.

ADDING CLERK: She doesn't belong in an office.

TELEPHONE GIRL: Who does?

STENOGRAPHER: I do!

ADDING CLERK: You said it!

FILING CLERK: Hot dog!

TELEPHONE GIRL: Hello—hello—George H. Jones Company—hello—hello—

STENOGRAPHER: I'm efficient. She's inefficient.

FILING CLERK: She's inefficient.

TELEPHONE GIRL: She's got J. going.

STENOGRAPHER: Going?

TELEPHONE GIRL: Going and coming.

FILING CLERK: Hot dog.
    (*Enter* JONES.)

JONES: Good morning, everybody.

TELEPHONE GIRL: Good morning.

FILING CLERK: Good morning.

ADDING CLERK: Good morning.

STENOGRAPHER: Good morning, Mr. J.

JONES: Miss A. isn't in yet?

TELEPHONE GIRL: Not yet, Mr. J.

FILING CLERK: Not yet.

ADDING CLERK: Not yet.

STENOGRAPHER: She's late.

JONES: I just wanted her to take a letter.

STENOGRAPHER: I'll take the letter.

JONES: One thing at a time and that done well.

ADDING CLERK (*yessing*): Done well.

STENOGRAPHER: I'll finish it later.

JONES: Hew to the line.

ADDING CLERK: Hew to the line.

STENOGRAPHER: Then I'll hurry.

JONES: Haste makes waste.

ADDING CLERK: Waste.

STENOGRAPHER: But if you're in a hurry.

JONES: I'm never in a hurry—That's how I get ahead! (*Laughs. They all laugh.*) First know you're right—then go ahead.

ADDING CLERK: Ahead.

JONES (*to* TELEPHONE GIRL): When Miss A. comes in tell her I want her to take a letter. (*Turns to go in—then.*) It's important.

TELEPHONE GIRL (*making a note*): Miss A.—important.

JONES (*starts up—then*): And I don't want to be disturbed.

TELEPHONE GIRL: You're in conference?

JONES: I'm in conference. (*Turns—then.*) Unless it's, A. B.—of course.

TELEPHONE GIRL: Of course—A. B.

JONES (*starts—turns again; attempts to be facetious*). Tell Miss A. the early bird catches the worm. (*Exit* JONES.)

TELEPHONE GIRL: The early worm gets caught.

ADDING CLERK: He's caught.

TELEPHONE GIRL: Hooked.

ADDING CLERK: In the pan.

FILING CLERK: Hot dog.

STENOGRAPHER: We beg leave to announce—
  (*Enter* YOUNG WOMAN. *Goes behind telephone booth to desk right.*)

STENOGRAPHER: You're late!

FILING CLERK: You're late.

ADDING CLERK: You're late.

STENOGRAPHER: And yesterday!

FILING CLERK: The day before.

ADDING CLERK: And the day before.

STENOGRAPHER: You'll lose your job.

YOUNG WOMAN: No!

STENOGRAPHER: No?
  (*Workers exchange glances.*)

YOUNG WOMAN: I can't!

STENOGRAPHER: Can't?
  (*Same business.*)

FILING CLERK: Rent—bills—installments—miscellaneous.

ADDING CLERK: A dollar ten—ninety-five—3.40—35—12.60.

STENOGRAPHER: Then why are you late?

YOUNG WOMAN: Why?

STENOGRAPHER: Excuse!

ADDING CLERK: Excuse!

FILING CLERK: Excuse.

TELEPHONE GIRL: Excuse it, please.

STENOGRAPHER: Why?

YOUNG WOMAN: The subway?

TELEPHONE GIRL: Long distance?

FILING CLERK: Old stuff!

ADDING CLERK: That stall!

STENOGRAPHER: Stalled?

YOUNG WOMAN: No—

STENOGRAPHER: What?

YOUNG WOMAN: I had to get out!

ADDING CLERK: Out!

FILING CLERK: Out?

STENOGRAPHER: Out where?

YOUNG WOMAN: In the air!

STENOGRAPHER: Air?

YOUNG WOMAN: All those bodies pressing.

FILING CLERK: Hot dog!

YOUNG WOMAN: I thought I would faint! I had to get out in the air!

FILING CLERK: Give her the air.

ADDING CLERK: Free air—

STENOGRAPHER: Hot air.

YOUNG WOMAN: Like I'm dying.

STENOGRAPHER: Same thing yesterday. (*Pause*). And the day before.

YOUNG WOMAN: Yes—what am I going to do?

ADDING CLERK: Take a taxi! (*They laugh*).

FILING CLERK: Call a cop!

TELEPHONE GIRL: Mr. J. wants you.

YOUNG WOMAN: Me?

TELEPHONE GIRL: You!

YOUNG WOMAN (*rises*): Mr. J.!

STENOGRAPHER: Mr. J.

TELEPHONE GIRL: He's bellowing for you!
  (YOUNG WOMAN *gives last pat to her hair—goes off into door—back.*)

STENOGRAPHER (*after her*): Get it just right.

FILING CLERK: She's always doing that to her hair.

TELEPHONE GIRL: It gives a line—it gives a line—

FILING CLERK: Hot dog.

ADDING CLERK: She's artistic.

STENOGRAPHER: She's inefficient.

FILING CLERK: She's inefficient.

STENOGRAPHER: Mr. J. knows she's inefficient.

ADDING CLERK: 46—23—84—2—2—2—1,492—678.

TELEPHONE GIRL: Hello—hello—George H. Jones Company—hello—Mr. Jones? He's in conference.

STENOGRAPHER (*sarcastic*): Conference!

ADDING CLERK: Conference.

FILING CLERK: Hot dog!

TELEPHONE GIRL: Do you think he'll marry her?

ADDING CLERK: If she'll have him.

STENOGRAPHER: If she'll have him!

FILING CLERK: Do you think she'll have him?

TELEPHONE GIRL: How much does he get?

ADDING CLERK: Plenty—5,000—10,000—15,000—20,000—25,000.

STENOGRAPHER: And plenty put away.

ADDING CLERK: Gas Preferred—4's—steel—5's—oil—6's.

FILING CLERK: Hot dog.

STENOGRAPHER: Will she have him? Will she have him? This agreement entered into—party of the first part—party of the second part—will he have her?

TELEPHONE GIRL: Well, I'd hate to get into bed with him. (*Familiar melting voice.*) Hello—humhum—hum—hum—hold the line a minute—will you—hum hum. (*Professional voice.*) Hell, hello—A.B., just a minute. Mr. A.B.—Mr. J.? Mr. A.B.—go ahead, Mr. A.B. (*Melting voice.*) We were interrupted—huh—huh—huh—huh-huh—hum—hum.

(*Enter* YOUNG WOMAN—*she goes to her chair, sits with folded hands.*)

FILING CLERK: That's all you ever say to a guy—

STENOGRAPHER: Hum—hum—or uh huh—(*Negative.*)

TELEPHONE GIRL: That's all you have to. (*To phone.*) Hum—hum—hum hum—hum hum.

STENOGRAPHER: Mostly hum hum.

ADDING CLERK: You've said it!

FILING CLERK: Hot dog.

TELEPHONE GIRL: Hum hum huh hum hum-humhum—tonight? She's got a date—she told me last night—humhumhuh—hum—all

right. (*Disconnects*) Too bad—my boy friend's got a friend—but my girl friend's got a date.

YOUNG WOMAN: You have a good time.

TELEPHONE GIRL: Big time.

STENOGRAPHER: Small time.

ADDING CLERK: A big time on the small time.

TELEPHONE GIRL: I'd ask you, kid, but you'd be up to your neck!

STENOGRAPHER: Neckers!

ADDING CLERK: Petters!

FILING CLERK: Sweet papas.

TELEPHONE GIRL: Want to come?

YOUNG WOMAN: Can't.

TELEPHONE GIRL: Date?

YOUNG WOMAN: My mother.

STENOGRAPHER: Worries?

TELEPHONE GIRL: Nags—hello—George H. Jones Company—Oh hello—

(young woman *sits before her machine—hands in lap, looking at them.*)

STENOGRAPHER: Why don't you get to work?

YOUNG WOMAN (*dreaming*): What?

ADDING CLERK: Work!

YOUNG WOMAN: Can't.

STENOGRAPHER: Can't?

YOUNG WOMAN: My machine's out of order.

STENOGRAPHER: Well, fix it!

YOUNG WOMAN: I can't—got to get somebody.

STENOGRAPHER: Somebody! Somebody! Always somebody! Here, sort the mail, then!

YOUNG WOMAN (*rises*): All right.

STENOGRAPHER: And hurry! You're late.

YOUNG WOMAN (*sorting letters*): George H. Jones and Company—George H. Jones Inc. George H. Jones—

STENOGRAPHER: You're always late.

ADDING CLERK: You'll lose your job.

YOUNG WOMAN (*hurrying*): George H. Jones—George H. Jones Personal—

TELEPHONE GIRL: Don't let 'em get your goat, kid—tell 'em where to get off.

YOUNG WOMAN: What?

TELEPHONE GIRL: Ain't it all set?

YOUNG WOMAN: What?

TELEPHONE GIRL: You and Mr. J.

STENOGRAPHER: You and the boss.

FILING CLERK: You and the big chief.

ADDING CLERK: You and the big cheese.

YOUNG WOMAN: Did he tell you?

TELEPHONE GIRL: I told you!

ADDING CLERK: I told you!

STENOGRAPHER: I don't believe it.

ADDING CLERK: 5,000—10,000—15,000.

FILING CLERK: Hot dog.

YOUNG WOMAN: No—it isn't so.

STENOGRAPHER: Isn't it?

YOUNG WOMAN: No.

TELEPHONE GIRL: Not yet.

ADDING CLERK: But soon.

FILING CLERK: Hot dog.

    (*Enter* JONES.)

TELEPHONE GIRL (*busy*): George H. Jones Company—Hello—Hello.

STENOGRAPHER: Awaiting your answer—

ADDING CLERK: 5,000—10,000—15,000—

JONES (*crossing to* YOUNG WOMAN—*puts hand on her shoulder, all stop and stare*): That letter done?

YOUNG WOMAN: No. (*She pulls away.*)

JONES: What's the matter?

STENOGRAPHER: She hasn't started.

JONES: O.K.—want to make some changes.

YOUNG WOMAN: My machine's out of order.

JONES: O.K.—use the one in my room.

YOUNG WOMAN: I'm sorting the mail.

STENOGRAPHER (*sarcastic*): One thing at a time!

JONES (*retreating—goes back center*): O.K. (*To* YOUNG WOMAN.) When you're finished. (*Starts back to his room.*)

STENOGRAPHER: Haste makes waste.

JONES (*at door*): O.K.—don't hurry.

    (*Exits.*)

STENOGRAPHER: Hew to the line!

TELEPHONE GIRL: He's hewing.

CLERK: Hot dog.

TELEPHONE GIRL: Why did you flinch, kid?

YOUNG WOMAN: Flinch?

TELEPHONE GIRL: Did he pinch?

YOUNG WOMAN: No.

TELEPHONE GIRL: Then what?

YOUNG WOMAN: Nothing!—Just his hand.

TELEPHONE GIRL: Oh—just his hand—(*Shakes her head thoughtfully.*) Uhhuh. (*Negative.*) Uhhuh. (*Decisively.*) No! Tell him no.

STENOGRAPHER: If she does she'll lose her job.

ADDING CLERK: Fired.

FILING CLERK: The sack!

TELEPHONE GIRL (*on the defensive*): And if she doesn't?

ADDING CLERK: She'll come to work in a taxi!

TELEPHONE GIRL: Work?

FILING CLERK: No work.

STENOGRAPHER: No worry.

ADDING CLERK: Breakfast in bed.

STENOGRAPHER (*sarcastic*): Did Madame ring?

FILING CLERK: Lunch in bed!

TELEPHONE GIRL: A double bed! (*In phone.*) Yes, Mr. J. (*To* YOUNG WOMAN.) J. wants you.

YOUNG WOMAN (*starts to get to her feet—but doesn't*): I can't—I'm not ready—in a minute. (*Sits staring ahead of her.*)

ADDING CLERK: 5,000—10,000—15,000—

FILING CLERK: Profits—plans—purchase—

STENOGRAPHER: Call your attention our prices are fixed.

TELEPHONE GIRL: Hello—hello—George H. Jones Company—hello—hello—

YOUNG WOMAN (*thinking her thoughts aloud—to the subdued accompaniment of the office sounds and voices*): Marry me—wants to marry me—George H. Jones—George H. Jones and Company—Mrs. George H. Jones—Mrs. George H. Jones. Dear Madame—marry—do you take this man to be your wedded husband—I do—to love, honor and to love—kisses—no—I can't—George H. Jones—How would you like to marry me—What do you say—Why Mr. Jones I—let me look at your little hands—you have such pretty little hands—let me hold your pretty little hands—George H. Jones—Fat hands—flabby hands—don't touch me—please—fat hands are never weary—please don't—married—all girls—most girls—married—babies—a baby—curls—little curls all over its head—George H. Jones—straight—thin—bald—don't touch me—please—no—can't—must—somebody—something—no rest—must rest—no rest—must rest—no rest—late today—yesterday—before—late—subway—air—pressing—bodies pressing—bodies—trembling—air—stop—air—late—job—no job—fired—late—alarm clock—alarm clock—alarm clock—hurry—job—ma—nag—nag—nag—ma—hurry—job—no job—no money—installments due—no money—money—George H. Jones—money—Mrs. George H. Jones—money—

no work—no worry—free!—rest—sleep till nine—sleep till ten—sleep till noon—now you take a good rest this morning—don't get up till you want to—thank you—oh thank you—oh don't!—please don't touch me—I want to rest—no rest—earn—got to earn—married— earn—no—yes—earn—all girls—most girls— ma—pa—ma—all women—most women—I can't—must—maybe—must—somebody— something—ma—pa—ma—can I, ma? Tell me, ma—something—somebody.

(*The scene blacks out. The sounds of the office machines continue until the scene lights into Episode 2—and the office sounds become the sound of a radio, offstage.*)

EPISODE 2

AT HOME

Scene: A kitchen: table, chairs, plates and food, garbage can, a pair of rubber gloves. The door at the back now opens on a hall—the window, on an apartment house court.

Sounds: Buzzer, radio (voice of announcer; music and singer).

Characters: YOUNG WOMAN; MOTHER

Outside voices: characters heard, but not seen: A JANITOR; A BABY; A MOTHER AND A SMALL BOY; A YOUNG BOY AND YOUNG GIRL; A HUSBAND AND A WIFE; ANOTHER HUSBAND AND A WIFE

At rise: YOUNG WOMAN *and* MOTHER *eating—radio off-stage—radio stops.*

YOUNG WOMAN: Ma—I want to talk to you.
MOTHER: Aren't you eating a potato?
YOUNG WOMAN: No.
MOTHER: Why not?
YOUNG WOMAN: I don't want one.
MOTHER: That's no reason. Here! Take one.
YOUNG WOMAN: I don't want it.
MOTHER: Potatoes go with stew—here!
YOUNG WOMAN: Ma, I don't want it!
MOTHER: Want it! Take it!
YOUNG WOMAN: But I—oh, all right. (*Takes it—then.*) Ma, I want to ask you something.

MOTHER: Eat your potato.
YOUNG WOMAN (*takes a bite—then*): Ma, there's something I want to ask you—something important.
MOTHER: Is it mealy?
YOUNG WOMAN: S'all right. Ma—tell me.
MOTHER: Three pounds for a quarter.
YOUNG WOMAN: Ma—tell me (*Buzzer.*)
MOTHER (*her dull voice brightening*): There's the garbage. (*Goes to door—or dumbwaiter—opens it. Stop radio.*)
JANITOR'S VOICE (*offstage*): Garbage.
MOTHER (*pleased—busy*): All right. (*Gets garbage can—puts it out.* YOUNG WOMAN *walks up and down.*) What's the matter now?
YOUNG WOMAN: Nothing.
MOTHER: That jumping up from the table every night the garbage is collected! You act like you're crazy.
YOUNG WOMAN: Ma, do all women—
MOTHER: I suppose you think you're too nice for anything so common! Well, let me tell you, my lady, that it's a very important part of life.
YOUNG WOMAN: Oh, Ma!
MOTHER: Well, are you?
YOUNG WOMAN: Am I what?
MOTHER: Glad! Grateful.
YOUNG WOMAN: Yes!
MOTHER: You don't act like it!
YOUNG WOMAN: Oh, Ma, don't talk!
MOTHER: You just said you wanted to talk.
YOUNG WOMAN: Well now—I want to think. I got to think.
MOTHER: Aren't you going to finish your potato?
YOUNG WOMAN: Oh, Ma!
MOTHER: Is there anything the matter with it?
YOUNG WOMAN: No—
MOTHER: Then why don't you finish it?
YOUNG WOMAN: Because I don't want it.
MOTHER: Why don't you?
YOUNG WOMAN: Oh, Ma! Let me alone!
MOTHER: Well, you've got to eat! If you don't eat—
YOUNG WOMAN: Ma! Don't nag!
MOTHER: Nag! Just because I try to look out for you— nag! Just because I try to care for you—nag! Why, you haven't sense enough to eat! What should become of you I'd like to know—if I didn't nag! (*Offstage—a sound of window opening—all these offstage sounds come in through the court window at the back.*)

WOMAN'S VOICE: Johnny—Johnny—come in now!

A SMALL BOY'S VOICE: Oh, Ma!

WOMAN'S VOICE: It's getting cold.

A SMALL BOY'S VOICE: Oh, Ma!

WOMAN'S VOICE: You heard me! (*Sound of window slamming.*)

YOUNG WOMAN: I'm grown up, Ma.

MOTHER: Grown up! What do you mean by that?

YOUNG WOMAN: Nothing much—I guess. (*Offstage sound of* BABY *crying.* MOTHER *rises, clatters dishes.*) Let's not do the dishes right away, Ma. Let's talk—I gotta.

MOTHER: Well, I can't talk with dirty dishes around—you may be able to but—(*Clattering—clattering.*)

YOUNG WOMAN: Ma! Listen! Listen!—There's a man wants to marry me.

MOTHER (*stops clattering—sits*): What man?

YOUNG WOMAN: He says he fell in love with my hands.

MOTHER: In love! Is that beginning again! I thought you were over that!
(*Offstage* boy's voice—*whistles*—girl's voice *answers.*)

BOY'S VOICE: Come on out.

GIRL'S VOICE: Can't.

BOY'S VOICE: Nobody'll see you.

GIRL'S VOICE: I can't.

BOY'S VOICE: It's dark now—come on.

GIRL'S VOICE: Well—just for a minute.

BOY'S VOICE: Meet you round the corner.

YOUNG WOMAN: I got to get married, Ma.

MOTHER: What do you mean?

YOUNG WOMAN: I gotta.

MOTHER: You haven't got in trouble, have you?

YOUNG WOMAN: Don't talk like that!

MOTHER: Well, you say you got to get married—what do you mean?

YOUNG WOMAN: Nothing.

MOTHER: Answer me!

YOUNG WOMAN: All women get married, don't they?

MOTHER: Nonsense!

YOUNG WOMAN: You got married, didn't you?

MOTHER: Yes, I did!
(*Offstage voices.*)

WOMAN'S VOICE: Where you going?

MAN'S VOICE: Out.

WOMAN'S VOICE: You were out last night.

MAN'S VOICE: Was I?

WOMAN'S VOICE: You're always going out.

MAN'S VOICE: Am I?

WOMAN'S VOICE: Where you going?

MAN'S VOICE: Out.
(*End of offstage voices.*)

MOTHER: Who is he? Where did you come to know him?

YOUNG WOMAN: In the office.

MOTHER: In the office!

YOUNG WOMAN: It's Mr. J.

MOTHER: Mr. J.?

YOUNG WOMAN: The Vice-President.

MOTHER: Vice-President! His income must be—Does he know you've got a mother to support?

YOUNG WOMAN: Yes.

MOTHER: What does he say?

YOUNG WOMAN: All right.

MOTHER: How soon you going to marry him?

YOUNG WOMAN: I'm not going to.

MOTHER: Not going to!

YOUNG WOMAN: No! I'm not going to.

MOTHER: But you just said—

YOUNG WOMAN: I'm not going to.

MOTHER: Are you crazy?

YOUNG WOMAN: I can't, Ma! I can't!

MOTHER: Why can't you?

YOUNG WOMAN: I don't love him.

MOTHER: Love!—what does that amount to! Will it clothe you? Will it feed you? Will it pay the bills?

YOUNG WOMAN: No! But it's real just the same!

MOTHER: Real!

YOUNG WOMAN: If it isn't—what can you count on in life?

MOTHER: I'll tell you what you can count on! You can count that you've got to eat and sleep and get up and put clothes on your back and take 'em off again—that you got to get old—and that you got to die. That's what you can count on! All the rest is in your head!

YOUNG WOMAN: But Ma—didn't you love Pa?

MOTHER: I suppose I did—I don't know—I've forgotten—what difference does it make—now?

YOUNG WOMAN: But then!—oh Ma, tell me!

MOTHER: Tell you what?

YOUNG WOMAN: About all that—love!
(*Offstage voices.*)

WIFE'S VOICE: Don't.

HUSBAND'S VOICE: What's the matter—don't you want me to kiss you?

WIFE'S VOICE: Not like that.

HUSBAND'S VOICE: Like what?

WIFE'S VOICE: That silly kiss!

HUSBAND'S VOICE: Silly kiss?

WIFE'S VOICE: You look so silly—oh I know what's coming when you look like that—and kiss me like that—don't—go away—
(*End of offstage voices.*)

MOTHER: He's a decent man, isn't he?

YOUNG WOMAN: I don't know. How should I know—yet.

MOTHER: He's a Vice-President—of course he's decent.

YOUNG WOMAN: I don't care whether he's decent or not. I won't marry him.

MOTHER: But you just said you wanted to marry—

YOUNG WOMAN: Not him.

MOTHER: Who?

YOUNG WOMAN: I don't know—I don't know—I haven't found him yet!

MOTHER: You talk like you're crazy!

YOUNG WOMAN: Oh, Ma—tell me!

MOTHER: Tell you what?

YOUNG WOMAN: Tell me—(*Words suddenly pouring out.*) Your skin oughtn't to curl—ought it—when he just comes near you—ought it? That's wrong, ain't it? You don't get over that, do you—ever, do you or do you? How is it, Ma—do you?

MOTHER: Do you what?

YOUNG WOMAN: Do you get used to, it—so after a while it doesn't matter? Or don't you? Does it always matter? You ought to be in love, oughtn't you, Ma? You must be in love, mustn't you, Ma? That changes everything, doesn't it—or does it? Maybe if you just like a person it's all right—is it? When he puts a hand on me, my blood turns cold. But your blood oughtn't to run cold, ought it? His hands are—his hands are fat, Ma—don't you see—his hands are fat—and they sort of press—and they're fat—don't you see?—Don't you see?

MOTHER (*stares at her bewildered*): See what?

YOUNG WOMAN (*rushing on*): I've always thought I'd find somebody—somebody young—and—and attractive—with wavy hair—wavy hair—I always think of children with curls—little curls all over their head—somebody young—and attractive—that I'd like—that I'd love—But I haven't found anybody like that yet—I haven't found anybody—I've hardly known anybody—you'd never let me go with anybody and—

MOTHER: Are you throwing it up to me that—

YOUNG WOMAN: No—let me finish, Ma! No—let me finish! I just mean I've never found any-body—anybody—nobody's ever asked me—till now—he's the only man that's ever asked me—And I suppose I got to marry some-body—all girls do—

MOTHER: Nonsense.

YOUNG WOMAN: But, I can't go on like this, Ma—I don't know why—but I can't—it's like I'm all tight inside—sometimes I feel like I'm sti-fling!—You don't know—stifling. (*Walks up and down.*) I can't go on like this much lon-ger—going to work—coming home—going to work—coming home—I can't—Sometimes in the subway I think I'm going to die—some-times even in the office if something don't happen—I got to do something—I don't know—it's like I'm all tight inside.

MOTHER: You're crazy.

YOUNG WOMAN: Oh, Ma!

MOTHER: You're crazy.

YOUNG WOMAN: Ma—if you tell me that again I'll kill you! I'll kill you!

MOTHER: If that isn't crazy!

YOUNG WOMAN: I'll kill you—Maybe I am crazy—I don't know. Sometimes I think I am—the thoughts that go on in my mind—sometimes I think I am—I can't help it if I am—I do the best I can—I do the best I can and I'm nearly crazy! (MOTHER *rises and sits.*) Go away! Go away! You don't know anything about anything! And you haven't got any pity—no pity—you just take it for granted that I go to work every day—and come home every night and bring my money every week—and just take it for granted—you'd let me go on forever—and never feel any pity—

(*Offstage radio—a voice singing a sentimental mother song or popular home song.* MOTHER *begins to cry—crosses to chair left—sits.*)

Oh Ma—forgive me! Forgive me!

MOTHER: My own child! To be spoken to like that by my own child!

YOUNG WOMAN: I didn't mean it, Ma—I didn't mean it! (*She goes to her mother—crosses to left.*)

MOTHER (*clinging to her hand*): You're all I've got in the world—and you don't want me—you want to kill me.

YOUNG WOMAN: No—no, I don't, Ma! I just said that!

MOTHER: I've worked for you and slaved for you!

YOUNG WOMAN: I know, Ma.

MOTHER: I brought you into the world.

YOUNG WOMAN: I know, Ma.

MOTHER: You're flesh of my flesh and—

YOUNG WOMAN: I know, Ma, I know.

MOTHER: And—

YOUNG WOMAN: You rest now, Ma—you rest—

MOTHER (*struggling*): I got to do the dishes.

YOUNG WOMAN: I'll do the dishes—You listen to the music, Ma—I'll do the dishes.

(ma *sits.* YOUNG WOMAN *crosses to behind screen. Takes a pair of rubber gloves and begins to put them on. The* MOTHER *sees them—they irritate her—there is a return of her characteristic mood.*)

MOTHER: Those gloves! I've been washing dishes for forty years and I never wore gloves! But my lady's hands! My lady's hands!

YOUNG WOMAN: Sometimes you talk to me like you're jealous, Ma.

MOTHER: Jealous?

YOUNG WOMAN: It's my hands got me a husband.

MOTHER: A husband? So you're going to marry him now?

YOUNG WOMAN: I suppose so.

MOTHER: If you ain't the craziest—

(*The scene blacks out. In the darkness, the mother song goes into jazz—very faint—as the scene lights into*)

EPISODE 3

HONEYMOON

Scene: Hotel bedroom: bed, chair, mirror. The door at the back now opens on a bathroom; the window, on a dancing casino opposite.

Sounds: A small jazz band (violin, piano, saxophone—very dim, at first, then louder).

Characters: young woman; husband; bellboy

Offstage: Seen not not heard, MEN AND WOMEN *dancing in couples.*

At rise: Set dark. BELLBOY, HUSBAND, *and* YOUNG WOMAN *enter.* BELLBOY *carries luggage. He switches on light by door. Stop music.*

HUSBAND: Well, here we are. (*Throws hat on bed;* BELLBOY *puts luggage down, crosses to window; raises shade three inches. Opens window three inches. Sounds of jazz music louder. Offstage.*)

BELLBOY (*comes to man for tip*): Anything else, Sir? (*Receives tip. Exits.*)

HUSBAND: Well, here we are.

WOMAN: Yes, here we are.

HUSBAND: Aren't you going to take your hat off—stay a while? (YOUNG WOMAN *looks around as though looking for a way out, then takes off her hat, pulls the hair automatically around her ears.*) This is all right, isn't it? Huh? Huh?

YOUNG WOMAN: It's very nice.

HUSBAND: Twelve bucks a day! They know how to soak you in these pleasure resorts. Twelve bucks! (*Music.*) Well—we'll get our money's worth out of it all right. (*Goes toward bathroom.*) I'm going to wash up. (*Stops at door.*) Don't you want to wash up?

(young woman *shakes head "No".*)

I do! It was a long trip! I want to wash up!

(*Goes off—closes door; sings in bathroom.* YOUNG WOMAN *goes to window—raises shade—sees the dancers going round and round in couples. Music is louder. Re-enter* HUSBAND.)

Say, pull that blind down! They can see in!

YOUNG WOMAN: I thought you said there'd be a view of the ocean!

HUSBAND: Sure there is.

YOUNG WOMAN: I just see people—dancing.

HUSBAND: The ocean's beyond.

YOUNG WOMAN (*desperately*): I was counting on seeing it!

HUSBAND: You'll see it tomorrow—what's eating you? We'll take in the boardwalk—Don't you want to wash up?

YOUNG WOMAN: No!

HUSBAND: It was a long trip. Sure you don't? (YOUNG WOMAN *shakes her head "No".* HUSBAND *takes off his coat—puts it over chair.*) Better make yourself at home. I'm going to. (*She stares at him—moves away from the window.*) Say, pull down that blind! (*Crosses to chair down left—sits.*)

YOUNG WOMAN: It's close—don't you think it's close?

HUSBAND: Well—you don't want people looking in, do you? (*Laughs.*) Huh—Huh?

YOUNG WOMAN: No.

HUSBAND (*laughs*): I guess not. Huh? (*Takes off shoes.* YOUNG WOMAN *leaves the window, and crosses down to the bed.*) Say—you look a little white around the gills! What's the matter?

YOUNG WOMAN: Nothing.

HUSBAND: You look like you're scared.

YOUNG WOMAN: No.

HUSBAND: Nothing to be scared of. You're with your husband, you know. (*Takes her to chair, left.*)

YOUNG WOMAN: I know.

HUSBAND: Happy?

YOUNG WOMAN: Yes.

HUSBAND (*sitting*): Then come here and give us a kiss. (*He puts her on his knee.*) That's the girlie. (*He bends her head down, and kisses her along the back of her neck.*) Like that? (*She tries to get to her feet.*) Say—stay there! What you moving for?—You know—you got to learn to relax, little girl—(*Dancers go off. Dim lights. Pinches her above knee.*) Say, what you got under there?

YOUNG WOMAN: Nothing.

HUSBAND: Nothing! (*Laughs.*) That's a good one! Nothing, huh? Huh? That reminds me of the story of the pullman porter and the—what's the matter—did I tell you that one? (*Music dims off and out.*)

YOUNG WOMAN: I don't know.

HUSBAND: The pullman porter and the tart?

YOUNG WOMAN: No.

HUSBAND: It's a good one—well—the train was just pulling out and the tart—

YOUNG WOMAN: You did tell that one!

HUSBAND: About the—

YOUNG WOMAN: Yes! Yes! I remember now!

HUSBAND: About the—

YOUNG WOMAN: Yes!

HUSBAND: All right—if I did. You're sure it was the one about the—

YOUNG WOMAN: I'm sure.

HUSBAND: When he asked her what she had underneath her seat and she said—

YOUNG WOMAN: Yes! Yes! That one!

HUSBAND: All right—But I don't believe I did. (*She tries to get up again, and he holds her.*) You know you have got something under there—what is it?

YOUNG WOMAN: Nothing—just—just my garter.

HUSBAND: Your garter! Your garter! Say did I tell you the one about—

YOUNG WOMAN: Yes! Yes!

HUSBAND (*with dignity*): How do you know which one I mean?

YOUNG WOMAN: You told me them all!

HUSBAND (*pulling her back to his knee*): No, I didn't! Not by a jugful! I got a lot of 'em up my sleeve yet—that's part of what I owe my success to—my ability to spring a good story—You know—you got to learn to relax, little girl—haven't you?

YOUNG WOMAN: Yes.

HUSBAND: That's one of the biggest things to learn in life. That's part of what I owe my success to. Now you go and get those heavy things off—and relax.

YOUNG WOMAN: They're not heavy.

HUSBAND: You haven't got much on—have you? But you'll feel better with 'em off. (*Gets up.*) Want me to help you?

YOUNG WOMAN: No.

HUSBAND: I'm your husband, you know.

YOUNG WOMAN: I know.

HUSBAND: You aren't afraid of your husband, are you?

YOUNG WOMAN: No—of course not—but I thought maybe—can't we go out for a little while?

HUSBAND: Out? What for?

YOUNG WOMAN: Fresh air—walk—talk.

HUSBAND: We can talk here—I'll tell you all about myself. Go along now. (YOUNG WOMAN *goes toward bathroom door. Gets bag.*) Where are you going?

YOUNG WOMAN: In here.

HUSBAND: I thought you'd want to wash up.

YOUNG WOMAN: I just want to—get ready.

HUSBAND: You don't have to go in there to take your clothes off!

YOUNG WOMAN: I want to.

HUSBAND: What for?

YOUNG WOMAN: I always do.

HUSBAND: What?

YOUNG WOMAN: Undress by myself.

HUSBAND: You've never been married till now—have you? (*Laughs.*) Or have you been pulling something over on me?

YOUNG WOMAN: No.

HUSBAND: I understand—kind of modest—huh? Huh?

YOUNG WOMAN: Yes.

HUSBAND: I understand women—(*Indulgently.*) Go along.

(*She goes off—starts to close door.* YOUNG WOMAN *exits.*)

Don't close the door—thought you wanted to talk.

(*He looks around the room with satisfaction—after a pause—rises—takes off his collar.*)

You're awful quiet—what are you doing in there?

YOUNG WOMAN: Just—getting ready—

HUSBAND (*still in his mood of satisfaction*): I'm going to enjoy life from now on—I haven't had such an easy time of it. I got where I am by hard work and self denial—now I'm going to enjoy life—I'm going to make up for all I missed—aren't you about ready?

YOUNG WOMAN: Not yet.

HUSBAND: Next year maybe we'll go to Paris. You can buy a lot of that French underwear—and Switzerland—all my life I've wanted a Swiss watch—that I bought right there—I coulda' got a Swiss watch here, but I always wanted one that I bought right there—Isn't that funny—huh? Isn't it? Huh? Huh?

YOUNG WOMAN: Yes.

HUSBAND: All my life I've wanted a Swiss watch that I bought right there. All my life I've counted on having that some day—more than anything—except one thing—you know what?

YOUNG WOMAN: No.

HUSBAND: Guess.

YOUNG WOMAN: I can't.

HUSBAND: Then I'm coming in and tell you.

YOUNG WOMAN: No! Please! Please don't.

HUSBAND: Well hurry up then! I thought you women didn't wear much of anything these days—huh? Huh? I'm coming in!

YOUNG WOMAN: No—no! Just a minute!

HUSBAND: All right. Just a minute. (YOUNG WOMAN *is silent.* HUSBAND *laughs and takes out watch.*) 13—

14—I'm counting the seconds on you—that's what you said, didn't you—just a minute!—49—50—51—52—53—

(*Enter* YOUNG WOMAN.)

YOUNG WOMAN (*at the door*): Here I am. (*She wears a little white gown that hangs very straight. She is very still, but her eyes are wide with a curious, helpless, animal terror.*)

HUSBAND (*starts toward her—stops. The room is in shadow except for one dim light by the bed. Sound of girl weeping*): You crying? (*Sound of weeping.*) What are you crying for? (*Crosses to her.*)

YOUNG WOMAN (*crying out*): Ma! Ma! I want my mother!

HUSBAND: I thought you were glad to get away from her.

YOUNG WOMAN: I want her now—I want somebody.

HUSBAND: You got me, haven't you?

YOUNG WOMAN: Somebody—somebody—

HUSBAND: There's nothing to cry about. There's nothing to cry about.

(*The scene blacks out. The music continues until the lights go up for Episode 4. Rhythm of the music is gradually replaced by the sound of steel riveting for Episode 4.*)

EPISODE 4

MATERNAL

Scene: A room in a hospital: bed, chair. The door in the back now opens on a corridor; the window on a tall building going up.

Sounds: Outside window—riveting.

Characters in the scene: YOUNG WOMAN; DOCTORS; NURSES; HUSBAND

Characters seen but not heard: WOMAN IN WHEEL CHAIR; WOMAN IN BATHROBE; STRETCHER WAGON; NURSE WITH TRAY; NURSE WITH COVERED BASIN

At rise: YOUNG WOMAN *lies still in bed. The door is open. In the corridor, a stretcher wagon goes by. Enter* NURSE.

NURSE: How are you feeling today? (*No response from* YOUNG WOMAN.) Better? (*No response.*) No pain? (*No response.* NURSE *takes her watch in one hand,* YOUNG WOMAN's *wrist in the other—stands, then goes to chart at foot of bed—writes.*) You're getting along fine. (*No response.*) Such a sweet baby you have, too. (*No response.*) Aren't you glad it's a girl? (YOUNG WOMAN *makes sign with her head "No."*) You're not! Oh, my! That's no way to talk! Men want boys—woman ought to want girls. (*No response.*) Maybe you didn't want either, eh? (YOUNG WOMAN *signs "No." Riveting machine.*) You'll feel different when it begins to nurse. You'll just love it then. Your milk hasn't come yet—has it? (*Sign—"No".*) It will! (*Sign—"No."*) Oh, you don't know Doctor! (*Goes to door—turns.*) Anything else you want? (YOUNG WOMAN *points to window.*) Draft? (*Sign—"No."*) The noise? (YOUNG WOMAN *signs "Yes."*) Oh, that can't be helped. Hospital's got to have a new wing. We've the biggest Maternity Hospital in the world. I'll close the window, though. (YOUNG WOMAN *signs "No."*) No?

YOUNG WOMAN (*whispers*): I smell everything then.

NURSE (*starting out the door—riveting machine*): Here's your man!

(*Enter* HUSBAND *with large bouquet. Crosses to bed.*)

HUSBAND: Well, how are we today? (YOUNG WOMAN—*no response.*)

NURSE: She's getting stronger!

HUSBAND: Of course she is!

NURSE (*taking flowers*): See what your husband brought you.

HUSBAND: Better put 'em in water right away. (*Exit nurse.*) Everything O.K.? (YOUNG WOMAN *signs "No."*) Now see here, my dear, you've got to brace up, you know! And—and face things! Everybody's got to brace up and face things! That's what makes the world go round. I know all you've been through but—(YOUNG WOMAN *signs "No."*) Oh, yes I do! I know all about it! I was right outside all the time! (YOUNG WOMAN *makes violent gestures of "No." Ignoring.*) Oh yes! But you've got to brace up now! Make an effort! Pull yourself together! Start the up-hill climb! Oh I've been down—but I haven't stayed down. I've been licked but I haven't stayed licked! I've pulled myself up by my own bootstraps, and that's what you've got to do! Will power! That's what conquers! Look at me! Now you've got to brace up! Face the music! Stand the gaff! Take life by

the horns! Look it in the face!—Having a baby's natural! Perfectly natural thing—why should— (young woman *chokes—points wildly to door. Enter* NURSE *with flowers in a vase.*)

NURSE: What's the matter?

HUSBAND: She's got that gagging again—like she had the last time I was here.
(young woman *gestures him out.*)

NURSE: Better go, sir.

HUSBAND (*at door*): I'll be back.
(young woman *gasping and gesturing.*)

NURSE: She needs rest.

HUSBAND: Tomorrow then. I'll be back tomorrow—tomorrow and every day—goodbye. (*Exits.*)

NURSE: You got a mighty nice husband, I guess you know that? (*Writes on chart.*) Gagging.
(*Corridor life—*WOMAN IN A BATHROBE *passes door. Enter* DOCTOR, YOUNG DOCTOR, NURSE, *wheeling surgeon's wagon with bottles, instruments, etc.*)

DOCTOR: How's the little lady today? (*Crosses to bed.*)

NURSE: She's better, Doctor.

DOCTOR: Of course she's better! She's all right—aren't you? (YOUNG WOMAN *does not respond.*) What's the matter? Can't you talk? (*Drops her hand. Takes chart.*)

NURSE: She's a little weak yet, Doctor.

DOCTOR (*at chart*): Milk hasn't come yet?

NURSE: No, Doctor.

DOCTOR: Put the child to breast. (YOUNG WOMAN—*"No—no"!—Riveting machine.*) No? Don't you want to nurse your baby? (YOUNG WOMAN *signs "No."*) Why not? (*No response.*) These modern neurotic women, eh, Doctor? What are we going to do with 'em? (YOUNG DOCTOR *laughs.* NURSE *smiles.*) Bring the baby!

YOUNG WOMAN: No!

DOCTOR: Well—that's strong enough. I thought you were too weak to talk—that's better. You don't want your baby?

YOUNG WOMAN: No.

DOCTOR: What do you want?

YOUNG WOMAN: Let alone—let alone.

DOCTOR: Bring the baby.

NURSE: Yes, Doctor—she's behaved very badly every time, Doctor—very upset—maybe we better not.

DOCTOR: I decide what we better and better not here, Nurse!

NURSE: Yes, doctor.

DOCTOR: Bring the baby.

NURSE: Yes, Doctor.

DOCTOR (*with chart*): Gagging—you mean nausea.

NURSE: Yes, Doctor, but—

DOCTOR: No buts, nurse.

NURSE: Yes, Doctor.

DOCTOR: Nausea!—Change the diet!—What is her diet?

NURSE: Liquids.

DOCTOR: Give her solids.

NURSE: Yes, Doctor. She says she can't swallow solids.

DOCTOR: Give her solids.

NURSE: Yes, Doctor. (*Starts to go—riveting machine.*)

DOCTOR: Wait—I'll change her medicine. (*Takes pad and writes prescription in Latin. Hands it to* NURSE.) After meals. (*To door.*) Bring her baby. (*Exit* DOCTOR, *followed by* YOUNG DOCTOR *and* NURSE *with surgeon's wagon.*)

NURSE: Yes, Doctor.

(*Exits.*)

YOUNG WOMAN (*alone*): Let me alone—let me alone—let me alone—I've submitted to enough—I won't submit to any more—crawl off—crawl off in the dark—Vixen crawled under the bed—way back in the corner under the bed—they were all drowned—puppies don't go to heaven—heaven—golden stairs—long stairs—long—too long—long golden stairs—climb those golden stairs—stairs—stairs—climb—tired—too tired—dead—no matter—nothing matters—dead—stairs—long stairs—all the dead going up—going up—to be in heaven—heaven—golden stairs—all the children coming down—coming down to be born—dead going up—children coming down—going up—coming down—going up—coming down—going up—coming down—going up—stop—stop—no—no traffic cop—no—no traffic cop in heaven—traffic cop—traffic cop—can't you give us a smile—tired—too tired—no matter—it doesn't matter—St. Peter—St. Peter at the gate—you can't come in—no matter—it doesn't matter—I'll rest—I'll lie down—down—all written down—down in a big book—no matter—it doesn't matter—I'll lie down—it weighs me—it's over me—it weighs—weighs—it's heavy—it's a heavy book—no matter—

lie still—don't move—can't move—rest—forget—they say you forget—a girl—aren't you glad it's a girl—a little girl—with no hair—none—little curls all over his head—a little bald girl—curls—curls all over his head—what kind of hair had God? No matter—it doesn't matter—everybody loves God—they've got to—got to—got to love God—God is love—even if he's bad they got to love him—if he's got fat hands—fat hands—no no—he wouldn't be God—His hands make you well—He lays on his hands—well—and happy—no matter—doesn't matter—far—too far—tired—too tired Vixen crawled off under bed—eight—there were eight—a woman crawled off under the bed—a woman has one—two three four—one two three four—one two three four—two plus two is four—two times two is four—two times four is eight—Vixen had eight—one two three four five six seven eight—eight—Puffie had eight—all drowned—drowned—drowned in blood—blood—Oh God! God—God never had one—Mary had one—in a manger—the lowly manger—God's on a high throne—far—too far—no matter—it doesn't matter—God Mary Mary God Mary—Virgin Mary—Mary had one—the Holy Ghost—the Holy Ghost—George H. Jones—oh don't—please don't! Let me rest—now I can rest—the weight is gone—inside the weight is gone—it's only outside—outside—all around—weight—I'm under it—Vixen crawled under the bed—there were eight—I'll not submit any more—I'll not submit—I'll not submit—

(*The scene blacks out. The sound of riveting continues until it goes into the sound of an electric piano and the scene lights up for Episode 5.*)

EPISODE 5

PROHIBITED

Scene: Bar: bottles, tables, chairs, electric piano.

Sound: Electric piano.

Characters: man behind the bar; POLICEMAN AT BAR; WAITER; *At Table 1:* A MAN AND A WOMAN; *at Table 2:* A

MAN AND A BOY; *at Table 3:* TWO MEN *waiting for* TWO GIRLS, *who are;* TELEPHONE GIRL *of Episode 1 and* YOUNG WOMAN.

At rise: Everyone except the GIRLS *on. Of the characters, the* MAN *and* WOMAN *at Table 1 are an ordinary man and woman. The* MAN *at Table 2 is a middle-aged fairy; the* BOY *is young, untouched. At Table 3,* FIRST MAN *is pleasing, common, vigorous. He has coarse wavy hair.* SECOND MAN *is an ordinary salesman type.*

(*At Table 3.*)
FIRST MAN: I'm going to beat it.
SECOND MAN: Oh, for the love of Mike.
FIRST MAN: They ain't going to show.
SECOND MAN: Sure they'll show.
FIRST MAN: How do you know they'll show?
SECOND MAN: I tell you you can't keep that baby away from me—just got to—(*Snaps fingers.*)—She comes running.
FIRST MAN: Looks like it.
SECOND MAN (*to* WAITER *makes sign "2" with his fingers*): The same. (WAITER *goes to the bar.*)
(*At Table 2.*)
MAN: Oh, I'm sorry I brought you here.
BOY: Why?
MAN: This Purgatory of noise! I brought you here to give you pleasure—let you taste pleasure. This sherry they have here is bottled—heaven. Wait till you taste it.
BOY: I don't drink.
MAN: Drink! This isn't drink! Real amontillado is sunshine and orange groves—it's the Mediterranean and blue moonlight and—love? Have you ever been in love?
BOY: No.
MAN: Never in love with—a woman?
BOY: No—not really.
MAN: What do you mean really?
BOY: Just—that.
MAN: Ah! (*Makes sign to* WAITER.) To—you know what I want—Two. (WAITER *goes to the bar.*)
(*At Table 1.*)
MAN: Well, are you going through with it, or ain't you?
WOMAN: That's what I want to do—go through with it.
MAN: But you can't.

WOMAN: Why can't I?
MAN: How can yuh? (*Silence.*) It's nothing—most women don't think anything about it—they just—Bert told me a doctor to go to—gave me the address—
WOMAN: Don't talk about it!
MAN: Got to talk about it—you got to get out of this. (*Silence*—MAN *makes sign to* WAITER.) What you having?
WOMAN: Nothing—I don't want anything. I had enough.
MAN: Do you good. The same?
WOMAN: I suppose so.
MAN (*makes sign "2" to* WAITER): The same. (WAITER *goes to the bar.*)
(*At Table 3.*)
FIRST MAN: I'm going to beat it.
SECOND MAN: Oh say, listen! I'm counting on you to take the other one off my hands.
FIRST MAN: I'm going to beat it.
SECOND MAN: For the love of Mike have a heart! Listen—as a favor to me—I got to be home by six—I promised my wife—sure. That don't leave me no time at all if we got to hang around—entertain some dame. You got to take her off my hands.
FIRST MAN: Maybe she won't fall for me.
SECOND MAN: Sure she'll fall for you! They all fall for you—even my wife likes you—tries to kid herself it's your brave exploits, but I know what it is—sure she'll fall for you.
(*Enter two girls*—TELEPHONE GIRL *and* YOUNG WOMAN.)
GIRL (*coming to table*): Hello—
SECOND MAN (*grouch*): Good night.
GIRL: Good night? What's eatin' yuh?
SECOND MAN (*same*): Nothin's eatin' me—thought somethin' musta swallowed you.
GIRL: Why?
SECOND MAN: You're late!
GIRL (*unimpressed*): Oh—(*Brushing it aside.*) Mrs. Jones—Mr. Smith.
SECOND MAN: Meet my friend, Mr. Roe. (*They all sit. To the* WAITER.) The same and two more. (WAITER *goes.*)
GIRL: So we kept you waiting, did we?
SECOND MAN: Only about an hour.
YOUNG WOMAN: Was it that long?

SECOND MAN: We been here that long—ain't we Dick?

FIRST MAN: Just about, Harry.

SECOND MAN: For the love of God what delayed yuh?

GIRL: Tell Helen that one.

SECOND MAN (*to* YOUNG WOMAN): The old Irish woman that went to her first race? Bet on the skate that came in last—she went up to the jockey and asked him, "For the love of God, what delayed yuh".
(*All laugh.*)

YOUNG WOMAN: Why, that's kinda funny!

SECOND MAN: Kinda!—What do you mean kinda?

YOUNG WOMAN: I just mean there are not many of 'em that are funny at all.

SECOND MAN: Not if you haven't heard the funny ones.

YOUNG WOMAN: Oh I've heard 'em all.

FIRST MAN: Not a laugh in a carload, eh?

GIRL: Got a cigarette?

SECOND MAN (*with package*): One of these?

GIRL (*taking one*): Uhhuh.
(*He offers the package to* YOUNG WOMAN.)

YOUNG WOMAN (*taking one*): Uhhuh.

SECOND MAN (*to* FIRST MAN): One of these?

FIRST MAN (*showing his own package*): Thanks—I like these.
(*He lights* YOUNG WOMAN'*s cigarette.*)

SECOND MAN (*lighting* GIRL'*s cigarette*): Well—baby—how they comin', huh?

GIRL: Couldn't be better.

SECOND MAN: How's every little thing?

GIRL: Just great.

SECOND MAN: Miss me?

GIRL: I'll say so—when did you get in?

SECOND MAN: Just a coupla hours ago.

GIRL: Miss me?

SECOND MAN: Did I? You don't know the half of it.

YOUNG WOMAN (*interrupting restlessly*): Can we dance here?

SECOND MAN: Not here.

YOUNG WOMAN: Where do we go from here?

SECOND MAN: Where do we go from here! You just got here!

FIRST MAN: What's the hurry?

SECOND MAN: What's the rush?

YOUNG WOMAN: I don't know.

GIRL: Helen wants to dance.

YOUNG WOMAN: I just want to keep moving.

FIRST MAN (*smiling*): You want to keep moving, huh?

SECOND MAN: You must be one of those restless babies! Where do we go from here!

YOUNG WOMAN: It's only some days—I want to keep moving.

FIRST MAN: You want to keep moving, huh? (*He is staring at her smilingly.*)

YOUNG WOMAN (*nods*): Uhhuh.

FIRST MAN (*quietly*): Stick around a while.

SECOND MAN: Where do we go from here! Say, what kind of a crowd do you run with, anyway?

GIRL: Helen don't run with any crowd—do you, Helen?

YOUNG WOMAN (*embarrassed*): No.

FIRST MAN: Well, I'm not a crowd—run with me.

SECOND MAN (*gratified*): All set, huh?—Dick was about ready to beat it.

FIRST MAN: That's before I met the little lady.
(WAITER *serves drinks.*)

FIRST MAN: Here's how.

SECOND MAN: Here's to you.

GIRL: Here's looking at you.

YOUNG WOMAN: Here's—happy days.
(*They all drink.*)

FIRST MAN: That's good stuff!

SECOND MAN: Off a boat.

FIRST MAN: Off a boat?

SECOND MAN: They get all their stuff here—off a boat.

GIRL: That's what *they* say.

SECOND MAN: No! Sure! Sure they do! Sure!

GIRL: It's all right with me.

SECOND MAN: But they do! Sure!

GIRL: I believe you, darling!

SECOND MAN: Did you miss me?

GIRL: Uhhuh. (*Affirmative.*)

SECOND MAN: Any other daddies?

GIRL: Uhhuh. (*Negative.*)

SECOND MAN: Love any daddy but daddy?

GIRL: Uhhuh. (*Negative.*)

SECOND MAN: Let's beat it!

GIRL (*a little self-conscious before* YOUNG WOMAN): We just got here.

SECOND MAN: Don't I know it—Come on!

GIRL: But—(*Indicates* YOUNG WOMAN.)

SECOND MAN (*not understanding*): They're all set—aren't you?

FIRST MAN (*to* YOUNG WOMAN): Are we? (*She doesn't answer.*)

SECOND MAN: I got to be out to the house by six—come on—(*Rising—to* GIRL.) Come on, kid—let's us beat it! (GIRL *indicates* YOUNG WOMAN. *Now understanding—very elaborate.*) Business is business, you know! I got a lot to do yet this afternoon—thought you might go along with me—help me out—how about it?

GIRL (*rising, her dignity preserved.*): Sure—I'll go along with you—help you out. (*Both rise.*)

SECOND MAN: All right with you folks?

FIRST MAN: All right with me.

SECOND MAN: All right with you? (*To* YOUNG WOMAN.)

YOUNG WOMAN: All right with me.

SECOND MAN: Come on, kid. (*They rise.*) Where's the damage?

FIRST MAN: Go on!

SECOND MAN: No!

FIRST MAN: Go on!

SECOND MAN: I'll match you.

YOUNG WOMAN: Heads win!

GIRL: Heads I win—tails you lose.

SECOND MAN (*impatiently*): He's matching me.

FIRST MAN: Am I matching you or are you matching me?

SECOND MAN: I'm matching you. (*They match.*) You're stung!

FIRST MAN (*contentedly*): Not so you can notice it. (*Smiles at* YOUNG WOMAN.)

GIRL: That's for you, Helen.

SECOND MAN: She ain't dumb! Come on.

GIRL (*to* FIRST MAN): You be nice to her now. She's very fastidious.—Goodbye.
(*Exit* SECOND MAN *and* GIRL.)

YOUNG WOMAN: I know what business is like.

FIRST MAN: You do—do yuh?

YOUNG WOMAN: I used to be a business girl myself before—

FIRST MAN: Before what?

YOUNG WOMAN: Before I quit.

FIRST MAN: What did you quit for?

YOUNG WOMAN: I just quit.

FIRST MAN: You're married, huh?

YOUNG WOMAN: Yes—I am.

FIRST MAN: All right with me.

YOUNG WOMAN: Some men don't seem to like a woman after she's married—

(WAITER *comes to the table.*)

FIRST MAN: What's the difference?

YOUNG WOMAN: Depends on the man, I guess.

FIRST MAN: Depends on the woman, I guess. (*To* WAITER, *makes sign of "2".*) The same. (WAITER *goes to the bar.*)
(*At Table 1.*)

MAN: It don't amount to nothing. God! Most women just—

WOMAN: I know—I know—I know.

MAN: They don't think nothing of it. They just—

WOMAN: I know—I know—I know.
(*Re-enter* SECOND MAN *and* GIRL. *They go to Table 3.*)

SECOND MAN: Say, I forgot—I want you to do something for me, will yuh?

FIRST MAN: Sure—what is it?

SECOND MAN: I want you to telephone me out home tomorrow—and ask me to come into town—will yuh?

FIRST MAN: Sure—why not?

SECOND MAN: You know—business—get me?

FIRST MAN: I get you.

SECOND MAN: I've worked the telegraph gag to death—and my wife likes you.

FIRST MAN: What's your number?

SECOND MAN: I'll write it down for you. (*Writes.*)

FIRST MAN: How is your wife?

SECOND MAN: She's fine.

FIRST MAN: And the kid?

SECOND MAN: Great. (*Hands him the card. To* GIRL.) Come on, kid. (*Turns back to* YOUNG WOMAN.) Get this bird to tell you about himself.

GIRL: Keep him from it.

SECOND MAN: Get him to tell you how he killed a couple of spig down in Mexico.

GIRL: You been in Mexico?

SECOND MAN: He just came up from there.

GIRL: Can you teach us the tango?

YOUNG WOMAN: You killed a man?

SECOND MAN: Two of 'em! With a bottle! Get him to tell you—with a bottle. Come on, kid. Goodbye.
(*Exit* SECOND MAN *and* GIRL.)

YOUNG WOMAN: Why did you?

FIRST MAN: What?

YOUNG WOMAN: Kill 'em?

FIRST MAN: To get free.

YOUNG WOMAN: Oh.
(*At Table 2.*)

MAN: You really must taste this—just taste it. It's a real amontillado, you know.

BOY: Where do they get it here?

MAN: It's always down the side streets one finds the real pleasures, don't you think?

BOY: I don't know.

MAN: Learn. Come, taste this! Amontillado! Or don't you like amontillado?

BOY: I don't know. I never had any before.

MAN: Your first taste! How I envy you! Come, taste it! Taste it! And die.

(BOY *tastes wine—finds it disappointing.*)

MAN (*gliding it*): Poe was a lover of amontillado. He returns to it continually, you remember— or are you a lover of Poe?

BOY: I've read a lot of him.

MAN: But are you a lover?

(*At Table 3.*)

FIRST MAN: There were a bunch of bandidos—bandits, you know, took me into the hills—holding me there—what was I to do? got the two birds that guarded me drunk one night, and then I filled the empty bottle with small stones—and let 'em have it!

YOUNG WOMAN: Oh!

FIRST MAN: I had to get free, didn't I? I let 'em have it—

YOUNG WOMAN: Oh—then what did you do?

FIRST MAN: Then I beat it.

YOUNG WOMAN: Where to—?

FIRST MAN: Right here. (*Pause.*) Glad?

YOUNG WOMAN (*nods*): Yes.

FIRST MAN (*makes sign to* WAITER *of* "2"): The same.

(WAITER *goes to the bar.*)

(*At Table 1.*)

MAN: You're just scared because this is the first time and—

WOMAN: I'm not scared.

MAN: Then what are you for Christ's sake?

WOMAN: I'm not scared. I want it—I want to have it—that ain't being scared, is it?

MAN: It's being goofy.

WOMAN: I don't care.

MAN: What about your folks?

WOMAN: I don't care.

MAN: What about your job? (*Silence.*) You got to keep your job, haven't you? (*Silence.*) Haven't you?

WOMAN: I suppose so.

MAN: Well—there you are!

WOMAN (*silence—then*): All right—let's go now— You got the address?

MAN: Now you're coming to.

(*They get up and go off. Exit* MAN *and* WOMAN.)

(*At Table 3.*)

YOUNG WOMAN: A bottle like that? (*She picks it up.*)

FIRST MAN: Yeah—filled with pebbles.

YOUNG WOMAN: What kind of pebbles?

FIRST MAN: Pebbles! Off the ground.

YOUNG WOMAN: Oh.

FIRST MAN: Necessity, you know, mother of invention. (*As* YOUNG WOMAN *handles the bottle.*) Ain't a bad weapon—first you got a sledge hammer—then you got a knife.

YOUNG WOMAN: Oh. (*Puts bottle down.*)

FIRST MAN: Women don't like knives, do they? (*Pours drink.*)

YOUNG WOMAN: No.

FIRST MAN: Don't mind a hammer so much, though, do they?

YOUNG WOMAN: No—

FIRST MAN: I didn't like it myself—any of it—but I had to get free, didn't I? Sure I had to get free, didn't I? (*Drinks.*) Now I'm damn glad I did.

YOUNG WOMAN: Why?

FIRST MAN: You know why. (*He puts his hand over hers.*)

(*At Table 2.*)

MAN: Let's go to my rooms—and I'll show them to you—I have a first edition of Verlaine that will simply make your mouth water. (*They stand up.*) Here—there's just a sip at the bottom of my glass—

(BOY *takes it.*)

That last sip's the sweetest—Wasn't it?

BOY (*laughs*): And I always thought that was dregs.

(*Exit* MAN *followed by* BOY.)

(*At Table 3.*)

(*The* MAN *is holding her hand across the table.*)

YOUNG WOMAN: When you put your hand over mine! When you just touch me!

FIRST MAN: Yeah? (*Pause.*) Come on, kid, let's go!

YOUNG WOMAN: Where?

FIRST MAN: You haven't been around much, have you, kid?

YOUNG WOMAN: No.

FIRST MAN: I could tell that just to look at you.

YOUNG WOMAN: You could?

FIRST MAN: Sure I could. What are you running around with a girl like that other one for?

YOUNG WOMAN: I don't know. She seems to have a good time.

FIRST MAN: So that's it?

YOUNG WOMAN: Don't she?

FIRST MAN: Don't you?

YOUNG WOMAN: No.

FIRST MAN: Never?

YOUNG WOMAN: Never.

FIRST MAN: What's the matter?

YOUNG WOMAN: Nothing—just me, I guess.

FIRST MAN: You're all right.

YOUNG WOMAN: Am I?

FIRST MAN: Sure. You just haven't met the right guy—that's all—girl like you—you got to meet the right guy.

YOUNG WOMAN: I know.

FIRST MAN: You're different from girls like that other one—any guy'll do her. You're different.

YOUNG WOMAN: I guess I am.

FIRST MAN: You didn't fall for that business gag—did you—when they went off?

YOUNG WOMAN: Well, I thought they wanted to be alone probably, but—

FIRST MAN: And how!

YOUNG WOMAN: Oh—so that's it.

FIRST MAN: That's it. Come along—let's go—

YOUNG WOMAN: Oh, I couldn't! Like this?

FIRST MAN: Don't you like me?

YOUNG WOMAN: Yes.

FIRST MAN: Then what's the matter?

YOUNG WOMAN: Do—you—like me?

FIRST MAN: Like yuh? You don't know the half of it—listen—you know what you seem like to me?

YOUNG WOMAN: What?

FIRST MAN: An angel. Just like an angel.

YOUNG WOMAN: I do?

FIRST MAN: That's what I said! Let's go!

YOUNG WOMAN: Where?

FIRST MAN: Where do you live?

YOUNG WOMAN: Oh, we can't go to my place.

FIRST MAN: Then come to my place.

YOUNG WOMAN: Oh I couldn't—is it far?

FIRST MAN: Just a step—come on—

YOUNG WOMAN: Oh I couldn't—what is it—a room?

FIRST MAN: No—an apartment—a one room apartment.

YOUNG WOMAN: That's different.

FIRST MAN: On the ground floor—no one will see you—coming or going.

YOUNG WOMAN (*getting up*): I couldn't.

FIRST MAN (*rises*): Wait a minute—I got to pay the damage—and I'll get a bottle of something to take along.

YOUNG WOMAN: No—don't.

FIRST MAN: Why not?

YOUNG WOMAN: Well—don't bring any pebbles.

FIRST MAN: Say—forget that! Will you?

YOUNG WOMAN: I just meant I don't think I'll need anything to drink.

FIRST MAN (*leaning to her eagerly*): You like me—don't you, kid?

YOUNG WOMAN: Do you me?

FIRST MAN: Wait!

(*He goes to the bar. She remains, her hands outstretched on the table, staring ahead. Enter a* MAN *and a* GIRL. *They go to one of the empty tables. The* WAITER *goes to them.*)

MAN (*to* GIRL): What do you want?

GIRL: Same old thing.

MAN (*to the* WAITER): The usual. (*Makes a sign "2".*)

(*The* FIRST MAN *crosses to* YOUNG WOMAN *with a wrapped bottle under his arm. She rises and starts out with him. As they pass the piano, he stops and puts in a nickel—the music starts as they exit. The scene blacks out.*)

(*The music of the electric piano continues until the lights go up for Episode 6, and the music has become the music of a hand organ, very very faint.*)

EPISODE 6

INTIMATE

Scene: A dark room.

Sounds. A hand organ; footbeats, of passing feet.

Characters: MAN; YOUNG WOMAN

At Rise: Darkness. Nothing can be discerned. From the outside comes the sound of a hand organ, very faint, and the irregular rhythm of passing feet. The hand organ is playing Cielito Lindo, *that Spanish song that has been on every hand organ lately.*

MAN: You're awful still, honey. What you thinking about?

WOMAN: About sea shells. (*The sound of her voice is beautiful.*)

MAN: Sheshells? Gee! I can't say it!

WOMAN: When I was little my grandmother used to have a big pink sea shell on the mantle behind the stove. When we'd go to visit her they'd let me hold it, and listen. That's what I was thinking about now.

MAN: Yeah?

WOMAN: You can hear the sea in 'em, you know.

MAN: Yeah, I know.

WOMAN: I wonder why that is?

MAN: Search me. (*Pause.*)

WOMAN: You going? (*He has moved.*)

MAN: No. I just want a cigarette.

WOMAN (*glad, relieved*): Oh.

MAN: Want one?

WOMAN: No. (*Taking the match.*) Let me light it for you.

MAN: You got mighty pretty hands, honey. (*The match is out.*) This little pig went to market. This little pig stayed home. This little pig went—

WOMAN (*laughs*): Diddle diddle dee. (*Laughs again.*)

MAN: You got awful pretty hands.

WOMAN: I used to have. But I haven't taken much care of them lately. I will now—(*Pause. The music gets clearer.*) What's that?

MAN: What?

WOMAN: That music?

MAN: A dago hand organ. I gave him two bits the first day I got here—so he comes every day.

WOMAN: I mean—what's that he's playing?

MAN: *Cielito Lindo.*

WOMAN: What does that mean?

MAN: Little Heaven.

WOMAN: Little Heaven?

MAN: That's what lovers call each other in Spain.

WOMAN: Spain's where all the castles are, ain't it?

MAN: Yeah.

WOMAN: Little Heaven—sing it!

MAN (*singing to the music of the hand organ*): Da la sierra morena viene, bajando viene, bajando; un par de ojitos negros—cielito lindo—da contrabando.

WOMAN: What does it mean?

MAN: From the high dark mountains.

WOMAN: From the high dark mountains—?

MAN: Oh it doesn't mean anything. It doesn't make sense. It's love. (*Taking up the song.*) Ay-ay-ay-ay.

WOMAN: I know what that means.

MAN: What?

WOMAN: Ay-ay-ay-ay. (*They laugh.*)

MAN (*taking up the song*): Canta non llores—Sing don't cry—

WOMAN (*taking up the song*): La-la-la-la-la-la-la-la-la-la—Little Heaven!

MAN: You got a nice voice, honey.

WOMAN: Have I? (*Laughs—tickles him.*)

MAN: You bet you have—hey!

WOMAN (*laughing*): You ticklish?

MAN: Sure I am! Hey! (*They laugh.*) Go on, honey, sing something.

WOMAN: I couldn't.

MAN: Go on—you got a fine voice.

WOMAN (*laughs and sings*): Hey, diddle, diddle, the cat and the fiddle, The cow jumped over the moon, The little dog laughed to see the sport, And the dish ran away with the spoon— (*Both laugh.*)

   I never thought that had any sense before—now I get it.

MAN: You got me beat.

WOMAN: It's you and me—La-lalalalalala—lalalalalala—Little Heaven. You're the dish and I'm the spoon.

MAN: You're a little spoon all right.

WOMAN: And I guess I'm the little cow that jumped over the moon. (*A pause.*) Do you believe in sorta guardian angels?

MAN: What?

WOMAN: Guardian angels?

MAN: I don't know. Maybe.

WOMAN: I do. (*Taking up the song again.*) Lalalalala—lalalalala—lalalala—Little Heaven. (*Talking.*) There must be something that looks out for you and brings you your happiness, at last—look at us! How did we both happen to go to that place today if there wasn't something!

MAN: Maybe you're right.

WOMAN: Look at us!

MAN: Everything's us to you, kid—ain't it?

WOMAN: Ain't it?

MAN: All right with me.

WOMAN: We belong together! We belong together! And we're going to stick together, ain't we?

MAN: Sing something else.

WOMAN: I tell you I can't sing!

MAN: Sure you can!

WOMAN: I tell you I hadn't thought of singing since I was a little bit of a girl.

MAN: Well sing anyway.

WOMAN (*singing*): And every little wavelet had its night cap on—its night cap on—its night cap on—and every little wave had its night cap on—so very early in the morning. (*Talking.*) Did you used to sing that when you were a little kid?

MAN: Nope.

WOMAN: Didn't you? We used to—in the first grade—little kids—we used to go round and round in a ring—and flop our hands up and down—supposed to be the waves. I remember it used to confuse me—because we did just the same thing to be little angels.

MAN: Yeah?

WOMAN: You know why I came here?

MAN: I can make a good guess.

WOMAN: Because you told me I looked like an angel to you! That's why I came.

MAN: Jeez, honey, all women look like angels to me—all white women. I ain't been seeing nothing but Indians, you know for the last couple a years. Gee, when I got off the boat here the other day—and saw all the women—gee I pretty near went crazy—talk at looking like angels—why—

WOMAN: You've had a lot of women, haven't you?

MAN: Not so many—real ones.

WOMAN: Did you—like any of 'em—better than me?

MAN: Nope—there wasn't one of 'em any sweeter than you, honey—not as sweet—no—not as sweet.

WOMAN: I like to hear you say it. Say it again—

MAN (*protesting good humoredly*): Oh—

WOMAN: Go on—tell me again!

MAN: Here! (*Kisses her.*) Does that tell you?

WOMAN: Yes. (*Pause.*) We're going to stick together—always—aren't we?

MAN (*honestly*): I'll have to be moving on, kid—some day, you know.

WOMAN: When?

MAN: Quien sabe?

WOMAN: What does that mean?

MAN: Quien sabe? You got to learn that, kid, if you're figuring on coming with me. It's the answer to everything—below the Rio Grande.

WOMAN: What does it mean?

MAN: It means—who knows?

WOMAN: Keen sabe?

MAN: Yep—don't forget it—now.

WOMAN: I'll never forget it!

MAN: Quien sabe.

WOMAN: And I'll never get used to it.

MAN: Quien sabe.

WOMAN: I'll never get—below the Rio Grande—I'll never get out of here.

MAN: Quien sabe.

WOMAN: (*change of mood*): That's right! Keen sabe? Who knows?

MAN: That's the stuff.

WOMAN: You must like it down there.

MAN: I can't live anywhere else—for long.

WOMAN: Why not?

MAN: Oh—you're free down there! You're free! (*A street light is lit outside. The outlines of a window take form against this light. There are bars across it, and from outside it, the sidewalk cuts across almost at the top. It is a basement room. The constant going and coming of passing feet, mostly feet of couples, can be dimly seen. Inside, on the ledge, there is a lily blooming in a bowl of rocks and water.*)

WOMAN: What's that?

MAN: Just the street light going on.

WOMAN: Is it as late as that?

MAN: Late as what?

WOMAN: Dark.

MAN: It's been dark for hours—didn't you know that?

WOMAN: No!—I must go! (*Rises.*)

MAN: Wait—the moon will be up in a little while—full moon.

WOMAN: It isn't that! I'm late! I must go! (*She comes into the light. She wears a white chemise that might be the tunic of a dancer, and as*

she comes into the light she fastens about her waist a little skirt. She really wears almost exactly the clothes that women wear now, but the finesse of their cut, and the grace and ease with which she puts them on, must turn this episode of her dressing into a personification, an idealization of a woman clothing herself. All her gestures must be unconscious, innocent, relaxed, sure and full of natural grace. As she sits facing the window pulling on a stocking.)
What's that?

MAN: What?

WOMAN: On the window ledge.

MAN: A flower.

WOMAN: Who gave it to you?

MAN: Nobody gave it to me. I bought it.

WOMAN: For yourself?

MAN: Yeah—Why not?

WOMAN: I don't know.

MAN: In Chinatown—made me think of Frisco where I was a kid—so I bought it.

WOMAN: Is that where you were born—Frisco?

MAN: Yep. Twin Peaks.

WOMAN: What's that?

MAN: A couple of hills—together.

WOMAN: One for you and one for me.

MAN: I bet you'd like Frisco.

WOMAN: I knew a woman went out there once!

MAN: The bay and the hills! Jeez, that's the life! Every Saturday we used to cross the Bay—get a couple nags and just ride—over the hills. One would have a blanket on the saddle—the other, the grub. At night, we'd make a little fire and eat—and then roll up in the old blanket and—

WOMAN: Who? Who was with you?

MAN (*indifferently*): Anybody. (*Enthusiastically.*) Jeez, that dry old grass out there smells good at night—full of tar weed—you know—

WOMAN: Is that a good smell?

MAN: Tar weed? Didn't you ever smell it? (*She shakes her head "No".*) Sure it's a good smell! The Bay and the hills.
(*She goes to the mirror of the dresser, to finish dressing. She has only a dress to put on that is in one piece—with one fastening on the side. Before slipping it on, she stands before the mirror and stretches. Appreciatively but indifferently.*)

You look in good shape, kid. A couple of months riding over the mountains with me, you'd be great.

WOMAN: Can I?

MAN: What?

WOMAN: Some day—ride mountains with you?

MAN: Ride mountains? Ride donkeys!

WOMAN: It's the same thing!—with you!—Can I—some day? The high dark mountains?

MAN: Who knows?

WOMAN: It must be great!

MAN: You ever been off like that, kid?—high up? On top of the world?

WOMAN: Yes.

MAN: When?

WOMAN: Today.

MAN: You're pretty sweet.

WOMAN: I never knew anything like this way! I never knew that I could feel like this! So,—so purified! Don't laugh at me!

MAN: I ain't laughing, honey.

WOMAN: Purified.

MAN: It's a hell of a word—but I know what you mean. That's the way it is—sometimes.

WOMAN (*she puts on a little hat, then turns to him*): Well—goodbye.

MAN: Aren't you forgetting something? (*Rises.*)
(*She looks toward him, then throws her head slowly back, lifts her right arm—this gesture that is in so many statues of women—Volupte. He comes out of the shadow, puts his arm around her, kisses her. Her head and arm go further back—then she brings her arm around with a wide encircling gesture, her hand closes over his head, her fingers spread. Her fingers are protective, clutching. When he releases her, her eyes are shining with tears. She turns away. She looks back at him—and the room—and her eyes fasten on the lily.*)

WOMAN: Can I have that?

MAN: Sure—why not?
(*She takes it—goes. As she opens the door, the music is louder. The scene blacks out.*)

WOMAN: Goodbye. And—(*Hesitates.*) And—thank you.

CURTAIN

(*The music continues until the curtain goes up for Episode 7. It goes up on silence.*)

EPISODE 7

DOMESTIC

Scene: A sitting room: a divan, a telephone, a window.

Characters: HUSBAND; YOUNG WOMAN

They are seated on opposite ends of the divan. They are both reading papers—to themselves.

HUSBAND: Record production.
YOUNG WOMAN: Girl turns on gas.
HUSBAND: Sale hits a millions—
YOUNG WOMAN: Woman leaves all for love—
HUSBAND: Market trend steady—
YOUNG WOMAN: Young wife disappears—
HUSBAND: Owns a life interest—
> (*Phone rings.* YOUNG WOMAN *looks toward it.*)
> That's for me. (*In phone.*) Hello—oh hello, A.B. It's all settled?—Everything signed? Good. Good! Tell R.A. to call me up. (*Hangs up phone—to* YOUNG WOMAN.) Well, it's all settled. They signed!—aren't you interested? Aren't you going to ask me?

YOUNG WOMAN (*by rote*): Did you put it over?
HUSBAND: Sure I put it over.
YOUNG WOMAN: Did you swing it?
HUSBAND: Sure I swung it.
YOUNG WOMAN: Did they come through?
HUSBAND: Sure they came through.
YOUNG WOMAN: Did they sign?
HUSBAND: I'll say they signed.
YOUNG WOMAN: On the dotted line?
HUSBAND: On the dotted line.
YOUNG WOMAN: The property's yours?
HUSBAND: The property's mine. I'll put a first mortgage. I'll put a second mortgage and the property's mine. Happy?
YOUNG WOMAN (*by rote*): Happy.
HUSBAND (*going to her*): The property's mine! It's not all that's mine! (*Pinching her cheek—happy and playful.*) I got a first mortgage on her—I got a second mortgage; on her—and she's mine!
> (YOUNG WOMAN *pulls away swiftly.*)
> What's the matter?

YOUNG WOMAN: Nothing—what?
HUSBAND: You flinched when I touched you.
YOUNG WOMAN: No.

HUSBAND: You haven't done that in a long time.
YOUNG WOMAN: Haven't I?
HUSBAND: You used to do it every time I touched you.
YOUNG WOMAN: Did I?
HUSBAND: Didn't know that, did you?
YOUNG WOMAN (*unexpectedly*): Yes. Yes, I know it.
HUSBAND: Just purity.
YOUNG WOMAN: No.
HUSBAND: Oh, I liked it. Purity.
YOUNG WOMAN: No.
HUSBAND: You're one of the purest women that ever lived.
YOUNG WOMAN: I'm just like anybody else only— (*Stops.*)
HUSBAND: Only what?
YOUNG WOMAN (*pause*): Nothing.
HUSBAND: It must be something.
> (*Phone rings. She gets up and goes to window.*)

HUSBAND (*in phone*): Hello—hello, R.A.—well, I put it over—yeah, I swung it—sure they came through—did they sign? On the dotted line! The property's mine. I made the proposition. I sold them the idea. Now watch me. Tell D.D. to call me up. (*Hangs up.*) That was R.A. What are you looking at?
YOUNG WOMAN: Nothing.
HUSBAND: You must be looking at something.
YOUNG WOMAN: Nothing—the moon.
HUSBAND: The moon's something, isn't it?
YOUNG WOMAN: Yes.
HUSBAND: What's it doing?
YOUNG WOMAN: Nothing.
HUSBAND: It must be doing something.
YOUNG WOMAN: It's moving—moving—(*She comes down restlessly.*)
HUSBAND: Pull down the shade, my dear.
YOUNG WOMAN: Why?
HUSBAND: People can look in.
> (*Phone rings.*)
> Hello—hello D.D.—Yes—I put it over—they came across—I put it over on them—yep—yep—yep—I'll say I am—yep—on the dotted line—Now you watch me—yep. Yep yep. Tell B.M. to phone me. (*Hangs up.*) That was D.D. (*To* YOUNG WOMAN *who has come down to davenport and picked up a paper.*) Aren't you listening?

YOUNG WOMAN: I'm reading.

HUSBAND: What you reading?

YOUNG WOMAN: Nothing.

HUSBAND: Must be something. (*He sits and picks up his paper.*)

YOUNG WOMAN (*reading*): Prisoner escapes—lifer breaks jail—shoots way to freedom—

HUSBAND: Don't read that stuff—listen—here's a first rate editorial. I agree with this. I agree absolutely. Are you listening?

YOUNG WOMAN: I'm listening.

HUSBAND (*importantly*): All men are born free and entitled to the pursuit of happiness. (young woman *gets up*.) My, you're nervous tonight.

YOUNG WOMAN: I try not to be.

HUSBAND: You inherit that from your mother. She was in the office today.

YOUNG WOMAN: Was she?

HUSBAND: To get her allowance.

YOUNG WOMAN: Oh—

HUSBAND: Don't you know it's the *first*.

YOUNG WOMAN: Poor Ma.

HUSBAND: What would she do without me?

YOUNG WOMAN: I know. You're very good.

HUSBAND: One thing—she's grateful.

YOUNG WOMAN: Poor Ma—poor Ma.

HUSBAND: She's got to have care.

YOUNG WOMAN: Yes. She's got to have care.

HUSBAND: A mother's a very precious thing—a good mother.

YOUNG WOMAN (*excitedly*): I try to be a good mother.

HUSBAND: Of course you're a good mother.

YOUNG WOMAN: I try! I try!

HUSBAND: A mother's a very precious thing—(*Resuming his paper.*) And a child's a very precious thing. Precious jewels.

YOUNG WOMAN (*reading*): Sale of jewels and precious stones.
(young woman *puts her hand to throat.*)

HUSBAND: What's the matter?

YOUNG WOMAN: I feel as though I were drowning.

HUSBAND: Drowning?

YOUNG WOMAN: With stones around my neck.

HUSBAND: You just imagine that.

YOUNG WOMAN: Stifling.

HUSBAND: You don't breathe deep enough—breathe now—look at me. (*He breathes.*) Breath is life. Life is breath.

YOUNG WOMAN (*suddenly*): And what is death?

HUSBAND (*smartly*): Just—no breath!

YOUNG WOMAN (*to herself*): Just no breath.
(*Takes up paper.*)

HUSBAND: All right?

YOUNG WOMAN: All right.

HUSBAND (*reads as she stares at her paper. Looks up after a pause.*): I feel cold air, my dear.

YOUNG WOMAN: Cold air?

HUSBAND: Close the window, will you?

YOUNG WOMAN: It isn't open.

HUSBAND: Don't you feel cold air?

YOUNG WOMAN: No—you just imagine it.

HUSBAND: I never imagine anything. (YOUNG WOMAN *is staring at the paper.*) What are you reading?

YOUNG WOMAN: Nothing.

HUSBAND: You must be reading something.

YOUNG WOMAN: Woman finds husband dead.

HUSBAND (*uninterested*): Oh. (*Interested.*) Here's a man says "I owe my success to a yeast cake a day—my digestion is good—I sleep very well—and—"(*His wife gets up, goes toward door.*) Where you going?

YOUNG WOMAN: No place.

HUSBAND: You must be going some place.

YOUNG WOMAN: Just—to bed.

HUSBAND: It isn't even eleven yet. Wait.

YOUNG WOMAN: Wait?

HUSBAND: It's only ten-forty-six—wait! (*Holds out his arms to her.*) Come here!

YOUNG WOMAN (*takes a step toward him—recoils*): Oh—I want to go away!

HUSBAND: Away? Where?

YOUNG WOMAN: Anywhere—away.

HUSBAND: Why, what's the matter?

YOUNG WOMAN: I'm scared.

HUSBAND: What of?

YOUNG WOMAN: I can't sleep—I haven't slept.

HUSBAND: That's nothing.

YOUNG WOMAN: And the moon—when it's full moon.

HUSBAND: That's nothing.

YOUNG WOMAN: I can't sleep.

HUSBAND: Of course not. It's the light.

YOUNG WOMAN: I don't see it! I feel it! I'm afraid.

HUSBAND (*kindly*): Nonsense—come here.

YOUNG WOMAN: I want to go away.

HUSBAND: But I can't get away now.

YOUNG WOMAN: Alone!

HUSBAND: You've never been away alone.

YOUNG WOMAN: I know.

HUSBAND: What would you do?

YOUNG WOMAN: Maybe I'd sleep.

HUSBAND: Now you wait.

YOUNG WOMAN (*desperately*): Wait?

HUSBAND: We'll take a trip—we'll go to Europe—I'll get my watch—I'll get my Swiss watch—I've always wanted a Swiss watch that I bought right there—isn't that funny? Wait—wait. (YOUNG WOMAN *comes down to davenport—sits.* HUSBAND *resumes his paper.*) Another revolution below the Rio Grande.

YOUNG WOMAN: Below the Rio Grande?

HUSBAND: Yes—another—

YOUNG WOMAN: Anyone—hurt?

HUSBAND: No.

YOUNG WOMAN: Any prisoners?

HUSBAND: No.

YOUNG WOMAN: All free?

HUSBAND: All free.

(*He resumes his paper.* YOUNG WOMAN *sits, staring ahead of her. The music of the hand organ sounds off very dimly, playing* Cielito Lindo. *Voices begin to sing it—'Ay-ay-ay-ay'—and then the words—the music and voices get louder.*)

THE VOICE OF HER LOVER: They were a bunch of bandidos—bandits you know—holding me there—what was I to do—I had to get free—didn't I? I had to get free—

VOICES: Free—free—free—

LOVER: I filled an empty bottle with small stones—

VOICES: Stones—stones—precious stones—mill-stones—stones—stones—millstones

LOVER: Just a bottle with small stones.

VOICES: Stones—stones—small stones

VOICE OF A HUCKSTER: Stones for sale—stones—stones—small stones—precious stones—

VOICES: Stones—stones—precious stones—

LOVER: Had to get free, didn't I? Free?

VOICES: Free? Free?

LOVER: Quien sabe? Who knows? Who knows?

VOICES: Who'd know? Who'd know? Who'd know?

HUCKSTER: Stones—stones—small stones—big stones—millstones—cold stones—head stones—

VOICES: Head stones—head stones—head stones.

(*The music—the voices—mingle—increase—the* YOUNG WOMAN *flies from her chair and cries out in terror.*)

YOUNG WOMAN: Oh! Oh!

(*The scene blacks out—the music and the dim voices, 'Stones—stones—stones,' continue until the scene lights for Episode 8.*)

EPISODE 8

THE LAW

Scene: Courtroom

Sounds: Clicking of telegraph instruments offstage.

Characters: JUDGE; JURY; LAWYERS; SPECTATORS; REPORTERS; MESSENGER BOYS; LAW CLERKS; BAILIFF; COURT REPORTER; YOUNG WOMAN

The words and movements of all these people except the YOUNG WOMAN *are routine—mechanical. Each is going through the motions of his own game.*

At rise: All assembled, except JUDGE.

(*Enter* JUDGE)

BAILIFF (*mumbling*): Hear ye—hear ye—! (*All rise.* JUDGE *sits. All sit.* LAWYER FOR DEFENSE *gets to his feet—He is the verbose, "eloquent" typical criminal defense lawyer.* JUDGE *signs to him to wait—turns to* LAW CLERKS, *grouped at foot of the bench.*)

FIRST CLERK (*handing up a paper—routine voice*): State versus Kling—stay of execution.

JUDGE: Denied.

(FIRST CLERK *goes.*)

CLERK: Bing vs. Ding—demurrer.

(JUDGE *signs.* SECOND CLERK *goes.*)

THIRD CLERK: Case of John King—habeas corpus.

(JUDGE *signs.* THIRD CLERK *goes.* JUDGE *signs to* BAILIFF.)

BAILIFF (*mumbling*): People of the State of _____ versus Helen Jones.

JUDGE (*to* LAWYER FOR DEFENSE): Defense ready to proceed?

LAWYER FOR DEFENSE: We're ready, your Honor.

JUDGE: Proceed.

LAWYER FOR DEFENSE: Helen Jones.

BAILIFF: Helen Jones!

(YOUNG WOMAN *rises.*)

LAWYER FOR DEFENSE: Mrs. Jones, will you take the stand?

(YOUNG WOMAN *goes to witness stand.*)

FIRST REPORTER (*writing rapidly*): The defense sprang a surprise at the opening of court this morning by putting the accused woman on the stand. The prosecution was swept off its feet by this daring defense strategy and—(*Instruments get louder.*)

SECOND REPORTER: Trembling and scarcely able to stand, Helen Jones, accused murderess, had to be almost carried to the witness stand this morning when her lawyer—

BAILIFF (*mumbling—with Bible*): Do you swear to tell the truth, the whole truth and nothing but the truth—so help you God?

YOUNG WOMAN: I do.

JUDGE: You may sit.

(*She sits in witness chair.*)

COURT REPORTER: What is your name?

YOUNG WOMAN: Helen Jones.

COURT REPORTER: Your age?

YOUNG WOMAN (*hesitates—then*): Twenty-nine.

COURT REPORTER: Where do you live?

YOUNG WOMAN: In prison.

LAWYER FOR DEFENSE: This is my client's legal address.

(*Hands a scrap of paper.*)

LAWYER FOR PROSECUTION (*jumping to his feet*): I object to this insinuation on the part of counsel of any illegality in the holding of this defendant in jail when the law—

LAWYER FOR DEFENSE: I made no such insinuation.

LAWYER FOR PROSECUTION: You implied it—

LAWYER FOR DEFENSE: I did not!

LAWYER FOR PROSECUTION: You're a—

JUDGE: Order!

BAILIFF: Order!

LAWYER FOR DEFENSE: Your Honor, I object to counsel's constant attempt to—

LAWYER FOR PROSECUTION: I protest—I—

JUDGE: Order!

BAILIFF: Order!

JUDGE: Proceed with the witness.

LAWYER FOR DEFENSE: Mrs. Jones, you are the widow of the late George H. Jones, are you not?

YOUNG WOMAN: Yes.

LAWYER FOR DEFENSE: How long were you married to the late George H. Jones before his demise?

YOUNG WOMAN: Six years.

LAWYER FOR DEFENSE: Six years! And it was a happy marriage, was it not? (YOUNG WOMAN *hesitates.*) Did you quarrel?

YOUNG WOMAN: No sir.

LAWYER FOR DEFENSE: Then it was a happy marriage, wasn't it?

YOUNG WOMAN: Yes, sir.

LAWYER FOR DEFENSE: In those six years of married life with your late husband, the late George H. Jones, did you EVER have a quarrel?

YOUNG WOMAN: No, sir.

LAWYER FOR DEFENSE: Never one quarrel?

LAWYER FOR PROSECUTION: The witness has said—

LAWYER FOR DEFENSE: Six years without one quarrel! Six years! Gentlemen of the jury, I ask you to consider this fact! Six years of married life without a quarrel. (*The* JURY *grins.*) I ask you to consider it seriously! Very seriously! Who of us—and this is not intended as any reflection on the sacred institution of marriage—no—but!

JUDGE: Proceed with your witness.

LAWYER FOR DEFENSE: You have one child—have you not, Mrs. Jones?

YOUNG WOMAN: Yes, sir.

LAWYER FOR DEFENSE: A little girl, is it not?

YOUNG WOMAN: Yes, sir.

LAWYER FOR DEFENSE: How old is she?

YOUNG WOMAN: She's five—past five.

LAWYER FOR DEFENSE: A little girl of past five. Since the demise of the late Mr. Jones you are the only parent she has living, are you not?

YOUNG WOMAN: Yes, sir.

LAWYER FOR DEFENSE: Before your marriage to the late Mr. Jones, you worked and supported your mother, did you not?

LAWYER FOR PROSECUTION: I object, your honor! Irrelevant—immaterial—and—

JUDGE: Objection sustained!

LAWYER FOR DEFENSE: In order to support your mother and yourself as a girl, you worked, did you not?

YOUNG WOMAN: Yes, sir.

LAWYER FOR DEFENSE: What did you do?

YOUNG WOMAN: I was a stenographer.

LAWYER FOR DEFENSE: And since your marriage you have continued as her sole support, have you not?

YOUNG WOMAN: Yes, sir.

LAWYER FOR DEFENSE: A devoted daughter, gentlemen of the jury! As well as a devoted wife and a devoted mother!

LAWYER FOR PROSECUTION: Your Honor!

LAWYER FOR DEFENSE (*quickly*): And now, Mrs. Jones, I will ask you—the law expects me to ask you—it demands that I ask you—did you—or did you not—on the night of June 2nd last or the morning of June 3rd last—kill your husband, the late George H. Jones—did you, or did you not?

YOUNG WOMAN: I did not.

LAWYER FOR DEFENSE: You did not?

YOUNG WOMAN: I did not.

LAWYER FOR DEFENSE: Now, Mrs. Jones, you have heard the witnesses for the State—They were not many—and they did not have much to say—

LAWYER FOR PROSECUTION: I object.

JUDGE: Sustained.

LAWYER FOR DEFENSE: You have heard some police and you have heard some doctors. None of whom was present! The prosecution could not furnish any witness to the crime—not one witness!

LAWYER FOR PROSECUTION: Your Honor!

LAWYER FOR DEFENSE: Nor one motive.

LAWYER FOR PROSECUTION: Your Honor—I protest! I—

JUDGE: Sustained.

LAWYER FOR DEFENSE: But such as these witnesses were, you have heard them try to accuse you of deliberately murdering your own husband, this husband with whom, by your own statement, you had never had a quarrel—not one quarrel in six years of married life, murdering him, I say, or rather—they say, while he slept, by brutally hitting him over the head with a bottle—a bottle filled with small stones—Did you, I repeat this, or did you not?

YOUNG WOMAN: I did not.

LAWYER FOR DEFENSE: You did not! Of course you did not! (*Quickly.*) Now, Mrs. Jones, will you tell the jury in your own words exactly what happened on the night of June 2nd or the morning of June 3rd last, at the time your husband was killed.

YOUNG WOMAN: I was awakened by hearing somebody—something—in the room, and I saw two men standing by my husband's bed.

LAWYER FOR DEFENSE: Your husband's bed—that was also your bed, was it not, Mrs. Jones?

YOUNG WOMAN: Yes.

LAWYER FOR DEFENSE: You hadn't the modern idea of separate beds, had you, Mrs. Jones?

YOUNG WOMAN: Mr. Jones objected.

LAWYER FOR DEFENSE: I mean you slept in the same bed, did you not?

YOUNG WOMAN: Yes.

LAWYER FOR DEFENSE: Then explain just what you mean by saying 'my husband's bed'.

YOUNG WOMAN: Well—I—

LAWYER FOR DEFENSE: You meant his side of the bed, didn't you?

YOUNG WOMAN: Yes, His side.

LAWYER FOR DEFENSE: That is what I thought, but I wanted the jury to be clear on that point. (*To the* JURY.) Mr. and Mrs. Jones slept in the same bed. (*To her.*) Go on, Mrs. Jones. (*As she is silent.*) You heard a noise and—

YOUNG WOMAN: I heard a noise and I awoke and saw two men standing beside my husband's side of the bed.

LAWYER FOR DEFENSE: Two men?

YOUNG WOMAN: Yes.

LAWYER FOR DEFENSE: Can you describe them?

YOUNG WOMAN: Not very well—I couldn't see them very well.

LAWYER FOR DEFENSE: Could you say whether they were big or small—light or dark, thin or—

YOUNG WOMAN: They were big dark looking men.

LAWYER FOR DEFENSE: Big dark looking men?

YOUNG WOMAN: Yes.

LAWYER FOR DEFENSE: And what did you do, Mrs. Jones, when you suddenly awoke and saw two big dark looking men standing beside your bed?

YOUNG WOMAN: I didn't do anything!

LAWYER FOR DEFENSE: You didn't have time to do anything—did you?

YOUNG WOMAN: No. Before I could do anything—one of them raised—something in his hand and struck Mr. Jones over the head with it.

LAWYER FOR DEFENSE: And what did Mr. Jones do? (*Spectators laugh.*)

JUDGE: Silence.

BAILIFF: Silence.

LAWYER FOR DEFENSE: What did Mr. Jones do, Mrs. Jones?

YOUNG WOMAN: He gave a sort of groan and tried to raise up.

LAWYER FOR DEFENSE: Tried to raise up!

YOUNG WOMAN: Yes!

LAWYER FOR DEFENSE: And then what happened?

YOUNG WOMAN: The man struck him again and he fell back.

LAWYER FOR DEFENSE: I see. What did the men do then? The big dark looking men.

YOUNG WOMAN: They turned and ran out of the room.

LAWYER FOR DEFENSE: I see. What did you do then, Mrs. Jones?

YOUNG WOMAN: I saw Mr. Jones was bleeding from the temple. I got towels and tried to stop it, and then I realized he had—passed away.

LAWYER FOR DEFENSE: I see. What did you do then?

YOUNG WOMAN: I didn't know what to do. But I thought I'd better call the police. So I went to the telephone and called the police.

LAWYER FOR DEFENSE: What happened then?

YOUNG WOMAN: Nothing. Nothing happened.

LAWYER FOR DEFENSE: The police came, didn't they?

YOUNG WOMAN: Yes—they came.

LAWYER FOR DEFENSE (quickly): And that is all you know concerning the death of your husband in the late hours of June 2nd or the early hours of June 3rd last, isn't it?

YOUNG WOMAN: Yes sir.

LAWYER FOR DEFENSE: All?

YOUNG WOMAN: Yes sir.

LAWYER FOR DEFENSE (to LAWYER FOR PROSECUTION): Take the witness.

FIRST REPORTER (writing): The accused woman told a straightforward story of—

SECOND REPORTER: The accused woman told a rambling, disconnected story of—

LAWYER FOR PROSECUTION: You made no effort to cry out, Mrs. Jones, did you, when you saw those two big dark men standing over your helpless husband, did you?

YOUNG WOMAN: No sir. I didn't. I—

LAWYER FOR PROSECUTION: And when they turned and ran out of the room, you made no effort to follow them or cry out after them, did you?

YOUNG WOMAN: No sir.

LAWYER FOR PROSECUTION: Why didn't you?

YOUNG WOMAN: I saw Mr. Jones was hurt.

LAWYER FOR PROSECUTION: Ah! You saw Mr. Jones was hurt! You saw this—how did you see it?

YOUNG WOMAN: I just saw it.

LAWYER FOR PROSECUTION: Then there was a light in the room?

YOUNG WOMAN: A sort of light.

LAWYER FOR PROSECUTION: What do you mean—a sort of light? A bed light?

YOUNG WOMAN: No. No, there was no light on.

LAWYER FOR PROSECUTION: They where did it come from—this sort of light?

YOUNG WOMAN: I don't know.

LAWYER FOR PROSECUTION: Perhaps—from the window.

YOUNG WOMAN: Yes—from the window.

LAWYER FOR PROSECUTION: Oh, the shade was up!

YOUNG WOMAN: No—no, the shade was down.

LAWYER FOR PROSECUTION: You're sure of that?

YOUNG WOMAN: Yes. Mr. Jones always wanted the shade down.

LAWYER FOR PROSECUTION: The shade was down—there was no light in the room—but the room was light—how do you explain this?

YOUNG WOMAN: I don't know.

LAWYER FOR PROSECUTION: You don't know!

YOUNG WOMAN: I think where the window was open—under the shade—light came in.

LAWYER FOR PROSECUTION: There is a street light there?

YOUNG WOMAN: No—there's no street light.

LAWYER FOR PROSECUTION: Then where did this light come from—that came in under the shade?

YOUNG WOMAN (desperately): From the moon!

LAWYER FOR PROSECUTION: The moon!

YOUNG WOMAN: Yes! It was a bright moon!

LAWYER FOR PROSECUTION: It was a bright moon—you are sure of that!

YOUNG WOMAN: Yes.

LAWYER FOR PROSECUTION: How are you sure?

YOUNG WOMAN: I couldn't sleep—I never can sleep in the bright moon. I never can.

LAWYER FOR PROSECUTION: It was bright moon. Yet you could not see two big dark looking men—but you could see your husband bleeding from the temple.

YOUNG WOMAN: Yes sir.

LAWYER FOR PROSECUTION: And did you call a doctor?

YOUNG WOMAN: No.

LAWYER FOR PROSECUTION: Why didn't you?

YOUNG WOMAN: The police did.

LAWYER FOR PROSECUTION: But you didn't?

YOUNG WOMAN: No.

LAWYER FOR PROSECUTION: Why didn't you? (*No answer.*) Why didn't you?

YOUNG WOMAN (*whispers*): I saw it was—useless.

LAWYER FOR PROSECUTION: Ah! You saw that! You saw that—very clearly.

YOUNG WOMAN: Yes.

LAWYER FOR PROSECUTION: And you didn't call a doctor.

YOUNG WOMAN: It was—useless.

LAWYER FOR PROSECUTION: What did you do?

YOUNG WOMAN: It was useless—there was no use of anything.

LAWYER FOR PROSECUTION: I asked you what you did?

YOUNG WOMAN: Nothing.

LAWYER FOR PROSECUTION: Nothing!

YOUNG WOMAN: I just sat there.

LAWYER FOR PROSECUTION: You sat there! A long while, didn't you?

YOUNG WOMAN: I don't know.

LAWYER FOR PROSECUTION: You don't know? (*Showing her the neck of a broken bottle.*) Mrs. Jones, did you ever see this before?

YOUNG WOMAN: I think so.

LAWYER FOR PROSECUTION: You think so.

YOUNG WOMAN: Yes.

LAWYER FOR PROSECUTION: What do you think it is?

YOUNG WOMAN: I think it's the bottle that was used against Mr. Jones.

LAWYER FOR PROSECUTION: Used against him—yes—that's right. You've guessed right. This neck and these broken pieces and these pebbles were found on the floor and scattered over the bed. There were no fingerprints, Mrs. Jones, on this bottle. None at all. Doesn't that seem strange to you?

YOUNG WOMAN: No.

LAWYER FOR PROSECUTION: It doesn't seem strange to you that this bottle held in the big dark hand of one of those big dark men left no mark! No print! That doesn't seem strange to you?

YOUNG WOMAN: No.

LAWYER FOR PROSECUTION: You are in the habit of wearing rubber gloves at night, Mrs. Jones—are you not? To protect—to soften your hands—are you not?

YOUNG WOMAN: I used to.

LAWYER FOR PROSECUTION: Used to—when was that?

YOUNG WOMAN: Before I was married.

LAWYER FOR PROSECUTION: And after your marriage you gave it up?

YOUNG WOMAN: Yes.

LAWYER FOR PROSECUTION: Why?

YOUNG WOMAN: Mr. Jones did not like the feeling of them.

LAWYER FOR PROSECUTION: You always did everything Mr. Jones wanted?

YOUNG WOMAN: I tried to—Anyway I didn't care any more—so much—about my hands.

LAWYER FOR PROSECUTION: I see—so after your marriage you never wore gloves at night any more?

YOUNG WOMAN: No.

LAWYER FOR PROSECUTION: Mrs. Jones, isn't it true that you began wearing your rubber gloves again—in spite of your husband's expressed dislike—about a year ago—a year ago this spring?

YOUNG WOMAN: No.

LAWYER FOR PROSECUTION: You did not suddenly begin to care particularly for your hands again—about a year ago this spring?

YOUNG WOMAN: No.

LAWYER FOR PROSECUTION: You're quite sure of that?

YOUNG WOMAN: Yes.

LAWYER FOR PROSECUTION: Quite sure?

YOUNG WOMAN: Yes.

LAWYER FOR PROSECUTION: Then you did not have in your possession, on the night of June 2nd last, a pair of rubber gloves?

YOUNG WOMAN (*shakes her head*): No.

LAWYER FOR PROSECUTION (*to* JUDGE): I'd like to introduce these gloves as evidence at this time, your Honor.

JUDGE: Exhibit 24.

LAWYER FOR PROSECUTION: I'll return to them later—now, Mrs. Jones—this nightgown—you recognize it, don't you?

YOUNG WOMAN: Yes.

LAWYER FOR PROSECUTION: Yours, is it not?

YOUNG WOMAN: Yes.

LAWYER FOR PROSECUTION: The one you were wearing the night your husband was murdered, isn't it?

YOUNG WOMAN: The night he died—yes.

LAWYER FOR PROSECUTION: Not the one you wore under your peignoir—I believe that it's what you call it, isn't it? A peignoir? When you received the police—but the one you wore before that—isn't it?

YOUNG WOMAN: Yes.

LAWYER FOR PROSECUTION: This was found—not where the gloves were found—no—but at the bottom the soiled clothes hamper in the bathroom—rolled up and wet—why was it wet, Mrs. Jones?

YOUNG WOMAN: I had tried to wash it.

LAWYER FOR PROSECUTION: Wash it? I thought you had just sat?

YOUNG WOMAN: First—I tried to make things clean.

LAWYER FOR PROSECUTION: Why did you want to make this—clean—as you say?

YOUNG WOMAN: There was blood on it.

LAWYER FOR PROSECUTION: Spattered on it?

YOUNG WOMAN: Yes.

LAWYER FOR PROSECUTION: How did that happen?

YOUNG WOMAN: The bottle broke—and the sharp edge cut.

LAWYER FOR PROSECUTION: Oh, the bottle broke and the sharp edge cut!

YOUNG WOMAN: Yes. That's what they told me afterwards.

LAWYER FOR PROSECUTION: Who told you?

YOUNG WOMAN: The police—that's what they say happened.

LAWYER FOR PROSECUTION: Mrs. Jones, why did you try so desperately to wash that blood away—before you called the police?

LAWYER FOR DEFENSE: I object!

JUDGE: Objection overruled.

LAWYER FOR PROSECUTION: Why, Mrs. Jones?

YOUNG WOMAN: I don't know. It's what anyone would have done, wouldn't they?

LAWYER FOR PROSECUTION: That depends, doesn't it? (*Suddenly taking up bottle.*) Mrs. Jones—when did you first see this?

YOUNG WOMAN: The night my husband was—done away with.

LAWYER FOR PROSECUTION: Done away with! You mean killed?

YOUNG WOMAN: Yes.

LAWYER FOR PROSECUTION: Why don't you say killed?

YOUNG WOMAN: It sounds so brutal.

LAWYER FOR PROSECUTION: And you never saw this before then?

YOUNG WOMAN: No sir.

LAWYER FOR PROSECUTION: You're quite sure of that?

YOUNG WOMAN: Yes.

LAWYER FOR PROSECUTION: And these stones—when did you first see them?

YOUNG WOMAN: The night my husband was done away with.

LAWYER FOR PROSECUTION: Before that night your husband was murdered—you never saw them? Never before then?

YOUNG WOMAN: No sir.

LAWYER FOR PROSECUTION: You are quite sure of that!

YOUNG WOMAN: Yes.

LAWYER FOR PROSECUTION: Mrs. Jones, do you remember about a year ago, a year ago this spring, bringing home to your house—a lily, a Chinese water lily?

YOUNG WOMAN: No—I don't think so.

LAWYER FOR PROSECUTION: You don't think you remember bringing home a water lily growing in a bowl filled with small stones?

YOUNG WOMAN: No—No I don't.

LAWYER FOR PROSECUTION: I'll show you this bowl, Mrs. Jones. Does that refresh your memory?

YOUNG WOMAN: I remember the bowl—but I don't remember—the lily.

LAWYER FOR PROSECUTION: You recognize the bowl then?

YOUNG WOMAN: Yes.

LAWYER FOR PROSECUTION: It is yours, isn't it?

YOUNG WOMAN: It was in my house—yes.

LAWYER FOR PROSECUTION: How did it come there?

YOUNG WOMAN: How did it come there?

LAWYER FOR PROSECUTION: Yes—where did you get it?

YOUNG WOMAN: I don't remember.

LAWYER FOR PROSECUTION: You don't remember?

YOUNG WOMAN: No.

LAWYER FOR PROSECUTION: You don't remember about a year ago bringing this bowl into your bedroom filled with small stones and some water and a lily? You don't remember tending very carefully that lily till it died? And when it died you don't remember hiding the bowl full of little stones away on the top shelf of your closet—and keeping it there until—you don't remember?

YOUNG WOMAN: No, I don't remember.

LAWYER FOR PROSECUTION: You may have done so?

YOUNG WOMAN: No—no—I didn't! I didn't! I don't know anything about all that.

LAWYER FOR PROSECUTION: But you do remember the bowl?

YOUNG WOMAN: Yes. It was in my house—you found it in my house.

LAWYER FOR PROSECUTION: But you don't remember the lily or the stones?

YOUNG WOMAN: No—No I don't!

(LAWYER FOR PROSECUTION *turns to look among his papers in a brief case.*)

FIRST REPORTER (*writing*): Under the heavy artillery fire of the State's attorney's brilliant cross-questioning, the accused woman's defense was badly riddled. Pale and trembling she—

SECOND REPORTER (*writing*): Undaunted by the Prosecution's machine-gun attack, the defendant was able to maintain her position of innocence in the face of rapid-fire questioning that threatened, but never seriously menaced her defense. Flushed but calm she—

LAWYER FOR PROSECUTION (*producing paper*): Your Honor, I'd like to introduce this paper in evidence at this time.

JUDGE: What is it?

LAWYER FOR PROSECUTION: It is an affidavit taken in the State of Guanajato, Mexico.

LAWYER FOR DEFENSE: Mexico? Your Honor, I protest. A Mexican affidavit! Is this the United States of America or isn't it?

LAWYER FOR PROSECUTION: It's properly executed—sworn to before a notary—and certified by an American Consul.

LAWYER FOR DEFENSE: Your Honor! I protest! In the name of this great United States of America—I

protest—are we to permit our sacred institutions to be thus—

JUDGE: What is the purpose of this document—who signed it?

LAWYER FOR PROSECUTION: It is signed by one Richard Roe, and its purpose is to refresh the memory of the witness on the point at issue—and incidentally supply a motive for this murder—this brutal and cold-blooded murder of a sleeping man by—

LAWYER FOR DEFENSE: I protest, your Honor! I object!

JUDGE: Objection sustained. Let me see the document. (*Takes paper which is handed to him—looks at it.*) Perfectly regular. Do you offer this affidavit as evidence at this time for the purpose of refreshing the memory of the witness at this time?

LAWYER FOR PROSECUTION: Yes, your Honor.

JUDGE: You may introduce the evidence.

LAWYER FOR DEFENSE: I object! I object to the introduction of this evidence at this time as irrelevant, immaterial, illegal, biased, prejudicial, and—

JUDGE: Objection overruled.

LAWYER FOR DEFENSE: Exception.

JUDGE: Exception noted. Proceed.

LAWYER FOR PROSECUTION: I wish to read the evidence to the jury at this time.

JUDGE: Proceed.

LAWYER FOR DEFENSE: I object.

JUDGE: Objection overruled.

LAWYER FOR DEFENSE: Exception.

JUDGE: Noted.

LAWYER FOR DEFENSE: Why is this witness himself not brought into court—so he can be cross-questioned?

LAWYER FOR PROSECUTION: The witness is a resident of the Republic of Mexico and as such not subject to subpoena as a witness to this court.

LAWYER FOR DEFENSE: If he was out of the jurisdiction of this court how did you get this affidavit out of him?

LAWYER FOR PROSECUTION: This affidavit was made voluntarily by the deponent in the furtherance of justice.

LAWYER FOR DEFENSE: I suppose you didn't threaten him with extradition on some other trumped-up charge so that—

JUDGE: Order!

BAILIFF: Order!

JUDGE: Proceed with the evidence.

LAWYER FOR PROSECUTION (*reading*): In the matter of the State of _____ vs. Helen Jones, I Richard Roe, being of sound mind, do herein depose and state that I know the accused, Helen Jones, and have known her for a period of over one year immediately preceding the date of the signature on this affidavit. That I first met the said Helen Jones in a so-called speak-easy somewhere in the West 40s in New York City. That on the day I met her, she went with me to my room, also somewhere in the West 40s in New York City, where we had intimate relations—

YOUNG WOMAN (*moans*): Oh!

LAWYER FOR PROSECUTION (*continues reading*): —and where I gave her a bowl filled with pebbles, also containing a flowering lily. That from the first day we met until I departed for Mexico in the Fall, the said Helen Jones was an almost daily visitor to my room where we continued to—

YOUNG WOMAN: No! No! (*Moans.*)

LAWYER FOR PROSECUTION: What is it, Mrs. Jones— what is it?

YOUNG WOMAN: Don't read any more! No more!

LAWYER FOR PROSECUTION: Why not?

YOUNG WOMAN: I did it! I did it! I did it!

LAWYER FOR PROSECUTION: You confess?

YOUNG WOMAN: Yes—I did it!

LAWYER FOR DEFENSE: I object, your Honor.

JUDGE: You confess you killed your husband?

YOUNG WOMAN: I put him out of the way—yes.

JUDGE: Why?

YOUNG WOMAN: To be free.

JUDGE: To be free? Is that the only reason?

YOUNG WOMAN: Yes.

JUDGE: If you just wanted to be free—why didn't you divorce him?

YOUNG WOMAN: Oh I couldn't do that!! I couldn't hurt him like that!

(*Burst of laughter from all in the court. The* YOUNG WOMAN *stares out at them, and then seems to go rigid.*)

JUDGE: Silence!

BAILIFF: Silence!

(*There is a gradual silence.*)

JUDGE: Mrs. Jones, why—

(*young woman begins to moan—suddenly—as though the realization of the enormity of her isolation had just come upon her. It is a sound of desolation, of agony, of human woe. It continues until the end of the scene.*)

Why—?

(YOUNG WOMAN *cannot speak.*)

LAWYER FOR DEFENSE: Your Honor, I ask a recess to—

JUDGE: Court's adjourned.

(*Spectators begin to file out. The* YOUNG WOMAN *continues in the witness box, unseeing, unheeding.*)

FIRST REPORTER: Murderess confesses.

SECOND REPORTER: Paramour brings confession.

THIRD REPORTER: I did it! Woman cries!

(*There is a great burst of speed from the telegraphic instruments. They keep up a constant accompaniment to the woman's moans. The scene blacks out as the courtroom empties, and two policemen go to stand by the woman. The sound of the telegraph instruments continues until the scene lights into Episode 9—and the prayers of the* PRIEST.)

EPISODE 9

A MACHINE

Scene: A prison room. The front bars face the audience. They are set back far enough to permit a clear passageway across the stage.

Sounds: The voice of a Negro singing; the whir of an aeroplane flying.

Characters: YOUNG WOMAN; A PRIEST; A JAILER; TWO BARBERS; A MATRON; MOTHER; TWO GUARDS

At rise: In front of the bars, at one side, sits a MAN; *at the opposite side, a* WOMAN—*the* JAILER *and the* MATRON.

Inside the bars, a MAN *and a* WOMAN—*the* YOUNG WOMAN *and a* PRIEST. *The* YOUNG WOMAN *sits still with folded hands. The* PRIEST *is praying.*

PRIEST: Hear, oh Lord, my prayer; and let my cry come to Thee. Turn not away Thy face from me; in the day when I am in trouble, incline thy ear to me. In what day soever I shall call upon Thee, hear me speedily. For my days are vanished like smoke; and my bones are grown dry, like fuel for the fire. I am smitten as grass, and my heart is withered; because I forgot to eat my bread. Through the voice of my groaning, my bone hath cleaved to my flesh. I am become like to a pelican of the wilderness. I am like a night raven in the house. I have watched and become as a sparrow all alone on the housetop. All the day long my enemies reproach me; and they that praised me did swear against me. My days have declined like a shadow, and I am withered like grass. But Thou, oh Lord, end rest forever. Thou shalt arise and have mercy, for it is time to have mercy. The time is come.

(*Voice of Negro offstage—begins to sing a Negro spiritual.*)

PRIEST: The Lord hath looked upon the earth, that He might hear the groans of them that are in fetters, that He might release the children of—

(*Voice of Negro grown louder.*)

JAILER: Stop that nigger yelling.

YOUNG WOMAN: No, let him sing. He helps me.

MATRON: You can't hear the Father.

YOUNG WOMAN: He helps me.

PRIEST: Don't I help you, daughter?

YOUNG WOMAN: I understand him. He is condemned. I understand him.

(*The voice of the Negro goes on louder, drowning out the voice of the* PRIEST.)

PRIEST (*chanting in Latin*): Gratiam tuum, quaesumus, Domine, metibus nostris infunde, ut qui, angelo nuntiante, Christifilii tui incamationem cognovimus, per passionem eius et crucem ad ressurectionis gloriam perducamus. Per eudem Christum Dominum nostrum.

(*Enter* TWO BARBERS. *There is a rattling of keys.*)

FIRST BARBER: How is she?

MATRON: Calm.

JAILER: Quiet.

YOUNG WOMAN (*rising*): I am ready.

FIRST BARBER: Then sit down.

YOUNG WOMAN (*in a steady voice*): Aren't you the death guard come to take me?

FIRST BARBER: No, we ain't the death guard. We're the barbers.

YOUNG WOMAN: The barbers.

MATRON: Your hair must be cut.

JAILER: Must be shaved.

BARBER: Just a patch.

(*The* BARBERS *draw near her.*)

YOUNG WOMAN: No!

PRIEST: Daughter, you're ready. You know you are ready.

YOUNG WOMAN (*crying out*): Not for this! Not for this!

MATRON: The rule.

JAILER: Regulations.

BARBER: Routine.

(*The* BARBERS *take her by the arms.*)

YOUNG WOMAN: No! No! Don't touch me—touch me!

(*They take her and put her down in the chair, cut a patch from her hair.*)

I will not be submitted—this indignity! No! I will not be submitted!—Leave me alone! Oh my God am I never to be let alone! Always to have to submit—to submit! No more—not now—I'm going to die—I won't submit! Not now!

BARBER (*finishing cutting a patch from her hair*): You'll submit, my lady. Right to the end, you'll submit! There, and a neat job too.

JAILER: Very neat.

MATRON: Very neat.

(*Exit* BARBERS.)

YOUNG WOMAN (*her calm shattered*): Father, Father! Why was I born?

PRIEST: I came forth from the Father and have come into the world—I leave the world and go onto the Father.

YOUNG WOMAN (*weeping*): Submit! Submit! Is nothing mine? The hair on my head! The very hair on my head—

PRIEST: Praise God.

YOUNG WOMAN: Am I never to be let alone! Never to have peace! When I'm dead, won't I have peace?

PRIEST: Ye shall indeed drink of my cup.

YOUNG WOMAN: Won't I have peace tomorrow?

PRIEST: I shall raise Him up at the last day.

YOUNG WOMAN: Tomorrow! Father! Where shall I be tomorrow?

PRIEST: Behold the hour cometh. Yea, is now come. Ye shall be scattered every man to his own.

YOUNG WOMAN: In Hell! Father! Will I be in Hell!

PRIEST: I am the Resurrection and the Life.

YOUNG WOMAN: Life has been hell to me, Father!

PRIEST: Life has been hell to you, daughter, because you never knew God! Gloria in excelsis Deo.

YOUNG WOMAN: How could I know Him, Father? He never was around me.

PRIEST: You didn't seek Him, daughter. Seek and ye shall find.

YOUNG WOMAN: I sought something—I was always seeking something.

PRIEST: What? What were you seeking?

YOUNG WOMAN: Peace. Rest and peace. Will I find it tonight, Father? Will I find it?

PRIEST: Trust in God.
(*A shadow falls across the passage in the front of the stage—and there is a whirring sound.*)

YOUNG WOMAN: What is that? Father! Jailer! What is that?

JAILER: An aeroplane.

MATRON: Aeroplane.

PRIEST: God in his Heaven.

YOUNG WOMAN: Look, Father! A man flying! He has wings! But he is not an angel!

JAILER: Hear his engine.

MATRON: Hear the engine.

YOUNG WOMAN: He has wings—but he isn't free! I've been free, Father! For one moment—down here on earth—I have been free! When I did what I did I was free! Free and not afraid! How is that, Father? How can that be? A great sin—a mortal sin—for which I must die and go to hell—but it made me free! One moment I was free! How is that, Father? Tell me that?

PRIEST: Your sins are forgiven.

YOUNG WOMAN: And that other sin—the other sin—that sin of love—That's all I ever knew of Heaven—heaven on earth! How is that, Father? How can that be—a sin—a mortal sin—all I know of heaven?

PRIEST: Confess to Almighty God.

YOUNG WOMAN: Oh, Father, pray for me—a prayer—that I can understand!

PRIEST: I will pray for you, daughter, the prayer of desire. Behind the King of Heaven, behold thy Redeemer and God, Who is even now coming; prepare thyself to receive Him with love, invite him with the ardor of thy desire; come, oh my Jesus, come to thy soul which desires Thee! Before Thou givest Thyself to me, I desire to give Thee my miserable heart. Do Thou accept it, and come quickly to take possession of it! Come my God, hasten! Delay no longer! My only and Infinite Good, my Treasure, my Life, my Paradise, my Love, my all, my wish is to receive thee with the love with which—
(*Enter the* MOTHER. *She comes along the passageway and stops before the bars.*)

YOUNG WOMAN (*recoiling*): Who's that woman?

JAILER: Your Mother.

MATRON: Your Mother.

YOUNG WOMAN: She's a stranger—take her away—she's a stranger.

JAILER: She's come to say goodbye to you—

MATRON: To say goodbye.

YOUNG WOMAN: But she's never known me—never known me—ever—(*To the* MOTHER.) Go away! You're a stranger! Stranger! Stranger! (MOTHER *turns and starts away. Reaching out her hands to her.*) Oh Mother! Mother! (*They embrace through the bars.*)
(*Enter* TWO GUARDS.)

PRIEST: Come, daughter.

FIRST GUARD: It's time.

SECOND GUARD: Time

YOUNG WOMAN: Wait! Mother, my child; my little strange child! I never knew her! She'll never know me! Let her live, Mother. Let her live! Live! Tell her—

PRIEST: Come, daughter.

YOUNG WOMAN: Wait! Wait! Tell her—
(*The* JAILER *takes the* MOTHER *away.*)

GUARD: It's time.

YOUNG WOMAN: Wait! Wait! Tell her! Wait! Just a minute more! There's so much I want to tell her—Wait—
(*the* JAILER *takes the* MOTHER *off. The* TWO GUARDS *take the* YOUNG WOMAN *by the arms, and start through the door in the bars and down the passage, across stage and off: the* PRIEST *follows; the* MATRON *follows the priest; the* PRIEST *is praying. The scene blacks out. The voice of the* PRIEST *gets dimmer and dimmer.*)

PRIEST: Lord have mercy—Christ have mercy—Lord have mercy—Christ hear us! God the Father of Heaven! God the Son, Redeemer of the World, God the Holy Ghost—Holy Trinity one God—Holy Mary—Holy Mother of God—Holy Virgin of Virgins—St. Michael—St. Gabriel—St. Raphael—

(*His voice dies out. Out of the darkness come the voices of* REPORTERS.)

FIRST REPORTER: What time is it now?

SECOND REPORTER: Time now.

THIRD REPORTER: Hush.

FIRST REPORTER: Here they come.

THIRD REPORTER: Hush.

PRIEST (*his voice sounds dimly gets louder—continues until the end*): St. Peter pray for us—St. Paul pray for us—St. James pray for us—St. John pray for us—all ye holy Angels and Archangels—all ye blessed orders of holy spirits—St. Joseph—St. John the Baptist—St. Thomas—

FIRST REPORTER: Here they are!

SECOND REPORTER: How little she looks! She's gotten smaller.

THIRD REPORTER: Hush.

PRIEST: St. Phillip pray for us. All you Holy Patriarchs and prophets—St. Phillip—St. Matthew—St. Simon—St. Thaddeus—All ye holy apostles—all ye holy disciples—all ye holy innocents—Pray for us—Pray for us—Pray for us—

FIRST REPORTER: Suppose the machine shouldn't work!

SECOND REPORTER: It'll work!—It always works!

THIRD REPORTER: Hush!

PRIEST: Saints of God make intercession for us—Be merciful—Spare us, oh Lord—be merciful—

FIRST REPORTER: Her lips are moving—what is she saying?

SECOND REPORTER: Nothing.

THIRD REPORTER: Hush!

PRIEST: Oh Lord deliver us from all evil—from all sin—from Thy wrath—from the snares of the devil—from anger and hatred and every evil will—from—

FIRST REPORTER: Did you see that? She fixed her hair under the cap—pulled her hair out under the cap.

THIRD REPORTER: Hush!

PRIEST: —Beseech Thee—hear us—that Thou would'st spare us—that Thou would'st pardon us—Holy Mary—pray for us—

SECOND REPORTER: There—

YOUNG WOMAN (*calling out*): Somebody! Somebod— (*Her voice is cut off.*)

PRIEST: Christ have mercy—Lord have mercy—Christ have mercy—

CURTAIN

Introduction to *Death of a Salesman*

WHEN THE PLAY WAS NEW

When Arthur Miller's most famous play, *Death of a Salesman*, premiered on February 10, 1949, in New York, the United States was still undergoing social, political, and economic adjustment after the massive changes wrought by World War II. This Pulitzer Prize–winning play enthralled audiences for some 742 performances, not only for its poignant, tragic story of a modern American failure, but for the remarkable acting ensemble led by Lee J. Cobb in the role of Willy Loman, for the sensitive directing of Elia Kazan who was emerging as America's most accomplished stage director, for the brilliant scenic and lighting designs by Jo Mielziner, and for a timely message from a playwright determined to challenge his audiences with dramatized problems that cut to the bone. Post–World War II America desperately wanted to believe the American Dream, and Arthur Miller was challenging the popular notions of U.S. prosperity and the road to success and happiness. The domestic environment was his battle ground and he presented an unblinking examination of our weaknesses.

Many of the most famous American plays of the twentieth century emerged between 1945 and 1960, and most of them were written by Miller and Tennessee Williams and directed by Kazan. The kind of psychologically realistic acting presented in these plays had begun with actors of the Group Theatre in the 1930s who in turn were inspired by the teachings of Konstantin Stanislavsky, the Russian exemplar of what became known in America at mid-century as "Method" acting. The style of Miller's dialogue and family conflict made *Death of a Salesman* an excellent vehicle for such acting. Kazan's production of Tennessee Williams' *A Streetcar Named Desire* also used emotional, realistic performance to explore family conflict and characters' illusions.

Although Miller did not write *Death of a Salesman* with stylization in mind, except for flashbacks recalled and played out by Willy Loman, Mielziner and Kazan envisioned the play in a space not entirely realistic. They exaggerated the smallness of the rooms in Willy's house, abstracted the cityscape behind the little house, changed to nonrealistic lighting for flashbacks, and simply moved other locations into neutral spaces on each side of the house interior. Therefore, Willy could step in and out of the present and the past. Realistic characterization and action prevailed, however. Since the 1940s such partial stylization of realistically drawn plays has been commonplace on the American stage.

THE PLAYWRIGHT

Arthur Miller (1915–2005) was born in New York City, came of age during the Great Depression, and was educated at the University of Michigan where he began seriously writing plays. He had his first professional productions in 1944, but first success came with *All My Sons* (1947), a moving play about family lies and business corruption at the expense of military pilots. This production also marked the beginning of a series of frequent collaborations of Miller with Kazan. One of Miller's most revived plays, *The Crucible* (1953), is set in Salem, Massachusetts, during the witchcraft hysteria of the seventeenth century. The play was a direct response to the excesses and frenzy of McCarthyism and the activities of the U.S. House Un-American Activities Committee, which investigated Miller in 1956 as part of its own witch hunt. Many artists and writers were harassed or ruined by this committee. It convicted Miller for contempt of Congress in 1957 because he refused to give names of other artists and writers suspected of being communists or communist sympathizers. Fortunately, this ruling was overturned by the courts in 1958. By the 1960s much of what had been launched by reactionaries in America waned. Miller continued to write successfully for the stage and has often been seen as America's moral conscience in the theatre. He adapted Ibsen's *An Enemy of the People* in 1950 and created *A View from the Bridge* (1955), a study in jealousy, inappropriate sexual attraction, and betrayal; *After the Fall* (1964) about Miller's ill-fated marriage to Marilyn Monroe and guilt over the Holocaust; *The Price* (1968), a fraternal conflict in the wake of a father's death; and many other searching plays up to the 1970s. In this decade plays continued to appear, but many critics began to consider Miller's plays old-fashioned, while still acknowledging the playwright's importance to the history of American theatre. Miller proved this assessment wrong by a resurgence of successful activity in the 1990s that continued until his death. Ironically this new wave of activity began with a production in London—*The Ride Down Mount Morgan* (1991), a study of bigamy—and continued both in the United States and abroad with *Broken Glass* (1994), a study in a marriage falling apart; *Resurrection Blues* (2002), a disturbing politico-religious drama; and *Finishing the Picture* (2004) a revised examination of Miller's experiences with Marilyn Monroe.

GENRE, STRUCTURE, AND STYLE

Structurally, *Death of a Salesman* is a modern tragedy. The protagonist is not the usual tragic figure of greatness or worldly stature, but a little man, a failed salesman who never carved out a meaningful place for himself. Yet, Miller treats him with respect because he is a human being—a man with big dreams but little accomplishment. Willy Loman (note the significance of his last name), wants great things for his sons, but his lessons for them either never took or they backfired. His son Biff showed significant athletic talent, but threw it away after feeling betrayed by his father's petty extramarital affair. In this tragedy we do not see a fall from the heights, but a fall nonetheless. The demise has already taken place at the start of the play, but the final humiliation and destruction have yet to come.

Through flashbacks and Willy's memories we see the development of his mistakes and the collapse of trust between father and son that stands at the center of the conflict. By juxtaposing the past with the present, Miller shows us all the mistakes and misguided dreams of the past that are still burning brightly in Willy's stubborn insistence on the validity of his misconceptions of both his own life and the lives of his sons.

The style is lyrical without being poetic in any literal sense. Miller calls for flute music and often a dreamy quality to the flashbacks that lend the present-day scenes a prosaic counterpoint to some of Willy's wishful thinking throughout much of the play. The result is a slow but relentless unraveling of the past that leads to the inevitable tragic conclusion of Willy's sad life.

IMPORTANT ELEMENTS OF CONTENT

Death of a Salesman asks us to question the value of the so-called American Dream and takes a hard look at what this kind of thinking has done to many Americans who have not found a way to make such a dream come true in their own lives. In this case we see the dream of financial success and achieving some kind of notoriety in the community through the distorted lens of a dysfunctional family. In the wake of *Death of a Salesman* such a condition has continued to pervade much domestic drama throughout the twentieth century, receiving many interpretations—often dark ones—in successful plays by writers such as Edward Albee, Sam Shepard, and David Mamet. *Death of a Salesman* is a nearly perfect example of the consequences of living a lie.

THE PLAY IN REVIVAL

Death of a Salesman has become an enduring modern classic and is almost always in production somewhere in the world. After the initial production in 1949, it was filmed for television and broadcast on radio in the 1950s. Some of the most significant revivals include George C. Scott's production in 1975 at Circle-in-the-Square in New York, for which Scott both directed and played Willy Loman. The play was revived in Beijing, China, with an all-Chinese cast under the direction of Miller in 1983. Miller shared his experiences with this production in his book, *Salesman in Beijing* (1984). Dustin Hoffman performed Loman with much notoriety in 1984 in New York with John Malkovich as Biff. This production was subsequently made into a TV film (1985). For the 50th anniversary of the first production, Robert Falls directed the play at the Goodman Theatre in Chicago and moved it to Broadway in 1999, starring Brian Dennehy as Loman. This play continues as a staple item in many regional professional theatres, universities, and community theatres. It is read and taught in many classrooms. There are few American plays that rival its popularity and recognition.

SPECIAL FEATURE

The appearance of *Death of a Salesman* in 1949 soon led to arguments among critics over the nature of tragedy, and the validity of tragedy in the modern world. Miller himself took on the critics and effectively defended his position in creating a tragedy with such a protagonist at the center. Much of this criticism is included in the bibliography below.

FURTHER READING ABOUT THE PLAY, PLAYWRIGHT, AND CONTEXT

For other plays by Arthur Miller: All of his produced plays remain in print in many editions, both singly and collected. The amount of material available on Miller is enormous.

For examinations of Miller's life and times, see Arthur Miller, *Timebends: A Life* (his autobiography); Martin Gottfried, *Arthur Miller: His Life and Work*; and Arthur Miller, *The Portable Arthur Miller*.

For collections of Miller's criticism and essays, see Matthew Roudané, *Conversations with Arthur Miller*; Arthur Miller, *The Theatre Essays of Arthur Miller*; Steve Centola, *Arthur Miller in Conversation*; and Arthur Miller, *Echoes Down the Corridor*.

For criticism of Miller's plays, see C. W. E. Bigsby, *The Cambridge Companion to Arthur Miller*, and Helene Koone, *Twentieth Century Interpretations of* Death of a Salesman.

Death of a Salesman

BY ARTHUR MILLER

The action takes place in Willy Loman's house and yard and in various places he visits in the New York and Boston of today.

Throughout the play, in the stage directions, left and right mean stage left and stage right.

ACT ONE

A melody is heard, played upon a flute. It is small and fine, telling of grass and trees and the horizon. The curtain rises.

Before us is the Salesman's house. We are aware of towering, angular shapes behind it, surrounding it on all sides. Only the blue light of the sky falls upon the house and forestage; the surrounding area shows an angry glow of orange. As more light appears, we see a solid vault of apartment houses around the small, fragile-seeming home. An air of the dream clings to the place, a dream rising out of reality. The kitchen at center seems actual enough, for there is a kitchen table with three chairs, and a refrigerator. But no other fixtures are seen. At the back of the kitchen there is a draped entrance, which leads to the living-room. To the right of the kitchen, on a level raised two feet, is a bedroom furnished only with a brass bedstead and a straight chair. On a shelf over the bed a silver athletic trophy stands. A window opens onto the apartment house at the side.

Behind the kitchen, on a level raised six and a half feet, is the boys' bedroom, at present barely visible. Two beds are dimly seen, and at the back of the room a dormer window. (This bedroom is above the unseen living-room.) At the left a stairway curves up to it from the kitchen.

The entire setting is wholly, or, in some places, partially transparent. The roof-line of the house is one-dimensional; under and over it we see the apartment buildings. Before the house lies an apron, curving beyond the forestage into the orchestra. This forward area serves as the back yard as well as the locale of all WILLY's imaginings and of his city scenes. Whenever the action is in the present the actors observe the imaginary wall-lines, entering the house only through its door at the left. But in the scenes of the past these boundaries are broken, and characters enter or leave a room by stepping "through" a wall onto the forestage.

From the right, WILLY LOMAN, the Salesman, enters, carrying two large sample cases. The flute plays on. He hears but is not aware of it. He is past sixty years of age, dressed quietly. Even as he crosses the stage to the doorway of the house, his exhaustion is apparent. He unlocks the door, comes into the kitchen, and thankfully lets his burden down, feeling the soreness of his palms. A word-sigh escapes his lips—it might be "Oh, boy, oh, boy." He closes the door, then carries his cases out into the living-room, through the draped kitchen doorway.

LINDA, his wife, has stirred in her bed at the right. She gets out and puts on a robe, listening. Most often jovial, she has developed an iron repression of her exceptions to WILLY's behavior—she more than loves him, she admires him, as though his mercurial nature, his temper, his massive dreams and little cruelties, served her only as sharp reminders of the turbulent longings within him, longings which she shares but lacks the temperament to utter and follow to their end.

LINDA (hearing WILLY outside the bedroom, calls with some trepidation): Willy!

WILLY: It's all right. I came back.

LINDA: Why? What happened? (Slight pause.) Did something happen, Willy?

WILLY: No, nothing happened.

LINDA: You didn't smash the car, did you?

WILLY (with casual irritation): I said nothing happened. Didn't you hear me?

LINDA: Don't you feel well?

WILLY: I'm tired to the death. (The flute has faded away. He sits on the bed beside her, a little numb.) I couldn't make it. I just couldn't make it, Linda.

LINDA (*very carefully, delicately*): Where were you all day? You look terrible.

WILLY: I got as far as a little above Yonkers. I stopped for a cup of coffee. Maybe it was the coffee.

LINDA: What?

WILLY (*after a pause*): I suddenly couldn't drive any more. The car kept going off onto the shoulder, y'know?

LINDA (*helpfully*): Oh. Maybe it was the steering again. I don't think Angelo knows the Studebaker.

WILLY: No, it's me, it's me. Suddenly I realize I'm goin' sixty miles an hour and I don't remember the last five minutes. I'm—I can't seem to—keep my mind to it.

LINDA: Maybe it's your glasses. You never went for your new glasses.

WILLY: No, I see everything. I came back ten miles an hour. It took me nearly four hours from Yonkers.

LINDA (*resigned*): Well, you'll just have to take a rest, Willy, you can't continue this way.

WILLY: I just got back from Florida.

LINDA: But you didn't rest your mind. Your mind is overactive, and the mind is what counts, dear.

WILLY: I'll start out in the morning. Maybe I'll feel better in the morning. (*She is taking off his shoes.*) These goddam arch supports are killing me.

LINDA: Take an aspirin. Should I get you an aspirin? It'll soothe you.

WILLY (*with wonder*): I was driving along, you understand? And I was fine. I was even observing the scenery. You can imagine, me looking at scenery, on the road every week of my life. But it's so beautiful up there, Linda, the trees are so thick, and the sun is warm. I opened the windshield and just let the warm air bathe over me. And then all of a sudden I'm goin' off the road! I'm tellin' ya, I absolutely forgot I was driving. If I'd've gone the other way over the white line I might've killed somebody. So I went on again—and five minutes later I'm dreamin' again, and I nearly— (*He presses two fingers against his eyes.*) I have such thoughts, I have such strange thoughts.

LINDA: Willy, dear. Talk to them again. There's no reason why you can't work in New York.

WILLY: They don't need me in New York. I'm the New England man. I'm vital in New England.

LINDA: But you're sixty years old. They can't expect you to keep traveling every week.

WILLY: I'll have to send a wire to Portland. I'm supposed to see Brown and Morrison tomorrow morning at ten o'clock to show the line. Goddammit, I could sell them! (*He starts putting on his jacket.*)

LINDA (*taking the jacket from him*): Why don't you go down to the place tomorrow and tell Howard you've simply got to work in New York? You're too accommodating, dear.

WILLY: If old man Wagner was alive I'd a been in charge of New York now! That man was a prince, he was a masterful man. But that boy of his, that Howard, he don't appreciate. When I went north the first time, the Wagner Company didn't know where New England was!

LINDA: Why don't you tell those things to Howard, dear?

WILLY (*encouraged*): I will, I definitely will. Is there any cheese?

LINDA: I'll make you a sandwich.

WILLY: No, go to sleep. I'll take some milk. I'll be up right away. The boys in?

LINDA: They're sleeping. Happy took Biff on a date tonight.

WILLY (*interested*): That so?

LINDA: It was so nice to see them shaving together, one behind the other, in the bathroom. And going out together. You notice? The whole house smells of shaving lotion.

WILLY: Figure it out. Work a lifetime to pay off a house. You finally own it, and there's nobody to live in it.

LINDA: Well, dear, life is a casting off. It's always that way.

WILLY: No, no, some people—some people accomplish something. Did Biff say anything after I went this morning?

LINDA: You shouldn't have criticized him, Willy, especially after he just got off the train. You mustn't lose your temper with him.

WILLY: When the hell did I lose my temper? I simply asked him if he was making any money. Is that a criticism?

LINDA: But, dear, how could he make any money?

WILLY (*worried and angered*): There's such an undercurrent in him. He became a moody man. Did he apologize when I left this morning?

LINDA: He was crestfallen, Willy. You know how he admires you. I think if he finds himself, then you'll both be happier and not fight any more.

WILLY: How can he find himself on a farm? Is that a life? A farmhand? In the beginning, when he was young, I thought, well, a young man, it's good for him to tramp around, take a lot of different jobs. But it's more than ten years now and he has yet to make thirty-five dollars a week!

LINDA: He's finding himself, Willy.

WILLY: Not finding yourself at the age of thirty-four is a disgrace!

LINDA: Shh!

WILLY: The trouble is he's lazy, goddammit!

LINDA: Willy, please!

WILLY: Biff is a lazy bum!

LINDA: They're sleeping. Get something to eat. Go on down.

WILLY: Why did he come home? I would like to know what brought him home.

LINDA: I don't know. I think he's still lost, Willy. I think he's very lost.

WILLY: Biff Loman is lost. In the greatest country in the world a young man with such—personal attractiveness, gets lost. And such a hard worker. There's one thing about Biff—he's not lazy.

LINDA: Never.

WILLY (*with pity and resolve*): I'll see him in the morning; I'll have a nice tally with him. I'll get him a job selling. He could be big in no time. My God! Remember how they used to follow him around in high school? When he smiled at one of them their faces lit up. When he walked down the street . . . (*He loses himself in reminiscences.*)

LINDA (*trying to bring him out of it*): Willy, dear, I got a new kind of American-type cheese today. It's whipped.

WILLY: Why do you get American when I like Swiss?

LINDA: I just thought you'd like a change—

WILLY: I don't want a change! I want Swiss cheese. Why am I always being contradicted?

LINDA (*with a covering laugh*): I thought it would be a surprise.

WILLY: Why don't you open a window in here, for God's sake?

LINDA (*with infinite patience*): They're all open, dear.

WILLY: The way they boxed us in here. Bricks and windows, windows and bricks.

LINDA: We should've bought the land next door.

WILLY: The street is lined with cars. There's not a breath of fresh air in the neighborhood. The grass don't grow any more, you can't raise a carrot in the back yard. They should've had a law against apartment houses. Remember those two beautiful elm trees out there? When I and Biff hung the swing between them?

LINDA: Yeah, like being a million miles from the city.

WILLY: They should've arrested the builder for cutting those down. They massacred the neighborhood. (*Lost*) More and more I think of those days, Linda. This time of year it was lilac and wisteria. And then the peonies would come out, and the daffodils. What fragrance in this room!

LINDA: Well, after all, people had to move somewhere.

WILLY: No, there's more people now.

LINDA: I don't think there's more people. I think—

WILLY: There's more people! That's what's ruining this country! Population is getting out of control. The competition is maddening! Smell the stink from that apartment house! And another one on the other side . . . How can they whip cheese?

(*On* WILLY's *last line,* BIFF *and* HAPPY *raise themselves up in their beds, listening.*)

LINDA: Go down, try it. And be quiet.

WILLY (*turning to* LINDA, *guiltily*): You're not worried about me, are you, sweetheart?

BIFF: What's the matter?

HAPPY: Listen!

LINDA: You've got too much on the ball to worry about.

WILLY: You're my foundation and my support, Linda.

LINDA: Just try to relax, dear. You make mountains out of molehills.

WILLY: I won't fight with him any more. If he wants to go back to Texas, let him go.

LINDA: He'll find his way.

WILLY: Sure. Certain men just don't get started till later in life. Like Thomas Edison, I think. Or B. F. Goodrich. One of them was deaf. (*He starts for the bedroom doorway.*) I'll put my money on Biff.

LINDA: And Willy—if it's warm Sunday we'll drive in the country. And we'll open the windshield, and take lunch.

WILLY: No, the windshields don't open on the new cars.

LINDA: But you opened it today.

WILLY: Me? I didn't. (*He stops.*) Now isn't that peculiar! Isn't that a remarkable—(*He breaks off in amazement and fright as the flute is heard distantly.*)

LINDA: What, darling?

WILLY: That is the most remarkable thing.

LINDA: What, dear?

WILLY: I was thinking of the Chevvy. (*Slight pause.*) Nineteen twenty-eight . . . when I had that red Chevvy—(*Breaks off.*) That funny? I coulda sworn I was driving that Chevvy today.

LINDA: Well, that's nothing. Something must've reminded you.

WILLY: Remarkable. Ts. Remember those days? The way Biff used to simonize that car? The dealer refused to believe there was eighty thousand miles on it. (*He shakes his head.*) Heh! (*To* LINDA): Close your eyes, I'll be right up. (*He walks out of the bedroom.*)

HAPPY (*to* BIFF): Jesus, maybe he smashed up the car again!

LINDA (*calling after* WILLY): Be careful on the stairs, dear! The cheese is on the middle shelf! (*She turns, goes over to the bed, takes his jacket, and goes out of the bedroom.*)

(*Light has risen on the boys' room. Unseen,* WILLY *is heard talking to himself, "Eighty thousand miles," and a little laugh.* BIFF *gets out of bed, comes downstage a bit, and stands attentively.* BIFF *is two years older than his brother* HAPPY, *well built, but in these days bears a worn air and seems less self-assured. He has succeeded less, and his dreams are stronger and less acceptable than* HAPPY'S. HAPPY *is tall, powerfully made. Sexuality is like a visible color on him,* or a scent that many women have discovered. He, like his brother, is lost, but in a different way, for he has never allowed himself to turn his face toward defeat and is thus more confused and hard-skinned, although seemingly more content.*)

HAPPY (*getting out of bed*): He's going to get his license taken away if he keeps that up. I'm getting nervous about him, y'know, Biff?

BIFF: His eyes are going.

HAPPY: No, I've driven with him. He sees all right. He just doesn't keep his mind on it. I drove into the city with him last week. He stops at a green light and then it turns red and he goes. (*He laughs.*)

BIFF: Maybe he's color-blind.

HAPPY: Pop? Why he's got the finest eye for color in the business. You know that.

BIFF (*sitting down on his bed*): I'm going to sleep.

HAPPY: You're not still sour on Dad, are you, Biff?

BIFF: He's all right, I guess.

WILLY (*underneath them, in the living-room*): Yes, sir, eighty thousand miles—eighty-two thousand!

BIFF: You smoking?

HAPPY (*holding out a pack of cigarettes*): Want one?

BIFF (*taking a cigarette*): I can never sleep when I smell it.

WILLY: What a simonizing job, heh!

HAPPY (*with deep sentiment*): Funny, Biff, y'know? Us sleeping in here again? The old beds. (*He pats his bed affectionately.*) All the talk that went across those two beds, huh? Our whole lives.

BIFF: Yeah. Lotta dreams and plans.

HAPPY (*with a deep and masculine laugh*): About five hundred women would like to know what was said in this room.

(*They share a soft laugh.*)

BIFF: Remember that big Betsy something—what the hell was her name—over on Bushwick Avenue?

HAPPY (*combing his hair*): With the collie dog!

BIFF: That's the one. I got you in there, remember?

HAPPY: Yeah, that was my first time—I think. Boy, there was a pig! (*They laugh, almost crudely.*) You taught me everything I know about women. Don't forget that.

BIFF: I bet you forgot how bashful you used to be. Especially with girls.

HAPPY: Oh, I still am, Biff.

BIFF: Oh, go on.

HAPPY: I just control it, that's all. I think I got less bashful and you got more so. What happened, Biff? Where's the old humor, the old confidence? (*He shakes* BIFF's *knee.* BIFF *gets up and moves restlessly about the room.*) What's the matter?

BIFF: Why does Dad mock me all the time?

HAPPY: He's not mocking you, he—

BIFF: Everything I say there's a twist of mockery on his face. I can't get near him.

HAPPY: He just wants you to make good, that's all. I wanted to talk to you about Dad for a long time, Biff. Something's—happening to him. He—talks to himself.

BIFF: I noticed that this morning. But he always mumbled.

HAPPY: But not so noticeable. It got so embarrassing I sent him to Florida. And you know something? Most of the time he's talking to you.

BIFF: What's he say about me?

HAPPY: I can't make it out.

BIFF: What's he say about me?

HAPPY: I think the fact that you're not settled, that you're still kind of up in the air . . .

BIFF: There's one or two other things depressing him, Happy.

HAPPY: What do you mean?

BIFF: Never mind. Just don't lay it all to me.

HAPPY: But I think if you just got started—I mean—is there any future for you out there?

BIFF: I tell ya, Hap, I don't know what the future is. I don't know—what I'm supposed to want.

HAPPY: What do you mean?

BIFF: Well, I spent six or seven years after high school trying to work myself up. Shipping clerk, salesman, business of one kind or another. And it's a measly manner of existence. To get on that subway on the hot mornings in summer. To devote your whole life to keeping stock, or making phone calls, or selling or buying. To suffer fifty weeks of the year for the sake of a two-week vacation, when all you really desire is to be outdoors, with your shirt off. And always to have to get ahead of the next fella. And still—that's how you build a future.

HAPPY: Well, you really enjoy it on a farm? Are you content out there?

BIFF (*with rising agitation*): Hap, I've had twenty or thirty different kinds of jobs since I left home before the war, and it always turns out the same. I just realized it lately. In Nebraska when I herded cattle, and the Dakotas, and Arizona, and now in Texas. It's why I came home now, I guess, because I realized it. This farm I work on, it's spring there now, see? And they've got about fifteen new colts. There's nothing more inspiring or—beautiful than the sight of a mare and a new colt. And it's cool there now, see? Texas is cool now, and it's spring. And whenever spring comes to where I am, I suddenly get the feeling, my God, I'm not gettin' anywhere! What the hell am I doing, playing around with horses, twenty-eight dollars a week! I'm thirty-four years old, I oughta be makin' my future. That's when I come running home. And now, I get here, and I don't know what to do with myself. (*After a pause*): I've always made a point of not wasting my life, and everytime I come back here I know that all I've done is to waste my life.

HAPPY: You're a poet, you know that, Biff? You're a—you're an idealist!

BIFF: No, I'm mixed up very bad. Maybe I oughta get married. Maybe I oughta get stuck into something. Maybe that's my trouble. I'm like a boy. I'm not married, I'm not in business, I just—I'm like a boy. Are you content, Hap? You're a success, aren't you? Are you content?

HAPPY: Hell, no!

BIFF: Why? You're making money, aren't you?

HAPPY (*moving about with energy, expressiveness*): All I can do now is wait for the merchandise manager to die. And suppose I get to be merchandise manager? He's a good friend of mine, and he just built a terrific estate on Long Island. And he lived there about two months and sold it, and now he's building another one. He can't enjoy it once it's finished. And I know that's just what I would do. I don't know what the hell I'm workin' for. Sometimes I sit in my apartment—all alone. And I think of the rent I'm paying. And it's crazy. But then, it's what I always wanted. My own apartment, a car, and plenty of women. And still, goddammit, I'm lonely.

BIFF (*with enthusiasm*): Listen, why don't you come out West with me?

HAPPY: You and I, heh?

BIFF: Sure, maybe we could buy a ranch. Raise cattle, use our muscles. Men built like we are should be working out in the open.

HAPPY (*avidly*): The Loman Brothers, heh?

BIFF (*with vast affection*): Sure, we'd be known all over the counties!

HAPPY (*enthralled*): That's what I dream about, Biff. Sometimes I want to just rip my clothes off in the middle of the store and outbox that goddam merchandise manager. I mean I can outbox, out-run, and outlift anybody in that store, and I have to take orders from those common, petty sons-of-bitches till I can't stand it any more.

BIFF: I'm tellin' you, kid, if you were with me I'd be happy out there.

HAPPY (*enthused*): See, Biff, everybody around me is so false that I'm constantly lowering my ideals . . .

BIFF: Baby, together we'd stand up for one another, we'd have someone to trust.

HAPPY: If I were around you—

BIFF: Hap, the trouble is we weren't brought up to grub for money. I don't know how to do it.

HAPPY: Neither can I!

BIFF: Then let's go!

HAPPY: The only thing is—what can you make out there?

BIFF: But look at your friend. Builds an estate and then hasn't the peace of mind to live in it.

HAPPY: Yeah, but when he walks into the store the waves part in front of him. That's fifty-two thousand dollars a year coming through the revolving door, and I got more in my pinky finger than he's got in his head.

BIFF: Yeah, but you just said—

HAPPY: I gotta show some of those pompous, self-important executives over there that Hap Lo-man can make the grade. I want to walk into the store the way he walks in. Then I'll go with you, Biff. We'll be together yet, I swear. But take those two we had tonight. Now weren't they gorgeous creatures?

BIFF: Yeah, yeah, most gorgeous I've had in years.

HAPPY: I get that any time I want, Biff. Whenever I feel disgusted. The only trouble is, it gets like bowling or something. I just keep knockin' them over and it doesn't mean anything. You still run around a lot?

BIFF: Naa. I'd like to find a girl—steady, somebody with substance.

HAPPY: That's what I long for.

BIFF: Go on! You'd never come home.

HAPPY: I would! Somebody with character, with resistance! Like Mom, y'know? You're gonna call me a bastard when I tell you this. That girl Charlotte I was with tonight is engaged to be married in five weeks. (*He tries on his new hat.*)

BIFF: No kiddin'!

HAPPY: Sure, the guy's in line for the vice-presidency of the store. I don't know what gets into me, maybe I just have an overdeveloped sense of competition or something, but I went and ruined her, and furthermore I can't get rid of her. And he's the third executive I've done that to. Isn't that a crummy characteristic? And to top it all, I go to their weddings! (*Indignantly, but laughing.*) Like I'm not supposed to take bribes. Manufacturers offer me a hundred-dollar bill now and then to throw an order their way. You know how honest I am, but it's like this girl, see. I hate myself for it. Because I don't want the girl, and, still, I take it and—I love it!

BIFF: Let's go to sleep.

HAPPY: I guess we didn't settle anything, heh?

BIFF: I just got one idea that I think I'm going to try.

HAPPY: What's that?

BIFF: Remember Bill Oliver?

HAPPY: Sure, Oliver is very big now. You want to work for him again?

BIFF: No, but when I quit he said something to me. He put his arm on my shoulder, and he said, "Biff, if you ever need anything, come to me."

HAPPY: I remember that. That sounds good.

BIFF: I think I'll go to see him. If I could get ten thousand or even seven or eight thousand dollars I could buy a beautiful ranch.

HAPPY: I bet he'd back you. 'Cause he thought highly of you, Biff. I mean, they all do. You're well liked, Biff. That's why I say to come back here, and we both have the apartment. And I'm tellin' you, Biff, any babe you want . . .

BIFF: No, with a ranch I could do the work I like and still be something. I just wonder though. I wonder if Oliver still thinks I stole that carton of basketballs.

HAPPY: Oh, he probably forgot that long ago. It's almost ten years. You're too sensitive. Anyway, he didn't really fire you.

BIFF: Well, I think he was going to. I think that's why I quit. I was never sure whether he knew or not. I know he thought the world of me, though. I was the only one he'd let lock up the place.

WILLY (*below*): You gonna wash the engine, Biff?

HAPPY: Shh!

(BIFF *looks at* HAPPY, *who is gazing down, listening.* WILLY *is mumbling in the parlor.*)

HAPPY: You hear that?

(*They listen.* WILLY *laughs, warmly.*)

BIFF (*growing angry*): Doesn't he know Mom can hear that?

WILLY: Don't get your sweater dirty, Biff!

(*A look of pain crosses* BIFF's *face.*)

HAPPY: Isn't that terrible? Don't leave again, will you? You'll find a job here. You gotta stick around. I don't know what to do about him, it's getting embarrassing.

WILLY: What a simonizing job!

BIFF: Mom's hearing that!

WILLY: No kiddin', Biff, you got a date? Wonderful!

HAPPY: Go on to sleep. But talk to him in the morning, will you?

BIFF (*reluctantly getting into bed*): With her in the house. Brother!

HAPPY (*getting into bed*): I wish you'd have a good talk with him.

(*The light on their room begins to fade.*)

BIFF (*to himself in bed*): That selfish, stupid . . .

HAPPY: Sh . . . Sleep, Biff.

(*Their light is out. Well before they have finished speaking,* WILLY's *form is dimly seen below in the darkened kitchen. He opens the refrigerator, searches in there, and takes out a bottle of milk. The apartment houses are fading out, and the entire house and surroundings become covered with leaves. Music insinuates itself as the leaves appear.*)

WILLY: Just wanna be careful with those girls, Biff, that's all. Don't make any promises. No prom-

ises of any kind. Because a girl, y'know, they always believe what you tell 'em, and you're very young, Biff, you're too young to be talking seriously to girls.

(*Light rises on the kitchen.* WILLY, *talking, shuts the refrigerator door and comes downstage to the kitchen table. He pours milk into a glass. He is totally immersed in himself, smiling faintly.*)

WILLY: Too young entirely, Biff. You want to watch your schooling first. Then when you're all set, there'll be plenty of girls for a boy like you. (*He smiles broadly at a kitchen chair.*) That so? The girls pay for you? (*He laughs.*) Boy, you must really be makin' a hit.

(WILLY *is gradually addressing—physically—a point offstage, speaking through the wall of the kitchen, and his voice has been rising in volume to that of a normal conversation.*)

WILLY: I been wondering why you polish the car so careful. Ha! Don't leave the hubcaps, boys. Get the chamois to the hubcaps. Happy, use newspaper on the windows, it's the easiest thing. Show him how to do it, Biff! You see, Happy? Pad it up, use it like a pad. That's it, that's it, good work. You're doin' all right, Hap. (*He pauses, then nods in approbation for a few seconds, then looks upward.*) Biff, first thing we gotta do when we get time is clip that big branch over the house. Afraid it's gonna fall in a storm and hit the roof. Tell you what. We get a rope and sling her around, and then we climb up there with a couple of saws and take her down. Soon as you finish the car, boys, I wanna see ya. I got a surprise for you, boys.

BIFF (*offstage*): Whatta ya got, Dad?

WILLY: No, you finish first. Never leave a job till you're finished—remember that. (*Looking toward the "big trees"*) Biff, up in Albany I saw a beautiful hammock. I think I'll buy it next trip, and we'll hang it right between those two elms. Wouldn't that be something? Just swingin' there under those branches. Boy, that would be . . .

(YOUNG BIFF *and* YOUNG HAPPY *appear from the direction* WILLY *was addressing.* HAPPY *carries rags and a pail of water.* BIFF, *wearing a sweater with a block "S," carries a football.*)

BIFF (*pointing in the direction of the car onstage*): How's that, Pop, professional?

WILLY: Terrific. Terrific job, boys. Good work, Biff.

HAPPY: Where's the surprise, Pop?

WILLY: In the back seat of the car.

HAPPY: Boy! (*He runs off.*)

BIFF: What is it, Dad? Tell me, what'd you buy?

WILLY (*laughing, cuffs him*): Never mind, something I want you to have.

BIFF (*turns and starts off*): What is it, Hap?

HAPPY (*offstage*): It's a punching bag!

BIFF: Oh, Pop!

WILLY: It's got Gene Tunney's signature on it!
  (HAPPY *runs onstage with a punching bag.*)

BIFF: Gee, how'd you know we wanted a punching bag?

WILLY: Well, it's the finest thing for the timing.

HAPPY (*lies down on his back and pedals with his feet*): I'm losing weight, you notice, Pop?

WILLY (*to* HAPPY): Jumping rope is good too.

BIFF: Did you see the new football I got?

WILLY (*examining the ball*): Where'd you get a new ball?

BIFF: The coach told me to practice my passing.

WILLY: That so? And he gave you the ball, heh?

BIFF: Well, I borrowed it from the locker room. (*He laughs confidentially.*)

WILLY (*laughing with him at the theft*): I want you to return that.

HAPPY: I told you he wouldn't like it!

BIFF (*angrily*): Well, I'm bringing it back!

WILLY (*stopping the incipient argument, to* HAPPY): Sure, he's gotta practice with a regulation ball, doesn't he? (*To* BIFF): Coach'll probably congratulate you on your initiative!

BIFF: Oh, he keeps congratulating my initiative all the time, Pop.

WILLY: That's because he likes you. If somebody else took that ball there'd be an uproar. So what's the report, boys, what's the report?

BIFF: Where'd you go this time, Dad? Gee we were lonesome for you.

WILLY (*pleased, puts an arm around each boy and they come down to the apron*): Lonesome, heh?

BIFF: Missed you every minute.

WILLY: Don't say? Tell you a secret, boys. Don't breathe it to a soul. Someday I'll have my own business, and I'll never have to leave home any more.

HAPPY: Like Uncle Charley, heh?

WILLY: Bigger than Uncle Charley! Because Charley is not—liked. He's liked, but he's not—well liked.

BIFF: Where'd you go this time, Dad?

WILLY: Well, I got on the road, and I went north to Providence. Met the Mayor.

BIFF: The Mayor of Providence!

WILLY: He was sitting in the hotel lobby.

BIFF: What'd he say?

WILLY: He said, "Morning!" And I said, "You got a fine city here, Mayor." And then he had coffee with me. And then I went to Waterbury. Waterbury is a fine city. Big clock city, the famous Waterbury clock. Sold a nice bill there. And then Boston—Boston is the cradle of the Revolution. A fine city. And a couple of other towns in Mass., and on to Portland and Bangor and straight home!

BIFF: Gee, I'd love to go with you sometime, Dad.

WILLY: Soon as summer comes.

HAPPY: Promise?

WILLY: You and Hap and I, and I'll show you all the towns. America is full of beautiful towns and fine, upstanding people. And they know me, boys, they know me up and down New England. The finest people. And when I bring you fellas up, there'll be open sesame for all of us, 'cause one thing, boys: I have friends. I can park my car in any street in New England, and the cops protect it like their own. This summer, heh?

BIFF AND HAPPY (*together*): Yeah! You bet!

WILLY: We'll take our bathing suits.

HAPPY: We'll carry your bags, Pop!

WILLY: Oh, won't that be something! Me comin' into the Boston stores with you boys carryin' my bags. What a sensation!
  (BIFF *is prancing around, practicing passing the ball.*)

WILLY: You nervous, Biff, about the game?

BIFF: Not if you're gonna be there.

WILLY: What do they say about you in school, now that they made you captain?

HAPPY: There's a crowd of girls behind him everytime the classes change.

BIFF (*taking* WILLY'S *hand*): This Saturday, Pop, this Saturday—just for you, I'm going to break through for a touchdown.

HAPPY: You're supposed to pass.

BIFF: I'm takin' one play for Pop. You watch me, Pop, and when I take off my helmet, that means I'm breakin' out. Then you watch me crash through that line!

WILLY (*kisses* BIFF): Oh, wait'll I tell this in Boston!

(BERNARD *enters in knickers. He is younger than* BIFF, *earnest and loyal, a worried boy.*)

BERNARD: Biff, where are you? You're supposed to study with me today.

WILLY: Hey, looka Bernard. What're you lookin' so anemic about, Bernard?

BERNARD: He's gotta study, Uncle Willy. He's got Regents next week.

HAPPY (*tauntingly, spinning* BERNARD *around*): Let's box, Bernard!

BERNARD: Biff! (*He gets away from* HAPPY.) Listen, Biff, I heard Mr. Birnbaum say that if you don't start studyin' math he's gonna flunk you, and you won't graduate. I heard him!

WILLY: You better study with him, Biff. Go ahead now.

BERNARD: I heard him!

BIFF: Oh, Pop, you didn't see my sneakers! (*He holds up a foot for* WILLY *to look at.*)

WILLY: Hey, that's a beautiful job of printing!

BERNARD (*wiping his glasses*): Just because he printed University of Virginia on his sneakers doesn't mean they've got to graduate him, Uncle Willy!

WILLY (*angrily*): What're you talking about? With scholarships to three universities they're gonna flunk him?

BERNARD: But I heard Mr. Birnbaum say—

WILLY: Don't be a pest, Bernard! (*To his boys*): What an anemic!

BERNARD: Okay, I'm waiting for you in my house, Biff.

(BERNARD *goes off.* THE LOMANS *laugh.*)

WILLY: Bernard is not well liked, is he?

BIFF: He's liked, but he's not well liked.

HAPPY: That's right, Pop.

WILLY: That's just what I mean. Bernard can get the best marks in school, y'understand, but when he gets out in the business world, y'understand, you are going to be five times ahead of him. That's why I thank Almighty God you're both built like Adonises. Because the man who makes an appearance in the business world, the man who creates personal interest, is the man who gets ahead. Be liked and you will never want. You take me, for instance. I never have to wait in line to see a buyer. "Willy Loman is here!" That's all they have to know, and I go right through.

BIFF: Did you knock them dead, Pop?

WILLY: Knocked 'em cold in Providence, slaughtered 'em in Boston.

HAPPY (*on his back, pedaling again*): I'm losing weight, you notice, Pop?

(LINDA *enters, as of old, a ribbon in her hair, carrying a basket of washing.*)

LINDA (*with youthful energy*): Hello, dear!

WILLY: Sweetheart!

LINDA: How'd the Chevvy run?

WILLY: Chevrolet, Linda, is the greatest car ever built. (*To the boys*): Since when do you let your mother carry wash up the stairs?

BIFF: Grab hold there, boy!

HAPPY: Where to, Mom?

LINDA: Hang them up on the line. And you better go down to your friends, Biff. The cellar is full of boys. They don't know what to do with themselves.

BIFF: Ah, when Pop comes home they can wait!

WILLY (*laughs appreciatively*): You better go down and tell them what to do, Biff.

BIFF: I think I'll have them sweep out the furnace room.

WILLY: Good work, Biff.

BIFF (*goes through wall-line of kitchen to doorway at back and calls down*): Fellas! Everybody sweep out the furnace room! I'll be right down!

VOICES: All right! Okay, Biff.

BIFF: George and Sam and Frank, come out back! We're hangin' up the wash! Come on, Hap, on the double! (*He and* HAPPY *carry out the basket.*)

LINDA: The way they obey him!

WILLY: Well, that's training, the training. I'm tellin' you, I was sellin' thousands and thousands, but I had to come home.

LINDA: Oh, the whole block'll be at that game. Did you sell anything?

WILLY: I did five hundred gross in Providence and seven hundred gross in Boston.

LINDA: No! Wait a minute, I've got a pencil. (*She pulls pencil and paper out of her apron pocket.*) That makes your commission . . . Two hundred—my God! Two hundred and twelve dollars!

WILLY: Well, I didn't figure it yet, but . . .

LINDA: How much did you do?

WILLY: Well, I—I did—about a hundred and eighty gross in Providence. Well, no—it came to—roughly two hundred gross on the whole trip.

LINDA (*without hesitation*): Two hundred gross. That's . . . (*She figures.*)

WILLY: The trouble was that three of the stores were half closed for inventory in Boston. Otherwise I woulda broke records.

LINDA: Well, it makes seventy dollars and some pennies. That's very good.

WILLY: What do we owe?

LINDA: Well, on the first there's sixteen dollars on the refrigerator—

WILLY: Why sixteen?

LINDA: Well, the fan belt broke, so it was a dollar eighty.

WILLY: But it's brand new.

LINDA: Well, the man said that's the way it is. Till they work themselves in, y'know.

(*They move through the wall-line into the kitchen.*)

WILLY: I hope we didn't get stuck on that machine.

LINDA: They got the biggest ads of any of them!

WILLY: I know, it's a fine machine. What else?

LINDA: Well, there's nine-sixty for the washing machine. And for the vacuum cleaner there's three and a half due on the fifteenth. Then the roof, you got twenty-one dollars remaining.

WILLY: It don't leak, does it?

LINDA: No, they did a wonderful job. Then you owe Frank for the carburetor.

WILLY: I'm not going to pay that man! That goddam Chevrolet, they ought to prohibit the manufacture of that car!

LINDA: Well, you owe him three and a half. And odds and ends, comes to around a hundred and twenty dollars by the fifteenth.

WILLY: A hundred and twenty dollars! My God, if business don't pick up I don't know what I'm gonna do!

LINDA: Well, next week you'll do better.

WILLY: Oh, I'll knock 'em dead next week. I'll go to Hartford. I'm very well liked in Hartford. You know, the trouble is, Linda, people don't seem to take to me.

(*They move onto the forestage.*)

LINDA: Oh, don't be foolish.

WILLY: I know it when I walk in. They seem to laugh at me.

LINDA: Why? Why would they laugh at you? Don't talk that way, Willy.

(WILLY *moves to the edge of the stage.* LINDA *goes into the kitchen and starts to darn stockings.*)

WILLY: I don't know the reason for it, but they just pass me by. I'm not noticed.

LINDA: But you're doing wonderful, dear. You're making seventy to a hundred dollars a week.

WILLY: But I gotta be at it ten, twelve hours a day. Other men—I don't know—they do it easier. I don't know why—I can't stop myself—I talk too much. A man oughta come in with a few words. One thing about Charley. He's a man of few words, and they respect him.

LINDA: You don't talk too much, you're just lively.

WILLY (*smiling*): Well, I figure, what the hell, life is short, a couple of jokes. (*To himself*) I joke too much! (*The smile goes.*)

LINDA: Why? You're—

WILLY: I'm fat. I'm very—foolish to look at, Linda. I didn't tell you, but Christmas time I happened to be calling on F. H. Stewarts, and a salesman I know, as I was going in to see the buyer I heard him say something about—walrus. And I—I cracked him right across the face. I won't take that. I simply will not take that. But they do laugh at me. I know that.

LINDA: Darling . . .

WILLY: I gotta overcome it. I know I gotta overcome it. I'm not dressing to advantage, maybe.

LINDA: Willy, darling, you're the handsomest man in the world—

WILLY: Oh, no, Linda.

LINDA: To me you are. (*Slight pause.*) The handsomest. (*From the darkness is heard the laughter of a woman.* WILLY *doesn't turn to it, but it continues through* LINDA's *lines.*)

LINDA: And the boys, Willy. Few men are idolized by their children the way you are.

(*Music is heard as behind a scrim, to the left of the house,* THE WOMAN, *dimly seen, is dressing.*)

WILLY (*with great feeling*): You're the best there is, Linda, you're a pal, you know that? On the

road—on the road I want to grab you sometimes and just kiss the life outa you.
(*The laughter is loud now, and he moves into a
brightening area at the left, where* THE WOMAN *has
come from behind the scrim and is standing, putting
on her hat, looking into a "mirror" and laughing.*)

WILLY: 'Cause I get so lonely—especially when
business is bad and there's nobody to talk to.
I get the feeling that I'll never sell anything
again, that I won't making a living for you, or
a business, a business for the boys. (*He talks
through* THE WOMAN's *subsiding laughter;* THE
WOMAN *primps at the "mirror."*) There's so much
I want to make for—

THE WOMAN: Me? You didn't make me, Willy. I
picked you.

WILLY (*pleased*): You picked me?

THE WOMAN (*who is quite proper-looking,* WILLY's *age*):
I did. I've been sitting at that desk watching
all the salesmen go by, day in, day out. But
you've got such a sense of humor, and we do
have such a good time together, don't we?

WILLY: Sure, sure. (*He takes her in his arms.*) Why do
you have to go now?

THE WOMAN: It's two o'clock . . .

WILLY: No, come on in! (*He pulls her.*)

THE WOMAN: . . . my sisters'll be scandalized.
When'll you be back?

WILLY: Oh, two weeks about. Will you come up
again?

THE WOMAN: Sure thing. You do make me laugh.
It's good for me. (*She squeezes his arm, kisses
him.*) And I think you're a wonderful man.

WILLY: You picked me, heh?

THE WOMAN: Sure. Because you're so sweet. And
such a kidder.

WILLY: Well, I'll see you next time I'm in Boston.

THE WOMAN: I'll put you right through to the buyers.

WILLY (*slapping her bottom*): Right. Well, bottoms up!

THE WOMAN (*slaps him gently and laughs*): You just
kill me, Willy. (*He suddenly grabs her and kisses
her roughly.*) You kill me. And thanks for the
stockings. I love a lot of stockings. Well, good
night.

WILLY: Good night. And keep your pores open!

THE WOMAN: Oh, Willy!

(THE WOMAN *bursts out laughing, and* LINDA's
laughter blends in. THE WOMAN *disappears into the
dark. Now the area at the kitchen table brightens.*
LINDA *is sitting where she was at the kitchen table,
but now is mending a pair of her silk stockings.*)

LINDA: You are, Willy. The handsomest man. You've
got no reason to feel that—

WILLY (*coming out of the woman's dimming area and
going over to* LINDA): I'll make it all up to you,
Linda, I'll—

LINDA: There's nothing to make up, dear. You're
doing fine, better than—

WILLY (*noticing her mending*): What's that?

LINDA: Just mending my stockings. They're so
expensive—

WILLY (*angrily, taking them from her*): I won't have
you mending stockings in this house! Now
throw them out!

(LINDA *puts the stockings in her pocket.*)

BERNARD (*entering on the run*): Where is he? If he
doesn't study!

WILLY (*moving to the forestage, with great agitation*):
You'll give him the answers!

BERNARD: I do, but I can't on a Regents! That's a
state exam! They're liable to arrest me!

WILLY: Where is he? I'll whip him, I'll whip him!

LINDA: And he'd better give back that football, Willy, it's not nice.

WILLY: Biff! Where is he? Why is he taking everything?

LINDA: He's too rough with the girls, Willy. All the
mothers are afraid of him!

WILLY: I'll whip him!

BERNARD: He's driving the car without a license!

(THE WOMAN's *laugh is heard.*)

WILLY: Shut up!

LINDA: All the mothers—

WILLY: Shut up!

BERNARD (*backing quietly away and out*): Mr. Birnbaum says he's stuck up.

WILLY: Get outa here!

BERNARD: If he doesn't buckle down he'll flunk
math! (*He goes off.*)

LINDA: He's right, Willy, you've gotta—

WILLY (*exploding at her*): There's nothing the matter with him! You want him to be a worm like
Bernard? He's got spirit, personality . . .

(*As he speaks,* LINDA, *almost in tears, exits into
the living-room.* WILLY *is alone in the kitchen, wilt-
ing and staring. The leaves are gone. It is night*

again, and the apartment houses look down from behind.)

WILLY: Loaded with it. Loaded! What is he stealing? He's giving it back, isn't he? Why is he stealing? What did I tell him? I never in my life told him anything but decent things.

(HAPPY *in pajamas has come down the stairs,* WILLY *suddenly becomes aware of* HAPPY's *presence.*)

HAPPY: Let's go now, come on.

WILLY (*sitting down at the kitchen table*): Huh! Why did she have to wax the floors herself? Everytime she waxes the floors she keels over. She knows that!

HAPPY: Shh! Take it easy. What brought you back tonight?

WILLY: I got an awful scare. Nearly hit a kid in Yonkers. God! Why didn't I go to Alaska with my brother Ben that time! Ben! That man was a genius, that man was success incarnate! What a mistake! He begged me to go.

HAPPY: Well, there's no use in—

WILLY: You guys! There was a man started with the clothes on his back and ended up with diamond mines!

HAPPY: Boy, someday I'd like to know how he did it.

WILLY: What's the mystery? The man knew what he wanted and went out and got it! Walked into a jungle, and comes out, the age of twenty-one, and he's rich! The world is an oyster, but you don't crack it open on a mattress!

HAPPY: Pop, I told you I'm gonna retire you for life.

WILLY: You'll retire me for life on seventy goddam dollars a week? And your women and your car and your apartment, and you'll retire me for life! Christ's sake, I couldn't get past Yonkers today! Where are you guys, where are you? The woods are burning! I can't drive a car!

(CHARLEY *has appeared in the doorway. He is a large man, slow of speech, laconic, immovable. In all he says, despite what he says, there is pity, and, now, trepidation. He has a robe over pajamas, slippers on his feet. He enters the kitchen.*)

CHARLEY: Everything all right?

HAPPY: Yeah, Charley, everything's . . .

WILLY: What's the matter?

CHARLEY: I heard some noise. I thought something happened. Can't we do something about the walls? You sneeze in here, and in my house hats blow off.

HAPPY: Let's go to bed, Dad. Come on.

(CHARLEY *signals to* HAPPY *to go.*)

WILLY: You go ahead, I'm not tired at the moment.

HAPPY (*to* WILLY): Take it easy, huh? (*He exits.*)

WILLY: What're you doin' up?

CHARLEY (*sitting down at the kitchen table opposite* WILLY): Couldn't sleep good. I had a heartburn.

WILLY: Well, you don't know how to eat.

CHARLEY: I eat with my mouth.

WILLY: No, you're ignorant. You gotta know about vitamins and things like that.

CHARLEY: Come on, let's shoot. Tire you out a little.

WILLY (*hesitantly*): All right. You got cards?

CHARLEY (*taking a deck from his pocket*): Yeah, I got them. Someplace. What is it with those vitamins?

WILLY (*dealing*): They build up your bones. Chemistry.

CHARLEY: Yeah, but there's no bones in a heartburn.

WILLY: What are you talkin' about? Do you know the first thing about it?

CHARLEY: Don't get insulted.

WILLY: Don't talk about something you don't know anything about.

(*They are playing. Pause.*)

CHARLEY: What're you doin' home?

WILLY: A little trouble with the car.

CHARLEY: Oh. (*Pause.*) I'd like to take a trip to California.

WILLY: Don't say.

CHARLEY: You want a job?

WILLY: I got a job, I told you that. (*After a slight pause.*) What the hell are you offering me a job for?

CHARLEY: Don't get insulted.

WILLY: Don't insult me.

CHARLEY: I don't see no sense in it. You don't have to go on this way.

WILLY: I got a good job. (*Slight pause.*) What do you keep comin' in here for?

CHARLEY: You want me to go?

WILLY (*after a pause, withering*): I can't understand it. He's going back to Texas again. What the hell is that?

CHARLEY: Let him go.

WILLY: I got nothin' to give him, Charley, I'm clean, I'm clean.

CHARLEY: He won't starve. None a them starve. Forget about him.

WILLY: Then what have I got to remember?

CHARLEY: You take it too hard. To hell with it. When a deposit bottle is broken you don't get your nickel back.

WILLY: That's easy enough for you to say.

CHARLEY: That ain't easy for me to say.

WILLY: Did you see the ceiling I put up in the living-room?

CHARLEY: Yeah, that's a piece of work. To put up a ceiling is a mystery to me. How do you do it?

WILLY: What's the difference?

CHARLEY: Well, talk about it.

WILLY: You gonna put up a ceiling?

CHARLEY: How could I put up a ceiling?

WILLY: Then what the hell are you bothering me for?

CHARLEY: You're insulted again.

WILLY: A man who can't handle tools is not a man. You're disgusting.

CHARLEY: Don't call me disgusting, Willy.

(UNCLE BEN, *carrying a valise and an umbrella, enters the forestage from around the right corner of the house. He is a stolid man, in his sixties, with a mustache and an authoritative air. He is utterly certain of his destiny, and there is an aura of far places about him. He enters exactly as* WILLY *speaks.*)

WILLY: I'm getting awfully tired, Ben.

(BEN'S *music is heard.* BEN *looks around at everything.*)

CHARLEY: Good, keep playing; you'll sleep better. Did you call me Ben?

(BEN *looks at his watch.*)

WILLY: That's funny. For a second there you reminded me of my brother Ben.

BEN: I only have a few minutes. (*He strolls, inspecting the place.* WILLY *and* CHARLEY *continue playing.*)

CHARLEY: You never heard from him again, heh? Since that time?

WILLY: Didn't Linda tell you? Couple of weeks ago we got a letter from his wife in Africa. He died.

CHARLEY: That so.

BEN (*chuckling*): So this is Brooklyn, eh?

CHARLEY: Maybe you're in for some of his money.

WILLY: Naa, he had seven sons. There's just one opportunity I had with that man . . .

BEN: I must make a train, William. There are several properties I'm looking at in Alaska.

WILLY: Sure, sure! If I'd gone with him to Alaska that time, everything would've been totally different.

CHARLEY: Go on, you'd froze to death up there.

WILLY: What're you talking about?

BEN: Opportunity is tremendous in Alaska, William. Surprised you're not up there.

WILLY: Sure, tremendous.

CHARLEY: Heh?

WILLY: There was the only man I ever met who knew the answers.

CHARLEY: Who?

BEN: How are you all?

WILLY (*taking a pot, smiling*): Fine, fine.

CHARLEY: Pretty sharp tonight.

BEN: Is Mother living with you?

WILLY: No, she died a long time ago.

CHARLEY: Who?

BEN: That's too bad. Fine specimen of a lady, Mother.

WILLY (*to* CHARLEY): Heh?

BEN: I'd hoped to see the old girl.

CHARLEY: Who died?

BEN: Heard anything from Father, have you?

WILLY (*unnerved*): What do you mean, who died?

CHARLEY (*taking a pot*): What're you talkin' about?

BEN (*looking at his watch*): William, it's half-past eight!

WILLY (*as though to dispel his confusion he angrily stops* CHARLEY'S *hand*): That's my build!

CHARLEY: I put the ace—

WILLY: If you don't know how to play the game I'm not gonna throw my money away on you!

CHARLEY (*rising*): It was my ace, for God's sake!

WILLY: I'm through, I'm through!

BEN: When did Mother die?

WILLY: Long ago. Since the beginning you never knew how to play cards.

CHARLEY (*picks up the cards and goes to the door*): All right! Next time I'll bring a deck with five aces.

WILLY: I don't play that kind of game!

CHARLEY (*turning to him*): You ought to be ashamed of yourself!

WILLY: Yeah?

CHARLEY: Yeah! (*He goes out.*)

WILLY (*slamming the door after him*): Ignoramus!

BEN (*as* WILLY *comes toward him through the wall-line of the kitchen*): So you're William.

WILLY (*shaking* BEN's *hand*): Ben! I've been waiting for you so long! What's the answer? How did you do it?

BEN: Oh, there's a story in that.

(LINDA *enters the forestage, as of old, carrying the wash basket.*)

LINDA: Is this Ben?

BEN (*gallantly*): How do you do, my dear.

LINDA: Where've you been all these years? Willy's always wondered why you—

WILLY (*pulling* BEN *away from her impatiently*): Where is Dad? Didn't you follow him? How did you get started?

BEN: Well, I don't know how much you remember.

WILLY: Well, I was just a baby, of course, only three or four years old—

BEN: Three years and eleven months.

WILLY: What a memory, Ben!

BEN: I have many enterprises, William, and I have never kept books.

WILLY: I remember I was sitting under the wagon in—was it Nebraska?

BEN: It was South Dakota, and I gave you a bunch of wild flowers.

WILLY: I remember you walking away down some open road.

BEN (*laughing*): I was going to find Father in Alaska.

WILLY: Where is he?

BEN: At that age I had a very faulty view of geography, William. I discovered after a few days that I was heading due south, so instead of Alaska, I ended up in Africa.

LINDA: Africa!

WILLY: The Gold Coast!

BEN: Principally diamond mines.

LINDA: Diamond mines!

BEN: Yes, my dear. But I've only a few minutes—

WILLY: No! Boys! Boys! (YOUNG BIFF *and* HAPPY *appear.*) Listen to this. This is your Uncle Ben, a great man! Tell my boys, Ben!

BEN: Why, boys, when I was seventeen I walked into the jungle, and when I was twenty-one I walked out. (*He laughs.*) And by God I was rich.

WILLY (*to the boys*): You see what I been talking about? The greatest things can happen!

BEN (*glancing at his watch*): I have an appointment in Ketchikan Tuesday week.

WILLY: No, Ben! Please tell about Dad. I want my boys to hear. I want them to know the kind of stock they spring from. All I remember is a man with a big beard, and I was in Mamma's lap, sitting around a fire, and some kind of high music.

BEN: His flute. He played the flute.

WILLY: Sure, the flute, that's right!

(*New music is heard, a high, rollicking tune.*)

BEN: Father was a very great and a very wild-hearted man. We would start in Boston, and he'd toss the whole family into the wagon, and then he'd drive the team right across the country; through Ohio, and Indiana, Michigan, Illinois, and all the Western states. And we'd stop in the towns and sell the flutes that he'd made on the way. Great inventor, Father. With one gadget he made more in a week than a man like you could make in a lifetime.

WILLY: That's just the way I'm bringing them up, Ben—rugged, well liked, all-around.

BEN: Yeah? (*To* BIFF): Hit that, boy—hard as you can. (*He pounds his stomach.*)

BIFF: Oh, no, sir!

BEN (*taking boxing stance*): Come on, get to me! (*He laughs.*)

WILLY: Go to it, Biff! Go ahead, show him!

BIFF: Okay! (*He cocks his fists and starts in.*)

LINDA (*to* WILLY): Why must he fight, dear?

BEN (*sparring with* BIFF): Good boy! Good boy!

WILLY: How's that, Ben, heh?

HAPPY: Give him the left, Biff!

LINDA: Why are you fighting?

BEN: Good boy! (*Suddenly comes in, trips* BIFF, *and stands over him, the point of his umbrella poised over* BIFF's *eye.*)

LINDA: Look out, Biff!

BIFF: Gee!

BEN (*patting* BIFF's *knee*): Never fight fair with a stranger, boy. You'll never get out of the jungle that way. (*Taking* LINDA's *hand and bowing.*) It was an honor and a pleasure to meet you, Linda.

LINDA (*withdrawing her hand coldly, frightened*): Have a nice—trip.

BEN (*to* WILLY): And good luck with your—what do you do?

WILLY: Selling.

BEN: Yes. Well . . . (*He raises his hand in farewell to all.*)

WILLY: No, Ben, I don't want you to think . . . (*He takes Ben's arm to show him.*) It's Brooklyn, I know, but we hunt too.

BEN: Really, now.

WILLY: Oh, sure, there's snakes and rabbits and—that's why I moved out here. Why, Biff can fell any one of these trees in no time! Boys! Go right over to where they're building the apartment house and get some sand. We're gonna rebuild the entire front stoop right now! Watch this, Ben!

BIFF: Yes, sir! On the double, Hap!

HAPPY (*as he and* BIFF *run off*): I lost weight, Pop, you notice?

(CHARLEY *enters in knickers, even before the boys are gone.*)

CHARLEY: Listen, if they steal any more from that building the watchman'll put the cops on them!

LINDA (*to* WILLY): Don't let Biff . . .

(BEN *laughs lustily.*)

WILLY: You shoulda seen the lumber they brought home last week. At least a dozen six-by-tens worth all kinds a money.

CHARLEY: Listen, if that watchman—

WILLY: I gave them hell, understand. But I got a couple of fearless characters there.

CHARLEY: Willy, the jails are full of fearless characters.

BEN (*clapping* WILLY *on the back, with a laugh at* CHARLEY): And the stock exchange, friend!

WILLY (*joining in* BEN's *laughter*): Where are the rest of your pants?

CHARLEY: My wife bought them.

WILLY: Now all you need is a golf club and you can go upstairs and go to sleep. (*To* BEN): Great athlete! Between him and his son Bernard they can't hammer a nail!

BERNARD (*rushing in*): The watchman's chasing Biff!

WILLY (*angrily*): Shut up! He's not stealing anything!

LINDA (*alarmed, hurrying off left*): Where is he? Biff, dear! (*She exits.*)

WILLY (*moving toward the left, away from* BEN): There's nothing wrong. What's the matter with you?

BEN: Nervy boy. Good!

WILLY (*laughing*): Oh, nerves of iron, that Biff!

CHARLEY: Don't know what it is. My New England man comes back and he's bleedin', they murdered him up there.

WILLY: It's contacts, Charley, I got important contacts!

CHARLEY (*sarcastically*): Glad to hear it, Willy. Come in later, we'll shoot a little casino. I'll take some of your Portland money. (*He laughs at* WILLY *and exits.*)

WILLY (*turning to* BEN): Business is bad, it's murderous. But not for me, of course.

BEN: I'll stop by on my way back to Africa.

WILLY (*longingly*): Can't you stay a few days? You're just what I need, Ben, because I—I have a fine position here, but I—well, Dad left when I was such a baby and I never had a chance to talk to him and I still feel—kind of temporary about myself.

BEN: I'll be late for my train.

(*They are at opposite ends of the stage.*)

WILLY: Ben, my boys—can't we talk? They'd go into the jaws of hell for me, see, but I—

BEN: William, you're being first-rate with your boys. Outstanding, manly chaps!

WILLY (*hanging on to his words*): Oh, Ben, that's good to hear! Because sometimes I'm afraid that I'm not teaching them the right kind of—Ben, how should I teach them?

BEN (*giving great weight to each word, and with a certain vicious audacity*): William, when I walked into the jungle, I was seventeen. When I walked out I was twenty-one. And, by God, I was rich! (*He goes off into the darkness around the right corner of the house.*)

WILLY: . . . was rich! That's just the spirit I want to imbue them with! To walk into a jungle! I was right! I was right! I was right!

(BEN *is gone, but* WILLY *is still speaking to him as* LINDA, *in nightgown and robe, enters the kitchen, glances around for* WILLY, *then goes to the door of the house, looks out and sees him. Comes down to his left. He looks at her.*)

LINDA: Willy, dear? Willy?

WILLY: I was right!

LINDA: Did you have some cheese? (*He can't answer.*) It's very late, darling. Come to bed, heh?

WILLY (*looking straight up*): Gotta break your neck to see a star in this yard.

LINDA: You coming in?

WILLY: Whatever happened to that diamond watch fob? Remember? When Ben came from Africa that time? Didn't he give me a watch fob with a diamond in it?

LINDA: You pawned it, dear. Twelve, thirteen years ago. For Biff's radio correspondence course.

WILLY: Gee, that was a beautiful thing. I'll take a walk.

LINDA: But you're in your slippers.

WILLY (*starting to go around the house at the left*): I was right! I was! (*Half to* LINDA, *as he goes, shaking his head.*) What a man! There was a man worth talking to. I was right!

LINDA (*calling after* WILLY): But in your slippers, Willy!

(WILLY *is almost gone when* BIFF, *in his pajamas, comes down the stairs and enters the kitchen.*)

BIFF: What is he doing out there?

LINDA: Sh!

BIFF: God Almighty, Mom, how long has he been doing this?

LINDA: Don't, he'll hear you.

BIFF: What the hell is the matter with him?

LINDA: It'll pass by morning.

BIFF: Shouldn't we do anything?

LINDA: Oh, my dear, you should do a lot of things, but there's nothing to do, so go to sleep.

(HAPPY *comes down the stair and sits on the steps.*)

HAPPY: I never heard him so loud, Mom.

LINDA: Well, come around more often; you'll hear him. (*She sits down at the table and mends the lining of* WILLY'S *jacket.*)

BIFF: Why didn't you ever write me about this, Mom?

LINDA: How would I write to you? For over three months you had no address.

BIFF: I was on the move. But you know I thought of you all the time. You know that, don't you, pal?

LINDA: I know, dear, I know. But he likes to have a letter. Just to know that there's still a possibility for better things.

BIFF: He's not like this all the time, is he?

LINDA: It's when you come home he's always the worst.

BIFF: When I come home?

LINDA: When you write you're coming, he's all smiles, and talks about the future, and—he's just wonderful. And then the closer you seem to come, the more shaky he gets, and then, by the time you get here, he's arguing, and he seems angry at you. I think it's just that maybe he can't bring himself to—to open up to you. Why are you so hateful to each other? Why is that?

BIFF (*evasively*): I'm not hateful, Mom.

LINDA: But you no sooner come in the door than you're fighting!

BIFF: I don't know why. I mean to change. I'm tryin', Mom, you understand?

LINDA: Are you home to stay now?

BIFF: I don't know. I want to look around, see what's doin'.

LINDA: Biff, you can't look around all your life, can you?

BIFF: I just can't take hold, Mom. I can't take hold of some kind of a life.

LINDA: Biff, a man is not a bird, to come and go with the springtime.

BIFF: Your hair . . . (*He touches her hair.*) Your hair got so gray.

LINDA: Oh, it's been gray since you were in high school. I just stopped dyeing it, that's all.

BIFF: Dye it again, will ya? I don't want my pal looking old. (*He smiles.*)

LINDA: You're such a boy! You think you can go away for a year and . . . You've got to get it into your head now that one day you'll knock on this door and there'll be strange people here—

BIFF: What are you talking about? You're not even sixty, Mom.

LINDA: But what about your father?

BIFF (*lamely*): Well, I meant him too.

HAPPY: He admires Pop.

LINDA: Biff, dear, if you don't have any feeling for him, then you can't have any feeling for me.

BIFF: Sure I can, Mom.

LINDA: No. You can't just come to see me, because I love him. (*With a threat, but only a threat, of tears.*) He's the dearest man in the world to me, and I won't have anyone making him feel unwanted and low and blue. You've got to make up your mind now, darling, there's no leeway any more. Either he's your father and you pay him that respect, or else you're not to come here. I know he's not easy to get along with—nobody knows that better than me—but . . .

WILLY (*from the left, with a laugh*): Hey, hey, Biffo!

BIFF (*starting to go out after* WILLY): What the hell is the matter with him? (HAPPY *stops him.*)

LINDA: Don't—don't go near him!

BIFF: Stop making excuses for him! He always, always wiped the floor with you. Never had an ounce of respect for you.

HAPPY: He's always had respect for—

BIFF: What the hell do you know about it?

HAPPY (*surlily*): Just don't call him crazy!

BIFF: He's got no character—Charley wouldn't do this. Not in his own house—spewing out that vomit from his mind.

HAPPY: Charley never had to cope with what he's got to.

BIFF: People are worse off than Willy Loman. Believe me, I've seen them!

LINDA: Then make Charley your father, Biff. You can't do that, can you? I don't say he's a great man. Willy Loman never made a lot of money. His name was never in the paper. He's not the finest character that ever lived. But he's a human being, and a terrible thing is happening to him. So attention must be paid. He's not to be allowed to fall into his grave like an old dog. Attention, attention must be finally paid to such a person. You called him crazy—

BIFF: I didn't mean—

LINDA: No, a lot of people think he's lost his—balance. But you don't have to be very smart to know what his trouble is. The man is exhausted.

HAPPY: Sure!

LINDA: A small man can be just as exhausted as a great man. He works for a company thirty-six years this March, opens up unheard-of territories to their trademark, and now in his old age they take his salary away.

HAPPY (*indignantly*): I didn't know that, Mom.

LINDA: You never asked, my dear! Now that you get your spending money someplace else you don't trouble your mind with him.

HAPPY: But I gave you money last—

LINDA: Christmas time, fifty dollars! To fix the hot water it cost ninety-seven fifty! For five weeks he's been on straight commission, like a beginner, an unknown!

BIFF: Those ungrateful bastards!

LINDA: Are they any worse than his sons? When he brought them business, when he was young, they were glad to see him. But now his old friends, the old buyers that loved him so and always found some order to hand him in a pinch—they're all dead, retired. He used to be able to make six, seven calls a day in Boston. Now he takes his valises out of the car and puts them back and takes them out again and he's exhausted. Instead of walking he talks now. He drives seven hundred miles, and when he gets there no one knows him any more, no one welcomes him. And what goes through a man's mind, driving seven hundred miles home without having earned a cent? Why shouldn't he talk to himself? Why? When he has to go to Charley and borrow fifty dollars a week and pretend to me that it's his pay? How long can that go on? How long? You see what I'm sitting here and waiting for? And you tell me he has no character? The man who never worked a day but for your benefit? When does he get the medal for that? Is this his reward—to turn around at the age of sixty-three and find his sons, who he loved better than his life, one a philandering bum—

HAPPY: Mom!

LINDA: That's all you are, my baby! (*To* BIFF.) And you! What happened to the love you had for him? You were such pals! How you used to talk to him on the phone every night! How lonely he was till he could come home to you!

BIFF: All right, Mom. I'll live here in my room, and I'll get a job. I'll keep away from him, that's all.

LINDA: No, Biff. You can't stay here and fight all the time.

BIFF: He threw me out of this house, remember that.

LINDA: Why did he do that? I never knew why.

BIFF: Because I know he's a fake and he doesn't like anybody around who knows!

LINDA: Why a fake? In what way? What do you mean?

BIFF: Just don't lay it all at my feet. It's between me and him—that's all I have to say. I'll chip in from now on. He'll settle for half my pay check. He'll be all right. I'm going to bed. (*He starts for the stairs.*)

LINDA: He won't be all right.

BIFF (*turning on the stairs, furiously*): I hate this city and I'll stay here. Now what do you want?

LINDA: He's dying, Biff.

(HAPPY *turns quickly to her, shocked.*)

BIFF (*after a pause*): Why is he dying?

LINDA: He's been trying to kill himself.

BIFF (*with great horror*): How?

LINDA: I live from day to day.

BIFF: What're you talking about?

LINDA: Remember I wrote you that he smashed up the car again? In February?

BIFF: Well?

LINDA: The insurance inspector came. He said that they have evidence. That all these accidents in the last year—weren't—weren't—accidents.

HAPPY: How can they tell that? That's a lie.

LINDA: It seems there's a woman . . . (*She takes a breath as*)

{ BIFF (*sharply but contained*): What woman?

{ LINDA (*simultaneously*): . . . and this woman . . .

LINDA: What?

BIFF: Nothing. Go ahead.

LINDA: What did you say?

BIFF: Nothing. I just said what woman?

HAPPY: What about her?

LINDA: Well, it seems she was walking down the road and saw his car. She says that he wasn't driving fast at all, and that he didn't skid. She says he came to that little bridge, and then deliberately smashed into the railing, and it was only the shallowness of the water that saved him.

BIFF: Oh, no, he probably just fell asleep again.

LINDA: I don't think he fell asleep.

BIFF: Why not?

LINDA: Last month . . . (*With great difficulty*): Oh, boys, it's so hard to say a thing like this! He's just a big stupid man to you, but I tell you there's more good in him than in many other people. (*She chokes, wipes her eyes.*) I was looking for a fuse. The lights blew out, and I went down the cellar. And behind the fuse box—it happened to fall out—was a length of rubber pipe—just short.

HAPPY: No kidding?

LINDA: There's a little attachment on the end of it. I knew right away. And sure enough, on the bottom of the water heater there's a new little nipple on the gas pipe.

HAPPY (*angrily*): That—jerk.

BIFF: Did you have it taken off?

LINDA: I'm—I'm ashamed to. How can I mention it to him? Every day I go down and take away that little rubber pipe. But, when he comes home, I put it back where it was. How can I insult him that way? I don't know what to do. I live from day to day, boys. I tell you, I know every thought in his mind. It sounds so old-fashioned and silly, but I tell you he put his whole life into you and you've turned your backs on him. (*She is bent over in the chair, weeping, her face in her hands.*) Biff, I swear to God! Biff, his life is in your hands!

HAPPY (*to* BIFF): How do you like that damned fool!

BIFF (*kissing her*): All right, pal, all right. It's all settled now. I've been remiss. I know that, Mom. But now I'll stay, and I swear to you, I'll apply myself. (*Kneeling in front of her, in a fever of self-reproach*): It's just you see, Mom, I don't fit in business. Not that I won't try. I'll try, and I'll make good.

HAPPY: Sure you will. The trouble with you in business was you never tried to please people.

BIFF: I know, I—

HAPPY: Like when you worked for Harrison's. Bob Harrison said you were tops, and then you go and do some damn fool thing like whistling whole songs in the elevator like a comedian.

BIFF (*against* HAPPY): So what? I like to whistle sometimes.

HAPPY: You don't raise a guy to a responsible job who whistles in the elevator!

LINDA: Well, don't argue about it now.

HAPPY: Like when you'd go off and swim in the middle of the day instead of taking the line around.

BIFF (*his resentment rising*): Well, don't you run off? You take off sometimes, don't you? On a nice summer day?

HAPPY: Yeah, but I cover myself!

LINDA: Boys!

HAPPY: If I'm going to take a fade the boss can call any number where I'm supposed to be and they'll swear to him that I just left. I'll tell you something that I hate to say, Biff, but in the business world some of them think you're crazy.

BIFF (*angered*): Screw the business world!

HAPPY: All right, screw it! Great, but cover yourself!

LINDA: Hap, Hap!

BIFF: I don't care what they think! They've laughed at Dad for years, and you know why? Because we don't belong in this nuthouse of a city! We should be mixing cement on some open plain, or—or carpenters. A carpenter is allowed to whistle!

(WILLY *walks in from the entrance of the house, at left.*)

WILLY: Even your grandfather was better than a carpenter. (*Pause. They watch him.*) You never grew up. Bernard does not whistle in the elevator, I assure you.

BIFF (*as though to laugh* WILLY *out of it*): Yeah, but you do, Pop.

WILLY: I never in my life whistled in an elevator! And who in the business world thinks I'm crazy?

BIFF: I didn't mean it like that, Pop. Now don't make a whole thing out of it, will ya?

WILLY: Go back to the West! Be a carpenter, a cowboy, enjoy yourself!

LINDA: Willy, he was just saying—

WILLY: I heard what he said!

HAPPY (*trying to quiet* WILLY): Hey, Pop, come on now . . .

WILLY (*continuing over* HAPPY's *line*): They laugh at me, heh? Go to Filene's, go to the Hub, go to Slattery's, Boston. Call out the name Willy Loman and see what happens! Big shot!

BIFF: All right, Pop.

WILLY: Big!

BIFF: All right!

WILLY: Why do you always insult me?

BIFF: I didn't say a word. (*To* LINDA): Did I say a word?

LINDA: He didn't say anything, Willy.

WILLY (*going to the doorway of the living-room*): All right, good night, good night.

LINDA: Willy, dear, he just decided . . .

WILLY (*to* BIFF): If you get tired hanging around tomorrow, paint the ceiling I put up in the living-room.

BIFF: I'm leaving early tomorrow.

HAPPY: He's going to see Bill Oliver, Pop.

WILLY (*interestedly*): Oliver? For what?

BIFF (*with reserve, but trying, trying*): He always said he'd stake me. I'd like to go into business, so maybe I can take him up on it.

LINDA: Isn't that wonderful?

WILLY: Don't interrupt. What's wonderful about it? There's fifty men in the City of New York who'd stake him. (*To* BIFF.) Sporting goods?

BIFF: I guess so. I know something about it and—

WILLY: He knows something about it! You know sporting goods better than Spalding, for God's sake! How much is he giving you?

BIFF: I don't know, I didn't even see him yet, but—

WILLY: Then what're you talkin' about?

BIFF (*getting angry*): Well, all I said was I'm gonna see him, that's all!

WILLY (*turning away*): Ah, you're counting your chickens again.

BIFF (*starting left for the stairs*): Oh, Jesus, I'm going to sleep!

WILLY (*calling after him*): Don't curse in this house!

BIFF (*turning*): Since when did you get so clean?

HAPPY (*trying to stop them*): Wait a . . .

WILLY: Don't use that language to me! I won't have it!

HAPPY (*grabbing* BIFF, *shouts*): Wait a minute! I got an idea. I got a feasible idea. Come here, Biff, let's talk this over now, let's talk some sense here. When I was down in Florida last time, I thought of a great idea to sell sporting goods. It just came back to me. You and I, Biff we have a line, the Loman Line. We train a couple of weeks, and put on a couple of exhibitions, see?

WILLY: That's an idea!

HAPPY: Wait! We form two basketball teams, see? Two water-polo teams. We play each other. It's a million dollars' worth of publicity. Two brothers, see? The Loman Brothers. Displays in the Royal Palms—all the hotels. And banners over the ring and the basketball court: "Loman Brothers." Baby, we could sell sporting goods!

WILLY: That is a one-million-dollar idea!

LINDA: Marvelous!

BIFF: I'm in great shape as far as that's concerned.

HAPPY: And the beauty of it is, Biff, it wouldn't be like a business. We'd be out playin' ball again . . .

BIFF (*enthused*): Yeah, that's . . .

WILLY: Million-dollar . . .

HAPPY: And you wouldn't get fed up with it, Biff. It'd be the family again. There'd be the old honor, and comradeship, and if you wanted to go off for a swim or somethin'—well, you'd do it! Without some smart cooky gettin' up ahead of you!

WILLY: Lick the world! You guys together could absolutely lick the civilized world.

BIFF: I'll see Oliver tomorrow. Hap, if we could work that out . . .

LINDA: Maybe things are beginning to—

WILLY (*wildly enthused, to* LINDA): Stop interrupting! (*To* BIFF): But don't wear sport jacket and slacks when you see Oliver.

BIFF: No, I'll—

WILLY: A business suit, and talk as little as possible, and don't crack any jokes.

BIFF: He did like me. Always liked me.

LINDA: He loved you!

WILLY (*To* LINDA): Will you stop! (*To* BIFF): Walk in very serious. You are not applying for a boy's job. Money is to pass. Be quiet, fine, and serious. Everybody likes a kidder, but nobody lends him money.

HAPPY: I'll try to get some myself, Biff. I'm sure I can.

WILLY: I see great things for you kids, I think your troubles are over. But remember, start big and you'll end big. Ask for fifteen. How much you gonna ask for?

BIFF: Gee, I don't know—

WILLY: And don't say "Gee." "Gee" is a boy's word. A man walking in for fifteen thousand dollars does not say "Gee!"

BIFF: Ten, I think, would be top though.

WILLY: Don't be so modest. You always started too low. Walk in with a big laugh. Don't look worried. Start off with a couple of your good stories to lighten things up. It's not what you say, it's how you say it—because personality always wins the day.

LINDA: Oliver always thought the highest of him—

WILLY: Will you let me talk?

BIFF: Don't yell at her, Pop, will ya?

WILLY (*angrily*): I was talking, wasn't I?

BIFF: I don't like you yelling at her all the time, and I'm tellin' you, that's all.

WILLY: What're you, takin' over this house?

LINDA: Willy—

WILLY (*turning on her*): Don't take his side all the time, goddammit!

BIFF (*furiously*): Stop yelling at her!

WILLY (*suddenly pulling on his cheek, beaten down, guilt ridden*): Give my best to Bill Oliver—he may remember me. (*He exits through the living-room doorway.*)

LINDA (*her voice subdued*): What'd you have to start that for? (BIFF *turns away.*) You see how sweet he was as soon as you talked hopefully? (*She goes over to* BIFF.) Come up and say good night to him. Don't let him go to bed that way.

HAPPY: Come on, Biff, let's buck him up.

LINDA: Please, dear. Just say good night. It takes so little to make him happy. Come. (*She goes through the living-room doorway, calling upstairs from within the living-room*): Your pajamas are hanging in the bathroom, Willy!

HAPPY (*looking toward where* LINDA *went out*): What a woman! They broke the mold when they made her. You know that, Biff?

BIFF: He's off salary. My God, working on commission!

HAPPY: Well, let's face it: he's no hot-shot selling man. Except that sometimes, you have to admit, he's a sweet personality.

BIFF (*deciding*): Lend me ten bucks, will ya? I want to buy some new ties.

HAPPY: I'll take you to a place I know. Beautiful stuff. Wear one of my striped shirts tomorrow.

BIFF: She got gray. Mom got awful old. Gee, I'm gonna go in to Oliver tomorrow and knock him for a—

HAPPY: Come on up. Tell that to Dad. Let's give him a whirl. Come on.

BIFF (*steamed up*): You know, with ten thousand bucks, boy!

HAPPY (*as they go into the living-room*): That's the talk, Biff, that's the first time I've heard the old confidence out of you! (*From within the living-room, fading off.*) You're gonna live with me, kid, and any babe you want just say the word . . . (*The last lines are hardly heard. They are mounting the stairs to their parents' bedroom.*)

LINDA (*entering her bedroom and addressing* WILLY, *who is in the bathroom. She is straightening the bed for him*): Can you do anything about the shower? It drips.

WILLY (*from the bathroom*): All of a sudden everything falls to pieces! Goddam plumbing, oughta be sued, those people. I hardly finished putting it in and the thing . . . (*His words rumble off.*)

LINDA: I'm just wondering if Oliver will remember him. You think he might?

WILLY (*coming out of the bathroom in his pajamas*): Remember him? Remember him? What's the matter with you, you crazy? If he'd've stayed with Oliver he'd be on top by now. Wait'll Oliver gets a look at him. You don't know the average caliber any more. The average young man today—(*he is getting into bed*)—is got a caliber of zero. Greatest thing in the world for him was to bum around.

(BIFF *and* HAPPY *enter the bedroom. Slight pause.*)

WILLY (*stops short, looking at* BIFF): Glad to hear it, boy.

HAPPY: He wanted to say good night to you, sport.

WILLY (*to* BIFF): Yeah. Knock him dead, boy. What'd you want to tell me?

BIFF: Just take it easy, Pop. Good night. (*He turns to go.*)

WILLY (*unable to resist*): And if anything falls off the desk while you're talking to him—like a package or something—don't you pick it up. They have office boys for that.

LINDA: I'll make a big breakfast—

WILLY: Will you let me finish? (*To* BIFF) Tell him you were in the business in the West. Not farm work.

BIFF: All right, Dad.

LINDA: I think everything—

WILLY (*going right through her speech*): And don't undersell yourself. No less than fifteen thousand dollars.

BIFF (*unable to bear him*): Okay. Good night, Mom. (*He starts moving.*)

WILLY: Because you got a greatness in you, Biff, remember that. You got all kinds a greatness . . . (*He lies back, exhausted.* BIFF *walks out.*)

LINDA (*calling after* BIFF): Sleep well, darling!

HAPPY: I'm gonna get married, Mom. I wanted to tell you.

LINDA: Go to sleep, dear.

HAPPY (*going*): I just wanted to tell you.

WILLY: Keep up the good work. (HAPPY *exits.*) God . . . remember that Ebbets Field game? The championship of the city?

LINDA: Just rest. Should I sing to you?

WILLY: Yeah. Sing to me. (LINDA *hums a soft lullaby.*) When that team came out—he was the tallest, remember?

LINDA: Oh, yes. And in gold.

(BIFF *enters the darkened kitchen, takes a cigarette, and leaves the house. He comes downstage into a golden pool of light. He smokes, staring at the night.*)

WILLY: Like a young god. Hercules—something like that. And the sun, the sun all around him. Remember how he waved to me? Right up from the field, with the representatives of three colleges standing by? And the buyers I brought, and the cheers when he came out—Loman, Loman, Loman! God Almighty, he'll be great yet. A star like that, magnificent, can never really fade away!

(*The light on* WILLY *is fading. The gas heater begins to glow through the kitchen wall, near the stairs, a blue flame beneath red coils.*)

LINDA (*timidly*): Willy dear, what has he got against you?

WILLY: I'm so tired. Don't talk any more.

(BIFF *slowly returns to the kitchen. He stops, stares toward the heater.*)

LINDA: Will you ask Howard to let you work in New York?

WILLY: First thing in the morning. Everything'll be all right.

(BIFF *reaches behind the heater and draws out a length of rubber tubing. He is horrified and turns his head toward* WILLY's *room, still dimly lit, from which the strains of* LINDA's *desperate but monotonous humming rise.*)

WILLY (*staring through the window into the moonlight*): Gee, look at the moon moving between the buildings!

(BIFF *wraps the tubing around his hand and quickly goes up the stairs.*)

CURTAIN

ACT TWO

Music is heard, gay and bright. The curtain rises as the music fades away. WILLY *in shirt sleeves, is sitting at the kitchen table, sipping coffee, his hat in his lap.* LINDA *is filling his cup when she can.*

WILLY: Wonderful coffee. Meal in itself.

LINDA: Can I make you some eggs?

WILLY: No. Take a breath.

LINDA: You look so rested, dear.

WILLY: I slept like a dead one. First time in months. Imagine, sleeping till ten on a Tuesday morning. Boys left nice and early, heh?

LINDA: They were out of here by eight o'clock.

WILLY: Good work!

LINDA: It was so thrilling to see them leaving together. I can't get over the shaving lotion in this house!

WILLY (*smiling*): Mmm—

LINDA: Biff was very changed this morning. His whole attitude seemed to be hopeful. He couldn't wait to get downtown to see Oliver.

WILLY: He's heading for a change. There's no question, there simply are certain men that take longer to get—solidified. How did he dress?

LINDA: His blue suit. He's so handsome in that suit. He could be a—anything in that suit!

(WILLY *gets up from the table.* LINDA *holds his jacket for him.*)

WILLY: There's no question, no question at all. Gee, on the way home tonight I'd like to buy some seeds.

LINDA (*laughing*): That'd be wonderful. But not enough sun gets back there. Nothing'll grow any more.

WILLY: You wait, kid, before it's all over we're gonna get a little place out in the country, and I'll raise some vegetables, a couple of chickens . . .

LINDA: You'll do it yet, dear.

(WILLY *walks out of his jacket.* LINDA *follows him.*)

WILLY: And they'll get married, and come for a weekend. I'd build a little guest house. 'Cause I got so many fine tools, all I'd need would be a little lumber, and some peace of mind.

LINDA (*joyfully*): I sewed the lining . . .

WILLY: I could build two guest houses, so they'd both come. Did he decide how much he's going to ask Oliver for?

LINDA (*getting him into the jacket*): He didn't mention it, but I imagine ten or fifteen thousand. You going to talk to Howard today?

WILLY: Yeah. I'll put it to him straight and simple. He'll just have to take me off the road.

LINDA: And Willy, don't forget to ask for a little advance, because we've got the insurance premium. It's the grace period now.

WILLY: That's a hundred . . . ?

LINDA: A hundred and eight, sixty-eight. Because we're a little short again.

WILLY: Why are we short?

LINDA: Well, you had the motor job on the car . . .

WILLY: That goddam Studebaker!

LINDA: And you got one more payment on the refrigerator . . .

WILLY: But it just broke again!

LINDA: Well, it's old, dear.

WILLY: I told you we should've bought a well-advertised machine. Charley bought a General Electric and it's twenty years old and it's still good, that son-of-a-bitch.

LINDA: But, Willy—

WILLY: Whoever heard of a Hastings refrigerator? Once in my life I would like to own something outright before it's broken! I'm always in a race with the junkyard! I just finished paying for the car and it's on its last legs. The refrigerator consumes belts like a goddam maniac. They time those things. They time them so when you finally paid for them, they're used up.

LINDA (*buttoning up his jacket as he unbuttons it*): All told, about two hundred dollars would carry us, dear. But that includes the last payment on the mortgage. After this payment, Willy, the house belongs to us.

WILLY: It's twenty-five years!

LINDA: Biff was nine years old when we bought it.

WILLY: Well, that's a great thing. To weather a twenty-five year mortgage is—

LINDA: It's an accomplishment.

WILLY: All the cement, the lumber, the reconstruction I put in this house! There ain't a crack to be found in it any more.

LINDA: Well, it served its purpose.

WILLY: What purpose? Some stranger'll come along, move in, and that's that. If only Biff would take this house, and raise a family . . . (*He starts to go.*) Good-by, I'm late.

LINDA (*suddenly remembering*): Oh, I forgot! You're supposed to meet them for dinner.

WILLY: Me?

LINDA: At Frank's Chop House on Forty-eighth near Sixth Avenue.

WILLY: Is that so! How about you?

LINDA: No, just the three of you. They're gonna blow you to a big meal!

WILLY: Don't say! Who thought of that?

LINDA: Biff came to me this morning, Willy, and he said, "Tell Dad, we want to blow him to a big meal." Be there six o'clock. You and your two boys are going to have dinner.

WILLY: Gee whiz! That's really somethin'. I'm gonna knock Howard for a loop, kid. I'll get an advance, and I'll come home with a New York job. Goddammit, now I'm gonna do it!

LINDA: Oh, that's the spirit, Willy!

WILLY: I will never get behind a wheel the rest of my life!

LINDA: It's changing, Willy, I can feel it changing!

WILLY: Beyond a question. G'by, I'm late. (*He starts to go again.*)

LINDA (*calling after him as she runs to the kitchen table for a handkerchief*): You got your glasses?

WILLY (*feels for them, then comes back in*): Yeah, yeah, got my glasses.

LINDA (*giving him the handkerchief*): And a handkerchief.

WILLY: Yeah, handkerchief.

LINDA: And your saccharine?

WILLY: Yeah, my saccharine.

LINDA: Be careful on the subway stairs.

(*She kisses him, and a silk stocking is seen hanging from her hand. WILLY notices it.*)

WILLY: Will you stop mending stockings? At least while I'm in the house. It gets me nervous. I can't tell you. Please.

(*LINDA hides the stocking in her hand as she follows WILLY across the forestage in front of the house.*)

LINDA: Remember, Frank's Chop House.

WILLY (*passing the apron*): Maybe beets would grow out there.

LINDA (*laughing*): But you tried so many times.

WILLY: Yeah. Well, don't work hard today. (*He disappears around the right corner of the house.*)

LINDA: Be careful!

(*As WILLY vanishes, LINDA waves to him. Suddenly the phone rings. She runs across the stage and into the kitchen and lifts it.*)

LINDA: Hello? Oh, Biff! I'm so glad you called, I just . . . Yes, sure, I just told him. Yes, he'll be there for dinner at six o'clock, I didn't forget. Listen, I was just dying to tell you. You know that little rubber pipe I told you about? That he connected to the gas heater? I finally decided to go down the cellar this morning and take it away and destroy it. But it's gone! Imagine? He took it away himself, it isn't there! (*She listens.*) When? Oh, then you took it. Oh—nothing, it's just that I'd hoped he'd taken it away himself. Oh, I'm not worried, darling, because this morning he left in such high spirits, it was like the old days! I'm not afraid any more. Did Mr. Oliver see you? . . . Well, you wait there then. And make a nice impression on him, darling. Just don't perspire too much before you see him. And have a nice time with Dad. He may have big news too! . . . That's right, a New York job. And be sweet to him tonight, dear. Be loving to him. Because he's only a little boat looking for a harbor. (*She is trembling with sorrow and joy.*) Oh, that's wonderful, Biff, you'll save his life. Thanks, darling. Just put your arm around him when he comes into the restaurant. Give him a smile. That's the boy . . . Good-by, dear . . . You got your comb? . . . That's fine. Good-by, Biff dear.

(*In the middle of her speech, HOWARD WAGNER, thirty-six, wheels on a small typewriter table on which is a wire-recording machine and proceeds to plug it in. This is on the left forestage. Light slowly fades on LINDA as it rises on HOWARD. HOWARD is intent on threading the machine and only glances over his shoulder as WILLY appears.*)

WILLY: Pst! Pst!

HOWARD: Hello, Willy, come in.

WILLY: Like to have a little talk with you, Howard.

HOWARD: Sorry to keep you waiting. I'll be with you in a minute.

WILLY: What's that, Howard?

HOWARD: Didn't you ever see one of these? Wire recorder.

WILLY: Oh. Can we talk a minute?

HOWARD: Records things. Just got delivery yesterday. Been driving me crazy, the most terrific machine I ever saw in my life. I was up all night with it.

WILLY: What do you do with it?

HOWARD: I bought it for dictation, but you can do anything with it. Listen to this. I had it home last night. Listen to what I picked up. The first one is my daughter. Get this. (*He flicks the switch and "Roll out the Barrel" is heard being whistled.*) Listen to that kid whistle.

WILLY: That is lifelike, isn't it?

HOWARD: Seven years old. Get that tone.

WILLY: Ts, ts. Like to ask a little favor if you . . .
(*The whistling breaks of, and the voice of* HOWARD'*s daughter is heard.*)

HIS DAUGHTER: "Now you, Daddy."

HOWARD: She's crazy for me! (*Again the same song is whistled.*) That's me! Ha! (*He winks.*)

WILLY: You're very good!
(*The whistling breaks off again. The machine runs silent for a moment.*)

HOWARD: Sh! Get this now, this is my son.

HIS SON: "The capital of Alabama is Montgomery; the capital of Arizona is Phoenix; the capital of Arkansas is Little Rock; the capital of California is Sacramento . . ." (*and on, and on.*)

HOWARD (*holding up five fingers*): Five years old, Willy!

WILLY: He'll make an announcer some day!

HIS SON (*continuing*): "The capital . . ."

HOWARD: Get that—alphabetical order! (*The machine breaks off suddenly.*) Wait a minute. The maid kicked the plug out.

WILLY: It certainly is a—

HOWARD: Sh, for God's sake!

HIS SON: "It's nine o'clock, Bulova watch time. So I have to go to sleep."

WILLY: That really is—

HOWARD: Wait a minute! The next is my wife.
(*They wait.*)

HOWARD'S VOICE: "Go on, say something." (*Pause.*) "Well, you gonna talk?"

HIS WIFE: "I can't think of anything."

HOWARD'S VOICE: "Well, talk—it's turning."

HIS WIFE (*shyly, beaten*): "Hello." (*Silence.*) "Oh, Howard, I can't talk into this . . ."

HOWARD (*snapping the machine off*): That was my wife.

WILLY: That is a wonderful machine. Can we—

HOWARD: I tell you, Willy, I'm gonna take my camera, and my bandsaw, and all my hobbies, and out they go. This is the most fascinating relaxation I ever found.

WILLY: I think I'll get one myself.

HOWARD: Sure, they're only a hundred and a half. You can't do without it. Supposing you wanna hear Jack Benny, see? But you can't be at home at that hour. So you tell the maid to turn the radio on when Jack Benny comes on, and this automatically goes on with the radio . . .

WILLY: And when you come home you . . .

HOWARD: You can come home twelve o'clock, one o'clock, any time you like, and you get yourself a Coke and sit yourself down, throw the switch, and there's Jack Benny's program in the middle of the night!

WILLY: I'm definitely going to get one. Because lots of time I'm on the road, and I think to myself, what I must be missing on the radio!

HOWARD: Don't you have a radio in the car?

WILLY: Well, yeah, but who ever thinks of turning it on?

HOWARD: Say, aren't you supposed to be in Boston?

WILLY: That's what I want to talk to you about, Howard. You got a minute? (*He draws a chair in from the wing.*)

HOWARD: What happened? What're you doing here?

WILLY: Well . . .

HOWARD: You didn't crack up again, did you?

WILLY: Oh, no. No . . .

HOWARD: Geez, you had me worried there for a minute. What's the trouble?

WILLY: Well, tell you the truth, Howard. I've come to the decision that I'd rather not travel any more.

HOWARD: Not travel! Well, what'll you do?

WILLY: Remember, Christmas time, when you had the party here? You said you'd try to think of some spot for me here in town.

HOWARD: With us?

WILLY: Well, sure.

HOWARD: Oh, yeah, yeah. I remember. Well, I couldn't think of anything for you, Willy.

WILLY: I tell ya, Howard. The kids are all grown up, y'know. I don't need much any more. If

I could take home well, sixty-five dollars a week, I could swing it.

HOWARD: Yeah, but Willy, see I—

WILLY: I tell ya why, Howard. Speaking frankly and between the two of us, y'know—I'm just a little tired.

HOWARD: Oh, I could understand that, Willy. But you're a road man, Willy, and we do a road business. We've only got a half-dozen salesmen on the floor here.

WILLY: God knows, Howard, I never asked a favor of any man. But I was with the firm when your father used to carry you in here in his arms.

HOWARD: I know that, Willy, but—

WILLY: Your father came to me the day you were born and asked me what I thought of the name of Howard, may he rest in peace.

HOWARD: I appreciate that, Willy, but there just is no spot here for you. If I had a spot I'd slam you right in, but I just don't have a single solitary spot.

(*He looks for his lighter.* WILLY *has picked it up and gives it to him. Pause.*)

WILLY (*with increasing anger*): Howard, all I need to set my table is fifty dollars a week.

HOWARD: But where am I going to put you, kid?

WILLY: Look, it isn't a question of whether I can sell merchandise, is it?

HOWARD: No, but it's a business, kid, and everybody's gotta pull his own weight.

WILLY (*desperately*): Just let me tell you a story, Howard—

HOWARD: 'Cause you gotta admit, business is business.

WILLY (*angrily*): Business is definitely business, but just listen for a minute. You don't understand this. When I was a boy—eighteen, nineteen—I was already on the road. And there was a question in my mind as to whether selling had a future for me. Because in those days I had a yearning to go to Alaska. See, there were three gold strikes in one month in Alaska, and I felt like going out. Just for the ride, you might say.

HOWARD (*barely interested*): Don't say.

WILLY: Oh, yeah, my father lived many years in Alaska. He was an adventurous man. We've got quite a little streak of self-reliance in our family. I thought I'd go out with my older brother and try to locate him, and maybe settle in the North with the old man. And I was almost decided to go, when I met a salesman in the Parker House. His name was Dave Singleman. And he was eighty-four years old, and he'd drummed merchandise in thirty-one states. And old Dave, he'd go up to his room, y'understand, put on his green velvet slippers—I'll never forget—and pick up his phone and call the buyers, and without ever leaving his room, at the age of eighty-four, he made his living. And when I saw that, I realized that selling was the greatest career a man could want. 'Cause what could be more satisfying than to be able to go, at the age of eighty-four, into twenty or thirty different cities, and pick up a phone, and be remembered and loved and helped by so many different people? Do you know? when he died—and by the way he died the death of a salesman, in his green velvet slippers in the smoker of the New York, New Haven and Hartford, going into Boston—when he died, hundreds of salesmen and buyers were at his funeral. Things were sad on a lotta trains for months after that. (*He stands up.* HOWARD *has not looked at him.*) In those days there was personality in it, Howard. There was respect, and comradeship, and gratitude in it. Today, it's all cut and dried, and there's no chance for bringing friendship to bear—or personality. You see what I mean? They don't know me any more.

HOWARD (*moving away, to the right*): That's just the thing, Willy.

WILLY: If I had forty dollars a week—that's all I'd need. Forty dollars, Howard.

HOWARD: Kid, I can't take blood from a stone, I—

WILLY (*desperation is on him now*): Howard, the year Al Smith was nominated, your father came to me and—

HOWARD (*starting to go off*): I've got to see some people, kid.

WILLY (*stopping him*): I'm talking about your father! There were promises made across this desk! You mustn't tell me you've got people to see— I put thirty-four years into this firm, Howard, and now I can't pay my insurance! You can't eat the orange and throw the peel away—a man is not a piece of fruit! (*After a pause*): Now pay attention. Your father—in 1928 I had a big year. I averaged a hundred and seventy dollars a week in commissions.

HOWARD (*impatiently*): Now, Willy, you never averaged—

WILLY (*banging his hand on the desk*): I averaged a hundred and seventy dollars a week in the year of 1928! And your father came to me—or rather, I was in the office here—it was right over this desk—and he put his hand on my shoulder—

HOWARD (*getting up*): You'll have to excuse me, Willy, I gotta see some people. Pull yourself together. (*Going out*): I'll be back in a little while.

(*On* HOWARD's *exit, the light on his chair grows very bright and strange.*)

WILLY: Pull myself together! What the hell did I say to him? My God, I was yelling at him! How could I! (WILLY *breaks off, staring at the light, which occupies the chair, animating it. He approaches this chair, standing across the desk from it.*) Frank, Frank, don't you remember what you told me that time? How you put your hand on my shoulder, and Frank . . . (*He leans on the desk and as he speaks the dead man's name he accidentally switches on the recorder, and instantly*)

HOWARD'S SON: " . . . of New York is Albany. The capital of Ohio is Cincinnati, the capital of Rhode Island is . . . " (*The recitation continues.*)

WILLY (*leaping away with fright, shouting*): Ha! Howard! Howard! Howard!

HOWARD (*rushing in*): What happened?

WILLY (*pointing at the machine, which continues nasally, childishly, with the capital cities*): Shut it off! Shut it off!

HOWARD (*pulling the plug out*): Look, Willy . . .

WILLY (*pressing his hands to his eyes*): I gotta get myself some coffee. I'll get some coffee . . .

(WILLY *starts to walk out.* HOWARD *stops him.*)

HOWARD (*rolling up the cord*): Willy, look . . .

WILLY: I'll go to Boston.

HOWARD: Willy, you can't go to Boston for us.

WILLY: Why can't I go?

HOWARD: I don't want you to represent us. I've been meaning to tell you for a long time now.

WILLY: Howard, are you firing me?

HOWARD: I think you need a good long rest, Willy.

WILLY: Howard—

HOWARD: And when you feel better, come back, and we'll see if we can work something out.

WILLY: But I gotta earn money, Howard. I'm in no position to—

HOWARD: Where are your sons? Why don't your sons give you a hand?

WILLY: They're working on a very big deal.

HOWARD: This is no time for false pride, Willy. You go to your sons and you tell them that you're tired. You've got two great boys, haven't you?

WILLY: Oh, no question, no question, but in the meantime . . .

HOWARD: Then that's that, heh?

WILLY: All right, I'll go to Boston tomorrow.

HOWARD: No, no.

WILLY: I can't throw myself on my sons. I'm not a cripple!

HOWARD: Look, kid, I'm busy this morning.

WILLY (*grasping* HOWARD's *arm*): Howard, you've got to let me go to Boston!

HOWARD (*hard, keeping himself under control*): I've got a line of people to see this morning. Sit down, take five minutes, and pull yourself together, and then go home, will ya? I need the office, Willy. (*He starts to go, turns, remembering the recorder, starts to push off the table holding the recorder.*) Oh, yeah. Whenever you can this week, stop by and drop off the samples. You'll feel better, Willy, and then come back and we'll talk. Pull yourself together, kid, there's people outside.

(HOWARD *exits, pushing the table off left.* WILLY *stares into space, exhausted. Now the music is heard*—BEN's *music—first distantly, then closer, closer. As* WILLY *speaks,* BEN *enters from the right. He carries valise and umbrella.*)

WILLY: Oh, Ben, how did you do it? What is the answer? Did you wind up the Alaska deal already?

BEN: Doesn't take much time if you know what you're doing. Just a short business trip. Boarding ship in an hour. Wanted to say good-by.

WILLY: Ben, I've got to talk to you.

BEN (*glancing at his watch*): Haven't the time, William.

WILLY (*crossing the apron to* BEN): Ben, nothing's working out. I don't know what to do.

BEN: Now, look here, William. I've bought timberland in Alaska and I need a man to look after things for me.

WILLY: God, timberland! Me and my boys in those grand outdoors!

BEN: You've a new continent at your doorstep, William. Get out of these cities, they're full of talk and time payments and courts of law. Screw on your fists and you can fight for a fortune up there.

WILLY: Yes, yes! Linda, Linda!

(LINDA *enters as of old, with the wash.*)

LINDA: Oh, you're back?

BEN: I haven't much time.

WILLY: No, wait! Linda, he's got a proposition for me in Alaska.

LINDA: But you've got—(*To* BEN): He's got a beautiful job here.

WILLY: But in Alaska, kid, I could—

LINDA: You're doing well enough, Willy!

BEN (*to* LINDA): Enough for what, my dear?

LINDA (*frightened of* BEN *and angry at him*): Don't say those things to him! Enough to be happy right here, right now. (*To* WILLY, *while* BEN *laughs*): Why must everybody conquer the world? You're well liked, and the boys love you, and someday—(*to* BEN)—why, old man Wagner told him just the other day that if he keeps it up he'll be a member of the firm, didn't he, Willy?

WILLY: Sure, sure. I am building something with this firm, Ben, and if a man is building something he must be on the right track, mustn't he?

BEN: What are you building? Lay your hand on it. Where is it?

WILLY (*hesitantly*): That's true, Linda, there's nothing.

LINDA: Why? (*To* BEN): There's a man eighty-four years old—

WILLY: That's right, Ben, that's right. When I look at that man I say, what is there to worry about?

BEN: Bah!

WILLY: It's true, Ben. All he has to do is go into any city, pick up the phone, and he's making his living and you know why?

BEN (*picking up his valise*): I've got to go.

WILLY (*holding* BEN *back*): Look at this boy!

(BIFF, *in his high school sweater, enters carrying suitcase.* HAPPY *carries* BIFF*'s shoulder guards, gold helmet, and football pants.*)

WILLY: Without a penny to his name, three great universities are begging for him, and from there the sky's the limit, because it's not what you do, Ben. It's who you know and the smile on your face! It's contacts, Ben, contacts! The whole wealth of Alaska passes over the lunch table at the Commodore Hotel, and that's the wonder, the wonder of this country, that a man can end with diamonds here on the basis of being liked! (*He turns to* BIFF.) And that's why when you get out on that field today it's important. Because thousands of people will be rooting for you and loving you. (*To* BEN, *who has again begun to leave*): And Ben! when he walks into a business office his name will sound out like a bell and all the doors will open to him! I've seen it, Ben, I've seen it a thousand times! You can't feel it with your hand like timber, but it's there!

BEN: Good-by, William.

WILLY: Ben, am I right? Don't you think I'm right? I value your advice.

BEN: There's a new continent at your doorstep, William. You could walk out rich. Rich! (*He is gone.*)

WILLY: We'll do it here, Ben! You hear me? We're gonna do it here!

(YOUNG BERNARD *rushes in. The gay music of the Boys is heard.*)

BERNARD: Oh, gee, I was afraid you left already!

WILLY: Why? What time is it?

BERNARD: It's half-past one!

WILLY: Well, come on, everybody! Ebbets Field next stop! Where's the pennants? (*He rushes through the wall-line of the kitchen and out into the living-room.*)

LINDA (*to* BIFF): Did you pack fresh underwear?

BIFF: (*who has been limbering up*): I want to go!

BERNARD: Biff, I'm carrying your helmet, ain't I?

HAPPY: No, I'm carrying the helmet.

BERNARD: Oh, Biff, you promised me.

HAPPY: I'm carrying the helmet.

BERNARD: How am I going to get in the locker room?

LINDA: Let him carry the shoulder guards. (*She puts her coat and hat on in the kitchen.*)

BERNARD: Can I, Biff? 'Cause I told everybody I'm going to be in the locker room.

HAPPY: In Ebbets Field it's the clubhouse.

BERNARD: I meant the clubhouse. Biff!

HAPPY: Biff!

BIFF (*grandly, after a slight pause*): Let him carry the shoulder guards.

HAPPY (*as he gives* BERNARD *the shoulder guards*): Stay close to us now.

(WILLY *rushes in with the pennants.*)

WILLY (*handing them out*): Everybody wave when Biff comes out on the field. (HAPPY *and* BERNARD *run off.*) You set now, boy?

(*The music has died away.*)

BIFF: Ready to go, Pop. Every muscle is ready.

WILLY (*at the edge of the apron*): You realize what this means?

BIFF: That's right, Pop.

WILLY (*feeling* BIFF's *muscles*): You're comin' home this afternoon captain of the All-Scholastic Championship Team of the City of New York.

BIFF: I got it, Pop. And remember, pal, when I take off my helmet, that touchdown is for you.

WILLY: Let's go! (*He is starting out, with his arm around* BIFF, *when* CHARLEY *enters, as of old, in knickers.*) I got no room for you, Charley.

CHARLEY: Room? For what?

WILLY: In the car.

CHARLEY: You goin' for a ride? I wanted to shoot some casino.

WILLY (*furiously*): Casino! (*Incredulously*): Don't you realize what today is?

LINDA: Oh, he knows, Willy. He's just kidding you.

WILLY: That's nothing to kid about!

CHARLEY: No, Linda, what's goin' on?

LINDA: He's playing in Ebbets Field.

CHARLEY: Baseball in this weather?

WILLY: Don't talk to him. Come on, come on! (*He is pushing them out.*)

CHARLEY: Wait a minute, didn't you hear the news?

WILLY: What?

CHARLEY: Don't you listen to the radio? Ebbets Field just blew up.

WILLY: You go to hell! (CHARLEY *laughs. Pushing them out*): Come on, come on! We're late.

CHARLEY (*as they go*): Knock a homer, Biff, knock a homer!

WILLY (*the last to leave, turning to* CHARLEY): I don't think that was funny, Charley. This is the greatest day of his life.

CHARLEY: Willy, when are you going to grow up?

WILLY: Yeah, heh? When this game is over, Charley, you'll be laughing out of the other side of your face. They'll be calling him another Red Grange. Twenty-five thousand a year.

CHARLEY (*kidding*): Is that so?

WILLY: Yeah, that's so.

CHARLEY: Well, then, I'm sorry, Willy. But tell me something.

WILLY: What?

CHARLEY: Who is Red Grange?

WILLY: Put up your hands. Goddam you, put up your hands!

(CHARLEY, *chuckling, shakes his head and walks away, around the left corner of the stage.* WILLY *follows him. The music rises to a mocking frenzy.*)

WILLY: Who the hell do you think you are, better than everybody else? You don't know everything, you big, ignorant, stupid . . . Put up your hands!

(*Light rises, on the right side of the forestage, on a small table in the reception room of* CHARLEY's *office. Traffic sounds are heard.* BERNARD, *now mature, sits whistling to himself. A pair of tennis rackets and an overnight bag are on the floor beside him.*)

WILLY (*offstage*): What are you walking away for? Don't walk away! If you're going to say something say it to my face! I know you laugh at me behind my back. You'll laugh out of the other side of your goddam face after this game. Touchdown! Touchdown! Eighty thousand people! Touchdown! Right between the goal posts.

(BERNARD *is a quiet, earnest, but self-assured young man.* WILLY's *voice is coming from right upstage now.* BERNARD *lowers his feet off the table and listens.* JENNY, *his father's secretary, enters.*)

JENNY (*distressed*): Say, Bernard, will you go out in the hall?

BERNARD: What is that noise? Who is it?

JENNY: Mr. Loman. He just got off the elevator.

BERNARD (*getting up*): Who's he arguing with?

JENNY: Nobody. There's nobody with him. I can't deal with him any more, and your father gets all upset everytime he comes. I've got a lot of typing to do, and your father's waiting to sign it. Will you see him?

WILLY (*entering*): Touchdown! Touch—(*He sees* JENNY.) Jenny, Jenny, good to see you. How're ya? Workin'? Or still honest?

JENNY: Fine. How've you been feeling?

WILLY: Not much any more, Jenny. Ha, ha! (*He is surprised to see the rackets.*)

BERNARD: Hello, Uncle Willy.

WILLY (*almost shocked*): Bernard! Well, look who's here! (*He comes quickly, guiltily, to* BERNARD *and warmly shakes his hand.*)

BERNARD: How are you? Good to see you.

WILLY: What are you doing here?

BERNARD: Oh, just stopped by to see Pop. Get off my feet till my train leaves. I'm going to Washington in a few minutes.

WILLY: Is he in?

BERNARD: Yes, he's in his office with the accountant. Sit down.

WILLY (*sitting down*): What're you going to do in Washington?

BERNARD: Oh, just a case I've got there, Willy.

WILLY: That so? (*Indicating the rackets*): You going to play tennis there?

BERNARD: I'm staying with a friend who's got a court.

WILLY: Don't say. His own tennis court. Must be fine people, I bet.

BERNARD: They are, very nice. Dad tells me Biff's in town.

WILLY (*with a big smile*): Yeah, Biff's in. Working on a very big deal, Bernard.

BERNARD: What's Biff doing?

WILLY: Well, he's been doing very big things in the West. But he decided to establish himself here. Very big. We're having dinner. Did I hear your wife had a boy?

BERNARD: That's right. Our second.

WILLY: Two boys! What do you know!

BERNARD: What kind of a deal has Biff got?

WILLY: Well, Bill Oliver—very big sporting-goods man—he wants Biff very badly. Called him in from the West. Long distance, carte blanche, special deliveries. Your friends have their own private tennis court?

BERNARD: You still with the old firm, Willy?

WILLY (*after a pause*): I'm—I'm overjoyed to see how you made the grade, Bernard, overjoyed. It's an encouraging thing to see a young man real-ly—really—Looks very good for Biff—very—(*He breaks off, then*): Bernard—(*He is so full of emotion, he breaks off again.*)

BERNARD: What is it, Willy?

WILLY (*small and alone*): What—what's the secret?

BERNARD: What secret?

WILLY: How—how did you? Why didn't he ever catch on?

BERNARD: I wouldn't know that, Willy.

WILLY (*confidentially, desperately*): You were his friend, his boyhood friend. There's something I don't understand about it. His life ended after that Ebbets Field game. From the age of seventeen nothing good ever happened to him.

BERNARD: He never trained himself for anything.

WILLY: But he did, he did. After high school he took so many correspondence courses. Radio mechanics; television; God knows what, and never made the slightest mark.

BERNARD (*taking off his glasses*): Willy, do you want to talk candidly?

WILLY (*rising, faces* BERNARD): I regard you as a very brilliant man, Bernard. I value your advice.

BERNARD: Oh, the hell with the advice, Willy. I couldn't advise you. There's just one thing I've always wanted to ask you. When he was supposed to graduate, and the math teacher flunked him—

WILLY: Oh, that son-of-a-bitch ruined his life.

BERNARD: Yeah, but, Willy, all he had to do was go to summer school and make up that subject.

WILLY: That's right, that's right.

BERNARD: Did you tell him not to go to summer school?

WILLY: Me? I begged him to go. I ordered him to go!

BERNARD: Then why wouldn't he go?

WILLY: Why? Why! Bernard, that question has been trailing me like a ghost for the last fifteen years. He flunked the subject, and laid down and died like a hammer hit him!

BERNARD: Take it easy, kid.

WILLY: Let me talk to you—I got nobody to talk to. Bernard, Bernard, was it my fault? Y'see? It keeps going around in my mind, maybe I did something to him. I got nothing to give him.

BERNARD: Don't take it so hard.

WILLY: Why did he lay down? What is the story there? You were his friend!

BERNARD: Willy, I remember, it was June, and our grades came out. And he'd flunked math.

WILLY: That son-of-a-bitch!

BERNARD: No, it wasn't right then. Biff just got very angry, I remember, and he was ready to enroll in summer school.

WILLY (*surprised*): He was?

BERNARD: He wasn't beaten by it at all. But then, Willy, he disappeared from the block for almost a month. And I got the idea that he'd gone up to New England to see you. Did he have a talk with you then?

(WILLY *stares in silence.*)

BERNARD: Willy?

WILLY (*with a strong edge of resentment in his voice*): Yeah, he came to Boston. What about it?

BERNARD: Well, just that when he came back—I'll never forget this, it always mystifies me. Because I'd thought so well of Biff, even though he'd always taken advantage of me. I loved him, Willy, y'know? And he came back after that month and took his sneakers—remember those sneakers with "University of Virginia" printed on them? He was so proud of those, wore them every day. And he took them down in the cellar, and burned them up in the furnace. We had a fist fight. It lasted at least half an hour. Just the two of us, punching each other down the cellar, and crying right through it. I've often thought of how strange it was that I knew he'd given up his life. What happened in Boston, Willy?

(WILLY *looks at him as at an intruder.*)

BERNARD: I just bring it up because you asked me.

WILLY (*angrily*): Nothing. What do you mean, "What happened?" What's that got to do with anything?

BERNARD: Well, don't get sore.

WILLY: What are you trying to do, blame it on me? If a boy lays down is that my fault?

BERNARD: Now, Willy, don't get—

WILLY: Well, don't—don't talk to me that way! What does that mean, "What happened?"

(CHARLEY *enters. He is in his vest, and he carries a bottle of bourbon.*)

CHARLEY: Hey, you're going to miss that train. (*He waves the bottle.*)

BERNARD: Yeah, I'm going. (*He takes the bottle.*) Thanks, Pop. (*He picks up his rackets and bag.*) Good-by, Willy, and don't worry about it. You know, "If at first you don't succeed . . ."

WILLY: Yes, I believe in that.

BERNARD: But sometimes, Willy, it's better for a man just to walk away.

WILLY: Walk away?

BERNARD: That's right.

WILLY: But if you can't walk away?

BERNARD (*after a slight pause*): I guess that's when it's tough. (*Extending his hand*): Good-by, Willy.

WILLY (*shaking* BERNARD's *hand*): Good-by, boy.

CHARLEY (*an arm on* BERNARD's *shoulder*): How do you like this kid? Gonna argue a case in front of the Supreme Court.

BERNARD (*protesting*): Pop!

WILLY (*genuinely shocked, pained, and happy*): No! The Supreme Court!

BERNARD: I gotta run. 'By, Dad!

CHARLEY: Knock 'em dead, Bernard!

(BERNARD *goes off.*)

WILLY (*as* CHARLEY *takes out his wallet*): The Supreme Court! And he didn't even mention it!

CHARLEY (*counting out money on the desk*): He don't have to—he's gonna do it.

WILLY: And you never told him what to do, did you? You never took any interest in him.

CHARLEY: My salvation is that I never took any interest in anything. There's some money—fifty dollars. I got an accountant inside.

WILLY: Charley, look . . . (*With difficulty*): I got my insurance to pay. If you can manage it—I need a hundred and ten dollars.

(CHARLEY *doesn't reply for a moment; merely stops moving.*)

WILLY: I'd draw it from my bank but Linda would know, and I . . .

CHARLEY: Sit down, Willy.

WILLY (*moving toward the chair*): I'm keeping an account of everything, remember. I'll pay every penny back. (*He sits.*)

CHARLEY: Now listen to me, Willy.

WILLY: I want you to know I appreciate . . .

CHARLEY (*sitting down on the table*): Willy, what're you doin'? What the hell is goin' on in your head?

WILLY: Why? I'm simply . . .

CHARLEY: I offered you a job. You can make fifty dollars a week. And I won't send you on the road.

WILLY: I've got a job.

CHARLEY: Without pay? What kind of a job is a job without pay? (*He rises.*) Now, look, kid, enough is enough. I'm no genius but I know when I'm being insulted.

WILLY: Insulted!

CHARLEY: Why don't you want to work for me?

WILLY: What's the matter with you? I've got a job.

CHARLEY: Then what're you walkin' in here every week for?

WILLY (*getting up*): Well, if you don't want me to walk in here—

CHARLEY: I am offering you a job.

WILLY: I don't want your goddam job!

CHARLEY: When the hell are you going to grow up?

WILLY (*furiously*): You big ignoramus, if you say that to me again I'll rap you one! I don't care how big you are! (*He's ready to fight.*)
(*Pause.*)

CHARLEY (*kindly, going to him*): How much do you need, Willy?

WILLY: Charley, I'm strapped, I'm strapped. I don't know what to do. I was just fired.

CHARLEY: Howard fired you?

WILLY: That snotnose. Imagine that? I named him. I named him Howard.

CHARLEY: Willy, when're you gonna realize that them things don't mean anything? You named him Howard, but you can't sell that. The only thing you got in this world is what you can sell. And the funny thing is that you're a salesman, and you don't know that.

WILLY: I've always tried to think otherwise, I guess. I always felt that if a man was impressive, and well liked, that nothing—

CHARLEY: Why must everybody like you? Who liked J. P. Morgan? Was he impressive? In a Turkish bath he'd look like a butcher. But with his pockets on he was very well liked. Now listen, Willy, I know you don't like me, and nobody can say I'm in love with you, but I'll give you a job because—just for the hell of it, put it that way. Now what do you say?

WILLY: I—I just can't work for you, Charley.

CHARLEY: What're you, jealous of me?

WILLY: I can't work for you, that's all, don't ask me why.

CHARLEY (*angered, takes out more bills*): You been jealous of me all your life, you damned fool! Here, pay your insurance. (*He puts the money in* WILLY's *hand.*)

WILLY: I'm keeping strict accounts.

CHARLEY: I've got some work to do. Take care of yourself. And pay your insurance.

WILLY (*moving to the right*): Funny, y'know? After all the highways, and the trains, and the appointments, and the years, you end up worth more dead than alive.

CHARLEY: Willy, nobody's worth nothin' dead. (*After a slight pause*): Did you hear what I said? (WILLY *stands still, dreaming.*)

CHARLEY: Willy!

WILLY: Apologize to Bernard for me when you see him. I didn't mean to argue with him. He's a fine boy. They're all fine boys, and they'll end up big—all of them. Someday they'll all play tennis together. Wish me luck, Charley. He saw Bill Oliver today.

CHARLEY: Good luck.

WILLY (*on the verge of tears*): Charley, you're the only friend I got. Isn't that a remarkable thing? (*He goes out.*)

CHARLEY: Jesus!
(CHARLEY *stares after him a moment and follows. All light blacks out. Suddenly raucous music is heard, and a red glow rises behind the screen at right.* STANLEY, *a young waiter, appears, carrying a table, followed by* HAPPY, *who is carrying two chairs.*)

STANLEY (*putting the table down*): That's all right, Mr. Loman, I can handle it myself. (*He turns and takes the chairs from* HAPPY *and places them at the table.*)

HAPPY (*glancing around*): Oh, this is better.

STANLEY: Sure, in the front there you're in the middle of all kinds a noise. Whenever you got a party, Mr. Loman, you just tell me and I'll put you back here. Y'know, there's a lotta people they don't like it private, because when they go out they like to see a lotta action around them because they're sick and tired to stay in the house by theirself. But I know you, you ain't from Hackensack. You know what I mean?

HAPPY (*sitting down*): So how's it coming, Stanley?

STANLEY: Ah, it's a dog's life. I only wish during the war they'd a took me in the Army. I coulda been dead by now.

HAPPY: My brother's back, Stanley.

STANLEY: Oh, he come back, heh? From the Far West.

HAPPY: Yeah, big cattle man, my brother, so treat him right. And my father's coming too.

STANLEY: Oh, your father too!

HAPPY: You got a couple of nice lobsters?

STANLEY: Hundred per cent, big.

HAPPY: I want them with the claws.

STANLEY: Don't worry, I don't give you no mice. (HAPPY *laughs.*) How about some wine? It'll put a head on the meal.

HAPPY: No. You remember, Stanley, that recipe I brought you from overseas? With the champagne in it?

STANLEY: Oh, yeah, sure. I still got it tacked up yet in the kitchen. But that'll have to cost a buck apiece anyways.

HAPPY: That's all right.

STANLEY: What'd you, hit a number or somethin'?

HAPPY: No, it's a little celebration. My brother is—I think he pulled off a big deal today. I think we're going into business together.

STANLEY: Great! That's the best for you. Because a family business, you know what I mean?—that's the best.

HAPPY: That's what I think.

STANLEY: 'Cause what's the difference? Somebody steals? It's in the family. Know what I mean? (*Sotto voce*) Like this bartender here. The boss is goin' crazy what kinda leak he's got in the cash register. You put it in but it don't come out.

HAPPY (*raising his head*): Sh!

STANLEY: What?

HAPPY: You notice I wasn't lookin' right or left, was I?

STANLEY: No.

HAPPY: And my eyes are closed.

STANLEY: So what's the—?

HAPPY: Strudel's comin'.

STANLEY (*catching on, looks around*): Ah, no, there's no—

(*He breaks off as a furred, lavishly dressed girl enters and sits at the next table. Both follow her with their eyes.*)

STANLEY: Geez, how'd ya know?

HAPPY: I got radar or something. (*Staring directly at her profile*): Ooooooooo . . . Stanley.

STANLEY: I think that's for you, Mr. Loman.

HAPPY: Look at that mouth. Oh, God. And the binoculars.

STANLEY: Geez, you got a life, Mr. Loman.

HAPPY: Wait on her.

STANLEY (*going to the girl's table*): Would you like a menu, ma'am?

GIRL: I'm expecting someone, but I'd like a—

HAPPY: Why don't you bring her—excuse me, miss, do you mind? I sell champagne, and I'd like you to try my brand. Bring her a champagne, Stanley.

GIRL: That's awfully nice of you.

HAPPY: Don't mention it. It's all company money. (*He laughs.*)

GIRL: That's a charming product to be selling, isn't it?

HAPPY: Oh, gets to be like everything else. Selling is selling, y'know.

GIRL: I suppose.

HAPPY: You don't happen to sell, do you?

GIRL: No, I don't sell.

HAPPY: Would you object to a compliment from a stranger? You ought to be on a magazine cover.

GIRL (*looking at him a little archly*): I have been. (STANLEY *comes in with a glass of champagne.*)

HAPPY: What'd I say before, Stanley? You see? She's a cover-girl.

STANLEY: Oh, I could see, I could see.

HAPPY (*to the* GIRL): What magazine?

GIRL: Oh, a lot of them. (*She takes the drink.*) Thank you.

HAPPY: You know what they say in France, don't you? "Champagne is the drink of the complexion"—Hya, Biff!

(BIFF *has entered and sits with* HAPPY.)

BIFF: Hello, kid. Sorry I'm late.

HAPPY: I just got here. Uh, Miss—?

GIRL: Forsythe.

HAPPY: Miss Forsythe, this is my brother.

BIFF: Is Dad here?

HAPPY: His name is Biff. You might've heard of him. Great football player.

GIRL: Really? What team?

HAPPY: Are you familiar with football?

GIRL: No, I'm afraid I'm not.

HAPPY: Biff is quarterback with the New York Giants.

GIRL: Well, that is nice, isn't it? (*She drinks.*)

HAPPY: Good health.

GIRL: I'm happy to meet you.

HAPPY: That's my name. Hap. It's really Harold, but at West Point they called me Happy.

GIRL (*now really impressed*): Oh, I see. How do you do? (*She turns her profile.*)

BIFF: Isn't Dad coming?

HAPPY: You want her?

BIFF: Oh, I could never make that.

HAPPY: I remember the time that idea would never come into your head. Where's the old confidence, Biff?

BIFF: I just saw Oliver—

HAPPY: Wait a minute. I've got to see that old confidence again. Do you want her? She's on call.

BIFF: Oh, no. (*He turns to look at the* GIRL.)

HAPPY: I'm telling you. Watch this. (*Turning to the* GIRL.) Honey? (*She turns to him.*) Are you busy?

GIRL: Well, I am . . . but I could make a phone call.

HAPPY: Do that, will you, honey? And see if you can get a friend. We'll be here for a while. Biff is one of the greatest football players in the country.

GIRL (*standing up*): Well, I'm certainly happy to meet you.

HAPPY: Come back soon.

GIRL: I'll try.

HAPPY: Don't try, honey, try hard.

(*The* GIRL *exits.* STANLEY *follows, shaking his head in bewildered admiration.*)

HAPPY: Isn't that a shame now? A beautiful girl like that? That's why I can't get married. There's not a good woman in a thousand. New York is loaded with them, kid!

BIFF: Hap, look—

HAPPY: I told you she was on call!

BIFF (*strangely unnerved*): Cut it out, will ya? I want to say something to you.

HAPPY: Did you see Oliver?

BIFF: I saw him all right. Now look, I want to tell Dad a couple of things and I want you to help me.

HAPPY: What? Is he going to back you?

BIFF: Are you crazy? You're out of your goddam head, you know that?

HAPPY: Why? What happened?

BIFF (*breathlessly*): I did a terrible thing today, Hap. It's been the strangest day I ever went through. I'm all numb, I swear.

HAPPY: You mean he wouldn't see you?

BIFF: Well, I waited six hours for him, see? All day. Kept sending my name in. Even tried to date his secretary so she'd get me to him, but no soap.

HAPPY: Because you're not showin' the old confidence, Biff. He remembered you, didn't he?

BIFF (*stopping* HAPPY *with a gesture*): Finally, about five o'clock, he comes out. Didn't remember who I was or anything. I felt like such an idiot, Hap.

HAPPY: Did you tell him my Florida idea?

BIFF: He walked away. I saw him for one minute. I got so mad I could've torn the walls down! How the hell did I ever get the idea I was a salesman there? I even believed myself that I'd been a salesman for him! And then he gave me one look and—I realized what a ridiculous lie my whole life has been! We've been talking in a dream for fifteen years. I was a shipping clerk.

HAPPY: What'd you do?

BIFF (*with great tension and wonder*): Well, he left, see. And the secretary went out. I was all alone in the waiting-room. I don't know what came over me, Hap. The next thing I know I'm in his office—paneled walls, everything. I can't explain it. I—Hap, I took his fountain pen.

HAPPY: Geez, did he catch you?

BIFF: I ran out. I ran down all eleven flights. I ran and ran and ran.

HAPPY: That was an awful dumb—what'd you do that for?

BIFF (*agonized*): I don't know, I just—wanted to take something, I don't know. You gotta help me, Hap, I'm gonna tell Pop.

HAPPY: You crazy? What for?

BIFF: Hap, he's got to understand that I'm not the man somebody lends that kind of money to. He thinks I've been spiting him all these years and it's eating him up.

HAPPY: That's just it. You tell him something nice.

BIFF: I can't.

HAPPY: Say you got a lunch date with Oliver tomorrow.

BIFF: So what do I do tomorrow?

HAPPY: You leave the house tomorrow and come back at night and say Oliver is thinking it over. And he thinks it over for a couple of weeks, and gradually it fades away and nobody's the worse.

BIFF: But it'll go on forever!

HAPPY: Dad is never so happy as when he's looking forward to something!

(WILLY *enters.*)

HAPPY: Hello, scout!

WILLY: Gee, I haven't been here in years!

(STANLEY *has followed* WILLY *in, and sets a chair for him.* STANLEY *starts off but* HAPPY *stops him.*)

HAPPY: Stanley!

(STANLEY *stands by, waiting for an order.*)

BIFF (*going to* WILLY *with guilt, as to an invalid*): Sit down, Pop. You want a drink?

WILLY: Sure, I don't mind.

BIFF: Let's get a load on.

WILLY: You look worried.

BIFF: N-no. (*To* STANLEY): Scotch all around. Make it doubles.

STANLEY: Doubles, right. (*He goes.*)

WILLY: You had a couple already, didn't you?

BIFF: Just a couple, yeah.

WILLY: Well, what happened, boy? (*Nodding affirmatively, with a smile*): Everything go all right?

BIFF (*takes a breath, then reaches out and grasps* WILLY'S *hand*): Pal . . . (*He is smiling bravely, and* WILLY *is smiling too.*) I had an experience today.

HAPPY: Terrific, Pop.

WILLY: That so? What happened?

BIFF (*high, slightly alcoholic, above the earth*): I'm going to tell you everything from first to last. It's been a strange day. (*Silence. He looks around, composes himself as best he can, but his breath keeps breaking the rhythm of his voice.*) I had to wait quite a while for him, and—

WILLY: Oliver?

BIFF: Yeah, Oliver. All day, as a matter of cold fact. And a lot of—instances—facts, Pop, facts about my life came back to me. Who was it, Pop? Who ever said I was a salesman with Oliver?

WILLY: Well, you were.

BIFF: No, Dad, I was a shipping clerk.

WILLY: But you were practically—

BIFF (*with determination*): Dad, I don't know who said it first, but I was never a salesman for Bill Oliver.

WILLY: What're you talking about?

BIFF: Let's hold on to the facts tonight, Pop. We're not going to get anywhere bullin' around. I was a shipping clerk.

WILLY (*angrily*): All right, now listen to me—

BIFF: Why don't you let me finish?

WILLY: I'm not interested in stories about the past or any crap of that kind because the woods are burning, boys, you understand? There's a big blaze going on all around. I was fired today.

BIFF (*shocked*): How could you be?

WILLY: I was fired, and I'm looking for a little good news to tell your mother, because the woman has waited and the woman has suffered. The gist of it is that I haven't got a story left in my head, Biff. So don't give me a lecture about facts and aspects. I am not interested. Now what've you got to say to me?

(STANLEY *enters with three drinks. They wait until he leaves.*)

WILLY: Did you see Oliver?

BIFF: Jesus, Dad!

WILLY: You mean you didn't go up there?

HAPPY: Sure he went up there.

BIFF: I did. I saw him. How could they fire you?

WILLY (*on the edge of his chair*): What kind of a welcome did he give you?

BIFF: He won't even let you work on commission?

WILLY: I'm out! (*Driving*) So tell me, he gave you a warm welcome?

HAPPY: Sure, Pop, sure!

BIFF (*driven*): Well, it was kind of—

WILLY: I was wondering if he'd remember you. (*To* HAPPY): Imagine, man doesn't see him for ten, twelve years and gives him that kind of a welcome!

HAPPY: Damn right!

BIFF (*trying to return to the offensive*): Pop, look—

WILLY: You know why he remembered you, don't you? Because you impressed him in those days.

BIFF: Let's talk quietly and get this down to the facts, huh?

WILLY (*as though* BIFF *had been interrupting*): Well, what happened? It's great news, Biff. Did he take you into his office or'd you talk in the waiting-room?

BIFF: Well, he came in, see, and—

WILLY (*with a big smile*): What'd he say? Betcha he threw his arm around you.

BIFF: Well, he kinda—

WILLY: He's a fine man. (*To* HAPPY): Very hard man to see, y'know.

HAPPY (*agreeing*): Oh, I know.

WILLY (*To* BIFF): Is that where you had the drinks?

BIFF: Yeah, he gave me a couple of—no, no!

HAPPY (*cutting in*): He told him my Florida idea.

WILLY: Don't interrupt. (*To* BIFF): How'd he react to the Florida idea?

BIFF: Dad, will you give me a minute to explain?

WILLY: I've been waiting for you to explain since I sat down here! What happened? He took you into his office and what?

BIFF: Well—I talked. And—and he listened, see.

WILLY: Famous for the way he listens, y'know. What was his answer?

BIFF: His answer was—(*He breaks off, suddenly angry.*) Dad, you're not letting me tell you what I want to tell you!

WILLY (*accusing, angered*): You didn't see him, did you?

BIFF: I did see him!

WILLY: What'd you insult him or something? You insulted him, didn't you?

BIFF: Listen, will you let me out of it, will you just let me out of it!

HAPPY: What the hell!

WILLY: Tell me what happened!

BIFF (*to* HAPPY): I can't talk to him!

(*A single trumpet note jars the ear. The light of green leaves stains the house, which holds the air of night and a dream.* YOUNG BERNARD *enters and knocks on the door of the house.*)

YOUNG BERNARD (*frantically*): Mrs. Loman, Mrs. Loman!

HAPPY: Tell him what happened!

BIFF (*To* HAPPY): Shut up and leave me alone!

WILLY: No, no! You had to go and flunk math!

BIFF: What math? What're you talking about?

YOUNG BERNARD: Mrs. Loman, Mrs. Loman! (LINDA *appears in the house, as of old.*)

WILLY (*wildly*): Math, math, math!

BIFF: Take it easy, Pop!

YOUNG BERNARD: Mrs. Loman!

WILLY (*furiously*): If you hadn't flunked you'd've been set by now!

BIFF: Now, look, I'm gonna tell you what happened, and you're going to listen to me.

YOUNG BERNARD: Mrs. Loman!

BIFF: I waited six hours—

HAPPY: What the hell are you saying?

BIFF: I kept sending in my name but he wouldn't see me. So finally he . . . (*He continues unheard as light fades low on the restaurant.*)

YOUNG BERNARD: Biff flunked math!

LINDA: No!

YOUNG BERNARD: Birnbaum flunked him! They won't graduate him!

LINDA: But they have to. He's gotta go to the university. Where is he? Biff! Biff!

YOUNG BERNARD: No, he left. He went to Grand Central.

LINDA: Grand—You mean he went to Boston!

YOUNG BERNARD: Is Uncle Willy in Boston?

LINDA: Oh, maybe Willy can talk to the teacher. Oh, the poor, poor boy!

(*Light on house area snaps out.*)

BIFF (*at the table, now audible, holding up a gold fountain pen*): . . . so I'm washed up with Oliver, you understand? Are you listening to me?

WILLY (*at a loss*): Yeah, sure. If you hadn't flunked—

BIFF: Flunked what? What're you talking about?

WILLY: Don't blame everything on me! I didn't flunk math—you did! What pen?

HAPPY: That was awful dumb, Biff, a pen like that is worth—

WILLY (*seeing the pen for the first time*): You took Oliver's pen?

BIFF (*weakening*): Dad, I just explained it to you.

WILLY: You stole Bill Oliver's fountain pen!

BIFF: I didn't exactly steal it! That's just what I've been explaining to you!

HAPPY: He had it in his hand and just then Oliver walked in, so he got nervous and stuck it in his pocket!

WILLY: My God, Biff!

BIFF: I never intended to do it, Dad!

OPERATOR'S VOICE: Standish Arms, good evening!

WILLY (*shouting*): I'm not in my room!

BIFF (*frightened*): Dad, what's the matter? (*He and* HAPPY *stand up.*)

OPERATOR: Ringing Mr. Loman for you!

WILLY: I'm not there, stop it!

BIFF (*horrified, gets down on one knee before* WILLY): Dad, I'll make good, I'll make good. (WILLY *tries to get to his feet.* BIFF *holds him down.*) Sit down now.

WILLY: No, you're no good, you're no good for anything.

BIFF: I am, Dad, I'll find something else, you understand? Now don't worry about anything. (*He holds up* WILLY's *face*): Talk to me, Dad.

OPERATOR: Mr. Loman does not answer. Shall I page him?

WILLY (*attempting to stand, as though to rush and silence the* OPERATOR): No, no, no!

HAPPY: He'll strike something, Pop.

WILLY: No, no . . .

BIFF (*desperately, standing over* WILLY): Pop, listen! Listen to me! I'm telling you something good. Oliver talked to his partner about the Florida idea. You listening? He—he talked to his partner, and he came to me . . . I'm going to be all right, you hear? Dad, listen to me, he said it was just a question of the amount!

WILLY: Then you . . . got it?

HAPPY: He's gonna be terrific, Pop!

WILLY (*trying to stand*): Then you got it, haven't you? You got it! You got it!

BIFF (*agonized, holds* WILLY *down*): No, no. Look, Pop. I'm supposed to have lunch with them tomorrow. I'm just telling you this so you'll know that I can still make an impression, Pop. And I'll make good somewhere, but I can't go tomorrow, see?

WILLY: Why not? You simply—

BIFF: But the pen, Pop!

WILLY: You give it to him and tell him it was an oversight!

HAPPY: Sure, have lunch tomorrow!

BIFF: I can't say that—

WILLY: You were doing a crossword puzzle and accidentally used his pen!

BIFF: Listen, kid, I took those balls years ago, now I walk in with his fountain pen? That clinches it, don't you see? I can't face him like that! I'll try elsewhere.

PAGE'S VOICE: Paging Mr. Loman!

WILLY: Don't you want to be anything?

BIFF: Pop, how can I go back?

WILLY: You don't want to be anything, is that what's behind it?

BIFF (*now angry at* WILLY *for not crediting his sympathy*): Don't take it that way! You think it was easy walking into that office after what I'd done to him? A team of horses couldn't have dragged me back to Bill Oliver!

WILLY: Then why'd you go?

BIFF: Why did I go? Why did I go! Look at you! Look at what's become of you!
(*Off left,* THE WOMAN *laughs.*)

WILLY: Biff, you're going to go to that lunch tomorrow, or—

BIFF: I can't go. I've got no appointment!

HAPPY: Biff, for . . . !

WILLY: Are you spiting me?

BIFF: Don't take it that way! Goddammit!

WILLY (*strikes* BIFF *and falters away from the table*): You rotten little louse! Are you spiting me?

THE WOMAN: Someone's at the door, Willy!

BIFF: I'm no good, can't you see what I am?

HAPPY (*separating them*): Hey, you're in a restaurant! Now cut it out, both of you! (*The girls enter.*) Hello, girls, sit down.
(THE WOMAN *laughs, off left.*)

MISS FORSYTHE: I guess we might as well. This is Letta.

THE WOMAN: Willy, are you going to wake up?

BIFF (*ignoring* WILLY): How're ya, miss, sit down. What do you drink?

MISS FORSYTHE: Letta might not be able to stay long.

LETTA: I gotta get up very early tomorrow. I got jury duty. I'm so excited! Were you fellows ever on a jury?

BIFF: No, but I been in front of them! (*The girls laugh.*) This is my father.

LETTA: Isn't he cute? Sit down with us, Pop.

HAPPY: Sit him down, Biff!

BIFF (*going to him*): Come on, slugger, drink us under the table. To hell with it! Come on, sit down, pal.
(*On* BIFF's *last insistence,* WILLY *is about to sit.*)

THE WOMAN (*now urgently*): Willy, are you going to answer the door!
(THE WOMAN's *call pulls* WILLY *back. He starts right, befuddled.*)

BIFF: Hey, where are you going?

WILLY: Open the door.

BIFF: The door?

WILLY: The washroom . . . the door . . . where's the door?

BIFF (*leading* WILLY *to the left*): Just go straight down. (WILLY *moves left.*)

THE WOMAN: Willy, Willy, are you going to get up, get up, get up, get up? (WILLY *exits left.*)

LETTA: I think it's sweet you bring your daddy along.

MISS FORSYTHE: Oh, he isn't really your father!

BIFF (*at left, turning to her resentfully*): Miss Forsythe, you've just seen a prince walk by. A fine, troubled prince. A hard-working, unappreciated prince. A pal, you understand? A good companion. Always for his boys.

LETTA: That's so sweet.

HAPPY: Well, girls, what's the program? We're wasting time. Come on, Biff. Gather round. Where would you like to go?

BIFF: Why don't you do something for him?

HAPPY: Me!

BIFF: Don't you give a damn for him, Hap?

HAPPY: What're you talking about? I'm the one who—

BIFF: I sense it, you don't give a good goddam about him. (*He takes the rolled-up hose from his pocket and puts it on the table in front of* HAPPY.) Look what I found in the cellar, for Christ's sake. How can you bear to let it go on?

HAPPY: Me? Who goes away? Who runs off and—

BIFF: Yeah, but he doesn't mean anything to you. You could help him—I can't! Don't you understand what I'm talking about? He's going to kill himself, don't you know that?

HAPPY: Don't I know it! Me!

BIFF: Hap, help him! Jesus . . . help him . . . Help me, help me, I can't bear to look at his face! (*Ready to weep, he hurries out, up right.*)

HAPPY (*starting after him*): Where are you going?

MISS FORSYTHE: What's he so mad about?

HAPPY: Come on, girls, we'll catch up with him.

MISS FORSYTHE (*as* HAPPY *pushes her out*): Say, I don't like that temper of his!

HAPPY: He's just a little overstrung, he'll be all right!

WILLY (*off left, as* THE WOMAN *laughs*): Don't answer! Don't answer!

LETTA: Don't you want to tell your father—

HAPPY: No, that's not my father. He's just a guy. Come on, we'll catch Biff, and, honey, we're going to paint this town! Stanley, where's the check! Hey, Stanley! (*They exit.* STANLEY *looks toward left.*)

STANLEY (*calling to* HAPPY *indignantly*): Mr. Loman! Mr. Loman! (STANLEY *picks up a chair and follows them off. Knocking is heard off left.* THE WOMAN *enters, laughing.* WILLY *follows her. She is in a black slip; he is buttoning his shirt. Raw, sensuous music accompanies their speech.*)

WILLY: Will you stop laughing? Will you stop?

THE WOMAN: Aren't you going to answer the door? He'll wake the whole hotel.

WILLY: I'm not expecting anybody.

THE WOMAN: Whyn't you have another drink, honey, and stop being so damn self-centered?

WILLY: I'm so lonely.

THE WOMAN: You know you ruined me, Willy? From now on, whenever you come to the office, I'll see that you go right through to the buyers. No waiting at my desk any more, Willy. You ruined me.

WILLY: That's nice of you to say that.

THE WOMAN: Gee, you are self-centered! Why so sad? You are the saddest, self-centeredest soul I ever did see-saw. (*She laughs. He kisses her.*) Come on inside, drummer boy. It's silly to be dressing in the middle of the night. (*As knocking is heard*): Aren't you going to answer the door?

WILLY: They're knocking on the wrong door.

THE WOMAN: But I felt the knocking. And he heard us talking in here. Maybe the hotel's on fire!

WILLY (*his terror rising*): It's a mistake.

THE WOMAN: Then tell him to go away!

WILLY: There's nobody there.

THE WOMAN: It's getting on my nerves, Willy. There's somebody standing out there and it's getting on my nerves!

WILLY (*pushing her away from him*): All right, stay in the bathroom here, and don't come out. I think there's a law in Massachusetts about it, so don't come out. It may be that new room clerk. He looked very mean. So don't come out. It's a mistake, there's no fire.

(*The knocking is heard again. He takes a few steps away from her, and she vanishes into the wing. The light follows him, and now he is facing* YOUNG BIFF, *who carries a suitcase.* BIFF *steps toward him. The music is gone.*)

BIFF: Why didn't you answer?

WILLY: Biff! What are you doing in Boston?

BIFF: Why didn't you answer? I've been knocking for five minutes, I called you on the phone—

WILLY: I just heard you. I was in the bathroom and had the door shut. Did anything happen home?

BIFF: Dad—I let you down.

WILLY: What do you mean?

BIFF: Dad . . .

WILLY: Biffo, what's this about? (*Putting his arm around* BIFF): Come on, let's go downstairs and get you a malted.

BIFF: Dad, I flunked math.

WILLY: Not for the term?

BIFF: The term. I haven't got enough credits to graduate.

WILLY: You mean to say Bernard wouldn't give you the answers?

BIFF: He did, he tried, but I only got a sixty-one.

WILLY: And they wouldn't give you four points?

BIFF: Birnbaum refused absolutely. I begged him, Pop, but he won't give me those points. You gotta talk to him before they close the school. Because if he saw the kind of man you are, and you just talked to him in your way, I'm sure he'd come through for me. The class came right before practice, see, and I didn't go enough. Would you talk to him? He'd like you, Pop. You know the way you could talk.

WILLY: You're on. We'll drive right back.

BIFF: Oh, Dad, good work! I'm sure he'll change it for you!

WILLY: Go downstairs and tell the clerk I'm check-in' out. Go right down.

BIFF: Yes, sir! See, the reason he hates me, Pop—one day he was late for class so I got up at the blackboard and imitated him. I crossed my eyes and talked with a lithp.

WILLY (*laughing*): You did? The kids like it?

BIFF: They nearly died laughing!

WILLY: Yeah? What'd you do?

BIFF: The thquare root of thixty twee is . . . (WILLY *bursts out laughing;* BIFF *joins him.*) And in the middle of it he walked in!

(WILLY *laughs and* THE WOMAN *joins in offstage.*)

WILLY (*without hesitation*): Hurry downstairs and—

BIFF: Somebody in there?

WILLY: No, that was next door.

(THE WOMAN *laughs offstage.*)

BIFF: Somebody got in your bathroom!

WILLY: No, it's the next room, there's a party—

THE WOMAN (*enters, laughing. She lisps this*): Can I come in? There's something in the bathtub, Willy, and it's moving!

(WILLY *looks at* BIFF, *who is staring open-mouthed and horrified at* THE WOMAN.)

WILLY: Ah—you better go back to your room. They must be finished painting by now. They're painting her room so I let her take a shower here. Go back, go back . . . (*He pushes her.*)

THE WOMAN (*resisting*): But I've got to get dressed, Willy, I can't—

WILLY: Get out of here! Go back, go back . . . (*Suddenly striving for the ordinary*): This is Miss Francis, Biff, she's a buyer. They're painting her room. Go back, Miss Francis, go back . . .

THE WOMAN: But my clothes, I can't go out naked in the hall!

WILLY (*pushing her offstage*): Get outa here! Go back, go back!

(BIFF *slowly sits down on his suitcase as the argument continues offstage.*)

THE WOMAN: Where's my stockings? You promised me stockings, Willy!

WILLY: I have no stockings here!

THE WOMAN: You had two boxes of size nine sheers for me, and I want them!

WILLY: Here, for God's sake, will you get outa here!

THE WOMAN (*enters holding a box of stockings*): I just hope there's nobody in the hall. That's all I hope. (*To* BIFF): Are you football or baseball?

BIFF: Football.

THE WOMAN (*angry, humiliated*): That's me too. G'night. (*She snatches her clothes from* WILLY, *and walks out.*)

WILLY (*after a pause*): Well, better get going. I want to get to the school first thing in the morning. Get my suits out of the closet. I'll get my valise. (BIFF *doesn't move.*) What's the matter? (BIFF *remains motionless, tears falling.*) She's a buyer. Buys for J. H. Simmons. She lives down the hall—they're painting. You don't imagine—(*He breaks off. After a pause*) Now listen, pal, she's just a buyer. She sees merchandise in her room and they have to keep it looking just so . . . (*Pause. Assuming command*) All right, get my suits. (BIFF *doesn't move.*) Now stop crying and do as I say. I gave you an order. Biff, I gave you an order! Is that what you do when I give you an order? How dare you cry! (*Putting his arm around* BIFF) Now look, Biff, when you grow up you'll understand about these things. You mustn't—you mustn't overemphasize a thing like this. I'll see Birnbaum first thing in the morning.

BIFF: Never mind.

WILLY (*getting down beside* BIFF): Never mind! He's going to give you those points. I'll see to it.

BIFF: He wouldn't listen to you.

WILLY: He certainly will listen to me. You need those points for the U. of Virginia.

BIFF: I'm not going there.

WILLY: Heh? If I can't get him to change that mark you'll make it up in summer school. You've got all summer to—

BIFF (*his weeping breaking from him*): Dad . . .

WILLY (*infected by it*): Oh, my boy . . .

BIFF: Dad . . .

WILLY: She's nothing to me, Biff. I was lonely, I was terribly lonely.

BIFF: You—you gave her Mama's stockings! (*His tears break through and he rises to go.*)

WILLY (*grabbing for* BIFF): I gave you an order!

BIFF: Don't touch me, you—liar!

WILLY: Apologize for that!

BIFF: You fake! You phony little fake! You fake! (*Overcome, he turns quickly and weeping fully goes out with his suitcase.* WILLY *is left on the floor on his knees.*)

WILLY: I gave you an order! Biff, come back here or I'll beat you! Come back here! I'll whip you! (STANLEY *comes quickly in from the right and stands in front of* WILLY.)

WILLY (*shouts at* STANLEY): I gave you an order . . .

STANLEY: Hey, let's pick it up, pick it up, Mr. Loman. (*He helps* WILLY *to his feet.*) Your boys left

with the chippies. They said they'll see you home.

(*A second waiter watches some distance away.*)

WILLY: But we were supposed to have dinner together.

(*Music is heard,* WILLY's *theme.*)

STANLEY: Can you make it?

WILLY: I'll—sure, I can make it. (*Suddenly concerned about his clothes*): Do I—I look all right?

STANLEY: Sure, you look all right. (*He flicks a speck off* WILLY's *lapel.*)

WILLY: Here—here's a dollar.

STANLEY: Oh, your son paid me. It's all right.

WILLY (*putting it in* STANLEY's *hand*): No, take it. You're a good boy.

STANLEY: Oh, no, you don't have to . . .

WILLY: Here—here's some more, I don't need it any more. (*After a slight pause*): Tell me—is there a seed store in the neighborhood?

STANLEY: Seeds? You mean like to plant?

(*As* WILLY *turns,* STANLEY *slips the money back into his jacket pocket.*)

WILLY: Yes. Carrots, peas . . .

STANLEY: Well, there's hardware stores on Sixth Avenue, but it may be too late now.

WILLY (*anxiously*): Oh, I'd better hurry. I've got to get some seeds. (*He starts off to the right.*) I've got to get some seeds, right away. Nothing's planted. I don't have a thing in the ground.

(WILLY *hurries out as the light goes down.* STANLEY *moves over to the right after him, watches him off. The other waiter has been staring at* WILLY.)

STANLEY (*to the* WAITER): Well, whatta you looking at?

(THE WAITER *picks up the chairs and moves off right.* STANLEY *takes the table and follows him. The light fades on this area. There is a long pause, the sound of the flute coming over. The light gradually rises on the kitchen, which is empty.* HAPPY *appears at the door of the house, followed by* BIFF. HAPPY *is carrying a large bunch of long-stemmed roses. He enters the kitchen, looks around for* LINDA. *Not seeing her, he turns to* BIFF, *who is just outside the house door, and makes a gesture with his hands, indicating "Not here, I guess." He looks into the living-room and freezes. Inside,* LINDA, *unseen, is seated,* WILLY's *coat on her lap. She rises ominously and quietly and moves toward* HAPPY, *who backs up into the kitchen, afraid.*)

HAPPY: Hey, what're you doing up? (LINDA *says nothing but moves toward him implacably.*) Where's Pop? (*He keeps backing to the right, and now* LINDA *is in full view in the doorway to the living-room.*) Is he sleeping?

LINDA: Where were you?

HAPPY (*trying to laugh it off*): We met two girls, Mom, very fine types. Here, we brought you some flowers. (*Offering them to her*): Put them in your room, Ma.

(*She knocks them to the floor at* BIFF's *feet. He has now come inside and closed the door behind him. She stares at* BIFF, *silent.*)

HAPPY: Now what'd you do that for? Mom, I want you to have some flowers—

LINDA (*cutting* HAPPY *off, violently to* BIFF): Don't you care whether he lives or dies?

HAPPY (*going to the stairs*): Come upstairs, Biff.

BIFF (*with a flare of disgust, to* HAPPY): Go away from me! (*To* LINDA): What do you mean, lives or dies? Nobody's dying around here, pal.

LINDA: Get out of my sight! Get out of here!

BIFF: I wanna see the boss.

LINDA: You're not going near him!

BIFF: Where is he? (*He moves into the living-room and* LINDA *follows.*)

LINDA (*shouting after* BIFF): You invite him for dinner. He looks forward to it all day—(BIFF *appears in his parents' bedroom, looks around, and exits*)—and then you desert him there. There's no stranger you'd do that to!

HAPPY: Why? He had a swell time with us. Listen, when I—(LINDA *comes back into the kitchen*)—desert him I hope I don't outlive the day!

LINDA: Get out of here!

HAPPY: Now look, Mom . . .

LINDA: Did you have to go to women tonight? You and your lousy rotten whores!

(BIFF *re-enters the kitchen.*)

HAPPY: Mom, all we did was follow Biff around trying to cheer him up! (*To* BIFF) Boy, what a night you gave me!

LINDA: Get out of here, both of you, and don't come back! I don't want you tormenting him any more. Go on now, get your things together! (*To* BIFF) You can sleep in his apartment. (*She starts to pick up the flowers and stops herself.*) Pick up this stuff, I'm not your maid any more. Pick it up, you bum, you!

(HAPPY *turns his back to her in refusal.* BIFF *slowly moves over and gets down on his knees, picking up the flowers.*)

LINDA: You're a pair of animals! Not one, not another living soul would have had the cruelty to walk out on that man in a restaurant!

BIFF (*not looking at her*): Is that what he said?

LINDA: He didn't have to say anything. He was so humiliated he nearly limped when he came in.

HAPPY: But, Mom, he had a great time with us—

BIFF (*cutting him off violently*): Shut up!

(*Without another word,* HAPPY *goes upstairs.*)

LINDA: You! You didn't even go in to see if he was all right!

BIFF (*still on the floor in front of* LINDA, *the flowers in his hand; with self-loathing*): No. Didn't. Didn't do a damned thing. How do you like that, heh? Left him babbling in a toilet.

LINDA: You louse. You . . .

BIFF: Now you hit it on the nose! (*He gets up, throws the flowers in the wastebasket.*) The scum of the earth, and you're looking at him!

LINDA: Get out of here!

BIFF: I gotta talk to the boss, Mom. Where is he?

LINDA: You're not going near him. Get out of this house!

BIFF (*with absolute assurance, determination*): No. We're gonna have an abrupt conversation, him and me.

LINDA: You're not talking to him!

(*Hammering is heard from outside the house, off right.* BIFF *turns toward the noise.*)

LINDA (*suddenly pleading*): Will you please leave him alone?

BIFF: What's he doing out there?

LINDA: He's planting the garden!

BIFF (*quietly*): Now? Oh, my God!

(BIFF *moves outside,* LINDA *following. The light dies down on them and comes up on the center of the apron as* WILLY *walks into it. He is carrying a flashlight, a hoe, and a handful of seed packets. He raps the top of the hoe sharply to fix it firmly, and then moves to the left, measuring off the distance with his foot. He holds the flashlight to look at the seed packets, reading off the instructions. He is in the blue of night.*)

WILLY: Carrots... quarter-inch apart. Rows... one-foot rows. (*He measures it off.*) One foot. (*He puts down a package and measures off.*) Beets. (*He puts down another package and measures again.*) Lettuce. (*He reads the package, puts it down.*) One foot—(*He breaks off as* BEN *appears at the right and moves slowly down to him.*) What a proposition, ts, ts. Terrific, terrific. 'Cause she's suffered, Ben, the woman has suffered. You understand me? A man can't go out the way he came in, Ben, a man has got to add up to something. You can't, you can't—(BEN *moves toward him as though to interrupt.*) You gotta consider, now. Don't answer so quick. Remember, it's a guaranteed twenty-thousand-dollar proposition. Now look, Ben, I want you to go through the ins and outs of this thing with me. I've got nobody to talk to, Ben, and the woman has suffered, you hear me?

BEN (*standing still, considering*): What's the proposition?

WILLY: It's twenty thousand dollars on the barrelhead. Guaranteed, gilt-edged, you understand?

BEN: You don't want to make a fool of yourself. They might not honor the policy.

WILLY: How can they dare refuse? Didn't I work like a coolie to meet every premium on the nose? And now they don't pay off? Impossible!

BEN: It's called a cowardly thing, William.

WILLY: Why? Does it take more guts to stand here the rest of my life ringing up a zero?

BEN (*yielding*): That's a point, William. (*He moves, thinking, turns.*) And twenty thousand—that is something one can feel with the hand, it is there.

WILLY (*now assured, with rising power*): Oh, Ben, that's the whole beauty of it! I see it like a diamond, shining in the dark, hard and rough, that I can pick up and touch in my hand. Not like—like an appointment! This would not be another damned-fool appointment, Ben, and it changes all the aspects. Because he thinks I'm nothing, see, and so he spites me. But the funeral—(*Straightening up*): Ben, that funeral will be massive! They'll come from Maine, Massachusetts, Vermont, New Hampshire! All the old-timers with the strange license plates—that boy will be thunder-struck, Ben, because he never realized—I am known! Rhode Island, New York, New Jersey—I am known, Ben, and he'll see it with his eyes once and for all. He'll see what I am, Ben! He's in for a shock, that boy!

BEN (*coming down to the edge of the garden*): He'll call you a coward.

WILLY (*suddenly fearful*): No, that would be terrible.

BEN: Yes. And a damned fool.

WILLY: No, no, he mustn't, I won't have that! (*He is broken and desperate.*)

BEN: He'll hate you, William.

(*The gay music of the* BOYS *is heard.*)

WILLY: Oh, Ben, how do we get back to all the great times? Used to be so full of light, and comradeship, the sleigh-riding in winter, and the ruddiness on his cheeks. And always some kind of good news coming up, always something nice coming up ahead. And never even let me carry the valises in the house, and simonizing, simonizing that little red car! Why, why can't I give him something and not have him hate me?

BEN: Let me think about it. (*He glances at his watch.*) I still have a little time. Remarkable proposition, but you've got to be sure you're not making a fool of yourself.

(BEN *drifts off upstage and goes out of sight.* BIFF *comes down from the left.*)

WILLY (*suddenly conscious of* BIFF, *turns and looks up at him, then begins picking up the packages of seeds in confusion*): Where the hell is that seed? (*Indignantly*): You can't see nothing out here! They boxed in the whole goddam neighborhood!

BIFF: There are people all around here. Don't you realize that?

WILLY: I'm busy. Don't bother me.

BIFF (*taking the hoe from* WILLY): I'm saying good-by to you, Pop. (WILLY *looks at him, silent, unable to move.*) I'm not coming back any more.

WILLY: You're not going to see Oliver tomorrow?

BIFF: I've got no appointment, Dad.

WILLY: He put his arm around you, and you've got no appointment?

BIFF: Pop, get this now, will you? Everytime I've left it's been a fight that sent me out of here.

Today I realized something about myself and I tried to explain it to you and I—I think I'm just not smart enough to make any sense out of it for you. To hell with whose fault it is or anything like that. (*He takes* WILLY's *arm*.) Let's just wrap it up, heh? Come on in, we'll tell Mom. (*He gently tries to pull* WILLY *to left*.)

WILLY (*frozen, immobile, with guilt in his voice*): No, I don't want to see her.

BIFF: Come on! (*He pulls again, and* WILLY *tries to pull away*.)

WILLY (*highly nervous*): No, no, I don't want to see her.

BIFF (*tries to look into* WILLY's *face, as if to find the answer there*): Why don't you want to see her?

WILLY (*more harshly now*): Don't bother me, will you?

BIFF: What do you mean, you don't want to see her? You don't want them calling you yellow, do you? This isn't your fault; it's me, I'm a bum. Now come inside! (WILLY *strains to get away*.) Did you hear what I said to you?
(WILLY *pulls away and quickly goes by himself into the house.* BIFF *follows*.)

LINDA (*to* WILLY): Did you plant, dear?

BIFF (*at the door, to* LINDA): All right, we had it out. I'm going and I'm not writing any more.

LINDA (*going to* WILLY *in the kitchen*): I think that's the best way, dear. 'Cause there's no use drawing it out, you'll just never get along.
(WILLY *doesn't respond*.)

BIFF: People ask where I am and what I'm doing, you don't know, and you don't care. That way it'll be off your mind and you can start brightening up again. All right? That clears it, doesn't it? (WILLY *is silent, and* BIFF *goes to him*.) You gonna wish me luck, scout? (*He extends his hand*.) What do you say?

LINDA: Shake his hand, Willy.

WILLY (*turning to her, seething with hurt*): There's no necessity to mention the pen at all, y'know.

BIFF (*gently*): I've got no appointment, Dad.

WILLY (*erupting fiercely*): He put his arm around . . . ?

BIFF: Dad, you're never going to see what I am, so what's the use of arguing? If I strike oil I'll send you a check. Meantime forget I'm alive.

WILLY (*to* LINDA): Spite, see?

BIFF: Shake hands, Dad.

WILLY: Not my hand.

BIFF: I was hoping not to go this way.

WILLY: Well, this is the way you're going. Good-by. (BIFF *looks at him a moment, then turns sharply and goes to the stairs*.)

WILLY (*stops him with*): May you rot in hell if you leave this house!

BIFF (*turning*): Exactly what is it that you want from me?

WILLY: I want you to know, on the train, in the mountains, in the valleys, wherever you go, that you cut down your life for spite!

BIFF: No, no.

WILLY: Spite, spite, is the word of your undoing! And when you're down and out, remember what did it. When you're rotting somewhere beside the railroad tracks, remember, and don't you dare blame it on me!

BIFF: I'm not blaming it on you!

WILLY: I won't take the rap for this, you hear? (HAPPY *comes down the stairs and stands on the bottom step, watching*.)

BIFF: That's just what I'm telling you!

WILLY (*sinking into a chair at the table, with full accusation*): You're trying to put a knife in me—don't think I don't know what you're doing!

BIFF: All right, phony! Then let's lay it on the line. (*He whips the rubber tube out of his pocket and puts it on the table*.)

HAPPY: You crazy—

LINDA: Biff! (*She moves to grab the hose, but* BIFF *holds it down with his hand*.)

BIFF: Leave it there! Don't move it!

WILLY (*not looking at it*): What is that?

BIFF: You know goddam well what that is.

WILLY (*caged, wanting to escape*): I never saw that.

BIFF: You saw it. The mice didn't bring it into the cellar! What is this supposed to do, make a hero out of you? This supposed to make me sorry for you?

WILLY: Never heard of it.

BIFF: There'll be no pity for you, you hear it? No pity!

WILLY (*to* LINDA): You hear the spite!

BIFF: No, you're going to hear the truth—what you are and what I am!

LINDA: Stop it!

WILLY: Spite!

HAPPY (*coming down toward* BIFF): You cut it now!

BIFF (*to* HAPPY): The man don't know who we are! The man is gonna know! (*To* WILLY): We never told the truth for ten minutes in this house!

HAPPY: We always told the truth!

BIFF (*turning on him*): You big blow, are you the assistant buyer? You're one of the two assistants to the assistant, aren't you?

HAPPY: Well, I'm practically—

BIFF: You're practically full of it! We all are! And I'm through with it. (*To* WILLY): Now hear this, Willy, this is me.

WILLY: I know you!

BIFF: You know why I had no address for three months? I stole a suit in Kansas City and I was in jail. (*To* LINDA, *who is sobbing*): Stop crying. I'm through with it.

(LINDA *turns away from them, her hands covering her face.*)

WILLY: I suppose that's my fault!

BIFF: I stole myself out of every good job since high school!

WILLY: And whose fault is that?

BIFF: And I never got anywhere because you blew me so full of hot air I could never stand taking orders from anybody! That's whose fault it is!

WILLY: I hear that!

LINDA: Don't, Biff!

BIFF: It's goddam time you heard that! I had to be boss big shot in two weeks, and I'm through with it!

WILLY: Then hang yourself! For spite, hang yourself!

BIFF: No! Nobody's hanging himself, Willy! I ran down eleven flights with a pen in my hand today. And suddenly I stopped, you hear me? And in the middle of that office building, do you hear this? I stopped in the middle of that building and I saw—the sky. I saw the things that I love in this world. The work and the food and time to sit and smoke. And I looked at the pen and said to myself, what the hell am I grabbing this for? Why am I trying to become what I don't want to be? What am I doing in an office, making a contemptuous, begging fool of myself, when all I want is out there, waiting for me the minute I say I know who I am! Why can't I say that, Willy? (*He tries to make* WILLY *face him, but* WILLY *pulls away and moves to the left.*)

WILLY (*with hatred, threateningly*): The door of your life is wide open!

BIFF: Pop! I'm a dime a dozen, and so are you!

WILLY (*turning on him now in an uncontrolled outburst*): I am not a dime a dozen! I am Willy Loman, and you are Biff Loman!

(BIFF *starts for* WILLY, *but is blocked by* HAPPY. *In his fury,* BIFF *seems on the verge of attacking his father.*)

BIFF: I am not a leader of men, Willy, and neither are you. You were never anything but a hardworking drummer who landed in the ash can like all the rest of them! I'm one dollar an hour, Willy! I tried seven states and couldn't raise it. A buck an hour! Do you gather my meaning? I'm not bringing home any prizes any more, and you're going to stop waiting for me to bring them home!

WILLY (*directly to* BIFF): You vengeful, spiteful mut!

(BIFF *breaks from* HAPPY. WILLY, *in fright, starts up the stairs.* BIFF *grabs him.*)

BIFF (*at the peak of his fury*): Pop, I'm nothing! I'm nothing, Pop. Can't you understand that? There's no spite in it any more. I'm just what I am, that's all.

(BIFF'*s fury has spent itself, and he breaks down, sobbing, holding on to* WILLY, *who dumbly fumbles for* BIFF'*s face.*)

WILLY (*astonished*): What're you doing? What're you doing? (*To* LINDA): Why is he crying?

BIFF (*crying, broken*): Will you let me go, for Christ's sake? Will you take that phony dream and burn it before something happens? (*Struggling to contain himself, he pulls away and moves to the stairs.*) I'll go in the morning. Put him—put him to bed. (*Exhausted,* BIFF *moves up the stairs to his room.*)

WILLY (*after a long pause, astonished, elevated*): Isn't that—isn't that remarkable? Biff—he likes me!

LINDA: He loves you, Willy!

HAPPY (*deeply moved*): Always did, Pop.

WILLY: Oh, Biff! (*Staring wildly*): He cried! Cried to me. (*He is choking with his love, and now cries out his promise*): That boy—that boy is going to be magnificent!

(BEN *appears in the light just outside the kitchen.*)

BEN: Yes, outstanding, with twenty thousand behind him.

LINDA (*sensing the racing of his mind, fearfully, carefully*): Now come to bed, Willy. It's all settled now.

WILLY (*finding it difficult not to rush out of the house*): Yes, we'll sleep. Come on. Go to sleep, Hap.

BEN: And it does take a great kind of a man to crack the jungle.

(*In accents of dread, BEN's idyllic music starts up.*)

HAPPY (*his arm around LINDA*): I'm getting married, Pop, don't forget it. I'm changing everything. I'm gonna run that department before the year is up. You'll see, Mom. (*He kisses her.*)

BEN: The jungle is dark but full of diamonds, Willy.

(WILLY *turns, moves, listening to* BEN.)

LINDA: Be good. You're both good boys, just act that way, that's all.

HAPPY: 'Night, Pop. (*He goes upstairs.*)

LINDA (*to* WILLY): Come, dear.

BEN (*with greater force*): One must go in to fetch a diamond out.

WILLY (*to* LINDA, *as he moves slowly along the edge of the kitchen, toward the door*): I just want to get settled down, Linda. Let me sit alone for a little.

LINDA (*almost uttering her fear*): I want you upstairs.

WILLY (*taking her in his arms*): In a few minutes, Linda. I couldn't sleep right now. Go on, you look awful tired. (*He kisses her.*)

BEN: Not like an appointment at all. A diamond is rough and hard to the touch.

WILLY: Go on now. I'll be right up.

LINDA: I think this is the only way, Willy.

WILLY: Sure, it's the best thing.

BEN: Best thing!

WILLY: The only way. Everything is gonna be—go on, kid, get to bed. You look so tired.

LINDA: Come right up.

WILLY: Two minutes.

(LINDA *goes into the living-room, then reappears in her bedroom.* WILLY *moves just outside the kitchen door.*)

WILLY: Loves me. (*Wonderingly*): Always loved me. Isn't that a remarkable thing? Ben, he'll worship me for it!

BEN (*with promise*): It's dark there, but full of diamonds.

WILLY: Can you imagine that magnificence with twenty thousand dollars in his pocket?

LINDA (*calling from her room*): Willy! Come up!

WILLY (*calling into the kitchen*): Yes! Yes. Coming! It's very smart, you realize that, don't you, sweetheart? Even Ben sees it. I gotta go, baby. 'By! 'By! (*Going over to* BEN, *almost dancing*): Imagine? When the mail comes he'll be ahead of Bernard again!

BEN: A perfect proposition all around.

WILLY: Did you see how he cried to me? Oh, if I could kiss him, Ben!

BEN: Time, William, time!

WILLY: Oh, Ben, I always knew one way or another we were gonna make it, Biff and I!

BEN (*looking at his watch*): The boat. We'll be late. (*He moves slowly off into the darkness.*)

WILLY (*elegiacally, turning to the house*): Now when you kick off, boy, I want a seventy-yard boot, and get right down the field under the ball, and when you hit, hit low and hit hard, because it's important, boy. (*He swings around and faces the audience.*) There's all kinds of important people in the stands, and the first thing you know . . . (*Suddenly realizing he is alone*): Ben! Ben, where do I . . . ? (*He makes a sudden movement of search.*) Ben, how do I . . . ?

LINDA (*calling*): Willy, you coming up?

WILLY (*uttering a gasp of fear, whirling about as if to quiet her*): Sh! (*He turns around as if to find his way; sounds, faces, voices, seem to be swarming in upon him and he flicks at them, crying*) Sh! Sh! (*Suddenly music, faint and high, stops him. It rises in intensity, almost to an unbearable scream. He goes up and down on his toes, and rushes off around the house.*) Shhh!

LINDA: Willy?

(*There is no answer.* LINDA *waits.* BIFF *gets up off his bed. He is still in his clothes.* HAPPY *sits up.* BIFF *stands listening.*)

LINDA (*with real fear*): Willy, answer me! Willy!

(*There is the sound of a car starting and moving away at full speed.*)

LINDA: No!

BIFF (*rushing down the stairs*): Pop!

(*As the car speeds off, the music crashes down in a frenzy of sound, which becomes the soft pulsation of a single cello string.* BIFF *slowly returns to his bedroom. He and* HAPPY *gravely don their jackets.* LINDA *slowly walks out of her room. The music has developed into a dead march. The leaves of day are appearing over everything.* CHARLEY *and* BERNARD, *somberly dressed, appear and knock on the kitchen door.* BIFF *and* HAPPY *slowly descend the stairs to the kitchen as* CHARLEY *and* BERNARD *enter. All stop a moment when* LINDA, *in clothes of mourning, bearing a little bunch of roses, comes through the draped doorway into the kitchen. She goes to* CHARLEY *and takes his arm. Now all move toward the audience, through the wall-line of the kitchen. At the limit of the apron,* LINDA *lays down the flowers, kneels, and sits back on her heels. All stare down at the grave.)*

REQUIEM

CHARLEY: It's getting dark, Linda.

(LINDA *doesn't react. She stares at the grave.*)

BIFF: How about it, Mom? Better get some rest, heh? They'll be closing the gate soon.

(LINDA *makes no move. Pause.*)

HAPPY (*deeply angered*): He had no right to do that. There was no necessity for it. We would've helped him.

CHARLEY (*grunting*): Hmmm.

BIFF: Come along, Mom.

LINDA: Why didn't anybody come?

CHARLEY: It was a very nice funeral.

LINDA: But where are all the people he knew? Maybe they blame him.

CHARLEY: Naa. It's a rough world, Linda. They wouldn't blame him.

LINDA: I can't understand it. At this time especially. First time in thirty-five years we were just about free and clear. He only needed a little salary. He was even finished with the dentist.

CHARLEY: No man only needs a little salary.

LINDA: I can't understand it.

BIFF: There were a lot of nice days. When he'd come home from a trip; or on Sundays, making the stoop; finishing the cellar; putting on the new porch; when he built the extra bathroom; and put up the garage. You know something,

Charley, there's more of him in that front stoop than in all the sales he ever made.

CHARLEY: Yeah. He was a happy man with a batch of cement.

LINDA: He was so wonderful with his hands.

BIFF: He had the wrong dreams. All, all, wrong.

HAPPY (*almost ready to fight* BIFF): Don't say that!

BIFF: He never knew who he was.

CHARLEY (*stopping* HAPPY's *movement and reply. To* BIFF): Nobody dast blame this man. You don't understand: Willy was a salesman. And for a salesman, there is no rock bottom to the life. He don't put a bolt to a nut, he don't tell you the law or give you medicine. He's a man way out there in the blue, riding on a smile and a shoeshine. And when they start not smiling back—that's an earthquake. And then you get yourself a couple of spots on your hat, and you're finished. Nobody dast blame this man. A salesman is got to dream, boy. It comes with the territory.

BIFF: Charley, the man didn't know who he was.

HAPPY (*infuriated*): Don't say that!

BIFF: Why don't you come with me, Happy?

HAPPY: I'm not licked that easily. I'm staying right in this city, and I'm gonna beat this racket! (*He looks at* BIFF, *his chin set.*) The Loman Brothers!

BIFF: I know who I am, kid.

HAPPY: All right, boy. I'm gonna show you and everybody else that Willy Loman did not die in vain. He had a good dream. It's the only dream you can have—to come out number-one man. He fought it out here, and this is where I'm gonna win it for him.

BIFF (*with a hopeless glance at* HAPPY, *bends toward his mother*): Let's go, Mom.

LINDA: I'll be with you in a minute. Go on, Charley. (*He hesitates.*) I want to, just for a minute. I never had a chance to say good-by.

(CHARLEY *moves away, followed by* HAPPY. BIFF *remains a slight distance up and left of* LINDA. *She sits there, summoning herself. The flute begins, not far away, playing behind her speech.*)

LINDA: Forgive me, dear. I can't cry. I don't know what it is, but I can't cry. I don't understand it. Why did you ever do that? Help me, Willy, I can't cry. It seems to me that you're just on another trip. I keep expecting you. Willy, dear, I can't cry. Why did you do it? I search and search and I search, and I can't understand it, Willy. I made the last payment on the house today. Today, dear. And there'll be nobody home. (*A sob rises in her throat.*) We're free and clear. (*Sobbing more fully, released*): We're free. (BIFF *comes slowly toward her.*) We're free . . . We're free . . .

(BIFF *lifts her to her feet and moves out up right with her in his arms.* LINDA *sobs quietly.* BERNARD *and* CHARLEY *come together and follow them, followed by* HAPPY. *Only the music of the flute is left on the darkening stage as over the house the hard towers of the apartment buildings rise into sharp focus, and*)

THE CURTAIN FALLS

Introduction to *The Caucasian Chalk Circle*

WHEN THE PLAY WAS NEW

When Bertolt Brecht wrote *The Caucasian Chalk Circle* in 1944–1945, he was an exile from his country of Germany. Vehemently opposed to the Nazi regime of Adolf Hitler, he left a successful theatrical career in his native land for near anonymity abroad. After World War II ended, Brecht found it uncomfortable to live and work in the United States because he was a communist. Like Arthur Miller a few years later, he was called before the House Un-American Activities Committee in 1947. Brecht soon returned to what was now East Berlin in communist-controlled East Germany, where he was given permission and subsidy to form the Berliner Ensemble in 1949. Under the direction of Brecht this company presented the first professional production of *The Caucasian Chalk Circle* in its original German language in 1954. Because of the great interest taken in Brecht's work by translator Eric Bentley in the United States, there was a college English-language production in the United States as early as 1948, but the prologue was omitted. Despite the energetic work of Bentley, Brecht's influence in the United States was minor until the 1960s, when he became a gigantic influence here as well as in Europe.

The Caucasian Chalk Circle addresses a number of issues critical to events and conditions leading up to World War II, especially mindless violence, land-grabbing, and victims of war. The play depicts nearly impossible attempts to maintain dignity during troubled times, oppression by those with political power, and oppression by those with only a little. As an exile, virtually unknown outside of Germany, Brecht experienced much grief and rebuke, and consequently took on difficult, hard-edged subjects. But his results were frequently satirical and often humorous as he depicted theatrical worlds on the brink of destruc-

tion. Most of his major characters (like himself) are unlikely survivors in an insane world.

THE PLAYWRIGHT

Bertolt Brecht (1898–1956), a world renowned playwright, theorist, and director, has been and continues to be one of the most powerful influences on theatrical activity. His career began with expressionism in 1919 with plays such as *Baal* (1919) and *Drums in the Night* (1922), but he quickly found this movement and style unsatisfying. While working with the experimental director Erwin Piscator, Brecht found a style of performance and a political voice of dissent called epic theatre, which he continued to modify and fine-tune throughout his career. His body of theory and large collection of plays (both original and adaptations) have come to represent the best in Epic Theatre. Most of his Epic plays incorporate music and song. Some of the early plays such as *Threepenny Opera* (1928) and *Mahagonny* (1930), written with music by Kurt Weill, are characterized as musicals, but most of his works are plays with music.

Brecht strove to create a theatre in which intellect was more important than emotionality. Humor was a key component of this approach. He wanted his audiences to remain objective in order to respond to his social critique, political messages, and call for action. Many of his early plays were also *leherstücke* (teaching plays). These short sketches and one-act plays demonstrated the need for revolution and used dramatized problems and the characters' attempts to solve them to express social and political lessons. One of the best of these is the one-act *The Measures Taken* (1930).

As a communist and anti-fascist in the 1930s, Brecht was quickly blacklisted by the Nazis and had to flee his country once Hitler rose to national control in 1933. In exile—first in western Europe and later the United States—he wrote some of his finest work, often in collaboration with many different writers and translators. The most famous of these plays are *Mother Courage and Her Children* (1939), a play about war, commercialism, and greed; *The Life of Galileo* (1938/1947), a reexamination of the conscience of the famous scientist; *The Good Person of Setzuan* (1940), one of several plays set by Brecht in Asian environments; and *The Caucasian Chalk Circle,* another "Asian" play. Brecht was fascinated by locations foreign to his experience, but once he visited the locations, he never wrote about them again. His "American" plays, for example, were written before his exile there.

After returning to Berlin in 1948, he opened the Berliner Ensemble, which he led until his death in 1956. The company was subsequently led by his wife, the actress Helene Weigel, who also played leading or major roles in many of his productions, such as the title role in *Mother Courage* and Natella, the governor's wife, in *The Caucasian Chalk Circle.* Although reorganized several times over the years, the Berliner Ensemble remains one of the world's leading theatre companies.

As a theatre practitioner Brecht was fond of saying, "the proof of the pudding is in the eating." He frequently cut and revised his plays and made radical changes when he found that a line, dramatic action, stage device, or scene did not work effectively in rehearsal or performance. This method of working is also evident in his published theory, which underwent serious revision as he placed his theory into practice.

GENRE, STRUCTURE, AND STYLE

The epic style evident in *The Caucasian Chalk Circle* and most of Brecht's plays is not reality-based even though he often drew very compelling characters. The presentation of events is episodic—we see only key moments in long-term development of the action. He often assigns titles to each scene and the titles are either projected on the stage or spoken by a narrator or singer. This narrative element is one of the reasons that the word "epic" was selected to distinguish this style from representational plays that typically encompass brief periods of time and create the illusion of real life on the stage. Most of the action in such a play is linear, but in *The Caucasian Chalk Circle* Brecht starts all over in Act II, backing up in time to introduce the story of Azdak (the drunken fake judge and principal character of the second act) until Azdak's development reaches the point where the action of Act I had concluded with the capture of Grusha (the poor palace maid and leading character of Act I). Late in Act II the two stories and lines of action become one in Grusha's trial, by means of which Azdak must resolve the conflict of Grusha's action with his perverse judgment.

A key element in Epic Theatre is *Verfremdungseffekt.* Although often translated in English as "alienation," "to make strange" is a more accurate (even if more awkward) meaning of the word. *Verfremdungseffekt* was Brecht's attempt to make strange things commonplace and the commonplace strange in order to compel his audience to analyze events and character decisions without losing objectivity through emotionality. To accomplish this he utilized many devices, such as songs unrelated to the story or character development but critical to the ideas in the play. Songs are introduced suddenly instead of creating emotional segues as we see in so many traditional musicals. Brecht would often project the lyrics on a screen or placard at the same time—the audience could thus read as well as listen. His settings are emblematic rather than realistic, matched by theatrical lighting and costumes that are often stylized as well. In his production of *The Caucasian Chalk Circle,* for example, the entire natural landscape surrounding Grusha on her journey into the mountains was represented by a large, silken cloth hanging from the flies decorated by a single tree painted in an Asian style.

Brecht used masks for many characters. In *The Caucasian Chalk Circle* many of the wicked or selfish characters, such as the governor's wife, wear masks; the sympathetic characters, such as Grusha and Simon, do not. Narrators often interrupt action to comment on it. The Prologue of *The Caucasian Chalk Circle* reminds us that the main action of the play is a play-within-a-play, a celebration of the prologue's satisfactory political conclusion. A large revolving stage, called for in many of Brecht's plays, was used very effectively in Brecht's first production for

Grusha's journeys. Also typical of Brecht is a large cast of characters and the expectation that doubling would occur in the casting.

In many of Brecht's plays, including *The Caucasian Chalk Circle*, the primary action is set in the distant past. Brecht called this distancing "historicization," not just because the play is set long ago, but because he wanted to demonstrate that the world has changed, but does so very slowly. He hoped to convince his audiences that social and political change could and should take place much more quickly.

IMPORTANT ELEMENTS OF CONTENT

Several ideas are critical to the action of the play. Brecht asserts that its world is so full of evil that corruption must be employed by the good in order to create any kind of justice. The only way for Grusha to get justice is through the illegalities of Azdak, the corrupt and unqualified judge. Brecht also seriously questions traditional notions of ownership; he claims that property should go to those who are good for it. In nearly every play, Brecht attacks the evils of the rich and powerful and sympathizes with the plight of the poor and oppressed. In his work Brecht often wrote lines such as "fill the belly first, then decide what is right."

THE PLAY IN REVIVAL

The Caucasian Chalk Circle has enjoyed many major revivals since its German premiere in 1956. The Berliner Ensemble kept it in its permanent repertory, and the play has been especially popular in Britain, Canada, and the United States. It has had one Broadway production at Lincoln Center in 1966, and many off-Broadway productions in the twentieth and twenty-first centuries. Many regional theatres have performed it, beginning with the inaugural production of Arena Stage in Washington, D.C., in 1961 under the powerful direction of Alan Schneider. This production was followed by that of the Guthrie Theatre in Minneapolis in 1965 and

by many more afterwards. In recent years the play has been remarkably popular at colleges and universities, with every season sporting several new productions. Interestingly, many productions, both early and recent, either cut the prologue or replaced it with a new scene intended to bring the issues more up-to-date and de-emphasize the Marxist philosophy. *The Caucasian Chalk Circle* remains one of Brecht's most popular and resilient works.

SPECIAL FEATURE

The Caucasian Chalk Circle is a play with music, not a musical. There is a singer (narrator) who, along with a chorus, is our guide through the action of the play. Some productions use more than one narrator, who in turn often play various characters in the action. The songs of the singer often provide commentary for the ideas of the play. Grusha sings periodically as well, and her songs are less about her story than about conditions in the world around her.

FURTHER READING ABOUT THE PLAY, PLAYWRIGHT, AND CONTEXT

For the largest collection of Brecht's plays that have been translated into English, see Bertolt Brecht, *Collected Plays*, a multi-volume collection edited by Ralph Manheim and John Willett.

For the life and times of Brecht, see John Fuegi, *Brecht and Company*; Frederic Ewen, *Bertolt Brecht: His Life, His Art, and His Times*; Martin Esslin, *Bertolt Brecht: A Choice of Evils*; and Ruth Berlau, *Living for Brecht*.

For criticism and production history, see Eric Bentley, *The Brecht Commentaries*, and John Fuegi, *Chaos According to Plan*.

For the collected dramatic and theatrical theory of Brecht, see *Brecht on Theatre*, edited by John Willett.

The Caucasian Chalk Circle

BY BERTOLT BRECHT

TRANSLATED BY ERIC BENTLEY

CHARACTERS

OLD MAN ON THE RIGHT
PEASANT WOMAN ON THE RIGHT
YOUNG PEASANT
A VERY YOUNG WORKER
OLD MAN ON THE LEFT
PEASANT WOMAN ON THE LEFT
AGRICULTURIST KATO
GIRL TRACTORIST
WOUNDED SOLDIER
THE DELEGATE   from the capital
THE SINGER
GEORGI ABASHWILI   the Governor
NATELLA   the Governor's wife
MICHAEL   their son
SHALVA   an adjutant
ARSEN KAZBEKI   a fat prince
MESSENGER   from the capital
NIKO MIKADZE AND MIKA LOLADZE   doctors
SIMON SHASHAVA   a soldier
GRUSHA VASHNADZE   a kitchen maid
OLD PEASANT   with the milk
CORPORAL AND PRIVATE
PEASANT AND HIS WIFE
LAVRENTI VASHNADZE   Grusha's brother
ANIKO   his wife
PEASANT WOMAN   for a while Grusha's mother-in-law
JUSSUP   her son
MONK
AZDAK   village recorder
SHAUWA   a policeman
GRAND DUKE
DOCTOR
INVALID
LIMPING MAN
BLACKMAILER
LUDOVICA
INNKEEPER   her father-in-law

STABLEBOY
POOR OLD PEASANT WOMAN
IRAKLI   her brother-in-law, a bandit
THREE WEALTHY FARMERS
ILLO SHUBOLADZE AND SANDRO OBOLADZE   lawyers
OLD MARRIED COUPLE
SOLDIERS, SERVANTS, PEASANTS, BEGGARS, MUSICIANS, MERCHANTS, NOBLES, ARCHITECTS

The time and the place: After a prologue, set in 1945, we move back perhaps 1000 years.

The action of The Caucasian Chalk Circle *centers on Nuka (or Nukha), a town in Azerbaijan. However, the capital referred to in the prologue is not Baku (capital of Soviet Azerbaijan) but Tiflis (or Tbilisi), capital of Georgia. When Azdak, later, refers to "the capital" he means Nuka itself, though whether Nuka was ever capital of Georgia I do not know: in what reading I have done on the subject I have only found Nuka to be the capital of a Nuka Khanate.*

The word "Georgia" has not been used in this English version because of its American associations: instead, the alternative name "Grusinia" (in Russian, Gruziya) has been used.

The reasons for resettling the old Chinese story in Trans-caucasia are not far to seek. The play was written when the Soviet chief of state, Joseph Stalin, was a Georgian, as was his favorite poet, cited in the Prologue, Mayakovsky. And surely there is a point in having this story acted out at the place where Europe and Asia meet, a place incomparably rich in legend and history. Here Jason found the Golden Fleece. Here Noah's Ark touched ground. Here the armies of both Genghis Khan and Tamerlane wrought havoc.

—E. B.

PROLOGUE

Summer, 1945.

Among the ruins of a war-ravaged Caucasian village the members of two Kolkhoz villages, mostly women and older men, are sitting in a circle, smoking and drinking wine. With them is a DELEGATE *of the State Reconstruction Commission from Nuka.*

PEASANT WOMAN, LEFT (*pointing*): In those hills over there we stopped three Nazi tanks, but the apple orchard was already destroyed.

OLD MAN, RIGHT: Our beautiful dairy farm: a ruin.

GIRL TRACTORIST: I laid the fire, Comrade.

(*Pause.*)

DELEGATE: Nuka, Azerbaijan S.S.R. Delegation received from the goat-breeding Kolkhoz "Rosa Luxemburg." This is a collective farm which moved eastwards on orders from the authorities at the approach of Hitler's armies. They are now planning to return. Their delegates have looked at the village and the land and found a lot of destruction. (DELEGATES *on the right nod.*) But the neighboring fruit farm— Kolkhoz (*to the left*) "Galinsk"—proposes to use the former grazing land of Kolkhoz "Rosa Luxemburg" for orchards and vineyards. This land lies in a valley where grass doesn't grow very well. As a delegate of the Reconstruction Commission in Nuka I request that the two Kolkhoz villages decide between themselves whether Kolkhoz "Rosa Luxemburg" shall return or not.

OLD MAN, RIGHT: First of all, I want to protest against the time limit on discussion. We of Kolkhoz "Rosa Luxemburg" have spent three days and three nights getting here. And now discussion is limited to half a day.

WOUNDED SOLDIER, LEFT: Comrade, we haven't as many villages as we used to have. We haven't as many hands. We haven't as much time.

GIRL TRACTORIST: All pleasures have to be rationed. Tobacco is rationed, and wine. Discussion should be rationed.

OLD MAN, RIGHT (*sighing*): Death to the fascists! But I will come to the point and explain why we want our valley back. There are a great many reasons, but I'll begin with one of the simplest.

Makinä Abakidze, unpack the goat cheese. (*A* PEASANT WOMAN FROM RIGHT *takes from a basket an enormous cheese wrapped in a cloth. Applause and laughter.*) Help yourselves, Comrades, start in!

OLD MAN, LEFT (*suspiciously*): Is this a way of influencing us?

OLD MAN, RIGHT (*amid laughter*): How could it be a way of influencing you, Surab, you valley-thief? Everyone knows you'll take the cheese and the valley, too. (*Laughter.*) All I expect from you is an honest answer. Do you like the cheese?

OLD MAN, LEFT: The answer is: yes.

OLD MAN, RIGHT: Really. (*Bitterly.*) I ought to have known you know nothing about cheese.

OLD MAN, LEFT: Why not? When I tell you I like it?

OLD MAN, RIGHT: Because you can't like it. Because it's not what it was in the old days. And why not? Because our goats don't like the new grass as they did the old. Cheese is not cheese because grass is not grass, that's the thing. Please put that in your report.

OLD MAN, LEFT: But your cheese is excellent.

OLD MAN, RIGHT: It isn't excellent. It's just passable. The new grazing land is no good, whatever the young people may say. One can't live there. It doesn't even smell of morning in the morning. (*Several people laugh.*)

DELEGATE: Don't mind their laughing: they understand you. Comrades, why does one love one's country? Because the bread tastes better there, the air smells better, voices sound stronger, the sky is higher, the ground is easier to walk on. Isn't that so?

OLD MAN, RIGHT: The valley has belonged to us from all eternity.

SOLDIER, LEFT: What does *that* mean—from all eternity? Nothing belongs to anyone from all eternity. When you were young you didn't even belong to yourself. You belonged to the Kazbeki princes.

OLD MAN, RIGHT: Doesn't it make a difference, though, what kind of trees stand next to the house you are born in? Or what kind of neighbors you have? Doesn't that make a difference? We want to go back just to have you as our neighbors, valley-thieves! Now you can all laugh again.

OLD MAN, LEFT (*laughing*): Then why don't you listen to what your neighbor, Kato Wachtang, our agriculturist, has to say about the valley?

PEASANT WOMAN, RIGHT: We've not said all we have to say about our valley. By no means. Not all the houses are destroyed. As for the dairy farm, at least the foundation wall is still standing.

DELEGATE: You can claim State support—here and there—you know that. I have suggestions here in my pocket.

PEASANT WOMAN, RIGHT: Comrade Specialist, we haven't come here to haggle. I can't take your cap and hand you another, and say "This one's better." The other one might *be* better, but you *like* yours better.

GIRL TRACTORIST: A piece of land is not a cap—not in our country, Comrade.

DELEGATE: Don't get mad. It's true we have to consider a piece of land as a tool to produce something useful, but it's also true that we must recognize love for a particular piece of land. As far as I'm concerned, I'd like to find out more exactly what you (*to those on the left*) want to do with the valley.

OTHERS: Yes, let Kato speak.

KATO (*rising; she's in military uniform*): Comrades, last winter, while we were fighting in these hills here as Partisans, we discussed how, once the Germans were expelled, we could build up our fruit culture to ten times its original size. I've prepared a plan for an irrigation project. By means of a cofferdam on our mountain lake, 300 hectares of unfertile land can be irrigated. Our Kolkhoz could not only cultivate more fruit, but also have vineyards. The project, however, would pay only if the disputed valley of Kolkhoz "Rosa Luxemburg" were also included. Here are the calculations. (*She hands* DELEGATE *a briefcase.*)

OLD MAN, RIGHT: Write into the report that our Kolkhoz plans to start a new stud farm.

GIRL TRACTORIST: Comrades, the project was conceived during days and nights when we had to take cover in the mountains. We were often without ammunition for our half-dozen rifles. Even finding a pencil was difficult. (*Applause from both sides.*)

OLD MAN, RIGHT: Our thanks to the Comrades of Kolkhoz "Galinsk" and all those who've defended our country! (*They shake hands and embrace.*)

PEASANT WOMAN, LEFT: In doing this our thought was that our soldiers—both your men and our men—should return to a still more productive homeland.

GIRL TRACTORIST: As the poet Mayakovsky said: "The home of the Soviet people shall also be the home of Reason"!

(*The delegates excluding the* OLD MAN *have got up, and with the* DELEGATE *specified proceed to study the Agriculturist's drawings. Exclamations such as. "Why is the altitude of fall 22 meters?"— "This rock will have to be blown up"— "Actually, all they need is cement and dynamite"— "They force the water to come down here, that's clever!"*)

A VERY YOUNG WORKER, RIGHT (*to* OLD MAN, RIGHT): They're going to irrigate all the fields between the hills, look at that, Aleko!

OLD MAN, RIGHT: I'm not going to look. I knew the project would be good. I won't have a pistol pointed at me!

DELEGATE: But they only want to point a pencil at you!

(*Laughter.*)

OLD MAN, RIGHT (*gets up gloomily, and walks over to look at the drawings*): These valley-thieves know only too well that we in this country are suckers for machines and projects.

PEASANT WOMAN, RIGHT: Aleko Bereshwili, you have a weakness for new projects. That's well known.

DELEGATE: What about my report? May I write that you will all support the cession of your old valley in the interests of this project when you get back to your Kolkhoz?

PEASANT WOMAN, RIGHT: I will. What about you, Aleko?

OLD MAN, RIGHT (*bent over drawings*): I suggest that you give us copies of the drawings to take along.

PEASANT WOMAN, RIGHT: Then we can sit down and eat. Once he has the drawings and he's ready to discuss them, the matter is settled. I know him. And it will be the same with the rest of us. (*Delegates laughingly embrace again.*)

OLD MAN, LEFT: Long live the Kolkhoz "Rosa Luxemburg" and much luck to your horse-breeding project!

PEASANT WOMAN, LEFT: In honor of the visit of the delegates from Kolkhoz "Rosa Luxemburg" and of the Specialist, the plan is that we all hear a presentation of the Singer Arkadi Tscheidse.

(*Applause.* GIRL TRACTORIST *has gone off to bring the* SINGER.)

PEASANT WOMAN, RIGHT: Comrades, your entertainment had better be good. It's going to cost us a valley.

PEASANT WOMAN, LEFT: Arkadi Tscheidse knows about our discussion. He's promised to perform something that has a bearing on the problem.

KATO: We wired Tiflis three times. The whole thing nearly fell through at the last minute because his driver had a cold.

PEASANT WOMAN, LEFT: Arkadi Tscheidse knows 21,000 lines of verse.

OLD MAN, LEFT: He's hard to get. You and the Planning Commission should persuade him to come north more often, Comrade.

DELEGATE: We are more interested in economics, I'm afraid.

OLD MAN, LEFT (*smiling*): You arrange the redistribution of vines and tractors, why not songs?

(*Enter the* SINGER *Arkadi Tscheidse, led by* GIRL TRACTORIST. *He is a well-built man of simple manners, accompanied by* FOUR MUSICIANS *with their instruments. The artists are greeted with applause.*)

GIRL TRACTORIST: This is the Comrade Specialist, Arkadi.

(*The* SINGER *greets them all.*)

DELEGATE: Honored to make your acquaintance. I heard about your songs when I was a boy at school. Will it be one of the old legends?

SINGER: A very old one. It's called "The Chalk Circle" and comes from the Chinese. But we'll do it, of course, in a changed version. Comrades, it's an honor for me to entertain you after a difficult debate. We hope you will find that the voice of the old poet also sounds well in the shadow of Soviet tractors. It may be a mistake to mix different wines, but old and new wisdom mix admirably. Now I hope we'll

get something to eat before the performance begins—it would certainly help.

VOICES: Surely. Everyone into the Club House!

(*While everyone begins to move,* DELEGATE *turns to* GIRL TRACTORIST.)

DELEGATE: I hope it won't take long. I've got to get back tonight.

GIRL TRACTORIST: How long will it last, Arkadi? The Comrade Specialist must get back to Tiflis tonight.

SINGER (*casually*): It's actually two stories. An hour or two.

GIRL TRACTORIST (*confidentially*): Couldn't you make it shorter?

SINGER: No.

VOICE: Arkadi Tscheidse's performance will take place here in the square after the meal.

(*And they all go happily to eat.*)

1

THE NOBLE CHILD

As the lights go up, the SINGER *is seen sitting on the floor, a black sheepskin cloak round his shoulders, and a little, well-thumbed notebook in his hand. A small group of listeners—the chorus—sits with him. The manner of his recitation makes it clear that he has told his story over and over again. He mechanically fingers the pages, seldom looking at them. With appropriate gestures, he gives the signal for each scene to begin.*

SINGER: In olden times, in a bloody time,
    There ruled in a Caucasian city—
    Men called it City of the Damned—
    A Governor.
    His name was Georgi Abashwili,
    He was rich as Croesus
    He had a beautiful wife
    He had a healthy baby.
    No other governor in Grusinia
    Had so many horses in his stable
    So many beggars on his doorstep
    So many soldiers in his service
    So many petitioners in his courtyard.
    Georgi Abashwili—how shall I describe
      him to you?
    He enjoyed his life.

On the morning of Easter Sunday
The Governor and his family went to
church.

(*At the left a large doorway, at the right an even larger gateway.* BEGGARS *and* PETITIONERS *pour from the gateway, holding up thin* CHILDREN, *crutches, and petitions. They are followed by* IRONSHIRTS, *and then, expensively dressed, the* GOVERNOR'S FAMILY.)

BEGGARS AND PETITIONERS: —Mercy! Mercy, Your Grace! The taxes are too high.
—I lost my leg in the Persian War, where can I get . . .
—My brother is innocent, Your Grace, a misunderstanding . . .
—The child is starving in my arms!
—Our petition is for our son's discharge from the army, our last remaining son!
—Please, Your Grace, the water inspector takes bribes.

(*One servant collects the petitions. Another distributes coins from a purse. Soldiers push the crowd back, lashing at them with thick leather whips.*)

SOLDIER: Get back! Clear the church door!

(*Behind the* GOVERNOR, *his* WIFE, *and the* ADJUTANT, *the* GOVERNOR'S CHILD *is brought through the gateway in an ornate carriage.*)

CROWD: —The baby!
—I can't see it, don't shove so hard!
—God bless the child, Your Grace!

SINGER (*while the crowd is driven back with whips*): For the first time on that Easter Sunday, the people saw the Governor's heir.
Two doctors never moved from the noble child, apple of the Governor's eye.
Even the mighty Prince Kazbeki bows before him at the church door.

(*The* FAT PRINCE *steps forwards and greets the* FAMILY.)

FAT PRINCE: Happy Easter, Natella Abashwili! What a day! When it was raining last night, I thought to myself, gloomy holidays! But this morning the sky was gay. I love a gay sky, a simple heart, Natella Abashwili. And little Michael is a governor from head to food! Titíti! (*He tickles the* CHILD.)

GOVERNOR'S WIFE: What do you think, Arsen, at last Georgi has decided to start building the east wing. All those wretched slums are to be torn down to make room for the garden.

FAT PRINCE: Good news after so much bad! What's the latest on the war, Brother Georgi? (*The* GOVERNOR *indicates a lack of interest.*) Strategical retreat, I hear. Well, minor reverses are to be expected. Sometimes things go well, sometimes not. Such is war. Doesn't mean a thing, does it?

GOVERNOR'S WIFE: He's coughing. Georgi, did you hear? (*She speaks sharply to the* DOCTORS, *two dignified men standing close to the little carriage.*) He's coughing!

FIRST DOCTOR (*to the* SECOND): May I remind you, Niko Mikadze, that I was against the lukewarm bath? (*To the* GOVERNOR'S WIFE:) There's been a little error over warming the bath water, Your Grace.

SECOND DOCTOR (*equally polite*): Mika Loladze, I'm afraid I can't agree with you. The temperature of the bath water was exactly what our great, beloved Mishiko Oboladze prescribed. More likely a slight draft during the night, Your Grace.

GOVERNOR'S WIFE: But do pay more attention to him. He looks feverish, Georgi.

FIRST DOCTOR (*bending over the* CHILD): No cause for alarm, Your Grace. The bath water will be warmer. It won't occur again.

SECOND DOCTOR (*with a venomous glance at the* FIRST): I won't forget that, my dear Mika Loladze. No cause for concern, Your Grace.

FAT PRINCE: Well, well, well! I always say: "A pain in my liver? Then the doctor gets fifty strokes on the soles of his feet." We live in a decadent age. In the old days one said: "Off with his head!"

GOVERNOR'S WIFE: Let's go into church. Very likely it's the draft here.

(*The procession of* FAMILY *and* SERVANTS *turns into the doorway. The* FAT PRINCE *follows, but the* GOVERNOR *is kept back by the* ADJUTANT, *a handsome young man. When the crowd of* PETITIONERS *has been driven off, a young dust-stained* RIDER, *his arm in a sling, remains behind.*)

ADJUTANT (*pointing at the* RIDER, *who steps forward*): Won't you hear the messenger from the capital, Your Excellency? He arrived this morning. With confidential papers.

GOVERNOR: Not before Service, Shalva. But did you hear Brother Kazbeki wish me a happy Easter? Which is all very well, but I don't believe it did rain last night.

ADJUTANT (*nodding*): We must investigate.

GOVERNOR: Yes, at once. Tomorrow.

(*They pass through the doorway. The* RIDER, *who has waited in vain for an audience, turns sharply round and, muttering a curse, goes of. Only one of the palace guards—*SIMON SHASHAVA—*remains at the door.*)

SINGER: The city is still.

> Pigeons strut in the church square.
> A soldier of the Palace Guard
> Is joking with a kitchen maid
> As she comes up from the river with a bundle.

(*A girl—*GRUSHA VASHNADZE—*comes through the gateway with a bundle made of large green leaves under her arm.*)

SIMON: What, the young lady is not in church? Shirking?

GRUSHA: I was dressed to go. But they needed another goose for the banquet. And they asked me to get it. I know about geese.

SIMON: A goose? (*He feigns suspicion.*) I'd like to see that goose. (GRUSHA *does not understand.*) One must be on one's guard with women. "I only went for a fish," they tell you, but it turns out to be something else.

GRUSHA (*walking resolutely toward him and showing him the goose*): There! If it isn't a fifteen-pound goose stuffed full of corn, I'll eat the feathers.

SIMON: A queen of a goose! The Governor himself will eat it. So the young lady has been down to the river again?

GRUSHA: Yes, at the poultry farm.

SIMON: Really? At the poultry farm, down by the river . . . not higher up maybe? Near those willows?

GRUSHA: I only go to the willows to wash the linen.

SIMON (*insinuatingly*): Exactly.

GRUSHA: Exactly what?

SIMON (*winking*): Exactly that.

GRUSHA: Why shouldn't I wash the linen by the willows?

SIMON (*with exaggerated laughter*): "Why shouldn't I wash the linen by the willows!" That's good, really good!

GRUSHA: I don't understand the soldier. What's so good about it?

SIMON (*slyly*): "If something I know someone learns, she'll grow hot and cold by turns!"

GRUSHA: I don't know what I could learn about those willows.

SIMON: Not even if there was a bush opposite? That one could see everything from? Everything that goes on there when a certain person is—"washing linen"?

GRUSHA: What does go on? Won't the soldier say what he means and have done?

SIMON: Something goes on. Something can be seen.

GRUSHA: Could the soldier mean I dip my toes in the water when it's hot? There's nothing else.

SIMON: There's more. Your toes. And more.

GRUSHA: More what? At most my foot?

SIMON: Your foot. And a little more. (*He laughs heartily.*)

GRUSHA (*angrily*): Simon Shashava, you ought to be ashamed of yourself! To sit in a bush on a hot day and wait till a girl comes and dips her legs in the river! And I bet you bring a friend along too! (*She runs off.*)

SIMON (*shouting after her*): I didn't bring any friend along!

(*As the* SINGER *resumes his tale, the* SOLDIER *steps into the doorway as though to listen to the service.*)

SINGER: The city lies still

> But why are there armed men?
> The Governor's palace is at peace
> But why is it a fortress?
> And the Governor returned to his palace
> And the fortress was a trap
> And the goose was plucked and roasted
> But the goose was not eaten this time
> And noon was no longer the hour to eat:
> Noon was the hour to die.

(*From the doorway at the left the* FAT PRINCE *quickly appears, stands still, looks around. Before the gateway at the right two* IRONSHIRTS *are squatting and playing dice. The* FAT PRINCE *sees them, walks slowly past, making a sign to them. They rise: one goes through the gateway, the other goes off at the right. Muffled voices are heard from various directions in the rear: "To your posts!" The palace is surrounded. The* FAT PRINCE *quickly goes off. Church bells in the distance. Enter, through the doorway, the* GOVERNOR'S FAMILY *and procession, returning from church.*)

GOVERNOR'S WIFE (*passing the* ADJUTANT): It's impossible to live in such a slum. But Georgi, of course, will only build for his little Michael. Never for me! Michael is all! All for Michael! (*The procession turns into the gateway. Again the* ADJUTANT *lingers behind. He waits. Enter the wounded* RIDER *from the doorway. Two* IRONSHIRTS *of the Palace Guard have taken up positions by the gateway.*)

ADJUTANT (*to the* RIDER): The Governor does not wish to receive military news before dinner—especially if it's depressing, as I assume. In the afternoon His Excellency will confer with prominent architects. They're coming to dinner too. And here they are! (*Enter three gentlemen through the doorway.*) Go to the kitchen and eat, my friend. (*As the* RIDER *goes, the* ADJUTANT *greets the* ARCHITECTS.) Gentlemen, His Excellency expects you at dinner. He will devote all his time to you and your great new plans. Come!

ONE OF THE ARCHITECTS: We marvel that His Excellency intends to build. There are disquieting rumors that the war in Persia has taken a turn for the worse.

ADJUTANT: All the more reason to build! There's nothing to those rumors anyway. Persia is a long way off, and the garrison here would let itself be hacked to bits for its Governor. (*Noise from the palace. The shrill scream of a woman. Someone is shouting orders. Dumbfounded, the* ADJUTANT *moves toward the gateway. An* IRONSHIRT *steps out, points his lance at him.*) What's this? Put down that lance, you dog.

ONE OF THE ARCHITECTS: It's the Princes! Don't you know the Princes met last night in the capital? And they're against the Grand Duke and his Governors? Gentlemen, we'd better make ourselves scarce. (*They rush off. The* ADJUTANT *remains helplessly behind.*)

ADJUTANT (*furiously to the* PALACE GUARD): Down with those lances! Don't you see the Governor's life is threatened? (*The* IRONSHIRTS *of the Palace Guard refuse to obey. They stare coldly and indifferently at the* ADJUTANT *and follow the next events without interest.*)

SINGER: O blindness of the great!
 They go their way like gods,

 Great over bent backs,
 Sure of hired fists,
 Trusting in the power
 Which has lasted so long.
 But long is not forever.
 O change from age to age!
 Thou hope of the people!

(*Enter the* GOVERNOR, *through the gateway, between two* SOLDIERS *armed to the teeth. He is in chains. His face is gray.*)

 Up, great sir, deign to walk upright!
 From your palace the eyes of many foes
  follow you!
 And now you don't need an architect, a
  carpenter will do.
 You won't be moving into a new palace
 But into a little hole in the ground.
 Look about you once more, blind man!

(*The arrested man looks round.*)

 Does all you had please you?
 Between the Easter Mass and the Easter
  meal
 You are walking to a place whence no one
  returns.

(*The* GOVERNOR *is led off. A horn sounds an alarm. Noise behind the gateway.*)

 When the house of a great one collapses
 Many little ones are slain.
 Those who had no share in the *good* fortunes of the mighty
 Often have a share in their *mis*fortunes.
 The plunging wagon
 Drags the sweating oxen down with it
 Into the abyss.

(*The* SERVANTS *come rushing through the gateway in panic.*)

SERVANTS (*among themselves*): —The baskets!
—Take them all into the third courtyard! Food for five days!
—The mistress has fainted! Someone must carry her down.
—She must get away.
—What about us? We'll be slaughtered like chickens, as always.
—Goodness, what'll happen? There's bloodshed already in the city, they say.
—Nonsense, the Governor has just been asked to appear at a Princes' meeting. All

very correct. Everything'll be ironed out. I heard this on the best authority . . .

(*The two* DOCTORS *rush into the courtyard.*)

FIRST DOCTOR (*trying to restrain the other*): Niko Mikadze, it is your duty as a doctor to attend Natella Abashwili.

SECOND DOCTOR: My duty! It's yours!

FIRST DOCTOR: Whose turn is it to look after the child today, Niko Mikadze, yours or mine?

SECOND DOCTOR: Do you really think, Mika Loladze, I'm going to stay a minute longer in this accursed house on that little brat's account? (*They start fighting. All one hears is: "You neglect your duty!" and "Duty, my foot!" Then the* SECOND DOCTOR *knocks the* FIRST *down.*) Go to hell! (*Exit.*)

(*Enter the soldier,* SIMON SHASHAVA. *He searches in the crowd for* GRUSHA.)

SIMON: Grusha! There you are at last! What are you going to do?

GRUSHA: Nothing. If worst comes to worst, I've a brother in the mountains. How about you?

SIMON: Forget about me. (*Formally again:*) Grusha Vashnadze, your wish to know my plans fills me with satisfaction. I've been ordered to accompany Madam Abashwili as her guard.

GRUSHA: But hasn't the Palace Guard mutinied?

SIMON (*seriously*): That's a fact.

GRUSHA: Isn't it dangerous to go with her?

SIMON: In Tiflis, they say: Isn't the stabbing dangerous for the knife?

GRUSHA: You're not a knife, you're a man, Simon Shashava, what has that woman to do with you?

SIMON: That woman has nothing to do with me. I have my orders, and I go.

GRUSHA: The soldier is pigheaded: he is running into danger for nothing—nothing at all. I must get into the third courtyard, I'm in a hurry.

SIMON: Since we're both in a hurry we shouldn't quarrel. You need time for a good quarrel. May I ask if the young lady still has parents?

GRUSHA: No, just a brother.

SIMON: As time is short—my second question is this: Is the young lady as healthy as a fish in water?

GRUSHA: I may have a pain in the right shoulder once in a while. Otherwise I'm strong enough for my job. No one has complained. So far.

SIMON: That's well known. When it's Easter Sunday, and the question arises who'll run for the goose all the same, she'll be the one. My third question is this: Is the young lady impatient? Does she want apples in winter?

GRUSHA: Impatient? No. But if a man goes to war without any reason and then no message comes—that's bad.

SIMON: A message will come. And now my final question . . .

GRUSHA: Simon Shashava, I must get to the third courtyard at once. My answer is yes.

SIMON (*very embarrassed*): Haste, they say, is the wind that blows down the scaffolding. But they also say: The rich don't know what haste is. I'm from . . .

GRUSHA: Kutsk . . .

SIMON: The young lady has been inquiring about me? I'm healthy, I have no dependents, I make ten piasters a month, as paymaster twenty piasters, and I'm asking—very sincerely—for your hand.

GRUSHA: Simon Shashava, it suits me well.

SIMON (*taking from his neck a thin chain with a little cross on it*): My mother gave me this cross, Grusha Vashnadze. The chain is silver. Please wear it.

GRUSHA: Many thanks, Simon.

SIMON (*hangs it round her neck*): It would be better to go to the third courtyard now. Or there'll be difficulties. Anyway, I must harness the horses. The young lady will understand?

GRUSHA: Yes, Simon.

(*They stand undecided.*)

SIMON: I'll just take the mistress to the troops that have stayed loyal. When the war's over, I'll be back. In two weeks. Or three. I hope my intended won't get tired, awaiting my return.

GRUSHA: Simon Shashava, I shall wait for you.

> Go calmly into battle, soldier
> The bloody battle, the bitter battle
> From which not everyone returns:
> When you return I shall be there.
> I shall be waiting for you under the
>   green elm
> I shall be waiting for you under the bare
>   elm
> I shall wait until the last soldier has
>   returned

And longer
When you come back from the battle
No boots will stand at my door
The pillow beside mine will be empty
And my mouth will be unkissed.
When you return, when you return
You will be able to say: It is just as it was.

SIMON: I thank you, Grusha Vashnadze. And good-bye!

(*He bows low before her. She does the same before him. Then she runs quickly off without looking round. Enter the* ADJUTANT *from the gateway.*)

ADJUTANT (*harshly*): Harness the horses to the carriage! Don't stand there doing nothing, scum! (SIMON SHASHAVA *stands to attention and goes off. Two* SERVANTS *crowd from the gateway, bent low under huge trunks. Behind them, supported by her women, stumbles* NATELLA ABASHWILI. *She is followed by a* WOMAN *carrying the* CHILD.)

GOVERNOR'S WIFE: I hardly know if my head's still on. Where's Michael? Don't hold him so clumsily. Pile the trunks onto the carriage. No news from the city, Shalva?

ADJUTANT: None. All's quiet so far, but there's not a minute to lose. No room for all those trunks in the carriage. Pick out what you need. (*Exit quickly.*)

GOVERNOR'S WIFE: Only essentials! Quick, open the trunks! I'll tell you what I need. (*The trunks are lowered and opened. She points at some brocade dresses.*) The green one! And, of course, the one with the fur trimming. Where are Niko Mikadze and Mika Loladze? I've suddenly got the most terrible migraine again. It always starts in the temples. (*Enter* GRUSHA.) Taking your time, eh? Go and get the hot water bottles this minute! (GRUSHA *runs off, returns later with hot water bottles; the* GOVERNOR'S WIFE *orders her about by signs.*) Don't tear the sleeves.

A YOUNG WOMAN: Pardon, madam, no harm has come to the dress.

GOVERNOR'S WIFE: Because I stopped you. I've been watching you for a long time. Nothing in your head but making eyes at Shalva Tzereteli. I'll kill you, you bitch! (*She beats the* YOUNG WOMAN.)

ADJUTANT (*appearing in the gateway*): Please make haste, Natella Abashwili. Firing has broken out in the city. (*Exit.*)

GOVERNOR'S WIFE (*letting go of the* YOUNG WOMAN): Oh dear, do you think they'll lay hands on us? Why should they? Why? (*She herself begins to rummage in the trunks.*) How's Michael? Asleep?

WOMAN WITH THE CHILD: Yes, madam.

GOVERNOR'S WIFE: Then put him down a moment and get my little saffron-colored boots from the bedroom. I need them for the green dress. (*The* WOMAN *puts down the* CHILD *and goes off.*) Just look how these things have been packed! No love! No understanding! If you don't give them every order yourself . . . At such moments you realize what kind of servants you have! They gorge themselves at your expense, and never a word of gratitude! I'll remember this.

ADJUTANT (*entering, very excited*): Natella, you must leave at once!

GOVERNOR'S WIFE: Why? I've got to take this silver dress—it cost a thousand piasters. And that one there, and where's the wine-colored one?

ADJUTANT (*trying to pull her away*): Riots have broken out! We must leave at once. Where's the baby?

GOVERNOR'S WIFE (*calling to the* YOUNG WOMAN *who was holding the baby*): Maro, get the baby ready! Where on earth are you?

ADJUTANT (*leaving*): We'll probably have to leave the carriage behind and go ahead on horseback.

(*The* GOVERNOR'S WIFE *rummages again among her dresses, throws some onto the heap of chosen clothes, then takes them off again. Noises, drums are heard. The* YOUNG WOMAN *who was beaten creeps away. The sky begins to grow red.*)

GOVERNOR'S WIFE (*rummaging desperately*): I simply cannot find the wine-colored dress. Take the whole pile to the carriage. Where's Asja? And why hasn't Maro come back? Have you all gone crazy?

ADJUTANT (*returning*): Quick! Quick!

GOVERNOR'S WIFE (*to the* FIRST WOMAN): Run! Just throw them into the carriage!

ADJUTANT: We're not taking the carriage. And if you don't come now, I'll ride off on my own.

GOVERNOR'S WIFE (*as the* FIRST WOMAN *can't carry everything*): Where's that bitch Asja? (*The* ADJUTANT *pulls her away.*) Maro, bring the baby!

(*To the* FIRST WOMAN:) Go and look for Masha. No, first take the dresses to the carriage. Such nonsense! I wouldn't dream of going on horseback!

(*Turning round, she sees the red sky, and starts back rigid. The fire burns. She is pulled out by the* ADJUTANT. *Shaking, the* FIRST WOMAN *follows with the dresses.*)

MARO (*from the doorway with the boots*): Madam! (*She sees the trunks and dresses and runs toward the* CHILD, *picks it up, and holds it a moment.*) They left it behind, the beasts. (*She hands it to* GRUSHA.) Hold it a moment. (*She runs off, following the* GOVERNOR'S WIFE.)

(*Enter* SERVANTS *from the gateway.*)

COOK: Well, so they've actually gone. Without the food wagons, and not a minute too early. It's time for us to clear out.

GROOM: This'll be an unhealthy neighborhood for quite a while. (*To one of the* WOMEN): Suliko, take a few blankets and wait for me in the foal stables.

GRUSHA: What have they done with the Governor?

GROOM (*gesturing throat cutting*): Ffffft.

A FAT WOMAN (*seeing the gesture and becoming hysterical*): Oh dear, oh dear, oh dear, oh dear! Our master Georgi Abashwili! A picture of health he was, at the morning Mass—and now! Oh, take me away, we're all lost, we must die in sin like our master, Georgi Abashwili!

OTHER WOMAN (*soothing her*): Calm down, Nina! You'll be taken to safety. You've never hurt a fly.

FAT WOMAN (*being led out*): Oh dear, oh dear, oh dear! Quick! Let's all get out before they come, before they come!

A YOUNG WOMAN: Nina takes it more to heart than the mistress, that's a fact. They even have to have their weeping done for them.

COOK: We'd better get out, all of us.

ANOTHER WOMAN (*glancing back*): That must be the East Gate burning.

YOUNG WOMAN (*seeing the* CHILD *in* GRUSHA's *arms*): The baby! What are you doing with it?

GRUSHA: It got left behind.

YOUNG WOMAN: She simply left it there. Michael, who was kept out of all the drafts!

(*The* SERVANTS *gather round the* CHILD.)

GRUSHA: He's waking up.

GROOM: Better put him down, I tell you. I'd rather not think what'd happen to anybody who was found with that baby.

COOK: That's right. Once they get started, they'll kill each other off, whole families at a time. Let's go.

(*Exeunt all but* GRUSHA, *with the* CHILD *on her arm, and* TWO WOMEN.)

TWO WOMEN: Didn't you hear? Better put him down.

GRUSHA: The nurse asked me to hold him a moment.

OLDER WOMAN: She's not coming back, you simpleton.

YOUNGER WOMAN: Keep your hands off it.

OLDER WOMAN (*amiably*): Grusha, you're a good soul, but you're not very bright, and you know it. I tell you, if he had the plague he couldn't be more dangerous.

GRUSHA (*stubbornly*): He hasn't got the plague. He looks at me! He's human!

OLDER WOMAN: Don't look at *him*. You're a fool—the kind that always gets put upon. A person need only say, "Run for the salad, you have the longest legs," and you run. My husband has an ox cart—you can come with us if you hurry! Lord, by now the whole neighborhood must be in flames.

(*Both women leave, sighing. After some hesitation,* GRUSHA *puts the sleeping* CHILD *down, looks at it for a moment, then takes a brocade blanket from the heap of clothes and covers it. Then both women return, dragging bundles.* GRUSHA *starts guiltily away from the* CHILD *and walks a few steps to one side.*)

YOUNGER WOMAN: Haven't you packed anything yet? There isn't much time, you know. The Ironshirts will be here from the barracks.

GRUSHA: Coming!

(*She runs through the doorway. Both women go to the gateway and wait. The sound of horses is heard. They flee, screaming. Enter the* FAT PRINCE *with drunken* IRONSHIRTS. *One of them carries the Governor's head on a lance.*)

FAT PRINCE: Here! In the middle! (*One soldier climbs onto the other's back, takes the head, holds it tentatively over the door.*) That's not the middle. Farther to the right. That's it. What I do, my friends, I do well. (*While with hammer and nail, the soldier fastens the head to the wall by its hair:*) This morning at the church door I said to Georgi Abashwili: "I love a gay sky." Actually, I prefer the lightning that comes out of a gay sky. Yes, indeed. It's a pity they took the brat along, though, I need him, urgently.

(*Exit With* IRONSHIRTS *through the gateway. Trampling of horses again. Enter* GRUSHA *through the doorway looking cautiously about her. Clearly she has waited for the* IRONSHIRTS *to go. Carrying a bundle, she walks toward the gateway. At the last moment, she turns to see if the* CHILD *is still there. Catching sight of the head over the doorway, she screams. Horrified, she picks up her bundle again, and is about to leave when the* SINGER *starts to speak. She stands rooted to the spot.*)

SINGER: As she was standing between courtyard and gate,
  She heard or she thought she heard a low voice calling.
  The child called to her,
  Not whining, but calling quite sensibly,
  Or so it seemed to her.
  "Woman," it said, "help me."
  And it went on, not whining, but saying quite sensibly:
  "Know, woman, he who hears not a cry for help
  But passes by with troubled ears will never hear
  The gentle call of a lover nor the blackbird at dawn
  Nor the happy sigh of the tired grapepicker as the Angelus rings."

(*She walks a few steps toward the* CHILD *and bends over it.*)
  Hearing this she went back for one more look at the child:
  Only to sit with him for a moment or two,
  Only till someone should come,
  His mother, or anyone.

(*Leaning on a trunk, she sits facing the* CHILD.)
  Only till she would have to leave, for the danger was too great,
  The city was full of flame and crying.

(*The light grows dimmer, as though evening and night were coming on.*)

Fearful is the seductive power of goodness!
(GRUSHA *now settles down to watch over the* CHILD *through the night. Once, she lights a small lamp to look at it. Once, she tucks it in with a coat. From time to time she listens and looks to see whether someone is coming.*)
  And she sat with the child a long time,
  Till evening came, till night came, till dawn came.
  She sat too long, too long she saw
  The soft breathing, the small clenched fists,
  Till toward morning the seduction was complete
  And she rose, and bent down and, sighing, took the child
  And carried it away.

(*She does what the* SINGER *says as he describes it.*)
  As if it was stolen goods she picked it up.
  As if she was a thief she crept away.

2

THE FLIGHT INTO THE NORTHERN MOUNTAINS

SINGER: When Grusha Vashnadze left the city
  On the Grusinian highway
  On the way to the Northern Mountains
  She sang a song, she bought some milk.
CHORUS: How will this human child escape
  The bloodhounds, the trap-setters?
  Into the deserted mountains she journeyed
  Along the Grusinian highway she journeyed
  She sang a song, she bought some milk.

(GRUSHA VASHNADZE *walks on. On her back she carries the* CHILD *in a sack, in one hand is a large stick, in the other a bundle. She sings.*)

THE SONG OF THE FOUR GENERALS
Four generals
Set out for Iran.
With the first one, war did not agree.
The second never won a victory.
For the third the weather never was right.
For the fourth the men would never fight.
Four generals

And not a single man!
Sosso Robakidse
Went marching to Iran
With him the war did so agree
He soon had won a victory.
For him the weather was always right.
For him the men would always fight.
Sosso Robakidse,
He is our man!

(*A peasant's cottage appears.*)

GRUSHA (*to the* CHILD): Noontime is meal time. Now we'll sit hopefully in the grass, while the good Grusha goes and buys a little pitcher of milk. (*She lays the* CHILD *down and knocks at the cottage door. An* OLD MAN *opens it.*) Grandfather, could I have a little pitcher of milk? And a corn cake, maybe?

OLD MAN: Milk? We have no milk. The soldiers from the city have our goats. Go to the soldiers if you want milk.

GRUSHA: But grandfather, you must have a little pitcher of milk for a baby?

OLD MAN: And for a God-bless-you, eh?

GRUSHA: Who said anything about a God-bless-you? (*She shows her purse.*) We'll pay like princes. "Head in the clouds, backside in the water." (*The peasant goes off, grumbling, for milk.*) How much for the milk?

OLD MAN: Three piasters. Milk has gone up.

GRUSHA: Three piasters for this little drop? (*Without a word the* OLD MAN *shuts the door in her face.*) Michael, did you hear that? Three piasters! We can't afford it! (*She goes back, sits down again, and gives the* CHILD *her breast.*) Suck. Think of the three piasters. There's nothing there, but you *think* you're drinking, and that's something. (*Shaking her head, she sees that the* CHILD *isn't sucking any more. She gets up, walks back to the door, and knocks again.*) Open, grandfather, we'll pay. (*Softly.*) May lightning strike you! (*When the* OLD MAN *appears:*) I thought it would be half a piaster. But the baby must be fed. How about one piaster for that little drop?

OLD MAN: Two.

GRUSHA: Don't shut the door again. (*She fishes a long time in her bag.*) Here are two piasters. The milk better be good. I still have two days' journey ahead of me. It's a murderous business you have here—and sinful, too!

OLD MAN: Kill the soldiers if you want milk.

GRUSHA (*giving the* CHILD *some milk*): This is an expensive joke. Take a sip, Michael, it's a week's pay. Around here they think we earned our money just sitting on our behinds. Oh, Michael, Michael, you're a nice little load for a girl to take on! (*Uneasy, she gets up, puts the* CHILD *on her back, and walks on. The* OLD MAN, *grumbling, picks up the pitcher and looks after her unmoved.*)

SINGER: As Grusha Vashnadze went northward
        The Princes' Ironshirts went after her.

CHORUS: How will the barefoot girl escape the Ironshirts,
        The bloodhounds, the trap-setters?
        They hunt even by night.
        Pursuers never tire.
        Butchers sleep little.

(*Two* IRONSHIRTS *are trudging along the highway.*)

CORPORAL: You'll never amount to anything, blockhead, your heart's not in it. Your senior officer sees this in little things. Yesterday, when I made the fat gal, yes, you grabbed her husband as I commanded, and you did kick him in the belly, at my request, but did you *enjoy* it, like a loyal Private, or were you just doing your duty? I've kept an eye on you blockhead, you're a hollow reed and a tinkling cymbal, you won't get promoted. (*They walk a while in silence.*) Don't think I've forgotten how insubordinate you are, either. Stop limping! I forbid you to limp! You limp because I sold the horses, and I sold the horses because I'd never have got that price again. You limp to show me you don't like marching. I know you. It won't help. You wait. Sing!

TWO IRONSHIRTS (*singing*): Sadly to war I went my way
        Leaving my loved one at her door.
        My friends will keep her honor safe
        Till from the war I'm back once more.

CORPORAL: Louder!

TWO IRONSHIRTS (*singing*): When 'neath a headstone I shall be
        My love a little earth will bring:
        "Here rest the feet that oft would run to me
        And here the arms that oft to me would cling."

(*They begin to walk again in silence.*)

CORPORAL: A good soldier has his heart and soul in it. When he receives an order, he gets a hard-on, and when he drives his lance into the enemy's guts, he comes. (*He shouts for joy.*) He lets himself be torn to bits for his superior officer, and as he lies dying he takes note that his corporal is nodding approval, and that is reward enough, it's his dearest wish. *You* won't get any nod of approval, but you'll croak all right. Christ, how'm I to get my hands on the Governor's bastard with the help of a fool like you! (*They stay on stage behind.*)

SINGER:

> When Grusha Vashnadze came to the River Sirra
> Flight grew too much for her, the helpless child too heavy.
> In the cornfields the rosy dawn
> Is cold to the sleepless one, only cold.
> The gay clatter of the milk cans in the farmyard where the smoke rises
> Is only a threat to the fugitive.
> She who carries the child feels its weight and little more.

(GRUSHA *stops in front of a farm. A fat* PEASANT WOMAN *is carrying a milk can through the door.* GRUSHA *waits until she has gone in, then approaches the house cautiously.*)

GRUSHA (*to the* CHILD): Now you've wet yourself again, and you know I've no linen. Michael, this is where we part company. It's far enough from the city. They wouldn't want you *so* much that they'd follow you all *this* way, little good-for-nothing. The peasant woman is kind, and can't you just smell the milk? (*She bends down to lay the* CHILD *on the threshold.*) So farewell, Michael, I'll forget how you kicked me in the back all night to make me walk faster. And you can forget the meager fare—it was meant well. I'd like to have kept you—your nose is so tiny—but it can't be. I'd have shown you your first rabbit, I'd have trained you to keep dry, but now I must turn around. My sweetheart the soldier might be back soon, and suppose he didn't find me? You can't ask that, can you? (*She creeps up to the door and lays the* CHILD *on the threshold. Then, hiding behind a tree, she waits until the* PEASANT WOMAN *opens the door and sees the bundle.*)

PEASANT WOMAN: Good heavens, what's this? Husband!

PEASANT: What is it? Let me finish my soup.

PEASANT WOMAN (*to the* CHILD): Where's your mother then? Haven't you got one? It's a boy. Fine linen. He's from a good family, you can see that. And they just leave him on our doorstep. Oh, these are times!

PEASANT: If they think we're going to feed it, they're wrong. You can take it to the priest in the village. That's the best we can do.

PEASANT WOMAN: What'll the priest do with him? He needs a mother. There, he's waking up. Don't you think we could keep him, though?

PEASANT (*shouting*): No!

PEASANT WOMAN: I could lay him in the corner by the armchair. All I need is a crib. I can take him into the fields with me. See him laughing? Husband, we have a roof over our heads. We can do it. Not another word out of you! (*She carries the* CHILD *into the house. The* PEASANT *follows protesting.* GRUSHA *steps out from behind the tree, laughs, and hurries off in the opposite direction.*)

SINGER: Why so cheerful, making for home?

CHORUS: Because the child has won new parents with a laugh,
> Because I'm rid of the little one, I'm cheerful.

SINGER: And why so sad?

CHORUS: Because I'm single and free, I'm sad
> Like someone who's been robbed
> Someone who's newly poor.

(*She walks for a short while, then meets the two* IRONSHIRTS *who point their lances at her.*)

CORPORAL: Lady, you are running straight into the arms of the Armed Forces. Where are you coming from? And when? Are you having illicit relations with the enemy? Where is he hiding? What movements is he making in your rear? How about the hills? How about the valleys? How are your stockings held in position? (GRUSHA *stands there frightened.*) Don't be scared, we always withdraw, if necessary . . . what, blockhead? I always withdraw. In that respect at least, I can be relied on. Why are you staring like that at my lance? In the field no soldier drops his lance, that's a rule. Learn it by heart, blockhead. Now, lady, where are you headed?

GRUSHA: To meet my intended, one Simon Shashava, of the Palace Guard in Nuka.

CORPORAL: Simon Shashava? Sure, I know him. He gave me the key so I could look you up once in a while. Blockhead, we are getting to be unpopular. We must make her realize we have honorable intentions. Lady, behind apparent frivolity I conceal a serious nature, so let me tell you officially: I want a child from you. (GRUSHA *utters a little scream.*) Blockhead, she understands me. Uh-huh, isn't it a sweet shock? "Then first I must take the noodles out of the oven, Officer. Then first I must change my torn shirt, Colonel." But away with jokes, away with my lance! We are looking for a baby. A baby from a good family. Have you heard of such a baby, from the city, dressed in fine linen, and suddenly turning up here?

GRUSHA: No, I haven't heard a thing. (*Suddenly she turns round and runs back, panic-stricken. The* IRONSHIRTS *glance at each other, then follow her, cursing.*)

SINGER: Run, kind girl! The killers are coming!
        Help the helpless babe, helpless girl!
        And so she runs!

CHORUS: In the bloodiest times
        There are kind people.

(*As* GRUSHA *rushes into the cottage, the* PEASANT WOMAN *is bending over the* CHILD'S *crib.*)

GRUSHA: Hide him. Quick! The Ironshirts are coming! I laid him on your doorstep. But he isn't mine. He's from a good family.

PEASANT WOMAN: Who's coming? What Ironshirts?

GRUSHA: Don't ask questions. The Ironshirts that are looking for it.

PEASANT WOMAN: They've no business in my house. But I must have a little talk with you, it seems.

GRUSHA: Take off the fine linen. It'll give us away.

PEASANT WOMAN: Linen, my foot! In this house I make the decisions! *"You* can't vomit in *my* room!"* Why did you abandon it? It's a sin.

GRUSHA (*looking out of the window*): Look, they're coming out from behind those trees! I shouldn't have run away, it made them angry. Oh, what shall I do?

PEASANT WOMAN (*looking out of the window and suddenly starting with fear*): Gracious! Ironshirts!

GRUSHA: They're after the baby.

PEASANT WOMAN: Suppose they come in!

GRUSHA: You mustn't give him to them. Say he's yours.

PEASANT WOMAN: Yes.

GRUSHA: They'll run him through if you hand him over.

PEASANT WOMAN: But suppose they ask for it? The silver for the harvest is in the house.

GRUSHA: If you let them have him, they'll run him through, right here in this room! You've got to say he's yours!

PEASANT WOMAN: Yes. But what if they don't believe me?

GRUSHA: You must be firm.

PEASANT WOMAN: They'll burn the roof over our heads.

GRUSHA: That's why you must say he's yours. His name's Michael. But I shouldn't have told you. (*The* PEASANT WOMAN *nods.*) Don't nod like that. And don't tremble—they'll notice.

PEASANT WOMAN: Yes.

GRUSHA: And stop saying yes, I can't stand it. (*She shakes the* WOMAN.) Don't you have any children?

PEASANT WOMAN (*muttering*): He's in the war.

GRUSHA: Then maybe *he's* an Ironshirt? Do you want *him* to run children through with a lance? You'd bawl him out. "No fooling with lances in my house!" you'd shout, "is that what I've reared you for? Wash your neck before you speak to your mother!"

PEASANT WOMAN: That's true, he couldn't get away with anything around here!

GRUSHA: So you'll say he's yours?

PEASANT WOMAN: Yes.

GRUSHA: Look! They're coming!

(*There is a knocking at the door. The women don't answer. Enter* IRONSHIRTS. *The* PEASANT WOMAN *bows low.*)

CORPORAL: Well, here she is. What did I tell you? What a nose I have! I *smelt* her. Lady, I have a question for you. Why did you run away? What did you think I would do to you? I'll bet it was something unchaste. Confess!

GRUSHA (*while the* PEASANT WOMAN *bows again and again*): I'd left some milk on the stove, and I suddenly remembered it.

CORPORAL: Or maybe you imagined I looked at you unchastely? Like there could be something between us? A carnal glance, know what I mean?

GRUSHA: I didn't see it.

CORPORAL: But it's possible, huh? You admit that much. After all, I might be a pig. I'll be frank with you: I could think of all sorts of things if we were alone. (*To the* PEASANT WOMAN:) Shouldn't you be busy in the yard? Feeding the hens?

PEASANT WOMAN (*falling suddenly to her knees*): Soldier, I didn't know a thing about it. Please don't burn the roof over our heads.

CORPORAL: What are you talking about?

PEASANT WOMAN: I had nothing to do with it. She left it on my doorstep, I swear it!

CORPORAL (*suddenly seeing the* CHILD *and whistling*): Ah, so there's a little something in the crib! Blockhead, I smell a thousand piasters. Take the old girl outside and hold on to her. It looks like I have a little cross-examining to do. (*The* PEASANT WOMAN *lets herself be led out by the* PRIVATE, *without a word.*) So, you've got the child I wanted from you! (*He walks toward the crib.*)

GRUSHA: Officer, he's mine. He's not the one you're after.

CORPORAL: I'll just take a look. (*He bends over the crib.*)

(GRUSHA *looks round in despair.*)

GRUSHA: He's mine! He's mine!

CORPORAL: Fine linen!

(GRUSHA *dashes at him to pull him away. He throws her off and again bends over the crib. Again looking round in despair, she sees a log of wood, seizes it, and hits the* CORPORAL *over the head from behind. The* CORPORAL *collapses. She quickly picks up the* CHILD *and rushes off.*)

SINGER: And in her flight from the Ironshirts
After twenty-two days of journeying
At the foot of the Janga-Tau Glacier
Grusha Vashnadze decided to adopt the child.

CHORUS: The helpless girl adopted the helpless child.

(GRUSHA *squats over a half-frozen stream to get the* CHILD *water in the hollow of her hand.*)

GRUSHA: Since no one else will take you, son,
I must take you.
Since no one else will take you, son,
You must take me.
O black day in a lean, lean year,

The trip was long, the milk was dear,
My legs are tired, my feet are sore:
But I wouldn't be without you any more.
I'll throw your silken shirt away
And wrap you in rags and tatters.
I'll wash you, son, and christen you in
glacier water.
We'll see it through together.

(*She has taken off the child's fine linen and wrapped it in a rag.*)

SINGER: When Grusha Vashnadze
Pursued by the Ironshirts
Came to the bridge on the glacier
Leading to the villages of the Eastern Slope
She sang the Song of the Rotten Bridge
And risked two lives.

(*A wind has risen. The bridge on the glacier is visible in the dark. One rope is broken and half the bridge is hanging down the abyss.* MERCHANTS, *two men and a woman, stand undecided before the bridge as* GRUSHA *and the* CHILD *arrive. One man is trying to catch the hanging rope with a stick.*)

FIRST MAN: Take your time, young woman. You won't get across here anyway.

GRUSHA: But I *have* to get the baby to the east side. To my brother's place.

MERCHANT WOMAN: Have to? How d'you mean, "have to"? I have to get there, too—because I have to buy carpets in Atum—carpets a woman had to sell because her husband had to die. But can *I* do what I have to? Can she? Andrei's been fishing for that rope for hours. And I ask you, how are we going to fasten it, even if he gets it up?

FIRST MAN (*listening*): Hush, I think I hear something.

GRUSHA: The bridge isn't quite rotted through. I think I'll try it.

MERCHANT WOMAN: I wouldn't—if the devil himself were after me. It's suicide.

FIRST MAN (*shouting*): Hi!

GRUSHA: Don't shout! (*To the* MERCHANT WOMAN:) Tell him not to shout.

FIRST MAN: But there's someone down there calling. Maybe they've lost their way.

MERCHANT WOMAN: Why shouldn't he shout? Is there something funny about you? Are they after you?

GRUSHA: All right, I'll tell. The Ironshirts are after me. I knocked one down.

SECOND MAN: Hide our merchandise!

(*The* WOMAN *hides a sack behind a rock.*)

FIRST MAN: Why didn't you say so right away? (*To the others:*) If they catch her they'll make mincemeat out of her!

GRUSHA: Get out of my way. I've got to cross that bridge.

SECOND MAN: You can't. The precipice is two thousand feet deep.

FIRST MAN: Even with the rope it'd be no use. We could hold it up with our hands. But then we'd have to do the same for the Ironshirts.

GRUSHA: Go away.

(*There are calls from the distance: "Hi, up there!"*)

MERCHANT WOMAN: They're getting near. But you can't take the child on that bridge. It's sure to break. And look!

(GRUSHA *looks down into the abyss. The* IRONSHIRTS *are heard calling again from below.*)

SECOND MAN: Two thousand feet!

GRUSHA: But those men are worse.

FIRST MAN: You can't do it. Think of the baby. Risk your life but not a child's.

SECOND MAN: With the child she's that much heavier!

MERCHANT WOMAN: Maybe she's *really* got to get across. Give *me* the baby. I'll hide it. Cross the bridge alone!

GRUSHA: I won't. We belong together. (*To the* CHILD:) "Live together, die together." (*She sings.*)

THE SONG OF THE ROTTEN BRIDGE
Deep is the abyss, son,
I see the weak bridge sway
But it's not for us, son,
To choose the way.

The way I know
Is the one you must tread,
And all you will eat
Is my bit of bread.

Of every four pieces
You shall have three.
Would that I knew
How big they will be!

Get out of my way, I'll try it without the rope.

MERCHANT WOMAN: You are tempting God!

(*There are shouts from below.*)

GRUSHA: Please, throw that stick away, or they'll get the rope and follow me. (*Pressing the* CHILD *to her, she steps onto the swaying bridge. The* MERCHANT WOMAN *screams when it looks as though the bridge is about to collapse. But* GRUSHA *walks on and reaches the far side.*)

FIRST MAN: She made it!

MERCHANT WOMAN (*who has fallen on her knees and begun to pray, angrily*): I still think it was a sin.

(*The* IRONSHIRTS *appear; the* CORPORAL's *head is bandaged.*)

CORPORAL: Seen a woman with a child?

FIRST MAN (*while the* SECOND MAN *throws the stick into the abyss*): Yes, there! But the bridge won't carry you!

CORPORAL: You'll pay for this, blockhead!

(GRUSHA, *from the far bank, laughs and shows the* CHILD *to the* IRONSHIRTS. *She walks on. The wind blows.*)

GRUSHA (*turning to the* CHILD): You mustn't be afraid of the wind. He's a poor thing too. He has to push the clouds along and he gets quite cold doing it. (*Snow starts falling.*) And the snow isn't so bad, either, Michael. It covers the little fir trees so they won't die in winter. Let me sing you a little song. (*She sings.*)

THE SONG OF THE CHILD
Your father is a bandit
A harlot the mother who bore you.
Yet honorable men
Shall kneel down before you.
Food to the baby horses
The tiger's son will take.
The mothers will get milk
From the son of the snake.

3

IN THE NORTHERN MOUNTAINS

SINGER: Seven days the sister, Grusha Vashnadze,
    Journeyed across the glacier
    And down the slopes she journeyed.
    "When I enter my brother's house," she
        thought,
    "He will rise and embrace me."
    "Is that you, sister?" he will say,

"I have long expected you.
This is my dear wife,
And this is my farm, come to me by
    marriage,
With eleven horses and thirty-one cows.
    Sit down.
Sit down with your child at our table and
    eat."
The brother's house was in a lovely valley.
When the sister came to the brother,
She was ill from walking.
The brother rose from the table.

(*A fat peasant couple rise from the table.* LAVRENTI VASHNADZE *still has a napkin round his neck, as* GRUSHA, *pale and supported by a* SERVANT, *enters with the* CHILD.)

LAVRENTI: Where've *you* come from, Grusha?

GRUSHA (*feebly*): Across the Janga-Tu Pass, Lavrenti.

SERVANT: I found her in front of the hay barn. She has a baby with her.

SISTER-IN-LAW: Go and groom the mare.

(*Exit the* SERVANT.)

LAVRENTI: This is my wife Aniko.

SISTER-IN-LAW: I thought you were in service in Nuka.

GRUSHA (*barely able to stand*): Yes, I was.

SISTER-IN-LAW: Wasn't it a good job? We were told it was.

GRUSHA: The Governor got killed.

LAVRENTI: Yes, we heard there were riots. Your aunt told us. Remember, Aniko?

SISTER-IN-LAW: Here with us, it's very quiet. City people always want something going on. (*She walks toward the door, calling:*) Sosso, Sosso, don't take the cake out of the oven yet, d'you hear? Where on earth are you? (*Exit, calling.*)

LAVRENTI (*quietly, quickly*): Is there a father? (*As she shakes her head:*) I thought not. We must think up something. She's religious.

SISTER-IN-LAW (*returning*): Those servants! (*to* GRUSHA:) You have a child.

GRUSHA: It's mine. (*She collapses.* LAVRENTI *rushes to her assistance.*)

SISTER-IN-LAW: Heavens, she's ill—what are we going to do?

LAVRENTI (*escorting her to a bench near the stove*): Sit down, sit. I think it's just weakness, Aniko.

SISTER-IN-LAW: As long as it's not scarlet fever!

LAVRENTI: She'd have spots if it was. It's only weakness. Don't worry, Aniko. (*To* GRUSHA:) Better, sitting down?

SISTER-IN-LAW: Is the child hers?

GRUSHA: Yes, mine.

LAVRENTI: She's on her way to her husband.

SISTER-IN-LAW: I see. Your meat's getting getting cold. (LAVRENTI *sits down and begins to eat.*) Cold food's not good for you, the fat mustn't get cold, you know your stomach's your weak spot. (*To* GRUSHA:) If your husband's not in the city, where is he?

LAVRENTI: She got married on the other side of the mountain, she says.

SISTER-IN-LAW: On the other side of the mountain. I see. (*She also sits down to eat.*)

GRUSHA: I think I should lie down somewhere, Lavrenti.

SISTER-IN-LAW: If it's consumption we'll all get it. (*She goes on cross-examining her.*) Has your husband got a farm?

GRUSHA: He's a soldier.

LAVRENTI: But he's coming into a farm—a small one—from his father.

SISTER-IN-LAW: Isn't he in the war? Why not?

GRUSHA (*with effort*): Yes, he's in the war.

SISTER-IN-LAW: Then why d'you want to go to the farm?

LAVRENTI: When he comes back from the war, he'll return to his farm.

SISTER-IN-LAW: But you're going there now?

LAVRENTI: Yes, to wait for him.

SISTER-IN-LAW (*calling shrilly*): Sosso, the cake!

GRUSHA (*murmuring feverishly*): A farm—a soldier—waiting—sit down, eat.

SISTER-IN-LAW: It's scarlet fever.

GRUSHA (*starting up*): Yes, he's got a farm!

LAVRENTI: I think it's just weakness, Aniko. Would you look after the cake yourself, dear?

SISTER-IN-LAW: But when will he come back if war's broken out again as people say? (*She waddles off, shouting:*) Sosso! Where on earth are you? Sosso!

LAVRENTI (*getting up quickly and going to* GRUSHA): You'll get a bed in a minute. She has a good heart. But wait till after supper.

GRUSHA (*holding out the* CHILD *to him*): Take him.

LAVRENTI (*taking it and looking around*): But you can't stay here long with the child. She's religious, you see.

(GRUSHA *collapses.* LAVRENTI *catches her.*)

SINGER: The sister was so ill,
　　　The cowardly brother had to give her shelter.
　　　Summer departed, winter came.
　　　The winter was long, the winter was short.
　　　People mustn't know anything.
　　　Rats mustn't bite.
　　　Spring mustn't come.

(GRUSHA *sits over the weaving loom in a workroom. She and the* CHILD, *who is squatting on the floor, are wrapped in blankets. She sings.*)

THE SONG OF THE CENTER
And the lover started to leave
And his betrothed ran pleading after him
Pleading and weeping, weeping and teaching:
"Dearest mine, dearest mine
When you go to war as now you do
When you fight the foe as soon you will
Don't lead with the front line
And don't push with the rear line
At the front is red fire
In the rear is red smoke
Stay in the war's center
Stay near the standard bearer
The first always die
The last are also hit
Those in the center come home."

Michael, we must be clever. If we make ourselves as small as cockroaches, the sister-in-law will forget we're in the house, and then we can stay till the snow melts.

(*Enter* LAVRENTI. *He sit down beside his sister.*)

LAVRENTI: Why are you sitting there muffled up like coachmen, you two? Is it too cold in the room?

GRUSHA (*hastily removing one shawl*): It's not too cold, Lavrenti.

LAVRENTI: If it's too cold, you shouldn't be sitting here with the child. Aniko would never forgive herself! (*Pause.*) I hope our priest didn't question you about the child?

GRUSHA: He did, but I didn't tell him anything.

LAVRENTI: That's good. I wanted to speak to you about Aniko. She has a good heart but she's very, very sensitive. People need only mention our farm and she's worried. She takes everything hard, you see. One time our milkmaid went to church with a hole in her stocking. Ever since, Aniko has worn two pairs of stockings in church. It's the old family in her. (*He listens.*) Are you sure there are no rats around? If there are rats, you couldn't live here. (*There are sounds as of dripping from the roof.*) What's that, dripping?

GRUSHA: It must be a barrel leaking.

LAVRENTI: Yes, it must be a barrel. You've been here six months, haven't you? Was I talking about Aniko? (*They listen again to the snow melting.*) You can't imagine how worried she gets about your soldier-husband. "Suppose he comes back and can't find her!" she says and lies awake. "He can't come before the spring," I tell her. The dear woman! (*The drops begin to fall faster.*) When d'you think he'll come? What do *you* think? (GRUSHA *is silent.*) Not before the spring, you agree? (GRUSHA *is silent.*) You don't believe he'll come at all? (GRUSHA *is silent.*) But when the spring comes and the snow melts here and on the passes, you can't stay on. They may come and look for you. There's already talk of an illegitimate child. (*The "glockenspiel" of the falling drops has grown faster and steadier.*) Grusha, the snow is melting on the roof. Spring is here.

GRUSHA: Yes.

LAVRENTI (*eagerly*): I'll tell you what we'll do. You need a place to go, and, because of the child (*he sighs*), you have to have a husband, so people won't talk. Now I've made cautious inquiries to see if we can find you a husband. Grusha, I *have* one. I talked to a peasant woman who has a son. Just the other side of the mountain. A small farm. And she's willing.

GRUSHA: But I *can't* marry! I must wait for Simon Shashava.

LAVRENTI: Of course. That's all been taken care of. You don't need a man in bed—you need a man on paper. And I've found you one. The son of this peasant woman is going to die. Isn't that wonderful? He's at his last gasp. And all in line with our story—a husband from the other side of the mountain! And when you met him he was at the last gasp. So you're a widow. What do you say?

GRUSHA: It's true I could use a document with stamps on it for Michael.

LAVRENTI: Stamps make all the difference. Without something in writing the Shah couldn't prove he's a Shah. And you'll have a place to live.

GRUSHA: How much does the peasant woman want?

LAVRENTI: Four hundred piasters.

GRUSHA: Where will you find it?

LAVRENTI (*guiltily*): Aniko's milk money.

GRUSHA: No one would know us there. I'll do it.

LAVRENTI (*getting up*): I'll let the peasant woman know.

(*Quick exit.*)

GRUSHA: Michael, you make a lot of work. I came by you as the pear tree comes by sparrows. And because a Christian bends down and picks up a crust of bread so nothing will go to waste. Michael, it would have been better had I walked quickly away on that Easter Sunday in Nuka in the second courtyard. Now I *am* a fool.

SINGER: The bridegroom was on his deathbed when the bride arrived.

The bridegroom's mother was waiting at the door, telling her to hurry.

The bride brought a child along.

The witness hid it during the wedding.

(*On one side the bed. Under the mosquito net lies a very sick man.* GRUSHA *is pulled in at a run by her future mother-in-law. They are followed by* LAVRENTI *and the* CHILD.)

MOTHER-IN-LAW: Quick! Quick! Or he'll die on us before the wedding. (*To* LAVRENTI:) I was never told she had a child already.

LAVRENTI: What difference does it make? (*Pointing toward the dying man.*) It can't matter to him—in his condition.

MOTHER-IN-LAW: To him? But I'll never survive the shame! We are honest people. (*She begins to weep.*) My Jussup doesn't have to marry a girl with a child!

LAVRENTI: All right, make it another two hundred piasters. You'll have it in writing that the farm will go to you: but she'll have the right to live here for two years.

MOTHER-IN-LAW (*drying her tears*): It'll hardly cover the funeral expenses. I hope she'll really lend a hand with the work. And what's happened to the monk? He must have slipped out through the kitchen window. We'll have the whole village on our necks when they hear Jussup's end is come! Oh dear! I'll go get the monk. But he mustn't see the child!

LAVRENTI: I'll take care he doesn't. But why only a monk? Why not a priest?

MOTHER-IN-LAW: Oh, he's just as good. I only made one mistake: I paid half his fee in advance. Enough to send him to the tavern. I only hope . . . (*She runs off.*)

LAVRENTI: She saved on the priest, the wretch! Hired a cheap monk.

GRUSHA: You *will* send Simon Shashava to see me if he turns up after all?

LAVRENTI: Yes. (*Pointing at the* SICK PEASANT.) Won't you take a look at him? (GRUSHA, *taking* MICHAEL *to her, shakes her head.*) He's not moving an eyelid. I hope we aren't too late.

(*They listen. On the opposite side enter neighbors who look around and take up positions against the walls, thus forming another wall near the bed, yet leaving an opening so that the bed can be seen. They start murmuring prayers. Enter the* MOTHER-IN-LAW *with a* MONK. *Showing some annoyance and surprise, she bows to the guests.*)

MOTHER-IN-LAW: I hope you won't mind waiting a few moments? My son's bride has just arrived from the city. An emergency wedding is about to be celebrated. (*To the* MONK *in the bedroom:*) I might have known you couldn't keep your trap shut. (*To* GRUSHA:) The wedding can take place at once. Here's the license. Me and the bride's brother (LAVRENTI *tries to hide in the background, after having quietly taken* MICHAEL *back from* GRUSHA. *The* MOTHER-IN-LAW *waves him away.*) are the witnesses.

(GRUSHA *has bowed to the* MONK. *They go to the bed. The* MOTHER-IN-LAW *lifts the mosquito net. The* MONK *starts reeling off the marriage ceremony in Latin. Meanwhile the* MOTHER-IN-LAW *beckons to* LAVRENTI *to get rid of the* CHILD, *but fearing that it will cry he draws its attention to the ceremony,*

GRUSHA *glances once at the* CHILD, *and* LAVRENTI *waves the* CHILD's *hand in a greeting.*)

MONK: Are you prepared to be a faithful, obedient, and good wife to this man, and to cleave to him until death you do part?

GRUSHA (*looking at the* CHILD): I am.

MONK (*to the* SICK PEASANT): Are you prepared to be a good and loving husband to your wife until death you do part? (*As the* SICK PEASANT *does not answer, the* MONK *looks inquiringly around.*)

MOTHER-IN-LAW: Of course he is! Didn't you hear him say yes?

MONK: All right. We declare the marriage contracted! How about extreme unction?

MOTHER-IN-LAW: Nothing doing! The wedding cost quite enough. Now I must take care of the mourners (*To* LAVRENTI:) Did we say seven hundred?

LAVRENTI: Six hundred. (*He pays.*) Now I don't want to sit with the guests and get to know people. So farewell, Grusha, and if my widowed sister comes to visit me, she'll get a welcome from my wife, or I'll show my teeth. (*Nods, gives the* CHILD *to* GRUSHA, *and leaves. The mourners glance after him without interest.*)

MONK: May one ask where this child comes from?

MOTHER-IN-LAW: Is there a child? I don't see a child. And you don't see a child either—you understand? Or it may turn out I saw all sorts of things in the tavern! Now come on.

(*After* GRUSHA *has put the* CHILD *down and told him to be quiet, they move over left,* GRUSHA *is introduced to the neighbors.*)

This is my daughter-in-law. She arrived just in time to find dear Jussup still alive.

ONE WOMAN: He's been ill now a whole year, hasn't he? When our Vassili was drafted he was there to say good-bye.

ANOTHER WOMAN: Such things are terrible for a farm. The corn all ripe and the farmer in bed! It'll really be a blessing if he doesn't suffer too long, I say.

FIRST WOMAN (*confidentially*): You know why we thought he'd taken to his bed? Because of the draft! And now his end is come!

MOTHER-IN-LAW: Sit yourselves down, please! And have some cakes!

(*She beckons to* GRUSHA *and both women go into the bedroom, where they pick up the cake pans off*

the floor. The guests, among them the MONK, sit on the floor and begin conversing in subdued voices.*)

ONE PEASANT (*to whom the* MONK *has handed the bottle which he has taken from his soutane*): There's a child, you say! How can that have happened to Jussup?

A WOMAN: She was certainly lucky to get herself married, with him so sick!

MOTHER-IN-LAW: They're gossiping already. And wolfing down the funeral cakes at the same time! If he doesn't die today, I'll have to bake some more tomorrow!

GRUSHA: I'll bake them for you.

MOTHER-IN-LAW: Yesterday some horsemen rode by, and I went out to see who it was. When I came in again he was lying there like a corpse! So I sent for you. It can't take much longer. (*She listens.*)

MONK: Dear wedding and funeral guests! Deeply touched, we stand before a bed of death and marriage. The bride gets a veil; the groom, a shroud: how varied, my children, are the fates of men! Alas! One man dies and has a roof over his head, and the other is married and the flesh turns to dust from which it was made. Amen.

MOTHER-IN-LAW: He's getting his own back. I shouldn't have hired such a cheap one. It's what you'd expect. A more expensive monk would behave himself. In Sura there's one with a real air of sanctity about him, but of course he charges a fortune. A fifty piaster monk like that has no dignity, and as for piety, just fifty piasters' worth and no more! When I came to get him in the tavern he'd just made a speech, and he was shouting: "The war is over, beware of the peace!" We must go in.

GRUSHA (*giving* MICHAEL *a cake*): Eat this cake, and keep nice and still, Michael.

(*The two women offer cakes to the guests. The dying man sits up in bed. He puts his head out from under the mosquito net, stares at the two women, then sinks back again. The* MONK *takes two bottles from his soutane and offers them to the peasant beside him. Enter three* MUSICIANS *who are greeted with a sly wink by the* MONK.*)

MOTHER-IN-LAW (*to the* MUSICIANS): What are you doing here? With instruments?

ONE MUSICIAN: Brother Anastasius here (*pointing at the* MONK) told us there was a wedding on.

MOTHER-IN-LAW: What? You brought them? Three more on my neck! Don't you know there's a dying man in the next room?

MONK: A very tempting assignment for a musician: something that could be either a subdued Wedding March or a spirited Funeral Dance.

MOTHER-IN-LAW: Well, you might as well play. Nobody can stop you eating in any case.

(*The* MUSICIANS *play a potpourri. The women serve cakes.*)

MONK: The trumpet sounds like a whining baby. And you, little drum, what have you got to tell the world?

DRUNKEN PEASANT (*beside the* MONK, *sings*):

There was a young woman who said:
I thought I'd be happier, wed.
But my husband is old
And remarkably cold
So I sleep with a candle instead.

(*The* MOTHER-IN-LAW *throws the* DRUNKEN PEASANT *out. The music stops. The guests are embarrassed.*)

GUESTS (*loudly*):

—Have you heard? The Grand Duke is back! But the Princes are against him.

—They say the Shah of Persia has lent him a great army to restore order in Grusinia.

—But how is that possible? The Shah of Persia is the enemy . . .

—The enemy of Grusinia, you donkey, not the enemy of the Grand Duke!

—In any case, the war's over, so our soldiers are coming back.

(GRUSHA *drops a cake pan.* GUESTS *help her pick up the cake.*)

AN OLD WOMAN (*to* GRUSHA): Are you feeling bad? It's just excitement about dear Jussup. Sit down and rest a while, my dear. (GRUSHA *staggers.*)

GUESTS: Now everything'll be the way it was. Only the taxes'll go up because now we'll have to pay for the war.

GRUSHA (*weakly*): Did someone say the soldiers are back?

A MAN: I did.

GRUSHA: It can't be true.

FIRST MAN (*to a* WOMAN): Show her the shawl. We bought it from a soldier. It's from Persia.

GRUSHA (*looking at the shawl*): They are here. (*She gets up, takes a step, kneels down in prayer, takes the silver cross and chain out of her blouse, and kisses it.*)

MOTHER-IN-LAW (*while the guests silently watch* GRUSHA): What's the matter with you? Aren't you going to look after our guests? What's all this city nonsense got to do with us?

GUESTS (*resuming conversation while* GRUSHA *remains in prayer*):

—You can buy Persian saddles from the soldiers too. Though many want crutches in exchange for them.

—The leaders on one side can win a war, the soldiers on both sides lose it.

—Anyway, the war's over. It's something they can't draft you any more.

(*The dying man sits bolt upright in bed. He listens.*)

—What we need is two weeks of good weather.

—Our pear trees are hardly bearing a thing this year.

MOTHER-IN-LAW (*Offering cakes*): Have some more cakes and welcome! There are more!

(*The* MOTHER-IN-LAW *goes to the bedroom with the empty cake pans. Unaware of the dying man, she is bending down to pick up another tray when he begins to talk in a hoarse voice.*)

PEASANT: How many more cakes are you going to stuff down their throats? D'you think I can shit money?

(*The* MOTHER-IN-LAW *starts, stares at him aghast, while he climbs out from behind the mosquito net.*)

FIRST WOMAN (*talking kindly to* GRUSHA *in the next room*): Has the young wife got someone at the front?

A MAN: It's good news that they're on their way home, huh?

PEASANT: Don't stare at me like that! Where's this wife you've saddled me with?

(*Receiving no answer, he climbs out of bed and in his nightshirt staggers into the other room. Trembling, she follows him with the cake pan.*)

GUESTS (*seeing him and shrieking*): Good God! Jussup!

(*Everyone leaps up in alarm. The women rush to the door.* GRUSHA, *still on her knees, turns round and stares at the man.*)

PEASANT: A funeral supper! You'd enjoy that, wouldn't you? Get out before I throw you out! (*As the guests stampede from the house, gloomily to* GRUSHA:) I've upset the apple cart, huh? (*Receiving no answer, he turns round and takes a cake from the pan which his mother is holding.*)

SINGER: O confusion! The wife discovers she has a husband.

> By day there's the child, by night there's the husband.
> The lover is on his way both day and night.
> Husband and wife look at each other.
> The bedroom is small.

(*Near the bed the* PEASANT *is sitting in a high wooden bathtub, naked, the* MOTHER-IN-LAW *is pouring water from a pitcher. Opposite* GRUSHA *cowers with* MICHAEL, *who is playing at mending straw mats.*)

PEASANT (*to his mother*): That's her work, not yours. Where's she hiding out now?

MOTHER-IN-LAW (*calling*): Grusha! The peasant wants you!

GRUSHA (*to* MICHAEL): There are still two holes to mend.

PEASANT (*when* GRUSHA *approaches*): Scrub my back!

GRUSHA: Can't the peasant do it himself?

PEASANT: "Can't the peasant do it himself?" Get the brush! To hell with you! Are you the wife here? Or are you a visitor? (*To the* MOTHER-IN-LAW:) It's too cold!

MOTHER-IN-LAW: I'll run for hot water.

GRUSHA: Let me go.

PEASANT: You stay here. (*The* MOTHER-IN-LAW *exits.*) Rub harder. And no shirking. You've seen a naked fellow before. That child didn't come out of thin air.

GRUSHA: The child was not conceived in joy, if that's what the peasant means.

PEASANT (*turning and grinning*): You don't look the type. (GRUSHA *stops scrubbing him, starts back. Enter the* MOTHER-IN-LAW.)

PEASANT: A nice thing you've saddled me with! A simpleton for a wife!

MOTHER-IN-LAW: She just isn't cooperative.

PEASANT: Pour—but go easy! Ow! Go easy, I said. (*To* GRUSHA:) Maybe you did something wrong in the city . . . I wouldn't be surprised. Why else should you be here? But I won't talk about that. I've not said a word about the illegitimate object you brought into my house either. But my patience has limits! It's against nature. (*To the* MOTHER-IN-LAW:) More! (*To* GRUSHA:) And even if your soldier does come back, you're married.

GRUSHA: Yes.

PEASANT: But your soldier won't come back. Don't you believe it.

GRUSHA: No.

PEASANT: You're cheating me. You're my wife and you're not my wife. Where you lie, nothing lies, and yet no other woman can lie there. When I go to work in the morning I'm tired—when I lie down at night I'm awake as the devil. God has given you sex—and what d'you do? I don't have ten piasters to buy myself a woman in the city. Besides, it's a long way. Woman weeds the fields and opens up her legs, that's what our calendar says. D'you hear?

GRUSHA (*quietly*): Yes. I didn't mean to cheat you out of it.

PEASANT: She didn't mean to cheat me out of it! Pour some more water! (*The* MOTHER-IN-LAW *pours.*) Ow!

SINGER: As she sat by the stream to wash the linen

> She saw his image in the water
> And his face grew dimmer with the passing moons.
> As she raised herself to wring the linen
> She heard his voice from the murmuring maple
> And his voice grew fainter with the passing moons.
> Evasions and sighs grew more numerous,
> Tears and sweat flowed.
> With the passing moons the child grew up.

(GRUSHA *sits by a stream, dipping linen into the water. In the rear, a few children are standing.*)

GRUSHA (*to* MICHAEL): You can play with them, Michael, but don't let them boss you around just because you're the littlest. (MICHAEL *nods and joins the children. They start playing.*)

BIGGEST BOY: Today it's the Heads-Off Game. (*To a* FAT BOY:) You're the Prince and you laugh. (*To* MICHAEL:) You're the Governor. (*To a* GIRL:) You're the Governor's wife and you cry when his head's cut off. And I do the cutting. (*He shows his wooden sword.*) With this. First, they lead the Governor into the yard. The Prince walks in front. The Governor's wife comes last.

(*They form a procession. The* FAT BOY *is first and laughs. Then comes* MICHAEL, *then the* BIGGEST BOY *and then the* GIRL, *who weeps.*)

MICHAEL (*standing still*): Me cut off head!

BIGGEST BOY: That's my job. You're the littlest. The Governor's the easy part. All you do is kneel down and get your head cut off—simple.

MICHAEL: Me want sword!

BIGGEST BOY: It's mine! (*He gives* MICHAEL *a kick.*)

GIRL (*shouting to* GRUSHA): He won't play his part!

GRUSHA (*laughing*): Even the little duck is a swimmer, they say.

BIGGEST BOY: You can be the Prince if you can laugh. (MICHAEL *shakes his head.*)

FAT BOY: I laugh best. Let him cut off the head just once. Then you do it, then me.

(*Reluctantly, the* BIGGEST BOY *hands* MICHAEL *the wooden sword and kneels down. The* FAT BOY *sits down, slaps his thigh, and laughs with all his might. The* GIRL *weeps loudly.* MICHAEL *swings the big sword and "cuts off" the head. In doing so, he topples over.*)

BIGGEST BOY: Hey! I'll show you how to cut heads off!

(MICHAEL *runs away. The children run after him.* GRUSHA *laughs, following them with her eyes. On looking back, she sees* SIMON SHASHAVA *standing on the opposite bank. He wears a shabby uniform.*)

GRUSHA: Simon!

SIMON: Is that Grusha Vashnadze?

GRUSHA: Simon!

SIMON (*formally*): A good morning to the young lady. I hope she is well.

GRUSHA (*getting up gaily and bowing low*): A good morning to the soldier. God be thanked he has returned in good health.

SIMON: They found better fish, so they didn't eat me, said the haddock.

GRUSHA: Courage, said the kitchen boy. Good luck, said the hero.

SIMON: How are things here? Was the winter bearable? The neighbor considerate?

GRUSHA: The winter was a trifle rough, the neighbor as usual, Simon.

SIMON: May one ask if a certain person still dips her toes in the water when rinsing the linen?

GRUSHA: The answer is no. Because of the eyes in the bushes.

SIMON: The young lady is speaking of soldiers. Here stands a paymaster.

GRUSHA: A job worth twenty piasters?

SIMON: And lodgings.

GRUSHA (*with tears in her eyes*): Behind the barracks under the date trees.

SIMON: Yes, there. A certain person has kept her eyes open.

GRUSHA: She has, Simon.

SIMON: And has not forgotten? (GRUSHA *shakes her head.*) So the door is still on its hinges as they say? (GRUSHA *looks at him in silence and shakes her head again.*) What's this? Is anything not as it should be?

GRUSHA: Simon Shashava, I can never return to Nuka. Something has happened.

SIMON: What can have happened?

GRUSHA: For one thing, I knocked an Ironshirt down.

SIMON: Grusha Vashnadze must have had her reasons for that.

GRUSHA: Simon Shashava, I am no longer called what I used to be called.

SIMON (*after a pause*): I do not understand.

GRUSHA: When do women change their names, Simon? Let me explain. Nothing stands between us. Everything is just as it was. You must believe that.

SIMON: Nothing stands between us and yet there's something?

GRUSHA: How can I explain it so fast and with the stream between us? Couldn't you cross the bridge there?

SIMON: Maybe it's no longer necessary.

GRUSHA: It is very necessary. Come over on this side, Simon, Quick!

SIMON: Does the young lady wish to say someone has come too late?

(GRUSHA *looks up at him in despair, her face streaming with tears.* SIMON *stares before him. He picks up a piece of wood and starts cutting it.*)

SINGER: So many words are said, so many left unsaid.

The soldier has come.

Where he comes from, he does not say.

Hear what he thought and did not say:
"The battle began, gray at dawn, grew
　　bloody at noon.
The first man fell in front of me, the
　　second behind me, the third at my
　　side.
I trod on the first, left the second behind,
　　the third was run through by the
　　captain.
One of my brothers died by steel, the
　　other by smoke.
My neck caught fire, my hands froze in
　　my gloves, my toes in my socks.
I fed on aspen buds, I drank maple juice,
　　I slept on stone, in water."

SIMON: I see a cap in the grass. Is there a little one already?

GRUSHA: There is, Simon. There's no keeping *that* from you. But please don't worry, it is not mine.

SIMON: When the wind once starts to blow, they say, it blows through every cranny. The wife need say no more. (GRUSHA *looks into her lap and is silent.*)

SINGER: There was yearning but there was no waiting.
The oath is broken. Neither could say why.
Hear what she thought but did not say:
"While you fought in the battle, soldier,
The bloody battle, the bitter battle
I found a helpless infant
I had not the heart to destroy him
I had to care for a creature that was lost
I had to stoop for breadcrumbs on the floor
I had to break myself for that which was not mine
That which was other people's.
Someone must help!
For the little tree needs water
The lamb loses its way when the shepherd is asleep
And its cry is unheard!"

SIMON: Give me back the cross I gave you. Better still, throw it in the stream. (*He turns to go.*)

GRUSHA (*getting up*): Simon Shashava, don't go away! He isn't mine! He isn't mine! (*She hears the children calling.*) What's the matter, children?

VOICES: Soldiers! And they're taking Michael away!

(GRUSHA *stands aghast as two* IRONSHIRTS, *with* MICHAEL *between them, come toward her.*)

ONE OF THE IRONSHIRTS: Are you Grusha? (*She nods.*) Is this your child?

GRUSHA: Yes. (SIMON *goes.*) Simon!

IRONSHIRT: We have orders, in the name of the law, to take this child, found in your custody, back to the city. It is suspected that the child is Michael Abashwili, son and heir of the late Governor Georgi Abashwili, and his wife, Natella Abashwili. Here is the document and the seal. (*They lead the* CHILD *away.*)

GRUSHA (*running after them, shouting*): Leave him here. Please! He's mine!

SINGER: The Ironshirts took the child, the beloved child.
The unhappy girl followed them to the city, the dreaded city.
She who had borne him demanded the child.
She who had raised him faced trial.
Who will decide the case?
To whom will the child be assigned?
Who will the judge be? A good judge? A bad?
The city was in flames.
In the judge's seat sat Azdak.[1]

4

THE STORY OF THE JUDGE

SINGER: Hear the story of the judge
How he turned judge, how he passed judgment, what kind of judge he was.
On that Easter Sunday of the great revolt, when the Grand Duke was overthrown
And his Governor Abashwili, father of our child, lost his head
The Village Scrivener Azdak found a fugitive in the woods and hid him in his hut.

(AZDAK, *in rags and slightly drunk, is helping an old beggar into his cottage.*)

---

1. The name Azdak should be accented on the second syllable.—E. B.

AZDAK: Stop snorting, you're not a horse. And it won't do you any good with the police to run like a snotty nose in April. Stand still, I say. (*He catches the* OLD MAN, *who has marched into the cottage as if he'd like to go through the walls.*) Sit down. Feed. Here's a hunk of cheese. (*From under some rags, in a chest, he fishes out some cheese, and the* OLD MAN *greedily begins to eat.*) Haven't eaten in a long time, huh? (*The* OLD MAN *growls.*) Why were you running like that, asshole? The cop wouldn't even have seen you.

OLD MAN: Had to! Had to!

AZDAK: Blue funk? (*The* OLD MAN *stares, uncomprehending.*) Cold feet? Panic? Don't lick your chops like a Grand Duke. Or an old sow. I can't stand it. We have to accept respectable stinkers as God made them, but not you! I once heard of a senior judge who farted at a public dinner to show an independent spirit! Watching you eat like that gives me the most awful ideas. Why don't you say something? (*Sharply.*) Show me your hand. Can't you hear? (*The* OLD MAN *slowly puts out his hand.*) White! So you're not a beggar at all! A fraud, a walking swindle! And I'm hiding you from the cops like you were an honest man! Why were you running like that if you're a landowner? For that's what you are. Don't deny it! I see it in your guilty face! (*He gets up.*) Get out! (*The* OLD MAN *looks at him uncertainly.*) What are you waiting for, peasant-flogger?

OLD MAN: Pursued. Need undivided attention. Make proposition . . .

AZDAK: Make what? A proposition? Well, if that isn't the height of insolence. He's making me a proposition! The bitten man scratches his fingers bloody, and the leech that's biting him makes him a proposition! Get out, I tell you!

OLD MAN: Understand point of view! Persuasion! Pay hundred thousand piasters one night! Yes?

AZDAK: What, you think you can buy me? For a hundred thousand piasters? Let's say a hundred and fifty thousand. Where are they?

OLD MAN: Have not them here. Of course. Will be sent. Hope do not doubt.

AZDAK: Doubt very much. Get out!

(*The* OLD MAN *gets up, waddles to the door. A* VOICE *is heard offstage.*)

VOICE: Azdak!

(*The* OLD MAN *turns, waddles to the opposite corner, stands still.*)

AZDAK (*calling out*): I'm not in! (*He walks to door.*) So you're sniffing around here again, Shauwa?

SHAUWA (*reproachfully*): You caught another rabbit, Azdak. And you'd promised me it wouldn't happen again!

AZDAK (*severely*): Shauwa, don't talk about things you don't understand. The rabbit is a dangerous and destructive beast. It feeds on plants, especially on the species of plants known as weeds. It must therefore be exterminated.

SHAUWA: Azdak, don't be so hard on me. I'll lose my job if I don't arrest you. I know you have a good heart.

AZDAK: I do not have a good heart! How often must I tell you I'm a man of intellect?

SHAUWA (*slyly*): I know, Azdak. You're a superior person. You say so yourself. I'm just a Christian and an ignoramus. So I ask you: When one of the Prince's rabbits is stolen, and I'm a policeman, what should I do with the offending party?

AZDAK: Shauwa, Shauwa, shame on you. You stand and ask me a question, than which nothing could be more seductive. It's like you were a woman—let's say that bad girl Nunowna, and you showed me your thigh—Nunowna's thigh, that would be—and asked me: "What shall I do with my thigh, it itches?" Is she as innocent as she pretends? Of course not. I catch a rabbit, but you catch a man. Man is made in God's image. Not so a rabbit, you know that. I'm a rabbit-eater, but you're a man-eater, Shauwa. And God will pass judgment on you. Shauwa, go home and repent. No, stop, there's something . . . (*He looks at the* OLD MAN *who stands trembling in the corner.*) No, it's nothing. Go home and repent. (*He slams the door behind* SHAUWA.) Now you're surprised, huh? Surprised I didn't hand you over? I couldn't hand over a bedbug to that animal. It goes against the grain. Now don't tremble because of a cop! So old and still so scared? Finish your cheese, but eat it like a poor man, or else they'll still catch you. Must I even explain how a poor man behaves? (*He pushes him down, and then gives him back the cheese.*) That box is the table. Lay your elbows on the table. Now, encircle the cheese on the plate like it might be snatched from you at any moment—what right have you to be safe, huh?—now, hold your knife like an undersized sickle, and give your cheese a troubled look because, like all beautiful things, it's already fading away. (AZDAK *watches him.*) They're after you, which speaks in your favor, but how can we be sure they're not mistaken about you? In Tiflis one time they hanged a landowner, a Turk, who could prove he quartered his peasants instead of merely cutting them in half, as is the custom, and he squeezed twice the usual amount of taxes out of them, his zeal was above suspicion. And yet they hanged him like a common criminal—because he was a Turk—a thing he couldn't do much about. What injustice! He got onto the gallows by a sheer fluke. In short, I don't trust you.

SINGER: Thus Azdak gave the old beggar a bed,
　　　　And learned that old beggar was the old
　　　　　　butcher, the Grand Duke himself,
　　　　And was ashamed.
　　　　He denounced himself and ordered the
　　　　　　policeman to take him to Nuka, to
　　　　　　court, to be judged.

(*In the court of justice three* IRONSHIRTS *sit drinking.*)
(*From a beam hangs a man in judge's robes. Enter* AZDAK, *in chains, dragging* SHAUWA *behind him.*)

AZDAK (*shouting*): I've helped the Grand Duke, the Grand Thief, the Grand Butcher, to escape! In the name of justice I ask to be severely judged in public trial!

FIRST IRONSHIRT: Who's this queer bird?

SHAUWA: That's our Village Scrivener, Azdak.

AZDAK: I am contemptible! I am a traitor! A branded criminal! Tell them, flatfoot, how I insisted on being tied up and brought to the capital. Because I sheltered the Grand Duke, the Grand Swindler, by mistake. And how I found out afterwards. See the marked man denounce himself! Tell them how I forced you to walk half the night with me to clear the whole thing up.

SHAUWA: And all by threats. That wasn't nice of you, Azdak.

AZDAK: Shut your mouth, Shauwa. You don't understand. A new age is upon us! It'll go thundering over you. You're finished. The police will be wiped out—poof! Everything will be gone into, everything will be brought into the open. The guilty will give themselves up. Why? They couldn't escape the people in any case. (*To* SHAUWA:) Tell them how I shouted all along Shoemaker Street (*with big gestures, looking at the* IRONSHIRTS) "In my ignorance I let the Grand Swindler escape! So tear me to pieces, brothers!" I wanted to get it in first.

FIRST IRONSHIRT: And what did your brothers answer?

SHAUWA: They comforted him in Butcher Street, and they laughed themselves sick in Shoemaker Street. That's all.

AZDAK: But with you it's different. I can see you're men of iron. Brothers, where's the judge? I must be tried.

FIRST IRONSHIRT (*pointing at the hanged man*): There's the judge. And please stop "brothering" us. It's rather a sore spot this evening.

AZDAK: "There's the judge." An answer never heard in Grusinia before. Townsman, where's His Excellency the Governor? (*Pointing to the ground.*) There's His Excellency, stranger. Where's the Chief Tax Collector? Where's the official Recruiting Officer? The Patriarch? The Chief of Police? There, there, there—all there. Brothers, I expected no less of you.

SECOND IRONSHIRT: What? *What* was it you expected, funny man?

AZDAK: What happened in Persia, brother, what happened in Persia?

SECOND IRONSHIRT: What did happen in Persia?

AZDAK: Everybody was hanged. Viziers, tax collectors. Everybody. Forty years ago now. My grandfather, a remarkable man by the way, saw it all. For three whole days. Everywhere.

SECOND IRONSHIRT: And who ruled when the Vizier was hanged?

AZDAK: A peasant ruled when the Vizier was hanged.

SECOND IRONSHIRT: And who commanded the army?

AZDAK: A soldier, a soldier.

SECOND IRONSHIRT: And who paid the wages?

AZDAK: A dyer. A dyer paid the wages.

SECOND IRONSHIRT: Wasn't it a weaver, maybe?

FIRST IRONSHIRT: And why did all this happen, Persian?

AZDAK: Why did all this happen? Must there be a special reason? Why do you scratch yourself, brother? War! Too long a war! And no justice! My grandfather brought back a song that tells how it was. I will sing it for you. With my friend the policeman. (*To* SHAUWA:) And hold the rope tight. Its very suitable. (*He sings, with* SHAUWA *holding the rope tight around him.*)

THE SONG OF INJUSTICE IN PERSIA
Why don't our sons bleed any more?
    Why don't our daughters weep?
Why do only the slaughterhouse cattle
    have blood in their veins?
Why do only the willows shed tears on
    Lake Urmia?
The king must have a new province, the
    peasant must give up his savings.
That the roof of the world might be
    conquered, the roof of the cottage is
    torn down.
Our men are carried to the ends of the
    earth, so that great ones can eat at
    home.
The soldiers kill each other, the marshals
    salute each other.
They bite the widow's tax money to see
    if it's good, their swords break.
The battle was lost, the helmets were
    paid for.
    Refrain: Is it so? Is it so?

SHAUWA (*refrain*): Yes, yes, yes, yes, yes it's so.
AZDAK: Want to hear the rest of it? (*The* FIRST IRONSHIRT *nods.*)
SECOND IRONSHIRT (*to* SHAUWA): Did he teach you that song?
SHAUWA: Yes, only my voice isn't very good.
SECOND IRONSHIRT: No. (*To* AZDAK:) Go on singing.
AZDAK: The second verse is about the peace. (*He sings.*)
    The offices are packed, the streets over-
      flow with officials.
    The rivers jump their banks and ravage
      the fields.
    Those who cannot let down their own
      trousers rule countries.

    They can't count up to four, but they
      devour eight courses.
    The corn farmers, looking round for
      buyers, see only the starving.
    The weavers go home from their looms
      in rags.
    Refrain: Is it so? Is it so?
SHAUWA (*refrain*): Yes, yes, yes, yes, yes it's so.
AZDAK: That's why our sons don't bleed any more,
      that's why our daughters don't weep.
    That's why only the slaughterhouse
      cattle have blood in their veins,
    And only the willows shed tears by Lake
      Urmia toward morning.
FIRST IRONSHIRT: Are you going to sing that song here in town?
AZDAK: Sure. What's wrong with it?
FIRST IRONSHIRT: Have you noticed that the sky's getting red? (*Turning round,* AZDAK *sees the sky red with fire.*) It's the people's quarters on the outskirts of town. The carpet weavers have caught the "Persian Sickness," too. And they've been asking if Prince Kazbeki isn't eating too many courses. This morning they strung up the city judge. As for us we beat them to pulp. We were paid one hundred piasters per man, you understand?
AZDAK (*after a pause*): I understand. (*He glances shyly round and, creeping away, sits down in a corner, his head in his hands.*)
IRONSHIRTS (*to each other*): If there ever was a troublemaker it's him—He must've come to the capital to fish in the troubled waters.
SHAUWA: Oh, I don't think he's a really bad character, gentlemen. Steals a few chickens here and there. And maybe a rabbit.
SECOND IRONSHIRT (*approaching* AZDAK): Came to fish in the troubled waters, huh?
AZDAK (*looking up*): I don't know why I came.
SECOND IRONSHIRT: Are you in with the carpet weavers maybe? (AZDAK *shakes his head.*) How about that song?
AZDAK: From my grandfather. A silly and ignorant man.
SECOND IRONSHIRT: Right. And how about the dyer who paid the wages?
AZDAK (*muttering*): That was in Persia.

FIRST IRONSHIRT: And this denouncing of yourself? Because you didn't hang the Grand Duke with your own hands?

AZDAK: Didn't I tell you I let him run? (*He creeps farther away and sits on the floor.*)

SHAUWA: I can swear to that: he let him run.

(*The* IRONSHIRTS *burst out laughing and slap* SHAUWA *on the back.* AZDAK *laughs loudest. They slap* AZDAK *too, and unchain him. They all start drinking as the* FAT PRINCE *enters with a young man.*)

FIRST IRONSHIRT (*to* AZDAK, *pointing at the* FAT PRINCE): There's your "new age" for you! (*More laughter.*)

FAT PRINCE: Well, my friends, what is there to laugh about? Permit me a serious word. Yesterday morning the Princes of Grusinia overthrew the warmongering government of the Grand Duke and did away with his Governors. Unfortunately the Grand Duke himself escaped. In this fateful hour our carpet weavers, those eternal troublemakers, had the effrontery to stir up a rebellion and hang the universally loved city judge, our dear Illo Orbeliani. Ts—ts—ts. My friends, we need peace, peace, peace in Grusinia! And justice! So I've brought along my dear nephew Bizergan Kazbeki. He'll be the new judge, hm? A very gifted fellow. What do you say? I want your opinion. Let the people decide!

SECOND IRONSHIRT: Does this mean *we* elect the judge?

FAT PRINCE: Precisely. Let the people propose some very gifted fellow! Confer among yourselves, my friends. (*The* IRONSHIRTS *confer.*) Don't worry, my little fox. The job's yours. And when we catch the Grand Duke we won't have to kiss this rabble's ass any longer.

IRONSHIRTS (*among themselves*):
—Very funny: they're wetting their pants because they haven't caught the Grand Duke.
—When the outlook isn't so bright, they say: "My friends!" and "Let the people decide!"
—Now he even wants justice for Grusinia! But fun is fun as long as it lasts! (*Pointing at* AZDAK.) *He* knows all about justice. Hey, rascal, would you like this nephew fellow to be the judge?

AZDAK: Are you asking me? You're not asking *me*?!

FIRST IRONSHIRT: Why not? Anything for a laugh!

AZDAK: You'd like to test him to the marrow, correct? Have you a criminal on hand? An experienced one? So the candidate can show what he knows?

SECOND IRONSHIRT: Let's see. We do have a couple of doctors downstairs. Let's use them.

AZDAK: Oh, no, that's no good, we can't take real criminals till we're sure the judge will be appointed. He may be dumb, but he must be appointed, or the law is violated. And the law is a sensitive organ. It's like the spleen, you mustn't hit it—that would be fatal. Of course you can hang those two without violating the law, because there was no judge in the vicinity. But judgment, when pronounced, must be pronounced with absolute gravity—it's all such nonsense. Suppose, for instance, a judge jails a woman—let's say she's stolen a corn cake to feed her child—and this judge isn't wearing his robes—or maybe he's scratching himself while passing sentence and half his body is uncovered—a man's thigh *will* itch once in a while—the sentence this judge passes is a disgrace and the law is violated. In short it would be easier for a judge's robe and a judge's hat to pass judgment than for a man with no robe and no hat. If you don't treat it with respect, the law just disappears on you. Now you don't try out a bottle of wine by offering it to a dog; you'd only lose your wine.

FIRST IRONSHIRT: Then what do you suggest, hairsplitter?

AZDAK: I'll be the defendant.

FIRST IRONSHIRT: You? (*He bursts out laughing.*)

FAT PRINCE: What have you decided?

FIRST IRONSHIRT: We've decided to stage a rehearsal. Our friend here will be the defendant. Let the candidate be the judge and sit there.

FAT PRINCE: It isn't customary, but why not? (*To the* NEPHEW:) A mere formality, my little fox. What have I taught you? Who got there first—the slow runner or the fast?

NEPHEW: The silent runner, Uncle Arsen.

(*The* NEPHEW *takes the chair. The* IRONSHIRTS *and the* FAT PRINCE *sit on the steps. Enter* AZDAK, *mimicking the gait of the* GRAND DUKE.)

AZDAK (*in the* GRAND DUKE'S *accent*): Is any here knows me? Am Grand Duke.

IRONSHIRTS:
—*What* is he?
—The Grand Duke. He knows him, too.
—Fine. So get on with the trial.

AZDAK: Listen! Am accused instigating war? Ridiculous! Am saying ridiculous! That enough? If not, have brought lawyers. Believe five hundred. (*He points behind him, pretending to be surrounded by lawyers.*) Requisition all available seats for lawyers! (*The* IRONSHIRTS *laugh; the* FAT PRINCE *joins in.*)

NEPHEW (*to the* IRONSHIRTS): You really wish me to try this case? I find it rather unusual. From the taste angle, I mean.

FIRST IRONSHIRT: Let's go!

FAT PRINCE (*smiling*): Let him have it, my little fox!

NEPHEW: All right. People of Grusinia versus Grand Duke. Defendant, what have you got to say for yourself?

AZDAK: Plenty. Naturally, have read war lost. Only started on the advice of patriots. Like Uncle Arsen Kazbeki. Call Uncle Arsen as witness.

FAT PRINCE (*to the* IRONSHIRTS, *delightedly*): What a madcap!

NEPHEW: Motion rejected. One cannot be arraigned for declaring a war, which every ruler has to do once in a while, but only for running a war badly.

AZDAK: Rubbish! Did not run it at all! Had it run! Had it run by Princes! Naturally, they messed it up.

NEPHEW: Do you by any chance deny having been commander-in-chief?

AZDAK: Not at all! Always *was* commander-in-chief. At birth shouted at wet nurse. Was trained drop turds in toilet, grew accustomed to command. Always commanded officials rob my cash box. Officers flog soldiers only on command. Landowners sleep with peasants' wives only on strictest command. Uncle Arsen here grew his belly at *my* command!

IRONSHIRTS (*clapping*): He's good! Long live the Grand Duke!

FAT PRINCE: Answer him, my little fox: I'm with you.

NEPHEW: I shall answer him according to the dignity of the law. Defendant, preserve the dignity of the law!

AZDAK: Agreed. Command you proceed with trial!

NEPHEW: It is not your place to command me. You claim that the Princes forced you to declare war. How can you claim, then, that they—er—"messed it up"?

AZDAK: Did not send enough people. Embezzled funds. Sent sick horses. During attack, drinking in whorehouse. Call Uncle Arsen as witness.

NEPHEW: Are you making the outrageous suggestion that the Princes of this country did not fight?

AZDAK: No. Princes fought. Fought for war contracts.

FAT PRINCE (*jumping up*): That's too much! This man talks like a carpet weaver!

AZDAK: Really? Told nothing but truth.

FAT PRINCE: Hang him! Hang him!

FIRST IRONSHIRT (*pulling the* PRINCE *down*): Keep quiet! Go on, Excellency!

NEPHEW: Quiet! I now render a verdict: You must be hanged! By the neck! Having lost war!

AZDAK: Young man, seriously advise not fall publicly into jerky clipped speech. Cannot be watchdog if howl like wolf. Got it? If people realize Princes speak same language as Grand Duke, may hang Grand Duke *and Princes,* huh? By the way, must overrule verdict. Reason? War lost, but not for Princes. Princes won their war. Got 3,863,000 piasters for horses not delivered, 8,240,000 piasters for food supplies not produced. Are therefore victors. War lost only for Grusinia, which is not present in this court.

FAT PRINCE: I think that will do, my friends. (*To* AZDAK:) You can withdraw, funny man. (*To the* IRONSHIRTS:) You may now ratify the new judge's appointment, my friends.

FIRST IRONSHIRT: Yes, we can. Take down the judge's gown. (*One* IRONSHIRT *climbs on the back of the other, pulls the gown off the hanged man.*) (*To the* NEPHEW:) Now you run away so the right ass can get on the right chair. (*To* AZDAK:) Step forward! Go to the judge's seat! Now sit in it! (AZDAK *steps up, bows, and sits down.*) The judge was always a rascal! Now the rascal shall be a judge! (*The judge's gown is placed round his shoulders, the hat on his head.*) And what a judge!

SINGER: And there was civil war in the land.
The mighty were not safe.

And Azdak was made a judge by the
Ironshirts.
And Azdak remained a judge for two
years.

SINGER AND CHORUS: When the towns were set
afire
And rivers of blood rose higher and
higher,
Cockroaches crawled out of every crack.
And the court was full of schemers
And the church of foul blasphemers.
In the judge's cassock sat Azdak.

(AZDAK *sits in the judge's chair, peeling an apple.*
SHAUWA *is sweeping out the hall. On one side an*
INVALID *in a wheelchair. Opposite, a young man
accused of blackmail. An* IRONSHIRT *stands guard,
holding the Ironshirts' banner.*)

AZDAK: In consideration of the large number of
cases, the Court today will hear two cases at
a time. Before I open the proceedings, a short
announcement—I accept. (*He stretches out his
hand. The* BLACKMAILER *is the only one to produce
any money. He hands it to* AZDAK.) I reserve the
right to punish one of the parties for contempt
of court. (*He glances at the* INVALID.) You (*to the*
DOCTOR) are a doctor, and you (*to the* INVALID)
are bringing a complaint against him. Is the
doctor responsible for your condition?

INVALID: Yes. I had a stroke on his account.

AZDAK: That would be professional negligence.

INVALID: Worse than negligence. I gave this man
money for his studies. So far, he hasn't paid
me back a cent. It was when I heard he was
treating a patient free that I had my stroke.

AZDAK: Rightly. (*To a* LIMPING MAN:) And what are
you doing here?

LIMPING MAN: I'm the patient, Your Honor.

AZDAK: He treated your leg for nothing?

LIMPING MAN: The wrong leg! My rheumatism was
in the left leg, he operated on the right. That's
why I limp.

AZDAK: And you were treated free?

INVALID: A five-hundred-piaster operation free! For
nothing! For a God-bless-you! And I paid for
this man's studies! (*To the* DOCTOR:) Did they
teach you to operate free?

DOCTOR: Your Honor, it is the custom to demand
the fee before the operation, as the patient

is more willing to pay before an operation
than after. Which is only human. In the case
in question I was convinced, when I started
the operation, that my servant had already received the fee. In this I was mistaken.

INVALID: He was mistaken! A good doctor doesn't
make mistakes! He examines before he operates!

AZDAK: That's right: (*To* SHAUWA:) Public Prosecutor, what's the other case about?

SHAUWA (*busily sweeping*): Blackmail.

BLACKMAILER: High Court of Justice, I'm innocent.
I only wanted to find out from the landowner
concerned if he really *had* raped his niece. He
informed me very politely that this was not
the case, and gave me the money only so I
could pay for my uncle's studies.

AZDAK: Hm. (*To the* DOCTOR:) You, on the other
hand, can cite no extenuating circumstances
for your offense, huh?

DOCTOR: Except that to err is human.

AZDAK: And you are aware that in money matters
a good doctor is a highly responsible person?
I once heard of a doctor who got a thousand
piasters for a sprained finger by remarking
that sprains have something to do with blood
circulation, which after all a less good doctor might have overlooked, and who, on another occasion made a real gold mine out of a
somewhat disordered gall bladder, he treated
it with such loving care. You have no excuse,
Doctor. The corn merchant Uxu had his son
study medicine to get some knowledge of
trade, our medical schools are so good. (*To
the* BLACKMAILER:) What's the landowner's
name?

SHAUWA: He doesn't want it mentioned.

AZDAK: In that case I will pass judgment. The Court
considers the blackmail proved. And you (*to
the* INVALID) are sentenced to a fine of one thousand piasters. If you have a second stroke, the
doctor will have to treat you free. Even if he
has to amputate. (*To the* LIMPING MAN:) As compensation, you will receive a bottle of rubbing
alcohol. (*To the* BLACKMAILER:) You are sentenced
to hand over half the proceeds of your deal to
the Public Prosecutor to keep the landowner's
name secret. You are advised, moreover, to
study medicine—you seem well suited to that

calling. (*To the* DOCTOR:) You have perpetrated an unpardonable error in the practice of your profession: you are acquitted. Next cases!

SINGER AND CHORUS: Men won't do much for a
  shilling.
  For a pound they may be willing.
  For twenty pounds the verdict's in the
    sack.
  As for the many, all too many,
  Those who've only got a penny—
  They've one single, sole recourse: Azdak.

(*Enter* AZDAK *from the caravansary on the highroad, followed by an old bearded* INNKEEPER. *The judge's chair is carried by a stableman and* SHAUWA. *An* IRONSHIRT, *with a banner, takes up his position.*)

AZDAK: Put me down. Then we'll get some air, maybe even a good stiff breeze from the lemon grove there. It does justice good to be done in the open: the wind blows her skirts up and you can see what she's got. Shauwa, we've been eating too much. These official journeys are exhausting. (*To the* INNKEEPER:) It's a question of your daughter-in-law?

INNKEEPER: Your Worship, it's a question of the family honor. I wish to bring an action on behalf of my son, who's away on business on the other side the mountain. This is the offending stableman, and here's my daughter-in-law.

(*Enter the* DAUGHTER-IN-LAW, *a voluptuous wench. She is veiled.*)

AZDAK (*sitting down*): I accept. (*Sighing, the* INNKEEPER *hands him some money.*) Good. Now the formalities are disposed of. This is a case of rape?

INNKEEPER: Your Honor, I caught the fellow in the act. Ludovica was in the straw on the stable floor.

AZDAK: Quite right, the stable. Lovely horses! I specially liked the little roan.

INNKEEPER: The first thing I did, of course, was to question Ludovica. On my son's behalf.

AZDAK (*seriously*): I said I specially liked the little roan.

INNKEEPER (*coldly*): Really? Ludovica confessed the stableman took her against her will.

AZDAK: Take your veil off, Ludovica. (*She does so.*) Ludovica, you please the Court. Tell us how it happened.

LUDOVICA (*well schooled*): When I entered the stable to see the new foal the stableman said to me on his own accord: "It's hot today!" and laid his hand on my left breast. I said to him: "Don't do that!" But he continued to handle me indecently, which provoked my anger. Before I realized his sinful intentions, he got much closer. It was all over when my father-in-law entered and accidentally trod on me.

INNKEEPER (*explaining*): On my son's behalf.

AZDAK (*to the* STABLEMAN): You admit you started it?

STABLEMAN: Yes.

AZDAK: Ludovica, you like to eat sweet things?

LUDOVICA: Yes, sunflower seeds!

AZDAK: You like to lie a long time in the bathtub?

LUDOVICA: Half an hour or so.

AZDAK: Public Prosecutor, drop your knife—there on the ground. (SHAUWA *does so.*) Ludovica, pick up that knife. (LUDOVICA, *swaying her hips, does so.*) See that? (*He points at her.*) The way it moves? The rape is now proven. By eating too much—sweet things, especially—by lying too long in warm water, by laziness and too soft a skin, you have raped that unfortunate man. Think you can run around with a behind like that and get away with it in court? This is a case of intentional assault with a dangerous weapon! You are sentenced to hand over to the Court the little roan which your father liked to ride "on his son's behalf." And now, come with me to the stables, so the Court can inspect the scene of the crime, Ludovica.

SINGER AND CHORUS: When the sharks the sharks
  devour
  Little fishes have their hour.
  For a while the load is off their back.
  On Grusinia's highways faring
  Fixed-up scales of justice bearing
  Strode the poor man's magistrate: Azdak.

  And he gave to the forsaken
  All that from the rich he'd taken.
  And a bodyguard of roughnecks was
    Azdak's.
  And our good and evil man, he
  Smiled upon Grusinia's Granny.
  His emblem was a tear in sealing wax.

All mankind should love each other
But when visiting your brother
Take an ax along and hold it fast.
Not in theory but in practice
Miracles are wrought with axes
And the age of miracles is not past.

(AZDAK's *judge's chair is in a tavern. Three rich* FARMERS *stand before* AZDAK. SHAUWA *brings him wine. In a corner stands an* OLD PEASANT WOMAN. *In the open doorway, and outside, stand villagers looking on. An* IRONSHIRT *stands guard with a banner.*)

AZDAK: The Public Prosecutor has the floor.

SHAUWA: It concerns a cow. For five weeks, the defendant has had a cow in her stable, the property of the farmer Suru. She was also found to be in possession of a stolen ham, and a number of cows belonging to Shutoff were killed after he asked the defendant to pay the rent on a piece of land.

FARMERS:
—It's a matter of my ham, Your Honor.
—It's a matter of my cow, Your Honor.
—It's a matter of my land, Your Honor.

AZDAK: Well, Granny, what have *you* got to say to all this?

OLD WOMAN: Your Honor, one night toward morning, five weeks ago, there was a knock at my door, and outside stood a bearded man with a cow. "My dear woman," he said, "I am the miracle-working Saint Banditus and because your son has been killed in the war, I bring you this cow as a souvenir. Take good care of it."

FARMERS:
—The robber, Irakli, Your Honor!
—Her brother-in-law, Your Honor!
—The cow-thief!
—The incendiary!
—He must be beheaded!

(*Outside, a woman screams. The crowd grows restless retreats. Enter the* BANDIT *Irakli with a huge ax.*)

BANDIT: A very good evening, dear friends! A glass of vodka!

FARMERS (*crossing themselves*): Irakli!

AZDAK: Public Prosecutor, a glass of vodka for our guest. And who are you?

BANDIT: I'm a wandering hermit, Your Honor. Thanks for the gracious gift. (*He empties the glass which* SHAUWA *has brought.*) Another!

AZDAK: I am Azdak. (*He gets up and bows. The* BANDIT *also bows.*) The Court welcomes the foreign hermit. Go on with your story, Granny.

OLD WOMAN: Your Honor, that first night I didn't yet know Saint Banditus could work miracles, it was only the cow. But one night, a few days later, the farmer's servants came to take the cow away again. Then they turned round in front of my door and went off without the cow. And bumps as big as a fist sprouted on their heads. So I knew that Saint Banditus had changed their hearts and turned them into friendly people.

(*The* BANDIT *roars with laughter.*)

FIRST FARMER: I know what changed them.

AZDAK: That's fine. You can tell us later. Continue.

OLD WOMAN: Your Honor, the next one to become a good man was the farmer Shutoff—a devil, as everyone knows. But Saint Banditus arranged it so he let me off the rent on the little piece of land.

SECOND FARMER: Because my cows were killed in the field.

(*The* BANDIT *laughs.*)

OLD WOMAN (*answering* AZDAK's *sign to continue*): Then one morning the ham came flying in at my window. It hit me in the small of the back. I'm still lame, Your Honor, look. (*She limps a few steps. The* BANDIT *laughs.*) Your Honor, was there ever a time when a poor old woman could get a ham *without* a miracle?

(*The* BANDIT *starts sobbing.*)

AZDAK (*rising from his chair*): Granny, that's a question that strikes straight at the Court's heart. Be so kind as to sit here. (*The* OLD WOMAN, *hesitating, sits in the judge's chair.*)

AZDAK (*sits on the floor, glass in hand, reciting*):
Granny
We could almost call you Granny Grusinia
The Woebegone
The Bereaved Mother
Whose sons have gone to war.
Receiving the present of a cow
She bursts out crying.
When she is beaten
She remains hopeful.
When she's not beaten

She's surprised.
On us
Who are already damned
May you render a merciful verdict
Granny Grusinia!

(*Bellowing at the* FARMERS:) Admit you don't believe in miracles, you atheists! Each of you is sentenced to pay five hundred piasters! For godlessness! Get out! (*The* FARMERS *slink out.*) And you Granny, and you (*to the* BANDIT) pious man, empty a pitcher of wine with the Public Prosecutor and Azdak!

SINGER AND CHORUS: And he broke the rules to save them.
    Broken law like bread he gave them.
    Brought them to shore upon his crooked back.
    At long last the poor and lowly
    Had someone who was not too holy
    To be bribed by empty hands: Azdak.

    For two years it was his pleasure
    To give the beasts of prey short measure:
    He became a wolf to fight the pack.
    From All Hallows to All Hallows
    On his chair beside the gallows
    Dispensing justice in his fashion sat Azdak.

SINGER: But the era of disorder came to an end.
    The Grand Duke returned.
    The Governor's wife returned.
    A trial was held.
    Many died.
    The people's quarters burned anew.
    And fear seized Azdak.

(ADZAK's *judge's chair stands, again in the court of justice.* AZDAK *sits on the floor, shaving and talking to* SHAUWA. *Noises outside. In the rear the* FAT PRINCE's *head is carried by on a lance.*)

AZDAK: Shauwa, the days of your slavery are numbered, maybe even the minutes. For a long time now I have held you in the iron curb of reason, and it has torn your mouth till it bleeds. I have lashed you with reasonable arguments, I have manhandled you with logic. You are by nature a weak man, and if one slyly throws an argument in your path, you *have* to snap it up, you can't resist. It is your nature

to lick the hand of some superior being. But superior beings can be of very different kinds. And now, with your liberation, you will soon be able to follow your natural inclinations, which are low. You will be able to follow your infallible instinct, which teaches you to plant your fat heel on the faces of men. Gone is the era of confusion and disorder, which I find described in the Song of Chaos. Let us now sing that song together in memory of those terrible days. Sit down and don't do violence to the music. Don't be afraid. It sounds all right. And it has a fine refrain. (*He sings.*)

THE SONG OF CHAOS
Sister, hide your face! Brother, take your knife!
The times are out of joint!
Big men are full of complaint
And small men full of joy.
The city says:
"Let us drive the mighty from our midst!"
Offices are raided. Lists of serfs are destroyed.
They have set Master's nose to the grindstone.
They who lived in the dark have seen the light.
The ebony poor box is broken.
Sesnem[2] wood is sawed up for beds.
Who had no bread have full barns.
Who begged for alms of corn now mete it out.

SHAUWA (*refrain*): Oh, oh, oh, oh.

---

2. I do not know what kind of wood this is, so I have left the word exactly as it stands in the German original. The song is based on an Egyptian papyrus which Brecht cites as such in his essay, "Five Difficulties in the Writing of the Truth." I should think he must have come across it in Adolf Erman's *Die Literatur der Aegypter*, 1923, p. 130 ff. Erman too gives the word as Sesnem. The same papyrus is quoted in Karl Jaspers' *Man in the Modern Age* (Anchor edition, pp. 18–19) but without the sentence about the Sesnem wood.—E. B.

AZDAK (*refrain*): Where are you, General, where are
you?

Please, please, please, restore order!

The nobleman's son can no longer be
recognized;

The lady's child becomes the son of her
slave-girl

The councilors meet in a shed.

Once, this man was barely allowed to
sleep on the wall;

Now, he stretches his limbs in a bed.

Once, this man rowed a boat; now, he
owns ships.

Their owner looks for them, but they're
his no longer.

Five men are sent on a journey by their
master.

"Go yourself," they say, "we have arrived."

SHAUWA (*refrain*): Oh, oh, oh, oh.

AZDAK (*refrain*): Where are you, General, where are
you?

Please, please, please, restore order!

Yes, so it might have been, had order been ne-
glected much longer. But now the Grand Duke
has returned to the capital, and the Persians
have lent him an army to restore order with.
The people's quarters are already aflame.
Go and get me the big book I always sit on.
(SHAUWA *brings the big book from the judge's chair.*
AZDAK *opens it.*) This is the Statute Book and
I've always used it, as you can testify. Now
I'd better look in this book and see what they
can do to me. I've let the down-and-outs get
away with murder, and I'll have to pay for it. I
helped poverty onto its skinny legs, so they'll
hang me for drunkenness. I peeped into the
rich man's pocket, which is bad taste. And I
can't hide anywhere—everybody knows me
because I've helped everybody.

SHAUWA: Someone's coming!

AZDAK (*in panic, he walks trembling to the chair*): It's the
end. And now they'd enjoy seeing what a Great
Man I am. I'll deprive them of that pleasure. I'll
beg on my knees for mercy. Spittle will slobber
down my chin. The fear of death is in me.
(*Enter Natella Abashwili, the* GOVERNOR'S WIFE,
followed by the ADJUTANT *and an* IRONSHIRT.)

GOVERNOR'S WIFE: What sort of a creature is that,
Shalva?

AZDAK: A willing one, Your Highness, a man ready
to oblige.

ADJUTANT: Natella Abashwili, wife of the late Governor, has just returned. She is looking for
her two-year-old son, Michael. She has been
informed that the child was carried off to the
mountains by a former servant.

AZDAK: The child will be brought back, Your Highness, at your service.

ADJUTANT: They say that the person in question is
passing it off as her own.

AZDAK: She will be beheaded, Your Highness, at
your service.

ADJUTANT: That is all.

GOVERNOR'S WIFE (*leaving*): I don't like that man.

AZDAK (*following her to door, bowing*): At your service, Your Highness, it will all be arranged

5

THE CHALK CIRCLE

SINGER: Hear now the story of the trial
Concerning Governor Abashwili's child
And the determination of the true
mother
By the famous test of the Chalk Circle.
(*Law court in Nuka.* IRONSHIRTS *lead* MICHAEL
across stage and out at the back. IRONSHIRTS *hold*
GRUSHA *back with their lances under the gateway
until the child has been led through. Then she is
admitted. She is accompanied by the former Governor's* COOK. *Distant noises and a fire-red sky.*)

GRUSHA (*trying to hide*): He's brave, he can wash
himself now.

COOK: You're lucky. It's not a real judge. It's Azdak,
a drunk who doesn't know what he's doing.
The biggest thieves have got by through him.
Because he gets everything mixed up and the
rich never offer him big enough bribes, the
like of us sometimes do pretty well.

GRUSHA: I *need* luck right now.

COOK: Touch wood. (*She crosses herself.*) I'd better
offer up another prayer that the judge may
be drunk. (*She prays with motionless lips, while*

GRUSHA *looks around, in vain, for the child.*) Why must you hold on to it at any price if it isn't yours? In days like these?

GRUSHA: He's mine. I brought him up.

COOK: Have you never thought what'd happen when she came back?

GRUSHA: At first I thought I'd give him to her. Then I thought she wouldn't come back.

COOK: And even a borrowed coat keeps a man warm, hm? (GRUSHA *nods.*) I'll swear to anything for you. You're a decent girl. (*She sees the soldier* SIMON SHASHAVA *approaching.*) You've done wrong by Simon, though. I've been talking with him. He just can't understand.

GRUSHA (*unaware of* SIMON's *presence*): Right now I can't be bothered whether he understands or not!

COOK: He knows the child isn't yours, but you married and not free "till death you do part"—he can't understand *that.*

(GRUSHA *sees* SIMON *and greets him.*)

SIMON (*gloomily*): I wish the lady to know I will swear I am the father of the child.

GRUSHA (*low*): Thank you, Simon.

SIMON: At the same time I wish the lady to know my hands are not tied—nor are hers.

COOK: You needn't have said that. You know she's married.

SIMON: And it needs no rubbing in.

(*Enter an* IRONSHIRT.)

IRONSHIRT: Where's the judge? Has anyone seen the judge?

ANOTHER IRONSHIRT (*stepping forward*): The judge isn't here yet. Nothing but a bed and a pitcher in the whole house!

(*Exeunt* IRONSHIRTS.)

COOK: I hope nothing has happened to him. With any other judge you'd have as much chance as a chicken has teeth.

GRUSHA (*who has turned away and covered her face*): Stand in front of me. I shouldn't have come to Nuka. If I run into the Ironshirt, the one I hit over the head . . .

(*She screams. An* IRONSHIRT *had stopped and, turning his back, had been listening to her. He now wheels around. It is the* CORPORAL, *and he has a huge scar across his face.*)

IRONSHIRT (*in the gateway*): What's the matter, Shotta? Do you know her?

CORPORAL (*after staring for some time*): No.

IRONSHIRT: She's the one who stole the Abashwili child, or so they say. If you know anything about it you can make some money, Shotta.

(*Exit the* CORPORAL, *cursing.*)

COOK: Was it him? (GRUSHA *nods.*) I think he'll keep his mouth shut, or he'd be admitting he was after the child.

GRUSHA: I'd almost forgotten him.

(*Enter the* GOVERNOR'S WIFE, *followed by the* ADJUTANT *and two* LAWYERS.)

GOVERNOR'S WIFE: At least there are no common people here, thank God. I can't stand their smell. It always gives me migraine.

FIRST LAWYER: Madam, I must ask you to be careful what you say until we have another judge.

GOVERNOR'S WIFE: But I didn't say anything, Illo Shuboladze. I love the people with their simple straightforward minds. It's only that their smell brings on my migraine.

SECOND LAWYER: There won't be many spectators. The whole population is sitting at home behind locked doors because of the riots in the people's quarters.

GOVERNOR'S WIFE (*looking at* GRUSHA): Is that the creature?

FIRST LAWYER: Please, most gracious Natella Abashwili, abstain from invective until it is certain the Grand Duke has appointed a new judge and we're rid of the present one, who's about the lowest fellow ever seen in judge's gown. Things are all set to move, you see.

(*Enter* IRONSHIRTS *from the courtyard.*)

COOK: Her Grace would pull your hair out on the spot if she didn't know Azdak is for the poor. He goes by the face.

(IRONSHIRTS *begin fastening a rope to a beam.* AZDAK, *in chains, is led in, followed by* SHAUWA, *also in chains. The three* FARMERS *bring up the rear.*)

AN IRONSHIRT: Trying to run away, were you? (*He strikes* AZDAK.)

ONE FARMER: Off with his judge's gown before we string him up!

(IRONSHIRTS *and* FARMERS *tear off* AZDAK's *gown. His torn underwear is visible. Then someone kicks him.*)

AN IRONSHIRT (*pushing him into someone else*): Want a load of justice? Here it is!

(*Accompanied by shouts of "You take it!" and "Let me have him, Brother!" they throw* AZDAK *back and forth until he collapses. Then he is lifted up and dragged under the noose.*)

GOVERNOR'S WIFE (*who, during this "ballgame," has clapped her hands hysterically*): I disliked that man from the moment I first saw him.

AZDAK (*covered with blood, panting*): I can't see. Give me a rag.

AN IRONSHIRT: What is it you want to see?

AZDAK: You, you dogs! (*He wipes the blood out of his eyes with his shirt.*) Good morning, dogs! How goes it, dogs! How's the dog world? Does it smell good? Got another boot for me to lick? Are you back at each other's throats, dogs? (*Accompanied by a* CORPORAL, *a dust-covered* RIDER *enters. He takes some documents from a leather case, looks at them, then interrupts.*)

RIDER: Stop! I bring a dispatch from the Grand Duke, containing the latest appointments.

CORPORAL (*bellowing*): Atten—shun!

RIDER: Of the new judge it says: "We appoint a man whom we have to thank for saving a life indispensable to the country's welfare—a certain Azdak of Nuka." Which is he?

SHAUWA (*pointing*): That's him, Your Excellency.

CORPORAL (*bellowing*): What's going on here?

AN IRONSHIRT: I beg to report that His Honor Azdak was already His Honor Azdak, but on these farmers' denunciation was pronounced the Grand Duke's enemy.

CORPORAL (*pointing at the* FARMERS): March them off! (*They are marched off. They bow all the time.*) See to it that His Honor Azdak is exposed to no more violence.

(*Exeunt* RIDER *and* CORPORAL.)

COOK (*to* SHAUWA): She clapped her hands! I hope he saw it!

FIRST LAWYER: It's a catastrophe.

(AZDAK *has fainted. Coming to, he is dressed again in judge's robes. He walks, swaying, toward the* IRONSHIRTS.)

AN IRONSHIRT: What does Your Honor desire?

AZDAK: Nothing, fellow dogs, or just an occasional boot to lick. (*To* SHAUWA) I pardon you. (*He is unchained.*) Get me some red wine, the sweet kind. (SHAUWA *stumbles off.*) Get out of here, I've got to judge a case. (*Exeunt* IRONSHIRTS.

SHAUWA *returns with a pitcher of wine.* AZDAK *gulps it down.*) Something for my backside. (SHAUWA *brings the Statute Book, puts it on the judge's chair.* AZDAK *sits on it.*) I accept.

(*The Prosecutors, among whom a worried council has been held, smile with relief. They whisper.*)

COOK: Oh dear!

SIMON: A well can't be filled with dew, they say.

LAWYERS (*approaching* AZDAK, *who stands up, expectantly*): A quite ridiculous case, Your Honor. The accused has abducted a child and refuses to hand it over.

AZDAK (*stretching out his hand, glancing at* GRUSHA): A most attractive person. (*He fingers the money, then sits down, satisfied.*) I declare the proceedings open and demand the whole truth. (*To* GRUSHA:) Especially from you.

FIRST LAWYER: High Court of Justice! Blood, as the popular saying goes, is thicker than water. This old adage . . .

AZDAK (*interrupting*): The Court wants to know the lawyers' fee.

FIRST LAWYER (*surprised*): I beg your pardon? (AZDAK, *smiling, rubs his thumb and index finger.*) Oh, I see. Five hundred piasters, Your Honor, to answer the Court's somewhat unusual question.

AZDAK: Did you hear? The question is unusual. I ask it because I listen in quite a different way when I know you're good.

FIRST LAWYER (*bowing*): Thank you, Your Honor. High Court of Justice, of all ties the ties of blood are strongest. Mother and child—is there a more intimate relationship? Can one tear a child from its mother? High Court of Justice, she has conceived it in the holy ecstasies of love. She has carried it in her womb. She has fed it with her blood. She has borne it with pain. High Court of Justice, it has been observed that the wild tigress, robbed of her young, roams restless through the mountains, shrunk to a shadow. Nature herself . . .

ADZAK (*interrupting, to* GRUSHA): What's your answer to all this and anything else that lawyer might have to say?

GRUSHA: He's mine.

AZDAK: Is that all? I hope you can prove it. Why should I assign the child to you in any case?

GRUSHA: I brought him up like the priest says "according to my best knowledge and conscience." I always found him something to eat. Most of the time he had a roof over his head. And I went to such trouble for him. I had expenses too. I didn't look out for my own comfort. I brought the child up to be friendly with everyone, and from the beginning taught him to work. As well as he could, that is. He's still very little.

FIRST LAWYER: Your Honor, it is significant that the girl herself doesn't claim any tie of blood between her and the child.

AZDAK: The Court takes note of that.

FIRST LAWYER: Thank you, Your Honor. And now permit a woman bowed in sorrow—who has already lost her husband and now has also to fear the loss of her child—to address a few words to you. The gracious Natella Abashwili is . . .

GOVERNOR'S WIFE (*quietly*): A most cruel fate, sir, forces me to describe to you the tortures of a bereaved mother's soul, the anxiety, the sleepless nights, the . . .

SECOND LAWYER (*bursting out*): Its outrageous the way this woman is being treated! Her husband's palace is closed to her! The revenue of her estates is blocked, and she is cold-bloodedly told that it's tied to the heir. She can't do a thing without that child. She can't even pay her lawyers!! (*To the* FIRST LAWYER, *who, desperate about this outburst, makes frantic gestures to keep him from speaking:*) Dear Illo Shuboladze, surely it can be divulged now that the Abashwili estates are at stake?

FIRST LAWYER: Please, Honored Sandro Oboladze! We agreed . . . (*To* AZDAK:) Of course it is correct that the trial will also decide if our noble client can take over the Abashwili estates, which are rather extensive. I say "also" advisedly, for in the foreground stands the human tragedy of a mother, as Natella Abashwili very properly explained in the fast words of her moving statement. Even if Michael Abashwili were not heir to the estates, he would still be the dearly beloved child of my client.

AZDAK: Stop! The Court is touched by the mention of estates. It's a proof of human feeling.

SECOND LAWYER: Thanks, Your Honor. Dear Illo Shuboladze, we can prove in any case that the woman who took the child is not the child's mother. Permit me to lay before the Court the bare facts. High Court of Justice, by an unfortunate chain of circumstances, Michael Abashwili was left behind on that Easter Sunday while his mother was making her escape. Grusha, a palace kitchen maid, was seen with the baby . . .

COOK: All her mistress was thinking of was what dresses she'd take along!

SECOND LAWYER (*unmoved*): Nearly a year later Grusha turned up in a mountain village with a baby and there entered into the state of matrimony with . . .

AZDAK: How'd you get to that mountain village?

GRUSHA: On foot, Your Honor. And he was mine.

SIMON: I'm the father, Your Honor.

COOK: I used to look after it for them, Your Honor. For five piasters.

SECOND LAWYER: This man is engaged to Grusha, High Court of Justice: his testimony is suspect.

AZDAK: Are you the man she married in the mountain village?

SIMON: No, Your Honor, she married a peasant.

AZDAK (*to* GRUSHA): Why? (*Pointing at* SIMON.) Is he no good in bed? Tell the truth.

GRUSHA: We didn't get that far. I married because of the baby. So he'd have a roof over his head. (*Pointing at* SIMON) He was in the war, Your Honor.

AZDAK: And now he wants you back again, huh?

SIMON: I wish to state in evidence . . .

GRUSHA (*angrily*): I am no longer free, Your Honor.

AZDAK: And the child, you claim, comes from whoring? (GRUSHA *doesn't answer.*) I'm going to ask you a question: What kind of child is he? A ragged little bastard? Or from a good family?

GRUSHA (*angrily*): He's an ordinary child.

AZDAK: I mean—did he have refined features from the beginning?

GRUSHA: He had a nose on his face.

AZDAK: A very significant comment! It has been said of me that I went out one time and sniffed at a rosebush before rendering a verdict—tricks like that are needed nowadays. Well, I'll make it short, and not listen to any more lies. (*To* GRU-SHA:) Especially not yours. (*To all the accused:*) I can imagine what you've cooked up to cheat me! I know you people. You're swindlers.

GRUSHA (*suddenly*): I can understand your wanting to cut it short, now I've seen what you accepted!

AZDAK: Shut up! Did I accept anything from you?

GRUSHA (*while the* COOK *tries to restrain her*): I haven't got anything.

AZDAK: True. Quite true. From starvelings I never get a thing. I might just as well starve, myself. You want justice, but do you want to pay for it, hm? When you go to a butcher you know you have to pay, but you people go to a judge as if you were off to a funeral supper.

SIMON (*loudly*): When the horse was shod, the horsefly held out its leg, as the saying is.

AZDAK (*eagerly accepting the challenge*): Better a treasure in manure than a stone in a mountain stream.

SIMON: A fine day. Let's go fishing, said the angler to the worm.

AZDAK: I'm my own master, said the servant, and cut off his foot.

SIMON: I love you as a father, said the Czar to the peasants, and had the Czarevitch's head chopped off.

AZDAK: A fool's worst enemy is himself.

SIMON: However, a fart has no nose.

AZDAK: Fined ten piasters for indecent language in court! That'll teach you what justice is.

GRUSHA (*furiously*): A fine kind of justice! You play fast and loose with us because we don't talk as refined as that crowd with their lawyers

AZDAK: That's true. You people are too dumb. It's only right you should get it in the neck.

GRUSHA: You want to hand the child over to her, and she wouldn't even know how to keep it dry, she's so "refined"! You know about as much about justice as I do!

AZDAK: There's something in that. I'm an ignorant man. Haven't even a decent pair of pants on under this gown. Look! With me, everything goes on food and drink—I was educated in a convent. Incidentally, I'll fine you ten piasters for contempt of court. And you're a very silly girl, to turn me against you, instead of making eyes at me and wiggling your backside a little to keep me in a good temper. Twenty piasters!

GRUSHA: Even if it was thirty, I'd tell you what I think of your justice, you drunken onion! (*Incoherently.*) How dare you talk to me like the cracked Isaiah on the church window? As if you were somebody? For you weren't born to this. You weren't born to rap your own mother on the knuckles if she swipes a little bowl of salt someplace. Aren't you ashamed of yourself when you see how I tremble before you? You've made yourself their servant so no one will take their houses from them—houses they had stolen! Since when have houses belonged to the bedbugs? But you're on the watch, or they couldn't drag our men into their wars! You bribetaker!

(AZDAK *half gets up, starts beaming. With his little hammer he halfheartedly knocks on the table as if to get silence. As* GRUSHA's *scolding continues, he only beats time with his hammer.*)

I've no respect for you. No more than for a thief or a bandit with a knife! You can do what you want. You can take the child away from me, a hundred against one, but I tell you one thing: only extortioners should be chosen for a profession like yours, and men who rape children! As punishment! Yes, let *them* sit in judgment on their fellow creatures. It is worse than to hang from the gallows.

AZDAK (*sitting down*): Now it'll be thirty! And I won't go on squabbling with you—we're not in a tavern. What'd happen to my dignity as a judge? Anyway, I've lost interest in your case. Where's the couple who wanted a divorce? (*To* SHAUWA:) Bring 'em in. This case is adjourned for fifteen minutes.

FIRST LAWYER (*to the* GOVERNOR'S WIFE): Even without using the rest of the evidence, Madam, we have the verdict in the bag.

COOK (*to* GRUSHA): You've gone and spoiled your chances with him. You won't get the child now.

GOVERNOR'S WIFE: Shalva, my smelling salts!

(*Enter a very old couple.*)

AZDAK: I accept. (*The old couple don't understand.*) I hear you want to be divorced. How long have you been together?

OLD WOMAN: Forty years, Your Honor.

AZDAK: And why do you want a divorce?

OLD MAN: We don't like each other, Your Honor.

AZDAK: Since when?

OLD WOMAN: Oh, from the very beginning, Your Honor.

AZDAK: I'll think about your request and render my verdict when I'm through with the other case. (SHAUWA *leads them back.*) I need the child. (*He beckons* GRUSHA *to him and bends not unkindly toward her.*) I've noticed you have a soft spot for justice. I don't believe he's your child, but if he *were* yours, woman, wouldn't you want him to be rich? You'd only have to say he wasn't yours, and he'd have a palace and many horses in his stable and many beggars on his doorstep and many soldiers in his service and many petitioners in his courtyard, wouldn't he? What do you say—don't you want him to be rich?

(GRUSHA *is silent.*)

SINGER: Hear now what the angry girl thought but did not say:

> Had he golden shoes to wear
> He'd be cruel as a bear
> Evil would his life disgrace.
> He'd laugh in my face.

> Carrying a heart of flint
> Is too troublesome a stint.
> Being powerful and bad
> Is hard on a lad.

> Then let hunger be his foe!
> Hungry men and women, no.
> Let him fear the darksome night
> But not daylight!

AZDAK: I think I understand you, woman.

GRUSHA (*suddenly and loudly*): I won't give him up. I've raised him, and he knows me.

(*Enter* SHAUWA *with the* CHILD.)

GOVERNOR'S WIFE: He's in rags!

GRUSHA: That's not true. But I wasn't given time to put his good shirt on.

GOVERNOR'S WIFE: He must have been in a pigsty.

GRUSHA (*furiously*): I'm not a pig, but there are some who are! Where did you leave your baby?

GOVERNOR'S WIFE: I'll show you, you vulgar creature! (*She is about to throw herself on* GRUSHA, *but is restrained by her lawyers.*) She's a criminal, she must be whipped. Immediately!

SECOND LAWYER (*holding his hand over her mouth*): Natella Abashwili, you promised... Your Honor, the plaintiff's nerves ...

AZDAK: Plaintiff and defendant! The Court has listened to your case, and has come to no decision as to who the real mother is; therefore, I, the judge, am obliged to *choose* a mother for the child. I'll make a test. Shauwa, get a piece of chalk and draw a circle on the floor. (SHAUWA *does so.*) Now place the child in the center. (SHAUWA *puts* MICHAEL, *who smiles at* GRUSHA, *in the center of the circle.*) Stand near the circle, both of you. (*The* GOVERNOR'S WIFE *and* GRUSHA *step up to the circle.*) Now each of you take the child by one hand. (*They do so.*) The true mother is she who can pull the child out of the circle.

SECOND LAWYER (*quickly*): High Court of Justice, I object! The fate of the great Abashwili estates, which are tied to the child, as the heir, should not be made dependent on such a doubtful duel. In addition, my client does not command the strength of this person, who is accustomed to physical work.

AZDAK: She looks pretty well fed to me. Pull! (*The* GOVERNOR'S WIFE *pulls the* CHILD *out of the circle on her side;* GRUSHA *has let go and stands aghast.*) What's the matter with you? You didn't pull.

GRUSHA: I didn't hold on to him.

FIRST LAWYER (*congratulating the* GOVERNOR'S WIFE): What did I say! The ties of blood!

GRUSHA (*running to* AZDAK): Your Honor, I take back everything I said against you. I ask your forgiveness. But could I keep him till he can speak all the words? He knows a few.

AZDAK: Don't influence the Court. I bet you only know about twenty words yourself. All right, I'll make the test once more, just to be certain. (*The two women take up their positions again.*) Pull! (*Again* GRUSHA *lets go of the* CHILD.)

GRUSHA (*in despair*): I brought him up! Shall I also tear him to bits? I can't!

AZDAK (*rising*): And in this manner the Court has determined the true mother. (*To* GRUSHA:) Take your child and be off. I advise you not to stay in the city with him. (*To the* GOVERNOR'S WIFE:)

And you disappear before I fine you for fraud. Your estates fall to the city. They'll be converted into a playground for the children. They need one, and I've decided it'll be called after me: Azdak's Garden.

(*The* GOVERNOR'S WIFE *has fainted and is carried out by the* LAWYERS *and the* ADJUTANT. GRUSHA *stands motionless.* SHAUWA *leads the* CHILD *toward her.*)

Now I'll take off this judge's gown—it's got too hot for me. I'm not cut out for a hero. In token of farewell I invite you all to a little dance in the meadow outside. Oh, I'd almost forgotten something in my excitement . . . to sign the divorce decree. (*Using the judge's chair as a table, he writes something on a piece of paper, and prepares to leave. Dance music has started.*)

SHAUWA (*having read what is on the paper*): But that's not right. You've not divorced the old people. You've divorced Grusha!

AZDAK: Divorced the wrong couple? What a pity! And I never retract! If I did, how could we keep order in the land? (*To the* OLD COUPLE:) I'll invite you to my party instead. You don't mind dancing with each other, do you? (*To* GRUSHA *and* SIMON:) I've got forty piasters coming from you.

SIMON (*pulling out his purse*): Cheap at the price, Your Honor. And many thanks.

AZDAK (*pocketing the cash*): I'll be needing this.

GRUSHA (*to* MICHAEL): So we'd better leave the city tonight, Michael? (*To* SIMON:) You like him?

SIMON: With my respects, I like him.

GRUSHA: Now I can tell you: I took him because on that Easter Sunday I got engaged to you. So he's a child of love. Michael, let's dance.

(*She dances with* MICHAEL, SIMON *dances with the* COOK, *the old couple with each other.* AZDAK *stands lost in thought. The dancers soon hide him from view. Occasionally he is seen, but less and less as more couples join the dance.*)

SINGER:

> And after that evening Azdak vanished
>   and was never seen again.
> The people of Grusinia did not forget
>   him but long remembered
> The period of his judging as a brief
>   golden age,
> Almost an age of justice.

(*All the couples dance off.* AZDAK *has disappeared.*)

> But you, you who have listened to the
>   Story of the Chalk Circle,
> Take note what men of old concluded:
> That what there is shall go to those who
>   are good for it,
> Children to the motherly, that they
>   prosper,
> Carts to good drivers, that they be driven
>   well,
> The valley to the waterers, that it yield
>   fruit.

Introduction to *Act without Words I*

WHEN THE PLAY WAS NEW

Act without Words I by Samuel Beckett was first performed in London at the Royal Court Theatre on April 3, 1957. Associated with Theatre of the Absurd and often considered that play category's most effective exponent, Beckett's work was one of the most profound expressions of the gripping anxiety in post-world-war Europe and America. The plays are undergirded by the horrors of the Holocaust, castastrophic casualities of war, and the looming threat of nuclear war. Many writers challenged traditional values, universality of thought, and the notion of any kind of spiritual or cosmic control. Drama of the period is full of pain, unanswered questions, uncertainty about the world, and the inability of characters to act on their anxiety. Beckett's plays of the 1950s and early 1960s are a perfect evocation of such a world dominated by the cold war and existential anguish.

THE PLAYWRIGHT

Samuel Beckett (1906–1989) was an Irish playwright, educated at Trinity College in Dublin. As a young man, however, he moved to France and eventually wrote most of his major plays in French. In most cases, he translated the plays himself into English. Beginning in 1928 Beckett became a protégé of the novelist James Joyce, who was undoubtedly a great influence on the novels and short stories of Beckett, many of which were written before any of the plays. Much of the prose work is dominated by stream-of-consciousness thinking—monologues or dialogues that grind on with few transitions.

Beckett's notoriety as a playwright began when he was middle-aged with the ground-breaking work *Waiting for Godot* (1953), one of the most famous and influential plays of the twentieth century. *Godot*, like many of his plays, explores the human condition in primary form, stripping away all but the essentials. The location is simply a road with a tree. Other important plays of Beckett include *Endgame* (1957), a study of human beings trapped in some kind of bunker approaching the end of their existence; *Krapp's Last Tape* (1958), about a brooding old man listening to an autobiographical tape he made some thirty years earlier; and *Happy Days* (1961), a play about a woman who in the first act is buried up to her waist in a mound, and in the second act, up to her neck. She seems oblivious to the confinement.

Although *Godot* and *Happy Days* are two-act plays, many of Beckett's plays are very short with little or no dialogue. (Sound, however, is very important in nearly all of Beckett's plays.) The dialogue he does use often sounds like characters speaking out of habit or because they are afraid of silence. We learn little about the characters and the characters' past. Typically, his plays are vague about location and time, but very specific about stage directions (especially action). Beckett's dramatic world is bleak, but the action is often clown-like and filled with physical humor, especially in the early plays. It is probably accurate to identify the basic Beckett character of the 1950s and early 1960s as a tramp who is also a clown.

Beckett also wrote radio plays and one film which characteristically is entitled *Film* (1964). His later plays like *Footfalls* (1976), *Quad* (1981), and *Ohio Impromptu* (1981) are more formal, abstracted, even sinister. Such pieces are often associated with postmodern experiment. In 1962 critic Martin Esslin identified Beckett's plays as belonging to the work of a group of playwrights including Eugène Ionesco, Jean Genet, and Harold Pinter. Esslin labeled their work Theatre of the Absurd. None of these playwrights were part of a conscious movement, but they did seem to be attracted to the philosophy of existentialism, which points to humanity's unsatisfying struggle to comprehend existence. All of these plays suggest that the human is a stranger to himself, that other people are unknowable, that meaningful communication is often difficult or impossible, and that we all suffer, often without knowing why. They dramatized a world without knowable cosmic control or purpose. Things occurred randomly and the condition of humanity was bound to be absurd.

A recluse in his later life, Beckett won the Nobel Prize for literature in 1969. Over the years he has had many remarkable theatrical interpreters internationally, such as directors Roger Blin in France and Alan Schneider in the United States, Irish actors Jack Macgowran and Patrick Magee, and actresses Irene Worth from the United States and Billie Whitelaw from England.

GENRE, STRUCTURE, AND STYLE

Many of Beckett's plays are structured around a condition rather than clearly defined action. The situation of waiting, for example, dominates several plays, and characters often keep themselves busy, but without accomplishing much of anything. *Act without Words I*, like many of Beckett's works, has no exposition about character or event, no specific location, no explanations, and of course no dialogue. The play is a brief mime played in one act, but it is not silent. Sound—especially the irritating whistle—is crucial to the play's development. Although stage directions are critical in all of Beckett's plays, in *Act without Words I* (and its "sequel" *Act without Words II*) they are vital. Stage directions as interpreted and offstage sound are everything.

Offstage action is suggested, but never seen. The character is frequently thrown onto the stage by an unseen character or force. The unseen controlling force is ominous, but never defined. In fact, the lack of definition lends the force mystery and danger, because we do not know what it is. There is manipulation in the dramatic world but without the puppet master. In fact, there is considerable action in the play that suggests the character as puppet or clown. This is a suffering clown, however—a clown with angst.

Although the location is vague, Beckett does call for scenery and properties, even if generic. He begins with an empty stage, but adds and sometimes takes away a tree, cubes, rope, scissors, and a carafe. The character is denied everything he tries to get, but he is never allowed to leave. He finally gives up, or can no longer stand to play the game, or maybe he has "learned" what his unsheltered life here will be.

IMPORTANT ELEMENTS OF CONTENT

The human is confined to a stark, harshly bright world he does not understand. He is subject to some kind of control outside himself which is not identified. This force teases and tantalizes the man, but also abuses and tortures him. Does it also test him? Does it expect him to learn? The answers to these questions are a matter of interpretation. In the man's little world (apparently not of his own choosing since he is thrown into it), he thinks at each new turn, pondering his condition—trying to make sense of the bizarre events that end in denial of desire or need.

The character does not find the simple, emblematic properties, but they come to him. In fact, the whistle must call his attention to their existence. The properties seem to represent sustenance (water), shade (tree), access (cubes and rope), and tools (scissors). All are offered to him but denied if he makes the effort to get or use them. Nothing is won, nothing is achieved. A bleak world indeed.

THE PLAY IN REVIVAL

Act without Words I is often performed with other Beckett short pieces, usually in small theatres, professional and amateur. This play is frequently seen at universities and Beckett festivals off-Broadway and all over the world. A very successful professional festival has been continuing in Athens, Greece, since 1993. The Beckett Project in Dublin revived the play in 2004 as did the Theatre Centre in Toronto.

SPECIAL FEATURE

The physical efforts of Beckett's clown-like characters are a staple of his early plays. They are probably a key to making the plays successful in the theatre. If the desolate world of the characters dominates performance and swamps characterization, then the plays can be tedious. If, however, the actors find humor in the physical action of the characters and bring the most dynamic attributes of the clown—specific gesture and movement, repetition, inablility to accomplish the simple, exaggerated trouble with objects—we laugh at the absurdity, and recognize what is ludicrous about the human condition. Consequently, the audience's emotional and intellectual responses to Beckett's plays (when well performed) are apt to be mixed. Perhaps that is why he called some of his plays *tragicomedies.*

FURTHER READING ABOUT THE PLAY, PLAYWRIGHT, AND CONTEXT

All of Beckett's plays remain in print and are readily available.

For studies of the life and times of Beckett, see John Fletcher, *About Beckett: The Playwright and the Work;* Gerry Dukes, *Samuel Beckett;* and Enoch Brater, *The Essential Samuel Beckett.*

For Beckett in production, see Alan Schneider, *Entrances: An American Director's Journey,* and Chris Ackerley, *The Grove Companion to Samuel Beckett.*

For criticism of Beckett's plays, see Martin Esslin, *The Theatre of the Absurd,* 3rd ed., and Linda Ben-Zvi, *Drawing on Beckett: Portraits, Performances, and Cultural Contexts.*

Act without Words I: A Mime for One Player

By Samuel Beckett

Desert. Dazzling light.

The man is flung backwards on stage from right wing. He falls, gets up immediately, dusts himself, turns aside, reflects.

Whistle from right wing.

He reflects, goes out right.

Immediately flung back on stage he falls, gets up immediately, dusts himself, turns aside, reflects.

Whistle from left wing.

He reflects, goes out left.

Immediately flung back on stage he falls, gets up immediately, dusts himself, turns aside, reflects.

Whistle from left wing.

He reflects, goes towards left wing, hesitates, thinks better of it, halts, turns aside, reflects.

A little tree descends from flies, lands. It has a single bough some three yards from ground and at its summit a meager tuft of palms casting at its foot a circle of shadow.

He continues to reflect.

Whistle from above.

He turns, sees tree, reflects, goes to it, sits down in its shadow, looks at his hands.

A pair of tailor's scissors descends from flies, comes to rest before tree, a yard from ground.

He continues to look at his hands.

Whistle from above.

He looks up, sees scissors, takes them and starts to trim his nails.

The palms close like a parasol, the shadow disappears.

He drops scissors, reflects.

A tiny carafe, to which is attached a huge label inscribed WATER, descends from flies, comes to rest some three yards from ground.

He continues to reflect.

Whistle from above.

He looks up, sees carafe, reflects, gets up, goes and stands under it, tries in vain to reach it, renounces, turns aside, reflects.

A big cube descends from flies, lands.

He continues to reflect.

Whistle from above.

He turns, sees cube, looks at it, at carafe, reflects, goes to cube, takes it up, carries it over and sets it down under carafe, tests its stability, gets up on it, tries in vain to reach carafe, renounces, gets down, carries cube back to its place, turns aside, reflects.

A second smaller cube descends from flies, lands.

He continues to reflect.

Whistle from above.

He turns, sees second cube, looks at it, at carafe, goes to second cube, takes it up, carries it over and sets it down under carafe, tests its stability, gets up on it, tries in vain to reach carafe, renounces, gets down, takes up second cube to carry it back to its place, hesitates, thinks better of it, sets it down, goes to big cube, takes it up, carries it over and puts it on small one, tests their stability, gets up on them, the cubes collapse, he falls, gets up immediately, brushes himself, reflects.

He takes up small cube, puts it on big one, tests their stability, gets up on them and is about to reach carafe when it is pulled up a little way and comes to rest beyond his reach.

He gets down, reflects, carries cubes back to their place, one by one, turns aside, reflects.

A third still smaller cube descends from flies, lands.

He continues to reflect.

Whistle from above.

He turns, sees third cube, looks at it, reflects, turns aside, reflects.

The third cube is pulled up and disappears in flies.

Beside carafe a rope descends from flies, with knots to facilitate ascent.

He continues to reflect.

Whistle from above.

He turns, sees rope, reflects, goes to it, climbs up it and is about to reach carafe when rope is let out and deposits him back on ground.

He reflects, looks around for scissors, sees them, goes and picks them up, returns to rope and starts to cut it with scissors.

The rope is pulled up, lifts him off ground, he hangs on, succeeds in cutting rope, falls back on ground, drops scissors, falls, gets up again immediately, brushes himself, reflects.

The rope is pulled up quickly and disappears in flies.

With length of rope in his possession he makes a lasso with which he tries to lasso carafe.

The carafe is pulled up quickly and disappears in flies.

He turns aside, reflects.

He goes with lasso in his hand to tree, looks at bough, turns and looks at cubes, looks again at bough, drops lasso, goes to cubes, takes up small one, carries it over and sets it down under bough, goes back for big one, takes it up and carries it over under bough, makes to put it on small one, hesitates, thinks better of it, sets it down, takes up small one and puts it on big one, tests their stability, turns aside and stoops to pick up lasso.

The bough folds down against trunk.

He straightens up with lasso in his hand, turns and sees what has happened.

He drops lasso, turns aside, reflects.

He carries back cubes to their place, one by one, goes back for lasso, carries it over to cubes and lays it in a neat coil on small one.

He turns aside, reflects.

Whistle from right wing.

He reflects, goes out right.

Immediately flung back on stage he falls, gets up immediately, brushes himself, turns aside, reflects.

Whistle from left wing.

He does not move.

He looks at his hands, looks around for scissors, sees them, goes and picks them up, starts to trim his nails, stops, reflects, runs his finger along blade of scissors, goes and lays them on small cube, turns aside, opens his collar, frees his neck and fingers it.

The small cube is pulled up and disappears in flies, carrying away rope and scissors.

He turns to take scissors, sees what has happened.

He turns aside, reflects.

He goes and sits down on big cube.

The big cube is pulled from under him. He falls. The big cube is pulled up and disappears in flies.

He remains lying on his side, his face towards auditorium, staring before him.

The carafe descends from flies and comes to rest a few feet from his body.

He does not move.

Whistle from above.

He does not move.

The carafe descends further, dangles and plays about his face.

He does not move.

The carafe is pulled up and disappears in flies.

The bough returns to horizontal, the palms open, the shadow returns.

Whistle from above.

He does not move.

The tree is pulled up and disappears in flies.

He looks at his hands.

CURTAIN

Introduction to *The Conduct of Life*

WHEN THE PLAY WAS NEW

The Conduct of Life by Maria Irene Fornes opened on February 21, 1985, at the Theatre of the New City in New York under the direction of the playwright, and won the Obie Award for best play. Although most of the action takes place in the home of Orlando, a Latin American military officer (the country is never identified), the play explores violence, torture, and uncontrolled power as it affects women who are nearly powerless to stop it. This play is still relevant and disturbing because we live in a world marked by terror, violence, torture, and uncertainty. The play was and is difficult to watch in performance because it includes rape and torture of an underage victim at the hands of an unscrupulous man more concerned about wielding power and moving upward in the chain of command than he is in exercising any significant moral code or social restraint.

It is difficult to read or witness this play in production without having a strong reaction to the disturbing events, the domestic ambiguities, and the breakdown in communication among the small cast of characters. Given recent events in Afghanistan and Iraq, perhaps this play is even more relevant to Americans at the present than it was at the time of writing, when the more obvious subject of attack was the kind of Latin American country in which such horrors were commonplace. Regardless of current political and military issues that could alter at any time, the play's exploration of the nature of power will always be a concern.

THE PLAYWRIGHT

Maria Irene Fornes was born in 1930 in Cuba, but emigrated to the United States in 1945 and became a U.S. citizen in 1951. She launched her artistic career as a painter around 1950, but after encountering *Waiting for Godot* by Samuel Beckett while studying in Europe, she altered her career path and started writing plays by the early 1960s. Since that time she has been identified primarily as an avant-garde playwright, but has also been very active as a director and designer, at first for her own plays, but in more recent years she has directed the plays of others as well. She is often labeled a feminist playwright, the tenets of which are evident in many of her plays.

Fornes has had so many off-Broadway productions since 1963, and has won so many Obie Awards since 1965, that she is sometimes seen as the queen of that venue. Of course her plays often appear in regional professional theatres (sometimes under the direction of Fornes) as well as at colleges and universities. Her professional productions began with *Tango Palace* (1963) followed by *Promenade* (1965), a musical about the intersection of prisoners' lives (an unusual subject for a musical). Another musical, *Molly's Dream* (1968) follows the struggles of a bar waitress. In the 1960s, Fornes produced work at many famous fringe theatres in New York such as Judson Poets' Theatre, the Open Theatre, and LaMama (all vital operations for off-Broadway). There was a six-year hiatus in her playwriting as she worked for an organization called Theatre Strategy and dedicated herself to helping other women get plays written and produced. By the late 1970s she was writing and directing again and she has remained prolific ever since. *Fefu and Her Friends* (1977), one of her most frequently revived and studied plays, is a feminist piece in which the action takes place in five different domestic spaces—the audience divides and moves to join four scenes of action played simultaneously four times until all audience members have experienced them before reuniting for the last scene. The play points up how behavior and communication change as the environment changes. Many of her plays are set several decades in the past. *The Danube* (1984) is set during World War II, *Sarita* (1984) examines a Cuban woman caught in a romantic triangle in New York City during the 1940s, and *Abingdon Square* (1987) is set in the early years of the twentieth century and follows the difficult choices of a young woman searching for independence. *Mud* (1983) is a bleak examination of the rural poor who can barely communicate; a woman and two men are cohabiting in a tiny house and are engaged in a power struggle that ends in murder.

Fornes has also adapted many famous plays from the past that she also directed, including *Life Is a Dream* by Calderón de la Barca, *Blood Wedding* by Federico Garcia Lorca, and *Hedda Gabler* by Henrik Ibsen. Fornes' new plays have continued to appear and be produced, including *Terra Incognita* (1991); *The Summer in Grossensas* (1997), a response to Ibsen; and *The Audition* (1998). These plays have not yet been published. Her work is certainly eclectic and bridges many different styles from the whimsical and gentle, to abstracted scenarios, to hard-hitting, sadistic realism. If there is a center to her work it is probably an insistence on exploring the human need for dignity and purpose in a world that often makes those goals difficult to achieve. She often finds humor in unexpected places.

Much of her work also experiments with theatrical space and challenges her audiences in terms of expectations and their relationship to the theatrical event. *The Conduct of Life* is no exception to this approach.

GENRE, STRUCTURE, AND STYLE

Like many of Fornes's plays, *The Conduct of Life* is episodic. The action is not meant to be broken by an intermission; it transpires in nineteen scenes, some of them quite short on the page. As is often the case in her plays, a scene with little or no dialogue might take much longer to perform than to read. We often do not know how much time is meant to have passed between scenes, but obviously some of the time gaps between scenes are considerable. Some critics have described the plays of Fornes as cinematic in structure.

At times the actual dramatized event is also ambiguous. Silence is important to the dramatic action, and many scenes do not allow effective communication between characters. In this respect some of her plays, including *The Conduct of Life*, bear a resemblance in theme and structure to the plays of Samuel Beckett, who inspired her profoundly at the beginning of her career.

IMPORTANT ELEMENTS OF CONTENT

Clearly Fornes is responding to real and specific conditions in some Latin American countries where people are oppressed by dictatorships and insensitive governments. The lives of the people are marked by turmoil, fear, and torture. Such issues are played out in *The Conduct of Life*, but the immediate sphere is domestic. We see the conditions either filtered through domestic inanities or shown to us in full-blown form even though Leticia, for example, is oblivious to the horrors transpiring in her own house for a long time. The play dramatizes flagrant disregard for the pain of others, and time and again requires that characters make ethical choices that are often horrific—especially in the torture scenes and at the play's end.

THE PLAY IN REVIVAL

Since the first production, Fornes has directed *The Conduct of Life* at other theatres. Professional avant-garde theatres across North America, as well as the Fringe Festival in Sydney, Australia, staged the play in the 1990s and the early years of this century. Many college and university theatres have been especially attracted to this play, which has had many productions between 2001 and 2005.

SPECIAL FEATURE

The Conduct of Life includes an intriguing spatial experiment. Fornes manipulates aesthetic distance for the audience by creating a setting with five levels, which simultaneously reveal many parts of the house of Orlando and Leticia as well as a military warehouse set at the greatest distance from the audience. At first the most torturous scenes are kept at a distance from the audience, but as the play progresses, the disturbing scenes get closer and eventually transpire in the closest space, the living room. Ironically, earlier in the play we see distressing scenes in the cellar, but seen through the foreground of the domestic interior spaces. The torture scenes are thus framed and modified by the presence of the living and dining rooms. In the play's final scene the underage victim, Nena; the abuser, Orlando; and his long-suffering wife, Leticia; are all sitting in the living room where yet one more act of violence will take place.

FURTHER READING ABOUT THE PLAY, PLAYWRIGHT, AND CONTEXT

A number of the plays written and produced by Fornes have not yet been published, but several collections as well as some single publications are available. See *Promenade and Other Plays* and *Plays: Mud, The Danube, The Conduct of Life, Sarita.*

For accounts of Fornes in production, see Marc Robinson, *The Theatre of Maria Irene Fornes;* and Diane Lynn Moroff, *Fornes: Theatre in Present Tense.*

For criticism of Fornes, see Assunta Kent, *Maria Irene Fornes and Her Critics,* and Maria Delgado and Caridad Svich, *Conducting a Life: Reflections on the Theatre of Maria Irene Fornes.*

For a biographical sketch, see Elaine T. Partnow, *The Female Dramatist.*

The Conduct of Life

BY MARIA IRENE FORNES

The floor is divided in four horizontal planes. Down-stage is the livingroom, which is about ten feet deep. Center stage, eighteen inches high, is the diningroom, which is about ten feet deep. Further upstage, eighteen inches high, is a hallway which is about four feet deep. At each end of the hallway there is a door. The one to the right leads to the servants' quarters, the one to the left to the basement. Upstage, three feet lower than the hall-way (same level as the livingroom), is the cellar, which is about sixteen feet deep. Most of the cellar is occupied by two platforms which are eight feet wide, eight feet deep, and three feet high. Upstage of the cellar are steps that lead up. Approximately ten feet above the cellar is another level, extending from the extreme left to the ex-treme right, which represents a warehouse. There is a door on the left of the warehouse. On the left and the right of the livingroom there are archways that lead to hallways or antechambers, the floors of these hallways are the same level as the diningroom. On the left and the right of the diningroom there is a second set of arch-ways that lead to hallways or antechambers, the floors of which are the same level as the hallways. All along the edge of each level there is a step that leads to the next level. All floors and steps are black marble. In the livingroom there are two chairs. One is to the left, next to a table with a telephone. The other is to the right. In the diningroom there are a large green marble table and three chairs. On the cellar floor there is a mattress to the right and a chair to the left. In the warehouse there is a table and a chair to the left, and a chair and some boxes and crates to the right.

SCENE 1

ORLANDO is doing jumping-jacks in the upper left corner of the diningroom in the dark. A light, slowly, comes up on him. He wears military breeches held by suspenders, and riding boots. He does jumping-jacks as long as it can be endured. He stops, the center area starts to be-come visible. There is a chair upstage of the table. There is a linen towel on the left side of the table. ORLANDO dries his face with the towel and sits as he puts the towel around his neck.

ORLANDO: Thirty three and I'm still a lieutenant. In two years I'll receive a promotion or I'll leave the military. I promise I will not spend time feeling sorry for myself.—Instead I will study the situation and draw an effective plan of action. I must eliminate all obstacles.—I will make the acquaintance of people in high pow-er. If I cannot achieve this on my own merit, I will marry a woman in high circles. Leticia must not be an obstacle.—Man must have an ideal, mine is to achieve maximum power. That is my destiny.—No other interest will deter me from this.—My sexual drive is detrimental to my ideals. I must no longer be overwhelmed by sexual passion or I will be degraded beyond hope of recovery. (Lights fade to black.)

SCENE 2

ALEJO sits to the right of the diningroom table. ORLANDO stands to ALEJO's left. He is now a lieutenant command-er. He wears an army tunic, breeches, and boots. LETICIA stands to the left. She wears a dress that suggests 1940s fashion.

LETICIA: What! Me go hunting? Do you think I'm going to shoot a deer, the most beautiful ani-mal in the world? Do you think I'm going to destroy a deer? On the contrary, I would run in the field and scream and wave my arms like a mad woman and try to scare them away so the hunters could not reach them. I'd run in front of the bullets and let the mad hunters kill me—stand in the way of the bullets—stop the bullets with my body. I don't see how anyone can shoot a deer.

ORLANDO (*To* ALEJO): Do you understand that? You, who are her friend, can you understand that? You don't think that is madness? She's mad. Tell her that—she'll think it's you who's mad. (*To* LETICIA.) Hunting is a sport! A skill! Don't talk about something you know nothing about. Must you have an opinion about every damn thing! Can't you keep your mouth shut when you don't know what you're talking about? (ORLANDO *exits right.*)

LETICIA: He told me that he didn't love me, and that his sole relationship to me was simply a marital one. What he means is that I am to keep this house, and he is to provide for it. That's what he said. That explains why he treats me the way he treats me. I never understood why he did, but now it's clear. He doesn't love me. I thought he loved me and that he stayed with me because he loved me and that's why I didn't understand his behavior. But now I know, because he told me that he sees me as a person who runs the house. I never understood that because I would have never—if he had said, "Would you marry me to run my house even if I don't love you." I would have never—I would have never believed what I was hearing. I would have never believed that these words were coming out of his mouth. Because I loved him.

(ORLANDO *has entered.* LETICIA *sees him and exits left.* ORLANDO *enters and sits center.*)

ORLANDO: I didn't say any of that. I told her that she's not my heir. That's what I said. I told her that she's not in my will, and she will not receive a penny of my money if I die. That's what I said. I didn't say anything about running the house. I said she will not inherit a penny from me because I didn't want to be humiliated. She is capable of foolishness beyond anyone's imagination. Ask her what she would do if she were rich and could do anything she wants with her money. (LETICIA *enters.*)

LETICIA: I would distribute it among the poor.

ORLANDO: She has no respect for money.

LETICIA: That is not true. If I had money I would give it to those who need it. I know what money is, what money can do. It can feed people, it can put a roof over their heads. Money can do that. It can clothe them. What do you know about money? What does it mean to you? What do you do with money? Buy rifles? To shoot deer?

ORLANDO: You're foolish!—You're foolish! You're a foolish woman! (ORLANDO *exits. He speaks from offstage.*)
Foolish. . . . Foolish. . . .

LETICIA: He has no respect for me. He is insensitive. He doesn't listen. You cannot reach him. He is deaf. He is an animal. Nothing touches him except sensuality. He responds to food, to the flesh. To music sometimes, if it is romantic. To the moon. He is romantic but he is not aware of what you are feeling. I can't change him.—I'll tell you why I asked you to come. Because I want something from you.— I want you to educate me. I want to study. I want to study so I am not an ignorant person. I want to go to the university. I want to be knowledgeable. I'm tired of being ignored. I want to study political science. Is political science what diplomats study? Is that what it is? You have to teach me elemental things because I never finished grammar school. I would have to study a great deal. A great deal so I could enter the university. I would have to go through all the subjects. I would like to be a woman who speaks in a group and have others listen.

ALEJO: Why do you want to worry about any of that? What's the use? Do you think you can change anything? Do you think anyone can change anything?

LETICIA: Why not? (*Pause.*) Do you think I'm crazy?— He can't help it.—Do you think I'm crazy?—Because I love him? (*He looks away from her. Lights fade to black.*)

SCENE 3

ORLANDO *enters the warehouse holding* NENA *close to him. She wears a gray overlarge uniform. She is barefoot. She resists him. She is tearful and frightened. She pulls away and runs to the right wall. He follows her.*

ORLANDO (*Softly*): You called me a snake.

NENA: No, I didn't. (*He tries to reach her. She pushes his hands away from her.*) I was kidding.—I swear I was kidding.

(*He grabs her and pushes her against the wall. He pushes his pelvis against her. He moves to the chair dragging her with him. She crawls to the left, pushes the table aside and stands behind it. He walks around the table. She goes under it. He grabs her foot and pulls her out toward the downstage side. He opens his fly and pushes his pelvis against her. Lights fade to black.*)

SCENE 4

OLIMPIA *is wiping crumbs off the diningroom table. She wears a plain gray uniform.* LETICIA *sits to the left of the table facing front. She wears a dressing gown. She writes in a notebook. There is some silverware on the table.* OLIMPIA *has a speech defect.*

LETICIA: Let's do this.

OLIMPIA: O.K. (*She continues wiping the table.*)

LETICIA (*Still writing*): What are you doing?

OLIMPIA: I'm doing what I always do.

LETICIA: Let's do this.

OLIMPIA (*In a mumble*): As soon as I finish doing this. You can't just ask me to do what you want me to do, and interrupt what I'm doing. I don't stop from the time I wake up in the morning to the time I go to sleep. You can't interrupt me whenever you want, not if you want me to get to the end of my work. I wake up at 5:30. I wash. I put on my clothes and make my bed. I go to the kitchen. I get the milk and the bread from outside and I put them on the counter. I open the icebox. I put one bottle in and take the butter out. I leave the other bottle on the counter. I shut the refrigerator door. I take the pan that I use for water and put water in it. I know how much. I put the pan on the stove, light the stove, cover it. I take the top off the milk and pour it in the milk pan except for a little. (*Indicating with her finger.*) Like this. For the cat. I put the pan on the stove, light the stove. I put coffee in the thing. I know how much. I light the oven and put bread in it. I come here, get the tablecloth and I lay it on the table. I shout "Breakfast." I get the napkins. I take the cups,

the saucers, and the silver out and set the table. I go to the kitchen. I put the tray on the counter, put the butter on the tray. The water and the milk are getting hot. I pick up the cat's dish. I wash it. I pour the milk I left in the bottle in the milk dish. I put it on the floor for the cat. I shout "Breakfast." The water boils. I pour it in the thing. When the milk boils I turn off the gas and cover the milk. I get the bread from the oven. I slice it down the middle and butter it. Then I cut it in pieces (*indicating*) this big. I set a piece aside for me. I put the rest of the bread in the bread dish and shout "Breakfast." I pour the coffee in the coffee pot and the milk in the milk pitcher, except I leave (*indicating*) this much for me. I put them on the tray and bring them here. If you're not in the diningroom I call again. "Breakfast." I go to the kitchen, I fill the milk pan with water and let it soak. I pour my coffee, sit at the counter and eat my breakfast. I go upstairs to make your bed and clean your bathroom. I come down here to meet you and figure out what you want for lunch and dinner. And try to get you to think quickly so I can run to the market and get it bought before all the fresh stuff is bought up. Then, I start the day.

LETICIA: So?

OLIMPIA: So I need a steam pot.

LETICIA: What is a steam pot?

OLIMPIA: A pressure cooker.

LETICIA: And you want a steam pot? Don't you have enough pots?

OLIMPIA: No.

LETICIA: Why do you want a steam pot?

OLIMPIA: It cooks faster.

LETICIA: How much is it?

OLIMPIA: Expensive.

LETICIA: How much?

OLIMPIA: Twenty.

LETICIA: Too expensive. (OLIMPIA *throws the silver on the floor.* LETICIA *turns her eyes up to the ceiling.*) Why do you want one more pot?

OLIMPIA: I don't have a steam pot.

LETICIA: A pressure cooker.

OLIMPIA: A pressure cooker.

LETICIA: You have too many pots. (OLIMPIA *goes to the kitchen and returns with an aluminum pan. She shows it to* LETICIA.)

OLIMPIA: Look at this. (LETICIA *looks at it.*)

LETICIA: What? (OLIMPIA *hits the pan against the back of a chair, breaking off a piece of the bottom.*)

OLIMPIA: It's no good.

LETICIA: All right! (*She takes money from her pocket and gives it to* OLIMPIA.) Here. Buy it!—What are we having for lunch?

OLIMPIA: Fish.

LETICIA: I don't like fish.—What else?

OLIMPIA: Boiled plantains.

LETICIA: Make something I like.

OLIMPIA: Avocados. (LETICIA *gives a look of resentment to* OLIMPIA.)

LETICIA: Why can't you make something I like?

OLIMPIA: Avocados.

LETICIA: Something that needs cooking.

OLIMPIA: Bread pudding.

LETICIA: And for dinner?

OLIMPIA: Pot roast.

LETICIA: What else?

OLIMPIA: Rice.

LETICIA: What else?

OLIMPIA: Salad.

LETICIA: What kind?

OLIMPIA: Avocado.

LETICIA: Again. (OLIMPIA *looks at* LETICIA.)

OLIMPIA: You like avocados.

LETICIA: Not again.—Tomatoes. (OLIMPIA *mumbles.*) What's wrong with tomatoes besides that you don't like them? (OLIMPIA *mumbles.*) Get some. (OLIMPIA *mumbles.*) What does that mean? (OLIMPIA *doesn't answer.*) Buy tomatoes.—What else?

OLIMPIA: That's all.

LETICIA: We need a green.

OLIMPIA: Watercress.

LETICIA: What else?

OLIMPIA: Nothing.

LETICIA: For dessert.

OLIMPIA: Bread pudding.

LETICIA: Again.

OLIMPIA: Why not?

LETICIA: Make a flan.

OLIMPIA: No flan.

LETICIA: Why not?

OLIMPIA: No good.

LETICIA: Why no good!—Buy some fruit then.

OLIMPIA: What kind?

LETICIA: Pineapple. (OLIMPIA *shakes her head.*) Why not? (OLIMPIA *shakes her head.*) Mango.

OLIMPIA: No mango.

LETICIA: Buy some fruit! That's all. Don't forget bread. (LETICIA *hands* OLIMPIA *some bills.* OLIMPIA *holds it and waits for more.* LETICIA *hands her one more bill. Lights fade to black.*)

SCENE 5

The warehouse table is propped against the door. The chair on the left faces right. The door is pushed and the table falls to the floor. ORLANDO *enters. He wears an undershirt with short sleeves, breeches with suspenders and boots. He looks around the room for* NENA. *Believing she has escaped, he becomes still and downcast. He turns to the door and stands there for a moment. He takes a few steps to the right and stands there for a moment staring fixedly. He hears a sound from behind the boxes, walks to them and takes a box off.* NENA *is there. Her head is covered with a blanket. He pulls the blanket off.* NENA *is motionless and staring into space. He looks at her for a while, then walks to the chair and sits facing right staring into space. A few moments pass. Lights fade to black.*

SCENE 6

LETICIA *speaks on the telephone to* MONA.

LETICIA: Since they moved him to the new department he's different. (*Brief pause.*) He's distracted. I don't know where he goes in his mind. He doesn't listen to me. He worries. When I talk to him he doesn't listen. He's thinking about the job. He says he worries. What is there to worry about? Do you think there is anything to worry about? (*Brief pause.*) What meeting? (*Brief pause.*) Oh, sure. When is it? (*Brief pause.*) At what time? What do you mean I knew? No one told me.—I don't remember. Would you pick me up? (*Brief pause.*) At one? Isn't one early? (*Brief pause.*) Orlando may still be home at one. Sometimes he's here a little longer than usual. After lunch he sits and smokes. Don't you think one thirty will give us enough time? (*Brief pause.*) No. I can't leave while he's smoking. . . . I'd rather not. I'd rather wait till he leaves. (*Brief pause.*). . . . One thirty, then. Thank you, Mona. (*Brief pause.*) See you then. Bye. (LETICIA *puts down the receiver and walks to stage right area.* ORLANDO'*s voice is heard offstage left. He and* ALEJO *enter halfway through the following speech.*)

ORLANDO: He made loud sounds not high-pitched like a horse. He sounded like a whale, like a wounded whale. He was pouring liquid from everywhere, his mouth, his nose, his eyes. He was not a horse but a sexual organ.—Helpless. A viscera.—Screaming. Making strange sounds. He collapsed on top of her. She wanted him off but he collapsed on top of her and stayed there on top of her. Like gum. He looked more like a whale than a horse. A seal. His muscles were soft. What does it feel like to be without shape like that. Without pride. She was indifferent. He stayed there for a while and then lifted himself off her and to the ground. (*Pause.*) He looked like a horse again.

LETICIA: Alejo, how are you? (ALEJO *kisses* LETICIA'*s hand.*)

ORLANDO (*As he walks to the livingroom. He sits left facing front.*): Alejo is staying for dinner.

LETICIA: Would you like some coffee?

ALEJO: Yes, thank you.

LETICIA: Would you like some coffee, Orlando?

ORLANDO: Yes, thank you.

LETICIA (*In a loud voice towards the kitchen*): Olimpia . . .

OLIMPIA: What?

LETICIA: Coffee . . . (LETICIA *sits to the right of the table.* ALEJO *sits center.*)

ALEJO: Have you heard?

LETICIA: Yes, he's dead and I'm glad he's dead. An evil man. I knew he'd be killed. Who killed him?

ALEJO: Someone who knew him.

LETICIA: What is there to gain? So he's murdered. Someone else will do the job. Nothing will change. To destroy them all is to say we destroy us all.

ALEJO: Do you think we're all rotten?

LETICIA: Yes.

ORLANDO: A bad germ?

LETICIA: Yes.

ORLANDO: In our hearts?

LETICIA: Yes.—In our eyes.

ORLANDO: You're silly.

LETICIA: We're blind. We can't see beyond an arm's reach. We don't believe our life will last beyond the day. We only know what we have in our hand to put in our mouth, to put in our stomach, and to put in our pocket. We take care of our pocket, but not of our country. We take care of our stomachs but not of our hungry. We are primitive. We don't believe in the future. Each night when the sun goes down we think that's the end of life—so we have one last fling. We don't think we have a future. We don't think we have a country. Ask anybody, "Do you have a country?" They'll say, "Yes." Ask them, "What is your country?" They'll say, "My bed, my dinner plate." But, things can change. They can. I have changed. You have changed. He has changed.

ALEJO: Look at me. I used to be an idealist. Now I don't have any feeling for anything. I used to be strong, healthy, I looked at the future with hope.

LETICIA: Now you don't?

ALEJO: Now I don't. I know what viciousness is.

ORLANDO: What is viciousness?

ALEJO: You.

ORLANDO: Me?

ALEJO: The way you tortured Felo.

ORLANDO: I never tortured Felo.

ALEJO: You did.

ORLANDO: Boys play that way. You did too.

ALEJO: I didn't.

ORLANDO: He was repulsive to us.

ALEJO: I never hurt him.

ORLANDO: Well, you never stopped me.

ALEJO: I didn't know how to stop you. I didn't know anyone could behave the way you did. It frightened me. It changed me. I became hopeless. (ORLANDO *walks to the diningroom.*)

ORLANDO: You were always hopeless. (*He exits.* OLIMPIA *enters carrying three demi-tasse coffees on a tray. She places them on the table and exits.*)

ALEJO: I am sexually impotent. I have no feelings. Things pass through me which resemble feelings but I know they are not. I'm impotent.

LETICIA: Nonsense.

ALEJO: It's not nonsense. How can you say it's nonsense?—How can one live in a world that festers the way ours does and take any pleasure in life? (*Lights fade to black.*)

SCENE 7

NENA *and* ORLANDO *stand against the wall in the warehouse. She is fully dressed. He is barebreasted. He pushes his pelvis against her gently. His lips touch her face as he speaks. The words are inaudible to the audience. On the table there is a tin plate with food and a tin cup with milk.*

ORLANDO: Look this way. I'm going to do something to you. (*She makes a move away from him.*) Don't do that. Don't move away. (*As he slides his hand along her side.*) I just want to put my hand here like this. (*He puts his lips on hers softly and speaks at the same time.*) Don't hold your lips so tight. Make them soft. Let them loose. So I can do this. (*She whimpers.*) Don't cry. I won't hurt you. This is all I'm going to do to you. Just hold your lips soft. Be nice. Be a nice girl. (*He pushes against her and reaches an orgasm. He remains motionless for a moment, then steps away from her still leaning his hand on the wall.*) Go eat. I brought you food. (*She goes to the table. He sits on the floor and watches her eat. She eats voraciously. She looks at the milk.*) Drink it. It's milk. It's good for you. (*She drinks the milk, then continues eating. Lights fade to black.*)

SCENE 8

LETICIA *stands left of the diningroom table. She speaks words she has memorized.* OLIMPIA *sits to the left of the table. She holds a book close to her eyes. Her head moves from left to right along the written words as she mumbles the sound of imaginary words. She continues doing this through the rest of the scene.*

LETICIA: The impact of war is felt particularly in the economic realm. The destruction of property, private as well as public may paralyze the country. Foreign investment is virtually . . . (*To* OLIMPIA.) Is that right? (*Pause.*) Is that right!

OLIMPIA: Wait a moment. (*She continues mumbling and moving her head.*)

LETICIA: What for? (*Pause.*) You can't read. (*Pause.*) You can't read!

OLIMPIA: Wait a moment. (*She continues mumbling and moving her head.*)

LETICIA (*Slapping the book off* OLIMPIA's *hand*): Why are you pretending you can read? (OLIMPIA *slaps* LETICIA's *hands. They slap each other's hands. Lights fade to black.*)

SCENE 9

ORLANDO *sits in the livingroom. He smokes. He faces front and is thoughtful.* LETICIA *and* OLIMPIA *are in the diningroom.* LETICIA *wears a hat and jacket. She tries to put a leather strap through the loops of a suitcase. There is a smaller piece of luggage on the floor.*

LETICIA: This strap is too wide. It doesn't fit through the loop. (ORLANDO *doesn't reply.*) Is this the right strap? Is this the strap that came with this suitcase? Did the strap that came with the suitcase break? If so, where is it? And when did it break? Why doesn't this strap fit the suitcase and how did it get here. Did you buy this strap, Orlando?

ORLANDO: I may have.

LETICIA: It doesn't fit.

ORLANDO: Hm.

LETICIA: It doesn't fit through the loops.

ORLANDO: Just strap it outside the loops. (LETICIA *stands.* OLIMPIA *tries to put the strap through the loop.*)

LETICIA: No. You're supposed to put it through the loops. That's what the loops are for. What happened to the other strap?

ORLANDO: It broke.

LETICIA: How?

ORLANDO: I used it for something.

LETICIA: What! (*He looks at her.*) You should have gotten me one that fit. What did you use it for?—Look at that.

ORLANDO: Strap it outside the loops.

LETICIA: That wouldn't look right.

ORLANDO (*Going to look at the suitcase*): Why do you need the straps?

LETICIA: Because they come with it.

ORLANDO: You don't need them.

LETICIA: And travel like this?

ORLANDO: Use another suitcase.

LETICIA: What other suitcase. I don't have another.
(ORLANDO *looks at his watch.*)

ORLANDO: You're going to miss your plane.

LETICIA: I'm not going. I'm not travelling like this.

ORLANDO: Go without it. I'll send it to you.

LETICIA: You'll get new luggage, repack it and send
it to me?—All right. (*She starts to exit left.*) It's
nice to travel light. (*Off stage.*) Do I have everything?—Come, Olimpia.
(OLIMPIA *follows with the suitcases.* ORLANDO *takes
the larger suitcase from* OLIMPIA. *She exits.* ORLAN-
DO *goes up the hallway and exits through the left
door. A moment later he enters holding* NENA *close
to him. She is pale, dishevelled and has black circles
around her eyes. She has a high fever and is almost
unconscious. Her dress is torn and soiled. She is
barefoot. He carries a new cotton dress on his arm.
He takes her to the chair in the livingroom. He
takes off the soiled dress and puts the new dress on
her over a soiled slip.*)

ORLANDO: That's nice. You look nice. (LETICIA*'s voice
is heard. He hurriedly takes* NENA *out the door,
closes it, and leans on it.*)

LETICIA (*Off stage.*): It would take but a second. You
run to the garage and get the little suitcase and
I'll take out the things I need. (LETICIA *and* OLIM-
PIA *enter left.* OLIMPIA *exits right.*) Hurry. Hurry.
It would take but a second. (*Seeing* ORLANDO.)
Orlando, I came back because I couldn't leave
without anything at all. I came to get a few
things because I have a smaller suitcase where
I can take a few things. (*She puts the suitcase
on the table, opens it and takes out the things she
mentions.*) A pair of shoes . . . (OLIMPIA *enters
right with a small suitcase.*)

OLIMPIA: Here.

LETICIA:	OLIMPIA:
A nightgown,	A robe,
a robe,	a dress,
underwear,	a nightgown,
a dress,	underwear,
a sweater.	a sweater,
	a pair of shoes.

(LETICIA *closes the large suitcase.* OLIMPIA *closes the
smaller suitcase.*)

LETICIA (*Starting to exit*): Goodbye.

OLIMPIA (*Following* LETICIA): Goodbye.

ORLANDO: Goodbye. (*Lights fade to black.*)

SCENE 10

NENA *is curled on the extreme right of the mattress.* OR-
LANDO *sits on the mattress using* NENA *as a back support.*
ALEJO *sits on the chair. He holds a green paper on his hand.*
OLIMPIA *sweeps the floor.*

ORLANDO: Tell them to check him. See if there's a
scratch on him. There's not a scratch on that
body. Why the fuss! Who was he and who's
making a fuss? Why is he so important.

ALEJO: He was in deep. He knew names.

ORLANDO: I was never told that. But it wouldn't
have mattered if they had because he died before I touched him.

ALEJO: You have to go to headquarters. They want
you there.

ORLANDO: He came in screaming and he wouldn't
stop. I had to wait for him to stop screaming
before I could even pose a question to him. He
wouldn't stop. I had put the poker to his neck
to see if he would stop. Just to see if he would
shut up. He just opened his eyes wide and started shaking and screamed even louder and fell
over dead. Maybe he took something. I didn't
do anything to him. If I didn't get anything from
him it's because he died before I could get to
him. He died of fear, not from anything I did to
him. Tell them to do an autopsy. I'm telling you
the truth. That's the truth. Why the fuss.

ALEJO (*Starting to put the paper in his pocket*): I'll tell
them what you said.

ORLANDO: Let me see that. (ALEJO *takes it to him.*
ORLANDO *looks at it and puts it back in* ALEJO*'s
hands.*) O.K. so it's a trap. So what side are you
on? (*Pause.* ALEJO *says nothing.*) So what do they
want? (*Pause.*) Who's going to question me?
That's funny. That's very funny. They want
to question me. They want to punch my eyes
out? I knew something was wrong because
they were getting nervous. Antonio was getting nervous. I went to him and I asked him
if something was wrong. He said, no, nothing
was wrong. But I could tell something was

wrong. He looked at Velez and Velez looked back at him. They are stupid. They want to conceal something from me and they look at each other right in front of me, as if I'm blind, as if I can't tell that they are worried about something. As if there's something happening right in front of my nose but I'm blind and I can't see it. (*He grabs the paper from* ALEJO'S *hand.*) You understand? (*He goes up the steps.*)

OLIMPIA: Like an alligator, big mouth and no brains. Lots of teeth but no brains. All tongue. (ORLANDO *enters through the left hallway door, and sits at the diningroom table.* ALEJO *enters a few moments later. He stands to the right.*)

ORLANDO: What kind of way is this to treat me?—After what I've done for them?—Is this a way to treat me?—I'll come up . . . as soon as I can—I haven't been well.—O.K. I'll come up. I get depressed because things are bad and they are not going to improve. There's something malignant in the world. Destructiveness, aggressiveness.—Greed. People take what is not theirs. There is greed. I am depressed, disillusioned . . . with life . . . with work . . . family. I don't see hope. (*He sits. He speaks more to himself than to* ALEJO.) Some people get a cut in a finger and die. Because their veins are right next to their skin. There are people who, if you punch them in their stomach the skin around the stomach bursts and the bowels fall out. Other people, you cut them open and you don't see any veins. You can't find their intestines. There are people who don't even bleed. There are people who bleed like pigs. There are people who have the nerves right on their skins. You touch them and they scream. They have their vital organs close to the surface. You hit them and they burst an organ. I didn't even touch this one and he died. He died of fear. (*Lights fade to black.*)

SCENE 11

NENA, ALEJO *and* OLIMPIA *sit crosslegged on the mattress in the basement.* NENA *sits right,* ALEJO *center,* OLIMPIA *left.* NENA *and* OLIMPIA *play patty-cake.* ORLANDO *enters. He goes close to them.*

ORLANDO: What are you doing?

OLIMPIA: I'm playing with her.

ORLANDO (*To* ALEJO): What are you doing here? (ALEJO *looks at* ORLANDO *as a reply.* ORLANDO *speaks sarcastically.*) They're playing pattycake. (*He goes near* NENA.) So? (*Short pause.* NENA *giggles.*) Stop laughing! (NENA *is frightened.* OLIMPIA *holds her.*)

OLIMPIA: Why do you have to spoil everything. We were having a good time.

ORLANDO: Shut up! (NENA *whimpers.*) Stop whimpering. I can't stand your whimpering. I can't stand it. (*Timidly, she tries to speak words as she whimpers.*) Speak up. I can't hear you! She's crazy! Take her to the crazy house!

OLIMPIA: She's not crazy! She's a baby!

ORLANDO: She's not a baby! She's crazy! You think she's a baby? She's older than you think! How old do you think she is—Don't tell me that.

OLIMPIA: She's sick. Don't you see she's sick? Let her cry! (*To* NENA.) Cry!

ORLANDO: You drive me crazy too with your . . . (*He imitates her speech defect. She punches him repeatedly.*)

OLIMPIA: You drive me crazy! (*He pushes her off.*) You drive me crazy! You are a bastard! One day I'm going to kill you when you're asleep! I'm going to open you up and cut your entrails and feed them to the snakes. (*She tries to strangle him.*) I'm going to tear your heart out and feed it to the dogs! I'm going to cut your head open and have the cats eat your brain! (*Reaching for his fly.*) I'm going to cut your peepee and hang it on a tree and feed it to the birds!

ORLANDO: Get off me! I'm getting rid of you too! (*He starts to exit.*) I can't stand you!

OLIMPIA: Oh, yeah! I'm getting rid of you.

ORLANDO: I can't stand you!

OLIMPIA: I can't stand you!

ORLANDO: Meddler! (*To* ALEJO.) I can't stand you either.

OLIMPIA (*Going to the stairs*): Tell the boss! Tell her! She won't get rid of me! She'll get rid of you! What good are you! Tell her! (*She goes to* NENA.) Don't pay any attention to him. He's a coward.—You're pretty. (ORLANDO *enters through the hallway left door. He sits center at the diningroom table and leans his head on it.* LETICIA *enters. He turns to look at her.*)

LETICIA: You didn't send it. (*Lights fade to black.*)

SCENE 12

LETICIA *sits next to the phone. She speaks to* MONA *in her mind.*

LETICIA: I walk through the house and I know where he's made love to her. I think I hear his voice making love to her. Saying the same things he says to me, the same words.—(*There is a pause.*) There is someone here. He keeps someone here in the house. (*Pause.*) I don't dare look. (*Pause.*) No, there's nothing I can do. I can't do anything. (*She walks to the hallway. She hears footsteps. She moves rapidly to left and hides behind a pillar.* OLIMPIA *enters from right. She takes a few steps down the hallway. She carries a plate of food. She sees* LETICIA *and stops. She takes a few steps in various directions, then stops.*)

OLIMPIA: Here kitty, kitty. (LETICIA *walks to* OLIMPIA, *looks closely at the plate, then up at* OLIMPIA.)

LETICIA: What is it?

OLIMPIA: Food.

LETICIA: Who is it for? (OLIMPIA *turns her eyes away and doesn't answer.* LETICIA *decides to go to the cellar door. She stops halfway there.*) Who is it?

OLIMPIA: A cat. (LETICIA *opens the cellar door.*)

LETICIA: It's not a cat. I'm going down. (*She opens the door to the cellar and starts to go down.*) I want to see who is there.

ORLANDO (*Offstage from the cellar.*): What is it you want? (*Lights fade to black.*)

SCENE 13

ORLANDO *leans back on the chair in the basement. His legs are outstretched. His eyes are bloodshot and leery. His tunic is open.* NENA *is curled on the floor.* ORLANDO *speaks quietly. He is deeply absorbed.*

ORLANDO: What I do to you is out of love. Out of want. It's not what you think. I wish you didn't have to be hurt. I don't do it out of hatred. It is not out of rage. It is love. It is a quiet feeling. It's a pleasure. It is quiet and it pierces my insides in the most internal way. It is my most private self. And this I give to you.—Don't be afraid.—It is a desire to destroy and to see things destroyed and to see the inside of

them.—It's my nature. I must hide this from others. But I don't feel remorse. I was born this way and I must have this.—I need love. I wish you did not feel hurt and recoil from me. (*Lights fade to black.*)

SCENE 14

ORLANDO *sits to the right and* LETICIA *sits to the left of the table.*

LETICIA: Don't make her scream. (*There is a pause.*)

ORLANDO: You're crazy.

LETICIA: Don't I give you enough?

ORLANDO (*He's calm.*): Don't start.

LETICIA: How long is she going to be here?

ORLANDO: Not long.

LETICIA: Don't make her cry. (*He looks at her.*) I can't stand it. (*Pause.*) Why do you make her scream?

ORLANDO: I don't make her scream.

LETICIA: She screams.

ORLANDO: I can't help it. (*Pause.*)

LETICIA: I tell you I can't stand it. I'm going to ask Mona to come and stay with me.

ORLANDO: No.

LETICIA: I want someone here with me.

ORLANDO: I don't want her here.

LETICIA: Why not?

ORLANDO: I don't.

LETICIA: I need someone here with me.

ORLANDO: Not now.

LETICIA: When?

ORLANDO: Soon enough.—She's going to stay here for a while. She's going to work for us. She'll be a servant here.

LETICIA: . . . No.

ORLANDO: She's going to be a servant here. (*Lights fade to black.*)

SCENE 15

OLIMPIA *and* NENA *are sitting at the diningroom table. They are separating stones and other matter from dry beans.*

NENA: I used to clean beans when I was in the home. And also string beans. I also pressed clothes. The days were long. Some girls did hand sewing. They spent the day doing that. I didn't like it. When I did that, the day was even longer and there were times when I couldn't move even if I tried. And they said I couldn't go there anymore, that I had to stay in the yard. I didn't mind sitting in the yard looking at the birds. I went to the laundry-room and watched the women work. They let me go in and sit there. And they showed me how to press. I like to press because my mind wanders and I find satisfaction. I can iron all day. I like the way the wrinkles come out and things look nice. It's a miracle isn't it? I could earn a living pressing clothes. And I could find my grandpa and take care of him.

OLIMPIA: Where is your grandpa?

NENA: I don't know. (*They work a little in silence.*) He sleeps in the streets. Because he's too old to remember where he lives. He needs a person to take care of him. And I can take care of him. But I don't know where he is.—He doesn't know where I am.—He doesn't know who he is. He's too old. He doesn't know any-thing about himself. He only knows how to beg. And he knows that, only because he's hungry. He walks around and begs for food. He forgets to go home. He lives in the camp for the homeless and he has his own box. It's not an ugly box like the others. It is a real box. I used to live there with him. He took me with him when my mother died till they took me to the home. It is a big box. It's big enough for two. I could sleep in the front where it's cold. And he could sleep in the back where it's warmer. And he could lean on me. The floor is hard for him because he's skinny and it's hard on his poor bones. He could sleep on top of me if that would make him feel comfortable. I wouldn't mind. Except that he may pee on me because he pees in his pants. He doesn't know not to. He is incontinent. He can't hold it. His box was a little smelly. But that doesn't matter because I could clean it. All I would need is some soap. I could get plenty of water from the public faucet. And I could borrow a brush. You know how clean I could get it? As clean as new. You know what I would do? I would make holes in the floor so the pee would go down to the ground. And you know what else I would do?

OLIMPIA: What?

NENA: I would get straw and put it on the floor for him and for me and it would make it comfort-able and clean and warm. How do you like that? Just as I did for my goat.

OLIMPIA: You have a goat?

NENA: . . . I did.

OLIMPIA: What happened to him?

NENA: He died. They killed him and ate him. Just like they did Christ.

OLIMPIA: Nobody ate Christ.

NENA: . . . I thought they did. My goat was eaten though.—In the home we had clean sheets. But that doesn't help. You can't sleep on clean sheets, not if there isn't someone watching over you while you sleep. And since my ma died there just wasn't anyone watching over me. Except you.—Aren't you? In the home they said guardian angels watch your sleep, but I didn't see any there. There weren't any. One day I heard my grandpa calling me and I went to look for him. And I didn't find him. I got tired and I slept in the street, and I was hungry and I was crying. And then he came to me and he spoke to me very softly so as not to scare me and he said he would give me some-thing to eat and he said he would help me look for my grandpa. And he put me in the back of his van. . . . And he took me to a place. And he hurt me. I fought with him but I stopped fighting—because I couldn't fight anymore and he did things to me. And he locked me in. And sometimes he brought me food and sometimes he didn't. And he did things to me. And he beat me. And he hung me on the wall. And I got sick. And sometimes he brought me medicine. And then he said he had to take me somewhere. And he brought me here. And I am glad to be here because you are here. I only wish my grandpa were here too. He doesn't beat me so much anymore.

OLIMPIA: Why does he beat you? I hear him at night. He goes down the steps and I hear you cry. Why does he beat you?

NENA: Because I'm dirty.

OLIMPIA: You are not dirty.

NENA: I am. That's why he beats me. The dirt won't go away from inside me.—He comes downstairs when I'm sleeping and I hear him coming and it frightens me. And he takes the covers off me and I don't move because I'm frightened and because I feel cold and I think I'm going to die. And he puts his hand on me and he recites poetry. And he is almost naked. He wears a robe but he leaves it open and he feels himself as he recites. He touches himself and he touches his stomach and his breasts and his behind. He puts his fingers in my parts and he keeps reciting. Then he turns me on my stomach and puts himself inside me. And he says I belong to him. (*There is a pause.*) I want to conduct each day of my life in the best possible way. I should value the things I have. And I should value all those who are near me. And I should value the kindness that others bestow upon me. And if someone should treat me unkindly, I should not blind myself with rage, but I should see them and receive them, since maybe they are in worse pain than me. (*Lights fade to black.*)

SCENE 16

LETICIA *speaks on the telephone with* MONA. *She speaks rapidly.*

LETICIA: He is violent. He has become more so. I sense it. I feel it in him.—I understand his thoughts. I know what he thinks.—I raised him. I practically did. He was a boy when I met him. I saw him grow. I was the first woman he loved. That's how young he was. I have to look after him, make sure he doesn't get into trouble. He's not wise. He's trusting. They are changing him.—He tortures people. I know he does. He tells me he doesn't but I know he does. I know it. How could I not. Sometimes he comes from headquarters and his hands are shaking. Why should he shake? What do they do there?—He should transfer. Why do that? He says he doesn't do it himself. That the officers don't do it. He says that people are not being tortured. That that is questionable.—Ev-

erybody knows it. How could he not know it when everybody knows it. Sometimes you see blood in the streets. Haven't you seen it? Why do they leave the bodies in the streets,—how evil, to frighten people? They tear their fingernails off and their poor hands are bloody and destroyed. And they mangle their genitals and expose them and they tear their eyes out and you can see the empty eyesockets in the skull. How awful, Mona. He musn't do it. I don't care if I don't have anything! What's money! I don't need a house as big as this! He's doing it for money! What other reason could he have! What other reason could he have!! He shouldn't do it. I cannot look at him without thinking of it. He's doing it. I know he's doing it.—Shhhh! I hear steps. I'll call you later. Bye, Mona. I'll talk to you. (*She hangs up the receiver. Lights fade to black.*)

SCENE 17

The livingroom. OLIMPIA *sits to the right,* NENA *to the left.*

OLIMPIA: I don't wear high heels because they hurt my feet. I used to have a pair but they hurt my feet and also (*Pointing to her calf.*) here in my legs. So I don't wear them anymore even if they were pretty. Did you ever wear high heels? (NENA *shakes her head.*) Do you have ingrown nails? (NENA *looks at her questioningly.*) Nails that grow twisted into the flesh. (NENA *shakes her head.*) I don't either. Do you have sugar in the blood? (NENA *shakes her head.*) My mother had sugar in the blood and that's what she died of but she lived to be eighty six which is very old even if she had many things wrong with her. She had glaucoma and high blood pressure. (LETICIA *enters and sits center at the table.* NENA *starts to get up.* OLIMPIA *signals her to be still.* LETICIA *is not concerned with them.*)

LETICIA: So, what are you talking about?

OLIMPIA: Ingrown nails. (NENA *turns to* LETICIA *to make sure she may remain seated there.* LETICIA *is involved with her own thoughts.* NENA *turns front. Lights fade to black.*)

SCENE 18

ORLANDO *is sleeping on the diningroom table. The telephone rings. He speaks as someone having a nightmare.*

ORLANDO: Ah! Ah! Ah! Get off me! Get off! I said get off! (LETICIA *enters.*)

LETICIA (*Going to him*): Orlando! What's the matter! What are you doing here!

ORLANDO: Get off me! Ah! Ah! Ah! Get off me!

LETICIA: Why are you sleeping here! On the table. (*Holding him close to her.*) Wake up.

ORLANDO: Let go of me. (*He slaps her hands as she tries to reach him.*) Get away from me. (*He goes to the floor on his knees and staggers to the telephone.*) Yes. Yes, it's me.—You did?—So?—It's true then.—What's the name?—Yes, sure.—Thanks.—Sure. (*He hangs up the receiver. He turns to look at* LETICIA. *Lights fade to black.*)

SCENE 19

Two chairs are placed side by side facing front in the center of the living room. LETICIA *sits on the right.* OR-LANDO *stands on the down left corner.* NENA *sits to the left of the dining room table facing front. She covers her face.* OLIMPIA *stands behind her, holding* NENA *and leaning her head on her.*

ORLANDO: Talk.

LETICIA: I can't talk like this.

ORLANDO: Why not?

LETICIA: In front of everyone.

ORLANDO: Why not?

LETICIA: It is personal. I don't need the whole world to know.

ORLANDO: Why not?

LETICIA: Because it's private. My life is private.

ORLANDO: Are you ashamed?

LETICIA: Yes, I am ashamed!

ORLANDO: What of . . . ? What of . . . ?—I want you to tell us—about your lover.

LETICIA: I don't have a lover. (*He grabs her by the hair.* OLIMPIA *holds on to* NENA *and hides her face.* NENA *covers her face.*)

ORLANDO: You have a lover.

LETICIA: That's a lie.

ORLANDO (*Moving closer to her*): It's not a lie. (*To* LET-ICIA.) Come on tell us. (*He pulls harder.*) What's his name? (*She emits a sound of pain. He pulls harder, leans toward her and speaks in a low tone.*) What's his name?

LETICIA: Albertico. (*He takes a moment to release her.*)

ORLANDO: Tell us about it. (*There is silence. He pulls her hair.*)

LETICIA: All right. (*He releases her.*)

ORLANDO: What's his name?

LETICIA: Albertico.

ORLANDO: Go on. (*Pause.*) Sit up! (*She does.*) Albertico what?

LETICIA: Estevez. (ORLANDO *sits next to her.*)

ORLANDO: Go on. (*Silence.*) Where did you first meet him?

LETICIA: At . . . I . . .

ORLANDO (*He grabs her by the hair.*): In my office.

LETICIA: Yes.

ORLANDO: Don't lie.—When?

LETICIA: You know when.

ORLANDO: When! (*Silence.*) How did you meet him?

LETICIA: You introduced him to me. (*He lets her go.*)

ORLANDO: What else? (*Silence.*) Who is he!

LETICIA: He's a lieutenant.

ORLANDO (*He stands.*): When did you meet with him?

LETICIA: Last week.

ORLANDO: When!

LETICIA: Last week.

ORLANDO: When!

LETICIA: Last week. I said last week.

ORLANDO: Where did you meet him?

LETICIA: . . . In a house of rendezvous . . .

ORLANDO: How did you arrange it?

LETICIA: . . . I wrote to him . . . !

ORLANDO: Did he approach you?

LETICIA: No.

ORLANDO: Did he!

LETICIA: No.

ORLANDO (*He grabs her hair again.*): He did! How!

LETICIA: I approached him.

ORLANDO: How!

LETICIA: (*Aggressively*): I looked at him! I looked at him! I looked at him! (*He lets her go.*)

ORLANDO: When did you look at him?

LETICIA: Please stop . . . !

ORLANDO: Where! When!

LETICIA: In your office!

ORLANDO: When?

LETICIA: I asked him to meet me!

ORLANDO: What did he say?

LETICIA (*Aggressively*): He walked away. He walked away! He walked away! I asked him to meet me.

ORLANDO: What was he like?

LETICIA: . . . Oh . . .

ORLANDO: Was he tender? Was he tender to you!

(*She doesn't answer. He puts his hand inside her blouse. She lets out an excruciating scream. He lets her go and walks to the right of the diningroom. She goes to the telephone table, opens the drawer, takes a gun and shoots* ORLANDO. ORLANDO *falls dead.* NENA *runs to downstage of the table.* LETICIA *is disconcerted, then puts the revolver in* NENA's *hand and steps away from her.*)

LETICIA: Please . . .

(NENA *is in a state of terror and numb acceptance. She looks at the gun. Then, up. The lights fade.*)

END

Introduction to *The Piano Lesson*

WHEN THE PLAY WAS NEW

The Piano Lesson by August Wilson opened at the Yale Repertory Theatre in New Haven, Connecticut, on November 26, 1987, with Samuel L. Jackson as Boy Willie. It was directed by Lloyd Richards, who directed all of the first productions of Wilson's plays between 1984 and 1995. When Richards's production of *The Piano Lesson* opened on Broadway in 1990, Boy Willie was played by Charles S. Dutton. This poignant play won many awards for Wilson, including his second Pulitzer Prize. *The Piano Lesson* was Wilson's fourth straight success, and it established beyond a doubt that a remarkable voice for the African American experience had arrived and was reaching popular audiences of all races.

Set in the 1930s, *The Piano Lesson* evokes unpleasant, often distressing memories of the Great Depression. But more importantly, the play depicts another dynamic variation on the effects of racism on African Americans in the United States. Like the plays of Tennessee Williams, this play joins remarkable characters, symbolism, and beauty of vocal expression with a dark, painful experience. It engages, challenges, and enlightens an audience still trying to come to terms with the legacy of slavery and segregation. With this and most of his other plays, Wilson has produced a remarkable array of studies of racism and its consequences—especially on African Americans—as prejudice and oppression paraded through the last century.

THE PLAYWRIGHT

August Wilson was born in 1945 in Pittsburgh, Pennsylvania, and was essentially self-educated after the age of sixteen when he dropped out of school due to racist treatment. In 1968 Wilson cofounded the Black Horizons on the Hill theatre company in Pittsburgh and worked there as a director and writer until 1978. His play *Jitney* is an examination of an estranged father and his son, who has just been released from prison. The two men attempt to reconnect in the setting of a jitney taxi service run by the long-suffering father. This play, along with many later ones, demonstrates Wilson's powerful dramatic facility when depicting family and generational conflict. *Jitney* was produced in Pittsburgh in 1982, but drew little attention. After later successes Wilson rewrote *Jitney*, and a series of successful productions began in 2000. Between 1982 and 2005, Wilson worked on a collection of ten plays—each set in a different decade—exploring the African American experience in the United States in the twentieth century.

Wilson's auspicious and internationally acclaimed career was launched in the professional American theatre with *Ma Rainey's Black Bottom* (1984), a conflict of race, power, and exploitation in the pop music world of the 1920s, set in a recording studio. *Ma Rainey* marks the beginning of Wilson's production collaboration with African American producer/director Lloyd Richards. Their association has some similarities to that of Elia Kazan with Arthur Miller and Tennessee Williams in the 1940s and 1950s. In Richard's case, the sensitive and talented director helped guide Wilson through script revisions to prepare the plays effectively for professional production. Typically their productions opened at the Yale Repertory Theatre and then moved to Broadway. Soon Wilson became the most commercially successful and the most well-known African American playwright in history. *Fences* (1985) won the Pulitzer Prize in 1987. The protagonist Troy, once a talented baseball player but now a garbage collector, is a victim of racist employment practices during the 1950s. Troy ends up oppressing his son and betraying his wife, thus undermining his own family.

Joe Turner's Come and Gone (1986, Broadway 1988) is set in the 1910s when many southern blacks were migrating to the north. A black man is imprisoned for seven years without knowing his crime. He goes in search of his past and his wife. *Two Trains Running* (1990/1992) takes place in a diner in the 1960s amidst social unrest over the war in Vietnam and civil rights. After *Seven Guitars,* which opened at the Goodman Theatre in Chicago in 1995, the pattern of collaboration was broken in the wake of the illness of Richards. Subsequent productions were directed by others. *Seven Guitars* is set in the 1940s at the end of the life of a blues guitarist. Also in 1995, *The Piano Lesson* was filmed for television. *King Hedley II* (2001) is set in the 1980s and *Gem of the Ocean* (2004) is set in the 1900s—the earliest historical setting of Wilson's plays. In 2005 Wilson completed his twentieth-century cycle with *Radio Golf,* set in the 1990s, which is his first play to explore the African American middle class. Fittingly, *Radio Golf* opened at the Yale Repertory Theatre where his cycle began in 1984.

Wilson is attracted to realistic settings and stories with an occasional touch of the supernatural or spiritual, especially at or near the end of plays such as *Fences* and *The Piano Lesson.* Most of his plays are set in Pittsburgh, and despite the ongoing theme of racism, most of his plays have only black characters. He was the first African American playwright to have two theatre productions running simultaneously on Broadway (*Fences* and *Joe Turner*).

In 1997 Wilson became embroiled in controversial arguments with critic/producer Robert Brustein, whom Wilson labeled a "cultural imperialist," over how black theatre companies should be funded and how black playwrights should be developed. Wilson is opposed to the typical American resident theatre practice of "colorblind" (or nontraditional) casting, calling it insulting. Wilson asserts that many black playwrights and companies are being held hostage by white producers and typical commercial practices in the contemporary theatre. This controversy has raged for a number of years. In recent times Wilson has taken to public speaking and even role-playing monologues to demonstrate his cultural and artistic position.

GENRE, STRUCTURE, AND STYLE

Like all of Wilson's major plays, *The Piano Lesson* is realistic in characterization, setting, and action. The play has a traditional, climactic structure in a realistic style. Somewhat like Ibsen and Miller, Wilson explores the domestic world of his characters in both their past and the present, although he keeps the dramatized action only in the present time of the setting of the play. Many of the dramatic scenes, including critical arguments, are delivered in the midst of everyday action; the argument between Boy Willie and Berniece in the final scene is punctuated by conversation and business as Berniece fixes the hair of her daughter, Maretha.

Ghosts, or memories from the characters' past (here evoked by the piano), invade the arguments, dilemmas, and suffering of the present. Unlike Ibsen, however, Wilson is more interested in racial and family heritage and dignity than in the destruction of his characters. Some of his plays end in death, however, as is the case in *Fences* and *Jitney. Seven Guitars* begins right after a death. Like so many American plays since the 1930s, family conflicts lie at the heart of *The Piano Lesson.* Yet Wilson offers touches of ambiguity and the supernatural. He does not like to tie everything up in a neat package at the end of the play. The conflict is over; the possibilities for the future remain hopeful but uncertain.

IMPORTANT ELEMENTS OF CONTENT

The Piano Lesson, like many of Wilson's plays, features generational conflict even when a generation is technically offstage—in the past. The struggle of Berniece and Boy Willie's great-grandfather, a plantation slave and the carver of the piano, is embodied in this family heirloom so near and dear to Berniece. The piano represents her family's past, but also suggests the ghosts of the great-grandfather's white masters. Boy Willie sees the piano as the key to economic freedom and the possibility of buying the land once belonging to the slave owners. The piano not only dominates the setting, but simultaneously stands as a symbol of slavery, remarkable accomplishment, and artistry in the midst of terrible times. The piano is a vehicle of memory.

In realistic plays such large issues must be tied up with the vicissitudes of the real world. The financial struggles of the characters are especially poignant since it is set in the 1930s, in the midst of the Great Depression. Economic limitations and the scarcity of opportunities drive much of the action of the play.

THE PLAY IN REVIVAL

The plays of August Wilson have been darlings of American resident theatres since their premieres. *Fences* has probably been the most frequently revived, but *The Piano Lesson* has enjoyed many productions across the continent in professional theatres and at universities. It was produced professionally at the Actors Theatre of Louisville in 2001, the Obsidian Theatre in Toronto in 2002, the Pittsburgh Public Theatre in 2003, and the Westcoast Black Theatre Troupe in Sarasota in 2004.

SPECIAL FEATURE

The haunting nature of the play goes beyond the ghost stories told by Boy Willie and becomes literal. Sutter's ghost is often talked about in the play, but is never seen—it is felt by the characters, heard by them and the audience, and finally becomes active as Boy Willie wrestles and fights with it. This action in the final scene brings on the climax of *The Piano Lesson* and is the most obvious use of the supernatural in Wilson's plays. It dynamically connects the spiritual world of his characters to the action of the play.

FURTHER READING ABOUT THE PLAY, PLAYWRIGHT, AND CONTEXT

All of Wilson's produced plays are published and readily available. There is one collection entitled *Three Plays*.

There is much criticism of Wilson's plays in articles and reviews, and Wilson is a very popular subject of doctoral dissertations.

For Wilson's placement in contemporary American theatre, see Don B. Wilmeth and Christopher Bigsby, *The Cambridge History of American Theatre*, Vol. 3.

For Wilson's own explanation of his artistic and professional position, see August Wilson, *The Ground on Which I Stand.*

For criticism on Wilson, see Harry Elam, *The Past as Present in the Drama of August Wilson;* Dana Williams, *August Wilson and Black Aesthetics;* Harold Bloom, *August Wilson;* and Marilyn Elkins, *August Wilson: A Casebook.*

The Piano Lesson

By August Wilson

THE SETTING

The action of the play takes place in the kitchen and parlor of the house where DOAKER CHARLES *lives with his niece,* BERNIECE, *and her eleven-year-old daughter,* MA-RETHA. *The house is sparsely furnished, and although there is evidence of a woman's touch, there is a lack of warmth and vigor.* BERNIECE *and* MARETHA *occupy the upstairs rooms.* DOAKER'S *room is prominent and opens onto the kitchen. Dominating the parlor is an old up-right piano. On the legs of the piano, carved in the man-ner of African sculpture, are mask-like figures resem-bling totems. The carvings are rendered with a grace and power of invention that lifts them out of the realm of craftsmanship and into the realm of art. At left is a staircase leading to the upstairs.*

ACT ONE

SCENE 1

The lights come up on the Charles household. It is five o'clock in the morning. The dawn is beginning to an-nounce itself, but there is something in the air that be-longs to the night. A stillness that is a portent, a gath-ering, a coming together of something akin to a storm. There is a loud knock at the door.

BOY WILLIE (*Off stage, calling*): Hey, Doaker . . . Doaker!
(*He knocks again and calls.*)
Hey, Doaker! Hey, Berniece! Berniece!
(DOAKER *enters from his room. He is a tall, thin man of forty-seven, with severe features, who has for all intents and purposes retired from the world though he works full-time as a railroad cook.*)

DOAKER: Who is it?

BOY WILLIE: Open the door, nigger! It's me . . . Boy Willie!

DOAKER: Who?

BOY WILLIE: Boy Willie! Open the door!

(DOAKER *opens the door and* BOY WILLIE *and* LYMON *enter.* BOY WILLIE *is thirty years old. He has an in-fectious grin and a boyishness that is apt for his name. He is brash and impulsive, talkative and somewhat crude in speech and manner.* LYMON *is twenty-nine.* BOY WILLIE'S *partner, he talks little, and then with a straightforwardness that is often disarming.*)

DOAKER: What you doing up here?

BOY WILLIE: I told you, Lymon. Lymon talking about you might be sleep. This is Lymon. You remember Lymon Jackson from down home? This my Uncle Doaker.

DOAKER: What you doing up here? I couldn't fig-ure out who that was. I thought you was still down in Mississippi.

BOY WILLIE: Me and Lymon selling watermelons. We got a truck out there. Got a whole truck-load of watermelons. We brought them up here to sell. Where's Berniece?
(*Calls.*)
Hey, Berniece!

DOAKER: Berniece up there sleep.

BOY WILLIE: Well, let her get up.
(*Calls.*)
Hey, Berniece!

DOAKER: She got to go to work in the morning.

BOY WILLIE: Well she can get up and say hi. It's been three years since I seen her.
(*Calls.*)
Hey, Berniece! It's me . . . Boy Willie.

DOAKER: Berniece don't like all that hollering now. She got to work in the morning.

BOY WILLIE: She can go on back to bed. Me and Ly-mon been riding two days in that truck . . . the least she can do is get up and say hi.

DOAKER (*Looking out the window*): Where you all get that truck from?

BOY WILLIE: It's Lymon's. I told him let's get a load of watermelons and bring them up here.

470

LYMON: Boy Willie say he going back, but I'm gonna stay. See what it's like up here.

BOY WILLIE: You gonna carry me down there first.

LYMON: I told you I ain't going back down there and take a chance on that truck breaking down again. You can take the train. Hey, tell him Doaker, he can take the train back. After we sell them watermelons he have enough money he can buy him a whole railroad car.

DOAKER: You got all them watermelons stacked up there no wonder the truck broke down. I'm surprised you made it this far with a load like that. Where you break down at?

BOY WILLIE: We broke down three times! It took us two and a half days to get here. It's a good thing we picked them watermelons fresh.

LYMON: We broke down twice in West Virginia. The first time was just as soon as we got out of Sunflower. About forty miles out she broke down. We got it going and got all the way to West Virginia before she broke down again.

BOY WILLIE: We had to walk about five miles for some water.

LYMON: It got a hole in the radiator but it runs pretty good. You have to pump the brakes sometime before they catch. Boy Willie have his door open and be ready to jump when that happens.

BOY WILLIE: Lymon think that's funny. I told the nigger I give him ten dollars to get the brakes fixed. But he thinks that funny.

LYMON: They don't need fixing. All you got to do is pump them till they catch.

(BERNIECE *enters on the stairs. Thirty-five years old, with an eleven-year-old daughter, she is still in mourning for her husband after three years.*)

BERNIECE: What you doing all that hollering for?

BOY WILLIE: Hey, Berniece. Doaker said you was sleep. I said at least you could get up and say hi.

BERNIECE: It's five o'clock in the morning and you come in here with all this noise. You can't come like normal folks. You got to bring all that noise with you.

BOY WILLIE: Hell, I ain't done nothing but come in and say hi. I ain't got in the house good.

BERNIECE: That's what I'm talking about. You start all that hollering and carry on as soon as you hit the door.

BOY WILLIE: Aw hell, woman, I was glad to see Doaker. You ain't had to come down if you didn't want to. I come eighteen hundred miles to see my sister I figure she might want to get up and say hi. Other than that you can go back upstairs. What you got, Doaker? Where your bottle? Me and Lymon want a drink.

(*To* BERNIECE.)

This is Lymon. You remember Lymon Jackson from down home.

LYMON: How you doing, Berniece. You look just like I thought you looked.

BERNIECE: Why you all got to come in hollering and carrying on? Waking the neighbors with all that noise.

BOY WILLIE: They can come over and join the party. We fixing to have a party. Doaker, where your bottle? Me and Lymon celebrating. The Ghosts of the Yellow Dog got Sutter.

BERNIECE: Say what?

BOY WILLIE: Ask Lymon, they found him the next morning. Say he drowned in his well.

DOAKER: When this happen, Boy Willie?

BOY WILLIE: About three weeks ago. Me and Lymon was over in Stoner County when we heard about it. We laughed. We thought it was funny. A great big old three-hundred-and-forty-pound man gonna fall down his well.

LYMON: It remind me of Humpty Dumpty.

BOY WILLIE: Everybody say the Ghosts of the Yellow Dog pushed him.

BERNIECE: I don't want to hear that nonsense. Somebody down there pushing them people in their wells.

DOAKER: What was you and Lymon doing over in Stoner County?

BOY WILLIE: We was down there working. Lymon got some people down there.

LYMON: My cousin got some land down there. We was helping him.

BOY WILLIE: Got near about a hundred acres. He got it set up real nice. Me and Lymon was down there chopping down trees. We was using Lymon's truck to haul the wood. Me and Lymon used to haul wood all around them parts.

(*To* BERNIECE.)

Me and Lymon got a truckload of watermelons out there.

(BERNIECE *crosses to the window to the parlor.*)
Doaker, where your bottle? I know you got a bottle stuck up in your room. Come on, me and Lymon want a drink.
(DOAKER *exits into his room.*)

BERNIECE: Where you all get that truck from?

BOY WILLIE: I told you it's Lymon's.

BERNIECE: Where you get the truck from, Lymon?

LYMON: I bought it.

BERNIECE: Where he get that truck from, Boy Willie?

BOY WILLIE: He told you he bought it. Bought it for a hundred and twenty dollars. I can't say where he got that hundred and twenty dollars from . . . but he bought that old piece of truck from Henry Porter. (*To* LYMON.) Where you get that hundred and twenty dollars from, nigger?

LYMON: I got it like you get yours. I know how to take care of money.
(DOAKER *brings a bottle and sets it on the table.*)

BOY WILLIE: Aw hell, Doaker got some of that good whiskey. Don't give Lymon none of that. He ain't used to good whiskey. He liable to get sick.

LYMON: I done had good whiskey before.

BOY WILLIE: Lymon bought that truck so he have him a place to sleep. He down there wasn't doing no work or nothing. Sheriff looking for him. He bought that truck to keep away from the sheriff. Got Stovall looking for him too. He down there sleeping in that truck ducking and dodging both of them. I told him come on let's go up and see my sister.

BERNIECE: What the sheriff looking for you for, Lymon?

BOY WILLIE: The man don't want you to know all his business. He's my company. He ain't asking you no questions.

LYMON: It wasn't nothing. It was just a misunderstanding.

BERNIECE: He in my house. You say the sheriff looking for him, I wanna know what he looking for him for. Otherwise you all can go back out there and be where nobody don't have to ask you nothing.

LYMON: It was just a misunderstanding. Sometimes me and the sheriff we don't think alike. So we just got crossed on each other.

BERNIECE: Might be looking for him about that truck. He might have stole that truck.

BOY WILLIE: We ain't stole no truck, woman. I told you Lymon bought it.

DOAKER: Boy Willie and Lymon got more sense than to ride all the way up here in a stolen truck with a load of watermelons. Now they might have stole them watermelons, but I don't believe they stole that truck.

BOY WILLIE: You don't even know the man good and you calling him a thief. And we ain't stole them watermelons either. Them old man Pitterford's watermelons. He give me and Lymon all we could load for ten dollars.

DOAKER: No wonder you got them stacked up out there. You must have five hundred watermelons stacked up out there.

BERNIECE: Boy Willie, when you and Lymon planning on going back?

BOY WILLIE: Lymon say he staying. As soon as we sell them watermelons I'm going on back.

BERNIECE (*Starts to exit up the stairs.*): That's what you need to do. And you need to do it quick. Come in here disrupting the house. I don't want all that loud carrying on around here. I'm surprised you ain't woke Maretha up.

BOY WILLIE: I was fixing to get her now.
(*Calls.*)
Hey, Maretha!

DOAKER: Berniece don't like all that hollering now.

BERNIECE: Don't you wake that child up!

BOY WILLIE: You going up there . . . wake her up and tell her her uncle's here. I ain't seen her in three years. Wake her up and send her down here. She can go back to bed.

BERNIECE: I ain't waking that child up . . . and don't you be making all that noise. You and Lymon need to sell them watermelons and go on back.
(BERNIECE *exits up the stairs.*)

BOY WILLIE: I see Berniece still try to be stuck up.

DOAKER: Berniece alright. She don't want you making all that noise. Maretha up there sleep. Let her sleep until she get up. She can see you then.

BOY WILLIE: I ain't thinking about Berniece. You hear from Wining Boy? You know Cleotha died?

DOAKER: Yeah, I heard that. He come by here about a year ago. Had a whole sack of money. He stayed here about two weeks. Ain't offered nothing. Berniece asked him for three dollars to buy some food and he got mad and left.

LYMON: Who's Wining Boy?

BOY WILLIE: That's my uncle. That's Doaker's brother. You heard me talk about Wining Boy. He play piano. He done made some records and everything. He still doing that, Doaker?

DOAKER: He made one or two records a long time ago. That's the only ones I ever known him to make. If you let him tell it he a big recording star.

BOY WILLIE: He stopped down home about two years ago. That's what I hear. I don't know. Me and Lymon was up on Parchman Farm doing them three years.

DOAKER: He don't never stay in one place. Now, he been here about eight months ago. Back in the winter. Now, you subject not to see him for another two years. It's liable to be that long before he stop by.

BOY WILLIE: If he had a whole sack of money you liable never to see him. You ain't gonna see him until he get broke. Just as soon as that sack of money is gone you look up and he be on your doorstep.

LYMON (*Noticing the piano*): Is that the piano?

BOY WILLIE: Yeah . . . look here, Lymon. See how it got all those carvings on it. See, that's what I was talking about. See how it's carved up real nice and polished and everything? You never find you another piano like that.

LYMON: Yeah, that look real nice.

BOY WILLIE: I told you. See how it's polished? My mama used to polish it every day. See all them pictures carved on it? That's what I was talking about. You can get a nice price for that piano.

LYMON: That's all Boy Willie talked about the whole trip up here. I got tired of hearing him talk about the piano.

BOY WILLIE: All you want to talk about is women. You ought to hear this nigger, Doaker. Talking about all the women he gonna get when he get up here. He ain't had none down there but he gonna get a hundred when he get up here.

DOAKER: How your people doing down there, Lymon?

LYMON: They alright. They still there. I come up here to see what it's like up here. Boy Willie trying to get me to go back and farm with him.

BOY WILLIE: Sutter's brother selling the land. He say he gonna sell it to me. That's why I come up here. I got one part of it. Sell them watermelons and get me another part. Get Berniece to sell that piano and I'll have the third part.

DOAKER: Berniece ain't gonna sell that piano.

BOY WILLIE: I'm gonna talk to her. When she see I got a chance to get Sutter's land she'll come around.

DOAKER: You can put that thought out your mind. Berniece ain't gonna sell that piano.

BOY WILLIE: I'm gonna talk to her. She been playing on it?

DOAKER: You know she won't touch that piano. I ain't never known her to touch it since Mama Ola died. That's over seven years now. She say it got blood on it. She got Maretha playing on it though. Say Maretha can go on and do everything she can't do. Got her in an extra school down at the Irene Kaufman Settlement House. She want Maretha to grow up and be a schoolteacher. Say she good enough she can teach on the piano.

BOY WILLIE: Maretha don't need to be playing on no piano. She can play on the guitar.

DOAKER: How much land Sutter got left?

BOY WILLIE: Got a hundred acres. Good land. He done sold it piece by piece, he kept the good part for himself. Now he got to give that up. His brother come down from Chicago for the funeral . . . he up there in Chicago got some kind of business with soda fountain equipment. He anxious to sell the land, Doaker. He don't want to be bothered with it. He called me to him and said cause of how long our families done known each other and how we been good friends and all, say he wanted to sell the land to me. Say he'd rather see me with it than Jim Stovall. Told me he'd let me have it for two thousand dollars cash money. He don't know I found out the most Stovall would give him for it was fifteen hundred dollars. He trying to get that extra five hundred out of me telling me he doing me a favor. I thanked him just as nice. Told him what a good man Sutter was and how he had my sympathy and all. Told him to give me two weeks. He said he'd wait on me. That's why I come up here. Sell them watermelons. Get Berniece to sell that piano. Put them two parts with the part I done saved. Walk in there. Tip my hat. Lay my money down on the table. Get my deed and walk on out. This time I get to keep all the cotton. Hire me some men to work it for me. Gin my cotton. Get my seed. And I'll see you again next year. Might even plant some tobacco or some oats.

DOAKER: You gonna have a hard time trying to get Berniece to sell that piano. You know Avery Brown from down there don't you? He up here now. He followed Berniece up here trying to get her to marry him after Crawley got killed. He been up here about two years. He call himself a preacher now.

BOY WILLIE: I know Avery. I know him from when he used to work on the Willshaw place. Lymon know him too.

DOAKER: He after Berniece to marry him. She keep telling him no but he won't give up. He keep pressing her on it.

BOY WILLIE: Avery think all white men is bigshots. He don't know there some white men ain't got as much as he got.

DOAKER: He supposed to come past here this morning. Berniece going down to the bank with him to see if he can get a loan to start his church. That's why I know Berniece ain't gonna sell that piano. He tried to get her to sell it to help him start his church. Sent the man around and everything.

BOY WILLIE: What man?

DOAKER: Some white fellow was going around to all the colored people's houses looking to buy up musical instruments. He'd buy anything. Drums. Guitars. Harmonicas. Pianos. Avery sent him past here. He looked at the piano and got excited. Offered her a nice price. She turned him down and got on Avery for sending him past. The man kept on her about two weeks. He seen where she wasn't gonna sell it, he gave her his number and told her if she ever wanted to sell it to call him first. Say he'd go one better than what anybody else would give her for it.

BOY WILLIE: How much he offer her for it?

DOAKER: Now you know me. She didn't say and I didn't ask. I just know it was a nice price.

LYMON: All you got to do is find out who he is and tell him somebody else wanna buy it from you. Tell him you can't make up your mind who to sell it to, and if he like Doaker say, he'll give you anything you want for it.

BOY WILLIE: That's what I'm gonna do. I'm gonna find out who he is from Avery.

DOAKER: It ain't gonna do you no good. Berniece ain't gonna sell that piano.

BOY WILLIE: She ain't got to sell it. I'm gonna sell it. I own just as much of it as she does.

BERNIECE (*Offstage, hollers*): Doaker! Go on get away. Doaker!

DOAKER (*Calling*): Berniece?
(DOAKER *and* BOY WILLIE *rush to the stairs*, BOY WILLIE *runs up the stairs, passing* BERNIECE *as she enters, running.*)

DOAKER: Berniece, what's the matter? You alright? What's the matter?
(BERNIECE *tries to catch her breath. She is unable to speak.*)

DOAKER: That's alright. Take your time. You alright. What's the matter?
(*He calls.*)
Hey, Boy Willie?

BOY WILLIE (*Offstage*): Ain't nobody up here.

BERNIECE: Sutter . . . Sutter's standing at the top of the steps.

DOAKER (*Calls*): Boy Willie!
(LYMON *crosses to the stairs and looks up.* BOY WILLIE *enters from the stairs.*)

BOY WILLIE: Hey Doaker, what's wrong with her? Berniece, what's wrong? Who was you talking to?

DOAKER: She say she seen Sutter's ghost standing at the top of the stairs.

BOY WILLIE: Seen what? Sutter? She ain't seen no Sutter.

BERNIECE: He was standing right up there.

BOY WILLIE (*Entering on the stairs*): That's all in Berniece's head. Ain't nobody up there. Go on up there, Doaker.

DOAKER: I'll take your word for it. Berniece talking about what she seen. She say Sutter's ghost standing at the top of the steps. She ain't just make all that up.

BOY WILLIE: She up there dreaming. She ain't seen no ghost.

LYMON: You want a glass of water, Berniece? Get her a glass of water, Boy Willie.

BOY WILLIE: She don't need no water. She ain't seen nothing. Go on up there and look. Ain't nobody up there but Maretha.

DOAKER: Let Berniece tell it.

BOY WILLIE: I ain't stopping her from telling it.

DOAKER: What happened, Berniece?

BERNIECE: I come out my room to come back down here and Sutter was standing there in the hall.

BOY WILLIE: What he look like?

BERNIECE: He look like Sutter. He look like he always look.

BOY WILLIE: Sutter couldn't find his way from Big Sandy to Little Sandy. How he gonna find his way all the way up here to Pittsburgh? Sutter ain't never even heard of Pittsburgh.

DOAKER: Go on, Berniece.

BERNIECE: Just standing there with the blue suit on.

BOY WILLIE: The man ain't never left Marlin County when be was living . . . and he's gonna come all the way up here now that he's dead?

DOAKER: Let her finish. I want to hear what she got to say.

BOY WILLIE: I'll tell you this. If Berniece had seen him like she think she seen him she'd still be running.

DOAKER: Go on, Berniece. Don't pay Boy Willie no mind.

BERNIECE: He was standing there . . . had his hand on top of his head. Look like he might have thought if he took his hand down his head might have fallen off.

LYMON: Did he have on a hat?

BERNIECE: Just had on that blue suit. . . . I told him to go away and he just stood there looking at me . . . calling Boy Willie's name.

BOY WILLIE: What he calling my name for?

BERNIECE: I believe you pushed him in the well.

BOY WILLIE: Now what kind of sense that make? You telling me I'm gonna go out there and hide, in the weeds with all them dogs and things he got around there. . . . I'm gonna hide and wait till I catch him looking down his well just right . . . then I'm gonna run over and push him in. A great big old three-hundred-and-forty-pound man.

BERNIECE: Well, what he calling your name for?

BOY WILLIE: He bending over looking down his well, woman . . . how he know who pushed him? It could have been anybody. Where was you when Sutter fell in his well? Where was Doaker? Me and Lymon was over in Stoner County. Tell her, Lymon. The Ghosts of the Yellow Dog got Sutter. That's what happened to him.

BERNIECE: You can talk all that Ghosts of the Yellow Dog stuff if you want. I know better.

LYMON: The Ghosts of the Yellow Dog pushed him. That's what the people say. They found him in his well and all the people say it must be the Ghosts of the Yellow Dog. Just like all them other men.

BOY WILLIE: Come talking about he looking for me. What he come all the way up here for? If he looking for me all he got to do is wait. He could have saved himself a trip if he looking for me. That ain't nothing but in Berniece's head. Ain't no telling what she liable to come up with next.

BERNIECE: Boy Willie, I want you and Lymon to go ahead and leave my house. Just go on somewhere. You don't do nothing but bring trouble with you everywhere you go. If it wasn't for you Crawley would still be alive.

BOY WILLIE: Crawley what? I ain't had nothing to do with Crawley getting killed. Crawley three time seven. He had his own mind.

BERNIECE: Just go on and leave. Let Sutter go somewhere else looking for you.

BOY WILLIE: I'm leaving. Soon as we sell them watermelons. Other than that I ain't going nowhere. Hell, I just got here. Talking about Sutter looking for me. Sutter was looking for that piano. That's what he was looking for. He had to die to find out where that piano was at . . . If I was you I'd get rid of it. That's the way to get rid of Sutter's ghost. Get rid of that piano.

BERNIECE: I want you and Lymon to go on and take all this confusion out of my house!

BOY WILLIE: Hey, tell her, Doaker. What kind of sense that make? I told you, Lymon, as soon as Berniece see me she was gonna start something.

Didn't I tell you that? Now she done made up that story about Sutter just so she could tell me to leave her house. Well, hell, I ain't going nowhere till I sell them watermelons.

BERNIECE: Well why don't you go out there and sell them! Sell them and go on back!

BOY WILLIE: We waiting till the people get up.

LYMON: Boy Willie say if you get out there too early and wake the people up they get mad at you and won't buy nothing from you.

DOAKER: You won't be waiting long. You done let the sun catch up with you. This the time everybody be getting up around here.

BERNIECE: Come on, Doaker, walk up here with me. Let me get Maretha up and get her started. I got to get ready myself. Boy Willie, just go on out there and sell them watermelons and you and Lymon leave my house. (BERNIECE *and* DO-AKER *exit up the stairs.*)

BOY WILLIE (*Calling after them*): If you see Sutter up there . . . tell him I'm down here waiting on him.

LYMON: What if she see him again?

BOY WILLIE: That's all in her head. There ain't no ghost up there.
(*Calls.*)
Hey, Doaker . . . I told you ain't nothing up there.

LYMON: I'm glad he didn't say he was looking for me.

BOY WILLIE: I wish I would see Sutter's ghost. Give me a chance to put a whupping on him.

LYMON: You ought to stay up here with me. You be down there working his land . . . he might come looking for you all the time.

BOY WILLIE: I ain't thinking about Sutter. And I ain't thinking about staying up here. You stay up here. I'm going back and get Sutter's land. You think you ain't got to work up here. You think this the land of milk and honey. But I ain't scared of work. I'm going back and farm every acre of that land.
(*DOAKER enters from the stairs.*)
I told you there ain't nothing up there, Doaker. Berniece dreaming all that.

DOAKER: I believe Berniece seen something. Berniece level-headed. She ain't just made all that up. She say Sutter had on a suit. I don't believe she ever seen Sutter in a suit. I believe that's what he was buried in, and that's what Berniece saw.

BOY WILLIE: Well, let her keep on seeing him then. As long as he don't mess with me.
(DOAKER *starts to cook his breakfast.*)
I heard about you, Doaker. They say you got all the women looking out for you down home. They be looking to see you coming. Say you got a different one every two weeks. Say they be fighting one another for you to stay with them.
(*To* LYMON.)
Look at him, Lymon. He know it's true.

DOAKER: I ain't thinking about no women. They never get me tied up with them. After Coreen I ain't got no use for them. I stay up on Jack Slattery's place when I be down there. All them women want is somebody with a steady payday.

BOY WILLIE: That ain't what I hear. I hear every two weeks the women all put on their dresses and line up at the railroad station.

DOAKER: I don't get down there but once a month. I used to go down there every two weeks but they keep switching me around. They keep switching all the fellows around.

BOY WILLIE: Doaker can't turn that railroad loose. He was working the railroad when I was walking around crying for sugartit. My mama used to brag on him.

DOAKER: I'm cooking now, but I used to line track. I pieced together the Yellow Dog stitch by stitch. Rail by rail. Line track all up around there. I lined track all up around Sunflower and Clarksdale. Wining Boy worked with me. He helped put in some of that track. He'd work it for six months and quit. Go back to playing piano and gambling.

BOY WILLIE: How long you been with the railroad now?

DOAKER: Twenty-seven years. Now, I'll tell you something about the railroad. What I done learned after twenty-seven years. See, you got North. You got West. You look over here you got South. Over there you got East. Now, you can start from anywhere. Don't care where you at. You got to go one of them four ways. And whichever way you decide to go they got a railroad that will take you there. Now, that's something simple. You think anybody would be able to understand that. But you'd be surprised how many people trying to go North get on a train going West. They think the train's supposed to go where they going rather than where it's going.

Now, why people going? Their sister's sick. They leaving before they kill somebody . . . and they sitting across from somebody who's leaving to keep from getting killed. They leaving cause they can't get satisfied. They going to meet someone. I wish I had a dollar for every time that someone wasn't at the station to meet them. I done seen that a lot. In between the time they sent the telegram and the time the person get there . . . they done forgot all about them.

They got so many trains out there they have a hard time keeping them from running into each other. Got trains going every whichaway. Got people on all of them. Somebody going where somebody just left. If everybody stay in one place I believe this would be a better world. Now what I done learned after twenty-seven years of railroading is this . . . if the train stays on the track . . . it's going to get where it's going. It might not be where you going. If it ain't, then all you got to do is sit and wait cause the train's coming back to get you. The train don't never stop. It'll come back every time. Now I'll tell you another thing . . .

BOY WILLIE: What you cooking over there, Doaker? Me and Lymon's hungry.

DOAKER: Go on down there to Wylie and Kirkpatrick to Eddie's restaurant. Coffee cost a nickel and you can get two eggs, sausage, and grits for fifteen cents. He even give you a biscuit with it.

BOY WILLIE: That look good what you got. Give me a little piece of that grilled bread.

DOAKER: Here . . . go on take the whole piece.

BOY WILLIE: Here you go, Lymon . . . you want a piece?

(*He gives* LYMON *a piece of toast.* MARETHA *enters from the stairs.*)

BOY WILLIE: Hey, sugar. Come here and give me a hug. Come on give Uncle Boy Willie a hug.

Don't be shy. Look at her, Doaker. She done got bigger. Ain't she got big?

DOAKER: Yeah, she getting up there.

BOY WILLIE: How you doing, sugar?

MARETHA: Fine.

BOY WILLIE: You was just a little old thing last time I seen you. You remember me, don't you? This your Uncle Boy Willie from down South. That there's Lymon. He my friend. We come up here to sell watermelons. You like watermelons? (MARETHA *nods.*)

We got a whole truckload out front. You can have as many as you want. What you been doing?

MARETHA: Nothing.

BOY WILLIE: Don't be shy now. Look at you getting all big. How old is you?

MARETHA: Eleven. I'm gonna be twelve soon.

BOY WILLIE: You like it up here? You like the North?

MARETHA: It's alright.

BOY WILLIE: That there's Lymon. Did you say hi to Lymon?

MARETHA: Hi.

LYMON: How you doing? You look just like your mama. I remember you when you was wearing diapers.

BOY WILLIE: You gonna come down South and see me? Uncle Boy Willie gonna get him a farm. Gonna get a great big old farm. Come down there and I'll teach you how to ride a mule. Teach you how to kill a chicken, too.

MARETHA: I seen my mama do that.

BOY WILLIE: Ain't nothing to it. You just grab him by his neck and twist it. Get you a real good grip and then you just wring his neck and throw him in the pot. Cook him up. Then you got some good eating. What you like to eat? What kind of food you like?

MARETHA: I like everything . . . except I don't like no black-eyed peas.

BOY WILLIE: Uncle Doaker tell me your mama got you playing that piano. Come on play something for me.

(BOY WILLIE *crosses over to the piano followed by* MARETHA.)

Show me what you can do. Come on now. Here . . . Uncle Boy Willie give you a dime . . .

show me what you can do. Don't be bashful now. That dime say you can't be bashful.

(MARETHA *plays. It is something any beginner first learns.*)

Here, let me show you something.

(BOY WILLIE *sits and plays a simple boogie-woogie.*)

See that? See what I'm doing? That's what you call the boogie-woogie. See now . . . you can get up and dance to that. That's how good it sound. It sound like you wanna dance. You can dance to that. It'll hold you up. Whatever kind of dance you wanna do you can dance to that right there. See that? See how it go? Ain't nothing to it. Go on you do it.

MARETHA: I got to read it on the paper.

BOY WILLIE: You don't need no paper. Go on. Do just like that there.

BERNIECE: Maretha! You get up here and get ready to go so you be on time. Ain't no need you trying to take advantage of company.

MARETHA: I got to go.

BOY WILLIE: Uncle Boy Willie gonna get you a guitar. Let Uncle Doaker teach you how to play that. You don't need to read no paper to play the guitar. Your mama told you about that piano? You know how them pictures got on there?

MARETHA: She say it just always been like that since she got it.

BOY WILLIE: You hear that, Doaker? And you sitting up here in the house with Berniece.

DOAKER: I ain't got nothing to do with that. I don't get in the way of Berniece's raising her.

BOY WILLIE: You tell your mama to tell you about that piano. You ask her how them pictures got on there. If she don't tell you I'll tell you.

BERNIECE: Maretha!

MARETHA: I got to get ready to go.

BOY WILLIE: She getting big, Doaker. You remember her, Lymon?

LYMON: She used to be real little.

(*There is a knock on the door.* DOAKER *goes to answer it.* AVERY *enters. Thirty-eight years old, honest and ambitious, he has taken to the city like a fish to water, finding in it opportunities for growth and advancement that did not exist for him in the rural South. He is dressed in a suit and tie with a gold cross around his neck. He carries a small Bible.*)

DOAKER: Hey, Avery, come on in. Berniece upstairs.

BOY WILLIE: Look at him . . . look at him . . . he don't know what to say. He wasn't expecting to see me.

AVERY: Hey, Boy Willie. What you doing up here?

BOY WILLIE: Look at him, Lymon.

AVERY: Is that Lymon? Lymon Jackson?

BOY WILLIE: Yeah, you know Lymon.

DOAKER: Berniece be ready in a minute, Avery.

BOY WILLIE: Doaker say you a preacher now. What . . . we supposed to call you Reverend? You used to be plain old Avery. When you get to be a preacher, nigger?

LYMON: Avery say he gonna be a preacher so he don't have to work.

BOY WILLIE: I remember when you was down there on the Willshaw place planting cotton. You wasn't thinking about no Reverend then.

AVERY: That must be your truck out there. I saw that truck with them watermelons, I was trying to figure out what it was doing in front of the house.

BOY WILLIE: Yeah, me and Lymon selling watermelons. That's Lymon's truck.

DOAKER: Berniece say you all going down to the bank.

AVERY: Yeah, they give me a half day off work. I got an appointment to talk to the bank about getting a loan to start my church.

BOY WILLIE: Lymon say preachers don't have to work. Where you working at, nigger?

DOAKER: Avery got him one of them good jobs. He working at one of them skyscrapers downtown.

AVERY: I'm working down there at the Gulf Building running an elevator. Got a pension and everything. They even give you a turkey on Thanksgiving.

LYMON: How you know the rope ain't gonna break? Ain't you scared the rope's gonna break?

AVERY: That's steel. They got steel cables hold it up. It take a whole lot of breaking to break that steel. Naw, I ain't worried about nothing like that. It ain't nothing but a little old elevator. Now, I wouldn't get in none of them airplanes. You couldn't pay me to do nothing like that.

LYMON: That be fun. I'd rather do that than ride in one of them elevators.

BOY WILLIE: How many of them watermelons you wanna buy?

AVERY: I thought you was gonna give me one seeing as how you got a whole truck full.

BOY WILLIE: You can get one, get two. I'll give you two for a dollar.

AVERY: I can't eat but one. How much are they?

BOY WILLIE: Aw, nigger, you know I'll give you a watermelon. Go on, take as many as you want. Just leave some for me and Lymon to sell.

AVERY: I don't want but one.

BOY WILLIE: How you get to be a preacher, Avery? I might want to be a preacher one day. Have everybody call me Reverend Boy Willie.

AVERY: It come to me in a dream. God called me and told me he wanted me to be a shepherd for his flock. That's what I'm gonna call my church . . . The Good Shepherd Church of God in Christ.

DOAKER: Tell him what you told me. Tell him about the three hobos.

AVERY: Boy Willie don't want to hear all that.

LYMON: I do. Lots a people say your dreams can come true.

AVERY: Naw. You don't want to hear all that.

DOAKER: Go on. I told him you was a preacher. He didn't want to believe me. Tell him about the three hobos.

AVERY: Well, it come to me in a dream. See . . . I was sitting out in this railroad yard watching the trains go by. The train stopped and these three hobos got off. They told me they had come from Nazareth and was on their way to Jerusalem. They had three candles. They gave me one and told me to light it . . . but to be careful that it didn't go out. Next thing I knew I was standing in front of this house. Something told me to go knock on the door. This old woman opened the door and said they had been waiting on me. Then she led me into this room. It was a big room and it was full of all kinds of different people. They looked like anybody else except they all had sheep heads and was making noise like sheep make. I heard somebody call my name. I looked around and there was these same three hobos. They told me to take off my clothes and they give me a blue robe with gold thread. They washed my feet and combed my hair. Then they showed me these three doors and told me to pick one.

I went through one of them doors and that flame leapt off that candle and it seemed like my whole head caught fire. I looked around and there was four or five other men standing there with these same blue robes on. Then we heard a voice tell us to look out across this valley. We looked out and saw the valley was full of wolves. The voice told us that these sheep people that I had seen in the other room had to go over to the other side of this valley and somebody had to take them. Then I heard another voice say, "Who shall I send?" Next thing I knew I said, "Here I am. Send me." That's when I met Jesus. He say, "If you go, I'll go with you." Something told me to say, "Come on. Let's go." That's when I woke up. My head still felt like it was on fire . . . but I had a peace about myself that was hard to explain. I knew right then that I had been filled with the Holy Ghost and called to be a servant of the Lord. It took me a while before I could accept that. But then a lot of little ways God showed me that it was true. So I became a preacher.

LYMON: I see why you gonna call it the Good Shepherd Church. You dreaming about them sheep people. I can see that easy.

BOY WILLIE: Doaker say you sent some white man past the house to look at that piano. Say he was going around to all the colored people's houses looking to buy up musical instruments.

AVERY: Yeah, but Berniece didn't want to sell that piano. After she told me about it . . . I could see why she didn't want to sell it.

BOY WILLIE: What's this man's name?

AVERY: Oh, that's a while back now. I done forgot his name. He give Berniece a card with his name and telephone number on it, but I believe she throwed it away.

(BERNIECE *and* MARETHA *enter from the stairs.*)

BERNIECE: Maretha, run back upstairs and get my pocket-book. And wipe that hair grease off your forehead. Go ahead, hurry up.

(MARETHA *exits up the stairs.*)

How you doing, Avery? You done got all dressed up. You look nice. Boy Willie, I thought you and Lymon was going to sell them watermelons.

BOY WILLIE: Lymon done got sleepy. We liable to get some sleep first.

LYMON: I ain't sleepy.

DOAKER: As many watermelons as you got stacked up on that truck out there, you ought to have been gone.

BOY WILLIE: We gonna go in a minute. We going.

BERNIECE: Doaker. I'm gonna stop down there on Logan Street. You want anything?

DOAKER: You can pick up some ham hocks if you going down there. See if you can get the smoked ones. If they ain't got that get the fresh ones. Don't get the ones that got all that fat under the skin. Look for the long ones. They nice and lean. (*He gives her a dollar.*)
Don't get the short ones lessen they smoked. If you got to get the fresh ones make sure that they the long ones. If they ain't got them smoked then go ahead and get the short ones. (*Pause.*)
You may as well get some turnip greens while you down there. I got some buttermilk . . . if you pick up some cornmeal I'll make me some cornbread and cook up them turnip greens. (MARETHA *enters from the stairs.*)

MARETHA: We gonna take the streetcar?

BERNIECE: Me and Avery gonna drop you off at the settlement house. You mind them people down there. Don't be going down there showing your color. Boy Willie, I done told you what to do. I'll see you later, Doaker.

AVERY: I'll be seeing you again, Boy Willie.

BOY WILLIE: Hey, Berniece . . . what's the name of that man Avery sent past say he want to buy the piano?

BERNIECE: I knew it. I knew it when I first seen you. I knew you was up to something.

BOY WILLIE: Sutter's brother say he selling the land to me. He waiting on me now. Told me he'd give me two weeks. I got one part. Sell them watermelons get me another part. Then we can sell that piano and I'll have the third part.

BERNIECE: I ain't selling that piano, Boy Willie. If that's why you come up here you can just forget about it.

(*To* DOAKER.)
Doaker, I'll see you later. Boy Willie ain't nothing but a whole lot of mouth. I ain't paying him no mind. If he come up here thinking he gonna sell that piano then he done come up here for nothing.

(BERNIECE, AVERY, *and* MARETHA *exit the front door.*)

BOY WILLIE: Hey, Lymon! You ready to go sell these watermelons.

(BOY WILLIE *and* LYMON *start to exit. At the door* BOY WILLIE *turns to* DOAKER.)
Hey, Doaker . . . if Berniece don't want to sell that piano . . . I'm gonna cut it in half and go on and sell my half.

(BOY WILLIE *and* LYMON *exit.*)

(*The lights go down on the scene.*)

SCENE 2

The lights come up on the kitchen. It is three days later. WINING BOY *sits at the kitchen table. There is a half-empty pint bottle on the table.* DOAKER *busies himself washing pots.* WINING BOY *is fifty-six years old.* DOAKER'S *older brother, he tries to present the image of a successful musician and gambler, but his music, his clothes, and even his manner of presentation are old. He is a man who looking back over his life continues to live it with an odd mixture of zest and sorrow.*

WINING BOY: So the Ghosts of the Yellow Dog got Sutter. That just go to show you I believe I always lived right. They say every dog gonna have his day and time it go around it sure come back to you. I done seen that a thousand times. I know the truth of that. But I'll tell you outright . . . if I see Sutter's ghost I'll be on the first thing I find that got wheels on it.

(DOAKER *enters from his room.*)

DOAKER: Wining Boy!

WINING BOY: And I'll tell you another thing . . . Berniece ain't gonna sell that piano.

DOAKER: That's what she told him. He say he gonna cut it in half and go on and sell his half. They been around here three days trying to sell them watermelons. They trying to get out to where the white folks live but the truck keep breaking down. They go a block or two and it break down again. They trying to get out to Squirrel Hill and can't get around the corner. He say soon as he can get that truck empty to where he can set the piano up in there he gonna take it out of here and go sell it.

WINING BOY: What about them boys Sutter got? How come they ain't farming that land?

DOAKER: One of them going to school. He left down there and come North to school. The other one ain't got as much sense as that frying pan over yonder. That is the dumbest white man I ever seen. He'd stand in the river and watch it rise till it drown him.

WINING BOY: Other than seeing Sutter's ghost how's Berniece doing?

DOAKER: She doing alright. She still got Crawley on her mind. He been dead three years but she still holding on to him. She need to go out here and let one of these fellows grab a whole handful of whatever she got. She act like it done got precious.

WINING BOY: They always told me any fish will bite if you got good bait.

DOAKER: She stuck up on it. She think it's better than she is. I believe she messing around with Avery. They got something going. He a preacher now. If you let him tell it the Holy Ghost sat on his head and heaven opened up with thunder and lightning and God was calling his name. Told him to go out and preach and tend to his flock. That's what he gonna call his church. The Good Shepherd Church.

WINING BOY: They had that joker down in Spear walking around talking about he Jesus Christ. He gonna live the life of Christ. Went through the Last Supper and everything. Rented him a mule on Palm Sunday and rode through the town. Did everything . . . talking about he Christ. He did everything until they got up to that crucifixion part. Got up to that part and told everybody to go home and quit pretending. He got up to the crucifixion part and changed his mind. Had a whole bunch of folks come down there to see him get nailed to the cross. I don't know who's the worse fool. Him or them. Had all them folks come down there . . . even carried the cross up this little hill. People standing around waiting to

see him get nailed to the cross and he stop everything and preach a little sermon and told everybody to go home. Had enough nerve to tell them to come to church on Easter Sunday to celebrate his resurrection.

DOAKER: I'm surprised Avery ain't thought about that. He trying every little thing to get him a congregation together. They meeting over at his house till he get him a church.

WINING BOY: Ain't nothing wrong with being a preacher. You got the preacher on one hand and the gambler on the other. Sometimes there ain't too much difference in them.

DOAKER: How long you been in Kansas City?

WINING BOY: Since I left here. I got tied up with some old gal down there.
(*Pause.*)
You know Cleotha died.

DOAKER: Yeah, I heard that last time I was down there. I was sorry to hear that.

WINING BOY: One of her friends wrote and told me. I got the letter right here.
(*He takes the letter out of his pocket.*)
I was down in Kansas City and she wrote and told me Cleotha had died. Name of Willa Bryant. She say she know cousin Rupert.
(*He opens the letter and reads.*)
Dear Wining Boy: I am writing this letter to let you know Miss Cleotha Holman passed on Saturday the first of May she departed this world in the loving arms of her sister Miss Alberta Samuels. I know you would want to know this and am writing as a friend of Cleotha. There have been many hardships since last you seen her but she survived them all and to the end was a good woman whom I hope have God's grace and is in His Paradise. Your cousin Rupert Bates is my friend also and he give me your address and I pray this reaches you about Cleotha. Miss Willa Bryant. A friend.
(*He folds the letter and returns it to his pocket.*)
They was nailing her coffin shut by the time I heard about it. I never knew she was sick. I believe it was that yellow jaundice. That's what killed her mama.

DOAKER: Cleotha wasn't but forty-some.

WINING BOY: She was forty-six. I got ten years on her. I met her when she was sixteen. You remember I used to run around there. Couldn't nothing keep me still. Much as I loved Cleotha I loved to ramble. Couldn't nothing keep me still. We got married and we used to fight about it all the time. Then one day she asked me to leave. Told me she loved me before I left. Told me, Wining Boy, you got a home as long as I got mine. And I believe in my heart I always felt that and that kept me safe.

DOAKER: Cleotha always did have a nice way about her.

WINING BOY: Man that woman was something. I used to thank the Lord. Many a night I sat up and looked out over my life. Said, well, I had Cleotha. When it didn't look like there was nothing else for me, I said, thank God, at least I had that. If ever I go anywhere in this life I done known a good woman. And that used to hold me till the next morning.

(*Pause.*)

What you got? Give me a little nip. I know you got something stuck up in your room.

DOAKER: I ain't seen you walk in here and put nothing on the table. You done sat there and drank up your whiskey. Now you talking about what you got.

WINING BOY: I got plenty money. Give me a little nip.

(DOAKER *carries a glass into his room and returns with it half-filled. He sets it on the table in front of* WINING BOY.)

WINING BOY: You hear from Coreen?

DOAKER: She up in New York. I let her go from my mind.

WINING BOY: She was something back then. She wasn't too pretty but she had a way of looking at you made you know there was a whole lot of woman there. You got married and snatched her out from under us and we all got mad at you.

DOAKER: She up in New York City. That's what I hear.

(*The door opens and* BOY WILLIE *and* LYMON *enter.*)

BOY WILLIE: Aw hell . . . look here! We was just talking about you. Doaker say you left out of here with a whole sack of money. I told him we wasn't going see you till you got broke.

WINING BOY: What you mean broke? I got a whole pocketful of money.

DOAKER: Did you all get that truck fixed?

BOY WILLIE: We got it running and got halfway out there on Centre and it broke down again. Lymon went out there and messed it up some more. Fellow told us we got to wait till tomorrow to get it fixed. Say he have it running like new. Lymon going back down there and sleep in the truck so the people don't take the watermelons.

LYMON: Lymon nothing. You go down there and sleep in it.

BOY WILLIE: You was sleeping in it down home, nigger! I don't know nothing about sleeping in no truck.

LYMON: I ain't sleeping in no truck.

BOY WILLIE: They can take all the watermelons. I don't care. Wining Boy, where you coming from? Where you been?

WINING BOY: I been down in Kansas City.

BOY WILLIE: You remember Lymon? Lymon Jackson.

WINING BOY: Yeah, I used to know his daddy.

BOY WILLIE: Doaker say you don't never leave no address with nobody. Say he got to depend on your whim. See when it strike you to pay a visit.

WINING BOY: I got four or five addresses.

BOY WILLIE: Doaker say Berniece asked you for three dollars and you got mad and left.

WINING BOY: Berniece try and rule over you too much for me. That's why I left. It wasn't about no three dollars.

BOY WILLIE: Where you getting all these sacks of money from? I need to be with you. Doaker say you had a whole sack of money . . . turn some of it loose.

WINING BOY: I was just fixing to ask you for five dollars.

BOY WILLIE: I ain't got no money. I'm trying to get some. Doaker tell you about Sutter? The Ghosts of the Yellow Dog got him about three weeks ago. Berniece done seen his ghost and everything. He right upstairs.

(*Calls.*)

Hey Sutter! Wining Boy's here. Come on, get a drink!

WINING BOY: How many that make the Ghosts of the Yellow Dog done got?

BOY WILLIE: Must be about nine or ten, eleven or twelve. I don't know.

DOAKER: You got Ed Saunders. Howard Peterson. Charlie Webb.

WINING BOY: Robert Smith. That, fellow that shot Becky's boy . . . say he was stealing peaches . . .

DOAKER: You talking about Bob Mallory.

BOY WILLIE: Berniece say she don't believe all that about the Ghosts of the Yellow Dog.

WINING BOY: She ain't got to believe. You go ask them white folks in Sunflower County if they believe. You go ask Sutter if he believe. I don't care if Berniece believe or not. I done been to where the Southern cross the Yellow Dog and called out their names. They talk back to you, too.

LYMON: What they sound like? The wind or something?

BOY WILLIE: You done been there for real, Wining Boy?

WINING BOY: Nineteen thirty. July of nineteen thirty I stood right there on that spot. It didn't look like nothing was going right in my life. I said everything can't go wrong all the time . . . let me go down there and call on the Ghosts of the Yellow Dog, see if they can help me. I went down there and right there where them two railroads cross each other . . . I stood right there on that spot and called out their names. They talk back to you, too.

LYMON: People say you can ask them questions. They talk to you like that?

WINING BOY: A lot of things you got to find out on your own. I can't say how they talked to nobody else. But to me it just filled me up in a strange sort of way to be standing there on that spot. I didn't want to leave. It felt like the longer I stood there the bigger I got. I seen the train coming and it seem like I was bigger than the train. I started not to move. But something told me to go ahead and get on out the way. The train passed and I started to go back up there and stand some more. But something told me not to do it. I walked away from there feeling like a king. Went on and had a stroke of luck that run on for three years. So I don't care if Berniece believe or not. Berniece ain't got to believe. I know cause I been there. Now Doaker'll tell you about the Ghosts of the Yellow Dog.

DOAKER: I don't try and talk that stuff with Berniece. Avery got her all tied up in that church. She just think it's a whole lot of nonsense.

BOY WILLIE: Berniece don't believe in nothing. She just think she believe. She believe in anything if it's convenient for her to believe. But when that convenience run out then she ain't got nothing to stand on.

WINING BOY: Let's not get on Berniece now. Doaker tell me you talking about selling that piano.

BOY WILLIE: Yeah . . . hey, Doaker, I got the name of that man Avery was talking about. The man what's fixing the truck gave me his name. Everybody know him. Say he buy up anything you can make music with. I got his name and his telephone number. Hey, Wining Boy, Sutter's brother say he selling the land to me. I got one part. Sell them watermelons get me the second part. Then . . . soon as I get them watermelons out that truck I'm gonna take and sell that piano and get the third part.

DOAKER: That land ain't worth nothing no more. The smart white man's up here in these cities. He cut the land loose and step back and watch you and the dumb white man argue over it.

WINING BOY: How you know Sutter's brother ain't sold it already? You talking about selling the piano and the man's liable to sold the land two or three times.

BOY WILLIE: He say he waiting on me. He say he give me two weeks. That's two weeks from Friday. Say if I ain't back by then he might gonna sell it to somebody else. He say he wanna see me with it.

WINING BOY: You know as well as I know the man gonna sell the land to the first one walk up and hand him the money.

BOY WILLIE: That's just who I'm gonna be. Look, you ain't gotta know he waiting on me. I know. Okay. I know what the man told me. Stoval already done tried to buy the land from him and he told him no. The man say he waiting on me . . . he waiting on me. Hey, Doaker . . . give me a drink. I see Wining Boy got his glass.

(DOAKER *exits into his room.*)

Wining Boy, what you doing in Kansas City? What they got down there?

LYMON: I hear they got some nice-looking women in Kansas City. I sure like to go down there and find out.

WINING BOY: Man, the women down there is something else.

(DOAKER *enters with a bottle of whiskey. He sets it on the table with some glasses.*)

DOAKER: You wanna sit up here and drink up my whiskey, leave a dollar on the table when you get up.

BOY WILLIE: You ain't doing nothing but showing your hospitality. I know we ain't got to pay for your hospitality.

WINING BOY: Doaker say they had you and Lymon down on the Parchman Farm. Had you on my old stomping grounds.

BOY WILLIE: Me and Lymon was down there hauling wood for Jim Miller and keeping us a little bit to sell. Some white fellows tried to run us off of it. That's when Crawley got killed. They put me and Lymon in the penitentiary.

LYMON: They ambushed us right there where that road dip down and around that bend in the creek. Crawley tried to fight them. Me and Boy Willie got away but the sheriff got us. Say we was stealing wood. They shot me in my stomach.

BOY WILLIE: They looking for Lymon down there now. They rounded him up and put him in jail for not working.

LYMON: Fined me a hundred dollars. Mr. Stovall come and paid my hundred dollars and the judge say I got to work for him to pay him back his hundred dollars. I told them I'd rather take my thirty days but they wouldn't let me do that.

BOY WILLIE: As soon as Stovall turned his back, Lymon was gone. He down there living in that truck dodging the sheriff and Stovall. He got both of them looking for him. So I brought him up here.

LYMON: I told Boy Willie I'm gonna stay up here. I ain't going back with him.

BOY WILLIE: Ain't nobody twisting your arm to make you go back. You can do what you want to do.

WINING BOY: I'll go back with you. I'm on my way down there. You gonna take the train? I'm gonna take the train.

LYMON: They treat you better up here.

BOY WILLIE: I ain't worried about nobody mistreating me. They treat you like you let them treat you. They mistreat me I mistreat them right back. Ain't no difference in me and the white man.

WINING BOY: Ain't no difference as far as how somebody supposed to treat you. I agree with that. But I'll tell you the difference between the colored man and the white man. Alright. Now you take and eat some berries. They taste real good to you. So you say I'm gonna go out and get me a whole pot of these berries and cook them up to make a pie or whatever. But you ain't looked to see them berries is sitting in the white fellow's yard. Ain't got no fence around them. You figure anybody want something they'd fence it in. Alright. Now the white man come along and say that's my land. Therefore everything that grow on it belong to me. He tell the sheriff, "I want you to put this nigger in jail as a warning to all the other niggers. Otherwise first thing you know these niggers have everything that belong to us."

BOY WILLIE: I'd come back at night and haul off his whole patch while he was sleep.

WINING BOY: Alright. Now Mr. So and So, he sell the land to you. And he come to you and say, "John, you own the land. It's all yours, now. But them is my berries. And come time to pick them I'm gonna send my boys over. You got the land . . . but them berries, I'm gonna keep them. They mine." And he go and fix it with the law that them is his berries. Now that's the difference between the colored man and the white man. The colored man can't fix nothing with the law.

BOY WILLIE: I don't go by what the law say. The law's liable to say anything. I go by if it's right or not. It don't matter to me what the law say. I take and look at it for myself.

LYMON: That's why you gonna end up back down there on the Parchman Farm.

BOY WILLIE: I ain't thinking about no Parchman Farm. You liable to go back before me.

LYMON: They work you too hard down there. All that weeding and hoeing and chopping down trees. I didn't like all that.

WINING BOY: You ain't got to like your job on Parchman. Hey, tell him, Doaker, the only one got to like his job is the waterboy.

DOAKER: If he don't like his job he need to set that bucket down.

BOY WILLIE: That's what they told Lymon. They had Lymon on water and everybody got mad at him cause he was lazy.

LYMON: That water was heavy.

BOY WILLIE: They had Lymon down there singing:
(*Sings.*)

> O Lord Berta Berta O Lord gal oh-ah
> O Lord Berta Berta O Lord gal well

(LYMON *and* WINING BOY *join in.*)

> Go 'head marry don't you wait on me
>   oh-ah
> Go 'head marry don't you wait on me well
> Might not want you when I go free oh-ah
> Might not want you when I go free well

BOY WILLIE: Come on, Doaker. Doaker know this one.
(*As* DOAKER *joins in the men stamp and clap to keep time. They sing in harmony with great fervor and style.*)

> O Lord Berta Berta O Lord gal oh-ah
> O Lord Berta Berta O Lord gal well
>
> Raise them up higher, let them drop on
>   down oh-ah
> Raise them up higher, let them drop on
>   down well
> Don't know the difference when the sun
>   go down oh-ah
> Don't know the difference when the sun
>   go down well
>
> Berta in Meridan and she living at ease
>   oh-ah
> Berta in Meridan and she living at ease
>   well
> I'm on old Parchman, got to work or
>   leave oh-ah
> I'm on old Parchman, got to work or
>   leave well
>
> O Alberta, Berta, O Lord gal oh-ah
> O Alberta, Berta, O Lord gal well
>
> When you marry, don't marry no farm-
>   ing man oh-ah
> When you marry, don't marry no farm-
>   ing man well

> Everyday Monday, hoe handle in your
>   hand oh-ah
> Everyday Monday, hoe handle in your
>   hand well
>
> When you marry, marry a railroad man,
>   oh-ah
> When you marry, marry a railroad man,
>   well
> Everyday Sunday, dollar in your hand
>   oh-ah
> Everyday Sunday, dollar in your hand well
>
> O Alberta, Berta, O Lord gal oh-ah
> O Alberta, Berta, O Lord gal well

BOY WILLIE: Doaker like that part. He like that railroad part.

LYMON: Doaker sound like Tangleye. He can't sing a lick.

BOY WILLIE: Hey, Doaker, they still talk about you down on Parchman. They ask me, "You Doaker Boy's nephew?" I say, "Yeah, me and him is family." They treated me alright soon as I told them that. Say, "Yeah, he my uncle."

DOAKER: I don't never want to see none of them niggers no more.

BOY WILLIE: I don't want to see them either. Hey, Wining Boy, come on play some piano. You a piano player, play some piano. Lymon wanna hear you.

WINING BOY: I give that piano up. That was the best thing that ever happened to me, getting rid of that piano. That piano got so big and I'm carrying it around on my back. I don't wish that on nobody. See, you think it's all fun being a recording star. Got to carrying that piano around and man did I get slow. Got just like molasses. The world just slipping by me and I'm walking around with that piano. Alright. Now, there ain't but so many places you can go. Only so many road wide enough for you and that piano. And that piano get heavier and heavier. Go to a place and they find out you play piano, the first thing they want to do is give you a drink, find you a piano, and sit you right down. And that's where you gonna be for the next eight hours. They ain't gonna let you get up! Now, the first three or four years of that is fun. You can't get enough whiskey and you can't get enough women and you don't never get tired of playing that piano. But that only last so long. You look up one day and you hate the whiskey, and you hate the women, and you hate the piano. But that's all you got. You can't do nothing else. All you know how to do is play that piano. Now, who am I? Am I me? Or am I the piano player? Sometime it seem like the only thing to do is shoot the piano player cause he the cause of all the trouble I'm having.

DOAKER: What you gonna do when your troubles get like mine?

LYMON: If I knew how to play it, I'd play it. That's a nice piano.

BOY WILLIE: Whoever playing better play quick. Sutter's brother say he waiting on me. I sell them watermelons. Get Berniece to sell that piano. Put them two parts with the part I done saved . . .

WINING BOY: Berniece ain't gonna sell that piano. I don't see why you don't know that.

BOY WILLIE: What she gonna do with it? She ain't doing nothing but letting it sit up there and rot. That piano ain't doing nobody no good.

LYMON: That's a nice piano. If I had it I'd sell it. Unless I knew how to play like Wining Boy. You can get a nice price for that piano.

DOAKER: Now I'm gonna tell you something, Lymon don't know this . . . but I'm gonna tell you why me and Wining Boy say Berniece ain't gonna sell that piano.

BOY WILLIE: She ain't got to sell it! I'm gonna sell it! Berniece ain't got no more rights to that piano than I do.

DOAKER: I'm talking to the man . . . let me talk to the man. See, now . . . to understand why we say that . . . to understand about that piano . . . you got to go back to slavery time. See, our family was owned by a fellow named Robert Sutter. That was Sutter's grandfather. Alright. The piano was owned by a fellow named Joel Nolander. He was one of the Nolander brothers from down in Georgia. It was coming up on Sutter's wedding anniversary and he was looking to buy his wife . . . Miss Ophelia was her name . . . he was looking to buy her an anniversary present. Only thing with him. . . . he ain't had no money. But he had some niggers. So he asked Mr. Nolander to see if maybe he could trade off some of his niggers for that piano. Told him he would give him one and a half niggers for it. That's the way he told him. Say he could have one full grown and one half grown. Mr. Nolander agreed only he say he had to pick them. He didn't want Sutter to give him just any old nigger. He say he wanted to have the pick of the litter. So Sutter lined up his niggers and Mr. Nolander looked them over and out of the whole bunch he picked my grandmother . . . her name was Berniece . . . same like Berniece . . . and he picked my daddy when he wasn't nothing but a little boy nine years old. They made the trade off and Miss Ophelia was so happy with that piano that it got to be just about all she would do was play on that piano.

WINING BOY: Just get up in the morning, get all dressed up and sit down and play on that piano.

DOAKER: Alright. Time go along. Time go along. Miss Ophelia got to missing my grandmother . . . the way she would cook and clean the house and talk to her and what not. And she missed having my daddy around the house to fetch things for her. So she asked to see if maybe she could trade back that piano and get her niggers back. Mr. Nolander said no. Said a deal was a deal. Him and Sutter had a big falling out about it and Miss Ophelia took sick to the bed. Wouldn't get out of the bed in the morning. She just lay there. The doctor said she was wasting away.

WINING BOY: That's when Sutter called our granddaddy up to the house.

DOAKER: Now, our granddaddy's name was Boy Willie. That's who Boy Willie's named after . . . only they called him Willie Boy. Now, he was a worker of wood. He could make you anything you wanted out of wood. He'd make you a desk. A table. A lamp. Anything you wanted. Them white fellows around there used to come up to Mr. Sutter and get him to make all kinds of things for them. Then they'd pay Mr. Sutter a nice price. See, everything my granddaddy made Mr. Sutter owned cause he owned him. That's why when Mr. Nolander offered to buy him to keep the family together Mr. Sutter wouldn't sell him. Told Mr. Nolander he didn't have enough money to buy him. Now . . . am I telling it right, Wining Boy?

WINING BOY: You telling it.

DOAKER: Sutter called him up to the house and told him to carve my grandmother and my daddy's picture on the piano for Miss Ophelia. And he took and carved this . . .

(DOAKER *crosses over to the piano.*)

See that right there? That's my grandmother, Berniece. She looked just like that. And he put a picture of my daddy when he wasn't nothing but a little boy the way he remembered him. He made them up out of his memory. Only thing . . . he didn't stop there. He carved all this. He got a picture of his mama . . . Mama Esther . . . and his daddy, Boy Charles.

WINING BOY: That was the first Boy Charles.

DOAKER: Then he put on the side here all kinds of things. See that? That's when him and Mama Berniece got married. They called it jumping the broom. That's how you got married in them days. Then he got here when my daddy was born . . . and here he got Mama Esther's funeral . . . and down here he got Mr. Nolander taking Mama Berniece and my daddy away down to his place in Georgia. He got all kinds of things what happened with our family. When Mr. Sutter seen the piano with all them carvings on it he got mad. He didn't ask for all that. But see . . . there wasn't nothing he could do about it. When Miss Ophelia seen it . . . she got excited. Now she had her piano and her niggers too. She took back to playing it and played on it right up till the day she died. Alright . . . now see, our brother Boy Charles . . . that's Berniece and Boy Willie's daddy . . . he was the oldest of us three boys. He's dead now. But he would have been fifty-seven if he had lived. He died in 1911 when he was thirty-one years old. Boy Charles used to talk about that piano all the time. He never could get it off his mind. Two or three months go by and he be talking about it again. He be talking about taking it out of Sutter's house.

Say it was the story of our whole family and as long as Sutter had it . . . he had us. Say we was still in slavery. Me and Wining Boy tried to talk him out of it but it wouldn't do any good. Soon as he quiet down about it he'd start up again. We seen where he wasn't gonna get it off his mind . . . so, on the Fourth of July, 1911 . . . when Sutter was at the picnic what the county give every year . . . me and Wining Boy went on down there with him and took that piano out of Sutter's house. We put it on a wagon and me and Wining Boy carried it over into the next county with Mama Ola's people. Boy Charles decided to stay around there and wait until Sutter got home to make it look like business as usual.

Now, I don't know what happened when Sutter came home and found that piano gone. But somebody went up to Boy Charles's house and set it on fire. But he wasn't in there. He must have seen them coming cause he went down and caught the 3:57 Yellow Dog. He didn't know they was gonna come down and stop the train. Stopped the train and found Boy Charles in the boxcar with four of them hobos. Must have got mad when they couldn't find the piano cause they set the boxcar afire and killed everybody. Now, nobody know who done that. Some people say it was Sutter cause it was his piano. Some people say it was Sheriff Carter. Some people say it was Robert Smith and Ed Saunders. But don't nobody know for sure. It was about two months after that that Ed Saunders fell down his well. Just upped and fell down his well for no reason. People say it was the ghost of them men who burned up in the boxcar that pushed him in his well. They started calling them the Ghosts of the Yellow Dog. Now, that's how all that got started and that why we say Berniece ain't gonna sell that piano. Cause her daddy died over it.

BOY WILLIE: All that's in the past. If my daddy had seen where he could have traded that piano in for some land of his own, it wouldn't be sitting up here now. He spent his whole life farming on somebody else's land. I ain't gonna do that. See, he couldn't do no better. When he come along he ain't had nothing he could build on. His daddy ain't had nothing to give him. The only thing my daddy had to give me was that piano. And he died over giving me that. I ain't gonna let it sit up there and rot without trying to do something with it. If Berniece can't see that, then I'm gonna go ahead and sell my half. And you and Wining Boy know I'm right.

DOAKER: Ain't nobody said nothing about who's right and who's wrong. I was just telling the man about the piano. I was telling him why we say Berniece ain't gonna sell it.

LYMON: Yeah, I can see why you say that now. I told Boy Willie he ought to stay up here with me.

BOY WILLIE: You stay! I'm going back! That's what I'm gonna do with my life! Why I got to come up here and learn to do something I don't know how to do when I already know how to farm? You stay up here and make your own way if that's what you want to do. I'm going back and live my life the way I want to live it.

(WINING BOY gets up and crosses to the piano.)

WINING BOY: Let's see what we got here. I ain't played on this thing for a while.

DOAKER: You can stop telling that. You was playing on it the last time you was through here. We couldn't get you off of it. Go on and play something.

(WINING BOY sits down at the piano and plays and sings. The song is one which has put many dimes and quarters in his pocket, long ago, in dimly remembered towns and way stations. He plays badly, without hesitation, and sings in a forceful voice.)

WINING BOY (Singing):

I am a rambling gambling man
I gambled in many towns
I rambled this wide world over
I rambled this world around
I had my ups and downs in life
And bitter times I saw
But I never knew what misery was
Till I lit on old Arkansas.

I started out one morning
to meet that early train
He said, "You better work for me
I have some land to drain.
I'll give you fifty cents a day,
Your washing, board and all

And you shall be a different man
In the state of Arkansas."

I worked six months for the rascal
Joe Herrin was his name
He fed me old corn dodgers
They was hard as any rock
My tooth is all got loosened
And my knees begin to knock
That was the kind of hash I got
In the state of Arkansas.

Traveling man
I've traveled all around this world
Traveling man
I've traveled from land to land
Traveling man
I've traveled all around this world
Well it ain't no use
writing no news
I'm a traveling man.

(The door opens and BERNIECE enters with MARETHA.)

BERNIECE: Is that . . . Lord, I know that ain't Wining Boy sitting there.

WINING BOY: Hey, Berniece.

BERNIECE: You all had this planned. You and Boy Willie had this planned.

WINING BOY: I didn't know he was gonna be here. I'm on my way down home. I stopped by to see you and Doaker first.

DOAKER: I told the nigger he left out of here with that sack of money, we thought we might never see him again. Boy Willie say he wasn't gonna see him till he got broke. I looked up and seen him sitting on the doorstep asking for two dollars. Look at him laughing. He know it's the truth.

BERNIECE: Boy Willie, I didn't see that truck out there. I thought you was out selling watermelons.

BOY WILLIE: We done sold them all. Sold the truck too.

BERNIECE: I don't want to go through none of your stuff. I done told you to go back where you belong.

BOY WILLIE: I was just teasing you, woman. You can't take no teasing?

BERNIECE: Wining Boy, when you get here?

WINING BOY: A little while ago. I took the train from Kansas City.

BERNIECE: Let me go upstairs and change and then I'll cook you something to eat.

BOY WILLIE: You ain't cooked me nothing when I come.

BERNIECE: Boy Willie, go on and leave me alone. Come on, Maretha, get up here and change your clothes before you get them dirty.

(BERNIECE *exits up the stairs, followed by* MARETHA.)

WINING BOY: Maretha sure getting big, ain't she, Doaker. And just as pretty as she want to be. I didn't know Crawley had it in him.

(BOY WILLIE *crosses to the piano.*)

BOY WILLIE: Hey, Lymon . . . get up on the other side of this piano and let me see something.

WINING BOY: Boy Willie, what is you doing?

BOY WILLIE: I'm seeing how heavy this piano is. Get up over there, Lymon.

WINING BOY: Go on and leave that piano alone. You ain't taking that piano out of here and selling it.

BOY WILLIE: Just as soon as I get them watermelons out that truck.

WINING BOY: Well, I got something to say about that.

BOY WILLIE: This my daddy's piano.

WINING BOY: He ain't took it by himself. Me and Doaker helped him.

BOY WILLIE: He died by himself. Where was you and Doaker at then? Don't come telling me nothing about this piano. This is me and Berniece's piano. Am I right, Doaker?

DOAKER: Yeah, you right.

BOY WILLIE: Let's see if we can lift it up, Lymon. Get a good grip on it and pick it up on your end. Ready? Lift!

(*As they start to move the piano, the sound of* SUT-TER'S GHOST *is heard.* DOAKER *is the only one to hear it. With difficulty they move the piano a little bit so it is out of place.*)

BOY WILLIE: What you think?

LYMON: It's heavy . . . but you can move it. Only it ain't gonna be easy.

BOY WILLIE: It wasn't that heavy to me. Okay, let's put it back.

(*The sound of* SUTTER'S GHOST *is heard again. They all hear it as* BERNIECE *enters on the stairs.*)

BERNIECE: Boy Willie . . . you gonna play around with me one too many times. And then God's gonna bless you and West is gonna dress you. Now set that piano back over there. I done told you a hundred times I ain't selling that piano.

BOY WILLIE: I'm trying to get me some land, woman. I need that piano to get me some money so I can buy Sutter's land.

BERNIECE: Money can't buy what that piano cost. You can't sell your soul for money. It won't go with the buyer. It'll shrivel and shrink to know that you ain't taken on to it. But it won't go with the buyer.

BOY WILLIE: I ain't talking about all that, woman. I ain't talking about selling my soul. I'm talking about trading that piece of wood for some land. Get something under your feet. Land the only thing God ain't making no more of. You can always get you another piano. I'm talking about some land. What you get something out the ground from. That's what I'm talking about. You can't do nothing with that piano but sit up there and look at it.

BERNIECE: That's just what I'm gonna do. Wining Boy, you want me to fry you some pork chops?

BOY WILLIE: Now, I'm gonna tell you the way I see it. The only thing that make that piano worth something is them carvings Papa Willie Boy put on there. That's what make it worth something. That was my great-grandaddy. Papa Boy Charles brought that piano into the house. Now, I'm supposed to build on what they left me. You can't do nothing with that piano sitting up here in the house. That's just like if I let them watermelons sit out there and rot. I'd be a fool. Alright now, if you say to me, Boy Willie, I'm using that piano. I give out lessons on it and that help me make my rent or whatever. Then that be something else. I'd have to go on and say, well, Berniece using that piano. She building on it. Let her go on and use it. I got to find another way to get Sutter's land. But Doaker say you ain't touched that piano the whole time it's been up here. So why you wanna stand in my way? See, you just looking at the sentimental value. See, that's good. That's alright. I take my hat off whenever somebody say my daddy's name. But I ain't gonna be no fool about no sentimental value. You can sit up here and look at the piano for the next hundred years and it's just gonna be a piano. You can't make more than that. Now I want to get Sutter's land with that piano. I get Sutter's land and I can go down and cash in the crop and get my seed. As long as I got the land and the seed then I'm alright. I can always get me a little something else. Cause that land give back to you. I can make me another crop and cash that in. I still got the land and the seed. But that piano don't put out nothing else. You ain't got nothing working for you. Now, the kind of man my daddy was he would have understood that. I'm sorry you can't see it that way. But that's why I'm gonna take that piano out of here and sell it.

BERNIECE: You ain't taking that piano out of my house.

(*She crosses to the piano.*)

Look at this piano. Look at it. Mama Ola polished this piano with her tears for seventeen years. For seventeen years she rubbed on it till her hands bled. Then she rubbed the blood in . . . mixed it up with the rest of the blood on it. Every day that God breathed life into her body she rubbed and cleaned and polished and prayed over it. "Play something for me, Berniece. Play something for me, Berniece." Every day. "I cleaned it up for you, play something for me, Berniece." You always talking about your daddy but you ain't never stopped to look at what his foolishness cost your mama. Seventeen years' worth of cold nights and an empty bed. For what? For a piano? For a piece of wood? To get even with somebody? I look at you and you're all the same. You, Papa Boy Charles, Wining Boy, Doaker, Crawley . . . you're all alike. All this thieving and killing and thieving and killing. And what it ever lead to? More killing and more thieving. I ain't never seen it come to nothing. People getting burned up. People getting shot. People falling down their wells. It don't never stop.

DOAKER: Come on now, Berniece, ain't no need in getting upset.

BOY WILLIE: I done a little bit of stealing here and there, but I ain't never killed nobody. I can't be speaking for nobody else. You all got to speak for yourself, but I ain't never killed nobody.

BERNIECE: You killed Crawley just as sure as if you pulled the trigger.

BOY WILLIE: See, that's ignorant. That's downright foolish for you to say something like that. You ain't doing nothing but showing your ignorance. If the nigger was here I'd whup his ass for getting me and Lymon shot at.

BERNIECE: Crawley ain't knew about the wood.

BOY WILLIE: We told the man about the wood. Ask Lymon. He knew all about the wood. He seen we was sneaking it. Why else we gonna be out there at night? Don't come telling me Crawley ain't knew about the wood. Them fellows come up on us and Crawley tried to bully them. Me and Lymon seen the sheriff with them and give in. Wasn't no sense in getting killed over fifty dollars' worth of wood.

BERNIECE: Crawley ain't knew you stole that wood.

BOY WILLIE: We ain't stole no wood. Me and Lymon was hauling wood for Jim Miller and keeping us a little bit on the side. We dumped our little bit down there by the creek till we had enough to make a load. Some fellows seen us and we figured we better get it before they did. We come up there and got Crawley to help us load it. Figured we'd cut him in. Crawley trying to keep the wolf from his door . . . we was trying to help him.

LYMON: Me and Boy Willie told him about the wood. We told him some fellows might be trying to beat us to it. He say let me go back and get my thirty-eight. That's what caused all the trouble.

BOY WILLIE: If Crawley ain't had the gun he'd be alive today.

LYMON: We had it about half loaded when they come up on us. We seen the sheriff with them and we tried to get away. We ducked around near the bend in the creek . . . but they was down there too. Boy Willie say let's give in. But Crawley pulled out his gun and started shooting. That's when they started shooting back.

BERNIECE: All I know is Crawley would be alive if you hadn't come up there and got him.

BOY WILLIE: I ain't had nothing to do with Crawley getting killed. That was his own fault.

BERNIECE: Crawley's dead and in the ground and you still walking around here eating. That's all I know. He went off to load some wood with you and ain't never come back.

BOY WILLIE: I told you, woman . . . I ain't had nothing to do with . . .

BERNIECE: He ain't here, is he? He ain't here!

(BERNIECE *hits* BOY WILLIE.)

I said he ain't here. Is he?

(BERNIECE *continues to hit* BOY WILLIE, *who doesn't move to defend himself, other than back up and turning his head so that most of the blows fall on his chest and arms.*)

DOAKER (*Grabbing* BERNIECE): Come on, Berniece . . . let it go, it ain't his fault.

BERNIECE: He ain't here, is he? Is he?

BOY WILLIE: I told you I ain't responsible for Crawley.

BERNIECE: He ain't here.

BOY WILLIE: Come on now, Berniece . . . don't do this now. Doaker get her. I ain't had nothing to do with Crawley . . .

BERNIECE: You come up there and got him!

BOY WILLIE: I done told you now. Doaker, get her. I ain't playing.

DOAKER: Come on. Berniece.

(MARETHA *is heard screaming upstairs. It is a scream of stark terror.*)

MARETHA: Mama! . . . Mama!

(*The lights go down to black. End of Act One.*)

ACT TWO

SCENE 1

The lights come up on the kitchen. It is the following morning. DOAKER *is ironing the pants to his uniform. He has a pot cooking on the stove at the same time. He is singing a song. The song provides him with the rhythm for his work and he moves about the kitchen with the ease born of many years as a railroad cook.*

DOAKER: Gonna leave Jackson Mississippi
　　　　and go to Memphis
　　　　and double back to Jackson
　　　　Come on down to Hattiesburg
　　　　Change cars on the Y.D.
　　　　coming through the territory to
　　　　Meridian
　　　　and Meridian to Greenville
　　　　and Greenville to Memphis
　　　　I'm on my way and I know where

　　　　Change cars on the Katy
　　　　Leaving Jackson
　　　　and going through Clarksdale
　　　　Hello Winona!
　　　　Courtland!
　　　　Bateville!
　　　　Como!
　　　　Senitobia!
　　　　Lewisberg!
　　　　Sunflower!
　　　　Glendora!
　　　　Sharkey!
　　　　And double back to Jackson
　　　　Hello Greenwood
　　　　I'm on my way Memphis
　　　　Clarksdale
　　　　Moorhead
　　　　Indianola
　　　　Can a highball pass through?
　　　　Highball on through sir
　　　　Grand Carson!
　　　　Thirty First Street Depot
　　　　Fourth Street Depot
　　　　Memphis!

(WINING BOY *enters carrying a suit of clothes.*)

DOAKER: I thought you took that suit to the pawnshop?

WINING BOY: I went down there and the man tell me the suit is too old. Look at this suit. This is one hundred percent silk! How a silk suit gonna get too old? I know what it was he just didn't want to give me five dollars for it. Best he wanna give me is three dollars. I figure a silk suit is worth five dollars all over the world. I wasn't gonna part with it for no three dollars so I brought it back.

DOAKER: They got another pawnshop up on Wylie.

WINING BOY: I carried it up there. He say he don't take no clothes. Only thing he take is guns and radios. Maybe a guitar or two. Where's Berniece?

DOAKER: Berniece still at work. Boy Willie went down there to meet Lymon this morning. I guess they got that truck fixed, they been out there all day and ain't come back yet. Maretha scared to sleep up there now. Berniece don't know, but I seen Sutter before she did.

WINING BOY: Say what?

DOAKER: About three weeks ago. I had just come back from down there. Sutter couldn't have been dead more than three days. He was sitting over there at the piano. I come out to go to work . . . and he was sitting right there. Had his hand on top of his head just like Berniece said. I believe he broke his neck when he fell in the well. I kept quiet about it. I didn't see no reason to upset Berniece.

WINING BOY: Did he say anything? Did he say he was looking for Boy Willie?

DOAKER: He was just sitting there. He ain't said nothing. I went on out the door and left him sitting there. I figure as long as be was on the other side of the room everything be alright. I don't know what I would have done if he had started walking toward me.

WINING BOY: Berniece say he was calling Boy Willie's name.

DOAKER: I ain't heard him say nothing. He was just sitting there when I seen him. But I don't believe Boy Willie pushed him in the well. Sutter here cause of that piano. I heard him playing on it one time. I thought it was Berniece but then she don't play that kind of music. I come out here and ain't seen nobody, but them piano keys was moving a mile a minute. Berniece need to go on and get rid of it. It ain't done nothing but cause trouble.

WINING BOY: I agree with Berniece. Boy Charles ain't took it to give it back. He took it cause he figure he had more right to it than Sutter did. If Sutter can't understand that . . . then that's just the way that go. Sutter dead and in the ground . . . don't care where his ghost is. He can hover around and play on the piano all he want. I want to see him carry it out the house. That's what I want to see. What time Berniece get home? I don't see how I let her get away from me this morning.

DOAKER: You up there sleep. Berniece leave out of here early in the morning. She out there in Squirrel Hill cleaning house for some bigshot down there at the steel mill. They don't like you to come late. You come late they won't give you your carfare. What kind of business you got with Berniece?

WINING BOY: My business. I ain't asked you what kind of business you got.

DOAKER: Berniece ain't got no money. If that's why you was trying to catch her. She having a hard enough time trying to get by as it is. If she go ahead and marry Avery . . . he working every day . . . she go ahead and marry him they could do alright for themselves. But as it stands she ain't got no money.

WINING BOY: Well, let me have five dollars.

DOAKER: I just give you a dollar before you left out of here. You ain't gonna take my five dollars out there and gamble and drink it up.

WINING BOY: Aw, nigger, give me five dollars. I'll give it back to you.

DOAKER: You wasn't looking to give me five dollars when you had that sack of money. You wasn't looking to throw nothing my way. Now you wanna come in here and borrow five dollars. If you going back with Boy Willie you need to be trying to figure out how you gonna get train fare.

WINING BOY: That's why I need the five dollars. If I had five dollars I could get me some money.
(DOAKER *goes into his pocket.*)
    Make it seven.

DOAKER: You take this five dollars . . . and you bring my money back here too.
(BOY WILLIE *and* LYMON *enter. They are happy and excited. They have money in all of their pockets and are anxious to count it.*)

DOAKER: How'd you do out there?

BOY WILLIE: They was lining up for them.

LYMON: Me and Boy Willie couldn't sell them fast enough. Time we got one sold we'd sell another.

BOY WILLIE: I seen what was happening and told Lymon to up the price on them.

LYMON: Boy Willie say charge them a quarter more. They didn't care. A couple of people give me a dollar and told me to keep the change.

BOY WILLIE: One fellow bought five. I say now what he gonna do with five watermelons? He can't eat them all. I sold him the five and asked him did he want to buy five more.

LYMON: I ain't never seen nobody snatch a dollar fast as Boy Willie.

BOY WILLIE: One lady asked me say, "Is they sweet?" I told her say, "Lady, where we grow these watermelons we put sugar in the ground." You know, she believed me. Talking about she had never heard of that before. Lymon was laughing his head off. I told her, "Oh, yeah, we put the sugar right in the ground with the seed." She say, "Well, give me another one." Them white folks is something else . . . ain't they, Lymon?

LYMON: Soon as you holler watermelons they come right out their door. Then they go and get their neighbors. Look like they having a contest to see who can buy the most.

WINING BOY: I got something for Lymon.

(WINING BOY *goes to get his suit.* BOY WILLIE *and* LYMON *continue to count their money.*)

BOY WILLIE: I know you got more than that. You ain't sold all them watermelons for that little bit of money.

LYMON: I'm still looking. That ain't all you got either. Where's all them quarters?

BOY WILLIE: You let me worry about the quarters. Just put the money on the table.

WINING BOY (*Entering with his suit*): Look here, Lymon . . . see this? Look at his eyes getting big. He ain't never seen a suit like this. This is one hundred percent silk. Go ahead . . . put it on. See if it fit you.

(LYMON *tries the suit coat on.*)

Look at that. Feel it. That's one hundred percent genuine silk. I got that in Chicago. You can't get clothes like that nowhere but New York and Chicago. You can't get clothes like that in Pittsburgh. These folks in Pittsburgh ain't never seen clothes like that.

LYMON: This is nice, feel real nice and smooth.

WINING BOY: That's a fifty-five-dollar suit. That's the kind of suit the bigshots wear. You need a pistol and a pocketful of money to wear that suit. I'll let you have it for three dollars. The women will fall out their windows they see you in a suit like that. Give me three dollars and go on and wear it down the street and get you a woman.

BOY WILLIE: That looks nice, Lymon. Put the pants on. Let me see it with the pants.

(LYMON *begins to try on the pants.*)

WINING BOY: Look at that . . . see how it fits you? Give me three dollars and go on and take it. Look at that, Doaker . . . don't he look nice?

DOAKER: Yeah . . . that's a nice suit.

WINING BOY: Got a shirt to go with it. Cost you an extra dollar. Four dollars you got the whole deal.

LYMON: How this look, Boy Willie?

BOY WILLIE: That look nice . . . if you like that kind of thing. I don't like them dress-up kind of clothes. If you like it, look real nice.

WINING BOY: That's the kind of suit you need for up here in the North.

LYMON: Four dollars for everything? The suit and the shirt?

WINING BOY: That's cheap. I should be charging you twenty dollars. I give you a break cause you a homeboy. That's the only way I let you have it for four dollars.

LYMON (*Going into his pocket*): Okay . . . here go the four dollars.

WINING BOY: You got some shoes? What size you wear?

LYMON: Size nine.

WINING BOY: That's what size I got! Size nine. I let you have them for three dollars.

LYMON: Where they at? Let me see them.

WINING BOY: They real nice shoes, too. Got a nice tip to them. Got pointy toe just like you want.

(WINING BOY *goes to get his shoes.*)

LYMON: Come on, Boy Willie, let's go out tonight. I wanna see what it looks like up here. Maybe we go to a picture show. Hey, Doaker, they got picture shows up here?

DOAKER: The Rhumba Theater. Right down there on Fullerton Street. Can't miss it. Got the speakers outside on the sidewalk. You can hear it a block away. Boy Willie know where it's at.

(DOAKER *exits into his room.*)

LYMON: Let's go to the picture show, Boy Willie. Let's go find some women.

BOY WILLIE: Hey, Lymon, how many of them watermelons would you say we got left? We got just under a half a load . . . right?

LYMON: About that much. Maybe a little more.

BOY WILLIE: You think that piano will fit up in there?

LYMON: If we stack them watermelons you can sit it up in the front there.

BOY WILLIE: I'm gonna call that man tomorrow.

WINING BOY (*Returns with his shoes*): Here you go . . . size nine. Put them on. Cost you three dollars. That's a Florsheim shoe. That's the kind Staggerlee wore.

LYMON (*Trying on the shoes*): You sure these size nine?

WINING BOY: You can look at my feet and see we wear the same size. Man, you put on that suit and them shoes and you got something there. You ready for whatever's out there. But is they ready for you? With them shoes on you be the King of the Walk. Have everybody stop to look at your shoes. Wishing they had a pair. I'll give you a break. Go on and take them for two dollars.

(LYMON *pays* WINING BOY *two dollars.*)

LYMON: Come on, Boy Willie . . . let's go find some women. I'm gonna go upstairs and get ready. I'll be ready to go in a minute. Ain't you gonna get dressed?

BOY WILLIE: I'm gonna wear what I got on. I ain't dressing up for these city niggers.

(LYMON *exits up the stairs.*)

That's all Lymon think about is women.

WINING BOY: His daddy was the same way. I used to run around with him. I know his mama too. Two strokes back and I would have been his daddy! His daddy's dead now . . . but I got the nigger out of jail one time. They was fixing to name him Daniel and walk him through the Lion's Den. He got in a tussle with one of them white fellows and the sheriff lit on him like white on rice. That's how the whole thing come about between me and Lymon's mama. She knew me and his daddy used to run together and he got in jail and she went down there and took the sheriff a hundred dollars. Don't get me to lying about where she got it from. I don't know. The sheriff looked at that hundred dollars and turned his nose up Told her, say, "That ain't gonna do him no good. You got to put another hundred on top of that." She come up there and got me where I was playing at this saloon . . . said she had all but fifty dollars and asked me if I could help. Now the way I figured it . . . without that fifty dollars the sheriff was gonna turn him over to Parchman. The sheriff turn him over to Parchman it be three years before anybody see him again. Now I'm gonna say it right. . . . I will give anybody fifty dollars to keep them out of jail for three years. I give her the fifty dollars and she told me to come over to the house. I ain't asked her. I figure if she was nice enough

to invite me I ought to go. I ain't had to say a word. She invited me over just as nice. Say, "Why don't you come over to the house?" She ain't had to say nothing else. Them words rolled off her tongue just as nice. I went on down there and sat about three hours. Started to leave and changed my mind. She grabbed hold to me and say, "Baby, it's all night long." That was one of the shortest nights I have ever spent on this earth! I could have used another eight hours. Lymon's daddy didn't even say nothing to me when he got out. He just looked at me funny. He had a good notion something had happened between me an' her. L. D. Jackson. That was one bad-luck nigger. Got killed at some dance. Fellow walked in and shot him thinking he was somebody else.

(DOAKER *enters from his room.*)

Hey, Doaker, you remember L. D. Jackson?

DOAKER: That's Lymon's daddy. That was one bad-luck nigger.

BOY WILLIE: Look like you ready to railroad some.

DOAKER: Yeah, I got to make that run.

(LYMON *enters from the stairs. He is dressed in his new suit and shoes, to which he has added a cheap straw hat.*)

LYMON: How I look?

WINING BOY: You look like a million dollars. Don't he look good, Doaker? Come on, let's play some cards. You wanna play some cards?

BOY WILLIE: We ain't gonna play no cards with you. Me and Lymon gonna find some women. Hey, Lymon, don't play no cards with Wining Boy. He'll take all your money.

WINING BOY (*To* LYMON): You got a magic suit there. You can get you a woman easy with that suit . . . but you got to know the magic words. You know the magic words to get you a woman?

LYMON: I just talk to them to see if I like them and they like me.

WINING BOY: You just walk right up to them and say, "If you got the harbor I got the ship." If that don't work ask them if you can put them in your pocket. The first thing they gonna say is, "It's too small." That's when you look them dead in the eye and say, "Baby, ain't nothing small about me." If that don't work then you move on to another one. Am I telling him right, Doaker?

DOAKER: That man don't need you to tell him nothing about no women. These women these days ain't gonna fall for that kind of stuff. You got to buy them a present. That's what they looking for these days.

BOY WILLIE: Come on, I'm ready. You ready, Lymon? Come on, let's go find some women.

WINING BOY: Here, let me walk out with you. I wanna see the women fall out their window when they see Lymon.

(*They all exit and the lights go down on the scene.*)

SCENE 2

The lights come up on the kitchen. It is late evening of the same day. BERNIECE *has set a tub for her bath in the kitchen. She is heating up water on the stove. There is a knock at the door.*

BERNIECE: Who is it?

AVERY: It's me, Avery.

(BERNIECE *opens the door and lets him in.*)

BERNIECE: Avery, come on in. I was just fixing to take my bath.

AVERY: Where Boy Willie? I see that truck out there almost empty. They done sold almost all them watermelons.

BERNIECE: They was gone when I come home. I don't know where they went off to. Boy Willie around here about to drive me crazy.

AVERY: They sell them watermelons . . . he'll be gone soon.

BERNIECE: What Mr. Cohen say about letting you have the place?

AVERY: He say he'll let me have it for thirty dollars a month. I talked him out of thirty-five and he say he'll let me have it for thirty.

BERNIECE: That's a nice spot next to Benny Diamond's store.

AVERY: Berniece . . . I be at home and I get to thinking you up here an' I'm down there. I get to thinking how that look to have a preacher that ain't married. It makes for a better congregation if the preacher was settled down and married.

BERNIECE: Avery . . . not now. I was fixing to take my bath.

AVERY: You know how I feel about you, Berniece. Now . . . I done got the place from Mr. Cohen. I get the money from the bank and I can fix it up real nice. They give me a ten cents a hour raise down there on the job . . . now Berniece, I ain't got much in the way of comforts. I got a hole in my pockets near about as far as money is concerned. I ain't never found no way through life to a woman I care about like I care about you. I need that. I need somebody on my bond side. I need a woman that fits in my hand.

BERNIECE: Avery, I ain't ready to get married now.

AVERY: You too young a woman to close up, Berniece.

BERNIECE: I ain't said nothing about closing up. I got a lot of woman left in me.

AVERY: Where's it at? When's the last time you looked at it?

BERNIECE (*Stunned by his remark*): That's a nasty thing to say. And you call yourself a preacher.

AVERY: Anytime I get anywhere near you . . . you push me away.

BERNIECE: I got enough on my hands with Maretha. I got enough people to love and take care of.

AVERY: Who you got to love you? Can't nobody get close enough to you. Doaker can't half say nothing to you. You jump all over Boy Willie. Who you got to love you, Berniece?

BERNIECE: You trying to tell me a woman can't be nothing without a man. But you alright, huh? You can just walk out of here without me—without a woman—and still be a man. That's alright. Ain't nobody gonna ask you, "Avery, who you got to love you?" That's alright for you. But everybody gonna be worried about Berniece. "How Berniece gonna take care of herself? How she gonna raise that child without a man? Wonder what she do with herself. How she gonna live like that?" Everybody got all kinds of questions for Berniece. Everybody telling me I can't be a woman unless I got a man. Well, you tell me, Avery—you know—how much woman am I?

AVERY: It wasn't me, Berniece. You can't blame me for nobody else. I'll own up to my own shortcomings. But you can't blame me for Crawley or nobody else.

BERNIECE: I ain't blaming nobody for nothing. I'm just stating the facts.

AVERY: How long you gonna carry Crawley with you, Berniece? It's been over three years.

At some point you got to let go and go on. Life's got all kinds of twists and turns. That don't mean you stop living. That don't mean you cut yourself off from life. You can't go through life carrying Crawley's ghost with you. Crawley's been dead three years. Three years, Berniece.

BERNIECE: I know how long Crawley's been dead. You ain't got to tell me that. I just ain't ready to get married right now.

AVERY: What is you ready for, Berniece? You just gonna drift along from day to day. Life is more than making it from one day to another. You gonna look up one day and it's all gonna be past you. Life's gonna be gone out of your hands—there won't be enough to make nothing with. I'm standing here now, Berniece— but I don't know how much longer I'm gonna be standing here waiting on you.

BERNIECE: Avery, I told you . . . when you get your church we'll sit down and talk about this. I got too many other things to deal with right now. Boy Willie and the piano . . . and Sutter's ghost. I thought I might have been seeing things, but Maretha done seen Sutter's ghost, too.

AVERY: When this happen, Berniece?

BERNIECE: Right after I came home yesterday. Me and Boy Willie was arguing about the piano and Sutter's ghost was standing at the top of the stairs. Maretha scared to sleep up there now. Maybe if you bless the house he'll go away.

AVERY: I don't know, Berniece. I don't know if I should fool around with something like that.

BERNIECE: I can't have Maretha scared to go to sleep up there. Seem like if you bless the house he would go away.

AVERY: You might have to be a special kind of preacher to do something like that.

BERNIECE: I keep telling myself when Boy Willie leave he'll go on and leave with him. I believe Boy Willie pushed him in the well.

AVERY: That's been going on down there a long time. The Ghosts of the Yellow Dog been pushing people in their wells long before Boy Willie got grown.

BERNIECE: Somebody down there pushing them people in their wells. They ain't just upped and fell. Ain't no wind pushed nobody in their well.

AVERY: Oh, I don't know. God works in mysterious ways.

BERNIECE: He ain't pushed nobody in their wells.

AVERY: He caused it to happen. God is the Great Causer. He can do anything. He parted the Red Sea. He say I will smite my enemies. Reverend Thompson used to preach on the Ghosts of the Yellow Dog as the hand of God.

BERNIECE: I don't care who preached what. Somebody down there pushing them people in their wells. Somebody like Boy Willie. I can see him doing something like that. You ain't gonna tell me that Sutter just upped and fell in his well. I believe Boy Willie pushed him so he could get his land.

AVERY: What Doaker say about Boy Willie selling the piano?

BERNIECE: Doaker don't want no part of that piano. He ain't never wanted no part of it. He blames himself for not staying behind with Papa Boy Charles. He washed his hands of that piano a long time ago. He didn't want me to bring it up here—but I wasn't gonna leave it down there.

AVERY: Well, it seems to me somebody ought to be able to talk to Boy Willie.

BERNIECE: You can't talk to Boy Willie. He been that way all his life. Mama Ola had her hands full trying to talk to him. He don't listen to nobody. He just like my daddy. He get his mind fixed on something and can't nobody turn him from it.

AVERY: You ought to start a choir at the church. Maybe if he seen you was doing something with it—if you told him you was gonna put it in my church—maybe he'd see it different. You ought to put it down in the church and start a choir. The Bible say "Make a joyful noise unto the Lord." Maybe if Boy Willie see you was doing something with it he'd see it different.

BERNIECE: I done told you I don't play on that piano. Ain't no need in you to keep talking this choir stuff. When my mama died I shut the top, on that piano and I ain't never opened it since. I was only playing it for her. When my daddy died seem like all her life went into that piano. She used to have me playing on it . . . had

Miss Eula come in and teach me . . . say when I played it she could hear my daddy talking to her. I used to think them pictures came alive and walked through the house. Sometime late at night I could hear my mama talking to them. I said that wasn't gonna happen to me. I don't play that piano cause I don't want to wake them spirits. They never be walking around in this house.

AVERY: You got to put all that behind you, Berniece.

BERNIECE: I got Maretha playing on it. She don't know nothing about it. Let her go on and be a schoolteacher or something. She don't have to carry all of that with her. She got a chance I didn't have. I ain't gonna burden her with that piano.

AVERY: You got to put all of that behind you, Berniece. That's the same thing like Crawley. Everybody got stones in their passway. You got to step over them or walk around them. You picking them up and carrying them with you. All you got to do is set them down by the side of the road. You ain't got to carry them with you. You can walk over there right now and play that piano. You can walk over there right now and God will walk over there with you. Right now you can set that sack of stones down by the side of the road and walk away from it. You don't have to carry it with you. You can do it right now.

(AVERY *crosses over to the piano and raises the lid.*)

Come on, Berniece . . . set it down and walk away from it. Come on, play "Old Ship of Zion." Walk over here and claim it as an instrument of the Lord. You can walk over here right now and make it into a celebration.

(BERNIECE *moves toward the piano.*)

BERNIECE: Avery . . . I done told you I don't want to play that piano. Now or no other time.

AVERY: The Bible say, "The Lord is my refuge . . . and my strength!" With the strength of God you can put the past behind you, Berniece. With the strength of God you can do anything! God got a bright tomorrow. God don't ask what you done . . . God ask what you gonna do. The strength of God can move mountains! God's got a bright tomorrow for you . . . all you got to do is walk over here and claim it.

BERNIECE: Avery, just go on and let me finish my bath. I'll see you tomorrow.

AVERY: Okay, Berniece. I'm gonna go home. I'm gonna go home and read up on my Bible. And tomorrow . . . if the good Lord give me strength tomorrow . . . I'm gonna come by and bless the house . . . and show you the power of the Lord.

(AVERY *crosses to the door.*)

It's gonna be alright, Berniece. God say he will soothe the troubled waters. I'll come by tomorrow and bless the house.

(*The lights go down to black.*)

SCENE 3

Several hours later. The house is dark. BERNIECE *has retired for the night.* BOY WILLIE *enters the darkened house with* GRACE.

BOY WILLIE: Come on in. This my sister's house. My sister live here. Come on, I ain't gonna bite you.

GRACE: Put some light on. I can't see.

BOY WILLIE: You don't need to see nothing, baby. This here is all you need to see. All you need to do is see me. If you can't see me you can feel me in the dark. How's that, sugar?

(*He attempts to kiss her.*)

GRACE: Go on now . . . wait!

BOY WILLIE: Just give me one little old kiss.

GRACE (*Pushing him away*): Come on, now. Where I'm gonna sleep at?

BOY WILLIE: We got to sleep out here on the couch. Come on, my sister don't mind. Lymon come back he just got to sleep on the floor. He run off with Dolly somewhere he better stay there. Come on, sugar.

GRACE: Wait now . . . you ain't told me nothing about no couch. I thought you had a bed. Both of us can't sleep on that little old couch.

BOY WILLIE: It don't make no difference. We can sleep on the floor. Let Lymon sleep on the couch.

GRACE: You ain't told me nothing about no couch.

BOY WILLIE: What difference it make? You just wanna be with me.

GRACE: I don't want to be with you on no couch. Ain't you got no bed?

BOY WILLIE: You don't need no bed, woman. My granddaddy used to take women on the backs of horses. What you need a bed for? You just want to be with me.

GRACE: You sure is country. I didn't know you was this country.

BOY WILLIE: There's a lot of things you don't know about me. Come on, let me show you what this country boy can do.

GRACE: Let's go to my place. I got a room with a bed if Leroy don't come back there.

BOY WILLIE: Who's Leroy? You ain't said nothing about no Leroy.

GRACE: He used to be my man. He ain't coming back. He gone off with some other gal.

BOY WILLIE: You let him have your key?

GRACE: He ain't coming back.

BOY WILLIE: Did you let him have your key?

GRACE: He got a key but he ain't coming back. He took off with some other gal.

BOY WILLIE: I don't wanna go nowhere he might come. Let's stay here. Come on, sugar.

(*He pulls her over to the couch.*)

Let me heist your hood and check your oil. See if your battery needs charged.

(*He pulls her to him. They kiss and tug at each other's clothing. In their anxiety they knock over a lamp.*)

BERNIECE: Who's that . . . Wining Boy?

BOY WILLIE: It's me . . . Boy Willie. Go on back to sleep. Everything's alright.

(*To* GRACE.)

That's my sister. Everything's alright, Berniece. Go on back to sleep.

BERNIECE: What you doing down there? What you done knocked over?

BOY WILLIE: It wasn't nothing. Everything's alright. Go on back to sleep.

(*To* GRACE.)

That's my sister. We alright. She gone back to sleep.

(*They begin to kiss.* BERNIECE *enters from the stairs dressed in a nightgown. She cuts on the light.*)

BERNIECE: Boy Willie, what you doing down here?

BOY WILLIE: It was just that there lamp. It ain't broke. It's okay. Everything's alright. Go on back to bed.

BERNIECE: Boy Willie, I don't allow that in my house. You gonna have to take your company someplace else.

BOY WILLIE: It's alright. We ain't doing nothing. We just sitting here talking. This here is Grace. That's my sister Berniece.

BERNIECE: You know I don't allow that kind of stuff in my house.

BOY WILLIE: Allow what? We just sitting here talking.

BERNIECE: Well, your company gonna have to leave. Come back and talk in the morning.

BOY WILLIE: Go on back upstairs now.

BERNIECE: I got an eleven-year-old girl upstairs. I can't allow that around here.

BOY WILLIE: Ain't nobody said nothing about that. I told you we just talking.

GRACE: Come on . . . let's go to my place. Ain't nobody got to tell me to leave but once.

BOY WILLIE: You ain't got to be like that, Berniece.

BERNIECE: I'm sorry, Miss. But he know I don't allow that in here.

GRACE: You ain't got to tell me but once. I don't stay nowhere I ain't wanted.

BOY WILLIE: I don't know why you want to embarrass me in front of my company.

GRACE: Come on, take me home.

BERNIECE: Go on, Boy Willie. Just go on with your company.

(BOY WILLIE *and* GRACE *exit.* BERNIECE *puts the light on in the kitchen and puts on the teakettle. Presently there is a knock at the door.* BERNIECE *goes to answer it.* BERNIECE *opens the door.* LYMON *enters.*)

LYMON: How you doing, Berniece? I thought you'd be asleep. Boy Willie been back here?

BERNIECE: He just left out of here a minute ago.

LYMON: I went out to see a picture show and never got there. We always end up doing something else. I was with this woman she just wanted to drink up all my money. So I left her there and came back looking for Boy Willie.

BERNIECE: You just missed him. He just left out of here.

LYMON: They got some nice-looking women in this city. I'm gonna like it up here real good. I like seeing them with their dresses on. Got them high heels. I like that. Make them look like they real precious. Boy Willie met a real nice one today. I wish I had met her before he did.

BERNIECE: He come by here with some woman a little while ago. I told him to go on and take all that out of my house.

LYMON: What she look like, the woman he was with? Was she a brown-skinned woman about this high? Nice and healthy? Got nice hips on her?

BERNIECE: She had on a red dress.

LYMON: That's her! That's Grace. She real nice. Laugh a lot. Lot of fun to be with. She don't be trying to put on. Some of these woman act like they the Queen of Sheba. I don't like them kind. Grace ain't like that. She real nice with herself.

BERNIECE: I don't know what she was like. He come in here all drunk knocking over the lamp, and making all kind of noise. I told them to take that somewhere else. I can't really say what she was like.

LYMON: She real nice. I seen her before he did. I was trying not to act like I seen her. I wanted to look at her a while before I said something. She seen me when I come into the saloon. I tried to act like I didn't see her. Time I looked around Boy Willie was talking to her. She was talking to him kept looking at me. That's when her friend Dolly came. I asked her if she wanted to go to the picture show. She told me to buy her a drink while she thought about it. Next thing I knew she done had three drinks talking about she too tired to go. I bought her another drink, then I left. Boy Willie was gone and I thought he might have come back here. Doaker gone, huh? He say he had to make a trip.

BERNIECE: Yeah, he gone on his trip. This is when I can usually get me some peace and quiet, Maretha asleep.

LYMON: She look just like you. Got them big eyes. I remember her when she was in diapers.

BERNIECE: Time just keep on. It go on with or without you. She going on twelve.

LYMON: She sure is pretty. I like kids.

BERNIECE: Boy Willie say you staying . . . what you gonna do up here in this big city? You thought about that?

LYMON: They never get me back down there. The sheriff looking for me. All because they gonna try and make me work for somebody when I don't want to. They gonna try and make me work for Stovall when he don't pay nothing. It ain't like that up here. Up here you more or less do what you want to. I figure I find me a job and try to get set up and then see what the year brings. I tried to do that two or three times down there . . . but it never would work out. I was always in the wrong place.

BERNIECE: This ain't a bad city once you get to know your way around.

LYMON: Up here is different. I'm gonna get me a job unloading boxcars or something. One fellow told me say he know a place. I'm gonna go over there with him next week. Me and Boy Willie finish selling them watermelons I'll have enough money to hold me for a while. But I'm gonna go over there and see what kind of jobs they have.

BERNIECE: You shouldn't have too much trouble finding a job. It's all in how you present yourself. See now, Boy Willie couldn't get no job up here. Somebody hire him they got a pack of trouble on their hands. Soon as they find that out they fire him. He don't want to do nothing unless he do it his way.

LYMON: I know. I told him let's go to the picture show first and see if there was any women down there. They might get tired of sitting at home and walk down to the picture show. He say he wanna look around first. We never did get down there. We tried a couple of places and then we went to this saloon where he met Grace. I tried to meet her before he did but he beat me to her. We left Wining Boy sitting down there running his mouth. He told me if I wear this suit I'd find me a woman. He was almost right.

BERNIECE: You don't need to be out there in them saloons. Ain't no telling what you liable to run into out there. This one liable to cut you as quick as that one shoot you. You don't need to be out there. You start out that fast life you can't keep it up. It makes you old quick. I don't know what them women out there be thinking about.

LYMON: Mostly they be lonely and looking for somebody to spend the night with them. Sometimes it matters who it is and sometimes it don't. I used to be the same way. Now it got to matter. That's why I'm here now. Dolly liable not to even recognize me if she sees me again. I don't like women like that. I like my women to be with me in a nice and easy way.

That way we can both enjoy ourselves. The way I see it we the only two people like us in the world. We got to see how we fit together. A woman that don't want to take the time to do that I don't bother with. Used to. Used to bother with all of them. Then I woke up one time with this woman and I didn't know who she was. She was the prettiest woman I had ever seen in my life. I spent the whole night with her and didn't even know it. I had never taken the time to look at her. I guess she kinda knew I ain't never really looked at her. She must have known that cause she ain't wanted to see me no more. If she had wanted to see me I believe we might have got married. How come you ain't married? It seem like to me you would be married. I remember Avery from down home. I used to call him plain old Avery. Now he Reverend Avery. That's kinda funny about him becoming a preacher. I like when he told about how that come to him in a dream about them sheep people and them hobos. Nothing ever come to me in a dream like that. I just dream about women. Can't never seem to find the right one.

BERNIECE: She out there somewhere. You just got to get yourself ready to meet her. That's what I'm trying to do. Avery's alright. I ain't really got nobody in mind.

LYMON: I get me a job and a little place and get set up to where I can make a woman comfortable I might get married. Avery's nice. You ought to go ahead and get married. You be a preacher's wife you won't have to work. I hate living by myself. I didn't want to be no strain on my mama so I left home when I was about sixteen. Everything I tried seem like it just didn't work out. Now I'm trying this.

BERNIECE: You keep trying it'll work out for you.

LYMON: You ever go down there to the picture show?

BERNIECE: I don't go in for all that.

LYMON: Ain't nothing wrong with it. It ain't like gambling and sinning. I went to one down in Jackson once. It was fun.

BERNIECE: I just stay home most of the time. Take care of Maretha.

LYMON: It's getting kind of late. I don't know where Boy Willie went off to. He's liable not to come back. I'm gonna take off these shoes. My feet hurt. Was you in bed? I don't mean to be keeping you up.

BERNIECE: You ain't keeping me up. I couldn't sleep after that Boy Willie woke me up.

LYMON: You got on that nightgown. I likes women when they wear them fancy nightclothes and all. It makes their skin look real pretty.

BERNIECE: I got this at the five-and-ten-cents store. It ain't so fancy.

LYMON: I don't too often get to see a woman dressed like that.

(*There is a long pause. LYMON takes off his suit coat.*) Well, I'm gonna sleep here on the couch. I'm supposed to sleep on the floor but I don't reckon Boy Willie's coming back tonight. Wining Boy sold me this suit. Told me it was a magic suit. I'm gonna put it on again tomorrow. Maybe it bring me a woman like he say.

(*He goes into his coat pocket and takes out a small bottle of perfume.*)

I almost forgot I had this. Some man sold me this for a dollar. Say it come from Paris. This is the same kind of perfume the Queen of France wear. That's what he told me. I don't know if it's true or not. I smelled it. It smelled good to me. Here . . . smell it see if you like it. I was gonna give it to Dolly. But I didn't like her too much.

BERNIECE (*Takes the bottle*): It smells nice.

LYMON: I was gonna give it to Dolly if she had went to the picture with me. Go on, you take it.

BERNIECE: I can't take it. Here . . . go on you keep it. You'll find somebody to give it to.

LYMON: I wanna give it to you. Make you smell nice.

(*He takes the bottle and puts perfume behind BERNIECE's ear.*)

They tell me you supposed to put it right here behind your ear. Say if you put it there you smell nice all day.

(*BERNIECE stiffens at his touch. LYMON bends down to smell her.*)

There . . . you smell real good now.

(*He kisses her neck.*)

You smell real good for Lymon.

(*He kisses her again. BERNIECE returns the kiss, then breaks the embrace and crosses to the stairs. She*

For our parents

Charles and Doris Fletcher
Harold and Adreene Wainscott

turns and they look silently at each other. LYMON *hands her the bottle of perfume.* BERNIECE *exits up the stairs.* LYMON *picks up his suit coat and strokes it lovingly with the full knowledge that it is indeed a magic suit. The lights go down on the scene.)*

SCENE 4

It is late the next morning. The lights come up on the parlor. LYMON *is asleep on the sofa.* BOY WILLIE *enters the front door.*

BOY WILLIE: Hey, Lymon! Lymon, come on get up.

LYMON: Leave me alone.

BOY WILLIE: Come on, get up, nigger! Wake up, Lymon.

LYMON: What you want?

BOY WILLIE: Come on, let's go. I done called the man about the piano.

LYMON: What piano?

BOY WILLIE (*Dumps* LYMON *on the floor*): Come on, get up!

LYMON: Why you leave, I looked around and you was gone.

BOY WILLIE: I come back here with Grace, then I went looking for you. I figured you'd be with Dolly.

LYMON: She just want to drink and spend up your money. I come on back here looking for you to see if you wanted to go to the picture show.

BOY WILLIE: I been up at Grace's house. Some nigger named Leroy come by but I had a chair up against the door. He got mad when he couldn't get in. He went off somewhere and I got out of there before he could come back. Berniece got mad when we came here.

LYMON: She say you was knocking over the lamp busting up the place.

BOY WILLIE: That was Grace doing all that.

LYMON: Wining Boy seen Sutter's ghost last night.

BOY WILLIE: Wining Boy's liable to see anything. I'm surprised he found the right house. Come on, I done called the man about the piano.

LYMON: What he say?

BOY WILLIE: He say to bring it on out. I told him I was calling for my sister, Miss Berniece Charles. I told him some man wanted to buy it for eleven hundred dollars and asked him

if he would go any better. He said yeah, he would give me eleven hundred and fifty dollars for it if it was the same piano. I described it to him again and he told me to bring it out.

LYMON: Why didn't you tell him to come and pick it up?

BOY WILLIE: I didn't want to have no problem with Berniece. This way we just take it on out there and it be out the way. He want to charge twenty-five dollars to pick it up.

LYMON: You should have told him the man was gonna give you twelve hundred for it.

BOY WILLIE: I figure I was taking a chance with that eleven hundred. If I had told him twelve hundred he might have run off. Now I wish I had told him twelve-fifty. It's hard to figure out white folks sometimes.

LYMON: You might have been able to tell him anything. White folks got a lot of money.

BOY WILLIE: Come on, let's get it loaded before Berniece come back. Get that end over there. All you got to do is pick it up on that side. Don't worry about this side. You wanna stretch you' back for a minute?

LYMON: I'm ready.

BOY WILLIE: Get a real good grip on it now.
(*The sound of* SUTTER'S GHOST *is heard. They do not hear it.*)

LYMON: I got this end. You get that end.

BOY WILLIE: Wait till I say ready now. Alright. You got it good? You got a grip on it?

LYMON: Yeah, I got it. You lift up on that end.

BOY WILLIE: Ready? Lift!
(*The piano will not budge.*)

LYMON: Man, this piano is heavy! It's gonna take more than me and you to move this piano.

BOY WILLIE: We can do it. Come on—we did it before.

LYMON: Nigger—you crazy! That piano weighs five hundred pounds!

BOY WILLIE: I got three hundred pounds of it! I know you can carry two hundred pounds! You be lifting them cotton sacks! Come on lift this piano!
(*They try to move the piano again without success.*)

LYMON: It's stuck. Something holding it.

BOY WILLIE: How the piano gonna be stuck? We just moved it. Slide you' end out.

LYMON: Naw—we gonna' need two or three more people. How this big old piano get in the house?

BOY WILLIE: I don't know how it got in the house. I know how it's going out though! You get on this end. I'll carry three hundred and fifty pounds of it. All you got to do is slide your end out. Ready?

(*They switch sides and try again without success.* DOAKER *enters from his room as they try to push and shove it.*)

LYMON: Hey, Doaker . . . how this piano get in the house?

DOAKER: Boy Willie, what you doing?

BOY WILLIE: I'm carrying this piano out the house. What it look like I'm doing? Come on, Lymon, let's try again.

DOAKER: Go on let the piano sit there till Berniece come home.

BOY WILLIE: You ain't got nothing to do with this, Doaker. This my business.

DOAKER: This is my house, nigger! I ain't gonna let you or nobody else carry nothing out of it. You ain't gonna carry nothing out of here without my permission!

BOY WILLIE: This is my piano. I don't need your permission to carry my belongings out of your house. This is mine. This ain't got nothing to do with you.

DOAKER: I say leave it over there till Berniece come home. She got part of it too. Leave it set there till you see what she say.

BOY WILLIE: I don't care what Berniece say. Come on, Lymon. I got this side.

DOAKER: Go on and cut it half in two if you want to. Just leave Berniece's half sitting over there. I can't tell you what to do with your piano. But I can't let you take her half out of here.

BOY WILLIE: Go on, Doaker. You ain't got nothing to do with this. I don't want you starting nothing now. Just go on and leave me alone. Come on, Lymon. I got this end.

(DOAKER *goes into his room.* BOY WILLIE *and* LYMON *prepare to move the piano.*)

LYMON: How we gonna get it in the truck?

BOY WILLIE: Don't worry about how we gonna get it on the truck. You got to get it out the house first.

LYMON: It's gonna take more than me and you to move this piano.

BOY WILLIE: Just lift up on that end, nigger!

(DOAKER *comes to the doorway of his room and stands.*)

DOAKER (*Quietly with authority*): Leave that piano set over there till Berniece come back. I don't care what you do with it then. But you gonna leave it sit over there right now.

BOY WILLIE: Alright . . . I'm gonna tell you this, Doaker. I'm going out of here . . . I'm gonna get me some rope . . . find me a plank and some wheels . . . and I'm coming back. Then I'm gonna carry that piano out of here . . . sell it and give Berniece half the money. See . . . now that's what I'm gonna do. And you . . . or nobody else is gonna stop me. Come on, Lymon . . . let's go get some rope and stuff. I'll be back, Doaker.

(BOY WILLIE *and* LYMON *exit. The lights go down on the scene.*)

SCENE 5

The lights come up. BOY WILLIE *sits on the sofa, screwing casters on a wooden plank.* MARETHA *is sitting on the piano stool.* DOAKER *sits at the table playing solitaire.*

BOY WILLIE (*To* MARETHA): Then after that them white folks down around there started falling down their wells. You ever seen a well? A well got a wall around it. It's hard to fall down a well. You got to be leaning way over. Couldn't nobody figure out too much what was making these fellows fall down their well . . . so everybody says the Ghosts of the Yellow Dog must have pushed them. That's what everybody called them four men what got burned up in the boxcar.

MARETHA: Why they call them that?

BOY WILLIE: Cause the Yazoo Delta railroad got yellow boxcars. Sometime the way the whistle blow sound like an old dog howling so the people call it the Yellow Dog.

MARETHA: Anybody ever see the Ghosts?

BOY WILLIE: I told you they like the wind. Can you see the wind?

MARETHA: No.

BOY WILLIE: They like the wind you can't see them. But sometimes you be in trouble they might be around to help you. They say if you go where the Southern cross the Yellow Dog . . . you go to where them two railroads cross each other . . . and call out their names . . . they say they talk back to you. I don't know, I ain't never done that. But Uncle Wining Boy he say he been down there and talked to them. You have to ask him about that part.

(BERNIECE *has entered from the front door.*)

BERNIECE: Maretha, you go on and get ready for me to do your hair.

(MARETHA *crosses to the steps.*)

Boy Willie, I done told you to leave my house. (*To* MARETHA.)

Go on, Maretha.

(MARETHA *is hesitant about going up the stairs.*)

BOY WILLIE: Don't be scared. Here, I'll go up there with you. If we see Sutter's ghost I'll put a whupping on him. Come on, Uncle Boy Willie going with you.

(BOY WILLIE *and* MARETHA *exit up the stairs.*)

BERNIECE: Doaker—what is going on here?

DOAKER: I come home and him and Lymon was moving the piano. I told them to leave it over there till you got home. He went out and got that board and them wheels. He say he gonna take that piano out of here and ain't nobody gonna stop him.

BERNIECE: I ain't playing with Boy Willie. I got Crawley's gun upstairs. He don't know but I'm through with it. Where Lymon go?

DOAKER: Boy Willie sent him for some rope just before you come in.

BERNIECE: I ain't studying Boy Willie or Lymon—or the rope. Boy Willie ain't taking that piano out this house. That's all there is to it.

(BOY WILLIE *and* MARETHA *enter on the stairs.* MARETHA *carries a hot comb and a can of hair grease.* BOY WILLIE *crosses over and continues to screw the wheels on the board.*)

MARETHA: Mama, all the hair grease is gone. There ain't but this little bit left.

BERNIECE (*Gives her a dollar*): Here . . . run across the street and get another can. You come straight back, too. Don't you be playing around out there. And watch the cars. Be careful when you cross the street.

(MARETHA *exits out the front door.*)

Boy Willie, I done told you to leave my house.

BOY WILLIE: I ain't in you' house. I'm in Doaker's house. If he ask me to leave then I'll go on and leave. But consider me done left your part.

BERNIECE: Doaker, tell him to leave. Tell him to go on.

DOAKER: Boy Willie ain't done nothing for me to put him out of the house. I told you if you can't get along just go on and don't have nothing to do with each other.

BOY WILLIE: I ain't thinking about Berniece.

(*He gets up and draws a line across the floor with his foot.*)

There! Now I'm out of your part of the house. Consider me done left your part. Soon as Lymon come back with that rope. I'm gonna take that piano out of here and sell it.

BERNIECE: You ain't gonna touch that piano.

BOY WILLIE: Carry it out of here just as big and bold. Do like my daddy would have done come time to get Sutter's land.

BERNIECE: I got something to make you leave it over there.

BOY WILLIE: It's got to come better than this thirty-two-twenty.

DOAKER: Why don't you stop all that! Boy Willie, go on and leave her alone. You know how Berniece get. Why you wanna sit there and pick with her?

BOY WILLIE: I ain't picking with her. I told her the truth. She the one talking about what she got. I just told her what she better have.

BERNIECE: That's alright, Doaker. Leave him alone.

BOY WILLIE: She trying to scare me. Hell, I ain't scared of dying. I look around and see people dying every day. You got to die to make room for somebody else. I had a dog that died. Wasn't nothing but a puppy. I picked it up and put it in a bag and carried it up there to Reverend C. L. Thompson's church. I carried it up there and prayed, and asked Jesus to make it live like he did the man in the Bible. I prayed real hard. Knelt down and everything. Say ask in Jesus' name. Well, I must have called Jesus' name two hundred times. I called his name till my mouth got sore. I got up and looked in the bag and the dog still dead. It ain't moved a muscle! I say, "Well, ain't nothing precious." And then I went out and killed me a cat. That's when I discovered the power of death. See, a nigger that ain't afraid to die is the worse kind of nigger for the white man. He can't hold that power over you. That's what I learned when I killed that cat. I got the power of death too. I can command him. I can call him up. The white man don't like to see that. He don't like for you to stand up and look him square in the eye and say, "I got it too." Then he got to deal with you square up.

BERNIECE: That's why I don't talk to him, Doaker. You try and talk to him and that's the only kind of stuff that comes out his mouth.

DOAKER: You say Avery went home to get his Bible?

BOY WILLIE: What Avery gonna do? Avery can't do nothing with me. I wish Avery would say something to me about this piano.

DOAKER: Berniece ain't said about that. Avery went home to get his Bible. He coming by to bless the house see if he can get rid of Sutter's ghost.

BOY WILLIE: Ain't nothing but a house full of ghosts down there at the church. What Avery look like chasing away somebody's ghost?

(MARETHA *enters the front door.*)

BERNIECE: Light that stove and set that comb over there to get hot. Get something to put around your shoulders.

BOY WILLIE: The Bible say an eye for an eye, a tooth for a tooth, and a life for a life. Tit for tat. But you and Avery don't want to believe that. You gonna pass up that part and pretend it ain't in there. Everything else you gonna agree with. But if you gonna agree with part of it you got to agree with all of it. You can't do nothing halfway. You gonna go at the Bible halfway. You gonna act like that part ain't in there. But you pull out the Bible and open it and see what it say. Ask Avery. He a preacher. He'll tell you it's in there. He the Good Shepherd. Unless he gonna shepherd you to heaven with half the Bible.

BERNIECE: Maretha, bring me that comb. Make sure it's hot.

(MARETHA *brings the comb.* BERNIECE *begins to do her hair.*)

BOY WILLIE: I will say this for Avery. He done figured out a path to go through life. I don't agree with it. But he done fixed it so he can go right through it real smooth. Hell, he liable to end up with a million dollars that he done got from selling bread and wine.

MARETHA: OWWWWWW!

BERNIECE: Be still, Maretha. If you was a boy I wouldn't be going through this.

BOY WILLIE: Don't you tell that girl that. Why you wanna tell her that?

BERNIECE: You ain't got nothing to do with this child.

BOY WILLIE: Telling her you wished she was a boy. How's that gonna make her feel?

BERNIECE: Boy Willie, go on and leave me alone.

DOAKER: Why don't you leave her alone? What you got to pick with her for? Why don't you go on out and see what's out there in the streets? Have something to tell the fellows down home.

BOY WILLIE: I'm waiting on Lymon to get back with that truck. Why don't you go on out and see what's out there in the streets? You ain't got to work tomorrow. Talking about me . . . why don't you go out there? It's Friday night.

DOAKER: I got to stay around here and keep you all from killing one another.

BOY WILLIE: You ain't got to worry about me. I'm gonna be here just as long as it takes Lymon to get back here with that truck. You ought to be talking to Berniece. Sitting up there telling Maretha she wished she was a boy. What kind of thing is that to tell a child? If you want to tell her something tell her about that piano. You ain't even told her about that piano. Like that's something to be ashamed of. Like she supposed to go off and hide somewhere about that piano. You ought to mark down on the calendar the day that Papa Boy Charles brought that piano into the house. You ought to mark that day down and draw a circle around it . . . and every year when it come up throw a party. Have a celebration. If you did that she wouldn't have no problem in life. She could walk around here with her head held high. I'm talking about a big party!

Invite everybody! Mark that day down with a special meaning. That way she know where she at in the world. You got her going out here thinking she wrong in the world. Like there ain't no part of it belong to her.

BERNIECE: Let me take care of my child. When you get one of your own then you can teach it what you want to teach it.

(DOAKER *exits into his room.*)

BOY WILLIE: What I want to bring a child into this world for? Why I wanna bring somebody else into all this for? I'll tell you this . . . If I was Rockefeller I'd have forty or fifty. I'd make one every day. Cause they gonna start out in life with all the advantages. I ain't got no advantages to offer nobody. Many is the time I looked at my daddy and seen him staring off at his hands. I got a little older I know what he was thinking. He sitting there saying, "I got these big old hands but what I'm gonna do with them? Best I can do is make a fifty-acre crop for Mr. Stovall. Got these big old hands capable of doing anything. I can take and build something with these hands. But where's the tools? All I got is these hands. Unless I go out here and kill me somebody and take what they got . . . it's a long row to hoe for me to get something of my own. So what I'm gonna do with these big old hands? What would you do?"

See now . . . if he had his own land, he wouldn't have felt that way. If he had something under his feet that belonged to him he could stand up taller. That's what I'm talking about. Hell, the land is there for everybody. All you got to do is figure out how to get you a piece. Ain't no mystery to life. You just got to go out and meet it square on. If you got a piece of land you'll find everything else fall right into place. You can stand right up next to the white man and talk about the price of cotton . . . the weather, and anything else you want to talk about. If you teach that girl that she living at the bottom of life, she's gonna grow up and hate you.

BERNIECE: I'm gonna teach her the truth. That's just where she living. Only she ain't got to stay there.

(*To* MARETHA.)

Turn you' head over to the other side.

BOY WILLIE: This might be your bottom but it ain't mine. I'm living at the top of life. I ain't gonna just take my life and throw it away at the bottom. I'm in the world like everybody else. The way I see it everybody else got to come up a little taste to be where I am.

BERNIECE: You right at the bottom with the rest of us.

BOY WILLIE: I'll tell you this . . . and ain't a living soul can put a come back on it. If you believe that's where you at then you gonna act that way. If you act that way then that's where you gonna be. It's as simple as that. Ain't no mystery to life. I don't know how you come to believe that stuff. Crawley didn't think like that. He wasn't living at the bottom of life. Papa Boy Charles and Mama Ola wasn't living at the bottom of life. You ain't never heard them say nothing like that. They would have taken a strap to you if they heard you say something like that.

(DOAKER *enters from his room.*)

Hey, Doaker . . . Berniece say the colored folks is living at the bottom of life. I tried to tell her if she think that . . . that's where she gonna be. You think you living at the bottom of life? Is that how you see yourself?

DOAKER: I'm just living the best way I know how. I ain't thinking about no top or no bottom.

BOY WILLIE: That's what I tried to tell Berniece. I don't know where she got that from. That sound like something Avery would say. Avery think cause the white man give him a turkey for Thanksgiving that makes him better than everybody else. That's gonna raise him out of the bottom of life. I don't need nobody to give me a turkey. I can get my own turkey. All you have to do is get out my way. I'll get me two or three turkeys.

BERNIECE: You can't even get a chicken let alone two or three turkeys. Talking about get out your way. Ain't nobody in your way.

(*To* MARETHA.)

Straighten your head, Maretha! Don't be bending down like that. Hold your head up!

(*To* BOY WILLIE.)

All you got going for you is talk. You' whole life that's all you ever had going for you.

BOY WILLIE: See now . . . I'll tell you something about me. I done strung along and strung along. Going this way and that. Whatever way would lead me to a moment of peace. That's all I want. To be as easy with everything. But I wasn't born to that. I was born to a time of fire.

The world ain't wanted no part of me. I could see that since I was about seven. The world say it's better off without me. See, Berniece accept that. She trying to come up to where she can prove something to the world. Hell, the world a better place cause of me. I don't see it like Berniece. I got a heart that beats here and it beats just as loud as the next fellow's. Don't care if he black or white. Sometime it beats louder. When it beats louder, then everybody can hear it. Some people get scared of that. Like Berniece. Some people get scared to hear a nigger's heart beating. They think you ought to lay low with that heart. Make it beat quiet and go along with everything the way it is. But my mama ain't birthed me for nothing. So what I got to do? I got to mark my passing on the road. Just like you write on a tree, "Boy Willie was here."

That's all I'm trying to do with that piano. Trying to put my mark on the road. Like my daddy done. My heart say for me to sell that piano and get me some land so I can make a life for myself to live in my own way. Other than that I ain't thinking about nothing Berniece got to say.

(*There is a knock at the door.* BOY WILLIE *crosses to it and yanks it open thinking it is* LYMON. AVERY *enters. He carries a Bible.*)

BOY WILLIE: Where you been, nigger? Aw . . . I thought you was Lymon. Hey, Berniece, look who's here.

BERNIECE: Come on in, Avery. Don't you pay Boy Willie no mind.

BOY WILLIE: Hey . . . Hey, Avery . . . tell me this . . . can you get to heaven with half the Bible?

BERNIECE: Boy Willie . . . I done told you to leave me alone.

BOY WILLIE: I just ask the man a question. He can answer. He don't need you to speak for him. Avery . . . if you only believe on half the Bible and don't want to accept the other half . . . you think God let you in heaven? Or do you got to have the whole Bible? Tell Berniece . . . if you only believe in part of it . . . when you see God he gonna ask you why you ain't believed in the other part . . . then he gonna send you straight to Hell.

AVERY: You got to be born again. Jesus say unless a man be born again he cannot come unto the Father and who so ever heareth my words and believeth them not shall be cast into a fiery pit.

BOY WILLIE: That's what I was trying to tell Berniece. You got to believe in it all. You can't go at nothing halfway. She think she going to heaven with half the Bible.
(*To* BERNIECE.)
You hear that . . . Jesus say you got to believe in it all.

BERNIECE: You keep messing with me.

BOY WILLIE: I ain't thinking about you.

DOAKER: Come on in, Avery, and have a seat. Don't pay neither one of them no mind. They been arguing all day.

BERNIECE: Come on in, Avery.

AVERY: How's everybody in here?

BERNIECE: Here, set this comb back over there on that stove.
(*To* AVERY.)
Don't pay Boy Willie no mind. He been around here bothering me since I come home from work.

BOY WILLIE: Boy Willie ain't bothering you. Boy Willie ain't bothering nobody. I'm just waiting on Lymon to get back. I ain't thinking about you. You heard the man say I was right and you still don't want to believe it. You just wanna go and make up anythin'. Well there's Avery . . . there's the preacher . . . go on and ask him.

AVERY: Berniece believe in the Bible. She been baptized.

BOY WILLIE: What about that part that say an eye for an eye a tooth for a tooth and a life for a life? Ain't that in there?

DOAKER: What they say down there at the bank, Avery?

AVERY: Oh, they talked to me real nice. I told Berniece . . . they say maybe they let me borrow the money. They done talked to my boss down at work and everything.

DOAKER: That's what I told Berniece. You working every day you ought to be able to borrow some money.

AVERY: I'm getting more people in my congregation every day. Berniece says she gonna be the Deaconess. I get me my church I can get married and settled down. That's what I told Berniece.

DOAKER: That be nice. You all ought to go ahead and get married. Berniece don't need to be by herself. I tell her that all the time.

BERNIECE: I ain't said nothing about getting married. I said I was thinking about it.

DOAKER: Avery get him his church you all can make it nice.

(*To* AVERY.)

Berniece said you was coming by to bless the house.

AVERY: Yeah, I done read up on my Bible. She asked me to come by and see if I can get rid of Sutter's ghost.

BOY WILLIE: Ain't no ghost in this house. That's all in Berniece's head. Go on up there and see if you see him. I'll give you a hundred dollars if you see him. That's all in her imagination.

DOAKER: Well, let her find that out then. If Avery blessing the house is gonna make her feel better . . . what you got to do with it?

AVERY: Berniece say Maretha seen him too. I don't know, but I found a part in the Bible to bless the house. If he is here then that ought to make him go.

BOY WILLIE: You worse than Berniece believing all that stuff. Talking about . . . if he here. Go on up there and find out. I been up there I ain't seen him. If you reading from that Bible gonna make him leave out of Berniece imagination, well, you might be right. But if you talking about . . .

DOAKER: Boy Willie, why don't you just be quiet? Getting all up in the man's business. This ain't got nothing to do with you. Let him go ahead and do what he gonna do.

BOY WILLIE: I ain't stopping him. Avery ain't got no power to do nothing.

AVERY: Oh, I ain't got no power. God got the power! God got power over everything in His creation. God can do anything. God say, "As I commandeth so it shall be." God said, "Let there be light," and there was light. He made the world in six days and rested on the seventh. God's got a wonderful power. He got power over life and death. Jesus raised Lazareth from the dead. They was getting ready to bury him and Jesus told him say, "Rise up and walk." He got up and walked and the people made great rejoicing at the power of God. I ain't worried about him chasing away a little old ghost!

(*There is a knock at the door.* BOY WILLIE *goes to answer it.* LYMON *enters carrying a coil of rope.*)

BOY WILLIE: Where you been? I been waiting on you and you run off somewhere.

LYMON: I ran into Grace. I stopped and bought her drink. She say she gonna go to the picture show with me.

BOY WILLIE: I ain't thinking about no Grace nothing.

LYMON: Hi, Berniece.

BOY WILLIE: Give me that rope and get up on this side of the piano.

DOAKER: Boy Willie, don't start nothing now. Leave the piano alone.

BOY WILLIE: Get that board there, Lymon. Stay out of this, Doaker.

(BERNIECE *exits up the stairs.*)

DOAKER: You just can't take the piano. How you gonna take the piano? Berniece ain't said nothing about selling that piano.

BOY WILLIE: She ain't got to say nothing. Come on, Lymon. We got to lift one end at a time up on the board. You got to watch so that the board don't slide up under there.

LYMON: What we gonna do with the rope?

BOY WILLIE: Let me worry about the rope. You just get up on this side over here with me.

(BERNIECE *enters from the stairs. She has her hand in her pocket where she has Crawley's gun.*)

AVERY: Boy Willie . . . Berniece . . . why don't you all sit down and talk this out now?

BERNIECE: Ain't nothing to talk out.

BOY WILLIE: I'm through talking to Berniece. You can talk to Berniece till you get blue in the face, and it don't make no difference. Get up on that side, Lymon. Throw that rope around there and tie it to the leg.

LYMON: Wait a minute . . . wait a minute, Boy Willie. Berniece got to say. Hey, Berniece . . . did you tell Boy Willie he could take this piano?

BERNIECE: Boy Willie ain't taking nothing out of my house but himself. Now you let him go ahead and try.

BOY WILLIE: Come on, Lymon, get up on this side with me.

(LYMON *stands undecided.*)

Come on, nigger! What you standing there for?

LYMON: Maybe Berniece is right, Boy Willie. Maybe you shouldn't sell it.

AVERY: You all ought to sit down and talk it out. See if you can come to an agreement.

DOAKER: That's what I been trying to tell them. Seem like one of them ought to respect the other one's wishes.

BERNIECE: I wish Boy Willie would go on and leave my house. That's what I wish. Now, he can respect that. Cause he's leaving here one way or another.

BOY WILLIE: What you mean one way or another? What's that supposed to mean? I ain't scared of no gun.

DOAKER: Come on, Berniece, leave him alone with that.

BOY WILLIE: I don't care what Berniece say. I'm selling my half. I can't help it if her half got to go along with it. It ain't like I'm trying to cheat her out of her half. Come on, Lymon.

LYMON: Berniece . . . I got to do this . . . Boy Willie say he gonna give you half of the money . . . say he want to get Sutter's land.

BERNIECE: Go on, Lymon. Just go on . . . I done told Boy Willie what to do.

BOY WILLIE: Here, Lymon . . . put that rope up over there.

LYMON: Boy Willie, you sure you want to do this? The way I figure it . . . I might be wrong . . . but I figure she gonna shoot you first.

BOY WILLIE: She just gonna have to shoot me.

BERNIECE: Maretha, get on out the way. Get her out the way, Doaker.

DOAKER: Go on, do what your mama told you.

BERNIECE: Put her in your room.

(MARETHA *exits to* DOAKER's *room.* BOY WILLIE *and* LYMON *try to lift the piano. The door opens and* WINING BOY *enters. He has been drinking.*)

WINING BOY: Man, these niggers around here! I stopped down there at Seefus . . . These folks standing around talking about Patchneck Red's coming. They jumping back and getting off the sidewalk talking about Patchneck Red this and Patchneck Red that. Come to find out . . . you know who they was talking about? Old John D. from up around Tyler! Used to run around with Otis Smith. He got everybody scared of him. Calling him Patchneck Red. They don't know I whupped the nigger's head in one time.

BOY WILLIE: Just make sure that board don't slide, Lymon.

LYMON: I got this side. You watch that side.

WINING BOY: Hey, Boy Willie, what you got? I know you got a pint stuck up in your coat.

BOY WILLIE: Wining Boy, get out the way!

WINING BOY: Hey, Doaker. What you got? Gimme a drink. I want a drink.

DOAKER: It look like you had enough of whatever it was. Come talking about "What you got?" You ought to be trying to find somewhere to lay down.

WINING BOY: I ain't worried about no place to lay down. I can always find me a place to lay down in Berniece's house. Ain't that right, Berniece?

BERNIECE: Wining Boy, sit down somewhere. You been out there drinking all day. Come in here smelling like an old polecat. Sit on down there, you don't need nothing to drink.

DOAKER: You know Berniece don't like all that drinking.

WINING BOY: I ain't disrespecting Berniece. Berniece, am I disrespecting you? I'm just trying to be nice. I been with strangers all day and they treated me like family. I come in here to family and you treat me like a stranger. I don't need your whiskey. I can buy my own. I wanted your company, not your whiskey.

DOAKER: Nigger, why don't you go upstairs and lay down? You don't need nothing to drink.

WINING BOY: I ain't thinking about no laying down. Me and Boy Willie fixing to party. Ain't that right, Boy Willie? Tell him. I'm fixing to play me some piano. Watch this.

(WINING BOY *sits down at the piano.*)

BOY WILLIE: Come on, Wining Boy! Me and Lymon fixing to move the piano.

WINING BOY: Wait a minute . . . wait a minute. This a song I wrote for Cleotha. I wrote this song in memory of Cleotha.

(*He begins to play and sing.*)

>Hey little woman what's the matter with you now
>Had a storm last night and blowed the line all down
>
>Tell me how long
>Is I got to wait
>Can I get it now
>Or must I hesitate
>
>It takes a hesitating stocking in her hesitating shoe
>It takes a hesitating woman wanna sing the blues
>
>Tell me how long
>Is I got to wait
>Can I kiss you now
>Or must I hesitate.

BOY WILLIE: Come on, Wining Boy, get up! Get up, Wining Boy! Me and Lymon's fixing to move the piano.

WINING BOY: Naw . . . Naw . . . you ain't gonna move this piano!

BOY WILLIE: Get out the way, Wining Boy.

(WINING BOY, *his back to the piano, spreads his arms out over the piano.*)

WINING BOY: You ain't taking this piano out the house. You got to take me with it!

BOY WILLIE: Get on out the way, Wining Boy! Doaker get him!

(*There is a knock on the door.*)

BERNIECE: I got him, Doaker. Come on, Wining Boy. I done told Boy Willie he ain't taking the piano.

(BERNIECE *tries to take* WINING BOY *away from the piano.*)

WINING BOY: He got to take me with it!

(DOAKER *goes to answer the door.* GRACE *enters.*)

GRACE: Is Lymon here?

DOAKER: Lymon.

WINING BOY: He ain't taking that piano.

BERNIECE: I ain't gonna let him take it.

GRACE: I thought you was coming back. I ain't gonna sit in that truck all day.

LYMON: I told you I was coming back.

GRACE (*Sees* BOY WILLIE): Oh, hi, Boy Willie. Lymon told me you was gone back down South.

LYMON: I said he was going back. I didn't say he had left already.

GRACE: That's what you told me.

BERNIECE: Lymon, you got to take your company someplace else.

LYMON: Berniece, this is Grace. That there is Berniece. That's Boy Willie's sister.

GRACE: Nice to meet you.

(*To* LYMON.)

I ain't gonna sit out in that truck all day. You told me you was gonna take me to the movie.

LYMON: I told you I had something to do first. You supposed to wait on me.

BERNIECE: Lymon, just go on and leave. Take Grace or whoever with you. Just go on get out my house.

BOY WILLIE: You gonna help me move this piano first, nigger!

LYMON (*To* GRACE): I got to help Boy Willie move the piano first.

(*Everybody but* GRACE *suddenly senses* SUTTER'S *presence.*)

GRACE: I ain't waiting on you. Told me you was coming right back. Now you got to move a piano. You just like all the other men.

(GRACE *now senses something.*)

Something ain't right here. I knew I shouldn't have come back up in this house.

(GRACE *exits.*)

LYMON: Hey, Grace! I'll be right back, Boy Willie.

BOY WILLIE: Where you going, nigger?

LYMON: I'll be back. I got to take Grace home.

BOY WILLIE: Come on, let's move the piano first!

LYMON: I got to take Grace home. I told you I'll be back.

(LYMON *exits.* BOY WILLIE *exits and calls after him.*)

BOY WILLIE: Come on, Lymon! Hey . . . Lymon! Lymon . . . come on!

(*Again, the presence of* SUTTER *is felt.*)

WINING BOY: Hey, Doaker, did you feel that? Hey, Berniece . . . did you get cold? Hey, Doaker . . .

DOAKER: What you calling me for?

WINING BOY: I believe that's Sutter.

DOAKER: Well, let him stay up there. As long as he don't mess with me.

BERNIECE: Avery, go on and bless the house.

DOAKER: You need to bless that piano. That's what you need to bless. It ain't done nothing but cause trouble. If you gonna bless anything go on and bless that.

WINING BOY: Hey, Doaker, if he gonna bless something let him bless everything. The kitchen . . . the upstairs. Go on and bless it all.

BOY WILLIE: Ain't no ghost in this house. He need to bless Berniece's head. That's what he need to bless.

AVERY: Seem like that piano's causing all the trouble. I can bless that. Berniece, put me some water in that bottle.

(AVERY *takes a small bottle from his pocket and hands it to* BERNIECE, *who goes into the kitchen to get water.* AVERY *takes a candle from his pocket and lights it. He gives it to* BERNIECE *as she gives him the water.*)

Hold this candle. Whatever you do make sure it don't go out.

O Holy Father we gather here this evening in the Holy Name to cast out the spirit of one James Sutter. May this vial of water be empowered with thy spirit. May each drop of it be a weapon and a shield against the presence of all evil and may it be a cleansing and blessing of this humble abode.

Just as Our Father taught us how to pray so He say, "I will prepare a table for you in the midst of mine enemies," and in His hands we place ourselves to come unto his presence. Where there is Good so shall it cause Evil to scatter to the Four Winds.

(*He throws water at the piano at each commandment.*)

AVERY: Get thee behind me, Satan! Get thee behind the face of Righteousness as we Glorify His Holy Name! Get thee behind the Hammer of Truth that breaketh down the Wall of Falsehood! Father. Father. Praise. Praise. We ask in Jesus' name and call forth the power of the Holy Spirit as it is written. . . .

(*He opens the Bible and reads from it.*)

I will sprinkle clean water upon thee and ye shall be clean.

BOY WILLIE: All this old preaching stuff. Hell, just tell him to leave.

(AVERY *continues reading throughout* BOY WILLIE's *outburst.*)

AVERY: I will sprinkle clean water upon you and you shall be clean: from all your uncleanliness, and from all your idols, will I cleanse you. A new heart also will I give you, and a new spirit will I put within you: and I will take out of your flesh the heart of stone, and I will give you a heart of flesh. And I will put my spirit within you, and cause you to walk in my statutes, and ye shall keep my judgments, and do them.

(BOY WILLIE *grabs a pot of water from the stove and begins to fling it around the room.*)

BOY WILLIE: Hey Sutter! Sutter! Get your ass out this house! Sutter! Come on and get some of this water! You done drowned in the well, come on and get some more of this water!

(BOY WILLIE *is working himself into a frenzy as he runs around the room throwing water and calling* SUTTER's *name.* AVERY *continues reading.*)

BOY WILLIE: Come on, Sutter!

(*He starts up the stairs.*)

Come on, get some water! Come on, Sutter!

(*The sound of* SUTTER's GHOST *is heard. As* BOY WILLIE *approaches the steps he is suddenly thrown back by the unseen force, which is choking him. As he struggles he frees himself, then dashes up the stairs.*)

BOY WILLIE: Come on, Sutter!

AVERY (*Continuing*): A new heart also will I give you and a new spirit will I put within you: and I will take out of your flesh the heart of stone, and I will give you a heart of flesh. And I will put my spirit within you, and cause you to walk in my statutes, and ye shall keep my judgments, and do them.

(*There are loud sounds heard from upstairs as* BOY WILLIE *begins to wrestle with* SUTTER's GHOST. *It is a life-and-death struggle fraught with perils and faultless terror.* BOY WILLIE *is thrown down the stairs.* AVERY *is stunned into silence.* BOY WILLIE *picks himself up and dashes back upstairs.*)

AVERY: Berniece, I can't do it.

(*There are more sounds heard from upstairs.* DOAKER *and* WINING BOY *stare at one another in stunned disbelief. It is in this moment, from somewhere old, that* BERNIECE *realizes what she must do. She crosses to the piano. She begins to play. The song is found piece by piece. It is an old urge to song that is both a commandment and a plea. With each repetition it gains in strength. It is intended as an exorcism and a dressing for battle. A rustle of wind blowing across two continents.)*

BERNIECE (*Singing*):

> I want you to help me
> I want you to help me
> I want you to help me
> I want you to help me
> I want you to help me
> I want you to help me
> Mama Berniece
> I want you to help me
> Mama Esther
> I want you to help me
> Papa Boy Charles
> I want you to help me
> Mama Ola
> I want you to help me
>
> I want you to help me
> I want you to help me
> I want you to help me
> I want you to help me
> I want you to help me
> I want you to help me
> I want you to help me
> I want you to help me

(The sound of a train approaching is heard. The noise upstairs subsides.)

BOY WILLIE: Come on, Sutter! Come back, Sutter!

(BERNIECE begins to chant:)

BERNIECE:

> Thank you.
> Thank you.
> Thank you.

(A calm comes over the house. MARETHA enters from DOAKER's room. BOY WILLIE enters on the stairs. He pauses a moment to watch BERNIECE at the piano.)

BERNIECE:

> Thank you.
> Thank you.

BOY WILLIE: Wining Boy, you ready to go back down home? Hey, Doaker, what time the train leave?

DOAKER: You still got time to make it.

(MARETHA crosses and embraces BOY WILLIE.)

BOY WILLIE: Hey Berniece . . . if you and Maretha don't keep playing on that piano . . . ain't no telling . . . me and Sutter both liable to be back.

(He exits.)

BERNIECE: Thank you.

(The lights go down to black.)

Introduction to *M. Butterfly*

WHEN THE PLAY WAS NEW

After premiering at the National Theatre in Washington, D.C., on February 10, David Henry Hwang's *M. Butterfly* opened on Broadway on March 20, 1988, at the Eugene O'Neill Theatre and ran for two years, amassing 777 performances. The play was directed by John Dexter with masterful theatricality and included stunning set and costume designs by Japanese artist Eiko Ishioka, who now frequently designs for feature films and the Cirque du Soleil. The production starred John Lithgow as Gallimard and B. D. Wong as Song Liling. Both actors have had successful stage, film, and television careers. *M. Butterfly* won the Tony Award for best play as well as numerous other awards. Although Hwang is prolific, this play remains his most famous creation.

The play is about many things topical both when the play was new and now. On one level the play is about international politics—especially espionage—and the political decisions and assumptions made about foreign cultures and governing systems. The play is also, and perhaps more tellingly, about gender confusion exacerbated by the cultural ignorance of the East by the West, which in turn is exploited by a Chinese spy to get close to a French diplomat and ultimately implicate him in the espionage as well. On another level, the play is about art—especially dramatic art—and how dramatic, operatic, and filmic stereotypes underscore cultural and personal decision making and behavior—often with disastrous results. We see the fallout from one culture co-opting the art or culture of another.

Not surprisingly, Hwang is a great advocate of cultural diversity in the theatre and a severe critic of cross-cultural conflicts in society. *M. Butterfly* is in part a response to the Puccini opera *Madama Butterfly*, which has been a staple of op-

era since 1904 and which, in turn, was based on the play *Madame Butterfly* (1900) by David Belasco. Hwang's play is a deconstruction of the source and becomes a radically new creation. The playwright was disturbed and offended by how the opera and play perpetuate stereotypes of the Asian woman as a naive, blushing flower, who pines away for the love of an absent white man. As an Asian-American of Chinese extraction, Hwang has spent a good portion of his artistic life fighting against racial and cultural stereotypes. In talking about the action of his play the playwright notes that his central French character fell in love with neither a man nor woman, but with a stereotypical fantasy. The play, therefore, is an exploration of East versus West in value systems, artistic endeavor, gender relations, and social expectations.

THE PLAYWRIGHT

David Henry Hwang was born in 1957 in Los Angeles, California, to immigrant Chinese parents. He graduated from Stanford and attended the Yale School of Drama. While still a student at Stanford in 1980 he wrote his first successful play, *F.O.B.* (an acronym for "fresh off the boat"). The play, about a Chinese immigrant confronted by more culturally savvy Chinese-Americans, was produced at the Public Theatre in New York. It won the Obie Award for best off-Broadway play. A number of his early plays such as *The Dance and the Railroad* (1981) and *Family Devotions* (1981) further explore Chinese immigrant problems. Hwang was very active in the 1980s producing plays with Japanese themes, including *Rich Relations* (1986) and the one-acts *The Sound of a Voice* (1983) and *The House of Sleeping Beauties* (1983) at the Public Theatre. After *M. Butterfly* he created the text for the visually stunning *1,000 Airplanes on the Roof* (1988), a science fiction music-drama, in collaboration with Philip Glass and Jerome Sirlin. *Trying to Find Chinatown* appeared in 1996 along with *Golden Child*, a play about generational conflicts, which became a Broadway production in 1998. Hwang's adaptation of Ibsen's *Peer Gynt* followed the same year. The playwright often writes about Asian-American issues, but many other topics as well. With Linda Woolverton and Robert Falls, Hwang co-wrote the book for the wildly popular musical *Aida* (2000) with music by Elton John and lyrics by Tim Rice. He also rewrote the book for a Broadway revival of Rodgers and Hammerstein's *Flower Drum Song* (2002). All along, Hwang has been very attracted to musicals, opera, and plays with music. As the play's afterword notes, when he first conceived the idea for *M. Butterfly*, he intended to make it a musical. Hwang has also been active with screenwriting, including the film adaptation of his own *M. Butterfly* and the screenplay for Neil LaBute's *Possession* (2002) starring Gwyneth Paltrow.

GENRE, STRUCTURE, AND STYLE

The basic structural approach to *M. Butterfly* is to deconstruct traditional Chinese Opera (music drama) and *Madame Butterfly* (opera and play). The criticism is intercultural layered with gender and sexual confusion. We see racism mixed with sexism. Politically, we see a deconstruction of the stereotypically "submissive" East and a dominant West. The East assumes the traditional female role, while the West assumes itself to be male.

Most of these conflicts are played out through a single relationship of a French man, Rene Gallimard, and a Chinese "woman," Song Liling. Most of the remaining roles are doubled, a device that enhances the close examination of the two principals who are also the dramatic and political agents of East and West. The action is set in the Paris prison cell of Gallimard but shifts backward in time and place from France to China as Gallimard remembers his bizarre past. The play is very loosely based on real events of espionage, sexual confusion, and duplicity. The action is presented episodically (not unlike the methods of Brecht) in 1947, 1960–63, 1966, 1968–1970, and 1986. Although the action shifts back and forth from present to past,

most of the past events appear chronologically. Gallimard in the prison cell thus becomes a frame for his memories of the crucial events leading up to his incarceration.

IMPORTANT ELEMENTS OF CONTENT

When encountering *M. Butterfly,* it is not necessary that the reader or theatergoer be familiar with *Madame Butterfly* already, but such a preparation enhances the experience considerably. Periodically the opera invades the play, most frequently at critical moments. Nonetheless, the stereotypes and cultural assumptions made by both "sides" in the play are likely to be very familiar to audiences because we see them in so many other venues such as television, movies, and perhaps life experiences in public, school, and the workplace.

Crucial to this play is the practice of cross-dressing, which ultimately is practiced by both leading characters, but for very different reasons. For one it is a device for exploitation and manipulation. For the other it is an emotional and desperate choice connecting him to his undying fantasy and demise.

THE PLAY IN REVIVAL

After a successful run on Broadway from 1988 to 1990, *M. Butterfly* was revived by many (probably most) regional theatres in the United States, and theatres in Canada and Europe. It continues to thrive in regional theatres such as Arena Stage in Washington, D.C., (2004), and Pac Rep in Carmel-by-the-Sea in California (2005). Interestingly the play has had, and continues to have, revivals in Asian and Asian-American theatres such as Singapore Repertory Theatre (1994) and East-West Players in Los Angeles (2004). Of course university theatres frequently revive this play as well and the play is often taught in university classes.

SPECIAL FEATURE

M. Butterfly requires some very difficult sequences based on Chinese opera—not only the traditional singing performance of Song Liling, but the addition of Chinese acrobats for authenticity. The result is a demanding production need, not easily met effectively by many theatres.

FURTHER READING ABOUT THE PLAY, PLAYWRIGHT, AND CONTEXT

All of David Henry Hwang's plays are published, usually in single editions. One collection of eight of the plays appeared in 2000. See David Henry Hwang, *Trying to Find Chinatown: Selected Plays.*

For biography and criticism of Hwang, see Douglas Street, *David Henry Hwang.*

For criticism of Hwang's plays, see James Moy, *Marginal Sights: Staging the Chinese American,* and Mira Wiegmann, *The Staging and Transformation of Gender Archetypes in* A Midsummer Night's Dream, M. Butterfly, *and* Kiss of the Spider Woman.

M. Butterfly

By David Henry Hwang

PLAYWRIGHT'S NOTES

"A former French diplomat and a Chinese opera singer have been sentenced to six years in jail for spying for China after a two-day trial that traced a story of clandestine love and mistaken sexual identity. . . . Mr. Bouriscot was accused of passing information to China after he fell in love with Mr. Shi, whom he believed for twenty years to be a woman."

—*The New York Times*, May 11, 1986

This play was suggested by international newspaper accounts of a recent espionage trial. For purposes of dramatization, names have been changed, characters created, and incidents devised or altered, and this play does not purport to be a factual record of real events or real people.

SETTING

The action of the play takes place in a Paris prison in the present, and in recall, during the decade 1960 to 1970 in Beijing, and from 1966 to the present in Paris.

ACT ONE

SCENE 1

M. GALLIMARD's *prison cell. Paris. Present.*

Lights fade up to reveal RENE GALLIMARD, *65, in a prison cell. He wears a comfortable bathrobe, and looks old and tired. The sparsely furnished cell contains a wooden crate upon which sits a hot plate with a kettle, and a portable tape recorder.* GALLIMARD *sits on the crate staring at the recorder, a sad smile on his face.*

Upstage SONG, *who appears as a beautiful woman in traditional Chinese garb, dances a traditional piece from the Peking Opera, surrounded by the percussive clatter of Chinese music.*

Then, slowly, lights and sound cross fade; the Chinese opera music dissolves into a Western opera, the "Love Duet" from Puccini's Madame Butterfly. SONG *continues dancing, now to the Western accompaniment. Though her movements are the same, the difference in music now gives them a balletic quality.*

GALLIMARD *rises, and turns upstage towards the figure of* SONG, *who dances without acknowledging him.*

GALLIMARD: Butterfly, Butterfly . . .

(*He forces himself to turn away, as the image of* SONG *fades out, and talks to us.*)

GALLIMARD: The limits of my cell are as such: four-and-a-half meters by five. There's one window against the far wall; a door, very strong, to protect me from autograph hounds. I'm responsible for the tape recorder, the hot plate, and this charming coffee table.

When I want to eat, I'm marched off to the dining room—hot, steaming slop appears on my plate. When I want to sleep, the light bulb turns itself off—the work of fairies. It's an enchanted space I occupy. The French—we know how to run a prison.

But, to be honest, I'm not treated like an ordinary prisoner. Why? Because I'm a celebrity. You see, I make people laugh.

I never dreamed this day would arrive. I've never been considered witty or clever. In fact, as a young boy, in an informal poll among my grammar school classmates, I was voted "least likely to be invited to a party." It's a title I managed to hold onto for many years. Despite some stiff competition.

But now, how the tables turn! Look at me: the life of every social function in Paris. Paris? Why be modest? My fame has spread to Amsterdam, London, New York. Listen to them! In the world's smartest parlors. I'm the one who lifts their spirits!

(*With a flourish,* GALLIMARD *directs our attention to another part of the stage.*)

SCENE 2
A party. Present.

Lights go up on a chic-looking parlor, where a well-dressed trio, two MEN *and one* WOMAN, *make conversation.* GALLIMARD *also remains lit; he observes them from his cell.*

WOMAN: And what of Gallimard?

MAN 1: Gallimard?

MAN 2: Gallimard!

GALLIMARD (*To us*): You see? They're all determined to say my name, as if it were some new dance.

WOMAN: He still claims not to believe the truth.

MAN 1: What? Still? Even since the trial?

WOMAN: Yes. Isn't it mad?

MAN 2 (*Laughing*): He says . . . it was dark . . . and she was very modest!

(*The trio break into laughter.*)

MAN 1: So—what? He never touched her with his hands?

MAN 2: Perhaps he did, and simply misidentified the equipment. A compelling case for sex education in the schools.

WOMAN: To protect the National Security—the Church can't argue with that.

MAN 1: That's impossible! How could he not know?

MAN 2: Simple ignorance.

MAN 1: For twenty years?

MAN 2: Time flies when you're being stupid.

WOMAN: Well, I thought the French were ladies' men.

MAN 2: It seems Monsieur Gallimard was overly anxious to live up to his national reputation.

WOMAN: Well, he's not very good-looking.

MAN 1: No, he's not.

MAN 2: Certainly not.

WOMAN: Actually, I feel sorry for him.

MAN 2: A toast! To Monsieur Gallimard!

WOMAN: Yes! To Gallimard!

MAN 1: To Gallimard!

MAN 2: Vive la différence!

(*They toast, laughing. Lights down on them.*)

SCENE 3
M. GALLIMARD'*s cell.*

GALLIMARD (*Smiling*): You see? They toast me. I've become patron saint of the socially inept. Can they really be so foolish? Men like that—they should be scratching at my door, begging to learn my secrets! For I, Rene Gallimard, you see, I have known, and been loved by . . . the Perfect Woman.

Alone in this cell, I sit night after night, watching our story play through my head, always searching for a new ending, one which redeems my honor, where she returns at last to my arms. And I imagine you—my ideal audience—who come to understand and even, perhaps just a little, to envy me.

(*He turns on his tape recorder. Over the house speakers, we hear the opening phrases of* Madame Butterfly.)

GALLIMARD: In order for you to understand what I did and why, I must introduce you to my favorite opera: *Madame Butterfly*. By Giacomo Puccini. First produced at La Scala, Milan, in 1904, it is now beloved throughout the Western world.

(*As* GALLIMARD *describes the opera, the tape segues in and out to sections he may be describing.*)

GALLIMARD: And why not? Its heroine, Cio-Cio-San, also known as Butterfly, is a feminine ideal, beautiful and brave. And its hero, the man for whom she gives up everything, is— (*He pulls out a naval officer's cap from under his crate, pops it on his head, and struts about*)—not very good-looking, not too bright, and pretty much a wimp: Benjamin Franklin Pinkerton of the U.S. Navy. As the curtain rises, he's just closed on two great bargains: one on a house, the other on a woman—call it a package deal.

Pinkerton purchased the rights to Butterfly for one hundred yen—in modern currency, equivalent to about . . . sixty-six cents. So, he's feeling pretty pleased with himself as Sharpless, the American consul, arrives to witness the marriage.

(MARC, *wearing an official cap to designate* SHARPLESS, *enters and plays the character.*)

SHARPLESS/MARC: Pinkerton!

PINKERTON/GALLIMARD: Sharpless! How's it hangin'? It's a great day, just great. Between my house, my wife, and the rickshaw ride in from town, I've saved nineteen cents just this morning.

SHARPLESS: Wonderful. I can see the inscription on your tombstone already: "I saved a dollar, here I lie." (*He looks around*) Nice house.

PINKERTON: It's artistic. Artistic, don't you think? Like the way the shoji screens slide open to reveal the wet bar and disco mirror ball? Classy, huh? Great for impressing the chicks.

SHARPLESS: "Chicks"? Pinkerton, you're going to be a married man!

PINKERTON: Well, sort of.

SHARPLESS: What do you mean?

PINKERTON: This country—Sharpless, it is okay. You got all these geisha girls running around—

SHARPLESS: I know! I live here!

PINKERTON: Then, you know the marriage laws, right? I split for one month, it's annulled!

SHARPLESS: Leave it to you to read the fine print. Who's the lucky girl?

PINKERTON: Cio-Cio-San. Her friends call her Butterfly. Sharpless, she eats out of my hand!

SHARPLESS: She's probably very hungry.

PINKERTON: Not like American girls. It's true what they say about Oriental girls. They want to be treated bad!

SHARPLESS: Oh, please!

PINKERTON: It's true!

SHARPLESS: Are you serious about this girl?

PINKERTON: I'm marrying her, aren't I?

SHARPLESS: Yes—with generous trade-in terms.

PINKERTON: When I leave, she'll know what it's like to have loved a real man. And I'll even buy her a few nylons.

SHARPLESS: You aren't planning to take her with you?

PINKERTON: Huh? Where?

SHARPLESS: Home!

PINKERTON: You mean, America? Are you crazy? Can you see her trying to buy rice in St. Louis?

SHARPLESS: So, you're not serious.
(*Pause.*)

PINKERTON/GALLIMARD (*As* PINKERTON): CONSUL, I AM A SAILOR IN PORT. (*As* GALLIMARD) They then proceed to sing the famous duet, "The Whole World Over."
(*The duet plays on the speakers.* GALLIMARD, *as* PINKERTON, *lip-syncs his lines from the opera.*)

GALLIMARD: To give a rough translation: "The whole world over, the Yankee travels, casting his anchor wherever he wants. Life's not worth living unless he can win the hearts of the fairest maidens, then hotfoot it off the premises ASAP." (*He turns towards* MARC) In the preceding scene, I played Pinkerton, the womanizing cad, and my friend Marc from school . . . (MARC *bows grandly for our benefit*) played Sharpless, the sensitive soul of reason. In life, however, our positions were usually—no, always—reversed.

SCENE 4
Ecole Nationale. Aix-en-Provence. 1947.

GALLIMARD: No, Marc, I think I'd rather stay home.

MARC: Are you crazy?! We are going to Dad's condo in Marseille! You know what happened last time?

GALLIMARD: Of course I do.

MARC: Of course you don't! You never know. . . . They stripped, Rene!

GALLIMARD: Who stripped?

MARC: The girls!

GALLIMARD: Girls? Who said anything about girls?

MARC: Rene, we're a buncha university guys goin' up to the woods. What are we gonna do—talk philosophy?

GALLIMARD: What girls? Where do you get them?

MARC: Who cares? The point is, they come. On trucks. Packed in like sardines. The back flips open, babes hop out, we're ready to roll.

GALLIMARD: You mean, they just—?

MARC: Before you know it, every last one of them—they're stripped and splashing around my pool. There's no moon out, they can't see what's going on, their boobs are flapping, right? You close your eyes, reach out—it's grab bag, get it? Doesn't matter whose ass is between whose legs, whose teeth are sinking into who. You're just in there, going at it, eyes closed, on and on for as long as you can stand. (*Pause*) Some fun, huh?

GALLIMARD: What happens in the morning?

MARC: In the morning, you're ready to talk some philosophy. (*Beat*) So how 'bout it?

GALLIMARD: Marc, I can't . . . I'm afraid they'll say no—the girls. So I never ask.

MARC: You don't have to ask! That's the beauty—don't you see? They don't have to say yes. It's perfect for a guy like you, really.

GALLIMARD: You go ahead . . . I may come later.

MARC: Hey, Rene—it doesn't matter that you're clumsy and got zits—they're not looking!

GALLIMARD: Thank you very much.

MARC: Wimp.

(MARC *walks over to the other side of the stage, and starts waving and smiling at women in the audience.*)

GALLIMARD (*To us*): We now return to my version of *Madame Butterfly* and the events leading to my recent conviction for treason.

(GALLIMARD *notices* MARC *making lewd gestures.*)

GALLIMARD: Marc, what are you doing?

MARC: Huh? (*Sotto voce*) Rene, there're a lotta great babes out there. They're probably lookin' at me and thinking, "What a dangerous guy."

GALLIMARD: Yes—how could they help but be impressed by your cool sophistication?

(GALLIMARD *pops the Sharpless cap on* MARC'S *head, and points him offstage.* MARC *exits, leering.*)

SCENE 5

M. GALLIMARD'S *cell.*

GALLIMARD: Next, Butterfly makes her entrance. We learn her age—fifteen . . . but very mature for her years.

(*Lights come up on the area where we saw* SONG *dancing at the top of the play. She appears there again, now dressed as Madame Butterfly, moving to the "Love Duet."* GALLIMARD *turns upstage slightly to watch, transfixed.*)

GALLIMARD: But as she glides past him, beautiful, laughing softly behind her fan, don't we who are men sigh with hope? We, who are not handsome, nor brave, nor powerful, yet somehow believe, like Pinkerton, that we deserve a Butterfly. She arrives with all her possessions in the folds of her sleeves, lays them all out, for her man to do with as he pleases. Even her life itself—she bows her head as she whispers that she's not even worth the hundred yen he paid for her. He's already given too much, when we know he's really had to give nothing at all.

(*Music and lights on* SONG *out.* GALLIMARD *sits at his crate.*)

GALLIMARD: In real life, women who put their total worth at less than sixty-six cents are quite hard to find. The closest we come is in the pages of these magazines. (*He reaches into his crate, pulls out a stack of girlie magazines, and begins flipping through them*) Quite a necessity in prison. For three or four dollars, you get seven or eight women.

I first discovered these magazines at my uncle's house. One day, as a boy of twelve. The first time I saw them in his closet . . . all lined up—my body shook. Not with lust—no, with power. Here were women—a shelfful—who would do exactly as I wanted.

(*The "Love Duet" creeps in over the speakers. Special comes up, revealing, not* SONG *this time, but a* PINUP GIRL *in a sexy negligee, her back to us.* GALLIMARD *turns upstage and looks at her.*)

GIRL: I know you're watching me.

GALLIMARD: My throat . . . it's dry.

GIRL: I leave my blinds open every night before I go to bed.

GALLIMARD: I can't move.

GIRL: I leave my blinds open and the lights on.

GALLIMARD: I'm shaking. My skin is hot, but my penis is soft. Why?

GIRL: I stand in front of the window.

GALLIMARD: What is she going to do?

GIRL: I toss my hair, and I let my lips part . . . barely.

GALLIMARD: I shouldn't be seeing this. It's so dirty. I'm so bad.

GIRL: Then, slowly, I lift off my nightdress.

GALLIMARD: Oh, god. I can't believe it. I can't—

GIRL: I toss it to the ground.

GALLIMARD: Now, she's going to walk away. She's going to—

GIRL: I stand there, in the light, displaying myself.

GALLIMARD: No. She's—why is she naked?

GIRL: To you.

GALLIMARD: In front of a window? This is wrong. No—

GIRL: Without shame.

GALLIMARD: No, she must . . . like it.

GIRL: I like it.

GALLIMARD: She . . . she wants me to see.

GIRL: I want you to see.

GALLIMARD: I can't believe it! She's getting excited!

GIRL: I can't see you. You can do whatever you want.

GALLIMARD: I can't do a thing. Why?

GIRL: What would you like me to do . . . next?

(*Lights go down on her. Music off. Silence, as* GAL-LIMARD *puts away his magazines. Then he resumes talking to us.*)

GALLIMARD: Act Two begins with Butterfly staring at the ocean. Pinkerton's been called back to the U.S., and he's given his wife a detailed schedule of his plans. In the column marked "return date," he's written "when the robins nest." This failed to ignite her suspicions. Now, three years have passed without a peep from him. Which brings a response from her faithful servant, Suzuki.

(COMRADE CHIN *enters, playing* SUZUKI.)

SUZUKI: Girl, he's a loser. What'd he ever give you? Nineteen cents and those ugly Day-Glo stockings? Look, it's finished! Kaput! Done! And you should be glad! I mean, the guy was a woofer! He tried before, you know—before he met you, he went down to geisha central and plunked down his spare change in front of the usual candidates—everyone else gagged! These are hungry prostitutes, and they were not interested, get the picture? Now, stop slathering when an American ship sails in, and let's make some bucks—I mean, yen! We are broke!

Now, what about Yamadori? Hey, hey—don't look away—the man is a prince—figuratively, and, what's even better, literally. He's rich, he's handsome, he says he'll die if you don't marry him—and he's even willing to overlook the little fact that you've been deflowered all over the place by a foreign devil. What do you mean, "But he's Japanese?" You're Japanese! You think you've been touched by the whitey god? He was a sailor with dirty hands!

(SUZUKI *stalks offstage.*)

GALLIMARD: She's also visited by Consul Sharpless, sent by Pinkerton on a minor errand.

(MARC *enters, as* SHARPLESS.)

SHARPLESS: I hate this job.

GALLIMARD: This Pinkerton—he doesn't show up personally to tell his wife he's abandoning her. No, he sends a government diplomat . . . at taxpayer's expense.

SHARPLESS: Butterfly? Butterfly? I have some bad—I'm going to be ill. Butterfly, I came to tell you—

GALLIMARD: Butterfly says she knows he'll return and if he doesn't she'll kill herself rather than go back to her own people. (*Beat*) This causes a lull in the conversation.

SHARPLESS: Let's put it this way . . .

GALLIMARD: Butterfly runs into the next room, and returns holding—

(*Sound cue: a baby crying.* SHARPLESS, *"seeing" this, backs away.*)

SHARPLESS: Well, good. Happy to see things going so well. I suppose I'll be going now. Ta ta. Ciao. (*He turns away. Sound cue out*) I hate this job. (*He exits*)

GALLIMARD: At that moment, Butterfly spots in the harbor an American ship—the *Abramo Lincoln!* (*Music cue: "The Flower Duet."* SONG, *still dressed as* BUTTERFLY, *changes into a wedding kimono, moving to the music.*)

GALLIMARD: This is the moment that redeems her years of waiting. With Suzuki's help, they cover the room with flowers—

(CHIN, *as* SUZUKI, *trudges onstage and drops a lone flower without much enthusiasm.*)

GALLIMARD: —and she changes into her wedding dress to prepare for Pinkerton's arrival.

(SUZUKI *helps* BUTTERFLY *change.* HELGA *enters, and helps* GALLIMARD *change into a tuxedo.*)

GALLIMARD: I married a woman older than myself—Helga.

HELGA: My father was ambassador to Australia. I grew up among criminals and kangaroos.

GALLIMARD: Hearing that brought me to the altar—

(HELGA *exits.*)

GALLIMARD: —where I took a vow renouncing love. No fantasy woman would ever want me, so, yes, I would settle for a quick leap up the career ladder. Passion, I banish, and in its place—practicality!

But my vows had long since lost their charm by the time we arrived in China. The sad truth is that all men want a beautiful woman, and the uglier the man, the greater the want.

(SUZUKI *makes final adjustments of* BUTTERFLY'S *costume, as does* GALLIMARD *of his tuxedo.*)

GALLIMARD: I married late, at age thirty-one. I was faithful to my marriage for eight years. Until the day when, as a junior-level diplomat in puritanical Peking, in a parlor at the German ambassador's house, during the "Reign of a Hundred Flowers," I first saw her . . . singing the death scene from *Madame Butterfly*.

(SUZUKI *runs offstage.*)

SCENE 6
German ambassador's house. Being. 1960.

*The upstage special area now becomes a stage. Several chairs face upstage, representing seating for some twenty guests in the parlor. A few "diplomats"—*RENEE, MARC, TOULON—*in formal dress enter and take seats.*

GALLIMARD *also sits down, but turns towards us and continues to talk. Orchestral accompaniment on the tape is now replaced by a simple piano.* SONG *picks up the death scene from the point where* BUTTERFLY *uncovers the hara-kiri knife.*

GALLIMARD: The ending is pitiful. Pinkerton, in an act of great courage, stays home and sends his American wife to pick up Butterfly's child. The truth, long deferred, has come up to her door.

(SONG, *playing* BUTTERFLY, *sings the lines from the opera in her own voice—which, though not classical, should be decent.*)

SONG: "Con onor muore/ chi non puo serbar/ vita con onore."

GALLIMARD (*Simultaneously*): "Death with honor/ Is better than life/ Life with dishonor."

(*The stage is illuminated; we are now completely within an elegant diplomat's residence.* SONG *proceeds to play out an abbreviated death scene. Everyone in the room applauds.* SONG, *shyly, takes her bows. Others in the room rush to congratulate her.* GALLIMARD *remains with us.*)

GALLIMARD: They say in opera the voice is everything. That's probably why I'd never before enjoyed opera. Here . . . here was a Butterfly with little or no voice—but she had the grace, the delicacy . . . I believed this girl. I believed her suffering. I wanted to take her in my arms—so delicate, even I could protect her, take her home, pamper her until she smiled.

(*Over the course of the preceeding speech,* SONG *has broken from the upstage crowd and moved directly upstage of* GALLIMARD.)

SONG: Excuse me. Monsieur . . . ?

(GALLIMARD *turns upstage, shocked.*)

GALLIMARD: Oh! Gallimard. Mademoiselle . . . ? A beautiful . . .

SONG: Song Liling.

GALLIMARD: A beautiful performance.

SONG: Oh, please.

GALLIMARD: I usually—

SONG: You make me blush. I'm no opera singer at all.

GALLIMARD: I usually don't like *Butterfly.*

SONG: I can't blame you in the least.

GALLIMARD: I mean, the story—

SONG: Ridiculous.

GALLIMARD: I like the story, but . . . what?

SONG: Oh, you like it?

GALLIMARD: I . . . what I mean is, I've always seen it played by huge women in so much bad makeup.

SONG: Bad makeup is not unique to the West.

GALLIMARD: But, who can believe them?

SONG: And you believe me?

GALLIMARD: Absolutely. You were utterly convincing. It's the first time—

SONG: Convincing? As a Japanese woman? The Japanese used hundreds of our people for medical experiments during the war, you know. But I gather such an irony is lost on you.

GALLIMARD: No! I was about to say, it's the first time I've seen the beauty of the story.

SONG: Really?

GALLIMARD: Of her death. It's a . . . a pure sacrifice. He's unworthy, but what can she do? She loves him . . . so much. It's a very beautiful story.

SONG: Well, yes, to a Westerner.

GALLIMARD: Excuse me?

SONG: It's one of your favorite fantasies, isn't it? The submissive Oriental woman and the cruel white man.

GALLIMARD: Well, I didn't quite mean . . .

SONG: Consider it this way: what would you say if a blonde homecoming queen fell in love with a short Japanese businessman? He treats her cruelly, then goes home for three years, during which time she prays to his picture and turns down marriage from a young Kennedy. Then, when she learns he has remarried, she kills herself. Now, I believe you would consider this girl to be a deranged idiot, correct? But because it's an Oriental who kills herself for a Westerner—ah!—you find it beautiful. (*Silence.*)

GALLIMARD: Yes . . . well . . . I see your point . . .

SONG: I will never do Butterfly again, Monsieur Gallimard. If you wish to see some real theatre, come to the Peking Opera sometime. Expand your mind.

(SONG *walks offstage.*)

GALLIMARD (*To us*): So much for protecting her in my big Western arms.

SCENE 7

M. GALLIMARD'*s apartment. Beijing. 1960.*

GALLIMARD *changes from his tux into a casual suit.* HELGA *enters.*

GALLIMARD: The Chinese are an incredibly arrogant people.

HELGA: They warned us about that in Paris, remember?

GALLIMARD: Even Parisians consider them arrogant. That's a switch.

HELGA: What is it that Madame Su says? "We are a very old civilization." I never know if she's talking about her country or herself.

GALLIMARD: I walk around here, all I hear every day, everywhere is how old this culture is. The fact that "old" may be synonymous with "senile" doesn't occur to them.

HELGA: You're not going to change them. "East is east, west is west, and . . . " whatever that guy said.

GALLIMARD: It's just that—silly. I met . . . at Ambassador Koening's tonight—you should've been there.

HELGA: Koening? Oh god, no. Did he enchant you all again with the history of Bavaria?

GALLIMARD: No. I met, I suppose, the Chinese equivalent of a diva. She's a singer in the Chinese opera.

HELGA: They have an opera, too? Do they sing in Chinese? Or maybe—in Italian?

GALLIMARD: Tonight, she did sing in Italian.

HELGA: How'd she manage that?

GALLIMARD: She must've been educated in the West before the Revolution. Her French is very good also. Anyway, she sang the death scene from *Madame Butterfly.*

HELGA: *Madame Butterfly!* Then I should have come. (*She begins humming, floating around the room as if dragging long kimono sleeves*) Did she have a nice costume? I think it's a classic piece of music.

GALLIMARD: That's what I thought, too. Don't let her hear you say that.

HELGA: What's wrong?

GALLIMARD: Evidently the Chinese hate it.

HELGA: She hated it, but she performed it anyway? Is she perverse?

GALLIMARD: They hate it because the white man gets the girl. Sour grapes if you ask me.

HELGA: Politics again? Why can't they just hear it as a piece of beautiful music? So, what's in their opera?

GALLIMARD: I don't know. But, whatever it is, I'm sure it must be *old.*

(HELGA *exits.*)

SCENE 8

Chinese opera house and the streets of Beijing. 1960. The sound of gongs clanging fills the stage.

GALLIMARD: My wife's innocent question kept ringing in my ears. I asked around, but no one knew anything about the Chinese opera. It took four weeks, but my curiosity overcame my cowardice. This Chinese diva—this unwilling Butterfly—what did she do to make her so proud?

The room was hot, and full of smoke. Wrinkled faces, old women, teeth missing—a man with a growth on his neck, like a human toad. All smiling, pipes falling from their mouths, cracking nuts between their teeth, a live chicken pecking at my foot—all looking, screaming, gawking . . . at her.

(*The upstage area is suddenly hit with a harsh white light. It has become the stage for the Chinese opera performance. Two dancers enter, along with* SONG. GALLIMARD *stands apart, watching.* SONG *glides gracefully amidst the two dancers. Drums suddenly slam to a halt.* SONG *strikes a pose, looking straight at* GALLIMARD. *Dancers exit. Light change. Pause, then* SONG *walks right off the stage and straight up to* GALLIMARD.)

SONG: Yes. You. White man. I'm looking straight at you.

GALLIMARD: Me?

SONG: You see any other white men? It was too easy to spot you. How often does a man in my audience come in a tie?

(SONG *starts to remove her costume. Underneath, she wears simple baggy clothes. They are now backstage. The show is over.*)

SONG: So, you are an adventurous imperialist?

GALLIMARD: I . . . thought it would further my education.

SONG: It took you four weeks. Why?

GALLIMARD: I've been busy.

SONG: Well, education has always been undervalued in the West, hasn't it?

GALLIMARD (*Laughing*): I don't think it's true.

SONG: No, you wouldn't. You're a Westerner. How can you objectively judge your own values?

GALLIMARD: I think it's possible to achieve some distance.

SONG: Do you? (*Pause*) It stinks in here. Let's go.

GALLIMARD: These are the smells of your loyal fans.

SONG: I love them for being my fans, I hate the smell they leave behind. I too can distance myself from my people. (*She looks around, then whispers in his ear*) "Art for the masses" is a shitty excuse to keep artists poor. (*She pops a cigarette in her mouth*) Be a gentleman, will you? And light my cigarette.

(GALLIMARD *fumbles for a match.*)

GALLIMARD: I don't . . . smoke.

SONG (*Lighting her own*): Your loss. Had you lit my cigarette, I might have blown a puff of smoke right between your eyes. Come.

(*They start to walk about the stage. It is a summer night on the Beijing streets. Sounds of the city play on the house speakers.*)

SONG: How I wish there were even a tiny cafe to sit in. With cappuccinos, and men in tuxedos and bad expatriate jazz.

GALLIMARD: If my history serves me correctly, you weren't even allowed into the clubs in Shanghai before the Revolution.

SONG: Your history serves you poorly, Monsieur Gallimard. True, there were signs reading "No dogs and Chinamen." But a woman, especially a delicate Oriental woman—we always go where we please. Could you imagine it otherwise? Clubs in China filled with pasty, big-thighed white women, while thousands of slender lotus blossoms wait just outside the door? Never. The clubs would be empty. (*Beat*) We have always held a certain fascination for you Caucasian men, have we not?

GALLIMARD: But . . . that fascination is imperialist, or so you tell me.

SONG: Do you believe everything I tell you? Yes. It is always imperialist. But sometimes . . . sometimes, it is also mutual. Oh—this is my flat.

GALLIMARD: I didn't even—

SONG: Thank you. Come another time and we will further expand your mind.

(SONG *exits.* GALLIMARD *continues roaming the streets as he speaks to us.*)

GALLIMARD: What was that? What did she mean, "Sometimes . . . it is mutual?" Women do not flirt with me. And I normally can't talk to them. But tonight, I held up my end of the conversation.

SCENE 9

GALLIMARD'*s bedroom. Beijing. 1960.* HELGA *enters.*

HELGA: You didn't tell me you'd be home late.

GALLIMARD: I didn't intend to. Something came up.

HELGA: Oh? Like what?

GALLIMARD: I went to the . . . to the Dutch ambassador's home.

HELGA: Again?

GALLIMARD: There was a reception for a visiting scholar. He's writing a six-volume treatise on the Chinese revolution. We all gathered that meant he'd have to live here long enough to actually write six volumes, and we all expressed our deepest sympathies.

HELGA: Well, I had a good night too. I went with the ladies to a martial arts demonstration. Some of those men—when they break those thick boards—(*She mimes fanning herself*) whoo-whoo!

(HELGA *exits. Lights dim.*)

GALLIMARD: I lied to my wife. Why? I've never had any reason to lie before. But what reason did I have tonight? I didn't do anything wrong. That night, I had a dream. Other people, I've been told, have dreams where angels appear. Or dragons, or Sophia Loren in a towel. In my dream, Marc from school appeared.

(MARC *enters, in a nightshirt and cap.*)

MARC: Rene! You met a girl!

(GALLIMARD *and* MARC *stumble down the Beijing streets. Night sounds over the speakers.*)

GALLIMARD: It's not that amazing, thank you.

MARC: No! It's so monumental, I heard about it halfway around the world in my sleep!

GALLIMARD: I've met girls before, you know.

MARC: Name one. I've come across time and space to congratulate you. (*He hands* GALLIMARD *a bottle of wine*)

GALLIMARD: Marc, this is expensive.

MARC: On those rare occasions when you become a formless spirit, why not steal the best?

(MARC *pops open the bottle, begins to share it with* GALLIMARD.)

GALLIMARD: You embarrass me. She . . . there's no reason to think she likes me.

MARC: "Sometimes, it is mutual"?

GALLIMARD: Oh.

MARC: "Mutual"? "Mutual"? What does that mean?

GALLIMARD: You heard!

MARC: It means the money is in the bank, you only have to write the check!

GALLIMARD: I am a married man!

MARC: And an excellent one too. I cheated after . . . six months. Then again and again, until now— three hundred girls in twelve years.

GALLIMARD: I don't think we should hold that up as a model.

MARC: Of course not! My life—it is disgusting! Phooey! Phooey! But, you—you are the model husband.

GALLIMARD: Anyway, it's impossible. I'm a foreigner.

MARC: Ah, yes. She cannot love you, it is taboo, but something deep inside her heart . . . she cannot help herself . . . she must surrender to you. It is her destiny.

GALLIMARD: How do you imagine all this?

MARC: The same way you do. It's an old story. It's in our blood. They fear us, Rene. Their women fear us. And their men—their men hate us. And, you know something? They are all correct.

(*They spot a light in a window.*)

MARC: There! There, Rene!

GALLIMARD: It's her window.

MARC: Late at night—it burns. The light—it burns for you.

GALLIMARD: I won't look. It's not respectful.

MARC: We don't have to be respectful. We're foreign devils.

(*Enter* SONG, *in a sheer robe. The "One Fine Day" aria creeps in over the speakers. With her back to us,* SONG *mimes attending to her toilette. Her robe comes loose, revealing her white shoulders.*)

MARC: All your life you've waited for a beautiful girl who would lay down for you. All your life you've smiled like a saint when it's happened to every other man you know. And you see them in magazines and you see them in movies. And you wonder, what's wrong with me? Will anyone beautiful ever want me? As the years pass, your hair thins and you struggle to hold onto even your hopes. Stop struggling, Rene. The wait is over. (*He exits*)

GALLIMARD: Marc? Marc?

(*At that moment,* SONG, *her back still towards us, drops her robe. A second of her naked back, then a sound cue: a phone ringing, very loud. Blackout, followed in the next beat by a special up on the bedroom area, where a phone now sits.* GALLIMARD *stumbles across the stage and picks up the phone. Sound cue out. Over the course of his conversation, area lights fill in the vicinity of his bed. It is the following morning.*)

GALLIMARD: Yes? Hello?

SONG (*Offstage*): Is it very early?

GALLIMARD: Why, yes.

SONG (*Offstage*): How early?

GALLIMARD: It's . . . it's 5:30. Why are you—?

SONG (*Offstage*): But it's light outside. Already.

GALLIMARD: It is. The sun must be in confusion today.
  (*Over the course of* SONG's *next speech, her upstage special comes up again. She sits in a chair, legs crossed, in a robe, telephone to her ear.*)

SONG: I waited until I saw the sun. That was as much discipline as I could manage for one night. Do you forgive me?

GALLIMARD: Of course . . . for what?

SONG: Then I'll ask you quickly. Are you really interested in the opera?

GALLIMARD: Why, yes. Yes I am.

SONG: Then come again next Thursday. I am playing *The Drunken Beauty*. May I count on you?

GALLIMARD: Yes. You may.

SONG: Perfect. Well, I must be getting to bed. I'm exhausted. It's been a very long night for me.
  (SONG *hangs up; special on her goes off.* GALLIMARD *begins to dress for work.*)

SCENE 10

SONG LILING's *apartment. Beijing. 1960.*

GALLIMARD: I returned to the opera that next week, and the week after that . . . she keeps our meetings so short—perhaps fifteen, twenty minutes at most. So I am left each week with a thirst which is intensified. In this way, fifteen weeks have gone by. I am starting to doubt the words of my friend Marc. But no, not really. In my heart, I know she has . . . an interest in me. I suspect this is her way. She is outwardly bold and outspoken, yet her heart is shy and afraid. It is the Oriental in her at war with her Western education.

SONG (*Offstage*): I will be out in an instant. Ask the servant for anything you want.

GALLIMARD: Tonight, I have finally been invited to enter her apartment. Though the idea is almost beyond belief, I believe she is afraid of me.
  (GALLIMARD *looks around the room. He picks up a picture in a frame, studies it. Without his noticing,* SONG *enters, dressed elegantly in a black gown from the twenties. She stands in the doorway looking like Anna May Wong.*)

SONG: That is my father.

GALLIMARD (*Surprised*): Mademoiselle Song . . .
  (*She glides up to him, snatches away the picture.*)

SONG: It is very good that he did not live to see the Revolution. They would, no doubt, have made him kneel on broken glass. Not that he didn't deserve such a punishment. But he is my father. I would've hated to see it happen.

GALLIMARD: I'm very honored that you've allowed me to visit your home.
  (SONG *curtsys.*)

SONG: Thank you. Oh! Haven't you been poured any tea?

GALLIMARD: I'm really not—

SONG (*To her offstage servant*): Shu-Fang! Cha! Kwai-lah! (*To* GALLIMARD) I'M SORRY. YOU WANT EVERYTHING TO BE PERFECT—

GALLIMARD: Please.

SONG: —and before the evening even begins—

GALLIMARD: I'm really not thirsty.

SONG: —it's ruined.

GALLIMARD (*Sharply*): Mademoiselle Song!
  (SONG *sits down.*)

SONG: I'm sorry.

GALLIMARD: What are you apologizing for now?
  (*Pause;* SONG *starts to giggle.*)

SONG: I don't know!
  (GALLIMARD *laughs.*)

GALLIMARD: Exactly my point.

SONG: Oh, I am silly. Lightheaded. I promise not to apologize for anything else tonight, do you hear me?

GALLIMARD: That's a good girl.
  (SHU-FANG, *a servant girl, comes out with a tea tray and starts to pour.*)

SONG (*To* SHU-FANG): No! I'LL POUR MYSELF FOR THE GENTLEMAN!
  (SHU-FANG, *staring at* GALLIMARD, *exits.*)

SONG: No, I . . . I don't even know why I invited you up.

GALLIMARD: Well, I'm glad you did.
  (SONG *looks around the room.*)

SONG: There is an element of danger to your presence.

GALLIMARD: Oh?

SONG: You must know.

GALLIMARD: It doesn't concern me. We both know why I'm here.

SONG: It doesn't concern me either. No . . . well perhaps . . .

GALLIMARD: What?

SONG: Perhaps I am slightly afraid of scandal.

GALLIMARD: What are we doing?

SONG: I'm entertaining you. In my parlor.

GALLIMARD: In France, that would hardly—

SONG: France. France is a country living in the modern era. Perhaps even ahead of it. China is a nation whose soul is firmly rooted two thousand years in the past. What I do, even pouring the tea for you now . . . it has . . . implications. The walls and windows say so. Even my own heart, strapped inside this Western dress . . . even it says things—things I don't care to hear.

(SONG *hands* GALLIMARD *a cup of tea.* GALLIMARD *puts his hand over both the teacup and* SONG's *hand.*)

GALLIMARD: This is a beautiful dress.

SONG: Don't.

GALLIMARD: What?

SORTS: I don't even know if it looks right on me.

GALLIMARD: Believe me—

SONG: You are from France. You see so many beautiful women.

GALLIMARD: France? Since when are the European women—?

SONG: Oh! What am I trying to do, anyway?!

(SONG *runs to the door, composes herself, then turns towards* GALLIMARD.)

SONG: Monsieur Gallimard, perhaps you should go.

GALLIMARD: But . . . why?

SONG: There's something wrong about this.

GALLIMARD: I don't see what.

SONG: I feel . . . I am not myself.

GALLIMARD: No. You're nervous.

SONG: Please. Hard as I try to be modern, to speak like a man, to hold a Western woman's strong face up to my own . . . in the end, I fail. A small, frightened heart beats too quickly and gives me away. Monsieur Gallimard, I'm a Chinese girl. I've never . . . never invited a man up to my flat before. The forwardness of my actions makes my skin burn.

GALLIMARD: What are you afraid of? Certainly not me, I hope.

SONG: I'm a modest girl.

GALLIMARD: I know. And very beautiful. (*He touches her hair*)

SONG: Please—go now. The next time you see me, I shall again be myself.

GALLIMARD: I like you the way you are right now.

SONG: You are a cad.

GALLIMARD: What do you expect? I'm a foreign devil.

(GALLIMARD *walks downstage.* SONG *exits.*)

GALLIMARD (*To us*): Did you hear the way she talked about Western women? Much differently than the first night. She does—she feels inferior to them—and to me.

SCENE 11

The French embassy. Beijing. 1960. GALLIMARD *moves towards a desk.*

GALLIMARD: I determined to try an experiment. In *Madame Butterfly*, Cio-Cio-San fears that the Western man who catches a butterfly will pierce its heart with a needle, then leave it to perish. I began to wonder: had I, too, caught a butterfly who would writhe on a needle?

(MARC *enters, dressed as a bureaucrat, holding a stack of papers. As* GALLIMARD *speaks,* MARC *hands papers to him. He peruses, then signs, stamps or rejects them.*)

GALLIMARD: Over the next five weeks, I worked like a dynamo. I stopped going to the opera, I didn't phone or write her. I knew this little flower was waiting for me to call, and, as I wickedly refused to do so, I felt for the first time that rush of power—the absolute power of a man.

(MARC *continues acting as the bureaucrat, but he now speaks as himself.*)

MARC: Rene! It's me!

GALLIMARD: Marc—I hear your voice everywhere now. Even in the midst of work.

MARC: That's because I'm watching you—all the time.

GALLIMARD: You were always the most popular guy in school.

MARC: Well, there's no guarantee of failure in life like happiness in high school. Somehow I knew I'd end up in the suburbs working for Renault and you'd be in the Orient picking exotic women off the trees. And they say there's no justice.

GALLIMARD: That's why you were my friend?

MARC: I gave you a little of my life, so that now you can give me some of yours (*Pause*) Remember Isabelle?

GALLIMARD: Of course I remember! She was my first experience.

MARC: We all wanted to ball her. But she only wanted me.

GALLIMARD: I had her.

MARC: Right. You balled her.

GALLIMARD: You were the only one who ever believed me.

MARC: Well, there's a good reason for that. (*Beat*) C'mon. You must've guessed.

GALLIMARD: You told me to wait in the bushes by the cafeteria that night. The next thing I knew, she was on me. Dress up in the air.

MARC: She never wore underwear.

GALLIMARD: My arms were pinned to the dirt.

MARC: She loved the superior position. A girl ahead of her time.

GALLIMARD: I looked up, and there was this woman . . . bouncing up and down on my loins.

MARC: Screaming, right?

GALLIMARD: Screaming, and breaking off the branches all around me, and pounding my butt up and down into the dirt.

MARC: Huffing and puffing like a locomotive.

GALLIMARD: And in the middle of all this, the leaves were getting into my mouth, my legs were losing circulation, I thought, "God. So this is *it?*"

MARC: You thought that?

GALLIMARD: Well, I was worried about my legs falling off.

MARC: You didn't have a good time?

GALLIMARD: No, that's not what I—I had a great time!

MARC: You're sure?

GALLIMARD: Yeah. Really.

MARC: 'Cuz I wanted you to have a good time.

GALLIMARD: I did.

(*Pause.*)

MARC: Shit. (*Pause*) When all is said and done, she was kind of a lousy lay, wasn't she? I mean, there was a lot of energy there, but you never

knew what she was doing with it. Like when she yelled "I'm coming!"—hell, it was so loud, you wanted to go "Look, it's not that big a deal."

GALLIMARD: I got scared. I thought she meant someone was actually coming. (*Pause*) But, Marc?

MARC: What?

GALLIMARD: Thanks.

MARC: Oh, don't mention it.

GALLIMARD: It was my first experience.

MARC: Yeah. You got her.

GALLIMARD: I got her.

MARC: Wait! Look at that letter again!

(GALLIMARD *picks up one of the papers he's been stamping, and rereads it.*)

GALLIMARD (*To us*): After six weeks, they began to arrive. The letters.

(*Upstage special on* SONG, *as* MADAME BUTTERFLY. *The scene is underscored by the "Love Duet."*)

SONG: Did we fight? I do not know. Is the opera no longer of interest to you? Please come—my audiences miss the white devil in their midst.

(GALLIMARD *looks up from the letter, towards us.*)

GALLIMARD (*To us*): A concession, but much too dignified. (*Beat; he discards the letter*) I skipped the opera again that week to complete a position paper on trade.

(*The bureaucrat hands him another letter.*)

SONG: Six weeks have passed since last we met. Is this your practice—to leave friends in the lurch? Sometimes I hate you, sometimes I hate myself, but always I miss you.

GALLIMARD (*To us*): Better, but I don't like the way she calls me "friend." When a woman calls a man her "friend," she's calling him a eunuch or a homosexual. (*Beat; he discards the letter*) I was absent from the opera for the seventh week, feeling a sudden urge to clean out my files.

(*Bureaucrat hands him another letter.*)

SONG: Your rudeness is beyond belief. I don't deserve this cruelty. Don't bother to call. I'll have you turned away at the door.

GALLIMARD (*To us*): I didn't. (*He discards the letter; bureaucrat hands him another*) And then finally, the letter that concluded my experiment.

SONG: I am out of words. I can hide behind dignity no longer. What do you want? I have already given you my shame.

(GALLIMARD *gives the letter back to* MARC, *slowly. Special on* SONG *fades out.*)

GALLIMARD (*To us*): Reading it, I became suddenly ashamed. Yes, my experiment had been a success. She was turning on my needle. But the victory seemed hollow.

MARC: Hollow?! Are you crazy?

GALLIMARD: Nothing, Marc. Please go away.

MARC (*Exiting, with papers*): Haven't I taught you anything?

GALLIMARD: "I have already given you my shame." I had to attend a reception that evening. On the way, I felt sick. If there is a God, surely he would punish me now. I had finally gained power over a beautiful woman, only to abuse it cruelly. There must be justice in the world. I had the strange feeling that the ax would fall this very evening.

SCENE 12

AMBASSADOR TOULON's *residence. Beijing. 1960.*

Sound cue: party noises. Light change. We are now in a spacious residence. TOULON, *the French ambassador, enters and taps* GALLIMARD *on the shoulder.*

TOULON: Gallimard? Can I have a word? Over here.

GALLIMARD (*To us*): Manuel Toulon. French ambassador to China. He likes to think of us all as his children. Rather like God.

TOULON: Look, Gallimard, there's not much to say. I've liked you. From the day you walked in. You were no leader, but you were tidy and efficient.

GALLIMARD: Thank you, sir.

TOULON: Don't jump the gun. Okay, our needs in China are changing. It's embarrassing that we lost Indochina. Someone just wasn't on the ball there. I don't mean you personally, of course.

GALLIMARD: Thank you, sir.

TOULON: We're going to be doing a lot more information-gathering in the future. The nature of our work here is changing. Some people are just going to have to go. It's nothing personal.

GALLIMARD: Oh.

TOULON: Want to know a secret? Vice-Consul LeBon is being transferred.

GALLIMARD (*To us*): My immediate superior!

TOULON: And most of his department.

GALLIMARD (*To us*): Just as I feared! God has seen my evil heart—

TOULON: But not you.

GALLIMARD (*To us*): —and he's taking her away just as . . . (*To* toulon) Excuse me, sir?

TOULON: Scare you? I think I did. Cheer up, Gallimard. I want you to replace LeBon as vice-consul.

GALLIMARD: You—? Yes, well, thank you, sir.

TOULON: Anytime.

GALLIMARD: I . . . accept with great humility.

TOULON: Humility won't be part of the job. You're going to coordinate the revamped intelligence division. Want to know a secret? A year ago, you would've been out. But the past few months, I don't know how it happened, you've become this new aggressive confident . . . thing. And they also tell me you get along with the Chinese. So I think you're a lucky man, Gallimard. Congratulations.

(*They shake hands.* TOULON *exits. Party noises out.* GALLIMARD *stumbles across a darkened stage.*)

GALLIMARD: Vice-consul? Impossible! As I stumbled out of the party, I saw it written across the sky: There is no God. Or, no—say that there is a God. But that God . . . understands. Of course! God who creates Eve to serve Adam, who blesses Solomon with his harem but ties Jezebel to a burning bed—that God is a man. And he understands! At age thirty-nine, I was suddenly initiated into the way of the world.

SCENE 13

SONG LILING's *apartment. Being. 1960.*

SONG *enters, in a sheer dressing gown.*

SONG: Are you crazy?

GALLIMARD: Mademoiselle Song—

SONG: To come here—at this hour? After . . . after eight weeks?

GALLIMARD: It's the most amazing—

SONG: You bang on my door? Scare my servants, scandalize the neighbors?

GALLIMARD: I've been promoted. To vice-consul. . . .
(*Pause.*)

SONG: And what is that supposed to mean to me?

GALLIMARD: Are you my Butterfly?

SONG: What are you saying?

GALLIMARD: I've come tonight for an answer: are you my Butterfly?

SONG: Don't you know already?

GALLIMARD: I want you to say it.

SONG: I don't want to say it.

GALLIMARD: So, that is your answer?

SONG: You know how I feel about—

GALLIMARD: I do remember one thing.

SONG: What?

GALLIMARD: In the letter I received today.

SONG: Don't.

GALLIMARD: "I have already given you my shame."

SONG: It's enough that I even wrote it.

GALLIMARD: Well, then—

SONG: I shouldn't have it splashed across my face.

GALLIMARD: —If that's all true—

SONG: Stop!

GALLIMARD: Then what is one more short answer?

SONG: I don't want to!

GALLIMARD: Are you my Butterfly? (*Silence; he crosses the room and begins to touch her hair*) I want from you honesty. There should be nothing false between us. No false pride.
(*Pause.*)

SONG: Yes, I am. I am your Butterfly.

GALLIMARD: Then let me be honest with you. It is because of you that I was promoted tonight. You have changed my life forever. My little Butterfly, there should be no more secrets: I love you.
(*He starts to kiss her roughly. She resists slightly.*)

SONG: No . . . no . . . gently . . . please, I've never . . .

GALLIMARD: No?

SONG: I've tried to appear experienced, but . . . the truth is . . . no.

GALLIMARD: Are you cold?

SONG: Yes. Cold.

GALLIMARD: Then we will go very, very slowly.
(*He starts to caress her; her gown begins to open.*)

SONG: No . . . let me . . . keep my clothes . . .

GALLIMARD: But . . .

SONG: Please . . . it all frightens me. I'm a modest Chinese girl.

GALLIMARD: My poor little treasure.

SONG: I am your treasure. Though inexperienced, I am not . . . ignorant. They teach us things, our mothers, about pleasing a man.

GALLIMARD: Yes?

SONG: I'll do my best to make you happy. Turn off the lights.
(GALLIMARD *gets up and heads for a lamp.* SONG, *propped up on one elbow, tosses her hair back and smiles.*)

SONG: Monsieur Gallimard?

GALLIMARD: Yes, Butterfly?

SONG: "Vieni, vieni!"

GALLIMARD: "Come, darling."

SONG: "Ah! Dolce notte!"

GALLIMARD: "Beautiful night."

SONG: "Tutto estatico d'amor ride il ciel!"

GALLIMARD: "All ecstatic with love, the heavens are filled with laughter."
(*He turns off the lamp. Blackout.*)

ACT TWO

SCENE 1

M. GALLIMARD's *cell. Paris. Present.*

Lights up on GALLIMARD. *He sits in his cell, reading from a leaflet.*

GALLIMARD: This, from a contemporary critic's commentary on *Madame Butterfly*: "Pinkerton suffers from . . . being an obnoxious bounder whom every man in the audience itches to kick." Bully for us men in the audience! Then, in the same note: "Butterfly is the most irresistibly appealing of Puccini's 'Little Women.' Watching the succession of her humiliations is like watching a child under torture." (*He tosses the pamphlet over his shoulder*) I suggest that, while we men may all want to kick Pinkerton, very few of us would pass up the opportunity to be Pinkerton.
(GALLIMARD *moves out of his cell.*)

SCENE 2

GALLIMARD *and* BUTTERFLY's *flat. Beijing. 1960.*

We are in a simple but well-decorated parlor. GALLIMARD *moves to sit on a sofa, while* SONG, *dressed in a chong sam, enters and curls up at his feet.*

GALLIMARD (*To us*): We secured a flat on the outskirts of Peking. Butterfly, as I was calling her now, decorated our "home" with Western furniture and Chinese antiques. And there, on a few stolen afternoons or evenings each week, Butterfly commenced her education.

SONG: The Chinese men—they keep us down.

GALLIMARD: Even in the "New Society"?

SONG: In the "New Society," we are all kept ignorant equally. That's one of the exciting things about loving a Western man. I know you are not threatened by a woman's education.

GALLIMARD: I'm no saint, Butterfly.

SONG: But you come from a progressive society.

GALLIMARD: We're not always reminding each other how "old" we are, if that's what you mean.

SONG: Exactly. We Chinese—once, I suppose, it is true, we ruled the world. But so what? How much more exciting to be part of the society ruling the world today. Tell me—what's happening in Vietnam?

GALLIMARD: Oh, Butterfly—you want me to bring my work home?

SONG: I want to know what you know. To be impressed by my man. It's not the particulars so much as the fact that you're making decisions which change the shape of the world.

GALLIMARD: Not the world. At best, a small corner.
(TOULON *enters, and sits at a desk upstage.*)

SCENE 3
French embassy. Beijing. 1961.

GALLIMARD *moves downstage, to* TOULON's *desk.* SONG *remains upstage, watching.*

TOULON: And a more troublesome corner is hard to imagine.

GALLIMARD: So, the Americans plan to begin bombing?

TOULON: This is very secret, Gallimard: yes. The Americans don't have an embassy here. They're asking us to be their eyes and ears. Say Jack Kennedy signed an order to bomb North Vietnam, Laos. How would the Chinese react?

GALLIMARD: I think the Chinese will squawk—

TOULON: Uh-huh.

GALLIMARD:—but, in their hearts, they don't even like Ho Chi Minh.
(*Pause.*)

TOULON: What a bunch of jerks. Vietnam was our colony. Not only didn't the Americans help us fight to keep them, but now, seven years later, they've come back to grab the territory for themselves. It's very irritating.

GALLIMARD: With all due respect, sir, why should the Americans have won our war for us back in '54 if we didn't have the will to win it ourselves?

TOULON: You're kidding, aren't you?
(*Pause.*)

GALLIMARD: The Orientals simply want to be associated with whoever shows the most strength and power. You live with the Chinese, Sir. Do you think they like Communism?

TOULON: I live in China. Not with the Chinese.

GALLIMARD: Well, I—

TOULON: *You* live with the Chinese.

GALLIMARD: Excuse me?

TOULON: I can't keep a secret.

GALLIMARD: What are you saying?

TOULON: Only that I'm not immune to gossip. So, you're keeping a native mistress. Don't answer. It's none of my business. (*Pause*) I'm sure she must be gorgeous.

GALLIMARD: Well . . .

TOULON: I'm impressed. You have the stamina to go out into the streets and hunt one down. Some of us have to be content with the wives of the expatriate community.

GALLIMARD: I do feel . . . fortunate.

TOULON: So, Gallimard, you've got the inside knowledge—what do the Chinese think?

GALLIMARD: Deep down, they miss the old days. You know, cappuccinos, men in tuxedos—

TOULON: So what do we tell the Americans about Vietnam?

GALLIMARD: Tell them there's a natural affinity between the West and the Orient.

TOULON: And that you speak from experience?

GALLIMARD: The Orientals are people too. They want the good things we can give them. If the Americans demonstrate the will to win, the Vietnamese will welcome them into a mutually beneficial union.

TOULON: I don't see how the Vietnamese can stand up to American firepower.

GALLIMARD: Orientals will always submit to a greater force.

TOULON: I'll note your opinions in my report. The Americans always love to hear how "welcome" they'll be. (*He starts to exit*)

GALLIMARD: Sir?

TOULON: Mmmm?

GALLIMARD: This . . . rumor you've heard.

TOULON: Uh-huh?

GALLIMARD: How . . . widespread do you think it is?

TOULON: It's only widespread within this embassy. Where nobody talks because everybody is guilty. We were worried about you, Gallimard. We thought you were the only one here without a secret. Now you go and find a lotus blossom . . . and top us all. (*He exits*)

GALLIMARD (*To us*): Toulon knows! And he approves! I was learning the benefits of being a man. We form our own clubs, sit behind thick doors, smoke—and celebrate the fact that we're still boys. (*He starts to move downstage, towards* SONG) So, over the—

(*Suddenly* COMRADE CHIN *enters.* GALLIMARD *backs away.*)

GALLIMARD (*To* SONG): No! Why does she have to come in?

SONG: Rene, be sensible. How can they understand the story without her? Now, don't embarrass yourself.

(GALLIMARD *moves down center.*)

GALLIMARD (*To us*): Now, you will see why my story is so amusing to so many people. Why they snicker at parties in disbelief. Please—try to understand it from my point of view. We are all prisoners of our time and place. (*He exits*)

SCENE 4
GALLIMARD *and* BUTTERFLY's *flat. Beijing. 1961.*

SONG (*To us*): 1961. The flat Monsieur Gallimard rented for us. An evening after he has gone.

CHIN: Okay, see if you can find out when the Americans plan to start bombing Vietnam. If you can find out what cities, even better.

SONG: I'll do my best, but I don't want to arouse his suspicions.

CHIN: Yeah, sure, of course. So, what else?

SONG: The Americans will increase troops in Vietnam to 170,000 soldiers with 120,000 militia and 11,000 American advisors.

CHIN (*Writing*): Wait, wait. 120,000 militia and—

SONG: —11,000 American—

CHIN: —American advisors. (*Beat*) How do you remember so much?

SONG: I'm an actor.

CHIN: Yeah. (*Beat*) Is that how come you dress like that?

SONG: Like what, Miss Chin?

CHIN: Like that dress! You're wearing a dress. And every time I come here, you're wearing a dress. Is that because you're an actor? Or what?

SONG: It's a . . . disguise, Miss Chin.

CHIN: Actors, I think they're all weirdos. My mother tells me actors are like gamblers or prostitutes or—

SONG: It helps me in my assignment.
(*Pause.*)

CHIN: You're not gathering information in any way that violates Communist Party principles, are you?

SONG: Why would I do that?

CHIN: Just checking. Remember: when working for the Great Proletarian State, you represent our Chairman Mao in every position you take.

SONG: I'll try to imagine the Chairman taking my positions.

CHIN: We all think of him this way. Good-bye, comrade. (*She starts to exit*) Comrade?

SONG: Yes?

CHIN: Don't forget: there is no homosexuality in China!

SONG: Yes, I've heard.

CHIN: Just checking. (*She exits*)

SONG (*To us*): What passes for a woman in modern China.
(GALLIMARD *sticks his head out from the wings.*)

GALLIMARD: Is she gone?

SONG: Yes, Rene. Please continue in your own fashion.

SCENE 5
Beijing. 1961–63.

GALLIMARD *moves to the couch where* SONG *still sits. He lies down in her lap, and she strokes his forehead.*

GALLIMARD (*To us*): And so, over the years 1961, '62, '63, we settled into our routine, Butterfly and I. She would always have prepared a light snack and then, ever so delicately, and only if I agreed, she would start to pleasure me. With her hands, her mouth . . . too many ways to explain, and too sad, given my present situation. But mostly we would talk. About my life. Perhaps there is nothing more rare than to find a woman who passionately listens.

(SONG *remains upstage, listening, as* HELGA *enters and plays a scene downstage with* GALLIMARD.)

HELGA: Rene, I visited Dr. Bolleart this morning.

GALLIMARD: Why? Are you ill?

HELGA: No, no. You see, I wanted to ask him . . . that question we've been discussing.

GALLIMARD: And I told you, it's only a matter of time. Why did you bring a doctor into this? We just have to keep trying—like a crapshoot, actually.

HELGA: I went, I'm sorry. But listen: he says there's nothing wrong with me.

GALLIMARD: You see? Now, will you stop—?

HELGA: Rene, he says he'd like you to go in and take some tests.

GALLIMARD: Why? So he can find there's nothing wrong with both of us?

HELGA: Rene, I don't ask for much. One trip! One visit! And then, whatever you want to do about it—you decide.

GALLIMARD: You're assuming he'll find something defective!

HELGA: No! Of course not! Whatever he finds—if he finds nothing, we decide what to do about nothing! But go!

GALLIMARD: If he finds nothing, we keep trying. Just like we do now.

HELGA: But at least we'll know! (*Pause*) I'm sorry. (*She starts to exit*)

GALLIMARD: Do you really want me to see Dr. Bolleart?

HELGA: Only if you want a child, Rene. We have to face the fact that time is running out. Only if you want a child. (*She exits*)

GALLIMARD (*To* SONG): I'm a modern man, Butterfly. And yet, I don't want to go. It's the same old voodoo. I feel like God himself is laughing at me if I can't produce a child.

SONG: You men of the West—you're obsessed by your odd desire for equality. Your wife can't give you a child, and *you're* going to the doctor?

GALLIMARD: Well, you see, she's already gone.

SONG: And because this incompetent can't find the defect, you now have to subject yourself to him? It's unnatural.

GALLIMARD: Well, what is the "natural" solution?

SONG: In Imperial China, when a man found that one wife was inadequate, he turned to another—to give him his son.

GALLIMARD: What do you—? I can't . . . marry you, yet.

SONG: Please. I'm not asking you to be my husband. But I am already your wife.

GALLIMARD: Do you want to . . . have my child?

SONG: I thought you'd never ask.

GALLIMARD: But, your career . . . your—

SONG: Phooey on my career! That's your Western mind, twisting itself into strange shapes again. Of course I love my career. But what would I love most of all? To feel something inside me—day and night—something I know is yours. (*Pause*) Promise me . . . you won't go to this doctor. Who is this Western quack to set himself as judge over the man I love? I know who is a man, and who is not. (*She exits*)

GALLIMARD (*To us*): Dr. Bolleart? Of course I didn't go. What man would?

SCENE 6
Beijing. 1963.

Party noises over the house speakers. RENEE *enters, wearing a revealing gown.*

GALLIMARD: 1963. A party at the Austrian embassy. None of us could remember the Austrian ambassador's name, which seemed somehow appropriate. (*To* RENEE) So, I tell the Americans, Diem must go. The U.S. wants to be respected by the Vietnamese, and yet they're propping up this nobody seminarian as her president. A man whose claim to fame is his sister-in-law imposing fanatic "moral order" campaigns? Oriental women—when they're good, they're very good, but when they're bad, they're Christians.

RENEE: Yeah.

GALLIMARD: And what do you do?

RENEE: I'm a student. My father exports a lot of useless stuff to the Third World.

GALLIMARD: How useless?

RENEE: You know. Squirt guns, confectioner's sugar, hula hoops . . .

GALLIMARD: I'm sure they appreciate the sugar.

RENEE: I'm here for two years to study Chinese.

GALLIMARD: Two years?

RENEE: That's what everybody says.

GALLIMARD: When did you arrive?

RENEE: Three weeks ago.

GALLIMARD: And?

RENEE: I like it. It's primitive, but . . . well, this is the place to learn Chinese, so here I am.

GALLIMARD: Why Chinese?

RENEE: I think it'll be important someday.

GALLIMARD: You do?

RENEE: Don't ask me when, but . . . that's what I think.

GALLIMARD: Well, I agree with you. One hundred percent. That's very farsighted.

RENEE: Yeah. Well of course, my father thinks I'm a complete weirdo.

GALLIMARD: He'll thank you someday.

RENEE: Like when the Chinese start buying hula hoops?

GALLIMARD: There're a billion bellies out there.

RENEE: And if they end up taking over the world—well, then I'll be lucky to know Chinese too, right?

(*Pause.*)

GALLIMARD: At this point, I don't see how the Chinese can possibly take—

RENEE: You know what I *don't* like about China?

GALLIMARD: Excuse me? No—what?

RENEE: Nothing to do at night.

GALLIMARD: You come to parties at embassies like everyone else.

RENEE: Yeah, but they get out at ten. And then what?

GALLIMARD: I'm afraid the Chinese idea of a dance hall is a dirt floor and a man with a flute.

RENEE: Are you married?

GALLIMARD: Yes. Why?

RENEE: You wanna . . . fool around?

(*Pause.*)

GALLIMARD: Sure.

RENEE: I'll wait for you outside. What's your name?

GALLIMARD: Gallimard. Rene.

RENEE: Weird. I'm Renee too. (*She exits*)

GALLIMARD (*To us*): And so, I embarked on my first extra-extramarital affair. Renee was picture perfect. With a body like those girls in the magazines. If I put a tissue paper over my eyes, I wouldn't have been able to tell the difference. And it was exciting to be with someone who wasn't afraid to be seen completely naked. But is it possible for a woman to be too uninhibited, too willing, so as to seem almost too . . . masculine?

(*Chuck Berry blares from the house speakers, then comes down in volume as* RENEE *enters, toweling her hair.*)

RENEE: You have a nice weenie.

GALLIMARD: What?

RENEE: Penis. You have a nice penis.

GALLIMARD: Oh. Well, thank you. That's very . . .

RENEE: What—can't take a compliment?

GALLIMARD: No, it's very . . . reassuring.

RENEE: But most girls don't come out and say it, huh?

GALLIMARD: And also . . . what did you call it?

RENEE: Oh. Most girls don't call it a "weenie," huh?

GALLIMARD: It sounds very—

RENEE: Small, I know.

GALLIMARD: I was going to say, "young."

RENEE: Yeah. Young, small, same thing. Most guys are pretty, uh, sensitive about that. Like, you know, I had a boyfriend back home in Denmark. I got mad at him once and called him a little weeniehead. He got so mad! He said at least I should call him a great big weeniehead.

GALLIMARD: I suppose I just say "penis."

RENEE: Yeah. That's pretty clinical. There's "cock," but that sounds like a chicken. And "prick" is painful, and "dick" is like you're talking about someone who's not in the room.

GALLIMARD: Yes. It's a . . . bigger problem than I imagined.

RENEE: I—I think maybe it's because I really don't know what to do with them—that's why I call them "weenies."

GALLIMARD: Well, you did quite well with . . . mine.

RENEE: Thanks, but I mean, really do with them. Like, okay, have you ever looked at one? I mean, really?

GALLIMARD: No, I suppose when it's part of you, you sort of take it for granted.

RENEE: I guess. But, like, it just hangs there. This little . . . flap of flesh. And there's so much fuss that we make about it. Like, I think the reason we fight wars is because we wear clothes. Because no one knows—between the men, I mean—who has the bigger . . . weenie. So, if I'm a guy with a small one, I'm going to build a really big building or take over a really big piece of land or write a really long book so the other men don't know, right? But, see, it never really works, that's the problem. I mean, you conquer the country, or whatever, but you're still wearing clothes, so there's no way to prove absolutely whose is bigger or smaller. And that's what we call a civilized society. The whole world run by a bunch of men with pricks the size of pins. (*She exits*)

GALLIMARD (*To us*): This was simply not acceptable. (*A high-pitched chime rings through the air.* SONG, *dressed as* BUTTERFLY, *appears in the upstage special. She is obviously distressed. Her body swoons as she attempts to clip the stems of flowers she's arranging in a vase.*)

GALLIMARD: But I kept up our affair, wildly, for several months. Why? I believe because of Butterfly. She knew the secret I was trying to hide. But, unlike a Western woman, she didn't confront me, threaten, even pout. I remembered the words of Puccini's *Butterfly*:

SONG: "Noi siamo gente avvezza/ alle piccole cose/ umili e silenziose."

GALLIMARD: "I come from a people/ Who are accustomed to little/ Humble and silent. " I saw Pinkerton and Butterfly, and what she would say if he were unfaithful . . . nothing. She would cry, alone, into those wildly soft sleeves, once full of possessions, now empty to collect her tears. It was her tears and her silence that excited me, every time I visited Renee.

TOULON (*Offstage*): Gallimard!

(TOULON *enters.* GALLIMARD *turns towards him. During the next section,* SONG, *up center, begins to dance with the flowers. It is a drunken dance, where she breaks small pieces off the stems.*)

TOULON: They're killing him.

GALLIMARD: Who? I'm sorry? What?

TOULON: Bother you to come over at this late hour?

GALLIMARD: No . . . of course not.

TOULON: Not after you hear my secret. Champagne?

GALLIMARD: Um . . . thank you.

TOULON: You're surprised. There's something that you've wanted, Gallimard. No, not a promotion. Next time. Something in the world. You're not aware of this, but there's an informal gossip circle among intelligence agents. And some of ours heard from some of the Americans—

GALLIMARD: Yes?

TOULON: That the U.S. will allow the Vietnamese generals to stage a coup . . . and assassinate President Diem.

(*The chime rings again.* TOULON *freezes.* GALLIMARD *turns up-stage and looks at* BUTTERFLY, *who slowly and deliberately clips a flower off its stem.* GALLIMARD *turns back towards* TOULON.)

GALLIMARD: I think . . . that's a very wise move!

(TOULON *unfreezes.*)

TOULON: It's what you've been advocating. A toast?

GALLIMARD: Sure. I consider this a vindication.

TOULON: Not exactly. "To the test. Let's hope you pass."

(*They drink. The chime rings again.* TOULON *freezes.* GALLIMARD *turns upstage, and* SONG *clips another flower.*)

GALLIMARD (*To* TOULON): THE TEST?

TOULON (*Unfreezing*): It's a test of everything you've been saying. I personally think the generals probably will stop the Communists. And you'll be a hero. But if anything goes wrong, then your opinions won't be worth a pig's ear. I'm sure that won't happen. But sometimes it's easier when they don't listen to you.

GALLIMARD: They're your opinions too, aren't they?

TOULON: Personally, yes.

GALLIMARD: So we agree.

TOULON: But my opinions aren't on that report. Yours are. Cheers.

(TOULON *turns away from* GALLIMARD *and raises his glass. At that instant* SONG *picks up the vase and hurls it to the ground. It shatters.* SONG *sinks down amidst the shards of the vase, in a calm, childlike trance. She sings softly, as if reciting a child's nursery rhyme.*)

SONG (*Repeat as necessary*): "The whole world over, the white man travels, setting anchor, wherever he likes. Life's not worth living, unless he finds, the finest maidens, of every land . . ."

(GALLIMARD *turns downstage towards us.* SONG *continues singing.*)

GALLIMARD: I shook as I left his house. That coward! That worm! To put the burden for his decisions on my shoulders!

I started for Renee's. But no, that was all I needed. A schoolgirl who would question the role of the penis in modern society. What I wanted was revenge. A vessel to contain my humiliation. Though I hadn't seen her in several weeks, I headed for Butterfly's.

(GALLIMARD *enters* SONG's *apartment.*)

SONG: Oh! Rene . . . I was dreaming!

GALLIMARD: You've been drinking?

SONG: If I can't sleep, then yes, I drink. But then, it gives me these dreams which—Rene, it's been almost three weeks since you visited me last.

GALLIMARD: I know. There's been a lot going on in the world.

SONG: Fortunately I am drunk. So I can speak freely. It's not the world, it's you and me. And an old problem. Even the softest skin becomes like leather to a man who's touched it too often. I confess I don't know how to stop it. I don't know how to become another woman.

GALLIMARD: I have a request.

SONG: Is this a solution? Or are you ready to give up the flat?

GALLIMARD: It may be a solution. But I'm sure you won't like it.

SONG: Oh well, that's very important. "Like it?" Do you think I "like" lying here alone, waiting, always waiting for your return? Please—don't worry about what I may not "like."

GALLIMARD: I want to see you . . . naked.

(*Silence.*)

SONG: I thought you understood my modesty. So you want me to—what—strip? Like a big cowboy girl? Shiny pasties on my breasts? Shall I fling my kimono over my head and yell "ya-hoo" in the process? I thought you respected my shame!

GALLIMARD: I believe you gave me your shame many years ago.

SONG: Yes—and it is just like a white devil to use it against me. I can't believe it. I thought myself so repulsed by the passive Oriental and the cruel white man. Now I see—we are al-ways most revolted by the things hidden within us.

GALLIMARD: I just mean—

SONG: Yes?

GALLIMARD:—that it will remove the only barrier left between us.

SONG: No, Rene. Don't couch your request in sweet words. Be yourself—a cad—and know that my love is enough, that I submit—submit to the worst you can give me. (*Pause*) Well, come. Strip me. Whatever happens, know that you have willed it. Our love, in your hands. I'm helpless before my man.

(GALLIMARD *starts to cross the room.*)

GALLIMARD: Did I not undress her because I knew, somewhere deep down, what I would find? Perhaps. Happiness is so rare that our mind can turn somersaults to protect it.

At the time, I only knew that I was seeing Pinkerton stalking towards his Butterfly, ready to reward her love with his lecherous hands. The image sickened me, pulled me to my knees, so I was crawling towards her like a worm. By the time I reached her, Pinkerton . . . had vanished from my heart. To be replaced by something new, something unnatural, that flew in the face of all I'd learned in the world—something very close to love.

(*He grabs her around the waist; she strokes his hair.*)

GALLIMARD: Butterfly, forgive me.

SONG: Rene . . .

GALLIMARD: For everything. From the start.

SONG: I'm . . .

GALLIMARD: I want to—

SONG: I'm pregnant. (*Beat*) I'm pregnant. (*Beat*) I'm pregnant.

(*Beat.*)

GALLIMARD: I want to marry you!

SCENE 7

GALLIMARD *and* BUTTERFLY's *flat. Beijing. 1963.*

Downstage, SONG *paces as* COMRADE CHIN *reads from her notepad. Upstage,* GALLIMARD *is still kneeling. He remains on his knees throughout the scene, watching it.*

SONG: I need a baby.

CHIN (*From pad*): He's been spotted going to a dorm.

SONG: I need a baby.

CHIN: At the Foreign Language Institute.

SONG: I need a baby.

CHIN: The room of a Danish girl . . . What do you mean, you need a baby?!

SONG: Tell Comrade Kang—last night, the entire mission, it could've ended.

CHIN: What do you mean?

SONG: Tell Kang—he told me to strip.

CHIN: *Strip?!*

SONG: Write!

CHIN: I tell you, I don't understand nothing about this case anymore. Nothing.

SONG: He told me to strip, and I took a chance. Oh, we Chinese, we know how to gamble.

CHIN (*Writing*): " . . . told him to strip."

SONG: My palms were wet, I had to make a split-second decision.

CHIN: Hey! Can you slow down?!
    (*Pause.*)

SONG: You write faster, I'm the artist here. Suddenly, it hit me—"All he wants is for her to submit. Once a woman submits, a man is always ready to become 'generous.' "

CHIN: You're just gonna end up with rough notes.

SONG: And it worked! He gave in! Now, if I can just present him with a baby. A Chinese baby with blond hair—he'll be mine for life!

CHIN: Kang will never agree! The trading of babies has to be a counterrevolutionary act!

SONG: Sometimes, a counterrevolutionary act is necessary to counter a counterrevolutionary act.
    (*Pause.*)

CHIN: Wait.

SONG: I need one . . . in seven months. Make sure it's a boy.

CHIN: This doesn't sound like something the Chairman would do. Maybe you'd better talk to Comrade Kang yourself.

SONG: Good. I will.
    (CHIN *gets up to leave.*)

SONG: Miss Chin? Why, in the Peking Opera, are women's roles played by men?

CHIN: I don't know. Maybe, a reactionary remnant of male—

SONG: No. (*Beat*) Because only a man knows how a woman is supposed to act.
    (CHIN *exits.* SONG *turns upstage, towards* GALLIMARD.)

GALLIMARD: (*Calling after* CHIN): Good riddance! (*To* SONG) I could forget all that betrayal in an in-

stant, you know. If you'd just come back and become Butterfly again.

SONG: Fat chance. You're here in prison, rotting in a cell. And I'm on a plane, winging my way back to China. Your President pardoned me of our treason, you know.

GALLIMARD: Yes, I read about that.

SONG: Must make you feel . . . lower than shit.

GALLIMARD: But don't you, even a little bit, wish you were here with me?

SONG: I'm an artist, Rene. You were my greatest . . . acting challenge. (*She laughs*) It doesn't matter how rotten I answer, does it? You still adore me. That's why I love you, Rene. (*She points to us*) So—you were telling your audience about the night I announced I was pregnant.
    (GALLIMARD *puts his arms around* SONG's *waist. He and* SONG *are in the positions they were in at the end of Scene 6.*)

SCENE 8
Same.

GALLIMARD: I'll divorce my wife. We'll live together here, and then later in France.

SONG: I feel so . . . ashamed.

GALLIMARD: Why?

SONG: I had begun to lose faith. And now, you shame me with your generosity.

GALLIMARD: Generosity? No, I'm proposing for very selfish reasons.

SONG: Your apologies only make me feel more ashamed. My outburst a moment ago!

GALLIMARD: Your outburst? What about my request?!

SONG: You've been very patient dealing with my . . . eccentricities. A Western man, used to women freer with their bodies—

GALLIMARD: It was sick! Don't make excuses for me.

SONG: I have to. You don't seem willing to make them for yourself.
    (*Pause.*)

GALLIMARD: You're crazy.

SONG: I'm happy. Which often looks like crazy.

GALLIMARD: Then make me crazy. Marry me.
    (*Pause.*)

SONG: No.

GALLIMARD: What?

SONG: Do I sound silly, a slave, if I say I'm not worthy?

GALLIMARD: Yes. In fact you do. No one has loved me like you.

SONG: Thank you. And no one ever will. I'll see to that.

GALLIMARD: So what is the problem?

SONG: Rene, we Chinese are realists. We understand rice, gold, and guns. You are a diplomat. Your career is skyrocketing. Now, what would happen if you divorced your wife to marry a Communist Chinese actress?

GALLIMARD: That's not being realistic. That's defeating yourself before you begin.

SONG: We must conserve our strength for the battles we can win.

GALLIMARD: That sounds like a fortune cookie!

SONG: Where do you think fortune cookies come from?

GALLIMARD: I don't care.

SONG: You do. So do I. And we should. That is why I say I'm not worthy. I'm worthy to love and even to be loved by you. But I am not worthy to end the career of one of the West's most promising diplomats.

GALLIMARD: It's not that great a career! I made it sound like more than it is!

SONG: Modesty will get you nowhere. Flatter yourself, and you flatter me. I'm flattered to decline your offer. (*She exits*)

GALLIMARD (*To us*): Butterfly and I argued all night. And, in the end, I left, knowing I would never be her husband. She went away for several months—to the countryside, like a small animal. Until the night I received her call.

(*A baby's cry from offstage.* SONG *enters, carrying a child.*)

SONG: He looks like you.

GALLIMARD: Oh! (*Beat; he approaches the baby*) Well, babies are never very attractive at birth.

SONG: Stop!

GALLIMARD: I'm sure he'll grow more beautiful with age. More like his mother.

SONG: "Chi vide mai/ a bimbo del Giappon . . . "

GALLIMARD: "What baby, I wonder, was ever born in Japan"—or China, for that matter—

SONG: " . . . occhi azzurrini?"

GALLIMARD: "With azure eyes"—they're actually sort of brown, wouldn't you say?

SONG: "E il labbro."

GALLIMARD: "And such lips!" (*He kisses* SONG) And such lips.

SONG: "E i ricciohni d'oro schietto?"

GALLIMARD: "And such a head of golden"—if slightly patchy—"curls?"

SONG: I'm going to call him "Peepee."

GALLIMARD: Darling, could you repeat that because I'm sure a rickshaw just flew by overhead.

SONG: You heard me.

GALLIMARD: "Song Peepee"? May I suggest Michael, or Stephan, or Adolph?

SONG: You may, but I won't listen.

GALLIMARD: You can't be serious. Can you imagine the time this child will have in school?

SONG: In the West, yes.

GALLIMARD: It's worse than naming him Ping Pong or Long Dong or—

SONG: But he's never going to live in the West, is he? (*Pause.*)

GALLIMARD: That wasn't my choice.

SONG: It is mine. And this is my promise to you: I will raise him, he will be our child, but he will never burden you outside of China.

GALLIMARD: Why do you make these promises? I want to be burdened! I want a scandal to cover the papers!

SONG (*To us*): Prophetic.

GALLIMARD: I'm serious.

SONG: So am I. His name is as I registered it. And he will never live in the West.

(SONG *exits with the child.*)

GALLIMARD (*To us*): It is possible that her stubbornness only made me want her more. That drawing back at the moment of my capitulation was the most brilliant strategy she could have chosen. It is possible. But it is also possible that by this point she could have said, could have done . . . anything, and I would have adored her still.

SCENE 9
Beijing. 1966.

A driving rhythm of Chinese percussion fills the stage.

GALLIMARD: And then, China began to change. Mao became very old, and his cult became very strong. And, like many old men, he entered his second childhood. So he handed over the reins of state to those with minds like his own. And children ruled the Middle Kingdom with complete caprice. The doctrine of the Cultural Revolution implied continuous anarchy. Contact between Chinese and foreigners became impossible. Our flat was confiscated. Her fame and my money now counted against us.

(*Two dancers in Mao suits and red-starred caps enter, and begin crudely mimicking revolutionary violence, in an agitprop fashion.*)

GALLIMARD: And somehow the American war went wrong too. Four hundred thousand dollars were being spent for every Viet Cong killed; so General Westmoreland's remark that the Oriental does not value life the way Americans do was oddly accurate. Why weren't the Vietnamese people giving in? Why were they content instead to die and die and die again?

(TOULON *enters.*)

TOULON: Congratulations, Gallimard.

GALLIMARD: Excuse me, sir?

TOULON: Not a promotion. That was last time. You're going home.

GALLIMARD: What?

TOULON: Don't say I didn't warn you.

GALLIMARD: I'm being transferred . . . because I was wrong about the American war?

TOULON: Of course not. We don't care about the Americans. We care about your mind. The quality of your analysis. In general, everything you've predicted here in the Orient . . . just hasn't happened.

GALLIMARD: I think that's premature.

TOULON: Don't force me to be blunt. Okay, you said China was ready to open to Western trade. The only thing they're trading out there are Western heads. And, yes, you said the Americans would succeed in Indochina. You were kidding, right?

GALLIMARD: I think the end is in sight.

TOULON: Don't be pathetic. And don't take this personally. You were wrong. It's not your fault.

GALLIMARD: But I'm going home.

TOULON: Right. Could I have the number of your mistress? (*Beat*) Joke! Joke! Eat a croissant for me.

(TOULON *exits.* SONG, *wearing a Mao suit, is dragged in from the wings as part of the upstage dance. They "beat" her, then lampoon the acrobatics of the Chinese opera, as she is made to kneel onstage.*)

GALLIMARD (*Simultaneously*): I don't care to recall how Butterfly and I said our hurried farewell. Perhaps it was better to end our affair before it killed her.

(GALLIMARD *exits.* COMRADE CHIN *walks across the stage with a banner reading: "The Actor Renounces His Decadent Profession!" She reaches the kneeling* SONG. *Percussion stops with a thud. Dancers strike poses.*)

CHIN: Actor-oppressor, for years you have lived above the common people and looked down on their labor. While the farmer ate millet—

SONG: I ate pastries from France and sweetmeats from silver trays.

CHIN: And how did you come to live in such an exalted position?

SONG: I was a plaything for the imperialists!

CHIN: What did you do?

SONG: I shamed China by allowing myself to be corrupted by a foreigner . . .

CHIN: What does this mean? The People demand a full confession!

SONG: I engaged in the lowest perversions with China's enemies!

CHIN: What perversions? Be more clear!

SONG: I let him put it up my ass!

(*Dancers look over, disgusted.*)

CHIN: Aaaa-ya! How can you use such sickening language?!

SONG: My language . . . is only as foul as the crimes I committed . . .

CHIN: Yeah. That's better. So—what do you want to do now?

SONG: I want to serve the people.

(*Percussion starts up, with Chinese strings.*)

CHIN: What?

SONG: I want to serve the people!

(*Dancers regain their revolutionary smiles, and begin a dance of victory.*)

CHIN: What?!

SONG: I want to serve the people!!

(*Dancers unveil a banner: "The Actor Is Rehabilitated!"* SONG *remains kneeling before* CHIN, *as the dancers bounce around them, then exit. Music out.*)

SCENE 10
A commune. Hunan Province. 1970.

CHIN: How you planning to do that?

SONG: I've already worked four years in the fields of Hunan, Comrade Chin.

CHIN: So? Farmers work all their lives. Let me see your hands.
(SONG *holds them out for her inspection.*)

CHIN: Goddamn! Still so smooth! How long does it take to turn you actors into good anythings? Hunh. You've just spent too many years in luxury to be any good to the Revolution.

SONG: I served the Revolution.

CHIN: Serve the Revolution? Bullshit! You wore dresses! Don't tell me—I was there. I saw you! You and your white vice-consul! Stuck up there in your flat, living off the People's Treasury! Yeah, I knew what was going on! You two . . . homos! Homos! Homos! (*Pause; she composes herself*) Ah! Well . . . you will serve the people, all right. But not with the Revolution's money. This time, you use your own money.

SONG: I have no money.

CHIN: Shut up! And you won't stink up China anymore with your pervert stuff. You'll pollute the place where pollution begins—the West.

SONG: What do you mean?

CHIN: Shut up! You're going to France. Without a cent in your pocket. You find your consul's house, you make him pay your expenses—

SONG: No.

CHIN: And you give us weekly reports! Useful information!

SONG: That's crazy. It's been four years.

CHIN: Either that, or back to rehabilitation center!

SONG: Comrade Chin, he's not going to support me! Not in France! He's a white man! I was just his plaything—

CHIN: Oh yuck! Again with the sickening language? Where's my stick?

SONG: You don't understand the mind of a man.
(*Pause.*)

CHIN: Oh no? No I don't? Then how come I'm married, huh? How come I got a man? Five, six years ago, you always tell me those kind of things, I felt very bad. But not now! Because what does the Chairman say? He tells us I'm now the smart one, you're now the nincompoop!
  You're the blackhead, the harebrain, the nitwit! You think you're so smart? You understand "The Mind of a Man"? Good! Then you go to France and be a pervert for Chairman Mao!
(CHIN *and* SONG *exit in opposite directions.*)

SCENE 11
Paris. 1968–70. GALLIMARD *enters.*

GALLIMARD: And what was waiting for me back in Paris? Well, better Chinese food than I'd eaten in China. Friends and relatives. A little accounting, regular schedule, keeping track of traffic violations in the suburbs. . . . And the indignity of students shouting the slogans of Chairman Mao at me—in French.

HELGA: Rene? Rene? (*She enters, soaking wet*) I've had a . . . a problem. (*She sneezes*)

GALLIMARD: You're wet.

HELGA: Yes, I . . . coming back from the grocer's. A group of students, waving red flags, they—
(GALLIMARD *fetches a towel.*)

HELGA: —they ran by, I was caught up along with them. Before I knew what was happening—
(GALLIMARD *gives her the towel.*)

HELGA: Thank you. The police started firing water cannons at us. I tried to shout, to tell them I was the wife of a diplomat, but you know how it is . . . (*Pause*) Needless to say, I lost the groceries. Rene, what's happening to France?

GALLIMARD: What's—? Well, nothing, really.

HELGA: Nothing?! The storefronts are in flames, there's glass in the streets, buildings are toppling—and I'm wet!

GALLIMARD: Nothing! . . . that I care to think about.

HELGA: And is that why you stay in this room?

GALLIMARD: Yes, in fact.

HELGA: With the incense burning? You know something? I hate incense. It smells so sickly sweet.

GALLIMARD: Well, I hate the French. Who just smell—period!

HELGA: And the Chinese were better?

GALLIMARD: Please—don't start.

HELGA: When we left, this exact same thing, the riots—

GALLIMARD: No, no . . .

HELGA: Students screaming slogans, smashing down doors—

GALLIMARD: Helga—

HELGA: It was all going on in China, too. Don't you remember?!

GALLIMARD: Helga! Please! (*Pause*) You have never understood China, have you? You walk in here with these ridiculous ideas, that the West is falling apart, that China was spitting in our faces. You come in, dripping of the streets, and you leave water all over my floor. (*He grabs* HELGA's *towel, begins mopping up the floor*)

HELGA: But it's the truth!

GALLIMARD: Helga, I want a divorce.

(*Pause;* GALLIMARD *continues, mopping the floor.*)

HELGA: I take it back. China is . . . beautiful. Incense, I like incense.

GALLIMARD: I've had a mistress.

HELGA: So?

GALLIMARD: For eight years.

HELGA: I knew you would. I knew you would the day I married you. And now what? You want to marry her?

GALLIMARD: I can't. She's in China.

HELGA: I see. You want to leave. For someone who's not here, is that right?

GALLIMARD: That's right.

HELGA: You can't live with her, but still you don't want to live with me.

GALLIMARD: That's right.

(*Pause.*)

HELGA: Shit. How terrible that I can figure that out. (*Pause*) I never thought I'd say it. But, in China, I was happy. I knew, in my own way, I knew that you were not everything you pretended to be. But the pretense—going on your arm to the embassy ball, visiting your office and the guards saying, "Good morning, good morning, Madame Gallimard"—the pretense . . . was very good indeed. (*Pause*) I hope everyone is mean to you for the rest of your life. (*She exits*)

GALLIMARD (*To us*): Prophetic.

(MARC *enters with two drinks.*)

GALLIMARD (*To* MARC): In China, I was different from all other men.

MARC: Sure. You were white. Here's your drink.

GALLIMARD: I felt . . . touched.

MARC: In the head? Rene, I don't want to hear about the Oriental love goddess. Okay? One night—can we just drink and throw up without a lot of conversation?

GALLIMARD: You still don't believe me, do you?

MARC: Sure I do. She was the most beautiful, et cetera, et cetera, blasé blasé.

(*Pause.*)

GALLIMARD: My life in the West has been such a disappointment.

MARC: Life in the West is like that. You'll get used to it. Look, you're driving me away. I'm leaving. Happy, now? (*He exits, then returns*) Look, I have a date tomorrow night. You wanna come? I can fix you up with—

GALLIMARD: Of course. I would love to come.

(*Pause.*)

MARC: Uh—on second thought, no. You'd better get a hold of yourself first.

(*He exits,* GALLIMARD *nurses his drink.*)

GALLIMARD (*To us*): This is the ultimate cruelty, isn't it? That I can talk and talk and to anyone listening, it's only air—too rich a diet to be swallowed by a mundane world. Why can't anyone understand? That in China, I once loved, and was loved by, very simply, the Perfect Woman.

(SONG *enters, dressed as* BUTTERFLY *in wedding dress.*)

GALLIMARD (*To* SONG): Not again. My imagination is hell. Am I asleep this time? Or did I drink too much?

SONG: Rene?

GALLIMARD: God, it's too painful! That you speak?

SONG: What are you talking about? Rene—touch me.

GALLIMARD: Why?

SONG: I'm real. Take my hand.

GALLIMARD: Why? So you can disappear again and leave me clutching at the air? For the entertainment of my neighbors who—?

(SONG *touches* GALLIMARD.)

SONG: Rene?

(GALLIMARD *takes* SONG's *hand. Silence.*)

GALLIMARD: Butterfly? I never doubted you'd return.

SONG: You hadn't . . . forgotten—?

GALLIMARD: Yes, actually, I've, forgotten everything. My mind, you see—there wasn't enough room in this hard head—not for the world *and* for you. No, there was only room for one. (*Beat*) Come, look. See? Your bed has been waiting, with the Klimt poster you like, and—see? The xiang lu [incense burner] you gave me?

SORTS: I . . . I don't know what to say.

GALLIMARD: There's nothing to say. Not at the end of a long trip. Can I make you some tea?

SONG: But where's your wife?

GALLIMARD: She's by my side. She's by my side at last.

(GALLIMARD *reaches to embrace* SONG. SONG *side-steps, dodging him.*)

GALLIMARD: Why?!

SONG (*To us*): So I did return to Rene in Paris. Where I found—

GALLIMARD: Why do you run away? Can't we show them how we embraced that evening?

SONG: Please. I'm talking.

GALLIMARD: You have to do what I say! I'm conjuring you up in *my* mind!

SONG: Rene, I've never done what you've said. Why should it be any different in your mind? Now split—the story moves on, and I must change.

GALLIMARD: I welcomed you into my home! I didn't have to, you know! I could've left you penniless on the streets of Paris! But I took you in!

SONG: Thank you.

GALLIMARD: So . . . please . . . don't change.

SONG: You know I have to. You know I will. And anyway, what difference does it make? No matter what your eyes tell you, you can't ignore the truth. You already know too much.

(GALLIMARD *exits.* SONG *turns to us.*)

SONG: The change I'm going to make requires about five minutes. So I thought you might want to take this opportunity to stretch your legs, enjoy a drink, or listen to the musicians. I'll be here, when you return, right where you left me.

(SONG *goes to a mirror in front of which is a wash basin of water. She starts to remove her makeup as stagelights go to half and houselights come up.*)

ACT THREE

SCENE 1
A courthouse in Paris. 1986.

As he promised, SONG *has completed the bulk of his transformation, onstage by the time the houselights go down and the stagelights come up full. He removes his wig and kimono, leaving them on the floor. Underneath, he wears a well-cut suit.*

SONG: So I'd done my job better than I had a right to expect. Well, give him some credit, too. He's right—I was in a fix when I arrived in Paris. I walked from the airport into town, then I located, by blind groping, the Chinatown district. Let me make one thing clear: whatever else may be said about the Chinese, they are stingy! I slept in doorways three days until I could find a tailor who would make me this kimono on credit. As it turns out, maybe I didn't even need it. Maybe he would've been happy to see me in a simple shift and mascara. But . . . better safe than sorry.

That was 1970, when I arrived in Paris. For the next fifteen years, yes, I lived a very comfy life. Some relief, believe me, after four years on a fucking commune in Nowheresville, China. Rene supported the boy and me, and I did some demonstrations around the country as part of my "cultural exchange" cover. And then there was the spying.

(SONG *moves upstage, to a chair.* TOULON *enters as a judge, wearing the appropriate wig and robes. He sits near* SONG. *It's 1986, and* SONG *is testifying in a courtroom.*)

SONG: Not much at first. Rene had lost all his high-level contacts. Comrade Chin wasn't very interested in parking-ticket statistics. But finally, at my urging, Rene got a job as a courier, handling sensitive documents. He'd photograph them for me, and I'd pass them on to the Chinese embassy.

JUDGE: Did he understand the extent of his activity?

SONG: He didn't ask. He knew that I needed those documents, and that was enough.

JUDGE: But he must've known he was passing classified information.

SONG: I can't say.

JUDGE: He never asked what you were going to do with them?

SONG: Nope.

(*Pause.*)

JUDGE: There is one thing that the court—indeed, that all of France—would like to know.

SONG: Fire away.

JUDGE: Did Monsieur Gallimard know you were a man?

SONG: Well, he never saw me completely naked. Ever.

JUDGE: But surely, he must've . . . how can I put this?

SONG: Put it however you like. I'm not shy. He must've felt around?

JUDGE: Mmmmm.

SONG: Not really. I did all the work. He just laid back. Of course we did enjoy more . . . complete union, and I suppose he *might* have wondered why I was always on my stomach, but. . . . But what you're thinking is. "Of course a wrist must've brushed . . . a hand hit . . . over twenty years!" Yeah. Well, Your Honor, it was my job to make him think I was a woman. And chew on this: it wasn't all that hard. See, my mother was a prostitute along the Bundt before the Revolution. And, uh, I think it's fair to say she learned a few things about Western men. So I borrowed her knowledge. In service to my country.

JUDGE: Would you care to enlighten the court with this secret knowledge? I'm sure we're all very curious.

SONG: I'm sure you are. (*Pause*) Okay, Rule One is: Men always believe what they want to hear. So a girl can tell the most obnoxious lies and the guys will believe them every time—"This is my first time"—"That's the biggest I've ever seen"—or *both*, which, if you really think about it, is not possible in a single lifetime. You've maybe heard those phrases a few times in your own life, yes, Your Honor?

JUDGE: It's not my life, Monsieur Song, which is on trial today.

SONG: Okay, okay, just trying to lighten up the proceedings. Tough room.

JUDGE: Go on.

SONG: Rule Two: As soon as a Western man comes into contact with the East—he's already confused. The West has sort of an international rape mentality towards the East. Do you know rape mentality?

JUDGE: Give us your definition, please.

SONG: Basically, "Her mouth says no, but her eyes say yes."

   The West thinks of itself as masculine—big guns, big industry, big money—so the East is feminine—weak, delicate, poor . . . but good at art, and full of inscrutable wisdom—the feminine mystique.

   Her mouth says no, but her eyes say yes. The West believes the East, deep down, *wants* to be dominated—because a woman can't think for herself.

JUDGE: What does this have to do with my question?

SONG: You expect Oriental countries to submit to your guns, and you expect Oriental women to be submissive to your men. That's why you say they make the best wives.

JUDGE: But why would that make it possible for you to fool Monsieur Gallimard? Please—get to the point.

SONG: One, because when he finally met his fantasy woman, he wanted more than anything to believe that she was, in fact, a woman. And second, I am an Oriental. And being an Oriental, I could never be completely a man.

(*Pause.*)

JUDGE: Your armchair political theory is tenuous, Monsieur Song.

SONG: You think so? That's why you'll lose in all your dealings with the East.

JUDGE: Just answer my question: did he know you were a man?

(*Pause.*)

SONG: You know, Your Honor, I never asked.

SCENE 2

Same.

Music from the "Death Scene" from Butterfly blares over the house speakers. It is the loudest thing we've heard in this play.

GALLIMARD *enters, crawling towards* SONG's *wig and kimono.*

GALLIMARD: Butterfly? Butterfly?

(SONG *remains a man, in the witness box, delivering a testimony we do not hear.*)

GALLIMARD (*To us*): In my moment of greatest shame, here, in this courtroom—with that . . . person up there, telling the world. . . . What strikes me especially is how shallow he is, how glib and obsequious . . . completely . . . without substance! The type that prowls around discos with a gold medallion stinking of garlic. So little like my Butterfly.

Yet even in this moment my mind remains agile, flip-flopping like a man on a trampoline. Even now, my picture dissolves, and I see that . . . witness . . . talking to me.

(SONG *suddenly stands straight up in his witness box, and looks at* GALLIMARD.)

SONG: Yes. You. White man.

(SONG *steps out of the witness box, and moves downstage towards* GALLIMARD. *Light change.*)

GALLIMARD (*To* SONG): WHO? ME?

SONG: Do you see any other white men?

GALLIMARD: Yes. There're white men all around. This is a French courtroom.

SONG: So you are an adventurous imperialist. Tell me, why did it take you so long? To come back to this place?

GALLIMARD: What place?

SONG: This theatre in China. Where we met many years ago.

GALLIMARD (*To us*): And once again, against my will, I am transported.

(*Chinese opera music comes up on the speakers.* SONG *begins to do opera moves, as he did the night they met.*)

SONG: Do you remember? The night you gave your heart?

GALLIMARD: It was a long time ago.

SONG: Not long enough. A night that turned your world upside down.

GALLIMARD: Perhaps.

SONG: Oh, be honest with me. What's another bit of flattery when you've already given me twenty years' worth? It's a wonder my head hasn't swollen to the size of China.

GALLIMARD: Who's to say it hasn't?

SONG: Who's to say? And what's the shame? In pride? You think I could've pulled this off if I wasn't already full of pride when we met? No, not just pride. Arrogance. It takes arrogance, really—to believe you can will, with your eyes and your lips, the destiny of another. (*He dances*) C'mon. Admit it. You still want me. Even in slacks and a button-down collar.

GALLIMARD: I don't see what the point of—

SONG: You don't? Well maybe, Rene, just maybe—I want you.

GALLIMARD: You do?

SONG: Then again, maybe I'm just playing with you. How can you tell? (*Reprising his feminine character, he sidles up to* GALLIMARD) "How I wish there were even a small cafe to sit in. With men in tuxedos, and cappuccinos, and bad expatriate jazz." Now you want to kiss me, don't you?

GALLIMARD (*Pulling away*): What makes you—?

SONG: —so sure? See? I take the words from your mouth. Then I wait for you to come and retrieve them. (*He reclines on the floor*)

GALLIMARD: Why?! Why do you treat me so cruelly?

SONG: Perhaps I *was* treating you cruelly. But now—I'm being nice. Come here, my little one.

GALLIMARD: I'm not your little one!

SONG: My mistake. It's I who am *your* little one, right?

GALLIMARD: Yes, I—

SONG: So come get your little one. If you like. I may even let you strip me.

GALLIMARD: I mean, you were! Before . . . but not like this!

SONG: I was? Then perhaps I still am. If you look hard enough. (*He starts to remove his clothes*)

GALLIMARD: What—what are you doing?

SONG: Helping you to see through my act.

GALLIMARD: Stop that! I don't want to! I don't—

SONG: Oh, but you asked me to strip, remember?

GALLIMARD: What? That was years ago! And I took it back!

SONG: No. You postponed it. Postponed the inevitable. Today, the inevitable has come calling.

(*From the speakers, cacophony: Butterfly mixed in with Chinese gongs.*)

GALLIMARD: No! Stop! I don't want to see!

SONG: Then look away.

GALLIMARD: You're only in my mind! All this is in my mind! I order you! To stop!

SONG: To what? To strip? That's just what I'm—

GALLIMARD: No! Stop! I want you—!

SONG: You want me?

GALLIMARD: To stop!

SONG: You know something, Rene? Your mouth says no, but your eyes say yes. Turn them away. I dare you.

GALLIMARD: I don't have to! Every night, you say you're going to strip, but then I beg you and you stop!

SONG: I guess tonight is different.

GALLIMARD: Why? Why should that be?

SONG: Maybe I've become frustrated. Maybe I'm saying "Look at me, you fool!" Or maybe I'm just feeling . . . sexy. (*He is down to his briefs*)

GALLIMARD: Please. This is unnecessary. I know what you are.

SONG: Do you? What am I?

GALLIMARD: A—a man.

SONG: You don't really believe that.

GALLIMARD: Yes I do! I knew all the time somewhere that my happiness was temporary, my love a deception. But my mind kept the knowledge at bay. To make the wait bearable.

SONG: Monsieur Gallimard—the wait is over.

(*SONG drops his briefs. He is naked. Sound cue out. Slowly, we and SONG come to the realization that what we had thought to be GALLIMARD's sobbing is actually his laughter.*)

GALLIMARD: Oh god! What an idiot! Of course!

SONG: Rene—what?

GALLIMARD: Look at you! You're a man! (*He bursts into laughter again*)

SONG: I fail to see what's so funny!

GALLIMARD: "You fail to see—!" I mean, you never did have much of a sense of humor, did you? I just think it's ridiculously funny that I've wasted so much time on just a man!

SONG: Wait. I'm not "just a man."

GALLIMARD: No? Isn't that what you've been trying to convince me of?

SONG: Yes, but what I mean—

GALLIMARD: And now, I finally believe you, and you tell me it's not true? I think you must have some kind of identity problem.

SONG: Will you listen to me?

GALLIMARD: Why?! I've been listening to you for twenty years. Don't I deserve a vacation?

SONG: I'm not just any man!

GALLIMARD: Then, what exactly are you?

SONG: Rene, how can you ask—? Okay, what about this?

(*He picks up Butterfly's robes, starts to dance around. No music.*)

GALLIMARD: Yes, that's very nice. I have to admit.

(*SONG holds out his arm to GALLIMARD.*)

SONG: It's the same skin you've worshiped for years. Touch it.

GALLIMARD: Yes, it does feel the same.

SONG: Now—close your eyes.

(*SONG covers GALLIMARD's eyes with one hand. With the other, SONG draws GALLIMARD's hand up to his face. GALLIMARD, like a blind man, lets his hands run over SONG's face.*)

GALLIMARD: This skin, I remember. The curve of her face, the softness of her cheek, her hair against the back of my hand . . .

SONG: I'm your Butterfly. Under the robes, beneath everything, it was always me. Now, open your eyes and admit it—you adore me. (*He removes his hand from GALLIMARD's eyes*)

GALLIMARD: You, who knew every inch of my desires—how could you, of all people, have made such a mistake?

SONG: What?

GALLIMARD: You showed me your true self. When all I loved was the lie. A perfect lie, which you let fall to the ground—and now, it's old and soiled.

SONG: So—you never really loved me? Only when I was playing a part?

GALLIMARD: I'm a man who loved a woman created by a man. Everything else—simply falls short.

(*Pause.*)

SONG: What am I supposed to do now?

GALLIMARD: You were a fine spy, Monsieur Song, with an even finer accomplice. But now I believe you should go. Get out of my life!

SONG: Go where? Rene, you can't live without me. Not after twenty years.

GALLIMARD: I certainly can't live with you—not after twenty years of betrayal.

SONG: Don't be so stubborn! Where will you go?

GALLIMARD: I have a date . . . with my Butterfly.

SONG: So, throw away your pride. And come . . .

GALLIMARD: Get away from me! Tonight, I've finally learned to tell fantasy from reality. And, knowing the difference, I choose fantasy.

SONG: I'm your fantasy!

GALLIMARD: You? You're as real as hamburger. Now get out! I have a date with my Butterfly and I don't want your body polluting the room! (He tosses SONG's suit at him) Look at these—you dress like a pimp.

SONG: Hey! These are Armani slacks and—! (He puts on his briefs and slacks) Let's just say . . . I'm disappointed in you, Rene. In the crush of your adoration, I thought you'd become something more. More like . . . a woman.

But no. Men. You're like the rest of them. It's all in the way we dress, and make up our faces, and bat our eyelashes. You really have so little imagination!

GALLIMARD: You, Monsieur Song? Accuse me of too little imagination? You, if anyone, should know—I am pure imagination. And in imagination I will remain. Now get out!

(GALLIMARD bodily removes SONG from the stage, taking his kimono.)

SONG: Rene! I'll never put on those robes again! You'll be sorry!

GALLIMARD: (To SONG): I'm already sorry! (Looking at the kimono in his hands) Exactly as sorry . . . as a Butterfly.

SCENE 3

M. GALLIMARD's prison cell. Paris. Present.

GALLIMARD: I've played out the events of my life night after night, always searching for a new ending to my story, one where I leave this cell and return forever to my Butterfly's arms.

Tonight I realize my search is over. That I've looked all along in the wrong place. And now, to you, I will prove that my love was not in vain—by returning to the world of fantasy where I first met her.

(He picks up the kimono; dancers enter.)

GALLIMARD: There is a vision of the Orient that I have. Of slender women in chong sams and kimonos who die for the love of unworthy foreign devils. Who are born and raised to be the perfect women. Who take whatever punishment we give them, and bounce back, strengthened by love, unconditionally. It is a vision that has become my life.

(Dancers bring the wash basin to him and help him make up his face.)

GALLIMARD: In public, I have continued to deny that Song Liling is a man. This brings me headlines, and is a source of great embarrassment to my French colleagues, who can now be sent into a coughing fit by the mere mention of Chinese food. But alone, in my cell, I have long since faced the truth.

And the truth demands a sacrifice. For mistakes made over the course of a lifetime. My mistakes were simple and absolute—the man I loved was a cad, a bounder. He deserved nothing but a kick in the behind, and instead I gave him . . . all my love.

Yes—love. Why not admit it all? That was my undoing, wasn't it? Love warped my judgment, blinded my eyes, rearranged the very lines on my face . . . until I could look in the mirror and see nothing but . . . a woman.

(Dancers help him put on the Butterfly wig.)

GALLIMARD: I have a vision. Of the Orient. That, deep within its almond eyes, there are still women. Women willing to sacrifice themselves for the love of a man. Even a man whose love is completely without worth.

(Dancers assist GALLIMARD in donning the kimono. They hand him a knife.)

GALLIMARD: Death with honor is better than life . . . life with dishonor. (He sets himself center stage, in a seppuku position) The love of a Butterfly can withstand many things—unfaithfulness, loss, even abandonment. But how can it face the one sin that implies all others? The devastating knowledge that, underneath it all, the object of her love was nothing more, nothing less than . . . a man. (He sets the tip of the knife against his body) It is 19__ And I have found her at last. In a prison on the outskirts of Paris. My name is Rene Gallimard—also known as Madame Butterfly.

(GALLIMARD turns upstage and plunges the knife into his body, as music from the "Love Duet" blares over the speakers. He collapses into the arms of the *dancers, who lay him reverently on the floor. The image holds for several beats. Then a tight special up on* SONG, *who stands as a man, staring at the dead* GALLIMARD. *He smokes a cigarette; the smoke filters up through the lights. Two words leave his lips.*)

SONG: Butterfly? Butterfly?

(*Smoke rises as lights fade slowly to black.*)

END OF PLAY

AFTERWORD

It all started in May of 1986, over casual dinner conversation. A friend asked, had I heard about the French diplomat who'd fallen in love with a Chinese actress, who subsequently turned out to be not only a spy, but a man? I later found a two-paragraph story in *The New York Times*. The diplomat, Bernard Bouriscot, attempting to account for the fact that he had never seen his "girlfriend" naked, was quoted as saying, "I thought she was very modest. I thought it was a Chinese custom."

Now, I am aware that this is *not* a Chinese custom, that Asian women are no more shy with their lovers than are women of the West. I am also aware, however, that Bouriscot's assumption was consistent with a certain stereotyped view of Asians as bowing, blushing flowers. I therefore concluded that the diplomat must have fallen in love, not with a person, but with a fantasy stereotype. I also inferred that, to the extent the Chinese spy encouraged these misperceptions, he must have played up to and exploited this image of the Oriental woman as demure and submissive. (In general, by the way, we prefer the term "Asian" to "Oriental," in the same way "Black" is superior to "Negro." I use the term "Oriental" specifically to denote an exotic or imperialistic view of the East.)

I suspected there was a play here. I purposely refrained from further research, for I was not interested in writing docudrama. Frankly, I didn't want the "truth" to interfere with my own speculations. I told Stuart Ostrow, a producer with whom I'd worked before, that I envisioned the story as a musical. I remember going so far as to speculate that it could be some "great *Madame Butterfly*–like tragedy." Stuart was very intrigued, and encouraged me with some early funding.

Before I can begin writing, I must "break the back of the story," and find some angle which compels me to set pen to paper. I was driving down Santa Monica Boulevard one afternoon, and asked myself, "What did Bouriscot think he was getting in this Chinese actress?" The answer came to me clearly: "He probably thought he had found Madame Butterfly."

The idea of doing a deconstructivist *Madame Butterfly* immediately appealed to me. This, despite the fact that I didn't even know the plot of the opera! I knew Butterfly only as a cultural stereotype; speaking of an Asian woman, we would sometimes say, "She's pulling a Butterfly," which meant playing the submissive Oriental number. Yet, I felt convinced that the libretto would include yet another lotus blossom pining away for a cruel Caucasian man, and dying for her love. Such a story has become too much of a cliché not to be included in the archtypal East-West romance that started it all. Sure enough, when I purchased the record, I discovered it contained a wealth of sexist and racist clichés, reaffirming my faith in Western culture.

Very soon after, I came up with the basic "arc" of my play: the Frenchman fantasizes that he is Pinkerton and his lover is Butterfly. By the end of the piece, he realizes that it is he who has been Butterfly, in that the Frenchman has been duped by love; the Chinese spy, who exploited that love, is therefore the real Pinkerton. I wrote a proposal to Stuart Ostrow, who found it very exciting. (On the night of the Tony Awards, Stuart produced my original two-page treatment, and we were gratified to see that it was, indeed, the play I eventually wrote.)

I wrote a play, rather than a musical, because, having "broken the back" of the story, I wanted to start immediately and not be hampered by the lengthy process of collaboration. I would like to think, however, that the play has retained many of its musical roots. So *Monsieur Butterfly* was completed in six weeks between September and mid-October, 1986. My wife, Ophelia, thought *Monsieur Butterfly* too obvious a title, and suggested I abbreviate it in the French fashion. Hence, *M. Butterfly*, far more mysterious and ambiguous, was the result.

I sent the play to Stuart Ostrow as a courtesy, assuming he would not be interested in producing what had become a straight play. Instead, he flew out to Los Angeles immediately for script conferences. Coming from a background in the not-for-profit theater, I suggested that we develop the work at a regional institution. Stuart, nothing if not bold, argued for bringing it directly to Broadway.

It was also Stuart who suggested John Dexter to direct. I had known Dexter's work only by its formidable reputation. Stuart sent the script to John, who called back the next day, saying it was the best play he'd read in twenty years. Naturally, this predisposed me to like him a great deal. We met in December in New York. Not long after, we persuaded Eiko Ishioka to design our sets and costumes. I had admired her work from afar ever since, as a college student, I had seen her poster for *Apocalypse Now* in Japan. By January, 1987, Stuart had optioned *M. Butterfly,* Dexter was signed to direct, and the normally sloth-like pace of commercial theater had been given a considerable prod.

On January 4, 1988, we commenced rehearsals. I was very pleased that John Lithgow had agreed to play the French diplomat, who I named Rene Gallimard. Throughout his tenure with us, Lithgow was every inch the center of our company, intelligent and professional, passionate and generous. B. D. Wong was forced to endure a five-month audition period before we selected him to play Song Liling. Watching B. D.'s growth was one of the joys of the rehearsal process, as he constantly attained higher levels of performance. It became clear that we had been fortunate enough to put together a company with not only great talent, but also wonderful camaraderie.

As for Dexter, I have never worked with a director more respectful of text and bold in the uses of theatricality. On the first day of rehearsal, the actors were given movement and speech drills. Then Dexter asked that everyone not required at rehearsal leave the room. A week later, we returned for an amazingly thorough run-through. It was not until that day that I first heard my play read, a note I direct at many regional theaters who "develop" a script to death.

We opened in Washington, D.C., at the National Theatre, where *West Side Story* and *Amadeus* had premiered. On the morning after opening night, most of the reviews were glowing, except for *The*

Washington Post. Throughout our run in Washington, Stuart never pressured us to make the play more "commercial" in reaction to that review. We all simply concluded that the gentleman was possibly insecure about his own sexual orientation and therefore found the play threatening. And we continued our work.

Once we opened in New York, the play found a life of its own. I suppose the most gratifying thing for me is that we had never compromised to be more "Broadway"; we simply did the work we thought best. That our endeavor should be rewarded to the degree it has is one of those all-too-rare instances when one's own perception and that of the world are in agreement.

Many people have subsequently asked me about the "ideas" behind the play. From our first preview in Washington, I have been pleased that people leaving the theater were talking not only about the sexual, but also the political, issues raised by the work.

From my point of view, the "impossible" story of a Frenchman duped by a Chinese man masquerading as a woman always seemed perfectly explicable; given the degree of misunderstanding between men and women and also between East and West, it seemed inevitable that a mistake of this magnitude would one day take place.

Gay friends have told me of a derogatory term used in their community: "Rice Queen"—a gay Caucasian man primarily attracted to Asians. In these relationships, the Asian virtually always plays the role of the "woman"; the Rice Queen, culturally and sexually, is the "man." This pattern of relationships had become so codified that, until recently, it was considered unnatural for gay Asians to date one another. Such men would be taunted with a phrase which implied they were lesbians.

Similarly, heterosexual Asians have long been aware of "Yellow Fever"—Caucasian men with a fetish for exotic Oriental women. I have often heard it said that "Oriental women make the best wives." (Rarely is this heard from the mouths of Asian men, incidentally.) This mythology is exploited by the Oriental mail-order bride trade which has flourished over the past decade. American men can now send away for catalogues of "obedient, domesticated" Asian women looking for husbands. Anyone who believes such stereotypes are a thing of the past need look no further than Manhattan cable television, which advertises call girls from "the exotic east, where men are king; obedient girls, trained in the art of pleasure."

In these appeals, we see issues of racism and sexism intersect. The catalogues and TV spots appeal to a strain in men which desires to reject Western women for what they have become—independent, assertive, self-possessed—in favor of a more reactionary model—the pre-feminist, domesticated geisha girl.

That the Oriental woman is penultimately feminine does not of course imply that she is always "good." For every Madonna there is a whore; for every lotus blossom there is also a dragon lady. In popular culture, "good" Asian women are those who serve the White protagonist in his battle against her own people, often sleeping with him in the process. Stallone's *Rambo II,* Cimino's *Year of the Dragon,* Clavell's *Shogun,* Van Lustbader's *The Ninja* are all familiar examples.

Now our considerations of race and sex intersect the issue of imperialism. For this formula—good natives serve Whites, bad natives rebel—is consistent with the mentality of colonialism. Because they are submissive and obedient, good natives of both sexes necessarily take on "feminine" characteristics in a colonialist world. Gunga Din's unfailing devotion to his British master, for instance, is not so far removed from Butterfly's slavish faith in Pinkerton.

It is reasonable to assume that influences and attitudes so pervasively displayed in popular culture might also influence our policymakers as they consider the world. The neo-Colonialist notion that good elements of a native society, like a good woman, desire submission to the masculine West speaks precisely to the heart of our foreign policy blunders in Asia and elsewhere.

For instance, Frances Fitzgerald wrote in *Fire in the Lake,* "The idea that the United States could not master the problems of a country as small and underdeveloped as Vietnam did not occur to Johnson as a possibility." Here, as in so many other cases, by dehumanizing the enemy, we dehumanize ourselves. We become the Rice Queens of *realpolitik.*

M. Butterfly has sometimes been regarded as an anti-American play, a diatribe against the stereotyping of the East by the West, of women by men. Quite to the contrary, I consider it a plea to all sides to cut through our respective layers of cultural and sexual misperception, to deal with one another truthfully for our mutual good, from the common and equal ground we share as human beings.

For the myths of the East, the myths of the West, the myths of men, and the myths of women—these have so saturated our consciousness that truthful contact between nations and lovers can only be the result of heroic effort. Those who prefer to bypass the work involved will remain in a world of surfaces, misperceptions running rampant. This is, to me, the convenient world in which the French diplomat and the Chinese spy lived. This is why, after twenty years, he had learned nothing at all about his lover, not even the truth of his sex.

D. H. H.

New York City
September, 1988

Introduction to *Marisol*

WHEN THE PLAY WAS NEW

José Rivera's *Marisol*, an apocalyptic fantasy, was first performed at the Humana Festival at the Actors Theatre of Louisville on March 13, 1992. Within its first year, *Marisol* had a number of professional productions, attesting to its timeliness and theatricality. After its New York production in 1993 at the New York Shakespeare Festival, *Marisol* won an Obie award for best new play. The urban horrors, paranoia, and displacement presented so effectively in the play continue to fascinate and disturb audiences. The play is still contemporary.

The play's import, however, is not just its depictions of terror, random street violence, and self-destruction, but in its cosmic themes and the title character's adamant search for not just safety, but fulfillment. There is a war in heaven waged by the angels against a senile god causing the guardian angels to abandon their posts on earth, thus allowing the violence and destruction to escalate in the cities. Rivera's dramatized window on the earth is the Bronx in New York, which turns into a war zone. Despite the almost-hopeless fix the characters find themselves in, surrounded by death, Rivera laces the play with bizarre humor, and creates a way to bring his heroine Marisol to a satisfying conclusion. Rivera always has hope and finds magical ways to extricate his good characters from destruction. In *Marisol* Rivera (a Latino playwright), brings together Hispanic and white characters for the first time in his body of plays.

THE PLAYWRIGHT

José Rivera was born in 1955 in Puerto Rico and moved to New York at the age of four. After graduating from Denison University in Ohio, he launched a writing career and soon found that playwriting was a natural outlet for him. He has also written success-

fully for television and film. An important early influence on his style and writing voice was his study with the novelist Gabriel Garcia Marquéz at the Sundance Festival. Rivera started getting professional theatrical productions in the early 1980s.

Among his early successes are *The House of Ramon Iglesias* (1983), a study of a Latino son in conflict with his immigrant parents (produced for television in 1986); *The Promise* (1988); and *Each Day Dies with Sleep* (1990). The term *magic realism* is often associated with his plays due to his mixture of the magical or impossible with reality. Rivera resists this term at times and refers to *alternative realities*. Whatever descriptive label one may wish to apply, his plays are undoubtedly highly theatrical and often dramatize both the seen and the unseen. The plays almost always tackle difficult contemporary problems such as a returning American soldier from the first Gulf War trying to reunite with his now-skeptical Hispanic wife in *References to Salvador Dali Make Me Hot* (1999). *Adoration of the Old Woman* (2002) presents an aging woman in a generational conflict with her great granddaughter, but both are haunted by the ghost of the old woman's past. Sometimes fantasy becomes more operative than reality as in Rivera's *Giants Have Us in Their Books* (1994), a collection of six short one-acts that he calls "children's plays for adults." Some of his plays experiment with form and delivery as in *Cloud Tectonics* (1995), in which time is impossibly compressed, and *Lovers of Red Hair* (2000), a three-minute telephone booth play. His *Sonnets for an Old Century* (2002) combines monologues, music, and dance. Rivera wrote the screenplay for the film *Motorcycle Diaries* (2004). He has also adapted Calderón's *Life Is a Dream* as *Sueño* and Lorca's *Blood Wedding* as a musical.

Rivera has been widely produced in off-Broadway theatres and leading regional theatres, as well as numerous theatres in Latin America and Europe. He has also had a number of writer's residencies in California, New York, and the Royal Court Theatre in London, where he wrote some of his early successes, including *Marisol*. He now resides in Los Angeles.

GENRE, STRUCTURE, AND STYLE

Typically, Rivera manipulates time in his plays. In *Marisol* the cosmic clock is very different than the worldly one, but the action still progresses in a linear, if episodic, fashion. Most of the title character's scenes have a reality base, although she converses with an angel and finds herself confused by events and character transformation. By calling for doubling of other characters, Rivera creates a powerful focus on his protagonist, who carries the day both in terms of the play's emotional journey and structural development. The play imitates chaos.

Rivera's dramatic result is an episodic tragicomedy. A happy ending is provided, but happiness is only possible in death. Earthly death is instantaneous (no suffering), and it transforms the victim so that she will never suffer again. The horrors end with renewal and a magical moment that is forward-looking, prophetic, and dreamlike. The term *magic realism* seems fitting for *Marisol*.

IMPORTANT ELEMENTS OF CONTENT

Marisol is one of the most powerful plays of the twentieth century in its evocation of paranoia, random violence, the urban nightmare, and simultaneous presence of the real and the invisible. The play juxtaposes images of traditional Christianity with strange variants of the supernatural and worlds usually seen only in our dreams or daydreams. A war in heaven runs a parallel path to the urban war on earth. Marisol searches for a safe haven, which becomes increasingly difficult until she finds herself completely exposed on the street. The only haven possible lies beyond the grave. Note that just before the final earthly moments of Marisol, she is examining the gravestones of children.

THE PLAY IN REVIVAL

After the first production at Actors Theatre of Louisville, *Marisol* was soon produced at LaJolla

Playhouse in California (1992), Hartford Stage Company in Connecticut (1993), and the New York Shakespeare Festival (1993). After the first wave of productions, a second began about 1998 in Vancouver and San Francisco and escalated after September 11, 2001. Between 2001 and 2005 many university productions have appeared along with periodic professional productions in Dallas, Chicago, and California.

SPECIAL FEATURE

The presentation of the angel is an intriguing production problem: In some scenes she is overheard, indicating heaven, but in other scenes she is face-to-face with Marisol on the earth. She must transform and lose her wings, which at one point melt in the hands of Marisol. She goes from guardian angel to an angel of war. The angel's presence is very physical and real for Marisol, yet for other characters she exists in another plane.

FURTHER READING ABOUT THE PLAY, PLAYWRIGHT, AND CONTEXT

Most of the plays of Rivera have been published as individual editions, or if short, in collections of his plays. See *Marisol and Other Plays, Plays from the South Coast Repertory* and *Giants Have Us in Their Books*.

No books have yet appeared on Rivera, but there are articles on his plays and stagecraft. See his description of his playwriting process outlined in an interview by Lucia Mauro at www.performink.com/Archives/stagepersonae/2003/RiveraJose.html.

See also Lynn Jacobson, "An Interview with José Rivera," *Studies in American Drama*, vol. 6, pp. 49–58; John Antush, "An Anthology of Puerto Rican Plays," in John R. Woolcott and Michael L. Quinn, eds., *Staging Diversity;* and José Rivera, "Poverty and Magic in Each Day Dies with Sleep," *Studies in American Drama*, vol. 7, pp. 163–232.

Marisol

By José Rivera

CHARACTERS

ANGEL
MARISOL
MAN WITH GOLF CLUB
MAN WITH ICE CREAM   *All can be*
LENNY   *played by the*
MAN WITH SCAR TISSUE   *same actor*
JUNE
WOMAN WITH FURS
RADIO ANNOUNCER
HOMELESS PEOPLE
Place: New York City.
Time: The present.

ACT ONE

SCENE ONE
New York City. The present.

Lights up on an upstage brick wall running the width of the stage and going as high as the theatre will allow. The windows in the wall are shielded by iron security gates. The highest windows are boarded up.

Spray painted on the wall is this graffiti poem:

> The moon carries the souls of dead
>   people to heaven.
> The new moon is dark and empty.
> It fills up every month
> with new glowing souls
> then it carries its silent burden to God.
>   WAKE UP.

The "WAKE UP" looks like it was added to the poem by someone else.

Downstage of the wall is a tall ladder coming down at an angle. Sitting on the ladder is MARISOL'S GUARDIAN ANGEL.

The ANGEL *is a young black woman in ripped jeans, sneakers, and black T-shirt. Crude silver wings hang limply from the back of the* ANGEL'S *diamond-studded black leather jacket. Though she radiates tremendous heat and light, there's something tired and lonely about the* ANGEL: *she looks like an urban warrior, a suffering burnt-out soldier of some lost cause. She watches the scene below with intense concern.*

Floating in the sky is a small gold crown inside a clear glass box.

Lights up on the subway car: a filth-covered bench.

It's late night. Late winter.

MARISOL PEREZ, *an attractive Puerto Rican woman of twenty-six, sits in the subway car.* MARISOL *has dark hair and deep, smart, dark eyes. She is a young urban professional: smartly dressed, reading the* New York Times, *returning to her Bronx apartment after a long day at her Manhattan job. She wears heavy winter clothing. She has no idea she's being watched by an angel.*

SUBWAY ANNOUNCER: . . . and a pleasant evening to all the ladies. 180th Street will be the next and last stop. Step lively, guard your valuables, trust no one.
(The MAN WITH GOLF CLUB *enters the subway car. He's a young white man, twenties, in a filthy black T-shirt and ripped jeans; his long matted hair hangs over blazing eyes. His shoes are rags and his mind is shot. The man looks at* MARISOL *and "shoots" the club like an Uzi.*

MARISOL has taught herself not to show fear or curiosity on the subway. She digs deeper into her paper. THE MAN *talks to* MARISOL.)

GOLF CLUB: It was the shock that got me. I was so shocked all I could see was pain all around me: little spinning starlights of pain 'cause of the shocking thing the angel just told me.

(*He waits for a reaction.* MARISOL *refuses to look at him.*)

You see, she was always *there* for me. I could *count* on her. She was my very own god-blessed little angel! My own gift from God!

(*No response. He makes a move toward* MARISOL. *She looks at him, quickly sizing him up . . .*)

MARISOL: God help you, you get in my face.

GOLF CLUB: But last night she crawled into the box I occupy on 180th Street in the Bronx. I was sleeping: nothing special walking through my thoughts 'cept the usual panic over my empty stomach, and the windchill factor, and how, oh *how,* was I *ever* gonna replace my lost Citibank MasterCard?

MARISOL: I have no money.

(MARISOL *tries to slide away from the* MAN, *trying to show no fear. He follows.*)

GOLF CLUB: She folded her hot silver angelwings under her leather jacket and creeped into my box last night, reordering the air, waking me up with the shock, the bad news that she was gonna *leave me forever . . .*

MARISOL (*Getting freaked*): Man, why don't you just get a job?!

GOLF CLUB: *Don't you see?* She once stopped Nazi skinheads from setting me on fire in Van Cordandt Park! Do you get it now, lady?! I live on the street! I am dead meat without my guardian angel! I'm gonna be *food . . .* a fucking *appetizer* for all the Hitler youth and their cans of *gasoline . . .*

(*The* MAN *lunges at* MARISOL *and rips the newspaper from her. She's on her feet, ready for a fight.*)

MARISOL (*To God*): Okay, God! Kill him now! Take him out!

GOLF CLUB (*Truly worried*): That means you don't have any protection either. Your guardian angel is gonna leave you too. That means, in the next *four or five seconds,* I could change the entire course of your life . . .

MARISOL (*To God*): Blast him into little bits! Turn him into salt!

GOLF CLUB (*Calm, almost pitying*): I could turn you into one of me. I could fix it so every time you look in the mirror . . . every time you dream . . .

or close your eyes in some hopeless logic that closed eyes are a shield against nightmares . . . *you're gonna think you turned into me . . .*

(*The* MAN *makes a move toward* MARISOL. *The* ANGEL *reacts. There's an earsplitting scream as the subway stops.* MARISOL *and the* MAN *are thrown violently across the subway car. The* MAN *falls.* MARISOL *seizes her chance, pushes the disoriented* MAN *away, and runs out of the subway car into the street. Lights to black on the subway. The* MAN *exits in the dark.*)

SCENE TWO

Lights up on the street: a small empty space with a battered city trash can. It's snowing lightly. The shivering MARISOL *stops to look up at the sky. She crosses herself.*

MARISOL: Thank you.

(*No response from the* ANGEL. *It stops snowing as* MARISOL *leaves the street and enters:*)

SCENE THREE

Lights up on MARISOL's *apartment: bed, table, lamp, clock, off-stage bathroom, and large romanticized picture of a traditional Catholic guardian angel on the wall.*

MARISOL *quickly runs in, slamming and locking the door behind her. She runs to the window to make sure the security gates are locked.*

She tries to catch her breath. She takes off her coat. She notices an army of cockroaches on the floor. She stomps them angrily until every last one is dead. This seems to make her feel a little better.

She collapses into bed. She pounds her pillow angrily. Exhausted, she checks a knife she keeps under her pillow. She puts it back and lies on her bed, trying to calm herself and just breathe.

As she changes her clothes she fixes herself a drink and downs it.

She checks the crucifix, horseshoe, rabbit's foot, prayer cards, milagros, medicine bundles, statuettes of Buddha and other good-luck charms kept under the bed. She crosses herself and closes her eyes.

MARISOL: Matthew, Mark, Luke and John.
Bless the bed that I lie on.
Four corners to my bed.
Four angels 'round my head.
One to watch and one to pray.
And two to bear my soul away.

(MARISOL *crosses herself, opens her eyes and lies down. Then the noises begin. They come at* MARISOL *from apartments all around her. Doors are slammed, bottles smashed, radiator pipes pounded, stereos played loud. Then the voices join in.*)

VOICE #1 (*Female*): *Ave Maria purisima, donde esta el* heat?

(MARISOL *sits up. She can't believe this bullshit is starting again . . .*)

VOICE #2 (*Female, a high-decibel shriek*): Matthew? It's Sandy! I KNOW YOU'RE IN THERE. STOP HIDING FROM ME, YOU MALIGNANT FUCK!

(MARISOL *starts rubbing her pounding head.*)

VOICE #3 (*Male*): Ah yeah yeah man you gotta help me man they broke my fuckin' *head* open . . .

(MARISOL *runs to her window, shakes the iron gates.*)

MARISOL: *Mira,* people are trying to sleep!

VOICE #2: YOU'RE PISSING ME OFF, MATTHEW, OPEN THE DOOR!

VOICE #1: *Donde esta el* heat?? *NO TENGO* HEAT, *coño!*

VOICE #2: MATTHEEEEEEEEEEEEEEEEW!

(MARISOL *dives back into bed, covering her head, trying not to hear. The noises increase and the voices come faster, louder, over-lapping . . .*)

VOICE #3: . . . I was jus' tryin' to sell 'em some dope man . . .

VOICE #2: MATTHEW, GODDAMMIT ITS SANDY! SANDY. YOUR *GIRLFRIEND,* YOU WITLESS *COCK!*

VOICE #1: *Me vas a matar* without *el* fucking heat!!

VOICE #2: MATTHEEEEEEEEWWWWWWW! OPEN THIS DOOOOOOOOOOOOR!

VOICE #3: . . . so they hadda go bust my fuckin' head open oh look haha there go my busted brains floppin' 'round the floor I'm gonna step right on 'em I'm not careful man I shouldda got their fuckin' *badge* numbers . . .

(MARISOL *bangs on the floor with a shoe.*)

MARISOL: Some people work in the morning!!

VOICE #3: . . . think I'll pick up my brains right now man get a shovel 'n' scoop up my soakin' brainbag off this messy linoleum floor man sponge up my absentee motherfuckin' *mind* . . .

VOICE #2: THAT'S IT, MATTHEW! YOU'RE DEAD. I'M COMING BACK WITH A GUN AND I'M GONNA KILL YOU AND THEN I'M GONNA KILL EVERYONE IN THIS APARTMENT BUILDING INCLUDING THE CHILDREN!

(*The voices stop.* MARISOL *waits. Thinking it's over,* MARISOL *gets into bed and tries to sleep. Beat.* MARISOL *starts to nod off. There's suddenly furious knocking at* MARISOL's *door.*)

VOICE #2: MATTHEW! I'M BACK I'VE GOT MY DADDY'S GUN! AND YOU'RE GONNA DIE RIGHT NOW.

(MARISOL *runs to the door.*)

MARISOL: Matthew doesn't live here! You have the wrong apartment!

VOICE #2: Matthew, *who's that???*

MARISOL: Matthew lives next door!!

VOICE #2: IS THAT YOUR NEW GIRLFRIEND, MATTHEW???! OH YOU'RE DEAD. YOU'RE REALLY DEAD NOW!!

(*A gun is cocked.* MARISOL *dives for cover. the* ANGEL *reacts. Suddenly, the stage is blasted with white light.*

There's complete silence. the rattling, banging, screaming all stop. We hear crickets.

MARISOL, *amazed by the instant calm, goes to the door, looks through the peephole. She cautiously opens the door.*

There's a small pile of salt on the floor. At first, MARISOL *just looks at it, too amazed to move. Then she bends down to touch the salt, letting it run through her fingers.*)

MARISOL: Salt?

(*Frightened, not sure she knows what this means,* MARISOL *quickly closes and locks the door. She gets into bed and turns out the light. Lights down everywhere except on the* ANGEL.)

SCENE FOUR

Lights shift in MARISOL's *apartment as the Angel climbs down the ladder to* MARISOL's *bed.*

MARISOL *feels the tremendous heat given off by the* ANGEL. *The* ANGEL *backs away from* MARISOL *so as not to burn her. The* ANGEL *goes to the window and looks out. Her voice is slightly amplified. She speaks directly to* MARISOL, *who sleeps.*

Throughout the scene, the light coming in through MARISOL's *window goes up slowly, until, by the end, it's the next morning.*

ANGEL: A man is worshiping a fire hydrant on Taylor Avenue, Marisol. He's draping rosaries on it, genuflecting hard. An old woman's selling charmed chicken blood in see-through Ziplock bags for a buck. They're setting another homeless man on fire in Van Cortlandt Park.
(*The* ANGEL *rattles the metal gate.*)
Cut that shit out you fucking Nazis!
(*The* ANGEL *goes to* MARISOL's *door and checks the lock. She stomps cockroaches. She straightens up a little.*)
I swear, best thing that could happen to this city is immediate evacuation followed by fire on a massive scale. Melt it all down. Consume the ruins. Then put the ashes of those evaporated dreams into a big urn and sit the urn on the desks of a few thousand oily politicians. Let them smell the disaster like we do.
(*The* ANGEL *goes to* MARISOL's *bed and looks at her.* MARISOL's *heart beats faster and she starts to hyperventilate.*)
So what do you believe in, Marisol? *You believe in me? Or do you believe your senses? If so, what's that taste in your mouth?*
(*The* ANGEL *clicks her fingers. Although* MARISOL *responds, she remains sleeping throughout the following scene.*)
MARISOL (*Tasting*): Oh my God, *arroz con gandules!* Yum!
ANGEL: What's your favorite smell, Marisol?
(*Click!*)
MARISOL (*Sniffing*): The ocean! I smell the ocean!
ANGEL: Do you like sex, Marisol?
(*Click!* MARISOL *is seized by powerful sexual spasms that wrack her body and nearly throw her off the bed. When they end,* MARISOL *stretches out luxuriously: exhausted but happy.*)
MARISOL (*Laughing*): I've got this wild energy running through my body!
(*The* ANGEL *gets closer to her.*)

ANGEL: Here's your big chance, baby. What would you like to ask the Angel of the Lord?
MARISOL (*Energized*): Are you real? Are you true? Are you gonna make the Bronx safe for me? Are you gonna make miracles and reduce my rent? Is it true angels' favorite food is Thousand Island dressing? Is it true your shit smells like mangoes and when you're drunk you speak Portuguese?!
ANGEL: Honey, last time *I* was drunk . . .
(MARISOL *gets a sudden, horrifying realization.*)
MARISOL: *Wait a minute—am I dead?* Did I die tonight? How did I miss that? Was it the man with the golf club? Did he beat me to death? Oh my God. I've been dead all night. And when I look around I see that Death is my ugly apartment in the Bronx. No this can't be Death! Death can't have this kind of furniture!
ANGEL: God, you're so cute, I could eat you up. No. You're still alive.
(MARISOL *is momentarily relieved—then she suddenly starts touching her stomach as she gets a wild, exhilarating idea:*)
MARISOL: *Am I pregnant with the Lord's baby?!* Is the new Messiah swimming in my electrified womb? Is the supersperm of God growing a mythic flower deep in the secret greenhouse inside me? Will my morning sickness taste like communion wine? This is amazing—*billions* of women on earth, and I get knocked up by God!
ANGEL: No baby, no baby, no baby, no baby—No. Baby.
(*Beat.* MARISOL *is a little disappointed.*)
MARISOL: No? Then what is it? Are you real or not? 'Cause if you're real and God is real and the Gospels are real, this would be the perfect time to tell me. 'Cause I once looked for angels, I did, in every shadow of my childhood—but I never found any. I thought I'd find you hiding inside the notes I sang to myself as a kid. The songs that put me to sleep and kept me from killing myself with fear. But I didn't see you then.
(*The* ANGEL *doesn't answer. Her silence—her very presence—starts to unhinge* MARISOL.)
C'mon! Somebody up there has to tell me why I live the way I do! What's going *on* here, any-

way? Why is there a war on children in this city? Why are apples extinct? Why are they planning to drop human insecticide on over-populated areas of the Bronx? Why has the color blue disappeared from the sky? Why does common rainwater turn your skin bright red? Why do cows give salty milk? Why did the Plague kill half my friends? AND WHAT HAPPENED TO THE MOON? Where did the moon go? How come nobody's seen it in nearly *nine months . . . ?*

(MARISOL *is trying desperately to keep from crying. The* ANGEL *gets into bed with* MARISOL. *Contact with the* ANGEL *makes* MARISOL *gasp. She opens her mouth to scream, but nothing comes out.* MARISOL *collapses—her whole body goes limp.*

MARISOL *rests her head on the* ANGEL'*s lap. Electricity surges gently through* MARISOL'*s body. She is feeling no pain, fear, or loneliness. The* ANGEL *strokes her hair.*)

ANGEL: I kick-started your heart, Marisol. I wired your nervous system. I pushed your fetal blood in the right direction and turned the foam in your infant lungs to oxygen. When you were six and your parents were fighting, I helped you pretend you were underwater: that you were a cold-blooded fish, in the bottom of the black ocean, far away and safe. When racists ran you out of school at ten, screaming . . .

MARISOL: . . . "kill the spik" . . .

ANGEL: . . . I turned the monsters into little columns of salt! At last count, one plane crash, one collapsed elevator, one massacre at the hands of a right-wing fanatic with an Uzi, and sixty-six-thousand-six-hundred-and-three separate sexual assaults never happened because of me.

MARISOL: Wow. Now I don't have to be so paranoid . . . ?

(*The* ANGEL *suddenly gets out of bed.* MARISOL *curls up in a fetal position. The* ANGEL *is nervous now, full of hostile energy, anxious.*)

ANGEL: Now the bad news.

(*The* ANGEL *goes to the window. She's silent a moment as she contemplates the devastated Bronx landscape.*)

MARISOL (*Worried*): What?

(*The* ANGEL *finds it very hard to tell* MARISOL *what's on her mind.*)

ANGEL: I can't expect you to understand the political ins and outs of what's going on. But you have eyes. You asked me questions about children and water and war and the moon: the same questions I've been asking myself for a thousand years.

(*We hear distant explosions.* MARISOL'*s body responds with a jolt.*)

MARISOL (*Quiet*): What's that noise?

ANGEL: The universal body is sick, Marisol. Constellations are wasting away, the nauseous stars are full of blisters and sores, the infected earth is running a temperature, and everywhere the universal mind is wracked with amnesia, boredom, and neurotic obsessions.

MARISOL (*Frightened*): Why?

ANGEL: Because God is old and dying and taking the rest of us with Him. And for too long, much too long, I've been looking the other way. Trying to stop the massive hemorrhage with my little hands. With my prayers. But it didn't work and I knew if I didn't do something soon, it would be too late.

MARISOL (*Frightened*): What did you do?

ANGEL: I called a meeting. And I urged the Heavenly Hierarchies—the Seraphim, Cherubim, Thrones, Dominions, Principalities, Powers, Virtues, Archangels and Angels—to vote to stop the universal ruin . . . by slaughtering our senile God. And they did. Listen well, Marisol: angels are going to kill the King of Heaven and restore the vitality of the universe with His blood. And I'm going to lead them.

(MARISOL *takes this in silently—then suddenly erupts—her body shaking with fear and energy.*)

MARISOL: Okay, I wanna wake up now!

ANGEL: There's going to be war. A revolution of angels.

MARISOL: GOD IS GREAT! GOD IS GOOD! THANK YOU FOR OUR NEIGHBORHOOD!

ANGEL: Soon we're going to send out spies, draft able-bodied celestial beings, raise taxes . . .

MARISOL: THANK YOU FOR THE BIRDS THAT SING! THANK YOU GOD FOR EVERYTHING!

ANGEL: Soon we're going to take off our wings of peace, Marisol, and put on our wings of war. Then we're going to spread blood and vigor across the sky and reawaken the dwindling stars!

MARISOL (*Reciting fast*): "And there was war in Heaven; Michael and his angels fought against the dragon; and the dragon fought—"

ANGEL: It could be suicide. A massacre. He's better armed. Better organized. And, well, a little omniscient. But we *have* to win. (*Beat*) And when we do win . . . when we crown the new God, and begin the new millennium . . . the earth will be restored. The moon will return. The degradation of the animal kingdom will end. Men and women will be elevated to a higher order. All children will speak Latin. And Creation will finally be perfect.
(*Distant thunder and lightning. The* ANGEL *quickly goes to the window to read the message in the lightning. She turns to* MARISOL, *who is struggling to wake up.*)
It also means I have to leave you. I can't stay. I can't protect you anymore.
(*Beat.*)

MARISOL: What? You're *leaving* me?

ANGEL: I don't want to. I love you. I thought you had to know. But now I have to go and fight—

MARISOL: I'm going to be alone?

ANGEL: And that's what you have to do, Marisol. You have to fight. You can't *endure* anymore. You can't trust luck or prayer or mercy or other people. When I drop my wings, all hell's going to break loose and soon you're not going to recognize the world—so get yourself some *power*, Marisol, whatever you do.

MARISOL: What's going to happen to me without you . . . ?
(*The* ANGEL *goes to* MARISOL *and tries to kiss her.*)

ANGEL: I don't know.
(MARISOL *lashes out, trying to hit the Angel.* MARISOL *spits at the Angel. The* ANGEL *grabs* MARISOL's *hands.*)

MARISOL: *I'm gonna be meat!* I'M GONNA BE FOOD!!
(*By now the lights are nearly up full: it's the next morning. The* ANGEL *holds the struggling* MARISOL.)

ANGEL: Unless you want to join us—

MARISOL: NOOOOO!!
(MARISOL *fights. Her alarm clock goes off.*
The ANGEL *lets* MARISOL *go and climbs up the ladder and disappears.*
MARISOL *wakes up violently—she looks around in a panic—instantly goes for the knife under her pillow.*

It takes her a few moments to realize she's home in her bed. She puts the knife away. Turns off the alarm clock. She thinks: "I must have been dreaming." She shakes her head, catches her breath and tries to calm down. She wipes the sweat from her face.
MARISOL *gets out of bed. She goes to the window and looks down at the street—her eyes filled with new terror. She runs to her offstage bathroom.*)

SCENE FIVE

Lights up on MARISOL's *office in Manhattan: two metal desks facing each other covered in books and papers. One desk has a small radio.*

JUNE *enters the office. She's an Irish-American, thirty-six: bright, edgy, hyper, dressed in cool East Village clothes. Her wild red hair and all-American freckles provide a vivid contrast to* MARISOL's *Latin darkness.* JUNE *tries to read the* New York Post *but she can't concentrate. She keeps waiting for* MARISOL *to appear.* JUNE *turns on the radio.*

RADIO VOICE: . . . sources indicate the president's psychics believe they know where the moon has gone to. They claim to see the moon hovering over the orbit of Saturn, looking lost. Pentagon officials are considering plans to spend billions on a space tug to haul the moon back to earth. The tug would attach a long chain to the moon so it never strays from its beloved earth again. One insider has been quoted as saying the White House hopes to raise revenues for Operation Moon Rescue by taxing lunatics. Responding to allegations that cows are giving salty milk because grass is contaminated, government scientists are drafting plans to develop a new strain of cow that lives by eating Astroturf.
(JUNE *turns of the radio.* MARISOL *enters the office in a change of clothes.* JUNE *sees her and lets out a yell of joy. She goes to* MARISOL *and embraces her.*)

JUNE: Marisol! Thank God! I couldn't sleep all night because of you!
(MARISOL, *still shaken by the night's strange visions, is dazed, unhappy. She pulls away from* JUNE.)

MARISOL (*Wary*): What's the matter?

JUNE (*Grabbing her*): You died! You died! It was all over the networks last night! You're on the front page of the *Post*!

(JUNE *shows* MARISOL *the paper. On the cover is a close-up of a young woman's battered corpse.* JUNE *reads:*)

"*Twenty-six*-year-old *Marisol Perez* of 180th Street in the Bronx was bludgeoned to death on the IRT Number Two last night. The attack occurred 11:00 P.M.*"

(MARISOL *tries to remain calm as she looks at the hideous picture.*)

I thought it was you. And I tried to call you last night but do you have any idea how many Marisol Perezes there are in the Bronx phone book? Only seven pages. I couldn't sleep.

MARISOL (*Barely calm*): How did he kill her?

JUNE: Fucking barbarian beat her with a *golf club*, can you believe that? Like a caveman kills its dinner, fucking freak. I'm still upset.

(MARISOL, *numb, gives the paper back to* JUNE.)

MARISOL: It wasn't me, June.

JUNE: It could have been you, living alone in that marginal neighborhood, all the chances you take. Like doesn't this scare you? Isn't it past time to leave the Bronx behind?

(MARISOL *looks at* JUNE *fully for the first time, trying to focus her thoughts.*)

MARISOL: But it wasn't me. I didn't die last night.

(MARISOL *sits at her desk.* JUNE *looks at the paper.*)

JUNE (*Not listening*): Goddamn vultures are having a field day with this, vast close-ups of Marisol Perez's pummeled face on TV, I mean what's the *point*? There's a prevailing sickness out there, I'm telling you, the Dark Ages are here, Visigoths are climbing the city walls, and I've never felt more like raw food in my life. Am I upsetting you with this?

(MARISOL *rubs her throbbing head.*)

MARISOL: Yeah.

JUNE: Good. Put the fear of God in you. Don't let them catch you not ready, okay? You gotta be prepared to really *fight* now!

MARISOL (*Looks at her, surprised*): Why do you say that? Did somebody tell you to say that?

(JUNE *gives* MARISOL *a long look.*)

JUNE: Something wrong with you today? You look like shit. You, Miss Puerto Rican Yuppy Princess of the Universe, you never look like shit.

(MARISOL *tries to smile, to shake off her fear.*)

MARISOL: It's nothing. Let's get to work. If I don't get this manuscript off my desk . . .

(MARISOL *opens up a manuscript and tries to read it.* JUNE *closes the manuscript.*)

JUNE: Something happen to you last night?

MARISOL: No—it's—nothing—it's—*my body*—it feels like. Like it fits into my clothes all wrong today. Every person on the subway this morning gave me the shivers. They all looked so hungry. I keep hearing children crying. I keep smelling burnt flesh. And now there's a woman with my exact name killed on my exact street last night. (*Beat*) And I had this dream. A winged woman. A black angel with beautiful wings. She came to my bed and said she loved me.

JUNE (*Very interested*): Oh?

MARISOL: She seemed so real. So absolute. Virtuous and powerful, incapable of lying, exalted, sublime, radiant, pure, perfect, fulgent.

JUNE: Fulgent?

(JUNE *takes* MARISOL *by the shoulders and looks in her eyes.*)

Whoa! Marisol! Yo! That didn't happen. You dreamed it. It's Roman Catholic bullshit.

MARISOL: . . . now I feel sorry. I just feel so sorry for everything . . .

(MARISOL *goes downstage and looks up at the sky, expecting to see something but not knowing what. She's fighting tears.* JUNE *looks at her:* MARISOL's *definitely not herself today.*

JUNE *goes to her, embraces her.* MARISOL *holds* JUNE *for dear life.* JUNE *tries to cheer* MARISOL *up.*)

JUNE: Lookit, I think your dream is like the moon's disappearance. It's all a lot of premillennium jitters. I've never seen so much nervousness. It's still up there but paranoia has clouded our view. That shit can happen you know.

(MARISOL *pulls away from* JUNE.)

MARISOL: I don't think the moon's disappearance is psychological. It's like the universe is senile, June. Like we're at the part of history where everything breaks down. Do you smell smoke?

(*The lights begin to subtly go down.* JUNE *notices the darkness right away. She looks at her watch.*)

JUNE: Wait! It's nine-thirty! They're expecting the smoke from that massive fire in Ohio to reach New York by nine-thirty.

(JUNE *and* MARISOL *look out the window. The lights go darker and darker.*)

Jesus! Those are a million trees burning!
(JUNE *and* MARISOL *calmly watch the spectacle.*)
Christ, you can smell the polyester . . . the
burnt malls . . . the defaulted loans . . . the un-
employment . . . the flat vowels . . .
(*Lights begin to go up.* MARISOL *and* JUNE *stand
at the window and watch the black smoke begin
to drift toward Europe. Silence. They look at each
other. The whole thing suddenly strikes them as
absurd—they laugh.*)
Fuck it, I'm going on break. You want something from downstairs? Coffee? I'm going for
coffee.

MARISOL: Coffee's extinct, June.

JUNE (*She hates tea*): Tea—I meant *tea*. I'll get us
both a cup of tea, try to carry on like normal.
I swear, one more natural cataclysm like that
and I'm going home. Are you okay?
(MARISOL *nods yes.* JUNE *leaves the office.* MARISOL
quickly starts reading from her manuscript.)

MARISOL (*With growing surprise*): " . . . Salt is in the
food and mythology of cultures old and new.
Ancient writers believed that angels in heaven
turned into salt when they died. Popular mythology holds that during the Fall of Satan,
angels who were killed in battle fell into the
primordial ocean, which was then fresh water. Today, the oceans are salted by the decom-
posed bodies of fallen angels . . . "
(*The* MAN WITH ICE CREAM *enters the office.*

   *He wears a business suit and licks an ice
cream cone.*

   He smiles at MARISOL, *who looks at him, instantly sensing trouble.*)

ICE CREAM: I was in the movie *Taxi Driver* with Robert De Niro and the son-of-a-gun never paid
me.

MARISOL: Uhm. Are you looking for someone?

ICE CREAM: The Second A. D. said this is where I go
to collect my pay for my work in *Taxi Driver.*

MARISOL: This isn't a film company, sir. We publish
science books. I think there's a film company
on the tenth floor.

ICE CREAM: No, this is the place. I'm sure this is the
place.

MARISOL: Well . . . you know, sir . . . maybe if I
called security for you . . .

ICE CREAM: I worked real hard on that picture. It
was my big break. And of course, working

with a genius like De Niro is like Actor Heav-
en, but, c'mon, I still need the money!

MARISOL: I'm a busy woman, sir, I have a department to run—

ICE CREAM: I mean, I don't want to get tempera-
mental, but *Taxi Driver* came out a long time
ago and I still haven't been paid!

MARISOL: Yeah, I'll call security for you—

ICE CREAM (*In despair*): Christ, I have bills! I have
rent! I have a toddler in a Catholic preschool!
I have an agent screaming for his ten percent!
*And how the fuck am I supposed to pay for this ice
cream cone? Do you think ice cream is free? Do
you think Carvel gives this shit out for nothing?*

MARISOL (*Calling out*): June?! Is somebody on this
floor?!

ICE CREAM: Don't fuck with me, lady. I once played
a Nazi skinhead in a TV movie-of-the-week. I
once set a man on fire in Van Cortlandt Park
for CBS! *And I really liked that role!*
(*The* MAN *throws the ice cream into* MARISOL's *face.*
JUNE *runs on.*)

JUNE: LEAVE HER ALONE YOU SCUMBAG!
(JUNE *hits the* MAN *as hard as she can. She pummels
him. He howls like a dog and runs out of the office.*
JUNE *runs after him. Off:*)
SOMEBODY HELP ME GET HIM!
(*As* MARISOL *wipes the ice cream from her face, we
hear footsteps going into the distance. Then foot-
steps returning.* JUNE *runs back in, panting.*)
He's gone. (*She picks up the phone*) Security?
*YOU FUCKING BOZOS! WHY DON'T YOU
DO YOUR JOB AND STOP LETTING MANI-
ACS INTO THE BUILDING?!*
(JUNE *slams down the phone. She goes to* MARISOL,
*who is still wiping ice cream from her clothes. She's
trembling.*)

MARISOL: Vanilla almond. I'll never be able to eat
vanilla almond again.

JUNE: Okay, that's IT, you and I are taking the rest
of the day off, going to my house where it's
safe, fuck everybody, I've had it with this death
trap . . .
(JUNE *starts to hustle* MARISOL *out of the office.*
   MARISOL *looks up—she's frozen by a vision.*
   Lights up, far above MARISOL. *The* ANGEL *is
there, cleaning an Uzi submachine gun, humming quietly.* MARISOL *isn't sure she's really seeing what she's seeing.*

JUNE *looks up, sees nothing, and pulls* MARISOL *offstage. Lights down on the* ANGEL, *who disappears in the dark.*)

SCENE SIX

Lights up on JUNE's *apartment: a marbleized Formica table and matching red chairs.*

It's later that day. JUNE *and* MARISOL *enter.* JUNE *automatically stomps cockroaches as she enters.*

JUNE: . . . so we agitated for them to install metal detectors in all the buildings on this block. That'll definitely cut down on the random homicides.

MARISOL: That's civilized.

JUNE (*Brightly*): That's Brooklyn.

MARISOL: What's that huge ugly windowless building with the smokestacks and armed guards across the street?

JUNE: Me? I think it's where they bring overthrown brutal rightwing dictators from Latin America to live, 'cause a friend's a friend, right?

MARISOL: I really appreciate this, June.

JUNE: Good, 'cause now I have to issue you a warning about my fucked-up brother who lives with me.

MARISOL: You do?

JUNE: Uhm. Lenny's a little weird about women. His imagination? It takes off on him on the slightest provocation and, uh, he doesn't know, you know, a reasonable way to channel his turbulent sexual death fantasies . . .

MARISOL: This is a long warning, June.

JUNE: He knows about you. Shit I've told him for two years. And so he's developed this *thing* for you, like he draws *pictures* of you, in crayon, covering every inch of his bedroom. He's thirty-four, you know, but he has the mental capacity of a child.

(LENNY *enters.* LENNY *has uncontrollable hair that makes him look a little crazy. He can stand very, very still for a very long time. He goes immediately to the window without looking at* JUNE *or* MARISOL.)

LENNY (*Indicating window*): Wrong. It's a federally funded torture center where they violate people who have gone over their credit card limit.

JUNE (*Wary*): Marisol, this is Lenny, the heat-seeking device. Lenny, this is Marisol Perez and you're *wrong*.

LENNY (*At window*): I've seen them bring the vans, June. So shut up. People tied up. Guards with truncheons. Big fat New York City police with dogs. It happens late at night. But you can hear the screams. They cremate the bodies. That's why Brooklyn smells so funny.

MARISOL (*Nervous*): I owe a lot of money to the MasterCard people.

(LENNY *suddenly turns to* MARISOL. *He is utterly focused on her.*)

JUNE (*To* MARISOL): What he says is not proven.

LENNY: *Everybody* knows, June. It's a political *issue*. If you weren't so right wing—

JUNE: I am not right wing, you punk, don't EVER call me that! I happen to be the last true practicing communist in New York!

(LENNY *keeps staring at* MARISOL.)

LENNY: You were on the news. You died on the news. But that was a different one.

MARISOL: She and I have the same name. Had.

LENNY (*Approaching* MARISOL): I'm so glad you didn't die before I got a chance to meet you.

(LENNY *suddenly takes* MARISOL's *hand and kisses it.* JUNE *tries to step in between them.*)

JUNE: That's enough, Lenny—I didn't bring her here to feed on . . .

LENNY (*Holding* MARISOL's *hand*): I went to your neighborhood this morning. To see the kind of street that would kill a Marisol Perez. I walked through Van Cortlandt Park. I played in the winter sunlight, watched perverts fondling snowmen, and at high noon, the dizziest time of the day, I saw a poor homeless guy being set on fire by Nazi skinheads—

JUNE: That's *it*, Lenny.

(JUNE *pulls* LENNY *aside. He knows he's in for a lecture.*)

LENNY: What?

JUNE: We had a hard day. We came here to relax. So take a deep breath—

LENNY: She talked to me first—

JUNE: Listen to me before you say anything more. Are you listening?

LENNY: *Yes. Okay.*

JUNE: Let's cool our hormones, okay? Before the psychodrama starts in earnest?

LENNY: Yes. All right.

JUNE: Are we really?

(LENNY *pulls away from* JUNE.)

LENNY (*To* MARISOL): Hey, honey, you wanna see my sculpture?

(LENNY *runs to his offstage bedroom before* MARISOL *can reply.* JUNE *grabs her coat angrily.*)

JUNE: You wanna get outta here? He's raving.

LENNY (*Off*): I'm an accomplished sculptor, Marisol. Before that I was a Life and Growth Empowerment Practitioner. Before that I worked for the Brooklyn Spiritual Emergence Network.

(LENNY *quickly reenters with his sculpture, a ball of nails welded together in a formless shape: it's an ugly little work of art and everyone knows it.*)

This one's called "Marisol Perez." The nails symbolize all the things I know about you. Spaces between the nails are all the things I don't know about you. As you see, you're a great mystery . . .

(MARISOL *looks at the sculpture, trying hard to see some beauty in it.*)

No one else is working like this. It's totally new. But it's only a small step in my career. I'm going to need a lot more *money* if I'm going to evolve past this point.

(LENNY *looks hard at* JUNE. JUNE *buttons up her coat, hoping to avoid a confrontation.*)

JUNE (*Tight*): I don't think Marisol wants to hear us talk about money.

LENNY: Well, I'm not gonna get a job, June, so you can fuck that noise.

JUNE (*To* MARISOL): Who said "job"? When did I say "job"?

LENNY (*To* MARISOL): I promised myself to never work for anyone again. She heard me say that—

JUNE: Gee Lenny, fuck you, we're going—

(JUNE *starts to go.* LENNY *blocks her path to the door.*)

LENNY (*To* JUNE): Why do you hate my sculpture? Why do you hate everything I do?!

JUNE (*Trying to control herself*): Man, man . . . Lenny . . . you don't want to learn *anything* from me, do you? You want to be a pathetic inver-

tebrate your whole life long. Fine. Just don't waste my precious time!

LENNY: Who gives a fuck about your time, I HAVE PROJECTS!

JUNE: Yeah? What ever happened to the CIA, Lenny? Didn't they want you for something *really special* in Nicaragua? What about the electric guitars you were gonna design for the Stones? What about *Smegma, the Literary Magazine of Brooklyn?* Huh?

(LENNY *runs back into his off stage room.*)

I swear, the cadavers of your dead projects are all over this goddamn apartment like Greenwood Cemetery. I can't eat a bowl of cereal in the morning without the ghosts of your old ideas begging me for a glass of milk!

(LENNY *reenters with stacks of homemade magazines and several unusual homemade guitars. He throws this trash at June's feet.*)

LENNY: *You wish Mom had drowned me!* I know that's what you wish! Well, you don't have to feel sorry for me anymore!

JUNE: Sure I do. You're pathetic. The only thing separating you from a concrete bed on Avenue D is *me*.

LENNY (*To* MARISOL): She thinks I'm a loser, Marisol! Can you believe that? Sometimes I want to kill her!

JUNE: Oh get out of my face, Lenny. You're never gonna kill me. You're never gonna get it together to kill *anybody*—

(LENNY *exits into his off stage room again.* JUNE *turns to* MARISOL *angrily.*)

Can I list for you just a few of the things I don't have because I have him? Lasting friendships. A retirement account. A house. A career. A nightlife. Winter clothing. Interest on checking. Regular real sex.

(LENNY *returns with a long kitchen knife and tries to cut* JUNE *'s throat.* JUNE *and* MARISOL *scream.*)

LENNY: *I was supposed to be somebody!* That's what I learned right after I died!

JUNE: YOU NEVER DIED!

(JUNE *scrambles from* LENNY *and goes for the door. There's chaos as* MARISOL *starts throwing things at* LENNY *and* LENNY *continues to chase* JUNE. LENNY *pulls* JUNE *from the door and throws her back in the room.*)

LENNY: The doctors all said I died! There's medical evidence! It's on the charts! My heart stopped for seven minutes and my soul was outta Lenox Hill at the speed of light!

(LENNY *is almost out of control as he stalks* JUNE, *slashing the air.*)

JUNE: Your whole *life*, everything I do is to *bolster* you, build you up—

LENNY: After my death . . . my soul was cruising up and up . . . and it was intercepted by angels and sucked back into my body, *and I lived!*

MARISOL: Give me that knife!

LENNY: . . . I was resurrected, I returned to the living to warn the world that big changes are coming . . . and we have to be ready . . . (*Fighting tears*) I've been warning people for years, but no one listens to me . . .

(LENNY *starts to cry.* MARISOL *and* JUNE *jump him, grabbing the knife away.* LENNY *throws himself on the ground like a toddler in a rage and cries.* JUNE *and* MARISOL *look at him.*

It takes JUNE *a moment to catch her breath and gather her thoughts.*)

JUNE: I can't do this shit no more. I can't mother you. Carry you around protected in my Epic Uterus anymore. This is final. Biology says you're a grown man. I don't love the law of the jungle, Lenny, but you're adult, you're leaving the nest and living in the real world from now on, eat or be eaten, I'm sorry, that's the way my emotions are built right now 'cause you *architectured* it that way! (*Beat*) I'm calling our mother, tell her not to take you in either. This is not a transition, Leonard. This is a break. A severing. So get up. Collect your mutant trash. Give me your fucking keys. Leave right now. And don't look back at me or I'll turn you to salt right where you stand with my eyes, so help me God.

(LENNY *stands, gathers his trash and exits to his room.* MARISOL *goes to comfort* JUNE *but she's interrupted by* LENNY *reentering, wearing a coat, carrying a bag of golf clubs.*

JUNE *gives* LENNY *all the money she has on her.* MARISOL *is unable to look at* LENNY. *He turns angrily to* JUNE.)

LENNY: I almost had Marisol married to me, June. We practically had babies! Now I'm alone.

Whatever happens to me out there, it's totally, specifically, on you.

(LENNY *leaves the apartment.* JUNE *sits at the table.* MARISOL *looks at* JUNE.)

MARISOL: So where do you want to have dinner?

(*No answer.* MARISOL *sits with* JUNE, *takes her hand. Tears on* JUNE's *face.*)

JUNE: You think I'm a shit for throwing him out . . . ?

MARISOL: Maybe people will throw him some change. Maybe this will force him to get a job.

JUNE: . . . is he gonna dissolve in the fucking street air . . . ?

(JUNE *runs to the door. She calls out.*)

Lenny! I'm SORRY! Come back, I'm sorry!!

(*No answer.* JUNE *sits.*)

Shit.

(JUNE *looks at* MARISOL *wiping her tears, getting an idea.*)

You wanna live with me? 'Cause if you wanna live with me, in Lenny's empty bedroom, I'll rent it to you, it's available right away.

(MARISOL *smiles, surprised.*)

MARISOL: Wait—where did that come from?

JUNE: Hey c'mon girlfriend, they're killing Marisol Perezes left and right today, we gotta stick together!

MARISOL (*Wanting to*): Wow. I don't know what to say . . .

JUNE: You think the Bronx needs you? It doesn't. It needs blood. It needs to feed. You *wanna* be the blood supply for its filthy habits?

MARISOL: But the Bronx is where I'm from.

JUNE: So friggin' what? Come here. We'll survive the millennium as a team. I'll shop. You can clean the chemicals off the food. I know where to buy gas masks. You know the vocabulary on the street. We'll walk each other through land mines and sharpen each other's wits.

(MARISOL *smiles and looks at* JUNE.)

MARISOL: You're not saying that just because you're scared to be alone, right? You really want me here, right?

JUNE: Of course I do, hey.

MARISOL: Then let's do it, girlfriend.

(*Delighted,* JUNE *embraces* MARISOL.)

JUNE: Oh great!

(JUNE *and* MARISOL *hold each other.* JUNE *is about ready to cry.* MARISOL *gently rocks her a little bit, then looks at* JUNE.)

MARISOL: I'm gonna go home and pack right now. We have to be fast. This town knows when you're alone. That's when it sends out the ghouls and the death squads.

(JUNE *nods understandingly, kisses* MARISOL *and gives her* LENNY's *keys.*)

JUNE: What a day I'm having, huh?

(MARISOL *takes the keys, leaves, goes back to her own apartment and immediately starts packing.*)

SCENE SEVEN

Later that night. MARISOL *is in the Bronx, packing. Her singing is heard underneath the others' dialogue.*

MARISOL (*Softly*): *Madre que linda noche*
  cuantas estrellas
  abreme la ventana
  que quiero verlas . . .

(JUNE *sits at the table in her apartment, facing downstage. She talks to herself.*)

JUNE: Maybe someone'll throw Lenny some change, right?

(LENNY *appears upstage, on the street, warming his hands at a burning trash can. His clothes are filthy and his eyes are glazed. The golf club is at his side. He looks at* MARISOL.)

LENNY: I've been on the street, Marisol. I know what it's like.

JUNE: Yeah, maybe people will throw him some change.

MARISOL (*Smiling, remembering*): "The flat vowels . . ."

LENNY: It's incredible there. Logic was executed by firing squad. People tell passionate horror stories and other people stuff their faces and go on. The street breeds new species. And new silence. No spoken language works there. There are no verbs to describe the cold air as it sucks on your hands. And if there *were* words to describe it, Marisol, you wouldn't believe it anyway, because, in fact, it's literally unbelievable, it's another reality, and it's actually happening *right now*. And *that* fact—the fact that it's happening right *now*—compounds the unbelievable nature of the street, Marisol, adds to its lunacy, its per-

manent deniability. (*Beat*) But I know it's real. I've been bitten by it. I have its rabies.

JUNE: I know someone will throw him some change.

(LENNY *raises the golf club over* JUNE's *head.* JUNE *is frozen. Blackout everywhere but* MARISOL's *apartment.* JUNE *and* LENNY *exit in the dark.*)

SCENE EIGHT

There's loud knocking at MARISOL's *door.* MARISOL *stops packing and looks at the door. The knocking continues—loud, violent—louder.*

MARISOL: Who is it?

(*Before* MARISOL *can move, her door is kicked open.* LENNY *comes in wielding a bloody golf club and holding an armful of exotic wildflowers.*)

LENNY: So how can you live in this neighborhood? Huh? You got a death wish, you stupid woman?

MARISOL: What are you doing here?

(MARISOL *goes to her bed and scrambles for the knife underneath her pillow.*)

LENNY: Don't you love yourself? Is that why you stay in this ghetto? Jesus, I almost got killed getting here!

(MARISOL *points the knife at* LENNY.)

MARISOL: Get out or I'll rip out both your fucking eyes, Lenny!

LENNY: God, I missed you.

(LENNY *closes the door and locks all the locks.*)

MARISOL: This is not going to happen to me in my own house! I still have God's protection!

(LENNY *holds out the flowers.*)

LENNY: Here. I hadda break into the Bronx Botanical Garden for them, but they match your eyes . . .

(LENNY *hands* MARISOL *the flowers.*)

MARISOL: Okay—thank you—okay—why don't we—turn around—and go—down to Brooklyn—okay?—let's go talk to June—

LENNY: We can't. Impossible. June *isn't. Is not*. I don't know who she is anymore! She's out walking the streets of Brooklyn! Babbling like an idiot! Looking for her lost mind!

MARISOL: What do you mean? Where is she?

LENNY: She had an accident. Her head had an accident. With the golf club. It was weird.

MARISOL (*Looking at the bloody club*): What did you do to her?

LENNY: She disappeared! I don't know!

MARISOL (*Panicking*): Please tell me June's okay, Lenny. Tell me she's not in some body bag somewhere—

LENNY: Oh man, you saw what it's like! June *controlled* me. She had me *neutered*. I squatted, and stooped and served like a goddamn house eunuch!

MARISOL: Did you hurt her?

(LENNY *starts to cry. He sobs like a baby, his body wracked with grief and self-pity.*)

LENNY: There are whole histories of me you can't guess. Did you know I was a medical experiment? To fix my asthma when I was five, my mother volunteered me for a free experimental drug on an army base in Nevada. I *was a shrieking experiment in army medicine for six years!* Isn't that funny? (*He laughs, trying to fight his tears*) And that drug's made me so friggin' loopy, I can't hold down a job, make friends, get a degree, *nothing*—and June?— June's had *everything*. She loved you. That's why she never brought you home to meet me *even after I begged her for two years.*

(MARISOL *is silent—and that silence nearly makes him explode.*)

DON'T BE THIS WAY. We don't have to be enemies. We can talk to each other the right way—

MARISOL: We have no right way, Lenny.

(LENNY *jumps up and down, very happy.*)

LENNY: We do! We do! 'Cause we have *God*, Marisol. We have God in common. Maybe it's God's will I'm with you now. On this frontier. Out in this lawless city, I'm what he designed for you.

MARISOL: I don't know what you're talking about . . .

LENNY: It's why God brought me here tonight—to offer you a way to survive. I know you don't love me. But you can't turn your back on God's gift.

MARISOL (*Exhausted*): Jesus Christ, just tell me what you want . . .

(LENNY *moves closer.*)

LENNY: I want to offer you a deal. (*Beat*) You controlled your life until now. But your life's in shambles! Ruins! So I'm gonna let you give *me* control over your life. That means I'll do everything for you. I'll take responsibility. I'll get a job and make money. I'll name our children. Okay? And what you get in return is my protection.

(*Beat.* LENNY *gives* MARISOL *the golf club.*)

I can protect you like June did. I can keep out the criminals and carry the knife for you. I can be your guardian angel, Marisol.

MARISOL: You're asking—

LENNY: A small price. Your faith. Your pretty Puerto Rican smile. No. I don't even want to sleep with you anymore. I don't want your affection. Or your *considerable* sexual mystery. I just want you to look up to me. Make me big. Make me central. Praise me, feed me, and believe everything I tell you.

(LENNY *steps closer to* MARISOL.)

You once tried to give these things to June. And June would have said yes because she loved you. Well, I'm June. June and I are here, together, under this hungry skin. You can love us both, Marisol.

(MARISOL *looks at* LENNY *a long moment, studying him, thinking of a way out. She makes a decision. She tosses her knife on the bed and drops the golf club.*

She takes a step toward LENNY. *They stare at each other.* MARISOL *lets herself be embraced.* LENNY, *amazed, revels in the feel of her body against his.*)

MARISOL: Okay. I'll believe what you say. I'll live inside you.

(LENNY *is oblivious to everything but* MARISOL'S *warm hands. She kisses him. It's the most electrifying feeling* LENNY'S *ever known. He closes his eyes.*) But. Before we set up house—live happily ever after—we're going to go outside—you and me—and we're going to find out what happened to your sister . . .

LENNY (*Oblivious*): She's lost. She can't be found.

MARISOL (*Kissing him*): . . . that's my condition . . .

(LENNY *starts to push* MARISOL *to the bed. She starts to resist.*)

LENNY: It's too dangerous for a girl out there.

MARISOL: . . . but if you don't help me find her, Lenny . . . there's no deal . . .

(*He pushes her. She resists.* LENNY *looks at her, hurt, a little confused.*)

LENNY: But I don't want to share you.

(*Beat.*)

MARISOL: Too bad. That's the deal.

(*Beat.*)

LENNY (*Hurt, realizing*): You don't love me. You're just fucking with me. That's not okay! WELL, I'M GLAD I HIT HER!

(LENNY *grabs* MARISOL, MARISOL *tries to escape. He holds her tightly trying to kiss her. He throws her to the floor. He rips at her clothes, trying to tear them off.* MARISOL *struggles with all her strength—until she finally pulls free and goes for the golf club. He tries to grab it from her and she swings at him.*)

You're lying to me! Why are you always lying to me?!

MARISOL: Because you're the enemy, Lenny. I will always be your enemy, because you will always find a way to be out there, hiding in stairwells, behind doors, under the blankets in my bed, in the cracks of every bad dream I've had since I've known there were savage differences between girls and boys! And I know you'll always be hunting for me. And I'll never be able to relax, or stop to look at the sky, or smile at something beautiful on the street—

LENNY: But I'm just a guy trying to be happy too—

MARISOL: I want you to tell me, RIGHT NOW, where June is—*right now!*

(MARISOL *swings at* LENNY. *He panics and falls to his knees in front of her.* MARISOL *pounds the floor with the golf club.*)

LENNY: She's on the street.

MARISOL: Where?

LENNY: Brooklyn.

MARISOL: Where?

LENNY: I don't know!

MARISOL: What happened?

LENNY: I hit her on the head. She doesn't know who she is. She went out there to look for you.

(MARISOL *stands over him, poised to strike him. He's shaking with fear.*)

Look at me. I'm a mess on the floor. Just asking you to look at me. To give me compassion and let me live like a human being for once. Marisol, we could have a baby . . . and love it so much . . .

(MARISOL *only shakes her head in disgust and turns to the door.* LENNY *springs to his feet and lunges at her. She turns and swings the club and hits* LENNY.

He falls to the ground.

MARISOL *looks at* LENNY'S *fallen body. Has she killed him? She panics and runs out of the apartment with the golf club.*

Blackout everywhere except on the street area.)

SCENE NINE

MARISOL *runs to the street area.*

It starts to snow there. There's blood on MARISOL'S *clothes. She's extremely cold. She shivers. She kneels on the ground, alone, not knowing what to do or where to go.*

Lights up over MARISOL'S *head, against the brick wall. The* ANGEL *appears. The* ANGEL *wears regulation military fatigues, complete with face camouflage and medals. She looks like a soldier about to go into battle. The Uzi is strapped to her back.*

MARISOL *sees her and gasps.*

There's blood coming down the ANGEL'S *back: the* ANGEL *has taken off her silver wings—her wings of peace. She holds the bloody wings out to the audience, like an offering. Then she drops the wings. They float down to the street.*

MARISOL *picks them up.*

MARISOL: War?

(*The wings dissolve in* MARISOL'S *hands. Blackout everywhere.*)

ACT TWO

Darkness. All the interiors are gone. The entire set now consists of the brick wall and a huge surreal street that covers the entire stage.

The ANGEL *is gone. The gold crown is still there.*

Street lighting comes up but there's something very different about this light. On this street, reality has been altered—and this new reality is reflected in the lighting.

We see a metal trash bin, overflowing with trash, and a fire hydrant covered in rosaries. There are several large mounds of rags on stage; underneath each mound is a sleeping homeless person.

MARISOL *is onstage exactly where she was at the end of Act One. She's holding out her hands as if holding the* ANGEL'S *wings but they're gone now; she holds air.*

She looks around and notices that the street she's now on is nothing like the street she remembers. She registers this weird difference and picks up the golf club, ready to defend herself.

She looks up to see the ANGEL, *but she's gone.*

She thinks she hears a sound behind her. She swings the club. There's nothing there. She tries to orient herself but she can't tell north from south.

And even though it's the dead of winter, it's also much warmer than it was before. Startled, MARISOL *fans herself.*

Bright sparkling lights streak across the sky like tracers or comets. The lights are followed by distant rumblings. Is that a thunderclap?

Or an explosion? MARISOL *hits the ground. Then the lights stop. Silence.*

The WOMAN WITH FURS *enters. The* WOMAN *is prosperous: long fur coat and high heels—but there are subtle bruises and cuts on her face and it looks like there's dried blood on her coat. She stands to the side, very, very still. She holds an open news-paper, but she stares past it, no emotion on her shell-shocked face.*

MARISOL *looks at the Woman With Furs, hesitates, then goes to her.*

MARISOL: Excuse me. Miss?
   (*No answer from the* WOMAN WITH FURS, *who doesn't look at her.*)
   Where the hell are we?
   (*The* WOMAN WITH FURS *ignores her.* MARISOL *gets closer.*)
   I'm—supposed to be on 180th Street. In the Bronx. There's supposed to be a bodega right *here*. A public school *there*. They sold crack on that corner. It was cold this morning!
   (*The* WOMAN WITH FURS *speaks out to the air, as if in a trance.*)
WOMAN WITH FURS: God help you, you get in my face.
   (MARISOL *begins to examine the altered space with growing fear.*)

MARISOL: No buildings. No streets. No cars. No noise. No cops. There are no subway tokens in my pocket!
WOMAN WITH FURS: I have no money.
MARISOL (*Realizing*): It's what she said would happen, isn't it? She said she'd drop her wings of peace . . . and I wouldn't recognize the world . . .
WOMAN WITH FURS: Don't you know where you are either?
MARISOL (*Trying to think it through*): . . . I have to . . . I have to . . . reclaim what I know: I need June. Where's June? Brooklyn. South. I gotta go south, find my friend, and restore her broken mind.
   (MARISOL *tries to run away hoping to find the subway to Brooklyn, but it's impossible to find anything familiar in this radically altered landscape.*)
WOMAN WITH FURS: I had tickets to *Les Misérables*. But I took a wrong turn. Followed bad advice. Ended up on this weird street.
   (MARISOL *sees something in the distance that makes her freeze in her tracks.*)
MARISOL (*To herself*): The Empire State Building? . . . what's it doing over there? It's supposed to be south. But that's . . . north . . . I'm sure it is . . . isn't it?
   (*In her panic,* MARISOL *runs to the* WOMAN WITH FURS *and tries to grab her arm.*)
   You have to help me!
   (*The* WOMAN WITH FURS *instantly recoils from* MARISOL's *touch. She starts to wander away.*)
WOMAN WITH FURS: I have to go. But I can't find a cab. I can't seem to find any transportation.
MARISOL: You're not listening! There's no transportation; forget that; the city's *gone*. You have to help me. We have to go south together and protect each other.
   (MARISOL *grabs the* WOMAN WITH FURS's *arm roughly, trying to pull her offstage. The* WOMAN WITH FURS *seems to snap out of her trance and pull back. The* WOMAN WITH FURS *is suddenly shaking, tearful, like a caged animal.*)
WOMAN WITH FURS: Oh God, I thought you were a nice person!
MARISOL (*Grabbing the* WOMAN): I am a nice person, but I've had some bad luck—
WOMAN WITH FURS (*Struggling*): Oh God, you're hurting me—

MARISOL (*Letting go*): No, no, no, I'm okay; I don't belong out here; I have a job in publishing; I'm middle-class—

WOMAN WITH FURS (*Freaking out, pointing at golf club*): Oh please don't kill me like that barbarian killed Marisol Perez!

(MARISOL *lets the* WOMAN WITH FURS *go. The* WOMAN WITH FURS *is almost crying.*)

MARISOL: I'm not what you think.

WOMAN WITH FURS: . . . Oh God, why did I have to buy that fucking hat?! God . . . God . . . why?

MARISOL: Please. June's not used to the street, she's an indoor animal, like a cat . . .

WOMAN WITH FURS: I bought a fucking hat on credit and everything disintegrated!

MARISOL: South. Protection.

(*The* WOMAN WITH FURS *takes off her fur coat. Underneath, she wears ripped pajamas. We can see the bruises and cuts on her arms clearly.*)

WOMAN WITH FURS: There is no protection. I just got out of hell. Last month, I was two hundred dollars over my credit card limit because I bought a hat on sale. And you know they're cracking down on that kind of thing. I used to do it all the time. It didn't matter. But now it matters. Midnight. The police came. Grabbed me out of bed, waving my credit statement in my face, my children screaming, they punched my husband in the stomach. I told them I was a lawyer! With a house in Cos Cob! And personal references a mile long! But they hauled me to this . . . huge windowless brick building in Brooklyn . . . where they tortured me . . . they . . .

(*The* WOMAN WITH FURS *cries.* MARISOL *goes to her and covers her up with the fur coat.* MARISOL *holds her.*)

MARISOL: That can't happen.

WOMAN WITH FURS: A lot of things can't happen that are happening. Everyone I know's had terrible luck this year. Losing condos. Careers cut in half. Ending up on the street. I thought I'd be immune. I thought I'd be safe.

MARISOL: This is going to sound crazy. But I think I know why this is happening.

(*The* WOMAN WITH FURS *looks at* MARISOL, *suddenly very afraid.*)

WOMAN WITH FURS: No. No.

(*The* WOMAN WITH FURS *tries to get away from* MARISOL. MARISOL *stops her.*)

MARISOL: It's angels, isn't it? It's the war.

WOMAN WITH FURS (*Panicking*): God is great! God is good! It didn't happen! It didn't happen! I dreamed it! I lied!

MARISOL: It did! It happened to me!

WOMAN WITH FURS: I'm not going to talk about this! You're going to think I'm crazy too! You're going to tell the Citibank MasterCard people where I am so they can pick me up and torture me some more!

MARISOL: I wouldn't!

(*The* WOMAN WITH FURS *grabs the golf club out of* MARISOL's *hand.*)

WOMAN WITH FURS: I know what I'm going to do now. I'm going to turn *you* in. I'm going to tell the Citibank police you stole my plastic! They'll like me for that. They'll like me a lot. They'll restore my banking privileges!

(*The* WOMAN WITH FURS *starts swinging wildly at* MARISOL. MARISOL *dodges the* WOMAN WITH FURS.)

MARISOL: I am not an animal! I am not a barbarian! I don't fight at this level!

WOMAN WITH FURS (*Swinging*): Welcome to the new world order, babe!

(*The* MAN WITH SCAR TISSUE *enters in a wheelchair. He's a homeless man in shredded, burnt rags. He wears a hood that covers his head and obscures his face. He wears sunglasses and gloves. His wheelchair is full of plastic garbage bags, clothes, books, newspapers, bottles, junk.*)

SCAR TISSUE: It's getting so bad, a guy can't sleep under the stars anymore.

(*The* WOMAN WITH FURS *sees the* MAN WITH SCAR TISSUE *and stops swinging.*)

WOMAN WITH FURS (*Indicating* MARISOL): This brown piece of shit is mine! *I'm* going to turn her in! Not you!

SCAR TISSUE: I was sleeping under the constellations one night and my whole life changed, took *seconds*: I had a life—then bingo—I *didn't* have a life . . . (*He moves toward the* WOMAN WITH FURS) . . . maybe you got it, huh? You got the thing I need . . .

WOMAN WITH FURS: Homelessness is against the law in this city. I'm going to have you two arrested! They'll like that. I'll get big points for that! I'll be revitalized!

(*The* WOMAN WITH FURS *runs off with the golf club.* MAN WITH SCAR TISSUE *looks at* MARISOL. *He waves hello. She looks at him—wary, but grateful—and tries to smile. She's instantly aware of his horrendous smell.*)

MARISOL: She, she was trying to kill me . . . thank you . . .

SCAR TISSUE: Used to be able to sleep under the moon *unmolested*. Moon was a shield. Catching all the bad karma before it fell to earth. All those crater holes in the moon? Those ain't rocks! That's bad karma crashing to the moon's surface!

MARISOL (*Really shaken*): She thinks I belong out here, but I don't. I'm well educated . . . anyone can see that . . .

SCAR TISSUE: Now the moon's gone. The shield's been lifted. Shit falls on you randomly. Sleep outside, you're fucked. That's why I got this! Gonna *yank* the moon back!

(*From inside his wheelchair,* SCAR TISSUE *pulls out a magnet. He aims his magnet to the sky and waits for the moon to appear.*)

MARISOL: She's crazy, that's all! I have to go before she comes back.

(MARISOL *starts going back and forth, looking for south.*)

SCAR TISSUE: Good thing I'm not planning to get married. What would a honeymoon be like now? Some stupid cardboard cut-out dangling out your hotel window? What kind of inspiration is that? How's a guy supposed to get it up for *that*?

(SCAR TISSUE *fondles himself, hoping to manufacture a hard-on, but nothing happens and he gives up.*)

MARISOL (*Noticing what he's doing*): I have to get to Brooklyn. I'm looking for my friend. She has red hair.

SCAR TISSUE: And did you know the moon carries the souls of dead people up to Heaven? Uh-huh. The new moon is dark and empty and gets filled with new glowing souls—until it's a bright full moon—then it carries its silent burden to God . . .

MARISOL: Do you know which way is south?!

(MARISOL *continues to walk around and around the stage, looking hopelessly for any landmark that will tell her which way is south.* SCAR TISSUE *watches her, holding his magnet up.*)

SCAR TISSUE: Give it up, princess. Time is crippled. Geography's deformed. You're permanently lost out here!

MARISOL: Bullshit. Even if God is senile, He still cares, He doesn't play dice you know. I read that.

SCAR TISSUE: Shit, what century do *you* live in?

(MARISOL *keeps running around the stage.*)

MARISOL: June and I had plans. Gonna live together. Survive together. I gotta get her fixed! I gotta get Lenny buried!

(SCAR TISSUE *laughs and suddenly drops his magnet and jumps out of his wheelchair. He runs to* MARISOL, *stopping her in her tracks. He looks at the shocked* MARISOL *fully for the first time. He smiles, very pleased.*)

SCAR TISSUE: You look pretty nice. You're kinda cute, in fact. What do you think this all means, us two, a man and woman, bumping into each other like this?

MARISOL (*Wary*): I don't know. But thank you for helping me. Maybe my luck hasn't run out.

SCAR TISSUE (*Laughs*): Oh, don't trust luck! Fastest way to die around here. Trust gunpowder. Trust plutonium. Don't trust divine intervention or you're fucked. My name is Elvis Presley, beautiful, what's yours?

MARISOL (*Wary*): . . . Marisol Perez.

(SCAR TISSUE *nearly jumps out of his rags.*)

SCAR TISSUE: *What?!!* No! Your name can't be that! Can't be Marisol Perez!

MARISOL: It is. It has to be.

SCAR TISSUE: You're confused! Or are the goddamn graves coughing up the dead?!

MARISOL: I'm not dead! That was her! I'm—me!

SCAR TISSUE: You can't prove it!

MARISOL: I was born in the Bronx. But—but—I can't remember the street!

SCAR TISSUE: A-ha! Dead!

MARISOL (*A recitation, an effort*): Born 1966—lived on East Tremont—then Taylor Avenue—Grand Concourse—Mami died—Fordham—English major—Phi Beta Kappa—I went into science publishing—I'm a head copywriter—I make good money—I work with words—I'm clean . . . (*She holds her head and closes her eyes*) I lived in the Bronx . . . I commuted light-

years to this other planet called—Manhattan!
I learned new vocabularies . . . wore weird
native dress . . . mastered arcane rituals . . .
and amputated neat sections of my psyche,
my cultural heritage . . . yeah, clean easy
amputations . . . with no pain expressed at
all—none!—but so much pain kept inside I
almost choked on it . . . so far deep inside my
Manhattan bosses and Manhattan friends and
my broken Bronx consciousness never even
suspected . . .

(*As* MARISOL *recites facts,* SCAR TISSUE *starts going
through his bag, pulling out old magazines and
newspapers. He reads from the* New York Post.)

SCAR TISSUE: "Memorial services for Marisol Perez
were held this morning in Saint Patrick's Ca-
thedral. The estimated fifty thousand mourners included the Mayor of New York, the Bronx
Borough President, the Guardian Angels, and
the cast of the popular daytime soap opera *As
the World Turns* . . . "

MARISOL: She wasn't me! I'm me! And I'm outta
here!

(MARISOL *starts to run off—but is stopped as, far
upstage, in the dark, a Nazi skinhead walks by,
holding a can of gasoline, goose-stepping ominously toward a sleeping homeless person.* MARISOL *runs
back and hides behind* SCAR TISSUE's *wheelchair. The
Skinhead doesn't see them.*

*SCAR TISSUE sees the Skinhead and suddenly hides
behind* MARISOL, *shaking. He starts to whine and cry
and moan. The homeless person runs off. The Skinhead exits, chasing the person. When the Skinhead is
gone,* SCAR TISSUE *turns angrily to* MARISOL.)

SCAR TISSUE: Who are you for real and why do you
attract so much trouble?! I hope you don't let
those Nazis come near me!

MARISOL: I don't mean to—

(*He grabs* MARISOL.)

SCAR TISSUE: What are you!? Are you protection?
Are you benign? Or are you some kind of angel of death?

MARISOL: I'm a good person.

SCAR TISSUE: Then why don't you do something
about those Nazis?! They're all over the place.
I'm getting out of here—

(SCAR TISSUE *tries to leave.* MARISOL *stops him.*)

MARISOL: Don't leave me!

SCAR TISSUE: Why? You're not alone, are you? You
got your faith still intact. You still believe God
is good. You still think you can glide through
the world and not be part of it.

MARISOL: I'm not a Nazi!

SCAR TISSUE: I can't trust you. Ever since the angels
went into open revolt, you can't trust your
own mother . . . oops.

(MARISOL *looks at him.*)

MARISOL: What did you say? You too? Did angels
talk to you too?

SCAR TISSUE (*Worried*): No. Never mind. I don't
know a thing. Just talking out my ass.

MARISOL: You didn't dream it—

SCAR TISSUE (*Scared*): I had enough punishment! I
don't wanna get in the middle of some celestial Vietnam! I don't want any more angelic
napalm dropped on me!

MARISOL: But I saw one too—I did—*what do all these
visitations mean?*

(MARISOL *suddenly grabs* SCAR TISSUE's *hands—and
he screams, pulls away, and cowers on the ground
like a beaten dog.*)

SCAR TISSUE: NOT MY HANDS! Don't touch my
hands!

(SCAR TISSUE *rips his gloves off. His hands are
covered in burn scars. He blows on his boiling
hands.*)

MARISOL: Oh my God.

SCAR TISSUE (*Nearly crying*): Heaven erupts but who
pays the price? The fucking innocent do . . . !

MARISOL: What happened to you?

SCAR TISSUE (*Crying*): I was an air-traffic controller,
Marisol Perez. I had a life. Then I saw angels
in the radar screen and I started to drink.

(MARISOL *gets closer to the whimpering* SCAR TIS-
SUE. *She has yet to really see his face.*

MARISOL *reaches out to him and pulls the hood
back and removes his sunglasses.* SCAR TISSUE's *face
has been horribly burned. She tries not to gasp but
she can't help it.*)

MARISOL: Ay Dios, ay Dios mio, ay Dios . . .

SCAR TISSUE: You're looking for your friend . . . everyone here is looking for something . . . I'm
looking for something too . . .

MARISOL: What is it? Maybe I can help?

SCAR TISSUE: I'm looking for my lost skin. Have you seen my lost skin? It was once very pretty. We were very close. I was really attached to it.
(SCAR TISSUE *runs to the trash bin and starts looking through it.*)

MARISOL: I haven't seen anything like that.

SCAR TISSUE: It's got to be somewhere . . . it must be looking for me . . . it must be lonely too, don't you think . . . ?

MARISOL: Look, I'm sorry I bothered you, I'm, I'm going to go now . . .
(SCAR TISSUE *looks at* MARISOL)

SCAR TISSUE: I was just sleeping under the stars. It was another night when I couldn't find shelter. The places I went to, I got beat up. They took my clothes. Urinated in my mouth. Fucking blankets they gave me were laced with DDT. I said Fuck It, I took my shit outside and went up to some dick-head park in the Bronx . . .

MARISOL (*Remembering*): Van Cortlandt Park?

SCAR TISSUE: . . . just to be near some shriveled trees and alone and away from the massive noise, just for a little nap . . . my eyes closed . . . I vaguely remember the sound of goose-stepping teenagers from Staten Island with a can of gasoline, shouting orders in German . . .
(MARISOL *walks away from* SCAR TISSUE.)

MARISOL: June's waiting for me . . .

SCAR TISSUE: A flash of light. I exploded outward. My bubbling skin divorced my suffering nerves and ran away, looking for some coolness, some paradise, some other body to embrace! (*Laughs bitterly*) Now I smell like barbecue! I could have eaten myself! I could have charged money for pieces of my broiled meat!

MARISOL: Please stop. I get the picture.
(SCAR TISSUE *stops, looks at* MARISOL *sadly. He motions to her that he needs help. She helps him with his gloves, sunglasses, hood.*)

SCAR TISSUE: The angel was Japanese. Dressed in armor. Dressed in iron. Dressed to endure the fire of war. She had a scimitar.

MARISOL (*Can't believe it; wanting to*): She?

SCAR TISSUE: Kissed me. I almost exploded. I kept hearing Jimi Hendrix in my middle ear as those lips, like two *brands*, nearly melted me. She was radiant. Raw.

MARISOL AND SCAR TISSUE: Fulgent.

SCAR TISSUE: She told me when angels are bored at night, they write your nightmares. She said the highest among the angels carry God's throne on their backs for eternity, singing, "Glory, glory, glory!" But her message was terrible and after she kissed me . . .

MARISOL AND SCAR TISSUE: . . . I spit at her.

SCAR TISSUE: Was that the right thing to do, Marisol?

MARISOL: I thought it was . . . but I don't know.
(MARISOL *looks gently at Scar Tissue. She kisses him softly. He smiles and pats her on the head like a puppy. He goes to his wheelchair and pulls out an old bottle of Kentucky bourbon. He smiles and offers the bottle to* MARISOL.
    MARISOL *drinks greedily.* SCAR TISSUE *applauds her. She smiles as the hot liquid burns down her throat. She laughs long and loud: in this barren landscape, it's a beautiful sound.
    As they both laugh,* SCAR TISSUE *motions that they should embrace.* MARISOL *holds her breath and embraces him.*)

SCAR TISSUE (*Hopeful*): So? Feelin' horny? Can I hope?
(MARISOL *quickly lets him go, and gives him back his bottle.*)

MARISOL: Let's not push it, okay Elvis?
(SCAR TISSUE *laughs. He goes to his wheelchair and prepares to hit the road again.*)

SCAR TISSUE: Word on the street is, water no longer seeks its own level, there are fourteen inches to the foot, six days in the week, seven planets in the solar system, and the French are polite. I also hear the sun rises in the north and sets in the South. I think I saw the sun setting over there . . . instinct tells me south is over there . . .
(MARISOL *turns to face south.*)

MARISOL: Thank you.
(*The* SKINHEAD *crosses the stage again, with the can of gasoline, chasing the frightened homeless person.* MARISOL *and* SCAR TISSUE *hit the ground.
    The homeless person falls. The* SKINHEAD *pours the gasoline on the homeless person and lights a match. There's a scream as the homeless person burns to death.* MARISOL *covers her ears so she can't hear.
    The* SKINHEAD *exits.* MARISOL *and* SCAR TISSUE *quickly get up.* MARISOL *tries to run to the burnt homeless person.* SCAR TISSUE *stops her.*)

SCAR TISSUE: No! There's nothing you can do! Don't even look!

MARISOL: Oh my God . . .

SCAR TISSUE: I gotta get outta here. Look—if you see some extra skin laying around somewhere . . . pick it up for me, okay? I'll be exceedingly grateful. Bye.

(SCAR TISSUE *gets back into his wheelchair.*)

MARISOL: Why don't we stay together—protect each other?

SCAR TISSUE: There is no protection. That Nazi is after me. He works for TRW. If I stay . . . you're gonna have torturers and death squads all over you.

(MARISOL *goes toward him.*)

MARISOL: I'm not afraid—

SCAR TISSUE: No, I said! *Get away from me! Just get away from me! Are you fucking CRAZY OR WHAT?* Just—just if you see my skin, beautiful . . . have some good sex with it and tell it to come home quick. (*He's gone. From offstage:*) I'll always love you, Marisol!

(MARISOL *is alone. More odd streaking lights rake the sky.* MARISOL *hits the ground again, looking up, hoping that the barrage will end.*)

MARISOL (*To herself*): South—that way—I'll go south that way, where the sun sets, to look for June until I hit Miami—then—I'll know I passed her.

(*The streaking lights stop.* MARISOL *gets up. She takes a step. Then another step. With each step, the lights change as if she were entering a new part of the city or time has suddenly jumped forward. She finds some homeless person's old coat and puts it on.*)

I'm getting dirty . . . and my clothes smell bad . . . I'm getting dirty and my clothes smell bad . . . my fucking stomach's grumbling . . .

(MARISOL *runs up to the metal trash bin. She ducks behind it. She takes a piss. She finishes and comes out from behind the trash bin, relieved. Grabbing her empty stomach,* MARISOL *tries to think through her predicament. To the gold crown:*)

Okay, I just wanna go home. I just wanna live with June—want my boring nine-to-five back—my two-weeks-out-of-the-year vacation—my intellectual detachment—my ability to read about the misery of the world and not lose a moment out of my busy day. To believe you really knew what you were doing, God—please—if the sun would just come *up!* (*Beat. To herself:*) But what if the sun doesn't come *up?* And this is it? It's the deadline. I'm against the wall. I'm at the rim of the apocalypse . . .

(MARISOL *looks up. To the angel:*)

Blessed guardian angel! Maybe you were right. God has stopped looking. We can't live life as if nothing's changed. To live in the sweet past. To look backwards for our instructions. We have to reach up, beyond the debris, past the future, spit in the eye of the sun, make a fist, and say *no,* and say *no,* and say *no,* and say . . . (*Beat. Doubts. To herself*) . . . no, what if she's wrong?

(*She hurriedly gets on her knees to pray. Vicious, to the crown:*)

Dear God, All-Powerful, All-Beautiful, what do I do now? How do I get out of this? Do I have to make a deal? Arrange payment and bail myself out? *What about it!?* I'll do anything! I'll spy for you. I'll steal for you. I'll decipher strange angelic codes and mine harbors and develop germ bombs and poison the angelic food supply. DEAR GOD, WHO DO I HAVE TO BETRAY TO GET OUT OF THIS FUCKING MESS?!

(*It starts to snow lightly.* MARISOL *can't believe it. She holds out her hand.*)

Snow? It's eighty degrees!

(*We hear the sound of bombs, heavy artillery, very close.* MARISOL *is suddenly, violently, gripped by hunger pains. She grabs her stomach.*)

Oh God!

(MARISOL *scrambles to the trash bin and starts burrowing into it like an animal searching for food. She finally finds a paper bag. She tears it open. She finds a bunch of moldy French fries. She closes her eyes and prepares to eat them.*)

LENNY'S VOICE: Marisol you don't want to eat that!

(MARISOL *throws the food down.*)

MARISOL (*To herself*): Lenny?

(LENNY *comes in pushing a battered baby carriage full of junk.* LENNY *is nine months pregnant: huge belly, swollen breasts.* MARISOL *is stunned by the transformation.*)

Holy shit.

LENNY: Don't eat anything in that pile, Marisol. It's lethal.

MARISOL: You're alive and you're . . . bloated—

LENNY: Man who owned the restaurant on the other side of that wall put rat poison in the trash to discourage the homeless from picking through the pile. God bless the child that's got his own, huh? It's nice to see you again, Marisol.

(*It stops snowing. Staring at his stomach,* MARISOL *goes over to* LENNY.)

MARISOL (*Amazed*): I thought I killed you.

LENNY: Almost. But I forgive you. I forgive my sister, too.

MARISOL: You've seen her?

LENNY: I haven't seen her, sorry. Hey, you want food? I have a little food. I'll prepare you some secret edible food.

(MARISOL *goes to* LENNY, *wide-eyed.*)

MARISOL: Okay . . . but . . . Lenny . . . you're immense . . .

(MARISOL *helps* LENNY *sit. He motions for her to sit next to him.*)

LENNY: I'm fucking enormous. Got the worst hemorrhoids. The smell of Chinese food makes me puke my guts.

MARISOL (*Embarrassed*): I just don't know . . . what to think about this . . . and what would June say . . . ?

LENNY (*Chuckles*): I have something you're gonna like, Marisol. Took me great pains to get. Lots of weaseling around the black market, greasing palms, you know, giving blow jobs—*the things a parent will do for their fetus!*—until I got it . . .

(LENNY *produces a bag. In the bag,* LENNY *reveals a scrawny little apple wrapped lovingly in layer after layer of delicate colored paper.* MARISOL *can't believe what she sees.*)

MARISOL: That's an apple. But that's extinct.

LENNY: Only if you believe the networks. Powers that be got the very last tree. It's in the Pentagon. In the center of the five-sided beast.

(LENNY *bites the apple, relishing its flavor. He pats his stomach approvingly.* MARISOL *hungrily watches him eat.*)

I was on a terrible diet 'til I got knocked up. Eating cigarette butts, old milk cartons, cat food,

raw shoelaces, roach motels. It's nice to be able to give my baby a few essential vitamins.

MARISOL: You're really gonna be a mother?

LENNY: Baby's been kicking. It's got great aim. Always going for my bladder. I'm pissing every five minutes.

MARISOL (*Tentative*): Can I feel?

(MARISOL *puts her hand on* LENNY's *belly. She feels movement and pulls her hand away.*)

LENNY: It's impossible to sleep. Lying on my back, I'm crushed. On my side, I can't breathe. The baby's heartbeat keeps me up at night. The beating is dreadful. Sounds like a bomb. I know when it goes, it's gonna go BIG.

MARISOL (*Frightened, unsure*): Something's moving in there . . .

LENNY: When it's in a good mood it does back flips and my fucking kidneys end up in my throat. Did I tell you about my hemorrhoids? Here, eat.

(LENNY *gives* MARISOL *the apple. She bites into it— chews—then quickly spits it all out. Livid,* LENNY *takes the apple away from* MARISOL.)

Don't waste my FOOD, *you dumb shit!*

(LENNY *starts picking up the bits of half-chewed apple spit out by* MARISOL *and eats them greedily.* MARISOL *continues to spit.*)

MARISOL (*Angry*): It's just salt inside there . . . just salt . . .

LENNY: My baby's trying to build a brain! My baby needs all the minerals it can get!

MARISOL: It's not an apple! It's not food!

LENNY: Get outta here if you're gonna be ungrateful! My baby and I don't need you! (*He devours the apple and tries to keep from crying.*) There isn't a single food group in the world that isn't pure salt anymore! Where the fuck have you been?! (*He holds his stomach for comfort.*)

MARISOL: This is your old bullshit, Lenny. That's a fucking pumpkin you got under your clothes. A big bundle of deceit and sexual CONFUSION. You're trying to *dislodge* me. Finally push me over the *edge*. Contradict all I know so I won't be able to say my own *name*.

(MARISOL *angrily pushes* LENNY *and he topples over, holding his stomach.*)

LENNY: There isn't much food left in the PENTAGON, you know!

MARISOL: Oh, give me a break. When the sun comes up in the morning, all this will be gone! The city will come back! People will go back to work. You'll be a myth. A folktale. (*Bitter*) Maybe you should stop pretending you're pregnant and find a job.

LENNY: *How can you say that when this is your baby!?*

MARISOL: It's not my baby!

LENNY: For days and days all I did was think about you and think about you and the more I thought about you, the bigger I got! Of course it's yours!

MARISOL: I don't know what you're saying!

LENNY: I shouldda had a fucking *abortion . . .*

MARISOL (*Trying not to lose control*): I think you're a freak, Lenny. I'm supposed to know that men don't have babies. But I don't know that anymore, do I? If you're really pregnant, then we have to start at the beginning, don't we? Well I'm not ready to do that!

(LENNY *gets to his feet, indignant.*)

LENNY: I'm no freak. Every man should have this experience. There'd be fewer wars. *This* is power. *This* is energy. I guard my expanding womb greedily. I worship my new organs . . . the violent bloodstream sending food and oxygen . . . back and forth . . . *between two hearts.* One body. Two surging hearts! *That's* a revolution!

(*He starts off. He stops in his tracks. He drops everything. He grabs his stomach. Pain knocks out his breathing.*)

MARISOL: Now what is it?

LENNY: Oh shit . . . I think it's time. I think this is it.

MARISOL: Get outta here.

(LENNY's *pants are suddenly wet.*)

LENNY: My water's burst. Oh God, it can't be now . . .

MARISOL: I'm telling you to stop this!

LENNY (*Panicking*): I'm not ready. Feel my breasts! They're empty! I can't let this baby be born yet! What if my body can't make enough milk to feed my baby?!

(LENNY *shrieks with pain, falls to his knees.* MARISOL *helps him lie down. She kneels beside him.*)

MARISOL: Okay, Lenny, breathe—breathe—breathe—

LENNY (*Incredible pain*): I'm breathing, you ASSHOLE, I'm breathing!

MARISOL: Breathe more!

LENNY: Jesus and I thought *war* was hell!

MIRASOL: Oh my God—oh Jesus . . .

LENNY: If I pull off this birth thing, *it'll be a miracle!*

MIRASOL: . . . *Angel of God please help him!*

(MARISOL *quickly covers* LENNY's *abdomen with her coat.* LENNY *starts the final stage of labor. He bears down.*

LENNY *lets out a final, cataclysmic scream.*

The baby is born. MARISOL *"catches" the baby.*

MARISOL *holds the silent baby in the coat, wrapping it tight. She examines the baby.* LENNY's *huge stomach has disappeared. He breathes hard. Short silence.*

LENNY *sits up slowly, wiping sweat from his face, happy the ordeal is over. All* LENNY *wants to do is hold his child.* MARISOL *stands up holding the baby, looking at it a long time, a troubled look on her face.*

LENNY *holds out his arms for the baby.* MARISOL *looks at* LENNY *and shakes her head, sadly, no.* LENNY *looks at* MARISOL, *all hope drained from his face.*)

LENNY: Dead?

MIRASOL: I'm sorry.

(MARISOL *nods yes and wraps the baby tighter.*

MARISOL *gives* LENNY *his baby.* LENNY *takes the bundle, kisses it, holds back tears.* MARISOL *looks at him.*)

LENNY: C'mon. There's something we have to do now.

(*Holding the baby,* LENNY *starts to walk around and around the stage.* MARISOL *follows.*

They come to the downstage corner where the rosary-covered fire hydrant is. Special lighting on this area. MARISOL *looks down and notices little crucifixes scratched into the sidewalk in rows.*

Dazzling, frenetic lights rip the air above MARISOL *and* LENNY.)

Do you know where you are, Marisol?

(MARISOL *shakes her head no.*)

You're in Brooklyn.

MARISOL (*Empty*): Wow. I finally made it. I'm here.

LENNY: Everybody comes to this street eventually.

MARISOL: Why?

LENNY: People are buried here. It looks like a sidewalk. But it's not. It's a tomb.

MARISOL: For who?

LENNY: For babies. *Angelitos.*

(LENNY *removes a slab of sidewalk concrete and starts digging up the dirt beneath it. There's a tiny wooden box there.*)

The city provides these coffins. There are numbers on them. The city knows how we live.

(LENNY *gently places the baby's body in the box.*)

These are babies born on the street. Little girls of the twilight hours who never felt warm blankets around their bodies. Never drank their mothers' holy milk. Little boys born with coke in their blood. This is where babies who die on the street are taken to rest. You never heard of it?

MARISOL: Never.

(LENNY *puts the box in the ground and covers it up with dirt.*)

LENNY: Everyone who sleeps and begs in the open air knows this address. We come with flowers, with crucifixes, with offerings. The wind plays organ music. Hard concrete turns into gentle moss so the babies can decompose in grace. We all come here sooner or later to pay respects to the most fragile of the street people.

(LENNY *replaces the concrete slab and scratches the name of the child into the concrete. He says a prayer. If there are other homeless people onstage, they pick up the prayer and repeat it softly underneath* LENNY.)

> Matthew, Mark, Luke, and John.
> Bless the bed that I lie on.
> Four corners to my bed.
> Four angels round my head.
> One to watch and one to pray.
> And two to bear your soul away.

(LENNY *kisses the ground.*)

'Night, little Marisol.

(LENNY *lies on the ground and falls asleep. Exhausted,* MARISOL *looks at the tiny cemetery. She reads the names scratched into the sidewalk.*)

MARISOL: Fermin Rivera . . . born March 14, died March 16 . . . Jose Amengual . . . born August 2, died August 2 . . . Delfina Perez . . . born December 23, died January 6 . . . Jonathan Sand . . . born July 1, died July 29 . . . Wilfredo Terron . . . dates unknown . . . no name . . . no name . . . no name . . .

(MARISOL *can't read anymore. She sits in the middle of the child cemetery, exhausted, notable to think, feel, or react anymore. For all she knows, this could be the end of the world.*

MARISOL *lies on the street, in* LENNY'S *arms, and falls asleep.*

Upstage there's the sound of marching feet. The SKINHEAD *enters and marches toward the sleeping* MARISOL *and* LENNY *and stops. Only as the light comes up on the* SKINHEAD *do we realize it's* JUNE.)

JUNE (*To herself, indicating* MARISOL): Look at this goddamn thing, this waste, this fucking parasite. God, I'm so sick of it. Sick of the eyesore. Sick of the diseases. Sick of the drugs. Sick of the homelessness. Sick of the border babies. Sick of the dark skin. Sick of that compassion thing! That's where it all started! When they put in that fucking compassion thing! (*Furious*) I mean, why can't they just go AWAY? I mean, okay, if you people want to kill yourselves, fine, do it: kill yourselves with your crack and your incest and your promiscuity and your homo anal intercourse . . . just leave me to take care of myself and my own. Leave me to my gardens. I'm good in my gardens. I'm good on my acres of green grass. God distributes green grass in just the right way! Take care of your own. Take care of your family. If everybody did that . . . I swear on my gold Citibank MasterCard . . . there wouldn't be any problems, anywhere, in the next millennium . . .

(JUNE *looks down at* MARISOL. *She unscrews the can of gasoline and starts pouring gasoline on* MARISOL *and* LENNY. MARISOL *wakes up.* JUNE *strikes a match.* MARISOL *jumps at* JUNE, *grabbing her.*)

MARISOL: Cut that shit out you fucking Nazi!

(JUNE *tries to throw the match on* MARISOL.)

JUNE: Stay still so I can burn you!

(MARISOL *grabs* JUNE *and tries to push her away from* LENNY. *They're face-to face for the first time.*)

What a day I'm having, huh?

MARISOL (*Startled*): . . . June?

JUNE: I started out burning hobos and ended up torching half the city! The entire Upper West Side up in ashes!

MARISOL (*Overjoyed*): Oh God, I found you.

JUNE: You got anything for me?!

MARISOL: I thought Lenny killed you—

JUNE: You got nothing for me? Get outta my way, asshole!

MARISOL: Don't you remember me?

JUNE: You should see what I did! It's fire on a massive scale! Buildings melted all down! Consumed! Ashes of those evaporated dreams are all over the fucking place!

MARISOL: June—it's Marisol . . .

(MARISOL *throws both arms around* JUNE, *embraces her tightly, and kisses her.* JUNE *tries to escape.*)

JUNE: We could be picked up real fast by the police . . . they've built great big facilities for us . . . 'cause our numbers are swelling . . .

(MARISOL *tries to hold* JUNE. JUNE *resists. But the prolonged and violent contact with* MARISOL'S *body has started to awaken* JUNE'S *memory. She begins to sound a little like her old self.*)

But they won't take me! I have a strategy now! I burn bag people! The troop likes that!

MARISOL: No more! That's not you!

(MARISOL *throws the can of gasoline into the trash bin. She grabs* JUNE'S *hand and pulls* JUNE *toward* LENNY. JUNE *resists.*)

JUNE: The Citicorp building was a great place to hide. A man would pull your teeth for free in Port Authority—

MARISOL: Lenny's right here . . .

JUNE: I hear the water in the Central Park reservoir is salty 'cause angels are falling outta the sky, Marisol . . .

MARISOL (*Astonished*): You said my name. You said Marisol.

(MARISOL *joyfully embraces* JUNE *and kisses her. That pushes* JUNE *over the edge and she collapses.* MARISOL *catches her and lays her gently on the ground.* MARISOL *sits with* JUNE'S *head on her lap. This time* JUNE *does not resist.*)

JUNE (*Weak, rubbing her head*): I can't understand these nightmares I'm having . . .

(MARISOL *holds* JUNE. JUNE *and* LENNY *quietly start to cry.*)

MARISOL: We survived. We survived, June.

(MARISOL *looks around her—at her two crippled, sobbing friends—at the distorted world—all too aware of the graveyard that has become the site of their reunion.*)

For what? To do what?

(MARISOL *looks up at the crown—a long, still moment.*)

Fuck you. Just *fuck* you!

(*Loud machine-gunfire rips the air.* MARISOL *hits the ground and covers* JUNE *and* LENNY *with her body.*)

June, Lenny . . . don't you guys worry . . . I have a clear vision for us. I know what I want to do.

(*The machine-gun firing stops.* MARISOL *kisses her friends.*)

Listen to me. We're going to find the angels. And I'm going to ask them to touch your foreheads. To press their angelic fingers into your temples. Fire your minds with instant light. Blow up your bad dreams. And resurrect you.

(MARISOL *looks up at the crown.*)

And then we're going to join them. Then we're going to fight with the angels.

(MARISOL *helps* JUNE *and* LENNY *to their feet.* JUNE *and* LENNY *see each other and embrace.*)

LENNY (*To* JUNE): I'm sorry for everything I did . . .

JUNE (*To* LENNY, *kissing him*): I'm sorry, too, Lenny . . .

(*As* MARISOL *takes their hands to start their new journey, the* WOMAN WITH FURS *enters, unseen, behind them. She is completely still. She is holding an Uzi.*)

MARISOL: What a time to be alive, huh? On one hand, we're nothing. We're dirt. On the other hand, we're the reason the universe was made.

(*The* WOMAN WITH FURS *loads the Uzi. Bombs are heard.*)

JUNE: What's that noise?

MARISOL: Right now, thousands upon millions of angels are dying on our behalf. Isn't that amazing? The silver cities of Heaven are burning for us. Attacks and counterattacks are ruining galaxies. The ripped-up planets are making travel impossible. And triumphant angels are taking over the television stations. All for us. All for me.

(*The* WOMAN WITH FURS *points the Uzi at* MARISOL, JUNE, *and* LENNY.)

WOMAN WITH FURS: Sorry, Marisol. We don't need revolution here. We can't have upheaval at the drop of a hat. No demonstrations here! No putting up pamphlets! No shoving daisies into the rifles of militiamen! No stopping tanks by standing in their way!

(MARISOL *turns to look at the* WOMAN WITH FURS.)

MARISOL: . . . Unless you want to join us—?

WOMAN WITH FURS: Traitors! Credit risks!

(MARISOL *goes to the* WOMAN WITH FURS *and the* WOMAN WITH FURS *blasts* MARISOL *pumping hundreds of rounds into her. She dies instantly and falls to the ground. The* WOMAN WITH FURS *exits.*

There's a blackout.

Suddenly, the stage is bathed in strange light. We hear the strange, indecipherable sounds of the angelic war.

JUNE *and* LENNY *kneel where* MARISOL *has fallen.* MARISOL *is standing apart, alone, in her own light.* MARISOL'S *voice is slightly amplified:*)

MARISOL: I'm killed instantly. Little blazing lead meteors enter my body. My blood cells ride those bullets into outer space. My soul surges up the oceans of the Milky Way at the speed of light. At the moment of death, I see the invisible war.

(*Beautiful music.*

The stage goes black, except for a light on MARISOL.)

Thousands of years of fighting pass in an instant. New and terrible forms of warfare, monstrous weapons, and unimagined strains of terror are created and destroyed in billionths of a second. Galaxies spring from a single drop of angel's sweat while hundreds of armies fight and die on the fingertips of children in the Bronx.

(*Light upstage reveals the* ANGEL. *She's dressed in a filthy, tattered uniform: the war has ravaged her. She also has huge magnificent wings: her wings of war. She's got an Uzi machine gun.*

The ANGEL *fires her Uzi into the air, at the invisible legions of God's loyal warriors. The terrible sounds of war.*

The angelic vision lasts only seconds. The stage once again goes to black. A spotlight on MARISOL.)

Three hundred million million beautiful angels die in the first charge of the Final Battle. The oceans are salty with rebel blood. Angels drop like lightning from the dying sky. The rebels are in full retreat. There's chaos. There's blood and fire and ambulances and Heaven's soldiers scream and fight and die in beautiful, beautiful light. It looks like the revolution is doomed . . .

(*Light upstage reveals a single homeless person angrily throwing rocks at the sky. The homeless person is joined by* LENNY *and* JUNE.)

. . . then, as if one body, one mind, the innocent of the earth take to the streets with anything they can find—rocks, sticks, screams—and aim their displeasure at the senile sky and fire into the tattered wind on the side of the angels . . . billions of poor, of homeless, of peaceful, of silent, of angry . . . fighting and fighting as no species has ever fought before. Inspired by the earthly noise, the rebels advance!

(*A small moon appears in the sky, far, far away.*)

New ideas rip the Heavens. New powers are created. New miracles are signed into law. It's the first day of the new history . . .

(*There's a few seconds of tremendous noise as the war hits its climax.*

Then silence.

The ANGEL *appears next to* MARISOL, *wingless, unarmed, holding the gold crown in her hands. The* ANGEL *holds the crown out to the audience as* MARISOL *looks at her.*)

Oh God. What light. What possibilities. What hope.

(*The* ANGEL *kisses* MARISOL.

Bright, bright light begins to shine directly into the audience's eyes for several seconds—and MARISOL, *the* ANGEL, JUNE, LENNY, *and the homeless people seem to be turned into light. Then, all seem to disappear in the wild light of the new millennium—blackout.*)

Introduction to *Venus*

WHEN THE PLAY WAS NEW

Venus by Suzan-Lori Parks opened on March 28, 1996, at the Yale Repertory Theatre, then moved to the Joseph Papp Public Theatre of the New York Shakespeare Festival in April and May. In the same year *Venus* won Parks her second Obie Award for best off-Broadway play. It was directed by the imaginative avant-garde playwright/director Richard Foreman, who also designed the set.

This play focuses on three themes common in African American criticism and post-modern theatrical work with which we can identify Parks: racism, sexism, and deconstruction of history (the play begins in 1810). Parks also makes generous use of repetition, especially images. She repeats lines of dialogue and snatches of words that become choric and underscore the distress of the protagonist, Venus. Such repetition tends to ritualize the presentation of the Venus Hottentot's dilemma and suffering. Her agony becomes a show. The central image is the human being trapped in a freak show and made the object of the gaze of audiences wanting to experience the titillating, the impossible, the grotesque. Although set in the early nineteenth century, the play is also about the world in which we continue to live.

THE PLAYWRIGHT

Suzan-Lori Parks was born in 1964 in Fort Knox, Kentucky, but lived in many different states and even in Germany during high school because her father was a U.S. Army colonel. While attending Mount Holyoke College, where she received her bachelor's degree in 1985, she studied creative writing with James Baldwin, who encouraged her to pursue playwriting. Parks' first production in New York was *Betting on the Dust Commander* (1987), performed in a garage bar. By 1989, however, she was working off-Broadway with *Imperceptible Mutabilities in the Third Kingdom*, which won her first Obie Award in 1990. *Death of the Last Black Man in the Entire World* (1990) followed, and *Devotees in the Garden of Love* (1992), a violent examination of courtship ritual, premiered at the Humana Festival of Actors Theatre of Louisville.

A breakthrough play for Parks was *America Play* (1994), an intriguing re-examination of America's fascination with the assassination of Abraham Lincoln, explored through a black carnival performer who plays Lincoln in whiteface while people line up to pretend to assassinate him. She revisited this deadly theme in a dynamically different way with *Topdog/Underdog* (2001), a tale of two African American brothers named Lincoln and Booth. *Topdog/Underdog* was first performed at the Joseph Papp Public Theatre before moving to Broadway. It was the first play by a black woman produced on Broadway for twenty-five years. Parks was also awarded the Pulitzer Prize for playwriting for *Topdog/Underdog*, the first to go to an African American woman. The playwright explored the world of *The Scarlet Letter* in two plays that are radical departures from the famous Hawthorne novel: *In the Blood* (1999) and *Fucking A* (2000) are modern studies in adultery, poverty, and racial oppression. Both plays have been professionally produced and published together as *The Red Letter Plays*.

Parks' work in other genres includes screenplays (*Girl 6* directed by Spike Lee, as well as others in production) and a novel, *Getting Mother's Body* (2003). She has also written at least three radio plays. Parks was awarded a MacArthur Foundation Genius Grant in 2001.

GENRE, STRUCTURE, AND STYLE

Venus is the most discursive and structurally complicated play in this anthology. Created and performed in a presentational style, the play incorporates frequent transformations of time, place, and character. Frequent character doubling feeds or is fed by a chorus that provides commentary, an onstage audience, and vocal underscoring and counterpoint for the primary action of the play. Instead of numbering the scenes in the order the audience expects, Parks creates an episodic countdown from 31 to 1, but a chronology is only faintly present. The numbering system lets the audience keep track of the action as it moves inexorably toward the demise of Venus.

The scenes are labeled in a way reminiscent of the Epic Theatre of Brecht. Parks also uses the epic devices of narration and stylization; the audience is always reminded that it is in a theatre. Even when the action and characterization are emotional and disturbing, some distance is created. The play at times seems to become the form that it deconstructs; it doesn't just present the sideshow, the freak show, but often imitates it. The language is alternately schematic and poetic, emblematic and abbreviated, profane and clinical. Parks is fond of modern musical forms and often uses riffs and snatches of music both literally and figuratively. She is one of America's most successful eclectic dramatic authors.

IMPORTANT ELEMENTS OF CONTENT

Parks frequently revisits history, deconstructs it, even tears it apart, asking us to reconsider what we think we know. *Venus* explores the life and persecution of a real person from the early nineteenth century, the so-called Venus Hottentot from South Africa, whose real name was Sartje or Sara Baartman. *Venus* is not only an account of the young woman who becomes the Venus Hottentot, but an exploration of how people today respond to usury and redefinitions of slavery. Venus becomes the "other" in terms of gender, sexuality, race, and perceptions of physical abnormality for the onstage audience, as well as for many in the real audience viewing Parks' play. *Venus* is about colonization—both literal and figurative. Most of all, it asks the audience to analyze its own gaze, its own inclination to become the voyeur. It is intended to make the audience of all races and both genders feel uncomfortable, maybe guilty, as Venus is paraded and exhibited, mistreated and ultimately dissected. The play is in part a commentary on nineteenth-century medicine, but at the same time it asks how far we have really progressed. Aren't we still fascinated by freak shows of all sorts—and not just at a sideshow that may now seem anachronistic? The sideshow has been nearly supplanted by television (with reality shows and talk shows) and by a multitude of sites on the Internet. With many of her plays, including *Venus*, Parks seems to ask how history defines famous people, and how those definitions inform the way others define us or the way we define ourselves.

THE PLAY IN REVIVAL

Since 2000, many professional European, American, and university theatres have tackled this challenging work. Between 2002 and 2005 at least ten universities and colleges mounted productions of *Venus*, including Mount Holyoke (Parks' alma mater). The Olney Theatre in Maryland and the Potomac Theatre Festival in Virginia produced it in 2004, and the Cleveland Public Theatre produced it in 2005. In the wake of Parks winning the Pulitzer Prize in 2002, the number of productions of her plays, not just *Topdog/Underdog*, has increased significantly.

SPECIAL FEATURE

A fascinating part of *Venus* is the presentation of the medical profession in the early nineteenth century. The crude and sexist behavior of doctors in the world of premodern medicine is of course horrific, but the doctors in the play fall prey to the same curiosities of most human beings when they encounter that which they have never seen, never expected, or cannot understand. The play may make us happy for the current state of the medical profession, but also reminds us that not so very long ago the play's conditions were commonplace.

FURTHER READING ABOUT THE PLAY, PLAYWRIGHT, AND CONTEXT

All of Parks' professionally produced plays are published singly and some are collected. Two collections include Parks, *The Red Letter Plays,* and *The America Play and Other Works.*

For an account on the real Venus Hottentot, see Richard D. Altick, *The Shows of London.*

For Parks on her own methods, see Parks, "How I Write: Suzan-Lori Parks," *The Writer,* 2004.

As of yet, there are no books of criticism or biography of Parks (she was in her early forties at this writing), but there are many articles about her in journals and magazines. For representative articles, see Shawn-Marie Garrett, "The Possession of Suzan-Lori Parks," *American Theatre,* 2000; and S. E. Wilmer, "Restaging the Nations: The Work of Suzan-Lori Parks," *Modern Drama,* Fall 2000.

Venus

By Suzan-Lori Parks

THE ROLES

MISS SAARTJIE BAARTMAN, a.k.a. THE GIRL, and later THE VENUS HOTTENTOT

THE MAN, later THE BARON DOCTEUR

THE MANS BROTHER, later THE MOTHER-SHOWMAN, later THE GRADE-SCHOOL CHUM

THE NEGRO RESURRECTIONIST

THE CHORUS as:

    THE CHORUS OF THE 8 HUMAN WONDERS

    THE CHORUS OF THE SPECTATORS

    THE CHORUS OF THE COURT

    THE CHORUS OF THE 8 ANATOMISTS

    THE PLAYERS OF "FOR THE LOVE OF THE VENUS"

Within *Venus* are scenes from *"For the Love of the Venus,"* a Drama in 3 Acts.

THE CHARACTERS

The roles should be cast from THE CHORUS.

THE FATHER

THE MOTHER

THE YOUNG MAN

THE UNCLE

THE BRIDE-TO-BE (later, guised as "THE HOTTENTOT VENUS")

AUTHOR'S NOTES: FROM *"THE ELEMENTS OF STYLE"*
In *Venus* I'm continuing the use of my slightly unconventional theatrical elements. Here's a road map.

—*(Rest)*
Take a little time, a pause, a breather; make a transition.

—A Spell
An elongated and heightened *(Rest)*. Denoted by repetition of figures' names with no dialogue. Has sort of an architectural look:

THE VENUS

THE BARON DOCTEUR

THE VENUS

THE BARON DOCTEUR

This is a place where the figures experience their pure true simple state. While no action or stage business is necessary, directors should fill this moment as they best see fit.

—[Brackets in the text indicate optional cuts for production.]

—(Parentheses around dialogue indicate softly spoken passages (asides; sotto voce).)

> Le travail humain
> Ressucite les choses
> D'entre les mortes.
> —Jean-luc Godard
> *Masculin*Feminin*

> "You don't believe in history,"
> said William.
> —Virginia Woolf
> *Between the Acts*

OVERTURE

THE VENUS *facing stage right. She revolves, counterclockwise. 270 degrees. She faces upstage.*

THE NEGRO RESURRECTIONIST: The Venus Hottentot!

THE MANS BROTHER, LATER THE MOTHER-SHOWMAN, LATER THE GRADE-SCHOOL CHUM: The Venus Hottentot!

THE MAN, LATER THE BARON DOCTEUR: The Venus Hottentot!
(*Rest*)
(THE VENUS *revolves 90 degrees. She faces stage right.*)
(*Rest*)

THE CHORUS: The Chorus of the 8 Human Wonders!

THE MAN, LATER THE BARON DOCTEUR: The Man, later
The Baron Docteur!

THE NEGRO RESURRECTIONIST: The Negro Resurrectionist!

THE MANS BROTHER, LATER THE MOTHER-SHOWMAN, LATER THE GRADE-SCHOOL CHUM: The Brother, later
The Mother-Showman! Later
The Grade-School Chum

THE NEGRO RESURRECTIONIST: The Negro Resurrectionist!

THE CHORUS: The Chorus of the 8 Anatomists!
(*Rest*)
(THE VENUS *revolves 180 degrees. She faces stage left.*)
(*Rest*)

THE MAN, LATER THE BARON DOCTEUR: The Chorus of the 8 Anatomists!

THE NEGRO RESURRECTIONIST: The Man, later
The Baron Docteur!

THE MAN, LATER THE BARON DOCTEUR: The Negro Resurrectionist!

THE MANS BROTHER, LATER THE MOTHER-SHOWMAN, LATER THE GRADE-SCHOOL CHUM: The Chorus of the Spectators!

THE NEGRO RESURRECTIONIST AND THE MAN, LATER THE BARON DOCTEUR: The Brother, later
The Mother-Showman! Later
The Grade-School Chum!

THE MAN AND THE MANS BROTHER: The Negro Resurrectionist!

THE MANS BROTHER, LATER THE MOTHER-SHOWMAN, LATER THE GRADE-SCHOOL CHUM: The Chorus of the Court!

ALL: The Venus Hottentot!
(*Rest*)

THE VENUS: The Venus Hottentot.
(*Rest*)
(*Rest*)

THE NEGRO RESURRECTIONIST: I regret to inform you that thuh Venus Hottentot iz dead.

ALL: Dead?

THE MANS BROTHER, LATER THE MOTHER-SHOWMAN, LATER THE GRADE-SCHOOL CHUM: There wont b inny show tonite.

THE CHORUS: Dead!

THE NEGRO RESURRECTIONIST: Exposure iz what killed her, nothin on
and our cold weather. 23 days in a row it rained.
Thuh doctor says she drank too much. It was thuh cold I think.

THE MAN, LATER THE BARON DOCTEUR: Dead?

THE NEGRO RESURRECTIONIST: Deh-duh.

THE MANS BROTHER, LATER THE MOTHER-SHOWMAN, LATER THE GRADE-SCHOOL CHUM: I regret to inform you that the Venus Hottentot iz dead.
There wont b inny show tonite.

THE NEGRO RESURRECTIONIST: Diggidy-diggidy-diggidy-diggidy.

THE MANS BROTHER, LATER THE MOTHER-SHOWMAN, LATER THE GRADE-SCHOOL CHUM: Im sure yr disappointed.
We hate to let you down.
But 23 days in a row it rained.

THE NEGRO RESURRECTIONIST: Diggidy-diggidy-diggidy-dawg.

THE MAN, LATER THE BARON DOCTEUR: I say:
Perhaps,
she died of drink.

THE NEGRO RESURRECTIONIST: It was thuh cold I think.

THE VENUS: Uhhhh!

THE CHORUS: Turn uhway. Dont look. Cover her face. Cover yr eyes.

THE VENUS: Uhhhh!

[THE CHORUS: (Drum. Drum. Drum. Drum.)
(Drum. Drum. Drum. Drum.)

A CHORUS MEMBER: They came miles and miles and miles and miles and miles.
Comin in from all over to get themselves uh look-see.
They heard the drum.

THE MANS BROTHER, LATER THE MOTHER-SHOWMAN, LATER THE GRADE-SCHOOL CHUM: Drum. Drum.

THE CHORUS: (Drum. Drum.)]

THE MANS BROTHER/ MOTHER-SHOWMAN/CHUM	THE CHORUS
DRUM	(drum)
DRUM	(drum)
DRUM	(drum)
DRUM.	(drum.)

THE VENUS: (I regret to inform you that thuh Venus Hottentot iz dead.
There wont b inny show tuhnite.)

THE CHORUS: (Outrage! Its an outrage!)

THE MAN, LATER THE BARON DOCTEUR: Dead?

THE NEGRO RESURRECTIONIST: Deh-duh.

THE MANS BROTHER, LATER THE MOTHER-SHOWMAN, LATER THE GRADE-SCHOOL CHUM: Tail end of r tale for there must be an end
is that Venus, Black Goddess, was shameles, she sinned or else
completely unknowing of r godfearin ways she stood
totally naked in her iron cage.

THE CHORUS: Shes thuh main attraction she iz
loves thuh sideshows center ring.
Whats thuh show without thuh star?

THE VENUS: Hum Drum Hum Drum.

THE CHORUS: Outrage! Its an outrage!
Gimmie gimmie back my buck!

THE MANS BROTHER, LATER THE MOTHER-SHOWMAN, LATER THE GRADE-SCHOOL CHUM: Behind that curtain just yesterday awaited:
Wild Female Jungle Creature. Of singular anatomy. Physiqued
in such a backward rounded way that she out-shapes
all others. Behind this curtain just yesterday alive uhwaits
a female—creature
an out—of towner
whos all undressed awaiting you
to take yr peek. So youve heard.

ALL: We've come tuh see your Venus.

THE MAN AND THE MANS BROTHER: We know youre disuhpointed.
We hate tuh let you down.

THE NEGRO RESURRECTIONIST: A scene of Love:

THE VENUS: *Kiss* me
Kiss me
Kiss me *Kiss*

[THE MAN, LATER THE BARON DOCTEUR: I look at you, V and I see Love

THE VENUS: Uhhhhhh!
Uhhhhhh!

THE CHORUS: Turn uhway. Dont look. Cover yr face.
  Cover yr eyes.

THE MANS BROTHER, LATER THE MOTHER-SHOWMAN,
  LATER THE GRADE-SCHOOL CHUM: She gained
  fortune and fame by not wearing a scrap
  hiding only the privates that lipped in her lap.

THE CHORUS AND THE MAN, LATER THE BARON DOCTEUR:
  Good God. Golly. Lookie-Lookie-Look-at-her.
  Ooh-la-la. What-a-find. Hubba-hubba-hubba.

A CHORUS MEMBER: They say that if I pay uh little
  more
  I'll get tuh look uh little longer
  and for uh little more on top uh that
  I'll get tuh stand
  stand off tuh thuh side
  in thuh special looking place.

A CHORUS MEMBER: (*And from there if Im really quick
  I'll stick
  my hand inside her
  cage and have a feel
  (if no ones looking*).)

ALL: Hubba-hubba-hubba-hubba.

THE VENUS: Hum Drum Hum Drum.]

ALL: THE VENUS HOTTENTOT
  THE ONLY LIVING CREATURE OF HER KIND
  IN THE WORLD
  AND ONLY ONE STEP UHWAY FROM YOU
  RIGHT NOW
  COME SEE THE HOT MISS HOTTENTOT
  STEP IN STEP IN.

THE VENUS: Hur-ry! Hur-ry!

ALL: Hur-ry! Hur-ry!

THE VENUS: But I regret to inform you that thuh Venus Hottentot iz dead.
  There wont b inny show tuhnite.

ALL: Outrage Its an outrage!
  Gimmie Gimmie back my buck!

THE NEGRO RESURRECTIONIST: Hear ye Hear ye Order Order!

ALL: The Venus Hottentot iz dead.

THE NEGRO RESURRECTIONIST: All rise.

A CHORUS MEMBER: Thuh gals got bottoms like hot
  air balloons.
  Bottoms and bottoms and bottoms pilin up like
  like 2 mountains. Magnificent. And endless.
  An ass to write home about.
  Well worth the admission price.

A spectacle a debacle a priceless prize, thuh
  filthy slut.
  Coco candy colored and dressed all in *au naturel*
  she likes when people peek and poke.

THE VENUS: Hum drum hum drum.

THE MANS BROTHER, LATER THE MOTHER-SHOWMAN,
  LATER THE GRADE-SCHOOL CHUM: Step in step in
  step in step in.

THE VENUS: There wont b inny show tuhnite.

THE MAN, LATER THE BARON DOCTEUR AND THE CHO-
  RUS: Hubba-hubba-hubba-hubba.

THE VENUS: She gained fortune and fame by not
  wearin uh scrap
  hidin only thuh privates that lipped inner
  lap.

A CHORUS MEMBER: I look at you, Venus, and see:
  Science. You
  in uh pickle
  on my library shelf.

THE VENUS: Uhhhhhh!
  Uhhhhhh!
  Uhhhhhh!
  Uhhhhhh!

ALL: Order Order Order Order! (*Rest*)

THE NEGRO RESURRECTIONIST: Tail end of our tale
  for there must be an end
  is that Venus, Black Goddess, was shameles, she
  sinned or else
  completely unknowing of r godfearin ways she
  stood
  totally naked in her iron cage.
  She gaind fortune and fame by not wearin a
  scrap
  hidin only the privates lippin down from her
  lap.
  When Death met her Death deathd her and left
  her to rot
  au naturel end for our hot Hottentot.
  And rot yes she would have right down to the
  bone
  had not The Docteur put her corpse in his
  home.
  Sheed a soul which iz mounted on Satans warm
  wall
  while her flesh has been pickled in Sciences
  Hall.

CURTAIN. APPLAUSE.

SCENE 31

MAY I PRESENT TO YOU "THE AFRICAN DANCING PRINCESS"/SHE'D MAKE A SPLENDID FREAK

Southern Africa, early 1800s. THE GIRL *on hands and knees with scrub brush and bucket scrubs a vast tile floor. She is meticulous and vigorous. The floor shines.* THE MAN *and his* BROTHER *walk about. They are deep in conversation.*

THE BROTHER: So yll finance me?
  Yes or No.
THE MAN: Last time you wanted money lets see
    what wuz it.
  Damn, it slips my mind nope Ive got it now:
  A Menagerie:
  "Gods Entire Kingdom All Under One Roof."
  A miserable failure.
THE BROTHER: I didnt know theyd die in captivity.
THE MAN: Should of figured on that, Brother.
THE BROTHER: I fed and watered them.
THE MAN: An animal needs more than that but God
    you never were a farmer.
THE BROTHER: Never was never will be.
    (*Rest*)
  Girl, you missed a spot.
    (*Rest*)
THE NEGRO RESURRECTIONIST: Scene 31:
  May I Present to You "The African Dancing
    Princess"/
  She'd Make a Splendid Freak.
    (*Rest*)
THE BROTHER: So yll finance me? Yes or No.
THE MAN: I need to think on it.
THE BROTHER: Whats there to think on?
  A simple 2 year investment. Back me
  and I'll double yr money no lets think big:
  I'll triple it.
THE MAN: You need a girl. Wholl go all that way to
    be a dancer?
THE BROTHER: Finding the girls the easy part.
    (*Rest*)
  That girl for instance.
  Shes good. Vigorous and meticulous.
THE MAN: (You dont know her?)
THE BROTHER: Cant say I do.
  Yll back me, Man? Say yes.

THE MAN: Scheme #3 remember?
  You went to Timbuktu.
THE BROTHER: What of it.
THE MAN: Timbuktu to collect wild flowers?
  Wild flowers to bring back here.
  "Garden Exotica" admission 2 cents.
THE BROTHER: They didnt take. Our soils too rich.
THE MAN: I lost my shirt!
THE BROTHER: And like a lizard anothers grown
    back in its place. Back me!
  This time Ive got a sure thing.
  Ive done tons of background research. This
    schemell bite!
THE MAN: A "Dancing African Princess?"
THE BROTHER: The English like that sort of thing.
THE MAN: (You really dont remember that girl?)
THE BROTHER: Not from this angle.
    (*Rest*)
  Theres a street over there lined with Freak Acts
  but not many dark ones, thats how we'll cash
    in.
THE MAN: A "Dancing African Princess."
THE BROTHER: Im begging on my knees!
THE MAN: Get up. Youve got it.
THE BROTHER: Just like a brother!
THE MAN: I am yr brother.
THE MAN AND THE BROTHER: Heh heh. Heh heh.
THE MAN: (You really dont remember her?)
THE BROTHER: Enlighten me.
THE MAN: (Scheme #1?)
THE BROTHER: (Marriage with the Hottentot—thats
    her?)
THE MAN: Father recognized the joke straight off
  but Mother poor thing she still gives you funny
    looks.
  You were barely 12.
THE BROTHER: Shes grown.
THE MAN: As they all do.
  Big Bottomed Girls. Thats their breed.
  You were at one time very into it.
THE BROTHER: Big Bottomed Girl. A novelty.
  Shes vigorous and meticulous.
  (Watch this, Brother!)
  (Oh, whats her name?)
THE MAN: Her—? Saartjie. "Little Sarah."
THE BROTHER: Saartjie. Lovely. Girl! GIRL!?
THE GIRL: Sir?

THE BROTHER: Dance.

THE GIRL: Dance?

THE BROTHER: Dance! Come on!

I'll clap time.

(THE BROTHER *claps time.* THE GIRL *dances.*)

THE MAN: An "African Dancing Princess?"

THE BROTHER: The Britsll eat it up.

Oh, she'd make a splendid freak.

THE MAN: A freak?

THE BROTHER: Thats what they call em

"freaks," "oddities," "curiosities."

THE MAN: Of course. Of course.

THE GIRL: Can I stop, Sir?

THE BROTHER: No no keep up.

Faster! Ha ha!

(I still dont recognize her.)

THE MAN: (She might know you though.

Their kind remember everything.)

THE BROTHER: (Ive grown a beard since then.)

THE MAN: Thats true.

THE BROTHER: Stop dancing. Stop!

THE GIRL: Stopped.

THE BROTHER: Girl?

THE GIRL: Sir.

THE BROTHER: How would you like to go to

England?

THE GIRL: England! Well.

"England." Whats that?

THE BROTHER: A big town. A boat ride away.

Where the streets are paved with gold.

THE GIRL: Gold, Sir?

THE BROTHER: Come to England. Dance a little.

THE GIRL: Dance?

THE BROTHER: Folks watch. Folks clap. Folks pay

you gold.

THE GIRL: Gold.

THE BROTHER: We'll split it 50–50.

THE GIRL: 50–50?

THE BROTHER: Half for me half for you.

May I present to you: "The African Dancing

Princess!"

THE GIRL: A Princess. Me?

THE BROTHER: Like Cinderella.

Shes heard of Cinderella, right?

THE GIRL: A princess overnight.

THE MAN: Thats it.

THE BROTHER: Yd be a sensation!

THE GIRL: Im a little shy.

THE BROTHER: Say yes and we'll go tomorrow!

THE GIRL: Will I be the only one?

THE BROTHER: Oh no, therell be a whole street

full.

THE GIRL: Im shy.

THE BROTHER: Think of it: Gold!

THE GIRL: Gold!

THE BROTHER: 2 yrs of work yd come back rich!

THE GIRL: Id come back rich!

THE BROTHER: Yd make a mint!

THE GIRL: A mint! A "mint."

How much is that?

THE MAN: You wouldnt have to work no more.

THE GIRL: I would have a house.

I would hire help.

I would be rich. Very rich.

Big bags of money!

THE MAN: Exactly.

THE GIRL: I like it.

THE BROTHER: Its settled then!

THE MAN: Yr a rascal, Brother.

THE GIRL: Do I have a choice? Id like to think on it.

THE BROTHER: Whats there to think on? Think of it

as a vacation!

2 years of work take half the take.

Come back here rich. Its settled then.

THE MAN: Think it over, Girl. Go on.

Think it all over.

THE BROTHER

THE GIRL

THE MAN

THE BROTHER

THE GIRL

THE MAN

(Rest)

(Rest)

THE GIRL: Hahahaha!

THE MAN: What an odd laugh.

THE GIRL: Just one question:

When do we go?

THE BROTHER: Next stop England!

THE GIRL: "England?"

THE BROTHER: England England England HO!

THE GIRL: "England?"

THE NEGRO RESURRECTIONIST: Scene #30

She Looks Like Shes Fresh Off the Boat:

SCENE 30

SHE LOOKS LIKE SHES
FRESH OFF THE BOAT

THE CHORUS OF THE 8 HUMAN WONDERS: Whos
    that?
Who knows?
Not from these parts.
She looks like shes fresh off the boat.
She looks like shes about to cry.
Go up to her say something nice. Cheer her up
    make her feel welcome.
I remember my first day here.
I didnt know which end was up.
And I had jet lag to boot.
Go to her, go on, be kind.
Go to her say something nice.
    (Rest)
I dunno maybe its better to stay quiet
what can anyone say at a time like this?
"Greetings"? "Salutations"? "Everythings com-
    ing up roses"?
Right, good luck.
We could stand here and tell her some lies
or the bald truth: That her lifell go from rough
    to worse.
Or we could say nothing at all.
What difference will it make?
Shes sunk. Theres no escape from this place.
THE GIRL: Whos there.
THE CHORUS OF THE 8 HUMAN WONDERS: No one in
    particular.
No one you wanna know.
THE GIRL: Yr not the other dancing cinderellas are
    you?
THE CHORUS OF THE 8 HUMAN WONDERS: Hardly,
    Girl. We've got talents
but none youd pay to see.
THE GIRL: Yr singers?
    Yr magicians!
THE CHORUS OF THE 8 HUMAN WONDERS: Yll find out
    soon enough.
THE GIRL: Its dark in here.
    (Rest)
    So this is "England."
THE CHORUS OF THE 8 HUMAN WONDERS: Bingo.

THE GIRL: Youve seen the golden avenues.
THE CHORUS OF THE 8 HUMAN WONDERS: Oh boy.
    Youve bit the big one.
I dunno maybe its better to stay quiet
What can anyone say at a time like this?
"Greetings!" "Salutations!" "Everythings com-
    ing up roses!"
THE GIRL: So happy to make yr aquaintance.
    Ive come here to get rich.
    Im an exotic dancer. Very well known at home.
    My manager is at this very moment securing us
        a proper room.
    We're planning to construct a mint, he and me
        together.
THE CHORUS OF THE 8 HUMAN WONDERS: Right, Girl,
    good luck.
We could stand here and tell her some lies
or the bald truth: That her lifell go from rough
    to worse.
Yr a fool, Girl!
THE GIRL: Yr the fools.
    Yr the fools!
    Huddled in the dark.
    Keep yr distance! You smell!
    I'd rather sit here by myself than be called names.
THE CHORUS OF THE 8 HUMAN WONDERS: I remem-
    ber my first day here.
I didnt know which end was up.
And I had jet lag to boot.
Poor girl. We shoulda said nothing. Nothing at
    all.
What difference could it make?
Shes sunk. Sunk like the rest of us.
Welcome welcome to the club, sweetheart.
Theres no escape from this place.
    (THE BROTHER enters with food.)
THE BROTHER: Here, Girl. Eat this.
    It isnt much but things right now are tight.
    Take it.
THE GIRL: Thank you.
THE BROTHER: Here. Have some water.
THE GIRL: Thank you.
THE BROTHER: Hungry?
THE GIRL: A little.
THE BROTHER: Thingsll pick up soon.
THE GIRL: When do we get to England, Sir?
THE BROTHER: This is England! Cant you tell?

THE GIRL: I wasnt sure.

> (*Rest*)

Where are the golden streets?

THE BROTHER: Just around that bend there.
You cant see them from here.

THE GIRL: Can I go out and take a look?

THE BROTHER: No no. Dont budge.
You cant. At least not yet.

THE GIRL: How long will we live in this room, Sir?

THE BROTHER: 2 or 3 days at the most.
Theres an overweight bureaucrat a real fatso
who dont want you in his country.
Im oiling his palms.
Here have more water.

THE GIRL: Its dark in here.

THE BROTHER: Tomorrow I'll show you the golden
streets.

THE GIRL: Im hungry and I'm cold.
Its dark in here.

THE BROTHER: Remember me? From way back
when?
About 12 yrs ago?

THE GIRL: Youve growd a beard other than that
you havent changed.

THE BROTHER: I wanted you then and I want you now.
Thats partly why we've come here.
So I can love you properly.
Not like at home.

THE GIRL: Home?
Love?
You oughta take me shopping. I need a new
dress.
I cant be presented to society in this old thing.

THE BROTHER: Tomorrow I'll buy you the town.
For now lift up yr skirt.
There. Thats good.

> (*She lifts her skirts showing her ass. He gropes her.*)

THE GIRL: I dont—

THE BROTHER: Relax.
Presenting "The African Dancing Princess!"

THE GIRL: Hahahaha!
I dont think I like it here.

THE BROTHER: Relax.
Relax.
Its going to be fantastic.

> (*They kiss and touch each other. He is more amo-rous than she.*)

> (*Rest*)

THE NEGRO RESURRECTIONIST:
Footnote #1:

> (*Rest*)

Historical Extract. Category: Theatrical.

> (*Rest*)

The year was 1810. On one end of town, in
somewhat shabby circumstances, a young
woman, native of the dark continent, bares
her bottoms. At the same time but in a
very different place, on the other end of town
in fact, we witness a very different performance.
Scene 29:
Presenting: "For the Love of the Venus."
A Drama in 3 Acts. Act I, Scene 3:

SCENE 29

"FOR THE LOVE OF THE VENUS." ACT I, SCENE 3

A play on a stage. THE BARON DOCTEUR *is the only per-son in the audience. Perhaps he sits in a chair. It's al-most as if he's watching TV.* THE VENUS *stands off to the side. She watches* THE BARON DOCTEUR.

THE BRIDE-TO-BE: Coffee, darling.

THE YOUNG MAN: No thank you.

THE BRIDE-TO-BE: Tea.

THE YOUNG MAN: No thank you.

THE BRIDE-TO-BE: Chocolate.

THE YOUNG MAN: Chocolate. Mmmmm.

THE BRIDE-TO-BE: Mmmmm?

THE YOUNG MAN: No *thank* you. ·

THE BRIDE-TO-BE: Look! Oh, what a treasure:
Bah-nah-nah.

THE YOUNG MAN: You *peel* it.

THE BRIDE-TO-BE: *Peel* it. Novelty.

THE YOUNG MAN: Uncle took Dad to Africa.
Showed Dad stuff. Blew Dads mind.

> (*Rest*)

> (THE YOUNG MAN *reads from his notebook.*)

THE YOUNG MAN: "The Man who has never been
from his own home is no *Man*. For how can a
Man call himself *Man* if he has not stepped off

his own doorstep and wandered out into the
world . . . Visit the world and *Man* he will be."
[THE BRIDE-TO-BE: Canasta.
Whist?
Crazy 8s?
THE YOUNG MAN: "When a Man takes his jour-
ney beyond all that to him was hitherto the
Known, when a Man packs his baggage and
walks himself beyond the Familiar, then sees
he his true I; not in the eyes of the Known but
in the eyes of the Known-Not."]
THE BRIDE-TO-BE: You wrote me once
such lovely poetry.
THE YOUNG MAN: "His place in the Great Chain of
Being is then to him and to all that set their
eyes upon him, thus revealed."
THE BRIDE-TO-BE: "My Love for you is artificial
Fabricated much like this epistle."
(*Rest*)
Such poetry you used to write me.
THE YOUNG MAN: "Beholding and Beheld as he is
seen through the eyes of the Great Known-
Not—taking his rightful place among the
Splendors of the Universe."
(*Rest*)
(*Rest*)
"Among the Splendors of *Gods* Universe" it
should be.
Dontcha think?
THE BRIDE-TO-BE: Aaahh me:
Unloved.
(*Curtain.* THE BARON DOCTEUR *applauds.*)

SCENE 28

FOOTNOTE #2

THE NEGRO RESURRECTIONIST *holds fast to* THE VENUS's
arm. He reads through THE BARON DOCTEUR's *notebook.*

THE NEGRO RESURRECTIONIST: Footnote #2:
(*Rest*)
Historical Extract. Category: Medical. Autopsy
report:
(*Rest*)
"Her brain, immediately after removal, deprived
of the greater part of its membranes, weighed
38 ounces."

(*Rest*)
"Her spinal cord was not examined, as it was
considered more desirable to preserve the
vertebral column intact. The dissection of her
nerves, although carefully made, revealed
no important deviations from the ordinary
arrangement."
(*Rest*)
"Her liver weighed 54 and ¾ ounces and was of
a ruinous color and slightly fatty."
(*Rest*)
"Her gallbladder was small and a little dilated
at the *fundus,* being almost cylindrical when
distendid with air. Length 4 inches."
(*Rest*)
"Her stomach was of the usual form. Small intestines measured 15 feet. Spleen was pale in
color and weighed 2 and ¼ ounces. Her pan-
creas weighed 1 and ¾ ounces. Her kidneys
were large."
(*Rest*)
(*He releases* THE VENUS's *arm. She flees but doesn't
get far. She runs smack into* THE MOTHER-SHOWMAN.)

SCENE 27

PRESENTING THE MOTHER-SHOWMAN
AND HER GREAT CHAIN OF BEING

THE MOTHER-SHOWMAN: Strip down.
Strip down come on yr filthy, Girl.
Come on lets move, thats it take off every stitch
and hand it here and pronto!
I'll clean em for ya.
Damn its dark in here.
That scrap too around yr womans parts hand
that here too.
THE GIRL: It dont come off
it stays. Its custom.
THE MOTHER-SHOWMAN: Fine.
God. He wasnt lying.
You got enough here to make em come
running.
Todays my lucky day.
THE GIRL: Whats that?
THE MOTHER-SHOWMAN: You smell.
So smelly yll make em go running I said.
Good God.

Heres a bucket and a brush.
Take a bath its yr big day today.
Yr gonna be presented to society so to speak.
Scrub down you smell I said.
THE GIRL: Maam. Who are you.
THE NEGRO RESURRECTIONIST: Scene 27:
    Presenting The Mother-Showman
    and Her Great Chain of Being:
THE MOTHER-SHOWMAN: Im yr new boss.
    Mother-Showman and her 8 Amazing Human
        Wonders!
    Yr Number 9.
THE GIRL: Wheres my Man?
    He had a beard.
THE MOTHER-SHOWMAN: Him? Girl, he skipped town.
    Yr lucky I was passing through
    good God girl he wasnt lying, you woulda
        starved to death or worse, been throwd in jail
        for heh
    indecency. But its alright now, dear. Mother-
        Showmanll guard yr Interests.
    Yr Secrets are safe with me.
    Scrub.
    SCRUB!
        (THE GIRL, *apart from the others, scrubs herself. The*
        MOTHER-SHOWMAN *introduces her* WONDERS.)
THE MOTHER-SHOWMAN: Sound the drum.
        (WONDER #3 *sounds the drum.*)
THE MOTHER-SHOWMAN: Step right up come on
    come in.
    Step inside come on come see
    the most lowly and unfortunate beings in Gods
        Universe:
    Mother-Showmans 9 Human Wonders will dazzle
    surprise intrigue horrify and disgust.
    The 9 lowest links in Gods Great Chain of Being.
THE CHORUS OF THE 8 HUMAN WONDERS: *Chain Chain*
    Chain.
THE MOTHER-SHOWMAN: Look sad like yr misfit-
    ness hangs heavy on yr mind.
        (*Rest*)
    Come on in in see with yr own eyes what never
        ever
    should have been allowed to live.
    The 9 lowest links in Gods Great Bein Chain.
THE CHORUS OF THE 8 HUMAN WONDERS: *Chain Chain*
    Chain.
THE MOTHER-SHOWMAN: See one for the price of a
    penny and a half

or all these 8 for a song!
Step inside come on come see
the ugliest creatures in creativity. Alive!
Alive! And waiting for you just inside.
Come on in in take a look
see a living misfit with yr own eyes.
Take a look at one for just a penny and a
    half
you can gawk as long as you like.
Waiting for yr gaze here inside
theyre all freaks and all alive.
[THE CHORUS OF THE 8 HUMAN WONDERS: When I
    was birthed intuh this world
    our Father cursed our Mother spat.
    SPAT!
THE MOTHER-SHOWMAN: Sing!
THE CHORUS OF THE 8 HUMAN WONDERS: This face
    of mine thats scary
    these blemishes this crooked back
    this extra arm uhtop my head
    this extra ear this extra leg
    this fin that swims out of my rear
    these blisters circling my eyes
    passed down tuh me from who knows
        where
    my existence is a curse
    you can gawk for a small purse!
        (*Rest*)
    We wonder thuh world.
THE MOTHER-SHOWMAN: Step up step in to see
    what God hisself dont wanna look at.
    Every day all day theyre on display!
    All Alive!
        (*Rest*)
    Uh hehm.
    8th being from the bottom, what I call my Won-
        der 1: The Bearded Gal.
    Uh woman furrier than most.
    By her Mom and Pop she was rejected.
    Shes thuh first freak I collected.
WONDER #1: Pull on my beard!
    Its real! Its real!
THE CHORUS OF THE 8 HUMAN WONDERS: We wonder
    thuh world.
THE MOTHER-SHOWMAN: After 1 comes Wonder 2
    one step closer to the monkeys.
    Uh Fireman who dines on flame.
    He claims thuh Devil his creator
    but really hails from thuh Equator.

WONDER #2: I am her most Flame-boyant child!
    Im goin tuh Hell! Hell in uh handbasket!
THE MOTHER-SHOWMAN: Next rung closer to thuh
    lowest: Wonder 3: Thuh Spotted Boy.
    Hes covered black and white all patchy
    thuh Lord could not make up his mind.
    Dont get too close tuh him its catchy.
WONDER #3: The Good Lord is indecisive!
    Im thuh proof!
THE CHORUS OF THE 8 HUMAN WONDERS: We wander
    thuh world.
THE MOTHER-SHOWMAN: Thuh Fat Mans next: 12
    hundred pounds, uh warnin to us all.
WONDER #4: *Feed* me.
THE MOTHER-SHOWMAN: And if his girth does not
    impress
    Ive 2 ladies here joined at thuh hip.
    Bornd that way theyll die that way
    mano a mano lip tuh lip.
WONDERS #5 AND #6: *Mano a mano lip tuh lip.*
THE CHORUS OF THE 8 HUMAN WONDERS: We wander
    thuh world.
THE MOTHER-SHOWMAN: Chain.
THE CHORUS OF THE 8 HUMAN WONDERS: Chain.
    We wander thuh world: Here is thuh Reason:
    Our funny looks read as High Treason.
THE MOTHER-SHOWMAN: *Jawohl Jawohl!*
    Step up my Wandering Wunderfuls
    and show how Nature takes her toll.
    Almost thuh lowest to thuh bottom is a freak
    called "Mr. Privates."
    Hes from thuh South
    what we carry *down here* he wears up here
    in thuh place of his eyes and his nose and his
    mouth.
WONDER #7: Horror! Horror!
    Horror! Horror!
THE CHORUS OF THE 8 HUMAN WONDERS: *Chain!
    Chain!*
THE MOTHER-SHOWMAN: On the bottom yesterday
    was the Whatsit, people, #8.
    So backward that her cyclops eye
    will see into yr future.
WONDER #8: Black its black!
    Myeye sees black!
THE CHORUS OF THE 8 HUMAN WONDERS: Howuh-
    bouthat?!

Howuhbouthat?!
WONDER #8: Black its black!
    Myeye sees black!
THE CHORUS OF THE 8 HUMAN WONDERS: Howuh-
    bouthat?!
    Howuhbouthat?!
THE MOTHER-SHOWMAN:] Foam rage tear at yr
    clothes, kids!
    Show yr stuff! Dont be shy!
    Pull out all thuh stops! Big Finish!
    Thats it! Thats it! Make yr Mama proud!
        (THE WONDERS *pull out all the stops, then they pose
        in a freakish tableau.* THE GIRL *has finished her bath.*
        THE NEGRO RESURRECTIONIST *watches her.*)
THE VENUS: What you lookin at?
THE NEGRO RESURRECTIONIST: You.
    (*Rest*)
    Yr lovely.
THE VENUS
THE NEGRO RESURRECTIONIST
THE VENUS
THE NEGRO RESURRECTIONIST
THE MOTHER-SHOWMAN: With yr appreciative
    permission
    for a seperate admission
    we've got a new girl: #9
    "The Venus Hottentot."
    She bottoms out at the bottom of the ladder
    yr not a man—until youve hadder.
    But truly, folks, before she showd up our little
    show was in the red
    but her big bottoms friendsll surely put us safely
    in the black!
        (THE GIRL *stands in the semidarkness. Lights blaze
        on her. She is now* THE VENUS HOTTENTOT. THE WON-
        DERS *become* THE CHORUS OF THE SPECTATORS *and
        gather round.*)
THE MOTHER-SHOWMAN: THE VENUS HOTTENTOT
    THE ONLY LIVNG CREATURE OF HER KIND
        IN THE WORLD
    STEPSISTER-MONKEY TO THE GREAT
        VENAL
    LOVE
    GODDESS
    AND ONLY ONE STEP UHWAY FROM YOU
        RIGHT NOW
    COME SEE THE HOT MISS HOTTENTOT

STEP IN STEP IN
HUR-RY! HUR-RY!
HUR-RY! HUR-RY!

THE VENUS

THE CHORUS OF THE SPECTATOR

THE VENUS

THE CHORUS OF THE SPECTATOR

THE VENUS

THE CHORUS OF THE SPECTATOR

THE VENUS

THE CHORUS OF THE SPECTATORS
(*Rest*)

THE VENUS: Oh, God:
Unloved.
(*Rest*)

THE NEGRO RESURRECTIONIST: Footnote #3:
Historical Extract. Category: Literary. From Robert Chambers's *Book of Days:*
(*Rest*)
"Early in the present century a poor wretched woman was exhibited in England under the appellation of *The Hottentot Venus.* The year was 1810. With an intensely ugly figure, distorted beyond all European notions of beauty, she was said by those to whom she belonged to possess precisely the kind of shape which is most admired among her countrymen, the Hottentots."
(*Rest*)
The year was 1810, three years after the Bill for the Abolition of the Slave-Trade had been passed in Parliament, and among protests and denials, horror and fascination, The Venus show went on.
(*Rest*)

THE VENUS

THE CHORUS OF THE SPECTATORS

THE VENUS

THE CHORUS OF THE SPECTATORS

THE VENUS

SPECTATOR #1: Eeeeeeeeeeeeeeeeeeeeeeeeeeeeeee
eeeeeeeeeeeeee!

THE MOTHER-SHOWMAN: Get used to it, Girl.
(*Rest*)

THE NEGRO RESURRECTIONIST: Scene 26:
From "For the Love of the Venus." Act II, Scene 9:

SCENE 26

"FOR THE LOVE OF THE VENUS."
ACT II, SCENE 9

As before, THE BARON DOCTEUR *is its only audience, and* THE VENUS *watches him.*

THE BRIDE-TO-BE: Eeeeeeeeeeeeeeeeeeeeee
he doesnt care
uh whit uhbout meeee.

THE MOTHER: Dont be a gumball, child.

THE BRIDE-TO-BE: He turns down tea.
He turns down coffee.
He will not take a turn in the park with me.
He will not hold my hand.

THE MOTHER: Have you tried whist? He loves his whist.

THE BRIDE-TO-BE: He used to leave me
poetry
in thuh knot of thuh tree in thuh front of my house.

THE MOTHER: Have you tried canasta?

THE BRIDE-TO—BE: "My love for you, My Love, is artificial
Fabricated much like this epistle . . . "
(*Rest*)
"My Love, My Love, My Love, My Love—"
No more rhymes.
Now he writes *tracts.*
Prose essays on (*Africaaaaah!*)

THE MOTHER: There there Girl dont cry.
Have faith in Love. Wipe your nose.
There there thats nice.

THE BRIDE-TO-BE: Aaaah me: Unloved.
(*Tableau.* THE BARON DOCTEUR *applauds. Curtain.*)

THE NEGRO RESURRECTIONIST: Counting Down/ Counting the Take:

SCENE 25

COUNTING DOWN/COUNTING THE TAKE

SPECTATOR #1: Eeeeeeeeeeeeeeeeeeeeeeeeeeee!

THE MOTHER-SHOWMAN: Get used to it, Girl
we're gonna be rich.
(*Rest*)

Can you count?

THE VENUS: I can count.

THE MOTHER-SHOWMAN: That puts you a bit above
the rest.

But thats our secret.

THE NEGRO RESURRECTIONIST: Scene 25:

THE MOTHER-SHOWMAN: 10–20–30–40
50–60–70–80–90.

THE VENUS: 1.

THE MOTHER-SHOWMAN: 10–20–30–40
50–60–70–80–90:

THE VENUS: 2.

THE MOTHER-SHOWMAN: 10–20–30–40
50–60–70–80–90:

THE VENUS: 3.

THE MOTHER-SHOWMAN: 10–20–30–40
50–60–70–80–90:

THE VENUS: 4.

THE MOTHER-SHOWMAN: 10–20–30–40
50–60–70–80–90:

THE VENUS: 5.

THE MOTHER-SHOWMAN: 10–20–30–40
50–60–70–80–90:

THE VENUS: 6.
   (*Rest*)

THE MOTHER-SHOWMAN: 9 ugly mouths to feed.
Plus my own.
We didnt do too bad today.
Hottentot, yr a godsend!

THE NEGRO RESURRECTIONIST: 31
30
29
28
27
26
25
24:

SCENE 24

"BUT NO ONE EVER NOTICED/HER FACE WAS STREAMED WITH TEARS"

THE CHORUS OF THE 8 HUMAN WONDERS: Ive been in
this line of work for years
and yet everytime the crowds gather and the
lights flash up
I freak out.

My first 5 months in this racket were like hell.
I didnt sleep I didnt eat my teeth were chatter-
ing nonstop.
That girl they call The Venus H. is holding up
holding up pretty well I think. And her crowds
have been stupendous.
(Some audience is better than none at all and
since shes come
we're in another economic bracket.) Stupendous!
Stupendous! Still: Shes got that far away look in
her eye
that look of someone who dont know thuh score.
She signed on for 2 years "only 19 months to go"
shes thinking.
But should I tell her? Uh uhnn, I havent got the
heart to say:
"Oh, Venus H., there is absolutely no escape."
   (*Rest*)
   (*Rest*)
   (*An enormous banner unfurls. It reads "The Venus Hottentot" and bears her likeness.* THE VENUS
   center stage. THE WONDERS *in the background.*)

THE MOTHER-SHOWMAN: Turn to the side, Girl.
Let em see! Let em see!
   (*Rest*)
What a fat ass, huh?!
Oh yes, this girls thuh Missin Link herself.
Come on inside and allow her to reveal to you
the Great and Horrid Wonder
of her great heathen buttocks.
Thuh Missing Link, Ladies and Gentlemen:
Thuh Venus Hottentot:
Uh warnin tuh us all.
Right this way.
   (*Rest*)
Sure is slow today.
No one around for miles.
Lets see:
   (*Rest*)
Plucked her from thuh Fertile Crescent
from thuh Fertile Crescent with my own bare
hands!
Ripped her off thuh mammoth lap of uh mam-
moth ape!
She was uh (((*keeping house for him*))). Folks, The
Venus Hottentot!
   (*Rest*)
Yr standing there with yr lips pokin out

like uh wooden lady on uh wooden ship
look uhlive
smile or somethin
jesus
stroke yr feathers
smoke yr pipe.
  (*Rest*)
Been with us in civilization for a mere 5 months.
  Teached her all she knows.
Look! Shes got talents!
  (*Rest*)
Walk, Girl.
  (THE VENUS *walks about.*)

THE MOTHER-SHOWMAN: WHAT A BLACKSIDE!
  OOOH LA LA!
  STEP IN!
  STEP IN STEP IN STEP IN STEP IN!
  (*Rest*)
  (*Rest*)
  Dry as a bone today.
  (*Rest*)
  Dance or something.

THE VENUS: Dance?

THE MOTHER-SHOWMAN: Dance. Go on Girl and the
  other uglies you all too.
  I'll clap time.
  DANCE!
  (THE MOTHER-SHOWMAN *claps time.* THE VENUS *and*
  THE WONDERS *dance.*)
  (*Suddenly* THE WONDERS *disappear.*)

THE NEGRO RESURRECTIONIST: Footnote #4:
  Historical Extract. Category: Newspaper Advertisements.
  AN ADVERTISING BILL:
  From Daniel Lysons *Collectanea: A Collection of
  Advertisements and Paragraphs from the Newspapers Relating to Various Subjects* (London,
  1809).
  "Parties of 12 and upwards, may be accommodated with a Private Exhibition of The Hottentot . . . between 7 and 8 o'clock in the evening,
  by giving notice to the Door-Keeper the day
  previous.
  "The Hottentot may also be viewed by single
  parties with no advance notice from 10 in
  the morning until 10 in the evening. Mon-
  days through Saturdays. No advance notice is
  necessary.

"A Woman will attend (if required)."
  (THE MOTHER-SHOWMAN: *is still clapping time.* THE
  VENUS *is still dancing.* SPECTATOR #2 *wanders in to
  watch. He hands over a coin.*)

THE MOTHER-SHOWMAN: Good morning, Sir!
  Good morning!
  A thousand thanks a million pleasantries
  we do appreciate yr audience.
  (THE MOTHER-SHOWMAN *out of breath stops clapping.* THE VENUS *stops dancing.* SPECTATOR #2 *pays
  some more.*)

THE MOTHER-SHOWMAN: What a bucket!
  What a bum!
  What a spanker!
  Never seen the likes of that, I'll bet.
  Go on Sir, go on.
  Feel her if you like.
  (*He takes a feel. He wanders off.* THE MOTHER-SHOW-
  MAN *wets her finger and tests the wind direction.*)

THE MOTHER-SHOWMAN: Look extra pitiful, Girl.
  Yeah thats it.
  (*Rest*)
  Ladies and Gents are you feeling lowly?
  Down in the dumps?
  Perhaps yr feelin that yr life is all for naught?
  Ive felt that way myself at times.
  Come on inside and get yr spirits lifted.
  One look at thisll make you feel like a
  King!
  (*Several* SPECTATORS *wander in.*)

THE MOTHER-SHOWMAN: Ladies and Gents: The
  Venus Hottentot
  Shes been in civilization a whole year and still
  hasnt learnd nothin!
  The very lowest rung on Our Lords Great Evo-
  lutionary Ladder!
  Observe: I kick her like I kick my dog!
  (THE MOTHER-SHOWMAN *kicks* THE VENUS *repeat-
  edly. The act has the feel of professional wrestling
  but also looks real.*)

THE MOTHER-SHOWMAN:	THE VENUS:
Aaaah!	Oh!
Aaaah!	Ah!
Aaaah!	Oh!

  (*Out of breath again,* THE MOTHER-SHOWMAN *stops
  to rest.*)

THE MOTHER-SHOWMAN: Whew. Thats hard work
  lemmie tell ya.

I need a rest. Hhh.
Paw her folks. Hands on. Go on have yr pleasure.
Her heathen shame is real.
(THE SPECTATORS *paw* THE VENUS.)

THE MOTHER-SHOWMAN: Thuh kicks is native for
    them Hottentots.
When I was down there in their hot home.
As Gods my witness Kickin Kickin
Kickin all day Kickin at eachother
thats just their way!
They do one kick for our "move uhbout."
2 kicks means uh well "pass thuh meat."
They mix it with thuh toes n heel: Uh whole lan-
    guage of kicks
very sophisticated
for them of course.
    (*Rest*)
Verify me, Venus.
(Go on, Girl, nod and back me up.)
See? I speak the truth!
Mother-Showman does not lie.
Stand up now, Girl.
Let em see you in yr alltogether.
Stand up thats it let Mother help ya.
Lets give these folks their moneys worth.
Stand still. In profile. There thats nice.
Ladies and Gents:
The Hottentots best angle.

THE CHORUS OF THE SPECTATORS

THE VENUS

THE MOTHER-SHOWMAN

THE CHORUS OF THE SPECTATORS

THE VENUS

THE MOTHER-SHOWMAN

THE CHORUS OF THE SPECTATORS

THE VENUS

THE MOTHER-SHOWMAN
    (*Rest*)
    (THE CHORUS OF THE SPECTATORS *errupts in wild*
    laughter.)

THE CHORUS OF THE SPECTATORS: HAHAHAHAHA
    HAHAHAHAHAHAHHAHAHAHA
    HAHAHHAHAHAHAHHAHAHAHAH
    HAHAHAHAHAHAHAHAHAHAHA
    HAHAHAHAHAHAHAHHAHAHHAHA.

THE VENUS

THE VENUS

THE VENUS

THE VENUS: Hahahahahahahaha!

THE NEGRO RESURRECTIONIST: Footnote #5:
    Historical Extract. Category: Literary. From *The*
      Life of One
    Called the Venus Hottentot As Told By Herself:
      (*Rest*)
    "The things they noticed were quite various
      but no one ever noticed that her face was
      streamed with tears."
      (*Rest*)
    Scene 23:
    From "For the Love of the Venus." Act II, Scene
    10:

SCENE 23

"FOR THE LOVE OF THE VENUS."
ACT II, SCENE 10
Again, THE BARON DOCTEUR *is the only audience.* THE
VENUS *watches him.*

THE FATHER: Youre in uh pickle Young Man
    an absolute pickle

THE UNCLE: Nabsolute pickle no question Boy.

THE FATHER: Marry yr girl, Boy and then
    Unclell take ya to Timbuktu
    if Timbuktus yr yen.

THE YOUNG MAN: Timbuktu?
    (*Rest*)
    A Man to be a Man must know Unknowns!
    So
    if The Man cant sail to the Unknown I guess
    the Unknown will sail to The Man. So!
    Im all decided:
    Before I wed, Uncle, I'd like you to procure for
      me an oddity.
    I wanna love
    something Wild.

THE FATHER

THE UNCLE

THE YOUNG MAN

THE UNCLE: Be a little more specific.

THE YOUNG MAN: In the paper yesterday:
    "In 2 weeks time
    for one week only"
    something called "The Hottentot Venus"
    Uncle. Get her for me somehow.

THE FATHER AND THE UNCLE: Heh. Heh.
Heh. Heh.
THE YOUNG MAN: Im all decided.
THE FATHER: (Make sure shes not *too* strange, Brother.
Brother, make sure shes clean.)
THE UNCLE: In 2 weeks time!
I will present to you, Young Man:
New Love!

(THE FATHER, THE UNCLE *and* THE YOUNG MAN *in*
Tableau. THE BARON DOCTEUR *applauds. Curtain.*)

SCENE 22

COUNTING THE TAKE/
THE DEAL THAT WAS
THE VENUS: 10–20–30–40
50–60–70–80–90:
THE MOTHER-SHOWMAN: 22.
THE VENUS: 10–20–30–40
50–60–70–80–90:
THE MOTHER-SHOWMAN: 23.
THE VENUS: 10–20–30–40
50–60–70–80–90:
THE MOTHER-SHOWMAN: 24.
THE VENUS: 10–20–30–40
50–60–70–80–90:
THE MOTHER-SHOWMAN: 25.
THE VENUS: You hit me hard the other day.
THE MOTHER-SHOWMAN: Mothers sorry.
THE VENUS: We should spruce up our act.
I could speak for them.
Say a little poem or something.
THE MOTHER-SHOWMAN: Count!
THE VENUS: You could pretend to teach me and I
would learn
before their very eyes.
THE MOTHER-SHOWMAN: Yr a Negro native with a
most remarkable spanker.
Thats what they pay for.
Their eyes are hot for yr tot-tot.
Theres the poetry.
THE VENUS: We should expand.
THE MOTHER-SHOWMAN: Count!!
THE VENUS: (Rest)
10–20–30–40
50–60–70–80–90:
THE MOTHER-SHOWMAN: 26.

THE VENUS: 10–20–30–40
50–60–70–80–90:
THE MOTHER-SHOWMAN: 27.
THE VENUS: 10–20–30–40
50–60–70–80–90:
THE MOTHER-SHOWMAN: 28.
THE VENUS: 10–20–30–40
50–60–70–80–90:
THE MOTHER-SHOWMAN: 29.
THE VENUS: 10–20–30–40
50–60–70–80–90:
THE MOTHER-SHOWMAN: 30.
THE VENUS: 10–20–30–40
50–60–70–80–90:
THE MOTHER-SHOWMAN: 31. And change.
Hhhhh.
We didnt do too bad today.
(Rest)
(Rest)
Lets see now:

(THE MOTHER-SHOWMAN *consults her map.*)

THE MOTHER-SHOWMAN: Town X to Town Y Town
Y to Town Z.
Town Z to Town A Town A to Town B.
Town B to Town C then back to Town X then off
to Town hmmmmm.
THE VENUS
THE MOTHER-SHOWMAN
THE VENUS
THE MOTHER-SHOWMAN: Dont steal from me, Girl.
Yll go to hell for it.
THE VENUS: Hell?
THE MOTHER-SHOWMAN: Christian talk. Fire and
brimstone and Satan himself.
Very hot.
THE VENUS: Oh.
THE MOTHER-SHOWMAN: Put thuh money back.
THE VENUS: You pay us each 5 coins a week.
We're all paid equal
but we dont draw equal.
THE MOTHER-SHOWMAN: Its past yr bedtime, Daughter.
THE VENUS: Im thuh one they come to see.
Im thuh main attraction.
Yr other freaks r 2nd fiddles.
THE MOTHER-SHOWMAN: Oh boy: Uh Diva.
THE VENUS: I should get 50 uh week.
Plus better food, uh lock on my door and uh
new dress now n then.

THE MOTHER-SHOWMAN: You should get some sleep,
  Girl.
  I wake you up early and you never like it.
THE VENUS: 50 uh week good food locked door new
  clothes say its a deal.
THE MOTHER-SHOWMAN: Go to hell.
THE VENUS: 40 then, the clothes and my own room.
  Forget the food.
THE MOTHER-SHOWMAN: Nothin doin, Lovely.
THE VENUS: 30.
THE MOTHER-SHOWMAN: Nope.
THE VENUS: Im leaving then.
THE MOTHER-SHOWMAN: Where to?
THE VENUS: Home.
THE MOTHER-SHOWMAN: But yr not yet rich and
  famous.
THE VENUS: Im not?
THE MOTHER-SHOWMAN: Yr a little known in cer-
  tain circles but you havent made yr fortune.
  Go back home and folks will laugh.
  Hahahaha.
  Stay.
THE VENUS: No.
  I'll set up shop and show myself.
  Be my own Boss make my own mint.
THE MOTHER-SHOWMAN: Youd walk out on yr
  mother?
THE VENUS: My time with you is spent.
  2 yrs work
  half the take for take-home pay, Im due at least
    a thousand coins!
  That was the deal.
THE MOTHER-SHOWMAN: That deal you didnt make
  with me, Love.
  You made yr bargin with a man Ive never met!
  For all I know youve made him up.
  Yeah, yr lyin and tryin to swindle yr poor Mother
  out of her retirement.
THE VENUS: 2 yrs, work
  half the take
  him and me were agreed.
  Hand it over.
THE MOTHER-SHOWMAN: Nothin doin.
THE VENUS: Im out of here.
  I'll make my own mark.
  Im all decided.
THE MOTHER-SHOWMAN: "Im all decided" oooh la la.
  Could it be Ive been showing you all wrong?

Christ I thought yr name was "Venus" but, Lord
    of mercy,
  yr the Queen of Fucking Sheeba.
THE VENUS: Hand it over.
THE MOTHER-SHOWMAN: Nope.
  Go to bed.
THE VENUS: I want whats mine!
THE MOTHER-SHOWMAN: They dont let your kind
  run loose in the streets
  much less set up their own shops.
THE VENUS: Gimmie!
THE MOTHER-SHOWMAN: You could be arrested.
  You need Mothers protection.
THE VENUS: GIMMMMMIE!
THE MOTHER-SHOWMAN: Dont push me, Sweetie.
  Next doors a smoky pub
  full of drunken men.
  I just may invite them in
  one at a time
  and let them fuck yr brains out.
THE VENUS: They do it anyway.
  (Rest)
  (Rest)
THE MOTHER-SHOWMAN: Well.
  Its the same
  for all of us, Love.
  (Rest)
  I love you like a daughter.
  We're yr family now.
  If you go off we'd miss you
  and besides we may go under.
THE VENUS: They come in drunken when yr
  sleeping.
  (Rest)
  I wanna go.
  Please.
THE MOTHER-SHOWMAN: Home?
THE VENUS: No.
  Not home.
THE MOTHER-SHOWMAN: Where to, then?
THE VENUS: Innywhere.
THE MOTHER-SHOWMAN: Sad to say, Girl, but you
  cant
  and its the same for all of us.
  The Law wants to shut us down
  we create too many "disturbances" so
  we gotta move about go hopping you know
  town to town.

A Whirlwind Tour! 100 cities in as many nights!
   Ive planned it out.
It looks like fun.
Yll see the world!

THE VENUS: No—

THE MOTHER-SHOWMAN: Relax.
   Relax.
   Its going to be fantastic.

SCENE 21

THE WHIRLWIND TOUR

During this scene THE BARON DOCTEUR *watches* THE VE-
NUS *and the others from his chair. He grows more and
more interested and watches more and more intently.*
THE VENUS, THE MOTHER-SHOWMAN *and* THE CHORUS
OF THE 8 HUMAN WONDERS *stand in a knot. They are
traveling.*

THE NEGRO RESURRECTIONIST: Town A! Town B!
   Town C! Town E!
   Town 25! Town 36! Town 42! Town 69!

[THE CHORUS OF THE 8 HUMAN WONDERS: Legend
   has it that The Girl was sent away from
   home.
   Those who sent her said she couldnt return for
   a thousand yrs.
   Even though she was strong of heart even she
   doubted she would live that long.
   After 500 years they allowed her to ask a question.
   She wanted to know what her crime had been.
   Simple: You wanted to go away once.
   9 hundred 99 of the years were finally up
   just one more year to go.
   She had in all that time circled the globe twice
   on foot
   saw 12 hundred thousand cities
   and had a lover or 2 in every port.
   She spent her last year of banishment living in a
   cave carved out
   outside the city wall.
   She spent that whole year longing not looking
   but longing not looking.
   They let her go home right on time
   all of her friends had died and well
   she didnt recognize the place.]

(THE CHORUS OF THE 8 HUMAN WONDERS *disappears.*
THE VENUS *and* THE MOTHER-SHOWMAN *remain.*)

THE NEGRO RESURRECTIONIST:

Town R! Town U!	THE VENUS
Town E! Town Q!	THE MOTHER-SHOWMAN
Town 58! Town 64!	THE VENUS
Town 85! Town 99!	THE MOTHER-SHOWMAN
(*Rest*)	THE VENUS
(*Rest*)	THE MOTHER-SHOWMAN
Town A! Town B!	THE VENUS
Town C! Town E!	THE MOTHER-SHOWMAN
Town 25! Town 36!	THE VENUS
Town 42! Town 69!	THE MOTHER-SHOWMAN
(*Rest*)	THE VENUS
Town R! Town U!	THE MOTHER-SHOWMAN
Town E! Town Q!	THE VENUS
Town 58! Town 64!	THE MOTHER-SHOWMAN
Town 85! Town 99!	THE VENUS

THE VENUS: How many towns till we get home?!
   (*A knot of* SPECTATORS *appears.*)

THE MOTHER-SHOWMAN: Presenting:
   Presenting:
   Presenting:
   THE VENUS HOTTENTOT!
   Love gone all wrong, if you will.
   Uh warning to us all.
   Gentlemen, Ladies, get yrselves a good long look.
   Kiddies push yr ways up front.

THE CHORUS OF THE SPECTATORS

THE VENUS

THE CHORUS OF THE SPECTATORS: (*Rest*)
   Oooooooooooooooooooooooooooh!
   (*Rest*)
   (*Rest*)
   Aaaaaaaaaaaaaaaaaaaaaaaaaaaaaaaaah!
   (*Rest*)
   (*Rest*)

THE NEGRO RESURRECTIONIST: Town 10! Town 3!
   Town R! Town Z!
   Town X!

THE MOTHER-SHOWMAN: Uh gift of chocklut is
   customary.
   Place yr treats at her feets and watch her feed.

THE NEGRO RESURRECTIONIST:

Town R! Town U!	THE VENUS
Town E! Town Q!	THE MOTHER-SHOWMAN
Town 58! Town 64!	THE VENUS
Town 85! Town 99!	THE MOTHER-SHOWMAN

(*Rest*)   THE VENUS
(*Rest*)   THE MOTHER-SHOWMAN
Town A! Town B!   THE VENUS
Town C! Town E!   THE MOTHER-SHOWMAN
Town 25! Town 36!   THE VENUS
Town 42! Town 69!   THE MOTHER-SHOWMAN
(*Rest*)   THE VENUS
Town R! Town U!   THE MOTHER-SHOWMAN
Town E! Town Q!   THE VENUS
Town 58! Town 64!   THE MOTHER-SHOWMAN
Town 85! Town 99!   THE VENUS

THE VENUS: How many towns till we get home?

[THE CHORUS OF THE SPECTATORS: Legend has it that The Girl was sent away from home.

Those who sent her said she couldnt return for a thousand yrs.

Even though she was strong of heart even she doubted she would live that long.

After 500 years they allowed her to ask a question.

She wanted to know what her crime had been.

Simple: You wanted to go away once.

9 hundred 98 of the years were finally up

just 2 short years to go.

She had in all that time circled the globe twice on foot

saw 12 hundred thousand cities

and had a lover or 2 in every port.

She spent her last 2 years of banishment living in a cave carved out

outside the city wall.

She spent those 2 years longing not looking but longing not looking.

They let her go home right on time

all of her friends had died and well

she didnt recognize the place.]

THE NEGRO RESURRECTIONIST: Town R! Town U! Town E! Town Q!

Town 58! Town 64! Town 85! Town 99!

(*Rest*)

Town M! Town 0! Town P! Town S!

Town 3! Town 5! Town 4! Town 9!

(THE BARON DOCTEUR *is out of his chair and watching* THE VENUS. *He is transfixed.*)

THE VENUS

THE CHORUS OF THE SPECTATORS

(THE CHORUS OF THE SPECTATORS *bursts into riot. They beat* THE VENUS's *cage with sticks. They also beat* THE MOTHER-SHOWMAN.)

THE BARON DOCTEUR: Order! Order! Order! Order!

SCENE 20A

THE VENUS HOTTENTOT BEFORE THE LAW (FOOTNOTE #6: HISTORICAL EXTRACT: MUSICAL. FROM R. TOOLE-SCOTT'S "THE CIRCUS AND THE ALLIED ARTS")

THE NEGRO RESURRECTIONIST: (*Rest*)

A Song of The Hottentot ladie and her day in court and what the judges did therein.

(*As* THE NEGRO RESURRECTIONIST *sings,* THE CHORUS OF THE SPECTATORS *leads* THE VENUS *to a jail cell and then transforms themselves into* THE CHORUS OF THE COURT.)

THE NEGRO RESURRECTIONIST: Have you heard about the rump she has (though strange it be).

Large as a cauldron pot?

This is why men go to see

The Venus Hottentot.

She showd her butts for many a day,

and eke for many a night;

till fights broke out in our dear streets

now, this was not alright.

Some said this was with her goodwill

some said that this was not.

All asked why they did use so ill

this lady Hottentot.

At last the sober folks stood forth

And into Court they took her.

To thus determine if she liked

for everyone to look her.

So they questioned the girl in court

along with many more

to learn if she did money get

and what xactly was the score?

Who having finished their intent

they visited the spot

and said twas done with full consent

of the fair Hottentot.

When speaking free from all alarm
the whole she does deride
and says she thinks there is no great harm
in showing her backside.

And now good people let us go
to see this wondrous sight.
We'll have uh gawk, toss her uh sweet
such recreation cant be beat.
Lets not be critical of what Loves got
cause lookin at her past-tense end
delights so much The Hottentot.
    (THE CHORUS is now THE CHORUS OF THE COURT.)

SCENE 20B

**THE VENUS HOTTENTOT BEFORE THE LAW
(CONTINUED) (HISTORICAL EXTRACT)**

THE CHORUS OF THE COURT: We representatives of
    the Law
have hauled into Court the case
of a most unfortunate female, who has been
    known to exhibit herself
to the view of the Public
in a manner offensive to decency and disgrace-
    ful to our country.
This Court wonders if she is at inny time
under the control of others, or some dark force,
    some say, black magic
making her exhibition against her will.
We ask 2 questions: Is she or was she ever inde-
    cent? And at inny time held against her will?
We do not wish to send her adrift in the world
    without asylum of a friend
a friend ready to receive and protect her.
But to the honor and credit of this country,
she will not find herslf without friends and pro-
    tection
even if she may be employed to expose herself
in a most disgraceful manner, however,
the Court intends to interfere and
receive her immediately under its protection;
for the purpose of restoring her to her own
    friends and her own country
so that she not become a burden to the state and
    contribute to our growing social ills.

(*Rest*)
Lets get this show on the road.
We begin with a writ of *Habeas Corpus.*

SCENE 20C

**THE VENUS HOTTENTOT BEFORE THE LAW
(CONTINUED) (DICTIONARY EXTRACT:
FROM WEBSTER'S NINTH NEW COLLE-
GIATE DICTIONARY, PAGE 545)**
Apart from the "courtroom" THE VENUS *sits in a jail cell.*

THE VENUS: (*Rest*)
    Habeas Corpus. Literally: "You should have the
    body" for submitting. Any of several com-
    mon-law writs issued to bring the body before
    the court or the judge.

SCENE 20D

**THE VENUS HOTTENTOT BEFORE THE LAW
(CONTINUED) (FIRST WITNESS)**
THE CHORUS OF THE COURT: First Witness!
THE CHORUS LEADER: We call for the testimony of
    her present Keeper
one called "The Mother-Showman."
    Mother-Showman, take the stand!
THE MOTHER-SHOWMAN: The one called The Mother-
    Showman is
unavailable for comment.
THE CHORUS OF THE COURT: Where is she? Find her!
THE MOTHER-SHOWMAN: Shes got 9 ugly mouths to
    feed.
    She works day in day out, folks.
    As to any questions
    concerning the Goddess Venus H.
    if Mothers been unkind she swears to mend her
        evil ways!
THE CHORUS OF THE COURT: Haul her in here!
THE MOTHER-SHOWMAN: Mama submits
    a certificate of baptism of the so-called Venus
        Hottentot
    as proof that I take good care of her.
THE CHORUS LEADER: Hmmmmmm. Interesting.
    Submit the certificate of baptism as Exhibit A.

SCENE 20E

THE VENUS HOTTENTOT BEFORE THE LAW (CONTINUED) (HISTORICAL EXTRACT: EXHIBIT A)

THE NEGRO RESURRECTIONIST: Exhibit A: The Certificate of Baptism

THE VENUS: (*Rest*)

Baptised 1 December 1811. The ceremony took place in Manchester, the clergyman being Reverend Joshua Brookes. The certificate of baptism is preserved in Paris. It states: "December 1. Sarah Baartman a Female Hottentot from the Colony of the Cape of Good Hope, born on the Borders of Caffraria, baptized this day by Permission of the Lord Bishop."

SCENE 20F

THE VENUS HOTTENTOT BEFORE THE LAW (CONTINUED) (WITNESS 1 AND WITNESS 2)

THE CHORUS OF THE COURT: Lets get uh witness on the stand!

(THE CHORUS *ejects one of its members:* WITNESS #1.)

THE NEGRO RESURRECTIONIST: 1st Witness:

Historical Extract: From a Mr. Hall, Member of Society:

WITNESS #1: I saw her, oh several times.

Call me and my Mrs. her regulars. She was always standing on a stage, 2 feet high, clothed in a light dress,

a dress thuh color of her own skin.

She looked, well, naked, kin I say that?

The whole place smelled of shit.

She didnt speak at all.

My Mrs. always fainted.

(THE CHORUS *ejects another member:* WITNESS #2. WITNESS #1 *rejoins* THE CHORUS.

THE CHORUS OF THE COURT: Whos next?! Whos next!?

THE NEGRO RESURRECTIONIST: 2nd Witness:

Historical Extract: Mr. Charles Mathewes visited The Venus

and related this scene to his now widow:

WITNESS #2: Im a widow.

THE CHORUS OF THE COURT: Widow, tell us whatcha seen.

WITNESS #2: I saw nothin.

Hearsay only.

2nd hand.

THE CHORUS OF THE COURT: Thatll do.

Spit it out.

WITNESS #2: Good people, Im uh Widow.

My dear man was fond of sights and before he died

he viewd The Venus H.

He related it to me this way:

"She was surrounded by many persons, some *females!*

One pinched her, another walked round her;

one gentleman *poked* her with his cane;

uh *lady* used her parasol to see if all was, as she called it, 'natural.'

Through all of this the creature didnt speak.

Maybe uh sigh or 2 maybe when she seemed inclined to protest the pawing."

She once handed my man a feather from her head.

Theyre said to bring good luck.

"A fight ensued. 3 men died. Uh little boy went mad. Uh woman lost her child."

My man escaped with thuh feather intact.

"Poor Creature."

"Very extraordinary indeed!"

"This is a sight which makes me melancholy!"

My husbands words exactly.

He was home standing by the window. I can see him now.

And then he walked away from me, deep in thought,

and then, totally forgetting his compassion, shouted loud:

"Good God what butts!"

(*Rest*)

Thuh shock of her killed him, I think,

cause 2 days later he was dead.

Ive thrown thuh feather away.

SCENE 20G

THE VENUS HOTTENTOT BEFORE THE LAW (CONTINUED) (EXHIBIT B)

THE VENUS: Exhibit B:

A feather from the head of the so-called Venus H.

The feathers were said to bring good luck—

when stroked such feathers cured infertility.
When ground and ingested these same feathers
   proved
a brilliant aphrodisiac.

SCENE 20H

**THE VENUS HOTTENTOT BEFORE THE LAW
(CONTINUED) (WITNESS 3 AND WITNESS 4)**
THE CHORUS LEADER: Let the Widow step down.
   Who's next? Who's next?
THE CHORUS OF THE COURT: We call to the stand
   the man who watches her from afar:
   The Baron Docteur.
THE BARON DOCTEUR: The Baron Docteur is
   unavailable for comment.
THE CHORUS OF THE COURT: Outrage! ItsanOutrage!
THE BARON DOCTEUR: Im speaking on The Venus
   subject at a conference.
   Yll have to wait till then.
THE CHORUS OF THE COURT: Outrage! ItsanOutrage!
   Lets get someone anyone on the stand!
   (*They eject another member:* WITNESS #3.)
THE CHORUS LEADER: We call to the stand
   a noted Abolitionist.
WITNESS #3: I am a noted abolitionist.
THE NEGRO RESURRECTIONIST: Historical Extract.
   Category: Journalistic.
   A letter of protest appearing in *The Morning
   Chronicle, Friday, 12 October 1810:*
WITNESS #3: "Sir,
   As a friend to liberty, in every situation of life,
   I cannot help calling your attention to a sub-
   ject, which I am sure need only be noticed by
   you to insure your immediate obesevation
   and comment. I allude to that wretched object
   advertised and publicly shown for money—
   'The Hottentot Venus.' This, Sir, is a wretched
   creature—an inhabitant of the interior of Africa, who has been brought here as a subject
   for the curiosity of this country, for 2 cents
   a-head. Her keeper is the only gainer. I am
   no advocate of these sights, on the contrary,
   I think it base in the extreme, that *any* human
   beings should be thus exposed! It is contrary
   to every principle of morality and good order
   as this exhibition connects the same offense

to public decency with that most horrid of all
   situations, *Slavery."*
WITNESS #4: Equal time! Equal time!
   I represent a man who knows!
THE NEGRO RESURRECTIONIST: A reply appearing in
   The Morning Chronicle, 23 October 1810.
WITNESS #4: "Since the English last took possession
   of the colonies, we have been consistently so-
   licited to bring to this country, subjects well
   worthy of the attention of the Virtuoso, and the
   curious in general. The girl in question fits this
   description and interest in her has been fully
   proved by the approbation of some of the First
   Rank and Chief Literati of the kingdom, who
   saw her previous to her being publicly exhibited. And pray, has she not as good a right to
   exhibit herself as the Famous Irish Giant or the
   renowned Dogfaced Dancing Dwarf?!?!"
THE CHORUS OF THE COURT: Thank you, Sirs.
   You may step down.
   The Court grants the writ of *Habeas Corpus.*
   Bring up the body of this female.

SCENE 20I

**THE VENUS HOTTENTOT BEFORE THE LAW
(CONTINUED) (HISTORICAL EXTRACT)**
THE VENUS *comes out of her cage.*

THE CHORUS OF THE COURT: We call The Venus Hot-
   tentot.
THE VENUS: Im called The Venus Hottentot.
THE CHORUS OF THE COURT: She speaks!!
   (*Rest*)
   Simple questions first.
   Who are you?
   Where are you from?
   Any family?
   Are you happy?
   Are you a witch?
   Were you ever beaten?
   Did you like it was it good?
   Do you wanna go home?
   If so, when?! If so, when?!
   Answer, come on, spit it out!
THE VENUS
THE VENUS
THE VENUS

THE VENUS: The Venus Hottentot
is unavailable for comment.
THE CHORUS OF THE COURT: Dont push us, Girl!
We could lock you up for life!
Answer this:
Are you here of yr own free will
or are you under some restraint?
THE VENUS: Im here to make a mint.
THE CHORUS OF THE COURT: Hubba-Hubba-Hubba-
Hubba.
(Order-order-order-order.)
THE VENUS: After all Ive gone through so far
to go home penniless would be disgraceful.
THE CHORUS OF THE COURT: Is poverty more dis-
graceful than nakedness?
We think not!
THE CHORUS LEADER: Shut her down!
Send her home!
THE VENUS: Good people. Let me stay.
THE CHORUS LEADER: No way!
Her kind bear Gods bad mark and, baptised or not,
they blacken-up the honor of our fair country.
Get her out of here!
THE CHORUS OF THE COURT: Shut her down!
Send her home!
THE VENUS: No!
Please. Good good honest people.
If I bear thuh bad mark what better way to
cleanse it off?
Showing my sinful person as a caution to you
all could,
in the Lords eyes, be a sort of repentance
and I could wash off my dark mark.
I came here black.
Give me the chance to leave here white.
THE CHORUS OF THE COURT: Hmmmmmmmmmm.
Her words strike a deep chord.
(Rest)
One more question, Girl, uh:
Have you ever been indecent?
THE CHORUS OF THE COURT
THE VENUS
THE CHORUS OF THE COURT
THE VENUS: (Rest)
"Indecent?"
THE CHORUS OF THE COURT: Nasty.
THE VENUS: Never.
No. I am just me.

THE CHORUS OF THE COURT: Whats that supposed
to mean?!?!
THE VENUS: To hide yr shame is evil.
I show mine. Would you like to see?
THE CHORUS OF THE COURT: Outrage! Ssanoutrage!
Outrage! Ssanoutrage!
(Order order order order.)
(Order order order order.)
God! Weve got
a lot to think about.
Recess! Recess!
Lets take uh break.
(They huddle in a knot.)
THE NEGRO RESURRECTIONIST: The year was 1810,
three years after the Bill for the Abolition of
the Slave-Trade had been passed in Parlia-
ment. Among protests and denials, horror and
fascination the show went on.
(Rest)
Scene 20J:

SCENE 20J

THE VENUS HOTTENTOT BEFORE THE LAW (CONCLUSION) (HISTORICAL EXTRACT)

THE CHORUS OF THE COURT: Hear ye hear ye hear
All rise and hear our ruling:
It appears to the Court
that the person on whose behalf this suit was
brought
lives under no restraint.
Her exhibition sounds indecent
but look at her now, shes nicely dressed.
It is clear shes got grand plots and plans
to make her mark and her mint by playing outside the bounds so that we find
her person much depraved but she sez her show
is part of Gods great plan
and we buy that.
Besides she has the right to make her mark just
like the Dancing Irish Dwarf
and she seems well fed.
At this time the Court rules
not to rule.
(Rest)
In closing, whatever happens to her
we should note that

it is very much to the credit of our great country
that even a female Hottentot can find a court to
review her status.
(*Rest*)
(*Rest*)
HAHAHAHAHAHAHAHAHHAHAHA-
HAHHAHAHAHAHAHAHAHAHA-
HAHAHAHAHAHAHHAHAHHAHAHA.
THE BARON DOCTEUR: Order! Order!
Order! Order!
(THE CHORUS OF THE COURT *vanishes*.)
THE NEGRO RESURRECTIONIST: Scene 19:
A Scene of Love
(?):

SCENE 19

A SCENE OF LOVE (?)
THE VENUS
THE BARON DOCTEUR
THE VENUS
THE BARON DOCTEUR
THE VENUS
THE BARON DOCTEUR
THE VENUS
THE BARON DOCTEUR
THE VENUS

SCENE 18

SHE ALWAYS WAS MY FAVORITE CHILD
THE BARON DOCTEUR: You show The Venus Hottentot?
THE MOTHER-SHOWMAN: Thats right.
Thought up her name and everything.
Im always by her side.
THE BARON DOCTEUR: I'd like to take her off yr
hands.
THE MOTHER-SHOWMAN: You would, huh?
To what purpose?
THE BARON DOCTEUR: Thats none of yr business.
THE MOTHER-SHOWMAN: You want her for a servant,
right?
Shes got talents but not on that line.
Besides. Shes wild. Pure heathen.
May revert as they call it inny minute.
Bite you square in thuh face.

My ears thuh proof of that.
Shes no servin girl, Sir. Sorry.
THE BARON DOCTEUR: Im a doctor.
THE MOTHER-SHOWMAN: Shes my prize Doe.
THE BARON DOCTEUR: She must be a handful to
maintain.
THE MOTHER-SHOWMAN: That she is.
THE BARON DOCTEUR: Her appeal wont last much
longer.
The crowds are looking skimpy.
THE MOTHER-SHOWMAN: Thats my business.
THE BARON DOCTEUR: Come on. How much.
THE MOTHER-SHOWMAN: Long term
or short term rental?
THE BARON DOCTEUR: Permanent.
Name yr price.
THE MOTHER-SHOWMAN
THE MOTHER-SHOWMAN
THE MOTHER-SHOWMAN: I might retire afterall.
What do you want her for?
THE BARON DOCTEUR: Thats not yr concern.
How much?
THE MOTHER-SHOWMAN
THE BARON DOCTEUR
THE BARON DOCTEUR: Ive watched you with her,
woman.
You kick her like I kick my dog!
THE MOTHER-SHOWMAN
THE BARON DOCTEUR
THE MOTHER-SHOWMAN
THE BARON DOCTEUR
(*Rest*)
THE MOTHER-SHOWMAN: We seem to have an under-
standing.
THE BARON DOCTEUR: How much.
THE MOTHER-SHOWMAN: A lot.
THE BARON DOCTEUR: Ok.
THE MOTHER-SHOWMAN: A ton.
THE BARON DOCTEUR: Alright.
THE MOTHER-SHOWMAN: A mint!
A fortune!
Fort Knox!
THE BARON DOCTEUR: Here here take it take it.
THE MOTHER-SHOWMAN: My retirement!
(*Rest*)
Whatll you do with her? Im curious.
THE BARON DOCTEUR: Get her out of that filthy cage
for one.

Teach her French. Who knows.
THE MOTHER-SHOWMAN: Be good to her, Sir.
  We sure will miss her.
  She always was my favorite child.

SCENE 17

YOU LOOK LIKE YOU NEED A VACATION

THE NEGRO RESURRECTIONIST: Scene 17:
THE CHORUS OF THE 8 HUMAN WONDERS: Ive been in
    this line of work for years and years
  and every time the crowds gather
  and the lights flash on me
  I freak out.
  That girl they call The Venus, The Venus Hot-
    tentot, shes holding up, well,
  pretty well: Stupendous. Stupendous. Still:
  Shes got that far away look in her eye.
  That look of someone who dont know whats in
    store.
  She signed on for 2 years. "One more month,"
    shes thinking.
  "One more month one more month one more
    month."
  But should I tell her? No, I havent got the balls
    to say:
  Lovely Venus, with yr looks theres absolutely no
    escape.
THE VENUS: Whos there.
THE BARON DOCTEUR: A friend.
  Im yr biggest fan.
THE VENUS: No—
THE BARON DOCTEUR: I find you fascinating.
THE VENUS: No—
THE BARON DOCTEUR: Not like that, Girl.
  Im a doctor.
  "Doctor."
  Understand?
THE VENUS
THE BARON DOCTEUR
  (Rest)
THE VENUS: I understand.
THE BARON DOCTEUR: Ive brought you chockluts.
  Here.
  You like?
    (He gives her a red heart box of chocolates.)
THE VENUS: I like.
THE BARON DOCTEUR: Well.

Lets have a look.
Stand still stand still, sweetheart
I'll orbit.
Dont start Ive doctors eyes and hands.
Well.
Extraordinary.
  (Rest)
  (Rest)
Sweetheart, how would you like to go to Paris?
THE VENUS: "Paris." Well.
  "Paris."
  Whats that?
THE BARON DOCTEUR: A big town!
  Only a short boat ride away!
THE VENUS: "Paris."
THE BARON DOCTEUR: "The City of Lights!"
  I'd teach you French.
THE VENUS: "French."
THE BARON DOCTEUR: Ive paid yr Mother off.
  Yd have a clean room.
  Mix with my associates.
  Move in a better circle.
THE VENUS: "Circle"
    (Rest)
  Yr hands. Theyre clean.
  Are you rich?
THE BARON DOCTEUR: Very.
THE VENUS: I like rich.
THE BARON DOCTEUR: Its settled then.
  I find you quite phenomenal.
  Hell, you look like you need a vacation. Say "yes!"
  Say "yes" and we'll leave this minute.
THE VENUS: Do I have a choice?
THE BARON DOCTEUR: Yes. God. Of course.
THE VENUS: Will you pay me?
THE BARON DOCTEUR: I could pay you, yes.
THE VENUS: 100 a week.
THE BARON DOCTEUR: Deal.
THE VENUS: New clothes and good meals.
THE BARON DOCTEUR: Whatever you want.
THE VENUS: My own room.
THE BARON DOCTEUR: (Rest)
  Yll sleep with me.
  Say "yes."
THE VENUS
THE BARON DOCTEUR
THE BARON DOCTEUR: Think it over. I'll stand by.
THE VENUS
THE BARON DOCTEUR

(*Rest*)

(THE BARON DOCTEUR *steps out of sight to let her think it over. Enter* THE MOTHER-SHOWMAN. *She rattles a stick along the bars of the cage.*)

THE MOTHER-SHOWMAN: Not gone yet?! Shit.
  I guess he changed his mind.
  He'll be back inny minute wanting his money
  and if I dont fork it over he'll gun me down most
    likely Christ!
  What a business this is.
  9 ugly mouths to feed plus my own.
  Hup Ho, Girl! Come on!
  We got a crowd out there.
THE VENUS: (yes.)
THE MOTHER-SHOWMAN: Theyre fresh from the pubs
    and I hate to say it
  but the stench of liquor on their collective
    breaths
THE VENUS: (yes.)
  (THE BARON DOCTEUR *takes* THE VENUS *from her cage.* THE MOTHER-SHOWMAN *continues her rant.*)
THE MOTHER-SHOWMAN: is only matched by
  the stench of yr shit in this pen, Girl! Jesus!
THE VENUS: (yes.)
THE MOTHER-SHOWMAN: Jesus! *Yr an animal!*
THE VENUS: Yes.
THE BARON DOCTEUR: Come on then.
  Lets get going.
THE VENUS: Yes.
THE BARON DOCTEUR: Paris! Paris! Paris! HO!
THE VENUS: Yes.
THE NEGRO RESURRECTIONIST: Scene 16:
  The Intermission:

INTERMISSION

SCENE 16

SEVERAL YEARS FROM NOW: IN THE ANA-TOMICAL THEATRE OF TUBINGEN. THE DIS(-RE-)MEMBERMENT OF THE VENUS HOTTENTOT, PART I

Scene 16 runs during the Intermission. House lights should come up and the audience should be encouraged to walk out of the theatre, take their intermission break, and then return. THE BARON DOCTEUR *stands at a podium. He reads from his notebook.* THE BRIDE-TO-BE *sits off to the side reading from her love letters.*

THE BRIDE-TO-BE: "My love for you, My Love, is
    artificial
  Fabricated much like this epistle."
THE BARON DOCTEUR: The height, measured after
    death,
  was 4 feet 11 and ½ inches.
  The total weight of the body was 98 pounds
    avoirdupois.
  As an aside I should say
  that as to the *value* of the information that I present
  to you today there can be no doubt.
  Their significance
  will be felt far beyond our seect community. All
    that in mind
  I understand that my yield is
  long in length.
  And while my finds are complete compensation
  for the amount of labor expended upon them
  I do invite you, Distinguished Gentlemen,
  Collegues and yr Distinguished Guests,
  if you need *relief*
  please take yourselves uh breather in thuh lobby.
  My voice will surely carry beyond these walls
    and if not
  my finds are published. Forthcoming in *The
    Royal College
  Journal of Anatomy.*
  Merely as an aside, Gentlemen.
  (*Rest*)
THE NEGRO RESURRECTIONIST: Scene 16:
  Several Years from Now:
  In the Anatomical Theatre of Tubingen:
  The Dis(-re-)memberment of the Venus Hotten-
    tot, Part I:
THE BRIDE-TO-BE: "My Love for you, My Love, is
    artificial
  Fabricated much like this epistle."
THE BARON DOCTEUR: The height, measured after
    death,
  was 4 feet 11 and ½ inches.
  The total weight of the body was 98 pounds
    avoirdupois.
  In the following notes my attention is chiefly
    directed
  to the more perishable soft structures of the body.

A glossary of medical terms can be found at the back of this [play].

The skeleton will form the subject of future examination.
  (Rest)
External Characteristics:
The great amounts of subcutaneous fat were
quite surprising. On the front of the thigh for
  instance
fat measured 1 inch in thickness.
On the thighs reverse the measure of fat was
4 inches deep.
On the buttocks proper, rested the fatty cushion,
  a.k.a.
Steatopygia the details of which I'll relate in due
  course.
  (Rest)
The Skin:
Prevaling color: Orange-brown tolerably uniform in tint
on all parts of the body save on abdomen and
  thighs:
2 shades darker.
  (Rest)
The palms of the hands
and soles of the feet
were almost white.
  (Rest)
The Face:
Remarkable for its great breadth and flatness
presenting to me resemblances to Mongolian
  and Simian
(previously noted by several other scholars).
The Face's Outline:
Both peculiar and characteristic
being broad in the malar region
contracting above the forehead but tapering
  suddenly
to form a narrow chin.
The great space between the eyes was 1.8:
  Remarkable.
The eyelids horizontal apertures were a full .95.
Irises dark brown with olive brown conjunctiva.
In profile the nose was nearly straight, straight
  on it was broad
and much depressed.
One and a half across the base and but one-half
  inch
one-half inch from tip to septum.
Nostrils, Gentlemen, were patulous,

of regular oval form: .5 in length, .3 in breadth.
Septum narium short and broad.
Aperture of mouth: 1.7 inches in width
with lips
broad and overted especially the upper one.
Chin was flat and angularish.
Ear 2.3 in its vertical diameter
the lobe quite underdeveloped.
  (Rest)
The hair on the scalp was black.
Arranged in numerous separate tufts
each tuft composed of a bunch of spirally
curled hairs. Much interwoven.
The length of the tufts atop the head were from
  1 inch to 1.5
becoming shorter and smaller at the scalps edge.
Several of the individual hairs when pulled out
  straight
were found to measure a full 7 inches.
On the scalp were several spots completely
  bald:
The subject when alive wore wigs which
could have produced the bare patches.
(A warning, Gentlemen, to us all.)
Eyebrows were very scanty.
Eyelashes short: .2 inch hairs.
On the pubes and labia majora
a few small scattered tufts
of crisply curled black hairs were present.
When pulled out straight these stretched out
over 3 inches long.
  (Rest)
  (Rest)
THE BRIDE-TO-BE: "My Love for you, My Love, is
  artificial
Fabricated much like this epistle.
Constructed with mans finest powrs
Will last through the days and the years and the
  hours."
  (Rest)
THE BARON DOCTEUR: The mammae, situated exactly
  over the fourth and fifth ribs,
  were a full 6 inches apart at the inner edge of
    their bases.
They were soft
soft, flaccid and subpendulous:
4 inches in diameter at the base
and about the same from base to apex.

Nipple very prominent of blackish-brownish hue
and 1 inch in diameter. An areola
darker than the neighbor skin
extended around for 1 and a ½ inches
from the nipple's center.
   (*Rest*)
What remains of the external characters, the information,
perhaps, of greatest interest,
will be revealed toward the end of my presentation
under the head of *Generative or Reproductive
   Organs.*
   (*Rest*)
The Muscular System:
   (*Rest*)
THE BRIDE-TO-BE: "Not to a rose not to a pansy not
   to daffodil
Compares my Love, My Love, which will Stretch
   back."
   (*Rest*)
THE BARON DOCTEUR: Presenting here, in the interest of time,
only those special points of interest.
You look, Distinguished Collegue, as if you need
   relief
or sleep.
Please, Sir, indulge yourself. Go take uh break.
Ive got strong lungs:
So please, if you need air, excuse yrself.
Youll hear me in the hallway.
Uh hehm:
The *Depressor anguli oris* and the *Depressor labii
   inferioris,*
that is, the muscles of the mouth, were both unusually
well developed, the latter
forming a distinct prominence causing
that protuberant under lip
so characteristic of the Negro tribe.
Our Anthropological scholars present will remember that
although, while during her stay with us, she
   picked up
uh bit of English, French and even Dutch all *patois,*
the native language of this woman is said
to have consisted entirely
of an almost uninterrupted succession
of clicks and explosives.

   (*Rest*)
A language of *clicks,* Gentlemen.
   (*Rest*)
The attachment of these mouth muscles was as
   usual.
Ear muscles, that is, *Retrahens aurem,*
were only moderately developed. They arose
by 2 slips from the base and middle of the *mastoid process*
and had the usual insertion.
The *Attollens* and *Attrahens aurem*
were injured in removing the *calvarium.*
The *Sterno-mastoid,* the muscles of the front of
   the neck,
and the muscles of the abdomen were distinct
in their attachments.
The former arose by a long and slender tendon,
   the latter
by muscular fibers from the inner end of the
   clavicle
breadth measured 1.7 inches. The *Omo-hyoid*
   muscle presented
a peculiarity on both sides having no origin
   from the *scapula.*
Its inferior extremity spread out to form a somewhat
widened attachment to the *clavicle*—
about an inch from the outer end and behind the
   trapezius.
In the muscles of the back of the neck and trunk
there was no trace of any fibers continued from
   the
normal *Latissimus dorsi* to represent
the *Dorso-epitrochlear* of the lower mammalia.
   (*Rest*)
The *Levator anguli scapulae* arose from the posterior *tubercles*
of the 1st, 2nd and 4th cervical vertebrae
and had the usual insertion but with an
   addition:
A small slip which passed downwards
to the middle of the *Serratus magnus.*
This small slip may be an indication of the *Levator claviculae*
as noted by Dr. McWhinnie and now well known
   to all anatomists,
though the name was first recognized in human
   myology

by Dr. Wood. The *Splenius colli*
was inserted by a double tendon into the *transverse process*
of the 2 upper cervical vertebrae, the lower tendon
being somewhat larger. The *Cervicalis Ascendens* was
distinctly separate from the *Sacro-lumbalis.*
It arose by delicate tendons from the posterior angles
of the 1st, 2nd, 3rd and 4th ribs
which joined in a muscular belly sending off similar slips
to the *transverse process* of the 6th and 7th
hhhh cervical vertebrae.
The *Trachelo-mastoid* was divided into two portions . . .
thin delicate and membranous sprung by delicate
delicate tendons from the *transverse process* of
the 4th and lst dorsal . . .
The *occipital* group of muscles were
all strongly developed . . .
As for the triceps, the 2 usual *humeral origins* were fused
into a single head
which reached as high as the insertion of the *Teres minor.*
Scapular origin normal.
(*Rest*)
The tendon of the *Extensor minimi digiti* in the right hand
divided above the annular ligament
into 2 distinct tendons
which passed under the ligament in separate grooves
and, proceeding over the *Metacarpo phalangeal* articulation,
were reunited, and joining
with the tendon of the *Extensor communis digitorum,* formed
the tendinous expansion upon the *dorsum* of the 5th digit.
In the left hand the tendon was also split, but the 2 divisions
(*Rest*)
passed through the same groove.
THE BRIDE-TO-BE: "Not to a rose not to a pansy not to daffodil

Compares my Love, My Love, which will
Stretch back and forth reach all through all Time
Deep from my heart, to pri-mordial slime."
THE BARON DOCTEUR: The *Extensor primi internodii pollicis*
was normal in its development and attachments.
(*Rest*)
On removing the *fascia* from the superior border
of the *Gluteus maximus* a considerable portion of the
Gluteus medius was exposed.
The condition of the *Flexor brevis digitorum pedis* presented
rather anomalous characters
it might be said to form 2 distinct muscles.
This condition interests us
because of the well-known fact that in the chimpanzee,
and all inferior Primates, a considerable portion of this muscle
always arises from the long *flexor* tendon while in man alone
the whole of it commonly takes orgin from the *Os calcis.*
(An arrangement recently described by Dr. Wood.)
The relation of the arrangements of the muscular system of Man
to that of the inferior Primates as we know
was first clearly described by Dr. Huxley
in his Hunterian Lectures
delivered at the Royal College of Surgeons earlier this year.
Unfortunately only a brief abstract has hitherto been published.
(*Rest*)
Her shoulders back and chest had grace.
Her charming hands . . . *uh hehm.*
Where was I?
Oh, of course: On referring to the absolutely different characters
. . . there laid down
we find that in no case does our subject
pass over the boundary line.
(*Rest*)
Thank you.
(*He exits.*)

[INTERMISSION
(*CONTINUED*):

Historical Extract. Musical: The Song of Jack Higgen-bottom

WONDER #7 *sings a song.*

WONDER #7: A song on behalf of myself and The Hottentot Venus, to the Ladies of New York:
"Fair Ladies, Ive saild, in obedience to you
from New York, since the last Masquerade, to Peru.
There, to guard gainst all possible scandal tonight
I turnd Priest and have conjurd my Black-a-moor white.
A strange Metamorphosis!—who that had seen us
tother night, would take this for *The Hottentot Venus.*
Or me for poor Jack? Now Im Priest of the Sun
and she, a queer kind of Peruvian Nun.
Though in this our Novitiate, we *preach* but so, so
youll grant that at least we *appear* comme il faut.
In pure Virgin robes, full of fears and alarms
how demurely she veils her protuberant charms!
Thus oft, to atone for absurdities past
Tom Foll turns a Methodist Preacher at last.
Yet the *Critics* not *we* were to blame—for od rot em
there was nothing but innocent fun *at the bottom!*"
(WONDER #7 *exits.*)]
(*End of Intermission.*)

SCENE 15

COUNTING DOWN
THE NEGRO RESURRECTIONIST: 31
30
29
28
27
26
25
24
23
22
21
20

19
18
17
16
15
14
   (*Rest*)
Scene 14:

SCENE 14

IN THE ORBITAL PATH OF THE BARON DOCTEUR
The lovers in bed.

THE BARON DOCTEUR: *Quatorze*
Treize
Douze
Onze
Dix
Neuf
Huit
Sept
Six
Cinq
Quatre
Trois
Deux
Un
   (*Rest*)
Its dark in here. Spooky.
Lets have light.
THE VENUS: Keep it dark.
Are yr eyes closed?
THE BARON DOCTEUR: Theyre closed.
Hurry up. Im eager.
THE NEGRO RESURRECTIONIST: Scene #14:
In the Orbital Path of the Baron Docteur:
VENUS: *Voilà.* Open yr eyes.
THE BARON DOCTEUR
THE VENUS
THE BARON DOCTEUR: Too dark to see.
Lie here beside me, Sweetheart.
Mmmm. Thats good.
THE VENUS: Love me?
THE BARON DOCTEUR: I do.
Ah, this is the life.
   (*He recites a poem.*)

THE BARON DOCTEUR: "My love for you is artificial
  Fabricated much like this epistle.
  Its crafted with my finest powers
  To last through the days and the weeks and the
    hours."
    (*Rest*)
  I made it up myself.
  Just this morning.
  You like it?
THE VENUS: I love it.
THE BARON DOCTEUR AND THE VENUS: Mmmmm-
  mmm.
THE VENUS
THE BARON DOCTEUR
    (*Rest*)
THE BARON DOCTEUR: You know what I want more
  than anything?
THE VENUS: Me.
  Lets have some love.
THE BARON DOCTEUR: After you. Guess what I want.
THE VENUS: More me.
  Kiss?
THE BARON DOCTEUR: Im an everyday anatomist.
  One in a crowd of millions.
THE VENUS: Another kiss.
  Mmmm thats good.
  Sweetheart, lie back down.
THE BARON DOCTEUR: You were just yrself and
  crowds came running.
  I was fascinated and a little envious but just a
    little.
  A doctor cant just be himself
  no onell pay a cent for that.
  Imagine me just being me.
THE VENUS: Hahahahahahaha.
THE BARON DOCTEUR: What a strange laugh.
THE VENUS: Lie back down.
  Hold me close to you. Its cold.
  Love me?
THE BARON DOCTEUR: I do.
THE VENUS
THE BARON DOCTEUR
THE VENUS
    (*Rest*)
THE BARON DOCTEUR: Most great minds discover
  something.
  Ive had ideas for things but.
  My ideas r—

(You wouldnt understand em anyway.)
THE VENUS: Touch me
  down here.
THE BARON DOCTEUR: In you, Sweetheart, Ive met
  my opposite-exact.
  Now if I could only match you.
THE VENUS: That feels good.
  Now touch me here.
THE BARON DOCTEUR: Crowds of people screamd yr
  name! "Venus Hottentot!!"
  You were a sensation! I wouldnt mind a bit of
    that.
  Known. Like you!
  Only, of course, in my specific circle.
THE VENUS: You could be whatshisname: Columbus.
THE BARON DOCTEUR: Thats been done.
THE VENUS: Columbus II?
THE BARON DOCTEUR: Dont laugh at me.
    (*Rest*)
THE VENUS
THE BARON DOCTEUR
THE VENUS
    (*Rest*)
THE BARON DOCTEUR: Here. Yr favorite: Chockluts.
  Have some.
    (THE BARON DOCTEUR *turns his back to her.*)
THE VENUS: *Petits Coeurs*
  Rhum Caramel
  Pharaon
  Bouchon Fraise
  Escargot Lait
  Enfant de Bruxelles.
    (*Rest*)
  Do you think I look like
  one of these little chocolate brussels infants?
THE BARON DOCTEUR: You cant stay here forever
  you know.
THE VENUS: *Capezzoli di Venere.*
  The nipples of Venus. Mmmmm. My favorite.
THE BARON DOCTEUR: Ive got a wife. Youve got a
  homeland and a family back there.
THE VENUS: I dont wanna go back inny more.
  I like yr company too much.
  Besides, it was a shitty life.
    (*Rest*)
  Whatre you doing?

A glossary of chocolate can be found at the back of this [play].

THE BARON DOCTEUR: Nothing.

THE VENUS: Lemmie see.

THE BARON DOCTEUR: Dont look! Dont look at me.
Look off
somewhere.
Eat yr chockluts
eat em slow
thats it.
Touch yrself.
Good.
Good.
  (*He's masturbating. He has his back to her. He sneaks little looks at her over his shoulder. He cums.*)

THE VENUS: Whyd you do that?

THE BARON DOCTEUR: Im polite.
  (*Rest*)

THE VENUS: Love me?

THE BARON DOCTEUR: Do I ever.

THE VENUS: More than yr wife?

THE BARON DOCTEUR: More than my life.
And my wife.
She and I are childless you know.

THE VENUS: I know.
These are yummy.
  (*Rest*)
Wear this uhround yr neck and never take it off.
Its uh good luck feather. Uh sort of amulet.
It might help.

THE BARON DOCTEUR: It smells of you.

THE VENUS: Love me?

THE BARON DOCTEUR: Yes.
You dont want to go home?

THE VENUS: Not inny more.
  (*Rest*)
Love me?

THE BARON DOCTEUR: I do.

THE VENUS: Lie down.
And kiss me.
Here.
And here.
And here.
And here.
And here, you missed a spot,
Dearheart.

THE BARON DOCTEUR: Dearheart.

THE VENUS: You could discover *me*.

THE BARON DOCTEUR

THE VENUS

THE BARON DOCTEUR
  (*Rest*)

THE BARON DOCTEUR

THE VENUS

THE BARON DOCTEUR
  (*Rest*)

THE BARON DOCTEUR: I love you, Girl.

THE VENUS: Lights out.

SCENE 13

FOOTNOTE #7

THE NEGRO RESURRECTIONIST *reads from* THE BARON DOCTEUR's *notebook.*

THE NEGRO RESURRECTIONIST: Footnote #7:
Historical Extract. Category: Medical.
  (*Rest*)
A DETAILED PHYSICAL DESCRIPTION OF THE SO-CALLED VENUS HOTTENTOT:
  (*Rest*)
"Her hair was black and wooly, much like that of the common Negro, the slits of the eyes horizontal as in Mongols, not oblique; the brows straight, wide apart and very much flattened close to the top of the nose, but jutting out at the temple above the cheekbones; her eyes were dark and lively: her lips blackish, terribly thick; her complexion very dark."
  (*Rest*)
"Her ears were much like those found in monkeys: Small, weakly formed at the *tragus,* and vanishing behind almost completely."
  (*Rest*)
"Her breasts she usually lifted and tightened beneath the middle part of her dress, but, left free, they hung bulkily and terminated obliquely in a blackish areola about 1 and ½ inches in diameter pitted with radiating wrinkles, near the center of what was a nipple so flattened and obliterated as to be barely visible: The color of her skin was on the whole a yellowish brown, almost as dark as her face."
  (*Rest*)
"Her movements had rapidity and came unexpected calling to mind well, with all respect to her, the movements of a monkey. Above

all, she had a way of pushing out her lips just like the monkeys do. Her personality was sprightly, her memory good. She spoke low Dutch, tolerably good English—the men at the Academy and I tried to teach her French. She danced after the fashion of her own country and played with a fairly good ear upon a little instrument she called a Jew's Harp."
(Rest)
"She had no body hair apart from a few short flecks of wool like that on her head, scattered about her pubic parts."
(Rest)
"The wonders of her lower regions, will be fleshed out in greater detail at a later date."
(Rest)
"This information was gleaned, as has been said, upon the first and subsequent examinations which were performed in the office of her personal physician. As stated for the record, she submitted to these examinations as willingly as a patient submits to his doctors eyes and hands."
(Rest)
Scene #12:

SCENE 12

LOVE IDUHNT WHAT/SHE USED TO BE
THE VENUS *stands alone. She's dressed in a beautiful dress and looks fabulous.* THE CHORUS OF THE 8 ANATOMISTS *wanders in one by one. They get to work.* THE BARON DOCTEUR *wanders in. He watches. He wears his feather amulet.*

ANATOMIST #8: "The book is on the table!"
THE VENUS: *Le livre est*
   sur la table!
ANATOMIST #8: "The book is on the floor!"
THE VENUS: *Le livre est*
   par terre!
ANATOMIST #8: "And now the book is on my shoulder!"
THE VENUS: *Et maintenant, le livre est*
   sur mon épaule!
ANATOMIST #8: "And now the book is on my head!"
THE VENUS: *Et maintenant, le livre est*
   sur ma tête!

(THE CHORUS OF THE 8 ANATOMISTS *applauds most respectfully.*)
ANATOMIST #8: Thats excellent! And shes only been here
what, Sir, 6 months?
THE BARON DOCTEUR: 6 months thats right.
ANATOMIST #8: Throws all of those throw-back theories back in the lake, I'd say.
Throw em back in the lake!
THE BARON DOCTEUR: Not entirely, Gentlemen.
We study a people as a group
and dont throw away our years of labor
because of one most glorious exception.
THE CHORUS OF THE 8 ANATOMISTS: Hahahahaha hahahahaha.
(THE ANATOMISTS *and* THE BARON DOCTEUR *laugh good-naturedly.* THE VENUS *joins in. While they laugh a new Anatomist wanders onstage. He is* THE BARON DOCTEUR'S GRADE-SCHOOL CHUM. *He surreptitiously hands* THE BARON DOCTEUR *a letter and wanders off.*)
THE BARON DOCTEUR: Enough play, Gentlemen!
Lets get to work!
(THE VENUS *denudes. Perhaps 2 of the female* ANATOMISTS *assist her. She is lightly clothed in a sheer fabric.*)
THE BARON DOCTEUR: We'll start with simple figure drawing.
An important skill for any promising Anatomist.
(Rest)
Sweetheart, stand here where the light is perfect on you.
Just relax.
Only doctors here.
Thats beautiful.
(Rest)
Alright, Gentlemen! Pose #1.
(THE VENUS *stands in profile as they sketch her.* THE BARON DOCTEUR *stands apart and reads his letter.*)
THE BARON DOCTEUR: ("Dear Sir:
I am a friend of yrs from way back.
Im sure you remember at least my face
we went to school together. How interesting
that we're both in the doctoring business.
But no time for reminiscing, old friend,
I must cut straight to the point:
In yr liason with that Negress, Sir, you disgrace yrself.

Not to mention the pain yr causing yr sweet
  lovely wife.
A year in her bed is plenty, Sir. Surely yve tired
  of her heathen charms by now.
Send the Thing back where she came from
and return yrself to the bosom of yr senses.
Im speaking plain because as an old friend Ive
made it my responsiblilty to bring you back.
Sincerly yrs,
A Grade-School Chum.")
  (*Rest*)
  (*Rest*)
Gentlemen!
On to pose #2!
  (*Rest*)
Sweetheart, reverse profile, if you please.
  (THE VENUS *stands in reverse profile.* THE CHORUS
  OF THE 8 ANATOMISTS *draws busily.* THE BARON
  DOCTEUR *stands apart.*)
THE BARON DOCTEUR: "Sincerely yrs, A Grade-
  School Chum."
  (*Rest*)
  (*Rest*)
"I'm sure you remember at least my face."
  (*Rest*)
  (*Rest*)
"A Grade-School Chum."
Ah, ridiculous!
"A Grade-School Chum." Ha!
Just some busy eager beaver
trying to beat my time, I'll bet.
  (*Rest*)
  (*Rest*)
THE VENUS
THE BARON DOCTEUR
THE VENUS
THE BARON DOCTEUR
  (*Rest*)
THE VENUS: Love me?
THE BARON DOCTEUR: How couldnt I?
  Yr lovelier than ever.
THE VENUS
THE BARON DOCTEUR
  (*Rest*)
  (*Rest*)
THE BARON DOCTEUR: Gentlemen!
  Time to practice Measurements!
  (THE CHORUS OF THE 8 ANATOMISTS *measures* THE
  VENUS. THE BARON DOCTEUR *stands apart.*)

THE BARON DOCTEUR: From thuh *vertex* to thuh
  chin:
THE CHORUS OF THE 8 ANATOMISTS: 8.0 inches.
THE BARON DOCTEUR: *Vertex* to
  the top of shoulder in inches:
THE CHORUS OF THE 8 ANATOMISTS: 9.0.
THE BARON DOCTEUR: To thuh upper part of thuh
  sternum:
THE CHORUS OF THE 8 ANATOMISTS: 10.5.
THE BARON DOCTEUR: To thuh *formal cartilages tip:*
THE CHORUS OF THE 8 ANATOMISTS: 16.3.
THE BARON DOCTEUR: To the *umbilicus:*
THE CHORUS OF THE 8 ANATOMISTS: To the *umbilicus:*
  23.5.
THE BARON DOCTEUR: To the *perineum:*
THE CHORUS OF THE 8 ANATOMISTS: To the *perineum:*
  30.0.
THE BARON DOCTEUR: To the middle fingers tip
  the arm being placed by the side:
THE CHORUS OF THE 8 ANATOMISTS: 32.2.
THE BARON DOCTEUR: To the middle fingers tip
  the arm being extended from the side:
THE CHORUS OF THE 8 ANATOMISTS: 32.1.
  (*Again,* THE GRADE-SCHOOL CHUM *wanders in and
  surreptitiously hands* THE BARON DOCTEUR *another
  letter. This time* THE GRADE-SCHOOL CHUM *joins the
  group of measurers.*)
THE BARON DOCTEUR: To the middle fingers tip
  the arm being extended towards the viewer
  full front:
THE CHORUS OF THE 8 ANATOMISTS: 32.1.
THE BARON DOCTEUR: To the lower edge
  of the *patella:*
THE CHORUS OF THE 8 ANATOMISTS: 41.3.
THE BARON DOCTEUR: To the sole of the foot:
THE CHORUS OF THE 8 ANATOMISTS: To the sole of the
  foot: 55.9.
  (*Rest*)
THE BARON DOCTEUR: ("Dear Sir:
  Perhaps my first letter went unnoticed,
  one scrap of paper
  one among the several thousands littering yr
  desk and yr hot bed.")
  (*Rest*)
Transverse breadth of the head:
THE CHORUS OF THE 8 ANATOMISTS: 5.2.
THE BARON DOCTEUR: Transverse breadth of the
  shoulders:
THE CHORUS OF THE 8 ANATOMISTS: 12.0.

THE BARON DOCTEUR: Transverse breadth, *thorax* at
  the lower part:
THE CHORUS OF THE 8 ANATOMISTS: 8.4.
THE BARON DOCTEUR: *Thorax* at *axilla*:
THE CHORUS OF THE 8 ANATOMISTS: 8.7.
THE BARON DOCTEUR: ("Another year has passed
  since I first wrote.
  And although youve not married yr pet Hottentot
  And play a good part with yr dear wife . . . ")
    (*Rest*)
  Pelvis at the crest of the ilium:
THE CHORUS OF THE 8 ANATOMISTS: 8.6.
THE BARON DOCTEUR: *Pelvis* at the great *trochanters:*
THE CHORUS OF THE 8 ANATOMISTS: *Pelvis* at the great
    trochanters:
  11.0.
    (*Rest*)
THE BARON DOCTEUR: Length of the *humerus:*
THE CHORUS OF THE 8 ANATOMISTS: 10.0.
THE BARON DOCTEUR: Of the *radius:*
THE CHORUS OF THE 8 ANATOMISTS: 7.3.
THE BARON DOCTEUR: Of the *ulna:*
THE CHORUS OF THE 8 ANATOMISTS: 7.9.
THE BARON DOCTEUR: Of the *femur:*
THE CHORUS OF THE 8 ANATOMISTS: Length of the *femur:*
  14.5.
THE BARON DOCTEUR: Of the *tibia:*
THE CHORUS OF THE 8 ANATOMISTS: 11.3.
THE BARON DOCTEUR: (("I'd like to think its my note
    thats moved you to return home although
  you reek of Hottentot-amour, Sir, and as a col-
    legue its my duty to speak plain, Sir:
  we all smell it!"))
    (*Rest*)
    (*Rest*)
  (THE CHORUS OF THE 8 ANATOMISTS *sniffs the air.*)
THE BARON DOCTEUR: (*Rest*)
  Of the spine from the upper border of the *atlas*
  to the tip of the *coccyx:*
THE CHORUS OF THE 8 ANATOMISTS: 23.8.
THE BARON DOCTEUR
THE BARON DOCTEUR
THE BARON DOCTEUR
THE BARON DOCTEUR
    (THE BARON DOCTEUR *is lost in thought.* THE CHORUS
    OF THE 8 ANATOMISTS *waits patiently for him to re-*
    sume, then, turning their backs to THE VENUS, *they*
    steal looks over their shoulders at her and jerk off
    (*much like* THE BARON DOCTEUR *did in Scene 14.*).)

THE BARON DOCTEUR: (*Rest*)
  Of the spine to the last lumbar vertebra:
THE CHORUS OF THE 8 ANATOMISTS: 19.2.
THE BARON DOCTEUR: (*Rest*)
  Circumference of the chest at the lower margin
  of the 6th rib:
THE CHORUS OF THE 8 ANATOMISTS: 27.5.
THE BARON DOCTEUR: (*Rest*)
  Span of the arms when extended:
  Pull em all the way out, Gentlemen!
THE CHORUS OF THE 8 ANATOMISTS: Span of the arms
  all the way out:
  58.9.
THE GRADE-SCHOOL CHUM: The measurements of
    her limb-bones
  will of course
  be corrected
  after maceration, Sir?
THE BARON DOCTEUR
THE GRADE-SCHOOL CHUM
THE VENUS: "Maceration?"
THE NEGRO RESURRECTIONIST: Footnote #8:
  Definition: Medical: *Maceration:*
    (*Rest*)
  "A process performed on the subject after the
    subjects death. The subjects body parts are
    soaked in a chemical solution to separate the
    flesh from the bones so that the bones may be
    measured with greater accuracy."
    (*Rest*)
THE BARON DOCTEUR: Thats enough for now.
  Gentlemen: Thats plenty for today and Im sure
    our lovely subjects
  all exhausted.
  Put yr hands together, Sirs.
  Show The Venus yr appreciation.
    (*They applaud politely.*)
THE NEGRO RESURRECTIONIST: Scene 11:
  From "For the Love of the Venus." Act II, Scene 12:

SCENE 11

"FOR THE LOVE OF THE VENUS."
ACT II, SCENE 12
THE BARON DOCTEUR'S *chair is empty.* THE NEGRO RESUR-
RECTIONIST *takes a seat and watches halfheartedly.*

THE BRIDE-TO-BE: He sez he loves a Hottentot.

THE MOTHER: Dont snuffle.
THE BRIDE-TO-BE: A *Hottentot!*
THE MOTHER: Blow yr nose.
THE BRIDE-TO-BE: *Hottentot Venus!*
THE MOTHER: Wipe yr eyes.
  My Sons gone wild
  but I have a plan.
  Listen up!
    (*Rest*)
  His head has turned from yr bright sun.
  He roams in thuh dark.
  Let me speak plain:
  He dudhnt love you inny more.
THE BRIDE-TO-BE: Aaah me!
THE MOTHER: [Uh multitude of responses are
    available.
  Thuh antiquity response would be thuh Asp.
  Get yrself uh poison-snake. Clasp it tuh yr bosom.
  On thuh left side. Let it fill yr heart with death.
  Cleopatra. Very moving. Old hat now though.
  Thuh classical response would be tuh hang yrself.
  Phaedra did that.
  Elizabethan response would be tuh drown yrself.
  A la little wassername.
THE BRIDE-TO-BE: Ophelia.
THE MOTHER: Good girl.
  They also drank poison. Fell on their swords.
  In modern dress they slit their wrists.
  Fill their pockets with rocks.
  Jump from bridges.
  Infront of trains.
  Sleeping pills. Take one or two too many. Thatll
    do it.
  Hunger strike: Turn yr face tuh thuh wall dont
    eat for weeks.
  Thats like pining. But more dramatic.
  To simply waste uhway—]
  But none of that.
  I have uh plan.
  Get this:
  Our young man wants uh Hottentot tuh love.
  Uh Hottentot yr not, my dear.
  But with some skill you can pretend.
THE BRIDE-TO-BE: Pretend?
THE MOTHER: Lets get to work.
  I'll get that Uncle on our side.
  We'll get you up, make you look wild
  Get you up like a Hottentot.
THE BRIDE-TO-BE: Like a Hottentot?

THE MOTHER: Bring my Son to his knees.
  Lets get to work.
THE BRIDE-TO-BE: Lets get to work.
    (*Curtain.* THE CHORUS *applauds.*)

SCENE 10

FOOTNOTE #9

THE NEGRO RESURRECTIONIST *reads from* THE BARON
DOCTEUR's *notebook.*

THE NEGRO RESURRECTIONIST: (*Rest*)
  Footnote #9:
  Historical Extract. Category: Medical.
    (*Rest*)
  "The female Hottentot under my care has the
    usual falling off of appearance common in
    women of 30 years old. Her *mammae* are flac-
    cid and elongated. While her *glutei* muscles
    along with their coverings, the 2 prominent
    peculiar hemispherical cushions of fat, are
    quite remarkable, more remarkable still are
    the long appendages which hang down from
    her *pudendum!*"
    (THE BARON DOCTEUR *snatches his notebook from*
    THE NEGRO RESURRECTIONIST's *hands.*)
THE BARON DOCTEUR
THE NEGRO RESURRECTIONIST
THE NEGRO RESURRECTIONIST: Scene #9:
  Her Charming Hands/
  An Anatomical Columbus:

SCENE 9

HER CHARMING HANDS/AN
ANATOMICAL COLUMBUS

THE VENUS *sits in the chair wrapped up to her chin in a
large cloth.* THE BARON DOCTEUR *stands above her wielding a shiny and sharp pair of scissors. He is giving her
a haircut.*

THE BARON DOCTEUR: Hold still.
  There now.
  Open yr eyes and take a look.
THE VENUS: Uh uhnn.
THE BARON DOCTEUR: Its almost perfect.
THE VENUS: Im nervous.
  I could be bald.

THE BARON DOCTEUR: Ive got the steadiest hands in
   the business.
   Dearheart. Look.
THE VENUS: Mmm.
   Not bad.
   A little uneven on the left.
   Just there.
      (*He evens out her haircut.*)
THE BARON DOCTEUR: Did yr dresses come today?
THE VENUS: They did.
THE BARON DOCTEUR: Wear the yellow one tonight.
THE VENUS: We're having company?
THE BARON DOCTEUR: No.
   Tonights dinner is just you and me.
THE VENUS: Its always only you and me.
   You and me this room that table.
   We dont go out.
   No one visits.
   You dont want me seen.
THE BARON DOCTEUR: Yr seen enough at the Academy.
THE VENUS: That dont count.
THE BARON DOCTEUR: We go for rides.
THE VENUS: In a closed coach!
THE BARON DOCTEUR: Ok Ok I confess: I wanna keep
   my Sweets
   all to myself.
   Im very greedy.
      (*Rest*)
   Take another look.
THE VENUS: Looks alright.
   Love me?
THE BARON DOCTEUR: Mmm.
THE VENUS
THE BARON DOCTEUR
      (*Rest*)
THE BARON DOCTEUR: Ok, up up!
   Ive got some work to do
   before we eat.
THE VENUS: Put yr hand here.
THE BARON DOCTEUR: Yr warm.
THE VENUS: Yes.
THE BARON DOCTEUR: Upset stomach? I'll fix you
   something.
   You eat too many chockluts you know.
   I give em to you by the truckload but
   you dont have to eat them all.
   Practice some restraint.
   Drink this.
THE VENUS: Put yr hand here, Sweetheart.

THE BARON DOCTEUR: Drink this first.
THE VENUS: No. Feel me.
THE BARON DOCTEUR: Fine.
THE VENUS
THE BARON DOCTEUR
THE VENUS
THE BARON DOCTEUR
      (*Rest*)
THE BARON DOCTEUR: What am I feeling?
THE VENUS: Guess.
THE VENUS
THE BARON DOCTEUR
THE VENUS
THE BARON DOCTEUR
      (*She's pregnant.*)
      (*Rest*)
THE BARON DOCTEUR: God. Is there anything we can
   do about it.
   Ive a wife. A career.
   A reputation. Is there anything
   we can do about it we together in
   the privacy of my office.
   Ive got various equipments in here
   we could figure something out.
THE VENUS
THE VENUS
THE VENUS
THE VENUS: Where I come from
   its cause for celebration.
THE BARON DOCTEUR: A simple yes or no will do, Girl.
      (*Rest*)
THE VENUS: Yes.
THE BARON DOCTEUR: Fine.
   We'll take care of it this evening.
   After dinner.
   Is that alright?
THE VENUS: Yes thats fine.
THE BARON DOCTEUR: Fine.
THE VENUS
THE BARON DOCTEUR
      (*Rest*)
      (*She exits.*)
THE BARON DOCTEUR
THE BARON DOCTEUR
      (*Rest*)
      (THE GRADE-SCHOOL CHUM *appears as if out of thin
      air.*)
THE GRADE-SCHOOL CHUM
THE BARON DOCTEUR

THE GRADE-SCHOOL CHUM

THE BARON DOCTEUR

THE GRADE-SCHOOL CHUM: The door was wide open.
  I walked right in.
  You 2 should keep yr voices down.
  Everyone kin hear yr business.
       (*Rest*)
  Dont you recognize me?
THE BARON DOCTEUR: Cant say I do.
THE GRADE-SCHOOL CHUM: We went to school
    together.
  Remember?
       (*Rest*)
THE BARON DOCTEUR
THE GRADE-SCHOOL CHUM
       (*Rest*)
THE BARON DOCTEUR: Vaguely.
THE GRADE-SCHOOL CHUM: I was the one who ripped
    the wings off the flies.
  We were like brothers.
  Hug me!
THE BARON DOCTEUR: Beat it.
THE GRADE-SCHOOL CHUM: Whats that thing around
    yr neck.
THE BARON DOCTEUR: None of yr business.
THE GRADE-SCHOOL CHUM: Get rid of her.
  Shes not yr type.
THE BARON DOCTEUR: Good evening, Sir.
  I'll show you out.
THE GRADE-SCHOOL CHUM: Yr wifes distraught.
THE BARON DOCTEUR: No she is not!
THE GRADE-SCHOOL CHUM: Yr reputation is in
    shambles.
THE BARON DOCTEUR: My discoveriesll right that.
THE GRADE-SCHOOL CHUM: You better dissect her
    soon, Old Friend,
  the Academy wont wait for ever.
THE BARON DOCTEUR: I'll dissect her soon enough!
THE GRADE-SCHOOL CHUM: Ive come as a friend.
  Giving friendly advice.
THE BARON DOCTEUR: Friend.
  I am to her a mere
  Anatomical Columbus.
  Lemmie read you a little
  of what Ive written so far.
  Where to begin? *Uh hehm*
  (*He reads from his notebook.*)
  ((" . . . the vast protuberance of her buttocks . . .
  The somewhat brutish appearance of her face."))

THE GRADE-SCHOOL CHUM: So get rid of her!
  Break with her!
  Kick her out on her fat ass!
THE BARON DOCTEUR: But, l
  I love her.
  I love her!!

SCENE 8

"FOR THE LOVE OF THE VENUS."
ACT III, SCENE 9

THE NEGRO RESURRECTIONIST *is the only audience.* THE
UNCLE *presents* THE BRIDE-TO-BE *disguised as* THE HOT-
TENTOT VENUS.

THE UNCLE: Presenting:
  Presenting:
  Young Man, to you for love alone
  the Wild Thing of yr hearts desire:
  From the darkest jungles may I present: "The
    Hottentot Venus!"
THE YOUNG MAN
THE HOTTENTOT VENUS
THE YOUNG MAN
THE HOTTENTOT VENUS
       (*Rest*)
THE FATHER: Young Man, say something.
THE YOUNG MAN: Good God good God.
  She is so odd.
  Love?
  Youre Love?
THE HOTTENTOT VENUS
THE YOUNG MAN
THE HOTTENTOT VENUS
THE YOUNG MAN
       (*Rest*)
THE YOUNG MAN: She doesnt speak?
THE UNCLE: Not many words we understand.
  Her hometown lingos uh strange one
  Therefore, Hottentot Venus, darling,
  allow me to interpret.
       (*Rest*)
  Hottentot Venus, you speak first.
       (*Rest*)
       (*They click and cluck at each other.*)
THE UNCLE
THE HOTTENTOT VENUS
       (*Rest*)

THE UNCLE: Young Man, she says shes Love.

THE YOUNG MAN: Whisper, ask her, if shes wild.

>   (*More clicking. More clucking.*)

THE UNCLE

THE HOTTENTOT VENUS

>   (*Rest*)

THE UNCLE: She sez she comes from far away where
>   its quite hot.
>
>   She sez shes pure bred Hottentot.
>
>   She sez if Wilds your desire
>
>   she comes from The Wilds and she carries them
>   behind her.
>
>   [Wild is her back-ground her fundament so to
>   speak
>
>   and although shes grown accustomed to our
>   civil ways
>
>   she still holds The Wilds within her
>
>   behind, inside, infront
>
>   which is to say, that all yr days
>
>   with her will be a lively lovely bliss.]

THE YOUNG MAN: Let me look at her!

THE UNCLE: Circle around
>   get all her angles.
>
>   (THE YOUNG MAN *orbits briefly.*)

THE YOUNG MAN

THE HOTTENTOT VENUS

THE YOUNG MAN

>   (*He stares hard at her.*)
>
>   (THE YOUNG MAN *and* THE HOTTENTOT VENUS *stand
>   in tableau.*)

THE NEGRO RESURRECTIONIST: "The height, mea-
>   sured after death,
>
>   was 4 feet 11 and ½ inches.
>
>   The total weight of the body was 98 pounds *av-
>   oirdupois* . . .
>
>   The great amounts of subcutaneous fat were
>   quite surprising."
>
>   (*Rest*)
>
>   Scene #7:

SCENE 7

SHE'LL MAKE A SPLENDID CORPSE

Bright sunshine. THE VENUS *in her bedroom daydream-
ing. She wears a wig.*

THE VENUS: He spends all his time with me because
>   he loves me.

He hardly visits her at all.

She may be his wife all right but shes all dried up.

He is not thuh most thrilling lay Ive had

but his gold makes up thuh difference and hhhh

I love him.

He will leave that wife for good and we'll get
>   married

(we better or I'll make a scene) oh, we'll get
>   married.

And we will lie in bed and make love all day
>   long.

Hahahaha.

We'll set tongues wagging for the rest of the
>   century.

The Docteur will introduce me to Napoléon
>   himself: Oh,

yes yr Royal Highness the Negro question does
>   keep me

awake at night oh yes it does.

Servant girl! Do this and that!

When Im Mistress I'll be a tough cookie.

I'll rule the house with an iron fist and have the
>   most fabulous parties.

Society will seek me out: Wheres Venus? Right
>   here!

Hhhhh. I need a new wig.

Every afternoon I'll take a 3 hour bath. In hot
>   rosewater.

After my bath theyll pat me down.

Theyll rub my body with the most expensive
>   oils

perfume my big buttocks and sprinkle them
>   with gold dust!

>   (THE BARON DOCTEUR *enters and watches her. She
>   does not see him.*)

THE VENUS: Come here quick, slave and attend me!
>   Fetch my sweets! Fix my hair!
>
>   Do this do that do this do that!
>
>   Hahahahahahah! Mmmmmmm.

THE BARON DOCTEUR: What are you doing?

THE VENUS: Oh.
>   Im sunning myself.

THE BARON DOCTEUR: Then you should have a parasol.

THE VENUS: No thanks.
>   Kiss me.

THE BARON DOCTEUR: Little Hotsey-Totsey.

THE VENUS: Come to bed.

THE BARON DOCTEUR: Its the middle of the day.

THE VENUS: So?

THE BARON DOCTEUR: Mmmm.

THE VENUS

THE BARON DOCTEUR

THE VENUS: I dont think I wanna go to yr Academy
    inny more.

THE BARON DOCTEUR: Dont be silly.
    They all love you there.
    And yr French is brilliant.
    Its only been 2 years and yr sounding like a
        native.
    Yr a linguistic genius!
    Everybody agrees.

THE VENUS: They touch me sometimes.
    When yr not looking.

THE BARON DOCTEUR: How could they not?
    Touching you is—well, its their job.

THE VENUS: Theyre lascivious.

THE BARON DOCTEUR: Jesus.
    Dont be hyperbolic.

THE VENUS: You seem half there.
    Love me?
    (Rest)

THE BARON DOCTEUR

THE VENUS
    (Rest)

THE BARON DOCTEUR: Im here arent I?

THE VENUS: I'll wake up one day youll be gone.

THE BARON DOCTEUR: Wrong.
    Im here to stay.
    Things are just a little off at work thats all.

THE VENUS: Touch me
    down here.

THE BARON DOCTEUR: What is it?

THE VENUS

THE BARON DOCTEUR
    (She's pregnant again.)
    (Rest)

THE BARON DOCTEUR: Can we do anything? Oh
    God.

THE VENUS: Oh God.

THE BARON DOCTEUR: A simple yes or no will do.

THE VENUS: Im not feeling very well.
    Its hot in here.
    Love me?

THE BARON DOCTEUR: A simple yes or no will do,
    Girl!

THE VENUS: Yes.
    Yes.

THE BARON DOCTEUR: Good. Now get some sleep.

THE VENUS

THE BARON DOCTEUR

THE VENUS

THE BARON DOCTEUR
    (Rest)

THE VENUS: Whats "maceration."

THE BARON DOCTEUR: Huh?

THE VENUS: "Maceration."

THE BARON DOCTEUR: Whyd you ask?

THE VENUS: They always say:
    "The measurementsll be corrected after
    'maceration.'" Whats it mean?

THE BARON DOCTEUR: "Macerations" French for
    "lunch."
    "After lunch" we also say.
    (Rest)
    Yr my true Love.
    Now get some sleep.
        (They sleep. Enter THE GRADE-SCHOOL CHUM, as if in a
        dream. THE BARON DOCTEUR wakes up with a start.)

THE GRADE-SCHOOL CHUM: Ready now:
    Cough.

THE BARON DOCTEUR: Uhh!

THE GRADE-SCHOOL CHUM: Turn yr head.
    Cough uhgain.

THE BARON DOCTEUR: Uhh!
    Yr not my regular physician.

THE GRADE-SCHOOL CHUM: Nope.
    Say "Aaaah."

THE BARON DOCTEUR: "Aaaah."

THE GRADE-SCHOOL CHUM: Bigger.

THE BARON DOCTEUR: "Aaaaaaah?"
    (Rest)
    Shes my True Love.
    She'd make uh splendid wife.

THE GRADE-SCHOOL CHUM: Yr sick.

THE BARON DOCTEUR: Thatsright.

THE GRADE-SCHOOL CHUM: Whatwith?

THE BARON DOCTEUR: True Love.

THE GRADE-SCHOOL CHUM: Yr reputation is in
    shambles.

THE BARON DOCTEUR: So?

THE GRADE-SCHOOL CHUM: Yr wifes distraught.

THE BARON DOCTEUR: Oh, she is not!

THE GRADE-SCHOOL CHUM: Whats so great about the
    black girl tell me.

THE BARON DOCTEUR: Get lost.

THE GRADE-SCHOOL CHUM: Yr still childless with the
    Mrs. arent you.

THE BARON DOCTEUR: Beat it.

THE GRADE-SCHOOL CHUM: And a laughing stock of
    the Academy to boot.

  Whats that uhround yr neck?

THE BARON DOCTEUR: Uh charm. For luck. Get lost.

THE GRADE-SCHOOL CHUM: Here: A pill. Take it.
    Doctors orders.

  Itll clear yr head.

  Go on. Doctors orders.

  Take it now.

  Wash it down.

  Aaaah?

THE BARON DOCTEUR: Aaah.

    (THE GRADE-SCHOOL CHUM *tosses a pill in* THE BAR-
    ON DOCTEUR's *mouth and he swallows it down.*)

THE GRADE-SCHOOL CHUM: Yr breath is off. Smells
    like—woah: Fuck.

  I wouldnt wear that. Looks like bad luck.

THE BARON DOCTEUR: You think?

THE GRADE-SCHOOL CHUM: I do. Lets take it off.

  Im doing you a favor, Man:

  Im packing yr bags and Im bringing you with me.

THE BARON DOCTEUR: Do I have a choice?

THE GRADE-SCHOOL CHUM: Sure.

  But you know, of course,

  yr not the only Doc

  whos got hisself uh Hottentot.

THE BARON DOCTEUR

THE GRADE-SCHOOL CHUM

    (*Rest*)

THE GRADE-SCHOOL CHUM

THE BARON DOCTEUR

    (*Rest*)

    (*Rest*)

THE BARON DOCTEUR: Speak plainly, Friend.

THE GRADE-SCHOOL CHUM: Some chap in Germany
    or somethin

  got his hands on one.

  He performed the autopsy today.

  Word is he'll publish inny minute.

THE BARON DOCTEUR: He'll beat me to the punch!

THE GRADE-SCHOOL CHUM: What do you care
    yr in Luv.

THE BARON DOCTEUR

THE GRADE-SCHOOL CHUM

THE BARON DOCTEUR: Shes not feeling so well.
  Said so herself.

THE GRADE-SCHOOL CHUM: She'll probably outlive
    us all.

THE BARON DOCTEUR: Shes—

  Shes got the clap.

THE GRADE-SCHOOL CHUM: The clap?

  From you?

THE BARON DOCTEUR: Perhaps.

    (*Rest*)

  It makes my work with her

  indecent somehow.

THE GRADE-SCHOOL CHUM: "Indecency!"

  We could clap her into jail for that.

THE BARON DOCTEUR: We could?

THE GRADE-SCHOOL CHUM: Its up to you of course.

    (*Rest*)

  Remember who you are, Sir,

  and make the right decision.

  Say yes and we'll have her gone by morning.

THE BARON DOCTEUR: There must be some other
    solution.

THE GRADE-SCHOOL CHUM: We'll clap her into jail.

  And if her clap runs its course, well,

  thats fate, Friend.

THE BARON DOCTEUR: Oh God.

THE GRADE-SCHOOL CHUM: A simple yes or no will
    do, Doctor.

  Come on.

THE BARON DOCTEUR: Such a lovely creature in her
    way.

  She has a grace—

THE GRADE-SCHOOL CHUM: Come on.

  Say yes.

  Before she wakes.

THE BARON DOCTEUR: Her charming hands—

THE GRADE-SCHOOL CHUM: Shes just a 2-bit side-
    show freak.

THE BARON DOCTEUR: She would have made uh
    splendid wife.

THE GRADE-SCHOOL CHUM: Oh, please.

  She'll make uh splendid corpse.

    (THE GRADE-SCHOOL CHUM *exits leading* THE BARON
    DOCTEUR *by the hand.* THE VENUS *wakes up with a
    start. She is alone.*)

THE VENUS

THE VENUS

THE VENUS

THE VENUS

    (*Rest*)

THE VENUS: Is it uh little hot in here

  or is it just me?

    (*Rest*)

THE VENUS

THE VENUS

THE VENUS

THE VENUS
   (*A knot of* SPECTATORS *gathers around her.*)
THE CHORUS OF THE SPECTATORS: Lookie-Lookie-
   Lookie-Lookie
   Hubba-Hubba-Hubba-Hubba
   Lookie-Lookie-Lookie-Lookie
   Hubba-Hubba-Hubba-Hubba.
   (*Rest*)
THE CHORUS OF THE SPECTATORS
THE VENUS
THE CHORUS OF THE SPECTATORS
   (*Rest*)
   (THE CHORUS OF THE SPECTATORS *bursts into a riot.*
   THE VENUS *flees.*)
THE NEGRO RESURRECTIONIST: Order!
   Order!
   Order!
   Order!
   (*Suddenly* THE VENUS *is again imprisoned. Not caged
   but chained like a dog in the yard.* THE NEGRO RESUR-
   RECTIONIST *seats himself beside her. He is her guard.*)
THE VENUS
THE NEGRO RESURRECTIONIST
THE VENUS
THE NEGRO RESURRECTIONIST
THE GRADE-SCHOOL CHUM: Indecency?
   Clap her into jail for that!
THE BARON DOCTEUR: Clap her into jail for that?
   (THE CHORUS OF THE SPECTATORS *applauds.*)

SCENE 6

SOME YEARS LATER IN TUBINGEN (REPRISE)

THE CHORUS OF THE SPECTATORS *applauds.* THE BARON
DOCTEUR *reads from his notebook.*

THE BARON DOCTEUR: *Uh hehm*
   (*Rest*)
   "In regards to the formation of her buttocks
   we make the following remarks:
   The fatty cushion, a.k.a.
   Steatopygia was 9 inches deep. Her buttocks—"
   Uh hehm.
THE NEGRO RESURRECTIONIST: Scene #6:
   Several Years Later, at a Conference in Tübingen:

The Dis(-re-)memberment of the Venus Hottentot, Part II:
THE BARON DOCTEUR: "Her buttocks had nearly
   nearly the usual origin and insertion
   but the muscular fibers were surprisingly thin
   and flabby
   and very badly developed thus showing that
   the protuberance of the buttocks
   so peculiar to the Bushman race
   is not the result of any muscular development
   but rather
   totally dependent
   on the accumulation of fat."
   (*Rest*)
   (THE VENUS *is chained.* THE NEGRO RESURRECTIONIST
   stands watch.)
THE VENUS: You ever Love?
THE NEGRO RESURRECTIONIST: Naw.
THE VENUS: No?
THE NEGRO RESURRECTIONIST: Nope.
THE VENUS: Ever been loved?
THE NEGRO RESURRECTIONIST: Uh uhnnn.
   (*Rest*)
   (*He gives her a red heart box of chocolates.*)
   Chockluts. Here.
   Theyre not from me.
   Theyre from a man who sez he knew you when.
   Doctor I think he sed.
THE VENUS: "Doctor?"
THE NEGRO RESURRECTIONIST: Maybe once when
   you were sick?
   (*Rest*)
   (THE BARON DOCTEUR *continues with great difficulty.*)
THE BARON DOCTEUR: Oh God my mind was
   wandering
   Where was I?
   Uh hehm:
   "While the uterus had the ordinary form of that
   organ in a
   once or twice impregnated female,
   the external characters,
   especially of the reproductive organs,
   form, in this view, the centerpiece of Study.
   (*Rest*)
   The *labia majora* were small.
   The clitoris sized moderate to large
   and had a well-developed *prepuce*
   all situated far more conspicuously
   than in the European female.

Her most remarkable feature
were the long appendages
which hung down from her *pudendum.*
They resembled 2 thongs
each about the thickness of a cedar-wood pencil
exactly like strips of sheepskin slightly twisted
and apparently vascular.
On separating her *labia* I found these *appendages*
to be the *nymphae* elongated.
I took up her appendages
and led the right one round her right side
above her gluteal projection, similarly
I led her left appendage round her left side
and their ends *met at her spine.*
     (*Rest*)
There was no trace of hymen.
     (*Rest*)
     (*Rest*)
The remarkable development of the *labia minora*
which heretofore is so general a characteristic of
the Hottentot or Bushman race
was so sufficiently well marked that it well dis-
     tinguished itself
from those of any of the ordinary varieties of the
     human species.
Again, their difference was so marked
their formation so distinguished
that they formed this studies centerpiece.
This author recommends further examination of
     said formation."
     (*Rest*)
Thank you.
     (*He stands there holding his notebook and hanging
     his head.*)

SCENE 5

WHO IS SHE TO ME?

THE VENUS *sleeps.* THE NEGRO RESURRECTIONIST *stands
watch.*

THE GRADE-SCHOOL CHUM: You watch The Venus
     Hottentot?
THE NEGRO RESURRECTIONIST: Im her Watchman,
     thats right.
     And I'll put her safely in the ground when she
     dies too.

Whats that to you?
THE GRADE-SCHOOL CHUM: I recognize you, Man
     I know you from way back.
     Youve got a memorable face.
THE NEGRO RESURRECTIONIST: So what.
THE GRADE-SCHOOL CHUM: You used to unearth bodies
     for my postmortem class.
     An illegal craft as I remember.
THE NEGRO RESURRECTIONIST: I quit that line years
     ago.
THE GRADE-SCHOOL CHUM: Once a *digger* always one.
THE NEGRO RESURRECTIONIST: Get to the point.
THE GRADE-SCHOOL CHUM: A friend of mine in the
     medical profession
     is very interested in the body of yr ward.
     After she "goes on."
     For scientific analysis only of course.
THE NEGRO RESURRECTIONIST: No thank you.
THE GRADE-SCHOOL CHUM: I'll have to call the cops
     on you.
     Theyll lock you up.
THE NEGRO RESURRECTIONIST: I quit that buisiness!
THE GRADE-SCHOOL CHUM: Yd be surprised at how
     the legal system works.
     (*Rest*)
     Shes gonna kick it inny minute.
     We'll pay you for yr trouble.
     Its not for me but for a friend.
     He doesnt got the balls to ask.
          (THE GRADE-SCHOOL CHUM *knees* THE NEGRO RESUR-
          RECTIONIST *in the balls.*)
THE GRADE-SCHOOL CHUM: We'll pay you well. In
     gold. Say yes.
THE NEGRO RESURRECTIONIST
THE GRADE-SCHOOL CHUM
     (*Rest*)
THE NEGRO RESURRECTIONIST: Uh uhnn.
THE GRADE-SCHOOL CHUM: Then its thuh slammer,
     Stupid.
     I gotcha by thuh throat, admit it.
THE NEGRO RESURRECTIONIST
THE GRADE-SCHOOL CHUM
THE NEGRO RESURRECTIONIST
THE GRADE-SCHOOL CHUM
     (*Rest*)
THE NEGRO RESURRECTIONIST: Ok.
     I mean, whatever.
     Yr uh bastards bastard.

But fine. Alright, I guess.
I mean, who is she to me?
THE GRADE-SCHOOL CHUM
THE NEGRO RESURRECTIONIST
THE GRADE-SCHOOL CHUM: Theres a good boy.
  Heh-Heh-Heh.
Heres a little in advance.
  (THE GRADE-SCHOOL CHUM *tosses him a single gold*
  coin. He takes the coin but feels like shit.)

SCENE 4

"FOR THE LOVE OF THE
VENUS" (CONCLUSION)

THE BARON DOCTEUR *watches from one place,* THE VENUS
from another. THE BRIDE-TO-BE, *masquerading as a* HOTTEN-
TOT VENUS, *and* THE YOUNG MAN *stare at each other.*

THE HOTTENTOT VENUS
THE YOUNG MAN
THE HOTTENTOT VENUS
THE YOUNG MAN
  (*Rest*)
THE YOUNG MAN: Tell her Im smitten.
THE UNCLE: I think she knows.
THE YOUNG MAN: By these knees Im bending on
  True Venus
  Im forever thine.
  I'll never change.
  Promise me the same.
  Uncle, put that on yr tongue then in her tongue
  then in her ear.
  (*Rest*)
  What is her answer?
THE UNCLE: She promises constancy but
  as we lose uh skin layer every day
  so will she shrug her old self off.
THE YOUNG MAN: Shrug all you want but keep
  thuh core.
  (*Rest*)
  Answer.
  (*She removes her disguise and again becomes* THE
  BRIDE-TO-BE.)
THE BRIDE-TO-BE: Dearheart: Your true love stands
  before you.
  (*He gives her a red heart box of chocolates. Love*
  Tableau. Curtain. THE BARON DOCTEUR *applauds.*)

SCENE 3

A BRIEF HISTORY OF CHOCOLATE
The planets align.

THE VENUS:
  (*Rest*)
A BRIEF HISTORY OF CHOCOLATE:
It is written in the ancient chronicles
that the Gods one day looked down with pity
pity on the people as they struggled.
The Gods resolved to visit the people
and teach them the ways of Love
for Love helps in times of hardship.
As an act of Love one God gives to the people
a little shrub that had, until then, belonged
only to the Gods.
This was the cacao tree.
  (*Rest*)
Time passed.
Time passed uhgain:
We find ourselves in the 19th century.
The Aztec word *cacao* literally "food of the Gods"
becomes *chocolate* and *cocoa.*
The *cacao* bean, once used as money
becomes an exotic beverage.
The Spanish were known to die for their choco-
  late.
In the New World, they were also known to kill
  for it.
In Europe the church wages a campaign against
  chocolate
on the grounds that it was tainted by the char-
  acter
of its heathen inventors.
"Chocolate is the damnable agent of necroman-
  cers and sorcerers,
said one French cleric circa 1620.
The Pilgrims in America. Some said they fled
  England because of chocolate.
But thats another story.
  (*Rest*)
Chocolate was soon mixed with milk and sugar
and formed into lozenges which one could eat
  on the run.
Chocolate lozenges are now found in a variety
  of shapes

mixed with everything from nuts to brandy.
Chocolate is a recognized emotional stimulant,
for doctors have recently noticed the tendency
    of some persons,
especially women,
to go on chocolate binges
binges either *after* emotionally upsetting incidents
or in an effort to allow themselves *to handle* an
    incident
which may be emotionally upsetting.
This information is interesting in that it has be-
    come the practice
to present a gift of chocolates when professing
    Love.
This practice, begun some time ago, continues
    to this day.
    (*Rest*)
While chocolate was once used as a stimulant
    and source of nutrition
it is primarily today a great source of fat,
and, of course, pleasure.
    (*Rest*)

SCENE 2

THE VENUS HOTTENTOT TELLS
THE STORY OF HER LIFE

THE NEGRO RESURRECTIONIST *fingers his new gold coin.*

THE VENUS: Whered ya get that?
THE NEGRO RESURRECTIONIST: I found it.
   Just this morning on the street.
THE VENUS: Yr lucky.
THE NEGRO RESURRECTIONIST: Im not lying!!
THE VENUS: I didnt say you were.
THE VENUS
THE NEGRO RESURRECTIONIST
THE VENUS
THE NEGRO RESURRECTIONIST
    (*Rest*)
THE VENUS: How long you lived here?
THE NEGRO RESURRECTIONIST: Me? Ive lived in this
    town all my life.
   I used to dig up people
   dead ones. You know,
   after theyd been buried.
   Doctors pay a lot for corpses
   but "Resurrection" is illegal

and I was always this close to getting arrested.
   This Jail-Watchmans jobs much more carefree.
THE VENUS: You dont have anything you miss?
   Yr lucky, Watchman.
   I always dream of home
   in every spare minute.
   It was a shitty shitty life but oh I miss it.
   Whats that sound outside, crowds?
THE NEGRO RESURRECTIONIST: Yes.
   Yr still a star.
THE VENUS: Dont let them in.
THE NEGRO RESURRECTIONIST: Dont worry.
THE VENUS
THE NEGRO RESURRECTIONIST
THE VENUS
THE NEGRO RESURRECTIONIST
    (*Rest*)
THE VENUS: Whats that outside?
   Crowds?
THE NEGRO RESURRECTIONIST: Just rain.
   We're having lousy weather.
   Its just rain.
THE VENUS: I was born near the coast, Watchman.
   Journeyed some worked some
   ended up here.
   I would live here I thought but only for uh minute!
   Make a mint.
   Had plans to.
   He had a beard.
   Big bags of money!
   Where wuz I?
   Fell in love. Hhh.
   Tried my hand at French.
   Gave me a haircut
   and thuh claps.
   You get thuh picture, huh?
   Dont look at me
   dont look . . .
    (*Rest*)
    (*She dies.*)
THE NEGRO RESURRECTIONIST:
    (*Rest*)
"Early in the 19th century a poor wretched woman
   was exhibited in England under the appella-
   tion of *The Hottentot Venus.* With an intensely
   ugly figure, distorted beyond all European
   notions of beauty, she was said to possess precisely the kind of shape which is most admired
   among her countrymen, the Hottentots."

The year was 1810, three years after the Bill for the Abolition of the Slave-Trade had been passed in Parliament, and among protests and denials, horror and fascination her show went on. She died in Paris 5 years later: A plaster cast of her body was once displayed, along with her skeleton, in the *Musee de l'Homme.* (*Rest*)

SCENE 1

FINAL CHORUS

THE NEGRO RESURRECTIONIST: I regret to inform you that thuh Venus Hottentot iz dead.

ALL: Dead!

THE NEGRO RESURRECTIONIST: There wont be inny show tuhnite.

THE VENUS: Miss me Miss me Miss me

THE GRADE-SCHOOL CHUM: Exposure iz what killed her

nothin on in our cold weather.

THE NEGRO RESURRECTIONIST: 23 days in uh row it rained.

THE BARON DOCTEUR: I say she died of drink.

THE NEGRO RESURRECTIONIST: It was the cold I think.

THE VENUS: Hear ye hear ye hear ye

thuh Venus Hottentot iz dead.

There wont be inny show tuhnite.

THE GRADE-SCHOOL CHUM: I know yr dissuhpointed.

I hate tuh let you down.

ALL: Gimmie gimmie back my buck!

THE VENUS: I come from miles and miles and miles and miles

ALL: Hotsey-Totsey!

THE NEGRO RESURRECTIONIST: Diggidy-diggidy-diggidy-diggidy.

ALL: Diggidy-diggidy-diggidy-dawg.

THE CHORUS OF THE 8 HUMAN WONDERS: Turn away dont look

cover yr face

cover yr eyes.

ALL: Drum Drum Drum Drum.

Hur-ry Hur-ry Step in Step in.

(*Rest*)

Thuh Venus Hottentot iz dead.

THE VENUS: Tail end of the tale for there must be uh end

is that Venus, Black Goddess, was shameless, she sinned or else

completely unknowing thuh Godfearin ways, she stood

showing her ass off in her iron cage.

When Death met Love Death deathd Love

and left Love tuh rot

au naturel end for thuh Miss Hottentot.

Loves soul, which was tidy, hides in heaven, yes, thats it

Loves corpse stands on show in museum. Please visit.

ALL: Diggidy-diggidy-diggidy

Diggidy-diggidy-diggidy-dawg!

THE NEGRO RESURRECTIONIST: A Scene of Love:

THE VENUS: *Kiss* me *Kiss* me *Kiss* me *Kiss*

END OF PLAY

A GLOSSARY OF MEDICAL TERMS

Annular ligament—a large muscle in the wrist

Atlas—the part of the spine that supports the head

Attolens and **Attrahens Aurem**—the muscles of the ear

Avoirdupois—personal weight

Axilla—the armpit

Calvarium—the skull lacking the lower jaw

Cervicalis ascendens—a neck muscle near the upper ribs

Clavicle—the collar bone

Coccyx—the tail bone

Conjunctiva—mucous membrane lining the eyeball

Dorso-epitrochlear muscle—a muscle similar to the **Latissimus dorsi** found in nonhuman animals

Dorsum—the back surface of an area

Extensor communis digitorum—a muscle of the forearm

Extensor minimi digiti—a slender muscle running through the arm and into the hand

Extensor primi internodii pollicis—the smallest muscle of the arm

Fascia—a sheet of connective tissue

Femur—the thigh bone (the longest, largest and strongest bone in the skeleton)

Flexor brevis digitorum pedis—a muscle in the middle of the sole of the foot

Formal cartilage's tip—a.k.a. the xyphoid process, the cartilage at the tip of the breastbone

Fundus—part of the aperture of an organ

Gluteus maximus—the muscle of the buttocks

Gluteus medius—the muscle on the outer surface of the pelvis covered by **Gluteus maximus**

Humeral bone—the upper arm bone

Labia majora—the outer vaginal lips

Labia minora—the inner vaginal lips

Latissimus dorsi muscle—a large flat muscle covering the lumbar and lower half of the dorsal region

Levator anguli scapulae—a muscle at the back and side of the neck

Levator claviculae—a muscle of the clavicle area first noted by Dr. McWhinnie

Malar—two small bones forming the prominence of the cheek

Mammae—the breasts

Mastoid process—the bone behind the ear, part of the jaw

Metacarpo-phalangeal—the hand and finger bones

Nymphae—the inner lips of the vulva

Occipitalis muscle—the muscle at the back of the skull

Omo-hyoid—a muscle of the neck, passing across the side of the neck

Os calcis—the heel bone

Patella—the knee bone

Pelvis at crest of ilium—the top crest of the hip bone

Perineum—the muscle between genitals and anus

Prepuce—the folds of skin enveloping the clitoris

Pubes—the pubic region

Pudendum—external genital organs, especially of a woman

Radius—the arm bone on the thumb side

Sacro-lumbalis muscle—located in the external portion of the erector (lower) spine

Scapula—the bone comprising the back part of the shoulder

Septum—the inner wall of the nose separating the nostrils

Septum narium/nares—the inner nasal area

Serratus magnus—a muscle in the chest

Splenius colli—a muscle at the back of the neck

Steatopygia—an excessive developement of fat on the buttocks especially of females, which is common among the so-called Hottentots and some Negro peoples

Sterno-mastoid—a large muscle passing downwards along the front of the neck

Sternum—the breastbone

Teres minor—the narrow muscle of the shoulder area

Thorax—the chest cavity

Tibia—the leg bone between the knee and ankle

Trachelo-mastoid—a muscle running from the jaw area around to the back

Tragus—the prominence at the front of the opening of the ear

Transverse process—a muscular-like lever which serves as the attachment of muscles which move the different parts of the spine

Trapezius—a muscle covering the upper and back part of the neck and shoulders

Triceps—muscles situated on the back of the arm

Trochanters—the upper part of the thigh bone

Tubercle—the protuberance near the head of the rib

Ulna—the arm bone on the little finger side

Umbilicus—the belly button

Vertex—the top of the head

A GLOSSARY OF CHOCOLATES

Bouchon Fraise—cupcake-shaped, either dark chocolate or buttercream, filled with either strawberry crème fraîche or cognac flavor, respectively

Capezzoli di Venere—"the nipples of Venus," breast-shaped mounds in dark or light chocolate with a red or white iced "nipple" on top; crème fraîche often inside

Enfant de Bruxelles—dark chocolate lozenge with an image of a little African child stamped upon it; coffee and chocolate crème fraîche inside

Escargot Lait—fashioned in the shape of a snail's shell; milk chocolate with praliné inside

Petits coeurs—"little hearts" of solid chocolate

Pharaon—a solid lozenge, either dark or buttercream, with the image of a pharaoh's head stamped upon it

Rhum Caramel—cube-shaped, dark chocolate with light caramel; crème fraîche and rum flavor inside

Index

Credits